A SELECT LIBRARY

OF

NICENE AND POST-NICENE FATHERS

OF

THE CHRISTIAN CHURCH.

Second Series.

TRANSLATED INTO ENGLISH WITH PROLEGOMENA AND EXPLANATORY NOTES

UNDER THE EDITORIAL SUPERVISION OF

PHILIP SCHAFF, D.D., LL.D., AND HENRY WACE, D.D.,

Professor of Church History in the Union Theological Seminary,
New York.

Principal of King's College,
London.

IN CONNECTION WITH A NUMBER OF PATRISTIC SCHOLARS OF EUROPE AND AMERICA.

VOLUME I.

EUSEBIUS:

CHURCH HISTORY,

LIFE OF CONSTANTINE THE GREAT,

AND

ORATION IN PRAISE OF CONSTANTINE.

T&T CLARK
EDINBURGH

WM. B. EERDMANS PUBLISHING COMPANY
GRAND RAPIDS, MICHIGAN

British Library Cataloguing in Publication Data

Nicene & Post-Nicene Fathers. — 2nd series
1. Fathers of the church
I. Schaff, Philip   II. Mace, Henry
230'.11   BR60.A62

T&T Clark ISBN 0 567 09410 3

Eerdmans ISBN 0-8028-8115-7

Reprinted 1997

CONTENTS OF VOLUME I.

PREFACE.

———

THE First Series of the Nicene and Post-Nicene Library of the Christian Fathers, containing, in fourteen volumes, the principal works of St. Augustin and St. Chrysostom, has been completed in less than four years, according to the Prospectus of the Publisher issued in 1886.

I am happy to state that the Second Series, containing the chief works of the Fathers from Eusebius to John of Damascus, and from Ambrose to Gregory the Great, will be issued on the same liberal terms, as announced by the Publisher.

The present volume opens the Second Series with a new translation and critical commentary of the historical works of Eusebius, by my friends, Dr. Arthur C. McGiffert and Dr. Ernest C. Richardson, who have bestowed a vast amount of labor of love on their tasks for several years past. I desired them to make these works a reliable and tolerably complete Church History of the first three centuries for the English reader. I think they have succeeded. Every scholar will at once see the great value and superiority of this over every other previous edition of Eusebius.

The next two volumes will contain the Church Histories of Socrates, Sozomen, Theodoret, and Evagrius. For further details the reader is referred to the Publisher's announcement at the end of this volume.

PHILIP SCHAFF.

NEW YORK, March, 1890.

THE CHURCH HISTORY OF EUSEBIUS

———▸•◂———

TRANSLATED WITH PROLEGOMENA AND NOTES

BY

THE REV. ARTHUR CUSHMAN McGIFFERT, Ph.D.,

PROFESSOR OF CHURCH HISTORY IN LANE THEOLOGICAL SEMINARY, CINCINNATI.

PREFACE

THE present translation of the Church History of Eusebius has been made from Heinichen's second edition of the Greek text, but variant readings have been adopted without hesitation whenever they have approved themselves to my judgment. In all such cases the variation from Heinichen's text has been indicated in the notes. A simple revision of Crusè's English version was originally proposed, but a brief examination of it was sufficient to convince me that a satisfactory revision would be an almost hopeless task, and that nothing short of a new and independent translation ought to be undertaken. In the preparation of that translation invaluable assistance has been rendered by my father, the Rev. Joseph N. McGiffert, D.D., for whose help and counsel I desire thus publicly to give expression to my profound gratitude. The entire translation has been examined by him and owes much to his timely suggestions and criticisms; while the translation itself of a considerable portion of the work (Bks. V.–VIII. and the Martyrs of Palestine) is from his hand. The part thus rendered by him I have carefully revised for the purpose of securing uniformity in style and expression throughout the entire work, and I therefore hold myself alone responsible for it as well as for the earlier and later books. As to the principle upon which the translation has been made, little need be said. The constant endeavor has been to reproduce as nearly as possible, both the substance and form of the original, and in view of the peculiar need of accuracy in such a work as the present, it has seemed better in doubtful cases to run the risk of erring in the direction of over-literalness rather than in that of undue license.

A word of explanation in regard to the notes which accompany the text may not be out of place. In view of the popular character of the series of which the present volume forms a part, it seemed important that the notes should contain much supplementary information in regard to persons, places, and events mentioned in the text which might be quite superfluous to the professional historian as well as to the student enjoying access to libraries rich in historical and bibliographical material, and I have therefore not felt justified in confining myself to such questions as might interest only the critical scholar. Requested by the general editor to make the work in some sense a general history of, or historical commentary upon, the first three centuries of the Christian Church, I have ventured to devote considerable space to a fuller presentation of various subjects but briefly touched upon or merely referred to by Eusebius. At the same time my chief endeavor has been, by a careful study of difficult and disputed points, to do all that I could for their elucidation, and thus to perform as faithfully as possible the paramount duty of a commentator. The number and fulness of the notes needed in such a work must of course be matter of dispute, but annoyed as I have repeatedly been by the fragmentary character of the annotations in the existing editions of the work, I have been anxious to avoid that defect, and have therefore passed by no passage which seemed to me to need discussion, nor consciously evaded any difficulty. Working with historical students constantly in mind I have felt it due to them to fortify all my statements by references to the authorities upon which they have been based, and to indicate at the same time with sufficient fullness the sources whose examination a fuller investigation of the subject on their part might render necessary. The modern works which have been most helpful are mentioned in the notes, but I cannot in justice refrain from making especial reference at this point to Smith and Wace's *Dictionary of Christian Biography* which has been constantly at my side, and to the first and second volumes of Schaff's *Church History*, whose bibliographies have been especially serviceable. Many of Valesius' notes have been found very suggestive and must always remain valuable in spite of the great advance made in historical knowledge since his day. For the commentary of Heinichen less can be said. Richardson's *Bibliographical Synopsis*, published as a supplement to the Ante-Nicene Library, did not come into my hands until the greater part of the work was completed. In the preparation of the notes upon the latter portion it proved helpful, and its existence has enabled me throughout the work to omit extended lists of books which it would otherwise have been necessary to give.

It was my privilege some three years ago to study portions of the fourth and fifth books of Eusebius' Church History with Professor Adolf Harnack in his *Seminar* at Marburg. Especial thanks are due for the help and inspiration gained from that eminent scholar, and for the light thrown by him upon many difficult passages in those portions of the work.

It gives me pleasure also to express my obligation to Dr. Isaac G. Hall, of New York, and to Dr. E. C. Richardson, of Hartford, for information furnished by them in regard to certain editions of the History, also to the Rev. Charles R. Gillett, Librarian of Union Theological Seminary, and to the Rev. J. H. Dulles, Librarian of Princeton Theological Seminary, for their kindness in granting me the privileges of the libraries under their charge, and for their unfailing courtesy shown me in many ways. To Mr. James McDonald, of Shelbyville, Ky., my thanks are due for his translation of the Testimonies for and against Eusebius, printed at the close of the Prolegomena, and to Mr. F. E. Moore, of New Albany, Ind., for assistance rendered in connection with the preparation of the indexes.

ARTHUR CUSHMAN McGIFFERT.

LANE THEOLOGICAL SEMINARY,
    April 15, 1890.

CONTENTS OF THE PROLEGOMENA.

PROLEGOMENA.

THE LIFE AND WRITINGS OF

EUSEBIUS OF CÆSAREA.

CHAPTER I.

THE LIFE OF EUSEBIUS.

§ 1. *Sources and Literature.*

ACACIUS, the pupil and successor of Eusebius in the bishopric of Cæsarea, wrote a life of the latter (Socr. *H. E.* II. 4) which is unfortunately lost. He was a man of ability (Sozomen *H. E.* III. 2, IV. 23) and had exceptional opportunities for producing a full and accurate account of Eusebius' life; the disappearance of his work is therefore deeply to be regretted.

Numerous notices of Eusebius are found in the works of Socrates, Sozomen, Theodoret, Athanasius, Jerome, and other writers of his own and subsequent ages, to many of which references will be made in the following pages. A collection of these notices, made by Valesius, is found in English translation on p. 57 sq. of this volume. The chief source for a knowledge of Eusebius' life and character is to be found in his own works. These will be discussed below, on p. 26 sq. Of the numerous modern works which treat at greater or less length of the life of Eusebius I shall mention here only those which I have found most valuable.

VALESIUS: *De vita scriptisque Eusebii Diatribe* (in his edition of Eusebius' *Historia Eccles.;* English version in Cruse's translation of the same work).

CAVE: *Lives of the Fathers*, II. 95–144 (ed. H. Cary, Oxf. 1840).

TILLEMONT: *Hist. Eccles.* VII. pp. 39–75 (compare also his account of the Arians in vol. VI.).

STROTH: *Leben und Schriften des Eusebius* (in his German translation of the *Hist. Eccles.*).

CLOSS: *Leben und Schriften des Eusebius* (in his translation of the same work).

DANZ: *De Eusebio Cæsariensi, Historiæ Eccles. Scriptore, ejusque fide historica recte æstimanda*, Cap. II.: *de rebus ad Eusebii vitam pertinentibus* (pp. 33–75).

STEIN: *Eusebius Bischof von Cæsarea. Nach seinem Leben, seinen Schriften, und seinem dogmatischen Charakter dargestellt* (Würzburg, 1859; full and valuable).

BRIGHT, in the introduction to his edition of Burton's text of the *Hist. Eccles.* (excellent).

LIGHTFOOT (Bishop of Durham): *Eusebius of Cæsarea*, in Smith and Wace's *Dictionary of Christian Biography*, vol. II. pp. 308–348. Lightfoot's article is a magnificent monument of patristic scholarship and contains the best and most exhaustive treatment of the life and writings of Eusebius that has been written.

The student may be referred finally to all the larger histories of the Church (*e.g.* Schaff, vol. III. 871 sqq. and 1034 sq.), which contain more or less extended accounts of Eusebius.

§ 2. *Eusebius' Birth and Training.   His Life in Cæsarea until the Outbreak of the Persecution.*

Our author was commonly known among the ancients as Eusebius of Cæsarea or Eusebius Pamphili. The former designation arose from the fact that he was bishop of the church in Cæsarea for many years; the latter from the fact that he was the intimate friend and devoted admirer of Pamphilus, a presbyter of Cæsarea and a martyr. Some such specific appellation was necessary to distinguish him from others of the same name. Smith and Wace's *Dictionary of Christian Biography* mentions 137 men of the first eight centuries who bore the name Eusebius, and of these at least forty were contemporaries of our author. The best known among them were Eusebius of Nicomedia (called by Arius the brother of Eusebius of Cæsarea), Eusebius of Emesa, and Eusebius of Samosata.

The exact date of our author's birth is unknown to us, but his *Ecclesiastical History* contains notices which enable us to fix it approximately. In *H. E.* V. 28 he reports that Paul of Samosata attempted to revive again in his day (καθ' ἡμᾶς) the heresy of Artemon. But Paul of Samosata was deposed from the episcopate of Antioch in 272, and was condemned as a heretic at least as early as 268, so that Eusebius must have been born before the latter date, if his words are to be strictly interpreted. Again, according to *H. E.* III. 28, Dionysius was bishop of Alexandria in Eusebius' time (καθ' ἡμᾶς). But Dionysius was bishop from 247 or 248 to 265, and therefore if Eusebius' words are to be interpreted strictly here as in the former case, he must have been born before 265. On the other hand, inasmuch as his death occurred about 340, we cannot throw his birth much earlier than 260. It is true that the references to Paul and to Dionysius do not prove conclusively that Eusebius was alive in their day, for his words may have been used in a loose sense. But in *H. E.* VII. 26, just before proceeding to give an account of Paul of Samosata, he draws the line between his own and the preceding generation, declaring that he is now about to relate the events of his own age (τὴν καθ' ἡμᾶς). This still further confirms the other indications, and we shall consequently be safe in concluding that Eusebius was born not far from the year 260 A.D. His birthplace cannot be determined with certainty. The fact that he is called "Eusebius the Palestinian" by Marcellus (*Euseb. lib. adv. Marcell.* I. 4), Basil (*Lib. ad. Amphil. de Spir. Sancto*, c. 29), and others, does not prove that he was a Palestinian by birth; for the epithet may be used to indicate merely his place of residence (he was bishop of Cæsarea in Palestine for many years). Moreover, the argument urged by Stein and Lightfoot in support of his Palestinian birth, namely, that it was customary to elect to the episcopate of any church a native of the city in preference to a native of some other place, does not count for much. All that seems to have been demanded was that a man should have been already a member of the particular church over which he was to be made bishop, and even this rule was not universal (see Bingham's *Antiquities*, II. 10, 2 and 3). The fact that he was bishop of Cæsarea therefore would at most warrant us in concluding only that he had made his residence in Cæsarea for some time previous to his election to that office. Nevertheless, although neither of these arguments proves his Palestinian birth, it is very probable that he was a native of that country, or at least of that section. He was acquainted with Syriac as well as with Greek, which circumstance taken in connection with his ignorance of Latin (see below, p. 47) points to the region of Syria as his birthplace. Moreover, we learn from his own testimony that he was in Cæsarea while still a youth (*Vita Constantini*, I. 19), and in his epistle to the church of Cæsarea (see below, p. 16) he says that he was taught the creed of the Cæsarean church in his childhood (or at least at the beginning of his Christian life: ἐν τῇ κατηχήσει), and that he accepted it at baptism. It would seem therefore that he must have lived while still a child either in Cæsarea itself, or in the neighborhood, where its creed was in use. Although no one therefore (except Theodorus Metochita of the fourteenth century, in his *Cap. Miscell.* 17; Migne, *Patr. Lat.* CXLIV. 949) directly states that Eusebius was a Palestinian by birth, we have every reason to suppose him such.

His parents are entirely unknown. Nicephorus Callistus (*H. E.* VI. 37) reports that his mother was a sister of Pamphilus. He does not mention his authority for this statement, and it is extremely unlikely, in the face of the silence of Eusebius himself and of all other writers, that it is true. It is far more probable that the relationship was later assumed to account for the close intimacy of the two men. Arius, in an epistle addressed to Eusebius of Nicomedia (contained in Theodoret's *Hist. Eccles.* I. 5), calls Eusebius of Cæsarea the latter's brother. It is objected to this that Eusebius of Nicomedia refers to Eusebius of Cæsarea on one occasion as his "master" (τοῦ δεσπότου μου, in his epistle to Paulinus contained in Theodoret's *Hist. Eccles.* I. 6), and that on the other hand Eusebius of Cæsarea calls Eusebius of Nicomedia, "the great Eusebius" (*Euseb. lib. adv. Marcell.* I. 4), both of which expressions seem inconsistent with brotherhood. Lightfoot justly remarks that neither the argument itself nor the objections carry much weight. The term ἀδελφός may well have been used to indicate merely theological or ecclesiastical association, while on the other hand, brotherhood would not exclude the form of expression employed by each in speaking of the other. Of more weight is the fact that neither Eusebius himself nor any historian of that period refers to such a relationship, and also the unlikelihood that two members of one family should bear the same name.

From Eusebius' works we gather that he must have received an extensive education both in secular philosophy and in Biblical and theological science. Although his immense erudition was doubtless the result of wide and varied reading continued throughout life, it is highly probable that he acquired the taste for such reading in his youth. Who his early instructors were we do not know, and therefore cannot estimate the degree of their influence over him. As he was a man, however, who cherished deep admiration for those whom he regarded as great and good men, and as he possessed an unusually acquisitive mind and a pliant disposition, we should naturally suppose that his instructors must have possessed considerable influence over him, and that his methods of study in later years must have been largely molded by their example and precept. We see this exemplified in a remarkable degree in the influence exerted over him by Pamphilus, his dearest friend, and at the same time the preceptor, as it were, of his early manhood. Certainly this great bibliopholist must have done much to strengthen Eusebius' natural taste for omnivorous reading, and the opportunities afforded by his grand library for the cultivation of such a taste were not lost. To the influence of Pamphilus, the devoted admirer and enthusiastic champion of Origen, was doubtless due also in large measure the deep respect which Eusebius showed for that illustrious Father, a respect to which we owe one of the most delightful sections of his Church History, his long account of Origen in the sixth book, and to which in part antiquity was indebted for the elaborate *Defense of Origen*, composed by Pamphilus and himself, but unfortunately no longer extant. Eusebius certainly owed much to the companionship of that eager student and noble Christian hero, and he always recognized with deep gratitude his indebtedness to him. (Compare the account of Pamphilus given below in Bk. VII. chap. 32, § 25 sq.) The names of his earlier instructors, who were eminently successful, at least in fostering his thirst for knowledge, are quite unknown to us. His abiding admiration for Plato, whom he always placed at the head of all philosophers (see Stein, p. 6), would lead us to think that he received at least a part of his secular training from some ardent Platonist, while his intense interest in apologetics, which lasted throughout his life, and which affected all his works, seems to indicate the peculiar bent of his early Christian education. Trithemius concluded from a passage in his *History* (VII. 32) that Eusebius was a pupil of the learned Dorotheus of Antioch, and Valesius, Lightfoot and others are apparently inclined to accept his conclusion. But, as Stroth remarks (*Eusebii Kirchengeschichte*, p. xix), all that Eusebius says is that he had heard Dorotheus expound the Scriptures in the church (τούτου μετρίως τὰς γραφὰς ἐπὶ τῆς ἐκκλησίας διηγουμένου κατηκούσαμεν), that is, that he had heard him preach. To conclude from this statement that he was a pupil of Dorotheus is certainly quite unwarranted.

Stroth's suggestion that he probably enjoyed the instruction of Meletius for seven years during the persecution rests upon no good ground, for the passage which he relies upon to sustain his opinion (*H. E.* VII. 32. 28) says only that Eusebius "observed Meletius well" (κατενοήσαμεν) during those seven years.

In Cæsarea Eusebius was at one time a presbyter of the church, as we may gather from his words in the epistle to that church already referred to, where, in speaking of the creed, he says, "As we believed and taught in the presbytery and in the episcopate itself." But the attempt to fix the date of his ordination to that office is quite vain. It is commonly assumed that he became presbyter while Agapius was bishop of Cæsarea, and this is not unlikely, though we possess no proof of it (upon Agapius see below, *H. E.* VII. 32, note 39). In his *Vita Constantini*, I. 19, Eusebius reports that he saw Constantine for the first time in Cæsarea in the train of the Emperor Diocletian. In his *Chron.* Eusebius reports that Diocletian made an expedition against Egypt, which had risen in rebellion in the year 296 A.D., and Theophanes, in his *Chron.*, says that Constantine accompanied him. It is probable therefore that it was at this time that Eusebius first saw Constantine in Cæsarea, when he was either on his way to Egypt, or on his way back (see Tillemont's *Hist. des Emp.*, IV. p. 34).

During these years of quiet, before the great persecution of Diocletian, which broke out in 303 A.D., Eusebius' life must have been a very pleasant one. Pamphilus' house seems to have been a sort of rendezvous for Christian scholars, perhaps a regular divinity school; for we learn from Eusebius' *Martyrs in Palestine* (Cureton's edition, pp. 13 and 14) that he and a number of others, including the martyr Apphianus, were living together in one house at the time of the persecution, and that the latter was instructed in the Scriptures by Pamphilus and acquired from him virtuous habits and conduct. The great library of Pamphilus would make his house a natural center for theological study, and the immense amount of work which was done by him, or under his direction, in the reproduction of copies of the Holy Scriptures, of Origen's works (see Jerome's *de vir. ill.* 75 and 81, and *contra Ruf.* I. 9), and in other literary employments of the same kind, makes it probable that he had gathered about him a large circle of friends and students who assisted him in his labors and profited by his counsel and instruction. Amidst these associations Eusebius passed his early manhood, and the intellectual stimulus thus given him doubtless had much to do with his future career. He was above all a literary man, and remained such to the end of his life. The pleasant companionships of these days, and the mutual interest and sympathy which must have bound those fellow-students and fellow-disciples of Pamphilus very close together, perhaps had much to do with that broad-minded spirit of sympathy and tolerance which so characterized Eusebius in later years. He was always as far as possible from the character of a recluse. He seems ever to have been bound by very strong ties to the world itself and to his fellow-men. Had his earlier days been filled with trials and hardships, with the bitterness of disappointed hopes and unfulfilled ambitions, with harsh experiences of others' selfishness and treachery, who shall say that the whole course of his life might not have been changed, and his writings have exhibited an entirely different spirit from that which is now one of their greatest charms? Certainly he had during these early years in Cæsarea large opportunities for cultivating that natural trait of admiration for other men, which was often so strong as to blind him even to their faults, and that natural kindness which led him to see good wherever it existed in his Christian brethren. At the same time these associations must have had considerable influence in fostering the apologetic temper. The pursuits of the little circle were apparently exclusively Christian, and in that day when Christianity stood always on its defense, it would naturally become to them a sacred duty to contribute to that defense and to employ all their energies in the task. It has been remarked that the apologetic temper is very noticeable in Eusebius' writings. It is more than that; we may say indeed in general terms that everything he wrote was an apology for the faith. His *History* was written avowedly with an apologetic purpose, his *Chronicle* was composed with the same end in view. Even when pronouncing a eulogy upon a deceased emperor he seized every possible opportunity to draw from that emperor's career, and from the circumstances of his reign, arguments for the truth and grandeur of the Christian religion. His natural temper of mind and his early training may have had much to do with this habit of thought, but certainly those years with Pamphilus and his friends in Cæsarea must have emphasized and developed it.

Another characteristic which Pamphilus and the circle that surrounded him doubtless did something to develop in our author was a certain superiority to the trammels of mere traditionalism, or we might perhaps better say that they in some measure checked the opposite tendency of slavishness to the traditional which seems to have been natural to him. Pamphilus' deep reverence for Origen proclaims him at once superior to that kind of narrow conservatism which led many men as learned and doubtless as conscientious as himself to pass severe and unconditional condemnation upon Origen and all his teaching. The effect of championing his cause must have fostered in this little circle, which was a very hotbed of Origenism, a contempt for the narrow and unfair judgments of mere traditionalists, and must have led them to seek in some degree the truth solely for its own sake, and to become in a measure careless of its relation to the views of any school or church. It could hardly be otherwise than that the free and fearless spirit of Origen should leave its impress through his writings upon a circle of followers so devoted to him as were these Cæsarean students. Upon the impressionable Eusebius these influences necessarily operated. And yet he brought to them no keen speculative powers, no deep originality such as Origen himself possessed. His was essentially an acquisitive, not a productive mind, and hence it was out of the question that he should become a second Origen. It was quite certain that Origen's influence over him would weaken somewhat his confidence in the traditional as such, — a confidence which is naturally great in such minds as his, — but at the same time would do little to lessen the real power of the past over him. He continued to get his truth from others, from the great men of the past with whom he had lived and upon whose thought he had feasted. All that he believed he had drawn from them; he produced nothing new for himself, and his creed was a traditional creed. And yet he had at the same time imbibed from his surroundings the habit of questioning and even criticising the past, and, in spite of his abiding respect for it, had learned to feel that the voice of the many is not always the voice of truth, and that the widely and anciently accepted is sometimes to be corrected by the clearer sight of a single man. Though he therefore depended for all he believed so completely upon the past, his associations had helped to free him from a slavish adherence to all that a particular school had accepted, and had made him in some small measure an eclectic in his relations to doctrines and opinions of earlier generations. A notable instance of this eclecticism on his part is seen in his treatment of the Apocalypse of John. He felt the force of an almost universal tradition in favor of its apostolic origin, and yet in the face of that he could listen to the doubts of Dionysius, and could be led by his example, in a case where his own dissatisfaction with the book acted as an incentive, almost, if not quite, to reject it and to ascribe it to another John. Instances of a similar mode of conduct on his part are quite numerous. While he is always a staunch apologist for Christianity, he seldom, if ever, degenerates into a mere partisan of any particular school or sect.

One thing in fact which is particularly noticeable in Eusebius' works is the comparatively small amount of time and space which he devotes to heretics. With his wide and varied learning and his extensive acquaintance with the past, he had opportunities for successful heresy hunting such as few possessed, and yet he never was a heresy hunter in any sense. This is surprising when we remember what a fascination this employment had for so many scholars of his own age, and when we realize that his historical tastes and talents would seem to mark him out as just the man for that kind of work. May it not be that the lofty spirit of Origen, animating that Cæsarean school, had something to do with the happy fact that he became an apologist instead of a mere polemic, that he chose the honorable task of writing a history of the Church instead of anticipating Epiphanius' Panarium?

It was not that he was not alive to the evils of heresy. He shared with nearly all good churchmen of his age an intense aversion for those who, as he believed, had corrupted the true Gospel of Christ. Like them he ascribed heresy to the agency of the evil one, and was no more able than they to see any good in a man whom he looked upon as a real heretic, or to do justice in any degree to the error which he taught. His condemnations of heretics in his *Church History* are most severe. Language is hardly strong enough to express his aversion for them. And yet, although he is thus most thoroughly the child of his age, the difference between him and most of his contemporaries is very apparent. He mentions these heretics only to dismiss them with disapproval or condemnation. He seldom, if ever, discusses and refutes their views. His interests lie evidently in other directions; he is concerned with higher things. A still more strongly marked difference between himself and many churchmen of his age lies in his large liberality towards those of his own day who differed with him in minor points of faith, and his comparative indifference to the divergence of views between the various parties in the Church. In all this we believe is to be seen not simply the inherent nature of the man, but that nature as trained in the school of Pamphilus, the disciple of Origen.

§ 3. *The Persecution of Diocletian.*

In this delightful circle and engaged in such congenial tasks, the time must have passed very happily for Eusebius, until, in 303, the terrible persecution of Diocletian broke upon the Church almost like a thunderbolt out of a clear sky. The causes of the sudden change of policy on Diocletian's part, and the terrible havoc wrought in the Church, it is not my intention to discuss here (see below, Bk. VIII. chap. 2, note 3 sq.). We are concerned with the persecution only in so far as it bears upon the present subject. In the first year of the persecution Procopius, the first martyr of Palestine, was put to death at Cæsarea (Eusebius' *Martyrs of Palestine*, Cureton's ed. p. 4), and from that time on that city, which was an important Christian center, was the scene of a tempest which raged with greater or less violence, and with occasional cessations, for seven years. Eusebius himself was an eyewitness of many martyrdoms there, of which he gives us an account in his *Martyrs of Palestine*. The little circle which surrounded Pamphilus did not escape. In the third year of the persecution (*Mart. of Pal.* p. 12 sq.) a youth named Apphianus, or Epiphanius (the former is given in the Greek text, the latter in the Syriac), who "resided in the same house with us, confirming himself in godly doctrine, and being instructed by that perfect martyr, Pamphilus" (as Eusebius says), committed an act of fanatical daring which caused his arrest and martyrdom. It seems that without the knowledge of his friends, concealing his design even from those who dwelt in the same house with him, he laid hold of the hand of the governor, Arbanus, who was upon the point of sacrificing, and endeavored to dissuade him from offering to "lifeless idols and wicked devils." His arrest was of course the natural consequence, and he had the glory of witnessing a good profession and suffering a triumphant death. Although Eusebius speaks with such admiration of his conduct, it is quite significant of the attitude of himself, and of most of the circle of which he was one, that Apphianus felt obliged to conceal his purpose from them. He doubtless feared that they would not permit him to perform the rash act which he meditated, and we may conclude from that, that the circle in the main was governed by the precepts of good common sense, and avoided that fanaticism which so frequently led men, as in the present case it led Apphianus, to expose themselves needlessly, and even to court martyrdom. It is plain enough from what we know of Eusebius' general character that he himself was too sensible to act in that way. It is true that he speaks with admiration of Apphianus' conduct, and in *H. E.* VIII. 5, of the equally rash procedure of a Nicomedian Christian; but that does not imply that he considered their course the wisest one, and that he would not rather recommend the employment of all proper and honorable precautions for the preservation of life. Indeed, in *H. E.* IV. 15, he speaks with evident approval of the prudent course pursued by Polycarp in preserving his life so long as he could without violating his Christian profession, and with manifest disapproval of the rash act of the Phrygian Quintus, who presumptuously courted martyrdom, only to fail when the test itself came. Pamphilus also possessed too much sound Christian sense to advocate any such fanaticism, or to practice it himself, as is plain enough from the fact that he was not arrested until the fifth year of the persecution. This unhealthy temper of mind in the midst of persecution was indeed almost universally condemned by the wisest men of the Church, and yet the boldness and the very rashness of those who thus voluntarily and needlessly threw their lives away excited widespread admiration and too often a degree

of commendation which served only to promote a wider growth of the same unhealthy sentiment.

In the fifth year of the persecution Pamphilus was arrested and thrown into prison, where he
remained for two years, when he finally, in the seventh year of the persecution, suffered martyrdom with eleven others, some of whom were his disciples and members of his own household.
(*Pal. Mart.* Cureton's ed. p. 36 sq.; *H. E.* App. chap. 11.)   During the two years of Pamphilus' imprisonment Eusebius spent a great deal of time with him, and the two together composed five books of an *Apology for Origen,* to which Eusebius afterward added a sixth (see below,
p. 36).   Danz (p. 37) assumes that Eusebius was imprisoned with Pamphilus, which is not an
unnatural supposition when we consider how much they must have been together to compose the
Apology as they did.   There is, however, no other evidence that he was thus imprisoned, and
in the face of Eusebius' own silence it is safer perhaps to assume (with most historians) that he
simply visited Pamphilus in his prison.   How it happened that Pamphilus and so many of his
followers were imprisoned and martyred, while Eusebius escaped, we cannot tell.   In his *Martyrs
of Palestine,* chap. 11, he states that Pamphilus was the only one of the company of twelve martyrs
that was a presbyter of the Cæsarean church ; and from the fact that he nowhere mentions the
martyrdom of others of the presbyters, we may conclude that they all escaped.   It is not surprising, therefore, that Eusebius should have done the same.   Nevertheless, it is somewhat
difficult to understand how he could come and go so frequently without being arrested and
condemned to a like fate with the others.   It is possible that he possessed friends among the
authorities whose influence procured his safety.   This supposition finds some support in the fact
that he had made the acquaintance of Constantine (the Greek in *Vita Const.* I. 19 has ἔγνωμεν,
which implies, as Danz remarks, that he not only saw, but that he became acquainted with Constantine) some years before in Cæsarea.   He could hardly have made his acquaintance unless
he had some friend among the high officials of the city.   Influential family connections may
account in part also for the position of prominence which he later acquired at the imperial court
of Constantine.   If he had friends in authority in Cæsarea during the persecution his exemption
from arrest is satisfactorily accounted for.   It has been supposed by some that Eusebius denied
the faith during the terrible persecution, or that he committed some other questionable and com-
promising act of concession, and thus escaped martyrdom.   In support of this is urged the fact
that in 335, at the council of Tyre, Potamo, bishop of Heraclea, in Egypt, addressed Eusebius in
the following words : " Dost thou sit as judge, O Eusebius ; and is Athanasius, innocent as he
is, judged by thee?   Who can bear such things?   Pray tell me, wast thou not with me in prison
during the persecution?   And I lost an eye in behalf of the truth, but thou appearest to have
received no bodily injury, neither hast thou suffered martyrdom, but thou hast remained alive
with no mutilation.   How wast thou released from prison unless thou didst promise those that
put upon us the pressure of persecution to do that which is unlawful, or didst actually do it ? "
Eusebius, it seems, did not deny the charge, but simply rose in anger and dismissed the council
with the words, " If ye come hither and make such accusations against us, then do your accusers
speak the truth.   For if ye tyrannize here, much more do ye in your own country " (Epiphan.
Hær. LXVIII. 8).   It must be noticed, however, that Potamo does not directly charge Eusebius
with dishonorable conduct, he simply conjectures that he must have acted dishonorably in order
to escape punishment ; as if every one who was imprisoned with Potamo must have suffered as
he did !   As Stroth suggests, it is quite possible that his peculiarly excitable and violent temperament was one of the causes of his own loss.   He evidently in any case had no knowledge of
unworthy conduct on Eusebius' part, nor had any one else so far as we can judge.   For in that
age of bitter controversy, when men's characters were drawn by their opponents in the blackest
lines, Eusebius must have suffered at the hands of the Athanasian party if it had been known
that he had acted a cowardly part in the persecution.   Athanasius himself refers to this incident
(*Contra Arian.* VIII. 1), but he only says that Eusebius was " accused of sacrificing," he does

not venture to affirm that he did sacrifice; and thus it is evident that he knew nothing of such an act. Moreover, he never calls Eusebius "the sacrificer," as he does Asterius, and as he would have been sure to do had he possessed evidence which warranted him in making the accusation (cf. Lightfoot, p. 311). Still further, Eusebius' subsequent election to the episcopate of Cæsarea, where his character and his conduct during the persecution must have been well known, and his appointment in later life to the important see of Antioch, forbid the supposition that he had ever acted a cowardly part in time of persecution. And finally, it is psychologically impossible that Eusebius could have written works so full of comfort for, and sympathy with, the suffering confessors, and could have spoken so openly and in such strong terms of condemnation of the numerous defections that occurred during the persecution, if he was conscious of his own guilt. It is quite possible, as remarked above, that influential friends protected him without any act of compromise on his part; or, supposing him to have been imprisoned with Potamo, it may be, as Lightfoot suggests, that the close of the persecution brought him his release as it did so many others. For it would seem natural to refer that imprisonment to the latter part of the persecution, when in all probability he visited Egypt, which was the home of Potamo. We must in any case vindicate Eusebius from the unfounded charge of cowardice and apostasy; and we ask, with Cave, "If every accusation against any man at any time were to be believed, who would be guiltless?"

From his *History* and his *Martyrs in Palestine* we learn that Eusebius was for much of the time in the very thick of the fight, and was an eyewitness of numerous martyrdoms not only in Palestine, but also in Tyre and in Egypt.

The date of his visits to the latter places (*H. E.* VIII. 7, 9) cannot be determined with exactness. They are described in connection with what seem to be the earlier events of the persecution, and yet it is by no means certain that chronological order has been observed in the narratives. The mutilation of prisoners — such as Potamo suffered — seems to have become common only in the year 308 and thereafter (see Mason's *Persecution of Diocletian*, p. 281), and hence if Eusebius was imprisoned with Potamo during his visit to Egypt, as seems most probable, there would be some reason for assigning that visit to the later years of the persecution. In confirmation of this might be urged the improbability that he would leave Cæsarea while Pamphilus was still alive, either before or after the latter's imprisonment, and still further his own statement in *H. E.* VII. 32, that he had observed Meletius escaping the fury of the persecution for seven years in Palestine. It is therefore likely that Eusebius did not make his journey to Egypt, which must have occupied some time, until toward the very end of the persecution, when it raged there with exceeding fierceness during the brief outburst of the infamous Maximin.

§ 4. *Eusebius' Accession to the Bishopric of Cæsarea.*

Not long after the close of the persecution, Eusebius became bishop of Cæsarea in Palestine, his own home, and held the position until his death. The exact date of his accession cannot be ascertained, indeed we cannot say that it did not take place even before the close of the persecution, but that is hardly probable; in fact, we know of no historian who places it earlier than 313. His immediate predecessor in the episcopate was Agapius, whom he mentions in terms of praise in *H. E.* VII. 32. Some writers have interpolated a bishop Agricolaus between Agapius and Eusebius (see *e.g.* Tillemont, *Hist. Eccles.* VII. 42), on the ground that his name appears in one of the lists of those present at the Council of Ancyra (c. 314), as bishop of Cæsarea in Palestine (see *Labbei et Cossartii Conc.* I. 1475). But, as Hefele shows (*Conciliengesch.* I. 220), this list is of late date and not to be relied upon. On the other hand, as Lightfoot points out, in the *Libellus Synodicus* (*Conc.* I. 1480), where Agricolaus is said to have been present at the Council of Ancyra, he is called bishop of Cæsarea in Cappadocia; and this statement is confirmed by a Syriac list given in Cowper's *Miscellanies*, p. 41. Though perhaps no great reliance is to be placed upon the correctness of any of these lists, the last two may at any rate be set over against the first, and we may conclude that there exists no ground for assuming that Agapius, who is the last Cæsarean bishop mentioned by Eusebius, was not the latter's immediate predecessor. At what time Agapius died we do not know. That he suffered martyrdom is hardly likely, in view of Eusebius' silence on the subject. It would seem more likely that he outlived the persecution. However that may be, Eusebius was already bishop at the time of the dedication of a new and elegant church at Tyre under the direction of his friend Paulinus, bishop of that city. Upon this occasion he delivered an address of considerable length, which he has inserted in his *Ecclesiastical History*, Bk. X. chap. 4. He does not name himself as its author, but the way in which he introduces it, and the very fact that he records the whole speech without giving the name of the man who delivered it, make its origin perfectly plain. Moreover, the last sentence of the preceding chapter makes it evident that the speaker was a bishop : " Every one of the rulers (ἀρχόντων) present delivered panegyric discourses." The date of the dedication of this church is a matter of dispute, though it is commonly put in the year 315. It is plain from Eusebius' speech that it was uttered before Licinius had begun to persecute the Christians, and also, as Görres remarks, at a time when Constantine and Licinius were at least outwardly at peace with each other. In the year 314 the two emperors went to war, and consequently, if the persecution of Licinius began soon after that event, as it is commonly supposed to have done, the address must have been delivered before hostilities opened ; that is, at least as early as 314, and this is the year in which Görres places it (*Kritische Untersuchungen ueber die licinianische Christenverfolgung*, p. 8). But if Görres' date (319 A.D.) for the commencement of the persecution be accepted (and though he can hardly be said to have proved it, he has urged some strong grounds in support of it), then the address may have been delivered at almost any time between 315 and 319, for, as Görres himself shows, Licinius and Constantine were outwardly at peace during the greater part of that time (*ib*. p. 14 sq.). There is nothing in the speech itself which prevents this later date, nor is it intrinsically improbable that the great basilica reached completion only in 315 or later. In fact, it must be admitted that Eusebius may have become bishop at any time between about 311 and 318.

The persecution of Licinius, which continued until his defeat by Constantine, in 323, was but local, and seems never to have been very severe. Indeed, it did not bear the character of a bloody persecution, though a few bishops appear to have met their death on one ground or another. Palestine and Egypt seem not to have suffered to any great extent (see Görres, *ib*. p. 32 sq.).

§ 5. *The Outbreak of the Arian Controversy. The Attitude of Eusebius.*

About the year 318, while Alexander was bishop of Alexandria, the Arian controversy broke out in that city, and the whole Eastern Church was soon involved in the strife. We cannot enter here into a discussion of Arius' views ; but in order to understand the rapidity with which the Arian party grew, and the strong hold which it possessed from the very start in Syria and Asia Minor, we must remember that Arius was not himself the author of that system which we know as Arianism, but that he learned the essentials of it from his instructor Lucian. The latter was one of the most learned men of his age in the Oriental Church, and founded an exegetico-theological school in Antioch, which for a number of years stood outside of the communion of the orthodox Church in that city, but shortly before the martyrdom of Lucian himself (which took place in 311 or 312) made its peace with the Church, and was recognized by it. He was held in the highest reverence by his disciples, and exerted a great influence over them even after his death. Among them were such men as Arius, Eusebius of Nicomedia, Asterius, and others who were afterward known as staunch Arians. According to Harnack the chief points in the system of Lucian and his disciples were the creation of the Son, the denial of his co-eternity with the Father, and his immutability acquired by persistent progress and steadfastness. His doctrine, which differed from that of Paul of Samosata chiefly in the fact that it was not a man but a created heavenly being who became "Lord," was evidently the result of a combination of the teaching of Paul and of Origen. It will be seen that we have here, at least in germ, all the essential elements of Arianism proper: the creation of the Son out of nothing, and consequently the conclusion that there was a time when he was not; the distinction of his essence from that of the Father, but at the same time the emphasis upon the fact that he "was not created as the other creatures," and is therefore to be sharply distinguished from them. There was little for Arius to do but to combine the elements given by Lucian in a more complete and well-ordered system, and then to bring that system forward clearly and publicly, and endeavor to make it the faith of the Church at large. His christology was essentially opposed to the Alexandrian, and it was natural that he should soon come into conflict with that church, of which he was a presbyter (upon Lucian's teaching and its relation to Arianism, see Harnack's *Dogmengeschichte*, II. p. 183 sq.).

Socrates (*H. E.* I. 5 sq.), Sozomen (*H. E.* I. 15) and Theodoret (*H. E.* I. 2 sq.), all of whom give accounts of the rise of Arianism, differ as to the immediate occasion of the controversy, but agree that Arius was excommunicated by a council convened at Alexandria, and that both he and the bishop Alexander sent letters to other churches, the latter defending his own course, the former complaining of his harsh treatment, and endeavoring to secure adherents to his doctrine. Eusebius of Nicomedia at once became his firm supporter, and was one of the leading figures on the Arian side throughout the entire controversy. His influential position as bishop of Nicomedia, the imperial residence, and later of Constantinople, was of great advantage to the Arian cause, especially toward the close of Constantine's reign. From a letter addressed by this Eusebius to Paulinus of Tyre (Theodoret, *H. E.* I. 6) we learn that Eusebius of Cæsarea was quite zealous in behalf of the Arian cause. The exact date of the letter we do not know, but it must have been written at an early stage of the controversy. Arius himself, in an epistle addressed to Eusebius of Nicomedia (Theodoret, *H. E*, I. 5), claims Eusebius of Cæsarea among others as accepting at least one of his fundamental doctrines ("And since Eusebius, your brother in Cæsarea, and Theodotus, and Paulinus, and Athanasius, and Gregory, and Ætius, and all the bishops of the East say that God existed before the Son, they have been condemned," etc.). More than this, Sozomen (*H. E.* I. 15) informs us that Eusebius of Cæsarea and two other bishops, having been appealed to by Arius for "permission for himself and his adherents, as he had already attained the rank of presbyter, to form the people who were with them into a church," concurred with others "who were assembled in Palestine," in granting the petition of Arius, and permitting him to assemble the people as before; but they "enjoined submission to Alexander, and commanded Arius to strive incessantly to be restored to peace and communion with him." The addition of the last sentence is noticeable, as showing that they did not care to support a presbyter in open and persistent rebellion against his bishop. A fragment of a letter written by our Eusebius to Alexander is still extant, and is preserved in the proceedings of the Second Council of Nicæa, Act. VI. Tom. V. (*Labbei et Cossartii Conc.* VII. col. 497). In this epistle Eusebius strongly remonstrates with Alexander for having misrepresented the views of Arius. Still further, in his epistle to Alexander of Constantinople, Alexander of Alexandria (Theodoret, *H. E.* I. 4) complains of three Syrian bishops "who side with them [*i.e.* the Arians] and excite them to plunge deeper and deeper into iniquity." The reference here is commonly supposed to be to Eusebius of Cæsarea, and his two friends Paulinus of Tyre and Theodotus of Laodicea, who are known to have shown favor to Arius. It is probable, though not certain, that our Eusebius is one of the persons meant. Finally, many of the Fathers (above all Jerome and Photius), and in addition to them the Second Council of Nicæa, directly accuse Eusebius of holding the Arian heresy, as may be seen by examining the testimonies quoted below on p. 67 sq. In agreement with these early Fathers, many modern historians have attacked Eusebius with great severity, and have endeavored to show that the opinion that he was an Arian is supported by his own writings. Among those who have judged him most harshly are Baronius (*ad ann.* 340, c. 38 sq.), Petavius

(*Dogm. Theol. de Trin.* I. c. 11 sq.), Scaliger (*In Elencho Trihæresii,* c. 27, and *De emendatione temporum,* Bk. VI. c. 1), Mosheim (*Ecclesiastical History,* Murdock's translation, I. p. 287 sq.), Montfaucon (*Prælim. in Comment. ad Psalm.* c. VI.), and Tillemont (*H. E.* VII. p. 67 sq. 2d ed.).

On the other hand, as may be seen from the testimonies in Eusebius' favor, quoted below on p. 57 sq., many of the Fathers, who were themselves orthodox, looked upon Eusebius as likewise sound on the subject of the Trinity. He has been defended in modern times against the charge of Arianism by a great many prominent scholars ; among others by Valesius in his *Life of Eusebius,* by Bull (*Def. Fid. Nic.* II. 9. 20, III. 9. 3, 11), Cave (*Lives of the Fathers,* II. p. 135 sq.), Fabricius (*Bibl. Græc.* VI. p. 32 sq.), Dupin (*Bibl. Eccles.* II. p. 7 sq.), and most fully and carefully by Lee in his prolegomena to his edition of Eusebius' *Theophania,* p. xxiv. sq. Lightfoot also defends him against the charge of heresy, as do a great many other writers whom it is not necessary to mention here. Confronted with such diversity of opinion, both ancient and modern, what are we to conclude ? It is useless to endeavor, as Lee does, to clear Eusebius of all sympathy with and leaning toward Arianism. It is impossible to explain such widespread and continued condemnation of him by acknowledging only that there are many expressions in his works which are in themselves perfectly orthodox but capable of being wrested in such a way as to produce a suspicion of possible Arianistic tendencies, for there are such expressions in the works of multitudes of ancient writers whose orthodoxy has never been questioned. Nor can the widespread belief that he was an Arian be explained by admitting that he was for a time the personal friend of Arius, but denying that he accepted, or in any way sympathized with his views (cf. Newman's *Arians,* p. 262). There are in fact certain fragments of epistles extant, which are, to say the least, decidedly Arianistic in their modes of expression, and these must be reckoned with in forming an opinion of Eusebius' views ; for there is no reason to deny, as Lee does, that they are from Eusebius' own hand. On the other hand, to maintain, with some of the Fathers and many of the moderns, that Eusebius was and continued through life a genuine Arian, will not do in the face of the facts that contemporary and later Fathers were divided as to his orthodoxy, that he was honored highly by the Church of subsequent centuries, except at certain periods, and was even canonized (see Lightfoot's article, p. 348), that he solemnly signed the Nicene Creed, which contained an express condemnation of the distinctive doctrines of Arius, and finally that at least in his later works he is thoroughly orthodox in his expressions, and is explicit in his rejection of the two main theses of the Arians, — that there *was a time when the Son of God was not,* and that he was *produced out of nothing.* It is impossible to enter here into a detailed discussion of such passages in Eusebius' works as bear upon the subject under dispute. Lee has considered many of them at great length, and the reader may be referred to him for further information.

A careful examination of them will, I believe, serve to convince the candid student that there is a distinction to be drawn between those works written before the rise of Arius, those written between that time and the Council of Nicæa, and those written after the latter. It has been very common to draw a distinction between those works written before and those written after the Council, but no one, so far as I know, has distinguished those productions of Eusebius' pen which appeared between 318 and 325, and which were caused by the controversy itself, from all his other writings. And yet such a distinction seems to furnish the key to the problem. Eusebius' opponents have drawn their strongest arguments from the epistles which Eusebius wrote to Alexander and to Euphration ; his defenders have drawn their arguments chiefly from the works which he produced subsequent to the year 325 ; while the exact bearing of the expressions used in his works produced before the controversy broke out has always been a matter of sharp dispute. Lee has abundantly shown his *Contra Marcel.,* his *De Eccl. Theol.,* his *Theophania* (which was written after the Council of Nicæa, and not, as Lee supposes, before it), and other later works, to be thoroughly orthodox and to contain nothing which a trinitarian might not have written. In his *Hist. Eccl., Præparatio Evang., Demonstratio Evang.,* and other earlier works, although we find some expressions employed which it would not have been possible for an orthodox trinitarian to use after the Council of Nicæa, at least without careful limitation to guard against misapprehension, there is nothing even in these works which requires us to believe that he accepted the doctrines of Arius' predecessor, Lucian of Antioch; that is, there is nothing distinctly and positively Arianistic about them, although there are occasional expressions which might lead the reader to expect that the writer would become an Arian if he ever learned of Arius' doctrines. But if there is seen to be a lack of emphasis upon the divinity of the Son, or rather a lack of clearness in the conception of the nature of that divinity, it must be remembered that there was at this time no especial reason for emphasizing and defining it, but there was on the contrary very good reason for laying particular stress upon the subordination of the Son over against Sabellianism, which was so widely prevalent during the third century, and which was exerting an influence even over many orthodox theologians who did not consciously accept Sabellianistic tenets. That Eusebius was a decided subordinationist must be plain to every one that reads his works with care, especially his earlier ones. It would be surprising if he had not been, for he was born at a time when Sabellianism (monarchianism) was felt to be the greatest danger to which orthodox christology was exposed, and he was trained under the influence of the followers of Origen, who had made it one of his chief aims to emphasize the subordination of the Son over against that very monarchianism.[1] The same subordinationism may be clearly seen in the writings of Dionysius of Alexandria and of Gregory Thaumaturgus, two of Origen's greatest disciples. It must not be forgotten that at the beginning of the fourth century the problem of how to preserve the Godhood of Christ and at the same time his subordination to the Father (in opposition to the monarchianists) had not been solved. Eusebius in his earlier writings shows that he holds both (he cannot be convicted of denying Christ's divinity), but that he is as far from a solution of the problem, and is just as uncertain in regard to the exact relation of Father and Son, as Tertullian, Hippolytus, Origen, Dionysius, and Gregory Thaumaturgus were; is just as inconsistent in his modes of expression as they, and yet no more so (see Harnack's *Dogmengeschichte*, I. pp. 628 sq. and 634 sq., for an exposition of the opinions of these other Fathers on the subject). Eusebius, with the same immature and undeveloped views which were held all through the third century, wrote those earlier works which have given rise to so much dispute between those who accuse him of Arianism and those who defend him against the charge. When he wrote them he was neither Arian nor Athanasian, and for that reason passages may be found in them which if written after the Council of Nicaea might prove him an Arian, and other passages which might as truly prove him an Athanasian, just as in the writings of Origen were found by both parties passages to support their views, and in Gregory Thaumaturgus passages apparently teaching Arianism, and others teaching its opposite, Sabellianism (see Harnack, *ib.* p. 646).

Let us suppose now that Eusebius, holding fast to the divinity of Christ, and yet convinced just as firmly of his subordination to the Father, becomes acquainted through Arius, or other like-minded disciples of Lucian of Antioch, with a doctrine which seems to preserve the Godhood, while at the same time emphasizing strongly the subordination of the Son, and which formulates the relation of Father and Son in a clear and rational manner. That he should accept such a doctrine eagerly is just what we should expect, and just what we find him doing. In his epistles to Alexander and Euphration, he shows himself an Arian, and Arius and his followers were quite

---

[1] It is interesting to notice that the creed of the Cæsarean church which Eusebius presented at the Council of Nice contains a clause which certainly looks as if it had been composed in opposition to the familiar formula of the Sabellians: "The same one is the Father, the same one the Son, the same one the Holy Spirit"(τὸν αὐτὸν εἶναι πατέρα, τὸν αὐτὸν εἶναι υἱὸν, τὸν αὐτὸν εἶναι ἅγιον πνεῦμα; see Epiphan. *Hær.* LXII. 1; and compare the statement made in the same section, that the Sabellians taught that God acts in three forms: in the form of the Father, as creator and law-giver; in the form of the Son, as redeemer; and in the form of the Spirit, as life-giver, etc.). The clause of the Cæsarean creed referred to runs as follows: "That the Father is truly Father, the Son truly Son, and the Holy Spirit truly Holy Spirit" (πατέρα ἀληθῶς πατέρα, καὶ υἱὸν ἀληθῶς υἱὸν, καὶ πνεῦμα ἅγιον ἀληθῶς ἅγιον). It is significant that in the revised creed adopted by the Council these words are omitted, evidently because the occasion for them no longer existed, since not Sabellianism but Arianism was the heresy combated; and because, more than that, the use of them would but weaken the emphasis which the Council wished to put upon the essential divinity of all three persons.

right in claiming him as a supporter. There is that in the epistles which is to be found nowhere in his previous writings, and which distinctly separates him from the orthodox party. How then are we to explain the fact that a few years later he signed the Nicene creed and anathematized the doctrines of Arius? Before we can understand his conduct, it is necessary to examine carefully the two epistles in question. Such an examination will show us that what Eusebius is defending in them is not genuine Arianism. He evidently thinks that it is, evidently supposes that he and Arius are in complete agreement upon the subjects under discussion; but he is mistaken. The extant fragments of the two epistles are given below on p. 70. It will be seen that Eusebius in them defends the Arian doctrine that there was a time when the Son of God was not. It will be seen also that he finds fault with Alexander for representing the Arians as teaching that the "Son of God was made out of nothing, like all creatures," and contends that Arius teaches that the Son of God was *begotten*, and that he was not produced like all creatures. We know that the Arians very commonly applied the word "begotten" to Christ, using it in such cases as synonymous with "created," and thus not implying, as the Athanasians did when they used the word, that he was of one substance with the Father (compare, for instance, the explanation of the meaning of the term given by Eusebius of Nicomedia in his epistle to Paulinus; Theod. *H. E.* I. 6). It is evident that the use of this word had deceived our Eusebius, and that he was led by it to think that they taught that the Son was of the Father in a peculiar sense, and did in reality partake in some way of essential Godhood. And indeed it is not at all surprising that the words of Arius, in his epistle to Alexander of Alexandria (see Athan. *Ep. de conc. Arim. et Seleuc.*, chap. II. § 3; Oxford edition of Athanasius' *Tracts against Arianism*, p. 97), quoted by Eusebius in his epistle to the same Alexander, should give Eusebius that impression. The words are as follows: "The God of the law, and of the prophets, and of the New Testament before eternal ages begat an only-begotten Son, through whom also He made the ages and the universe. And He begat him not in appearance, but in truth, and subjected him to his own will, unchangeable and immutable, a perfect creature of God, but not as one of the creatures." Arius' use here of the word "begat," and his qualification of the word "creature" by the adjective "perfect," and by the statement that he was "not as one of the creatures" naturally tended to make Eusebius think that Arius acknowledged a real divinity of the Son, and that appeared to him to be all that was necessary. Meanwhile Alexander in his epistle to Alexander of Constantinople (Theod. *H. E.* I. 4) had, as Eusebius says, misstated Arius' opinion, or at least had attributed to him the belief that Christ was "made like all other men that have ever been born," whereas Arius expressly disclaims such a belief. Alexander undoubtedly thought that that was the legitimate result to which the other views of Arius must lead; but Eusebius did not think so, and felt himself called upon to remonstrate with Alexander for what seemed to him the latter's unfairness in the matter.

When we examine the Cæsarean creed[1] which Eusebius presented to the Council as a fair statement of his belief, we find nothing in it inconsistent with the acceptance of the kind of Arianism which he defends in his epistle to Alexander, and which he evidently supposed to be practically the Arianism of Arius himself. In his epistle to Euphration, however, Eusebius seems at first glance to go further and to give up the real divinity of the Son. His words are, "Since the Son is himself God, but not true God." But we have no right to interpret these words, torn as they are from the context which might make their meaning perfectly plain, without due regard to Eusebius' belief expressed elsewhere in this epistle, and in his epistle to Alexander which was evidently written about the same time. In the epistle to Alexander he clearly reveals a belief in the real divinity of the Son, while in the other fragment of his epistle to Euphration he dwells upon the subordination of the Son and approves the Arian opinion, which he had defended also in the other epistle, that the "Father was before the Son." The expression, "not true God" (a very common Arian expression; see Athan. *Orat. c. Arian.* I. 6) seems therefore to have been

---

[1] For a translation of the creed see below, p. 16, where it is given as a part of Eusebius' epistle to the Church of Cæsarea.

used by Eusebius to express a belief, not that the Son did not possess real divinity (as the genuine Arians used it), but that he was not equal to the Father, who, to Eusebius' thought, was "true God." He indeed expressly calls the Son θεός, which shows — when the sense in which he else-where uses the word is considered — that he certainly did believe him to partake of Godhood, though, in some mysterious way, in a smaller degree, or in a less complete manner than the Father. That Eusebius misunderstood Arius, and did not perceive that he actually denied all real deity to the Son, was due doubtless in part to his lack of theological insight (Eusebius was never a great theologian), in part to his habitual dread of Sabellianism (of which Arius had accused Alexander, and toward which Eusebius evidently thought that the latter was tending), which led him to look with great favor upon the pronounced subordinationism of Arius, and thus to overlook the dangerous extreme to which Arius carried that subordinationism.

We are now, the writer hopes, prepared to admit that Eusebius, after the breaking out of the Arian controversy, became an Arian, as he understood Arianism, and supported that party with considerable vigor; and that not as a result of mere personal friendship, but of theological conviction. At the same time, he was then, as always, a peace-loving man, and while lending Arius his approval and support, he united with other Palestinian bishops in enjoining upon him submission to his bishop (Sozomen, *H. E.* I. 15). As an Arian, then, and yet possessed with the desire of securing, if it were possible, peace and harmony between the two factions, Eusebius appeared at the Council of Nicæa, and there signed a creed containing Athanasian doctrine and anathematizing the chief tenets of Arius. How are we to explain his conduct? We shall, perhaps, do best to let him explain his own conduct. In his letter to the church of Cæsarea (preserved by Socrates, *H. E.* I. 8, as well as by other authors), he writes as follows: —

"What was transacted concerning ecclesiastical faith at the Great Council assembled at Nicæa you have probably learned, Beloved, from other sources, rumour being wont to precede the accurate account of what is doing. But lest in such reports the circumstances of the case have been misrepresented, we have been obliged to transmit to you, first, the formula of faith presented by ourselves; and next, the second, which the Fathers put forth with some additions to our words. Our own paper, then, which was read in the presence of our most pious Emperor, and declared to be good and unexceptionable, ran thus: —

"'As we have received from the Bishops who preceded us, and in our first catechisings, and when we received the Holy Laver, and as we have learned from the divine Scriptures, and as we believed and taught in the presbytery, and in the Episcopate itself, so believing also at the time present, we report to you our faith, and it is this: —

"'We believe in One God, the Father Almighty, the Maker of all things visible and invisible. And in One Lord Jesus Christ, the Word of God, God from God, Light from Light, Life from Life, Son Only-begotten, first-born of every creature, before all the ages, begotten from the Father, by whom also all things were made; who for our salvation was made flesh, and lived among men, and suffered, and rose again the third day, and ascended to the Father, and will come again in glory to judge quick and dead. And we believe also in One Holy Ghost; believing each of These to be and to exist, the Father truly Father, and the Son truly Son, and the Holy Ghost truly Holy Ghost, as also our Lord, sending forth His disciples for the preaching, said, *Go, teach all nations, baptizing them in the Name of the Father, and of the Son, and of the Holy Ghost.* Concerning whom we confidently affirm that so we hold, and so we think, and so we have held aforetime, and we maintain this faith unto the death, anathematizing every godless heresy. That this we have ever thought from our heart and soul, from the time we recollect ourselves, and now think and say in truth, before God Almighty and our Lord Jesus Christ do we witness, being able by proofs to show and to convince you, that, even in times past, such has been our belief and preaching.'

"On this faith being publicly put forth by us, no room for contradiction appeared; but our most pious Emperor, before any one else, testified that it comprised most orthodox statements. He confessed, moreover, that such were his own sentiments; and he advised all present to agree to it, and to subscribe its articles and to assent to them, with the insertion of the single word, 'One in substance' (ὁμοούσιος), which, moreover, he interpreted as not in the sense of the affections of bodies, nor as if the Son subsisted from the Father, in the way of division, or any severance; for that the immaterial and intellectual and incorporeal nature could not be the subject of any corporeal affection, but that it became us to conceive of such things in a divine and ineffable manner. And such were the theological remarks of our most wise and most religious Emperor; but they, with a view to the addition of 'One in substance,' drew up the following formula :—

"' We believe in One God, the Father Almighty, Maker of all things visible and invisible:— And in One Lord Jesus Christ, the Son of God, begotten of the Father, Only-begotten, that is, from the Substance of the Father; God from God, Light from Light, very God from very God, begotten, not made, One in substance with the Father, by whom all things were made, both things in heaven and things in earth; who for us men and for our salvation came down and was made flesh, was made man, suffered, and rose again the third day, ascended into heaven, and cometh to judge quick and dead.

"' And in the Holy Ghost. But those who say, "Once He was not," and "Before His generation He was not," and "He came to be from nothing," or those who pretend that the Son of God is "Of other subsistence or substance," or "created," or "alterable," or "mutable," the Catholic Church anathematizes.'

"On their dictating this formula, we did not let it pass without inquiry in what sense they introduced 'of the substance of the Father,' and 'one in substance with the Father.' Accordingly questions and explanations took place, and the meaning of the words underwent the scrutiny of reason. And they professed that the phrase 'of the substance' was indicative of the Son's being indeed from the Father, yet without being as if a part of Him. And with this understanding we thought good to assent to the sense of such religious doctrine, teaching, as it did, that the Son was from the Father, not, however, a part of His substance. On this account we assented to the sense ourselves, without declining even the term 'One in substance,' peace being the object which we set before us, and steadfastness in the orthodox view. In the same way we also admitted 'begotten, not made'; since the Council alleged that 'made' was an appellative common to the other creatures which came to be through the Son, to whom the Son had no likeness. Wherefore, said they, He was not a work resembling the things which through Him came to be, but was of a substance which is too high for the level of any work, and which the Divine oracles teach to have been generated from the Father, the mode of generation being inscrutable and incalculable to every generated nature. And so, too, on examination there are grounds for saying that the Son is 'one in substance' with the Father; not in the way of bodies, nor like mortal beings, for He is not such by division of substance, or by severance; no, nor by any affection, or alteration, or changing of the Father's substance and power (since from all such the ingenerate nature of the Father is alien), but because 'one in substance with the Father' suggests that the Son of God bears no resemblance to the generated creatures, but that to His Father alone who begat Him is He in every way assimilated, and that He is not of any other subsistence and substance, but from the Father.

"To which term also, thus interpreted, it appeared well to assent; since we were aware that, even among the ancients, some learned and illustrious Bishops and writers have used the term 'one in substance' in their theological teaching concerning the Father and Son. So much, then, be said concerning the faith which was published; to which all of us assented, not without inquiry, but according to the specified senses, mentioned before the most religious Emperor himself, and justified by the fore-mentioned considerations. And as to the anathematism published by them at the end of the Faith, it did not pain us, because it forbade to use words not in Scripture, from which almost all the confusion and disorder of the Church have come. Since, then, no divinely inspired Scripture has used the phrases, 'out of nothing' and 'once He was not,' and the rest which follow, there appeared no ground for using or teaching them; to which also we assented as a good decision, since it had not been our custom hitherto to use these terms. Moreover, to anathematize 'Before His generation He was not' did not seem preposterous, in that it is confessed by all that the Son of God was before the generation according to the flesh. Nay, our most religious Emperor did at the time prove, in a speech, that He was in being even according to His divine generation which is before all ages, since even before he was generated in energy, He was in virtue with the Father ingenerately, the Father being always Father, as King always and Saviour always, having all things in virtue, and being always in the same respects and in the same way. This we have been forced to transmit to you, Beloved, as making clear to you the deliberation of our inquiry and assent, and how reasonably we resisted even to the last minute, as long as we were offended at statements which differed from our own, but received without contention what no longer pained us, as soon as, on a candid examination of the sense of the words, they appeared to us to coincide with what we ourselves have professed in the faith which we have already published." [1]

It will be seen that while the expressions "of the substance of the Father," "begotten, not made," and "One in substance," or "consubstantial with the Father," are all explicitly anti-Arianistic, yet none of them contradicts the doctrines held by Eusebius before the Council, so far as we can learn them from his epistles to Alexander and Euphration and from the Cæsarean creed. His own explanation of those expressions, which it is to be observed was the explanation given by the Council itself, and which therefore he was fully warranted in accepting, — even though it may not have been so rigid as to satisfy an Athanasius, — shows us how this is. He had believed before that the Son partook of the Godhood in very truth, that He was "begotten," and therefore "not made," if "made" implied something different from "begotten," as the Nicene Fathers held that it did ; and he had believed before that the "Son of God has no resemblance to created things, but is in every respect like the Father only who begat him, and that He is of no other substance or essence than the Father," and therefore if that was what the word "Consubstantial" (ὁμοούσιος) meant he could not do otherwise than accept that too.

It is clear that the dread of Sabellianism was still before the eyes of Eusebius, and was the cause of his hesitation in assenting to the various changes, especially to the use of the word ὁμοούσιος, which had been a Sabellian word and had been rejected on that account by the Synod of Antioch, at which Paul of Samosata had been condemned some sixty years before.

It still remains to explain Eusebius' sanction of the anathemas attached to the creed which expressly condemn at least one of the beliefs which he had himself formerly held, viz. : that the "Father was before the Son," or as he puts it elsewhere, that "He who is begat him who was not." The knot might of course be simply cut by supposing an act of hypocrisy on his part, but the writer is convinced that such a conclusion does violence to all that we know of Eusebius and of his subsequent treatment of the questions involved in this discussion. It is quite possible to suppose that a real change of opinion on his part took place during the sessions of the Council. Indeed when we realize how imperfect and incorrect a conception of Arianism he had before the Council began, and how clearly its true bearing was there brought out by its enemies, we can see that he could not do otherwise than change ; that he must have become either an out-and-out Arian, or an opponent of Arianism as he did. When he learned, and learned for the first time, that Arianism meant the denial of all essential divinity to Christ, and when he saw that it involved the ascription of mutability and of other finite attributes to him, he must either change entirely his views on those points or he must leave the Arian party. To him who with all his subordinationism had laid in all his writings so much stress on the divinity of the Word (even though he had not realized exactly what that divinity involved) it would have been a revolution in his Christian life and faith to have admitted what he now learned that Arianism involved. Sabellianism had been his dread, but now this new fear, which had aroused so large a portion of the Church, seized him too, and he felt that stand must be made against this too great separation of Father and Son, which was leading to dangerous results. Under the pressure of this fear it is not surprising that he should become convinced that the Arian formula—"there was a time when the Son was not"—involved serious consequences, and that Alexander and his followers should have succeeded in pointing out to him its untruth, because it led necessarily to a false conclusion. It is not surprising, moreover, that they should have succeeded in explaining to him at least

---

[1] The translation is that of Newman, as given in the Oxford edition of Athanasius' *Select Treatises against Arianism*, p. 59 sq.

partially their belief, which, as his epistle to Alexander shows, had before been absolutely incomprehensible, that the Son was generated from all eternity, and that therefore the Father did not exist before him in a temporal sense.

He says toward the close of his epistle to the Cæsarean church that he had not been accustomed to use such expressions as "There was a time when he was not," "He came to be from nothing," etc. And there is no reason to doubt that he speaks the truth. Even in his epistles to Alexander and Euphration he does not use those phrases (though he does defend the doctrine taught by the first of them), nor does Arius himself, in the epistle to Alexander upon which Eusebius apparently based his knowledge of the system, use those expressions, although he too teaches the same doctrine. The fact is that in that epistle Arius studiously avoids such favorite Arian phrases as might emphasize the differences between himself and Alexander, and Eusebius seems to have avoided them for the same reason. We conclude then that Eusebius was not an Arian (nor an adherent of Lucian) before 318, that soon after that date he became an Arian in the sense in which he understood Arianism, but that during the Council of Nicæa he ceased to be one in any sense. His writings in later years confirm the course of doctrinal development which we have supposed went on in his mind. He never again defends Arian doctrines in his works, and yet he never becomes an Athanasian in his emphasis upon the ὁμοούσιον. In fact he represents a mild orthodoxy, which is always orthodox — when measured by the Nicene creed as interpreted by the Nicene Council — and yet is always mild. Moreover, he never acquired an affection for the word ὁμοούσιος, which to his mind was bound up with too many evil associations ever to have a pleasant sound to him. He therefore studiously avoided it in his own writings, although clearly showing that he believed fully in what the Nicene Council had explained it to mean. It must be remembered that during many years of his later life he was engaged in controversy with Marcellus, a thorough-going Sabellian, who had been at the time of the Council one of the strongest of Athanasius' colleagues. In his contest with him it was again anti-Sabellianistic polemics which absorbed him and increased his distaste for ὁμοούσιον and minimized his emphasis upon the distinctively anti-Arianistic doctrines formulated at Nicæa. For any except the very wisest minds it was a matter of enormous difficulty to steer between the two extremes in those times of strife ; and while combating Sabellianism not to fall into Arianism, and while combating the latter not to be engulfed in the former. That Eusebius under the constant pressure of the one fell into the other at one time, and was in occasional danger of falling into it again in later years, can hardly be cited as an evidence either of wrong heart or of weak head. An Athanasius he was not, but neither was he an unsteady weather-cock, or an hypocritical time-server.

§ 6. The Council of Nicæa.

At the Council of Nicæa, which met pursuant to an imperial summons in the year 325 A.D., Eusebius played a very prominent part. A description of the opening scenes of the Council is given in his *Vita Constantini*, III. 10 sq. After the Emperor had entered in pomp and had taken his seat, a bishop who sat next to him upon his right arose and delivered in his honor the opening oration, to which the Emperor replied in a brief Latin address. There can be no doubt that this bishop was our Eusebius. Sozomen (*H. E.* I. 19) states it directly ; and Eusebius, although he does not name the speaker, yet refers to him, as he had referred to the orator at the dedication of Paulinus' church at Tyre, in such a way as to make it clear that it was himself ; and moreover in his *Vita Constantini*, I. 1, he mentions the fact that he had in the midst of an assembly of the servants of God addressed an oration to the Emperor on the occasion of the latter's *vicennalia*, i.e. in 325 A.D. On the other hand, however, Theodoret (*H. E.* I. 7) states that this opening oration was delivered by Eustathius, bishop of Antioch ; while Theodore of Mopsuestia and Philostorgius (according to Nicetas Choniates, *Thes. de orthod. fid.* V. 7) assign it to Alexander of Alexandria. As Lightfoot suggests, it is possible to explain the discrepancy in the reports by supposing that Eustathius and Alexander, the two great patriarchs, first addressed a few words to the Emperor and that then Eusebius delivered the regular oration. This supposition is not at all unlikely, for it would be quite proper for the two highest ecclesiastics present to welcome the Emperor formally in behalf of the assembled prelates, before the regular oration was delivered by Eusebius. At the same time, the supposition that one or the other of the two great patriarchs must have delivered the opening address was such a natural one that it may have been adopted by Theodoret and the other writers referred to without any historical basis. It is in any case certain that the regular oration was delivered by Eusebius himself (see the convincing arguments adduced by Stroth, p. xxvii. sq.). This oration is no longer extant, but an idea of its character may be formed from the address delivered by Eusebius at the Emperor's *tricennalia* (which is still extant under the title *De laudibus Constantini;* see below, p. 43) and from the general tone of his Life of Constantine. It was avowedly a panegyric, and undoubtedly as fulsome as it was possible to make it, and his powers in that direction were by no means slight.

That Eusebius, instead of the bishop of some more prominent church, should have been selected to deliver the opening address, may have been in part owing to his recognized standing as the most learned man and the most famous writer in the Church, in part to the fact that he was not as pronounced a partisan as some of his distinguished brethren; for instance, Alexander of Alexandria, and Eusebius of Nicomedia; and finally in some measure to his intimate relations with the Emperor. How and when his intimacy with the latter grew up we do not know. As already remarked, he seems to have become personally acquainted with him many years before, when Constantine passed through Cæsarea in the train of Diocletian, and it may be that a mutual friendship, which was so marked in later years, began at that time. However that may be, Eusebius seems to have possessed special advantages of one kind or another, enabling him to come into personal contact with official circles, and once introduced to imperial notice, his wide learning, sound common sense, genial temper and broad charity would insure him the friendship of the Emperor himself, or of any other worthy officer of state. We have no record of an intimacy between Constantine and Eusebius before the Council of Nicæa, but many clear intimations of it after that time. In fact, it is evident that during the last decade at least of the Emperor's life, few, if any, bishops stood higher in his esteem or enjoyed a larger measure of his confidence. Compare for instance the records of their conversations (contained in the *Vita Constantini,* I. 28 and II. 9), of their correspondence (*ib.* II. 46, III. 61, IV. 35 and 36), and the words of Constantine himself (*ib.* III. 60). The marked attention paid by him to the speeches delivered by Eusebius in his presence (*ib.* IV. 33 and 46) is also to be noticed. Eusebius' intimacy with the imperial family is shown likewise in the tone of the letter which he wrote to Constantia, the sister of Constantine and wife of Licinius, in regard to a likeness of Christ which she had asked him to send her. The frankness and freedom with which he remonstrates with her for what he considers mistaken zeal on her part, reveal a degree of familiarity which could have come only from long and cordial relations between himself and his royal correspondent. Whatever other reasons therefore may have combined to indicate Eusebius as the most fitting person to deliver the oration in honor of the Emperor at the Council of Nicæa, there can be little doubt that Constantine's personal friendship for him had much to do with his selection. The action of the Council on the subject of Arianism, and Eusebius' conduct in the matter, have already been discussed. Of the bishops assembled at the Council, not far from three hundred in number (the reports of eye-witnesses vary from two hundred and fifty to three hundred and eighteen), all but two signed the Nicene creed as adopted by the Council. These two, both of them Egyptians, were banished with Arius to Illyria, while Eusebius of Nicomedia, and Theognis of Nicæa, who subscribed the creed itself but refused to assent to its anathemas, were also banished for a time, but soon yielded, and were restored to their churches.

Into the other purposes for which the Nicene Council was called,—the settlement of the dispute respecting the time of observing Easter and the healing of the Meletian schism,—it is not necessary to enter here. We have no record of the part which Eusebius took in these transactions. Lightfoot has abundantly shown (p. 313 sq.) that the common supposition that Eusebius was the author of the paschal cycle of nineteen years is false, and that there is no reason to suppose that he had anything particular to do with the decision of the paschal question at this Council.

§ 7. *Continuance of the Arian Controversy. Eusebius' Relations to the Two Parties.*

The Council of Nicæa did not bring the Arian controversy to an end. The orthodox party was victorious, it is true, but the Arians were still determined, and could not give up their enmity against the opponents of Arius, and their hope that they might in the end turn the tables on their antagonists. Meanwhile, within a few years after the Council, a quarrel broke out between our Eusebius and Eustathius, bishop of Antioch, a resolute supporter of Nicene orthodoxy. According to Socrates (*H. E.* I. 23) and Sozomen (*H. E.* II. 18) Eustathius accused Eusebius of perverting the Nicene doctrines, while Eusebius denied the charge, and in turn taxed Eustathius with Sabellianism. The quarrel finally became so serious that it was deemed necessary to summon a Council for the investigation of Eustathius' orthodoxy and the settlement of the dispute. This Council met in Antioch in 330 A.D. (see Tillemont, VII. p. 651 sq., for a discussion of the date), and was made up chiefly of bishops of Arian or semi-Arian tendencies. This fact, however, brings no discredit upon Eusebius. The Council was held in another province, and he can have had nothing to do with its composition. In fact, convened, as it was, in Eustathius' own city, it must have been legally organized ; and indeed Eustathius himself acknowledged its jurisdiction by appearing before it to answer the charges made against him. Theodoret's absurd account of the origin of the synod and of the accusations brought against Eustathius (*H. E.* I. 21) bears upon its face the stamp of falsehood, and is, as Hefele has shown (*Conciliengeschichte*, I. 451), hopelessly in error in its chronology. It is therefore to be rejected as quite worthless. The decision of the Council doubtless fairly represented the views of the majority of the bishops of that section, for we know that Arianism had a very strong hold there. To think of a packed Council and of illegal methods of procedure in procuring the verdict against Eustathius is both unnecessary and unwarrantable. The result of the Council was the deposition of Eustathius from his bishopric and his banishment by the Emperor to Illyria, where he afterward died. There is a division of opinion among our sources in regard to the immediate successor of Eustathius. All of them agree that Eusebius was asked to become bishop of Antioch, but that he refused the honor, and that Euphronius was chosen in his stead. Socrates and Sozomen, however, inform us that the election of Eusebius took place immediately after the deposition of Eustathius, while Theodoret (*H. E.* I. 22) names Eulalius as Eustathius' immediate successor, and states that he lived but a short time, and that Eusebius was then asked to succeed him. Theodoret is supported by Jerome (*Chron.*, year of Abr. 2345) and by Philostorgius (*H. E.* III. 15), both of whom insert a bishop Eulalius between Eustathius and Euphronius. It is easier to suppose that Socrates and Sozomen may have omitted so unimportant a name at this point than that the other three witnesses inserted it without warrant. Socrates indeed implies in the same chapter that his knowledge of these affairs is limited, and it is not surprising that Eusebius' election, which caused a great stir, should have been connected in the mind of later writers immediately with Eustathius' deposition, and the intermediate steps forgotten. It seems probable, therefore, that immediately after the condemnation of Eustathius, Eulalius was appointed in his place, perhaps by the same Council, and that after his death, a few months later, Eusebius, who had meanwhile gone back to Cæsarea, was elected in due order by another Council of neighboring bishops summoned for the purpose, and that he was supported by a large party of citizens. It is noticeable that the letter written by the Emperor to the Council, which wished to transfer Eusebius to Antioch (see *Vita Const.* III. 62), mentions in its salutation the names of five bishops, but among them is only one (Theodotus who is elsewhere named as present at the Council which deposed Eustathius, while Eusebius of Nicomedia, and Theognis of Nicæa, as well as others whom we know to have been on hand on that occasion, are not referred to by the Emperor. This fact certainly seems to point to a different council.

It is greatly to Eusebius' credit that he refused the call extended to him. Had he been governed simply by selfish ambition he would certainly have accepted it, for the patriarchate of Antioch stood at that time next to Alexandria in point of honor in the Eastern Church. The Emperor commended him very highly for his decision, in his epistles to the people of Antioch and to the Council (*Vita Const.* III. 60, 62), and in that to Eusebius himself (*ib.* III. 61). He saw in it a desire on Eusebius' part to observe the ancient canon of the Church, which forbade the transfer of a bishop from one see to another. But that in itself can hardly have been sufficient to deter the latter from accepting the high honor offered him, for it was broken without scruple on all sides. It is more probable that he saw that the schism of the Antiochenes would be embittered by the induction into the bishopric of that church of Eustathius' chief opponent, and that he did not feel that he had a right so to divide the Church of God. Eusebius' general character, as known to us, justifies us in supposing that this high motive had much to do with his decision. We may suppose also that so difficult a place can have had no very great attractions for a man of his age and of his peace-loving disposition and scholarly tastes. In Cæsarea he had spent his life ; there he had the great library of Pamphilus at his disposal, and leisure to pursue his literary work. In Antioch he would have found himself compelled to plunge into the midst of quarrels and seditions of all kinds, and would have been obliged to devote his entire·attention to the performance of his official duties. His own tastes therefore must have conspired with his sense of duty to lead him to reject the proffered call and to remain in the somewhat humbler station which he already occupied.

Not long after the deposition of Eustathius, the Arians and their sympathizers began to work more energetically to accomplish the ruin of Athanasius, their greatest foe. He had become Alexander's successor as bishop of Alexandria in the year 326, and was the acknowledged head of the orthodox party. If he could be brought into discredit, there might be hopes of restoring Arius to his position in Alexandria, and of securing for Arianism a recognition, and finally a dominating influence in the church at large. To the overthrow of Athanasius therefore all good Arians bent their energies. They found ready accomplices in the schismatical Meletians of Egypt, who were bitter enemies of the orthodox church of Alexandria. It was useless to accuse Athanasius of heterodoxy ; he was too widely known as the pillar of the orthodox faith. Charges must be framed of another sort, and of a sort to stir up the anger of the Emperor against him. The Arians therefore and the Meletians began to spread the most vile and at the same time absurd stories about Athanasius (see especially the latter's *Apol. c. Arian.* § 59 sq.). These at last became so notorious that the Emperor summoned Athanasius to appear and make his defense before a council of bishops to be held in Cæsarea (Sozomen, *H. E.* II. 25 ; Theodoret, *H. E.* I. 28). Athanasius, however, fearing that the Council would be composed wholly of his enemies, and that it would therefore be impossible to secure fair play, excused himself and remained away. But in the following year (see Sozomen, *H. E.* II. 25) he received from the Emperor a summons to appear before a council at Tyre. The summons was too peremptory to admit of a refusal, and Athanasius therefore attended, accompanied by many of his devoted adherents (see Sozomen, *ib.;* Theodoret, *H. E.* I. 30 ; Socrates, *H. E.* I. 28 ; Athanasius, *Apol. c. Arian.* § 71 sq. ; Eusebius, *Vita Const.* IV. 41 sq., and Epiphanius, *Hær.* LXVIII. 8). After a time, perceiving that he had no chance of receiving fair play, he suddenly withdrew from the Council and proceeded directly to Constantinople, in order to lay his case before the Emperor himself, and to induce the latter to allow him to meet his accusers in his presence, and plead his cause before him. There was nothing for the Synod to do after his flight but to sustain the charges brought against him, some of which he had not stayed to refute, and to pass condemnation upon him. Besides various immoral and sacrilegious deeds of which he was accused, his refusal to appear before the Council of

Cæsarea the previous year was made an important item of the prosecution. It was during this Council that Potamo flung at Eusebius the taunt of cowardice, to which reference was made above, and which doubtless did much to confirm Eusebius' distrust of and hostility to the Athanasian party. Whether Eusebius of Cæsarea, as is commonly supposed, or Eusebius of Nicomedia, or some other bishop, presided at this Council we are not able to determine. The account of Epiphanius seems to imply that the former was presiding at the time that Potamo made his untimely accusation. Our sources are, most of them, silent on the matter, but according to Valesius, Eusebius of Nicomedia is named by some of them, but which they are I have not been able to discover. We learn from Socrates (*H. E.* I. 28), as well as from other sources, that this Synod of Tyre was held in the thirtieth year of Constantine's reign, that is, between July, 334, and July, 335. As the Council was closed only in time for the bishops to reach Jerusalem by July, 335, it is probable that it was convened in 335 rather than in 334. From Sozomen (*H. E.* II. 25) we learn also that the Synod of Cæsarea had been held the preceding year, therefore in 333 or 334 (the latter being the date commonly given by historians). While the Council of Tyre was still in session, the bishops were commanded by Constantine to proceed immediately to Jerusalem to take part in the approaching festival to be held there on the occasion of his *tricennalia.* The scene was one of great splendor. Bishops were present from all parts of the world, and the occasion was marked by the dedication of the new and magnificent basilica which Constantine had erected upon the site of Calvary (Theodoret, I. 31 ; Socrates, I. 28 and 33 ; Sozomen, II. 26 ; Eusebius, *Vita Const.* IV. 41 and 43). The bishops gathered in Jerusalem at this time held another synod before separating. In this they completed the work begun at Tyre, by re-admitting Arius and his adherents to the communion of the Church (see Socrates, I. 33 and Sozomen, II. 27). According to Sozomen the Emperor, having been induced to recall Arius from banishment in order to reconsider his case, was presented by the latter with a confession of faith, which was so worded as to convince Constantine of his orthodoxy. He therefore sent Arius and his companion Euzoius to the bishops assembled in Jerusalem with the request that they would examine the confession, and if they were satisfied with its orthodoxy would re-admit them to communion. The Council, which was composed largely of Arius' friends and sympathizers, was only too glad to accede to the Emperor's request.

Meanwhile Athanasius had induced Constantine, out of a sense of justice, to summon the bishops that had condemned him at Tyre to give an account of their proceedings before the Emperor himself at Constantinople. This unexpected, and, doubtless, not altogether welcome summons came while the bishops were at Jerusalem, and the majority of them at once returned home in alarm, while only a few answered the call and repaired to Constantinople. Among these were Eusebius of Nicomedia, Theognis of Nicæa, Patrophilus of Scythopolis, and other prominent Arians, and with them our Eusebius (Athanasius, *Apol. c. Arian.* §§ 86 and 87 ; Socrates, I. 33–35 ; Sozomen, II. 28). The accusers of Athanasius said nothing on this occasion in regard to his alleged immoralities, for which he had been condemned at Tyre, but made another equally trivial accusation against him, and the result was his banishment to Gaul. Whether Constantine banished him because he believed the charge brought against him, or because he wished to preserve him from the machinations of his enemies (as asserted by his son Constantine, and apparently believed by Athanasius himself; see his *Apol. c. Arian.* § 87), or because he thought that Athanasius' absence would allay the troubles in the Alexandrian church we do not know. The latter supposition seems most probable. In any case he was not recalled from banishment until after Constantine's death. Our Eusebius has been severely condemned by many historians for the part taken by him in the Eustathian controversy and especially in the war against Athanasius. In justice to him a word or two must be spoken in his defense. So far as his relations to Eustathius are concerned, it is to be noticed that the latter commenced the controversy by accusing Eusebius of heterodoxy. Eusebius himself did not begin the quarrel, and very likely had no desire to engage in any such doctrinal strife ; but he was compelled to defend himself, and in doing so he could not do otherwise than accuse Eustathius of Sabellianism; for if the latter was not satisfied with Eusebius' orthodoxy, which Eusebius himself believed to be truly Nicene, then he must be leaning too far toward the other extreme; that is, toward Sabellianism. There is no reason to doubt that Eusebius was perfectly straightforward and honorable throughout the whole controversy, and at the Council of Antioch itself. That he was not actuated by unworthy motives, or by a desire for revenge, is evinced by his rejection of the proffered call to Antioch, the acceptance of which would have given him so good an opportunity to triumph over his fallen enemy. It must be admitted, in fact, that Eusebius comes out of this controversy without a stain of any kind upon his character. He honestly believed Eustathius to be a Sabellian, and he acted accordingly.

Eusebius has been blamed still more severely for his treatment of Athanasius. But again the facts must be looked at impartially. It is necessary always to remember that Sabellianism was in the beginning and remained throughout his life the heresy which he most dreaded, and which he had perhaps most reason to dread. He must, even at the Council of Nicæa, have suspected Athanasius, who laid so much stress upon the unity of essence on the part of Father and Son, of a leaning toward Sabellianistic principles; and this suspicion must have been increased when he discovered, as he believed, that Athanasius' most staunch supporter, Eustathius, was a genuine Sabellian. Moreover, on the other side, it is to be remembered that Eusebius of Nicomedia, and all the other leading Arians, had signed the Nicene creed and had proclaimed themselves thoroughly in sympathy with its teaching. Our Eusebius, knowing the change that had taken place in his own mind upon the controverted points, may well have believed that their views had undergone even a greater change, and that they were perfectly honest in their protestations of orthodoxy. And finally, when Arius himself presented a confession of faith which led the Emperor, who had had a personal interview with him, to believe that he had altered his views and was in complete harmony with the Nicene faith, it is not surprising that our Eusebius, who was naturally unsuspicious, conciliatory and peace-loving, should think the same thing, and be glad to receive Arius back into communion, while at the same time remaining perfectly loyal to the orthodoxy of the Nicene creed which he had subscribed. Meanwhile his suspicions of the Arian party being in large measure allayed, and his distrust of the orthodoxy of Athanasius and of his adherents being increased by the course of events, it was only natural that he should lend more or less credence to the calumnies which were so industriously circulated against Athanasius. To charge him with dishonesty for being influenced by these reports, which seem to us so absurd and palpably calumnious, is quite unwarranted. Constantine, who was, if not a theologian, at least a clear-headed and sharp-sighted man, believed them, and why should Eusebius not have done the same? The incident which took place at the Council of Tyre in connection with Potamo and himself was important; for whatever doubts he may have had up to that time as to the truth of the accusations made against Athanasius and his adherents, Potamo's conduct convinced him that the charges of tyranny and high-handed dealing brought against the whole party were quite true. It could not be otherwise than that he should believe that the good of the Alexandrian church, and therefore of the Church at large, demanded the deposition of the seditious and tyrannous archbishop, who was at the same time quite probably Sabellianistic in his tendencies. It must in justice be noted that there is not the slightest reason to suppose that our Eusebius had anything to do with the dishonorable intrigues of the Arian party throughout this controversy. Athanasius, who cannot say enough in condemnation of the tactics of Eusebius of Nicomedia and his supporters, never mentions Eusebius of Cæsarea in a tone of bitterness. He refers to him occasionally as a member of the opposite party, but he has no complaints to utter against him, as he has against the others. This is very significant, and should put an end to all suspicions of unworthy conduct on Eusebius' part. It is to be observed that the latter, though having good cause as he believed to condemn Athanasius and his adherents, never acted as a leader in the war against them. His name, if mentioned at all, occurs always toward the end of the list as one of the minor combatants, although his position and his learning would have entitled him to take the most prominent position in the whole affair, if he had cared to. He was but true to his general character in shrinking from such a controversy, and in taking part in it only in so far as his conscience compelled him to. We may suspect indeed that he would not have made one of the small party that repaired to Constantinople in response to the Emperor's imperious summons had it not been for the celebration of Constantine's *tricennalia*, which was taking place there at the time, and at which he delivered, on the special invitation of the Emperor and in his presence, one of his greatest orations. Certain it is, from the account which he gives in his *Vita Constantini*, that both in Constantinople and in Jerusalem the festival of the *tricennalia*, with its attendant ceremonies, interested him much more than did the condemnation of Athanasius.

§ 8. *Eusebius and Marcellus.*

It was during this visit to Constantinople that another synod was held, at which Eusebius was present, and the result of which was the condemnation and deposition of the bishop Marcellus of Ancyra (see Socrates, I. 36 ; Sozomen, II. 33 ; Eusebius, *Contra Marc.* II. 4). The attitude of our Eusebius toward Marcellus is again significant of his theological tendencies. Marcellus had written a book against Asterius, a prominent Arian, in which, in his zeal for the Nicene orthodoxy, he had laid himself open to the charge of Sabellianism. On this account he was deposed by the Constantinopolitan Synod, and our Eusebius was urged to write a work exposing his errors and defending the action of the Council. As a consequence he composed his two works against Marcellus which will be described later. That Eusebius, if not in the case of Athanasius and possibly not in that of Eustathius, had at least in the present case good ground for the belief that Marcellus was a Sabellian, or Sabellianistic in tendency, is abundantly proved by the citations which he makes from Marcellus' own works ; and, moreover, his judgment and that of the Synod was later confirmed even by Athanasius himself. Though not suspecting Marcellus for some time, Athanasius finally became convinced that he had deviated from the path of orthodoxy, and, as Newman has shown (in his introduction to Athanasius' fourth discourse against the Arians, *Oxford Library of the Fathers*, vol. 19, p. 503 sq.), directed that discourse against his errors and those of his followers.

The controversy with Marcellus seems to have been the last in which Eusebius was engaged, and it was opposition to the dreaded heresy of Sabellius which moved him here as in all the other cases. It is important to emphasize, however, what is often overlooked, that though Eusebius during these years was so continuously engaged in controversy with one or another of the members of the anti-Arian party, there is no evidence that he ever deviated from the doctrinal position which he took at the Council of Nicæa. After that date it was never Arianism which he consciously supported ; it was never the Nicene orthodoxy which he opposed. He supported those members of the old Arian party who had signed the Nicene creed and protested that they accepted its teaching, against those members of the opposite party whom he believed to be drifting toward Sabellianism, or acting tyrannously and unjustly toward their opponents. The anti-Sabellianistic interest influenced him all the time, but his post-Nicene writings contain no evidence that he had fallen back into the Arianizing position which he had held before 325. They reveal, on the contrary, a fair type of orthodoxy, colored only by its decidedly anti-Sabellian emphasis.

§ 9. *The Death of Eusebius.*

In less than two years after the celebration of his *tricennalia*, on May 22, 337 A.D., the great Constantine breathed his last, in Nicomedia, his former Capital. Eusebius, already an old man, produced a lasting testimonial of his own unbounded affection and admiration for the first Christian emperor, in his *Life of Constantine*. Soon afterward he followed his imperial friend at the advanced age of nearly, if not quite, eighty years. The exact date of his death is unknown, but it can be fixed approximately. We know from Sozomen (*H. E.* III. 5) that in the summer of 341, when a council was held at Antioch (on the date of the Council, which we are able to fix with great exactness, see Hefele, *Conciliengesch.* I. p. 502 sq.) Acacius, Eusebius' successor, was already bishop of Cæsarea. Socrates (*H. E.* II. 4) and Sozomen (*H. E.* III. 2) both mention the death of Eusebius and place it shortly before the death of Constantine the younger, which took place early in 340 (see Tillemont's *Hist. des Emp.* IV. p. 327 sq.), and after the intrigues had begun which resulted in Athanasius' second banishment. We are thus led to place Eusebius' death late in the year 339, or early in the year 340 (cf. Lightfoot's article, p. 318).

CHAPTER II.

THE WRITINGS OF EUSEBIUS.

§ 1. *Eusebius as a Writer.*

EUSEBIUS was one of the most voluminous writers of antiquity, and his labors covered almost every field of theological learning. In the words of Lightfoot he was "historian, apologist, topographer, exegete, critic, preacher, dogmatic writer, in turn." It is as an historian that he is best known, but the importance of his historical writings should not cause us to overlook, as modern scholars have been prone to do, his invaluable productions in other departments. Lightfoot passes a very just judgment upon the importance of his works in the following words : " If the permanent utility of an author's labors may be taken as a test of literary excellence, Eusebius will hold a very high place indeed. The *Ecclesiastical History* is absolutely unique and indispensable. The *Chronicle* is the vast storehouse of information relating to the ancient monarchies of the world. The *Preparation* and *Demonstration* are the most important contributions to theology in their own province. Even the minor works, such as the *Martyrs of Palestine*, the *Life of Constantine*, the *Questions addressed to Stephanus and to Marinus*, and others, would leave an irreparable blank, if they were obliterated. And the same permanent value attaches also to his more technical treatises. The *Canons* and *Sections* have never yet been superseded for their particular purpose. The *Topography of Palestine* is the most important contribution to our knowledge in its own department. In short, no ancient ecclesiastical writer has laid posterity under heavier obligations."

If we look in Eusebius' works for evidences of brilliant genius we shall be disappointed. He did not possess a great creative mind like Origen's or Augustine's. His claim to greatness rests upon his vast erudition and his sterling sense. His powers of acquisition were remarkable and his diligence in study unwearied. He had at his command undoubtedly more acquired material than any man of his age, and he possessed that true literary and historical instinct which enabled him to select from his vast stores of knowledge those things which it was most worth his while to tell to the world. His writings therefore remain valuable while the works of many others, perhaps no less richly equipped than himself for the mission of adding to the sum of human knowledge, are entirely forgotten. He thus had the ability to do more than acquire ; he had the ability to impart to others the very best of that which he acquired, and to make it useful to them. There is not in his writings the brilliancy which we find in some others, there is not the same sparkle and freshness of new and suggestive thought, there is not the same impress of an overmastering individuality which transforms everything it touches. There is, however, a true and solid merit which marks his works almost without exception, and raises them above the commonplace. His exegesis is superior to that of most of his contemporaries, and his apologetics is marked by fairness of statement, breadth of treatment, and instinctive appreciation of the difference between the important and the unimportant points under discussion, which give to his apologetic works a permanent value. His wide acquaintance, too, with other systems than his own, and with the products of Pagan as well as Christian thought, enabled him to see things in their proper relations and to furnish a treatment of the great themes of Christianity adapted to the wants of those who had looked beyond the confines of a single school. At the same time it must be acknowledged that he was not always equal to the grand opportunities which his acquaintance with the works and lives of other men and other peoples opened before him. He does not always reveal the possession of that high quality of genius which is able to interpret the most various forces and to discover the higher principles of unity which alone make them intelligible ; indeed, he often loses himself completely in a wilderness of thoughts and notions which have come to him from other men and other ages, and the result is dire confusion.

We shall be disappointed, too, if we seek in the works of Eusebius for evidences of a refined literary taste, or for any of the charms which attach to the writings of a great master of composition. His style is, as a rule, involved and obscure, often painfully rambling and incoherent. This quality is due in large part to the desultoriness of his thinking. He did not often enough clearly define and draw the boundaries of his subject before beginning to write upon it. He apparently did much of his thinking after he had taken pen in hand, and did not subject what he had thus produced to a sufficiently careful revision, if to any revision at all. Thoughts and suggestions poured in upon him while he was writing ; and he was not always able to resist the temptation to insert them as they came, often to the utter perversion of his train of thought, and to the ruin of the coherency and perspicuity of his style. It must be acknowledged, too, that his literary taste was, on the whole, decidedly vicious. Whenever a flight of eloquence is attempted by him, as it is altogether too often, his style becomes hopelessly turgid and pretentious. At such times his skill in mixing metaphors is something astounding (compare, for instance, *H. E.* II. 14). On the other hand, his works contain not a few passages of real beauty. This is especially true of his *Martyrs of Palestine*, where his enthusiastic admiration for and deep sympathy with the heroes of the faith cause him often to forget himself and to describe their sufferings in language of genuine fire or pathos. At times, too, when he has a sharply defined and absorbing aim in mind, and when the subject with which he is dealing does not seem to him to demand rhetorical adornment, he is simple and direct enough in his language, showing in such cases that his commonly defective style is not so much the consequence of an inadequate command of the Greek tongue as of desultory thinking and vicious literary taste.

But while we find much to criticise in Eusebius' writings, we ought not to fail to give him due credit for the conscientiousness and faithfulness with which he did his work. He wrote often, it is true, too rapidly for the good of his style, and he did not always revise his works as carefully as he should have done ; but we seldom detect undue haste in the collection of materials or carelessness and negligence in the use of them. He seems to have felt constantly the responsibilities which rested upon him as a scholar and writer, and to have done his best to meet those responsibilities. It is impossible to avoid contrasting him in this respect with the most learned man of the ancient Latin Church, St. Jerome. The haste and carelessness with which the latter composed his *De Viris Illustribus,* and with which he translated and continued Eusebius' *Chronicle,* remain an everlasting disgrace to him. An examination of those and of some others of Jerome's works must tend to raise Eusebius greatly in our esteem. He was at least conscientious and honest in his work, and never allowed himself to palm off ignorance as knowledge, or to deceive his readers by sophistries, misstatements, and pure inventions. He aimed to put the reader into possession of the knowledge which he had himself acquired, but was always conscientious enough to stop there, and not attempt to make fancy play the *rôle* of fact.

One other point, which was mentioned some pages back, and to which Lightfoot calls particular attention, should be referred to here, because of its bearing upon the character of Eusebius' writings. He was, above all things, an apologist ; and the apologetic aim governed both the selection of his subjects and method of his treatment. He composed none of his works with a purely scientific aim. He thought always of the practical result to be attained, and his selection of material and his choice of method were governed by that. And yet we must recognize the fact that this aim was never narrowing in its effects. He took a broad view of apologetics, and in his lofty conception of the Christian religion he believed that every field of knowledge might be laid under tribute to it. He was bold enough to be confident that history, philosophy, and science all contribute to our understanding and appreciation of divine truth; and so history and philosophy and science were studied and handled by him freely and fearlessly. He did not feel the need of distorting truth of any kind because it might work injury to the religion which he professed. On the contrary, he had a sublime faith which led him to believe that all truth must have its place and its mission, and that the cause of Christianity will be benefited by its discovery and diffusion. As an apologist, therefore, all fields of knowledge had an interest for him; and he was saved that pettiness of mind and narrowness of outlook which are sometimes characteristic of those who write with a purely practical motive.

§ 2. *Catalogue of his Works.*

There is no absolutely complete edition of Eusebius' extant works. The only one which can lay claim even to relative completeness is that of Migne: *Eusebii Pamphili, Cæsareæ Palestinæ Episcopi, Opera omnia quæ extant, curis variorum, nempe: Henrici Valesii, Francisci Vigeri, Bernardi Montfauconii, Card. Angelo Maii edita; collegit et denuo recognovit J. P. Migne.* Par. 1857. 6 vols (tom. XIX.–XXIV. of Migne's *Patrologia Græca*). This edition omits the works which are extant only in Syriac versions, also the *Topica*, and some brief but important Greek fragments (among them the epistles to Alexander and Euphration). The edition, however, is invaluable and cannot be dispensed with. References to it (under the simple title *Opera*) will be given below in connection with those works which it contains. Many of Eusebius' writings, especially the historical, have been published separately. Such editions will be mentioned in their proper place in the Catalogue.

More or less incomplete lists of our author's writings are given by Jerome (*De vir. ill.* 87); by Nicephorus Callistus (*H. E.* VI. 37); by Ebedjesu (in Assemani's *Bibl. Orient.* III. p. 18 sq.); by Photius (*Bibl.* 9–13, 27, 39, 127); and by Suidas (who simply copies the Greek version of Jerome). Among modern works all the lives of Eusebius referred to in the previous chapter give more or less extended catalogues of his writings. In addition to the works mentioned there, valuable lists are also found in Lardner's *Credibility*, Part II. chap. 72, and especially in Fabricius' *Bibl. Græca* (ed. 1714), vol. VI. p. 30 sq.

The writings of Eusebius that are known to us, extant and non-extant, may be classified for convenience' sake under the following heads: I. Historical. II. Apologetic. III. Polemic. IV. Dogmatic. V. Critical and Exegetical. VI. Biblical Dictionaries. VII. Orations. VIII. Epistles. IX. Spurious or doubtful works. The classification is necessarily somewhat artificial, and claims to be neither exhaustive nor exclusive.[1]

I. Historical Works.

Life of Pamphilus (ἡ τοῦ Παμφίλου βίου ἀναγραφή; see *H. E.* VI. 32). Eusebius himself refers to this work in four passages (*H. E.* VI. 32, VII. 32, VIII. 13, and *Mart. Pal.* c. 11). In the last he informs us that it consisted of three books. The work is mentioned also more than once by Jerome (*De vir. ill.* 81; *Ep. ad Marcellam*, Migne's ed. *Ep.* 34; *Contra Ruf.* I. 9), who speaks of it in terms of praise, and in the last passage gives a brief extract from the third book, which is, so far as known, the only extant fragment of the work. The date of its composition can be fixed within comparatively narrow limits. It must of course have been written before the shorter recension of the *Martyrs of Palestine*, which contains a reference to it (on its relation to the

---

[1] In the preparation of the following Catalogue of Eusebius' writings Stein, and especially Lightfoot, have been found most helpful.

longer recension, which does not mention it, see below, p. 30), and also before the *History* (i.e. as early as 313 A.D. (?), see below, p. 45). On the other hand, it was written after Pamphilus' death (see *H. E.* VII. 32, 25), which occurred in 310.

Martyrs of Palestine (περὶ τῶν ἐν Παλαιστίνῃ μαρτυρησάντων). This work is extant in two recensions, a longer and a shorter. The longer has been preserved entire only in a Syriac version, which was published, with English translation and notes, by Cureton in 1861. A fragment of the original Greek of this work as preserved by Simeon Metaphrastes had previously been published by Papebroch in the *Acta Sanctorum* (June, tom. I. p. 64; reprinted by Fabricius, *Hippolytus*, II. p. 217), but had been erroneously regarded as an extract from Eusebius' *Life of Pamphilus*. Cureton's publication of the Syriac version of the *Martyrs of Palestine* showed that it was a part of the original of that work. There are extant also, in Latin, the *Acts of St. Procopius*, which were published by Valesius (in his edition of Eusebius' *Hist. Eccles.* in a note on the first chapter of the *Mart. Pal.;* reprinted by Cureton, *Mart. Pal.* p. 50 sq.). Moreover, according to Cureton, Assemani's *Acta SS. Martyrum Orient. et Occidentalium*, part II. p. 169 sq. (Romæ, 1748) contains another Syriac version of considerable portions of this same work. The Syriac version published by Cureton was made within less than a century after the composition of the original work (the manuscript of it dates from 411 A.D.; see Cureton, *ib.*, preface, p. i.), perhaps within a few years after it, and there is every reason to suppose that it represents that original with considerable exactness. That Eusebius himself was the author of the original cannot be doubted. In addition to this longer recension there is extant in Greek a shorter form of the same work which is found attached to the *Ecclesiastical History* in most MSS. of the latter. In some of them it is placed between the eighth and ninth books, in others at the close of the tenth book, while one MS. inserts it in the middle of VIII. 13. In some of the most important MSS. it is wanting entirely, as likewise in the translation of Rufinus, and, according to Lightfoot, in the Syriac version of the *History*. Most editions of Eusebius' *History* print it at the close of the eighth book. Migne gives it separately in *Opera*, II. 1457 sq. In the present volume the translation of it is given as an appendix to the eighth book, on p. 342 sq.

There can be no doubt that the shorter form is younger than the longer. The mention of the *Life of Pamphilus* which is contained in the shorter, but is not found in the corresponding passage of the longer form would seem to indicate that the former was a remodeling of the latter rather than the latter of the former (see below, p. 30). Moreover, as Cureton and Lightfoot both point out, the difference between the two works both in substance and in method is such as to make it clear that the shorter form is a revised abridgment of the longer. That Eusebius himself was the author of the shorter as well as of the longer form is shown by the fact that not only in the passages common to both recensions, but also in those peculiar to the shorter one, the author speaks in the same person and as an eye-witness of many of the events which he records. And still further, in Chap. 11 he speaks of having himself written the *Life of Pamphilus* in three books, a notice which is wanting in the longer form and therefore must emanate from the hand of the author of the shorter. It is interesting to inquire after Eusebius' motive in publishing an abridged edition of this work. Cureton supposes that he condensed it simply for the purpose of inserting it in the second edition of his *History*. Lightfoot, on the other hand, suggests that it may have formed " part of a larger work, in which the sufferings of the martyrs were set off against the deaths of the persecutors," and he is inclined to see in the brief appendix to the eighth book of the *History* (translated below on p. 340) " a fragment of the second part of the treatise of which the *Martyrs of Palestine* in the shorter recension formed the first." The suggestion is, to say the least, very plausible. If it be true, the attachment of the shorter form of the *Martyrs of Palestine* to the *Ecclesiastical History* was probably the work, not of Eusebius himself, but of some copyist or copyists, and the disagreement among the various MSS. as to its position in the *History* is more easily explained on this supposition than on Cureton's theory that it was attached to a later edition of the latter work by Eusebius himself.

The date at which the *Martyrs of Palestine* was composed cannot be determined with certainty. It was at any rate not published until after the first nine books of the *Ecclesiastical History* (i.e. not before 313, see below, p. 45), for it is referred to as a projected work in *H. E.* VIII. 13. 7. On the other hand, the accounts contained in the longer recension bear many marks of having been composed on the spot, while the impressions left by the martyrdoms witnessed by the author were still fresh upon him. Moreover, it is noticeable that in connection with the account of Pamphilus' martyrdom, given in the shorter recension, reference is made to the *Life of Pamphilus* as a book already published, while in the corresponding account in the longer recension no such book is referred to. This would seem to indicate that the *Life of Pamphilus* was written after the longer, but before the shorter recension of the *Martyrs*. But on the other hand the *Life* was written before the *Ecclesiastical History* (see above, p. 29), and consequently before the publication of either recension of the *Martyrs*. May it not be that the accounts of the various martyrdoms were written, at least some of them, during the persecution, but that they were not arranged, completed, and published until 313, or later? If this be admitted we may suppose that the account of Pamphilus' martyrdom was written soon after his death and before the *Life* was begun. When it was later embodied with the other accounts in the one work *On the Martyrs of Palestine* it may have been left just as it was, and it may not have occurred to the author to insert a reference to the *Life of Pamphilus* which had meanwhile been published. But when he came to abridge and in part rewrite for a new edition the accounts of the various martyrdoms contained in the work *On Martyrs* he would quite naturally refer the reader to the *Life* for fuller particulars.

If we then suppose that the greater part of the longer recension of the *Martyrs* was already complete before the end of the persecution, it is natural to conclude that the whole work was published at an early date, probably as soon as possible after the first edition of the *History*. How much later the abridgment was made we cannot tell.[1]

The differences between the two recensions lie chiefly in the greater fullness of detail on the part of the longer one. The arrangement and general mode of treatment is the same in both. They contain accounts of the Martyrs that suffered in Palestine during the years 303–310, most of whom Eusebius himself saw.

Collection of Ancient Martyrdoms (ἀρχαίων μαρτυρίων συναγωγή). This work is mentioned by Eusebius in his *H. E.* IV. 15, V. præf., 4, 21. These notices indicate that it was not an original

---

[1] Since the above section was written, another possibility has suggested itself to me. As remarked below, on p. 45, it is possible that Eusebius issued a second edition of his *History* in the year 324 or 325, with a tenth book added, and that he inserted at that time two remarks not contained in the first edition of the first nine books. It is possible, therefore, to suppose that the references to the *Vita Pamphili*, as an already published book, found in *H. E.* VI. 32 and VII. 32, may have been added at the same time. Turning to the latter passage we find our author saying, "It would be no small matter to show what sort of man he [Pamphilus] was, and whence he came. But we have described in a separate work devoted to him all the particulars of his life, and of the school which he established, and the trials which he endured in many confessions during the persecution, and the crown of martyrdom with which he was finally honored. *But* of all who were there he was the most admirable" (ἀλλ' οὗτος μὲν τῶν τῇδε θαυμασιωτάτος). The ἀλλά, *but*, seems very unnatural after the paragraph in regard to the work which Eusebius had already written. In fact, to give the word its proper adversative force after what precedes is quite impossible, and it is therefore commonly rendered (as in the translation of the passage on p. 321, below) simply "indeed." If we suppose the passage in regard to the Biography of Pamphilus to be a later insertion, the use of the ἀλλά becomes quite explicable. "It would be no small matter to show what sort of man he was and whence he came. *But* (this much I can say here) he was the most admirable of all who were there." Certainly the reference at this point to the *Vita*

Pamphili thus has something of the look of a later insertion. In VI. 32, the reference to that work might be struck out without in the least impairing the continuity of thought. Still further, in VIII. 13, where the *Vita* is mentioned, although the majority of the MSS. followed by most of the modern editions have the past tense ἀνεγράψαμεν "we have written," three of the best MSS. read ἀναγράψομεν "we shall write." Might not this confusion have arisen from the fact that Eusebius, in revising the *History*, instead of rewriting this whole passage simply substituted in the copy which he had before him the word ἀνεγράψαμεν for the earlier ἀναγράψομεν, and that some copyist, or copyists, finding the earlier form still legible, preferred that to the substituted form, thinking the latter to be an insertion by some unauthorized person? If we were then to suppose that the *Vita Pamphili* was written after the first edition of the *History*, but before the issue of the complete work in its revised form, we should place its composition later than the longer recension of the *Martyrs*, but earlier than the shorter recension, and thus explain quite simply the lack of any reference to the *Vita* in the former. Against the theory stated in this note might be urged the serious objection that the reference to the *Martyrs of Palestine* in VIII. 13 is allowed to remain in the future tense even in the revised edition of the *History*, a fact which of course argues against the change of ἀναγράψομεν to ἀνεγράψαμεν in the reference to the *Vita* in the same chapter. Indeed, I do not wish to be understood as maintaining this theory, or as considering it more probable than the one stated in the text. I suggest it simply as an alternative possibility.

composition, but simply a compilation; a collection of extant accounts of martyrdoms which had taken place before Eusebius' day. The work is no longer extant, but the accounts of the martyrdom of Pamphilus and others at Smyrna, of the persecution in Lyons and Vienne, and of the defense of Apollonius in Rome, which Eusebius inserts in his *Ecclesiastical History* (IV. 15, V. 1, V. 21), are taken, as he informs us, from this collection. As to the time of compilation, we can say only that it antedates the composition of the earlier books of the *History* (on whose date, see below, p. 45).

Chronicle (χρονικοὶ κανόνες). Eusebius refers to this work in his *Church History* (I. 1), in his *Præparatio Evang.* X. 9, and at the beginning of his *Eclogæ propheticæ*. It is divided into two books, the first of which consists of an epitome of universal history drawn from various sources, the second of chronological tables, which "exhibit in parallel columns the succession of the rulers of different nations in such a way that the reader can see at a glance with whom any given monarch was contemporary." The tables "are accompanied by notes, marking the years of some of the more remarkable historical events, these notes also constituting an epitome of history." Eusebius was not the first Christian writer to compose a work on universal chronology. Julius Africanus had published a similar work early in the third century, and from that Eusebius drew his model and a large part of the material for his own work. At the same time his *Chronicle* is more than a simple revision of Africanus' work, and contains the result of much independent investigation on his own part. The work of Africanus is no longer extant, and that of Eusebius was likewise lost for a great many centuries, being superseded by a revised Latin edition, issued by Jerome. Jerome's edition, which comprises only the second book of Eusebius' *Chronicle*, is a translation of the original work, enlarged by notices taken from various writers concerning human history, and containing a continuation of the chronology down to his own time. This, together with numerous Greek fragments preserved by various ancient writers, constituted our only source for a knowledge of the original work, until late in the last century an Armenian translation of the whole work was discovered and published in two volumes by J. B. Aucher: Venice, 1818. The Armenian translation contains a great many errors and not a few *lacunæ*, but it is our most valuable source for a knowledge of the original work.

The aim of the *Chronicle* was, above all, apologetic, the author wishing to prove by means of it that the Jewish religion, of which the Christian was the legitimate continuation, was older than the oldest of heathen cults, and thus deprive pagan opponents of their taunt of novelty, so commonly hurled against Christianity. As early as the second century, the Christian apologists had emphasized the antiquity of Judaism; but Julius Africanus was the first to devote to the matter scientific study, and it was with the same idea that Eusebius followed in his footsteps. The *Chronology*, in spite of its errors, is invaluable for the light it throws on many otherwise dark periods of history, and for the numerous extracts it contains from works no longer extant.

There are good and sufficient reasons (as is pointed out by Salmon in his article in Smith and Wace's *Dictionary of Christian Biography*) for supposing that two editions of the *Chronicle* were published by Eusebius. But two of these reasons need be stated here: first, the chronology of the Armenian version differs from that of Jerome's edition in many important particulars, divergencies which can be satisfactorily accounted for only on the supposition of a difference in the sources from which they respectively drew; secondly, Jerome states directly that the work was brought down to the *vicennalia* of Constantine, — that is, to the year 325, — but the *Chronicle* is referred to as an already published work in the *Eclogæ propheticæ* (I. 1), and in the *Præparatio Evang.* (X. 9), both of which were written before 313. We may conclude, then, that a first edition of the work was published during, or more probably before, the great persecution, and that a second and revised edition was issued probably in 325, or soon thereafter.

For further particulars in regard to the *Chronicle* see especially the article of Salmon already referred to. The work has been issued separately a great many times. We may refer here to the edition of Scaliger, which was published in 1606 (2d ed. 1658), in which he attempted to restore the Greek text from the fragments of Syncellus and other ancient writers, and to the new edition of Mai, which was printed in 1833 in his *Scriptorum veterum nova collectio*, Tom. VIII., and reprinted by Migne, *Eusebii Opera*, I. 99–598. The best and most recent edition, however, and the one which supersedes all earlier editions, is that of Alfred Schoene, in two volumes : Berlin, 1875 and 1866.

Ecclesiastical History (ἐκκλησιαστικὴ ἱστορία). For a discussion of this work see below, p. 45 sq.

Life of Constantine (εἰς τὸν βίον τοῦ μακαρίου Κωνσταντίνου τοῦ βασιλέως). For particulars in regard to this work, see the prolegomena of Dr. Richardson, on pp.   sq., of this volume.

II. Apologetic Works.

Against Hierocles (πρὸς τοὺς ὑπὲρ Ἀπολλωνίου τοῦ τυανέως Ἱεροκλέους λόγους, as Photius calls it in his *Bibl.* 39). Hierocles was governor of Bithynia during the early years of the Diocletian persecution, and afterwards governor of Egypt. In both places he treated the Christians with great severity, carrying out the edicts of the emperors to the fullest extent, and even making use of the most terrible and loathsome forms of persecution (see Lactantius, *De Mort. Pers.* 16, and Eusebius, *Mart. Pal.* 5, Cureton's ed. p. 18). He was at the same time a Neo-Platonic philosopher, exceedingly well versed in the Scriptures and doctrines of the Christians. In a work against the Christians entitled λόγος φιλαλήθης πρὸς τοὺς χριστιανούς, he brought forward many scriptural difficulties and alleged contradictions, and also instituted a comparison between Christ and Apollonius of Tyana, with the intention of disparaging the former. Eusebius feels called upon to answer the work, but confines himself entirely to that part of it which concerned Christ and Apollonius, leaving to some future time a refutation of the remainder of the work, which indeed, he says, as a mere reproduction of the arguments of Celsus, had been already virtually answered by Origen (see chap. 1). Eusebius admits that Apollonius was a good man, but refuses to concede that he was anything more, or that he can be compared with Christ. He endeavors to show that the account of Apollonius given by Philostratus is full of contradictions and does not rest upon trustworthy evidence. The tone of the book is mild, and the arguments in the main sound and well presented. It is impossible to fix the date of the work with any degree of certainty. Valesius assigns it to the later years of the persecution, when Eusebius visited Egypt ; Stein says that it may have been written about 312 or 313, or even earlier ; while Lightfoot simply remarks, "It was probably one of the earliest works of Eusebius." There is no ground for putting it at one time rather than another except the intrinsic probability that it was written soon after the work to which it was intended to be a reply. In fact, had a number of years elapsed after the publication of Hierocles' attack, Eusebius would doubtless, if writing against it at all, have given a fuller and more complete refutation of it, such as he suggests in the first chapter that he may yet give. The work of Hierocles, meanwhile, must have been written at any rate some time before the end of the persecution, for it is mentioned in Lactantius' *Div. Inst.* V. 2.

Eusebius' work has been published by Gaisford : *Eusebii Pamph. contra Hieroclem et Marcellum libri*, Oxon. 1852 ; and also in various editions of the works of Philostratus. Migne, *Opera* IV. 795 sq., reprints it from Olearius' edition of Philostratus' works (Lips. 1709).

Against Porphyry (κατὰ Πορφυρίου). Porphyry, the celebrated Neo-Platonic philosopher, regarded by the early Fathers as the bitterest and most dangerous enemy of the Church, wrote toward the end of the third century a work against Christianity in fifteen books, which was looked upon as the most powerful attack that had ever been made, and which called forth refutations from some of the greatest Fathers of the age : from Methodius of Tyre, Eusebius of Cæsarea, and Apollinaris of Laodicea ; and even as late as the end of the fourth or beginning of the fifth century the historian Philostorgius thought it necessary to write another reply to it (see his *H. E.* X. 10). Porphyry's work is no longer extant, but the fragments of it which remain show us that it was both learned and skillful. He made much of the alleged contradictions in the Gospel records, and suggested difficulties which are still favorite weapons in the hands of skeptics.   Like the work of Porphyry, and all the other refutations of it, the Apology of Eusebius has entirely perished.   It is mentioned by Jerome (*de vir. ill.* 81 and *Ep. ad Magnum*, § 3, Migne's ed. *Ep.* 70), by Socrates (*H. E.* III. 23), and by Philostorgius (*H. E.* VIII. 14).   There is some dispute as to the number of books it contained. In his *Ep. ad Magn.* Jerome says that "Eusebius et Apollinaris viginti quinque, et triginta volumina condiderunt," which implies that it was composed of twenty-five books; while in his *de vir. ill.* 81, he speaks of thirty books, of which he had seen only twenty.   Vallarsi says, however, that all his MSS. agree in reading "twenty-five" instead of "thirty" in the latter passage, so that it would seem that the vulgar text is incorrect.

It is impossible to form an accurate notion of the nature and quality of Eusebius' refutation. Socrates speaks of it in terms of moderate praise ("which [i.e. the work of Porphyry] has been ably answered by Eusebius"), and Jerome does the same in his *Ep. ad Magnum* ("Alteri [i.e. Porphyry] Methodius, Eusebius, et Apollinaris fortissime responderunt").   At the same time the fact that Apollinaris and others still thought it necessary to write against Porphyry would seem to show that Eusebius' refutation was not entirely satisfactory.   In truth, Jerome (*Ep. ad Pammachium et Oceanum*, § 2, Migne's ed. *Ep.* 84) appears to rank the work of Apollinaris above that of Eusebius, and Philostorgius expressly states that the former far surpassed the latter (ἐπὶ πολὺ κρατεῖν ἠγωνισμένων Ἐυσεβίῳ κατ᾽ αὐτοῦ).   The date of Eusebius' work cannot be determined.   The fact that he never refers to it, although he mentions the work of Porphyry a number of times, has been urged by Valesius and others as proof that he did not write it until after 325 A.D.; but it is quite possible to explain his silence, as Lardner does, by supposing that his work was written in his earlier years, and that afterward he felt its inferiority and did not care to mention it.   It seems, in fact, not unlikely that he wrote it as early, or even earlier than his work against Hierocles, at any rate before his attention was occupied with the Arian controversy and questions connected with it.

On the Numerous Progeny of the Ancients (περὶ τῆς τῶν παλαιῶν ἀνδρῶν πολυπαιδίας).   This work is mentioned by Eusebius in his *Praep. Evang.* VII. 8. 20 (Migne, *Opera*, III. 525), but by no one else, unless it be the book to which Basil refers in his *De Spir. Sancto*, 29, as *Difficulties respecting the Polygamy of the Ancients*.   The work is no longer extant, but we can gather from the connection in which it is mentioned in the *Praeparatio*, that it aimed at accounting for the polygamy of the Patriarchs and reconciling it with the ascetic ideal of the Christian life which prevailed in the Church of Eusebius' lifetime.   It would therefore seem to have been written with an apologetic purpose.

Praeparatio Evangelica (προπαρασκευὴ εὐαγγελική) and *Demonstratio Evangelica* (Ἐυαγγελικὴ ἀπόδειξις).   These two treatises together constitute Eusebius' greatest apologetic work.   The former is directed against heathen, and aims to show that the Christians are justified in accepting the sacred books of the Hebrews and in rejecting the religion and philosophy of the Greeks. The latter endeavors to prove from the sacred books of the Hebrews themselves that the Christians do right in going beyond the Jews, in accepting Jesus as their Messiah, and in adopting another mode of life.   The former is therefore in a way a preparation for the latter, and the two together constitute a defense of Christianity against all the world, Jews as well as heathen.   In grandeur of conception, in comprehensiveness of treatment, and in breadth of learning, this apology undoubtedly surpasses all other apologetic works of antiquity.   Lightfoot justly says, " This great apologetic work exhibits the same merits and defects which we find elsewhere in Eusebius.   There is the same greatness of conception marred by the same inadequacy of execution, the same profusion of learning combined with the same inability to control his materials, which we have seen in his *History*.   The divisions are not kept distinct; the topics start up unexpectedly and out of season.   But with all its faults this is probably the most important apologetic work of the early Church.   It necessarily lacks the historical interest of the apologetic writings of the second century; it falls far short of the thoughtfulness and penetration which give a permanent value to Origen's treatise against Celsus as a defense of the faith; it lags behind the Latin apologists in rhetorical vigor and expression. But the forcible and true conceptions which it exhibits from time to time, more especially bearing on the theme which may be briefly designated 'God in history,' arrest our attention now, and must have impressed his contemporaries still more strongly; while in learning and comprehensiveness it is without a rival." The wide acquaintance with classical literature exhibited by Eusebius in the *Præparatio* is very remarkable. Many writers are referred to whose names are known to us from no other source, and many extracts are given which constitute our only fragments of works otherwise totally lost. The *Præparatio* thus does for classical much what the *History* does for Christian literature.

A very satisfactory summary of the contents of the *Præparatio* is given at the beginning of the fifteenth book. In the first, second, and third books, the author exposes the absurdities of heathen mythology, and attacks the allegorical theology of the Neo-Platonists; in the fourth and fifth books he discusses the heathen oracles; in the sixth he refutes the doctrine of fate; in the seventh he passes over to the Hebrews, devoting the next seven books to an exposition of the excellence of their system, and to a demonstration of the proposition that Moses and the prophets lived before the greatest Greek writers, and that the latter drew their knowledge from the former; in the fourteenth and fifteenth books he exposes the contradictions among Greek philosophers and the vital errors in their systems, especially in that of the Peripatetics. The *Præparatio* is complete in fifteen books, all of which are still extant.

The *Demonstratio* consisted originally of twenty books (see Jerome's *de vir. ill.* 81, and Photius' *Bibl.* 10). Of these only ten are extant, and even in the time of Nicephorus Callistus no more were known, for he gives the number of the books as ten (*H. E.* VI. 37). There exists also a fragment of the fifteenth book, which was discovered and printed by Mai (*Script. vet. nova coll.* I. 2, p. 173). In the first book, which is introductory, Eusebius shows why the Christians pursue a mode of life different from that of the Jews, drawing a distinction between Hebraism, the religion of all pious men from the beginning, and Judaism, the special system of the Jews, and pointing out that Christianity is a continuation of the former, but a rejection of the latter, which as temporary has passed away. In the second book he shows that the calling of the Gentiles and the repudiation of the Jews are foretold in Scripture. In books three to nine he discusses the humanity, divinity, incarnation, and earthly life of the Saviour, showing that all were revealed in the prophets. In the remainder of the work we may assume that the same general plan was followed, and that Christ's death, resurrection, and ascension, and the spread of his Church, were the subjects discussed in this as in nearly all works of the kind.

There is much dispute as to the date of these two works. Stroth and Cave place them after the Council of Nicæa, while Valesius, Lightfoot, and others, assign them to the ante-Nicene period. In two passages in the *History* Eusebius has been commonly supposed to refer to the *Demonstratio* (*H. E.* I. 2 and 6), but it is probable that the first, and quite likely the second also, refers to the *Eclogæ Proph.* We can, therefore, base no argument upon those passages. But in *Præp. Evang.* XII. 10 (*Opera*, III. 969) there is a reference to the persecution, which seems clearly to imply that it was still continuing; and in the *Demonstratio* (III. 5 and IV. 6; *Opera*, IV. 213 and 307), which was written after the *Præparatio*, are still more distinct indications of the continuance of the persecution. On the other hand, in V. 3 and VI. 20 (*Opera*, IV. 364 and 474) there are passages which imply that the persecution has come to an end. It seems necessary then to conclude, with Lightfoot, that the *Demonstratio* was begun during the persecution, but not completed until peace had been established. The *Præparatio*, which was completed before the *Demonstratio* was begun (see the *proœmium* to the latter), must have been finished during the persecution. It contains in X. 9 (*Opera*, III. 807) a reference to the *Chronicle* as an already published work (see above, p. 31).

The *Præparatio* and *Demonstratio* are found in Migne's edition of the *Opera*, III. and IV.
9 sq. A more recent text is that of Dindorf in Teubner's series, 1867. The *Præparatio* has been
published separately by Heinichen, 2 vols., Lips. 1842, and by Gaisford, 4 vols., Oxon. 1843.
The latter contains a full critical apparatus with Latin translation and notes, and is the most
useful edition which we have. Seguier in 1846 published a French translation with notes. The
latter are printed in Latin in Migne's edition of the *Opera*, III. 1457 sq. The French translation
I have not seen.

The *Demonstratio* was also published by Gaisford in 2 vols., Oxon. 1852, with critical apparatus and Latin translation. Hænell has made the two works the subject of a monograph entitled
De Eusebio Cæsariensi religionis Christianæ Defensore (Gottingæ, 1843) which I know only
from the mention of it by Stein and Lightfoot.

Præparatio Ecclesiastica (Ἐκκλησιαστικὴ Προπαρασκευή), and *Demonstratio Ecclesiastica*
(Ἐκκλησιαστικὴ Ἀπόδειξις). These two works are no longer extant. We know of the former only
from Photius' reference to it in *Bibl.* 11, of the latter from his mention of it in *Bibl.* 12.

Lightfoot says that the latter is referred to also in the *Jus Græco-Romanum* (lib. IV. p. 295 ;
ed. Leunclav.). We know nothing about the works (except that the first according to Photius
contained extracts), and should be tempted to think them identical with the *Præparatio* and
Demonstratio Evang. were it not that Photius expressly mentions the two latter in another part
of his catalogue (*Bibl.* 10). Lightfoot supposes that the two lost works did for the society what
the *Præp.* and *Dem. Evang.* do for the doctrines of which the society is the depositary, and he
suggests that those portions of the *Theophania* (Book IV.) which relate to the foundation of the
Church may have been adopted from the *Dem. Ecclesiastica*, as other portions of the work (Book
V.) are adopted from the *Dem. Evang.*

If there is a reference in the *Præp. Evang.* I. 3 (*Opera*, III. 33) to the *Demonstratio Eccles.*,
as Lightfoot thinks there may be, and as is quite possible, the latter work, and consequently in
all probability the *Præp. Eccles.* also, must have been written before 313 A.D.

Two Books of Objection and Defense (Ἐλέγχου καὶ Ἀπολογίας λόγοι δύο). These are no
longer extant, but are mentioned by Photius in his *Bibl.* 13. We gather from Photius' language
that two editions of the work were extant in his time. The books, as Photius clearly indicates,
contained an apology for Christianity against the attacks of the heathen, and not, as Cave supposed,
a defense of the author against the charge of Arianism. The tract mentioned by Gelasius of
Cyzicus (see below, p. 64) is therefore not to be identified with this work, as Cave imagined
that it might be.

Theophania or *Divine Manifestation* (θεοφάνεια). A Syriac version of this work is extant in
the same MS. which contains the *Martyrs of Palestine*, and was first published by Lee in 1842.
In 1843 the same editor issued an English translation with notes and extended prolegomena
(Cambridge, 1 vol.). The original work is no longer extant in its entirety, but numerous Greek
fragments were collected and published by Mai in 1831 and 1833 (*Script. vet. nov. coll.* I.
and VIII.), and again with additions in 1847 (*Bibl. Nova Patrum*, IV. 110 and 310; reprinted
by Migne, *Opera*, VI. 607–690. Migne does not give the Syriac version). The manuscript
which contains the Syriac version was written in 411, and Lee thinks that the translation itself
may have been made even during the lifetime of Eusebius. At any rate it is very old and, so
far as it is possible to judge, seems to have reproduced the sense of the original with comparative
accuracy. The subject of the work is the manifestation of God in the incarnation of the Word.
It aims to give, with an apologetic purpose, a brief exposition of the divine authority and influence of Christianity. It is divided into five books which handle successively the subject and
the recipients of the revelation, that is, the Logos on the one hand, and man on the other; the
necessity of the revelation; the proof of it drawn from its effects; the proof of it drawn from
its fulfillment of prophecy; finally, the common objections brought by the heathen against Christ's
character and wonderful works. Lee says of the work: "As a brief exposition of Christianity,

particularly of its Divine authority, and amazing influence, it has perhaps never been surpassed."
" When we consider the very extensive range of inquiry occupied by our author, the great variety
both of argument and information which it contains, and the small space which it occupies ; we
cannot, I think, avoid coming to the conclusion, that it is a very extraordinary work, and one
which is as suitable to our own times as it was to those for which it was written. Its chief
excellency is, that it is argumentative, and that its arguments are well grounded, and logically
conducted."

The *Theophania* contains much that is found also in other works of Eusebius. Large portions
of the first, second, and third books are contained in the *Oratio de Laudibus Constantini*, nearly
the whole of the fifth book is given in the *Dem. Evang.*, while many passages occur in the *Præp.
Evang.*

These coincidences assist us in determining the date of the work. That it was written after
persecution had ceased and peace was restored to the Church, is clear from II. 76, III. 20, 79,
V. 52. Lee decided that it was composed very soon after the close of the Diocletian persecution,
but Lightfoot has shown conclusively (p. 333) from the nature of the parallels between it and other
writings of Eusebius, that it must have been written toward the end of his life, certainly later than
the *De Laud. Const.* (335 A.D.), and indeed it is not improbable that it remained unfinished at
the time of his death.

III. POLEMIC WORKS.

Defense of Origen ('Απολογία ὑπὲρ Ὠριγένους). This was the joint work of Eusebius and
Pamphilus, as is distinctly stated by Eusebius himself in his *H. E.* VI. 33, by Socrates, *H. E.* III. 7, by
the anonymous collector of the *Synodical Epistles* (*Ep.* 198), and by Photius, *Bibl.* 118. The last
writer informs us that the work consisted of six books, the first five of which were written by Eusebius and Pamphilus while the latter was in prison, the last book being added by the former after
Pamphilus' death (see above, p. 9). There is no reason to doubt the statement of Photius, and we
may therefore assign the first five books to the years 307–309, and assume that the sixth was written
soon afterward. The *Defense* has perished, with the exception of the first book, which was
translated by Rufinus (*Rufin. ad Hieron.* I. 582), and is still extant in his Latin version. Rufinus
ascribed this book expressly to Pamphilus, and Pamphilus' name alone appears in the translation.
Jerome (*Contra Ruf.* I. 8 ; II. 15, 23 ; III. 12) maintains that the whole work was written by
Eusebius, not by Pamphilus, and accuses Rufinus of having deliberately substituted the name of
the martyr Pamphilus for that of the Arianizing Eusebius in his translation of the work, in order
to secure more favorable acceptance for the teachings of Origen. Jerome's unfairness and
dishonesty in this matter have been pointed out by Lightfoot (p. 340). In spite of his endeavor
to saddle the whole work upon Eusebius, it is certain that Pamphilus was a joint author of it, and
it is quite probable that Rufinus was true to his original in ascribing to Pamphilus all the explanations which introduce and connect the extracts from Origen, which latter constitute the greater
part of the book. Eusebius may have done most of his work in connection with the later books.

The work was intended as a defense of Origen against the attacks of his opponents (see
Eusebius' *H. E.* VI. 33, and the Preface to the *Defense* itself). According to Socrates (*H. E.*
VI. 13), Methodius, Eustathius, Apollinaris, and Theophilus all wrote against Origen. Of these
only Methodius had written before the composition of the *Defense,* and he was expressly attacked in the sixth book of that work, according to Jerome (*Contra Ruf.* I. 11). The wide
opposition aroused against Origen was chiefly in consequence not of his personal character, but
of his theological views. The *Apology*, therefore, seems to have been devoted in the main to
a defense of those views over against the attacks of the men that held and taught opposite
opinions, and may thus be regarded as in some sense a regular polemic. The extant book is
devoted principally to a discussion of Origen's views on the Trinity and the Incarnation. It is
not printed in Migne's edition of Eusebius' *Opera*, but is published in the various editions of

Origen's works (in Lommatzsch's edition, XXIV. 289–412). For further particulars in regard to the work, see Delarue's introduction to it (Lommatzsch, XXIV. 263 sq.), and Lightfoot's article on Eusebius, pp. 340 and 341.

Against Marcellus, Bishop of Ancyra (κατὰ Μαρκέλλου τοῦ 'Αγκύρας ἐπισκόπου). The occasion of this work has been already described (see p. 25), and is explained by Eusebius himself in Book II. chap. 4. The work must have been written soon after the Council at which Marcellus was condemned. It aims simply to expose his errors, exegetical as well as theological. The work consists of two books, and is still extant (*Opera*, VI. 707–824).

On the Theology of the Church, a Refutation of Marcellus (οἱ πρὸς Μάρκελλον ἔλεγχοι περὶ τῆς ἐκκλησιαστικῆς Θεολογίας). The occasion of this work is stated in the first chapter. In the previous work Eusebius had aimed merely to expose the opinions of Marcellus, but in this he devotes himself to their refutation, fearing that some might be led astray by their length and plausibility. The work, which consists of three books, is still extant, and is given by Migne in the *Opera*, VI. 825–1046. Both it and the preceding are published with the *Contra Hieroclem* in Gaisford's *Euseb. Pamph. contra Hieroclem et Marcellum*, Oxon. 1852. Zahn has written a valuable monograph entitled *Marcellus von Ancyra* (Gotha, 1867).

Against the Manicheans. Epiphanius (*Hær.* LXVI. 21) mentions, among other refutations of the Manicheans, one by our Eusebius. The work is referred to nowhere else, and it is possible that Epiphanius was mistaken in his reference, or that the refutation he has in mind formed only a part of some other work, but we are hardly justified in asserting, as Lightfoot does, that the work cannot have existed.

IV. DOGMATIC WORKS.

General Elementary Introduction ('Η καθόλου στοιχειώδης εἰσαγωγή). This work consisted of ten books, as we learn from a reference to it in the *Eclogæ Propheticæ*, IV. 35. It was apparently a general introduction to the study of theology, and covered a great variety of subjects. Five brief fragments have been preserved, all of them apparently from the first book, which must have dealt largely with general principles of ethics. The fragments were published by Mai (*Bibl. Nova Patrum*, IV. 316), and are reprinted by Migne (*Opera*, IV. 1271 sq.). In addition to these fragments, the sixth, seventh, eighth, and ninth books of the work are extant under the title:

Prophetical Extracts (Προφητικαὶ 'Εκλογαί). Although this formed a part of the larger work, it is complete in itself, and circulated independently of the rest of the *Introduction*. It contains extracts of prophetical passages from the Old Testament relating to the person and work of Christ, accompanied by explanatory notes. It is divided into four books, the first containing extracts from the historical Scriptures, the second from the Psalms, the third from the other poetical books and from the prophets, the fourth from Isaiah alone. The personality of the Logos is the main topic of the work, which is thus essentially dogmatic, rather than apologetic, as it might at first glance seem to be. It was composed during the persecution, which is clearly referred to in Book I. chap. 8 as still raging; it must have been written therefore between 303 and 313. The date of these books, of course, fixes the date of the *General Introduction*, of which they formed a part. The *Eclogæ* are referred to in the *History*, I. 2. On the other hand, they mention the *Chronicle* as a work already written (I. 1 : *Opera*, p. 1023) ; a reference which goes to prove that there were two editions of the *Chronicle* (see above, p. 31). The four books of the *Prophetical Extracts* were first published by Gaisford in 1842 (Oxford) from a Vienna MS. The MS. is mutilated in many places, and the beginning, including the title of the work, is wanting. Migne has reprinted Gaisford's edition in the *Opera*, IV. 1017 sq.

On the Paschal Festival (περὶ τῆς τοῦ πάσχα ἑορτῆς). This work, as Eusebius informs us in his *Vita Const.* IV. 34, was addressed to the Emperor Constantine, who commends it very highly in an epistle to Eusebius preserved in the *Vita Const.* IV. 35. From this epistle we learn, moreover, that the work had been translated into Latin. It is no longer extant in its entirety, but a considerable fragment of it was discovered by Mai in Nicetas' *Catena on Luke*, and published by him in his *Bibl. Nova Patrum*, IV. p. 208 sq. The extant portion of it contains twelve chapters, devoted partly to a discussion of the nature of the Passover and its typical significance, partly to an account of the settlement of the paschal question at the Council of Nicæa, and partly to an argument against the necessity of celebrating the paschal feast at the time of the Jewish Passover, based on the ground that Christ himself did not keep the Passover on the same day as the Jews.

Jerome, although he does not mention this work in his catalogue of Eusebius' writings (*de vir. ill.* 81), elsewhere (*ib.* 61) states that Eusebius composed a paschal canon with a cycle of nineteen years. This cycle may have been published (as Lightfoot remarks) as a part of the writing under discussion. The date of the work cannot be determined with exactness. It was written after the Council of Nicæa, and, as would seem from the connection in which it is mentioned in the *Vita Constantini*, before the Emperor's *tricennalia* (335 A.D.), but not very long before. The extant fragment, as published by Mai, is reprinted by Migne in the *Opera*, VI. 693–706.

V. Critical and Exegetical Works.

Biblical Texts. We learn from Jerome (*Præf. in librum Paralip.*) that Eusebius and Pamphilus published a number of copies of Origen's edition of the LXX., that is, of the fifth column of the Hexapla. A colophon found in a Vatican MS., and given in fac-simile in Migne's *Opera*, IV. 875, contains the following account of their labors (the translation is Lightfoot's) : " It was transcribed from the editions of the Hexapla, and was corrected from the Tetrapla of Origen himself, which also had been corrected and furnished with scholia in his own handwriting ; whence I, Eusebius, added the scholia, Pamphilus and Eusebius corrected [this copy]." Compare also Field's *Hexapla*, I. p. xcix.

Taylor, in the *Dictionary of Christian Biography*, III. p. 21, says : " The whole work [i.e. the Hexapla] was too massive for multiplication ; but many copies of its fifth column alone were issued from Cæsarea under the direction of Pamphilus the martyr and Eusebius, and this recension of the LXX. came into common use. Some of the copies issued contained also marginal scholia, which gave *inter alia* a selection of readings from the remaining versions in the Hexapla. The oldest extant MS. of this recension is the Leiden *Codex Sarravianus* of the fourth or fifth century." These editions of the LXX. must have been issued before the year 309, when Pamphilus suffered martyrdom, and in all probability before 307, when he was imprisoned (see Lardner's *Credibility*, Part II. chap. 72.

In later years we find Eusebius again engaged in the publication of copies of the Scriptures. According to the *Vita Const.* IV. 36, 37, the Emperor wrote to Eusebius, asking him to prepare fifty sumptuous copies of the Scriptures for use in his new Constantinopolitan churches. The commission was carefully executed, and the MSS. prepared at great cost. It has been thought that among our extant MSS. may be some of these copies which were produced under Eusebius' supervision, but this is extremely improbable (see Lightfoot, p. 334).

Ten Evangelical Canons, with the Letter to Carpianus prefixed (κανόνες δέκα ; *Canones decem harmoniæ evangeliorum præmissa ad Carpianum epistola*). Ammonius of Alexandria early in the third century had constructed a harmony of the Gospels, in which, taking Matthew as the standard, he placed alongside of that Gospel the parallel passages from the three others. Eusebius' work was suggested by this *Harmony*, as he tells us in his epistle to Carpianus. An inconvenient feature of Ammonius' work was that only the Gospel of Matthew could be read continuously, the sequence of the other Gospels being broken in order to bring their parallel sections into the order followed by Matthew. Eusebius, desiring to remedy this defect, constructed his work on a different principle. He made a table of ten canons, each containing a list of passages as follows : Canon I. passages common to all four Gospels ; II. those common to Matthew, Mark, and Luke ; III. those common to Matt., Luke, and John ; IV. those common to Matt., Mark, and John; V. those common to Matthew and Luke; VI. those common to Matt. and Mark; VII. those common to Matt. and John; VIII. those common to Luke and Mark; IX. those common to Luke and John; X. those peculiar to each Gospel: first to Matthew, second to Mark, third to Luke, and fourth to John.

Each Gospel was then divided into sections, which were numbered continuously. The length of the section was determined, not by the sense, but by the table of canons, each section comprising a passage common to four, to three, to two Gospels, or peculiar to itself, as the case might be. A single section therefore might comprise even less than a verse, or it might cover more than a chapter. The sections were numbered in black, and below each number was placed a second figure in red, indicating the canon to which the section belonged. Upon glancing at that canon the reader would find at once the numbers of the parallel sections in the other Gospels, and could turn to them readily. The following is a specimen of a few lines of the first canon : —

MT.	MP.	Λ.	IΩ.
η	β	ζ	ι
ια	δ	ι	ϛ
ια	δ	ι	ιβ
ια	δ	ι	ιδ

Thus, opposite a certain passage in John, the reader finds ιβ (12) written, and beneath it, A (1). He therefore turns to the first canon (A) and finds that sections ια (11) in Matthew, δ (4) in Mark, and ι (10) in Luke are parallel with ιβ in John. The advantage and convenience of such a system are obvious, and the invention of it shows great ingenuity. It has indeed never been superseded, and the sections and canons are still indicated in the margins of many of our best Greek Testaments (e.g., in those of Tregelles and of Tischendorf). The date of the construction of these canons it is quite impossible to determine. For further particulars in regard to them, see Lightfoot's article on Eusebius, p. 334 sq., and Scrivener's *Introduction to the Criticism of the New Testament*, 2d ed. p. 54 sq. The canons, with the letter to Carpianus prefixed, are given by Migne, *Opera*, IV. 1275-1292.

Gospel Questions and Solutions. This work consists of two parts, or of two separate works combined. The first bears the title *Gospel Questions and Solutions addressed to Stephanus* (πρὸς Στέφανον περὶ τῶν ἐν εὐαγγελίοις ζητημάτων καὶ λύσεων), and is referred to by Eusebius in his *Dem. Evang.* VII. 3, as *Questions and Solutions on the Genealogy of our Saviour* (τῶν εἰς τὴν γενεαλογίαν τοῦ σωτῆρος ἡμῶν ζητημάτων καὶ λύσεων). The second part is entitled *Gospel Questions and Solutions addressed to Marinus* (πρὸς Μαρῖνον). The first work consisted of two books, as we learn from the opening of the second work. In that passage, referring to the previous work, Eusebius says that having discussed there the difficulties which beset the beginning of the Gospels, he will now proceed to consider questions concerning the latter part of them, the intermediate portions being omitted. He thus seems to regard the two works as in a sense forming parts of one whole. In his *de vir. ill.* 81, Jerome mentions among the writings of Eusebius one *On the Discrepancy of the Gospels* (*De Evangeliorum Diaphonia*), and in his *Comm. in Matt.* chap. I. vers. 16, he refers to Eusebius' *libri διαφωνίας εὐαγγελίων*. Ebed-jesu also remarks, " Eusebius Cæsariensis composuit librum solutionis contradictionum evangelii." In the sixteenth century there were found in Sicily, according to the announcement of Latino Latini, " libri tres Eusebii Cæsariensis de Evangeliorum diaphonia," but nothing more has been heard or seen of this Sicilian MS. There can be no doubt that the work referred to under the title *De Evangeliorum Diaphonia* is identical with the *Gospel Questions and Solutions*, for the discrepancies in the Gospels occupy a considerable space in the *Questions and Solutions* as we have it, and the word διαφωνία occurs frequently. The three books mentioned by Latino Latini were therefore the two books addressed to Stephanus which Eusebius himself refers to, and the one book addressed to Marinus. The complete work is no longer extant, but an epitome of it was discovered and published by Mai, together with numerous fragments of the unabridged work, two of them in Syriac (*Bibl. Nova Patrum*, IV. 217 sq.; reprinted by Migne, *Opera*, IV. 879–1016). In the epitome the work addressed to Stephanus consists of sixteen chapters, and the division into two books is not retained. The work addressed to Marinus consists of only four chapters.

The work purports to have been written in answer to questions and difficulties suggested by Stephanus and Marinus, who are addressed by Eusebius in terms of affection and respect. The first work is devoted chiefly to a discussion of the genealogies of Christ, as given by Matthew and Luke; the second work deals with the apparent discrepancies between the accounts of the resurrection as given by the different evangelists. Eusebius does not always reach a solution of the difficulties, but his work is suggestive and interesting. The question as to the date of the work is complicated by the fact that there is in the *Dem. Evang.* VII. 3 a reference to the *Questions and Solutions addressed to Stephanus*, while in the epitome of the latter work (*Quaest.* VII. § 7) there is a distinct reference to the *Demonstratio Evang.* This can be satisfactorily explained only by supposing, with Lightfoot, that the Epitome was made at a later date than the original work, and that then Eusebius inserted this reference to the *Demonstratio*. We are thus led to assume two editions of this work, as of others of Eusebius' writings, the second edition being a revised abridgment of the first. The first edition, at least of the *Quæstiones ad Stephanum*, must have been published before the *Demonstratio Evangelica*. We cannot fix the date of the epitome, nor of the *Quæstiones ad Marinum*.

Commentary on the Psalms (εἰς τοὺς ψαλμούς). This commentary is extant entire as far as the 118th psalm, but from that point to the end only fragments of it have been preserved. It was first published in 1707, by Montfaucon, who, however, knew nothing of the fragments of the latter part of the work. These were discovered and published by Mai, in 1847 (*Bibl. Nov. Patrum*, IV. 65 sq.), and the entire extant work, including these fragments, is printed by Migne, *Opera*, V. and VI. 9–76. According to Lightfoot, notices of extant Syriac extracts from it are found in Wright's *Catal. Syr. MSS. Brit. Mus.* pp. 35 sq. and 125. Jerome (*de vir. ill.* 96 and *Ep. ad Vigilantium*, § 2; Migne's ed. *Ep.* 61) informs us that Eusebius of Vercellæ translated this commentary into Latin, omitting the heretical passages. This version is no longer extant. The commentary had a high reputation among the Fathers, and justly so. It is distinguished for its learning, industry, and critical acumen. The *Hexapla* is used with great diligence, and the author frequently corrects the received LXX. text of his day upon the authority of one of the other versions. The work betrays an acquaintance with Hebrew, uncommon among the Fathers, but by no means extensive or exact. Eusebius devotes considerable attention to the historical relations of the Psalms, and exhibits an unusual degree of good judgment in their treatment, but the allegorical method of the school of Origen is conspicuous, and leads him into the mystical extravagances so common to patristic exegesis.

The work must have been written after the close of the persecution and the death of the persecutors (*in Psal.* XXXVI. 12). In another passage (*in Psal.* LXXXVII. 11) there seems to be a reference to the discovery of the site of the Holy Sepulchre and the erection of Constantine's basilica upon it (see *Vita Const.* III. 28, 30, &c.). The basilica was dedicated in the year 335 (see above, p. 24), and the site of the sepulchre was not discovered until the year 326, or later (see Lightfoot, p. 336). The commentary must have been written apparently after the basilica was begun, and probably after its completion. If so, it is to be placed among the very latest of Eusebius' works.

Commentary on Isaiah (ὑπομνήματα εἰς Ἡσαΐαν). This work is also extant almost entire, and was first published in 1706, by Montfaucon (*Coll. Nova Patrum et Script. Græc.* II.; reprinted by Migne, *Opera*, VI. 77–526). In his *de vir. ill.* 81 Jerome refers to it as containing ten books (*in Isaiam libri decem*), but in the preface to his *Comment. in Isaiam* he speaks of it as composed of fifteen (*Eusebius quoque Pamphili juxta historicam explanationem quindecim edidit volumina*). In its present form there is no trace of a division into books. The commentary is marked by the same characteristics which were noticed in connection with the one on the Psalms, though it does not seem to have acquired among the ancients so great a reputation as that work. It must have been written after the close of the persecution (*in Is.* XLIV. 5), and apparently after the accession of Constantine to sole power (*in Is.* XLIX. 23 compared with *Vita Const.* IV. 28). If the commentary on the Psalms was written toward the close of Eusebius' life, as assumed above, it is natural to conclude that the present work preceded that.

Commentary on Luke (εἰς τὸ κατὰ Λουκᾶν εὐαγγέλιον). This work is no longer extant, but considerable fragments of it exist and have been published by Mai (*Bibl. Nova Patrum*, IV. 159 sq.; reprinted by Migne, *Opera*, VI. 529–606). Although the fragments are all drawn from Catenæ on Luke, there are many passages which seem to have been taken from a commentary on Matthew (see the notes of the editor). A number of extracts from the work are found in Eusebius' *Theophania* (see Mai's introduction to his fragments of the latter work).

The date of the commentary cannot be fixed with certainty, but I am inclined to place it before the persecution of Diocletian, for the reason that there appears in the work, so far as I have discovered, no hint of a persecution, although the passages expounded offer many opportunities for such a reference, which it is difficult to see how the author could have avoided making if a persecution were in progress while he was writing; and further, because in discussing Christ's prophecies of victory and dominion over the whole world, no reference is made to the triumph gained by the Church in the victories of Constantine. A confirmation of this early date may be found in the extreme simplicity of the exegesis, which displays neither the wide learning, nor the profound study that mark the commentaries on the Psalms and on Isaiah.

Commentary on the First Epistle to the Corinthians. This work is no longer extant, and we know of it only from a reference in Jerome's *Ep. ad Pammachium*, § 3 (Migne's ed. *Ep.* 49): "Origenes, Dionysius, Pierius, Eusebius Cæsariensis, Didymus, Apollinaris latissime hanc Epistolam interpretati sunt."

Exegetical Fragments. Mai has published brief fragments containing expositions of passages from *Proverbs* (*Bibl. Nova Patrum*, IV. 316; reprinted by Migne, *Opera*, VI. 75–78), from *Daniel* (*ib.* p. 314; Migne, VI. 525–528), and from the *Epistle to the Hebrews* (*ib.* p. 207; Migne, VI. 605). Fabricius mentions also fragments from a commentary on the *Song of Songs* as published by Meursius, and says that other commentaries are referred to by Montfaucon in his *Epistola de Therapeutis*, p. 151. We have no references in the works of the ancients to any such commentaries, so far as I am aware, and it is quite possible that the various fragments given by Mai, as well as those referred to by Fabricius may have been taken not from continuous commentaries, but from Eusebius' *General Elementary Introduction*, or others of his lost works. According to Migne (VI. 527) some Greek Catenæ published by Cramer in Oxford in the year 1884 contain extensive fragments on Matthew and John, which, however, have been taken from Eusebius' *Quæst. Evang.* Other fragments in Catenæ on the same Evangelists and on Mark, have been taken, according to Migne, from the *Quæstiones ad Stephanum*, or from the *Commentary on Luke*.

It is, however, quite possible, as it seems to me, that Eusebius wrote a commentary on Daniel. At any rate, the exegetical fragments which we have, taken with the extended discussions of certain passages found in the *Dem. Evang.* VIII. 2 and in the *Eclogæ Proph.* III. 40 sq., show that he expounded at one time or another a considerable portion of the book.

VI. Biblical Dictionaries.

Interpretation of the Ethnological Terms in the Hebrew Scriptures. This work is no longer extant, but is known to us from Eusebius' reference to it in the preface to his work *On the Names of Places*, where he writes as follows: τῶν ἀνὰ τὴν οἰκουμένην ἐθνῶν ἐπὶ τὴν ἑλλάδα φωνὴν μεταβαλὼν τὰς ἐν τῇ θείᾳ γραφῇ κειμένας ἑβραίοις ὀνόμασι προσρήσεις. Jerome, in the preface to his Latin version of the same work, also refers to it in the following words: ". . . diversarum

vocabula nationum, quæ quomodo olim apud Hebræos dicta sint, et nunc dicantur, exposuit."
No other ancient authority mentions the work so far as I am aware.

Chorography of Ancient Judea with the Inheritances of the Ten Tribes. This work too is lost,
but is referred to by Eusebius in the same preface in the following words : τῆς πάλαι Ἰουδαίας ἀπὸ
πάσης Βίβλου καταγραφὴν πεποιημένος καὶ τὰς ἐν αὐτῇ τῶν δώδεκα φυλῶν διαιρῶν κλήρους. Jerome
(*ib.*) says : ". . . Chorographiam terrae Judaeae, et distinctas tribuum sortes . . . laboravit."

It is remarked by Fabricius that this work is evidently intended by Ebedjesu in his catalogue,
where he mentions among the writings of Eusebius a *Librum de Figura Mundi* (cf. Assemani's
Bibl. Orient. III. p. 18, note 7).

*A Plan of Jerusalem and of the Temple, accompanied with Memoirs relating to the Various
Localities.* This too is lost, but is referred to by Eusebius (*ib.*) in the following words : ὡς ἐν
γραφῆς τύπῳ τῆς πάλαι διαβοήτου μητροπόλεως αὐτῆς (λέγω δὲ τὴν Ἰερουσαλήμ) τοῦ τε ἐν αὐτῇ ἱεροῦ
τὴν εἰκόνα διαχαράξας μετὰ παραθέσεως τῶν εἰς τοὺς τύπους ὑπομνημάτων. Jerome (*ib.*) says : "ipsius
quoque Jerusalem templique in ea cum brevissima expositione picturam, ad extremum in hoc
opusculo laboravit."

On the Names of Places in Holy Scripture (περὶ τῶν τοπικῶν ὀνομάτων τῶν ἐν τῇ θείᾳ
γραφῇ). In Jerome's version this work bears the title *Liber de Situ et Nominibus Locorum
Hebraicorum*, but in his *de vir. ill.* 81, he refers to it as τοπικῶν, *liber unus*, and so it is commonly
called simply *Topica*. It is still extant, both in the original Greek and in a revised and partly
independent Latin version by Jerome. Both are published by Vallarsi in *Hieronymi Opera*, III.
122 sq. Migne, in his edition of Eusebius' works, omits the *Topica* and refers to his edition of
Jerome's works, where, however, he gives only Jerome's version, not the original Greek (III.
859–928). The best editions of the Greek text are by Larsow and Parthey (*Euseb. Pamph. Episc.
Cæs. Onomasticon,* &c., Berolini, 1862), and by Lagarde (*Onomastica Sacra*, I. 207–304, Gottingæ, 1870). The work aims to give, in the original language, in alphabetical order, the names
of the cities, villages, mountains, rivers, &c., mentioned in the· Scriptures, together with their
modern designations and brief descriptions of each. The work is thus of the same character as
a modern dictionary or Biblical geography. The other three works were narrower than this
one in their scope, but seem also to have been arranged somewhat on the dictionary plan. The
work is dedicated to Paulinus, a fact which leads us to place its composition before 325 A.D.,
when Paulinus was already dead (see below, p. 369). Jerome, in the preface to his version,
says that Eusebius wrote the work after his *History* and *Chronicle*. We are to conclude, then,
either that the work was published in 324 or early in 325, within a very few months after the
History, or, what is more probable, that Jerome is mistaken in his statement. He is proverbially
careless and inaccurate, and Eusebius, neither in his preface — from which Jerome largely quotes
in his own — nor in the work itself, gives any hint of the fact that his *History* and *Chronicle* were
already written.

On the Nomenclature of the Book of the Prophets (περὶ τῆς τοῦ βιβλίου τῶν προφητῶν
ὀνομασίας καὶ ἀπὸ μέρους τί περιέχει ἕκαστος). This work contains brief accounts of the several
prophets and notes the subjects of their prophecies. It is thus, so far as it goes, a sort of
biographical dictionary. It was first published by Curterius in his *Procopii Sophistæ Christianæ
variarum in Isaiam Prophetam commentationum epitome* (Paris, 1850, under the title *De
vitis Prophetarum*, by which it is commonly known. We have no means of determining the date
of its composition. Curterius' text has been reprinted by Migne, *Opera*, IV. 1261–1272.

VII. Orations.

Panegyric on the Building of the Churches, addressed to Paulinus, Bishop of Tyre (Πανη-
γυρικὸς ἐπὶ τῇ τῶν ἐκκλησιῶν οἰκοδομῇ, Παυλίνῳ Τυρίων ἐπισκόπῳ προσπεφωνημένος). This oration
was delivered at the dedication of Paulinus' new church in Tyre, to which reference has already
been made (see above, p. 11). It has been preserved in Eusebius' *History*, Book X. chap. 4 (see
below, p. 370 sq.).

Oration delivered at the Vicennalia of Constantine. Eusebius refers to this in the Preface to his *Vita Constantini* as εἰκοσαετηρικοὶ ὕμνοι. It is to be identified with the oration delivered at the opening of the Council of Nicæa (*Vita Const.* III. 11), as stated above, on p. 19. It is unfortunately no longer extant.

Oration on the Sepulchre of the Saviour. In his *Vita Const.* IV. 33 Eusebius informs us that he delivered an oration on this subject (ἀμφὶ τοῦ σωτηρίου μνήματος λόγος) in the presence of the Emperor at Constantinople. In the same work, IV. 46, he says that he wrote a description of the church of the Saviour and of his sepulchre, as well as of the splendid presents given by the Emperor for their adornment. This description he gave in a special work which he addressed to the Emperor (ἐν οἰκείῳ συγγράμματι παραδόντες, αὐτῷ βασιλεῖ προσεφωνήσαμεν). If these two are identical, as has always been assumed, the *Oration on the Sepulchre* must have been delivered in 335, when Eusebius went to Constantinople, just after the dedication of the Church of the Holy Sepulchre in Jerusalem (see above, p. 23), and just before the *Oratio de laudibus Constantini* (see *ib.* IV. 46). That the two are identical has always been assumed, and seems most probable. At the same time it is worthy of notice that in IV. 33 Eusebius speaks as if he returned to Cæsarea immediately after delivering his oration, and gives no hint of the delivery of his *De laud. Const.* at that time. It is noticeable also that he speaks in IV. 46 of a *work* (σύγγραμμα) not of an *oration* (λόγος), and that in IV. 45 he mentions the fact that he has described the splendid edifice and gifts of the Emperor *in writing* (διὰ γράμματος), which would seem to imply something else than an address. Finally, it is to be observed that, whereas, in IV. 46, he expressly refers to the church erected by Constantine and to his rich gifts in connection with its construction, in IV. 33 he refers only to the sepulchre. It appears to me, in fact, quite possible that Eusebius may be referring to two entirely different compositions, the one an oration delivered after the discovery of the sepulchre and before the Emperor had built the church (perhaps containing the suggestion of such a building), the other a descriptive work written after the completion of that edifice. I present this only as a possibility, for I realize that against it may be urged the unlikelihood that two separate works should have been composed by Eusebius upon subjects so nearly, if not quite, identical, and also the probability that, if there were two, both, and not one only, would have been attached to the end of the *Vita Const.* with the *De laud Const.* (see IV. 46). Neither the *Oration on the Sepulchre of the Saviour* nor the *Work on the Church and the Sepulchre* (whether the two are same or not) is now extant.

Oration delivered at the Tricennalia of Constantine (εἰς Κωνσταντῖνον τὸν βασιλέα τριακονταετηρικός), commonly known under the title *Oratio de laudibus Constantini.* In his *Vita Const.* IV. 46, Eusebius promised to append this oration, together with the writing *On the Church and the Sepulchre*, to that work. The *de laudibus* is still found at the end of the MSS. of the *Vita*, while the other writing is lost. It was delivered in Constantinople in 335 on the occasion of the Emperor's *tricennalia*, very soon after the dedication of the church of the Holy Sepulchre in Jerusalem (see above, p. 25). It is highly panegyrical, but contains a great deal of theology, especially in regard to the person and work of the Logos. Large portions of it were afterward incorporated into the *Vita Constantini* and the *Theophania*. The oration is published in most, if not all, editions of the *Vita Constantini;* in Migne, *Opera*, II. 1315–1440.

Oration in Praise of the Martyrs. This oration is mentioned in the catalogue of Ebedjesu (*et orationem de laudibus eorum* [i.e. Martyrum Occidentalium] ; see Assemani, *Bibl. Orient.* III. p. 19), and, according to Lightfoot, is still extant in a Syriac version, which has been published in the *Journal of Sacred Literature*, N. S., Vol. V. p. 403 sq., with an English translation by B. H. Cowper, *ib.* VI. p. 129 sq. Lightfoot finds in it an indication that it was delivered at Antioch, but pronounces it of little value or importance.

On the Failure of Rain. This is no longer extant, and is known to us only from a reference in the catalogue of Ebedjesu (*et orationem de defectu pluviæ;* see Assemani, *ib.*).

VIII. EPISTLES.

To Alexander, bishop of Alexandria. The purpose and the character of this epistle have been already discussed (see above, p. oo). A fragment of it has been preserved in the Proceedings of the Second Council of Nicæa, Act VI., Tom. V. (*Labbei et Cossartii Conc.* VII. col. 497). For a translation of the epistle, see below, p. 70. This and the following epistle were written after the outbreak of the Arian controversy, but before the Nicene Council.

To Euphration, bishop of Balaneæ in Syria, likewise a strong opponent of the Arians (see Athan. *de Fuga,* 3; *Hist. Ar. ad Mon.* 5). · Athanasius states that this epistle declared plainly that Christ is not God (Athan. *de Synod.* 17). A brief fragment of it has been preserved in the Acts of the Second Council of Nicæa (*l.c.*), which probably contains the very passage to which Athanasius refers. Upon the interpretation and significance of the fragment, see above, p. 15.

To Constantia Augusta, the sister of Constantine and wife of Licinius. Constantia had written to Eusebius requesting him to send her a certain likeness of Christ of which she had heard. Eusebius, in this epistle, rebukes her, and speaks strongly against the use of such representations, on the ground that it tends toward idolatry. The tone of the letter is admirable. Numerous fragments of it have been discovered, so that we have it now almost entire. It is printed in Migne, *Opera,* II. 1545-1550. We have no means of ascertaining the date at which it was written.

To the Church of Cæsarea. This epistle was written from Nicæa in 325 A.D., during or immediately after the Council. Its purpose and character have been discussed above on p. 16 sq., where a translation of it is given. The epistle is preserved by Athanasius (*de Decret. Syn. Nic.* app.); by Socrates, *H. E.* I. 8; by Theodoret, *H. E.* I. 11, and others. It is printed by Migne, *Opera,* II. 1535-1544.

In the Acts of the Second Council of Nicæa (*l.c.*) we find a mention of "all the epistles" of Eusebius, as if many were at that time extant. We know, however, only of those which have been mentioned above.

IX. SPURIOUS OR DOUBTFUL WORKS.

Fourteen Latin *opuscula* were discovered and published by Sirmond in 1643, and have been frequently reprinted (Migne, *Opera,* VI. 1047-1208). They are of a theological character, and bear the following titles : —

De fide adv. Sabellium, libri duo.
De Resurrectione, libri duo.
De Incorporali et invisibili Deo.
De Incorporali.
De Incorporali Anima.
De Spiritali Cogitatu hominis.
De eo quod Deus Pater incorporalis est, libri duo.
De eo quod ait Dominus, Non veni pacem, etc.
De Mandato Domini, Quod ait, Quod dico vobis in aure, etc.
De operibus bonis et malis.
De operibus bonis, ex epist. II. ad Corinth.

Their authenticity is a matter of dispute. Some of them may be genuine, but Lardner is doubtless right in denying the genuineness of the two Against Sabellius, which are the most important of all (see Lardner's *Credibility,* Part II. chap. 72).

Lightfoot states that a treatise, *On the Star which appeared to the Magi,* was published by Wright in the *Journal of Sacred Literature* (1866) from a Syriac MS. It is ascribed to Eusebius, but its genuineness has been disputed, and good reasons have been given for supposing that it was written originally in Syriac (see Lightfoot, p. 345).

Fabricius (*Bibl. Gr.* VI. 104) reports that the following works are extant in MS.: *Fragmentum de Mensuris ac Ponderibus* (MSS. Is. Vossii, n. 179); *De Morte Herodis* (MS. in Bibl. Basil.); *Præfatio ad Canticum Mosis in Exodo* (Lambec. III. p. 35).

CHAPTER III.

EUSEBIUS' CHURCH HISTORY.

§ 1.   *Date of its Composition.*

THE work with which we are especially concerned at this time is the *Church History*, the original Greek of which is still extant in numerous MSS. It consists of ten books, to which is added in most of the MSS. the shorter form of the *Martyrs of Palestine* (see above, p. 29). The date of the work can be determined with considerable exactness. It closes with a eulogy of Constantine and his son Crispus; and since the latter was put to death by his father in the summer of 326, the *History* must have been completed before that time. On the other hand, in the same chapter Eusebius refers to the defeat of Licinius, which took place in the year 323 A.D.   This gives a fixed *terminus a quo.* It is not quite certain from Eusebius' words whether the death of Licinius had already taken place at the time he wrote, but it seems probable that it had, and if so, the completion of the work must be put as late as the summer of 324. On the other hand, not the slightest reference is made to the Council of Nicæa, which met in the summer of 325; and still further the tenth book is dedicated to Paulinus, at one time bishop of Tyre and afterward bishop of Antioch (see Euseb. *Contra Marc.* I. 4, and Philost. *H. E.* III. 15), who was already dead in the summer of 325: for at the Nicene Council, Zeno appears as bishop of Tyre, and Eustathius as bishop of Antioch (see for further particulars Lightfoot, p. 322). We are thus led to place the completion of the *History* in the year 324, or, to give the widest possible limits, between the latter part of 323 and the early part of 325 A.D.

But the question has been raised whether the earlier books may not have been composed some years before this.   Lightfoot (following Westcott) supposes that the first nine books were completed not long after the edict of Milan and before the outbreak of the quarrel between Constantine and Licinius in 314.   There is considerable to be said in favor of this theory.   The language used in the dedication of the tenth book seems to imply that the nine books had been completed some time before, and that the tenth is added as a sort of postscript.   The close of the ninth book strengthens that conclusion.   Moreover, it would seem from the last sentences of that book that Constantine and Licinius were in perfect harmony at the time it was written, a state of affairs which did not exist after 314.   On the other hand, it must be noticed that in Book IX. chap. 9 Licinius' "madness" is twice referred to as having "not yet" seized him (in § 1 οὔπω μανέντος τοτε, and in § 12 οὔπω τότε ἐφ᾽ ἣν ὕστερον ἐκπέπτωκε μανίαν, τὴν διάνοιαν ἐκτραπείς). It is necessary either to interpret both these clauses as later insertions (possibly by Eusebius' own hand at the time when he added the tenth book; cf. also p. 30, above), or to throw the composition of the ninth book down to the year 319 or later.   It is difficult to decide between these alternatives, but I am inclined on the whole to think that Westcott's theory is probably correct, and that the two clauses can best be interpreted as later insertions.   The very nature of his *History* would at any rate lead us to think that Eusebius spent some years in the composition of it, and that the earlier books, if not published, were at least completed long before the issue of the ten books as a whole.   The *Chronicle* is referred to as already written in I. 1; the *Ecloga Proph.* (? see below, p. 85) in I. 2 and 6; the *Collection of Ancient Martyrdoms* in IV. 15, V. preface, 4, and 22; the *Defense of Origen* in VI. 23, 33, and 36; the *Life of Pamphilus* in VI. 32, VII. 32, and VIII. 13.   In VIII. 13 Eusebius speaks also of his intention of relating the sufferings of the martyrs in another work (but see above, p. 30).

§ 2. *The Author's Design.*

That the composition of a history of the Church was Eusebius' own idea, and was not due to any suggestion from without, seems clear, both from the absence of reference to any one else as prompting it, and from the lack of a dedication at the beginning of the work. The reasons which led him to undertake its composition seem to have been both scientific and apologetic. He lived, and he must have realized the fact, at the opening of a new age in the history of the Church. He believed, as he frequently tells us, that the period of struggle had come to an end, and that the Church was now about entering upon a new era of prosperity. He must have seen that it was a peculiarly fitting time to put on record for the benefit of posterity the great events which had taken place within the Church during the generations that were past, to sum up in one narrative all the trials and triumphs which had now emerged in this final and greatest triumph, which he was witnessing. He wrote, as any historian of the present day would write, for the information and instruction of his contemporaries and of those who should come after, and yet there was in his mind all the time the apologetic purpose, the desire to exhibit to the world the history of Christianity as a proof of its divine origin and efficacy. The plan which he proposed to himself is stated at the very beginning of his work : " It is my purpose to write an account of the successions of the holy apostles, as well as of the times which have elapsed from the days of our Saviour to our own ; and to relate how many and how important events are said to have occurred in the history of the Church ; and to mention those who have governed and presided over the Church in the most prominent parishes, and those who in each generation have proclaimed the divine word either orally or in writing. It is my purpose also to give the names and the number and the times of those who through love of innovation have run into the greatest errors, and proclaiming themselves discoverers of knowledge, falsely so-called, have, like fierce wolves, unmercifully devastated the flock of Christ. It is my intention, moreover, to recount the misfortunes which immediately came upon the whole Jewish nation in consequence of their plots against our Saviour, and to record the ways and the times in which the divine word has been attacked by the Gentiles, and to describe the character of those who at various periods have contended for it in the face of blood and tortures, as well as the confessions which have been made in our own days, and finally the gracious and kindly succour which our Saviour afforded them all." It will be seen that Eusebius had a very comprehensive idea of what a history of the Church should comprise, and that he was fully alive to its importance.

§ 3. *Eusebius as a Historian. The Merits and Defects of his History.*

The whole Christian world has reason to be thankful that there lived at the opening of the fourth century a man who, with his life spanning one of the greatest epochs that has occurred in the history of the Church, with an intimate experimental knowledge of the old and of the new condition of things, was able to conceive so grand a plan and possessed the means and the ability to carry it out. Had he written nothing else, Eusebius' *Church History* would have made him immortal ; for if immortality be a fitting reward for large and lasting services, few possess a clearer title to it than the author of that work. The value of the *History* to us lies not in its literary merit, but in the wealth of the materials which it furnishes for a knowledge of the early Church. How many prominent figures of the first three centuries are known to us only from the pages of Eusebius ; how many fragments, priceless on account of the light which they shed upon movements of momentous and far-reaching consequence, have been preserved by him alone ; how often a hint dropped, a casual statement made in passing, or the mention of some apparently trifling event, gives the clue which enables us to unravel some perplexing labyrinth, or to fit into one whole various disconnected and apparently unrelated elements, and thus to trace the steps in the development of some important historical movement whose rise and whose bearing must otherwise remain an unsolved riddle.   The work reveals no sympathy with Ebionism, Gnosticism, and Montanism, and little appreciation of their real nature, and yet our knowledge of their true significance and of their place in history is due in considerable part to facts respecting the movements or their leaders which Eusebius alone has recorded or preserved.   To understand the development of the Logos Christology we must comprehend the significance of the teaching of Paul of Samosata, and how inadequate would our knowledge of the nature of that teaching be without the epistle quoted in Book VII. chap. 30.   How momentous were the consequences of the paschal controversies, and how dark would they be were it not for the light shed upon them by our author.   How important, in spite of their tantalizing brevity and obscurity, the fragments of Papias' writings ; how interesting the extracts from the memoirs of Hegesippus ; how suggestive the meager notices from Dionysius of Corinth, from Victor of Rome, from Melito, from Caius ; how instructive the long and numerous quotations from the epistles of Dionysius of Alexandria !   He may often fail to appreciate the significance of the events which he records, he may in many cases draw unwarranted conclusions from the premises which he states, he may sometimes misinterpret his documents and misunderstand men and movements, but in the majority of cases he presents us with the material upon which to form our own judgments, and if we differ with him we must at the same time thank him for the data which have enabled us independently to reach other results.

But the value of Eusebius' *Church History* does not lie solely in the fact that it contains so many original sources which would be otherwise unknown to us.   It is not merely a thesaurus, it is a history in the truest sense, and it possesses an intrinsic value of its own, independent of its quotations from other works.   Eusebius possessed extensive sources of knowledge no longer accessible to us.   His *History* contains the results of his extended perusal of many works which are now irrecoverably lost, of his wide acquaintance with the current traditions of his day, of his familiar intercourse with many of the chief men of the age.   If we cut out all the documents which he quotes, there still remains an extensive history whose loss would leave an irreparable blank in our knowledge of the early Church.   How invaluable, for instance, to mention but one matter, are the researches of our author in regard to the circulation of the books of the New Testament : his testimony to the condition of the canon in his own time, and to the more or less widespread use of particular writings by the Fathers of preceding centuries.   Great as is the value of the sources which Eusebius quotes, those that he does not give are still more extensive, and it is the knowledge gained from them which he has transmitted to us.

The worth of these portions of his *History* must depend in the first place upon the extent and reliability of his sources, and in the second place upon the use which he made of them.

A glance at the list of his authorities given in the index, reveals at once the immense range of his materials.   The number of books which he either quotes or refers to as read is enormous.   When to these are added the works employed by him in the composition of his *Præp. Evang.*, as well as the great number which he must have perused, but does not mention, we are amazed at the extent of his reading.   He must have been a voracious reader from his earliest years, and he must have possessed extraordinary acquisitive powers.   It is safe to say that there was among the Fathers, with the possible exception of Origen, no more learned man than he.   He thus possessed one of the primary qualifications of the historian.   And yet even in this respect he had his limitations.   He seems to have taken no pains to acquaint himself with the works of heretics, but to have been content to take his knowledge of them at second hand.   And still further, he was sadly ignorant of Latin literature and of the Latin Church in general (see below, p. 106); in fact, we must not expect to glean from his *History* a very thorough or extended knowledge of western Christendom.

But his sources were not confined to literary productions.   He had a wide acquaintance with the world, and he was enabled to pick up much from his intercourse with other men and with different peoples that he could not have found upon the shelves of the Cæsarean or of any other library. Moreover, he had access to the archives of state, and gathered from them much information quite inaccessible to most men. He was thus peculiarly fitted, both by nature and by circumstances, for the task of acquiring material, the first task of the genuine historian.

But the value of his work must depend in the second place upon the wisdom and honesty with which he used his sources, and upon the faithfulness and accuracy with which he reproduced the results thus reached. We are therefore led to enquire as to his qualifications for this part of his work.

We notice, in the first place, that he was very diligent in the use of his sources. Nothing seems to have escaped him that might in any way bear upon the particular subject in hand. When he informs us that a certain author nowhere mentions a book or an event, he is, so far as I am aware, never mistaken. When we realize how many works he read entirely through for the sake of securing a single historical notice, and how many more he must have read without finding anything to his purpose, we are impressed with his untiring diligence. To-day, with our convenient indexes, and with the references at hand which have been made by many other men who have studied the writings of the ancients, we hardly comprehend what an amount of labor the production of a *History* like Eusebius' must have cost him, a pioneer in that kind of work.

In the second place, we are compelled to admire the sagacity which our author displays in the selection of his materials. He possessed the true instinct of the historian, which enabled him to pick out the salient points and to present to the reader just that information which he most desires. We shall be surprised upon examining his work to see how little it contains which it is not of the utmost importance for the student of early Church history to know, and how shrewdly the author has anticipated most of the questions which such a student must ask. He saw what it was in the history of the first three centuries of the Church which posterity would most desire to know, and he told them. His wisdom in this respect is all the more remarkable when compared with the unwisdom of most of his successors, who filled their works with legends of saints and martyrs, which, however fascinating they may have been to the readers of that age, possess little either of interest or of value for us. When he wishes to give us a glimpse of the persecutions of those early days, his historical and literary instinct leads him to dwell especially upon two thoroughly representative cases, — the martyrdom of Polycarp and the sufferings of the churches of Lyons and Vienne, — and to preserve for posterity two of the noblest specimens of martyrological literature which the ancient Church produced. It is true that he sometimes erred in his judgment as to the wants of future readers; we could wish that he had been somewhat fuller and clearer on many points, and that he had not so entirely neglected some others; but on the whole I am of the opinion that few historical works, ancient or modern, have in the same compass better fulfilled their mission in this respect.

In the third place, we can hardly fail to be impressed by the wisdom with which Eusebius discriminated between reliable and unreliable sources. Judged by the modern standard he may fall short as a literary critic, but judged by the standard of antiquity he must be given a very high rank. Few indeed are the historians of ancient times, secular or ecclesiastical, who can compare with Eusebius for sound judgment in this matter. The general freedom of his work from the fables and prodigies, and other improbable or impossible tales which disfigure the pages of the great majority even of the soberest of ancient historians, is one of its most marked features. He shows himself uncommonly particular in demanding good evidence for the circumstances which he records, and uncommonly shrewd in detecting spurious and unreliable sources. When we remember the great number of pseudonymous works which were current in his day we are compelled to admire his care and his discrimination. Not that he always succeeded in detecting the false. More than once he was sadly at fault (as for instance in regard to the Abgarus correspondence and Josephus' testimony to Christ), and has in consequence been severely denounced or held up to unsparing ridicule by many modern writers. But the wonder certainly is not that he erred as often as he did, but that he did not err oftener; not that he was sometimes careless in regard to the reliability of his sources, but that he was ever as careful as, in the majority of cases, he has proved himself to be. In fact, comparing him with other writers of antiquity, we cannot commend too highly the care and the skill with which he usually discriminated between the true and the false.

In the fourth place, he deserves all praise for his constant sincerity and unfailing honesty. I believe that emphasis should be laid upon this point for the reason that Eusebius' reputation has often suffered sadly in consequence of the unjust imputations, and the violent accusations, which it was for a long time the fashion to make against him, and which lead many still to treat his statements with distrust, and his character with contempt. Gibbon's estimate of his honesty is well known and has been unquestioningly accepted in many quarters, but it is none the less unjust, and in its implications quite untrue to the facts. Eusebius does dwell with greater fullness upon the virtues than upon the vices of the early Church, upon its glory than upon its shame, and he tells us directly that it is his intention so to do (*H. E.* VIII. 2), but he never undertakes to conceal the sins of the Christians, and the chapter immediately preceding contains a denunciation of their corruptness and wickedness uttered in no faint terms. In fact, in the face of these and other candid passages in his work, it is the sheerest injustice to charge him with dishonesty and unfairness because he prefers, as almost any Christian historian must, to dwell with greater fullness of detail upon the bright than upon the dark side of the picture. Scientific, Eusebius' method, in this respect, doubtless is not; but dishonest, no one has a right to call it. The most severe attack which has been made upon Eusebius in recent years is found in an article by Jachmann (see below, p. 55). The evident animus which runs through his entire paper is very unpleasant; the conclusions which he draws are, to say the least, strained. I cannot enter here into a consideration of his positions; most of them are examined below in the notes upon the various passages which he discusses. The whole article, like most similar attacks, proceeds upon the supposition that our author is guilty, and then undertakes simply to find evidence of that which is already presupposed. I submit that few writers could endure such an ordeal. If Eusebius is tried according to the principles of common justice, and of sound literary criticism, I am convinced, after long and careful study, that his sincerity and honesty of purpose cannot be impeached. The particular instances which have been urged as proving his dishonesty will be discussed below in the notes upon the respective passages, and to those the reader is referred (compare especially pp. 88, 98, 100, 111, 112, 114, 127, 194).

Eusebius' critics are wont to condemn him severely for what they are pleased to call the dishonesty displayed by him in his *Vita Constantini*. Such critics forget, apparently, that that work pretends to be, not a history, but a panegyric. Judging it as such, I am unable to find anything in it which leads me to entertain for a moment a suspicion of the author's honesty. It is true that Eusebius emphasizes the Emperor's good qualities, and fails to mention the darker spots in his character; but so far as I am aware he misstates no facts, and does only what those who eulogize deceased friends are accustomed to do the world over. For a discussion of this matter the reader is referred to the prolegomena of Dr. Richardson, pp. 467 sq. of this volume. I am pleased to learn from him that his study of the *Vita* has shown him nothing which justifies the charge of dishonesty brought against Eusebius.

One of the most decisive marks of veracity upon the part of our author is the frankness with which he confesses his lack of knowledge upon any subject (cf. IV. 5), and the care with which he distinguishes between the different kinds of evidence upon which he bases his statements. How frequently the phrases λόγος ἔχει, φασί, λέγεται, &c., occur in connection with accounts which a less scrupulous historian would not hesitate to record as undoubted fact. How particular he is to mention his sources for any unusual or startling event. If the authorities seem to him quite inadequate, he simply omits all reference to an occurrence which most of his contemporaries and successors would have related with the greatest gusto; if the testimony seems to him strong, he records the circumstance and expressly mentions his authority, whether oral tradition, the testimony of eye-witnesses, or written accounts, and we are thus furnished the material from which to form our own judgments.

He is often blamed by modern writers for what they are pleased to call his excessive credulity. Those who accuse him thus seem to forget that he lived in the fourth, not in the nineteenth century. That he believed many things which we now declare to be incredible is perfectly true, but that he believed things that other Christians of his day pronounced incredible is not true. Judged, in fact, according to the standard of his age — and indeed of eleven succeeding centuries — he must be pronounced remarkably free from the fault of over-credulity, in truth uncommonly skeptical in his attitude toward the marvelous. Not that he denies the occurrence of prodigies and wonders in his own and other ages, but that he always demands the strongest testimony before he allows himself to be convinced of their truth. Compare, e.g., the care with which he gives his authorities for the anecdote in regard to the Thundering Legion (V. 5), and his final suspension of judgment in the matter; compare also the emphasis which he lays upon the personal testimony of the Emperor in the matter of the appearance of the sign of the cross in the sky (*Vita Const.* I. 28 sq.), a phenomenon which he himself tells us that he would have believed upon no ordinary evidence. His conduct in this matter is a sign rather of a skepticism uncommon in his age than of an excessive and unusual credulity. Gibbon himself gives our author due credit in this respect, when he speaks of his character as " less tinctured with credulity, and more practiced in the arts of courts, than that of almost any of his contemporaries " (*Decline and Fall*, chap. XVI.).

On the other hand, Eusebius as an historian had many very grave faults which it is not my wish in the least to palliate or conceal. One of the most noticeable of these is his complete lack of any conception of historiography as a fine art. His work is interesting and instructive because of the facts which it records, but that interest is seldom if ever enhanced by his mode of presentation. There is little effective grouping, almost no sense of perspective, utter ignorance of the art of suggesting by a single line or phrase a finished picture of a man or of a movement. He was not, in other words, a Thucydides or a Tacitus; but the world has seen not many such as they.

A second and still more serious fault is our author's want of depth, if I may so express myself, his failure to look beneath the surface and to grasp the real significance of things, to trace the influence of opinions and events. We feel this defect upon every page. We read the annals, but we are conscious of no masterful mind behind them, digesting and comprehending them into one organic and imposing whole. This radical weakness in our author's method is revealed perhaps most clearly in his superficial and transcendental treatment of heretics and heresies, his failure to appreciate their origin and their bearing upon the progress of Christian thought. Of a development in theology, in fact, he knows nothing, and hence his work lacks utterly that which we now look upon as the most instructive part of Church history, — the history of doctrine.

In the third place, severe censure must be passed upon our author for his carelessness and inaccuracy in matters of chronology. We should expect that one who had produced the most extensive chronological work that had ever been given to the world, would be thoroughly at home in that province, but in truth his chronology is the most defective feature of his work. The difficulty is chiefly due to his inexcusable carelessness, we might almost say slovenliness, in the use of different and often contradictory sources of information. Instead of applying himself to the discrepancies, and endeavoring to reach the truth by carefully weighing the respective merits of the sources, or by testing their conclusions in so far as tests are possible, he adopts in many cases the results of both, apparently quite unsuspicious of the confusion consequent upon such a course. In fact, the critical spirit which actuates him in dealing with many other matters seems to leave him entirely when he is concerned with chronology; and instead of proceeding with the care and circumspection of an historian, he accepts what he finds with the unquestioning faith of a child. There is no case in which he can be convicted of disingenuousness, but at times his obtuseness is almost beyond belief. An identity of names, or a resemblance between events recorded by different authors, will often be enough to lead him all unconsciously to himself into the most absurd and contradictory conclusions. Instances of this may be seen in Book I. chap. 5, and in II. 11. His confusion in regard to the various Antonines (see especially the note on the preface to Book V.) is not at all unusual among the writers of his day, and in view of the frequent and perplexing use of the same names by the different emperors, might be quite excusable in a less scholarly man than Eusebius, but in his case it is evidence of unpardonable want of care. This serious defect in our author's method is not peculiar to him. Many historians, critical almost to a fault in most matters, accept the received chronology without question, and build upon it as if it were the surest of foundations. Such a consideration does not excuse Eusebius; it relieves him, however, of the stigma of peculiarity.

Finally, the character of the *History* is greatly impaired by our author's desultory method. This is a characteristic of his literary work in general, and• was referred to in the previous chapter. All his works are marred by it, but few suffer more noticeably than the *History*. The author does not confine himself as strictly as he should to the logical limits of the subject which he is treating, but allows himself to be led away from the main point by the suggestions that pour in upon him from all sides. As Lightfoot remarks, " We have not unfrequently to pick out from various parts of his work the notices bearing on one definite and limited subject. He relates a fact, or quotes an authority bearing upon it, in season or out of season, according as it is recalled to his memory by some accidental connexion." This unfortunate habit of Eusebius' is one into which men of wide learning are very apt to fall. The richness of their acquisitions embarrasses them, and the immense number of facts in their possession renders a comprehension of them all into one logical whole very difficult ; and yet unless the facts be thus comprehended, unless they be thoroughly digested and arranged, the result is confusion and obscurity. To exclude is as necessary as to include, if one would write history with the highest measure of success ; to exclude rigidly at one time what it is just as necessary to include at another. To men like Eusebius there is perhaps nothing more difficult than this. Only a mind as intensive as it is extensive, with a grasp as strong as its reach is wide, can accomplish it, and few are the minds that are blessed with both qualities. Few are the writers whose histories stand upon our shelves that fail not sadly in the one or in the other ; and in few perhaps does the failure seem more marked than in our author.

And yet, though it is apparent that the value of Eusebius' work is greatly impaired by its desultory method of treatment, I am confident that the defect is commonly exaggerated. The paragraph which Lightfoot quotes from Westcott on this subject leaves a false impression. Altogether too often our author introduces irrelevant matters, and repeats himself when repetition " mars the symmetry of his work " ; and yet on the whole he follows a fairly well ordered plan with fairly good success. He endeavors to preserve a strictly chronological sequence in his arrangement of the books, and he adheres for the most part to his purpose. Though there may be disorder and confusion within the various periods, for instance within the apostolic age, the age of Trajan, of Hadrian, of the Antonines, &c., yet the periods themselves are kept reasonably distinct from one another, and having finished his account of one of them the author seldom returns to it. Even in his treatment of the New Testament canon, which is especially desultory, he says most of what he has to say about it in connection with the apostles themselves, and before passing on to the second century. I would not overlook the exceeding flagrancy of his desultoriness and repetitiousness in his accounts of the writings of many of the Fathers, especially of the two Clements, and yet I would emphasize the fact that he certainly had an outline plan which he designed to follow, and for which due credit should be given him. He compares favorably in this respect with at least most of the writers of antiquity. Only with our modern method of dividing history into periods, separated by natural boundary lines, and of handling it under clearly defined rubrics, have we become able wholly to avoid the confused and illogical treatment of Eusebius and of others like him.

§ 4. *Editions and Versions.*

The original Greek of Eusebius' *History* has been published in many editions.

1. The *editio princeps* is that of Robert Stephanus, which appeared at Paris in 1544, and again, with a few changes, and with the Latin translation of Christophorsonus and the notes of Suffridus Petrus, at Geneva in 1612.

2. Henr. Valesius (de Valois) published his first edition of the Greek text, with a new Latin translation and with copious critical and explanatory notes, at Paris in 1659. His edition was reprinted at Mainz in 1672, but the reprint is full of errors. In 1677, after Valesius' death, a revised edition was issued at Paris, which in 1695 was reprinted with some corrections at Amsterdam. In 1720 Valesius' edition of Eusebius, together with his edition of Socrates, Sozomen, and the other Greek historians, was republished at Cambridge by William Reading, in three folio volumes. This is the best edition of Valesius, the commentary being supplemented by MS. notes which he had left among his papers, and increased by large additions from other writers under the head of *Variorum.* A reprint of Reading's edition was issued in 1746–1748, but according to Heinichen it is not as accurate as that of 1720. For the elucidation of Eusebius' *History* we owe more to Valesius than to any other man. His edition of the text was an immense advance upon that of Stephanus, and has formed the basis of all subsequent editions, while his notes are a perfect storehouse of information from which all annotators of Eusebius have extensively drawn. Migne's edition (*Opera*, II. 45–906) is a reprint of Valesius' edition of 1659.

3. F. A. Stroth (Halle, 1779). A new edition of the Greek text, of which, however, only the first volume appeared, comprising Books I.–VII.

4. E. Zimmermann (Frankfort-on-the-Main, 1822). A new edition of the Greek text, containing also the Latin translation of Valesius, and a few critical notes.

5. F. A. Heinichen (Leipzig, 1827 and 1828). An edition of the Greek text in three volumes, with a reprint of the entire commentary of Valesius, and with the addition of *Variorum* notes. The critical apparatus, printed in the third volume, is very meager. A few valuable excursuses close the work. Forty years later Heinichen published a second edition of the *History* in his *Eusebii Pamphili Scripta Historica* (Lips. 1868–1870, 3 vols.). The first volume contains the Greek text of the *History*, with valuable prolegomena, copious critical apparatus and very useful indices; the second volume contains the *Vita Constantini*, the *Panegyricus* or *De laudibus Constantini*, and Constantine's *Oratio ad Sanctorum coetum*, also accompanied with critical apparatus and indices; the third volume contains an extensive commentary upon the works included in the first two volumes, together with twenty-nine valuable excursuses. This entirely supersedes the first, and is on the whole the most complete and useful edition of the *History* which we have. The editor made diligent use of the labors of his predecessors, especially of Laemmer's. He did no independent work, however, in the way of collecting material for the criticism of the text, and was deficient in critical judgment. As a consequence his text has often to be amended on the basis of the variant readings, which he gives with great fullness. His commentary is made up largely of quotations from Valesius and other writers, and is valuable for the material it thus contains as well as for its references to other works. It labors under the same incompleteness, however, that mars Valesius' commentary, and, moreover, contains almost nothing of independent value.

6. E. Burton (Oxford, 1838). The Greek text in two volumes, with the translation of Valesius and with critical apparatus; and again in 1845, with the critical apparatus omitted, but with the notes of Valesius, Heinichen and others added. Burton made large contributions to the criticism of the text, and had he lived to superintend the issue of the second edition, would perhaps have succeeded in giving us a better text than any which we now possess, for he was a far more

sagacious critic than Heinichen. As it is, his edition is marred by numerous imperfections, largely caused by the inaccuracy of those who collated MSS. for him. His text, with the translation, notes, and critical apparatus omitted, was reprinted by Bright at Oxford in 1872, and again in 1881, in a single volume. This is a very handy edition, and for school use is unsurpassed. The typography is superb, and the admirable plan is followed of discarding quotation marks and printing all citations in smaller type, thus making plain to the eye at a glance what is Eusebius' own and what is another's. The text is preceded by a very interesting and graphic life of the historian.

7. Schwegler (Tübingen, 1852, in one volume). The Greek text with critical apparatus, but without translation and notes. An accurate and useful edition.

8. Laemmer (Schaffhausen, 1859–1862). The Greek text in one volume, with extensive critical apparatus, but without explanatory notes. Laemmer had unusual opportunities for collecting material, and has made larger additions to the critical apparatus than any one else. His edition was issued, however, in a most slovenly manner, and swarms with mistakes. Great care should therefore be exercised in the use of it.

9. Finally must be mentioned the text of Dindorf (Lips. 1871), which is published in the Teubner series, and like most of the volumes of that series is handy and convenient, but of little value to the critical student.

There are few writings of the Fathers which more sadly need and more richly deserve a new critical edition than the *History* of Eusebius. The material for the formation of a reliable text is extensive and accessible, but editors have contented themselves too much in the past with the results of their predecessors' labors, and unfortunately those labors have not always been accurate and thorough. As a consequence a new and more careful collation of most of the MSS. of the original, together with those of Rufinus' translation, must lie at the foundation of any new work which is to be done in this line. The publication of the Syriac version will doubtless furnish much valuable material which the next editor of the *History* will be able to use to advantage. Anything less than such a thorough work as I have indicated will be of little worth. Unless the new edition be based upon extensive and independent labors, it will be little if any improvement upon that of Heinichen. It is to be hoped that a critical text, up to the standard of those of some other patristic works which we already possess, may yet be issued, which shall give us this, one of the noblest productions of the ancient Church, in a fitting and satisfactory form.

Translations of Eusebius' *History* are very numerous. Probably the earliest of all is the ancient Syriac version which is preserved in great part in two MSS., one of which is at St. Petersburg and contains the entire *History* with the exception of Book VI. and large portions of Books V. and VII. The MS. is dated 462 A.D. (see Wright's description of it in his *Catalogue of the Syriac MSS. in the British Museum acquired since the year 1838*, Part III. p. xv. sq.). The second MS. is in the British Museum, and contains Books I.–V., with some mutilations at the beginning of the first book. The MS. dates from the sixth century (see Wright's description of it in his *Catalogue*, p. 1039). From these MSS. Wright was engaged in preparing an edition of the Syriac, which remained unfinished at the time of his death. Whether he left his work in such shape that it can soon be issued by some one else I have not yet learned. The version was probably made at a very early date, possibly within the lifetime of Eusebius himself, though of that we can have no assurance. I understand that it confirms in the main the Greek text as now printed in our best editions.

The original Latin version was made by Rufinus in the early years of the fifth century. He translated only nine books, and added to them two of his own, in which he brought the history down to the death of Theodosius the Great. He allowed himself his customary license in translating, and yet, although his version is by no means exact, it is one of our best sources for a knowledge of the true text of Eusebius, for it is possible, in many doubtful cases where our MSS. are hopelessly divided, to ascertain from his rendering what stood in the original Greek.

The version of Rufinus had a large circulation, and became in the Western Church a substitute for the original throughout the Middle Ages. It was first printed, according to Fabricius (*ib.* p. 59), in 1476 at Rome, afterward a great many times there and elsewhere. The first critical edition, which still remains the best, is that of Cacciari (Rome, 1740), which has become rare, and is very difficult to find. A new edition is a great desideratum. An important work upon Rufinus' version is Kimmel's *De Rufino Eusebii Interprete*, Geræ, 1838.

A new Latin translation, by Wolfgang Musculus, was published in Basle, in 1549, and again in 1557, 1562, and 1611, according to Fabricius (*Bibl. Gr.* VI. p. 60). I have myself seen only the edition of 1562.

Still another Latin version, from the hand of Christophorsonus, was published at Louvain in 1570. This is the only edition of Christophorsonus which I have seen, but I have notices of Cologne editions of 1570, 1581 and 1612, and of a Paris edition of 1571. According to Fabricius the Paris edition, and according to Brunnet the Cologne edition of 1581, contain the notes of Suffridus Petrus. A revision of Christophorsonus' version is said by Crusè to have been published by Curterius, but I have not seen it, nor am I aware of its date.

Another translation, by Grynæus, was published at Basle in 1611. This is the only edition of Grynæus' version which I have seen, and I find in it no reference to an earlier one. I have been informed, however, that an edition appeared in 1591. Hanmer seems to imply, in his preface, that Grynæus' version is only a revision of that of Musculus, and if that were so we should have to identify the 1611 edition with the 1611 edition of Musculus mentioned by Fabricius (see above). I am able, however, to find no hint in Grynæus' edition itself that his version is a revision of that of Musculus.

The translation of Valesius, which was first published in 1659 (see above), was a great improvement upon all that had preceded it, and has been many times reprinted in other editions of Eusebius, as well as in his own.

The first German translation was published by Caspar Hedio. The date of publication is given by Fabricius as 1545, but the copy which I have seen is dated 1582, and contains no reference to an earlier edition. It comprises only nine books of Eusebius, supplemented by the two of Rufinus. The title runs as follows: *Chronica, das ist: wahrhaftige Beschreibunge aller alten Christlichen Kirchen;* zum ersten, die *hist. eccles.* Eusebii Pamphili Cæsariensis, Eilff Bücher; zum andern, die *hist. eccles. tripartita* Sozomeni, Socratis und Theodoreti, Zwölff Bücher; zum dritten die *hist. eccles.* sampt andern treffenlichen Geschichten, die zuvor in Teutscher Sprache wenig gelesen sind, auch Zwölff Bücher. Von der Zeit an da die *hist. eccles. tripartita* aufhöret: das ist, von der jarzal an, vierhundert nach Christi geburt, biss auff das jar MDXLV, durch D. Caspar Hedion zu Strassburg verteutscht und zusamen getragen. Getruckt zu Franckfurt am Mayn, im jar 1582.

A second German translation of the entire *History* (with the exception of the *Martyrs of Palestine*, and the *Oration on the Building of the Churches*, X. 4), together with the *Life of Constantine*, was published by F. A. Stroth in Quedlinburg in 1777, in two volumes. Stroth prefaced the translation with a very valuable Life of Eusebius, and added a number of excellent notes of his own. The translation is reasonably accurate.

A much more elegant German version (including the *Oration*, but omitting the *Martyrs of Palestine*) was published by Closs in Stuttgart in 1839, in one volume. This is in my opinion the best translation of the *History* that exists. Its style is admirable, but pure German idiom is sometimes secured at the expense of faithfulness. In fact the author has aimed to produce a free, rather than a literal translation, and has occasionally allowed himself to depart too far from the original. A few brief notes, most of them taken from Valesius or Stroth, accompany the translation.

More recently a German translation has been published by Stigloher (Kempten, 1880) in the Kempten *Bibliothek der Kirchenväter*. It purports to be a new translation, but is practically nothing more than a poorly revised edition of Closs' version. The changes which are made are seldom improvements.

Fabricius mentions a French translation by Claudius Seysselius, but does not give the date of it, and I have not myself seen it. Dr. Richardson, however, informs me that he has a copy of this translation (which is from the Latin, not from the Greek) bearing the following title : *L'Histoire ecclesiastique translatie de Latin au Français, par M. Claude de Seyssel, evesque lors de Marseille, et depuis archevesque de Thurin.* Paris, 1532 [or '33], f°. He informs me also that there exist editions of the years 1537 and 1567.

More than a century later appeared a new French translation by Louis Cousin, bearing the following title : *Histoire de l'Eglise écrité par Eusèbe de Césarée, Socrate, Sozomène, Theodoret et Evagre, avec l'abrégé de Philostorge par Photius, et de Théodore par Nicephore Calliste.* Paris, 1675-1676. 4 vol. 4°. Another edition appeared in Holland in 1686, 5 vol. 12°.

The first English translation was made by Hanmer, and was issued in 1584, and, according to Crusè, passed through five editions. The fourth edition, which lies before me, was published in London in 1636. The volume contains the *Histories* of Eusebius, of Socrates, and of Evagrius ; Dorotheus' *Lives*, and Eusebius' *Life of Constantine.*

Another translation is said by Crusè to have been published about a century later by T. Shorting, and to be a decided improvement upon that of Hanmer. I have seen no copy bearing Shorting's name, but have examined an anonymous translation which bears the following title : *The Ecclesiastical History of Eusebius Pamphilus in ten books.* Made into English from that edition set forth by Valesius, and printed at Paris in the year 1659 ; together with Valesius' notes on the said historian, which are done into English and set at their proper place in the margin. Hereto also is annexed an account of the life and writings of the aforesaid historian, collected by Valesius and rendered into English. Cambridge : John Hayes, 1683. This is evidently the translation of Shorting referred to by Crusè, for it answers perfectly the description which he gives of it.

An abridgment of this version, made by Parker, is mentioned both by Fabricius (*ib.* p. 62) and by Crusè, but I have not myself seen it. Fabricius gives its date as 1703, and Dr. Richardson informs me that he has seen an edition bearing the date 1729, and that he has a note of another published in 1703 or 1720.

The latest English translation was made by the Rev. C. F. Crusè, an American Episcopalian of German descent, and was published first in Philadelphia in 1833, with a translation, by Parker, of Valesius' *Life of Eusebius* prefixed. It has been reprinted a great many times both in England and America, and is included in Bohn's Ecclesiastical Library. In Bohn's edition are printed a few scattered notes from Valesius' commentary, and in some other editions an historical account of the Council of Nicæa, by Isaac Boyle, is added. The translation is an improvement upon its predecessors, but is nevertheless very faulty and unsatisfactory. The translator is not thoroughly at home in the English, and, moreover, his version is marred by many serious omissions and interpolations which reveal an inexcusable degree of carelessness on his part.

§ 5. *Literature.*

The literature upon Eusebius' *History* is very extensive. Many of the editions already mentioned discuss, in their prolegomena, the *History* itself and Eusebius' character as a historian, as do also all the lives of Eusebius referred to above, and all the larger histories of the Church. In addition to these we have numerous important monographs and essays, of which the following may be mentioned here : Möller, *de Fide Eusebii in rebus christianis enarrandis*, Havn. 1813 ; Danz, *de Eusebio Cæsariensi Hist. Ecclesiasticæ Scriptore*, Jenæ, 1815. This was mentioned in Chapter I. as containing a valuable discussion of the life of Eusebius. Its chief importance lies in its treatment of the sources of the *Church History*, to which the author devotes the whole of

Chap. III. which bears the title, *de fontibus, quibus usus, historiam ecclesiasticam conscripsit Eusebius*, pp. 76–144. Kestner, *de Eusebii Historiæ Eccles. conditoris auctoritate, et fide diplomatica, sive de ejus Fontibus et Ratione qua eis usus est*, Gottingæ, 1816; and by the same author, *Ueber die Einseitigkeit und Partheiligkeit des Eusebius als Geschichtschreibers*, Jenæ, 1819; Reuterdahl, *de Fontibus Historiæ Eccles. Eusebianæ*, Londini Gothorum, 1826; Reinstra, *de Fontibus, ex quibus Historiæ Eccles. opus hausit Eusebius Pamphili, et de Ratione, qua iis usus est*, Trajecti ad Rhenum, 1833; F. C. Baur, *Comparatur Eusebius Historiæ Eccles. Parens cum Parente Historiæ Herodoto*, Tüb. 1834; and pp. 9–26 of the same author's *Epochen der kirchlichen Geschichtschreibung*, Tüb. 1852; Dowling, *Introduction to the Critical Study of Eccles. History*, London, 1838, pp. 11–18; Hély, *Eusèbe de Césarée, premier Historien de l'Église*, Paris, 1877; J. Burckhardt, *Zeit Constantins*, 2d ed. 1880, pp. 307 sq. Burckhardt depreciates Eusebius' value and questions his veracity. The review articles that have been written on Eusebius' *History* are legion. I shall mention only Engelhardt's *Eusebius als Kirchengeschichtschreiber*, in the *Zeitschrift für hist. Theol.* 1852, pp. 652–657; and Jachmann's *Bemerkungen über die Kirchengeschichte des Eusebius, ib.* 1839, II. pp. 10–60. The latter contains one of the most unsparing attacks upon Eusebius' honesty that has ever been made (see above, p. 49).

TESTIMONIES OF THE ANCIENTS IN FAVOR OF EUSEBIUS.[1]

From Constantine's Letter to the Antiochians (in Eusebius' *Life of Constantine*, Book III. chap. 60).

" I confess, then, that on reading your records I perceived, by the highly eulogistic testimony which they bear to Eusebius, bishop of Cæsarea (whom I have myself long well known and esteemed for his learning and moderation), that you are strongly attached to him and desire to appropriate him as your own prelate. What thoughts then do you suppose that I entertain on this subject, desirous as I am to seek for and act on the strict principles of right? What anxiety do you imagine this desire of yours has caused me? O holy faith, who givest us in our Saviour's words and precepts a model, as it were, of what our life should be, how hardly wouldst thou thyself resist the course of sin were it not that thou refusest to subserve the purposes of gain! In my own judgment, he whose first object is the maintenance of peace seems to be superior to Victory herself; and where a right and honorable course lies open to one's choice, surely no one would hesitate to adopt it. I ask then, brethren, why do we so decide as to inflict an injury on others by our choice? Why do we covet those objects which will destroy the credit of our own character? I myself highly esteem the individual whom ye judge worthy of your respect and affection; notwithstanding, it cannot be right that those principles should be entirely disregarded which should be authoritative and binding on all alike; for example, that each should be content with the limits assigned them, and that all should enjoy their proper privileges; nor can it be right in considering the claims of rival candidates to suppose but that not one only, but many, may appear worthy of comparison with this person. For as long as no violence or harshness are suffered to disturb the dignities of the Church, they continue to be on an equal footing, and worthy of the same consideration everywhere. Nor is it reasonable that an enquiry into the qualifications of one person should be made to the detriment of others; since the judgment of all churches, whether reckoned of greater importance in themselves, is equally capable of receiving and maintaining the divine ordinances, so that one is in no way inferior to another (if we will but boldly declare the truth), in regard to that standard of practice which is common to all. If this be so, we must say that you will be chargeable, not with retaining this prelate, but with wrongfully removing him; your conduct will be characterized rather by violence than justice; and whatever may be generally thought by others, I dare clearly and boldly affirm that this measure will furnish ground of accusation against you, and will provoke factious disturbances of the most mischievous kind; for even timid flocks can show the use and power of their teeth when the watchful care of their shepherd declines, and they find themselves bereft of his accustomed guidance. If this then be really so, if I am not deceived in my judgment, let this, brethren, be your first consideration (for many and important considerations will immediately present themselves, if you adopt my advice), whether, should you persist in your intention, that mutual kindly feeling and affection which should subsist among you will suffer no diminution? In the next place remember that Eusebius, who came among you for the purpose of offering disinterested counsel, now enjoys the reward which is due to him in the judgment of heaven; for he has received no ordinary recompense in the high testimony you have borne to his equitable conduct. Lastly, in accordance with your usual sound judgment, do ye exhibit a becoming diligence in selecting the person of whom you stand in need, carefully avoiding all factious and tumultuous clamor: for such clamor is always wrong, and from the collision of discordant elements both sparks and flame will arise."

---

[1] The following *Testimonies of the Ancients* were collected by Valesius, and are printed in the original languages in his edition of Eusebius' *Historia Ecclesiastica*, at the close of his *Vita Eusebii*. The order of Valesius has been preserved in the following pages, but occasionally a passage, for the sake of greater clearness, has been given more fully than by him. A few extracts have been omitted (as noted below), and one or two, overlooked by him, have been added. The extracts have all been translated from the original for this edition, with the exception of the quotations from the *Life of Constantine*, and from the Greek Ecclesiastical Historians,— Socrates, Sozomen, Theodoret, and Evagrius,—which have been copied, with a few necessary corrections, from the version found in Bagster's edition of the *Greek Ecclesiastical Historians*. The translation has been made at my request by Mr. James McDonald, of Shelbyville, Ky., a member of the senior class (1890) of Lane Theological Seminary.

From the Emperor's Letter to Eusebius (in Eusebius' *Life of Constantine*, Book III. chap. 61).

" I have most carefully perused your letter, and perceive that you have strictly conformed to the rule enjoined by the discipline of the Church. Now to abide by that which appears at the same time pleasing to God, and accordant with apostolic tradition, is a proof of true piety : and you have reason to deem yourself happy on this behalf, that you are counted worthy, in the judgment, I may say, of all the world, to have the oversight of the whole Church. For the desire which all feel to claim you for their own, undoubtedly enhances your enviable fortune in this respect. Notwithstanding, your Prudence, whose resolve it is to observe the ordinances of God and the apostolic rule of the Church, has done excellently well in declining the bishopric of the Church at Antioch, and desiring to continue in that Church of which you first received the oversight by the will of God."

From Constantine's Letter to the Council (in Eusebius' *Life of Constantine*, Book III. chap. 62).

" I have perused the letters written by your Prudences, and highly approve of the wise resolution of your colleague in the ministry, Eusebius. Having, moreover, been informed of the circumstances of the case, partly by your letters, partly by those of our illustrious friends Acacius and Strategius, after sufficient investigation I have written to the people at Antioch, suggesting the course which will be at once pleasing to God and advantageous for the Church. A copy of this I have ordered to be subjoined to this present letter, in order that ye yourselves may know what I thought fit, as an advocate of the cause of justice, to write to that people : since I find in your letter this proposal, that, in consonance with the choice of the people, sanctioned by your own desire, Eusebius the holy bishop of Cæsarea should preside over and take the charge of the Church at Antioch. Now the letters of Eusebius himself on this subject appeared to be strictly accordant with the order prescribed by the Church."

From a Letter of Constantine to Eusebius (in Eusebius' *Life of Constantine*, Book IV. chap. 35).

" It is indeed an arduous task, and beyond the power of language itself, worthily to treat of the mysteries of Christ, and to explain in a fitting manner the controversy respecting the feast of Easter, its origin as well as its precious and toilsome accomplishment. For it is not in the power even of those who are able to apprehend them, adequately to describe the things of God. I am, notwithstanding, filled with admiration of your learning and zeal, and have not only myself read your work with pleasure, but have given directions, according to your own desire, that it be communicated to many sincere followers of our holy religion. Seeing, then, with what pleasure we receive favors of this kind from your Sagacity, be pleased to gladden us more frequently with those compositions, to the practice of which, indeed, you confess yourself to have been trained from an early period, so that I am urging a willing man (as they say), in exhorting you to your customary pursuits. And certainly the high and confident judgment we entertain is a proof that the person who has translated your writings into the Latin tongue is in no respect incompetent to the task, impossible though it be that such version should fully equal the excellence of the works themselves."

From a Letter of Constantine to Eusebius (in Eusebius' *Life of Constantine*, Book IV. chap. 36).

" It happens, through the favoring providence of God our Saviour, that great numbers have united themselves to the most holy Church in the city which is called by my name. It seems, therefore, highly requisite, since that city is rapidly advancing in prosperity in all other respects, that the number of Churches should also be increased. Do you, therefore, receive with all readiness my determination on this behalf. I have thought it expedient to instruct your Prudence to order fifty copies of the sacred scriptures (the provision and use of which you know to be most needful for the instruction of the Church) to be written on prepared parchment in a legible manner, and in a commodious and portable form, by transcribers thoroughly practiced in their art. The procurator of the diocese has also received instructions by letter from our Clemency to be careful to furnish all things necessary for the preparation of such copies ; and it will be for you to take special care that they be completed with as little delay as possible. You have authority also, in virtue of this letter, to use two of the public carriages for their conveyance, by which arrangement the copies when fairly written will most easily be forwarded for my personal inspection ; and one of the deacons of your Church may be intrusted with this service, who, on his arrival here, shall experience my liberality. God preserve you, beloved brother ! "

From the Epistle of Eusebius of Nicomedia, to Paulinus, Bishop of Tyre (given by Theodoret in his *Eccles. Hist.* I. 6).

"Neither has the zeal of my lord Eusebius concerning the truth, nor thy silence in this matter been unknown, but has reached even us. And, as was fitting, on the one hand we have rejoiced on account of my lord Eusebius; but on the other, we are grieved on thy account, since we look upon the silence of such a man as a condemnation of our cause."

From the Book of Basil, to Amphilochius, on the Holy Spirit (chap. 29).

"If to any one Eusebius of Palestine seem trustworthy on account of his great experience, we give his own words in the *Difficulties concerning the Polygamy of the Ancients.*"

From the Book of Questions on the Old and New Testaments, which is published among the Works of Augustine (chap. 125).

"We remember to have read in a certain pamphlet of Eusebius, a man formerly distinguished among the rest of men, that not even the Holy Spirit knows the mystery of the nativity of our Lord Jesus Christ; and I wonder that a man of so great learning should have imposed this stigma upon the Holy Spirit."

From Jerome's Epistle to Pammachius and Oceanus (*Ep.* 65).

"Apollinarius wrote the very strongest books against Porphyry; Eusebius has excellently composed his *Ecclesiastical History.* Of these men, one taught an incomplete human nature in Christ; the other was a most open defender of the heresy of Arius."

From the Apology of Jerome against Rufinus (Book I. chap. 8).

"As I have already said, Eusebius, bishop of Cæsarea, formerly leader of the Arian party, has written six books in defense of Origen — a very extensive and elaborate work; with much evidence he has proved that Origen was, from his point of view, a Catholic, that is, from ours, an Arian."

From the same book (chap. 9).

"For Eusebius himself, a friend, eulogist and companion of Pamphilus, has written three very elegant books comprising a life of Pamphilus. In these, after extolling other things with wondrous praises and exalting his humility to the skies, he also adds this in the third book," &c.

And a little farther on in the same book (chap. 11).

"I have praised Eusebius in his *Ecclesiastical History*, in his *Chronological Canons*, in his *Description of the Holy Land;* and turning these same little works into Latin I have given them to those of my own tongue. Am I therefore an Arian, because Eusebius who wrote these books is an Arian?"

From Jerome's second book against Rufinus (chap. 16).

"Eusebius, a very learned man (I have said learned, not Catholic; lest after the usual manner, even in this thing, thou heap calumny upon me), in six volumes does nothing else than show Origen to be of his own faith; that is, of the Arian heresy."

From the Preface of Jerome's Book on Hebrew Topography.

"Eusebius, who took his surname from the blessed martyr Pamphilus, after the ten books of his *Ecclesiastical History*, after his *Chronological Canons*, which we have published in the Latin tongue, after his *Names of Various Nations*, in which he showed how these were formerly, and are now, called among the Hebrews; after his *Topography of the Land of Judea, with the inheritances of the tribes;* after his *Jerusalem*, also, and his *Plan of the Temple, with a very brief explanation,* — after all these he has finally in this little work labored that he might collect for us from Holy Scripture the names of almost all the cities, mountains, rivers, villages, and divers places, which either remain the same, or have since been changed, or else have become corrupted from some source, wherefore we also, following the zeal of this admirable man," &c.

From Jerome's Book on Ecclesiastical Writers (chap. 61).

" Hippolytus, bishop of a certain church (I have not indeed been able to find out the name of the city), wrote a reckoning of Easter, and chronological tables up to the first year of the Emperor Alexander, and hit upon a cycle of sixteen years which the Greeks call ἐκκαιδεκαετηρίδα ; and gave an occasion to Eusebius, who also composed an Easter canon, with a cycle of nineteen years, that is ἐννεαδεκαετηρίδα."

From the same book (chap. 81).

" Eusebius, bishop of Cæsarea in Palestine, a man most studious in the sacred Scriptures, and along with Pamphilus the martyr a most diligent investigator of sacred literature, has edited an infinite number of volumes, some of which are these : of the *Demonstratio Evangelica*, twenty books ; of the *Præparatio Evangelica*, fifteen books ; of the *Theophania*, five books ; of the *Ecclesiastical History*, ten books ; a *General History in Chronological Tables*, and an *Epitome* of them ; also, *On the Discrepancies of the Gospels; On Isaiah*, ten books ; and *Against Porphyry* (who at the same time was writing in Sicily, as some think), thirty books, of which only twenty have come to my notice ; of his *Topica*, one book ; of the *Apologia*, in defense of Origen, six books ; *On the Life of Pamphilus*, three books ; *Concerning the Martyrs*, other small works ; also very learned commentaries on the hundred and fifty Psalms, and many other writings. He flourished chiefly under the emperors Constantine and Constantius ; and on account of his friendship with Pamphilus the martyr, he took from him his surname."

From the same book (chap. 96).

" Eusebius, by nation a Sardinian, and, after being reader in Rome, bishop of Vercellæ, on account of his confession of the faith banished by the Prince Constantius to Scythopolis, and thence to Cappadocia, under Julian the emperor sent back to the Church, has published the *Commentaries on the Psalms* of Eusebius of Cæsarea, which he had translated from Greek into Latin."

Jerome in the Preface to his Commentaries on Daniel.

" Against the prophet Daniel Porphyry wrote a twelfth volume, denying that that book was composed by him with whose name it is inscribed, &c. To him Eusebius, bishop of Cæsarea, has replied very skillfully in three volumes, that is, in volumes XVIII., XIX., and XX. Apollinarius also in one large volume, that is, in the twenty-sixth volume, and before these, in part, Methodius."

Jerome on the Twenty-fourth Chapter of Matthew.

" Concerning this place, that is, concerning the abomination of desolation which was spoken of by the prophet Daniel, standing in the holy place, Porphyry has uttered many blasphemies against us in the thirteenth volume of his work. To whom Eusebius, bishop of Cæsarea, has replied in three volumes, that is, in volumes XVIII., XIX., and XX."

The same, in his Epistle to Magnus (Ep. 84).

" Celsus and Porphyry have written against us. To the former Origen, to the latter Methodius, Eusebius, and Apollinarius have very vigorously replied. Of whom Origen wrote eight books, Methodius proceeded as far as ten thousand lines, Eusebius and Apollinarius composed twenty-five and thirty volumes respectively."

The same, in his Epistle to Pammachius and Oceanus (Ep. 65).

" What more skillful, more learned, more eloquent men can be found than Eusebius and Didymus, the advocates of Origen? The former of whom, in the six volumes of his *Apologia*, proves that he [Origen] was of the same opinion as himself."

Jerome, in the Preface to his Commentaries on Isaiah.

" Eusebius Pamphili also has published an historical commentary in fifteen volumes."

The same, in the Preface to the Fifth Book of his Commentaries on Isaiah.

" Shall I take upon myself a work at which the most learned men have labored hard? I speak of Origen and Eusebius Pamphili. Of these the former wanders afar in the free spaces of allegory, and his genius so interprets single names as to make out of them the sacred things of the Church. The latter, while promising in his title an historical exposition, meanwhile forgets his purpose, and yields himself up to the tenets of Origen."

The same, in the fifth book of his Commentaries on Isaiah.

"Eusebius of Cæsarea, while promising in his title an historical exposition, strays off in divers notions : while reading his books ᐧI found much else than what he gave promise of in his title. For wherever history has failed him, he has crossed over into allegory ; and in such a manner does he unite things that are distinct, that I wonder at his joining together by a new art of discourse stone and iron into one body."

Jerome on the first chapter of Matthew.

"This [chapter] also Africanus, a writer of chronology, and Eusebius of Cæsarea, in his books on the *Discrepancies of the Gospels*, have discussed more fully."

Rufinus in his Epistle to the Bishop Chromatius.

"You charge me to translate into Latin the *Ecclesiastical History*, which the very learned Eusebius of Cæsarea wrote in the Greek tongue."

Augustine, in his Book on Heresies (chap. 83).

"When I had searched through the *History* of Eusebius, to which Rufinus, after having himself translated it into the Latin tongue, has also added two books of subsequent history, I did not find any heresy which I had not read among these very ones, except that one which Eusebius inserts in his sixth book, stating that it had existed in Arabia. Therefore these heretics, since he assigns them no founder, we may call Arabians, who declared that the soul dies and is destroyed along with the body, and that at the end of the world both are raised again. But he states that they were very quickly corrected, these by the disputation of Origen in person, and those by his exhortation."

Antipater, Bishop of Bostra, in his First Book against Eusebius of Cæsarea's Apology for Origen.

"Since now this man was very learned, having searched out and traced back all the books and writings of the more ancient writers, and having set forth the opinions of almost all of them, and having left behind very many writings, some of which are worthy of all acceptation, making use of such an estimation as this of the man, they attempt to lead away some, saying, that Eusebius would not have chosen to take this view, unless he had accurately ascertained that all the opinions of the ancients required it. I, indeed, agree and admit that the man was very learned, and that not anything of the more ancient writings escaped his knowledge ; for, taking advantage of the imperial co-operation, he was enabled easily to collect for his use material from whatever quarter."

From the First Book of Extracts from the Ecclesiastical History of Philostorgius.

"Philostorgius, while praising Eusebius Pamphili both as to whatever of worth belongs to his histories and as to other things, yet declares that with regard to religion he has fallen into great error ; and that he impiously sets forth this error of his in detail, holding that the Deity is unknowable and incomprehensible. Moreover, he holds that he has also gone astray on other such things. But he unites with others in attesting that he brought his *History* down to the accession of the sons of Constantine the Great."

Socrates in the First Book of his Ecclesiastical History (chap. 1).

"Eusebius, surnamed Pamphilus (i.e. universally beloved), has composed a History of the Church in ten books, brought down to the time of the Emperor Constantine, when the persecution ceased which Diocletian had commenced against the Christians. But, in writing the life of Constantine, this author has very slightly treated of the Arian controversy, being evidently more intent on a highly wrought eulogium of the emperor than an accurate statement of facts."

The same Socrates in the Eighth Chapter of the same Book, speaking of Sabinus, Bishop of Macedonia, who had written a History of the Synod, says: —

"Yet he commends Eusebius Pamphilus as a witness worthy of credit, and praises the Emperor as capable in stating Christian doctrines ; but he still brands the faith which was declared at Nice as having been set forth by ignorant men, and such as had no intelligence in the matter.   Thus he voluntarily contemns the testimony of a man whom he himself pronounces a wise and true witness ; for Eusebius declares that of the ministers of God who were present at the Nicene Synod, some were eminent for the word of wisdom, others for the strictness of their life ; and that the Emperor himself being present, leading all into unanimity, established unity of judgment, and conformity of opinion among them."

The same Socrates, in Book II. chap. 21.

" But since some have attempted to stigmatize Eusebius Pamphilus as having favored the Arian views in his works, it may not be irrelevant here to make a few remarks respecting him.   In the first place, then, he was present at the council of Nice, and gave his assent to what was there determined in reference to the consubstantiality of the Son with the Father, and in the third book of the *Life of Constantine*, he thus expressed himself : ' *The Emperor incited all to unanimity, until he had rendered them united in judgment on those points on which they were previously at variance : so that they were quite agreed at Nice in matters of faith.*'   Since, therefore, Eusebius, in mentioning the Nicene Synod, says that all differences were composed, and that unanimity of sentiment prevailed, what ground is there for assuming that he was himself an Arian ?   The Arians are certainly deceived in supposing him to be a favorer of their tenets.   But some one will perhaps say that in his discourses he seems to have adopted the opinions of Arius, because of his frequently saying *by Christ*.   Our answer is that ecclesiastical writers often use this mode of expression, and others of a similar kind denoting the *economy* of our Saviour's humanity : and that before all these the apostle made use of such expressions without ever being accounted a teacher of false doctrine.   Moreover, inasmuch as Arius has dared to say that the Son is a creature, as one of the others, observe what Eusebius says on this subject in his first book against Marcellus :

"' *He alone, and no other, has been declared to be, and is the only-begotten Son of God ; whence any one would justly censure those who have presumed to affirm that he is a Creature made of nothing, like the rest of the creatures ; for how then would he be a Son ? and how could he be God's only-begotten, were he assigned the same nature as the other creatures, and were he one of the many created things, seeing that he, like them, would in that case be partaker of a creation from nothing ?   The sacred Scriptures do not thus instruct us concerning these things.*'   He again adds a little afterwards : ' *Whoever then determines that the Son is made of things that are not, and that he is a creature produced from nothing pre-existing, forgets that while he concedes the name of Son, he denies him to be so in reality.   For he that is made of nothing cannot truly be the Son of God, any more than the other things which have been made : but the true Son of God, forasmuch as he is begotten of the Father, is properly denominated the only-begotten and beloved of the Father.   For this reason also, he himself is God : for what can the offspring of God be but the perfect resemblance of him who begat him ?   A sovereign, indeed, builds a city, but does not beget it ; and is said to beget a son, not to build one.   An artificer may be called the framer, but not the father of his work ; while he could by no means be styled the framer of him whom he had begotten.   So also the God of the Universe is the father of the Son ; but would be fitly termed the Framer and Maker of the world.   And although it is once said in Scripture, The Lord created me the beginning of his ways on account of his works, yet it becomes us to consider the import of this phrase, which I shall hereafter explain ; and not, as Marcellus has done, from a single passage to subvert one of the most important doctrines of the Church.*'

" These and many other such expressions are found in the first book of Eusebius Pamphilus against Marcellus ; and in his third book, declaring in what sense the term *creature* is to be taken, he says : ' *Accordingly these things being established, it follows that in the same sense as that which preceded, these words also are to be understood,* The Lord created me in the beginning of his ways on account of his works.   *For although he says that he was created, it is not as if he should say that he had arrived at existence from what was not, nor that he himself also was made of nothing like the rest of the creatures, which some have erroneously supposed : but as subsisting, living, pre-existing, and being before the constitution of the whole world ; and having been appointed to rule the universe by his Lord and Father : the word created being here used instead of* ordained *or* constituted.   *Certainly the apostle expressly called the rulers and governors among men* creature, *when he said,* Submit yourselves to every human *creature* for the Lord's sake ;

whether to the king as supreme, or to governors as those sent by him. *The prophet also does not use the word ἔκτισεν created in the sense of made of that which had no previous existence, when he says, Prepare, Israel, to invoke thy God.* For behold he who confirms the thunder, creates the Spirit, and announces his Christ unto men. *For God did not then create the Spirit when he declared his Christ to all men, since* There is nothing new under the sun; *but the Spirit was, and subsisted before: but he was sent at what time the apostles were gathered together, when like thunder,* There came a sound from heaven as of a rushing mighty wind: and they were filled with the Holy Spirit. *And thus they declared unto all men the Christ of God in accordance with that prophecy which says,* Behold he who confirms the thunder, creates the spirit, and announces his Christ unto men: *the word* creates *being used instead of* sends down, *or* appoints; *and* thunder *in a similar way implying* the preaching of the Gospel. *Again he that says,* Create in me a clean heart, O God, *said not this as if he had no heart; but prayed that his mind might be purified. Thus also it is said,* That he might create the two into one new man, *instead of* unite. *Consider also whether this passage is not of the same kind,* Clothe yourselves with the new man, which is created according to God; *and this,* If, therefore, any one be in Christ, he is a new creature, *and whatever other expressions of a similar nature any one may find who shall carefully search the divinely-inspired Scripture. Wherefore one should not be surprised if in this passage,* The Lord created me the beginning of his ways, *the term* created *is used metaphorically, instead of* appointed, *or* constituted.'

"These quotations from the books of Eusebius against Marcellus have been adduced to confute those who have slanderously attempted to traduce and criminate him. Neither can they prove that Eusebius attributes a beginning of subsistence to the Son of God, although they may find him often using the expressions of dispensation: and especially so, because he was an emulator and admirer of the works of Origen, in which those who are able to comprehend that author's writings, will perceive it to be everywhere stated that the Son was begotten of the Father. These remarks have been made in passing, in order to refute those who have misrepresented Eusebius."

Sozomen in the First Book of his Ecclesiastical History (chap. 1.).

" I at first felt strongly inclined to trace the course of events from the very commencement; but on reflecting that similar records of the past, up to their own time, had been compiled by the learned Clemens and Hegesippus, successors of the apostles, by Africanus the historian and Eusebius surnamed Pamphilus, a man intimately acquainted with the sacred Scriptures and the writings of the Greek poets and historians, I merely drew up an epitome in two books of all that is recorded to have happened to the churches, from the ascension of Christ to the deposition of Licinius."

Victorius in the Paschal Canon.

" Reviewing therefore the trustworthy histories of the ancients, namely the *Chronicles* and prologue of the blessed Eusebius, bishop of Cæsarea, a city in Palestine, a man pre-eminently accomplished and learned; and likewise those things which have been added to these same *Chronicles* by Jerome of sacred memory."

Jerome, in his Epistle to Chromatius and Heliodorus, prefixed to the Martyrology which bears Jerome's Name.

" It is evident that our Lord Jesus Christ obtains triumphs at every martyrdom of his saints, whose sufferings we find described by the saintly Eusebius, bishop of Cæsarea. For when Constantine Augustus came to Cæsarea and told the celebrated bishop to ask some favors which should benefit the church at Cæsarea, it is said that Eusebius answered: That a church enriched by its own resources was under no necessity of asking favors, yet that he himself had an unalterable desire, that whatever had been done in the Roman republic against God's saints by successive judges in the whole Roman world they should search out by a careful examination of the public records; and that they should draw from the archives themselves and send to Eusebius himself, by royal command, the names of the martyrs: under what judge, in what province or city, upon what day, and with what steadfastness, they had obtained the reward of their suffering. Whence it has come about that, being an able narrator and a diligent historiographer, he has both composed an *Ecclesiastical History* and has set forth the triumphs of nearly all of the martyrs of all the Roman provinces."

Pope Gelasius in his Decree concerning the Apocryphal Books.

"Likewise as to the *Chronicles* of Eusebius and the books of his *Ecclesiastical History*, although in the first book of his narration he has grown cold, and has afterwards written one book in praise and in defense of Origen the schismatic, yet on account of his singular knowledge of things which pertain to instruction, we do not say that they ought to be rejected."

The same in his book On the Two Natures.

"That saying the same thing with one heart and one mouth we may also believe what we have received from our forefathers, and, God giving them to us, that we may hand them down to posterity to be believed in, with which things the adduced testimony of the Catholic masters, being summed up, bear witness that a united faith in a gracious God endures."

And a little farther on.

"From the exposition of the seventh psalm, by Eusebius, bishop in Palestine, by surname Pamphili, etc. Likewise from his *Præparatio Evangelica*, Book VII."

Pope Pelagius II. in his Third Epistle to Elias of Aquileia and other Bishops of Istria.

"For, indeed, among hæresiarchs who can be found worse than Origen, and among historiographers who more honorable than Eusebius? And who of us does not know with how great praises Eusebius extols Origen in his books? But because the holy Church deals more kindly with the hearts of her faithful ones than she does severely with their words, neither could the testimony of Eusebius remove him from his proper place among heretics, nor on the other hand has she condemned Eusebius for the fault of praising Origen."

Evagrius, in the First Book of his Ecclesiastical History (chap. 1).

"Eusebius Pamphili — an especially able writer, to the extent, in particular, of inducing his readers to embrace our religion, though failing to perfect them in the faith — and Sozomen, Theodoret, and Socrates have produced a most excellent record of the advent of our compassionate God, and his ascension into heaven, and of all that has been achieved in the endurance of the divine Apostles, as well as of the other martyrs," etc.

Gregory the Great in his Epistle to Eulogius, Bishop of Alexandria.

"I have now become one of the number of hearers, to whom your Holiness has taken the pains to write, that we ought to transmit the deeds of all the martyrs which have been collected by Eusebius of Cæsarea in the age of Constantine of holy memory. But I was not aware before receiving your Holiness' letter whether these things had been collected or not. I therefore am thankful that being informed by the writings of your most holy learning, I have begun to know what I did not know before. For excepting these things which are contained in the books of this same Eusebius *On the deeds of the holy martyrs*, I have met with nothing else in the archives of this our church, nor in the libraries of Rome, except some few collected in a single volume."

Gelasius of Cyzicus in his Second Book On the Council of Nicæa (chap. 1).

"Let us hear now what says this the most illustrious husbandman in ecclesiastical farming, the most truth-loving Eusebius, surnamed after the celebrated Pamphilus. Licinius, indeed, he says, having followed the same path of impiety with the ungodly tyrants, has justly been brought to the same precipice with them, etc. (which may be found at the end of the tenth book of the *Ecclesiastical History*). As to Eusebius Pamphili, the most trustworthy of ancient ecclesiastical historians, who has investigated and set forth so many struggles, having made a choice from among his simply written works, we say that in all ten books of his *Ecclesiastical History* he has left behind an accurately written work. Beginning with the advent of our Lord he has, not without much labor, proceeded as far as those times. For how else could it be with him who took so great care to preserve for us the harmony of this collection? But as I have just said, he brought to bear upon it much study and an untold amount of labor. But let no one suppose, from those things which have been alleged with regard to him, that this man ever adopted the heresy of Arius; but let him be sure, that even if he did speak somewhat of, and did write briefly concerning the conjectures of Arius, he certainly did not do it on account of his entertaining the impious notion of that man, but from artless simplicity, as indeed he himself fully assures us in his Apology, which he distributed generally among orthodox bishops."

The author of the Alexandrian Chronicle (p. 582).

" The very learned Eusebius Pamphili has written thus : As the Jews crucified Christ at the feast, so they all perished at their own feast."

Nicephorus in the Sixth Book of his History (chap. 37).

" Upon whose authority also we know of the divine Pamphilus as both living the life of a philosopher and wearing the dignity of presbyter in that place. His life and every event in it, also his establishing in that place the study of sacred and profane philosophy, also his confession of his religion in divers persecutions, his struggles, and at last his wearing the martyr's crown, Eusebius his nephew, who had such a regard for him as to take from him his surname, has comprehended in detail in one separate book ; to this we refer those who may wish to find out accurately concerning him. This Eusebius, indeed, although having prosecuted many studies, especially excels in the study of sacred literature. His life extended until the time of Constantius. Being. a man pre-eminently Christian, and endowed with great zeal for Christ, he has written the *Præparatio Evangelica* in fifteen books, and in ten more the *Demonstratio Evangelica*. He was also the first one to take in hand this subject, having been the first to call his book an *Ecclesiastical History;* this work is contained in ten volumes. There is also another book of his extant which he entitled *Canons*, in which he accurately investigates chronological matters. He has also composed five books *On the Life of Constantine*, and another addressed to him which he calls τριακονταετή-ρικον. To Stephanus he also dedicates another concerning those things in the sacred Gospels which have been called in question ; and he has also left behind divers other works which are of great benefit to the Church. Apart from being such a man as this, he in many ways seems to uphold the opinions of Arius," etc.

From the MS. Acts of Pope Silvester.

" Eusebius Pamphili, in writing his *Ecclesiastical History*, has in every case omitted to mention those things which he has pointed out in other works ; for he has put into eleven books the sufferings of the martyrs, bishops, and confessors, who have suffered in almost all the provinces. But indeed as to the sufferings of women and maidens, such as with manly fortitude suffered for the sake of Christ the Lord, he records nothing. He is, moreover, the only one who has set forth in their order the sufferings of the bishops, from the Apostle Peter down. Moreover, he drew up for the benefit of the public a catalogue of the pontiffs of those cities and apostolic seats ; that is, of the great city of Rome, and the cities of Alexandria and Antioch. Of the number then of those of whom, up to his own times, the above-mentioned author wrote in the Greek tongue, this man's life he was unable to paraphrase ; that is, the life of the saint Silvester," etc.

An ancient author in the Passion of the Holy Valerian.

" The glorious struggles of the most blessed martyrs, for the honor of Christ the Lord and of our God, are celebrated by perpetual services and an annual solemnity, that while our faithful people know the faith of the martyrs, they may also rejoice in their triumphs, and may rest assured that it is by the protection of these that they themselves are to be protected. For it is held in repute that Eusebius the historian, of sacred memory, bishop of the city of Cæsarea, a most blessed priest of excellent life, very learned also in ecclesiastical matters, and to be venerated for his extraordinary carefulness, set forth for every city, in so far as the truth was able to be ascertained, the Holy Spirit announcing the deeds that had been done, — inasmuch as the cities of single provinces and localities or towns have merited being made famous by the heavenly triumphs of martyrs, — set forth, I say, in the time of what rulers the innumerable persecutions were inflicted at the command of officials. Who, although he has not described entire the sufferings of individual martyrs, yet has truly intimated why they ought to be described or celebrated by faithful and devoted Christians. Thus this faithful husbandman has cultivated the grace of God, which has been scattered abroad in all the earth, while, as it were, from a single grain of wheat, plenteous harvests are produced on account of the fertility of the field, and go on in multiplied abundance. So through the narration of the above-mentioned man, diffused from the fountain of a single book, with the ever-spreading writings of the faithful, the celebrating of the sufferings of the martyrs has watered all the earth."

Usuardus in his Martyrology.

" On the twenty-first day of June, in Palestine, the holy Eusebius, bishop and confessor, a man of most excellent genius, and a historiographer."

Notker in his Martyrology.

"On the twenty-first day of June, the deposition in Cæsarea of the holy bishop Eusebius."

Manecharius in his Epistle to Ceraunius, Bishop of Paris.

"Unceasing in thy continual efforts to equal in merit the very excellent persons of the most blessed bishops in all the conversation of the priesthood, zealous to adorn thyself every day with holy religion, by thy zeal for reading thou hast searched through the whole of the doctrines of the sacred Scriptures. Now as an addition to thy praiseworthiness thou dost faithfully purpose, in the city of Paris, to gather together for the love of religion, the deeds of the holy martyrs. Wherefore thou art worthy of being compared in zeal with Eusebius of Cæsarea, and art worthy of being remembered perpetually with an equal share of glory."

From an old Manuscript Breviary of the Lemovicensian Church.

"Of the holy Eusebius, bishop and confessor.

"Lesson 1. Eusebius, bishop of Cæsarea in Palestine, on account of his friendship with Pamphilus the martyr, took from him the surname of Pamphili ; inasmuch as along with this same Pamphilus he was a most diligent investigator of sacred literature. The man indeed is very worthy of being remembered in these times, both for his skill in many things, and for his wonderful genius, and by both Gentiles and Christians he was held distinguished and most noble among philosophers. This man, after having for a time labored in behalf of the Arian heresy, coming to the council of Nicæa, inspired by the Holy Spirit, followed the decision of the Fathers, and thereafter up to the time of his death lived in a most holy manner in the orthodox faith.

"Lesson 2. He was, moreover, very zealous in the study of the sacred Scriptures, and along with Pamphilus the martyr was a most diligent investigator of sacred literature. At the same time he has written many things, but especially the following books : The *Præparatio Evangelica*, the *Ecclesiastical History*, *Against Porphyry*, a very bitter enemy of the Christians ; he has also composed *Six Apologies in Behalf of Origen*, a *Life of Pamphilus the Martyr*, from whom on account of friendship he took his surname, in three books; likewise very learned *Commentaries on the hundred and fifty Psalms.*

"Lesson 3. Moreover, as we read, after having ascertained the sufferings of many holy martyrs in all the provinces, and the lives of confessors and virgins, he has written concerning these saints twenty books ; while on account of these books therefore, and especially on account of his *Præparatio Evangelica*, he was held most distinguished among the Gentiles, because of his love of truth he contemned the ancestral worship of the gods. He has written also a *Chronicle*, extending from the first year of Abraham up to the year 300 A.D., which the divine Hieronymus has continued. Finally this Eusebius, after the conversion of Constantine the Great, was united to him by strong friendship as long as he lived."

In the Breviary of the same church, June twenty-first.

"Omnipotent, eternal God, who dost permit us to take part in the festivities in honor of Eusebius, thy holy confessor and priest, bring us, we pray thee, through his prayers, into the society of heavenly joys, through our Lord Jesus Christ," etc.[1]

From the book On the Lights of the Church.

"Eusebius of Cæsarea, the key of the Scriptures and custodian of the New Testament, is proved by the Greeks to be greater than many in his treatises. There are three celebrated works of his which truly testify to this : the *Canons of the Four Gospels*, which set forth and defend the New Testament, ten books of *Ecclesiastical History*, and the *Chronicon*, that is, a chronological summary. We have never found any one who has been able to follow in all his foot-prints."

From the Miscellanies of Theodore Metochita (chap. 19).

"Eusebius Pamphili was also a Palestinian by birth, but as he himself says, he sojourned for quite a long time in Egypt. He was a very learned man, and it is evident indeed that he published many books, and that he used language thus."

---

[1] Valesius adds brief extracts from other missals of the same church, which it is not necessary to quote here.

TESTIMONIES OF THE ANCIENTS AGAINST EUSEBIUS.

From the Epistle of Arius to Eusebius, Bishop of Nicomedia (in Theodoret's *Eccles. Hist.* I. 5).[1]

" Eusebius, your brother bishop of Cæsarea, Theodotius, Paulinus, Athanasius, Gregory, Ætius, and all the bishops of the East, have been condemned because they say that God had an existence prior to that of his Son."

From the Book of Marcellus of Ancyra against the Arians.

" Having happened upon a letter of Narcissus, bishop of Neronias, which he wrote to one Chrestus and to Euphronius and to Eusebius, in which it seems that Hosius, the bishop, had asked him whether or not like Eusebius of Palestine he believed in the existence of two essences, I read in the writing that he answered that he believed in the existence of three essences."

From the Synodical Epistle of the Bishops of Egypt, met in the City of Alexandria, to All the Bishops of the Catholic Church (which Athanasius gives in his second apology against the Arians).

" For what sort of a council of bishops was that? What sort of an assembly having truth for its aim? Who out of the great majority of them was not our enemy? Did not the followers of Eusebius rise up against us on account of the Arian madness? Did not they bring forward the others who held the same opinions as themselves? Were we not continually writing against them as against those who held the opinions of Arius? Was not Eusebius of Cæsarea in Palestine accused by our confessors of sacrificing?"

Epiphanius in the Heresy of the Meletians (Hær. LXVIII.).

" The emperor upon hearing these things becomes very angry and orders that a synod be convoked in Phœnicia in the city of Tyre ; he also gave orders that Eusebius and some others should act as judges : these persons moreover had leaned somewhat too far toward the vulgarity of the Arians. There were also summoned the bishops of the Catholic Church in Egypt, also certain men subject to Athanasius, who were likewise great and who kept their lives transparent before God, among whom was the great Potamo of blessed memory, bishop and confessor of Heraclea. But there were also present Meletians, the chief accusers of Athanasius. Being zealous for truth and for orthodoxy, the above-mentioned Potamo of blessed memory, a free-spoken man, who regarded the person of no man, — for he had been deprived of an eye in the persecution for the truth, — seeing Eusebius sitting down and acting as judge, and Athanasius standing up, overcome by grief and weeping, as is the wont with true men, he addressed Eusebius in a loud voice, saying, ' Dost thou sit down, Eusebius, and is Athanasius, an innocent man, judged by thee? Who could bear such things? Do thou tell me, wert thou not in confinement with me at the time of the persecution? I have parted with an eye for the sake of the truth, but thou neither seemest to be maimed at all in body, nor hast thou suffered martyrdom, but art alive, and in no part mutilated. How didst thou escape from the confinement unless that thou didst promise those who have inflicted upon us the violence of persecution to perform the ungodly act, or didst actually perform it? '"

From the Epistle of the Catholic Bishops of Egypt to the Synod of Tyre (which Athanasius gives in the above-mentioned Apology).

" For ye also know, as we have said before, that they are our enemies, and ye know why Eusebius of Cæsarea has become our enemy since last year."

Athanasius in his Epistle on the Decrees of the Council of Nicæa.

" The strange thing is that Eusebius of Cæsarea in Palestine, who had denied on one day, but on the next day had subscribed, sent to his church, saying that this is the faith of the Church,

---

[1] This extract is not given by Valesius.

and that this is the tradition of the Fathers. He plainly showed to all that before they had been in error, and had been vainly striving after the truth; for although he was then ashamed to write in just these terms, and excused himself to the Church as he himself wished, yet he plainly wishes to imply this in his Epistle, by his not denying the 'Homoöusion,' 'one in substance,' and 'of the substance.' He got into serious difficulty, for in defending himself, he went on to accuse the Arians, because, having written that 'the Son did not exist before that he was begotten,' they thereby denied that he existed before his birth in the flesh."

The same, in his Treatise on the Synods of Ariminum and Seleucia.

"Most of all, what would Acacius say to Eusebius his own teacher? who not only signed in the synod at Nicæa, but also made it known by letter to the people under him that that was the true faith, which had been agreed upon at the council of Nicæa; for although he defended himself as he pleased through the letter, yet he did not deny the grounds taken. But he also accused the Arians, since, in saying that 'the Son did not exist before that he was begotten,' they also deny that he existed before Mary."

The same, in his Epistle to the Bishops of Africa.

"This also was known all the while to Eusebius, bishop of Cæsarea, who, at first identifying himself with the Arian heresy, and having afterwards signed at the self-same synod of Nicæa, wrote to his own particular friends, firmly maintaining that, 'We have known of certain learned and renowned bishops and writers among the ancients who have used the term ὁμοούσιος in reference to the divinity of the Father and Son.'"

The same, in his Treatise on the Synods of Ariminum and Seleucia.

"Eusebius of Cæsarea in Palestine, writing to Euphration the bishop, did not fear to say openly that Christ is not true God."

Jerome, in his Epistle to Ctesiphon against the Pelagians.

"He did this in the name of the holy martyr Pamphilus, that he might designate with the name of the martyr Pamphilus the first of the six books in defense of Origen which were written by Eusebius of Cæsarea, whom every one knows to have been an Arian."

The same, in his Second Book against Rufinus.

"As soon as he leaves the harbor he runs his ship aground. For, quoting from the *Apology* of Pamphilus the Martyr (which we have proved to be the work of Eusebius, prince of Arians)," etc.

The same, in his First Book against Rufinus.

"Eusebius, bishop of Cæsarea, of whom I have made mention above, in the sixth book of his *Apology* in behalf of Origen, lays this same charge against Methodius the bishop and martyr, which you lay against me in my praises [of him]; he says: 'How did Methodius dare to write against Origen after having said this and that concerning his opinions?' This is no place to speak in behalf of a martyr, for not all things ought to be discussed in all places. Now let it suffice to have barely touched upon the matter, that this same thing was charged against a most renowned and most eloquent martyr by an Arian, which you as a friend praise in me, and, being offended, censure me for."

The same, in his Epistle to Minervius and Alexander.

"I both in manhood and in extreme old age am of the same opinion, that Origen and Eusebius of Cæsarea were indeed very learned men, but went astray in the truth of their opinions."

Socrates, in the First Book of his Ecclesiastical History (chap. 23).

"Eusebius Pamphilus says that immediately after the Synod Egypt became agitated by intestine divisions; but as he does not assign the reason for this, some have accused him of disingenuousness, and have even attributed his failure to specify the causes of these dissensions to a determination on his part not to give his sanction to the proceedings at Nice."

Again, in the same chapter.

"Eustathius, bishop of Antioch, accuses Eusebius Pamphilus of perverting the Nicene Creed ; but Eusebius denies that he violates that exposition of the faith, and recriminates, saying that Eustathius was a defender of the opinion of Sabellius. In consequence of these misunderstandings, each of them wrote volumes as if contending against adversaries : and although it was admitted on both sides that the Son of God has a distinct person and existence, and all acknowledged that there is one God in a Trinity of Persons ; yet, from what cause I am unable to divine, they could not agree among themselves, and therefore were never at peace."

Theodoritus, in his Interpretation of the Epistle of Paul to the Hebrews, speaking of the Arians, writes as follows :

"If not even this is sufficient to persuade them, it at least behooves them to believe Eusebius of Palestine, whom they call the chief advocate of their own doctrines."

Nicetas, in his Thesaurus of the Orthodox Faith, Book V. Chap. 7.

"Moreover, Theodore of Mopsuestia relates that there were only nine persons out of all whom the decrees of the Synod did not please, and that their names are as follows : Theognis of Nicæa, Eusebius of Nicomedia, Patrophilus of Scythopolis, Eusebius of Cæsarea in Palestine, Narcissus of Neronias in Cilicia, which is now called Irenopolis, Paulinus of Tyre, Menophantus of Ephesus, Secundus of Ptolemaïs, which borders upon Egypt, and Theonas of Marmarica."[1]

Antipater, Bishop of Bostra, in his First Book against Eusebius' Apology for Origen.

"I deny that the man has yet arrived at an accurate knowledge of the doctrines ; wherefore he ought to be given place to so far as regards his great learning, but as regards his knowledge of doctrine he ought not. But, moreover, we know him to have been altogether lacking in such accurate knowledge."

And a little farther on.

"So now, that we may not seem to be trampling upon the man, — concerning whom it is not our purpose for the present to speak, — examining into the accuracy of his *Apology*, we may go on to show that both were heretics, both he who composed the *Apology*, and he in whose behalf it was composed."

And farther on.

"For as to your attempting to show that others as well as he [Origen] have spoken of the subordination of the Son to the Father, we may not at first wonder at it, for such is your opinion and that of your followers ; wherefore we say nothing concerning this matter for the present, since it was long ago submitted and condemned at the general Council."

From the Acts of the Seventh Œcumenical Council.

"For who of the faithful ones in the Church, and who of those who have obtained a knowledge of true doctrine, does not know that Eusebius Pamphili has given himself over to false ways of thinking, and has become of the same opinion and of the same mind with those who follow after the opinions of Arius? In all his historical books he calls the Son and Word of God a creature, a servant, and to be adored as second in rank. But if any speaking in his defense say that he subscribed in the council, we may admit that is true ; but while with his lips he has respected the truth, in his heart he is far from it, as all his writings and epistles go to show. But if from time to time, on account of circumstances or from different causes, he has become confused or has changed around, sometimes praising those who hold to the doctrines of Arius, and at other times feigning the truth, he shows himself to be, according to James the brother of our Lord, a double-minded man, unstable in all his ways ; and let him not think that he shall receive anything of the Lord. For if with the heart he had believed unto righteousness, and with the mouth had confessed the truth unto salvation, he would have asked forgiveness for his writings, at the same time correcting them. But this he has by no means done, for he remained like Æthiops with his skin unchanged. In interpreting the verse ' I said to the Lord, Thou art my Lord,' he has strayed far away from the true sense, for this is what he says : ' By the laws of nature every son's father

---

[1] Valesius inserts after this extract a brief and unimportant quotation from Eulogius of Alexandria, which, however, is so obscure, — severed as it is from its context, which is not accessible to me, — that no translation of it has been attempted.

must be his lord; wherefore God who begat him must be at the same time God, Lord, and Father of the only-begotten Son of God.' So also in his epistle to the holy Alexander, the teacher of the great Athanasius, which begins thus: 'With what anxiety and with what care have I set about writing this letter,' in most open blasphemy he speaks as follows concerning Arius and his followers: 'Thy letter accuses them of saying that the Son was made out of nothing, like all men. But they have produced their own epistle which they wrote to thee, in which they give an account of their faith, and expressly confess that "the God of the law and of the prophets and of the New Testament, before eternal ages begat an only-begotten Son, through whom also he made the ages and the universe; and that he begat him not in appearance, but in truth, and subjected him to his own will, unchangeable and immutable, a perfect creature of God, but not as one of the creatures." If, therefore, the letter received from them tells the truth, they wholly contradict thee, in that they confess that the Son of God who existed before eternal ages, and through whom he made the world, is unchangeable and a perfect creature of God, but not as one of the creatures. But thy epistle accuses them of saying that the Son was made as one of the creatures. They do not say this, but clearly declare that he was not as one of the creatures. See if cause is not immediately given them again to attack and to misrepresent whatever they please. Again thou findest fault with them for saying that He who is begat him who was not. I wonder if any one is able to say anything else than that. For if He who is is one, it is plain that everything has been made by Him and after Him. But if He who is is not the only one, but there was also a Son existing, how did He who is beget him who was existing? For thus those existing would be two.' These things then Eusebius wrote to the illustrious Alexander; but there are also other epistles of his directed to the same holy man, in which are found various blasphemies in defense of the followers of Arius. So also, in writing to the bishop Euphration, he blasphemes most openly; his letter begins thus: 'I return to my Lord all thanks'; and farther on: 'For we do not say that the Son was with the Father, but that the Father was before the Son. But the Son of God himself, knowing well that he was greater than all, and knowing that he was other than the Father, and less than and subject to Him, very piously teaches this to us also when he says, "The Father who sent me is greater than I."' And farther on: 'Since the Son also is himself God, but not true God.' So then from these writings of his he shows that he holds to the doctrines of Arius and his followers. And with this rebellious heresy of theirs the inventors of that Arian madness hold to one nature in hypostatic union, and affirm that our Lord took upon himself a body without soul, in his scheme of redemption, affirming that the divine nature supplied the purposes and movements of the soul: that, as Gregory the Divine says, they may ascribe suffering to the Deity; and it is evident that those who ascribe suffering to the Deity are Patripassians. Those who share in this heresy do not allow images, as the impious Severus did not, and Peter Cnapheus, and Philoxenus of Hierapolis, and all their followers, the many-headed yet headless hydra. So then Eusebius, who belongs to this faction, as has been shown from his epistles and historical writings, as a Patripassian rejected the image of Christ," etc.[1]

Photius, in his 144th Epistle to Constantine.

"That Eusebius (whether slave or friend of Pamphilus I know not) was carried off by Arianism, his books loudly proclaim. And he, feeling repentance as he pretends, and against his will, confesses to his infirmity; although by his repentance he rather shows that he has not repented. For he cannot show, by means of those writings in which he would seem to be defending himself, that he has withdrawn from his former heretical doctrines, nor can he show that he agreed with the holy and Œcumenical Synod. But he speaks of it as a marvel that the upholders of the Homoousion should concur with him in sentiment and agree with him in opinion: and this fact both many other things and the epistle written by him to his own people at Cæsarea accurately confirm. But that from the beginning he inwardly cherished the Arian doctrines, and that up to the end of his life he did not cease following them, many know, and it is easy to gather it from many sources; but that he shared also in the infirmity of Origen, namely, the error with regard to the common resurrection of us all, is to most persons unknown. But if thou thyself examine carefully his books, thou shalt see that he was none the less truly overcome by that deadly disease than he was by the Arian madness."

Photius, in his Bibliotheca (chap. 13).

"Of the *Objection and Defense* of Eusebius two books have been read; also other two, which although differing in some respects from the former two, are in other respects the same with regard

---

[1] This extract is translated from the original Greek of the Acts of the Second Nicene Council, Act VI. Tom. V. (as given by Labbe and Cossartius in their *Concilia*, Tom. VII. p. 495 sq.). Valesius gives only a Latin translation, and that in a fragmentary form.

to both diction and thought. But he presents certain difficulties with regard to our blameless religion as having originated with the Greeks. These he correctly solves, although not in all cases. But as regards his diction, it is by no means either pleasing or brilliant. The man is indeed very learned, although as regards shrewdness of mind and firmness of character, as well as accuracy in doctrine, he is deficient. For also in many places in these books it is plain to be seen that he blasphemes against the Son, calling him a second cause, and general-in-chief, and other terms which have had their origin in the Arian madness. It seems that he flourished in the time of Constantine the Great. He was also an ardent admirer of the excellences of the holy martyr Pamphilus, for which cause some say that he took from him the surname Pamphili."

Photius, in the Same Work (chap. 127).

"There has been read the work of Eusebius Pamphili *In praise of the great emperor Constantine*, consisting of four books. In this is contained the whole life of the man, starting with his very boyhood, also whatever deeds of his belong to ecclesiastical history, until he departed from life at the age of sixty-four. Eusebius is, however, even in this work, like himself in diction, except that his discourse has risen to a somewhat more than usual brilliancy, and that sometimes he has made use of more flowery expressions than he is wont. However, of pleasantness and beauty of expression there is little, as indeed is the case in his other works. He inserts, moreover, in this work of his in four books very many passages from the whole decalogue of his *Ecclesiastical History*. He says that Constantine the Great himself also was baptized in Nicomedia, he having put off his baptism until then, because he desired to be baptized in the Jordan. Who baptized him he does not clearly show. However, as to the heresy of Arius, he does not definitely state whether he holds that opinion, or whether he has changed; or even whether Arius held correct or incorrect views, although he ought to have made mention of these things, because the synod occupied an important place among the deeds of Constantine the Great, and it again demands a detailed account of them. But he does state that a 'controversy' arose between Arius and Alexander (this is the name he cunningly gives to the heresy), and that the God-fearing prince was very much grieved at this controversy, and strove by epistles and through Hosius, who was then bishop of Cordova, to bring back the dissenting parties into peace and concord, they having laid aside the strife existing between them with regard to such questions ; and that when he could not persuade them to do this he convoked a synod from all quarters, and that it dissolved into peace the strife that had arisen. These things, however, are not described accurately or clearly; it would seem then that he is ashamed, as it were, and does not wish to make public the vote cast against Arius in the Synod, and the just retribution of those who were his companions in impiety and who were cast out together with him. Finally, he does not even mention the terrible fate which was inflicted by God upon Arius in the sight of all. None of these things he brings to the light, nor has he drawn up an account of the Synod and the things that were done in it. Whence, also, when about to write a narrative concerning the divine Eustathius, he does not even mention his name, nor what things were threatened and executed against him ; but referring these things also to sedition and tumult, he again speaks of the calmness of the bishops, who having been convened in Antioch by the zeal and coöperation of the Emperor, changed the sedition and tumult into peace. Likewise as to what things were maliciously contrived against the ever-conquering Athanasius, when he set about making his history cover these things, he says that Alexandria again was filled with sedition and tumult, and that this was calmed by the coming of the bishops, who had the imperial aid. But he by no means makes it clear who was the leader of the sedition, what sort of sedition it was, or by what means the strife was settled. He also keeps up almost the same mode of dissimulating in his account of the contentions existing among bishops with respect to doctrines, and their disagreements on other matters."

Joannes Zonaras, in his Third Volume, in which he relates the Deeds of Constantine.

"Even Eusebius Pamphili, bishop of Cæsarea in Palestine, was at that time one of those who upheld the doctrines of Arius. He is said to have afterwards withdrawn from the opinion of Arius, and to have become of like mind with those who hold that the Son is coëqual and of the same nature with the Father, and to have been received into communion by the holy Fathers. Moreover, in the Acts of the first Synod, he is found to have defended the faithful. These things are found thus narrated by some ; but he makes them to appear doubtful by certain things which he is seen to have written in his *Ecclesiastical History*. For in many places in the above-mentioned work he seems to be following after Arius. In the very beginning of his book, where he quotes David as saying, 'He spake and they were made, he commanded and they were established,' he says that the Father and Maker is to be considered as maker and universal ruler, governing by a kingly nod, and that the second after him in authority, the divine Word, is subject to the commands of the Father. And farther on he says, that he, as being the power and wisdom of the Father, is entrusted with the second place in the kingdom and rule over all. And again, a little farther on, that there is also a certain essence, living and subsisting before the world, which ministers to the God and Father of the universe for the creation of things that are created. Also Solomon, in the person of the wisdom of God, says, 'The Lord created me in the beginning of his ways,' etc., and farther on he says: And besides all this, as the preexistent word of God, who also preëxisted before all ages created, he received divine honor from the Father, and is worshipped as God. These and other things show that Eusebius agreed with Arian doctrines, unless some one say that they were written before his conversion."

Suidas, under the word Διόδωρος.

" Diodorus, a monk, who was bishop of Tarsus in Cilicia, in the times of Julian and Valens, wrote divers works, as Theodorus Lector states in his *Ecclesiastical History.* These are as follows: A *Chronicle,* which corrects the error of Eusebius Pamphilus with regard to chronology," etc.

The same Suidas, from Sophronius.

"Eusebius Pamphili, a devotee of the Arian heresy, bishop of Cæsarea in Palestine, a man zealous in the study of the holy Scriptures, and along with Pamphilus the martyr a most careful investigator of sacred literature, has published many books, among which are the following." [1]

---

[1] The remainder of this extract from Sophronius is a translation of the chapter of Jerome's *de viris illustribus,* which is quoted above, on p. 60, and is therefore omitted at this point. Valesius adds some extracts from Baronius and Scaliger; but inasmuch as they are to be classed with modern rather than with ancient writers, it has seemed best to omit the quotations from their works.

CONTENTS OF THE CHURCH HISTORY.

BOOK I.

BOOK II.

BOOK III.

BOOK VI.

BOOK VII.

BOOK VIII.

MARTYRS OF PALESTINE.

BOOK IX.

BOOK X.

THE CHURCH HISTORY OF EUSEBIUS.

BOOK I.

CHAPTER I.

The Plan of the Work.

1   It is my purpose to write an account of the successions of the holy apostles, as well as of the times which have elapsed from the days of our Saviour to our own; and to relate the many important events which are said to have occurred in the history of the Church; and to mention those who have governed and presided over the Church in the most prominent parishes, and those who in each generation have proclaimed the divine word either orally or in writing. It is my purpose also to give the names and number and times of those who through **2** love of innovation have run into the greatest errors, and, proclaiming themselves discoverers of knowledge falsely so-called,[1] have like fierce wolves unmercifully devastated the flock of Christ. It is my intention, moreover, to recount the misfortunes which immediately came upon the whole Jewish nation in conse- **3** quence of their plots against our Saviour, and to record the ways and the times in which the divine word has been attacked by the Gentiles, and to describe the character of those who at various periods have contended for it in the face of blood and of tortures, as well as the confessions which have been made in our own days, and finally the gracious and kindly succor which our Saviour has afforded them all. Since I propose to write of all these things I shall commence my work with the beginning of the dispensation[2] of our Saviour and Lord Jesus Christ.[3]

But at the outset I must crave for my **4** work the indulgence of the wise,[4] for I confess that it is beyond my power to produce a perfect and complete history, and since I am the first to enter upon the subject, I am attempting to traverse as it were a lonely and untrodden path.[5] I pray that I may have God as my guide and the power of the Lord as my aid, since I am unable to find even the bare footsteps of those who have traveled the way before me, except in brief fragments, in which some in one way, others in another, have transmitted to us particular accounts of the times in which they lived. From afar they raise their voices like torches, and they cry out, as from some lofty and conspicuous watch-tower, admonishing us where to walk and how to direct the course of our work steadily and safely. Having gathered therefore from the matters mentioned **5** here and there by them whatever we consider important for the present work, and having plucked like flowers from a meadow the appropriate passages from ancient writers,[6] we shall endeavor to embody the whole in an historical narrative, content if we preserve the memory of

---

[1] Cf. 1 Tim. vi. 20.

[2] Greek οἰκονομία. Suicer (*Thesaurus Eccles.*) points out four uses of this word among ecclesiastical writers: (1) *Ministerium Evangelii.* (2) *Providentia et numen* (i.e. of God). (3) *Naturæ humanæ assumtio.* (4) *Totius redemptionis mysterium et passionis Christi sacramentum.* Valesius says, "The ancient Greeks use the word to denote whatever Christ did in the world to proclaim salvation for the human race, and thus the first οἰκονομία τοῦ χριστοῦ is the incarnation, as the last οἰκονομία is the passion." The word in the present case is used in its wide sense to denote not simply the act of incarnation, but the whole economy or dispensation of Christ upon earth. See the notes of Heinichen upon this passage, Vol. III. p. 4 sq., and of Valesius, Vol. I. p. 2.

[3] Five MSS., followed by nearly all the editors of the Greek text

and by the translators Stigloher and Crusè, read τοῦ θεοῦ after χριστόν. The words, however, are omitted by the majority of the best MSS. and by Rufinus, followed by Heinichen and Closs. (See the note of Heinichen, Vol. I. p. 4).

[4] All the MSS. followed by the majority of the editors read εὐγνωμονῶν, which must agree with λόγος. Heinichen, however, followed by Burton, Schwegler, Closs, and Stigloher, read εὐγνωμόνων, which I have also accepted. Closs translates *die Nachsicht der Kenner;* Stigloher, *wohlwollende Nachsicht.* Crusè avoids the difficulty by omitting the word; an omission which is quite unwarranted.

[5] Eusebius is rightly called the "Father of Church History." He had no predecessors who wrote, as he did, with a comprehensive historical plan in view; and yet, as he tells us, much had been written of which he made good use in his History. The one who approached nearest to the idea of a Church historian was Hegesippus (see Bk. IV. chap. 22, note 1), but his writings were little more than fragmentary memoirs, or collections of disconnected reminiscences. For instance, Eusebius, in Bk. II. chap 23, quotes from his fifth and last book the account of the martyrdom of James the Just, which shows that his work lacked at least all chronological arrangement. Julius Africanus (see Bk. VI. chap. 31, note 1) also furnished Eusebius with much material in the line of chronology, and in his *Chronicle* Eusebius made free use of him. These are the only two who can in any sense be said to have preceded Eusebius in his province, and neither one can rob him of his right to be called the "Father of Church History."

[6] One of the greatest values of Eusebius' History lies in the quotations which it contains from earlier ecclesiastical writers. The works of many of them are lost, and are known to us only through the extracts made by Eusebius. This fact alone is enough to make his History of inestimable worth.

the successions of the apostles of our Saviour ; if not indeed of all, yet of the most renowned of them in those churches which are the most noted, and which even to the present time are held in honor.

6   This work seems to me of especial importance because I know of no ecclesiastical writer who has devoted himself to this subject ; and I hope that it will appear most useful to those who are fond of historical research.

7   I have already given an epitome of these things in the Chronological Canons[7] which I have composed, but notwithstanding that, I have undertaken in the present work to write as full an account of them as I am able. My

8   work will begin, as I have said, with the dispensation[8] of the Saviour Christ, — which is loftier and greater than human conception, — and with a discussion of his divinity[9] ;

9   for it is necessary, inasmuch as we derive even our name from Christ, for one who proposes to write a history of the Church to begin with the very origin of Christ's dispensation, a dispensation more divine than many think.

CHAPTER II.

Summary View of the Pre-existence and Divinity of Our Saviour and Lord Jesus Christ.

1   SINCE in Christ there is a twofold nature, and the one — in so far as he is thought of as God — resembles the head of the body, while the other may be compared with the feet, — in so far as he, for the sake of our salvation, put on human nature with the same passions as our own, — the following work will be complete only if we begin with the chief and lordliest events of all his history. In this way will the antiquity and divinity of Christianity be shown to those who suppose it of recent and foreign origin,[1] and imagine that it appeared only yester-

2   day.[2] No language is sufficient to express

the origin and the worth, the being and the nature of Christ. Wherefore also the divine Spirit says in the prophecies, "Who shall declare his generation?"[3] For none knoweth the Father except the Son, neither can any one know the Son adequately except the Father alone who hath begotten him.[4] For who beside the Father could clearly understand the Light 3 which was before the world, the intellectual and essential Wisdom which existed before the ages, the living Word which was in the beginning with the Father and which was God, the first and only begotten of God which was before every creature and creation visible and invisible, the commander-in-chief of the rational and immortal host of heaven, the messenger of the great counsel, the executor of the Father's unspoken will, the creator, with the Father, of all things, the second cause of the universe after the Father, the true and only-begotten Son of God, the Lord and God and King of all created things, the one who has received dominion and power, with divinity itself, and with might and honor from the Father ; as it is said in regard to him in the mystical passages of Scripture which speak of his divinity : "In the beginning was the Word, and the Word was with God, and the Word was God."[5] "All things were made by him ; and without him was not anything made."[6] This, too, the great Moses teaches, 4 when, as the most ancient of all the prophets, he describes under the influence of the divine Spirit the creation and arrangement of the universe. He declares that the maker of the world and the creator of all things yielded to Christ himself, and to none other than his own clearly divine and first-born Word, the making of inferior things, and communed with him respecting the creation of man. "For," says he, "God said, Let us make man in our image and in our likeness."[7] And another of the prophets 5 confirms this, speaking of God in his hymns as follows : "He spake and they were made ; he commanded and they were created."[8] He here introduces the Father and Maker as Ruler of all, commanding with a kingly nod, and second to him the divine Word, none other than the one who is proclaimed by us, as carrying out

---

[7] On Eusebius' *Chronicle*, see the Prolegomena, p. 31, above.

[8] οἰκονομία. See above, note 2.

[9] θεολογία. Suicer gives four meanings for this word: (1) *Doctrina de Deo.* (2) *Doctrina de SS. Trinitate.* (3) *Divina Christi natura, seu doctrina de ea.* (4) *Scriptura sacra utriusque Testamenti.* The word is used here in its third signification (cf. also chap. 2, § 3, and Bk. V. chap. 28, § 5). It occurs very frequently in the works of the Fathers with this meaning, especially in connection with οἰκονομία, which is then quite commonly used to denote the "human nature" of Christ. In the present chapter οἰκονομία keeps throughout its more general signification of "the Dispensation of Christ," and is not confined to the mere act of incarnation, nor to his "human nature."

[1] νέαν αὐτὴν καὶ ἐκτετοπισμένην.

[2] This was one of the principal objections raised against Christianity. Antiquity was considered a prime requisite in a religion which claimed to be true, and no reproach was greater than the reproach of novelty. Hence the apologists laid great stress upon the antiquity of Christianity, and this was one reason why they appropriated the Old Testament as a Christian book. Compare, for instance, the apologies of Justin Martyr, Tatian, Athenagoras, Theophilus, Tertullian and Minucius Felix, and the works of Clement of Alexandria. See Engelhardt's article on Eusebius, in the *Zeitschrift für die hist. Theologie,* 1852, p. 652 sq.; Schaff's

Church History, Vol. II. p. 110; and Tzschirner's *Geschichte der Apologetik,* p. 99 sq.

[3] Isa. liii. 8.
[4] Cf. Matt. xi. 27.
[5] John i. 1.
[6] John i. 3.
[7] Gen. i. 26.
[8] Ps. xxxiii. 9. There is really nothing in this passage to imply that the Psalmist thinks, as Eusebius supposes, of the Son as the Father's agent in creation, who is here addressed by the Father. As Stroth remarks, "According to Eusebius, 'He spake' is equivalent to 'He said to the Son, Create'; and 'They were created' means, according to him, not 'They arose immediately upon this command of God,' but 'The Son was immediately obedient to the command of the Father and produced them.' For Eusebius connects this verse with the sixth, 'By the *word* of the Lord were the heavens made,' where he understands Christ to be referred to. Perhaps this verse has been omitted in the Greek through an oversight, for it is found in Rufinus."

6 the Father's commands.   All that are said
   to have excelled in righteousness and piety
since the creation of man, the great servant Moses and before him in the first place Abraham
and his children, and as many righteous men and
prophets as afterward appeared, have contemplated him with the pure eyes of the mind, and
have recognized him and offered to him the
   worship which is due him as Son of God.
7 But he, by no means neglectful of the reverence due to the Father, was appointed to
teach the knowledge of the Father to them all.
For instance, the Lord God, it is said, appeared
as a common man to Abraham while he was sitting at the oak of Mambre.[9] And he, immediately
falling down, although he saw a man with his
eyes, nevertheless worshiped him as God, and
sacrificed to him as Lord, and confessed that he
was not ignorant of his identity when he uttered
the words, " Lord, the judge of all the earth, wilt
   thou not execute righteous judgment?"[10]
8 For if it is unreasonable to suppose that the
   unbegotten and immutable essence of the
almighty God was changed into the form of man,
or that it deceived the eyes of the beholders
with the appearance of some created thing, and
if it is unreasonable to suppose, on the other
hand, that the Scripture should falsely invent such
things, when the God and Lord who judgeth all
the earth and executeth judgment is seen in the
form of a man, who else can be called, if it be
not lawful to call him the first cause of all things,
than his only pre-existent Word?[11]   Concerning whom it is said in the Psalms, " He sent his
   Word and healed them, and delivered them
9 from their destructions."[12]   Moses most
   clearly proclaims him second Lord after the
Father, when he says, " The Lord rained upon
Sodom and Gomorrah brimstone and fire from
the Lord."[13]   The divine Scripture also calls him
God, when he appeared again to Jacob in the
form of a man, and said to Jacob, " Thy name
shall be called no more Jacob, but Israel shall
be thy name, because thou hast prevailed with
God."[14]   Wherefore also Jacob called the name
of that place " Vision of God,"[15] saying, " For I
   have seen God face to face, and my life is
10 preserved."[16]   Nor is it admissible to suppose that the theophanies recorded were

appearances of subordinate angels and ministers
of God, for whenever any of these appeared
to men, the Scripture does not conceal the
fact, but calls them by name not God nor Lord,
but angels, as it is easy to prove by numberless testimonies. Joshua, also, the suc-   11
cessor of Moses, calls him, as leader of
the heavenly angels and archangels and of the
supramundane powers, and as lieutenant of
the Father,[17] entrusted with the second rank of
sovereignty and rule over all, " captain of the
host of the Lord," although he saw him not
otherwise than again in the form and appearance of a man.   For it is written : " And it
came to pass when Joshua was at Jericho[18]   12
that he looked and saw a man standing
over against him with his sword drawn in his
hand, and Joshua went unto him and said, Art
thou for us or for our adversaries? And he said
unto him, As captain of the host of the Lord am
I now come.   And Joshua fell on his face to the
earth and said unto him, Lord, what dost thou
command thy servant? and the captain of the
Lord said unto Joshua, Loose thy shoe from off
thy feet, for the place whereon thou standest
is holy."[19]   You will perceive also from the   13
same words that this was no other than he
who talked with Moses.[20]   For the Scripture
says in the same words and with reference to
the same one, " When the Lord saw that he
drew near to see, the Lord called to him out of
the bush and said, Moses, Moses. And he said,
What is it? And he said, Draw not nigh hither ;
loose thy shoe from off thy feet, for the place
whereon thou standest is holy ground. And he
said unto him, I am the God of thy fathers, the
God of Abraham, and the God of Isaac, and
the God of Jacob."[21]

And that there is a certain substance   14
which lived and subsisted[22] before the world,
and which ministered unto the Father and God
of the universe for the formation of all created
things, and which, is called the Word of God
and Wisdom, we may learn, to quote other
proofs in addition to those already cited, from
the mouth of Wisdom herself, who reveals most
clearly through Solomon the following mysteries
concerning herself : " I, Wisdom, have dwelt

---

[9] See Gen. xviii. 1 sq.   [10] Gen. xviii. 25.
[11] Eusebius accepts the common view of the early Church, that
the theophanies of the Old Testament were Christophanies; that is,
appearances of the second person of the Trinity. Augustine seems
to have been the first of the Fathers to take a different view, maintaining that such Christophanies were not consistent with the identity of essence between Father and Son, and that the Scriptures
themselves teach that it was not the Logos, but an angel, that appeared to the Old Testament worthies on various occasions (cf. De
Trin. III. 11). Augustine's opinion was widely adopted, but in
modern times the earlier view, which Eusebius represents, has been
the prevailing one (see Hodge, Systematic Theology, I. p. 490, and
Lange's article Theophany in Herzog).
[12] Ps. cvii. 20.
[13] Gen. xix. 24.   [15] εἶδος θεοῦ.
[14] Gen. xxxii. 28.   [16] Gen. xxxii. 30.

[17] The MSS. differ greatly at this point. A number of them,
followed by Valesius, Closs, and Crusè, read, ὡσανεὶ τοῦ πατρὸς
ὑπάρχοντα δύναμιν καὶ σοφίαν. Schwegler, Laemmer, Burton,
and Heinichen adopt another reading which has some MS. support,
and which we have followed in our translation: ὡσανεὶ τοῦ πατρὸς
ὕπαρχον. See Heinichen's edition, Vol. I. p. 10, note 41.
[18] ἐν Ἱεριχῶ.
[19] Josh. v. 13–15.
[20] Eusebius agrees with other earlier Fathers (e.g. Justin Martyr,
Origen, and Cyprian) in identifying the one that appeared to Joshua
with him that had appeared to Moses, on the ground that the same
words were used in both cases (cf. especially Justin's Dial. c.
Trypho, chap. 62). Many later Fathers (e.g. Theodoret) regard the
person that appeared to Joshua as the archangel Michael, who is
described by Daniel (x. 21 and xii. 1) as fighting for the people of
God. See Keil's Commentary on Joshua, chap. 5, vv. 13–15.
[21] Ex. iii. 4–6. Cf. Justin's Dial., chap. 63.
[22] οὐσία τις προκόσμιος ζῶσα καὶ ὑφεστῶσα.

with prudence and knowledge, and I have invoked understanding. Through me kings reign, and princes ordain righteousness. Through me the great are magnified, and through me 15 sovereigns rule the earth."[23] To which she adds: "The Lord created me in the beginning of his ways, for his works; before the world he established me, in the beginning, before he made the earth, before he made the depths, before the mountains were settled, before all hills he begat me. When he prepared the heavens I was present with him, and when he established the fountains of the region under heaven[24] I was with him, disposing. I was the one in whom he delighted; daily I rejoiced before him at all times when he was rejoicing 16 at having completed the world."[25] That the divine Word, therefore, pre-existed, and appeared to some, if not to all, has thus been briefly shown by us.

17   But why the Gospel was not preached in ancient times to all men and to all nations, as it is now, will appear from the following considerations.[26] The life of the ancients was not of such a kind as to permit them to receive the all-wise and all-virtuous teaching 18 of Christ. For immediately in the beginning, after his original life of blessedness, the first man despised the command of God, and fell into this mortal and perishable state, and exchanged his former divinely inspired luxury for this curse-laden earth. His descendants having filled our earth, showed themselves much worse, with the exception of one here and there, and entered upon a certain brutal and insupportable mode of life. They thought 19 neither of city nor state, neither of arts nor sciences. They were ignorant even of the name of laws and of justice, of virtue and of philosophy. As nomads, they passed their lives in deserts, like wild and fierce beasts, destroying, by an excess of voluntary wickedness, the natural reason of man, and the seeds of thought and of culture implanted in the human soul. They gave themselves wholly over to all kinds of profanity, now seducing one another, now slaying one another, now eating human flesh, and now daring to wage war with the Gods and to undertake those battles of the giants celebrated by all; now planning to fortify earth against heaven, and in the madness of un-

governed pride to prepare an attack upon the very God of all.[27]

On account of these things, when they 20 conducted themselves thus, the all-seeing God sent down upon them floods and conflagrations as upon a wild forest spread over the whole earth. He cut them down with continuous famines and plagues, with wars, and with thunderbolts from heaven, as if to check some terrible and obstinate disease of souls with more severe punishments. Then, when the 21 excess of wickedness had overwhelmed nearly all the race, like a deep fit of drunkenness, beclouding and darkening the minds of men, the first-born and first-created wisdom of God, the pre-existent Word himself, induced by his exceeding love for man, appeared to his servants, now in the form of angels, and again to one and another of those ancients who enjoyed the favor of God, in his own person as the saving power of God, not otherwise, however, than in the shape of man, because it was impossible to appear in any other way. And 22 as by them the seeds of piety were sown among a multitude of men and the whole nation, descended from the Hebrews, devoted themselves persistently to the worship of God, he imparted to them through the prophet Moses, as to multitudes still corrupted by their ancient practices, images and symbols of a certain mystic Sabbath and of circumcision, and elements of other spiritual principles, but he did not grant them a complete knowledge of the mysteries themselves. But when their law 23 became celebrated, and, like a sweet odor, was diffused among all men, as a result of their influence the dispositions of the majority of the heathen were softened by the lawgivers and philosophers who arose on every side, and their wild and savage brutality was changed into mildness, so that they enjoyed deep peace, friendship, and social intercourse.[28] Then, finally, at the time of the origin of the Roman Empire, there appeared again to all men and nations throughout the world, who had been, as it were, previously assisted, and were now fitted to receive the knowledge of the Father, that same teacher

---

[23] Prov. viii. 12, 15, 16.
[24] τῆς ὑπ' οὐρανόν, with all the MSS. and the LXX., followed by Schwegler, Burton, Heinichen, and others. Some editors, in agreement with the version of Rufinus (*fontes sub cœlo*), read τὰς ὑπ' οὐρανόν. Closs, Stigloher, and Crusè translate in the same way.
[25] Prov. viii. 22–25, 27, 28, 30, 31.
[26] Eusebius pursues much the same line of argument in his *Dem. Evang.*, Prœm. Bk. VIII.; and compare also Gregory of Nyssa's Third Oration on the birth of the Lord (at the beginning). The objection which Eusebius undertakes to answer here was an old one, and had been considered by Justin Martyr, by Origen in his work against Celsus, and by others (see Tzschirner's *Geschichte der Apologetik*, p. 25 ff.).

[27] The reference here seems to be to the building of the tower of Babel (Gen. xi. 1–9), although Valesius thinks otherwise. The fact that Eusebius refers to the battles of the giants, which were celebrated in heathen song, does not militate against a reference in this passage to the narrative recounted in Genesis. He illustrates the presumption of the human race by instances familiar to his readers whether drawn from Christian or from Pagan sources. Compare the *Præp. Evang.* ix. 14.
[28] It was the opinion of Eusebius, in common with most of the Fathers, that the Greek philosophers, lawgivers, and poets had obtained their wisdom from the ancient Hebrews, and this point was pressed very strongly by many of the apologists in their effort to prove the antiquity of Christianity. The assertion was made especially in the case of Plato and Pythagoras, who were said to have become acquainted with the books of the Hebrews upon their journey to Egypt. Compare among other passages Justin's *Apol.* I. 59 ff.; Clement of Alexandria's *Cohort. ad Gentes*, chap. 6; and Tertullian's *Apol.* chap. 47. Compare also Eusebius' *Præp. Evang.*, Bks. IX. and X.

of virtue, the minister of the Father in all good things, the divine and heavenly Word of God, in a human body not at all differing in substance from our own. He did and suffered the things which had been prophesied. For it had been foretold that one who was at the same time man and God should come and dwell in the world, should perform wonderful works, and should show himself a teacher to all nations of the piety of the Father. The marvelous nature of his birth, and his new teaching, and his wonderful works had also been foretold; so likewise the manner of his death, his resurrection from the dead, and, finally, his divine ascension into heaven.

24   For instance, Daniel the prophet, under the influence of the divine Spirit, seeing his kingdom at the end of time,[29] was inspired thus to describe the divine vision in language fitted to human comprehension: "For I beheld," he says, "until thrones were placed, and the Ancient of Days did sit, whose garment was white as snow and the hair of his head like pure wool; his throne was a flame of fire and his wheels burning fire. A river of fire flowed before him. Thousand thousands ministered unto him, and ten thousand times ten thousand stood before
25   him. He appointed judgment, and the books were opened."[30]   And again, "I saw," says he, "and behold, one like the Son of man came with the clouds of heaven, and he hastened unto the Ancient of Days and was brought into his presence, and there was given him the dominion and the glory and the kingdom; and all peoples, tribes, and tongues serve him. His dominion is an everlasting dominion which shall not pass away, and his
26   kingdom shall not be destroyed."[31]   It is clear that these words can refer to no one else than to our Saviour, the God Word who was in the beginning with God, and who was called the Son of man because of his final
27   appearance in the flesh. But since we have collected in separate books[32] the selections from the prophets which relate to our Saviour Jesus Christ, and have arranged in a more logical form those things which have been revealed concerning him, what has been said will suffice for the present.

CHAPTER III.

The Name Jesus and also the Name Christ were known from the Beginning, and were honored by the Inspired Prophets.

1   IT is now the proper place to show that the very name Jesus and also the name Christ were honored by the ancient proph-
2   ets beloved of God.[1]   Moses was the first to make known the name of Christ as a name especially august and glorious. When he delivered types and symbols of heavenly things, and mysterious images, in accordance with the oracle which said to him, "Look that thou make all things according to the pattern which was shown thee in the mount,"[2] he consecrated a man high priest of God, in so far as that was possible, and him he called Christ.[3]   And thus to this dignity of the high priesthood, which in his opinion surpassed the most honorable position among men, he attached for the sake of
3   honor and glory the name of Christ. He knew so well that in Christ was something divine. And the same one foreseeing, under the influence of the divine Spirit, the name Jesus, dignified it also with a certain distinguished privilege. For the name of Jesus, which had never been uttered among men before the time of Moses, he applied first and only to the one who he knew would receive after his death, again as a type and symbol, the supreme command.
4   His successor, therefore, who had not hitherto borne the name Jesus, but had been called by another name, Auses,[4] which had been given him by his parents, he now called Jesus, bestowing the name upon him as a gift of honor, far greater than any kingly diadem. For Jesus himself, the son of Nave, bore a resemblance to our Saviour in the fact that he alone, after Moses and after the completion of the symbolical worship which had been transmitted by him, succeeded to the government of the true and pure religion. Thus Moses bestowed
5   the name of our Saviour, Jesus Christ, as a mark of the highest honor, upon the two men who in his time surpassed all the rest of the people in virtue and glory; namely, upon the high priest and upon his own successor
6   in the government. And the prophets that came after also clearly foretold Christ by name, predicting at the same time the plots which the Jewish people would form against him, and the calling of the nations through him. Jeremiah, for instance, speaks as follows: "The

---

[29] The Greek has only ἐπὶ τέλει, which can refer, however, only to the end of time or to the end of the world.
[30] Dan. vii. 9, 10.   [31] Dan. vii. 13, 14.
[32] Eusebius refers here probably to his *Eclogæ propheticæ*, or *Prophetical Extracts*, possibly to his *Dem. Evang.*; upon these works see the Prolegomena, p. 34 and 37, above.

[1] Compare the *Dem. Evang.* iv. 17.
[2] Ex. xxv. 40.
[3] Eusebius here has in mind the passages Lev. iv. 5, 16, and vi. 22, where the LXX. reads ὁ ἱερεὺς ὁ χριστός: *The priest, the anointed one*" (Closs). The Authorized Version reads, *The priest that was anointed;* the Revised Version, *The anointed priest.*
[4] A few MSS. followed by Laemmer and Heinichen, read here Ναυῆ, but the best MSS. followed by the majority of editors read Ἀυσῆ, which is a corruption of the name *Oshea*, which means "Salvation," and which Joshua bore before his name was changed, by the addition of a syllable, to Jehoshua=Jesus, meaning "God's salvation" (Num. xiii. 16). Jerome (*de vir. ill.* c. I.) speaks of this corruption as existing in Greek and Latin MSS. of the Scriptures, and as having no sense, and contends that Osee is the proper form, Osee meaning "Salvator." The same corruption (Auses) occurs also in Tertullian, *Adv. Marc.* iii. 16, and *Adv. Jud.* 9 (where the English translator, as Crusè also does in the present passage, in both cases departs from the original, and renders 'Oshea,' *Ante-Nicene Fathers*, Am. Ed. III. p. 334, 335, and 163), and in Lactantius, *Institutes*, iv. 17.

Spirit before our face, Christ the Lord, was taken in their destructions; of whom we said, under his shadow we shall live among the nations."[5] And David, in perplexity, says, "Why did the nations rage and the people imagine vain things? The kings of the earth set themselves in array, and the rulers were gathered together against the Lord and against his Christ";[6] to which he adds, in the person of Christ himself, "The Lord said unto me, Thou art my Son, this day have I begotten thee. Ask of me, and I will give thee the nations for thine inheritance, and the uttermost parts of the earth for thy possession."[7]

7   And not only those who were honored with the high priesthood, and who for the sake of the symbol were anointed with especially prepared oil, were adorned with the name of Christ among the Hebrews, but also the kings whom the prophets anointed under the influence of the divine Spirit, and thus constituted, as it were, typical Christs. For they also bore in their own persons types of the royal and sovereign power of the true and only Christ, the 8 divine Word who ruleth over all. And we have been told also that certain of the prophets themselves became, by the act of anointing, Christs in type, so that all these have reference to the true Christ, the divinely inspired and heavenly Word, who is the only high priest of all, and the only King of every creature, and the Father's only supreme prophet of proph- 9 ets. And a proof of this is that no one of those who were of old symbolically anointed, whether priests, or kings, or prophets, possessed so great a power of inspired virtue as was ex- hibited by our Saviour and Lord Jesus, the 10 true and only Christ. None of them at least, however superior in dignity and honor they may have been for many generations among their own people, ever gave to their followers the name of Christians from their own typical name of Christ. Neither was divine honor ever rendered to any one of them by their subjects; nor after their death was the disposition of their followers such that they were ready to die for the one whom they honored. And never did so great a commotion arise among all the nations of the earth in respect to any one of that age; for the mere symbol could not act with such power among them as the truth itself which 11 was exhibited by our Saviour. He, although he received no symbols and types of high priesthood from any one, although he was not born of a race of priests, although he was not elevated to a kingdom by military guards, although he was not a prophet like those of old, although he obtained no honor nor pre-eminence among the Jews, nevertheless was adorned by the Father with all, if not with the symbols,

yet with the truth itself. And therefore, 12 although he did not possess like honors with those whom we have mentioned, he is called Christ more than all of them. And as himself the true and only Christ of God, he has filled the whole earth with the truly august and sacred name of Christians, committing to his followers no longer types and images, but the uncovered virtues themselves, and a heavenly life in the very doctrines of truth. And he was not 13 anointed with oil prepared from material substances, but, as befits divinity, with the divine Spirit himself, by participation in the unbegotten deity of the Father. And this is taught also again by Isaiah, who exclaims, as if in the person of Christ himself, "The Spirit of the Lord is upon me; therefore hath he anointed me. He hath sent me to preach the Gospel to the poor, to proclaim deliverance to captives, and re- covery of sight to the blind."[8] And not only 14 Isaiah, but also David addresses him, say- ing, "Thy throne, O God, is forever and ever. A scepter of equity is the scepter of thy king- dom. Thou hast loved righteousness and hast hated iniquity. Therefore God, thy God, hath anointed thee with the oil of gladness above thy fellows."[9] Here the Scripture calls him God in the first verse, in the second it honors him with a royal scepter. Then a little farther 15 on, after the divine and royal power, it rep- resents him in the third place as having become Christ, being anointed not with oil made of material substances, but with the divine oil of gladness. It thus indicates his especial honor, far superior to and different from that of those who, as types, were of old anointed in a more material way. And elsewhere the 16 same writer speaks of him as follows: "The Lord said unto my Lord, Sit thou at my right hand until I make thine enemies thy foot- stool";[10] and, "Out of the womb, before the morning star, have I begotten thee. The Lord hath sworn and he will not repent. Thou art a priest forever after the order of Melchize- dec."[11] But this Melchizedec is introduced 17 in the Holy Scriptures as a priest of the most high God,[12] not consecrated by any anoint- ing oil, especially prepared, and not even be- longing by descent to the priesthood of the Jews. Wherefore after his order, but not after the order of the others, who received symbols and types, was our Saviour proclaimed, with an appeal to an oath, Christ and priest. History, therefore, does not relate that he 18 was anointed corporeally by the Jews, nor

[8] Isa. lxi. 1. Eusebius as usual follows the LXX., which in this case differs somewhat from the Hebrew, and hence the translation differs from the English text. The LXX., however, contains an extra clause which Eusebius omits. See Heinichen's edition, Vol. I. p. 21, note 49.
[9] Ps. xlv. 6, 7.   [10] Ps. cx. 1.   [11] Ps. cx. 4.
[12] See Gen. xiv. 18; Heb. v. 6, 10; vi. 20; viii.

[5] Sam. iv. 20.   [6] Ps. ii. 1, 2.   [7] Ps. ii. 7, 8.

that he belonged to the lineage of priests, but that he came into existence from God himself before the morning star, that is before the organization of the world, and that he obtained an immortal and undecaying priesthood for

19 eternal ages. But it is a great and convincing proof of his incorporeal and divine unction that he alone of all those who have ever existed is even to the present day called Christ by all men throughout the world, and is confessed and witnessed to under this name, and is commemorated both by Greeks and Barbarians, and even to this day is honored as a King by his followers throughout the world, and is admired as more than a prophet, and is glorified as the true and only high priest of God.[13] And besides all this, as the pre-existent Word of God, called into being before all ages, he has received august honor from the Father, and is wor-

20 shiped as God. But most wonderful of all is the fact that we who have consecrated ourselves to him, honor him not only with our voices and with the sound of words, but also with complete elevation of soul, so that we choose to give testimony unto him rather than to preserve our own lives.

21 I have of necessity prefaced my history with these matters in order that no one, judging from the date of his incarnation, may think that our Saviour and Lord Jesus, the Christ, has but recently come into being.

CHAPTER IV.

The Religion proclaimed by him to All Nations was neither New nor Strange.

1 BUT that no one may suppose that his doctrine is new and strange, as if it were framed by a man of recent origin, differing in no respect from other men, let us now briefly

2 consider this point also. It is admitted that when in recent times the appearance of our Saviour Jesus Christ had become known to all men there immediately made its appearance a new nation ; a nation confessedly not small, and not dwelling in some corner of the earth, but the most numerous and pious of all nations,[1] indestructible and unconquerable, because it always receives assistance from God. This nation, thus suddenly appearing at the time appointed by the inscrutable counsel of God, is the one which has been honored by all with the name of

3 Christ. One of the prophets, when he saw beforehand with the eye of the Divine Spirit

that which was to be, was so astonished at it that he cried out, "Who hath heard of such things, and who hath spoken thus? Hath the earth brought forth in one day, and hath a nation been born at once?"[2] And the same prophet gives a hint also of the name by which the nation was to be called, when he says, "Those that serve me shall be called by a new name, which shall be blessed upon the earth."[3] But although

4 it is clear that we are new and that this new name of Christians has really but recently been known among all nations, nevertheless our life and our conduct, with our doctrines of religion, have not been lately invented by us, but from the first creation of man, so to speak, have been established by the natural understanding of divinely favored men of old. That this is so we shall show in the following way. That

5 the Hebrew nation is not new, but is universally honored on account of its antiquity, is known to all. The books and writings of this people contain accounts of ancient men, rare indeed and few in number, but nevertheless distinguished for piety and righteousness and every other virtue. Of these, some excellent men lived before the flood, others of the sons and descendants of Noah lived after it, among them Abraham, whom the Hebrews celebrate as their own founder and forefather. If any

6 one should assert that all those who have enjoyed the testimony of righteousness, from Abraham himself back to the first man, were Christians in fact if not in name, he would not go beyond the truth.[4] For that which

7 the name indicates, that the Christian man, through the knowledge and the teaching of Christ, is distinguished for temperance and righteousness, for patience in life and manly virtue, and for a profession of piety toward the one and only God over all — all that was zealously practiced by them not less than by us. They did not care about circumcision of

8 the body, neither do we. They did not care about observing Sabbaths, nor do we. They did not avoid certain kinds of food, neither did they regard the other distinctions which Moses first delivered to their posterity to be observed as symbols ; nor do Christians of the present day do such things. But they also clearly knew the very Christ of God ; for it has already been shown that he appeared unto Abraham, that he imparted revelations to Isaac, that he talked with Jacob, that he held converse with Moses and with the prophets that came after. Hence

9 you will find those divinely favored men honored with the name of Christ, according to the passage which says of them, "Touch not my Christs, and do my prophets no harm."[5]

[13] Eusebius, in this chapter and in the *Dem. Evang.* IV. 15, is the first of the Fathers to mention the three offices of Christ.
[1] Cf. Tertullian, *Apol.* XXXVII. (*Ante-Nicene Fathers,* Am. Ed. Vol. III. p. 45).

[2] Isa. lxvi. 8.
[3] Isa. lxv. 15, 16.
[4] Compare Justin Martyr's *Apol.* I. 46.
[5] 1 Chron. xvi. 22, and Ps. cv. 15.

10　So that it is clearly necessary to consider that religion, which has lately been preached to all nations through the teaching of Christ, the first and most ancient of all religions, and the one discovered by those divinely favored

11　men in the age of Abraham. If it is said that Abraham, a long time afterward, was given the command of circumcision, we reply that nevertheless before this it was declared that he had received the testimony of righteousness through faith ; as the divine word says, "Abraham believed in God, and it was counted

12　unto him for righteousness." [6]　And indeed unto Abraham, who was thus before his circumcision a justified man, there was given by God, who revealed himself unto him (but this was Christ himself, the word of God), a prophecy in regard to those who in coming ages should be justified in the same way as he. The prophecy was in the following words : "And in thee shall all the tribes of the earth be blessed." [7] And again, "He shall become a nation great and numerous ; and in him shall all the

13　nations of the earth be blessed." [8]　It is permissible to understand this as fulfilled in us. For he, having renounced the superstition of his fathers, and the former error of his life, and having confessed the one God over all, and having worshiped him with deeds of virtue, and not with the service of the law which was afterward given by Moses, was justified by faith in Christ, the Word of God, who appeared unto him. To him, then, who was a man of this character, it was said that all the tribes and all the nations of the earth should be blessed

14　in him. But that very religion of Abraham has reappeared at the present time, practiced in deeds, more efficacious than words, by Christians alone throughout the world.

15　What then should prevent the confession that we who are of Christ practice one and the same mode of life and have one and the same religion as those divinely favored men of old? Whence it is evident that the perfect religion committed to us by the teaching of Christ is not new and strange, but, if the truth must be spoken, it is the first and the true religion. This may suffice for this subject.

CHAPTER V.

The Time of his Appearance among Men.

1　AND now, after this necessary introduction to our proposed history of the Church, we can enter, so to speak, upon our journey, beginning with the appearance of our Saviour in the flesh. And we invoke God, the Father of the Word, and him, of whom we have been speaking, Jesus Christ himself our Saviour and Lord, the heavenly Word of God, as our aid and fellow-laborer in the narration of the truth.

2　It was in the forty-second year of the reign of Augustus [1] and the twenty-eighth after the subjugation of Egypt and the death of Antony and Cleopatra, with whom the dynasty of the Ptolemies in Egypt came to an end, that our Saviour and Lord Jesus Christ was born in Bethlehem of Judea, according to the prophecies which had been uttered concerning him. [2]　His birth took place during the first census, while Cyrenius was governor of Syria. [3]　Flavius Josephus, the most cele-

3　brated of Hebrew historians, also mentions this census, [4] which was taken during Cyrenius'

---

[1] Eusebius here makes the reign of Augustus begin with the death of Julius Cæsar (as Josephus does in chap. 9, § 1, below), and he puts the birth of Christ therefore into the year 752 U.C. (2 B.C.), which agrees with Clement of Alexandria's *Strom.* I. (who gives the twenty-eighth year after the conquest of Egypt as the birth-year of Christ), with Epiphanius, *Hær.* LI. 22, and Orosius, *Hist.* I. 1. Eusebius gives the same date also in his *Chron.* (ed. Schœne, II. p. 144). Irenæus, III. 25, and Tertullian, *Adv. Jud.* 8, on the other hand, give the forty-first year of Augustus, 751 U.C. (3 B.C.). But all these dates are certainly too late. The true year of Christ's birth has always been a matter of dispute. But it must have occurred before the death of Herod, which took place in the spring of 750 U.C. (4 B.C.). The most widely accepted opinion is that Christ was born late in the year 5, or early in the year 4 B.C., though some scholars put the date back as far as 7 B.C.

The time of the year is also uncertain, the date commonly accepted in the occident (Dec. 25th) having nothing older than a fourth century tradition in its favor. The date accepted by the Greek Church (Jan. 6th) rests upon a somewhat older tradition, but neither day has any claim to reliability.

For a full and excellent discussion of this subject, see the essay of Andrews in his *Life of our Lord*, pp. 1–22. See, also, Schaff's *Church Hist.* I. p. 98 sq.

[2] Micah v. 2.

[3] Cf. Luke ii. 2.
Quirinius is the original Latin form of the name of which Luke gives the Greek form κυρήνιος or Cyrenius (which is the form given also by Eusebius).

The statement of Luke presents a chronological difficulty which has not yet been completely solved. Quirinius we know to have been made governor of Syria in A.D. 6; and under him occurred a census or enrollment mentioned by Josephus, *Ant.* XVII. 13. 5, and XVIII. 1. 1. This is undoubtedly the same as that referred to in Acts v. 37. But this took place some ten years after the birth of Christ, and cannot therefore be connected with that event. Many explanations have been offered to account for the difficulty, but since the discovery of Zumpt, the problem has been much simplified. He, as also Mommsen, has proved that Quirinius was twice governor of Syria, the first time from B.C. 4 (autumn) to B.C. 1. But as Christ must have been born before the spring of B.C. 4, the governorship of Quirinius is still a little too late. A solution of the question is thus approached, however, though not all the difficulties are yet removed. Upon this question, see especially A. M. Zumpt, *Das Geburtsjahr Christi* (Leipzig, 1869), and compare Schaff's *Church Hist.*, I. 121–125, for a condensed but excellent account of the whole matter, and for the literature of the subject.

[4] Eusebius here identifies the census mentioned by Josephus (*Ant.* XVIII. 1. 1) and referred to in Acts v. 37, with the one mentioned in Luke ii. 2; but this is an obvious error, as an interval of ten years separated the two. Valesius considers it all one census, and hence regards Eusebius as correct in his statement; but this is very improbable. Jachmann (in Illgen's *Zeitschrift f. hist. Theologie*, 1839, II. p. 35 sq.), according to his custom, charges Eusebius with willful deception and perversion of the facts. But such a charge is utterly without warrant. Eusebius, in cases where we can control his statements, can be shown to have been always conscientious. Moreover, in his *Chron.* (ed. Schoene II. p. 144) he identifies the two censuses in the same way. But his *Chronicles* were written some years before his *History*, and he cannot have had any object to de-

---

[6] Gen. xv. 6.　　　　[8] Gen. xviii. 18.
[7] Gen. xii. 3.

term of office. In the same connection he gives an account of the uprising of the Galileans, which took place at that time, of which also Luke, among our writers, has made mention in the Acts, in the following words: "After this man rose up Judas of Galilee in the days of the taxing, and drew away a multitude[5] after him: he also perished; and all, even as many as obeyed him, were dispersed."[6]

4

The above-mentioned author, in the eighteenth book of his Antiquities, in agreement with these words, adds the following, which we quote exactly: "Cyrenius, a member of the senate, one who had held other offices and had passed through them all to the consulship, a man also of great dignity in other respects, came to Syria with a small retinue, being sent by Cæsar to be a judge of the nation and to make an assessment of their property."[7]

5

And after a little[8] he says: "But Judas,[9] a Gaulonite, from a city called Gamala, taking with him Sadduchus,[10] a Pharisee, urged the people to revolt, both of them saying that the taxation meant nothing else than downright slavery, and exhorting the nation to defend their liberty." And in the second book of his History of the Jewish War, he writes as follows concerning the same man: "At this time a certain Galilean, whose name was Judas, persuaded his countrymen to revolt, declaring that they were cowards if they submitted to pay tribute to the Romans, and if they endured,

6

besides God, masters who were mortal."[11] These things are recorded by Josephus.

CHAPTER VI.

About the Time of Christ, in accordance with Prophecy, the Rulers who had governed the Jewish Nation in Regular Succession from the Days of Antiquity came to an End, and Herod, the First Foreigner, became King.

WHEN Herod,[1] the first ruler of foreign blood, became King, the prophecy of Moses received its fulfillment, according to which there should "not be wanting a prince of Judah, nor a ruler from his loins, until he come for whom it is reserved."[2] The latter, he also shows, was to be the expectation of the nations.[3]

1

This prediction remained unfulfilled so long as it was permitted them to live under rulers from their own nation, that is, from the time of Moses to the reign of Augustus. Under the latter, Herod, the first foreigner, was given the Kingdom of the Jews by the Romans. As Josephus relates,[4] he was an Idumean[5] on his father's side and an Arabian on his mother's. But Africanus,[6] who was also no common writer, says that they who were more accurately informed about him report that he was a son of Antipater, and that the latter was the son of a certain Herod of Ascalon,[7] one of the so-called

2

---

ceive in them such as Jachmann assumes that he had in his *History*. It is plain that Eusebius has simply made a blunder, a thing not at all surprising when we remember how frequent his chronological errors are. He is guilty of an inexcusable piece of carelessness, but nothing worse. It was natural to connect the two censuses mentioned as taking place under the same governor, though a little closer attention to the facts would have shown him the discrepancy in date, which he simply overlooked.

[5] The New Testament (*Textus Rec.*) reads λαὸν ἱκανόν, with which Laemmer agrees in his edition of Eusebius. Two MSS., followed by Stephanus and Valesius, and by the English and German translators, read λαὸν πολύν. All the other MSS. and editors, as well as Rufinus, read λαόν alone.

[6] Acts v. 37.

[7] Josephus, *Ant.* XVIII. 1. 1. Upon Josephus and his works, see below, Bk. III. c. 9. [8] *Ibid.*

[9] Judas the Gaulonite. In Acts v. 37, and in Josephus, *B. J.* II. 8. 1 (quoted just below), and 17. 8, and in *Ant.* XVIII. 1. 6 and XX. 5. 2, he is called Judas of Galilee. But in the present section Josephus gives the fullest and most accurate account of him. Gaulonitis lay east of the Jordan, opposite Galilee. Judas of Galilee was probably his common designation, given to him either because his revolt took rise in Galilee, or because Galilee was used as a general term for the north country. He was evidently a man of position and great personal influence, and drew vast numbers to his standard, denouncing, in the name of religion, the payment of tribute to Rome and all submission to a foreign yoke. The revolt spread very rapidly, and the whole country was thrown into excitement and disorder; but the Romans proved too strong for him, and he soon perished, and his followers were dispersed, though many of them continued active until the final destruction of the city. The influence of Judas was so great and lasted so long that Josephus (*Ant.* XVIII. 1. 1 and 6) calls the tendency represented by him the "fourth philosophy of the Jews," ranking it with Pharisaism, Sadduceeism, and Essenism. The distinguishing characteristic of this "fourth philosophy" or sect was its love of freedom. For an excellent account of Judas and his revolt, see Ewald's *Geschichte des Volkes Israel*, V. p. 16 sq.

[10] Greek, Σάδδοχον; Rufinus, *Sadduchum*. He, too, must have been a man of influence and position. Later in the same paragraph he is made by Josephus a joint founder with Judas of the "fourth philosophy," but in § 6 of the same chapter, where the author of it is referred to, Judas alone is mentioned.

[11] Josephus, *B. J.* II. 8. 1.

[1] Herod the Great, son of Antipater, an Idumean, who had been appointed procurator of Judea by Cæsar in B.C. 47. Herod was made governor of Galilee at the same time, and king of Judea by the Roman Senate in B.C. 40.

[2] Gen. xlix. 10. The LXX., which Eusebius quotes here, according to his custom, is in the present instance somewhat different from the Hebrew. [3] *Ibid.*

[4] Eusebius refers here to *Ant.* XIV. 1. 3 and 7. 3. According to Josephus, Herod's father was Antipater, and his mother Cypros, an Arabian woman of noble birth.

[5] The Idumeans or Edomites were the descendants of Esau, and inhabited the Sinaitic peninsula south of the Dead Sea. Their principal city and stronghold was the famous rock city, Petra. They were constant enemies of the Jews, refused them free passage through their land (Num. xx. 20); were conquered by Saul and David, but again regained their independence, until they were finally completely subjugated by John Hyrcanus, who left them in possession of their land, but compelled them to undergo circumcision, and adopt the Jewish law. Compare Josephus, *Ant.* XIII. 9. 1; XV. 7. 9; *B. J.* IV. 5. 5.

[6] On Africanus, see Bk. VI. chap. 31. This account is given by Africanus in his epistle to Aristides, quoted by Eusebius in the next chapter. Africanus states there (§ 11) that the account, as he gives it, was handed down by the relatives of the Lord. But the tradition, whether much older than Africanus or not, is certainly incorrect. We learn from Josephus (*Ant.* XIV. 2), who is the best witness upon this subject, that Antipater, the father of Herod the Great, was the son of another Antipater, or Antipas, an Idumean who had been made governor of Idumea by the Jewish king Alexander Jannæus (of the Maccabæan family). In *Ant.* XVI. 11 Josephus informs us that a report had been invented by friends and flatterers of Herod that he was descended from Jewish ancestors. The report originated with Nicolai Damasceni, a writer of the time of the Herods. The tradition preserved here by Africanus had its origin, evidently, in a desire to degrade Herod by representing him as descended from a slave.

[7] Ascalon, one of the five cities of the Philistines (mentioned frequently in the Old Testament), lay upon the Mediterranean Sea, between Gaza and Joppa. It was beautified by Herod (although not belonging to his dominions), and after his death became the residence of his sister Salome. It was a prominent place in the Middle Ages, but is now in ruins. Of this Herod of Ascalon nothing is known. Possibly no such man existed.

3   servants[8] of the temple of Apollo. This
Antipater, having been taken a prisoner while
a boy by Idumean robbers, lived with them, because his father, being a poor man, was unable
to pay a ransom for him.   Growing up in their
practices he was afterward befriended by Hyrcanus,[9] the high priest of the Jews.   A son of his
was that Herod who lived in the times of
4   our Saviour.[10]   When the Kingdom of the
Jews had devolved upon such a man the
expectation of the nations was, according to
prophecy, already at the door.   For with him
their princes and governors, who had ruled in
regular succession from the time of Moses,
5   came to an end.   Before their captivity and
their transportation to Babylon they were
ruled by Saul first and then by David, and before the kings leaders governed them who were
called Judges, and who came after Moses
6   and his successor Jesus.   After their return
from Babylon they continued to have without interruption an aristocratic form of government, with an oligarchy.   For the priests had
the direction of affairs until Pompey, the Roman
general, took Jerusalem by force, and defiled
the holy places by entering the very innermost
sanctuary of the temple.[11]   Aristobulus,[12] who,
by the right of ancient succession, had been up
to that time both king and high priest, he sent
with his children in chains to Rome ; and gave
to Hyrcanus, brother of Aristobulus, the high
priesthood, while the whole nation of the Jews
was made tributary to the Romans from
7   that time.[13]   But Hyrcanus, who was the
last of the regular line of high priests, was
very soon afterward taken prisoner by the Parthians,[14] and Herod, the first foreigner, as I have

already said, was made King of the Jewish
nation by the Roman senate and by Augus-   8
tus.   Under him Christ appeared in bodily
shape, and the expected Salvation of the nations
and their calling followed in accordance with
prophecy.[15]   From this time the princes and
rulers of Judah, I mean of the Jewish nation,
came to an end, and as a natural consequence
the order of the high priesthood, which from
ancient times had proceeded regularly in closest
succession from generation to generation,
was immediately thrown into confusion.[16]   Of   9
these things Josephus is also a witness,[17] who
shows that when Herod was made King by the
Romans he no longer appointed the high priests
from the ancient line, but gave the honor to
certain obscure persons.   A course similar to
that of Herod in the appointment of the priests
was pursued by his son Archelaus,[18] and after
him by the Romans, who took the government into their own hands.[19]   The same   10
writer shows[20] that Herod was the first that
locked up the sacred garment of the high priest
under his own seal and refused to permit the
high priests to keep it for themselves.   The
same course was followed by Archelaus after
him, and after Archelaus by the Romans.

These things have been recorded by us   11
in order to show that another prophecy has
been fulfilled in the appearance of our Saviour
Jesus Christ.   For the Scripture, in the book of
Daniel,[21] having expressly mentioned a certain
number of weeks until the coming of Christ, of
which we have treated in other books,[22] most
clearly prophesies, that after the completion of
those weeks the unction among the Jews should
totally perish.   And this, it has been clearly
shown, was fulfilled at the time of the birth of
our Saviour Jesus Christ.   This has been neces-

---

[8] ἱερόδουλος, "a temple-slave."
[9] Hyrcanus II., eldest son of the King Alexander Jannæus of
the Maccabæan family, became high priest upon the death of his
father, in 78 B.C.; and upon the death of his mother, in 69 B.C., ascended the throne.   He gave up his kingdom afterward (66 B.C.) to
his younger brother, Aristobulus; but under the influence of Antipater the Idumean endeavored to regain it, and after a long war with
his brother, was re-established in power by Pompey, in 63 B.C., but
merely as high priest and governor, not with the title of king.   He
retained his position until 40 B.C., when he was driven out by his
nephew Antigonus.   He was murdered in 30 B.C., by command of
Herod the Great, who had married his grand-daughter Mariamne.
He was throughout a weak man, and while in power was completely
under the influence of his minister, Antipater.
[10] Herod the Great.
[11] In 63 B.C., when Pompey's curiosity led him to penetrate into
the Holy of Holies.   He was much impressed, however, by its simplicity, and went away without disturbing its treasures, wondering at
a religion which had no visible God.
[12] Aristobulus II., younger brother of Hyrcanus, a much abler
and more energetic man, assumed the kingdom by an arrangement
with his brother in 66 B.C. (see note 9, above).   In 63 B.C. he was
deposed, and carried to Rome by Pompey.   He died about 48 B.C.
Eusebius is hardly correct in saying that Aristobulus was king and
high priest by regular succession, as his elder brother Hyrcanus was
the true heir, and he had assumed the power only because of his
superior ability.
[13] The real independence of the Jews practically ceased at this
time.   For three years only, from 40 to 37 B.C., while Antigonus, son
of Aristobulus and nephew of Hyrcanus, was in power, Jerusalem
was independent of Rome, but was soon retaken by Herod the Great,
and remained from that time on in more or less complete subjection,
either as a dependent kingdom or as a province.
[14] 40 B.C., when Antigonus, by the aid of the Parthians took Jerusalem and established himself as king there, until conquered by

Herod in 37 B.C.   Hyrcanus returned to Jerusalem in 36 B.C., but
was no longer high priest.
[15] Compare Isa. ix. 2; xlii. 6; xlix. 6, etc.
[16] Eusebius' statement is perfectly correct.   The high priestly
lineage had been kept with great scrupulousness until Hyrcanus II.,
the last of the regular succession.   (His grandson Aristobulus, however, was high priest for a year under Herod, but was then slain by
him.)   Afterward the high priest was appointed and changed at
pleasure by the secular ruler.
Herod the Great first established the practice of removing a high
priest during his lifetime; and under him there were no less than six
different ones.
[17] Josephus, Ant. XX. 8.
[18] Archelaus, a son of Herod the Great by Malthace, a Samaritan
woman, and younger brother of Herod Antipas.   Upon the death of
his father, B.C. 4, he succeeded to the government of Idumea, Samaria, and Judea, with the title of Ethnarch.   Upon the death of
Archelaus (A.D. 7), Judea was made a
Roman province, and ruled by procurators until Herod Agrippa I.
came into power in 37 A.D. (see below, Bk. II. chap. 4, note 3).   The
changes in the high priesthood during the most of this time were
very rapid, one after another being appointed and removed according to the fancy of the procurator, or of the governor of Syria, who
held the power of appointment most of the time.   There were no
fewer than nineteen high priests between the death of Archelaus and
the fall of Jerusalem.
[20] Josephus, Ant. XV. 11. 4.   [21] Dan. ix. 26.
[22] It is commonly assumed that Eusebius refers here to the Dem.
Evang. VIII. 2 sq., where the prophecies of Daniel are discussed at
length.   But, as Lightfoot remarks, the reference is just as well satisfied by the Ecloga Proph. III. 45.   We cannot, in fact, decide
which work is meant.

CHAPTER VII.

The Alleged Discrepancy in the Gospels in regard to the Genealogy of Christ.

1   MATTHEW and Luke in their gospels have given us the genealogy of Christ differently, and many suppose that they are at variance with one another. Since as a consequence every believer, in ignorance of the truth, has been zealous to invent some explanation which shall harmonize the two passages, permit us to subjoin the account of the matter which has come down to us,[1] and which is given by Africanus, who was mentioned by us just above, in his epistle to Aristides,[2] where he discusses the harmony of the gospel genealogies. After refuting the opinions of others as forced and deceptive, he gives the account which he had received from tra-
2   dition[3] in these words : " For whereas the names of the generations were reckoned in Israel either according to nature or according to law, — according to nature by the succession of legitimate offspring, and according to law whenever another raised up a child to the name of a brother dying childless ;[4] for because a clear hope of resurrection was not yet given they had

a representation of the future promise by a kind of mortal resurrection, in order that the name of the one deceased might be perpetuated ; — whereas then some of those who are inserted   3 in this genealogical table succeeded by natural descent, the son to the father, while others, though born of one father, were ascribed by name to another, mention was made of both — of those who were progenitors in fact and of those who were so only in name. Thus   4 neither of the gospels is in error, for one reckons by nature, the other by law. For the line of descent from Solomon and that from Nathan[5] were so involved, the one with the other, by the raising up of children to the childless and by second marriages, that the same persons are justly considered to belong at one time to one, at another time to another ; that is, at one time to the reputed fathers, at another to the actual fathers. So that both these accounts are strictly true and come down to Joseph with considerable intricacy indeed, yet quite accurately. But in order that what I have   5 said may be made clear I shall explain the interchange of the generations. If we reckon the generations from David through Solomon, the third from the end is found to be Matthan, who begat Jacob the father of Joseph. But if, with Luke, we reckon them from Nathan the son of David, in like manner the third from the end is Melchi,[6] whose son Eli was the father of Joseph. For Joseph was the son of Eli, the son of Melchi. Joseph therefore being   6 the object proposed to us, it must be shown how it is that each is recorded to be his father, both Jacob, who derived his descent from Solomon, and Eli, who derived his from Nathan ; first how it is that these two, Jacob and Eli, were brothers, and then how it is that their fathers, Matthan and Melchi, although of different families, are declared to be grandfathers of Joseph. Matthan and Melchi having married   7 in succession the same woman, begat children who were uterine brothers, for the law did not prohibit a widow, whether such by divorce or by the death of her husband, from marrying another. By Estha[7] then (for this was the   8 woman's name according to tradition) Matthan, a descendant of Solomon, first begat Jacob.

---

[1] " Over against the various opinions of uninstructed apologists for the Gospel history, Eusebius introduces this account of Africanus with the words, τὴν περὶ τούτων κατελθοῦσαν εἰς ἡμᾶς ἱστορίαν." (Spitta.)

[2] On Africanus, see Bk. VI. chap. 31. Of this Aristides to whom the epistle is addressed we know nothing. He must not be confounded with the apologist Aristides, who lived in the reign of Trajan (see below, Bk. IV. c. 3). Photius (*Bibl.* 34) mentions this epistle, but tells us nothing about Aristides himself. The epistle exists in numerous fragments, from which Spitta (*Der Brief des Julius Africanus an Aristides kritisch untersucht und hergestellt,* Halle, 1877) attempts to reconstruct the original epistle. His work is the best and most complete upon the subject. Compare Routh, *Rel. Sacræ,* II. pp. 228–237 and pp. 329–356, where two fragments are given and discussed at length. The epistle (as given by Mai) is translated in the *Ante-Nicene Fathers,* Am. ed. VI. p. 125 ff.

The attempt of Africanus is, so far as we know, the first critical attempt to harmonize the two genealogies of Christ. The question had been the subject merely of guesses and suppositions until his time. He approaches the matter in a free critical spirit (such as seems always to have characterized him), and his investigations therefore deserve attention. He holds that both genealogies are those of Joseph, and this was the unanimous opinion of antiquity, though, as he says, the discrepancies were reconciled in various ways. Africanus himself, as will be seen, explains by the law of Levirate marriages, and his view is advocated by Mill (*On the Mythical Interpretation of the Gospel,* p. 201 sq.) ; but of this interpretation Rev. John Lightfoot justly says, " There is neither reason for it, nor, indeed, any foundation at all."

Upon the supposition that both genealogies relate to Joseph the best explanation is that Matthew's table represents the royal line of legal successors to the throne of David, while Luke's gives the line of actual descent. This view is ably advocated by Hervey in Smith's *Bible Dictionary* (article *Genealogy of Jesus*). Another opinion which has prevailed widely since the Reformation is that Luke gives the genealogy of Mary. The view is defended very ingeniously by Weiss (*Leben Jesu,* I. 205, 2d edition). For further particulars see, besides the works already mentioned, the various commentaries upon Matthew and Luke and the various lives of Christ, especially Andrews', p. 55 sq.

[3] Eusebius makes a mistake in saying that Africanus had received the explanation which follows from tradition. For Africanus himself says expressly (§ 15, below) that his interpretation is not supported by testimony. Eusebius' error has been repeated by most writers upon the subject, but is exposed by Spitta, *ibid.* p. 63.

[4] The law is stated in Deut. xxv. 5 sq.

[5] Nathan was a son of David and Bathsheba, and therefore own brother of Solomon.

[6] Melchi, who is here given as the third from the end, is in our present texts of Luke the fifth (Luke iii. 24), Matthat and Levi standing between Melchi and Eli. It is highly probable that the text which Africanus followed omitted the two names Matthat and Levi (see Westcott and Hort's Greek Testament, Appendix, p. 57). It is impossible to suppose that Africanus in such an investigation as this could have overlooked two names by mistake if they had stood in his text of the Gospels.

[7] We know nothing more of Estha. Africanus probably refers to the tradition handed down by the relatives of Christ, who had, as he says, preserved genealogies which agreed with those of the Gospels. He distinguishes here what he gives on tradition from his own interpretation of the Gospel discrepancy upon which he is engaged.

And when Matthan was dead, Melchi, who traced his descent back to Nathan, being of the same tribe[8] but of another family,[9] married her, as before said, and begat a son Eli. Thus **9** we shall find the two, Jacob and Eli, although belonging to different families, yet brethren by the same mother. Of these the one, Jacob, when his brother Eli had died childless, took the latter's wife and begat by her a son[10] Joseph, his own son by nature[11] and in accordance with reason. Wherefore also it is written : 'Jacob begat Joseph.'[12] But according to law[13] he was the son of Eli, for Jacob, being the brother of the latter, raised up seed to him. **10** Hence the genealogy traced through him will not be rendered void, which the evangelist Matthew in his enumeration gives thus : 'Jacob begat Joseph.' But Luke, on the other hand, says : 'Who was the son, as was supposed'[14] (for this he also adds), 'of Joseph, the son of Eli, the son of Melchi'; for he could not more clearly express the generation according to law. And the expression 'he begat' he has omitted in

his genealogical table up to the end, tracing the genealogy back to Adam the son of God. This interpretation is neither incapable of **11** proof nor is it an idle conjecture.[15] For the relatives of our Lord according to the flesh, whether with the desire of boasting or simply wishing to state the fact, in either case truly, have handed down the following account :[16] Some Idumean robbers,[17] having attacked Ascalon, a city of Palestine, carried away from a temple of Apollo which stood near the walls, in addition to other booty, Antipater, son of a certain temple slave named Herod. And since the priest[18] was not able to pay the ransom for his son, Antipater was brought up in the customs of the Idumeans, and afterward was befriended by Hyrcanus, the high priest of the Jews. And having been sent by Hyrcanus on an **12** embassy to Pompey, and having restored to

---

8 φυλή.

9 γένος. "In this place γένος is used to denote *family*. Matthan and Melchi were of different families, but both belonged to the same Davidic race which was divided into two families, that of Solomon and that of Nathan" (Valesius).

10 All the MSS. and editions of Eusebius read τρίτον instead of υἱόν here. But it is very difficult to make any sense out of the word τρίτον in this connection. We therefore prefer to follow Spitta (see *ibid.* pp. 87 sqq.) in reading υἱόν instead of τρίτον, an emendation which he has ventured to make upon the authority of Rufinus, who translates "genuit Joseph filium suum," showing no trace of a τρίτον. The word τρίτον is wanting also in three late Catenæ which contain the fragments of Africanus' Epistle (compare Spitta, *ibid.* p. 117, note 12).

11 κατὰ λόγον. These words have caused translators and commentators great difficulty, and most of them seem to have missed their significance entirely. Spitta proposes to alter by reading κατάλογον, but the emendation is unnecessary. The remarks which he makes (p. 89 sqq.) upon the relation between this sentence and the next are, however, excellent. It was necessary to Africanus' theory that Joseph should be allowed to trace his lineage through Jacob, his father "by nature," as well as through Eli, his father "by law," and hence the words κατὰ λόγον are added and emphasized. He was his son by nature and therefore "rightfully to be reckoned as his son." This explains the Biblical quotation which follows: "Wherefore"—because he was Jacob's son by nature and could rightfully be reckoned in his line, and not only in the line of Eli—"it is written," &c.

12 Matt. i. 6.

13 See Rev. John Lightfoot's remarks on Luke iii. 23, in his *Hebrew and Talmudical Exercitations on St. Luke.*

14 This passage has caused much trouble. Valesius remarks, "Africanus wishes to refer the words ὡς ἐνομίζετο ('as was supposed') not only to the words υἱὸς Ἰωσήφ, but also to the words τοῦ Ἡλί, which follow, which although it is acute is nevertheless improper and foolish; for if Luke indicates that legal generation or adoption by the words ὡς ἐνομίζετο, as Africanus claims, it would follow that Christ was the son of Joseph by legal adoption in the same way that Joseph was the son of Eli. And thus it would be said that Mary, after the death of Joseph, married his brother, and that Christ was begotten by him, which is impious and absurd. And besides, if these words, ὡς ἐνομίζετο, are extended to the words τοῦ Ἡλί, in the same way they can be extended to all which follow. For there is no reason why they should be supplied in the second grade and not in the others." But against Valesius, Stroth says that Africanus seeks nothing in the words ὡς ἐνομίζετο, but in the fact that Luke says "he was the son of," while Matthew says "he begat." Stroth's interpretation is followed by Closs, Heinichen, and others, but Routh follows Valesius. Spitta discusses the matter carefully (p. 91 sq.), agreeing with Valesius that Africanus lays the emphasis upon the words ὡς ἐνομίζετο, but by an emendation (introducing a second ὡς ἐνομίζετο, and reading "who was the son, as was supposed, of Joseph, the son of Jacob, who was himself also the son, as was supposed,—for this he also adds,—of Eli, the son of Melchi ") he applies the ὡς ἐνομίζετο only to the first and second members, and takes it in a more general sense to cover both cases, thus escaping Valesius' conclusions expressed above. The conjecture is ingenious, but is unwarranted and

unnecessary. The words which occur in the next sentence, "and the expression 'he begat' he has omitted," show that Africanus, as Stroth contends, lays the emphasis upon the difference of form in the two genealogies, "Son of" and "he begat." The best explanation seems to me to be that Africanus supposes Luke to have implied the legal generation in the words "the Son of," used in distinction from the definite expression "he begat," and that the words ὡς ἐνομίζετο, which "he also adds," simply emphasize this difference of expression by introducing a still greater ambiguity into Luke's mode of statement. He not only uses the words, the "Son of," which have a wide latitude, admitting *any* kind of sonship, but "he also adds," "as was supposed," showing, in Africanus' opinion, still more clearly that the list which follows is far from being a closely defined table of descent by "natural generation."

15 This seems the best possible rendering of the Greek, which reads τὴν ἀναφορὰν ποιησάμενος ἕως τοῦ Ἀδάμ, τοῦ θεοῦ κατ' ἀνάλυσιν. οὐδὲ μὴν ἀναπόδεικτον κ.τ.λ., which is very dark, punctuated thus, and it is difficult to understand what is meant by κατ' ἀνάλυσιν in connection with the preceding words. (Cruse translates, "having traced it back as far as Adam, 'who was the son of God,' he resolves the whole series by referring back to God. Neither is this incapable of proof, nor is it an idle conjecture.") The objections which Spitta brings against the sentence in this form are well founded. He contends (p. 63 sqq.), and that rightly, that Africanus could not have written the sentence thus. In restoring the original epistle of Africanus, therefore, he throws the words κατ' ἀνάλυσιν into the next sentence, which disposes of the difficulty, and makes good sense. We should then read, "having traced it back as far as Adam, the Son of God. This interpretation (more literally, 'as an interpretation,' or 'by way of interpretation') is neither incapable of proof, nor is it an idle conjecture." That Africanus wrote thus I am convinced. But as Spitta shows, Eusebius must have divided the sentences as they now stand, for, according to his idea, that Africanus' account was one which he had received by tradition, the other mode of reading would be incomprehensible, though he probably did not understand much better the meaning of κατ' ἀνάλυσιν as he placed it. In translating Africanus' epistle here, I have felt justified in rendering it as Africanus probably wrote it, instead of following Eusebius' incorrect reproduction of it.

16 The Greek reads: παρέδοσαν καὶ τοῦτο, "have handed down also." The καὶ occurs in all the MSS. and versions of Eusebius, and was undoubtedly written by him, but Spitta supposes it an addition of Eusebius, caused, like the change in the previous sentence, by his erroneous conception of the nature of Africanus' interpretation. The καὶ is certainly troublesome if we suppose that all that precedes is Africanus' own interpretation of the Biblical lists, and not a traditional account handed down by the "relatives of our Lord"; and this, in spite of Eusebius' belief, we must certainly insist upon. We may therefore assume with Spitta that the καὶ did not stand in the original epistle as Africanus wrote it. The question arises, if what precedes is not given upon the authority of the "relatives of our Lord," why then is this account introduced upon their testimony, as if confirming the preceding? We may simply refer again to Africanus' words at the end of the extract (§ 15 below) to prove that his interpretation did not rest upon testimony, and then we may answer with Spitta that their testimony, which is appealed to in § 14 below, was to the genealogies themselves, and in this Africanus wishes it to be known that they confirmed the Gospel lists.

17 See above, chap. VI. notes 5 and 6.

18 We should expect the word "temple-servant" again instead of "priest"; but, as Valesius remarks, "It was possible for the same person to be both priest and servant, if for instance it was a condition of priesthood that only captives should be made priests." And this was really the case in many places.

him the kingdom which had been invaded by his brother Aristobulus, he had the good fortune to be named procurator of Palestine.[19]   But Antipater having been slain by those who were envious of his great good fortune,[20] was succeeded by his son Herod, who was afterward, by a decree of the senate, made King of the Jews [21] under Antony and Augustus.   His sons were Herod and the other tetrarchs.[22]   These accounts agree

13   also with those of the Greeks.[23]   But as there had been kept in the archives [24] up to that time the genealogies of the Hebrews as well as of those who traced their lineage back to proselytes,[25] such as Achior [26] the Ammonite and Ruth the Moabitess, and to those who were mingled with the Israelites and came out of Egypt with them, Herod, inasmuch as the lineage of the Israelites contributed nothing to his advantage, and since he was goaded with the consciousness of his own ignoble extraction, burned all the genealogical records,[27] thinking that he might appear of noble origin if no one else were able, from the public registers, to trace back his lineage to the patriarchs or proselytes and to those mingled with them, who were called Geo-

14   rae.[28]   A few of the careful, however, having obtained private records of their own, either by remembering the names or by getting them in some other way from the registers, pride themselves on preserving the memory of their noble extraction.   Among these are those already mentioned, called Desposyni,[29] on account of their connection with the family of the Saviour.   Coming from Nazara and Cochaba,[30] villages of Judea,[31] into other parts of the world, they drew the aforesaid genealogy from memory [32] and from the book of daily records [33] as faithfully as possible.   Whether then the case stand thus

15   or not no one could find a clearer explanation, according to my own opinion and that of every candid person.   And let this suffice us,

---

[19] Appointed by Julius Cæsar in 47 B.C. (see chap. VI. note 1, above).

[20] He was poisoned by Malichus in 42 B.C. (see Josephus, *Ant.* XIV. 11. 4).

[21] Appointed king in 40 B.C. (see chap. VI. note 1, above).

[22] The ethnarch Archelaus (see chap. VI. note 18) and the tetrarchs Herod Antipas and Herod Philip II.

[23] Cf. Dion Cassius, XXXVII. 15 sqq. and Strabo, XVI. 2. 46.

[24] It was the custom of the Jews, to whom tribal and family descent meant so much, to keep copies of the genealogical records of the people in the public archives. Cf. e.g. Josephus, *De Vita*, § 1, where he draws his own lineage from the public archives; and cf. *Contra Apion.* I. 7.

[25] ἄχρι προσηλύτων. Heinichen and Burton read ἀρχιπροσηλύτων, "ancient proselytes." The two readings are about equally supported by MS. authority, but the same persons are meant here as at the end of the paragraph, where προσηλύτους, not ἀρχιπροσηλύτους, occurs (cf. Spitta, pp. 97 sq., and Routh's *Reliquiæ Sacræ* II. p. 347 sq., 2d ed.).

[26] Achior was a general of the Ammonites in the army of Holofernes, who, according to the Book of Judith, was a general of Nebuchadnezzar, king of the Assyrians, and was slain by the Jewish heroine, Judith. Achior is reported to have become afterward a Jewish proselyte.

[27] The Greek reads ἐνέπρησεν αὐτῶν τὰς ἀναγραφὰς τῶν γενῶν, but, with Spitta, I venture, against all the Greek MSS., to insert πάσας before τὰς ἀναγραφὰς upon the authority of Rufinus and the author of the Syriac version, both of whom reproduce the word (cf. Spitta, p. 99 sq.). Africanus certainly supposed that Herod destroyed *all* the genealogical records, and not simply those of the true Jews.

This account of the burning of the records given by Africanus is contradicted by history, for we learn from Josephus, *De Vita*, § 1, that he drew his own lineage from the public records, which were therefore still in existence more than half a century after the time at which Herod is said to have utterly destroyed them. It is significant that Rufinus translates *omnes Hebræorum generationes descriptæ in Archivis templi secretioribus habebantur.*

How old this tradition was we do not know; Africanus is the sole extant witness of it.

[28] τοὺς τε καλουμένους γειώρας. The word γειώρας occurs in the LXX. of Ex. xii. 19, where it translates the Hebrew גֵּר. The A. V. reads *stranger*, the R. V., *sojourner*, and Liddell and Scott give the latter meaning for the Greek word. See Valesius' note *in loco*, and Routh (II. p. 349 sq.), who makes some strictures upon Valesius' note. Africanus refers here to all those that came out from Egypt with the Israelites, whether native Egyptians, or foreigners resident in Egypt. Ex. xii. 38 tells us that a "mixed multitude" went out with the children of Israel (ἐπίμικτος πόλυς), and Africanus just above speaks of them in the same way (ἐπιμίκτων).

[29] δεσπόσυνοι: the persons called above (§ 11) the relatives of the Saviour according to the flesh (οἱ κατὰ σάρκα συγγενεῖς). The Greek word signifies "belonging to a master."

[30] Cochaba, according to Epiphanius (*Haer.* XXX. 2 and 16), was a village in Basanitide near Decapolis. It is noticeable that this region was the seat of Ebionism. There may therefore be significance in the care with which these *Desposyni* preserved the genealogy of Joseph, for the Ebionites believed that Christ was the real son of Joseph, and therefore Joseph's lineage was his.

[31] "Judea" is here used in the wider sense of Palestine as a whole, including the country both east and west of the Jordan. The word is occasionally used in this sense in Josephus; and so in Matt. xix. 1, and Mark x. 1, we read of "the coasts of Judea beyond Jordan." Ptolemy, Dion Cassius, and Strabo habitually employ the word in the wide sense.

[32] ἐκ μνήμης. These words are not found in any extant MSS., but I have followed Stroth and others in supplying them for the following reasons. The Greek, as we have it, runs: καὶ τὴν προκειμένην γενεαλογίαν ἔκ τε τῆς βίβλου τῶν ἡμερῶν κ.τ.λ. The particle τε indicates plainly that some phrase has fallen out. Rufinus translates *ordinem supra dictæ generationis partim memoriter partim etiam ex dierum libris in quantum erat perdocebant.* The words *partim memoriter* find no equivalent in the Greek as we have it, but the particle τε, which still remains, shows that words which Rufinus translated must have stood originally in the Greek. The Syriac version also confirms the conclusion that something stood in the original which has since disappeared, though the rendering which it gives rests evidently upon a corrupt text (cf. Spitta, p. 101). Valesius suggests the insertion of ἀπὸ μνήμης, though he does not place the phrase in his text. Heinichen supplies μνημονεύσαντες, and is followed by Closs in his translation. Stroth, Migne, Routh, and Spitta read ἐκ μνήμης. The sense is essentially the same in each case.

[33] It has been the custom since Valesius, to consider this "Book of daily records" (βίβλος τῶν ἡμερῶν) the same as the "private records" (ἰδιωτικὰς ἀπογραφάς) mentioned just above. But this opinion has been combated by Spitta, and that with perfect right. The sentence is, in fact, an exact parallel to the sentence just above, where it is said that a few of the careful, either by means of their memory or by means of copies, were able to have "private records of their own." In the present sentence it is said that "they drew the *aforesaid genealogy* (viz., 'the private records of their own') from memory, or from the *Book of daily records*" (which corresponds to the *copies* referred to above). This book of daily records is clearly, therefore, something other than the ἰδιωτικὰς ἀπογραφὰς, but exactly what we are to understand by it is not so easy to say. It cannot denote the regular public records (called the archives above), for these were completed, and would not need to be supplemented by memory; and apparently, according to Africanus' opinion, these private records were made after the destruction of the regular public ones. The "Book of daily records" referred to must have been at any rate an incomplete genealogical source needing to be supplemented by the memory. Private family record books, if such existed previous to the supposed destruction of the public records, of which we have no evidence, would in all probability have been complete for each family. Spitta maintains (p. 101 sq.) that the Book of Chronicles is meant: the Hebrew דִּבְרֵי הַיָּמִים, *words* or *records of the days*. This is a very attractive suggestion, as the book exactly corresponds to the book described: the genealogies which it gives are incomplete and require supplementing, and it is a book which was accessible to all; public, therefore, and yet not involved in the supposed destruction. The difficulty lies in the name given. It is true that Jerome calls the Books of Chronicles *Verba Dierum* and Hilary *Sermones Dierum*, &c.; but we should expect Africanus to use here the technical LXX. designation, Παραλειπομένων. But whatever this "Book of daily records" was, it cannot have been the "private records" which were formed "from memory and from copies," but was one of the sources from which those "private records" were drawn.

for, although we can urge no testimony in its support,[34] we have nothing better or truer to offer. In any case the Gospel states the truth." And at the end of the same epistle he adds these words: "Matthan, who was descended from Solomon, begat Jacob. And when Matthan was dead, Melchi, who was descended from Nathan, begat Eli by the same woman. Eli and Jacob were thus uterine brothers. Eli having died childless, Jacob raised up seed to him, begetting Joseph, his own son by nature, but by law the son of Eli. Thus Joseph was the son of

17 both." Thus far Africanus. And the lineage of Joseph being thus traced, Mary also is virtually shown to be of the same tribe with him, since, according to the law of Moses, intermarriages between different tribes were not permitted.[35] For the command is to marry one of the same family[36] and lineage,[37] so that the inheritance may not pass from tribe to tribe. This may suffice here.

CHAPTER VIII.

The Cruelty of Herod toward the Infants, and the Manner of his Death.

1   WHEN Christ was born, according to the prophecies, in Bethlehem of Judea, at the time indicated, Herod was not a little disturbed by the enquiry of the magi who came from the east, asking where he who was born King of the Jews was to be found, — for they had seen his star, and this was their reason for taking so long a journey; for they earnestly desired to worship the infant as God,[1] — for he imagined that his kingdom might be endangered; and he enquired therefore of the doctors of the law, who belonged to the Jewish nation, where they expected Christ to be born. When he learned

that the prophecy of Micah[2] announced that Bethlehem was to be his birthplace he commanded, in a single edict, all the male infants in Bethlehem, and all its borders, that were two years of age or less, according to the time which he had accurately ascertained from the magi, to be slain, supposing that Jesus, as was indeed likely, would share the same fate as the others of his own age. But the child   2 anticipated the snare, being carried into Egypt by his parents, who had learned from an angel that appeared unto them what was about to happen. These things are recorded by the Holy Scriptures in the Gospel.[3] It is   3 worth while, in addition to this, to observe the reward which Herod received for his daring crime against Christ and those of the same age. For immediately, without the least delay, the divine vengeance overtook him while he was still alive, and gave him a foretaste of what he was to receive after death. It is not   4 possible to relate here how he tarnished the supposed felicity of his reign by successive calamities in his family, by the murder of wife and children, and others of his nearest relatives and dearest friends.[4] The account, which casts every other tragic drama into the shade, is detailed at length in the histories of Josephus.[5] How, immediately after his crime against   5 our Saviour and the other infants, the punishment sent by God drove him on to his death, we can best learn from the words of that historian who, in the seventeenth book of his Antiquities of the Jews, writes as follows concerning his end:[6] "But the disease of Herod grew   6 more severe, God inflicting punishment for his crimes. For a slow fire burned in him which was not so apparent to those who touched him, but augmented his internal distress; for he had a terrible desire for food which it was not possible to resist. He was affected also with ulceration of the intestines, and with especially severe pains in the colon, while a watery and transparent humor settled about his feet. He   7 suffered also from a similar trouble in his abdomen. Nay more, his privy member was putrefied and produced worms. He found also excessive difficulty in breathing, and it was particularly disagreeable because of the offensive-

---

[34] Compare note 3, above. Africanus' direct statement shows clearly enough that he does not rest his interpretation of the genealogies (an interpretation which is purely a result of Biblical study) upon the testimony of the relatives of the Saviour. Their testimony is invoked with quite a different purpose, namely, in confirmation of the genealogies themselves, and the long story (upon the supposition that their testimony is invoked in support of Africanus' *interpretation*, introduced absolutely without sense and reason) thus has its proper place, in showing how the "relatives of the Saviour" were in a position to be competent witnesses upon this question of *fact* (not *interpretation*), in spite of the burning of the public records by Herod.

[35] The law to which Eusebius refers is recorded in Num. xxxvi. 6, 7. But the prohibition given there was not an absolute and universal one, but a prohibition which concerned only heiresses, who were not to marry out of their own tribe upon penalty of forfeiting their inheritance (cf. Josephus, *Ant.* IV. 7. 5). It is an instance of the limited nature of the law that Mary and Elizabeth were relatives, although Joseph and Mary belonged to the tribe of Judah and Zacharias, at least, was a Levite. This example lay so near at hand that Eusebius should not have overlooked it in making his assertion. His argument, therefore, in proof of the fact that Mary belonged to the tribe of Judah has no force, but the fact itself is abundantly established both by the unanimous tradition of antiquity (independent of Luke's genealogy, which was universally supposed to be that of Joseph), and by such passages as Ps. cxxxii. 11, Acts ii. 30, xiii. 23, Rom. i. 3.

[36] δήμου.   [37] πατριᾶς.

[1] οἶα θεῷ προσκυνῆσαι. Eusebius adds the words οἶα θεῷ, which are not found in Matt. ii. 2 and 11, where προσκυνῆσαι is used.

[2] Mic. v. 2.   [3] Matt. ii.

[4] Herod's reign was very successful and prosperous, and for most of the time entirely undisturbed by external troubles; but his domestic life was embittered by a constant succession of tragedies resulting from the mutual jealousies of his wives (of whom he had ten) and of their children. Early in his reign he slew Hyrcanus, the grandfather of his best-loved wife Mariamne, upon suspicion of treason; a little later, Mariamne herself was put to death; in 6 B.C. her sons, Alexander and Aristobulus, were condemned and executed; and in 4 B.C., but a few days before his death, Antipater, his eldest son, who had been instrumental in the condemnation of Alexander and Aristobulus, was also slain by his orders. These murders were accompanied by many others of friends and kindred, who were constantly falling under suspicion of treason.

[5] In the later books of the *Antiquities* and in the first book of the Jewish war.   [6] Josephus, *Ant.* XVII. 6. 5.

ness of the odor and the rapidity of respiration. He had convulsions also in every limb,
8 which gave him uncontrollable strength. It was said, indeed, by those who possessed the power of divination and wisdom to explain such events, that God had inflicted this punishment upon the King on account of his great impiety."

The writer mentioned above recounts these
9 things in the work referred to. And in the second book of his History he gives a similar account of the same Herod, which runs as follows :[7] "The disease then seized upon his whole body and distracted it by various torments. For he had a slow fever, and the itching of the skin of his whole body was insupportable. He suffered also from continuous pains in his colon, and there were swellings on his feet like those of a person suffering from dropsy, while his abdomen was inflamed and his privy member so putrefied as to produce worms. Besides this he could breathe only in an upright posture, and then only with difficulty, and he had convulsions in all his limbs, so that the diviners said that his diseases were a punishment.[8]
10 But he, although wrestling with such sufferings, nevertheless clung to life and hoped for safety, and devised methods of cure. For instance, crossing over Jordan he used the warm baths at Callirhoë,[9] which flow into the Lake Asphaltites,[10] but are themselves sweet enough
11 to drink. His physicians here thought that they could warm his whole body again by means of heated oil. But when they had let him down into a tub filled with oil, his eyes became weak and turned up like the eyes of a dead person. But when his attendants raised an outcry, he recovered at the noise ; but finally, despairing of a cure, he commanded about fifty drachms to be distributed among the soldiers, and great sums to be given to his generals
12 and friends. Then returning he came to Jericho, where, being seized with melancholy, he planned to commit an impious deed, as if challenging death itself. For, collecting from every town the most illustrious men of all Judea, he commanded that they be shut up in the so-called hippodrome. And having 13 summoned Salome,[11] his sister, and her husband, Alexander,[12] he said : ' I know that the Jews will rejoice at my death. But I may be lamented by others and have a splendid funeral if you are willing to perform my commands. When I shall expire surround these men, who are now under guard, as quickly as possible with soldiers, and slay them, in order that all Judea and every house may weep for me even against their will.' "[13]

And after a little Josephus says, "And again 14 he was so tortured by want of food and by a convulsive cough that, overcome by his pains, he planned to anticipate his fate. Taking an apple he asked also for a knife, for he was accustomed to cut apples and eat them. Then looking round to see that there was no one to hinder, he raised his right hand as if to stab himself."[14] In addition to these things the 15 same writer records that he slew another of his own sons[15] before his death, the third one slain by his command, and that immediately afterward he breathed his last, not without excessive pain.

Such was the end of Herod, who suffered 16 a just punishment for his slaughter of the children of Bethlehem,[16] which was the result of his plots against our Saviour. After this 17 an angel appeared in a dream to Joseph in Egypt and commanded him to go to Judea with the child and its mother, revealing to him that those who had sought the life of the child were dead.[17] To this the evangelist adds, "But when he heard that Archelaus did reign in the room of his father Herod he was afraid to go thither ; notwithstanding being warned of God in a dream he turned aside into the parts of Galilee."[18]

---

[7] B. J. I. 33. 5 and 6.

[8] ποινὴν εἶναι τὰ νοσήματα λέγειν. Josephus, according to the text of Hudson, reads ποινὴν εἶναι τῶν σοφιστῶν τὰ νοσήματα λέγειν, which is translated by Traill, "pronounced his maladies a judgment for his treatment of the Sophists." Nicephorus (H. E. I. 15) agrees with Eusebius in omitting the words τῶν σοφιστῶν, but he is not an independent witness. Whether Hudson's text is supported at this point by strong MS. authority I do not know. If the words stood in the original of Josephus, we may suppose that they were accidentally omitted by Eusebius or by one of his copyists, or that they were thrown out in order to make Josephus' statement better correspond with his own words in Ant. XVII. 6, quoted just above, where his disease is said to have been a result of his impiety in general, not of any particular exhibition of it. On the other hand, the omission of the words in Ant. XVII. 6 casts at least a suspicion on their genuineness, and if we were to assume that the words did not occur in the original text of Josephus, it would be very easy to understand their insertion by some copyist, for in the previous paragraph the historian has been speaking of the Sophists, and of Herod's cruel treatment of them.

[9] Callirhoë was a town just east of the Dead Sea.

[10] τὴν Ἀσφαλτῖτιν λίμνην. This is the name by which Josephus commonly designates the Dead Sea. The same name occurs also in Diodorus Siculus (II. 48, XIX. 98).

[11] Salome was own sister of Herod the Great, and wife in succession of Joseph, Costabarus, and Alexas. She possessed all the cruelty of Herod himself and was the cause, through her jealousy and envy, of most of the terrible tragedies in his family.

[12] Alexander, the third husband of Salome, is always called Alexas by Josephus.

[13] B. J. I. 13. 6 (cf. Ant. XVII. 6. 5). This terrible story rests upon the authority of Josephus alone, but is so in keeping with Herod's character that we have no reason to doubt its truth. The commands of Herod, however, were not carried out, the condemned men being released after his death by Salome (see ibid. § 8).

[14] B. J. I. 33. 7 (cf. Ant. XVII. 7). Herod's suicide was prevented by his cousin Achiabus, as Josephus informs us in the same connection.

[15] B. J. I. 33. 7 and 8 (cf. Ant. XVII. 7). Antipater, son of Herod and his first wife Doris, was intended by his father to be his successor in the kingdom. He was beheaded five days before the death of Herod, for plotting against his father. He richly deserved his fate.

[16] Eusebius gives here the traditional Christian interpretation of the cause of Herod's sufferings. Josephus nowhere mentions the slaughter of the innocents; whether through ignorance, or because of the insignificance of the tragedy when compared with the other bloody acts of Herod's reign, we do not know.

[17] See Matt. ii. 19, 20.

[18] Matt. ii. 22.

CHAPTER IX.

The Times of Pilate.

THE historian already mentioned agrees with the evangelist in regard to the fact that Archelaus[1] succeeded to the government after Herod. He records the manner in which he received the kingdom of the Jews by the will of his father Herod and by the decree of Cæsar Augustus, and how, after he had reigned ten years, he lost his kingdom, and his brothers Philip[2] and Herod the younger,[3] with Lysanias,[4] still ruled their own tetrarchies. The same writer, in the eighteenth book of his Antiquities,[5] says that about the twelfth year of the reign of Tiberius,[6] who had succeeded to the empire after Augustus had ruled fifty-seven years,[7] Pon-

tius Pilate was entrusted with the government of Judea, and that he remained there ten full years, almost until the death of Tiberius. Accordingly the forgery of those who have 2 recently given currency to acts against our Saviour[8] is clearly proved. For the very date given in them[9] shows the falsehood of their fabricators. For the things which they have 3 dared to say concerning the passion of the Saviour are put into the fourth consulship of Tiberius, which occurred in the seventh year of his reign; at which time it is plain that Pilate was not yet ruling in Judea, if the testimony of Josephus is to be believed, who clearly shows in the above-mentioned work[10] that Pilate was made procurator of Judea by Tiberius in the twelfth year of his reign.

CHAPTER X.

The High Priests of the Jews under whom Christ taught.

IT was in the fifteenth year of the reign 1 of Tiberius,[1] according to the evangelist, and in the fourth year of the governorship of Pontius Pilate,[2] while Herod and Lysanias and Philip were ruling the rest of Judea,[3] that our Saviour and Lord, Jesus the Christ of God, being about thirty years of age,[4] came to John for baptism and began the promulgation of the Gospel. The Divine Scripture says, more- 2 over, that he passed the entire time of his ministry under the high priests Annas and Caiaphas,[5] showing that in the time which be-

---

[1] Archelaus was a son of Herod the Great, and own brother of the Tetrarch Herod Antipas, with whom he was educated at Rome. Immediately after the death of Antipater he was designated by his father as his successor in the kingdom, and Augustus ratified the will, but gave him only the title of ethnarch. The title of King he never really received, although he is spoken of as king in Matt. ii. 22, the word being used in a loose sense. His dominion consisted of Idumea, Judea, Samaria, and the cities on the coast, comprising a half of his father's kingdom. The other half was divided between Herod Antipas and Philip. He was very cruel, and was warmly hated by most of his subjects. In the tenth year of his reign (according to Josephus, *Ant.* XVII. 13. 2), or in the ninth (according to *B. J.* II. 7. 3), he was complained against by his brothers and subjects on the ground of cruelty, and was banished to Vienne in Gaul, where he probably died, although Jerome says that he was shown his tomb near Bethlehem. Jerome's report, however, is too late to be of any value. The exact length of his reign it is impossible to say, as Josephus is not consistent in his reports. The difference may be due to the fact that Josephus reckoned from different starting-points in the two cases. He probably ruled a little more than nine years. His condemnation took place in the consulship of M. Æmilius Lepidus and L. Arruntius (i.e. in 6 A.D.) according to Dion Cassius, LV. 27. After the deposition of Archelaus Judea was made a Roman province and attached to Syria, and Coponius was sent as the first procurator. On Archelaus, see Josephus, *Ant.* XVII. 8, 9, 11 sq., and *B. J.* I. 33. 8 sq.; II. 6 sq.

[2] Philip, a son of Herod the Great by his wife Cleopatra, was Tetrarch of Batanea, Trachonitis, Aurinitis, &c., from B.C. 4 to A.D. 34. He was distinguished for his justice and moderation. He is mentioned only once in the New Testament, Luke iii. 1. On Philip, see Josephus, *Ant.* XVII. 8. 1; 11. 4; XVIII. 4. 6.

[3] Herod Antipas, son of Herod the Great by his wife Malthace, was Tetrarch of Galilee and Perea from B.C. 4 to A.D. 39. In 39 A.D. he went to Rome to sue for the title of King, which his nephew Herod Agrippa had already secured. But accusations against him were sent to the emperor by Agrippa, and he thereby lost his tetrarchy and was banished to Lugdunum (Lyons) in Gaul, and died (according to Josephus, *B. J.* II. 9. 6) in Spain. It was he who beheaded John the Baptist, and to him Jesus was sent by Pilate. His character is plain enough from the New Testament account. For further particulars of his life, see Josephus, *Ant.* XVII. 8. 1; 11. 4; XVIII. 2. 1; 5 and 7; *B. J.* II. 9.

[4] The Lysanias referred to here is mentioned in Luke iii. 1 as Tetrarch of Abilene. Eusebius, in speaking of Lysanias here, follows the account of Luke, not that of Josephus, for the latter nowhere says that Lysanias continued to rule his tetrarchy after the exile of Archelaus. Indeed he nowhere states that Lysanias ruled a tetrarchy at this period. He only refers (*Ant.* XVIII. 6. 10; XIX. 5. 1; XX. 7. 1; and *B. J.* II. 12. 8) to "the tetrarchy of Lysanias," which he says was given to Agrippa I. and II. by Caligula and Claudius. Eusebius thus reads more into Josephus than he has any right to do, and yet we cannot assume that he is guilty of willful deception, for he may quite innocently have interpreted Josephus in the light of Luke's account, without realizing that Josephus' statement is of itself entirely indefinite. That there is no real contradiction between the statements of Josephus and Luke has been abundantly demonstrated by Davidson, *Introduction to the New Testament*, I. p. 215 sq.

[5] Josephus, *Ant.* XVIII. 2. 2 and 4. 2.

[6] Josephus reckons here from the death of Augustus (14 A.D.), when Tiberius became sole emperor. Pilate was appointed procurator in 26 A.D. and was recalled in 36.

[7] Josephus dates the beginning of Augustus' reign at the time of the death of Julius Cæsar (as Eusebius also does in chap. 5, § 2), and calls him the second emperor. But Augustus did not actually become emperor until 31 B.C., after the battle of Actium.

[8] Eusebius refers here, not to the acts of Pilate written by Christians, of which so many are still extant (cf. Bk. II. chap. 2, note 1), but to those forged by their enemies with the approval of the emperor Maximinus (see below, Bk. IX. chap. 5).

[9] ὁ ὁ τῆς παρασημειώσεως χρόνος. "In this place παρασ. is the superscription or the designation of the time which was customarily prefixed to acts. For judicial acts were thus drawn up: *Consulatu Tiberii Augusti Septimo, inducto in judicium Jesu*, &c." (Val.)

[10] *Ant.* XVIII. 2. 2. Compare § 1, above.

[1] Luke iii. 1. Eusebius reckons the fifteenth year of Tiberius from 14 A.D., that is, from the time when he became sole emperor. There is a difference of opinion among commentators as to whether Luke began to reckon from the colleagueship of Tiberius (11 or 12 A.D.), or from the beginning of his reign as sole emperor. Either mode of reckoning is allowable, but as Luke says that Christ "began to be about thirty years of age" at this time, and as he was born probably about 4 B.C., the former seems to have been Luke's mode. Compare Andrew's *Life of our Lord*, p. 28.

[2] Luke says simply, "while Pontius Pilate was governor of Judea," and does not mention the year, as Eusebius does.

[3] See the previous chapter.

[4] Eusebius' reckoning would make Christ's birthday synchronize with the beginning of our Christian era, which is at least three years out of the way.

[5] Luke iii. 2 compared with John xi. 49 and 51, and xviii. 13. Stroth remarks: "Had I not feared acting contrary to the duty of a translator, I should gladly, for the sake of Eusebius' honor, have left out this entire chapter, which is full of historical inaccuracies and contradictions. Eusebius deduces from Josephus himself that the Procurator Gratus, whom Pilate succeeded, appointed Caiaphas high priest. Therefore Caiaphas became high priest before the twelfth year of Tiberius, for in that year Pilate became procurator. In the fifteenth year of Tiberius, Christ began his work when Caiaphas had already been high priest three years, and according to the false account of our author he became high priest for the first time in the nineteenth year of Tiberius. The whole structure of this chapter, therefore, falls to the ground. It is almost inconceivable how so prudent a man could have committed so great a mistake of the same

longed to the priesthood of those two men the whole period of his teaching was completed. Since he began his work during the high priesthood of Annas and taught until Caiaphas held the office, the entire time does not com-

3 prise quite four years. For the rites of the law having been already abolished since that time, the customary usages in connection with the worship of God, according to which the high priest acquired his office by hereditary descent and held it for life, were also annulled, and there were appointed to the high priesthood by the Roman governors now one and now another person who continued in office not

4 more than one year.[6] Josephus relates that there were four high priests in succession from Annas to Caiaphas. Thus in the same book of the Antiquities[7] he writes as follows: "Valerius Gratus[8] having put an end to the priesthood of Ananus[9] appoints Ishmael,[10] the son of Fabi, high priest. And having removed him after a little he appoints Eleazer,[11] the son of Ananus the high priest, to the same office. And having removed him also at the end of a year he gives the high priesthood to Simon,[12] the son of Camithus. But he likewise held the honor no more than a year, when Josephus, called also Caiaphas,[13] succeeded him." Ac-

cordingly the whole time of our Saviour's ministry is shown to have been not quite four full years, four high priests, from Annas to the accession of Caiaphas, having held office a year each. The Gospel therefore has rightly indicated Caiaphas as the high priest under whom the Saviour suffered. From which also we can see that the time of our Saviour's ministry does not disagree with the foregoing investigation.

Our Saviour and Lord, not long after the 5 beginning of his ministry, called the twelve apostles,[14] and these alone of all his disciples he named apostles, as an especial honor. And again he appointed seventy others whom he sent out two by two before his face into every place and city whither he himself was about to come.[15]

CHAPTER XI.

Testimonies in Regard to John the Baptist and Christ.

NOT long after this John the Baptist was 1 beheaded by the younger Herod,[1] as is stated in the Gospels.[2] Josephus also records the same fact,[3] making mention of Herodias[4] by name, and stating that, although she was the wife of his brother, Herod made her his own wife after divorcing his former lawful wife, who was the daughter of Aretas,[5] king of Petra, and separating Herodias from her husband while he was still alive. It was on her account also 2 that he slew John, and waged war with Aretas, because of the disgrace inflicted on the daughter of the latter. Josephus relates that in this war, when they came to battle, Herod's entire army was destroyed,[6] and that he suffered this calamity on account of his crime against John.

The same Josephus confesses in this ac- 3 count that John the Baptist was an exceedingly righteous man, and thus agrees with the things written of him in the Gospels. He records also that Herod lost his kingdom on account of

sort as that which he had denounced a little before in connection with the *Acts of Pilate.*"

The whole confusion is due to Eusebius' mistaken interpretation of the Gospel account, which he gives in this sentence. It is now universally assumed that Annas is named by the evangelists as ex-high-priest, and that Eusebius, not understanding this, supposed that a part of Christ's ministry must have fallen during the active administration of Annas, a part during that of Caiaphas, and therefore his ministry must have run from the one to the other, embracing the intermediate administrations of Ishmael, Eleazer, and Simon, and covering less than four years. In order to make this out he interprets the "not long after" in connection with Ishmael as meaning "one year," which is incorrect, as shown below in note 9. How Eusebius could have overlooked the plain fact that all this occurred under Valerius Gratus instead of Pilate, and therefore many years too early (when he himself states the fact), is almost incomprehensible. Absorbed in making out his interpretation, he must have thoughtlessly confounded the names of Gratus and Pilate while reading the account. He cannot have acted knowingly, with the intention to deceive, for he must have seen that anybody reading his account would discover the glaring discrepancy at once.

[6] It is true that under the Roman governors the high priests were frequently changed (cf. above, chap. 6, note 19), but there was no regularly prescribed interval, and some continued in office for many years; for instance, Caiaphas was high priest for more than ten years, during the whole of Pilate's administration, having been appointed by Valerius Gratus, Pilate's predecessor, and his successor being appointed by the Proconsul Vitellius in 37 A.D. (*vid.* Josephus, *Ant.* XVIII. 2. 2 and 4. 3).   [7] Josephus, *Ant.* XVIII. 2. 2.

[8] This Valerius Gratus was made procurator by Tiberius, soon after his accession, and ruled about eleven years, when he was succeeded by Pilate in 26 A.D.

[9] Ananus (or Annas) was appointed high priest by Quirinius, governor of Syria, in 6 or 7 A.D. (Josephus, *Ant.* XVIII. 2. 1), and remained in office until A.D. 14 or 15, when he was deposed by Valerius Gratus (*ib.* § 2). This forms another instance, therefore, of a term of office more than one year in length. Annas is a familiar personage from his connection with the Gospel history; but the exact position which he occupied during Christ's ministry is difficult to determine (cf. Wieseler's *Chronology of the Life of Christ*).

[10] Either this Ishmael must have held the office eight or ten years, or else Caiaphas that long before Pilate's time, for otherwise Gratus' period is not filled up. Josephus' statement is indefinite in regard to Ishmael, and Eusebius is wrong in confining his term of office to one year.

[11] According to Josephus, *Ant.* XX. 9. 1, five of the sons of Annas became high priests.

[12] This Simon is an otherwise unknown personage.

[13] Joseph Caiaphas, son-in-law of Annas, is well known from his connection with the Gospel history.

[14] See Matt. x. 1-4; Mark iii. 14-19; Luke vi. 13-16.

[15] See Luke x. 1.

[1] Herod Antipas.   [3] Josephus, *Ant.* XVIII. 5. 2.

[2] Matt. xiv. 1-12; Mark vi. 17 sq.

[4] Herodias, a daughter of Aristobulus and grand-daughter of Herod the Great, first married Herod Philip (whom Josephus calls Herod, and whom the Gospels call Philip), a son of Herod the Great, and therefore her uncle, who seems to have occupied a private station. Afterwards, leaving him during his lifetime, she married another uncle, Herod Antipas the Tetrarch. When her husband, Antipas, was banished to Gaul, she voluntarily shared his banishment and died there. Her character is familiar from the accounts of the New Testament.

[5] Aretas Æneas is identical with the Aretas mentioned in 2 Cor. xi. 32, in connection with Paul's flight from Jerusalem (cf. Wieseler, *Chron. des ap. Zeitalters*, p. 142 and 167 sq.). He was king of Arabia Nabatæa, whose capital was the famous rock city, Petra, which gave its name to the whole country, which was in consequence commonly called Arabia Petræa.

[6] In this emergency Herod appealed to Tiberius, with whom he was a favorite, and the emperor commanded Vitellius, the governor of Syria, to proceed against Aretas. The death of Tiberius interrupted operations, and under Caligula friendship existed between Aretas and the Romans.

the same Herodias, and that he was driven into banishment with her, and condemned to

4 live at Vienne in Gaul.[7] He relates these things in the eighteenth book of the Antiquities, where he writes of John in the following words:[8] "It seemed to some of the Jews that the army of Herod was destroyed by God, who most justly avenged John called the Baptist.

5 For Herod slew him, a good man and one who exhorted the Jews to come and receive baptism, practicing virtue and exercising righteousness toward each other and toward God; for baptism would appear acceptable unto Him when they employed it, not for the remission of certain sins, but for the purification of the body, as the soul had been already purified in righteous-

6 ness. And when others gathered about him (for they found much pleasure in listening to his words), Herod feared that his great influence might lead to some sedition, for they appeared ready to do whatever he might advise. He therefore considered it much better, before any new thing should be done under John's influence, to anticipate it by slaying him, and to repent after revolution had come, and when he found himself in the midst of difficulties.[9] On account of Herod's suspicion John was sent in bonds to the above-mentioned citadel of

7 Machæra,[10] and there slain." After relating these things concerning John, he makes mention of our Saviour in the same work, in the following words:[11] "And there lived at that time

Jesus, a wise man, if indeed it be proper to call him a man. For he was a doer of wonderful works, and a teacher of such men as receive the truth in gladness. And he attached to himself many of the Jews, and many also of the Greeks. He was the Christ. When Pilate, 8 on the accusation of our principal men, condemned him to the cross, those who had loved him in the beginning did not cease loving him. For he appeared unto them again alive on the third day, the divine prophets having told these and countless other wonderful things concerning him. Moreover, the race of Christians, named after him, continues down to the present day." Since an historian, who is one of the 9 Hebrews themselves, has recorded in his work these things concerning John the Baptist and our Saviour, what excuse is there left for not convicting them of being destitute of all shame, who have forged the acts against them?[12] But let this suffice here.

CHAPTER XII.

The Disciples of our Saviour.

THE names of the apostles of our Sa- 1 viour are known to every one from the Gospels.[1] But there exists no catalogue of the seventy disciples.[2] Barnabas, indeed, is said to have been one of them, of whom the Acts of the apostles makes mention in various places,[3]

---

[7] Josephus gives the account of Herod's banishment in his *Antiquities* XVIII. 7. 2, but names Lyons instead of Vienne as the place of his exile. Eusebius here confounds the fate of Herod with that of Archelaus, who was banished to Vienne (see above, chap. 9, note 1).

[8] *Ant.* XVIII. 5. 2. This passage upon John the Baptist is referred to by Origen in his *Contra Cels.* I. 47, and is found in all our MSS. of Josephus. It is almost universally admitted to be genuine, and there is no good reason to doubt that it is, for such a dispassionate and strictly impartial account of John could hardly have been written by a Christian interpolator.

[9] Josephus differs with the Evangelists as to the reason for John's imprisonment, but the accounts of the latter bear throughout the stamp of more direct and accurate knowledge than that of Josephus. Ewald remarks with truth, "When Josephus, however, gives as the cause of John's execution only the Tetrarch's general fear of popular outbreaks, one can see that he no longer had perfect recollection of the matter. The account of Mark is far more exact and instructive."

[10] Machæra was an important fortress lying east of the northern end of the Dead Sea. It was the same fortress to which the daughter of Aretas had retired when Herod formed the design of marrying Herodias; and the word "aforesaid" refers to Josephus' mention of it in that connection in the previous paragraph.

[11] *Ant.* XVIII. 3. 3. This account occurs before that of John the Baptist, not after it. It is found in all our MSS. of Josephus, and was considered genuine until the sixteenth century, but since then has been constantly disputed. Four opinions are held in regard to it; (1) It is entirely genuine. This view has at present few supporters, and is absolutely untenable. A Christian hand is unmistakably apparent, — if not throughout, certainly in many parts; and the silence in regard to it of all Christian writers until the time of Eusebius is fatal to its existence in the original text. Origen, for instance, who mentions Josephus' testimony to John the Baptist in *Contra Cels.* I. 47, betrays no knowledge of this passage in regard to Christ. (2) It is entirely spurious. Such writers as Hase, Keim, and Schürer adopt this view. (3) It is partly genuine and partly interpolated. This opinion has, perhaps, the most defenders, among them Gieseler, Weizsäcker, Renan, Edersheim, and Schaff. (4) It has been changed from a bitter Jewish calumny of Christ to a Christian eulogy of him. This is Ewald's view. The second opinion seems to me the correct one. The third I regard as untenable, for the reason that after the obviously Christian passages are omitted

there remains almost nothing; and it seems inconceivable that Josephus should have given so colorless a report of one whom the Jews regarded with such enmity, if he mentioned him at all. The fourth view might be possible, and is more natural than the third; but it seems as if some trace of the original calumny would have survived somewhere, had it ever existed. To me, however, the decisive argument is the decided break which the passage makes in the context; § 2 gives the account of a sedition of the Jews, and § 4 opens with the words, "About the same time also another sad calamity put the Jews into disorder"; while § 3, containing the account of Christ, gives no hint of sedition or disorder among the Jews.

It has been suggested that Eusebius himself, who is the first one to quote this passage, introduced it into the text of Josephus. This is possible, but there is no reason to suppose it true, for it is contrary to Eusebius' general reputation for honesty, and the manner in which he introduces the quotation both here and in his *Dem. Evang.* III. 5 certainly bears every mark of innocence; and he would scarcely have dared to insert so important an account in his *History* had it not existed in at least some MSS. of Josephus. We may be confident that the interpolation must have been made in the MSS. of Josephus before it appeared in the *History*. For a brief summary of the various views upon the subject, see Schaff's *Church History*, Vol. I. p. 9 sq., and Edersheim's article on Josephus in Smith and Wace's *Dict. of Christian Biography*. Compare also Heinichen's *Excursus* upon the passage in his edition of Eusebius, Vol. III. p. 623-654.

[12] See chap. 9, note 8, above.

[1] See Matt. x. 2-4; Luke vi. 13-16; Mark iii. 14-19.

[2] See Luke x. 1-20.

[3] See Acts iv. 36, xiii. 1 *et passim*. Clement of Alexandria (*Strom.* II. 20) calls Barnabas one of the Seventy. This tradition is not in itself improbable, but we can trace it back no further than Clement. The Clementine *Recognitions* and *Homilies* frequently mention Barnabas as an apostle active in Alexandria and in Rome. One tradition sends him to Milan and makes him the first bishop of the church there, but the silence of Ambrose in regard to it is a sufficient proof of its groundlessness. There is extant an apocryphal work, probably of the fifth century, entitled *Acta et Passio Barnabæ in Cypro*, which relates his death by martyrdom in Cyprus. The tradition may be true, but its existence has no weight. Barnabas came from Cyprus and labored there for at least a time. It would be natural, therefore, to assign his death (which was necessarily martyrdom, for no Christian writer of the early centuries could have admitted that he died a natural death) to that place.

and especially Paul in his Epistle to the Galatians.[4] They say that Sosthenes also, who wrote to the Corinthians with Paul, was one of them.[5]

2　This is the account of Clement[6] in the fifth book of his Hypotyposes, in which he also says that Cephas was one of the seventy disciples,[7] a man who bore the same name as the apostle Peter, and the one concerning whom Paul says,

3　"When Cephas came to Antioch I withstood him to his face."[8]　Matthias,[9] also, who was numbered with the apostles in the place of Judas, and the one who was honored by being made a candidate with him,[10] are likewise said to have been deemed worthy of the same calling with the seventy. They say that Thaddeus[11] also was one of them, concerning whom I shall presently relate an account which has come down to us.[12]　And upon examination you will find that our Saviour had more than seventy disciples, according to the testimony of Paul, who says that after his resurrection from the dead he appeared first to Cephas, then to the twelve, and after them to above five hundred brethren at once, of whom some had fallen asleep ;[13] but the majority were still living

4　at the time he wrote. Afterwards he says he appeared unto James, who was one of the so-called brethren of the Saviour.[14]　But,

since in addition to these, there were many others who were called apostles, in imitation of the Twelve, as was Paul himself, he adds : "Afterward he appeared to all the apostles."[15] So much in regard to these persons. But the story concerning Thaddeus is as follows.

---

puted matter. Three theories have been advanced, and are all widely represented.

The first is the full-brother hypothesis, according to which the brothers and sisters of Jesus were children of both Joseph and Mary. This was advocated strongly by the heretic Helvidius in Rome in 380, and is widely accepted in the Protestant Church. The only serious objection to it is the committal of Mary to the care of John by Christ upon the cross. But John was at any rate an own cousin of Jesus, and the objection loses its weight when we realize the spiritual sympathy which existed between Jesus and John, and the lack of belief exhibited by his own brothers. The second is the half-brother hypothesis, which regards the brethren and sisters of Jesus as children of Joseph by a former wife. This has the oldest tradition in its favor (though the tradition for none of the theories is old or universal enough to be of great weight), the apocryphal *Gospel of James*, chap. ix., recording that Joseph was a widower and had children before marrying Mary.　It is still the established theory in the Greek Church.　The greatest objection to it is that if it be true, Christ, as a younger son of Joseph, could not have been regarded as the heir to the throne of David.　That the objection is absolutely fatal cannot be asserted, for it is nowhere clearly stated that he was the heir-apparent to the throne; it is said only that he was of the line of David.　Both of these theories agree in distinguishing James, the brother of the Lord, from James, the son of Alphæus, the apostle, and thus assume at least three Jameses in the New Testament.　Over against both of them is to be mentioned a third, which assumes only two Jameses, regarding the brethren of the Lord as his cousins, and identifying them with the sons of Alphæus. This theory originated with Jerome in 383 A.D. with the confessedly dogmatic object of preserving the virginity both of Mary and of Joseph in opposition to Helvidius.　Since his time it has been the established theory in the Latin Church, and is advocated also by many Protestant scholars.　The original and common form of the theory makes Jesus and James maternal cousins: finding only three women in John xix. 25, and regarding Mary, the wife of Clopas, as the sister of the Virgin Mary.　But this is in itself improbable and rests upon poor exegesis.　It is far better to assume that four women are mentioned in this passage.　A second form of the cousin theory, which regards Jesus and James as paternal cousins — making Alphæus (Clopas) the brother of Joseph — originated with Lange. It is very ingenious, and urges in its support the authority of Hegesippus, who, according to Eusebius (*H. E.* III. 11), says that Clopas was the brother of Joseph and the father of Simeon, which would make the latter the brother of James, and thus just as truly the brother of the Lord as he.　But Hegesippus plainly thinks of James and of Simeon as standing in different relations to Christ, — the former his brother, the latter his cousin, — and therefore his testimony is against, rather than for Lange's hypothesis.　The statement of Hegesippus, indeed, expresses the cousinship of Christ with James the Little, the son of Clopas (if Alphæus and Clopas be identified), but does not identify this cousin with James the brother of the Lord.　Eusebius also is claimed by Lange as a witness to his theory, but his exegesis of the passage to which he appeals is poor (see below, Bk. IV. chap. 22, note 4).　Against both forms of the cousin theory may be urged the natural meaning of the word ἀδελφός, and also the statement of John vii. 5, "Neither did his brethren believe in him," which makes it impossible to suppose that his brothers were apostles.　From this fatal objection both of the brother hypotheses are free, and either of them is possible, but the former rests upon a more natural interpretation of the various passages involved, and would perhaps have been universally accepted had it not been for the dogmatic interest felt by the early Church in preserving the virginity of Mary.　Renan's complicated theory (see his *Les Évangiles*, p. 537 sqq.) does not help matters at all, and need not be discussed here.　There is much to be said, however, in favor of the separation of Alphæus and Clopas, upon which he insists and which involves the existence of four Jameses instead of only three.

For a fuller discussion of this whole subject, see Andrews (*Life of our Lord*, pp. 104-116), Schaff (*Church Hist.* I. 272-275), and Weiss (*Einleitung in das N.T.* p. 388 sqq.), all of whom defend the natural brother hypothesis; Lightfoot (Excursus upon " The Brethren of the Lord " in his *Commentary on Galatians*, 2d ed. p. 247-282), who is the strongest advocate of the half-brother theory; Mill (*The Accounts of our Lord's Brethren in the N. T. vindicated*, Cambridge, 1843), who maintains the maternal cousin theory; and Lange (in *Herzog*), who presents the paternal cousin hypothesis. Compare finally Holtzmann's article in the *Zeitschrift für Wiss. Theologie*, 1880, p. 198 sqq.

[15] 1 Cor. xv. 7.

---

[4] Gal. ii. 1, 9, and 13.

[5] Sosthenes is mentioned in 1 Cor. i. 1. From what source Eusebius drew this report in regard to him I cannot tell. He is the first to mention it, so far as I know.　A later tradition reports that he became Bishop of Colophon, a city in Ionia.　A Sosthenes is mentioned also in Acts xviii. 17, as ruler of the Jewish synagogue in Corinth.　Some wish to identify the two, supposing the latter to have been afterward converted, but in this case of course he cannot have been one of the Seventy.　Eusebius' tradition is one in regard to whose value we can form no opinion.

[6] On Clement and his works see Bk. V. chap. 11, note 1, and Bk. VI. chap. 13.

[7] Clement is, so far as I know, the first to make this distinction between Peter the Apostle, and Cephas, one of the Seventy.　The reason for the invention of a second Peter in the post-apostolic age is easy to understand as resulting from the desire to do away with the conflict between two apostles.　This Cephas appears frequently in later traditions, and is commemorated in the Menology of Basil on December 9, and in the Armenian calendar on September 25.　In the *Ecclesiastical Canons* he is made one of the twelve apostles, and distinguished from Peter.　　　　[8] Gal. ii. 11.

[9] We learn from Acts i. 21 sqq. that Matthias was a follower of Christ throughout his ministry, and therefore the tradition, which Eusebius is, so far as we know, the first to record, is not at all improbable.　Nicephorus (at the close of the first book of his *Hær.*, Dindorf's ed. I. p. 337) a half-century later records the same tradition. Nicephorus Callistus (II. 40) says that he labored and suffered martyrdom in Ethiopia (probably meaning Caucasian Ethiopia, east of the Black Sea).　Upon the *Gospel of Matthias* see below, III. 25, note 30.

[10] Joseph Barsabas, surnamed Justus.　He, too, had been with Christ from the beginning, and therefore may well have been one of the Seventy, as Eusebius reports.　Papias (quoted by Eusebius, III. 39, below) calls him Justus Barsabas, and relates that he drank a deadly poison without experiencing any injury.

[11] From a comparison of the different lists of apostles given by Matthew, Mark, and Luke, Thaddeus is seen to be one of the Twelve, apparently identical with Jude and Lebbæus (compare Jerome, *In Matt.* X.).　Eusebius here sunders him from the apostles and makes him one of the Seventy, committing an error similar to that which arose in the case of Peter and Cephas.　He perhaps records only an oral tradition, as he uses the word φασί.　He is, so far as is known, the first to mention the tradition.

[12] See the next chapter.　　　　[13] See 1 Cor. xv. 5-7.

[14] The relationship of James and Jesus has always been a dis-

CHAPTER XIII.

Narrative concerning the Prince of the Edessenes.

1   THE divinity of our Lord and Saviour Jesus Christ being noised abroad among all men on account of his wonder-working power, he attracted countless numbers from foreign countries lying far away from Judea, who had the hope of being cured of their diseases and 2 of all kinds of sufferings.   For instance, the King Abgarus,[1] who ruled with great glory the nations beyond the Euphrates, being afflicted with a terrible disease which it was beyond the power of human skill to cure, when he heard of the name of Jesus, and of his miracles, which were attested by all with one accord, sent a message to him by a courier and 3 begged him to heal his disease.   But he did not at that time comply with his request ; yet he deemed him worthy of a personal letter in which he said that he would send one of his disciples to cure his disease, and at the same time promised salvation to himself 4 and all his house.   Not long afterward his promise was fulfilled.   For after his resurrection from the dead and his ascent into heaven, Thomas,[2] one of the twelve apostles, under divine impulse sent Thaddeus, who was also numbered among the seventy disciples of Christ,[3] to Edessa,[4] as a preacher and evangelist of the teaching of Christ.   And all that our Saviour had promised received through him its 5 fulfillment.   You have written evidence of these things taken from the archives of Edessa,[5] which was at that time a royal city.

For in the public registers there, which contain accounts of ancient times and the acts of Abgarus, these things have been found preserved down to the present time.   But there is no better way than to hear the epistles themselves which we have taken from the archives and have literally translated from the Syriac language[6] in the following manner.

Copy of an epistle written by Abgarus the ruler to Jesus, and sent to him at Jerusalem by Ananias[7] the swift courier.

" Abgarus, ruler of Edessa, to Jesus the   6 excellent Saviour who has appeared in the country of Jerusalem, greeting.   I have heard the reports of thee and of thy cures as performed by thee without medicines or herbs.   For it is said that thou makest the blind to see and the lame to walk, that thou cleansest lepers and castest out impure spirits and demons, and that thou healest those afflicted with lingering disease, and raisest the dead.   And having heard all   7 these things concerning thee, I have concluded that one of two things must be true : either thou art God, and having come down from heaven thou doest these things, or else thou, who doest these things, art the Son of God.[8]   I have therefore written to thee   8 to ask thee that thou wouldest take the trouble to come to me and heal the disease which I have.   For I have heard that the Jews are murmuring against thee and are plotting to injure thee.   But I have a very small yet noble city which is great enough for us both."

---

[1] Abgarus was the name of several kings of Edessa, who reigned at various periods from B.C. 99 to A.D. 217.   The Abgar contemporary with Christ was called Abgar Ucomo, or " the Black."   He was the fifteenth king, and reigned, according to Gutschmid, from A.D. 13 to A.D. 50.   A great many ecclesiastical fictions have grown up around his name, the story, contained in its simplest form in the present chapter, being embellished with many marvelous additions. A starting-point for this tradition of the correspondence with Christ, — from which in turn grew all the later legends, — may be found in the fact that in the latter part of the second century there was a Christian Abgar, King of Edessa, at whose court Bardesanes, the Syrian Gnostic, enjoyed high favor, and it is certain that Christianity had found a foothold in this region at a much earlier period. Soon after the time of this Abgar the pretended correspondence was very likely forged, and foisted back upon the Abgar who was contemporary with Christ.   Compare Cureton's *Anc. Syriac Documents relative to the Earliest Establishment of Christianity in Edessa*, London, 1864.

[2] On the traditions in regard to Thomas, see Bk. III. chap 1.

[3] See chap. 12, note 11.

[4] Edessa, the capital of Abgar's dominions, was a city of Northern Mesopotamia, near the river Euphrates.   History knows nothing of the city before the time of the Seleucidæ, though tradition puts its origin back into distant antiquity, and some even identify it with Abraham's original home, Ur of the Chaldees.   In the history of the Christian Church it played an important part as a centre of Syrian learning.   Ephraem, the Syrian, founded a seminary there in the fourth century, which after his death fell into the hands of the Arians.

[5] We have no reason to doubt that Eusebius, who is the first to mention these apocryphal epistles, really found them in the public archives at Edessa.   Moses Chorenensis, the celebrated Armenian historian of the fifth century, who studied a long time in Edessa, is an independent witness to their existence in the Edessene archives. Eusebius has been accused of forging this correspondence himself;

but this unworthy suspicion has been refuted by the discovery and publication of the original Syriac (*The Doct. of Addai the Apostle, with an English Translation and Notes*, by G. Phillips, London, 1876; compare also *Contemp. Rev.*, May, 1877, p. 1137).   The epistles were forged probably long before his day, and were supposed by him to be genuine.   His critical insight, but not his honesty, was at fault.   The apocryphal character of these letters is no longer a matter of dispute, though Cave and Grabe defended their genuineness (so that Eusebius is in good company), and even in the present century Rinck (*Ueber die Echtheit des Briefwechsels des Königs Abgars mit Jesu, Zeitschrift für Hist. Theol.*, 1843, II. p. 3-26) has had the hardihood to enter the lists in their defense; but we know of no one else who values his critical reputation so little as to venture upon the task.

[6] Eusebius does not say directly that he translated these documents himself, but this seems to be the natural conclusion to be drawn from his words.   Ἡμῖν is used only with ἀναληφθεισῶν, and not with μεταβληθεισῶν.   It is impossible, therefore, to decide with certainty ; but the documents must have been in Syriac in the Edessene archives, and Eusebius' words imply that, if he did not translate them himself, he at least employed some one else to do it.   At the end of this chapter he again uses an indefinite expression, where perhaps it might be expected that he would tell us directly if he had himself translated the documents.

[7] In the greatly embellished narrative of Cedrenus (*Hist. Compendium*, p. 176; according to Wright, in his article on Abgar in the *Dict. of Christian Biog.*) this Ananias is represented as an artist who endeavored to take the portrait of Christ, but was dazzled by the splendor of his countenance; whereupon Christ, having washed his face, wiped it with a towel, which miraculously retained an image of his features.   The picture thus secured was carried back to Edessa, and acted as a charm for the preservation of the city against its enemies.   The marvelous fortunes of the miraculous picture are traced by Cedrenus through some centuries (see also Evagrius, *H. E.* IV. 27).

[8] The expression " Son of God " could not be used by a heathen prince as it is used here.

The answer of Jesus to the ruler Abgarus by the courier Ananias.

9   "Blessed art thou who hast believed in me without having seen me.[9] For it is written concerning me, that they who have seen me will not believe in me, and that they who have not seen me will believe and be saved.[10] But in regard to what thou hast written me, that I should come to thee, it is necessary for me to fulfill all things here for which I have been sent, and after I have fulfilled them thus to be taken up again to him that sent me. But after I have been taken up I will send to thee one of my disciples, that he may heal thy disease and give life to thee and thine."

10   To these epistles there was added the following account in the Syriac language. "After the ascension of Jesus, Judas,[11] who was also called Thomas, sent to him Thaddeus, an apostle,[12] one of the Seventy. When he was come he lodged with Tobias,[13] the son of Tobias. When the report of him got abroad, it was told Abgarus that an apostle of Jesus was come,

11   as he had written him. Thaddeus began then in the power of God to heal every disease and infirmity, insomuch that all wondered. And when Abgarus heard of the great and wonderful things which he did and of the cures which he performed, he began to suspect that he was the one of whom Jesus had written him, saying,

'After I have been taken up I will send to thee one of my disciples who will heal thee.' Therefore, summoning Tobias, with whom **12** Thaddeus lodged, he said, I have heard that a certain man of power has come and is lodging in thy house. Bring him to me. And Tobias coming to Thaddeus said to him, The ruler Abgarus summoned me and told me to bring thee to him that thou mightst heal him. And Thaddeus said, I will go, for I have been sent to him with power. Tobias **13** therefore arose early on the following day, and taking Thaddeus came to Abgarus. And when he came, the nobles were present and stood about Abgarus. And immediately upon his entrance a great vision appeared to Abgarus in the countenance of the apostle Thaddeus. When Abgarus saw it he prostrated himself before Thaddeus, while all those who stood about were astonished; for they did not see the vision, which appeared to Abgarus alone. **14** He then asked Thaddeus if he were in truth a disciple of Jesus the Son of God, who had said to him, 'I will send thee one of my disciples, who shall heal thee and give thee life.' And Thaddeus said, Because thou hast mightily believed in him that sent me, therefore have I been sent unto thee. And still further, if thou believest in him, the petitions of thy heart shall be granted thee as thou believest. And **15** Abgarus said to him, So much have I believed in him that I wished to take an army and destroy those Jews who crucified him, had I not been deterred from it by reason of the dominion of the Romans. And Thaddeus said, Our Lord has fulfilled the will of his Father, and having fulfilled it has been taken up to his Father. And Abgarus said to him, I too have believed in him and in his Father. And Thaddeus said **16** to him, Therefore I place my hand upon thee in his name. And when he had done it, immediately Abgarus was cured of the disease and of the suffering which he had. And **17** Abgarus marvelled, that as he had heard concerning Jesus, so he had received in very deed through his disciple Thaddeus, who healed him without medicines and herbs, and not only him, but also Abdus[14] the son of Abdus, who was afflicted with the gout; for he too came to him and fell at his feet, and having received a benediction by the imposition of his hands, he was healed. The same Thaddeus cured also many other inhabitants of the city, and did wonders and marvelous works, and preached

---

[9] Compare John xx. 29.

[10] γέγραπται, as used by Christ and his disciples, always referred to the Old Testament. The passage quoted here does not occur in the Old Testament; but compare Isa. vi. 9, Jer. v. 21, and Ezek. xii. 2; and also Matt. xiii. 14, Mark iv. 12, and especially Acts xxviii. 26–28 and Rom. xi. 7 sq.

[11] Thomas is not commonly known by the name of Judas, and it is possible that Eusebius, or the translator of the document, made a mistake, and applied to Thomas a name which in the original was given to Thaddeus. But Thomas is called Judas Thomas in the Apocryphal Acts of Thomas, and in the Syriac *Doctrina Apostolorum*, published by Cureton.

[12] The word "apostle" is by no means confined to the twelve apostles of Christ. The term was used very commonly in a much wider sense, and yet the combination, "the apostle, one of the Seventy," in this passage, does not seem natural, and we cannot avoid the conclusion that the original author of this account did not thus describe Thaddeus. The designation, "one of the Seventy," carries the mind back to Christ's own appointment of them, recorded by Luke, and the term "apostle," used in the same connection, would naturally denote one of the Twelve appointed by Christ,—that is, an apostle in the narrow sense. It might be suggested as possible that the original Syriac connected the word "apostle" with Thomas, reading, "Thomas the apostle sent Judas, who is also called Thaddeus, one of the Seventy," &c. Such a happy confusion is not beyond the power of an ancient translator, for most of whom little can be said in the way of praise. That this can have been the case in the present instance, however, is rendered extremely improbable by the fact that throughout this account Thaddeus is called an apostle, and we should therefore expect the designation upon the first mention of him. It seems to me much more probable that the words, "one of the Seventy," are an addition of Eusebius, who has already, in two places (§ 4, above, and chap. 12, § 3), told us that Thaddeus was one of them. It is probable that the original Syriac preserved the correct tradition of Thaddeus as one of the Twelve; while Eusebius, with his false tradition of him as one of the Seventy, takes pains to characterize him as such, when he is first introduced, but allows the word "apostle," so common in its wider sense, to stand throughout. He does not intend to correct the Syriac original; he simply defines Thaddeus, as he understands him, more closely.

[13] Tobias was very likely a Jew, or of Jewish extraction, the name being a familiar one among the Hebrews. This might have been the reason that Thaddeus (if he went to Edessa at all) made his home with him.

[14] Moses Chorenensis reads instead (according to Rinck), "Potagrus, the son of Abdas." Rinck thinks it probable that Eusebius or the translator made a mistake, confusing the Syrian name Potagrus with the Greek word ποδάγρα, "a sort of gout," and then inserting a second Abdas. The word "Podagra" is Greek and could not have occurred in the Armenian original, and therefore Eusebius is to be corrected at this point by Moses Chorenensis (Rinck, *ibid.* p. 18). The Greek reads Ἄβδον τὸν τοῦ Ἄβδου ποδάγραν ἔχοντα.

18   the word of God.   And afterward Abgarus
said, Thou, O Thaddeus, doest these things
with the power of God, and we marvel.   But, in
addition to these things, I pray thee to inform
me in regard to the coming of Jesus, how he
was born; and in regard to his power, by what
power he performed those deeds of which
19   I have heard.   And Thaddeus said, Now
indeed will I keep silence, since I have
been sent to proclaim the word publicly.   But
to-morrow assemble for me all thy citizens, and
I will preach in their presence and sow among
them the word of God, concerning the coming
of Jesus, how he was born; and concerning his
mission, for what purpose he was sent by the
Father; and concerning the power of his works,
and the mysteries which he proclaimed in the
world, and by what power he did these things;
and concerning his new preaching, and his
abasement and humiliation, and how he humbled himself, and died and debased his divinity
and was crucified, and descended into Hades,[15]

and burst the bars which from eternity had not
been broken,[16] and raised the dead; for he descended alone, but rose with many, and
thus ascended to his Father.[17]   Abgarus   20
therefore commanded the citizens to assemble early in the morning to hear the preaching
of Thaddeus, and afterward he ordered gold and
silver to be given him.   But he refused to take
it, saying, If we have forsaken that which was
our own, how shall we take that which is another's?   These things were done in the three
hundred and fortieth year." [18]

I have inserted them here in their proper
place, translated from the Syriac[19] literally, and
I hope to good purpose.

---

[15] This is probably the earliest distinct and formal statement of
the descent into Hades; but no special stress is laid upon it as a
new doctrine, and it is stated so much as a matter of course as to
show that it was commonly accepted at Edessa at the time of the
writing of these records, that is certainly as early as the third century.   Justin, Irenæus, Clement of Alexandria, Origen, Tertullian,
&c., all witness to the belief of the Church in this doctrine, though
it did not form an article in any of the older creeds, and appeared in
the East first in certain Arian confessions at about 360 A.D.   In the
West it appeared first in the Aquileian creed, from which it was
transferred to the Apostles' creed in the fifth century or later.
   The doctrine is stated in a very fantastic shape in the *Gospel of
Nicodemus*, part II. (*Ante-Nicene Fathers*, Am. ed. VIII. p.
435 sq.), which is based upon an apocryphal gospel of the second
century, according to Tischendorf.   In it the descent of Christ into
Hades and his ascent with a great multitude are dwelt upon at
length.   Compare Pearson, *On the Creed*, p. 340 sq.; Schaff's

Creeds of Christendom, I. p. 46; and especially, Plumptre's *Spirits
in Prison*, p. 77 sq.
   [16] Compare the *Gospel of Nicodemus*, II. 5.
   [17] καταβὰς γὰρ μόνος συνήγειρεν πολλοὺς, εἶθ' οὕτως ἀνέβη πρὸς
τὸν πατέρα αὐτοῦ.   Other MSS. read κατέβη μόνος, ἀνέβη δὲ μετὰ
πολλοῦ ὄχλου πρὸς τὸν πατέρα αὐτοῦ.   Rufinus translates *Qui de-
scendit quidem solus, ascendit autem cum grandi multi-
tudine ad patrem suum.*   Compare the words of Cyril of Jerusalem (*Catech.* IV. 11): κατῆλθεν εἰς τὰ καταχθόνια, ἵνα κἀκεῖθεν
λυτρώσηται τοὺς δικαίους, " He descended into the depths, that he
might ransom thence the just."
   [18] According to the *Chronicle* of Eusebius (ed. Schoene, II.
p. 116) the Edessenes dated their era from the year of Abraham
1706 (B.C. 310), which corresponded with the second year of the one
hundred and seventeenth Olympiad (or, according to the Armenian,
to the third year of the same Olympiad), the time when Seleucus Ni-
canor began to rule in Syria.   According to this reckoning the 340th
year of the Edessenes would correspond with the year of Abraham
2046, the reign of Tiberius 16 (A.D. 30); that is, the second year of the
two hundred and second Olympiad (or, according to the Armenian,
the third year of the same).   According to the *Chronicle* of Eusebius,
Jesus was crucified in the nineteenth year of Tiberius (year of Abraham 2048 = A.D. 32), according to Jerome's version in the eighteenth
year (year of Abraham 2047 = A.D. 31).   Thus, as compared with
these authorities, the 340th year of the Edessenes falls too early.
But Tertullian, Lactantius, Augustine, and others put Christ's death
in 783 U.C., that is in 30 A.D., and this corresponds with the Edessene
reckoning as given by Eusebius.   [19] See note 6.

BOOK II.

INTRODUCTION.

1   WE have discussed in the preceding book those subjects in ecclesiastical history which it was necessary to treat by way of introduction, and have accompanied them with brief proofs. Such were the divinity of the saving Word, and the antiquity of the doctrines which we teach, as well as of that evangelical life which is led by Christians, together with the events which have taken place in connection with Christ's recent appearance, and in connection with his passion and with the choice 2 of the apostles. In the present book let us examine the events which took place after his ascension, confirming some of them from the divine Scriptures, and others from such writings as we shall refer to from time to time.

CHAPTER I.

The Course pursued by the Apostles after the Ascension of Christ.

1   FIRST, then, in the place of Judas, the betrayer, Matthias,[1] who, as has been shown,[2] was also one of the Seventy, was chosen to the apostolate. And there were appointed to the diaconate,[2a] for the service of the congregation, by prayer and the laying on of the hands of the apostles, approved men,

---

although Luke had many opportunities to call the Seven "deacons" if he had considered them such; and finally, that according to Epiphanius (*Hær*. XXX. 18), the Ebionitic churches of Palestine in his time had only presbyters and Archisynagogi (*chiefs of the synagogue*). These Ebionites were the Jewish Christian reactionaries who refused to advance with the Church catholic in its normal development; it is therefore at least significant that there were no deacons among them in the fourth century.

In view of these considerations I feel compelled to doubt the traditional identification, although it is accepted without dissent by almost all scholars (cf. e.g. Lightfoot's article on *The Christian Ministry* in his *Commentary on Philippians*). There remain but two possibilities: either the Seven constituted a merely temporary committee (as held by Chrysostom, and in modern times, among others, by Vitringa, in his celebrated work on the Synagogue, and by Stanley in his *Essays on the Apostolic Age*); or they were the originals of permanent officers in the Church, other than deacons. The former alternative is possible, but the emphasis which Luke lays upon the appointment is against it, as also the fact that the very duties which these men were chosen to perform were such as would increase rather than diminish with the growth of the Church, and such as would therefore demand the creation of a new and similar committee if the old were not continued.

In favor of the second alternative there is, it seems to me, much to be said. The limits of this note forbid a full discussion of the subject. But it may be urged: First, that we find in the Acts frequent mention of a body of men in the Jerusalem church known as "elders." Of the appointment of these elders we have no account, and yet it is clear that they cannot have been in existence when the apostles proposed the appointment of the Seven. Secondly, although the Seven were such prominent and influential men, they are not once mentioned as a body in the subsequent chapters of the Acts, while, whenever we should expect to find them referred to with the apostles, it is always the "elders" that are mentioned. Finally, when the elders appear for the first time (Acts xi. 30), we find them entrusted with the same duties which the Seven were originally appointed to perform: *they* receive the alms sent by the church of Antioch. It is certainly, to say the least, a very natural conclusion that these "elders" occupy the office of whose institution we read in Acts vi.

Against this identification of the Seven with the elders of the Jerusalem church it might be urged: First, that Luke does not call them elders. But it is quite possible that they were not called by that name at first, and yet later acquired it; and in that case, in referring to them in later times, people would naturally call the first appointed "the Seven," to distinguish them from their successors, "the elders," — the well-known and frequently mentioned officers whose number may well have been increased as the church grew. It is thus easier to account for Luke's omission of the name "elder," than it would be to account for his omission of the name "deacon," if they were deacons. In the second place, it might be objected that the duties which the Seven were appointed to perform were not commensurate with those which fell to the lot of the elders as known to us. This objection, however, loses its weight when we realize that the same kind of a development went on in connection with the bishop, as has been most clearly pointed out by Hatch in his *Organization of the Early Christian Churches*, and by Harnack in his translation of that work and in his edition of the *Teaching of the Apostles*. Moreover, in the case of the Seven, who were evidently the chiefest men in the Jerusalem church after the apostles, and at the same time were "full of the Spirit," it was very natural that, as the apostles gradually scattered, the successors of these Seven should have committed to them other duties besides the purely financial ones.

The theory presented in this note is not a novel one. It was suggested first by Böhmer (in his *Diss. Juris eccles.*), who was followed by Ritschl (in his *Entstehung der alt-kath. Kirche*), and has been accepted in a somewhat modified form by Lange (in his *Apostolisches Zeitalter*), and by Lechler (in his *Apost. und Nachapost. Zeitalter*). Before learning that the theory had been proposed by others, I had myself adopted it and had embodied it in a more elaborate form in a paper read before a ministerial association in the spring of 1888. My confidence in its validity has of course been increased by the knowledge that it has been maintained by the eminent scholars referred to above.

---

[1] See Acts i. 23–26.   [2] Bk. I. chap. 12, § 2.

[2a] The view that the Seven were deacons appears first in Irenæus (*adv. Hær*. I. 26. 3; III. 12. 10; IV. 15. 1), then in Cyprian (*Ep*. 64. 3), and was the commonly accepted opinion of the Roman Church in the third century (for, while they had forty-six presbyters, they had only seven deacons; see below, Bk. VI. chap. 43), and has been ever since almost universally accepted. In favor of the identification are urged this early and unanimous tradition, the similarity of the duties assigned to the Seven and to later deacons, and the use of the words διακονία and διακονεῖν in connection with the "Seven" in Acts vi. It must be remarked, however, that ancient tradition is not unanimously in favor of the identification, for Chrysostom (*Homily XIV. on Acts*) denies it; still further, the functions of the Seven and of later deacons were not identical, for the former were put in charge of the financial affairs of the Jerusalem church, while the latter acted simply as bishops' assistants. In fact, it was the bishop of the second century, not the deacon, that had charge of the church finances. And finally, no weight can be laid upon the use of the terms διακονεῖν and διακονία in connection with the Seven, for these words are used always in a general, never in an official sense in other parts of the Acts and of the New Testament, and, what is still more decisive, the same word (διακονία) is used in the same passage in connection with the apostles; the Seven are "to serve tables" (διακονεῖν ταῖς τραπέζαις), the apostles are to give themselves to "the service of the word" (διακονία τοῦ λόγου). There is just as much reason, therefore, on linguistic grounds, for calling the apostles "deacons" as for giving that name to the Seven. On the other hand, against the opinion that the Seven were deacons, are to be urged the facts that they are never called "deacons" by Luke or by any other New Testament writer; that we are nowhere told, in the New Testament or out of it, that there were deacons in the Jerusalem church,

seven in number, of whom Stephen was one.[3] He first, after the Lord, was stoned to death at the time of his ordination by the slayers of the Lord, as if he had been promoted for this very purpose.[4] And thus he was the first to receive the crown, corresponding to his name,[5] which belongs to the martyrs of Christ, who are

2 worthy of the meed of victory. Then James, whom the ancients surnamed the Just[6] on account of the excellence of his virtue, is recorded to have been the first to be made bishop of the church of Jerusalem. This James was called the brother of the Lord[7] because he was known as a son of Joseph,[8] and Joseph was supposed to be the father of Christ, because the Virgin, being betrothed to him, "was found with child by the Holy Ghost before they came together,"[9] as the account of the holy

3 Gospels shows. But Clement in the sixth book of his Hypotyposes[10] writes thus: "For they say that Peter and James and John after the ascension of our Saviour, as if also preferred by our Lord, strove not after honor, but chose James the Just bishop of Jeru-

4 salem."[11] But the same writer, in the seventh book of the same work, relates also the following things concerning him: "The Lord after his resurrection imparted knowledge to James the Just and to John and Peter, and they imparted it to the rest of the apostles, and the rest of the apostles to the seventy, of whom Barnabas was one.[12] But there were two Jameses:[13] one called the Just, who was thrown

from the pinnacle of the temple and was beaten to death with a club by a fuller,[14] and another who was beheaded."[15] Paul also makes mention of the same James the Just, where he writes, "Other of the apostles saw I none,

5 save James the Lord's brother."[16] At that time also the promise of our Saviour to the king of the Osrhœnians was fulfilled. For Thomas, under a divine impulse, sent Thaddeus to Edessa as a preacher and evangelist of the religion of Christ, as we have shown a little above from the document found there.[17]

7 When he came to that place he healed Abgarus by the word of Christ; and after bringing all the people there into the right attitude of mind by means of his works, and leading them to adore the power of Christ, he made them disciples of the Saviour's teaching. And from that time down to the present the whole city of the Edessenes has been devoted to the name of Christ,[18] offering no common proof of the beneficence of our Saviour

8 toward them also. These things have been drawn from ancient accounts; but let us now turn again to the divine Scripture. When the first and greatest persecution was instigated by the Jews against the church of Jerusalem in connection with the martyrdom of Stephen, and when all the disciples, except the Twelve, were scattered throughout Judea and Samaria,[19] some, as the divine Scripture says, went as far as Phœnicia and Cyprus and Antioch, but could not yet venture to impart the word of faith to the nations, and therefore

9 preached it to the Jews alone.[20] During this time Paul was still persecuting the church, and entering the houses of believers was dragging men and women away and committing them to prison.[21] Philip also,

10 one of those who with Stephen had been entrusted with the diaconate, being among those who were scattered abroad, went down to Samaria,[22] and being filled with the divine power, he first preached the word to the inhabitants of that country. And divine grace worked so mightily with him that even Simon Magus with many others was attracted by his

---

[3] See Acts vi. 1-6.   [4] See Acts vii.
[5] στέφανος, "a crown."
[6] James is not called the "Just" in the New Testament, but Hegesippus (quoted by Eusebius, chap. 23) says that he was called thus by all from the time of Christ, on account of his great piety, and it is by this name that he is known throughout history.
[7] See above, Bk. I. chap. 12, note 13.
[8] Eusebius' testimony is in favor of the half-brother theory; for had he considered James the son of Mary, he could not have spoken in this way.   [9] Matt. i. 18.
[10] On Clement's Hypotyposes, see Bk. VI. chap. 13, note 3. On Clement's life and writings, see Bk. V. chap. 11.
[11] ἀλλ' Ἰάκωβον τὸν δίκαιον ἐπίσκοπον τῶν Ἱεροσολύμων ἐλεσθαι, as the majority of the MSS. and editions read. Laemmer, followed by Heinichen, substitutes γενέσθαι for ἐλεσθαι on the authority of two important codices. The other reading, however, is as well, if not better, supported.
How soon after the ascension of Christ, James the Just assumed a leading position in the church of Jerusalem, we do not know. He undoubtedly became prominent very soon, as Paul in 37 (or 40) A.D. sees him in addition to Peter on visiting Jerusalem. But we do not know of his having a position of leadership until the Jerusalem Council in 51 (Acts xv. and Gal. ii.), where he is one of the three pillars, standing at least upon an equality in influence with Peter and John. But this very expression "three pillars of the Church" excludes the supposition that he was bishop of the Church in the modern sense of the term — he was only one of the rulers of the Church. Indeed, we have abundant evidence from other sources that the monarchical episcopacy was nowhere known at that early age. It was the custom of all writers of the second century and later to throw back into the apostolic age their own church organization, and hence we hear of bishops appointed by the apostles in various churches where we know that the episcopacy was a second century growth.
[12] See above, Bk. I. chap. 12, note 3.
[13] Clement evidently identifies James, the brother of the Lord, with James, the son of Alphæus (compare the words just above: "These delivered it to the rest of the apostles," in which the word "apostles," on account of the "Seventy" just following, seems to be used in a narrow sense, and therefore this James to be one of the Twelve), and he is thus cited as a witness to the cousin hypothesis (see above, Bk. I. chap. 12, note 13). Papias, too, in a fragment

given by Routh (Rel. Sac. I. p. 16) identifies the two. But Hegesippus (quoted by Eusebius in chap. 23) expressly states that there were many of this name, and that he was therefore called James the Just to distinguish him from others. Eusebius quotes this passage of Clement with apparently no suspicion that it contradicts his own opinion in regard to the relationship of James to Christ. The contradiction, indeed, appears only upon careful examination.
[14] Josephus (Ant. XX. 9. 1) says he was stoned to death. The account of Clement agrees with that of Hegesippus quoted by Eusebius in chap. 23, below, which see.
[15] James, the son of Zebedee, who was beheaded by Herod Agrippa I., 44 A.D. See Acts xii. 2, and Bk. II. chap. 9, below.
[16] Gal. i. 19.   [17] See above, Bk. I. chap. 13.
[18] The date of the introduction of Christianity into Edessa is not known (see above, Bk. I. chap. 13, notes 1 and 3), but it was the seat of a bishop in the third century, and in Eusebius' time was filled with magnificent churches and monasteries.
[19] See Acts viii. 1.   [21] See Acts viii. 3.
[20] See Acts xi. 19.   [22] See Acts viii. 5.

11 words.[23] Simon was at that time so celebrated, and had acquired, by his jugglery,
such influence over those who were deceived
by him, that he was thought to be the great
power of God.[24] But at this time, being
amazed at the wonderful deeds wrought by
Philip through the divine power, he feigned and
counterfeited faith in Christ, even going so
12 far as to receive baptism.[25] And what is
surprising, the same thing is done even to
this day by those who follow his most impure
heresy.[26] For they, after the manner of their
forefather, slipping into the Church, like a
pestilential and leprous disease greatly afflict
those into whom they are able to infuse the
deadly and terrible poison concealed in themselves.[27] The most of these have been expelled
as soon as they have been caught in their
wickedness, as Simon himself, when detected by
Peter, received the merited punishment.[28]
13 But as the preaching of the Saviour's
Gospel was daily advancing, a certain providence led from the land of the Ethiopians an
officer of the queen of that country,[29] for Ethiopia even to the present day is ruled, according to ancestral custom, by a woman. He,
first among the Gentiles, received of the mysteries of the divine word from Philip in consequence of a revelation, and having become
the first-fruits of believers throughout the
world, he is said to have been the first on
returning to his country to proclaim the knowledge of the God of the universe and the life-

giving sojourn of our Saviour among men;[30]
so that through him in truth the prophecy
obtained its fulfillment, which declares that
"Ethiopia stretcheth out her hand unto
God."[31] In addition to these, Paul, that   14
"chosen vessel,"[32] "not of men neither
through men, but by the revelation of Jesus
Christ himself and of God the Father who
raised him from the dead,"[33] was appointed an
apostle, being made worthy of the call by a
vision and by a voice which was uttered in a
revelation from heaven.[34]

CHAPTER II.

*How Tiberius was affected when informed by
Pilate concerning Christ.*

AND when the wonderful resurrection and   1
ascension of our Saviour were already noised
abroad, in accordance with an ancient custom
which prevailed among the rulers of the provinces, of reporting to the emperor the novel
occurrences which took place in them, in order
that nothing might escape him, Pontius Pilate
informed Tiberius[1] of the reports which were
noised abroad through all Palestine concerning
the resurrection of our Saviour Jesus from
the dead. He gave an account also of   2
other wonders which he had learned of him,
and how, after his death, having risen from the
dead, he was now believed by many to be a
God.[2] They say that Tiberius referred the
matter to the Senate,[3] but that they rejected it,
ostensibly because they had not first examined
into the matter (for an ancient law prevailed

---

[23] See Acts viii. 9 sqq. Upon Simon, see chap. 13, note 3.
[24] τὴν μεγάλην δύναμιν τοῦ θεοῦ. Compare Acts viii. 10, which
has ἡ δύναμις τοῦ θεοῦ ἡ καλουμένη Μεγάλη. According to Irenæus (I. 23. 1) he was called "the loftiest of all powers, i.e. the
one who is father over all things" (*sublissimam virtutem, hoc est,
eum qui sit nuper omnia Pater*); according to Justin Martyr,
Apol. I. 26 (see below, chap. 13), τὸν πρῶτον θεόν; according to
the Clementine *Homilies* (II. 22) he wished to be called "a certain
supreme power of God" (ἀνωτάτη τις δύναμις). According to the
Clementine *Recognitions* (II. 7) he was called the "Standing one"
(*hinc ergo Stans appellatur*).
[25] Eusebius here utters the universal belief of the early Church,
which from the subsequent career of Simon, who was considered the
founder of all heresies, and the great arch-heretic himself, read back
into his very conversion the hypocrisy for which he was afterward
distinguished in Church history. The account of the Acts does not
say that his belief was hypocritical, and leaves it to be implied (if it
be implied at all) only from his subsequent conduct in endeavoring
to purchase the gift of God with money.
[26] Eusebius may refer here to the Simonians, an heretical sect
(mentioned by Justin, Irenæus, Clement of Alexandria, and others),
which recognized him as its founder and leader (though they originated probably at a later date), and even looked upon him as a God.
They were exceedingly licentious and immoral. Their teachings
gradually assumed a decidedly Gnostic character, and Simon came
to be looked upon as the father of all Gnostics (compare Irenæus,
I. 27. 4), and hence of heretics in general, and as himself the arch-
heretic. Eusebius, therefore, perhaps refers in this place simply to
the Gnostics, or to the heretics in general.
[27] Another instance of the external and artificial conception of
heresy which Eusebius held in common with his age.
[28] Acts viii. tells of no punishment which befell Simon further
than the rebuke of Peter which Hippolytus (*Phil.* vi. 15) calls a
curse, and which as such may have been regarded by Eusebius as a
deserved punishment, its effect clinging to him, and finally bringing
him to destruction (see below, chap. 14, note 8).
[29] Acts viii. 26 sqq. This queen was Candace, according to the
Biblical account; but Candace was the name, not of an individual,
but of a dynasty of queens who ruled in Meroë, an island formed by
two branches of the Nile, south of Egypt. See Pliny, *H. N.* VI. 35
(Delphin edition); Dion Cassius, LIV. 5; and Strabo, XVII. 1. 54
(Müller's edit., Paris, 1877).

[20] Irenæus (*Adv. Hær.* III. 12. 8) says that this Eunuch returned to Ethiopia and preached there. But by no one else, so far
as I know, is the origin of Christianity in Ethiopia traced back to
him. The first certain knowledge we have of the introduction of
Christianity into Ethiopia is in the fourth century, under Frumen-
tius and Ædesius, of whom Rufinus, I. 9, gives the original account;
and yet it is probable that Christianity existed there long before this
time. Compare Neander's *Kirchengeschichte*, I. p. 46. See also
H. R. Reynolds' article upon the "Ethiopian Church" in Smith
and Wace's *Dictionary of Christian Biography*, II. 232 sqq.
[31] Psa. xviii. 31.   [32] Acts ix. 15.   [33] Gal. i. 1.
[34] See Acts ix. 3 sqq.; xxii. 6 sqq.; xxvi. 12 sqq.; Gal. i. 16;
1 Cor. xv. 8-10.
[1] That Pilate made an official report to Tiberius is stated also by
Tertullian (*Apol.* 21), and is in itself quite probable. Justin Martyr (*Apol.* I. 35 and 48) mentions certain *Acts of Pilate* as well
known in his day, but the so-called *Acts of Pilate* which are still
extant in various forms are spurious, and belong to a much later
period. They are very fanciful and curious. The most important
of these *Acts* is that which is commonly known under the title of the
Gospel of Nicodemus. There are also extant numerous spurious
epistles of Pilate addressed to Herod, to Tiberius, to Claudius, &c.
The extant Acts and Epistles are collected in Tischendorf's *Evang.
Apoc.*, and most of them are translated by Cowper in his *Apocryphal
Gospels.* See also the *Ante-Nicene Fathers*, Am. ed., VIII. p.
416 sqq. Compare the excellent article of Lipsius upon the Apocryphal Gospels in the *Dict. of Christ. Biog.* II. p. 707 sqq., also
the Prolegomena of Tischendorf, p. lxii sqq.
[2] The existing *Report of Pilate* (translated in the *Ante-Nicene
Fathers, ibid.* p. 460, 461) answers well to Eusebius' description, containing as it does a detailed account of Christ's miracles and of his
resurrection. According to Tischendorf, however, it is in its present form of a much later date, but at the same time is very likely
based upon the form which Eusebius saw, and has been changed by
interpolations and additions. See the Prolegomena of Tischendorf
referred to in the previous note.   [3] See below, note 12.

that no one should be made a God by the Romans except by a vote and decree of the Senate), but in reality because the saving teaching of the divine Gospel did not need the confirmation and recommendation of men.

3   But although the Senate of the Romans rejected the proposition made in regard to our Saviour, Tiberius still retained the opinion which he had held at first, and contrived
4   no hostile measures against Christ.[4] These things are recorded by Tertullian,[5] a man well versed in the laws of the Romans,[6] and in other respects of high repute, and one of those especially distinguished in Rome.[7] In his apology for the Christians,[8] which was written by him in the Latin language, and has been translated into Greek,[9] he writes as fol-

lows:[10] "But in order that we may give an 5 account of these laws from their origin, it was an ancient decree[11] that no one should be consecrated a God by the emperor until the Senate had expressed its approval.   Marcus Aurelius did thus concerning a certain idol, Alburnus.[12]   And this is a point in favor of our doctrine,[13] that among you divine dignity is conferred by human decree.   If a God does not please a man he is not made a God.   Thus, according to this custom, it is necessary for man to be gracious to God.   Tiberius, 6 therefore, under whom the name of Christ made its entry into the world, when this doctrine was reported to him from Palestine, where it first began, communicated with the Senate, making it clear to them that he was pleased with the doctrine.[14]   But the Senate, since it had not itself proved the matter, rejected it.   But Tiberius continued to hold his own opinion, and threatened death to the accusers of the Christians."[15]   Heavenly providence had wisely instilled this into his mind in order that the doctrine of the Gospel, unhindered at its beginning, might spread in all directions throughout the world.

---

[4] That Tiberius did not persecute the Christians is a fact; but this was simply because they attracted no notice during his reign, and not because of his respect for them or of his belief in Christ.

[5] Tertullian was born in Carthage about the middle of the second century. The common opinion is that he was born about 160, but Lipsius pushes the date back toward the beginning of the fifties, and some even into the forties. For a recent study of the subject, see Ernst Nöldechen in the *Zeitschrift für wissenschaftliche Theologie*, 1886, Heft 2. He concludes that he was born about 150 and lived until about 230. Tertullian's father was a Roman centurion, and he himself became a lawyer and rhetorician in Rome. He was converted to Christianity probably between 180 and 190, and according to Jerome, became a presbyter and continued as such until middle life (whether in Rome or in Carthage we cannot tell; probably in the latter, for he certainly spent the later years of his life, while he was a Montanist, in Carthage, and also a considerable part of his earlier life, as his writings indicate), when he went over to Montanism (probably about 200 A.D.), and died at an advanced age (220+). That he was a presbyter rests only upon the authority of Jerome (*de vir. ill.* 53), and is denied by some Roman Catholic historians in the interest of clerical celibacy, for Tertullian was a married man. He wrote a great number of works, — apologetic, polemic, and practical — a few in Greek, but most of them in Latin, — and many of the Latin ones are still extant. The best edition of them is by Oehler, Leipzig, 1853, in three volumes. Vol. III. contains valuable dissertations upon the life and works of Tertullian by various writers. An English translation of his works is given in the *Ante-Nicene Fathers*, Vols. III. and IV. 1–125. Our main sources for a knowledge of his life are his own writings, and Jerome's *de vir. ill.* chap. 53. For a fuller account of Tertullian, see any of the larger Church histories, and especially a good monograph by A. Hauck, *Tertullian's Leben und Schriften*, Erlangen, 1877. For the literature, see Schaff's *Church Hist.* II. p. 818.

[6] His accurate acquaintance with the laws of the Romans is not very conspicuous in his writings. His books lead us to think that as a lawyer he must have been noted rather for brilliancy and fertility of resource than for erudition. And this conclusion is borne out by his own description of his life before his conversion, which seems to have been largely devoted to pleasure, and thus to have hardly admitted the acquirement of extensive and accurate learning.

[7] Καὶ τῶν μάλιστα ἐπὶ ᾿Ρώμης λαμπρῶν. Rufinus translates *inter nostros Scriptores celeberrimus,* and Valesius *inter Latinos Scriptores celeberrimus,* taking ἐπὶ ᾿Ρώμης to mean the *Latin language.* But this is not the literal translation of the words of Eusebius. He says expressly, *one of the especially distinguished men in Rome.* From his work *de cultu Feminarum,* Lib. I. chap. 7, we know that he had spent some time in Rome, and his acquaintance with the Roman records would imply a residence of some duration there. He very likely practiced law and rhetoric in Rome until his conversion.

[8] Tertullian's *Apology* ranks first among his extant works, and is "one of the most beautiful monuments of the heroic age of the Church" (Schaff). The date of its composition is greatly disputed, though it must have been written during the reign of Septimius Severus, and almost all scholars are agreed in assigning it to the years 197–204. Since the investigations of Bonwetsch (*Die Schriften Tertullian's,* Bonn, 1878), of Harnack (in the *Zeitschrift für Kirchengeschichte,* 1878, p. 572 sqq.), and of Nöldechen (in Gebhardt and Harnack's *Texte und Untersuchungen,* Band V. Heft 2), all of whom agree in assigning its composition to the latter part (summer or fall) of the year 197, its date may be accepted as practically established.

[9] Some have contended that Eusebius himself translated this passage from Tertullian, but his words show clearly enough that he quotes from an already existing translation. His knowledge of the Latin language appears to have been very limited. He must have had some acquaintance with it, for he translates Hadrian's rescript

to Fundanus from Latin into Greek, as he informs us in Bk. IV. chap. 8; but the translation of so brief and simple a piece of writing would not require a profound knowledge of the language, and there are good reasons for concluding that he was not a fluent Latin scholar. For instance, the only work of Tertullian's which he quotes is his *Apology,* and he uses only a Greek translation of that. It is not unnatural to conclude that the rest of Tertullian's works, or at least the most of them, were not translated, and that Eusebius was not enough of a Latin scholar to be able to read them in the original with any degree of ease. Moreover, this conclusion in regard to his knowledge of Latin is confirmed by the small acquaintance which he shows with the works of Latin writers in general. In fact, he does not once betray a personal acquaintance with any of the important Latin works which had been produced before his time, except such as existed in Greek translations. Compare Heinichen's note in his edition of Eusebius' *History,* Vol. III. p. 128 sqq. The translation of Tertullian's *Apology* used by Eusebius was very poor, as may be seen from the passage quoted here, and also from the one quoted in Bk. II. chap. 25, § 4. For the mistakes, however, of course not Eusebius himself, but the unknown translator, is to be held responsible.

[10] Tertullian's *Apology,* chap. 5.

[11] Havercamp remarks (in his edition of Tertullian's *Apology,* p. 56) that this law is stated in the second book of Cicero's *De Legibus* in the words: *Separatim nemo habessit deos, neve novos; sed ne advenas nisi publice adscitos privatim colunto.*

[12] Μάρκος ᾿Αιμίλιος οὕτως περί τινος εἰδώλου πεποίηκεν᾿Αλβούρνου. Latin: *Scit M. Æmilius de deo suo Alburno.* In *Adv. Marcionem,* I. 18, Tertullian says, *Alioquin si sic homo Deum commentabitur, quomodo Romulus Consum, et Tatius Cloacinam, et Hostilius Pavorem, et Metellus Alburnum, et quidam ante hoc tempus Antinoum; hoc aliis licebit; nos Marcionem naucleros novimus, non regem, nec imperatorem.*

I cannot discover that this εἴδωλος or *Deus* Alburnus is mentioned by any other writer than Tertullian, nor do I find a reference to him in any dictionary accessible to me.

[13] Literally, "This has been done in behalf of (or for the sake of) our doctrine" (καὶ τοῦτο ὑπὲρ τοῦ ἡμῶν λόγου πεποίηται); but the freer translation given in the text better expresses the actual sense. The original Latin reads: *facit et hoc ad causam nostram.*

[14] This entire account bears all the marks of untruthfulness, and cannot for a moment be thought of as genuine. Tertullian was probably, as Neander suggests, deceived by falsified or interpolated documents from some Christian source. He cannot have secured his knowledge from original state records. The falsification took place, probably, long after the time of Tiberius. Tertullian is the first writer to mention these circumstances, and Tertullian was not by any means a critical historian. Compare Neander's remarks in his *Church History,* Vol. I. p. 93 sqq. (Torrey's Translation).

[15] Were this conduct of Tiberius a fact, Trajan's rescript and all subsequent imperial action upon the subject would become inexplicable.

CHAPTER III.

The Doctrine of Christ soon spread throughout All the World.

1 THUS, under the influence of heavenly power, and with the divine co-operation, the doctrine of the Saviour, like the rays of the sun, quickly illumined the whole world;[1] and straightway, in accordance with the divine Scriptures,[2] the voice of the inspired evangelists and apostles went forth through all the earth, and their words to the end of the world. In 2 every city and village, churches were quickly established, filled with multitudes of people like a replenished threshing-floor. And those whose minds, in consequence of errors which had descended to them from their forefathers, were fettered by the ancient disease of idolatrous superstition, were, by the power of Christ operating through the teaching and the wonderful works of his disciples, set free, as it were, from terrible masters, and found a release from the most cruel bondage. They renounced with abhorrence every species of demoniacal polytheism, and confessed that there was only one God, the creator of all things, and him they honored with the rites of true piety, through the inspired and rational worship which has been planted by our Saviour 3 among men. But the divine grace being now poured out upon the rest of the nations, Cornelius, of Cæsarea in Palestine, with his whole house, through a divine revelation and the agency of Peter, first received faith in Christ;[3] and after him a multitude of other Greeks in Antioch,[4] to whom those who were scattered by the persecution of Stephen had preached the Gospel. When the church of Antioch was now increasing and abounding, and a multitude of prophets from Jerusalem were on the ground,[5] among them Barnabas and Paul, and in addition many other brethren, the name of Christians first sprang up there,[6] as from

a fresh and life-giving fountain.[7] And 4 Agabus, one of the prophets who was with them, uttered a prophecy concerning the famine which was about to take place,[8] and Paul and Barnabas were sent to relieve the necessities of the brethren.[9]

CHAPTER IV.

After the Death of Tiberius, Caius appointed Agrippa King of the Jews, having punished Herod with Perpetual Exile.

TIBERIUS died, after having reigned about 1 twenty-two years,[1] and Caius succeeded him in the empire.[2] He immediately gave the government of the Jews to Agrippa,[3] making him king over the tetrarchies of Philip and of Lysanias; in addition to which he bestowed upon him, not long afterward, the tetrarchy of Herod,[4] having punished Herod (the one under whom the Saviour suffered[5]) and his wife Herodias with perpetual exile[6] on account of numerous crimes. Josephus is a witness to these facts.[7] Under this emperor, Philo[8] became known; 2

common in the Greek of that day. It was probably originally given as a term of contempt, but accepted by the disciples as a term of the highest honor.
[7] ἀπ' εὐθαλοῦς καὶ γονίμου πηγῆς. Two MSS., followed by Stephanus, Valesius, Closs, and Crusè, read γῆς; but all the other MSS., together with Rufinus, support the reading πηγῆς, which is adopted by the majority of editors.
[8] See Acts xi. 28. Agabus is known to us only from this and one other passage of the Acts (xxi. 10), where he foretells the imprisonment of Paul. The famine here referred to took place in the reign of Claudius, where Eusebius puts it when he mentions it again in chap. 8. He cannot therefore be accused, as many accuse him, of putting the famine itself into the reign of Tiberius, and hence of committing a chronological error. He is following the account of the Acts, and mentions the prominent fact of the famine in that connection, without thinking of chronological order. His method is, to be sure, loose, as he does not inform his readers that he is anticipating by a number of years, but leaves them to discover it for themselves when they find the same subject taken up again after a digression of four chapters. Upon the famine itself, see below, chap. 8.
[9] See Acts xi. 29, 30.
[1] From Aug. 29, A.D. 14, to March 16, A.D. 37.
[2] Caius ruled from the death of Tiberius until Jan. 24, A.D. 41.
[3] Herod Agrippa I. He was a son of Aristobulus, and a grandson of Herod the Great. He was educated in Rome and gained high favor with Caius, and upon the latter's accession to the throne received the tetrarchies of Philip and Lysanias, and in A.D. 39 the tetrarchy of Galilee and Perea, which had belonged to Herod Antipas. After the death of Caius, his successor, Claudius, appointed him also king over the province of Judea and Samaria, which made him ruler of all Palestine, a dominion as extensive as that of Herod the Great. He was a strict observer of the Jewish law, and courted the favor of the Jews with success. It was by him that James the Elder was beheaded, and Peter imprisoned (Acts xii.). He died of a terrible disease in A.D. 44. See below, chap. 10.
[4] Herod Antipas.   [5] See Luke xxiii. 7-11.
[6] He was banished in A.D. 39 to Lugdunum in Gaul (according to Josephus, *Ant.* XVIII. 7. 2; or to Spain, according to his *B. J.* II. 9. 6), and died in Spain (according to *B. J.* II. 9. 6).
[7] See *Ant.* XVIII. 6 and 7, and *B. J.* II. 9.
[8] Philo was an Alexandrian Jew of high family, who was born probably about 20-10 B.C. (in his *Legat. ad Cajum*, he calls himself an old man). Very little is known about his life, and the time of his death is uncertain. The only fixed date which we have is the embassy to Caligula (A.D. 40), and he lived for at least some time after this. He is mentioned by Jerome (*de vir. ill.* 11), who says he was born of a priestly family; but Eusebius knows nothing of this, and there is probably no truth in the statement. He is mentioned also by Josephus in his *Ant.* XVIII. 8. 1. He was a Jewish philosopher, thoroughly imbued with the Greek spirit, who strove to unite Jewish beliefs with Greek culture, and exerted immense influence upon the thought of subsequent ages, especially upon Christian theology. His works (Biblical, historical, philosophical,

[1] Compare Col. i. 6. That Christianity had already spread over the whole world at this time is, of course, an exaggeration; but the statement is not a mere rhetorical flourish; it was believed as a historical fact. This conception arose originally out of the idea that the second coming of Christ was near, and the whole world must know of him before his coming. The tradition that the apostles preached in all parts of the world is to be traced back to the same cause.
[2] Ps. xix. 4.   [3] See Acts x. 1 sq.
[4] See Acts xi. 20. The Textus Receptus of the New Testament reads at this point Ἑλληνιστάς, a reading which is strongly supported by external testimony and adopted by Westcott and Hort. But the internal evidence seems to demand Ἑλληνας, and this reading is found in some of the oldest versions and in a few MSS., and is adopted by most modern critics, including Tischendorf. Eusebius is a witness for the latter reading. He takes the word Ἑλληνας in a broad sense to indicate all that are not Jews, as is clear from his insertion of the ἄλλων, "*other* Greeks," after speaking of Cornelius, who was not a Greek, but a Roman. Closs accordingly translates *Nichtjuden*, and Stigloher *Heiden*.   [5] See Acts xi. 22 sqq.
[6] See Acts xi. 26. This name was first given to the disciples by the heathen of Antioch, not by the Jews, to whom the word "Christ" meant too much; nor by the disciples themselves, for the word seldom appears in the New Testament, and nowhere in the mouth of a disciple. The word χριστιανός has a Latin termination, but this does not prove that it was invented by Romans, for Latinisms were

a man most celebrated not only among many of our own, but also among many scholars without the Church. He was a Hebrew by birth, but was inferior to none of those who held high dignities in Alexandria. How exceedingly he labored in the Scriptures and in the studies of his nation is plain to all from the work which he has done. How familiar he was with philosophy and with the liberal studies of foreign nations, it is not necessary to say, since he is reported to have surpassed all his contemporaries in the study of Platonic and Pythagorean philosophy, to which he particularly devoted his attention.[9]

CHAPTER V.

Philo's Embassy to Caius in Behalf of the Jews.

1   Philo has given us an account, in five books, of the misfortunes of the Jews under Caius.[1] He recounts at the same time the madness of Caius: how he called himself a god, and performed as emperor innumerable acts of tyranny; and he describes further the miseries of the Jews under him, and gives a report of the embassy upon which he himself was sent to Rome in behalf of his fellow-countrymen in Alexandria;[2] how when he appeared before

Caius in behalf of the laws of his fathers he received nothing but laughter and ridicule, and almost incurred the risk of his life. Jose- 2 phus also makes mention of these things in the eighteenth book of his Antiquities, in the following words:[3] "A sedition having arisen in Alexandria between the Jews that dwell there and the Greeks,[4] three deputies were chosen from each faction and went to Caius. One 3 of the Alexandrian deputies was Apion,[5] who uttered many slanders against the Jews; among other things saying that they neglected the honors due to Cæsar. For while all other subjects of Rome erected altars and temples to Caius, and in all other respects treated him just as they did the gods, they alone considered it disgraceful to honor him with statues and to swear by his name. And when Apion 4 had uttered many severe charges by which he hoped that Caius would be aroused, as indeed was likely, Philo, the chief of the Jewish embassy, a man celebrated in every respect, a brother of Alexander the Alabarch,[6] and not unskilled in philosophy, was prepared to enter

their side, followed the example of the Greeks, sending an embassy for their own defense, with Philo at its head. The result was as Eusebius relates, and the Jews were left in a worse condition than before, from which, however, they were speedily relieved by the death of Caius. Claudius, who succeeded Caius, restored to them for a time religious freedom and all the rights which they had hitherto enjoyed.

[3] Josephus, *Ant.* XVIII. 8. 1.

[4] This sedition, mentioned above, began in 38 A.D., soon after the accession of Caius. The Jews, since the time of Alexander the Great, when they had come in great numbers to the newly founded city, Alexandria, had enjoyed with occasional interruptions high favor there, and were among the most influential inhabitants. They possessed all the rights of citizenship and stood upon an equality with their neighbors in all respects. When Alexandria fell into the hands of the Romans, all the inhabitants, Jews as well as Greeks, were compelled to take a position subordinate to the conquerors, but their condition was not worse than that of their neighbors. They had always, however, been hated more or less by their fellow-citizens on account of their prosperity, which was the result of superior education and industry. This enmity came to a crisis under Caius, when the financial condition of Egypt was very bad, and the inhabitants felt themselves unusually burdened by the Roman demands. The old hatred for their more prosperous neighbors broke out afresh, and the terrible disturbance mentioned was the result. The refusal of the Jews to worship Caius as a God was made a pretext for attacking them, and it was this refusal which gained for them the hatred of Caius himself.

[5] Apion, chief of the Greek deputies, was a grammarian of Alexandria who had won great fame as a writer and Greek scholar. He seems to have been very unscrupulous and profligate, and was a bitter and persistent enemy of the Jews, whom he attacked very severely in at least two of his works—the *Egyptian History* and a special work *Against the Jews,* neither of which is extant. He was very unscrupulous in his attacks, inventing the most absurd and malicious falsehoods, which were quite generally believed, and were the means of spreading still more widely the common hatred of the Jews. Against him Josephus wrote his celebrated work, *Contra Apionem* (more fully *de antiquitate Judæorum contra Apionem*), which is still extant, and in the second book of which he exposes the ignorance and mendacity of Apion. In the Pseudo-Clementines he plays an important (but of course fictitious) role as an antagonist of the Gospel. The extant fragments of Apion's works are given, according to Lightfoot, in Müller's *Fragm. Hist. Græc.* II. 506 sq., and in Fabricius' *Bibl. Græc.* I. 503, and VII. 50. Compare Lightfoot's article in Smith and Wace's *Dict. of Christ. Biog.*

[6] The Alabarch was the chief magistrate of the Jews at Alexandria. Alexander was a very rich and influential Jew, who was widely known and held in high esteem. His son Tiberius Alexander was appointed procurator of Judea in 46 A.D., as successor of Cuspius Fadus. Philo thus belonged to a high and noble Jewish family. The accuracy of Josephus' statement that Philo was the brother of the Alabarch Alexander has been denied (e.g., by Ewald, *Gesch. des Jüdischen Volkes,* Vol. VI. p. 235), and the Alabarch has been assumed to have been the nephew of Philo, but this without sufficient ground (compare Schürer, *ibid.* p. 832, note 5).

---

practical, &c.) are very numerous, and probably the majority of them are still extant. For particulars, see chap. 18, below. For an excellent account of Philo, see Schürer, *Geschichte des Jüdischen Volkes im Zeitalter Jesu Christi;* zweite Auflage, Bd. II. p. 831 to 884 (Leipzig, 1886), where the chief literature upon the subject is given.

[9] Philo was thoroughly acquainted with Greek literature in all its departments, and shows great familiarity with it in his works. The influence of Plato upon him was very great, not only upon his philosophical system, but also upon his language; and all the Greek philosophers were studied and honored by him. He may, indeed, himself be called one of them. His system is eclectic, and contains not only Platonic, but also Pythagorean, and even Stoic, elements. Upon his doctrinal system, see especially Schürer, *ibid.* p. 836 sq.

[1] Upon this work, see Schürer, p. 855 sqq. According to him, the whole work embraced five books, and probably bore the title περὶ ἀρετῶν καὶ πρεσβείας πρὸς Γάιον. Eusebius cites what seems to be the same work under these two different titles in this and in the next chapter; and the conclusion that they were but one work is confirmed by the fact that Eusebius (in chap. 18) mentions the work under the title *On the Virtues,* which he says that Philo humorously prefixed to his work, describing the impiety of Caius. The omission of the title ἡ πρεσβεία in so complete a catalogue of Philo's works makes its identification with περὶ ἀρετῶν very probable. Of the five, only the third and fourth are extant, — εἰς Φλάκκον, *Adversus Flaccum,* and περὶ πρεσβείας πρὸς Γάιον, *de legatione ad Cajum* (found in Mangey's ed. Vol. II. p. 517–600). Book I., which is lost, contained, probably, a general introduction; Book II., which is also lost, contained an account of the oppression of the Jews during the time of Tiberius, by Sejanus in Rome, and by Pilate in Judea (see below, note 9); Book III., *Adversus Flaccum* (still extant), contains an account of the persecution of the Jews of Alexandria at the beginning of the reign of Caius; Book IV., *Legatio ad Cajum* (still extant), describes the sufferings which came upon the Jews as a result of Caius' command that divine honors should everywhere be paid him; Book V., the παλινῳδία (which is lost), contained an account of the change for the better in the Jews' condition through the death of Caius, and the edict of toleration published by Claudius. Upon the other works of Philo, see chap. 18, below.

[2] The occasion of this embassy was a terrible disturbance which had arisen between the Jews and Greeks in Alexandria, and had continued with occasional interruptions for more than a year. Much blood had been shed, and affairs were becoming constantly worse. All efforts to secure peace utterly failed, and finally, in 40 A.D., the Greeks dispatched an embassy to the emperor, hoping to secure from him an edict for the extermination of the Jews. The Jews, on

5 upon a defense in reply to his accusations. But Caius prevented him and ordered him to leave, and being very angry, it was plain that he meditated some severe measure against them. And Philo departed covered with insult, and told the Jews that were with him to be of good courage ; for while Caius was raging against them he was in fact already contending 6 with God." Thus far Josephus. And Philo himself, in the work *On the Embassy*[7] which he wrote, describes accurately and in detail the things which were done by him at that time. But I shall omit the most of them, and record only those things which will make clearly evident to the reader that the misfortunes of the Jews came upon them not long after their daring deeds against Christ and 7 on account of the same. And in the first place he relates that at Rome in the reign of Tiberius, Sejanus, who at that time enjoyed great influence with the emperor, made every effort to destroy the Jewish nation utterly ;[8] and that in Judea, Pilate, under whom the crimes against the Saviour were committed, attempted something contrary to the Jewish law in respect to the temple, which was at that time still standing in Jerusalem, and excited them to the greatest tumults.[9]

CHAPTER VI.

The Misfortunes which overwhelmed the Jews after their Presumption against Christ.

1 AFTER the death of Tiberius, Caius received the empire, and, besides innumerable other acts of tyranny against many people, he greatly afflicted especially the whole nation of the Jews.[1] These things we may learn briefly from the words of Philo, who writes as follows :[2] 2 "So great was the caprice of Caius in his conduct toward all, and especially toward the nation of the Jews. The latter he so bitterly hated that he appropriated to himself their places of worship in the other cities,[3] and beginning with Alexandria he filled them with images and statues of himself (for in permitting others to erect them he really erected them himself). The temple in the holy city, which had hitherto been left untouched, and had been regarded as an inviolable asylum, he altered and transformed into a temple of his own, that it might be called the temple of the visible Jupiter, the younger Caius."[4] Innumerable other terrible and 3 almost indescribable calamities which came upon the Jews in Alexandria during the reign of the same emperor, are recorded by the same author in a second work, to which he gave the title, *On the Virtues*.[5] With him agrees also Josephus, who likewise indicates that the misfortunes of the whole nation began with the time of Pilate, and with their daring crimes against the Saviour.[6] Hear what he says in 4 the second book of his Jewish War, where he writes as follows :[7] "Pilate being sent to Judea as procurator by Tiberius, secretly carried veiled images of the emperor, called ensigns,[8] to Jerusalem by night. The following day this caused the greatest disturbance among the Jews. For those who were near were confounded at the sight, beholding their laws, as it were, trampled under foot. For they allow no image to be set up in their city." Comparing 5 these things with the writings of the evangelists, you will see that it was not long before there came upon them the penalty for the exclamation which they had uttered under the same Pilate, when they cried out that they had no other king than Cæsar.[9] The same 6 writer further records that after this another calamity overtook them. He writes as follows :[10] "After this he stirred up another tumult by making use of the holy treasure, which is called Corban,[11] in the construction of an aqueduct

---

[7] See note 1, above. The work is cited here under the title ἡ πρεσβεία (*Legatio*).

[8] The Jews in Rome had enjoyed the favor of Augustus, and had increased greatly in numbers and influence there. They were first disturbed by Tiberius, who was very hostile to them, and to whose notice all the worst sides of Jewish character were brought by their enemies, especially by Sejanus, who had great influence with the emperor, and was moreover a deadly enemy of the Jews. The Jews were driven out of Rome, and suffered many acts of violence. After the death of Sejanus, which took place in 31 A.D., they were allowed to return, and their former rights were restored.

[9] Pilate proved himself exceedingly tyrannical, and was very obnoxious to the Jews, offending them greatly at different times during his administration by disregarding their religious scruples as no procurator before him had ventured to do. Soon after his accession he changed his quarters from Cæsarea to Jerusalem, and introduced the Roman standard into the Holy City. The result was a great tumult, and Pilate was forced to yield and withdraw the offensive ensigns (Josephus, *B. J.* II. 9. 2; see the next chapter). At another time he offended the Jews by hanging in his palace some shields inscribed with the names of heathen deities, which he removed only upon an express order of Tiberius (Philo, *ad Caium*, chap. 38). Again, he appropriated a part of the treasure of the temple to the construction of an aqueduct, which caused another terrible tumult which was quelled only after much bloodshed (Josephus, *B. J.* II. 9. 4; see the next chapter). For further particulars about Pilate, see chap. 7, below.

[1] Caius' hostility to the Jews resulted chiefly (as mentioned above, chap. 5, note 4) from their refusal to pay him divine honors, which he demanded from them as well as from his other subjects. His demands had caused terrible disturbances in Alexandria; and in Jerusalem, where he commanded the temple to be devoted to his worship, the tumult was very great and was quieted only by the yielding of the emperor, who was induced to give up his demands by the request of Agrippa, who was then at Rome and in high favor with him. Whether the Jews suffered in the same way in Rome we do not know, but it is probable that the emperor endeavored to carry out the same plan there as elsewhere.

[2] Philo, *Legat. ad Caium*, 43.

[3] ἐν ταῖς ἄλλαις πόλεσι. The reason for the use of the word "other" is not quite clear, though Philo perhaps means all the cities except Jerusalem, which he mentions a little below.

[4] "'Caius the younger,' to distinguish him from Julius Cæsar who bore the name Caius, and who was also deified" (Valesius).

[5] This work is probably the same as that mentioned in the beginning of chap. 5. (See chap. 5, note 1.) The work seems to have borne two titles ἡ πρεσβεία and περὶ ἀρετῶν. See Schürer, *ibid.* p. 859, who considers the δευτέρῳ here the addition of a copyist, who could not reconcile the two different titles given by Eusebius.

[6] This is rather an unwarranted assumption on the part of Eusebius, as Josephus is very far from intimating that the calamities of the nation were a consequence of their crimes against our Saviour.

[7] Josephus, *B. J.* II. 9. 2.   [9] John xix. 15.

[8] σημαίαι καλοῦνται.   [10] Josephus, *B. J.* II. 9. 4.

[11] Heb. קָרְבָּן ; Greek κορβᾶν and κορβανᾶς. The word denoted

7   three hundred stadia in length.[12] The multitude were greatly displeased at it, and when Pilate was in Jerusalem they surrounded his tribunal and gave utterance to loud complaints. But he, anticipating the tumult, had distributed through the crowd armed soldiers disguised in citizen's clothing, forbidding them to use the sword, but commanding them to strike with clubs those who should make an outcry. To them he now gave the preconcerted signal from the tribunal. And the Jews being beaten, many of them perished in consequence of the blows, while many others were trampled under foot by their own countrymen in their flight, and thus lost their lives. But the multitude, overawed by the fate of those who

8   were slain, held their peace." In addition to these the same author records [13] many other tumults which were stirred up in Jerusalem itself, and shows that from that time seditions and wars and mischievous plots followed each other in quick succession, and never ceased in the city and in all Judea until finally the siege of Vespasian overwhelmed them. Thus the divine vengeance overtook the Jews for the crimes which they dared to commit against Christ.

CHAPTER VII.

Pilate's Suicide.

IT is worthy of note that Pilate himself, who was governor in the time of our Saviour, is reported to have fallen into such misfortunes under Caius, whose times we are recording, that he was forced to become his own murderer and executioner ; [1] and thus divine vengeance, as it seems, was not long in overtaking him. This is stated

by those Greek historians who have recorded the Olympiads, together with the respective events which have taken place in each period.[2]

CHAPTER VIII.

The Famine which took Place in the Reign of Claudius.

CAIUS had held the power not quite four   1
years,[1] when he was succeeded by the emperor Claudius. Under him the world was visited with a famine,[2] which writers that are entire strangers to our religion have recorded in their histories.[3] And thus the prediction of Agabus recorded in the Acts of the Apostles,[4] according to which the whole world was to be visited by a famine, received its fulfillment. And   2
Luke, in the Acts, after mentioning the famine in the time of Claudius, and stating that the brethren of Antioch, each according to his ability, sent to the brethren of Judea by the hands of Paul and Barnabas,[5] adds the following account.

CHAPTER IX.

The Martyrdom of James the Apostle.

" [1] Now about that time " (it is clear that   1
he means the time of Claudius) " Herod the King [2] stretched forth his hands to vex certain of the Church. And he killed James the brother of John with the sword." And   2
concerning this James, Clement, in the seventh book of his Hypotyposes,[3] relates a story

---

originally any offering to God, especially an offering in fulfillment of a vow. The form κορβανᾶς, which Josephus has employed here, was used to denote the sacred treasure or the treasury itself. In Matt. xxvii. 6, the only place where this form of the word occurs in the New Testament, it is used with the latter meaning. Upon this act of Pilate's, see above, chap. 5, note 9.

[12] Josephus, in *Ant.* XVIII. 3. 2, says that the aqueduct was 200 stadia long. In the passage which Eusebius quotes the number given is 400, according to the Greek MSS. of Josephus, though the old Latin translation agrees with Eusebius in reading 300. The situation of the aqueduct we do not know, though the remains of an ancient aqueduct have been found to the south of Jerusalem, and it is thought that this may have been the same. It is possible that Pilate did not construct a new aqueduct, but simply restored one that had been built in the time of Solomon. Schultz (*Jerusalem*, Berlin, 1845) suggests the number 40, supposing that the aqueduct began at Bethlehem, which is 40 stadia from Jerusalem.

[13] See *B. J.* II. 10, 12 sqq.

[1] Pilate's downfall occurred in the following manner. A leader of the Samaritans had promised to disclose the sacred treasures which Moses was reported to have concealed upon Mt. Gerizim, and the Samaritans came together in great numbers from all quarters. Pilate, supposing the gathering to be with rebellious purpose, sent troops against them and defeated them with great slaughter. The Samaritans complained to Vitellius, governor of Syria, who sent Pilate to Rome (36 A.D.) to answer the charges brought against him. Upon reaching Rome he found Tiberius dead and Caius upon the throne. He was unsuccessful in his attempt to defend himself, and, according to tradition, was banished to Vienne in Gaul, where a monument is still shown as Pilate's tomb. According to another tradition he committed suicide upon the mountain near Lake Lucerne, which bears his name.

[2] Eusebius, unfortunately, does not mention his authority in this case, and the end of Pilate is recorded by no Greek historians known to us. We are unable, therefore, to form a judgment as to the trustworthiness of the account.

[1] Caius ruled from March 16, A.D. 37, to Jan. 24, A.D. 41, and was succeeded by his uncle Claudius.

[2] Several famines occurred during the reign of Claudius (cf. Dion Cassius, LX. 11, Tacitus, *Annal.* XII. 13, and Eusebius, *Chron.*, year of Abr. 2070) in different parts of the empire, but no universal famine is recorded such as Eusebius speaks of. According to Josephus (*Ant.* XX. 2. 5 and 5. 2), a severe famine took place in Judea while Cuspius Fadus and Tiberius Alexander were successively procurators. Fadus was sent to Judea upon the death of Agrippa (44 A.D.), and Alexander was succeeded by Cumanus in 48 A.D. The exact date of Alexander's accession we do not know, but it took place probably about 45 or 46. This famine is without doubt the one referred to by Agabus in Acts xi. 28. The exact meaning of the word οἰκουμένη, in that passage, is a matter of dispute. Whether it refers simply to Palestine, or is used to indicate a succession of famines in different parts of the world, or is employed only in a rhetorical sense, it is impossible to say. Eusebius understands the word in its widest sense, and therefore assumes a universal famine; but he is mistaken in his assumption.

[3] The only non-Christian historians, so far as we know, to record a famine during the reign of Claudius, are Dion Cassius and Tacitus, who mention a famine in Rome, and Josephus, who speaks of the famine in Judea (see the previous note for the references). Eusebius, in his *Chron.*, mentions famines both in Greece and in Rome during this reign, but upon what authority we do not know. As already remarked, we have no extant account of a general famine at this time.

[4] Acts xi. 28.   [5] Acts xi. 29, 30.   [1] Acts xii. 1, 2.

[2] Herod Agrippa I.; see above, chap. 4, note 3.

[3] On Clement's *Hypotyposes*, see below, Bk. VI. chap. 13, note 3. This fragment is preserved by Eusebius alone. The account was probably received by Clement from oral tradition. He had a great store of such traditions of the apostles and their immediate fol-

which is worthy of mention; telling it as he received it from those who had lived before him. He says that the one who led James to the judgment-seat, when he saw him bearing his testimony, was moved, and confessed that he
3 was himself also a Christian. They were both therefore, he says, led away together; and on the way he begged James to forgive him. And he, after considering a little, said, " Peace be with thee," and kissed him. And thus they were both beheaded at the same time.
4 And then, as the divine Scripture says,[4] Herod, upon the death of James, seeing that the deed pleased the Jews, attacked Peter also and committed him to prison, and would have slain him if he had not, by the divine appearance of an angel who came to him by night, been wonderfully released from his bonds, and thus liberated for the service of the Gospel. Such was the providence of God in respect to Peter.

CHAPTER X.

Agrippa, who was also called Herod, having persecuted the Apostles, immediately experienced the Divine Vengeance.

1 THE consequences of the king's undertaking against the apostles were not long deferred, but the avenging minister of divine justice overtook him immediately after his plots against them, as the Book of Acts records.[1] For when he had journeyed to Cæsarea, on a notable feast-day, clothed in a splendid and royal garment, he delivered an address to the people from a lofty throne in front of the tribunal. And when all the multitude applauded the speech, as if it were the voice of a god and not of a man, the Scripture relates that an angel of the Lord smote him, and being eaten of worms he
2 gave up the ghost.[2] We must admire the account of Josephus for its agreement with the divine Scriptures in regard to this wonderful event; for he clearly bears witness to the truth in the nineteenth book of his Antiquities, where he relates the wonder in the following
3 words:[3] " He had completed the third year of his reign over all Judea[4] when he came to Cæsarea, which was formerly called Strato's Tower.[5] There he held games in honor

of Cæsar, learning that this was a festival observed in behalf of Cæsar's safety.[6] At this festival was collected a great multitude of the highest and most honorable men in the province. And on the second day of the games
4 he proceeded to the theater at break of day, wearing a garment entirely of silver and of wonderful texture. And there the silver, illuminated by the reflection of the sun's earliest rays, shone marvelously, gleaming so brightly as to produce a sort of fear and terror in those who gazed upon him. And imme-
5 diately his flatterers, some from one place, others from another, raised up their voices in a way that was not for his good, calling him a god, and saying, ' Be thou merciful; if up to this time we have feared thee as a man, henceforth we confess that thou art superior to the nature of mortals.' The king did not re-
6 buke them, nor did he reject their impious flattery. But after a little, looking up, he saw an angel sitting above his head.[7] And this he quickly perceived would be the cause of evil as

---

lowers, — in how far true or false it is impossible to say; compare the story which he tells of John, quoted by Eusebius, Bk. III. chap. 23, below. This story of James is not intrinsically improbable. It may have been true, though external testimony for it is, of course, weak. The Latin legends concerning James' later labors in Spain and his burial in Compostella are entirely worthless. Epiphanius reports that he was unmarried, and lived the life of a Nazarite; but he gives no authority for his statement, and it is not improbable that the report originated through a confusion of this James with James the Just.
[1] See Acts xii. 19 sqq.   [2] Acts xii. 23.
[3] Josephus, *Ant.* XIX. 8. 2.
[4] 44 A.D. Agrippa began to reign over the whole kingdom in 41 A.D. See above, chap. 4, note 3.
[5] Cæsarea lay upon the Mediterranean Sea, northwest of Jerusa-

lem. In the time of Strabo there was simply a small town at this point, called " Strato's Tower "; but about 10 B.C. Herod the Great built the city of Cæsarea, which soon became the principal Roman city of Palestine, and was noted for its magnificence. It became, later, the seat of an important Christian school, and played quite a part in Church history. Eusebius himself was Bishop of Cæsarea. It was a city of importance, even in the time of the crusades, but is now a scene of utter desolation.
[6] The occasion of this festival is uncertain. Some have considered it the festival in honor of the birth of Claudius; others, a festival in honor of the return of Claudius from Britain. But neither of these suggestions is likely. It is more probable that the festival mentioned was the *Quinquennalia*, instituted by Herod the Great in honor of Augustus in 12 B.C. (see Josephus, *Ant.* XV. 8. 1; *B. J.* I. 21. 8), and celebrated regularly every five years. See Wieseler's *Chronologie des ap. Zeitalters*, p. 131 sqq., where this question is carefully discussed in connection with the date of Agrippa's death, which is fixed by Wieseler as Aug. 6, 44 A.D.
[7] The passage in Josephus reads: " But as he presently afterward looked up he saw an owl sitting on a certain rope over his head, and immediately understood that this bird was the messenger of evil tidings, as it had once been the messenger of good tidings to him." This conveys an entirely different sense, the owl being omitted in Eusebius. As a consequence most writers on Eusebius have made the gravest charges against him, accusing him of a willful perversion of the text of Josephus with the intention of producing a confirmation of the narrative of the Acts, in which the angel of God is spoken of, but in which no mention is made of an owl. The case certainly looks serious, but so severe an accusation — an accusation which impeaches the honesty of Eusebius in the most direct manner — should not be made except upon unanswerable grounds. Eusebius elsewhere shows himself to be a writer who, though not always critical, is at least honest in the use he makes of his materials. In this case, therefore, his general conduct ought to be taken into consideration, and he ought to be given the benefit of the doubt. Lightfoot, who defends his honesty, gives an explanation which appears to me sufficiently satisfactory. He says: " Doubtless also the omission of the owl in the account of Herod Agrippa's death was already in some texts of Josephus. The manner in which Eusebius deals with his very numerous quotations elsewhere, where we can test his honesty, is a sufficient vindication against this unjust charge." And in a note he adds: " It is not the *substitution* of an angel for an owl, as the case is not uncommonly stated. The result is produced mainly by the *omission* of some words in the text of Josephus, which runs thus: ἀνακύψας δ᾽ οὖν μετ᾽ ὀλίγον [τὸν βουβῶνα] τῆς ἑαυτοῦ κεφαλῆς ὑπὲρ καθεζόμενον εἶδεν [ἐπὶ σχοινίου τινός] ἄγγελόν [τε] τοῦτον εὐθὺς ἐνόησε κακῶν εἶναι, τὸν καί ποτε τῶν ἀγαθῶν γενόμενον. The words bracketed are omitted, and αἴτιον is added after εἶναι, so that the sentence runs, εἶδεν ἄγγελον τοῦτον εὐθὺς ἐνόησε κακῶν εἶναι αἴτιον κ.τ.λ. This being so, I do not feel at all sure that the change (by whomsoever made) was dictated by any disingenuous motive. A scribe unacquainted with Latin would stumble over τὸν βουβῶνα, which had a wholly different meaning and seems never to have been used of an owl in Greek; and he would alter the text in order to extract some sense out of it. In the previous mention of the bird (*Ant.* XVIII. 6, 7) Josephus, or his translator, gives it as a Latin name: βουβῶνα δὲ οἱ Ῥωμαῖοι τὸν ὄρνιν τοῦτον καλοῦσι. Möller (quoted by Bright, p. XLV.) calls this ' the one case '

it had once been the cause of good fortune,[8] and he was smitten with a heart-piercing pain.

7 And straightway distress, beginning with the greatest violence, seized his bowels. And looking upon his friends he said, 'I, your god, am now commanded to depart this life; and fate thus on the spot disproves the lying words you have just uttered concerning me. He who has been called immortal by you is now led away to die; but our destiny must be accepted as God has determined it. For we have passed our life by no means ingloriously, but in that splendor

8 which is pronounced happiness.'[9] And when he had said this he labored with an increase of pain. He was accordingly carried in haste to the palace, while the report spread among all that the king would undoubtedly soon die. But the multitude, with their wives and children, sitting on sackcloth after the custom of their fathers, implored God in behalf of the king, and every place was filled with lamentation and tears.[10] And the king as he lay in a lofty chamber, and saw them below lying prostrate on the ground, could not refrain from weeping himself. And after suffering continually

9 for five days with pain in the bowels, he departed this life, in the fifty-fourth year of his age, and in the seventh year of his reign.[11] Four years he ruled under the Emperor Caius — three of them over the tetrarchy of Philip, to which was added in the fourth year that of Herod[12] — and three years during the reign of the Emperor Claudius."

I marvel greatly that Josephus, in these

10 things as well as in others, so fully agrees with the divine Scriptures. But if there should seem to any one to be a disagreement in respect to the name of the king, the time at least and the events show that the same person is meant, whether the change of name has been caused by the error of a copyist, or is due to the fact that he, like so many, bore two names.[13]

CHAPTER XI.

The Impostor Theudas and his Followers.

LUKE, in the Acts, introduces Gamaliel

1 as saying, at the consultation which was held concerning the apostles, that at the time referred to,[1] "rose up Theudas boasting himself to be somebody; who was slain; and all, as many as obeyed him, were scattered."[2] Let us therefore add the account of Josephus concerning this man. He records in the work mentioned just above, the following circumstances:[3] "While Fadus was procurator of Judea[4] a

2 certain impostor called Theudas[5] persuaded

---

in which, so far as he recollects, 'a sinceritatis via paululum deflexit noster'; and even here the indictment cannot be made good. The severe strictures against Eusebius, made e.g. by Alford on Acts xii. 21, are altogether unjustifiable" (Smith and Wace's Dict. of Christian Biog. II. p. 325). The Greek word βουβών means, according to Liddell and Scott, (1) the groin, (2) a swelling in the groin. The Latin word Bubo signifies "an owl," and the word is here directly transferred by Josephus from the Latin into Greek without any explanation. A scribe unacquainted with Latin might easily stumble at the word, as Lightfoot suggests. In Ant. XVIII. 6, 7, where the bird is mentioned, the name is, to be sure, explained; but the alteration at this point was made apparently by a copyist of Eusebius, not of Josephus, and therefore by one who had probably never seen that explanation.

Whiston in his translation of Josephus inserts a note to the following effect: "We have a mighty cry made here by some writers, as if the great Eusebius had on purpose falsified this account of Josephus, so as to make it agree with the parallel account in the Acts of the Apostles, because the present copies of his citation of it, Hist. Eccles. Bk. II. chap. 10, omit the words βουβῶνα . . . ἐπὶ σχοινίου, τινος, i.e. 'an owl . . . on a certain rope,' which Josephus' present copies retain, and only have the explanatory word ἀγγελον, or 'angel,' as if he meant that 'angel of the Lord' which St. Luke mentions as smiting Herod, Acts xii. 23, and not that owl, which Josephus called 'an angel or messenger, formerly of good but now of bad news,' to Agrippa. This accusation is a somewhat strange one in the case of the great Eusebius, who is known to have so accurately and faithfully produced a vast number of other ancient records and particularly not a few out of our Josephus also, without any suspicion of prevarication. Now, not to allege how uncertain we are, whether Josephus' and Eusebius' copies of the fourth century were just like the present in this clause, which we have no distinct evidence of, the following words preserved still in Eusebius will not admit of any such exposition. 'This [bird] (says Eusebius) Agrippa presently perceived to be the cause of ill fortune, as it was once of good fortune'; which can belong only to that bird the 'owl,' which, as it had formerly foreboded his happy deliverance from imprisonment, Ant. XVIII. 6. 7, so was it then foretold to prove afterward the unhappy forewarner of his death in five days' time. If the improper word αἴτιον, or 'cause,' be changed for Josephus' proper word ἀγγελον, 'angel,' or 'messenger,' and the foregoing words, βουβῶνα ἐπὶ σχοινίου τινος, be inserted, Eusebius' text will truly represent that in Josephus."

[8] Josephus (Ant. XVIII. 6. 7) records that while Agrippa was in chains — having been condemned to imprisonment by Tiberius — an owl made its appearance and perched upon a tree near him. A fellow-prisoner interpreted the event as a good omen, prophesying that Agrippa would soon be released from his bonds and become king, but that the same bird would appear to him again five days before his death. Tiberius died in the following year, and the events prophesied came to pass. The story was apparently implicitly believed by Josephus, who relates it in good faith.

[9] The text of Josephus, as well as the majority of the MSS. of Eusebius, followed by Valesius, Stroth, Burton, and Schwegler, read ἐπὶ τῆς μακαριζομένης λαμπρότητος, which I have adopted in preference to the reading of Heinichen, who follows a few good MSS. in substituting μακαριότητος for λαμπρότητος.

[10] This shows the success with which Agrippa had courted the favor of the Jews. A far different feeling was shown at his death from that exhibited at the death of his grandfather, Herod the Great.

---

[11] He was born in 10 B.C., and began to reign as successor of Philip and Lysanias in 37 A.D. See above, chap. 4, note 3.

[12] Herod Antipas.

[13] Luke always calls the king, Herod, which was the family name, while Josephus calls him by his given name Agrippa. He is known to us under the name of Herod Agrippa I. It seems strange that Eusebius should not have known that he bore the two names, Herod Agrippa, instead of expressing doubt in the matter, as he does. In the heading of the chapter he gives the king both names, without intimating that he entertained any uncertainty in the matter.

[1] κατὰ τὸν δηλούμενον χρόνον, i.e. about the time of Agrippa's death. But Luke writes πρὸ γὰρ τούτων τῶν ἡμερῶν, "Before these days."

[2] Acts v. 36.   [3] Josephus, Ant. XX. 5. 1.

[4] About 44 A.D. See above, chap. 8, note 2.

[5] There is a chronological difficulty in connection with this Theudas which has caused much dispute. The Theudas mentioned by Josephus arose in the time of Claudius; but the Theudas referred to by Gamaliel in the Acts must have lived many years before that. Various solutions of greater or less plausibility have been offered, almost any one of which is possible, and abundantly sufficient to account for the alleged discrepancy, though none can be proved to be true. Compare Wieseler's Chron. des ap. Zeitalters, p. 138, note 1; Ewald's Gesch. des Jüdischen Volkes, Bd. VI. p. 532; Jost's Gesch. der Israeliten, Bd. II. Anhang, p. 86; and the various commentaries on the Acts in loco.

A question of more importance for us, in the present instance, is as to Eusebius' conduct in the case. He identifies the Theudas of Luke with the Theudas of Josephus, — an identification which is impossible, if both accounts are accepted as trustworthy. Eusebius has consequently been accused of an intentional perversion of facts for the sake of promoting the credibility of Luke's accounts. But a protest must again be entered against such grave imputations upon the honesty of Eusebius. A man with a very small allowance of common sense would certainly not have been so foolish as to consciously involve himself in such a glaring anachronism — an anacha very great multitude to take their possessions and follow him to the river Jordan. For he said that he was a prophet, and that the river should be divided at his command, and afford them an easy passage. And with these 3 words he deceived many. But Fadus did not permit them to enjoy their folly, but sent a troop of horsemen against them, who fell upon them unexpectedly and slew many of them and took many others alive, while they took Theudas himself captive, and cut off his head and carried it to Jerusalem." Besides this he also makes mention of the famine, which took place in the reign of Claudius, in the following words.

CHAPTER XII.

Helen, the Queen of the Osrhœnians.

1　　[1]"And at this time[2] it came to pass that the great famine[3] took place in Judea, in which the queen Helen,[4] having purchased grain from Egypt with large sums, distributed it to the needy."

2　　You will find this statement also in agreement with the Acts of the Apostles, where it is said that the disciples at Antioch, " each according to his ability, determined to send relief to the brethren that dwelt in Judea ; which also they did, and sent it to the elders by 3 the hands of Barnabas and Paul."[5] But splendid monuments[6] of this Helen, of whom the historian has made mention, are still shown in the suburbs of the city which is now called Ælia.[7] But she is said to have been queen of the Adiabeni.[8]

---

[1] Josephus, *Ant.* XX. 5. 2.

[2] In the times of these procurators, Cuspius Fadus and Tiberius Alexander

[3] Josephus had already mentioned this famine in the same book of his *Ant.*, chap. 2, § 5.

[4] Josephus gives an extensive account of this Helen and of her son Izates in the *Ant.* XX. 2. Helen was the wife of the king Monabazus of Adiabene, and the mother of Izates, his successor. Both Izates and Helen embraced the Jewish religion, and the latter happening to come to Jerusalem in the time of the famine, did a great deal to relieve the distress, and was seconded in her benefactions by her son. After their death the bones of both mother and son were brought to Jerusalem and buried just outside of the walls, where Helen had erected three pyramids (Jos. *Ant.* XX. 4. 3).

[5] Acts xi. 29, 30. The passage in Acts has Saul instead of Paul. But the change made by Eusebius is a very natural one.

[6] " Pausanias (*in Arcadicis*) speaks of these great monuments of Helen and compares them to the tomb of Mausolus. Jerome, too, testifies that they were standing in his time. Helen had besides a palace in Jerusalem " (Stroth).

[7] Ælia was the heathen city built on the site of Jerusalem by Hadrian (see below, Bk. IV. chap. 6).

CHAPTER XIII.

Simon Magus.[1]

But faith in our Saviour and Lord Jesus 1 Christ having now been diffused among all men,[2] the enemy of man's salvation contrived a plan for seizing the imperial city for himself. He conducted thither the above-mentioned Simon,[3] aided him in his deceitful arts, led many of the inhabitants of Rome astray, and thus brought them into his own power. This is 2 stated by Justin,[4] one of our distinguished writers who lived not long after the time of the apostles. Concerning him I shall speak in the proper place.[5] Take and read the work of this

---

[8] Adiabene was probably a small province lying between the Tigris, Lycus, and the Gordiæan Mountains (see Dion Cassius, LXVIII.), but before the time of Pliny, according to Vaux (in Smith's *Dict. of Greek and Roman Geography*), the word was used in a wider sense to indicate Assyria in general (see Pliny, *H. N.* VI. 12, and Ammianus Marcellinus, XXIII. 6). Izates was king of Adiabene in the narrower sense.

[1] It is justly remarked by Reuterdahl that no chapters of Eusebius' *History* are so imperfect and unsatisfactory as those which relate to heresies, but that this is to be ascribed more to the age than to the author. A right understanding of heresies and an appreciation of any truth which they might contain was utterly impossible to men who looked upon heresy as the work of the devil, and all heretics as his chosen tools. Eusebius has been condemned by some, because he gives his information about heretics only from second hand, and quotes none of them directly; but it must be remembered that this method was by no means peculiar to Eusebius, and, moreover, it is highly probable that he did not have access to any of their works. The accounts of the heretics given by Irenæus, Hippolytus, and others would of course be preserved, but the writings of heretics themselves would be piously excluded as completely as possible from all Christian libraries, and the knowledge of them cannot have remained long in the Church. The sources upon which we have to rely at the present day for a knowledge of these heresies furnish an illustration of this. We know them almost solely through their enemies, and Eusebius knew them in the same way and very likely for the same reason.　　[2] See chap. 3, note 1.

[3] Simon Magus, of whom mention is first made in Acts viii. 9 sqq. (quoted above, in chap. 1), played a very prominent rôle in early Church history. His life has been so greatly embellished with legends that it is very difficult to extract a trustworthy account of him. Indeed the Tübingen school, as well as some other modern critics, have denied altogether the existence of such a personage, and have resolved the account of him into a Jewish Christian fiction produced in hostility to the apostle Paul, who under the mask of Simon was attacked as the real heretic. But this identification of Paul and Simon rests upon a very slender foundation, as many passages can be adduced in which the two are expressly distinguished, and indeed the thought of identifying Paul and Simon seems never to have occurred to the writer of the *Recognitions*. The most that can be said is that the author of the *Homilies* gives, and without doubt purposely, some Pauline traits to his picture of Simon, but this does not imply that he makes Simon no more than a mask for Paul (cf. the words of Salmon in his article, *Clementine Literature*, in the *Dict. of Christ. Biog.* Vol. I. p. 576). The original of Simon then is not to be found in Paul. The third century fiction is based upon a real historic person whose actual existence must be assumed to account for the common notices of him in the Acts and in Justin Martyr, as well as the common tradition of him among all parties in the Church. Salmon considers Simon of Gitton — the basis of the account of Justin Martyr and of all the later Simon legends — a second century Gnostic distinct from the Simon mentioned in the Acts (see his excellent article *Simon Magus*, in the *Dict. of Christ. Biog.* IV. p. 681 sqq.). In the Pseudo-Clementines Simon is represented as traveling widely and spreading his errors in all directions, while Peter follows him for the purpose of exposing his impostures, and refutes him repeatedly in public disputations, until at length he conquers him completely in Rome, and Simon ends his life by suicide. His death, as well as his life, is recorded in various conflicting and fabulous traditions (see note 9, below). For ancient accounts of Simon, see Justin Martyr, *Apol.* I. 26 and 56 and *Dial. c. Trypho.* CXX.: the Pseudo-Clementine *Homilies* and *Recognitions ;* Irenæus, I. 23; Hippolytus, VI. 2 sq.; Tertullian's *Apology, On Idolatry, On the Soul*, etc.; *Apost. Constitutions*, VII. 7 sq.; Arnobius, *Adv. Gentes*, II. 12, &c.; *Acts of the Holy Apostles Peter and Paul* (*Ante-Nicene Fathers*, Am. ed. VIII. p. 477 sqq.); Epiphanius, *Hær.* XXI.: and Theodoret, *Hær. Fab.* I. 1. See also Lipsius, article in Schinkel's *Bibel-Lexicon*, Vol. V.

[4] In his *Apology*, I. 26, 56.

[5] In Bk. IV. chaps. 8, 11, 16-18.

---

ronism which every reader had the means of exposing — for the sake of making a point in confirmation of the narrative of Luke. Had he been conscious of the discrepancy, he would certainly have endeavored to reconcile the two accounts, and it would not have required a great amount of ingenuity or research to discover in the pages of Josephus himself a sufficiently plausible reconciliation. The only reasonable explanation of Eusebius' anachronism is his carelessness, which caused him to fall into many blunders as bad as the present, especially in questions of chronology. He read, in the Acts, of Theudas; he read, in Josephus, of a similar character of the same name; he identified the two hastily, and without a thought of any chronological difficulty in the case. He quotes the passage from the Acts very freely, and possibly without recollecting that it occurs several chapters before the account of the famine and of the other events which happened in the time of Claudius.

man, who in the first Apology[6] which he addressed
to Antonine in behalf of our religion writes
3   as follows:[7] "And after the ascension of
the Lord into heaven the demons put forward certain men who said they were gods,
and who were not only allowed by you to go
unpersecuted, but were even deemed worthy of
honors. One of them was Simon, a Samaritan
of the village of Gitto,[8] who in the reign of
Claudius Cæsar[9] performed in your imperial
city some mighty acts of magic by the art of
demons operating in him, and was considered
a god, and as a god was honored by you with a
statue, which was erected in the river Tiber,[10] between the two bridges, and bore this inscription in
the Latin tongue, *Simoni Deo Sancto*, that
4   is, *To Simon the Holy God*.[11] And nearly
all the Samaritans and a few even of other
nations confess and worship him as the first
God. And there went around with him at that
time a certain Helena[12] who had formerly been
a prostitute in Tyre of Phœnicia; and her they
call the first idea that proceeded from him."[13]

Justin relates these things, and Irenæus also   5
agrees with him in the first book of his work,
Against Heresies, where he gives an account of
the man[14] and of his profane and impure teaching. It would be superfluous to quote his account
here, for it is possible for those who wish to
know the origin and the lives and the false doctrines of each of the heresiarchs that have followed
him, as well as the customs practiced by them
all, to find them treated at length in the
above-mentioned work of Irenæus. We   6
have understood that Simon was the author
of all heresy.[15] From his time down to the
present those who have followed his heresy have
feigned the sober philosophy of the Christians,
which is celebrated among all on account of its
purity of life. But they nevertheless have embraced again the superstitions of idols, which
they seemed to have renounced; and they fall
down before pictures and images of Simon himself and of the above-mentioned Helena who
was with him; and they venture to worship
them with incense and sacrifices and libations. But those matters which they keep   7
more secret than these, in regard to which
they say that one upon first hearing them would
be astonished, and, to use one of the written
phrases in vogue among them, would be confounded,[16] are in truth full of amazing things,
and of madness and folly, being of such a sort
that it is impossible not only to commit them to
writing, but also for modest men even to utter
them with the lips on account of their excessive baseness and lewdness.[17] For what-   8
ever could be conceived of, viler than the
vilest thing — all that has been outdone by this
most abominable sect, which is composed of
those who make a sport of those miserable
females that are literally overwhelmed with all
kinds of vices.[18]

---

[6] On Justin's *Apology*, see below, Bk. IV. chap. 18, note 2.
[7] Justin's *Apology*, I. 26.
[8] Gitton was a village of Samaria, near Flavia Neapolis (the modern Nâblus), and is identified by Robinson with the present village
of Kuryet Jit (see Robinson's *Biblical Researches*, III. p. 144,
note). Some have doubted the accuracy of Justin's report, for the
reason that Josephus (*Ant.* XXII. 7. 2) mentions a magician named
Simon, of about the same date, who was born in Cyprus. There
was a town called Κίτιον in Cyprus, and it has been thought that
Justin may have mistaken this place for the Samaritan Gitton. But
even if we assume the identity of the two Simons, as many critics do,
it is less likely that Justin, a native of Samaria, was mistaken upon
a question concerning his own country, than that Josephus was.
Simon's activity may have extended to Cyprus, in which case Josephus might easily have mistaken his birthplace.
[9] Justin here assigns Simon's visit to Rome to the reign of
Claudius (41–54 A.D.), as Irenæus also does. Other accounts assign it to the reign of Nero, but all differ as to the details of his
death; suicide, death from injuries received while trying to fly, voluntary burial in expectation of rising again on the third day, &c.,
are reported in different traditions. All, however, agree that he
visited Rome at some time or another.
[10] That is, on the island which lies in the middle of the Tiber, a
short distance below the Vatican, and which now bears the name
Isola Tiberiana, or *di S. Sebastiano*.
[11] In 1574 a statue, bearing the inscription *Semoni Sanco deo
fidio*, &c., was found in the place described by Justin Martyr, but
this statue was erected to the Sabine divinity Semo Sancus. It is
therefore highly probable that Justin mistook this statue for a statue
of Simon Magus. This is now the commonly accepted view, though
the translator of Justin Martyr in the *Ante-Nicene Fathers* ventures to dispute it (see the Am. ed. Vol. I. p. 171, note). The report
is given a second time by Justin in his *Apol.* 56, and also by Irenæus, I. 23. 1 (who, however, simply says "It is said," and may
have drawn his knowledge only from Justin Martyr) and by Tertullian, *Apol.* chap. 13. The last named is in general a poor authority,
even if he be independent of Justin at this point, which is not probable. Hippolytus, who lived at Rome, and who gives us an account
of the death of Simon (Bk. VII. chap. 15), says nothing about the
statue, and his silence is a strong argument against it.
[12] A similar story is told of this Helen by Irenæus, I. 23; by
Hippolytus, VI. 15 (who adds some important particulars); by
Tertullian, *De Anima*, 34; by Epiphanius, *Hær.* 21; and by Theodoret, *Hær. Fab.* I. 1; compare also Origen, *Contra Celsum*, V. 62.
Simon taught that this Helen was the first conception of his mind,
the mother of all things, the impersonation of the divine intelligence,
&c. The Simonians, according to Irenæus (I. 23. 4), and Hippolytus
(VI. 15; see chap. 14, note 8), had images of Simon and Helen whom
they honored as Jupiter and Minerva. Simon's doctrines and practice, as recorded by these Fathers, show some of the general conceptions common to all the Gnostic systems, but exhibit a crude and
undeveloped form of Gnosticism. Upon Helen, see Salmon, in
the *Dict. of Christ. Biog.* II. p. 880 sq., and all the works upon
Simon Magus.
[13] This conception of the idea (ἔννοια) is thoroughly Gnostic,
and plays an important part in all the Gnostic systems. Most of
these systems had a dualistic element recognizing the δύναμις and
the ἔννοια as the original principles from whose union all beings

emanated. These general conceptions appeared in all varieties of
forms in the different systems.   [14] Irenæus *adv. Hær.* I. 23.
[15] See note 3, above.   [16] θαμβωθήσεσθαι.
[17] This was the general opinion of the early Fathers, all of whom
picture Gnosticism as a wilderness of absurdities and nonsense; and
Irenæus, Hippolytus, and others undertake its refutation only for the
purpose of exposing these absurdities. It is treated by none of them
as an intelligent speculation with a foundation in reason or sense.
This thorough misunderstanding of the nature and aim of Gnosticism
has been perpetuated in our day by many writers upon the subject.
Neander was the first to attempt a thoroughly philosophical treatment of it (in his *Genetische Entwickelung d. gnost. Systeme*, Berlin, 1818), and since that time the subject has been treated intelligently and discriminatingly by many writers, e.g. Baur, Lipsius,
Lightfoot, Salmon, and especially Harnack, who has grasped the
true principle of Gnosticism perhaps more fully than any one else.
See his *Dogmengeschichte*, I. p. 158 sqq.
[18] This was true of the Simonians, who were very immoral and
licentious, and of some other Gnostic sects, as e.g. the Ophites, the
Carpocratians, &c. But many of the Gnostics, e.g. Marcion (but
see below, IV. 11, note 24), Saturninus, Tatian, &c., went to the opposite extreme, teaching a rigid and gloomy asceticism. Underlying
both of these extremes we perceive the same principle — a dualism
of matter and spirit, therefore of body and mind — the former considered as the work of the devil, and therefore to be despised and
abused; the latter as divine, and therefore to be honored above all
else. The abhorrence of the body, and of matter and nature in general, logically led to one of the two opposite results, asceticism or
antinomianism, according to the character and instincts of the person himself. See Schaff, *Church Hist.* II. p. 457 sqq. The Fathers,
in their hatred of all forms of heresy, naturally saw no good in any

CHAPTER XIV.

The Preaching of the Apostle Peter in Rome.

1 THE evil power,[1] who hates all that is good and plots against the salvation of men, constituted Simon at that time the father and author of such wickedness,[2] as if to make him a mighty antagonist of the great, inspired 2 apostles of our Saviour. For that divine and celestial grace which co-operates with its ministers, by their appearance and presence, quickly extinguished the kindled flame of evil, and humbled and cast down through them "every high thing that exalted itself against the 3 knowledge of God."[3] Wherefore neither the conspiracy of Simon nor that of any of the others who arose at that period could accomplish anything in those apostolic times. For everything was conquered and subdued by the splendors of the truth and by the divine word itself which had but lately begun to shine from heaven upon men, and which was then flourishing upon earth, and dwelling in the apos-4 tles themselves. Immediately[4] the above-mentioned impostor was smitten in the eyes of his mind by a divine and miraculous flash, and after the evil deeds done by him had been first detected by the apostle Peter in Judea,[5] he fled and made a great journey across the sea from the East to the West, thinking that only thus could he live according to his mind. 5 And coming to the city of Rome,[6] by the mighty co-operation of that power which was lying in wait there, he was in a short time so successful in his undertaking that those who dwelt there honored him as a god by the 6 erection of a statue.[7] But this did not last long. For immediately, during the reign of Claudius, the all-good and gracious Providence, which watches over all things, led Peter, that strongest and greatest of the apostles, and the one who on account of his virtue was the

speaker for all the others, to Rome[8] against this great corrupter of life. He like a noble commander of God, clad in divine armor, carried the costly merchandise of the light of the understanding from the East to those who dwelt in the West, proclaiming the light itself, and the word which brings salvation to souls, and preaching the kingdom of heaven.[9]

CHAPTER XV.

The Gospel according to Mark.

AND thus when the divine word had 1 made its home among them,[1] the power of

[1] See the previous chapter, note 1.

[2] See chap. 1, note 25.   [3] 2 Cor. x. 5.

[4] The significance of the word "immediately" as employed here is somewhat dark. There is no event described in the preceding context with which it can be connected. I am tempted to think that Eusebius may have been using at this point some unknown source, and that the word "immediately" refers to an encounter which Simon had had with Peter (perhaps his Cæsarean encounter, mentioned in the Clementines), of which an account was given in the document employed by Eusebius. The figure employed here is most remarkable.

[5] Acts viii. 9 sqq. This occurred in Samaria, not in Judea proper, but Eusebius evidently uses the word "Judea" in a wide sense, to indicate the Roman province of Judea, which included also Samaria. It is not impossible, especially if Eusebius is quoting here from a written source, that some other encounter of Simon and Peter is referred to. Such a one e.g. as is mentioned in the *Apostolic Constitutions*, VI. 8.

[6] Rome was a great gathering place of heretics and schismatics. They were all attracted thither by the opportunities for propagandism which the city afforded, and therefore Eusebius, with his transcendental conception of heresy, naturally makes it the especial seat of the devil.

[7] See above, chap. 13, note 11.

[8] Upon the historic truth of Peter's visit to Rome, see below, chap. 25, note 7. Although we may accept it as certain that he did visit Rome, and that he met his death there, it is no less certain that he did not reach there until late in the reign of Nero. The tradition that he was for twenty-five years bishop of Rome is first recorded by Jerome (*de vir. ill.* c. 1), and since his time has been almost universally accepted in the Roman Catholic Church, though in recent years many more candid scholars of that communion acknowledge that so long an episcopate there is a fiction. The tradition undoubtedly took its rise from the statement of Justin Martyr (quoted in the previous chapter) that Simon Magus came to Rome during the reign of Claudius. Tradition, in the time of Eusebius, commonly connected the Roman visits of Simon and of Peter; and consequently Eusebius, accepting the earlier date for Simon's arrival in Rome, quite naturally assumed also the same date for Peter's arrival there, although Justin does not mention Peter in connection with Simon in the passage which Eusebius quotes. The assumption that Peter took up his residence in Rome during the reign of Claudius contradicts all that we know of Peter's later life from the New Testament and from other early writers. In 44 A.D. he was in Jerusalem (according to Acts xii. 3); in 51 he was again there (according to Acts xv.); and a little later in Antioch (according to Gal. i. 11 sq.). Moreover, at some time during his life he labored in various provinces in Asia Minor, as we learn from his first epistle, and probably wrote that epistle from Babylon on the Euphrates (see chap. 15, note 7). At any rate, he cannot have been in Rome when Paul wrote his epistle to the Romans (57 or 58 A.D.), for no mention is made of him among the brethren to whom greetings are sent. Nor can he have been there when Paul wrote from Rome during his captivity (61 or 62 to 63 or 64 A.D.). We have, in fact, no trace of him in Rome, except the extra-Biblical but well-founded tradition (see chap. 25, note 7) that he met his death there. We may assume, then, that he did not reach Rome at any rate until shortly before his death; that is, shortly before the summer of 64 A.D. As most of the accounts put Simon Magus' visit to Rome in the reign of Nero (see above, chap. 13, note 9), so they make him follow Peter thither (as he had followed him everywhere, opposing and attacking him), instead of precede him, as Eusebius does. Eusebius follows Justin in giving the earlier date for Simon's visit to Rome; but he goes beyond Justin in recording his encounter there with Peter, which neither Justin nor Irenæus mentions. The earlier date for Simon's visit is undoubtedly that given by the oldest tradition. Afterward, when Peter and Paul were so prominently connected with the reign of Nero, the visit of Simon was postponed to synchronize with the presence of the two apostles in Rome. A report of Simon's meeting with Peter in Rome is given first by Hippolytus (VI. 15); afterward by Arnobius (II. 12), who does not describe the meeting; by the *Ap. Const.*, the Clementine *Recognitions* and *Homilies*, and the *Acts of the Apostles Peter and Paul*. It is impossible to tell from what source Eusebius drew his information. Neither Justin, Irenæus, nor Tertullian mentions it. Hippolytus and Arnobius and the *App. Const.* give too much, as they give accounts of his death, which Eusebius does not follow. As to this, it might, however, be said that these accounts are so conflicting that Eusebius may have omitted them entirely, while yet recording the meeting. Still, if he had read Hippolytus, he could hardly have omitted entirely his interesting account. Arnobius and Tertullian, who wrote in Latin, he did not read, and the Clementines were probably too late for him; at any rate, they cannot have been the source of his account, which differs entirely from theirs. It is highly probable, therefore, that he followed Justin and Irenæus as far as they go, and that he recorded the meeting with Peter in Rome as a fact commonly accepted in his time, and one for which he needed no written authority; or it is possible that he had another source, unknown to us, as suggested above (note 4).

[9] A most amazing mixture of metaphors. This sentence furnishes an excellent illustration of Eusebius' rhetorical style.

[1] The origin of the Church at Rome is shrouded in mystery. Eusebius gives the tradition which rules in the Catholic Church, viz.: that Christianity was introduced into Rome by Peter, who

of them, and heretics were therefore indiscriminately accused of immorality and licentiousness in their worst forms.

Simon was quenched and immediately destroyed, together with the man himself.[2] And so greatly did the splendor of piety illumine the minds of Peter's hearers that they were not satisfied with hearing once only, and were not content with the unwritten teaching of the divine Gospel, but with all sorts of entreaties they besought Mark,[3] a follower of Peter, and the one whose Gospel is extant, that he would leave them a written monument of the doctrine which had been orally communicated to them. Nor did they cease until they had prevailed with the man, and had thus become the occasion of the written Gospel which bears the name of Mark.[4]

And they say that Peter, when he had **2** learned, through a revelation of the Spirit, of that which had been done, was pleased with the zeal of the men, and that the work obtained the sanction of his authority for the purpose of being used in the churches.[5] Clement in the eighth book of his Hypotyposes gives this account, and with him agrees the bishop of Hierapolis named Papias.[6] And Peter makes mention of Mark in his first epistle which they say that he wrote in Rome itself, as is indicated by him, when he calls the city, by a figure, Babylon, as he does in the following words : " The church that is at Babylon, elected together with you, saluteth you ; and so doth Marcus my son." [7]

CHAPTER XVI.

Mark first proclaimed Christianity to the Inhabitants of Egypt.

AND they say that this Mark was the first **1** that was sent to Egypt, and that he proclaimed the Gospel which he had written, and first established churches in Alexandria.[1] And the multitude of believers, both men **2** and women, that were collected there at the very outset, and lived lives of the most philosophical and excessive asceticism, was so great, that Philo thought it worth while to describe their pursuits, their meetings, their entertainments, and their whole manner of life." [2]

went there during the reign of Claudius. But this tradition is sufficiently disproved by history. The origin of the Church was due to unknown persons, though it is possible we may obtain a hint of them in the Andronicus and Junia of Romans xvi. 7, who are mentioned as apostles, and who were therefore, according to the usage of the word in Paul's writings, persons that introduced Christianity into a new place — missionaries proper, who did not work on others' ground.

[2] See chap. 12, note 9, and chap. 14, note 8.

[3] John Mark, son of Mary (Acts xii. 12), a sister of Barnabas (Col. iv. 10), was a companion of Paul and Barnabas in their missionary journeys, and afterward a companion of Barnabas alone (Acts xv. 39), and still later was with Paul again in Rome (Col. iv. 10 and Philemon 24), and with Peter when he wrote his first epistle (1 Pet. v. 13). For the later traditions concerning Mark, see the next chapter, note 1.

[4] That Mark wrote the second Gospel under the influence of Peter, or as a record of what he had heard from him, is the universal tradition of antiquity. Papias, in the famous and much-disputed passage (quoted by Eusebius, III. 39, below), is the first to record the tradition. Justin Martyr refers to Mark's Gospel under the name " Memoirs (ἀπομνημονεύματα) of Peter" (*Dial. c. Tryph.* 106; the translation in the *Ante-Nicene Fathers*, Am. Ed. Vol. I. p. 252, which refers the αὐτοῦ to Christ, is incorrect; compare Weiss, *N. T. Einleitung*, p. 44, note 4). Irenæus (*Adv. Hær.* III. 11. 1, quoted below, V. 8. 2), Tertullian (*Adv. Marcionem*, IV. 5), and Origen (quoted below, VI. 25) confirm the tradition, which is repeated over and over again by the Fathers.

The question as to the real authorship of our second Gospel, or rather as to its composition and its relation to Matthew and Luke, is a very difficult one. The relationship of the three synoptical Gospels was first discussed by Augustine (*De Consensu Evangelistarum*), who defended the traditional order, but made Mark dependent upon Matthew. This view prevailed until the beginning of the present century, when the problem was attacked anew, and since then it has been the crux of the literary criticism of the Bible. The three have been held to be dependent upon each other, and every possible order has found its advocates; a common source has been assumed for the three: the Hebrew Matthew, the *Gospel according to the Hebrews* (see Bk. III. chap. 25, note 24), our canonical Gospel of Mark, or an original Mark, resembling the present one; a number of fragmentary documents have been assumed; while others, finally, have admitted only oral tradition as the basis. According to Baur's tendency theory, Matthew (polemically Jewish-Christian) came first, followed by an original Luke (polemically Pauline-Christian), then by our Mark, which was based upon both and written in the interest of neutrality, and lastly by our present Luke, designed as a final irenicum. This view now finds few advocates. The whole matter is still unsettled, but criticism seems to be gradually converging toward a common ground type (or rather two independent types) for all three, while at the same time maintaining the relative independence of the three, one toward the other. What these ground types were, is a matter of still sharper dispute, although criticism is gradually drawing their larger features with more and more certainty and clearness. (The latest discussion upon the subject by Handmann, *das Hebräer-Evangelium*, makes the two types the " Ur-Marcus" and the *Gospel of the Hebrews*.) That in the last analysis, however, some space must still be left for floating tradition, or for documents irreducible to the one or two types, seems absolutely certain. For further information as to the state of discussion upon this intricate problem, see among recent works, especially Weiss, *Einleitung*, p. 473 sqq., Holtzmann, *Einleitung*, p. 328 sqq., and Schaff, *Ch. Hist.* I. 575 sqq., where the literature down to 1882 is given with great fullness. Conservative opinion puts the composition of all the synoptic Gospels before the destruction of Jerusalem (for the date of Luke, see III. 4, note 12); but the critical school, while throwing the original type back of that date, considers the composition of our present Gospels to have been the gradual work of years, assuming

that they were not finally crystallized into the form in which we have them before the second century.

[5] This mention of the " pleasure" of Peter, and the " authority" given by him to the work of Mark, contradicts the account of Clement to which Eusebius here appeals as his authority. In Bk. VI. chap. 14 he quotes from the *Hypotyposes* of Clement, a passage which must be identical with the one referred to in this place, for it is from the same work and the general account is the same; but there Clement says expressly, " which when Peter understood he neither directly hindered nor encouraged it."

[6] The passage from Papias is quoted below in Bk. III. chap. 39. Papias is a witness to the general fact that Mark wrote down what he had heard from Peter, but not (so far as he is extant) to the details of the account as given by Eusebius. Upon Papias himself, see Bk. III. chap. 39.

[7] 1 Pet. v. 13. Commentators are divided as to the place in which Peter wrote this epistle (compare Schaff's *Church Hist.* I. p. 744 sqq.). The interpretation given by Eusebius is the patristic and Roman Catholic opinion, and is maintained by many Protestant commentators. But on the other hand the literal use of the word " Babylon" is defended by a great number of the leading scholars of the present day. Compare Schaff, *N. T. Einleitung*, p. 433, note 1.

[1] That Mark labored in Egypt is stated also by Epiphanius (*Hær.* LI. 6), by Jerome (*de vir. ill.* 8), by Nicephorus (*H. E.* II. 43), and by the *Acta Barnabæ*, p. 26 (Tischendorf's *Acta Apost. Apocr.* p. 74), which were written probably in the third century. Eusebius gained his knowledge apparently from oral tradition, for he uses the formula, " they say" (φασὶν). In chap. 24, below, he says that Annianus succeeded Mark as a leader of the Alexandrian Church in the eighth year of Nero (62 A.D.), thus implying that Mark died in that year; and Jerome gives the same date for his death. But if the tradition that he wrote his Gospel in Rome under Peter (or after Peter's death, as the best tradition puts it, so e.g. Irenæus) be correct, then this date is hopelessly wrong. The varying traditions are at best very uncertain, and the whole career of Mark, so far as it is not recorded in the New Testament, is involved in obscurity.

[2] See the next chapter.

CHAPTER XVII.

Philo's Account of the Ascetics of Egypt.

1   It is also said that Philo in the reign of Claudius became acquainted at Rome with Peter, who was then preaching there.[1] Nor is this indeed improbable, for the work of which we have spoken, and which was composed by him some years later, clearly contains those rules of the Church which are even to this

2   day observed among us. And since he describes as accurately as possible the life of our ascetics, it is clear that he not only knew, but that he also approved, while he venerated and extolled, the apostolic men of his time, who were as it seems of the Hebrew race, and hence observed, after the manner of the Jews, the

3   most of the customs of the ancients. In the work to which he gave the title, *On a Contemplative Life or on Suppliants,*[2] after af-

firming in the first place that he will add to those things which he is about to relate nothing contrary to truth or of his own invention,[3] he says that these men were called Therapeutæ and the women that were with them Therapeutrides.[4] He then adds the reasons for such a name, explaining it from the fact that they applied remedies and healed the souls of those who came to them, by relieving them like physicians, of evil passions, or from the fact that they served and worshiped the Deity in purity and sincer-

4   ity. Whether Philo himself gave them this name, employing an epithet well suited to their mode of life, or whether the first of them really called themselves so in the beginning, since the name of Christians was not yet everywhere known, we need not discuss here.

5   He bears witness, however, that first of all they renounce their property. When they begin the philosophical[5] mode of life, he says, they give up their goods to their relatives, and then, renouncing all the cares of life, they go forth beyond the walls and dwell in lonely fields and gardens, knowing well that intercourse with people of a different character is unprofitable and harmful. They did this at that time, as seems probable, under the influence of a spirited and ardent faith, practicing in emulation the prophets' mode of life. For in the Acts of

6   the Apostles, a work universally acknowledged as authentic,[6] it is recorded that all the

---

[1] This tradition that Philo met Peter in Rome and formed an acquaintance with him is repeated by Jerome (*de vir. ill.* 11), and by Photius (*Cod.* 105), who even goes further, and says directly that Philo became a Christian. The tradition, however, must be regarded as quite worthless. It is absolutely certain from Philo's own works, and from the otherwise numerous traditions of antiquity that he never was a Christian, and aside from the report of Eusebius (for Jerome and Photius do not represent an independent tradition) there exists no hint of such a meeting between Peter and Philo; and when we realize that Philo was already an old man in the time of Caius (see above, chap. 4, note 8), and that Peter certainly did not reach Rome before the later years of Nero's reign, we may say that such a meeting as Eusebius records (only upon tradition, λόγος ἔχει is certainly not historical. Where Eusebius got the tradition we do not know. It may have been manufactured in the interest of the Philonic authorship of the *De vita contemplativa*, or it may have been a natural outgrowth of the ascription of that work to him, some such explanation suggesting itself to the reader of that work as necessary to explain Philo's supposed praise of Christian monks. Philo's visit to Rome during the reign of Caligula being a well-known historic fact, and Peter's visit to Rome during the reign of Claudius being assumed as likewise historic (see above, chap. 14, note 8), it was not difficult to suppose a meeting between them (the great Christian apostle and the great Jewish philosopher), and to invent for the purpose a second visit of Philo to Rome. It seems probable that the ascription of the work *De vita contemplativa* to Philo came before the tradition of his acquaintance with Peter in Rome (which is first mentioned by Eusebius); but in any case the two were mutually corroborative.

[2] περὶ βίου θεωρητικοῦ ἢ ἱκετῶν; *De Vita Contemplativa*. This work is still extant, and is given by Mangey, II. 471–486. Eusebius is the first writer to mention it, and he identifies the Therapeutæ described in it with the Christian monks, and assumes in consequence that monasticism in the form in which he knew it existed in the apostolic age, and was known and praised by Philo. This opinion was generally adopted by the Fathers (with the single exception of Photius, *Cod.* 105, who looked upon the Therapeutæ as a Jewish sect) and prevailed unquestioned until the Reformation, when in the Protestant reaction against monasticism it was denied that monks existed in the apostolic age, and that the Therapeutæ were Christians at all. Various opinions as to their identity have been held since that time, the commonest being that they were a Jewish sect or school, parallel with the Palestinian Essenes, or that they were an outgrowth of Alexandrian Neo-Pythagoreanism. The former opinion may be said to have been the prevailing one among Christian scholars until Lucius, in his work entitled *Die Therapeuten und ihre Stellung in der Gesch. der Askese* (Strassburg, 1879), proved (what had been asserted already by Grätz and Jost) that the Therapeutæ are really to be identified with Christian monks, and that the work *De Vita Contemplativa* is not a genuine work of Philo's. If the former proposition is proved, the latter follows of necessity, for it is absolutely impossible to suppose that monasticism can have existed in so developed a form (or indeed in any form) in the time of Philo. On the other hand it may be proved that the work is not Philonic, and yet it may not follow that the Therapeutæ are to be identified with Christian monks. And so some scholars reject the Philonic authorship while still maintaining the Jewish character of the Therapeutæ (e.g. Nicolas, Kuenen, and Weingarten; see Schürer, *Gesch. der Juden im Zeitalter Jesu Christi*, p. 863). In the opinion of the writer, who agrees therein with the great majority of scholars, Lucius has conclusively demonstrated both his propositions, and has shown that the work *De Vita Contemplativa* is the production of

some Christian of the latter part of the third century, who aimed to produce an apology for and a panegyric of monasticism as it existed in his day, and thus to secure for it wider recognition and acceptance. Lucius concludes with the following words: "Wir haben es demnach in D.V.C. mit einer Tendenzschrift zu thun, welche, da sie eine weit ausgebildete und in zahlreichen Ländern verbreitete Askese, so wie Zustände voraussetzt, genau wie dieselben nur in Christenthum des dritten Jahrhunderts vorhanden waren, kaum anders aufgefasst werden kann, als eine, etwa am Ende des dritten Jahrhunderts, unter dem Namen Philo's, zu Gunsten der Christlichen Askese, verfasste Apologie, als erstes Glied eines an derartigen Producte überaus reichen Litteratur-zweige der alten Kirche." Compare with Lucius' work the reviews of it by Hilgenfeld in the *Zeitschrift für wiss. Theol.*, 1880, pp. 423–440, and by Schürer in the *Theologische Literaturzeitung*, 1880, No. 5. The latter especially has added some important considerations with reference to the reasons for the composition of this work under the name of Philo. Assuming then the correctness of Lucius' conclusions, we see that Eusebius was quite right in identifying the Therapeutæ with the Christian monks as he knew them in his day, but that he was quite wrong in accepting the Philonic authorship of the work in question, and in concluding that the institution of monasticism as he knew it existed already in the apostolic age (compare note 19, below).

[3] It may fairly be doubted whether the work does not really contain considerable that is not in strict accordance with the facts observed by the author, whether his account is not to an extent idealized, and whether, in his endeavor to emphasize the Jewish character of the Therapeutæ, with the design of establishing the antiquity of monasticism (compare the review of Schürer referred to above), he has not allowed himself to introduce some imaginative elements. The strong asseveration which he makes of the truthfulness of his account would rather increase than allay this suspicion, and the account itself at certain points seems to bear it out. On the whole, however, it may be regarded as a reasonably accurate sketch. Were it not such, Eusebius would not have accepted it, so unreservedly as he does, as an account of Christian monks. Lucius' exhibition of the points of similarity between the practices of the Therapeutæ, as described here, and of early Christian monks, as known from other sources, is very interesting (see p. 158 sq.).

[4] θεραπευταί and θεραπευτρίδες, "worshipers" or "physicians"; from θεραπεύω, which means either to do service to the gods, or to tend the sick.

[5] See Bk. VI. chap. 3, note 9.

[6] See Bk. III. chap. 4, note 14.

companions of the apostles sold their possessions and their property and distributed to all according to the necessity of each one, so that no one among them was in want. "For as many as were possessors of lands or houses," as the account says, "sold them and brought the prices of the things that were sold, and laid them at the apostles' feet, so that distribution was made unto every man according as he had need." [7]

7   Philo bears witness to facts very much like those here described and then adds the following account: [8] "Everywhere in the world is this race [9] found. For it was fitting that both Greek [9a] and Barbarian should share in what is perfectly good. But the race particularly abounds in Egypt, in each of its so-called nomes, [10] and especially about Alexandria.

8   The best men from every quarter emigrate, as if to a colony of the Therapeutæ's fatherland, [11] to a certain very suitable spot which lies above the lake Maria [12] upon a low hill excellently situated on account of its security and the mildness of the atmosphere." And then a

9   little further on, after describing the kind of houses which they had, he speaks as follows concerning their churches, which were scattered about here and there: [13] "In each house there is a sacred apartment which is called a sanctuary and monastery, [14] where, quite alone, they perform the mysteries of the religious life. They bring nothing into it, neither drink nor food, nor any of the other things which contribute to the necessities of the body, but only the laws, and the inspired oracles of the prophets, and hymns and such other things as augment and make perfect their knowledge and piety."

10   And after some other matters he says: [15] "The whole interval, from morning to evening, is for them a time of exercise. For they read the holy Scriptures, and explain the philosophy of their fathers in an allegorical manner, regarding the written words as symbols of hidden truth which is communicated in obscure

11   figures. They have also writings of ancient men, who were the founders of their sect,

and who left many monuments of the allegorical method. These they use as models, and imitate their principles." These things **12** seem to have been stated by a man who had heard them expounding their sacred writings. But it is highly probable that the works of the ancients, which he says they had, were the Gospels and the writings of the apostles, and probably some expositions of the ancient prophets, such as are contained in the Epistle to the Hebrews, and in many others of Paul's Epistles. Then again he writes as **13** follows concerning the new psalms which they composed: [16] "So that they not only spend their time in meditation, but they also compose songs and hymns to God in every variety of metre and melody, though they divide them, of course, into measures of more than common solemnity." The same book contains an **14** account of many other things, but it seemed necessary to select those facts which exhibit the characteristics of the ecclesiastical mode of life. But if any one thinks that what **15** has been said is not peculiar to the Gospel polity, but that it can be applied to others besides those mentioned, let him be convinced by the subsequent words of the same author, in which, if he is unprejudiced, he will find undisputed testimony on this subject. Philo's words are as follows: [17] "Having laid down **16** temperance as a sort of foundation in the soul, they build upon it the other virtues. None of them may take food or drink before sunset, since they regard philosophizing as a work worthy of the light, but attention to the wants of the body as proper only in the darkness, and therefore assign the day to the former, but to the latter a small portion of the night. But **17** some, in whom a great desire for knowledge dwells, forget to take food for three days; and some are so delighted and feast so luxuriously upon wisdom, which furnishes doctrines richly and without stint, that they abstain even twice as long as this, and are accustomed, after six days, scarcely to take necessary food." These statements of Philo we regard as referring clearly and indisputably to those of our communion.

But if after these things any one still obsti- **18** nately persists in denying the reference, let him renounce his incredulity and be convinced by yet more striking examples, which are to be found nowhere else than in the evangelical religion of the Christians. [18] For they say **19** that there were women also with those of whom we are speaking, and that the most of them were aged virgins [19] who had preserved

---

[7] Acts ii. 45.   [8] De Vita Contemplativa, § 3.
[9] Namely, the Therapeutæ.
[9a] Heinichen omits, without explanation, the words καὶ τὴν Ἑλλάδα, which are found in all the other editions that I have examined. Inasmuch as Heinichen gives no hint of an alternate reading at this point, I can conclude only that the words were accidentally omitted by him.
[10] Egypt, exclusive of the cities Alexandria and Ptolemais, was divided into land districts, originally 36 in number, which were called νομοί (see Mommsen's *Provinces of the Roman Empire*, Scribner's ed. I. p. 255 sq.).
[11] πατρίδα. This word, as Schürer points out (*Theol. Literaturzeitung*, 1880, no. 5), is not a noun, as it is commonly regarded (and hence translated "fatherland"), but an adjective (and hence to be translated "eine vaterländische Colonie," "a colony of the fatherland"); the οἰκουμένη, mentioned in the previous paragraph, being the fatherland of the Therapeutæ.
[12] ὑπὲρ λίμνης Μαρίας. In Strabo the name is given as ἡ Μαρεῶτις or Μαρεία λίμνη. The Lake Mareotis (as it is most commonly called) lies in the northern part of the Delta, just south of Alexandria. It was in ancient times much more of a lake than it is now, and the description of the climate as given here is quite accurate.
[13] Ibid.   [14] σεμνεῖον καὶ μοναστήριον.

[15] Ibid.   [17] Ibid. § 4.
[16] Ibid.   [18] See Ibid. § 8.
[19] How Eusebius, who knew that Philo lived and wrote during

their chastity, not out of necessity, as some of the priestesses among the Greeks,[20] but rather by their own choice, through zeal and a desire for wisdom. And that in their earnest desire to live with it as their companion they paid no attention to the pleasures of the body, seeking not mortal but immortal progeny, which only the pious soul is able to bear of itself. Then after a little he adds still more emphatically:[21] "They expound the Sacred Scriptures figuratively by means of allegories. For the whole law seems to these men to resemble a living organism, of which the spoken words constitute the body, while the hidden sense stored up within the words constitutes the soul. This hidden meaning has first been particularly studied by this sect, which sees, revealed as in a mirror of names, the surpassing beauties of the thoughts." Why is it necessary to add to these things their meetings and the respective occupations of the men and of the women during those meetings, and the practices which are even to the present day habitually observed by us, especially such as we are accustomed to observe at the feast of the Saviour's passion, with fasting and night watching and study of the divine Word. These things the above-mentioned author has related in his own work, indicating a mode of life which has been preserved to the present time by us alone, recording especially the vigils kept in connection with the great festival, and the exercises performed during those vigils, and the hymns customarily recited by us, and describing how, while one sings regularly in time, the others listen in silence, and join in chanting only the close of the hymns; and how, on the days referred to, they sleep on the ground on beds of straw, and to use his own words,[22] "taste no wine at all, nor any flesh, but water is their only drink, and the relish with their bread is salt and hyssop." In addition to this Philo describes the order of dignities which exists among those who carry on the services of the church, mentioning the diaconate, and the office of bishop, which takes the precedence over all the others.[23] But

whosoever desires a more accurate knowledge of these matters may get it from the history already cited. But that Philo, when he wrote these things, had in view the first heralds of the Gospel and the customs handed down from the beginning by the apostles, is clear to every one.

CHAPTER XVIII.

The Works of Philo[1] *that have come down to us.*

Copious in language, comprehensive in thought, sublime and elevated in his views of divine Scripture, Philo has produced manifold and various expositions of the sacred books. On the one hand, he expounds in order the events recorded in Genesis in the books to which he gives the title *Allegories of the Sacred Laws;*[2] on the other hand, he makes successive divisions of the chapters in the Scriptures which are the subject of investigation, and gives objections and solutions, in the books which he quite suitably calls *Questions and Answers on Genesis and Exodus.*[3] There are, besides these, treatises expressly worked out by him on certain subjects, such as the two books *On Agriculture,*[4] and the same number *On Drunken-*

---

20. the reign of Claudius, could have overlooked the fact that Christianity had not at that time been long enough established to admit of virgins growing old within the Church, is almost inexplicable. It is but another example of his carelessness in regard to chronology which comes out so often in his history. Compare Stroth's words: "In der That ein wichtiger Beweis, der gerade der irrigen Meinung des Eusebius am meisten entgegen ist. Denn sie hätten alt zum Christenthum kommen müssen, sonst konnten sie ja zu Philo's Zeiten unmöglich im Christenthum alt geworden sein, dessen Schrift Eusebius selbst in die Regierung des Claudius setzt. Es ist beinahe unbegreiflich, wie ein so guter Kopf, wie Eusebius ist, in so grobe Irrthümer fallen konnte."

20. For a description of the religious cults among the Greeks and Romans, that demanded virginity in their priests or priestesses, see Döllinger's *Heidenthum und Judenthum,* p. 182 and 521 sq.

21. *De Vita Contemplativa,* § 10.

22. *Ibid.* § 9.

23. *Ibid.* §§ 8-10. The author of the *D. V. C.* mentions young men that serve at table (διακονοῦντες), and a president (πρόεδρος) who leads in the exposition of the Scriptures. Eusebius is quite right in finding in these persons deacons and bishops. The similarity is too

close to be merely accidental, and the comment of Stroth upon this passage is quite unwarranted: "Was einer doch alles in einer Stelle finden kann, wenn er es darin finden will! Philo sagt, dass bei ihren gemeinschaftlichen Gastmählern einige bei Tische dienten (διακο-νοῦντες), hieraus macht Eusebius Diakonate; und dass bei ihren Untersuchungen über die Bibel einer (πρόεδρος) den Vorsitz habe; hieraus macht Eusebius die bischöfliche würde (ἐπισκοπῆς προε-δρίαν)."

1. On Philo's works, see Schürer, *Gesch. des jüd. Volkes,* II. p. 831 sqq. The best (though it leaves much to be desired) complete edition of Philo's works is that of Mangey: 2 vols., folio, London, 1742; English translation of Philo's works by Yonge, 4 vols., London, 1854-55. Upon Philo's life, see chaps. 4-6, above. Eusebius, in his *Præp. Evang.,* quotes extensively from Philo's works and preserves some fragments of which we should otherwise be ignorant.

2. νόμων ἱερῶν ἀλληγορίαι. This work is still extant, and, according to Schürer, includes all the works contained in the first volume of Mangey's edition (except the *De Opificio Mundi,* upon which see Schürer, p. 846 sqq. and note 11, below), comprising 16 different titles. The work forms the second great group of writings upon the Pentateuch, and is a very full and allegorical commentary upon Genesis, beginning with the second chapter and following it verse by verse through the fourth chapter; but from that point on certain passages are selected and treated at length under special titles, and under those titles, in Schürer's opinion, were published by Philo as separate works, though really forming a part of one complete whole. From this much confusion has resulted. Eusebius embraces all of the works as far as the end of chap. 4 (including five titles in Mangey) under the one general title, but from that point on he too quotes separate works under special titles, but at the end (§ 5, below) he unites them all as the "extant works on Genesis." Many portions of the commentary are now missing. Compare Schürer, *ibid.* pp. 838-846.

3. ζητήματα καὶ λύσεις: *Quaestiones et solutiones.* According to Schürer (*ibid.* p. 836 sq.), a comparatively brief catechetical interpretation of the Pentateuch in the form of questions and answers, embracing probably six books on Genesis and five on Exodus, and forming the first great group of writings upon the Pentateuch. So far as Eusebius seems to have known, they covered only Genesis and Exodus, and this is all that we are sure of, though some think that they included also the remainder of the Pentateuch. About half of this work (four books on Genesis and two on Exodus) is extant in an Armenian version (published by Aucher in 2 vols., Venet. 1822 and '26, and in Latin by Ritter, vols. 6 and 7 of his edition of Philo's works); and numerous Latin and Greek fragments still exist (see Schürer, p. 837 sqq.).

4. περὶ γεωργίας δύο: *De Agricultura duo* (so Jerome, *de vir. ill.* 11). Upon Genesis ix. 20, forming a part (as do all the works mentioned in §§ 2-4 except *On the Three Virtues,* and *On the Unwritten Laws,* which belong to the third group of writings on the

ness ;[5] and some others distinguished by different titles corresponding to the contents of each ; for instance, *Concerning the things which the Sober Mind desires and execrates,*[6] *On the Confusion of Tongues,*[7] *On Flight and Discovery,*[8] *On Assembly for the sake of Instruction,*[9] *On the question, ‘ Who is heir to things divine ?’* or *On the division of things into equal and unequal,*[10] and still further the work *On the three Virtues which*

3　*with others have been described by Moses.*[11]

In addition to these is the work *On those whose Names have been changed and why they have been changed,*[12] in which he says that he had

4　written also two books *On Covenants.*[13] And

there is also a work of his *On Emigration,*[14] and one *On the life of a Wise Man made perfect in Righteousness,* or *On unwritten Laws ;*[15] and still further the work *On Giants* or *On the Immutability of God,*[16] and a first, second, third, fourth and fifth book *On the proposition, that Dreams according to Moses are sent by God.*[17] These are the books on Genesis that have come down to us. But on Exodus we are ac-　5 quainted with the first, second, third, fourth and fifth books of *Questions and Answers ;*[18] also with that *On the Tabernacle,*[19] and that *On the ten Commandments,*[20] and the four books

---

Pentateuch) of the large commentary, νόμων ἱερῶν ἀλληγορίαι, mentioned above (note 2). This work is still extant, and is given by Mangey, I. 300–356, as two works with distinct titles: περὶ γεωργίας and περὶ φυτουργίας Νῶε τὸ δεύτερον (Schürer, p. 843).

[5] περὶ μέθης τοσαῦτα: *De ebrietate duo* (so Jerome, *ibid.*). Upon Gen. ix. 21. Only the second book is extant (Mangey, I. 357–391), but from its beginning it is plain that another book originally preceded it (Schürer, p. 843).

[6] περὶ ὧν νήψας ὁ νοῦς εὔχεται καὶ καταρᾶται. Jerome, *de vir. ill.* 11, *de his quæ sensu precamur et detestamur.* Upon Gen. ix. 24. Still extant, and given by Mangey (I. 392–403), who, however, prints the work under the title περὶ τοῦ ἐξένηψε Νῶε: *De Sobrietate;* though in two of the best MSS. (according to Mangey, I. 392, note) the title agrees closely with that given by Eusebius (Schürer, p. 843).

[7] περὶ συγχύσεως τῶν διαλέκτων. Upon Gen. xi. 1–9. Still extant, and given by Mangey, I. 404–435 (Schürer, p. 844).

[8] περὶ φυγῆς καὶ εὑρέσεως. The same title is found in Johannes Monachus (Mangey, I. 546, note), and it is probably correct, as the work treats of the flight and the discovery of Hagar (Gen. xvi. 6–14). It is still extant, and is given by Mangey (I. 546–577) under the title περὶ φυγάδων, ‘On Fugitives.’ The text of Eusebius in this place has been very much corrupted. The reading which I give is supported by good MS. authority, and is adopted by Valesius, Stroth, and Laemmer. But Nicephorus reads περὶ φυγῆς καὶ αἱρέσεως καὶ ὁ περὶ φύσεως καὶ εὑρέσεως, which is also supported by MS. authority, and is adopted by Burton, Schwegler, and Heinichen. But upon comparing the title of the work, as given by Johannes Monachus and as found in the various MSS. of Philo, with the contents of the work itself, there can be little doubt of the correctness of the shorter reading. Of the second work, which the longer reading introduces into the text of Eusebius, we have no knowledge, and Philo can hardly have written it. Schürer, who adopts the shorter reading, expresses himself very strongly (p. 845, note 34).

[9] περὶ τῆς πρὸς τὰ παιδεύματα συνόδου, “On Assembly for the sake of instruction.” Upon Gen. xvi. 1–6, which is interpreted to mean that one must make himself acquainted with the lower branches of knowledge (Hagar) before he can get to the higher (Sarah), and from them obtain the fruit, viz.: virtue (Isaac). Still extant, and given by Mangey, I. 519–545 (Schürer, 844 sqq.).

[10] περὶ τῆς πρὸς τὰ παιδεύματα συνόδου, ἢ περὶ τῆς εἰς τὰ ἴσα καὶ ἐναντία τομῆς. From this double title Jerome (*de vir. ill.* 11) wrongly makes two works. The writing is still extant, and is given by Mangey (I. 473–518) under the title περὶ τοῦ τίς ὁ τῶν θείων πραγμάτων κληρονόμος (Schürer, 844).

[11] περὶ τῶν τριῶν ἀρετῶν, ἃς σὺν ἄλλαις ἀνέγραψε Μωυσῆς. This work is still extant, and is given by Mangey under the title περὶ τριῶν ἀρετῶν ἤτοι περὶ ἀνδρείας καὶ φιλανθρωπίας καὶ μετανοίας: περὶ ἀνδρείας, II. 375–383; περὶ φιλανθρωπίας, II. 383–405; περὶ μετανοίας, II. 405–407. Jerome gives the simple title *De tribus virtutibus liber unus.* According to Schürer (p. 852 sqq.) it forms an appendix to the third great group of works upon the Pentateuch, containing those laws which do not belong to any one of the ten commandments in particular, but fall under the head of general cardinal virtues. The third group, as Schürer describes it (p. 846), aims to give for non-Jews a complete view of the Mosaic legislation, and embraces, first, the work upon the Creation (which in the MSS. and editions of Philo is wrongly placed at the beginning in connection with the general *Allegorical Commentary,* and is thus included in that by Eusebius in his list of Philo's works, so that he does not make special mention of it); second, the lives of great and good men, the *living unwritten law ;* and third, the Mosaic legislation proper (1. The ten commandments; 2. The special laws connected with each of these); and finally an appendix treating of certain cardinal virtues, and of reward and punishments. This group is more historic and less allegoric than the two others, which are rather esoteric and scientific.

[12] περὶ τῶν μετονομαζομένων καὶ ὧν ἕνεκα μετονομάζονται, *De Mutatione nominum.* Upon Gen. xvii. 1–22. This work is still extant, and is given by Mangey, I. 578–619. See Schürer, p. 485.

[13] ἐν ᾧ φησι συντετάχεναι καὶ περὶ διαθηκῶν πρῶτον καὶ δεύτερον. Nearly all the MSS., followed by some of the editors, read

πρώτης καὶ δευτέρας instead of πρῶτον καὶ δεύτερον, thus making Eusebius mention a work “On the first and second covenants,” instead of a first and second book “On the covenants.” It is plain from Philo's own reference to the work (on p. 586 in Mangey's ed.) that he wrote two books “On covenants,” and not a work “On the two covenants.” I have therefore felt warranted in reading with Heinichen and some other editors πρῶτον καὶ δεύτερον, a reading which is more natural in view of the absence of an article with διαθηκῶν, and which is confirmed by Nicephorus Callistus. This reading must be correct unless we are to suppose that Eusebius misread Philo. Fabricius suggests that Eusebius probably wrote ἃ καὶ β′, which the copyists wrongly referred to the “ covenants ” instead of to the number of the books, and hence gave the feminine instead of the neuter form.

This work “On covenants,” or “ On the whole discussion concerning covenants ” (as Philo gives it), is now lost, as it was already in the time of Eusebius; at least he knew of it only from Philo's reference to it. See Schürer, p. 845.

[14] περὶ ἀποικίας: *De Migratione Abrahami.* Upon Gen. xii. 1–6. The work is still extant, and is given by Mangey, I. 436–472. See Schürer, p. 844.

[15] βίου σοφοῦ κατὰ δικαιοσύνην τελειωθέντος, ἢ νόμων ἀγράφων. (According to Schürer, δικαιοσύνην here is a mistake for διδασκαλίαν, which is the true reading in the original title.) This work, which is still extant, is given by Mangey, II. 1–40, under the same title (διδασκαλίαν, however, instead of δικαιοσύνην), with the addition, ὅ ἐστι περὶ Ἀβραάμ: *De Abrahamo.* It opens the second division of the third great group of writings on the Pentateuch (see note 11, above): the biographical division, mentioning Enos, Enoch and Noah, Abraham, Isaac and Jacob, but dealing chiefly with Abraham. The biographies of Isaac and Jacob probably followed, but they are lost, and we have no trace of them, so that the life of Joseph (see below, note 26) in the MSS. follows directly upon that of Abraham (Schürer, p. 848 sqq.).

[16] περὶ γιγάντων, ἢ περὶ τοῦ μὴ τρέπεσθαι τὸ θεῖον. Upon Gen. vi. 1–4 and 4–12. The two parts of this work, both of which are still extant, form really but one book; for instance, Johannes Monachus (*ineditus*) quotes from the latter part under the title περὶ γιγάντων (according to Mangey, I. 262, note, and 272, note). But the two are divided in Mangey's edition, where the first is given under the title περὶ γιγάντων (I. 262–272), the second under the title ὅτι ἄτρεπτον (I. 272–299). See Schürer, p. 843. The title is found in the form given at the beginning of this note in all the MSS. of Eusebius except two, which have καὶ instead of ἢ, thus making two separate works. This reading is adopted by Heinichen and by Closs, but is poorly supported by MS. authority, and since the two titles cover only one work, as already mentioned, the ἢ is more natural than the καὶ.

[17] περὶ τε τοῦ κατὰ Μωϋσέα θεοπέμπτους εἶναι τοὺς ὀνείρους πρῶτον, δεύτερον, κ.τ.λ. Two books are extant, the first upon Gen. xxviii. 12 sqq. and xxxi. 11 sqq. (given by Mangey, I. 620–658), the second upon Gen. xxxvii. and xl.–xli. (given by Mangey, I. 659–699). Jerome (*de vir. ill.* 11) follows Eusebius in mentioning five books, and there is no occasion to doubt the report. Schürer thinks that the two extant books are the second and third of the original five (Schürer, 845 sqq.).

[18] ζητήματα καὶ λύσεις; see above, note 3. Eusebius knew only five books upon Exodus, and there is no reason to think there were any more.

[19] Philo wrote a work entitled περὶ βίου Μωσέως: *Vita Mosis,* which is still extant, but is not mentioned in the catalogue of Eusebius. It contains a long description of the tabernacle, and consequently Schürer concludes that the work mentioned here by Eusebius (περὶ τῆς σκηνῆς) represents that portion of the larger work. If this be the case, it is possible that that section in the MSS. used by Eusebius was detached from the rest of the work and constituted an independent book. The omission of the title of the larger work is doubtless due, as Schürer remarks, to the imperfect transmission of the text of Eusebius' catalogue. See Schürer, p. 855.

[20] περὶ τῶν δέκα λογίων: *De Decalogo.* Still extant, and given by Mangey, II. 180–209. Jerome has the condensed title *de tabernaculo et decalogo libri quattuor,* and this introduces the third division of the third general group of works upon the Pentateuch (see note 11, above), and, according to Schürer, should be joined directly

On the laws which refer especially to the principal divisions of the ten Commandments,[21] and another *On animals intended for sacrifice* and *On the kinds of sacrifice,*[22] and another *On the rewards fixed in the law for the good, and on the punishments and curses fixed for the wicked.*[23]
6 In addition to all these there are extant also some single-volumed works of his; as for instance, the work *On Providence,*[24] and the book composed by him *On the Jews,*[25] and *The Statesman;*[26] and still further, *Alexander,* or *On the possession of reason by the irrational animals.*[27] Besides these there is a work *On the*

proposition that every wicked man is a slave, to which is subjoined the work *On the proposition that every good man is free.*[28] After 7 these was composed by him the work *On the contemplative life,* or *On suppliants,*[29] from which we have drawn the facts concerning the life of the apostolic men; and still further, the *Interpretation of the Hebrew names in the law and in the prophets* are said to be the result of his industry.[30] And he is said to have 8 read in the presence of the whole Roman Senate during the reign of Claudius[31] the work which he had written, when he came to Rome under Caius, concerning Caius' hatred of the gods, and to which, with ironical reference to its character, he had given the title *On the Virtues.*[32] And his discourses were so much admired as to be deemed worthy of a place in the libraries.

At this time, while Paul was completing 9 his journey "from Jerusalem and round about unto Illyricum,"[33] Claudius drove the Jews out of Rome; and Aquila and Priscilla, leaving Rome with the other Jews, came to Asia, and there abode with the apostle Paul, who was confirming the churches of that region whose

---

to the βίος πολιτικός, or *Life of Joseph*, and not separated from it by the insertion of the *Life of Moses* (as is done by Mangey), which does not belong to this group (Schürer, p. 849 sqq.).

[21] τὰ περὶ τῶν ἀναφερομένων ἐν εἴδει νόμων εἰς τὰ συντείνοντα κεφάλαια τῶν δέκα λόγων, α΄β΄γ΄δ΄: *De specialibus legibus.* A part of the third division of the third general group of works (see note 11, above). It is still extant in four books, each with a special title, and each containing many subdivisions. They are given by Mangey: first book, II. 210–269, in seven parts: *de circumcisione, de monarchia Liber I., de monarchia Liber II., de praemiis sacerdotum, de victimis, de sacrificantibus,* or *de victimis offerentibus, de mercede meretricis non accipienda in sacrarium;* second book, 270–298, incomplete in Mangey, but entire in Tischendorf's *Philonea,* p. 1–83; third book, 299–334; fourth book, 335–374: made up like the first of a number of tracts on special subjects. Philo, in this work, attempts to bring all the Mosaic laws into a system under the ten rubrics of the decalogue: for instance, under the first two commandments, the laws in regard to priests and sacrifices; under the fourth, the laws in regard to the Sabbath, &c. See Schürer, p. 850 sqq.

[22] περὶ τῶν εἰς τὰς ἱερουργίας ζῴων, καὶ τίνα τὰ τῶν θυσιῶν εἴδη. This is really only a portion of the first book of the work just mentioned, given in Mangey under the title *de victimis* (II. 237–250). It is possible that these various sections of books — or at least this one — circulated separately, and that thus Eusebius took it for an independent work. See Schürer, p. 851.

[23] περὶ τῶν προκειμένων ἐν τῷ νόμῳ τοῖς μὲν ἀγαθοῖς ἄθλων, τοῖς δὲ πονηροῖς ἐπιτιμίων καὶ ἀρῶν, still extant and given by Mangey (incorrectly under the titles περὶ ἄθλων καὶ ἐπιτιμίων, *de praemiis et poenis* (II. 408–428), and περὶ ἀρῶν, *de execrationibus* (II. 429–437). The writing forms a sort of epilogue to the work upon the Mosaic legislation. Schürer, p. 854.

[24] τὸ περὶ προνοίας, *De providentia.* This work is extant only in an Armenian version, and is published with a Latin translation by Aucher, Vol. I. p. 1–121 (see above, note 3), and in Latin by Ritter (Vol. VIII.). Two Greek fragments, one of considerable extent, are preserved by Eusebius in his *Praeparatio Evang.* VII. 21, and VIII. 14. In the Armenian the work consists of two books, but the first is of doubtful genuineness, and Eusebius seems to have known only one, for both quotations in the *Praep. Evang.* are from the present second book, and the work is cited in the singular, as also in the present passage, where τὸ is to be read instead of τά, though some MSS. have the latter. The work (which is not found in Mangey's ed.) is one of Philo's separate works which does not fall under any of the three groups upon the Pentateuch.

[25] περὶ Ἰουδαίων, which is doubtless to be identified with the ἡ ὑπὲρ Ἰουδαίων ἀπολογία, which is no longer extant, but which Eusebius mentions, and from which he quotes in his *Praep. Evang.* VIII. 2. The fragment given by Eusebius is printed by Mangey in Vol. II. p. 632–634, and in Dähne's opinion (*Theol. Studien und Kritiken,* 1883, p. 990) the two preceding fragments given by Mangey (p. 626 sqq.) also belong to this *Apology.* The work entitled *de nobilitate* (Mangey, II. 437–444) possibly formed a part of the *Apology.* This is Dähne's opinion (see *ibid.* p. 990, 1037), with whom Schürer agrees. The genuineness of the *Apology* is generally admitted, though it has been disputed on insufficient grounds by Grätz (*Gesch. der Juden,* III. p. 680, third ed.), who is followed by Hilgenfeld (in the *Zeitschrift für wiss. Theologie,* 1882, p. 275 sq. and in his *Ketzergesch. des Urchristenthums,* p. 87 sq.). This too, like the preceding, was one of the separate works of Philo. See Schürer, p. 861 sq.

[26] ὁ πολιτικός. Still extant, and given by Mangey (II. 41–79) under the title βίος πολιτικὸς ὅπερ ἐστὶ περὶ Ἰωσήφ: *De Josepho.* Photius, *Bib. Cod.* 103, gives the title περὶ βίου πολιτικοῦ. This forms a part of the second division of the third great group upon the Pentateuch (see above, note 11), and follows directly the Life of Abraham, the Lives of Isaac and Jacob probably having fallen out (compare note 15, above). The work is intended to show how the wise man should conduct himself in affairs of state or political life. See Schürer, p. 849.

[27] ὁ Ἀλέξανδρος ἢ περὶ τοῦ λόγον ἔχειν τὰ ἄλογα ζῶα, *De Alexandro et quod propriam rationem muta animalia habeant,* as the title is given by Jerome (*de vir. ill.* c. 11). The work is extant only in Armenian, and is given by Aucher, I. p. 123–172, and

in Latin by Ritter, Vol. VII. Two short Greek fragments are also found in the *Florilegium* of Leontius and Johannes, according to Schürer. This book is also one of the separate works of Philo, and belongs to his later writings. See Schürer, p. 860 sqq.

[28] ὁ περὶ τοῦ δοῦλον εἶναι πάντα φαῦλον, ᾧ ἑξῆς ἐστιν ὁ περὶ τοῦ πάντα σπουδαῖον ἐλεύθερον εἶναι. These two works formed originally the two halves of a single work, in which the subject was treated from its two sides, — the slavery of the wicked man and the freedom of the good man. The first half is lost; but the second half is extant, and is given by Mangey (II. 445–470). A long fragment of the extant second half is given also by Eusebius, in his *Praep. Evang.* VIII. 12. The genuineness of the work has been disputed by some, but is defended with success by Lucius, *Der Essenismus,* p. 13–23, Strasburg, 1881 (Schürer, p. 85).

[29] See the preceding chapter; and on the work, see note 2 on that chapter.

[30] τῶν ἐν νόμῳ δὲ καὶ προφήταις Ἑβραϊκῶν ὀνομάτων αἱ ἑρμηνεῖαι. The way in which Eusebius speaks of this work (τοῦ αὐτοῦ σπουδαῖ εἶναι λέγονται) shows that it lay before him as an anonymous work, which, however, was "said to be the result of Philo's industry." Jerome, too, in speaking of the same work (at the beginning of his own work, *De nominibus Hebraicis*), says that, according to the testimony of Origen, it was the work of Philo. For Jerome, too, therefore, it was an anonymous work. This testimony of Origen cannot, according to Schürer, be found in his extant works, but in his *Comment. in Joann.* II. 27 (ed. Lommatzsch, I. 50) he speaks of a work upon the same subject, the author of which he does not know. The book therefore in view of the existing state of the tradition in regard to it, is usually thought to be the work of some other writer than Philo. In its original form it is no longer extant (and in the absence of this original it is impossible to decide the question of authorship), though there exist a number of works upon the same subject which are probably based upon this lost original. Jerome, e.g., informs us that his *Liber de Nominibus Hebraicis* (Migne, III. 771) is a revision of it. See Schürer, p. 865 sq.

[31] "This report is very improbable, for a work full of hatred to the Romans and of derogatory references to the emperor Caligula could not have been read before the Roman Senate, especially when the author was a Jew" (Closs). It is in fact quite unlikely that Philo was in Rome during the reign of Claudius (see above, chap. 17, note 1). The report given here by Eusebius owes its origin perhaps to the imagination of some man who supposed that Philo was in Rome during the reign of Claudius (on the ground of the other tradition already referred to), and whose fancy led him to picture Philo as obtaining at that time his revenge upon the emperor Caligula in this dramatic way. It was not difficult to imagine that this bitterly sarcastic and vivid work might have been intended for public reading, and it was an attractive suggestion that the Senate might have constituted the audience.

[32] See above, chap. 5, note 1.

[33] Romans xv. 19.

foundations he had newly laid.   The sacred book of the Acts informs us also of these things.[34]

CHAPTER XIX.

The · Calamity which befell the Jews in Jerusalem on the Day of the Passover.

1   WHILE Claudius was still emperor, it happened that so great a tumult and disturbance took place in Jerusalem at the feast of the Passover, that thirty thousand of those Jews alone who were forcibly crowded together at the gate of the temple perished,[1] being trampled under foot by one another.   Thus the festival became a season of mourning for all the nation, and there was weeping in every house.   These things are related literally[2] by Josephus.

2   But Claudius appointed Agrippa,[3] son of Agrippa, king of the Jews, having sent Felix[4] as procurator of the whole country of

---

[34] See Acts xviii. 2, 18, 19 sqq.
[1] This disturbance (described by Jos. *B. J.* II. 12. 1, and *Ant.* XX. 5. 3) took place in 48 A.D. while Cumanus was procurator of Judea.   During the Passover feast the procurator, as was the custom, brought extra troops to Jerusalem to guard against any uproar which might arise among the great mass of people.   One of the soldiers, with the view of insulting the Jews, conducted himself indecently in their presence, whereupon so great an uproar arose that the procurator felt obliged to collect his troops upon the temple hill, but the appearance of the soldiers so greatly alarmed the multitude assembled there that they fled in all directions and crushed each other to death in their eagerness to escape. Josephus, in his *Jewish War*, gives the number of the slain as ten thousand, and in the *Antiquities* as twenty thousand.   The latter work was written last, but knowing Josephus' fondness for exaggerating numbers, we shall perhaps not accept the correction as any nearer the truth. That Josephus gives thirty thousand need not arouse suspicion as to his honesty, — he could have had no object for changing " twenty " to " thirty," when the former was certainly great enough, — we need simply remember how easily numbers become altered in transcription.   Valesius says that this disturbance took place under Quadratus in 52 A.D. (quoting Pearson's *Ann. Paull.* p. 11 sqq., and Tacitus, *Ann.* XII. 54).   But Eusebius, in his *Chron.*, gives the eighth year of Claudius (48 A.D.), and Orosius, VII. 4, gives the seventh year.   Jost and Ewald agree with Eusebius in regard to the date.
[2] Eusebius simply sums up in the one sentence what fills half a page in Josephus.
[3] Herod Agrippa II., son of Herod Agrippa I.   At the time of his father's death (44 A.D.) he was but seventeen years of age, and his youth deterred Claudius from giving him the kingdom of his father, which was therefore again converted into a Roman province, and Fadus was sent as procurator.   In 49 A.D. Agrippa was given the kingdom of Chalcis which had belonged to his uncle Herod (a brother of Agrippa I.), and in 53 A.D. he was transferred to the tetrarchies of Philip and Lysanias with the title of King.   He was never king of the Jews in the same sense in which his father was, as Judea remained a Roman province throughout his reign, while his dominion comprised only the northeastern part of Palestine.   He enjoyed, however, the right of appointing and removing the high priests, and under Nero his domain was somewhat increased by the addition of several cities of Galilee, and Perea.   He sided with the Romans in the Jewish war, and afterwards went to Rome, where he died in 100 A.D., the last prince of the Herodian line.   It was before this Agrippa that Paul made his defense recorded in Acts xxvi.
[4] Felix, a freedman of Claudius, succeeded Cumanus as procurator of Judea in 52 (or, according to Wieseler, 53) A.D.   The territory over which he ruled included Samaria and the greater part of Galilee and Perea, to which Judea was added by Nero, according to Josephus, *B. J.* II. 13. 2.   Ewald, in the attempt to reconcile Tacitus, *Ann.* XII. 54, and Josephus, *Ant.* XX. 5. 2–7. 1, — the former of whom makes Cumanus and Felix contemporary procurators, each over a part of the province, while the latter makes Felix the successor of Cumanus, — concludes that Felix was sent to Judea as the assistant of Cumanus, and became procurator upon the banishment of the latter.   This is not impossible, though we have no testimony to support it.   Compare Wieseler, p. 67 sqq.   Between 59 and 61 (according to Wieseler, in 60; see chap. 22, note 1, below) he was succeeded by Porcius Festus.   For the relations of these two procurators to the apostle Paul, see Acts xx. sqq.   Eusebius, in his

---

Samaria and Galilee, and of the land called Perea.[5]   And after he had reigned thirteen years and eight months[6] he died, and left Nero as his successor in the empire.

CHAPTER XX.

The Events which took Place in Jerusalem during the Reign of Nero.

JOSEPHUS again, in the twentieth book of   1 his Antiquities, relates the quarrel which arose among the priests during the reign of Nero, while Felix was procurator of Judea. His words are as follows[1] : " There arose a   2 quarrel between the high priests on the one hand and the priests and leaders of the people of Jerusalem on the other.[2]   And each of them collected a body of the boldest and most restless men, and put himself at their head, and whenever they met they hurled invectives and stones at each other.   And there was no one that would interpose ; but these things were done at will as if in a city destitute of a ruler.   And so great was the shame-   3 lessness and audacity of the high priests that they dared to send their servants to the threshing-floors to seize the tithes due to the priests ; and thus those of the priests that were poor were seen to be perishing of want.   In this way did the violence of the factions prevail over all justice."   And the same   4 author again relates that about the same time there sprang up in Jerusalem a certain kind of robbers,[3] " who by day," as he says, " and in the middle of the city slew those who met them."   For, especially at the feasts,   5 they mingled with the multitude, and with short swords, which they concealed under their garments, they stabbed the most distinguished men.   And when they fell, the murderers themselves were among those who expressed their indignation.   And thus on account of the con-

---

Chron., puts the accession of Felix in the eleventh year of Claudius (51 A.D.), and the accession of Festus in the fourteenth year (54 A.D.), but both of these dates are clearly incorrect (cf. Wieseler, p. 68, note).
[5] Eusebius evidently supposed the Roman province at this time to have been limited to Samaria, Galilee, and Perea; but in this he was wrong, for it included also Judea (see preceding note), Agrippa II. having under him only the tetrarchies mentioned above (note 3) and a few cities of Galilee and Perea.   He had, however, the authority over the temple and the power of appointing the high priests (see Jos. *Ant.* XX. 8. 11 and 9. 1, 4, 6, 7), which had been given by Claudius to his uncle, the king of Chalcis (Jos. *Ant.* XX. 1. 3).
[6] Claudius ruled from Jan. 24, 41 A.D., to Oct. 13, 54.
[1] Jos. *Ant.* XX. 8. 8.   Felix showed himself throughout very mean and cruel, and his procuratorship was marked with continual disturbances.
[2] This disturbance arose toward the end of Felix's term, under the high priest Ishmael, who had been appointed by Agrippa but a short time before.   No cause is given by Josephus for the quarrel.
[3] *B. J.* II. 13. 3.   These open robberies and murders, which took place in Jerusalem at this period, were in part a result of the conduct of Felix himself in the murder of Jonathan (see the next note).   At least his conduct in this case started the practice, which was kept up with zeal by the ruffians who were so numerous at that time.

fidence which was reposed in them by all,
6 they remained undiscovered. The first
that was slain by them was Jonathan the
high priest;[4] and after him many were killed
every day, until the fear became worse than
the evil itself, each one, as in battle, hourly
expecting death.

CHAPTER XXI.

*The Egyptian, who is mentioned also in the Acts
of the Apostles.*

1 AFTER other matters he proceeds as follows:[1] "But the Jews were afflicted with
a greater plague than these by the Egyptian
false prophet.[2] For there appeared in the land
an impostor who aroused faith in himself as a
prophet, and collected about thirty thousand
of those whom he had deceived, and led them
from the desert to the so-called Mount of Olives
whence he was prepared to enter Jerusalem by
force and to overpower the Roman garrison and
seize the government of the people, using those
who made the attack with him as body-
2 guards. But Felix anticipated his attack,
and went out to meet him with the Roman
legionaries, and all the people joined in the
defense, so that when the battle was fought the
Egyptian fled with a few followers, but the most
of them were destroyed or taken captive."
3 Josephus relates these events in the second
book of his History.[3] But it is worth while

comparing the account of the Egyptian given
here with that contained in the Acts of the
Apostles. In the time of Felix it was said to
Paul by the centurion in Jerusalem, when the
multitude of the Jews raised a disturbance
against the apostle, "Art not thou he who before
these days made an uproar, and led out into the
wilderness four thousand men that were murderers?"[4] These are the events which took
place in the time of Felix.[5]

CHAPTER XXII.

*Paul having been sent bound from Judea to
Rome, made his Defense, and was acquitted
of every Charge.*

FESTUS[1] was sent by Nero to be Felix's 1
successor. Under him Paul, having made his
defense, was sent bound to Rome.[2] Aristarchus
was with him, whom he also somewhere in his
epistles quite naturally calls his fellow-prisoner.[3]

reached thirty thousand, and that when attacked the rabble dispersed, but that Felix slew or took captive the six hundred robbers,
against whom his attack had been directed, while the Egyptian
escaped with a small number (i.e. small in comparison with the
thirty thousand), who may well have been the four thousand mentioned by the author of the Acts in the passage quoted below by
Eusebius. It is no more difficult therefore to reconcile the Acts and
Josephus in this case than to reconcile Josephus with himself, and
we have no reason to assume a mistake upon the part of either one,
though as already remarked, numbers are so treacherous in transcription that the difference may really have been originally less than
it is. Whenever the minute elements of two accounts are in substantial agreement, little stress can be laid upon a difference in figures.
Cf. Tholuck, *Glaubwürdigkeit*, p. 169 (quoted by Hackett, *Com.
on Acts*, p. 254).
4 Acts xxi. 38.
5 Valesius and Heinichen assert that Eusebius is incorrect in
assigning this uproar, caused by the Egyptian, to the reign of Nero,
as he seems to do. But their assertion is quite groundless, for Josephus in both of his accounts relates the uproar among events
which he expressly assigns to Nero's reign, and there is no reason
to suppose that the order of events given by him is incorrect. Valesius and Heinichen proceed on the erroneous assumption that Festus
succeeded Felix in the second year of Nero, and that therefore, since
Paul was two years in Cæsarea before the recall of Felix, the uprising of the Egyptian, which was referred to at the time of Paul's arrest
and just before he was carried to Cæsarea, must have taken place before the end of the reign of Claudius. But it happens to be a fact
that Felix was succeeded by Festus at the earliest not before the
sixth year of Nero (see chap. 22, note 2, below). There is, therefore, no ground for accusing either Josephus or Eusebius of a blunder in the present case.
1 The exact date of the accession of Festus is not known, but it
is known that his death occurred before the summer of 62 A.D.; for
at that time his successor, Albinus, was already procurator, as we
can see from Josephus, *B. J.* VI. 5. 3. But from the events recorded
by Josephus as happening during his term of office, we know he
must have been procurator at least a year; his accession, therefore,
took place certainly as early as 61 A.D., and probably at least a year
earlier, i.e. in 60 A.D., the date fixed by Wieseler. The widest possible margin for his accession is from 59-61. Upon this whole question, see Wieseler, p. 66 sqq. Festus died while in office. He seems
to have been a just and capable governor,—in this quite a contrast to his predecessor.
2 Acts xxv. sqq. The determination of the year in which Paul
was sent as a prisoner to Rome depends in part upon the determination of the year of Festus' accession. He was in Rome (which he
reached in the spring) at least two years before the Neronic persecution (June, 64 A.D.), therefore as early as 62 A.D. He was sent
from Cæsarea the previous autumn, therefore as early as the autumn
of 61. If Festus became procurator in 61, this must have been the
date. But if, as is probable, Festus became procurator in 60, then
Paul was sent to Rome in the autumn of the same year, and reached
Rome in the spring of 61. This is now the commonly accepted
date; but the year 62 cannot be shut out (cf. Wieseler, *ibid.*).
Wieseler shows conclusively that Festus cannot have become procurator before 60 A.D., and hence Paul cannot have been taken to Rome
before the fall of that year.
3 Col. iv. 10.

4 This high priest, Jonathan, had used his influence in procuring
the appointment of Felix as procurator, and was therefore upon intimate terms with him, and took the liberty of advising and rebuking
him at pleasure; until at last he became so burdensome to Felix
that he bribed a trusted friend of Jonathan to bring about his murder. The friend accomplished it by introducing a number of robbers
into the city, who, being unknown, mingled freely with the people
and slew Jonathan and many others with him, in order to turn away
suspicion as to the object of the crime. See Jos. *Ant.* XX. 8. 5.
Josephus has omitted to mention Jonathan's appointment to the
high priesthood, and this has led Valesius to conclude that he was
not really a high priest, but simply one of the upper class of priests.
But this conclusion is unwarranted, as Josephus expressly calls him
the high priest in the passage referred to (cf. also the remarks of
Reland, quoted in Havercamp's ed. of Josephus, p. 912). Wieseler
(p. 77, note) thinks that Jonathan was not high priest at this time,
but that he had been high priest and was called so on that account.
He makes Ananias high priest from 48 to 57, quoting Anger, *De
temporum in Act. Ap. ratione.*
1 Jos. *B. J.* II. 13. 5.
2 An Egyptian Jew; one of the numerous magicians and false
prophets that arose during this century. He prophesied that Jerusalem, which had made itself a heathen city, would be destroyed by
God, who would throw down the walls as he had the walls of
Jericho, and then he and his followers, as the true Israel and the
army of God, would gain the victory over the oppressors and rule
the world. For this purpose he collected his followers upon the
Mount of Olives, from whence they were to witness the falling of
the walls and begin their attack.
3 Josephus gives two different accounts of this event. In the
B. J. he says that this Egyptian led thirty thousand men out of the
desert to the Mount of Olives, but that Felix attacked them, and
the Egyptian "escaped with a few," while most of his followers
were either destroyed or captured. In *Ant.* XX. 8. 6, which was
written later, he states that the Egyptian led a multitude "out from
Jerusalem" to the Mount of Olives, and that when they were attacked by Felix, four hundred were slain and two hundred taken
captive. There seems to be here a glaring contradiction, but we
are able to reconcile the two accounts by supposing the Egyptian to
have brought a large following of robbers from the desert, which
was augmented by a great rabble from Jerusalem, until the number

And Luke, who wrote the Acts of the Apostles,[4] brought his history to a close at this point, after stating that Paul spent two whole years at Rome as a prisoner at large, and preached the 2 word of God without restraint.[5] Thus after he had made his defense it is said that the apostle was sent again upon the ministry of preaching,[6] and that upon coming to the same city a second time he suffered martyrdom.[7] In this imprisonment he wrote his second epistle to Timothy,[8] in which he mentions his first 3 defense and his impending death. But hear his testimony on these matters : "At my

first answer," he says, "no man stood with me, but all men forsook me : I pray God that it may not be laid to their charge. Notwithstanding the Lord stood with me, and strengthened me ; that by me the preaching might be fully known, and that all the Gentiles might hear : and I was delivered out of the mouth of the lion." [9]
He plainly indicates in these words that 4 on the former occasion, in order that the preaching might be fulfilled by him, he was rescued from the mouth of the lion, referring, in this expression, to Nero, as is probable on account of the latter's cruelty. He did not therefore afterward add the similar statement, "He will rescue me from the mouth of the lion " ; for he saw in the spirit that his end would not be long delayed. Wherefore he 5 adds to the words, "And he delivered me from the mouth of the lion," this sentence : "The Lord shall deliver me from every evil work, and will preserve me unto his heavenly kingdom," [10] indicating his speedy martyrdom ; which he also foretells still more clearly in the same epistle, when he writes, " For I am now ready to be offered, and the time of my departure is at hand." [11] In his second 6 epistle to Timothy, moreover, he indicates that Luke was with him when he wrote,[12] but at his first defense not even he.[13] Whence it is probable that Luke wrote the Acts of the Apostles at that time, continuing his history down to the period when he was with Paul.[14] But 7 these things have been adduced by us to show that Paul's martyrdom did not take place at the time of that Roman sojourn which Luke

---

[4] See below, Bk. III. chap. 4.   [5] See Acts xxviii. 30.
[6] Eusebius is the first writer to record the release of Paul from a first, and his martyrdom during a second Roman imprisonment. He introduces the statement with the formula λόγος ἔχει, which indicates probably that he has only an oral tradition as his authority, and his efforts to establish the fact by exegetical arguments show how weak the tradition was. Many maintain that Eusebius follows no tradition here, but records simply his own conclusion formed from a study of the Pastoral Epistles, which apparently necessitate a second imprisonment. But were this the case, he would hardly have used the formula λόγος ἔχει. The report may have arisen solely upon exegetical grounds, but it can hardly have originated with Eusebius himself. In accordance with this tradition, Eusebius, in his *Chron.*, gives the date of Paul's death as 67 A.D. Jerome (*de vir. ill.* 5) and other later writers follow Eusebius (though Jerome gives the date as 68 instead of 67), and the tradition soon became firmly established (see below, chap. 25, note 5). Scholars are greatly divided as to the fact of a second imprisonment. Nearly all that defend the genuineness of the Pastoral Epistles assume a second imprisonment, though some (e.g. Wieseler, Ebrard, Reuss and others) defend the epistles while assuming only one imprisonment; but this is very difficult. On the other hand, most opponents of the epistles (e.g. the Tübingen critics and the majority of the new critical school) deny the second imprisonment. As to the place where Paul spent the interval — supposing him to have been released — there is again a difference of opinion. The Pastoral Epistles, if assumed to be genuine, seem to necessitate another visit to the Orient. But for such a visit there is no ancient tradition, although Paul himself, in the Epistle to the Philippians, expresses his expectation of making such a visit. On the other hand, there is an old tradition that he visited Spain (which must of course have been during this interval, as he did not reach it before the first imprisonment). The Muratorian Fragment (from the end of the second century) records this tradition in a way to imply that it was universally known. Clement of Rome (*Epistle to the Corinthians*, c. 5.) is also claimed as a witness for such a visit, but the interpretation of his words is doubtful, so that little weight can be laid upon his statement. In later times the tradition of this visit to Spain dropped out of the Church. The strongest argument against the visit is the absence of any trace of it in Spain itself. If any church there could have claimed the great apostle to the Gentiles as its founder, it seems that it must have asserted its claim and the tradition have been preserved at least in that church. This appears to the writer a fatal argument against a journey to Spain. On the other hand, the absence of all tradition of another journey to the Orient does not militate against such a visit, for tradition at any place might easily preserve the fact of a visit of the apostle, without preserving an accurate account of the number of his visits if more than one were made. Of the defenders of the Pastoral Epistles, that accept a second imprisonment, some assume simply a journey to the Orient, others assume also the journey to Spain. Between the spring of 63 A.D., the time when he was probably released, if released, and the date of his death (at the earliest the summer of 64), there is time enough, but barely so, for both journeys. If the date of Paul's death be put later with Eusebius and Jerome (as many modern critics put it), the time is of course quite sufficient. Compare the various Lives of Paul, Commentaries, etc., and especially, among recent works, Schaff's *Church Hist.* I. p. 231 sqq.; Weiss' *Einleitung in das N. T.* p. 283 sqq.; Holtzmann's *Einleitung*, p. 295 sqq.; and Weizsäcker's *Apostolisches Zeitalter*, p. 453 sqq.
[7] See below, chap. 25, note 6.
[8] Eusebius looked upon the Pastoral Epistles as undoubtedly genuine, and placed them among the *Homologumena*, or undisputed writings (compare Bk. III. chaps. 3 and 25). The external testimony for them is very strong, but their genuineness has, during the present century, been quite widely denied upon internal grounds. The advanced critical scholars of Germany treat their non-Pauline authorship as completely established, and many otherwise conservative scholars follow their lead. It is impossible here to give the various arguments for or against their genuineness; we may refer the reader particularly to Holtzmann's *Die Pastoralbriefe, kritisch und exegetisch behandelt* (1880), and to his *Einleitung* (1886), for the most complete presentation of the case against the genuineness; and to Weiss' *Einleitung in das N. T.* (1886), p. 286 sqq.,

and to his Commentary on the Pastoral Epistles, in the fifth edition of the Meyer Series, for a defense of their genuineness, and also to Woodruff's article in the *Andover Review*, October, 1886, for a brief and somewhat popular discussion of the subject. The second epistle must have been written latest of all Paul's epistles, just before his death, — at the termination of his second captivity, or of his first, if his second be denied.
[9] 2 Tim. iv. 16, 17.
[10] 2 Tim. iv. 18.   [12] See 2 Tim. iv. 11.
[11] *Ibid.* iv. 6.   [13] See 2 Tim. iv. 16.
[14] This is a very commonly accepted opinion among conservative commentators, who thus explain the lack of mention of the persecution of Nero and of the death of Paul. On the other hand, some who accept Luke's authorship of the Acts, put the composition into the latter part of the century and explain the omission of the persecution and the death of Paul from the object of the work, e.g. Weiss, who dates the Gospel of Luke between 70 and 80, and thus brings the Acts down to a still later date (see his *Einleitung*, p. 585 sqq.). It is now becoming quite generally admitted that Luke's Gospel was written after the destruction of Jerusalem, and if this be so, the Acts must have been written still later. There is in fact no reason for supposing the book to have been written at the point of time at which its account of Paul ceases. The design of the book (its text is found in the eighth verse of the first chapter) was to give an account of the progress of the Church from Jerusalem to Rome, not to write the life of Paul. The record of Paul's death at the close of the book would have been quite out of harmony with this design, and would have formed a decided anti-climax, as the author was wise enough to understand. He was writing, not a life of Paul, nor of any apostle or group of apostles, but a history of the planting of the Church of Christ. The advanced critics, who deny that the Acts were written by a pupil of Paul, of course put its composition much later, — some into the time of Domitian, most into the second century. But even such critics admit the genuineness of certain portions of the book (the celebrated " We " passages), and the old Tübingen theory of intentional misrepresentation on the part of the author is finding less favor even among the most radical critics.

8 records. It is probable indeed that as Nero was more disposed to mildness in the beginning, Paul's defense of his doctrine was more easily received; but that when he had advanced to the commission of lawless deeds of daring, he made the apostles as well as others the subjects of his attacks.[15]

CHAPTER XXIII.

The Martyrdom of James, who was called the Brother of the Lord.

1 BUT after Paul, in consequence of his appeal to Cæsar, had been sent to Rome by Festus, the Jews, being frustrated in their hope of entrapping him by the snares which they had laid for him, turned against James, the brother of the Lord,[1] to whom the episcopal seat at Jerusalem had been entrusted by the apostles.[2] The following daring measures 2 were undertaken by them against him. Leading him into their midst they demanded of him that he should renounce faith in Christ in the presence of all the people. But, contrary to the opinion of all, with a clear voice, and with greater boldness than they had anticipated, he spoke out before the whole multitude and confessed that our Saviour and Lord Jesus is the Son of God. But they were unable to bear longer the testimony of the man who, on account of the excellence of ascetic virtue[3] and of piety which he exhibited in his life, was esteemed by all as the most just of men, and consequently they slew him. Opportunity for this deed of violence was furnished by the prevailing anarchy, which was caused by the fact that Festus had died just at this time in Judea, and that the province was thus without a governor 3 and head.[4] The manner of James' death has been already indicated by the above-quoted words of Clement, who records that he was thrown from the pinnacle of the temple, and was beaten to death with a club.[5] But Hegesippus,[6] who lived immediately after the apostles, gives the most accurate account in the fifth book of his Memoirs.[7] He writes 4 as follows : " James, the brother of the Lord,

succeeded to the government of the Church in conjunction with the apostles.[8] He has been called the Just[9] by all from the time of our Saviour to the present day; for there were many that bore the name of James. He was holy 5 from his mother's womb; and he drank no wine nor strong drink, nor did he eat flesh. No razor came upon his head; he did not anoint himself with oil, and he did not use the bath. He alone was permitted to enter 6 into the holy place; for he wore not woolen but linen garments. And he was in the habit of entering alone into the temple, and was frequently found upon his knees begging forgiveness for the people, so that his knees became hard like those of a camel, in consequence of his constantly bending them in his worship of God, and asking forgiveness for the people.[10] Because 7 of his exceeding great justice he was called the Just, and Oblias,[11] which signifies in Greek, 'Bulwark of the people' and 'Justice,'[12] in accordance with what the prophets declare concerning him.[13] Now some of the seven 8 sects, which existed among the people and which have been mentioned by me in the Memoirs,[14] asked him, 'What is the gate of Jesus?'[15]

---

[8] μετὰ τῶν ἀποστόλων, "with the apostles"; as Rufinus rightly translates, *cum apostolis*. Jerome, on the contrary, reads *post apostolos*, "after the apostles," as if the Greek were μετὰ τοὺς ἀποστόλους. This statement of Hegesippus is correct. James was a leader of the Jerusalem church, in company with Peter and John, as we see from Gal. ii. 9. But that is quite different from saying, as Eusebius does just above, and as Clement (quoted by Eusebius, chap. 1, § 3) does, that he was appointed Bishop of Jerusalem by the apostles. See chap. 1, note 11.   [9] See chap. 1, note 6.
[10] "The dramatic account of James by Hegesippus is an overdrawn picture from the middle of the second century, colored by Judaizing traits which may have been derived from the *Ascents of James*, and other Apocryphal sources. He turns James into a Jewish priest and Nazarite saint (cf. his advice to Paul, Acts xxi. 23, 24), who drank no wine, ate no flesh, never shaved nor took a bath, and wore only linen. But the Biblical James is Pharisaic and legalistic, rather than Essenic and ascetic" (Schaff, *Ch. Hist.* I. p. 268). For Peter's asceticism, see the Clementine *Recognitions*, VII. 6; and for Matthew's, see Clement of Alexandria's *Pædagogus*, II. 1.
[11] 'Ωβλίας : probably a corruption of the Heb. עַם אֹבֶל, which signifies "bulwark of the people." The same name is given to James by Epiphanius, by Dionysius the Areopagite, and others. See Suicer, *Thesaurus Ecclesiasticus*, s.v.
[12] περιοχὴ τοῦ λαοῦ καὶ δικαιοσύνη.
[13] To what Hegesippus refers I do not know, as there is no passage in the prophets which can be interpreted in this way. He may have been thinking of the passage from Isaiah quoted in § 15, below, but the reference is certainly very much strained.
[14] See Bk. IV. chap. 22.
[15] For a discussion of this very difficult question, whose interpretation has puzzled all commentators, see Routh' *Rel. Sac.* I. p. 434 sq., and Heinichen's Mel. IV., in his edition of Eusebius, Vol. III., p. 654 sqq. The explanation given by Grabe (in his *Spic. PP.* p. 254), seems to me the best. According to him, the Jews wish to ascertain James' opinion in regard to Christ, whether he considers him a true guide or an impostor, and therefore they ask, "What (of what sort) is the gate (or the way) of Christ? Is it a gate which opens into life (or a way which leads to life); or is it a gate which opens upon death (or a way which leads to death)?" Cf. Matt. vii. 13, 14, where the two ways and the two gates are compared. The Jews had undoubtedly often heard Christ called "the Way," and thus they might naturally use the expression in asking James' opinion about Jesus, "Is he the true or the false way?" or, "Is this way true or false?" The answer of James which follows is then perfectly consistent: "He is the Saviour," in which words he expresses as decidedly as he can his belief that the way or the gate of Christ led to salvation. And so below, in § 12, where he gives a second answer to the question, expressing his belief in Christ still more emphatically. This is somewhat similar to the explanation of Heinichen (*ibid.* p. 659 sq.), who construes the genitive 'Iησοῦ as in virtual apposition to θυρα: "What is this way, Jesus?" But Grabe seems to bring out most clearly the true meaning of the question.

---

[15] Whether Eusebius' conclusion be correct or not, it is a fact that Nero became much more cruel and tyrannical in the latter part of his reign. The famous "first five years," however exaggerated the reports about them, must at least have been of a very different character from the remainder of his reign. But those five years of clemency and justice were past before Paul reached Rome.
[1] See above, Bk. I. chap. 12, note 14.
[2] See above, chap. 1, note 11.
[3] φιλοσοφίας. See Bk. VI. chap. 3, note 9.
[4] See the preceding chapter, note 1, and below, note 40.
[5] See chap. 1, above.
[6] On Hegesippus, see Bk. IV. chap. 22.
[7] As the Memoirs of Hegesippus consisted of but five books, this account of James occurred in the last book, and this shows how entirely lacking the work was in all chronological arrangement (cf. Book IV. chap. 22). This fragment is given by Routh, *Rel. Sac.* I. p. 208 sqq., with a valuable discussion on p. 228 sqq.

and he replied that he was the Saviour.
9   On account of these words some believed
that Jesus is the Christ. But the sects mentioned above did not believe either in a resurrection or in one's coming to give to every
man according to his works.[16] But as many as
believed did so on account of James.
10   Therefore when many even of the rulers
believed, there was a commotion among
the Jews and Scribes and Pharisees, who said
that there was danger that the whole people
would be looking for Jesus as the Christ. Coming therefore in a body to James they said, 'We
entreat thee, restrain the people ; for they are
gone astray in regard to Jesus, as if he were the
Christ.[17] We entreat thee to persuade all that
have come to the feast of the Passover concerning Jesus ; for we all have confidence in thee.
For we bear thee witness, as do all the people,
that thou art just, and dost not respect per-
11   sons.[18] Do thou therefore persuade the
multitude not to be led astray concerning
Jesus. For the whole people, and all of us also,
have confidence in thee. Stand therefore upon
the pinnacle of the temple,[19] that from that high
position thou mayest be clearly seen, and that
thy words may be readily heard by all the people. For all the tribes, with the Gentiles also,
are come together on account of the Pass-
12   over.' The aforesaid Scribes and Pharisees
therefore placed James upon the pinnacle
of the temple, and cried out to him and said:
'Thou just one, in whom we ought all to have
confidence, forasmuch as the people are led
astray after Jesus, the crucified one, declare
13   to us, what is the gate of Jesus.'[20] And he answered with a loud voice, 'Why do ye ask me

concerning Jesus, the Son of Man? He himself
sitteth in heaven at the right hand of the great
Power, and is about to come upon the
clouds of heaven.'[21]   And when many were   14
fully convinced and gloried in the testimony
of James, and said, 'Hosanna to the Son of
David,' these same Scribes and Pharisees said
again to one another, 'We have done badly in
supplying such testimony to Jesus. But let us
go up and throw him down, in order that
they may be afraid to believe him.' And   15
they cried out, saying, 'Oh ! oh ! the just
man is also in error.' And they fulfilled the
Scripture written in Isaiah,[22] 'Let us take away[23]
the just man, because he is troublesome to us :
therefore they shall eat the fruit of their
doings.' So they went up and threw down   16
the just man, and said to each other, 'Let
us stone James the Just.' And they began to
stone him, for he was not killed by the fall ; but
he turned and knelt down and said, 'I entreat
thee, Lord God our Father,[24] forgive them,
for they know not what they do.'[25]   And   17
while they were thus stoning him one of
the priests of the sons of Rechab, the son of the
Rechabites,[26] who are mentioned by Jeremiah
the prophet,[27] cried out, saying, 'Cease, what
do ye? The just one prayeth for you.'[28]

[21] Cf. Matt. xxvi. 64 and Mark xiv. 62.
[22] Isa. iii. 10. Jess (p. 50) says, "Auch darin ist Hegesipp
nur ein Kind seiner Zeit, dass er in ausgedehntem Masse im Alten
Testamente Weissagungen auffindet. Aber mit Bezug darauf darf
man nicht vergessen, — dass dergleichen mehr oratorische Benut-
zung als exegetische Erklärungen sein sollen." Cf. the writer's
Dialogue between a Christian and a Jew (Papiscus and Philo),
chap. 1.
[23] ἄρωμεν. The LXX, as we have it to-day, reads δήσωμεν, but
Justin Martyr's Dial., chap. 136, reads ἄρωμεν (though in chaps.
17 and 133 it reads δήσωμεν). Tertullian also in his Adv. Marc.
Bk. III. chap. 22, shows that he read ἄρωμεν, for he translates
auferamus.
[24] Κύριε θεὲ πάτερ.   [25] Luke xxiii. 34.
[26] 'Ραχαβείμ, which is simply the reproduction in Greek letters
of the Hebrew plural, and is equivalent to "the Rechabites." But
Hegesippus uses it without any article as if it were the name of an
individual, just as he uses the name 'Ρηχάβ which immediately precedes. The Rechabites were a tribe who took their origin from Jehonadab, the son of Rechab, who appears from 1 Chron. ii. 55 to
have belonged to a branch of the Kenites, the Arabian tribe which
came into Palestine with the Israelites. Jehonadab enjoined upon
his descendants a nomadic and ascetic mode of life, which they
observed with great strictness for centuries, and received a blessing from God on account of their steadfastness (Jer. xxxv. 19).
That a Rechabite, who did not belong to the tribe of Judah, nor
even to the genuine people of Israel, should have been a priest
seems at first sight inexplicable. Different solutions have been offered. Some think that Hegesippus was mistaken, — the source
from which he took his account having confounded this ascetic
Rechabite with a priest, — but this is hardly probable. Plumptre,
in Smith's Bib. Dict. art. Rechabites (which see for a full account of
the tribe), thinks that the blessing pronounced upon them by God
(Jer. xxxv. 19) included their solemn adoption among the people of
Israel, and their incorporation into the tribe of Levi, and therefore into
the number of the priests. Others (e.g. Tillemont, H. E. I. p. 633)
have supposed that many Jews, including also priests, embraced the
practices and the institutions of the Rechabites and were therefore
identified with them. The language here, however, seems to imply
a native Rechabite, and it is probable that Hegesippus at least believed this person to be such, whether his belief was correct or not.
See Routh, I. p. 243 sq.   [27] See Jer. xxxv.
[28] In Epiphanius, Haer. LXXVIII. 14, these words are put into
the mouth of Simeon, the son of Clopas; from which some have
concluded that Simeon had joined the order of the Rechabites; but
there is no ground for such an assumption. The Simeon of Epiphanius and the Rechabite of Hegesippus are not necessarily identical. They represent simply varieties of the original account, and
Epiphanius', as the more exact, was undoubtedly the later tradition,
and an intentional improvement upon the vagueness of the original.

[16] Rufinus translates non crediderunt neque surrexisse eum,
&c., and he is followed by Fabricius (Cod. Apoc. N. T. II. p. 603).
This rendering suits the context excellently, and seems to be the
only rendering which gives any meaning to the following sentence.
And yet, as our Greek stands, it is impossible to translate thus, as
both ἀνάστασιν and ἐρχόμενον are left entirely indefinite. The
Greek runs, οὐκ ἐπίστευον ἀνάστασιν, οὔτε ἐρχόμενον ἀποδοῦναι,
κ.τ.λ. Cf. the notes of Valesius and of Heinichen on this passage.
Of these seven sects, so far as we know, only one, the Sadducees,
disbelieved in the resurrection from the dead. If Hegesippus' words,
therefore, be understood of a general resurrection, he is certainly in
error.
[17] This sentence sufficiently reveals the legendary character of
Hegesippus' account. James' position as a Christian must have
been well enough known to prevent such a request being made to
him in good faith (and there is no sign that it was made in any other
spirit); and at any rate, after his reply to them already recorded,
such a repetition of the question in public is absurd. Fabricius, who
does not think the account is true, says that, if it is, the Jews seem
to have asked him a second time, thinking that they could either
flatter or frighten him into denying Christ.
[18] Cf. Matt. xxii. 16.
[19] ἐπὶ τὸ πτερύγιον τοῦ ναοῦ. Some MSS. read τοῦ ἱεροῦ, and
in the preceding paragraph that phrase occurs, which is identical
with the phrase used in Matt. iv. 5, where the devil places Christ on
a pinnacle of the temple. ἱερός is the general name for the temple
buildings as a whole, while ναός is a specific name for the temple
proper.
[20] Some MSS., with Rufinus and the editions of Valesius and
Heinichen, add σταυρωθέντος, "who was crucified," and Stroth,
Closs, and Crusè follow this reading in their translations. But many
of the best MSS. omit the words, as do also Nicephorus, Burton,
Routh, Schwegler, Laemmer, and Stigloher, and I prefer to follow
their example, as the words seem to be an addition from the previous
line.

18 And one of them, who was a fuller, took the club with which he beat out clothes and struck the just man on the head. And thus he suffered martyrdom.[29] And they buried him on the spot, by the temple, and his monument still remains by the temple.[30] He became a true witness, both to Jews and Greeks, that Jesus is the Christ. And immediately Vespasian besieged them."[31]

19 These things are related at length by Hegesippus, who is in agreement with Clement.[32] James was so admirable a man and so celebrated among all for his justice, that the more sensible even of the Jews were of the opinion that this was the cause of the siege of Jerusalem, which happened to them immediately after his martyrdom for no other reason than 20 their daring act against him. Josephus, at least, has not hesitated to testify this in his writings, where he says,[33] "These things happened to the Jews to avenge James the Just, who was a brother of Jesus, that is called the Christ. For the Jews slew him, although 21 he was a most just man." And the same writer records his death also in the twentieth book of his Antiquities in the following words : [34] "But the emperor, when he learned of the death of Festus, sent Albinus [35] to be

procurator of Judea. But the younger Ananus,[36] who, as we have already said,[37] had obtained the high priesthood, was of an exceedingly bold and reckless disposition. He belonged, moreover, to the sect of the Sadducees, who are the most cruel of all the Jews in the execution of judgment, as we have already shown.[38] Ananus, 22 therefore, being of this character, and supposing that he had a favorable opportunity on account of the fact that Festus was dead, and Albinus was still on the way, called together the Sanhedrim, and brought before them the brother of Jesus, the so-called Christ, James by name, together with some others,[39] and accused them of violating the law, and condemned them to be stoned.[40] But those in the city who 23 seemed most moderate and skilled in the law were very angry at this, and sent secretly to the king,[41] requesting him to order Ananus to cease such proceedings. For he had not done right even this first time. And certain of them also went to meet Albinus, who was journeying from Alexandria, and reminded him that it was not lawful for Ananus to summon the Sanhedrim without his knowledge.[42] And Albinus, being 24

---

[29] Clement (in chap. 5, § 4, above), who undoubtedly used the account of Hegesippus as his source, describes the death of James as taking place in the same way, but omits the stoning which preceded. Josephus, on the other hand (quoted below), mentions only the stoning. But Hegesippus' account, which is the fullest that we have, gives us the means of reconciling the briefer accounts of Clement and of Josephus, and we have no reason to think either account incorrect.

[30] Valesius remarks that the monument (στήλη) could not have stood through the destruction of Jerusalem until the time of Hegesippus, nor could James have been buried near the temple, as the Jews always buried their dead without the city walls. Tillemont attempted to meet the difficulty by supposing that James was thrown from a pinnacle of the temple overlooking the Valley of Jehoshaphat, and therefore fell without the walls, where he was stoned and buried, and where his monument could remain undisturbed. Tillemont, however, afterward withdrew his explanation, which was beset with difficulties. Others have supposed that the monument mentioned by Hegesippus was erected after the destruction of Jerusalem (cf. Jerome, de vir. ill. 2), while his body was buried in another place. This is quite possible, as Hegesippus must have seen some monument of James which was reported to have been the original one, but which must certainly have been of later date. A monument, which is now commonly known as the tomb of St. James, is shown upon the east side of the Valley of Jehoshaphat, and therefore at a considerable distance from the temple. See Routh, Rel. Sac. I. p. 246 sqq.   [31] See below, note 40.

[32] See above, chap. 1, § 4. His agreement with Clement is not very surprising, inasmuch as the latter probably drew his knowledge from the account of the former.

[33] This passage is not found in our existing MSS. of Josephus, but is given by Origen (Contra Celsum, I. 47), which shows at any rate that Eusebius did not invent the words. It is probable therefore, that the copies of Josephus used by Origen and Eusebius contained this interpolation, while the copies from which our existing MSS. drew were without it. It is of course possible, especially since he does not mention the reference in Josephus, that Eusebius quoted these words from Origen. But this does not help matters any, as it still remains as difficult to account for the occurrence of the words in Origen, and even if Eusebius did take the passage from Origen instead of from Josephus himself, we still have no right with Jachmann (ib. p. 40) to accuse him of wilful deception. For with his great confidence in Origen, and his unbounded admiration for him, and with his naturally uncritical spirit, he would readily accept as true in all good faith a quotation given by Origen and purporting to be taken from Josephus, even though he could not find it in his own copy of the latter's works.   [34] Ant. XX. 9. 1.

[35] Albinus succeeded Festus in 61 or 62 A.D. He was a very corrupt governor and was in turn succeeded by Gessius Florus in 64 A.D. See Wieseler, Chron. d. Ap. Zeitalters, p. 89.

[36] Ananus was the fifth son of the high priest Annas mentioned in the N. T. His father and his four brothers had been high priests before him, as Josephus tells us in this same paragraph. He was appointed high priest by Agrippa II. in 61 or 62 A.D., and held the office but three months.

[37] Ananus' accession is recorded by Josephus in a sentence immediately preceding, which Eusebius, who abridges Josephus' account somewhat, has omitted in this quotation.

[38] I can find no previous mention in Josephus of the hardness of the Sadducees; but see Reland's note upon this passage in Josephus. It may be that we have lost a part of the account of the Sadducees and Pharisees.

[39] καὶ παραγαγὼν εἰς αὐτὸ [τὸν ἀδελφὸν Ἰησοῦ τοῦ χριστοῦ λεγομένου, Ἰάκωβος ὄνομα αὐτῷ, καί] τινας [ἑτέρους], κ.τ.λ. Some critics regard the bracketed words as spurious, but Neander, Gesch. der Pflanzung und Leitung der Christlichen Kirche, 5th ed., p. 445, note, contends for their genuineness, and this is now the common opinion of critics. It is in fact very difficult to suppose that a Christian in interpolating the passage, would have referred to James as the brother of the "so-called Christ." On the other hand, as the words stand there is no good reason to doubt their genuineness.

[40] The date of the martyrdom of James, given here by Josephus, is 61 or 62 A.D. (at the time of the Passover, according to Hegesippus, § 10, above). There is no reason for doubting this date which is given with such exactness by Josephus, and it is further confirmed by Eusebius in his Chron., who puts James's martyrdom in the seventh year of Nero, i.e. 61 A.D., while Jerome puts it in the eighth year of Nero. The Clementines and the Chronicon Paschale, which state that James survived Peter, and are therefore cited in support of a later date, are too late to be of any weight over against such an exact statement as that of Josephus, especially since Peter and James died at such a distance from one another. Hegesippus has been cited over and over again by historians as assigning the date of the martyrdom to 69 A.D., and as thus being in direct conflict with Josephus; as a consequence some follow his supposed date, others that of Josephus. But I can find no reason for asserting that Hegesippus assigns the martyrdom to 69. Certainly his words in this chapter, which are referred to, by no means necessitate such an assumption. He concludes his account with the words καὶ εὐθὺς Οὐεσπασιανὸς πολιορκεῖ αὐτούς. The πολιορκεῖ αὐτούς is certainly to be referred to the commencement of the war (not to the siege of the city of Jerusalem, which was undertaken by Titus, not by Vespasian), i.e. to the year 67 A.D., and in such an account as this, in which the overthrow of the Jews is designedly presented in connection with the death of James, it is hyper-criticism to insist that the word εὐθὺς must indicate a space of time of only a few months' duration. It is a very indefinite word, and the most we can draw from Hegesippus' account is that not long before Vespasian's invasion of Judea, James was slain. The same may be said in regard to Eusebius' report in Bk. III. chap. 11, § 1, which certainly is not definite enough to be cited as a contradiction of his express statement in his Chronicle. But however it may be with this report and that of Hegesippus, the date given by Josephus is undoubtedly to be accepted as correct.   [41] Agrippa II.

[42] ὡς οὐκ ἐξὸν ἦν Ἀνάνῳ χωρὶς τῆς αὐτοῦ γνώμης καθίσαι συνέ-

persuaded by their representations, wrote in anger to Ananus, threatening him with punishment. And the king, Agrippa, in consequence, deprived him of the high priesthood,[43] which he had held three months, and appointed Jesus, the son of
25 Damnæus." [44] These things are recorded in regard to James, who is said to be the author of the first of the so-called catholic [45] epistles. But it is to be observed that it is disputed ; [46] at least, not many of the ancients have mentioned it, as is the case likewise with the epistle that bears the name of Jude,[47] which is

also one of the seven so-called catholic epistles. Nevertheless we know that these also,[48] with the rest, have been read publicly in very many churches.[49]

CHAPTER XXIV.

Annianus the First Bishop of the Church of Alexandria after Mark.

WHEN Nero was in the eighth year of his reign,[1] Annianus [2] succeeded Mark the evangelist in the administration of the parish of Alexandria.[3]

CHAPTER XXV.

The Persecution under Nero in which Paul and Peter were honored at Rome with Martyrdom in Behalf of Religion.

WHEN the government of Nero was now 1 firmly established, he began to plunge into unholy pursuits, and armed himself even against the religion of the God of the universe. To describe the greatness of his depravity 2 does not lie within the plan of the present work. As there are many indeed that have recorded his history in most accurate narratives,[1] every one may at his pleasure learn from them the coarseness of the man's extraordinary madness, under the influence of which, after he had accomplished the destruction of so many myriads without any reason, he ran into such blood-guiltiness that he did not spare even his nearest relatives and dearest friends, but destroyed his mother and his brothers and his wife,[2] with very many others of his own family,

---

δριον. Jost reads ἐκείνου (referring to Agrippa) instead of αὐτοῦ (referring to Albinus), and consequently draws the conclusion that the Sanhedrim could be called only with the consent of Agrippa, and that therefore Ananus had acted contrary to the rights of Agrippa, but not contrary to the rights of Albinus. But the reading αυτου is supported by overwhelming MS. authority, and must be regarded as undoubtedly correct. Jost's conclusion, therefore, which his acceptance of the ἐκείνου forced upon him, is quite incorrect. The passage appears to imply that the Sanhedrim could be called only with the consent of the procurator, and it has been so interpreted; but as Schürer points out (*Gesch. der Juden im Zeitalter Jesu Christi*, p. 169 sq.), this conclusion is incorrect, and all that the passage implies is that the Sanhedrim could not hold a sovereign process, that is, could not meet for the purpose of passing sentence of death and executing the sentence, during the absence or without the consent of the procurator. For the transaction of ordinary business the consent of the procurator was not necessary. Compare the Commentaries on John xviii. 31, and the remarks of Schürer in the passage referred to above.

[43] Agrippa, as remarked above, chap. 19, note 4, exercised government over the temple, and enjoyed the power of appointing and removing the high priests.

[44] Of Jesus, the son of Damnæus, nothing further is known. He was succeeded, while Albinus was still procurator, by Jesus, the son of Gamaliel (*Ant.* XX. 9. 4).

[45] This term was applied to all or a part of these seven epistles by the Alexandrian Clement, Origen, and Dionysius, and since the time of Eusebius has been the common designation. The word is used in the sense of " general," to denote that the epistles are encyclical letters addressed to no particular persons or congregations, though this is not true of II. and III. John, which, however, are classed with the others on account of their supposed Johannine authorship, and consequent close connection with his first epistle. The word was not first used, as some have held, in the sense of " canonical," to denote the catholic or general acceptance of the epistle, — a meaning which Eusebius contradicts in this very passage, and which the history of the epistles themselves (five of the seven being among the antilegomena) sufficiently refutes. See Holtzmann's *Einleitung*, p. 472 sqq., and Weiss, *ibid.* p. 89 sqq.

[46] νοθεύεται. It is common to translate the word νόθος, " spurious" (and the kindred verb, " to be spurious"); but it is plain enough from this passage, as also from others, that Eusebius did not employ the word in that sense. He commonly used it, in fact, in a loose way, to mean " disputed," in the same sense in which he often employed the word ἀντιλεγόμενος. Lücke, indeed, maintained that Eusebius always used the words νόθος and ἀντιλεγόμενος as synonymous; but in Bk. III. chap. 25, as pointed out in note 1 on that chapter, he employed the words as respective designations of two distinct classes of books.

The Epistle of James is classed by Eusebius (in Bk. III. chap. 25) among the antilegomena. The ancient testimonies for it are very few: It was used by no one, except Hermas, down to the end of the second century. Irenæus seems to have known the epistle (his works exhibit some apparent reminiscences of it), but he nowhere directly cites it. The Muratorian Fragment omits it, but the Syriac Peshito contains it, and Clement of Alexandria shows a few faint reminiscences of it in his extant works, and according to Eusebius, VI. 14, wrote commentaries upon " Jude and the other catholic epistles." It is quoted frequently by Origen, who first connects it with the " Brother of the Lord," but does not express himself with decision as to its authenticity. From his time on it was commonly accepted as the work of " James, the Lord's brother." Eusebius throws it among the antilegomena; not necessarily because he considered it unauthentic, but because the early testimonies for it are too few to raise it to the dignity of one of the homologoumena (see Bk. III. chap. 25, note 1). Luther rejected the epistle upon purely dogmatic grounds. The advanced critical school are unanimous in considering it a post-apostolic work, and many conservative scholars agree with them. See Holtzmann's *Einleitung*, p. 475 sqq., and Weiss' *Einleitung*, p. 396 sqq. The latter defends its authenticity (i.e. the authorship of James, the brother of the Lord), and, in agreement with many other scholars of conservative tendencies, throws its origin back into the early part of the fifties.

[47] The authenticity of the Epistle of Jude (also classed among

the antilegomena by Eusebius in Bk. III. chap. 25) is about as well supported as that of the Epistle of James. The Peshito does not contain it, and the Syrian Church in general rejected it for a number of centuries. The Muratorian Fragment accepts it, and Tertullian evidently considered it a work of Jude, the apostle (see *De Cultu Fem.* I. 3). The first to quote from it is Clement of Alexandria, who wrote a commentary upon it in connection with the other catholic epistles, according to Eusebius, VI. 14. 1. Origen looked upon it much as he looked upon the Epistle of James, but did not make the " Jude, the brother of James," one of the twelve apostles. Eusebius treats it as he does James, and Luther, followed by many modern conservative scholars (among them Neander), rejects it. Its defenders commonly ascribe it to Jude, the brother of the Lord, in distinction from Jude the apostle, and put its composition before the destruction of Jerusalem. The advanced critical school unanimously deny its authenticity, and most of them throw its composition into the second century, although some put it back into the latter part of the first. See Holtzmann, p. 501.

[48] On the Epistles of Peter, see Bk. III. chap. 3, notes 1 and 2. On the Epistles of John, see *ibid.* chap. 44, notes 18 and 19.

[49] ἐν πλείσταις ἐκκλησίαις.

[1] 62 A.D. With this agrees Jerome's version of the *Chron.*, while the Armenian version gives the seventh year of Nero.

[2] Annianus, according to Bk. III. chap. 14, below, held his office twenty-two years. In *Apost. Const.* VII. 46 he is said to have been ordained by Mark as the first bishop of Alexandria. The *Chron. Orient.* 89 (according to Westcott in the *Dict. of Christ. Biog.*) reports that he was appointed by Mark after he had performed a miracle upon him. He is commemorated in the Roman martyrology with St. Mark, on April 25.

[3] Upon Mark's connection with Egypt, see above, chap. 16, note 1.

[1] Tacitus (*Ann.* XIII.-XVI.), Suetonius (*Nero*), and Dion Cassius (LXI.-LXIII.).

[2] Nero's mother, Agrippina the younger, daughter of Germani-

as he would private and public enemies,
3 with various kinds of deaths. But with
all these things this particular in the catalogue of his crimes was still wanting, that he
was the first of the emperors who showed
himself an enemy of the divine religion.
4 The Roman Tertullian is likewise a witness
of this. He writes as follows : [3] " Examine
your records. There you will find that Nero
was the first that persecuted this doctrine,[4]
particularly then when after subduing all the
east, he exercised his cruelty against all at
Rome.[5] We glory in having such a man the
leader in our punishment. For whoever knows
him can understand that nothing was condemned by Nero unless it was something
5 of great excellence." Thus publicly announcing himself as the first among God's
chief enemies, he was led on to the slaughter of
the apostles. It is, therefore, recorded that
Paul was beheaded in Rome itself,[6] and that

Peter likewise was crucified under Nero.[7] This
account of Peter and Paul is substantiated by the
fact that their names are preserved in the cemeteries of that place even to the present
day. It is confirmed likewise by Caius,[8]   6

the first quarter of the third century, is another witness to his death
in Rome, as is also Dionysius of Corinth (quoted below, § 8) of the
second century. Origen (quoted by Euseb. III. 1) states that he
was martyred in Rome under Nero. Tertullian (at the end of the
second century), in his *De præscriptione Hær.* chap. 36, is still
more distinct, recording that Paul was beheaded in Rome. Eusebius and Jerome accept this tradition unhesitatingly, and we may
do likewise. As a Roman citizen, we should expect him to meet
death by the sword.

[7] The tradition that Peter suffered martyrdom in Rome is as old
and as universal as that in regard to Paul, but owing to a great
amount of falsehood which became mixed with the original tradition
by the end of the second century the whole has been rejected as
untrue by some modern critics, who go so far as to deny that Peter
was ever at Rome. (See especially Lipsius' *Die Quellen der
römischen Petrus-Sage*, Kiel, 1872; a summary of his view is given
by Jackson in the *Presbyterian Quarterly and Princeton Review*,
1876, p. 265 sq. In Lipsius' latest work upon this subject, *Die
Acta Pauli und Petri*, 1887, he makes important concessions.)
The tradition is, however, too strong to be set aside, and there is
absolutely no trace of any conflicting tradition. We may therefore
assume it as overwhelmingly probable that Peter was in Rome and
suffered martyrdom there. His martyrdom is plainly referred to in
John xxi. 10, though the place of it is not given. The first extra-
biblical witness to it is Clement of Rome. He also leaves the place
of the martyrdom unspecified (*Ad Cor.* 5), but he evidently assumes the place as well known, and indeed it is impossible that the
early Church could have known of the death of Peter and Paul
without knowing where they died, and there is in neither case a
single opposing tradition. Ignatius (*Ad Rom.* chap. 4) connects
Paul and Peter in an especial way with the Roman Church, which
seems plainly to imply that Peter had been in Rome. Phlegon
(supposed to be the Emperor Hadrian writing under the name of a
favorite slave) is said by Origen (*Contra Celsum*, II. 14) to have
confused Jesus and Peter in his *Chronicles*. This is very significant as implying that Peter must have been well known in Rome.
Dionysius, quoted below, distinctly states that Peter labored in
Rome, and Caius is a witness for it. So Irenæus, Clement, Tertullian, and later Fathers without a dissenting voice. The first to mention Peter's death by crucifixion (unless John xxi. 18 be supposed
to imply it) is Tertullian (*De Præscrip. Hær.* chap. 36), but he
mentions it as a fact already known, and tradition since his time is
so unanimous in regard to it that we may consider it in the highest
degree probable. On the tradition reported by Origen, that Peter
was crucified head downward, see below, Bk. III. chap. 1, where
Origen is quoted by Eusebius.

[8] The history of Caius is veiled in obscurity. All that we know
of him is that he was a very learned ecclesiastical writer, who at
the beginning of the third century held a disputation with Proclus in
Rome (cf. Bk. VI. chap. 20, below). The accounts of him given
by Jerome, Theodoret, and Nicephorus are drawn from Eusebius
and furnish us no new data. Photius, however (*Bibl.* XLVIII.),
reports that Caius was said to have been a presbyter of the Roman
Church during the episcopates of Victor and Zephyrinus, and to
have been elected " Bishop of the Gentiles," and hence he is commonly spoken of as a presbyter of the Roman Church, though the
tradition rests certainly upon a very slender foundation, as Photius
lived some six hundred years after Caius, and is the first to mention
the fact. Photius also, although with hesitation, ascribes to Caius a
work *On the Cause of the Universe*, and one called *The Labyrinth*, and another *Against the Heresy of Artemon* (see below,
Bk. V. chap. 28, note 1). The first of these (and by some the
last also), is now commonly ascribed to Hippolytus. Though the
second may have been written by Caius it is no longer extant, and
hence all that we have of his writings are the fragments of the
Dialogue with Proclus preserved by Eusebius in this chapter and
in Bk. III. chaps. 28, 31. The absence of any notice of the personal
activity of so distinguished a writer has led some critics (e.g. Salmon
in Smith and Wace, I. p. 386, who refers to Lightfoot, *Journal of
Philology*, I. 98, as holding the same view) to assume the identity
of Caius and Hippolytus, supposing that Hippolytus in the *Dialogue with Proclus* styled himself simply by his prænomen Caius,
and that thus as the book fell into the hands of strangers the tradition arose of a writer Caius who in reality never had a separate existence. This theory is ingenious, and in many respects plausible, and
certainly cannot be disproved (owing chiefly to our lack of knowledge
about Caius), and yet in the absence of any proof that Hippolytus actually bore the prænomen Caius it can be regarded as no more than a
bare hypothesis. The two are distinguished by Eusebius and by all
the writers who mention them. On Caius' attitude toward the Apocalypse, see Bk. III. chap. 28, note 4; and on his opinion in regard
to the authorship of the Epistle to the Hebrews, see Bk. VI. chap.
20, and Bk. III. chap. 3, note 17. The fragments of Caius (including fragments from the *Little Labyrinth*, mentioned above) are
given with annotations in Routh's *Rel. Sacræ*, II. 125–158, and in
translation (with the addition of the Muratorian Fragment, wrongly
ascribed to Caius by its discoverer) in the *Ante-Nicene Fathers*,

cus and of Agrippina the elder, was assassinated at Nero's command
in 60 A.D. in her villa on Lake Lucrine, after an unsuccessful attempt
to drown her in a boat so constructed as to break to pieces while she
was sailing in it on the lake. His younger brother Britannicus was
poisoned by his order at a banquet in 55 A.D. His first wife Octavia
was divorced in order that he might marry Poppæa, the wife of his
friend Otho, and was afterward put to death. Poppæa herself died
from the effects of a kick given her by Nero while she was with
child.   [3] Tertullian, *Apol.* V.

[4] We learn from Tacitus, *Ann.* XV. 39, that Nero was suspected
to be the author of the great Roman conflagration, which took place
in 64 A.D. (Pliny, *H. N.* XVII. 1, Suetonius, 38, and Dion Cassius,
LXII. 18, state directly that he was the author of it), and that to
avert this suspicion from himself he accused the Christians of the
deed, and the terrible Neronian persecution which Tacitus describes
so fully was the result. Gibbon, and in recent times especially Schil-
ler (*Geschichte der Römischen Kaiserzeit unter der Regierung
des Nero*, p. 584 sqq.), have maintained that Tacitus was mistaken
in calling this a persecution of Christians, which was rather a persecution of the Jews as a whole. But we have no reason for impeaching Tacitus' accuracy in this case, especially since we remember
that the Jews enjoyed favor with Nero through his wife Poppæa.
What is very significant, Josephus is entirely silent in regard to a
persecution of his countrymen under Nero. We may assume as
probable (with Ewald and Renan) that it was through the suggestion of the Jews that Nero's attention was drawn to the Christians,
and he was led to throw the guilt upon them, as a people whose
habits would best give countenance to such a suspicion, and most
easily excite the rage of the populace against them. This was not
a persecution of the Christians in the strict sense, that is, it was not
aimed against their religion as such; and yet it assumed such proportions and was attended with such horrors that it always lived in
the memory of the Church as the first and one of the most awful of
a long line of persecutions instituted against them by imperial Rome,
and it revealed to them the essential conflict which existed between
Rome as it then was and Christianity.

[5] The Greek translator of Tertullian's *Apology*, whoever he may
have been (certainly not Eusebius himself; see chap. 2, note 9,
above), being ignorant of the Latin idiom *cum maxime*, has made
very bad work of this sentence, and has utterly destroyed the sense
of the original, which runs as follows: *illic reperietis primum
Neronem in hanc sectam cum maxime Romæ orientem Cæsa-
riano gladio ferocisse* ("There you will find that Nero was the
first to assail with the imperial sword the Christian sect, which was
then especially flourishing in Rome"). The Greek translation
reads: ἐκεῖ εὑρήσετε πρῶτον Νερῶνα τοῦτο τὸ δόγμα, ἡνίκα μάλιστα
ἐν Ῥώμῃ τὴν ἀνατολὴν πᾶσαν ὑποτάξας ὠμὸς ἦν εἰς πάντας, διώ-
ξοντα, in the rendering of which I have followed Cruse, who has reproduced the idea of the Greek translator with as much fidelity as
the sentence will allow. The German translators, Stroth and Closs,
render the sentence directly from the original Latin, and thus preserve the meaning of Tertullian, which is, of course, what the Greek
translator intended to reproduce. I have not, however, felt at liberty in the present case to follow their example.

[6] This tradition, that Paul suffered martyrdom in Rome, is early
and universal, and disputed by no counter-tradition, and may be
accepted as the one certain historical fact known about Paul outside
of the New Testament accounts. Clement (*Ad. Cor.* chap. 5) is the
first to mention the death of Paul, and seems to imply, though he
does not directly state, that his death took place in Rome during
the persecution of Nero. Caius (quoted below, § 7), a writer of

a member of the Church,[9] who arose [10] under Zephyrinus,[11] bishop of Rome. He, in a published disputation with Proclus,[12] the leader of the Phrygian heresy,[13] speaks as follows concerning the places where the sacred corpses

7 of the aforesaid apostles are laid : "But [14] I can show the trophies of the apostles. For if you will go to the Vatican [15] or to the Ostian way,[16] you will find the trophies of those who laid the foundations of this church." [17]

8 And that they both suffered martyrdom at the same time is stated by Dionysius,[18] bishop of Corinth,[18] in his epistle to the Romans,[19] in the following words : "You have thus by such an admonition bound together the planting of Peter and of Paul at Rome and Corinth. For both of them planted and likewise taught us in our Corinth.[20] And they

taught together in like manner in Italy, and suffered martyrdom at the same time." [21] I have quoted these things in order that the truth of the history might be still more confirmed.

CHAPTER XXVI.

The Jews, afflicted with Innumerable Evils, commenced the Last War against the Romans.

JOSEPHUS again, after relating many things   1 in connection with the calamity which came upon the whole Jewish nation, records,[1] in addition to many other circumstances, that a great many[2] of the most honorable among the Jews were scourged in Jerusalem itself and then crucified by Florus.[3] It happened that he was procurator of Judea when the war began to be kindled, in the twelfth year of Nero.[4]

V. 599–604. See also the article of Salmon in Smith and Wace, of Harnack, in Herzog (2d ed.), and Schaff's *Ch. Hist.* II. p. 775 sqq.

[9] ἐκκλησιαστικὸς ἀνήρ.
[10] γεγονώς. Crusè translates "born"; but Eusebius cannot have meant that, for in Bk. VI. chap. 20 he tells us that Caius' disputation with Proclus was held during the episcopate of Zephyrinus. He used γεγονώς, therefore, to indicate that at that time he came into public notice, as we use the word "arose."
[11] On Zephyrinus, see below, Bk. V. chap. 28, § 7.
[12] This Proclus probably introduced Montanism into Rome at the beginning of the third century. According to Pseudo-Tertullian (*Adv. omnes Hær.* chap. 7) he was a leader of one division of the Montanists, the other division being composed of followers of Æschines. He is probably to be identified with the *Proculus noster*, classed by Tertullian, in *Adv. Val.* chap. 5, with Justin Martyr, Miltiades, and Irenæus as a successful opponent of heresy.
[13] The sect of the Montanists. Called the "Phrygian heresy," from the fact that it took its rise in Phrygia. Upon Montanism, see below, Bk. IV. chap. 27, and especially Bk. V. chap. 16 sqq.
[14] The δὲ here makes it probable that Caius, in reply to certain claims of Proclus, was asserting over against him the ability of the Roman church to exhibit the true trophies of the greatest of all the apostles. And what these claims of Proclus were can perhaps be gathered from his words, quoted by Eusebius in Bk. III. chap. 31, § 4, in which Philip and his daughters are said to have been buried in Hierapolis. That these two sentences were closely connected in the original is quite possible.
[15] According to an ancient tradition, Peter was crucified upon the hill of Janiculum, near the Vatican, where the Church of San Pietro in Montorio now stands, and the hole in which his cross stood is still shown to the trustful visitor. A more probable tradition makes the scene of execution the Vatican hill, where Nero's circus was, and where the persecution took place. Baronius makes the whole ridge on the right bank of the Tiber one hill, and thus reconciles the two traditions. In the fourth century the remains of Peter were transferred from the Catacombs of San Sebastiano (where they are said to have been interred in 258 A.D.) to the Basilica of St. Peter, which occupied the sight of the present basilica on the Vatican.
[16] Paul was beheaded, according to tradition, on the Ostian way, at the spot now occupied by the Abbey of the Three Fountains. The fountains, which are said to have sprung up at the spots where Paul's head struck the ground three times after the decapitation, are still shown, as also the pillar to which he is supposed to have been bound! In the fourth century, at the same time that Peter's remains were transferred to the Vatican, Paul's remains are said to have been buried in the Basilica of St. Paul, which occupied the site now marked by the church of San Paolo fuori le mura. There is nothing improbable in the traditions as to the spot where Paul and Peter met their death. They are as old as the second century; and while they cannot be accepted as indisputably true (since there is always a tendency to fix the deathplace of a great man even if it is not known), yet on the other hand if Peter and Paul were martyred in Rome, it is hardly possible that the place of their death and burial could have been forgotten by the Roman church itself within a century and a half.
[17] Neither Paul nor Peter founded the Roman church in the strict sense, for there was a congregation of believers there even before Paul came to Rome, as his Epistle to the Romans shows, and Peter cannot have reached there until some time after Paul. It was, however, a very early fiction that Paul and Peter together founded the church in that city.
[18] On Dionysius of Corinth, see below, Bk. IV. chap. 23.
[19] Another quotation from this epistle is given in Bk. IV. chap. 23. The fragments are discussed by Routh, *Rel. Sac.* I. 179 sq.
[20] Whatever may be the truth of Dionysius' report as to Peter's

martyrdom at Rome, he is almost certainly in error in speaking as he does of Peter's work in Corinth. It is difficult, to be sure, to dispose of so direct and early a tradition, but it is still more difficult to accept it. The statement that Paul and Peter together planted the Corinthian church is certainly an error, as we know that it was Paul's own church, founded by him alone. The so-called Cephas party, mentioned in 1 Cor. i., is perhaps easiest explained by the previous presence and activity of Peter in Corinth, but this is by no means necessary, and the absence of any reference to the fact in the two epistles of Paul renders it almost absolutely impossible. It is barely possible, though by no means probable, that Peter visited Corinth on his way to Rome (assuming the Roman journey) and that thus, although the church had already been founded many years, he became connected in tradition with its early days, and finally with its origination. But it is more probable that the tradition is wholly in error and arose, as Neander suggests, partly from the mention of Peter in 1 Cor. i., partly from the natural desire to ascribe the origin of this great apostolic church to the two leading apostles, to whom in like manner the founding of the Roman church was ascribed. It is significant that this tradition is recorded only by a Corinthian, who of course had every inducement to accept such a report, and to repeat it in comparing his own church with the central church of Christendom. We find no mention of the tradition in later writers, so far as I am aware.
[21] κατὰ τὸν αὐτὸν καιρόν. The κατὰ allows some margin in time and does not necessarily imply the same day. Dionysius is the first one to connect the deaths of Peter and Paul chronologically, but later it became quite the custom. One tradition put their deaths on the same day, one year apart (Augustine and Prudentius, e.g., are said to support this tradition). Jerome (*de vir. ill.* 1) is the first to state explicitly that they suffered on the same day. Eusebius in his *Chron.* (Armen.) puts their martyrdom in 67, Jerome in 68. The Roman Catholic Church celebrates the death of Peter on the 29th and that of Paul on the 30th of June, but has no fixed tradition as to the year of the death of either of them.
[1] Josephus, *B. J.* II. 14. 9. He relates that Florus, in order to shield himself from the consequences of his misrule and of his abominable extortions, endeavored to inflame the Jews to rebel against Rome by acting still more cruelly toward them. As a result many disturbances broke out, and many bitter things were said against Florus, in consequence of which he proceeded to the severe measures referred to here by Eusebius.
[2] μυρίους ὅσους. Josephus gives the whole number of those that were destroyed, including women and children, as about thirty-six hundred (no doubt a gross exaggeration, like most of his figures). He does not state the number of noble Jews whom Florus whipped and crucified. The "myriads" of Eusebius is an instance of the exaggerated use of language which was common to his age, and which almost invariably marks a period of decline. In many cases "myriads" meant to Eusebius and his contemporaries twenty, or thirty, or even less. Any number that seemed large under the circumstances was called a "myriad."
[3] Gessius Florus was a Greek whose wife, Cleopatra, was a friend of the Empress Poppæa, through whose influence he obtained his appointment (Jos. *Ant.* XX. 11. 1). He succeeded Albinus in 64 A.D. (see above, chap. 23, note 35), and was universally hated as the most corrupt and unprincipled governor Judea had ever endured. Josephus (*B. J.* II. 14. 2 sqq. and *Ant.* XX. 11. 1) paints him in very black colors.
[4] Josephus (*B. J.* II. 14. 4) puts the beginning of the war in the twelfth year of the reign of Nero (i.e. A.D. 66) in the month of Artemision, corresponding to the month Iyar, the second month of

2   Josephus says[5] that at that time a terrible commotion was stirred up throughout all Syria in consequence of the revolt of the Jews, and that everywhere the latter were destroyed without mercy, like enemies, by the inhabitants of the cities, " so that one could see cities filled with unburied corpses, and the dead bodies of the aged scattered about with the bodies of infants, and women without even a covering for their nakedness, and the whole province full of indescribable calamities, while the dread of those things that were threatened was greater than the sufferings themselves which they anywhere endured."[6]   Such is the account of Josephus ; and such was the condition of the Jews at that time.

the Jewish year. According to Josephus (*Ant.* XX. 11. 1) this was in the second year of Gessius Florus. The war began at this time by repeated rebellious outbreaks among the Jews, who had been driven to desperation by the unprincipled and tyrannical conduct of Florus, — though Vespasian himself did not appear in Palestine until the spring of 67, when he began his operations in Galilee.

[5] Jos. *B. J.* II. 18. 2.

[6] *Ibid.*

BOOK III.

CHAPTER I.

The Parts of the World in which the Apostles preached Christ.

1 SUCH was the condition of the Jews. Meanwhile the holy apostles and disciples of our Saviour were dispersed throughout the world.[1] Parthia,[2] according to tradition, was allotted to Thomas as his field of labor, Scythia[3] to Andrew,[4] and Asia[5] to John,[6] who, after he had lived some time there,[7] died at Ephesus. Peter appears to have preached[8] in Pontus, Galatia, Bithynia, Cappadocia, and Asia[9] to the Jews of the dispersion. And at last, having come to Rome, he was crucified head-downwards;[10] for he had requested that he might suffer in this way. What do we need to say concerning Paul, who preached the Gospel of Christ from Jerusalem to Illyricum,[11] and afterwards suffered martyrdom in Rome under

2

---

[1] According to Lipsius, the legends concerning the labors of the apostles in various countries were all originally connected with that of their separation at Jerusalem, which is as old as the second century. But this separation was put at various dates by different traditions, varying from immediately after the Ascension to twenty-four years later. A lost book, referred to by the *Decretum Gelasii* as *Liber qui appellatus sortes Apostolorum apocryphus*, very likely contained the original tradition, and an account of the fate of the apostles, and was probably of Gnostic or Manichean origin. The efforts to derive from the varying traditions any trustworthy particulars as to the apostles themselves is almost wholly vain. The various traditions not only assign different fields of labor to the different apostles, but also give different lists of the apostles themselves. See Lipsius' article on the *Apocryphal Acts of the Apostles* in Smith and Wace's *Dict. of Christ. Biog.* I. p. 17 sqq. The extant Apocryphal Gospels, Acts, Apocalypses, &c., are translated in the *Ante-Nicene Fathers*, Vol. VIII. p. 361 sqq. Lipsius states that, according to the oldest form of the tradition, the apostles were divided into three groups: first, Peter and Andrew, Matthew and Bartholomew, who were said to have preached in the region of the Black Sea; second, Thomas, Thaddeus, and Simeon, the Canaanite, in Parthia; third, John and Philip, in Asia Minor.

[2] Parthia, in the time of the apostles, was an independent kingdom, extending from the Indus to the Tigris, and from the Caspian Sea to the Persian Gulf. This is the oldest form of the tradition in regard to Thomas (see preceding note). It is found also in the Clementine *Recognitions*, IX. 29, and in Socrates, *H. E.* I. 19. Rufinus (*H. E.* II. 5) and Socrates (*H. E.* IV. 18) speak of Edessa as his burial place. Later traditions extended his labors eastward as far as India, and made him suffer martyrdom in that land; and there his remains were exhibited down to the sixteenth century. According to the *Martyrium Romanum*, however, his remains were brought from India to Edessa, and from thence to Ortona, in Italy, during the Crusades. The Syrian Christians in India called themselves Thomas-Christians; but the name cannot be traced beyond the eighth century, and is derived, probably, from a Nestorian missionary.

[3] The name Scythia was commonly used by the ancients, in a very loose sense, to denote all the region lying north of the Caspian and Black Seas. But two Scythias were distinguished in more accurate usage: a European Scythia, lying north of the Black Sea, between the Danube and the Tanais, and an Asiatic Scythia, extending eastward from the Ural. The former is here meant.

[4] The traditions respecting Andrew are very uncertain and contradictory, though, as remarked above (note 1), the original form, represented everywhere, assigned as his field the region in the neighborhood of the Black Sea. His traditional activity in Scythia has made him the patron saint of Russia. He is also called the patron saint of Greece, where he is reported to have been crucified; but his activity there rests upon a late tradition. His body is said to have been carried to Constantinople in 357 (cf. Philostorgius, *Hist. Eccles.* III. 2), and during the Crusades transferred to Amalpæ in Italy, in whose cathedral the remains are still shown. Andrew is in addition the patron saint of Scotland; but the tradition of his activity there dates back only to the eighth century (cf. Skene's *Celtic Scotland*, II. 221 sq.). Numerous other regions are claimed, by various traditions, to have been the scene of his labors.

[5] Proconsular Asia included only a narrow strip of Asia Minor, lying upon the coast of the Mediterranean, and comprising Mysia, Lydia, and Caria.

[6] The universal testimony of antiquity assigns John's later life to Ephesus: e.g. Irenæus, *Adv. Hær.* III. 1. 1 and 3. 4, etc.; Clement of Alex., *Quis Dives Salvetur*, c. 42 (quoted by Eusebius, chap. 23, below); Polycrates in his Epistle to Victor (quoted by Eusebius in chap. 31, below, and in Bk. V. chap. 24); and many others. The testimony of Irenæus is especially weighty, for the series: Irenæus, the pupil of Polycarp, the pupil of John, forms a complete chain such as we have in no other case. Such testimony, when its force is broken by no adverse tradition, ought to be sufficient to establish John's residence in Ephesus beyond the shadow of a doubt, but it has been denied by many of the critics who reject the Johannine authorship of the fourth Gospel (e.g. Keim, Holtzmann, the author of *Supernat. Religion*, and others), though the denial is much less positive now than it was a few years ago. The chief arguments urged against the residence of John in Ephesus are two, both *a silentio*: first, Clement in his first Epistle to the Corinthians speaks of the apostles in such a way as to seem to imply that they were all dead; secondly, in the Ignatian Epistles, Paul is mentioned, but not John, which is certainly very remarkable, as one is addressed to Ephesus itself. In reply it may be said that such an interpretation of Clement's words is not necessary, and that the omission of John in the epistles of Ignatius becomes perfectly natural if the Epistles are thrown into the time of Hadrian or into the latter part of Trajan's reign, as they ought to be (cf. chap. 36, note 4). In the face of the strong testimony for John's Ephesian residence these two objections must be overruled. The traditional view is defended by all conservative critics as well as by the majority even of those who deny the Johannine authorship of the fourth Gospel (cf. especially Hilgenfeld in his *Einleitung*, and Weizsäcker in his *Apostolisches Zeitalter*). The silence of Paul's epistles and of the Acts proves that John cannot have gone to Ephesus until after Paul had permanently left there, and this we should naturally expect to be the case. Upon the time of John's banishment to Patmos, see Bk. III. chap. 18, note 1. Tradition reports that he lived until the reign of Trajan (98–117). Cf. Irenæus, II. 22. 5 and III. 3. 4.

[7] Origen in this extract seems to be uncertain how long John remained in Ephesus and when he died.

[8] The language of Origen (κεκηρυχέναι ἔοικεν, instead of λόγος ἔχει or παράδοσις περιέχει) seems to imply that he is recording not a tradition, but a conclusion drawn from the first Epistle of Peter, which was known to him, and in which these places are mentioned. Such a tradition did, however, exist quite early. Cf. e.g. the Syriac *Doctrina Apostolorum* (ed. Cureton) and the Gnostic *Acts of Peter and Andrew*. The former assigns to Peter, Antioch, Syria, and Cilicia, in addition to Galatia and Pontus, and cannot, therefore, rest solely upon the first Epistle of Peter, which does not mention the first three places. All the places assigned to Peter are portions of the field of Paul, who in all the traditions of this class is completely crowded out and his field given to other apostles, showing the Jewish origin of these traditions. Upon Peter's activity in Rome and his death there, see Bk. II. chap. 25, note 7.

[9] Five provinces of Asia Minor, mentioned in 1 Pet. i. 1.

[10] Origen is the first to record that Peter was crucified with his head downward, but the tradition afterward became quite common. It is of course not impossible, but the absence of any reference to it by earlier Fathers (even by Tertullian, who mentions the crucifixion), and its decidedly legendary character, render it exceedingly doubtful.

[11] Cf. Rom. xv. 19. Illyricum was a Roman province lying along the eastern coast of the Adriatic.

Nero?[12]　These facts are related by Origen in the third volume of his Commentary on Genesis.[13]

CHAPTER II.

The First Ruler of the Church of Rome.

AFTER the martyrdom of Paul and of Peter, Linus[1] was the first to obtain the episcopate of the church at Rome. Paul mentions him, when writing to Timothy from Rome, in the salutation at the end of the epistle.[2]

CHAPTER III.

The Epistles of the Apostles.

1　ONE epistle of Peter, that called the first, is acknowledged as genuine.[1] And this the ancient elders[2] used freely in their own writings as an undisputed work.[3] But we have learned that his extant second Epistle does not belong to the canon;[4] yet, as it has appeared profitable to many, it has been used with the other Scriptures.[5] The so-called Acts 2 of Peter,[6] however, and the Gospel[7] which bears his name, and the Preaching[8] and the

---

[12] See above, Bk. II. chap. 25, note 5.

[13] This fragment of Origen has been preserved by no one else. It is impossible to tell where the quotation begins — whether with the words "Thomas according to tradition received Parthia," as I have given it, or with the words "Peter appears to have preached," etc., as Bright gives it.

[1] The actual order of the first three so-called bishops of Rome is a greatly disputed matter. The oldest tradition is that given by Irenæus (Adv. Hær. III. 3. 3) and followed here by Eusebius, according to which the order was Linus, Anencletus, Clement. Hippolytus gives a different order, in which he is followed by many Fathers; and in addition to these two chief arrangements all possible combinations of the three names, and all sorts of theories to account for the difficulties and to reconcile the discrepancies in the earlier lists, have been proposed. In the second chapter of the so-called Epistle of Clement to James (a part of the Pseudo-Clementine Literature prefixed to the Homilies) it is said that Clement was ordained by Peter, and Salmon thinks that this caused Hippolytus to change the order, putting Clement first. Gieseler (Eccles. Hist., Eng. Trans., I. p. 107, note 10) explains the disagreements in the various traditions by supposing that the three were presbyters together at Rome, and that later, in the endeavor to make out a complete list of bishops, they were each successively elevated by tradition to the episcopal chair. It is at least certain that Rome at that early date had no monarchical bishop, and therefore the question as to the order of these first three so-called bishops is not a question as to a fact, but simply as to which is the oldest of various unfounded traditions. The Roman Church gives the following order: Linus, Clement, Cletus, Anacletus, following Hippolytus in making Cletus and Anacletus out of the single Anencletus of the original tradition. The apocryphal martyrdoms of Peter and Paul are falsely ascribed to Linus (see Tischendorf, Acta Apost. Apocr. p. xix. sq.). Eusebius (chap. 13, below) says that Linus was bishop for twelve years. In his Chron. (Armen.) he says fourteen years, while Jerome says eleven. These dates are about as reliable as the episcopal succession itself. We have no trustworthy information as to the personal character and history of Linus. Upon the subjects discussed in this note see especially Salmon's articles, Clemens Romanus, and Linus, in the Dict. of Christ. Biog.

[2] 2 Tim. iv. 21. The same identification is made by Irenæus, Adv. Hær. III. 3, and by Pseudo-Ignatius in the Epistle to the Trallians (longer version), chap. 7.

[1] The testimony of tradition is unanimous for the authenticity of the first Epistle of Peter. It was known to Clement of Rome, Polycarp, Papias, Hermas, &c. (the Muratorian Fragment, however, omits it), and was cited under the name of Peter by Irenæus, Tertullian, and Clement of Alexandria, from whose time its canonicity and Petrine authorship were established, so that Eusebius rightly puts it among the homologoumena. Semler, in 1784, was the first to deny its direct Petrine authorship, and Cludius, in 1808, pronounced it absolutely ungenuine. The Tübingen School followed, and at the present time the genuineness is denied by all the negative critics, chiefly on account of the strong Pauline character of the epistle (cf. Holtzmann, Einleitung, p. 487 sqq., also Weiss, Einleitung, p. 428 sqq., who confines the resemblances to the Epistles to the Romans and to the Ephesians, and denies the general Pauline character of the epistle). The great majority of scholars, however, maintain the Petrine authorship. A new opinion, expressed by Harnack, upon the assumption of the distinctively Pauline character of the epistle, is that it was written during the apostolic age by some follower of Paul, and that the name of Peter was afterward attached to it, so that it represents no fraud on the part of the writer,

but an effort of a later age to find an author for the anonymous epistle. In support of this is urged the fact that though the epistle is so frequently quoted in the second century, it is never connected with Peter's name until the time of Irenæus. (Cf. Harnack's Lehre der Zwölf Apostel, p. 106, note, and his Dogmengeschichte, I. p. 278, note 2.) This theory has found few supporters.

[2] οἱ πάλαι πρεσβύτεροι. On the use of the term "elders" among the Fathers, see below, chap. 39, note 6.

[3] ὡς ἀναμφιλέκτῳ.

[4] οὐκ ἐνδιάθηκον μὲν εἶναι παρειλήφαμεν. The authorship of the second Epistle of Peter has always been widely disputed. The external testimony for it is very weak, as no knowledge of it can be proved to have existed before the third century. Numerous explanations have been offered by apologists to account for this curious fact; but it still remains almost inexplicable, if the epistle be accepted as the work of the apostle. The first clear references to it are made by Firmilian, Bishop of Cæsarea in Cappadocia (third century), in his Epistle to Cyprian, § 6 (Ep. 74, in the collection of Cyprian's Epistles, Ante-Nicene Fathers, Am. ed., V. p. 391), and by Origen (quoted by Eusebius, VI. 25, below), who mentions the second Epistle as disputed. Clement of Alexandria, however, seems at least to have known and used it (according to Euseb. VI. 14). The epistle was not admitted into the Canon until the Council of Hippo, in 393, when all doubts and discussion ceased until the Reformation. It is at present disputed by all negative critics, and even by many otherwise conservative scholars. Those who defend its genuineness date it shortly before the death of Peter, while the majority of those who reject it throw it into the second century, — some as late as the time of Clement of Alexandria (e.g. Harnack, in his Lehre der Zwölf Apostel, p. 15 and 159, who assigns its composition to Egypt). Cf. Holtzmann, Einleitung, p. 495 sqq., and Weiss (who leaves its genuineness an open question), Einleitung, p. 436 sqq. For a defense of the genuineness, see especially Warfield, in the Southern Pres. Rev., 1883, p. 390 sqq., and Salmon's Introduction to the N. T., p. 512 sqq.

[5] Although disputed by many, as already remarked, and consequently not looked upon as certainly canonical until the end of the fourth century, the epistle was yet used, as Eusebius says, quite widely from the time of Origen on, e.g. by Origen, Firmilian, Cyprian, Hippolytus, Methodius, etc. The same is true, however, of other writings, which the Church afterward placed among the Apocrypha.

[6] These πράξεις (or περίοδοι, as they are often called) Πέτρου were of heretical origin, according to Lipsius, and belonged, like the heretical Acta Pauli (referred to in note 20, below), to the collection of περίοδοι τῶν ἀποστόλων, which were ascribed to Lucius Charinus, and, like them, formed also, from the end of the fourth century, a part of the Manichean Canon of the New Testament. The work, as a whole, is no longer extant, but a part of it is preserved, according to Lipsius, in a late Catholic redaction, under the title Passio Petri. Upon these Acts of Peter, their original form, and their relation to other works of the same class, see Lipsius, Apocryphen Apostelgeschichten, II. 1, p. 78 sq. The heretical Acta Pauli already referred to, this work, too, was used in the composition of the Catholic Acts of Paul and Peter, which are still extant, and which assumed their present form in the fifth century, according to Lipsius. These Catholic Acts of Peter and Paul have been published by Thilo (Acta Petri et Pauli, Halle, 1837), and by Tischendorf, in his Acta Apost. Apocr., p. 1–39. English translation in the Ante-Nicene Fathers (Am. ed.), VIII. p. 477.

[7] This Gospel is mentioned by Serapion as in use in the church of Rhossus (quoted by Eusebius, Bk. VI. chap. 12, below), but was rejected by him because of the heretical doctrines which it contained. It is mentioned again by Eusebius, III. 25, only to be rejected as heretical; also by Origen (in Matt. Vol. X. 17) and by Jerome (de vir. ill. 1), who follows Eusebius in pronouncing it an heretical work employed by no early teachers of the Christian Church. Lipsius regards it as probably a Gnostic recast of one of the Canonical Gospels. From Serapion's account of this Gospel (see below, Bk. VI. chap. 12), we see that it differs from the Canonical Gospels, not in denying their truth, or in giving a contradictory account of Christ's life, but rather in adding to the account given by them. This, of course, favors Lipsius' hypothesis; and in any case he is certainly quite right in denying that the Gospel was an original work made use of by Justin Martyr, and that it in any way lay at the base of our present Gospel of Mark. The Gospel (as we learn from the same chapter) was used by the Docetæ, but that does not imply that it contained what we call Docetic ideas of Christ's body (cf. note 8 on that chapter). The Gospel is no longer extant. See Lipsius, in Smith and Wace's Dict. of Christ. Biog. II. p. 712.

[8] This Preaching of Peter (Κήρυγμα Πέτρου, Prædicatio Petri), which is no longer extant, probably formed a part of a lost

Apocalypse,[9] as they are called, we know have not been universally accepted,[10] because no ecclesiastical writer, ancient or modern, has made use of testimonies drawn from them.[11]

3   But in the course of my history I shall be careful to show, in addition to the official succession, what ecclesiastical writers have from time to time made use of any of the disputed works,[12] and what they have said in regard to the canonical and accepted writings,[13] as well as in regard to those which are not

4   of this class. Such are the writings that bear the name of Peter, only one of which I know to be genuine[14] and acknowledged by the ancient elders.[15]

5   Paul's fourteen epistles are well known

and undisputed.[16] It is not indeed right to overlook the fact that some have rejected the Epistle to the Hebrews,[17] saying that it is dis-

[16] The thirteen Pauline Epistles of our present Canon, and the Epistle to the Hebrews. These formed for Eusebius an absolutely undisputed part of the Canon (cf. chap. 25, below, where he speaks of them with the same complete assurance), and were universally accepted until the present century. The external testimony for all of them is ample, going back (the Pastoral Epistles excepted) to the early part of the second century. The Epistles to the Romans, Corinthians, and Galatians have never been disputed (except by an individual here and there, especially during the last few years in Holland), even the Tübingen School accepting them as genuine works of Paul. The other epistles have not fared so well. The genuineness of Ephesians was first questioned by Usteri in 1824 and De Wette in 1826, and the Tübingen School rejected it. Scholars are at present greatly divided: the majority of negative critics reject it, while many liberal and all conservative scholars defend it. Colossians was first attacked by Mayerhoff in 1838, followed by the whole Tübingen School. It fares to-day somewhat better than Ephesians. It is still, however, rejected by many extreme critics, while others leave the matter in suspense (e.g. Weizsäcker in his *Apostolisches Zeitalter*). Since 1872, when the theory was proposed by Holtzmann, some scholars have held that our present Epistle contains a genuine Epistle of Paul to] the Colossians, of which it is a later revision and expansion. Baur and the Tübingen School were the first to attack Philippians as a whole, and it too is still rejected by many critics, but at the same time it is more widely accepted than either Ephesians or Colossians (e.g. Weizsäcker and even Hilgenfeld defend its genuineness). Second Thessalonians was first attacked by Schmidt in 1801, followed by a number of scholars, until Baur extended the attack to the first Epistle also. Second Thessalonians is still almost unanimously rejected by negative critics, and even by some moderates, while First Thessalonians has regained the support of many of the former (e.g. Hilgenfeld, Weizsäcker, and even Holtzmann), and is entirely rejected by comparatively few critics. Philemon — which was first attacked by Baur — is quite generally accepted, but the Pastoral Epistles are almost as generally rejected, except by the regular conservative school (upon the Pastorals, see Bk. II. chap. 22, note 8, above). For a concise account of the state of criticism upon each epistle, see Holtzmann's *Einleitung*. For a defense of them all, see the *Einleitung* of Weiss.

[17] τινες ἠθετήκασι. That the Epistle to the Hebrews was not written by Paul is now commonly acknowledged, and may be regarded as absolutely certain. It does not itself lay any claim to Pauline authorship; its theology and style are both non-Pauline; and finally, external testimony is strongly against its direct connection with Paul. The first persons to assign the epistle to Paul are Pantænus and Clement of Alexandria (see below, Bk. VI. chap. 14), and they evidently find it necessary to defend its Pauline authorship in the face of the objections of others. Clement, indeed, assumes a Hebrew original, which was translated into Greek by Luke. Origen (see below, Bk. VI. chap. 25) leaves its authorship undecided, but thinks it probable that the thoughts are Paul's, but the diction that of some one else, who has recorded what he heard from the apostle. He then remarks that one tradition assigned it to Clement of Rome, another to Luke. Eusebius himself, in agreement with the Alexandrians (who, with the exception of Origen, unanimously accept the Pauline authorship), looks upon it as a work of Paul, but accepts Clement of Alexandria's theory that it was written in Hebrew, and thinks it probable that Clement of Rome was its translator (see chap. 38, below). In the Western Church, where the epistle was known very early (e.g. Clement of Rome uses it freely), it is not connected with Paul until the fourth century. Indeed, Tertullian (*de pudicit.* 20) states that it bore the name of Barnabas, and evidently had never heard that it had been ascribed to any one else. The influence of the Alexandrians, however, finally prevailed, and from the fifth century on we find it universally accepted, both East and West, as an epistle of Paul, and not until the Reformation was its origin again questioned. Since that time its authorship has been commonly regarded as an insoluble mystery. Numerous guesses have been made (e.g. Luther guessed Apollos, and he has been followed by many), but it is impossible to prove that any of them are correct. For Barnabas, however, more can be said than for any of the others. Tertullian expressly connects the epistle with him; and its contents are just what we should expect from the pen of a Levite who had been for a time under Paul's influence, and yet had not received his Christianity from him; its standpoint, in fact, is Levitic, and decidedly non-Pauline, and yet reveals in many places the influence of Pauline ideas. Still further, it is noticeable that in the place where the Epistle to the Hebrews is first ascribed to Paul, there first appears an epistle which is ascribed (quite wrongly; see below, chap. 25, note 20) to Barnabas. May it not be (as has been suggested by Weiss and others) that the anonymous Epistle to the Hebrews was originally accepted in Alexandria as the work of Barnabas, but that later it was ascribed to Paul; and that the tradition that Barnabas had written an epistle, which must still have remained in the Church, led to the ascription of another anonymous epistle to him? We seem thus most easily to explain the false ascription of the one epistle to Paul, and the false ascription of the other to Barnabas. It may be said that the claims of both Barnabas and Apollos have many supporters, while still more attempt no decision. In regard to the canonicity of the epistle there seems never to-

Preaching of Peter and Paul (cf. Clement of Alexandria, *Strom.* VI. 5, and Lactantius, *Inst.* IV. 21). It was mentioned frequently by the early Fathers, and a number of fragments of it have been preserved by Clement of Alexandria, who quotes it frequently as a genuine record of Peter's teaching. (The fragments are collected by Grabe in his *Spic. Patr.* I. 55–71, and by Hilgenfeld in his *N. T. extra Can. rec.*, 2d ed., IV. p. 51 sqq.). It is mentioned twice by Origen (*in Johan.* XIII. 17, and *De Princ.* Præf. 8), and in the latter place is expressly classed among spurious works. It was probably, according to Lipsius, closely connected with the *Acts of Peter and Paul* mentioned in note 6, above. Lipsius, however, regards those *Acts* as a Catholic adaptation of a work originally Ebionitic, though he says expressly that the *Preaching* is not at all of that character, but is a Petro-Pauline production, and is to be distinguished from the Ebionitic κηρύγματα. It would seem therefore that he must put the *Preaching* later than the original of the *Acts*, into a time when the Ebionitic character of the latter had been done away with. Salmon meanwhile holds that the *Preaching* is as old as the middle of the second century and the most ancient of the works recording Peter's preaching, and hence (if this view be accepted) the Ebionitic character which Lipsius ascribes to the *Acts* did not (if it existed at all) belong to the original form of the record of Peter's preaching embodied in the *Acts* and in the *Preaching*. The latter (if it included also the *Preaching of Paul*, as seems almost certain) appears to have contained an account of some of the events of the life of Christ, and it may have been used by Justin. Compare the remarks of Lipsius in the *Dict. of Christ. Biog.* I. p. 28 (*Cath. Adaptations of Ebionitic Acts*), and Salmon's article on the *Preaching of Peter, ibid.* IV. 329.

[9] The *Apocalypse of Peter* enjoyed considerable favor in the early Church and was accepted by some Fathers as a genuine work of the apostle. It is mentioned in the Muratorian Fragment in connection with the Apocalypse of John, as a part of the Roman Canon, and is accepted by the author of the fragment himself; although he says that some at that time rejected it. Clement of Alexandria, in his *Hypotyposes* (according to Eusebius, IV. 14, below), commented upon it, thus showing that it belonged at that time to the Alexandrian Canon. It the third century it was still received in the North African Church (so Harnack, who refers to the stichometry of the Codex Claramontanus). The *Eclogæ* or *Prophetical Selections* of Clement of Alexandria give it as a genuine work of Peter (§§ 41, 48, 49, p. 1000 sq., Potter's ed.), and so Methodius of Tyre (*Sympos.* XI. 6, p. 16, ed. Jahn, according to Lipsius). After Eusebius' time the work seems to have been universally regarded as spurious, and thus, as its canonicity depended upon its apostolic origin (see chap. 24, note 19), it gradually fell out of the Canon. It nevertheless held its place for centuries among the semi-scriptural books, and was read in many churches. According to Sozomen, *H. E.* VII. 19, it was read at Easter, which shows that it was treated with especial respect. Nicephorus in his *Stichometry* puts it among the Antilegomena, in immediate connection with the Apocalypse of John. As Lipsius remarks, its "lay-recognition in orthodox circles proves that it could not have had a Gnostic origin, nor otherwise have contained what was offensive to Catholic Christians" (see Lipsius, *Dict. of Christ. Biog.* I. p. 130 sqq.). Only a few fragments of the work are extant, and these are given by Hilgenfeld, in his *Nov. Test. extra Can. receptum*, IV. 74 sq., and by Grabe, *Spic. Patr.* I. 71 sqq.

[10] οὐδ᾽ ὅλως ἐν καθολικαῖς ἴσμεν παραδεδομένα.

[11] Eusebius exaggerates in this statement. The *Apocalypse of Peter* was in quite general use in the second century, as we learn from the Muratorian Fragment; and Clement (as Eusebius himself says in VI. 14) wrote a commentary upon it in connection with the other Antilegomena.

[12] τῶν ἀντιλεγομένων.
[13] περὶ τῶν ἐνδιαθήκων καὶ ὁμολογουμένων.
[14] ὧν μόνην μίαν γνησίαν ἔγνων.
[15] As above; see note 2.

puted [18] by the church of Rome, on the ground that it was not written by Paul. But what has been said concerning this epistle by those who lived before our time I shall quote in the proper place.[19] In regard to the so-called Acts of Paul,[20] I have not found them among the undisputed writings.[21]

6　　But as the same apostle, in the salutations at the end of the Epistle to the Romans,[22] has made mention among others of Hermas, to whom the book called The Shepherd [23] is ascribed, it should be observed that this too has been disputed by some, and on their account cannot be placed among the acknowledged books; while by others it is considered quite indispensable, especially to those who need instruction in the elements of the faith. Hence, as we know, it has been publicly read in churches, and I have found that some of the most ancient writers used it.

This will serve to show the divine writ-　7 ings that are undisputed as well as those that are not universally acknowledged.

---

have been any serious dispute, and it is this fact doubtless which did most to foster the belief in its Pauline authorship from the third century on. For the criterion of canonicity more and more came to be looked upon as apostolicity, direct or indirect. The early Church had cared little for such a criterion. In only one place does Eusebius seem to imply that doubts existed as to its canonicity, — in Bk. VI. chap. 13, where he classes it with the Book of Wisdom, and the Epistles of Barnabas, Clement, and Jude, among the *antilegomena*. But in view of his treatment of it elsewhere it must be concluded that he is thinking in that passage not at all of its canonicity, but of its Pauline authorship, which he knows is disputed by some, and in reference to which he uses the same word, ἀντιλέγεσθαι, in the present sentence. Upon the canonicity of the epistle, see still further chap. 25, note 1. For a discussion of the epistle, see especially the N. T. Introductions of Weiss and Holtzmann.

[18] ἀντιλέγεσθαι.　　　　[19] See Bk. VI. chaps. 14, 20, 25.

[20] These πράξεις are mentioned also in chap. 25, below, where they are classed among the νόθοι, implying that they had been originally accepted as canonical, but were not at the time Eusebius wrote widely accepted as such. This implies that they were not, like the works which he mentions later in the chapter, of an heretical character. They were already known to Origen, who (*De Prin.* I. 2, 3) refers to them in such a way as to show that they were in good repute in the Catholic Church. They are to be distinguished from the Gnostic περίοδοι or πράξεις Παύλου, which from the end of the fourth century formed a part of the Manichean canon of the New Testament, and of which some fragments are still extant under various forms. The failure to keep these Catholic and heretical *Acta Pauli* always distinct has caused considerable confusion. Both of these Acts, the Catholic and the heretical, formed, according to Lipsius (*Apokr. Apostelgeschichten*, II. 1, p. 305 sq.) one of the sources of the Catholic *Acts of Peter and Paul*, which in their extant form belong to the fifth century. For a discussion of these Catholic *Acts of Paul* referred to by Eusebius, see Lipsius, *ibid.*, p. 70 sq.

[21] οὐδὲ μὴν τὰς λεγομένας αὐτοῦ πράξεις ἐν ἀναμφιλέκτοις παρείληφα.

[22] See Rom. xvi. 14. The greater part of this last chapter of Romans is considered by many a separate epistle addressed to Ephesus. This has been quite a common opinion since 1829, when it was first broached by David Schulz (*Studien und Kritiken*, p. 629 sq.), and is accepted even by many conservative scholars (e.g. Weiss), while on the other hand it is opposed by many of the opposite school. While Aquila and Priscilla, of verse 3, and Epænetus, of verse 5, seem to point to Ephesus, and the fact that so many personal friends are greeted, leads us to look naturally to the East as Paul's field of labor, where he had formed so many acquaintances, rather than to Rome, where he had not been; yet on the other hand such names as Junias, Narcissus, Rufus, Hermas, Nereus, Aristobulus, and Herodion point strongly to Rome. We must, however, be content to leave the matter undecided, but may be confident that the evidence for the Ephesian hypothesis is certainly, in the face of the Roman names mentioned, and of universal tradition (for which as for Eusebius the epistle is a unit), not strong enough to establish it.

[23] The *Shepherd* of Hermas was in circulation in the latter half of the second century, and is quoted by Irenæus (*Adv. Hær.* IV. 20. 2) as Scripture, although he omits it in his discussion of Scripture testimonies in Bk. III. chap. 9 sqq., which shows that he considered it not quite on a level with regular Scripture. Clement of Alexandria and Origen often quote it as an inspired book, though the latter expressly distinguishes it from the canonical books, admitting that it is disputed by many (cf. *De Prin.* IV. 11). Eusebius in chap. 25 places it among the νόθοι or spurious writings in connection with the *Acts of Paul* and the *Apocalypse of Peter*. According to the Muratorian Fragment it was "written very recently in our times in the city of Rome by Hermas, while his brother, Bishop Pius, sat in the chair of the Church of Rome. And therefore it also ought to be read; but it cannot be made public in the Church to the people, nor placed among the prophets, as their number is complete, nor among the apostles to the end of time." This shows the very high esteem in which the work was held in that age. It was very widely employed in private and in public, both in the East and the West, until about the fourth century, when it gradually passed out of use. Jerome (*de vir. ill.* 10) says that it was almost unknown among the Latins of his time. As to the date and authorship of the *Shepherd* opinions vary widely. The only direct testimony of antiquity is that of the Muratorian Fragment, which says that it was written by Hermas, the brother of Pius, during the episcopacy of the latter (139–154 A.D.). This testimony is accepted by the majority of scholars, most of whom date the book near the middle of the second century, or at least as late as the reign of Hadrian. This opinion received not long ago what was supposed to be a strong confirmation from the discovery of the fact that Hermas in all probability quoted from Theodotion's version of Daniel (see Hort's article in the *Johns Hopkins University Circular*, December, 1884), which has been commonly ascribed to the second century. But it must now be admitted that no one knows the *terminus a quo* for the composition of Theodotion's version, and therefore the discovery leaves the date of Hermas entirely undetermined (see Schürer, *Gesch. des jüdischen Volkes*, II. p. 709). Meanwhile Eusebius in this connection records the tradition, which he had read, that the book was written by the Hermas mentioned in Romans xvi. This tradition, however, appears to be no older than Origen, with whom it is no more than a mere guess. While in our absence of any knowledge as to this Hermas we cannot absolutely disprove his claim (unless we prove decisively the late date of the book), there is yet no ground for accepting it other than a mere coincidence in a very common name. In *Vis.* II. 4. 3 Hermas is told to give one copy of his book to Clement. From this it is concluded by many that the author must have been contemporary with the well-known Roman Clement, the author of the Epistle to the Corinthians. While this appears very likely, it cannot be called certain in the face of evidence for a considerably later date. Internal testimony helps us little, as there is nothing in the book which may not have been written at the very beginning of the second century, or, on the other hand, as late as the middle of it. Zahn dates it between 97 and 100, and assigns it to an unknown Hermas, a contemporary of the Roman Clement, in which he is followed by Salmon in a very clear and keen article in the *Dict. of Christ. Biog.* Critics are unanimously agreed that the book was written in Rome. It consists of three parts, Visions, Mandates, and Similitudes, and is of the nature of an apocalypse, written for the purpose of reforming the life of the Church, which seemed to the author to have become very corrupt. The work (especially the last part) is in the form of an allegory, and has been compared to the *Pilgrim's Progress*. Opinions are divided as to whether it is actually founded upon visions and dreams of the author, or is wholly a fiction. The former opinion seems to be the more probable.

Until recent years only a Latin translation of Hermas was known. In 1856 the first Greek edition was issued by Anger and Dindorf, being based upon a Mt. Athos MS. discovered shortly before by Simonides. Of the ten leaves of the MS. three were lost; three were sold by Simonides to the University of Leipsic, and the other six were transcribed by him in a very faulty manner. The Sinaitic Codex has enabled us to control the text of Simonides in part, but unfortunately it contains only the *Visions* and a small part of the *Mandates*. All recent editions have been obliged to take the faulty transcription of Simonides as their foundation. In 1880 the six leaves of the Athos Codex, which had been supposed to be lost, and which were known only through Simonides' transcription, were discovered by Lambros at Mt. Athos, and in 1888 *A Collation of the Athos Codex of the Shepherd of Hermas by Dr. Spyr Lambros* was issued in English translation by J. A. Robinson, at Cambridge, England. We thus have now a reliable Greek text of nine-tenths of the *Shepherd* of Hermas. Hilgenfeld, in his last edition (1887) of his *Novum Test. Extra Can. Rec.*, published also a Greek text of the lost part of the work, basing it upon a pretended transcription by Simonides from the lost Athos MS. But this has been conclusively shown to be a mere fraud on the part of Simonides, and we are therefore still without any MS. authority for the Greek text of the close of the work. Cf. Robinson's introduction to the *Collation of Lambros* mentioned above, and Harnack's articles in the *Theol. Literaturzeitung* (1887). The most useful edition of the original is that of Gebhardt and Harnack, *Patrum Apost. Opera*, Fasc. III. (Lips. 1877). The work is translated in the *Ante-Nicene Fathers*, Vol. II. The literature upon the subject is very extensive, but the reader should examine especially the Prolegomena of Harnack in his edition. Cf. Zahn's *Hirt des Hermas* (1868), and the article by Salmon in the *Dict. of Christ. Biog.* II. p. 912 sqq. Cf. also chap. 24, note 20, in regard to the reasons for the non-canonicity of the *Shepherd*.

CHAPTER IV.

The First Successors of the Apostles.

1   THAT Paul preached to the Gentiles and laid the foundations of the churches "from Jerusalem round about even unto Illyricum," is evident both from his own words,[1] and from the account which Luke has given in the Acts.[2]

2   And in how many provinces Peter preached Christ and taught the doctrine of the new covenant to those of the circumcision is clear from his own words in his epistle already mentioned as undisputed,[3] in which he writes to the Hebrews of the dispersion in Pontus, Galatia, Cappadocia, Asia, and Bithy-

3   nia.[4]   But the number and the names of those among them that became true and zealous followers of the apostles, and were judged worthy to tend the churches founded by them, it is not easy to tell, except those

4   mentioned in the writings of Paul.   For he had innumerable fellow-laborers, or "fellow-soldiers," as he called them,[5] and most of them were honored by him with an imperishable memorial, for he gave enduring testimony

5   concerning them in his own epistles.   Luke also in the Acts speaks of his friends, and mentions them by name.[6]

6   Timothy, so it is recorded, was the first to receive the episcopate of the parish in Ephesus,[7] Titus of the churches in Crete.[8]

---

[1] Rom. xv. 19.
[2] From Acts ix. on.
[3] In chap. 3, § 1.
[4] 1 Pet. i. 1.
[5] Phil. ii. 25; Philem. 2.
[6] Barnabas (Acts ix. 27, and often); John Mark (xii. 25; xiii. 13; xv. 37, 39); Silas (xv. 40); Timothy (xvi. 1 sqq. and often); Aquila and Priscilla (xviii.); Erastus (xix. 22); Gaius of Macedonia (xix. 29); Aristarchus (xix. 29; xx. 4; xxvii. 2); Sopater, Secundus, Gaius of Derbe (perhaps the same as the Gaius of Macedonia?), and Tychichus (xx. 4); Trophimus (xx. 4; xxi. 29).
[7] That Timothy was the first bishop of Ephesus is stated also by the *Apost. Const.* (VII. 46), and by Nicephorus (*H. E.* III. 11), who records (upon what authority we do not know) that he suffered martyrdom under Domitian.   Against the tradition that he labored during his later years in Ephesus there is nothing to be urged; though on the other hand the evidence for it amounts to little, as it seems to be no more than a conclusion drawn from the Epistles to Timothy, though hardly a conclusion drawn by Eusebius himself, for he uses the word ἱστορεῖται, which seems to imply that he had some authority for his statement.   According to those epistles, he was at the time of their composition in Ephesus, though they give us no hint as to whether he was afterward there or not.   From Heb. xiii. 23 (the date of which we do not know) we learn that he had just been released from some imprisonment, apparently in Italy, but whither he afterward went is quite uncertain.   Eusebius' report that he was bishop of Ephesus is the customary but unwarranted carrying back into the first century of the monarchical episcopate which was not known until the second.   According to the *Apost. Const.* VII. 46 both Timothy and John were bishops of Ephesus, the former appointed by Paul, the latter by himself.   Timothy is a saint in the Roman Catholic sense, and is commemorated January 24.
[8] Cf. Tit. i. 5.   Titus is commonly connected by tradition with Crete, of which he is supposed to have been the first bishop, — the later institution being again pushed back into the first century.   In the fragment *de Vita et Actis Titi,* by the lawyer Zenas (in Fabric. *Cod. Apoc. N. T.* II. 831 sqq., according to Howson in Smith's *Dict. of the Bible*), he is said to have been bishop of Gortyna, a city of Crete (where still stand the ruins of a church which bears his name), and of a royal Cretan family by birth.   This tradition is late, and, of course, of little authority, but at the same time, accords very well with all that we know of Titus; and consequently there is no reason for denying it *in toto.*   According to 2 Tim. iv. 10, he went, or was sent, into Dalmatia; but universal tradition ascribes his later life and his death to Crete.   Candia, the modern capital, claims the

---

But Luke,[9] who was of Antiochian parent-   7   age and a physician by profession,[10] and who was especially intimate with Paul and well acquainted with the rest of the apostles,[11] has left us, in two inspired books, proofs of that spiritual healing art which he learned from them. One of these books is the Gospel,[12] which he testifies that he wrote as those who were from the beginning eye-witnesses and ministers of the word delivered unto him, all of whom, as he says, he followed accurately from the first.[13]   The other book is the Acts of the Apostles[14] which he

---

honor of being his burial place (see Cave's *Apostolici,* ed. 1677, p. 63).   Titus is a saint, in the Roman Catholic sense, and is commemorated January 4.
[9] Of Luke personally we know very little.   He is not mentioned in the Acts, and only three times in Paul's epistles (Col. iv. 14; Philem. 24; 2 Tim. iv. 11), from which passages we learn that he was a physician, was one of Paul's fellow-workers who was very dear to him, and was with him during his last imprisonment.   Irenæus, who is the first to ascribe the third Gospel and the Acts to this Luke, seems to know nothing more about him personally.   Eusebius is the first to record that he was born at Antioch; but the tradition must have been universally accepted in his day, as he states it without any misgivings and with no qualifying phrase.   Jerome (*de vir. ill.* 7) and many later writers follow Eusebius in this statement. There is no intrinsic improbability in the tradition, which seems, in fact, to be favored by certain minor notices in the Acts (see Schaff, *Ch. Hist.* I. 651).   Gregory Nazianzen (*Orat.* 25) says that he labored in Achaia, and in *Orat.* 4 he calls him a martyr.   Jerome (*ibid.*) says that he was buried in Constantinople.   According to Nicephorus (*H. E.* II. 43) and later writers, Luke was a painter of great skill; but this late tradition, of which the earlier Fathers know nothing, is quite worthless.   Epiphanius (*Hær.* II. 11) makes him one of the Seventy, which does not accord with Luke's own words at the beginning of his Gospel, where he certainly implies that he himself was not an eye-witness of the events which he records.   In the same connection, Epiphanius says that he labored in Dalmatia, Gallia, Italy, and Macedonia, — a tradition which has about as much worth as most such traditions in regard to the fields of labor of the various apostles and their followers.   Theophylact (*On Luke* xxiv. 13–24) records that some supposed that he was one of the disciples with whom Christ walked to Emmaus, and this ingenious but unfounded guess has gained some modern supporters (e.g. Lange). He is a saint in the Roman Catholic sense, and is commemorated October 18.
[10] See Col. iv. 14.
[11] Of Luke's acquaintance with the other apostles we know nothing, although, if we suppose him to have been the author of the "We" sections in the Acts, he was with Paul in Jerusalem at the time he was taken prisoner (Acts xxi.), when he met James at least, and possibly others of the Twelve.   It is not at all improbable that in the course of his life he became acquainted with several of the apostles.
[12] The testimony to the existence of our third Gospel, although it is not so old as that for Matthew and Mark, is still very early. It was used by Marcion, who based upon it his own mutilated gospel, and is quoted very frequently by Justin Martyr.   The Gospel is first distinctly ascribed to Luke by Irenæus (III. 1. 1) and by the Muratorian Fragment.   From that time on tradition was unanimous both as to its authorship and its authority.   The common opinion — still defended by the great majority of conservative critics — has always been that the third Gospel was written before the destruction of Jerusalem.   The radical critics of the present century, however, bring its composition down to a latter date — ranging all the way from 70 to 140 (the latter is Baur's date, which is now universally recognized as very wild).   Many conservative critics put its composition after the destruction of Jerusalem on account of the peculiar form of its eschatological discourses — e.g. Weiss, who puts it between 70 and 80 (while putting Matthew and Mark before the destruction of Jerusalem).   The traditional and still prevalent opinion is that Luke's Gospel was written later than those of Matthew and Mark.   See the various commentaries and New Testament Introductions, and for a clear exhibition of the synoptical problem in general, see Schaff's *Ch. Hist.* I. p. 607 sqq.   On Luke in particular, p. 648 sqq.
[13] Luke i. 2, 3.
[14] Traces of a knowledge of the Acts are found in the Apostolic Fathers, in Justin, and in Tatian, and before the end of the second century the book occupied a place in the Canon, undisputed except by heretics, such as the Marcionites, Manicheans, &c.   The Muratorian Fragment and Irenæus (III. 14) are the first to mention Luke as the author of the Acts, but from that time on tradition has been unanimous in ascribing it to him.   The only exception occurs in the case of Photius (*ad Amphil. Quæst.* 123, ed. Migne), who states that the work was ascribed by some to Clement, by others to Barnabas, and by others to Luke; but it is probable, as Weiss remarks, that Photius, in this case, confuses the Acts with the Epistle to the Hebrews.   As to the date of its composition, Irenæus (III. 1. 1) seems (one cannot speak with certainty, as some have done) to put

composed not from the accounts of others,
8   but from what he had seen himself. And
they say that Paul meant to refer to Luke's
Gospel wherever, as if speaking of some gospel
of his own, he used the words, "according
9   to my Gospel."[15] As to the rest of his followers, Paul testifies that Crescens was sent
to Gaul;[16] but Linus, whom he mentions in the

Second Epistle to Timothy[17] as his companion
at Rome, was Peter's successor in the episcopate of the church there, as has already
been shown.[18] Clement also, who was ap-   10
pointed third bishop of the church at Rome,
was, as Paul testifies, his co-laborer and fellow-soldier.[19] Besides these, that Areopa-   11
gite, named Dionysius, who was the first to
believe after Paul's address to the Athenians in
the Areopagus (as recorded by Luke in the
Acts)[20] is mentioned by another Dionysius, an

it after the death of Peter and Paul, and therefore, necessarily, the Acts still later. The Muratorian Fragment implies that the work was written at least after the death of Peter. Later, however, the tradition arose that the work was written during the lifetime of Paul (so Jerome, *de vir. ill.* 7), and this has been the prevailing opinion among conservative scholars ever since, although many put the composition between the death of Paul and the destruction of Jerusalem; while some (e.g. Weiss) put it after the destruction of Jerusalem, though still assigning it to Luke. The opposite school of critics deny Luke's authorship, throwing the book into the latter part of the first century (Scholten, Hilgenfeld, &c.), or into the times of Trajan and Hadrian (e.g. Volkmar, Keim, Hausrath, &c.). The Tübingen School saw in the Acts a "tendency-writing," in which the history was intentionally perverted. This theory finds few supporters at present, even among the most extreme critics, all of whom, however, consider the book a source of the second rank, containing much that is legendary and distorted and irreconcilable with Paul's Epistles, which are looked upon as the only reliable source. The question turns upon the relation of the author of the "we" sections to the editor of the whole. Conservative scholars agree with universal tradition in identifying them (though this is not necessary in order to maintain the historical accuracy of the work), while the opposite school denies the identity, considering the "we" sections authentic historical accounts from the pen of a companion of Paul, which were afterward incorporated into a larger work by one who was not a pupil of Paul. The identity of the author of the third Gospel and of the Acts is now admitted by all parties. See the various Commentaries and New Testament Introductions; and upon the sources of the Acts, compare especially Weizsäcker's *Apost. Zeitalter*, p. 182 sqq., and Weiss' *Einleitung*, p. 569 sq.

[15] Rom. ii. 16, xvi. 25; 2 Tim. ii. 8. Eusebius uses the expression φασί, "they say," which seems to imply that the interpretation was a common one in his day. Schaff (*Ch. Hist.* I. p. 649) says that Origen also thus interpreted the passages in Romans and Timothy referred to, but he gives no references, and I have not been able to find in Origen's works anything to confirm the statement. Indeed, in commenting upon the passages in the Epistle to the Romans he takes the words "my Gospel" to refer to the gospel preached by Paul, not to the Gospel written by Luke. It is true, however, that in the passage from his Commentary on Matthew, quoted by Eusebius in VI. 25, below, Origen does suppose Paul to refer to Luke and his Gospel in 2 Cor. viii. 18. The interpretation of the words "according to my Gospel," which Eusebius represents as common in his day, is adopted also by Jerome (*de vir. ill.* chap. 7), but is a gross exegetical blunder. Paul never uses the word εὐαγγέλιον in such a sense, nor is it used by any New Testament writer to designate the gospel record, or any one of the written Gospels. It is used always in the general sense of "glad tidings," or to denote the scheme of salvation, or the substance of the gospel revelation. Eusebius is not the first to connect Luke's Gospel with Paul. The Muratorian Fragment speaks of Luke's connection with Paul, and Irenæus (III. 1. 1, quoted below in V. 8. § 2) says directly that Luke recorded the Gospel preached by Paul. Tertullian (*Adv. Marcion.* IV. 5) tells us that Luke's form of the Gospel is usually ascribed to Paul, and in the same work, IV. 2, he lays down the principle that the preaching of the disciples of the apostles needs the authority of the apostles themselves, and it is in accord with this principle that so much stress was laid by the early Church upon the connection of Mark with Peter and of Luke with Paul. In chap. 24 Eusebius refers again to Luke's relation to Paul in connection with his Gospel, and so, too, Origen, as quoted by Eusebius, Bk. VI. chap. 25. The Pauline nature of the Gospel has always been emphasized, and still is by the majority of scholars. This must not be carried so far, however, as to imply that Luke drew his materials from Paul; for Paul himself was not an eye-witness, and Luke expressly states in his preface the causes which induced him to write, and the sources from which he derived his material. The influence of Paul is seen in Luke's standpoint, and in his general spirit—his Gospel is the Gospel of universal salvation.

[16] 2 Tim. iv. 10, where the Greek word used is ἐπορεύθη, which means simply "went" or "is gone." That Paul had sent him as Eusebius states (using the word στειλάμενος) is not implied in the epistle. Instead of εἰς τὰς Γαλλίας (or τὴν Γαλλίαν) most of the ancient MSS. of the New Testament have εἰς Γαλατίαν, which is the reading of the Textus Receptus, of Tregelles, of Westcott and Hort and others. Some MSS., however (including the Sinaitic), have Γαλλίαν, which Tischendorf adopts; and some of the MSS. of Eusebius also have this form, though the majority read τὰς Γαλλίας. Christophorsonus in his edition of Eusebius reads ἐπὶ τὴν Γαλατίαν, but entirely without MS. authority. Epiphanius (*Hær.* LI. 11)

contends that in 2 Tim. iv. 10 should be read Γαλλία and not Γαλατία: οὐ γὰρ ἐν τῇ Γαλατίᾳ ὥς τινες πλανηθέντης νομίζουσιν, ἀλλὰ ἐν τῇ Γαλλίᾳ. Theodoret (in 2 Tim. IV. 10) reads Γαλατίαν, but interprets it as meaning τὰς Γαλλίας: οὕτω γὰρ ἐκαλοῦντο πάλαι.

[17] 2 Tim. iv. 21.   [18] See chap. 2, note 1, above.

[19] Clement is mentioned in Phil. iv. 3, but is not called a "fellow-soldier." Eusebius was evidently thinking of Paul's references to Epaphroditus (Phil. ii. 25) and to Archippus (Philem. 2), whom he calls his fellow-soldiers. The Clement to whom Eusebius here refers was a very important personage in the early Roman church, being known to tradition as one of its first three bishops. He has played a prominent part in Church history on account of the numerous writings which have passed under his name. We know nothing certain about his life. Eusebius identifies him with the Philippian Clement mentioned by Paul,—an identification apparently made first by Origen, and after him repeated by a great many writers. But the identification is, to say the least, very doubtful, and resting as it does upon an agreement in a very common name deserves little consideration. It was quite customary in the early Church to find Paul's companions, whenever possible, in responsible and influential positions during the latter part of the first century. A more plausible theory, which, if true, would throw an interesting light upon Clement and the Roman church of his day, is that which identifies him with the consul Flavius Clement, a relative of the emperor Domitian (see below, chap. 18, note 6). Some good reasons for the identification might be urged, and his rank would then explain well Clement's influential position in the Church. But as pointed out in chap. 18, note 6, it is extremely improbable that the consul Flavius Clement was a Christian; and in any case a fatal objection to the identification (which is nevertheless adopted by Hilgenfeld and others) is the fact that Clement is nowhere spoken of as a martyr until the time of Rufinus, and also that no ancient writer identifies him or connects him in any way with the consul, although Eusebius' mention of the latter in chap. 23 shows that he was a well-known person. When we remember the tendency of the early Church to make all its heroes martyrs, and to ascribe high birth to them, the omission in this case renders the identification, we may say, virtually impossible. More probable is the conjecture of Lightfoot, that he was a freedman belonging to the family of the consul Clement, whose name he bore. This is simply conjecture, however, and is supported by no testimony. Whoever Clement was, he occupied a very prominent position in the early Roman church, and wrote an epistle to the Corinthians which is still extant (see below, chap. 16; and upon the works falsely ascribed to him, see chap. 38). In regard to his place in the succession of Roman bishops, see chap. 2, note 1, above. For a full account of Clement, see especially Harnack's Prolegomena to his edition of Clement's Epistle (*Patrum Apost. Opera*, Vol. I.), Salmon's article, *Clemens Romanus*, in the *Dict. of Christ. Biog.*, Schaff's *Ch. Hist.* II. 636 sq., and Donaldson's *Hist. of Christ. Lit. and Doctrine*, I. p. 90 sq.

[20] Acts xvii. 34. This Dionysius has played an important part in Church history, as the pretended author of a series of very remarkable writings, which pass under the name of Dionysius, the Areopagite, but which in reality date from the fifth or sixth century, and probably owe their origin to the influence of Neo-Platonism. The first mention of these writings is in the records of the Council of Constantinople (532 A.D.); but from that time on they were constantly used and unanimously ascribed to Dionysius, the Areopagite, until, in the seventeenth century, their claims to so great antiquity were disputed. They are still defended, however, in the face of the most positive evidence, by many Roman Catholic writers. The influence of these works upon the theology of the Middle Ages was prodigious. Scholasticism may be said to be based upon them, for Thomas Aquinas used them, perhaps, more than any other source; so much so, that he has been said "to have drawn his whole theological system from Dionysius."

Our Dionysius has had the further honor of being identified by tradition with Dionysius (St. Denis), the patron saint of France,—an identification which we may follow the most loyal of the French in accepting, if we will, though we shall be obliged to suppose that our Dionysius lived to the good old age of two to three hundred years.

The statement of Dionysius of Corinth that the Areopagite was bishop of Athens (repeated by Eusebius again in Bk. IV. chap. 23) is the usual unwarranted throwing back of a second century conception into the first century. That Dionysius held a position of

ancient writer and pastor of the parish in Corinth,[21] as the first bishop of the church at
12 Athens. But the events connected with the apostolic succession we shall relate at the proper time. Meanwhile let us continue the course of our history.

CHAPTER V.

The Last Siege of the Jews after Christ.

1 AFTER Nero had held the power thirteen years,[1] and Galba and Otho had ruled a year and six months,[2] Vespasian, who had become distinguished in the campaigns against the Jews, was proclaimed sovereign in Judea and received the title of Emperor from the armies there.[3] Setting out immediately, therefore, for Rome, he entrusted the conduct of the war
2 against the Jews to his son Titus.[4] For the Jews after the ascension of our Saviour, in addition to their crime against him, had been devising as many plots as they could against his apostles. First Stephen was stoned to death by them,[5] and after him James, the son of Zebedee and the brother of John, was beheaded,[6] and finally James, the first that had obtained the episcopal seat in Jerusalem after the ascension of our Saviour, died in the manner already described.[7] But the rest of the apostles, who had been incessantly plotted against with a view to their destruction, and had been driven out of the land of Judea, went unto all nations to preach the Gospel,[8] relying upon the power of Christ, who had said to them, " Go ye and make disciples of all the nations in my name." [9]
3 But the people of the church in Jerusalem had been commanded by a revelation, vouchsafed to approved men there before the

war, to leave the city and to dwell in a certain town of Perea called Pella.[10] And when those that believed in Christ had come thither from Jerusalem, then, as if the royal city of the Jews and the whole land of Judea were entirely destitute of holy men, the judgment of God at length overtook those who had committed such outrages against Christ and his apostles, and totally destroyed that generation of impious men.
4 But the number of calamities which everywhere fell upon the nation at that time, the extreme misfortunes to which the inhabitants of Judea were especially subjected, the thousands of men, as well as women and children, that perished by the sword, by famine, and by other forms of death innumerable, — all these things, as well as the many great sieges which were carried on against the cities of Judea, and the excessive sufferings endured by those that fled to Jerusalem itself, as to a city of perfect safety, and finally the general·course of the whole war, as well as its particular occurrences in detail, and how at last the abomination of desolation, proclaimed by the prophets,[11] stood in the very temple of God, so celebrated of old, the temple which was now awaiting its total and final destruction by fire, — all these things any one that wishes may find accurately described in the history written by Josephus.[12]
5 But it is necessary to state that this writer records that the multitude of those who were assembled from all Judea at the time of the Passover, to the number of three million souls,[13] were shut up in Jerusalem " as in a prison,"
6 to use his own words. For it was right that in the very days in which they had inflicted suffering upon the Saviour and the Benefactor of all, the Christ of God, that in those days, shut up " as in a prison," they should meet with destruction at the hands of divine justice.
7 But passing by the particular calamities which they suffered from the attempts made upon them by the sword and by other means, I think it necessary to relate only the misfortunes which the famine caused, that those who read

influence among the few Christians whom Paul left in Athens is highly probable, and the tradition that later he was made the first bishop there is quite natural. The church of Athens plays no part in the history of the apostolic age, and it is improbable that there was any organization there until many years after Paul's visit; for even in the time of Dionysius of Corinth, the church there seems to have been extremely small and weak (cf. Bk. IV. chap. 23, § 2). Upon Dionysius and the writings ascribed to him, see especially the article of Lupton in the *Dict. of Christ. Biog.* I. p. 841–848.
21 Upon Dionysius of Corinth, see Bk. IV. chap. 23, below.
1 Nero was emperor from Oct. 16, 54; to June 9, 68 A.D.
2 Eusebius' figures are incorrect. He omits Vitellius entirely, while he stretches Galba's and Otho's reigns to make them cover a period of eighteen months, instead of nine (Galba reigned from June 9, 68, to Jan. 15, 69; and Otho from Jan. 15 to April 20, 69). The total of the three reigns of Galba, Otho, and Vitellius was about eighteen months.
3 Vespasian was proclaimed emperor by the prefect of Egypt at Alexandria, July 1, 69, while Vitellius was the acknowledged emperor in Italy. His choice was immediately ratified by his army in Judea, and then by all the legions in the East. Vitellius was conquered by Vespasian's generals, and slain in Italy, Dec. 20, 69, while Vespasian himself went to Alexandria. The latter was immediately recognized by the Senate, and reached Italy in the summer of 70. Eusebius is thus approximately correct, though he is not exact as to details.
4 Titus undertook the prosecution of the war against the Jews after his father's departure, and brought the siege of Jerusalem to an end, Sept. 8, 70 A.D.
5 See Acts vii. 8 sqq.		8 See chap. 1, note 1.
6 See Acts xii. 2.		9 See Matt. xxviii. 19.
7 See Bk. II. chap. 23.

10 Pella was a town situated beyond the Jordan, in the north of Perea, within the dominions of Herod Agrippa II. The surrounding population was chiefly Gentile. See Pliny V. 18, and Josephus, *B. J.* III. 3. 3, and I. 4. 8. Epiphanius (*De pond. et mens.* 15) also records this flight of the Christians to Pella.
11 Dan. ix. 27.		12 Josephus, *B. J.* Bks. V. and VI.
13 *B. J.* VI. 9, §§ 3 and 4. Eusebius simply gives round numbers. Josephus in § 3 puts the number at 2,700,000, exclusive of the " unclean and the strangers " who were not allowed to eat the Passover. In the same work, Bk. II. chap. 14, § 3, Josephus states that when Cestius Gallus, governor of Syria, came to Jerusalem at the time of the Passover in 65 A.D., no less than 3,000,000 persons came about him to enter complaint against the procurator Florus. These numbers are grossly exaggerated. Tacitus estimates the number in the city at the time of the siege as 600,000, but this, too, is far above the truth. The writer of the article *Jerusalem*, in Smith's *Bible Dict.*, estimates that the city can never have had a population of more than 50,000 souls, and he concludes that at the time of the siege there cannot have been more than 60,000 or 70,000 collected within the walls. This is probably too low an estimate, but shows how far out of the way the figures of Josephus and Tacitus must be.

this work may have some means of knowing that God was not long in executing vengeance upon them for their wickedness against the Christ of God.

CHAPTER VI.

The Famine which oppressed them.

1 TAKING the fifth book of the History of Josephus again in our hands, let us go through the tragedy of events which then 2 occurred.[1] " For the wealthy," he says, " it was equally dangerous to remain. For under pretense that they were going to desert men were put to death for their wealth. The madness of the seditions increased with the famine, and both the miseries were inflamed more 3 and more day by day. Nowhere was food to be seen ; but, bursting into the houses, men searched them thoroughly, and whenever they found anything to eat they tormented the owners on the ground that they had denied that they had anything ; but if they found nothing, they tortured them on the ground that they 4 had more carefully concealed it. The proof of their having or not having food was found in the bodies of the poor wretches. Those of them who were still in good condition they assumed were well supplied with food, while those who were already wasted away they passed by, for it seemed absurd to slay those who were 5 on the point of perishing for want. Many, indeed, secretly sold their possessions for one measure of wheat, if they belonged to the wealthier class, of barley if they were poorer. Then shutting themselves up in the innermost parts of their houses, some ate the grain uncooked on account of their terrible want, while others baked it according as necessity and 6 fear dictated. Nowhere were tables set, but, snatching the yet uncooked food from the fire, they tore it in pieces. Wretched was the fare, and a lamentable spectacle it was to see the more powerful secure an abundance while 7 the weaker mourned. Of all evils, indeed, famine is the worst, and it destroys nothing so effectively as shame. For that which under other circumstances is worthy of respect, in the midst of famine is despised. Thus women snatched the food from the very mouths of their husbands and children, from their fathers, and what was most pitiable of all, mothers from their babes. And while their dearest ones were wasting away in their arms, they were not ashamed to take away from them the last 8 drops that supported life. And even while they were eating thus they did not remain undiscovered. But everywhere the rioters appeared, to rob them even of these portions of food. For whenever they saw a house shut up, they regarded it as a sign that those inside were taking food. And immediately bursting open the doors they rushed in and seized what they were eating, almost forcing it out of their very throats. Qld men who clung to their 9 food were beaten, and if the women concealed it in their hands, their hair was torn for so doing. There was pity neither for gray hairs nor for infants, but, taking up the babes that clung to their morsels of food, they dashed them to the ground. But to those that anticipated their entrance and swallowed what they were about to seize, they were still more cruel, just as if they had been wronged by them. And 10 they devised the most terrible modes of torture to discover food, stopping up the privy passages of the poor wretches with bitter herbs, and piercing their seats with sharp rods. And men suffered things horrible even to hear of, for the sake of compelling them to confess to the possession of one loaf of bread, or in order that they might be made to disclose a single drachm of barley which they had concealed. But the tormentors themselves did not suf- 11 fer hunger. Their conduct might indeed have seemed less barbarous if they had been driven to it by necessity ; but they did it for the sake of exercising their madness and of providing sustenance for themselves for days to come. And when any one crept out of the 12 city by night as far as the outposts of the Romans to collect wild herbs and grass, they went to meet him ; and when he thought he had already escaped the enemy, they seized what he had brought with him, and even though oftentimes the man would entreat them, and, calling upon the most awful name of God, adjure them to give him a portion of what he had obtained at the risk of his life, they would give him nothing back. Indeed, it was fortunate if the one that was plundered was not also slain."

To this account Josephus, after relating other things, adds the following :[2] "The 13 possibility of going out of the city being brought to an end,[3] all hope of safety for the Jews was cut off. And the famine increased and devoured the people by houses and families. And the rooms were filled with dead women and children, the lanes of the city with the corpses of old men. Children and youths, 14 swollen with the famine, wandered about the market-places like shadows, and fell down wherever the death agony overtook them. The sick were not strong enough to bury even their own relatives, and those who had the strength

---

[1] Josephus, *B. J.* Bk. V. chap. 10, §§ 2 and 3.

[2] *Ibid.* chap. 12, §§ 3 and 4.
[3] Titus had just completed the building of a wall about the city by which all egress from the town was shut off. Josephus gives an account of the wall in the paragraph immediately preceding.

hesitated because of the multitude of the dead and the uncertainty as to their own fate. Many, indeed, died while they were burying others, and many betook themselves to their graves

15 before death came upon them. There was neither weeping nor lamentation under these misfortunes; but the famine stifled the natural affections. Those that were dying a lingering death looked with dry eyes upon those that had gone to their rest before them. Deep silence and death-laden night encircled the city.

16 But the robbers were more terrible than these miseries; for they broke open the houses, which were now mere sepulchres, robbed the dead and stripped the covering from their bodies, and went away with a laugh. They tried the points of their swords in the dead bodies, and some that were lying on the ground still alive they thrust through in order to test their weapons. But those that prayed that they would use their right hand and their sword upon them, they contemptuously left to be destroyed by the famine. Every one of these died with eyes fixed upon the temple; and they left the seditious

17 alive. These at first gave orders that the dead should be buried out of the public treasury, for they could not endure the stench. But afterward, when they were not able to do this, they threw the bodies from the walls

18 into the trenches. And as Titus went around and saw the trenches filled with the dead, and the thick blood oozing out of the putrid bodies, he groaned aloud, and, raising his hands, called God to witness that this was

19 not his doing." After speaking of some other things, Josephus proceeds as follows:[4] "I cannot hesitate to declare what my feelings compel me to. I suppose, if the Romans had longer delayed in coming against these guilty wretches, the city would have been swallowed up by a chasm, or overwhelmed with a flood, or struck with such thunderbolts as destroyed Sodom. For it had brought forth a generation of men much more godless than were those that suffered such punishment. By their madness indeed was the whole people brought to destruction."

20 And in the sixth book he writes as follows:[5] "Of those that perished by famine in the city the number was countless, and the miseries they underwent unspeakable. For if so much as the shadow of food appeared in any house, there was war, and the dearest friends engaged in hand-to-hand conflict with one another, and snatched from each other the most wretched supports of life. Nor would they believe

21 that even the dying were without food; but the robbers would search them while they

were expiring, lest any one should feign death while concealing food in his bosom. With mouths gaping for want of food, they stumbled and staggered along like mad dogs, and beat the doors as if they were drunk, and in their impotence they would rush into the same houses twice or thrice in one hour. Ne-

22 cessity compelled them to eat anything they could find, and they gathered and devoured things that were not fit even for the filthiest of irrational beasts. Finally they did not abstain even from their girdles and shoes, and they stripped the hides off their shields and devoured them. Some used even wisps of old hay for food, and others gathered stubble and sold the smallest weight of it for four Attic drachmæ.[6]

23 "But why should I speak of the shamelessness which was displayed during the famine toward inanimate things? For I am going to relate a fact such as is recorded neither by Greeks nor Barbarians; horrible to relate, incredible to hear. And indeed I should gladly have omitted this calamity, that I might not seem to posterity to be a teller of fabulous tales, if I had not innumerable witnesses to it in my own age. And besides, I should render my country poor service if I suppressed the account of the sufferings which she endured.

24 "There was a certain woman named Mary that dwelt beyond Jordan, whose father was Eleazer, of the village of Bathezor[7] (which signifies the *house of hyssop*). She was distinguished for her family and her wealth, and had fled with the rest of the multitude to Jerusalem and was shut up there with them during the siege. The tyrants had robbed her of the

25 rest of the property which she had brought with her into the city from Perea. And the remnants of her possessions and whatever food was to be seen the guards rushed in daily and snatched away from her. This made the woman terribly angry, and by her frequent reproaches and imprecations she aroused the anger of the rapacious villains against herself. But

26 no one either through anger or pity would slay her; and she grew weary of finding food for others to eat. The search, too, was already become everywhere difficult, and the famine was piercing her bowels and marrow, and resentment was raging more violently than famine. Taking, therefore, anger and necessity as her counsellors, she proceeded to a most unnatural thing.

27 Seizing her child, a boy which was sucking at her breast, she said, Oh, wretched child, in war, in famine, in sedition, for what do I pre-

---

[4] *Ibid.* chap. 13, § 6.
[5] *Ibid.* Bk. VI. chap. 3, §§ 3 and 4.

[6] Ἀττικῶν τεσσάρων; the word δραχμῶν is to be supplied. An Attic drachm, according to some authorities, was equal to about fifteen cents, according to others (among them Liddell and Scott) to about nineteen cents.
[7] βαθεζώρ. Some MSS. have βαθεχώρ, and the MSS. of Josephus have βηθεζώβ, which Whiston translates Bethezub.

serve thee? Slaves among the Romans we shall be even if we are allowed to live by them. But even slavery is anticipated by the famine, and the rioters are more cruel than both. Come, be food for me, a fury for these rioters,[8] and a bye-word to the world, for this is all that is wanting to complete the calamities of the Jews. And when she had said this she slew her son;

28 and having roasted him, she ate one half herself, and covering up the remainder, she kept it. Very soon the rioters appeared on the scene, and, smelling the nefarious odor, they threatened to slay her immediately unless she should show them what she had prepared. She replied that she had saved an excellent portion for them, and with that she uncovered the

29 remains of the child. They were immediately seized with horror and amazement, and stood transfixed at the sight. But she said, This is my own son, and the deed is mine. Eat, for I too have eaten. Be not more merciful than a woman, nor more compassionate than a mother. But if you are too pious and shrink from my sacrifice, I have already[9] eaten of

30 it; let the rest also remain for me. At these words the men went out trembling, in this one case being affrighted; yet with difficulty did they yield that food to the mother. Forthwith the whole city was filled with the awful crime, and as all pictured the terrible deed before their own eyes, they trembled as if they

31 had done it themselves. Those that were suffering from the famine now longed for death; and blessed were they that had died before hearing and seeing miseries like these."

32 Such was the reward which the Jews received for their wickedness and impiety against the Christ of God.

CHAPTER VII.

The Predictions of Christ.

1 It is fitting to add to these accounts the true prediction of our Saviour in which he

2 foretold these very events. His words are as follows:[1] " Woe unto them that are with child, and to them that give suck in those days! But pray ye that your flight be not in the winter, neither on the Sabbath day. For

there shall be great tribulation, such as was not since the beginning of the world to this time, no, nor ever shall be."

The historian, reckoning the whole num- 3 ber of the slain, says that eleven hundred thousand persons perished by famine and sword,[2] and that the rest of the rioters and robbers, being betrayed by each other after the taking of the city, were slain.[3] But the tallest of the youths and those that were distinguished for beauty were preserved for the triumph. Of the rest of the multitude, those that were over seventeen years of age were sent as prisoners to labor in the works of Egypt,[4] while still more were scattered through the provinces to meet their death in the theaters by the sword and by beasts. Those under seventeen years of age were carried away to be sold as slaves, and of these alone the number reached ninety thousand.[5] These things 4 took place in this manner in the second year of the reign of Vespasian,[6] in accordance with the prophecies of our Lord and Saviour Jesus Christ, who by divine power saw them beforehand as if they were already present, and wept and mourned according to the statement of the holy evangelists, who give the very words which he uttered, when, as if addressing Jerusalem herself, he said:[7] " If thou hadst 5 known, even thou, in this day, the things which belong unto thy peace! But now they are hid from thine eyes. For the days shall come upon thee, that thine enemies shall cast a rampart about thee, and compass thee round, and keep thee in on every side, and shall lay thee and thy children even with the ground." And 6 then, as if speaking concerning the people, he says,[8] " For there shall be great distress in the land, and wrath upon this people. And they shall fall by the edge of the sword, and shall be led away captive into all nations. And Jerusalem shall be trodden down of the Gentiles, until the times of the Gentiles be fulfilled." And again:[9] " When ye shall see Jerusalem com-

---

[8] " In accordance with the idea that the souls of the murdered tormented, as furies, those who were most guilty of their death" (Stroth).

[9] ἤδη. All the MSS. of Eusebius read ὑμῶν. Some of the MSS. of Josephus read ἤδη, and Rufinus translates *nam et ego prior comedi.* Valesius, without MS. authority (but apparently with the support of some MSS. of Josephus, for Whiston translates "one-half") reads ἥμισυ, a half, and he is followed by the English and German translators. Some change from the reading of the MSS. of Eusebius is certainly necessary; and though the alteration made by Valesius produces very good sense and seems quite natural, I have preferred to accept the reading which is given by many of the MSS. of Josephus, and which has the support of Rufinus.

[1] Matt. xxiv. 19–21.

[2] Josephus, *B. J.* Bk. VI. chap. 9, § 3. Josephus simply says that the whole number of those that perished during the siege was 1,100,000; he does not specify the manner of their death. On the accuracy of the numbers which he gives, see above, chap. 5, note 13.

[3] *Ibid.* § 2.

[4] εἰς τὰ κατ᾽ Ἀιγυπτον ἔργα. The works meant are the great stone quarries of Egypt (commonly called the mines of Egypt), which furnished a considerable part of the finest marble used for building purposes in Rome and elsewhere. The quarries were chiefly in the hands of the Roman government, and the work of quarrying was done largely by captives taken in war, as in the present case.

[5] Josephus does not say that the number of those sold as slaves was upward of 90,000, as Eusebius asserts, but simply (*ibid.* § 3) that the number of captives taken during the whole war was 97,000, a number which Eusebius, through an error, applies to the one class of prisoners that were sold as slaves.

[6] In *B. J.* Bk. VI. 8. 5 and 10. 1 Josephus puts the completion of the siege on the eighth of the month Elul (September), and in the second passage he puts it in the second year of Vespasian. Vespasian was proclaimed emperor in Egypt July 1, 69, so that Sept. 8 of his second year would be Sept. 8, A.D. 70. (Cf. Schürer, *N. T. Zeitgesch.* p. 347.)

[7] Luke xix. 42–44.

[8] *Ibid.* xxi. 23, 24.

[9] *Ibid.* verse 20.

passed with armies, then know that the desolation thereof is nigh."

7　　If any one compares the words of our Saviour with the other accounts of the historian concerning the whole war, how can one fail to wonder, and to admit that the foreknowledge and the prophecy of our Saviour were

8　　truly divine and marvellously strange.[10] Concerning those calamities, then, that befell the whole Jewish nation after the Saviour's passion and after the words which the multitude of the Jews uttered, when they begged the release of the robber and murderer, but besought that the Prince of Life should be taken from their midst,[11] it is not necessary to add anything to the

9　　account of the historian. But it may be proper to mention also those events which exhibited the graciousness of that all-good Providence which held back their destruction full forty years after their crime against Christ, — during which time many of the apostles and disciples, and James himself the first bishop there, the one who is called the brother of the Lord,[12] were still alive, and dwelling in Jerusalem itself, remained the surest bulwark of the place. Divine Providence thus still proved itself long-suffering toward them in order to see whether by repentance for what they had done they might obtain pardon and salvation; and in addition to such long-suffering, Providence also furnished wonderful signs of the things which were about to happen to them if they did not repent.

10　　Since these matters have been thought worthy of mention by the historian already cited, we cannot do better than to recount them for the benefit of the readers of this work.

CHAPTER VIII.

The Signs which preceded the War.

1　　TAKING, then, the work of this author, read what he records in the sixth book of his History. His words are as follows :[1] " Thus were the miserable people won over at this time by the impostors and false prophets ;[2] but they did not heed nor give credit to the visions and signs that foretold the approaching desolation. On the contrary, as if struck by lightning, and as if possessing neither eyes nor understanding, they slighted the proclamations of God. At

2　　one time a star, in form like a sword, stood over the city, and a comet, which lasted for a whole year ; and again before the revolt and before the disturbances that led to the war, when the people were gathered for the feast of unleavened bread, on the eighth of the month Xanthicus,[3] at the ninth hour of the night, so great a light shone about the altar and the temple that it seemed to be bright day ; and this continued for half an hour. This seemed to the unskillful a good sign, but was interpreted by the sacred scribes as portending those events which very soon took place. And at the same feast a cow, led

3　　by the high priest to be sacrificed, brought forth a lamb in the midst of the temple. And the eastern gate of the inner temple,

4　　which was of bronze and very massive, and which at evening was closed with difficulty by twenty men, and rested upon iron-bound beams, and had bars sunk deep in the ground, was seen at the sixth hour of the night to open of itself. And not many days after the feast,

5　　on the twenty-first of the month Artemisium,[4] a certain marvelous vision was seen which passes belief. The prodigy might seem fabulous were it not related by those who saw it, and were not the calamities which followed deserving of such signs. For before the setting of the sun chariots and armed troops were seen throughout the whole region in mid-air, wheeling through the clouds and encircling the cities. And at the feast which is called Pentecost,

6　　when the priests entered the temple at night, as was their custom, to perform the services, they said that at first they perceived a movement and a noise, and afterward a voice as of a great multitude, saying, ' Let us go hence.'[5] But what follows is still more

7　　terrible ; for a certain Jesus, the son of Ananias, a common countryman, four years before the war,[6] when the city was particularly

---

[10] It is but right to remark that not merely the negative school of critics, but even many conservative scholars (e.g. Weiss) put the composition of the Gospel of Luke after the year 70, because its eschatological discourses seem to bear the mark of having been recorded after the fulfillment of the prediction, differing as they do in many minor particulars from the accounts of the same discourses in Matthew and Mark. To cite a single instance: in the passage quoted just above from Luke xxi. 20, the armies encompassing Jerusalem are mentioned, while in parallel passages in the other Gospels (Matt. xxiv. 15 and Mark xiii. 14) not armies, but "the abomination of desolation standing in the holy place" is spoken of as the sign. Compare the various commentaries upon these passages.

[11] Compare Acts iii. 14, and see Matt. xvii. 20, Mark xv. 11, Luke xxii. 18.　　[12] See above, Bk. I. chap. 12, note 14.

[1] Josephus, *B. J.* Bk. VI. chap. 5, § 3.

[2] καταψευδόμενοι τοῦ θεοῦ. In the previous paragraph Josephus says that a great many false prophets were suborned by the tyrants to impose on the people. It is to these false prophets therefore that he refers here, and I have consequently felt at liberty thus to translate the Greek word given above, instead of rendering merely " liars

against God " (as Crusè does), which is indefinite, and might have various meanings.

[3] The feast referred to is the feast of the Passover. The Greek name of the month used here is ξανθικός, which was the name of a Macedonian month corresponding to our April. According to Whiston, Josephus regularly used this name for the Jewish month Nisan (the first month of the Jewish year), in which case this event took place six days before the Passover, which began on the 14th of Nisan.

[4] Ἀρτεμίσιος. According to Liddell and Scott, this was a Spartan and Macedonian month corresponding to a part of the ninth Attic month (ἐλαφηβολιών), which in turn corresponded to the latter part of our March and the early part of April. According to Wieseler, Josephus used the word to denote the second month of the Jewish year, the month Iyar.

[5] The majority of the MSS. of Eusebius read μεταβαίνομεν, " we go hence." But at least one of the best MSS. and a majority of the MSS. of Josephus, supported by Rufinus and Jerome (who render *migremus*), read μεταβαίνωμεν, " let us go hence," and I have followed Stephanus, Valesius, Stroth, and the English and German translators in adopting that reading.

[6] That is, in 62 A.D., for, according to Josephus, the war began

prosperous and peaceful, came to the feast, at which it was customary for all to make tents at the temple to the honor of God,[7] and suddenly began to cry out: 'A voice from the east, a voice from the west, a voice from the four winds, a voice against Jerusalem and the temple, a voice against bridegrooms and brides, a voice against all the people.' Day and night he went 8 through all the alleys crying thus. But certain of the more distinguished citizens, vexed at the ominous cry, seized the man and beat him with many stripes. But without uttering a word in his own behalf, or saying anything in particular to those that were present, he continued to cry out in the same words as before. 9 And the rulers, thinking, as was true, that the man was moved by a higher power, brought him before the Roman governor.[8] And then, though he was scourged to the bone, he neither made supplication nor shed tears, but, changing his voice to the most lamentable tone possible, he answered each stroke with the words, 'Woe, woe unto Jerusalem.'"

10   The same historian records another fact still more wonderful than this. He says[9] that a certain oracle was found in their sacred writings which declared that at that time a certain person should go forth from their country to rule the world. He himself understood 11 that this was fulfilled in Vespasian. But Vespasian did not rule the whole world, but only that part of it which was subject to the Romans. With better right could it be applied to Christ; to whom it was said by the Father, "Ask of me, and I will give thee the heathen for thine inheritance, and the ends of the earth for thy possession."[10] At that very time, indeed, the voice of his holy apostles "went throughout all the earth, and their words to the end of the world."[11]

CHAPTER IX.

Josephus and the Works which he has left.

1   AFTER all this it is fitting that we should know something in regard to the origin and family of Josephus, who has contributed so much to the history in hand. He himself gives us information on this point in the following words:[1]

"Josephus, the son of Mattathias, a priest of Jerusalem, who himself fought against the Romans in the beginning and was compelled to be present at what happened afterward." He 2 was the most noted of all the Jews of that day, not only among his own people, but also among the Romans, so that he was honored by the erection of a statue in Rome,[2] and his works were deemed worthy of a place in the library.[3] He wrote the whole of the Antiquities of 3 the Jews[4] in twenty books, and a history of the war with the Romans which took place in his time, in seven books.[5] He himself testifies that the latter work was not only written in Greek, but that it was also translated by himself

---

reference to himself, but also in his autobiography, which was written after the year 100. The work was occasioned by the *Chronicle* of Justus of Tiberias, which had represented him as more patriotic and more hostile to the Romans than he liked, and he therefore felt impelled to paint himself in the blackest of colors, as a traitor and renegade, — probably much blacker than he really was. It is devoted chiefly to an account of the intrigues and plots formed against him while he was governor of Galilee, and contains little of general biographical interest, except in the introduction and the conclusion. Josephus was of a priestly family, — his father Matthias belonging to the first of the twenty-four courses, — and he was born in the first year of Caius Cæsar; i.e. in the year beginning March 16, 37 A.D. He played a prominent part in the Jewish war, being entrusted with the duty, as governor of Galilee and commander of the forces there, of meeting and opposing Vespasian, who attacked that province first. He was, however, defeated, and gave himself up to the victors, in the summer of 67. He was treated with honor in the camp of the Romans, whom he served until the end of the war, and became a favorite and flatterer of the Vespasian house, incurring thereby the everlasting contempt of his countrymen. He went to Rome at the close of the war, and lived in prosperity there until early in the second century. His works are our chief source for a knowledge of Jewish affairs from the time of the Maccabees, and as such are, and will always remain, indispensable, and their author immortal, whatever his character. He was a man of learning and of talent, but of inordinate selfishness and self-esteem. He was formerly accused of great inaccuracy, and his works were considered a very poor historical source; but later investigations have increased his credit, and he seems, upon the whole, to have been a historian of unusual ability and conscientiousness.

[2] Eusebius is the only one, so far as we know, to mention this statue in Rome, and what authority there is for his statement we cannot tell.

[3] In § 64 of his *Life* Josephus tells us that Titus was so much pleased with his accounts of the Jewish war that he subscribed his name to them, and ordered them published (see the next chapter, § 8 sqq., where the passage is quoted). The first public library in Rome, according to Pliny, was founded by Pollio (76 B.C.–4 A.D.). The one referred to here is undoubtedly the imperial library, which, according to Suetonius, was originally established by Augustus in the temple of Apollo on the Palatine, and contained two sections, — one for Greek, and the other for Latin works. It was greatly enlarged by Tiberius and Domitian.

[4] 'Ιουδαϊκὴ 'Αρχαιολογία, *Antiquitates Judaicæ*. This work, which is still extant, is Josephus' most extensive work, and aims to give, in twenty books, a complete history of the Jews, from the time of Abraham to the beginning of the great war with Rome. The object of the work is mainly apologetic, the author aiming to place Judaism before Gentile readers in as favorable a light as possible. It contains much legendary matter, but is the main source for our knowledge of a long period of Jewish history, and as such is invaluable. The work was completed, according to his own statement (XX. 11. 2), in the thirteenth year of Domitian (93–94 A.D.), and frequently corrects erroneous statements made in his earlier work upon the Jewish war.

[5] 'Ιστορία 'Ιουδαϊκοῦ πολέμου πρὸς 'Ρωμαίους, *de Bello Judaico*. This work, in seven books, constitutes our most complete and trustworthy source for a knowledge of that great war, so momentous in its consequences both to Judaism and to Christianity. The author wrote from personal knowledge of many of the events described, and had, besides, access to extensive and reliable written sources; and the general accuracy of the work may therefore be accepted. He says that he undertook the work for the purpose of giving a true narrative of the war, in consequence of the many false and distorted accounts which had already appeared in various quarters. He presented the work, when finished, to Vespasian and Titus, and obtained their approval and testimony to its trustworthiness; and hence it must have been written during the reign of Vespasian, probably toward the end of it, as other works upon the war had preceded his (*B. J.*, Preface, § 1).

---

in 66 A.D. A little further on, Josephus says that he continued his cry for seven years and five months, when he was slain during the siege of Jerusalem. This shows that he is here, as well as elsewhere, reckoning the date of the beginning of the war as 66 A.D.

[7] That is, the Feast of Tabernacles, which began on the fifteenth day of the seventh month of the Jewish year, and continued seven days.

[8] This was Albinus, as we should know from the date of the event, and as Josephus directly states in the context. He was procurator from 61 or 62 to 64 A.D. See above, Bk. II. chap. 23, note 35, and chap. 22, note 1.

[9] See Josephus, *B. J.* VI. 5. 4, and cf. *ibid.* III. 8. 9.
[10] Ps. ii. 8.   [11] Ps. xix. 4.
[1] *B. J.*, Preface, § 1. We have an original source for the life of Josephus, not only in his various works, in which he makes frequent

into his native tongue.[6] He is worthy of credit here because of his truthfulness in other

4 matters. There are extant also two other books of his which are worth reading. They treat of the antiquity of the Jews,[7] and in them he replies to Apion the Grammarian, who had at that time written a treatise against the Jews, and also to others who had attempted to vilify the hereditary institutions of the Jewish people.

5 In the first of these books he gives the number of the canonical books of the so-called Old Testament. Apparently[8] drawing his information from ancient tradition, he shows what books were accepted without dispute among the Hebrews. His words are as follows.

CHAPTER X.

The Manner in which Josephus mentions the Divine Books.

1   [1] "WE have not, therefore, a multitude of books disagreeing and conflicting with one another; but we have only twenty-two, which contain the record of all time and are justly held to be divine. Of these, five are by 2 Moses, and contain the laws and the tradi-

11. Ezra and Nehemiah.	17. Twelve Minor Prophets.
12. Esther.	18. Job.
13. Isaiah.	19. Psalms.
14. Jeremiah and Lamentations.	20. Proverbs.
15. Ezekiel.	21. Ecclesiastes.
16. Daniel.	22. Song of Songs.

The earliest detailed list of Old Testament books is that of Melito (given by Eusebius, IV. 26), which is as follows: —

	Genesis.	Proverbs.
Books	Exodus.	Ecclesiastes.
of	Leviticus.	Song of Songs.
Moses	Numbers.	Job.
	Deuteronomy.	Isaiah.
	Joshua Nave.	Jeremiah.
	Judges.	Twelve Minor Prophets.
	Ruth.	Daniel.
	Four of Kings.	Ezekiel.
	Chronicles.	Ezra.
	Psalms.	

Melito says nothing of the number twenty-two, and, in fact, his list, as he gives it, numbers only twenty-one. His list really differs from Josephus' only in omitting the Book of Esther. This omission may be accidental, though it is omitted by Athanasius and Gregory Nazianzen. He makes no mention of Nehemiah, but that is doubtless included with Ezra, as in the case of Josephus' canon. His canon purports to be the Palestinian one, and hence we should expect it to be the same as that of Josephus, which makes it more probable that the omission of Esther was only accidental. Origen (in Eusebius, VI. 25) tells us that there were twenty-six books in the Hebrew canon; but his list differs somewhat from that of Josephus. It is as follows: —

1–5. Books of Moses.		15. Song of Songs.
6. Joshua.		16. [Twelve Minor Prophets (Rufinus).]
7. Judges and Ruth.		
8. Samuel.		17. Isaiah.
9. Kings.		18. Jeremiah, Lamentations, and Epistle.
10. Chronicles.		
11. Ezra I. and II.		19. Daniel.
12. Psalms.		20. Ezekiel.
13. Proverbs.		21. Job.
14. Ecclesiastes.		22. Esther.

"Besides these also the Maccabees."

The peculiar thing about the list is the omission of the Twelve Minor Prophets and the insertion of the Epistle of Jeremiah. The former were certainly looked upon by Origen as sacred books, for he wrote a commentary upon them (according to Eusebius, VI. 36). There is no conceivable reason for their omission, and indeed they are needed to make up the number twenty-two. We must conclude that the omission is simply an oversight on the part of Eusebius or of some transcriber. Rufinus gives them as number sixteen, as shown in the list, but the position there assigned to them is not the ordinary one. We should expect to find them in connection with the other prophets; but the various lists are by no means uniform in the order of the books. On the other hand, the Greek Epistle of Jeremiah (Baruch vi.) did not stand in the Hebrew canon, and can have been included by Origen here only because he had been used to seeing it in connection with Jeremiah in his copy of the LXX. (for in ancient MSS. of the LXX., which probably represent the original arrangement, it is given not as a part of Baruch, but as an appendix to Lamentations), and hence mentioned it in this book without thinking of its absence from the Hebrew canon. Origen adds the Maccabees to his list, but expressly excludes them from the twenty-two books (see Bk. VI. chap. 25, note 5). Meanwhile the Talmud and the Midrash divide the canon into twenty-four books, and this was probably the original Jewish division. The number twenty-two was gained by adding Ruth to Judges and Lamentations to Jeremiah. The number thus obtained agreed with the number of letters in the alphabet, and was therefore accepted as the number sanctioned by divine authority, and the division was commonly adopted by the Fathers. This is Strack's view, and seems better than the opposite opinion, which is advocated by many, that the number twenty-four might be changed to twenty-two than how the reverse should happen. So, for instance, Jerome, in his preface to the translation of Samuel and Kings, makes the number twenty-two, and gives a list which agrees with the canon of Josephus except in the three general divisions, which are differently composed. It will be seen that these various lists (with the exception of that of Origen, which includes the Epistle of Jeremiah and appends the Maccabees) include only the books of our canon. But the LXX. prints with the Old Testament a number of Books which we call Apocrypha and exclude from the canon. It has been commonly supposed, therefore, that there was a regular Alexandrian canon differing from the Palestinian. But this is not likely. An examination of Philo's use of the Old Testament shows us that his canon agreed with that of Josephus,

---

[6] The work, as Josephus informs us (*B. J.*, Preface, § 1; and *contra Apion.* I. 9), was written originally in his own tongue,— Aramaic, — and afterwards translated by himself into Greek, with the help of others. Eusebius inverts the fact, making the Greek the original.

[7] The full title of this work is the *Apology of Flavius Josephus on the Antiquities of the Jews against Apion* (περὶ ἀρχαιότητος Ἰουδαίων κατὰ Ἀπίωνος, *De Antiquitate Judæorum contra Apionem*). It is ordinarily cited simply as *contra Apionem* (*Against Apion*). It consists of two books, and is, in fact, nothing else than an apology for Judaism in general, and to a less extent, a defense of himself and his former work (the *Antiquities*) against hostile critics. The common title, *contra Apionem*, is rather misleading, as he is not once mentioned in the first book, although in the first part of the second book he is attacked with considerable bitterness and through him a large class of enemies and detractors of Judaism. (Upon Apion, the famous Alexandrian and the bitter enemy of the Jews, see above, Bk. II. chap. 5, note 5.) The work is Josephus' best effort from a literary point of view, and shows both learning and ability, and in spite of its brevity contains much of great value. It was written after his *Antiquities* (i.e. after 93 A.D.), how long afterward we cannot tell. These three works of Josephus, with his autobiography already mentioned (note 1), are all that are extant, although he seems to have written another work relating to the history of the Seleucidæ (cf. *Ant.* XIII. 2. 1, 2. 4, 4. 6, 5. 11) of which not a trace remains, and which is mentioned by no one else. The other works planned by Josephus — *On God and his Essence* (*Ant.* XX. 11. 3), and *On the Laws of the Jews* (*ibid.* and *Ant.* III. 5. 6, 8. 10) — seem never to have been written. (They are mentioned also by Eusebius in the next chapter.) Other compositions attributed to him are not from his hand. The best edition of the works of Josephus is that of Benedict Niese (Berlin, 1885 sq.), of which the first two volumes have been already issued, comprising ten books of the *Antiquities*. A good complete edition is that of Dindorf (Paris, 1845–47, 2 vols.). That of Bekker (Leipzig, 1855, 6 vols.) is very convenient. The only complete English translation is by Whiston, unfortunately uncritical and inaccurate. Traill's translation of the *Jewish War* (London, 1862) is a great improvement, but does not cover the remainder of Josephus' works. Upon Josephus and his writings, see the article of Edersheim in the *Dict. of Christ. Biog.* III. 441–460, and compare the literature given there.   [8] ὡσάν.

[1] *Against Apion*, I. 8. The common Christian tradition (since the first century, when it was stated in the fourth book of Ezra xiv. 44 sq.) is that Ezra was the compiler of the Old Testament canon. This, however, is a mistake, for the canon was certainly not completed before the time of Judas Maccabæus. Josephus is the earliest writer to give us a summary of the books of the Old Testament; and he evidently gives not merely his own private opinion, but the commonly accepted canon of his day. He does not name the separate books, but tells us that they were twenty-two in number (the number of the letters of the Hebrew alphabet), and gives us the three divisions, so that we are able to ascertain his canon in detail. It was doubtless as follows: —

1–5. Books of Moses.		8. Samuel.
6. Joshua.		9. Kings.
7. Judges and Ruth.		10. Chronicles.

tion respecting the origin of man, and continue the history[2] down to his own death. This period embraces nearly three thousand 3 years.[3] From the death of Moses to the death of Artaxerxes, who succeeded Xerxes as king of Persia, the prophets that followed Moses wrote the history of their own times in thirteen books.[4] The other four books contain hymns to God, and precepts for the regula-4 tion of the life of men. From the time of Artaxerxes to our own day all the events have been recorded, but the accounts are not worthy of the same confidence that we repose in those which preceded them, because there has not been during this time an exact 5 succession of prophets.[5] How much we

are attached to our own writings is shown plainly by our treatment of them. For although so great a period has already passed by, no one has ventured either to add to or to take from them, but it is inbred in all Jews from their very birth to regard them as the teachings of God, and to abide by them, and, if necessary, cheer-fully to die for them."

These remarks of the historian I have thought might advantageously be introduced in this connection. Another work of no little merit 6 has been produced by the same writer, On the Supremacy of Reason,[6] which some have called Maccabaicum,[7] because it contains an account of the struggles of those Hebrews who contended manfully for the true religion, as is related in the books called Maccabees. And at the end of the twentieth book of 7 his Antiquities[8] Josephus himself intimates that he had purposed to write a work in four books concerning God and his existence, accord-ing to the traditional opinions of the Jews, and also concerning the laws, why it is that they per-mit some things while prohibiting others.[9] And the same writer also mentions in his own works other books written by himself.[9] In 8 addition to these things it is proper to quote also the words that are found at the close of his Antiquities,[10] in confirmation of the testimony which we have drawn from his accounts. In that place he attacks Justus of Tiberias,[11] who, like himself, had attempted to write a history of contemporary events, on the ground that he had not written truthfully. Having brought many

---

comprising no apocryphal books. It is probable in fact that the LXX. included in their translation these other books which were held in high esteem, without intending to deliver any utterance as to the extent of the canon or to alter the common Jewish canon by declaring these a part of it. But however that was, the use of the LXX., which was much wider than that of the Hebrew, brought these books into general use, and thus we see them gradually acquir-ing canonical authority and used as a part of the canon by Augus-tine and later Fathers. Jerome was the only one in the West to utter a protest against such use of them. Both Athanasius and Cyril of Jerusalem added to the canon Baruch and the Epistle of Jeremiah; but opinion in the Orient was mostly against making any books not in the Hebrew canon of canonical authority, and from the fourth century the Eastern Fathers used them less and less. They were, however, officially recognized as a part of the canon by numer-ous medieval and modern synods until 1839, when the larger Cate-chism of the Orthodox Catholic Eastern Church, the most authorita-tive standard of the Græco-Russian Church, expressly excluded them. The Latin Church, meanwhile, has always regarded the Apocrypha as canonical, and by its action at the Council of Trent has made them a part of the official canon. See Strack's article in Herzog, trans-lated in Schaff-Herzog; also Harman's *Introduction to the Holy Scripture*, p. 33 sqq. The subject is discussed in all Old Testa-ment introductions.

[2] Literally, " the tradition respecting the origin of man (ἀνθρω-πογονίας) down to his own death." I have felt it necessary to in-sert the words, " and continue the history," which are not found in the Greek, but which are implied in the words, " down to his own death."

[3] Among the Jews in the time of Christ a world's era was in use, dating from the creation of the world; and it is this era which Jose-phus employs here and throughout his *Antiquities*. His figures are often quite inconsistent, — probably owing, in large part, to the corrupt state of the existing text, — and the confusion which results is considerable. See Destinon's *Chronologie des Josephus.*

[4] These thirteen books were: —

1. Joshua.	8. Isaiah.
2. Judges and Ruth.	9. Jeremiah and Lamentations.
3. Samuel.	10. Ezekiel.
4. Kings.	11. Daniel.
5. Chronicles.	12. Twelve Minor Prophets.
6. Ezra and Nehemiah.	13. Job.
7. Esther.	

As will be seen, Josephus divided the canon into three parts: first, the Law (five books of Moses); second, the Prophets (the thirteen just mentioned); third, the Hagiographa (Psalms, Proverbs, Eccle-siastes, and Canticles). The division of the canon into three such parts is older than Josephus; at the same time, his division is quite different from any other division known. Jerome's is as follows: —
   1. Law: five books of Moses.
   2. Prophets: Joshua, Judges and Ruth, Samuel, Kings, Isaiah, Jeremiah and Lamentations, Ezekiel, Twelve Minor Prophets (eight books).
   3. Hagiographa (Holy writings): Job, Psalms, Proverbs, Eccle-siastes, Canticles, Daniel, Chronicles, Ezra, Esther (nine books). The division which exists in our Hebrew Bibles differs from this of Jerome's only in transferring Ruth and Lamentations to the third division, and thus making twenty-four books. This is held by many to be a later form, as remarked above, but as Strack shows, it is rather the original. In the LXX., which is followed in our Eng-lish Bible, the books are arranged, without reference to the three divisions, solely according to their subject-matter. The peculiar division of Josephus was caused by his looking at the matter from the historical standpoint, which led him to include in the second division all the books which contained, as he says, an account of events from Moses to Artaxerxes.

[5] The Artaxerxes here referred to is Artaxerxes Longimanus who reigned B.C. 464 to 425. It was under him that Ezra and Nehemiah

carried on their work and that the later prophets flourished. Mala-chi — the last of them — uttered his prophecies at the end of Artax-erxes' or at the beginning of Darius' reign. It was commonly held among the Jews that with Haggai, Zachariah, and Malachi the pro-phetical spirit had departed from Israel, and the line was sharply drawn, as here by Josephus, between them and the writers of the Apocrypha who followed them.

[6] εἰς Μακκαβαίους λόγος ἢ περὶ αὐτοκράτορος λογισμοῦ: *De Maccabaeis, seu de rationis imperio liber*. This book is often called the Fourth Book of Maccabees, and was formerly ascribed to Josephus. As a consequence it is printed with his works in many editions. But it is now universally acknowledged to be spurious, although who the author is we cannot tell.

[7] Μακκαβαϊκόν.

[8] *Ant.* XX. 11. 3. See the previous chapter, note 7.

[9] See the same note.

[10] The passage referred to, which is quoted just below, is found in his *Life*, § 65, and not in the *Antiquities*. But we can see from the last paragraph of the *Antiquities* that he wrote his *Life* really as an appendix to that work, and undoubtedly, as Ewald suggests, issued it with a second edition of the *Antiquities* about twenty years after the first. In the MSS. it is always found with the *Antiquities*, and hence the whole might with justice be viewed as one work. It will be noticed that Eusebius mentions no separate *Life* of Josephus, which shows that he regarded it simply as a part of the *Antiquities*.

[11] Justus of Tiberias was the leader of one of the factions of that city during the troublous times before the outbreak of the war, while Josephus was governor of Galilee, and as an opponent he caused him considerable trouble. He is mentioned frequently in Josephus' *Life*, and we are thus enabled to gather a tolerably complete idea of him — though of course the account is that of an enemy. He wrote a work on the Jews which was devoted chiefly to the affairs of the Jewish war and in which he attacked Josephus very severely. This work, which is no longer extant, was read by Photius and is described by him in his *Bibl. Cod.* 33, under the title, βασιλεῖς Ἰουδαῖοι οἱ ἐν τοῖς στέμμασι. It was in consequence of this work that Josephus felt obliged to publish his *Life*, which is really little more than a defense of himself over against the attacks of Justus. See above, note 1.

other accusations against the man, he continues in these words:[12] "I indeed was not afraid
9 in respect to my writings as you were,[13] but, on the contrary, I presented my books to the emperors themselves when the events were almost under men's eyes. For I was conscious that I had preserved the truth in my account, and hence was not disappointed in my ex-
10 pectation of obtaining their attestation. And I presented my history also to many others, some of whom were present at the war, as, for instance, King Agrippa[14] and some of his
11 relatives. For the Emperor Titus desired so much that the knowledge of the events should be communicated to men by my history alone, that he indorsed the books with his own hand and commanded that they should be published. And King Agrippa wrote sixty-two epistles testifying to the truthfulness of my account." Of these epistles Josephus subjoins two.[15]
12 But this will suffice in regard to him. Let us now proceed with our history.

CHAPTER XI.

Symeon rules the Church of Jerusalem after James.

1 After the martyrdom of James[1] and the conquest of Jerusalem which immediately followed,[2] it is said that those of the apostles and disciples of the Lord that were still living came together from all directions with those that were related to the Lord according to the flesh[3] (for the majority of them also were still alive) to take counsel as to who was worthy to succeed James. They all with one 2
consent pronounced Symeon,[4] the son of Clopas, of whom the Gospel also makes mention,[5] to be worthy of the episcopal throne of that parish. He was a cousin, as they say, of the Saviour. For Hegesippus records that Clopas was a brother of Joseph.[6]

CHAPTER XII.

Vespasian commands the Descendants of David to be sought.

He also relates that Vespasian after the conquest of Jerusalem gave orders that all that belonged to the lineage of David should be sought out, in order that none of the royal race might be left among the Jews; and in consequence of this a most terrible persecution again hung over the Jews.[1]

---

12 *Vita*, § 65.

13 Josephus has just affirmed in a previous paragraph that Justus had had his *History* written for twenty years, and yet had not published it until after the death of Vespasian, Titus, and Agrippa, and he accuses him of waiting until after their death because he was afraid that they would contradict his statements. Josephus then goes on to say in the passage quoted that he was not, like Justus, afraid to publish his work during the lifetime of the chief actors in the war.

14 Agrippa II. See above, Bk. II. chap. 19, note 3. Agrippa sided with the Romans in the war and was with Vespasian and Titus in their camp much of the time, and in Galilee made repeated efforts to induce the people to give up their rebellion, that the war might be avoided.

15 These two epistles are still extant, and are given by Josephus in his *Vita*, immediately after the passage just quoted by Eusebius. The first of them reads as follows (according to Whiston's translation): "King Agrippa to Josephus, his dear friend, sendeth greeting. I have read over thy book with great pleasure, and it appears to me that thou hast done it much more accurately and with greater care than have the other writers. Send me the rest of these books. Farewell, my dear friend."

1 61 or 62 A.D. See above, Bk. II. chap. 23.

2 See *ibid.* note 40. The date of Symeon's accession (assuming that he did take charge of the Jerusalem church as James had done) cannot be fixed. Eusebius himself, as he informs us in Bk. IV. chap. 5, although he had a list of the Jerusalem bishops, had no information as to the dates of their accession, or the length of their incumbency. He puts Symeon's accession after the destruction of Jerusalem, but he evidently does that only because he supposed that it followed immediately upon the death of James. Some (e.g. Lightfoot) think it probable that Symeon was appointed immediately after James' death, therefore before the destruction of Jerusalem; others (e.g. Renan) suppose that in Pella they had no bishop and appointed Symeon only after the return of the church to Jerusalem.

3 λόγος κατέχει. Hegesippus (quoted in Bk. IV. chap. 22, below) says that "Symeon was appointed the second bishop, whom all proposed as the cousin of our Lord." Upon what authority Eusebius' more definite account rests we do not know. He introduces it with the formula λόγος κατέχει, and we know of no other author who has put it as he does. It may be that the simple statement of Hegesippus was the sole ground of the more detailed tradition which Eusebius repeats in this chapter. The reason of Symeon's appointment as given by Hegesippus is quite significant. It was the common Oriental custom to accord the highest honors to all the members of a prophet's or religious leader's family, and it was undoubtedly owing chiefly to his close physical relationship to Christ that James enjoyed such prominence and influence in the Jerusalem church, apparently exceeding even that of the apostles themselves.

4 This Symeon is to be distinguished from the apostle Simon, the Canaanite, and also from Simon, the brother of our Lord (mentioned in Matt. xiii. 55 and Mark vi. 3). It is noticeable that Hegesippus nowhere calls him the "brother of the Lord," though he does give James that title in Bk. II. chap. 23. Clopas is mentioned in John xix. 25, as the husband of Mary, who is without doubt identical with Mary the mother of James (the little) and of Joses; mentioned in Matt. xxvii. 56, Mark xv. 40, &c. If Hegesippus' account be accepted as trustworthy (and there is no reason for doubting it), Symeon was the son of Clopas and Mary, and therefore brother of James the Little and Joses. If, then, Alphæus and Clopas be the same, as many claim, James the Little is to be identified with James the son of Alphæus, the apostle, and hence the latter was the brother of Symeon. This identification, however, is entirely arbitrary, and linguistically difficult, and we shall do better therefore to keep the men separate, as Renan does (see above, Bk. I. chap. 12, note 14). Upon the martyrdom of Symeon, see below, chap. 32.

5 In John xix. 25.

6 Hegesippus, quoted below in Bk. IV. chap. 22, calls Clopas the uncle of the Lord, which would make him of course the brother or brother-in-law of Joseph. Eusebius evidently considered them own brothers. Whether Hegesippus elsewhere stated this directly, or whether Eusebius' opinion is simply an inference from the words of Hegesippus already referred to, we do not know. There is no objection to the conclusion that Clopas and Joseph were own brothers, although it cannot be proved from Hegesippus' words that they were more than brothers-in-law. From John xix. 25 it is at any rate plain that their wives cannot have been own sisters, as was formerly maintained by so many commentators. With the remaining possibilities of relationship we do not need to concern ourselves.

1 It is not certain that Eusebius intends to give Hegesippus as his authority for the statements of this chapter, inasmuch as he does not mention his name. He gives the account, however, upon the authority of some one else, and not as a direct historical statement, for the verb is in the infinitive, and it is much more natural to supply Ἡγήσιππος ἱστορεῖ, the last words of the preceding chapter, than to supply any other phrase, such as λόγος κατέχει, which occurs two chapters earlier. The translators are divided as to the words that are to be supplied, but it seems to me beyond doubt that this account rests upon the same authority as that of the previous chapter. There is in any case nothing at all unlikely in the report, as Vespasian and his successors kept a very close watch upon the Jews, and this would have been a very natural method of endeavoring to prevent future revolutions. The same course was pursued also by Domitian; see below, chaps. 19 and 20. We hear from no other source of a persecution raised against the Jews by Vespasian, and we may therefore conclude that it cannot have amounted to much, if indeed it deserves to be called a persecution at all.

CHAPTER XIII.

Anencletus, the Second Bishop of Rome.

AFTER Vespasian had reigned ten years Titus, his son, succeeded him.[1] In the second year of his reign, Linus, who had been bishop of the church of Rome for twelve years,[2] delivered his office to Anencletus.[3] But Titus was succeeded by his brother Domitian after he had reigned two years and the same number of months.[4]

CHAPTER XIV.

Abilius, the Second Bishop of Alexandria.

IN the fourth year of Domitian, Annianus,[1] the first bishop of the parish of Alexandria, died after holding office twenty-two years, and was succeeded by Abilius,[2] the second bishop.

CHAPTER XV.

Clement, the Third Bishop of Rome.

IN the twelfth year of the same reign Clement succeeded Anencletus[1] after the latter had been bishop of the church of Rome for twelve years. The apostle in his Epistle to the Philippians informs us that this Clement was his fellow-worker. His words are as follows :[2] "With Clement and the rest of my fellow-laborers whose names are in the book of life."

CHAPTER XVI.

The Epistle of Clement.

THERE is extant an epistle of this Clement[1] which is acknowledged to be genuine and is of considerable length and of remarkable merit.[2] He wrote it in the name of the church of Rome to the church of Corinth, when a sedition had arisen in the latter church.[3] We know that this epistle also has been publicly used in a great many churches both in former times and in our own.[4] And of the fact that a sedition did take place in the church of Corinth at the time referred to Hegesippus is a trustworthy witness.[5]

CHAPTER XVII.

The Persecution under Domitian.

DOMITIAN, having shown great cruelty toward many, and having unjustly put to death no small number of well-born and notable men at Rome, and having without cause exiled and confiscated the property of a great many other illustrious men, finally became a successor of Nero in his hatred and enmity toward God. He was in fact the second that stirred up a persecution against us,[1] although his father Vespasian had undertaken nothing prejudicial to us.[2]

MSS., and in a Syriac version, consists of fifty-nine chapters, and is found in all editions of the Apostolic Fathers. It purports to have been written from the church at Rome to the church at Corinth, but bears the name of no author. Unanimous tradition, however (beginning with Dionysius of Corinth, in Eusebius, IV. 23), ascribes it to Clement, Bishop of Rome, and scholars, with hardly an exception, accept it as his work. It was, in all probability, written immediately after the persecution of Domitian, in the last years of the first century, and is one of the earliest, perhaps the very earliest, post-biblical works which we have. It was held in very high repute in the early Church, and in the Alexandrian Codex it stands among the canonical books as a part of the New Testament (though this is exceptional; cf. chap. 3, above, and chap. 25, below, in both of which this epistle is omitted, though Eusebius is giving lists of New Testament books, both accepted and disputed). We have had the epistle complete only since 1875, when Bryennios discovered a MS. containing it and other valuable works. Previously a part of the epistle had been wanting. In consequence the older editions have been superseded by the more recent. See appendix to Lightfoot's edition (1877), which gives the recovered portions of the text; so, also, the later editions of Gebhardt and Harnack's, and of Hilgenfeld's Apostolic Fathers. The epistle is translated in the *Ante-Nicene Fathers*, I. p. 5–21.
[2] μεγάλη τε καὶ θαυμασία.
[3] See the epistle itself, especially chaps. 1 and 3. It was these seditions in the church at Corinth which occasioned the epistle.
[4] Compare the words of Dionysius of Corinth, in Bk. IV. chap. 23. Though the epistle was held in high esteem, it was not looked upon as a part of the New Testament canon.
[5] Hegesippus' testimony upon this point is no longer extant.
[1] The persecutions under Nero and Domitian were not undertaken by the state as such; they were simply personal matters, and established no precedent as to the conduct of the state toward Christianity. They were rather spasmodic outbursts of personal enmity, but were looked upon with great horror as the first to which the Church was subjected. There was no general persecution, which took in all parts of the empire, until the reign of Decius (249–251), but Domitian's cruelty and ferocity were extreme, and many persons of the highest rank fell under his condemnation and suffered banishment and even death, not especially on account of Christianity, though there were Christians among them, but on account of his jealousy, and for political reasons of various sorts. That Domitian's persecution of the Christians was not of long duration is testified by Tertullian, *Apol.* 5. Upon the persecutions of the Christians, see, among other works, Wieseler's *Die Christenverfolgungen der Cäsaren, hist. und chronolog. untersucht,* 1878; Uhlhorn's *Der Kampf des Christenthums mit dem Heidenthum,* English translation by Smyth and Ropes, 1879; and especially the keen essay of Overbeck, *Gesetze der römischen Kaiser gegen die Christen,* in his *Studien zur Gesch. der alten Kirche,* I. (1875).
[2] The fact that the Christians were not persecuted by Vespasian is abundantly confirmed by the absence of any tradition to the opposite effect. Compare Tertullian's *Apol.* chap. 5, where the persecutions of Nero and Domitian are recorded.

---

[1] Vespasian reigned from July 1 (if his reign be dated from the time he was proclaimed emperor in Egypt; if from the death of Vitellius, Dec. 20), 69, to June 24, 79 A.D.
[2] In his *Chron.* (Armenian) Eusebius gives the length of Linus' episcopate as fourteen years, while Jerome gives it as eleven years. Both figures are about equally reliable; see above, chap. 2, note 1.
[3] Of Anencletus, or Cletus, as he is also called, we know nothing more than that he was one of the traditional first three bishops of Rome. Hippolytus makes two bishops, Anencletus and Cletus, out of the one man, and he is followed by the Roman Catholic Church (see above, chap. 2, note 1). According to chap. 15, Anencletus held office twelve years.
[4] Titus died Dec. 13, A.D. 81. He therefore reigned two years and six months, instead of two years and two months as Eusebius states.
[1] 85 A.D.; on Annianus, see above, Bk. II. chap. 24, note 2.
[2] Ἀβίλιος. According to one tradition Abilius was ordained presbyter with his successor Cerdon by Mark himself (see Smith and Wace). According to another (*Ap. Const.* VII. 46) he was appointed bishop by Luke. He held office thirteen years according to chap. 21, below. Valesius claims that the name should be written Avilius, regarding it as a Latin name, and citing in support of his opinion the name of a prefect of Egypt, Avilius Flaccus, mentioned by Philo, and the fact that the name of Avilius' predecessor, Annianus, is also Latin.
[1] On Anencletus, see chap. 13, note 3.
[2] Phil. iv. 3. For an account of Clement, see above, chap. 4, note 19; and upon the order of succession of the Roman bishops, see chap. 2, note 1.
[1] This epistle of Clement, which is still extant in two Greek

CHAPTER XVIII.

The Apostle John and the Apocalypse.

1   IT is said that in this persecution the apostle and evangelist John, who was still alive, was condemned to dwell on the island of Patmos in consequence of his testimony to the
2   divine word.[1] Irenæus, in the fifth book of his work Against Heresies, where he discusses the number of the name of Antichrist which is given in the so-called Apocalypse of John,[2] speaks as follows concerning him:
3   [3] "If it were necessary for his name to be proclaimed openly at the present time, it would have been declared by him who saw the revelation. For it was seen not long ago, but almost in our own generation, at the end of the reign of Domitian."
4   To such a degree, indeed, did the teaching of our faith flourish at that time that even those writers who were far from our religion did not hesitate to mention in their histories the persecution and the martyrdoms which
5   took place during it.[4] And they, indeed, accurately indicated the time. For they recorded that in the fifteenth year of Domitian[5] Flavia Domitilla, daughter of a sister of Flavius Clement, who at that time was one of the consuls of Rome,[6] was exiled with many others to the island of Pontia in consequence of testimony borne to Christ.

---

[1] Unanimous tradition, beginning with Irenæus (V. 30. 3, quoted just below, and again in Eusebius V. 8) assigns the banishment of John and the apocalyptic visions to the reign of Domitian. This was formerly the common opinion, and is still held by some respectable writers, but strong internal evidence has driven most modern scholars to the conclusion that the Apocalypse must have been written before the destruction of Jerusalem, the banishment therefore (upon the assumption that John wrote the Apocalypse, upon which see chap. 24, note 19) taking place under Nero instead of Domitian. If we accept this, we have the remarkable phenomenon of an event taking place at an earlier date than that assigned it by tradition, an exceptional and inexplicable thing. We have too the difficulty of accounting for the erroneousness of so early and unanimous a tradition. The case thus stood for years, until in 1886 Vischer published his pamphlet *Die Offenbarung des Johannes, eine jüdische Apocalypse in Christlicher Bearbeitung* (Gebhardt and Harnack's *Texte und Untersuchungen*, Band II. Heft. 3), which if his theory were true, would reconcile external and internal evidence in a most satisfactory manner, throwing the original into the reign of Nero's successor, and the Christian recension into the reign of Domitian. Compare especially Harnack's appendix to Vischer's pamphlet; and upon the Apocalypse itself, see chap. 24, below.
[2] Rev. xiii. 18. It will be noticed that Eusebius is careful not to commit himself here on the question of the authorship of the Apocalypse. See below, chap. 24, note 20.
[3] Irenæus, *Adv. Hær.* V. 30. 3; quoted also below, in Bk. V. chap. 8.
[4] Jerome, in his version of the *Chron.* of Eusebius (year of Abr. 2112), says that the historian and chronographer Bruttius recorded that many of the Christians suffered martyrdom under Domitian. Since the works of Bruttius are not extant, we have no means of verifying the statement. Dion Cassius (LXVII. 14) relates some of the banishments which took place under Domitian, among them that of Flavia Domitilla, who was, as we know, a Christian; but he does not himself say that any of these people were Christians, nor does he speak of a persecution of the Christians.
[5] We learn from Suetonius (*Domit.* chap. 15) that the events referred to by Eusebius in the next sentence took place at the very end of Domitian's reign; that is, in the year 96 A.D., the fifteenth year of his reign, as Eusebius says here. Dion Cassius also (LXVII. 14) puts these events in the same year.
[6] Flavius Clemens was a cousin of Domitian, and his wife, Domitilla, a niece of the emperor. They stood high in favor, and their

CHAPTER XIX.

Domitian commands the Descendants of David to be slain.

BUT when this same Domitian had commanded that the descendants of David should be slain, an ancient tradition says[1] that some of the heretics brought accusation against the descendants of Jude (said to have been a brother of the Saviour according to the flesh), on the ground that they were of the lineage of David and were related to Christ himself. Hegesippus relates these facts in the following words.

CHAPTER XX.

The Relatives of our Saviour.

"OF the family of the Lord there were still   1 living the grandchildren of Jude, who is said to have been the Lord's brother according to the flesh.[1] Information was given that they belonged to the family of David, and they   2 were brought to the Emperor Domitian by the Evocatus.[2] For Domitian feared the com-

---

two sons were designated as heirs to the empire, while Flavius Clemens himself was made Domitian's colleague in the consulship. But immediately afterward Clemens was put to death and Domitilla was banished. Suetonius (*Domit.* chap. 15) accuses Clemens of *contemtissimæ inertiæ*, and Dion Cassius (LXVII. 14) of atheism (ἀθεότητος). These accusations are just such as heathen writers of that age were fond of making against the Christians (compare, for instance, Athenagoras' *Adv. Gent.* chap. 4, and Tertullian's *Apol.* chap. 42). Accordingly it has been very commonly held that both Flavius Clemens and Domitilla were Christians, and were punished on that account. But early tradition makes only Domitilla a Christian; and certainly if Clemens also — a man of such high rank — had been a Christian, an early tradition to that effect would be somewhere preserved. We must, therefore, conclude that his offense was something else than Christianity. The very silence of Christian tradition as to Clement is an argument for the truth of the tradition in regard to Domitilla, and the heathen historians referred to confirm its main points, though they differ in minor details. The *Acts of Martyrdom of Nereus and Achilles* represent Domitilla as the niece, not the wife, of Flavius Clemens, and Eusebius does the same. More than that, while the heathen writers report that Domitilla was banished to the island Pandateria, these *Acts*, as well as Eusebius and Jerome (*Ep. adv. Eustachium*, Migne's ed., *Ep.* CVIII. 7), give the island of Pontia as the place of banishment. Tillemont and other writers have therefore assumed that there were two Domitillas, — aunt and niece, — one banished to one island, the other to another. But this is very improbable, and it is easier to suppose that there was but one Domitilla and but one island, and that the discrepancies are due to carelessness or to the mistakes of transcribers. Pandateria and Pontia were two small islands in the Mediterranean, just west of central Italy, and were very frequently employed by the Roman emperors as places of exile for prisoners.
[1] παλαιὸς κατέχει λόγος. It is noticeable that, although Eusebius has the written authority of Hegesippus for this account, he still speaks of it as supported by "ancient tradition." This is different from his ordinary custom, and serves to make us careful in drawing conclusions as to the nature of Eusebius' authority for any statement from the expression used in introducing it.
[1] This Jude was the brother of James, "the brother of the Lord," who is mentioned in Jude 1, and is to be distinguished from Jude (Thaddeus-Lebbæus), one of the Twelve, whose name appears in the catalogues of Luke (Luke vi. 14 and Acts i. 13) as the son of James (not his brother, as the A. V. translates; the Greek words are 'Ιούδας 'Ιακώβου). For a discussion of the relationship of these men to Christ, see above, Bk. I. chap. 12, note 14. Of the son of Jude and father of the young men mentioned in this chapter we know nothing.
[2] According to Andrew's Lexicon, "An Evocatus was a soldier who, having served out his time, was called upon to do military duty as a volunteer."
This suspiciousness is perfectly in keeping with the character of Domitian. The same thing is told also of Vespasian, in chap. 12;

ing of Christ as Herod also had feared it. And he asked them if they were descendants of David, and they confessed that they were. Then he asked them how much property they had, or how much money they owned. And both of them answered that they had only nine thousand denarii,[3] half of which be-

4　longed to each of them ; and this property did not consist of silver, but of a piece of land which contained only thirty-nine acres, and from which they raised their taxes[4] and supported themselves by their own labor."[5]

5　Then they showed their hands, exhibiting the hardness of their bodies and the callousness produced upon their hands by continuous toil as evidence of their own labor.

6　And when they were asked concerning Christ and his kingdom, of what sort it was and where and when it was to appear, they answered that it was not a temporal nor an earthly kingdom, but a heavenly and angelic one, which would appear at the end of the world, when he should come in glory to judge the quick and the dead, and to give unto every one

7　according to his works. Upon hearing this, Domitian did not pass judgment against them, but, despising them as of no account, he let them go, and by a decree put a stop to

8　the persecution of the Church. But when they were released they ruled the churches, because they were witnesses[6] and were also relatives of the Lord.[7] And peace being established, they lived until the time of Trajan. These things are related by Hegesippus.

9　Tertullian also has mentioned Domitian in the following words :[8] "Domitian also, who possessed a share of Nero's cruelty, attempted once to do the same thing that the latter did. But because he had, I suppose, some intelligence,[9] he very soon ceased, and even

10　recalled those whom he had banished."

But after Domitian had reigned fifteen years,[10] and Nerva had succeeded to the empire, the Roman Senate, according to the writers that

record the history of those days,[11] voted that Domitian's honors should be cancelled, and that those who had been unjustly banished should return to their homes and have their property restored to them. It was at this time

11　that the apostle John returned from his banishment in the island and took up his abode at Ephesus, according to an ancient Christian tradition.[12]

CHAPTER XXI.

Cerdon becomes the Third Ruler of the Church of Alexandria.

AFTER Nerva had reigned a little more

1　than a year[1] he was succeeded by Trajan. It was during the first year of his reign that Abilius,[2] who had ruled the church of Alexandria for thirteen years, was succeeded by Cerdon.[3] He was the third that presided

2　over that church after Annianus,[4] who was the first. At that time Clement still ruled the church of Rome, being also the third that held the episcopate there after Paul and Peter. Linus was the first, and after him came

3　Anencletus.[5]

CHAPTER XXII.

Ignatius, the Second Bishop of Antioch.

AT this time Ignatius[1] was known as the second bishop of Antioch, Evodius having been the first.[2] Symeon[3] likewise was at that time second ruler of the church of Jerusalem, the brother of our Saviour having been the first.

---

[11] See Dion Cassius, LXVIII. 1 sq., and Suetonius' *Domitian*, chap. 23.

[12] Literally, "the word of the ancients among us" (ὁ τῶν παρ' ἡμῖν ἀρχαίων λόγος). On the tradition itself, see chap. 1, note 6.

[1] From Sept. 18, 96, to Jan. 27, 98 A.D.

[2] On Abilius, see chap. 14, note 2, above.

[3] According to the legendary *Acts of St. Mark*, Cerdo was one of the presbyters ordained by Mark. According to Eusebius (*H. E.* IV. 1 and *Chron.*) he held office until the twelfth year of Trajan.

[4] On Annianus, see Bk. II. chap. 24, note 2.

[5] On the order of succession of the early Roman bishops, see above, chap. 2, note 1. Paul and Peter are here placed together by Eusebius, as co-bishops of Rome. Compare the association of the two apostles by Caius, and by Dionysius of Corinth (quoted by Eusebius, in Bk. II. chap. 25).

[1] On Ignatius' life, writings, and martyrdom, see below, chap. 36.

[2] We cannot doubt that the earliest tradition made Evodius first bishop of Antioch, for otherwise we could not explain the insertion of his name before that of the great name of Ignatius. The tendency would be, of course, to connect Ignatius directly with the apostles, and to make him the first bishop. This tendency is seen in Athanasius and Chrysostom, who do not mention Evodius at all; also in the *Apost. Const.* VII. 46, where, however, it is said that Evodius was ordained by Peter, and Ignatius by Paul (as in the parallel case of Clement of Rome). The fact that the name of Evodius appears here shows that the tradition that he was the first bishop seemed to the author too old and too strong to be set aside. Origen (*in Luc. Hom.* VI.) is an indirect witness to the episcopacy of Evodius, since he makes Ignatius the second, and not the first, bishop of Antioch. As to the respective dates of the early bishops of Antioch, we know nothing certain. On their chronology, see Harnack, *Die Zeit des Ignatius*, and cf. Salmon's article *Evodius* in Smith and Wace's *Dict. of Christ. Biog.*

[3] On Symeon, see above, chap. 11, note 4.

---

but in his case the political situation was far more serious, and revolutions under the lead of one of the royal family might most naturally be expected just after the terrible destruction. The same act is also mentioned in connection with Trajan, in chap. 32, and there is no reason to doubt its truthfulness, for the Jews were well known as a most rebellious and troublesome people.

[3] A denarius was a Roman silver coin, in value about sixteen, or, according to others, about nineteen, cents.

[4] "Taxes or tributes were paid commonly in the products of the land" (Val.).

[5] Most editors (including Valesius, Heinichen, Crusè, &c.) regard the quotation from Hegesippus as extending through § 8; but it really ends here, and from this point on Eusebius reproduces the sense in his own words (and so Bright gives it in his edition). This is perfectly clear, for in the first place, the infinitive ἐπιδεικνύναι occurs in the next sentence, a form possible only in indirect discourse; and secondly, as Lightfoot has pointed out, the statement of § 8 is repeated in chap. 32, § 6, and there in the exact language of Hegesippus, which differs enough from the language of § 8 to show that the latter is a free reproduction.

[6] μάρτυρας. On the use of this word, see chap. 32, note 15.

[7] Compare Renan's *Les Evangiles*, p. 466.

[8] Tertullian, *Apol.* chap. 5.

[9] τι συνέσεως. Lat. *sed qua et homo.*

[10] Domitian reigned from Dec. 13, 81 A.D., to Sept. 18, 96.

CHAPTER. XXIII.

Narrative concerning John the Apostle.

1   At that time the apostle and evangelist John, the one whom Jesus loved, was still living in Asia, and governing the churches of that region, having returned after the death of Domitian from his exile on the island.[1]
2   And that he was still alive at that time[2] may be established by the testimony of two witnesses. They should be trustworthy who have maintained the orthodoxy of the Church; and such indeed were Irenæus and Clem-
3   ent of Alexandria.[3] The former in the second book of his work Against Heresies, writes as follows:[4] "And all the elders that associated with John the disciple of the Lord in Asia bear witness that John delivered it to them. For he remained among them until the
4   time of Trajan."[5] And in the third book of the same work he attests the same thing in the following words:[6] "But the church in Ephesus also, which was founded by Paul, and where John remained until the time of Trajan, is a faithful witness of the apostolic tradi-
5   tion." Clement likewise in his book entitled What Rich Man can be saved?[7] indicates the time,[8] and subjoins a narrative which is most attractive to those that enjoy hearing what is beautiful and profitable. Take and read the account which runs as follows:[9]
6   "Listen to a tale, which is not a mere tale, but a narrative[10] concerning John the apostle, which has been handed down and treasured up in memory. For when, after the tyrant's death,[11] he returned from the isle of Patmos to Ephesus, he went away upon their invitation to the neighboring territories of the Gentiles, to appoint bishops in some places, in other places to set in order whole churches, elsewhere to choose to the ministry some one[12] of those that were pointed out by the Spirit. When he
7   had come to one of the cities not far away (the name of which is given by some[13]), and had consoled the brethren in other matters, he finally turned to the bishop that had been appointed, and seeing a youth of powerful physique, of pleasing appearance, and of ardent temperament, he said, 'This one I commit to thee in all earnestness in the presence of the Church and with Christ as witness.' And when the bishop had accepted the charge and had promised all, he repeated the same injunction with an appeal to the same witnesses, and then departed for Ephesus. But the presbyter,[14] taking home the youth committed to him,

---

[1] See chap. 1, note 6, and chap. 18, note 1.
[2] That is, at the beginning of the reign of Trajan.
[3] The test of a man's trustworthiness in Eusebius' mind — and not in his alone — was his orthodoxy. Irenæus has always been looked upon as orthodox, and so was Clement, in the early Church, which reckoned him among the saints. His name, however, was omitted in the Martyrology issued by Clement VIII., on the ground that his orthodoxy was open to suspicion.
[4] Irenæus, *Adv. Hær.* II. 22. 5.
[5] It is in this immediate connection that Irenæus makes the extraordinary assertion, founding it upon the testimony of those who were with John in Asia, that Christ lived to the age of forty or fifty years. A statement occurring in connection with such a palpably false report might well fall under suspicion; but the fact of John's continuance at Ephesus until the time of Trajan is supported by other passages, and there is no reason to doubt it (cf. chap. 1, note 6). Irenæus himself repeats the statement as a well-known fact, in III. 3, 4 (quoted just below). It may also be said that the opinion as to Christ's age is founded upon subjective grounds (cf. the preceding paragraph of Irenæus) and upon a mistaken interpretation of John viii. 56, 57, rather than upon external testimony, and that the testimony (which itself may have been only the result of a subjective opinion) is dragged in only for the sake of confirming a view already adopted. Such a fact as John's own presence in Ephesus at a certain period could hardly be subject to such uncertainty and to the influence of dogmatic prepossessions. It is significant of Eusebius' method that he omits entirely Irenæus' assertion as to the length of Christ's ministry, with which he did not agree (as shown by his account in Bk. I. chap. 10), while extracting from his statement the single fact which he wishes here to establish. The falsity of the context he must have recognized, and yet, in his respect for Irenæus, the great maintainer of sound doctrine, he nowhere refers to it. The information which John is said, in this passage, to have conveyed to the "presbyters of Asia" is that Christ lived to old age. The whole passage affords an instance of how much of error may be contained in what, to all appearances, should be a very trustworthy tradition. Internal evidence must come to the support of external, and with all its alleged uncertainty and subjectivity, must play a great part in the determination of the truth of history.   [6] *Adv. Hær.* III. 3, 4.
[7] τίς ὁ σωζόμενος πλούσιος: *Quis Dives salvetur.* This able and interesting little treatise upon the proper use of wealth is still extant, and is found in the various editions of Clement's works; English translation in the *Ante-Nicene Fathers* (Am. ed.), II. p. 591–604. The sound common sense of the book, and its freedom from undue asceticism are conspicuous, and furnish a pleasing contrast to most of the writings of that age.
[8] He indicates the time only by saying "after the tyrant was dead," which might refer either to Domitian or to Nero. But the

mention of John a little below as "an aged man" would seem to point to the end of the century rather than to Nero's time. At any rate, Eusebius understood Clement as referring to Domitian, and in the presence of unanimous tradition for Domitian, and in the absence of any counter-tradition, we can hardly understand him otherwise.
[9] *Quis Dives salvetur*, chap. 42.
[10] μῦθον οὐ μῦθον, ἀλλὰ ὄντα λόγον. Clement in these words asserts the truth of the story which he relates. We cannot regard it as very strongly corroborated, for no one else records it, and yet we can hardly doubt that Clement gives it in good faith. It may have been an invention of some early Christian, but it is so fully in accord with what we know of John's character that there exists no reason for refusing to believe that at least a groundwork of truth underlies it, even though the story may have gained in the telling of it. It is certainly beautiful, and fully worthy of the "beloved disciple."
[11] See note 8.
[12] κλήρῳ ἕνα γέ τινα κληρώσων. Compare the note of Heinichen in his edition of Eusebius, Vol. I. p. 122. Upon the use of the word κλῆρος in the early Church, see Baur's *Das Christenthum und die christliche Kirche der drei ersten Jahrhunderte*, 2d ed., p. 266 sq., and especially Ritschl's *Entstehung der alt-kath. Kirche*, 2d ed., p. 388 sq. Ritschl shows that the word κλῆρος was originally used by the Fathers in the general sense of order or rank (*Reihe, Rang*), and that from this arose its later use to denote church officers as a class, — the clergy. As he remarks, the word is employed in this later specific sense for the first time in this passage of Clement's *Quis Dives salvetur*. Tertullian, Hippolytus, and Cyprian are the next ones to use it in the same sense. Ritschl remarks in connection with this passage: "Da für eine Wahl der Gemeindebeamten durch das Loos alle sonstigen Beweisen fehlen, und da in dem vorliegenden Satze die Einsetzung von einer Mehrzahl von ἐπίσκοποι durch den Apostel ohne jede Methode erwähnt wird, so fällt jeder Grund hinweg, dass bei der Wahl einzelner Beamten das Mittel des Loosens angewandt sein sollte, zumal bei dieser Deutung ein Pleonasmus vorausgesetzt würde. Es ist vielmehr zu erklären, dass Johannes an einzelnen Orten mehrere Beamte zugleich eingesetzt, an anderen Orten wo schon ein Collegium bestand, dem Beamtenstande je ein Mitglied eingereiht habe."
[13] According to Stroth the *Chronicon Paschale* gives Smyrna as the name of this city, and it has been suggested that Clement withholds the name in order to spare the reputation of Polycarp, who, according to tradition, was appointed bishop of that city by John.
[14] The same man that is called a bishop just above is here called a presbyter. It is such passages — and they are not uncommon in the early Fathers — that have seemed to many to demonstrate conclusively the original identity of presbyters and bishops, an identity which is maintained by most Presbyterians, and is admitted by many Episcopalians (e.g. by Lightfoot in his essay on the Christian Ministry, printed in his Commentary on Philippians). On the other

reared, kept, cherished, and finally baptized [15] him. After this he relaxed his stricter care and watchfulness, with the idea that in putting upon him the seal of the Lord [16] he had given him a perfect protection. But some youths **9** of his own age, idle and dissolute, and accustomed to evil practices, corrupted him when he was thus prematurely freed from restraint. At first they enticed him by costly entertainments; then, when they went forth at night for robbery, they took him with them, and finally they demanded that he should unite with them in some greater crime. He gradually **10** became accustomed to such practices, and on account of the positiveness of his character,[17] leaving the right path, and taking the bit in his teeth like a hard-mouthed and powerful horse, he rushed the more violently down into the depths. And finally despairing of salvation **11** in God, he no longer meditated what was insignificant, but having committed some great crime, since he was now lost once for all, he expected to suffer a like fate with the rest. Taking them, therefore, and forming a band of robbers, he became a bold bandit-chief, the most violent, most bloody, most cruel of them all. Time **12** passed, and some necessity having arisen, they sent for John. But he, when he had set in order the other matters on account of which he had come, said, 'Come, O bishop, restore us the deposit which both I and Christ committed to thee, the church, over which thou presidest, being witness.' But the bishop was **13** at first confounded, thinking that he was falsely charged in regard to money which he had not received, and he could neither believe the accusation respecting what he had not, nor could he disbelieve John. But when he said, 'I demand the young man and the soul of the brother,' the old man, groaning deeply and at the same time bursting into tears, said, 'He is dead.' 'How and what kind of death?' 'He is dead to God,' he said; 'for he turned wicked and abandoned, and at last a robber. And now, instead of the church, he haunts the mountain with a band like himself.' But the **14** apostle rent his clothes, and beating his head with great lamentation, he said, 'A fine guard I left for a brother's soul! But let a horse be brought me, and let some one show me the way.' He rode away from the church just as he was, and coming to the place, he was **15** taken prisoner by the robbers' outpost. He, however, neither fled nor made entreaty,

hand, the passages which reveal a distinction between presbyters and bishops are very early, and are adduced not merely by prelatists, but by such disinterested scholars as Harnack (in his translation of Hatch's *Organization of the Early Christian Churches*) as proving that there was from the beginning a difference of some sort between a bishop and a presbyter. I cannot enter here into a discussion of the various views in regard to the original relation between bishops and presbyters. I desire simply to suggest a theory of my own, leaving the fuller exposition of it for some future time. My theory is that the word πρεσβύτερος was originally employed in the most general sense to indicate any church officer, thus practically equivalent to the ἡγούμενος of Heb. xiii. 17, and the ποιμήν of Eph. iv. 11. The terms ἐπίσκοπος and διάκονος, on the other hand, were employed to designate specific church officers charged with the performance of specific duties. If this were so, we should expect the general term to be used before the particular designations, and this is just what we find in the New Testament. We should expect further that the general term and the specific terms might be used by the same person in the same context, according as he thought of the officers in general or of a particular division of the officers; on the other hand the general term and one of the specific terms could never be co-ordinated (we could never find " presbyter *and* bishop," " presbyter *and* deacon "), but we should expect to find the specific terms thus co-ordinated (" bishops *and* deacons "). An examination of the Epistle to the Philippians, of the Pastoral Epistles, of Clement's Epistle to the Corinthians, and of the Didache will show that our expectations are fully realized. This theory explains the fact that so frequently presbyters and bishops seem to be identical (the general and the specific term might of course in many cases be used interchangeably), and also the fact that so frequently they seem to be quite distinct. It explains still further the remarkable fact that while in the first century we never find a distinction in official rank between bishops and presbyters, that distinction appears early in the second. In many churches it must early have become necessary to appoint some of the officers as a special committee to take charge of the economic affairs of the congregation. The members of such a committee might very naturally be given the special name ἐπίσκοποι (see Hatch's discussion of the use of this word in his work already referred to). In some churches the duties might be of such a character that the bishops would need assistants (to whom it would be natural to give the name διάκονος), and such assistants would of course be closely associated with the bishops, as we find them actually associated with them in the second and following centuries (a fact which Hatch has emphasized). Of course where the bishops constituted a special and smaller committee of the general body, entrusted with such important duties, they would naturally acquire especial influence and power, and thus the chairman of the committee — the chairman of the bishops as such, not of the presbyters, though he *might* be that also — would in time, as a central authority was more and more felt to be necessary, gradually assume the supremacy, retaining his original name ἐπίσκοπος. As the power was thus concentrated in his hands, the committee of bishops as such would cease to be necessary, and he would require only the deacons, who should carry out his directions in economic matters, as we find them doing in the second century. The elevation of the bishop would of course separate him from the other officers in such a way that although still a presbyter (i.e. an officer), he would cease to be called longer by the general name. In the same way the deacons obliged to devote themselves to their specific duties, would cease to have much to do with the more general functions of the other officers, to whom finally the name presbyter — originally a general term — would be confined, and thus become a distinctive name for part of the officers. In their hands would remain the general disciplinary functions which had belonged from the beginning to the entire body of officers as such, and their rank would naturally be second only to that of the bishop, for the deacons as assistants only, not independent officers, could not outrank them (though they struggled hard in the third and fourth centuries to do so). It is of course likely that in a great many churches the simple undivided office would long remain, and that bishops and deacons as specific officers distinguished from the general body would not exist. But after the distinction between the three orders had been sharply drawn in one part of Christendom, it must soon spread throughout the Church and become established even in places where it had not been produced by a natural process of evolution. The Church organization of the second century is thus complete, and its further development need not concern us here, for it is not matter of controversy. Nor is this the place to show how the local church officers gradually assumed the spiritual functions which belonged originally to apostles, prophets, and teachers. The Didache is the document which has shed most light upon that process, and Harnack in his edition of it has done most to make the matter clear.

[15] ἐφώτισε: literally, " enlightened him." The verb φωτίζω was very commonly used among the Fathers, with the meaning " to baptize." See Suicer's *Thesaurus*, where numerous examples of this use of the word by Chrysostom, Gregory Nazianzen, and others, are given.

[16] τὴν σφραγῖδα κυρίου. The word σφραγίς was very widely used in the primitive Church to denote baptism. See Suicer's *The-* saurus for examples. Gregory Nazianzen, in his *Orat.* XL., gives the reason for this use of the word: " We call baptism a seal," he says, " because it is a preservative and a sign of ownership." Chrysostom, in his third Homily on 2 Cor. § 7, says, " So also art thou thyself made king and priest and prophet in the laver; a king, having dashed to earth all the deeds of wickedness and slain thy sins; a priest, in that thou offerest thyself to God, having sacrificed thy body and being thyself slain also: . . . a prophet, knowing what shall be, and being inspired by God, and sealed. For as upon soldiers a seal, so is also the Spirit put upon the faithful. And if thou desert, thou art manifest to all. For the Jews had circumcision for a seal, but we the earnest of the Spirit." (*Nicene and Post-Nicene Fathers*, First Series, Vol. XII. p. 293.)

[17] Literally, " greatness of his nature " (μέγεθος φύσεως).

but cried out, ' For this did I come ; lead
16   me to your captain.' The latter, meanwhile, was waiting, armed as he was.   But
when he recognized John approaching, he
17   turned in shame to flee.   But John, forgetting his age, pursued him with all his might,
crying out, ' Why, my son, dost thou flee from
me, thine own father, unarmed, aged ? Pity me,
my son ; fear not ; thou hast still hope of life.
I will give account to Christ for thee.   If need
be, I will willingly endure thy death as the Lord
suffered death for us.   For thee will I give up
my life.   Stand, believe ; Christ hath sent
18   me.'   And he, when he heard, first stopped
and looked down ; then he threw away his
arms, and then trembled and wept bitterly. And
when the old man approached, he embraced
him, making confession with lamentations as he
was able, baptizing himself a second time with
tears, and concealing only his right hand.
19   But John, pledging himself, and assuring
him on oath that he would find forgiveness
with the Saviour, besought him, fell upon his
knees, kissed his right hand itself as if now purified by repentance, and led him back to the
church.   And making intercession for him with
copious prayers, and struggling together with
him in continual fastings, and subduing his mind
by various utterances, he did not depart, as they
say, until he had restored him to the church,
furnishing a great example of true repentance
and a great proof of regeneration, a trophy of a
visible resurrection."

CHAPTER XXIV.

The Order of the Gospels.

1   THIS extract from Clement I have inserted
here for the sake of the history and for the
benefit of my readers.   Let us now point out
the undisputed writings of this apostle.
2   And in the first place his Gospel, which is
known to all the churches under heaven,
must be acknowledged as genuine.[1]   That it has

with good reason been put by the ancients in
the fourth place, after the other three Gospels,
may be made evident in the following way.
Those great and truly divine men, I mean   3
the apostles of Christ, were purified in their
life, and were adorned with every virtue of the
soul, but were uncultivated in speech. They were
confident indeed in their trust in the divine and
wonder-working power which was granted unto
them by the Saviour, but they did not know how,
nor did they attempt to proclaim the doctrines
of their teacher in studied and artistic language,
but employing only the demonstration of the
divine Spirit, which worked with them, and the
wonder-working power of Christ, which was displayed through them, they published the knowledge of the kingdom of heaven throughout the
whole world, paying little attention to the
composition of written works.   And this   4
they did because they were assisted in their
ministry by one greater than man.   Paul, for instance, who surpassed them all in vigor of expression and in richness of thought, committed to writing no more than the briefest epistles,[2] although
he had innumerable mysterious matters to communicate, for he had attained even unto the sights
of the third heaven, had been carried to the very
paradise of God, and had been deemed worthy
to ·hear unspeakable utterances there.[3]
And the rest of the followers of our Saviour,   5
the twelve apostles, the seventy disciples,
and countless others besides, were not ignorant
of these things.   Nevertheless, of all the disciples[4] of the Lord, only Matthew and John have
left us written memorials, and they, tradition
says, were led to write only under the pressure of necessity.   For Matthew, who had   6
at first preached to the Hebrews, when he
was about to go to other peoples, committed his
Gospel to writing in his native tongue,[5] and thus

---

[1] The testimony of antiquity, — both orthodox and heretical, —
to the authenticity of John's Gospel is universal, with the exception
of a single unimportant sect of the second century, the Alogi, who
denied the Johannine authorship on account of the Logos doctrine,
which they rejected, and very absurdly ascribed the Gospel to the
Gnostic Cerinthus ; though its absolute opposition to Cerinthus'
views is so apparent that Irenæus (III. 11. 1) even supposed John to
have written the Gospel against Cerinthus.   The writings of the second century are full of the spirit of John's Gospel, and exhibit frequent
parallels in language too close to be mistaken ; while from the last
quarter of the second century on it is universally and expressly ascribed to John (Theophilus of Antioch and the Muratorian Fragment
being the first to name him as its author).   The Church never entertained a doubt of its authenticity until the end of the seventeenth
century, when it was first questioned by the English Deists ; but its
genuineness was vindicated, and only scattering and occasional attacks were made upon it until the rise of the Tübingen school, since
which time its authenticity has been one of the most fiercely contested points in apostolic history.   Its opponents have been obliged
gradually to throw back the date of its origin, until now no sensible
critic thinks of assigning it to a time later than the early part of the

second century, which is a great gain over the position of Baur and
his immediate followers, who threw it into the latter half of the century.   See Schaff's *Ch. Hist.* I. 701-724 for a full defense of its
authenticity and a comprehensive account of the controversy ; also
p. 406-411 for the literature of the subject.   For the most complete
summary of the external evidence, see Ezra Abbott's *The Authorship of the Fourth Gospel,* 1880.   Among recent works, compare
Weiss' *Leben Jesu,* I. 84-124, and his *N. T. Einleitung,* 586-620,
for a defense of the Gospel, and upon the other side Holtzmann's
Einleitung, 413-460, and Weizsäcker's *Apost. Zeitalter,* p. 531-
558.
[2] Overbeck remarks that Eusebius in this passage is the first to
tell us that Paul wrote no more than what we have in the canon.
But this is a mistake, for Origen (quoted by Eusebius in VI. 25, below) states it just as distinctly as Eusebius does.   The truth is, neither
of them says it directly, and yet it is clear enough when this passage
is taken in connection with chapter 3, that it is what Eusebius meant,
and the same idea underlies the statement of the Muratorian Fragment.   Of course this does not prove that Paul wrote only the epistles which we have (which is indeed contrary to fact), but it shows
what the idea of the early Church was.
[3] See 2 Cor. xii. 2-4.
[4] The majority of the MSS., followed by Burton, Schwegler, and
Laemmer, read διατριβῶν instead of μαθητῶν ; and Burton therefore
translates, *sed tamen ex his omnibus sole Matthæus et Joannes
nobis reliquerunt commentarios de vita et sermonibus Domini,*
" but of all these only Matthew and John have left us commentaries
on the life and conversations of the Lord."   Two important MSS.,
however, read μαθητῶν, and this is confirmed by Rufinus and adopted by Heinichen, Closs, and Crusè.
[5] That Matthew wrote a gospel in Hebrew, although denied by

compensated those whom he was obliged
7   to leave for the loss of his presence. And
    when Mark and Luke had already published
their Gospels,[6] they say that John, who had employed all his time in proclaiming the Gospel
orally, finally proceeded to write for the following
reason.   The three Gospels already mentioned
having come into the hands of all and into his
own too, they say that he accepted them and
bore witness to their truthfulness ; but that there
was lacking in them an account of the deeds
    done by Christ at the beginning of his min-
8   istry.[7]   And this indeed is true.   For it is
    evident that the three evangelists recorded
only the deeds done by the Saviour for one year
after the imprisonment of John the Baptist,[8] and

indicated this in the beginning of their account.   For Matthew, after the forty days'   9
fast and the temptation which followed it,
indicates the chronology of his work when he
says : " Now when he heard that John was delivered up he withdrew from Judea into Galilee." [9]   Mark likewise says : " Now after   10
that John was delivered up Jesus came into
Galilee." [10]   And Luke, before commencing his
account of the deeds of Jesus, similarly marks
the time, when he says that Herod, " adding to
all the evil deeds which he had done, shut
up John in prison." [11]   They say, therefore,   11
that the apostle John, being asked to do it
for this reason, gave in his Gospel an account of
the period which had been omitted by the earlier
evangelists, and of the deeds done by the Saviour
during that period ; that is, of those which were
done before the imprisonment of the Baptist.
And this is indicated by him, they say, in the
following words : " This beginning of miracles
did Jesus " ; [12] and again when he refers to the
Baptist, in the midst of the deeds of Jesus, as
still baptizing in Ænon near Salim ; [13] where he
states the matter clearly in the words : " For
John was not yet cast into prison." [14]   John   12
accordingly, in his Gospel, records the deeds
of Christ which were performed before the Baptist was cast into prison, but the other three
evangelists mention the events which happened after that time.   One who under-   13
stands this can no longer think that the
Gospels are at variance with one another, inasmuch as the Gospel according to John contains
the first acts of Christ, while the others give an
account of the latter part of his life.   And the
genealogy of our Saviour according to the flesh
John quite naturally omitted, because it had
been already given by Matthew and Luke, and
began with the doctrine of his divinity, which
had, as it were, been reserved for him, as
their superior, by the divine Spirit.[15]   These   14
things may suffice, which we have said concerning the Gospel of John.   The cause which led
to the composition of the Gospel of Mark has
been already stated by us.[16]   But as for Luke,   15
in the beginning of his Gospel, he states
himself the reasons which led him to write it.

many, is at present the prevailing opinion among scholars, and may
be accepted as a fact both on account of its intrinsic probability and
of the testimony of the Fathers, which begins with the statement of
Papias, quoted by Eusebius in chap. 39, below, is confirmed by Irenæus (III. I. I, quoted below, V. 8, § 2),—whether independently
of Papias or not, we cannot say, — by Pantænus (but see below,
Bk. V. chap. 10), by Origen (see below, VI. 25), by Jerome (de vir.
ill. 3),—who says that a copy of it still existed in the library at
Cæsarea, — and by Epiphanius (Hær. XXIX. 9).   The question as
to the relation of this Hebrew original to our present Greek Matthew
is much more difficult.   That our Greek Matthew is a mere translation of the original Hebrew was once a prevailing theory, but is now
completely abandoned.   That Matthew himself wrote both is a common conservative position, but is denied by most critical scholars,
many of whom deny then the composition even of the Hebrew original.   Upon the theory that the original Hebrew Matthew was identical with the " Gospel according to the Hebrews," see chap. 27, note
8.   Upon the synoptic problem, see above, II. 15, note 4; and see
the works mentioned there for a discussion of this original Matthew,
and in addition the recent works by Gla, Original-Sprache des Matt.
Evang., 1887, and Resch, Agrapha, Leipzig, 1889.
    The very natural reason which Eusebius gives for the composi-
tion of Matthew's Gospel — viz. that, when on the point of going to
other nations, he committed it to writing, and thus compensated
them for the loss of his presence — occurs in none of the earlier reports of the composition of the Gospel which we now possess. It
was probably a fact which he took from common tradition, as he remarks in the previous sentence that tradition says " they undertook
it from necessity."
    [6] Upon the date and authorship of the Gospel of Luke, see above,
chap. 4, notes 12 and 15.   Upon Mark, see Bk. II. chap. 15, note 4.
    [7] No writer before Eusebius' time, so far as is known, assigned
the reason given by him for the composition of John's Gospel.
Jerome, de vir. ill. chap. 9, repeats the view, combining with it the
anti-heretical purpose.   The indefinite expression, " they say," shows
that Eusebius was recording tradition commonly received in his
time, and does not involve the authority of any particular writer.
This object — viz. the supplementing and filling out of the accounts
of the Synoptists — is assumed as the real object by some modern
scholars; but it is untenable, for though the book serves this purpose to a great extent, the author's real aim was much higher, — viz.
the establishment of belief in the Messiahship and divinity of Christ
(John xx. 31 sqq.), — and he chose his materials accordingly.   The
Muratorian Fragment says, " The Fourth Gospel is that of John,
one of the disciples.   When his fellow-disciples and bishops entreated
him, he said, ' Fast ye now with me for the space of three days, and
let us recount to each other whatever may be revealed to us.'   On
the same night it was revealed to Andrew, one of the apostles, that
John should narrate all things in his own name as they called them
to mind."   Irenæus (III. 11. 1) supposes John to have written his
Gospel as a polemic against Cerinthus.   Clement of Alexandria, in
his Hypotyposes (quoted by Eusebius, VI. 14), says that John wrote
a spiritual Gospel, as a supplement to the other Gospels, which had
sufficiently described the external facts.   The opinion of Eusebius
is very superficial.   Upon examination of the Gospels it will be seen
that, of the events which John relates independently of the synoptists, but a small portion occurred before the imprisonment of John
the Baptist.   John's Gospel certainly does incidentally supplement
the Synoptists in a remarkable manner, but not in any such intentional and artificial way as Eusebius supposes.   Compare Weiss'
Einleitung, p. 602 sqq., and Schaff's Ch. Hist. II. p. 680 sqq.
    [8] The Synoptic Gospels certainly give the impression that Christ's
public ministry lasted but a single year; and were it not for the additional light which John throws upon the subject, the one year
ministry would be universally accepted, as it was by many of the
early Fathers, — e.g. Clement of Alexandria, Tertullian, Origen,
Lactantius, &c.   John, however, expressly mentions three, perhaps
four, passovers, so that Christ's ministry lasted either two or three
years.   Upon comparison of the Synoptists with John, it will be

seen that the events which they record are not all comprised within
a single year, as Eusebius thought, but that they are scattered over
the whole period of his ministry, although confined to his work in
Galilee up to the time of his last journey to Judea, six months before his crucifixion.   The distinction between John and the Synoptists, as to the events recorded, is therefore rather that of place than
of time; but the distinction is not absolute.
    [9] Matt. iv. 12.   [10] Mark i. 14.   [11] Luke iii. 20.
    [12] John ii. 11.   The arguments of Eusebius, whether original or
borrowed from his predecessors, are certainly very ingenious, and
he makes out apparently quite a strong case for his opinion; but a
careful harmony of the four Gospels shows that it is untenable.
    [13] John iii. 23.   [14] ibid. verse 24.
    [15] Eusebius approaches here the opinion of Clement of Alexan-
dria, mentioned in note 7, above, who considered John's Gospel a
spiritual supplement to the others, — a position which the Gospel
certainly fills most admirably.
    [16] See Bk. II. chap. 15.

He states that since many others had more rashly undertaken to compose a narrative of the events of which he had acquired perfect knowledge, he himself, feeling the necessity of freeing us from their uncertain opinions, delivered in his own Gospel an accurate account of those events in regard to which he had learned the full truth, being aided by his intimacy and his

16   stay with Paul and by his acquaintance with the rest of the apostles.[17] So much for our own account of these things. But in a more fitting place we shall attempt to show by quotations from the ancients, what others have said concerning them.

17   But of the writings of John, not only his Gospel, but also the former of his epistles, has been accepted without dispute both now and in ancient times.[18] But the other two

18   are disputed.[19]   In regard to the Apoc-

alypse, the opinions of most men are still divided.[20] But at the proper time this question

character. But in spite of the slight external testimony to the epistles the conclusion of Weiss seems correct, that " inasmuch as the second and third clearly betray the same author, and inasmuch as the second is related to the first in such a manner that they must either be by the same author or the former be regarded as an entirely aimless imitation of the latter, so everything favors the ascription of them both to the author of the first, viz. to the apostle." (*ibid.* p. 469.)

[20] The Apocalypse is one of the best authenticated books of the New Testament. It was used by Papias and others of the earliest Fathers, and already by Justin Martyr was expressly ascribed to the apostle John. (Compare also the epistle of the Churches of Lyons and Vienne, Eusebius, V. 1.) Tradition, so far as we have it, is unanimous (with the exception of the Alogi, an insignificant heretical sect of the second century, who attributed the Apocalypse as well as the Gospel to Cerinthus. Caius is not an exception; see below, chap. 28, note 4) in ascribing the Apocalypse to the apostle John, until Dionysius of Alexandria, who subjected the book to severe literary criticism (see below, Bk. VII. chap. 25), and upon the assumption of the genuineness of the Gospel and the first Epistle, doubted its authenticity on account of its divergence from these writings both in spirit and in style. He says (VII. 25, § 2) that some others before him had denied the Johannine authorship and ascribed the book to Cerinthus, but the way in which he speaks of them shows that there cannot have been a ruling tradition to that effect. He may have referred simply to the Alogi, or he may have included others of whom we do not know. He himself rejects this hypothesis, and supposes the books to have been written by some John, not the apostle (by what John he does not decide), and does not deny the inspiration and prophetic character of the book. Dionysius was led to exercise criticism upon the Apocalypse (which was as well supported by tradition as any book of the New Testament) from dogmatic reasons. The supposed sensuous and materialistic conceptions of the Apocalypse were offensive to the spiritualizing tendencies of the Alexandrian school, and the offensiveness increased with time. Although Dionysius held the work as inspired and authoritative, yet his position would lead logically to the exclusion of the Apocalypse from the canon, just as Hermas had been already excluded, although Origen held it to be inspired and authoritative in the same sense in which Dionysius held the Apocalypse to be, — i.e. as composed by an apostle's pupil, not by an apostle. Apocalyptic literature did not belong properly to the New Testament, but rather to the prophetic portion of the Old Testament; but the number of the Old Testament prophets was already complete (according to the Muratorian Fragment), and therefore no prophetic writing (e.g. Hermas) could find a place there; nor, on the other hand, could it be made a part of the New Testament, for it was not apostolic. The same was true of the Apocalypse of Peter, and the only thing which kept the Apocalypse of John in the canon was its supposed apostolic authorship. It was received as a part of the New Testament not because it was apocalyptic, but because it was apostolic, and thus the criticism of Dionysius would lead logically to its rejection from the canon. John's Apocalypse is the only New Testament book cited by Justin as γραφή (so also by the Epistle of Vienne and Lyons, Eusebius, V. 1), and this because of its prophetic character. It must have been (according to their opinion) either a true prophecy (and therefore inspired by the Holy Spirit) or a forgery. Its authenticity being accepted, the former alternative necessarily followed, and it was placed upon a line with the Old Testament prophets, i.e. with the γραφή. After Dionysius' time doubts of its authenticity became quite widespread in the Eastern Church, and among the doubters was Eusebius, who evidently wished to ascribe it to the mysterious presbyter John, whose existence he supposed to be established by Papias in a passage quoted in chap. 39, § 4, below (compare the note on the passage). Eusebius' treatment of the book is hesitating. He evidently himself discredited its apostolic authority, but at the same time he realized (as a historian more keenly than Dionysius the theologian) the great weight of external testimony to its authenticity, and therefore he gives his readers the liberty (in the next chapter) of putting it either with the *Homologoumena* or with the νόθοι. It legitimately belonged among the *Homologoumena*, but Donysius' attitude toward it doubtless led Eusebius to think that it might at some time in the future be thrown out of the canon, and of course his own objections to its contents and his doubts as to its apostolicity caused him to contemplate such a possibility not without pleasure (see the next chapter, note 1). In chapter 18, above, he speaks of it as the " so-called" Apocalypse of John, but in other places he repeats many testimonies in favor of its authenticity (see the next note), and only in chapter 39 does he state clearly his own opinion in the matter, which even there he does not press as a fixed conviction. The reason for the doubts of the book's genuineness on the part of Eusebius and so many others lay evidently most of all in objections to the contents of the book, which seemed to favor chiliasm, and had been greatly abused for the advancement of the crassest chiliastic views. Many, like Dionysius of Alexandria, were no doubt influenced also by the idea that it was impossible that the Gospel and the Apocalypse could be the works of one author, and they preferred to sacrifice the latter rather than the former. The book has found objectors in almost every age of the Church, but has continued to hold its place in the canon (its position was never disturbed in the Western Church, and only for some two or three centuries after Eusebius in parts of the Eastern Church) as an authentic work of the apostle John. The Tübingen school exalted the Apocalypse to the honorable position of

---

[17] See Luke i. 1–4. Eusebius puts the case more strongly than Luke himself. Luke does not say that others had rashly undertaken the composition of their narratives, nor does he say that he himself writes in order to free his readers from the uncertain suppositions of others; but at the same time the interpretation which Eusebius gives is, though not an exact, yet certainly a natural one, and we have no right to accuse him, as has been done, of intentional falsification of the text of the Gospel. Eusebius also augments Luke's statement by the mention of the source from which the latter gained his knowledge, viz., "from his intimacy and stay with Paul, and from his acquaintance with the rest of the apostles." If Eusebius intended to convey the impression that Luke said this, he is of course inexcusable; but we have no reason to suppose this to be the case. It is simply the explanation on the part of Eusebius of an indefinite statement of Luke's by a fact which was universally assumed as true. That he was adding to Luke's own account probably never occurred to him. He does not pretend to quote Luke's exact words.

[18] The testimony to the first Epistle of John goes hand in hand with that to the fourth Gospel (cf. note 1, above). But we can find still clearer trace of the Epistle in the early part of the second century than of the Gospel (e.g. in Polycarp's Epistle, where traces of the Gospel are wanting; and so, too, in Papias, according to chap. 39, below). The writings of the second century are full of the spirit of the Epistle as well as of the Gospel, and exhibit frequent parallels in language too close to be mistaken. The first express testimony as to its authorship occurs in the Muratorian Fragment. The first systematic attack upon the Epistle was made by Bretschneider, in 1820, in connection with the attack upon the Gospel. The Tübingen school likewise rejected both. Before Bretschneider there had been a few critics (e.g. Lange, 1797) who had rejected the Epistle while accepting the Gospel, and since then a few have accepted the Epistle while rejecting the Gospel; but these are exceptional cases. The Gospel and Epistle have almost universally, and quite rightly, been regarded as the work of the same author, and may be said to stand or fall together. Cf. the works cited in note 1, and also Westcott's *Epistles of St. John.* (On the use of πρότερα instead of πρώτη, see p. 388, note.)

[19] The Muratorian Fragment expressly ascribes two epistles to John. Citations from the second Epistle appear first in Irenæus, though he does not distinguish it from the first. Clement of Alexandria (*Strom.* II. 15) quotes from 1 John under the formula "John says in his larger Epistle," showing that he knew of a second. The lack of citations from the second and third Epistles is easily explained by their brevity and the minor importance of their doctrinal contents. The second and third Epistles belong to the seven *Antilegomena.* Origen cites the first Epistle often, the second and third never, and of the latter he says "not all agree that they are genuine" (quoted by Eusebius, VI. 25), and apparently he himself did not consider them of apostolic origin (cf. Weiss' *Einleitung,* p. 87). Origen's treatment of the Catholic Epistles was implicitly followed by his pupil Dionysius and by succeeding generations. Eusebius himself does not express his own judgment in the matter, but simply records the state of tradition which was a mere repetition of Origen's position in regard to them. Jerome (*de vir. ill.* 9 and 18) says that most writers ascribe them to the presbyter John — an opinion which evidently arose upon the basis of the author's self-designation in 2 John 1, and 3 John 1, and some modern critics (among them Reuss and Wieseler) have done the same. Eusebius himself in the next chapter implies that such an opinion existed in his day, though he does not express his own view on the matter. He placed them, however, among the *Antilegomena.* (On the presbyter John, see below, chap. 39, note 4.) That the two epistles fell originally into the class of *Antilegomena* was due doubtless to the peculiar self-designation mentioned, which seemed to distinguish the author from the apostle, and also to their private and doctrinally unimportant

likewise shall be decided from the testimony of the ancients.[21]

CHAPTER XXV.

The Divine Scriptures that are accepted and those that are not.[1]

1   SINCE we are dealing with this subject it is proper to sum up the writings of the New Testament which have been already mentioned.   First then must be put the holy quaternion of the Gospels ;[2] following them the Acts of the Apostles.[3]   After this must   2 be reckoned the epistles of Paul ;[4] next in

---

one of the five genuine monuments of the apostolic age, and from it as a basis conducted their attacks upon the other Johannine writings. The more modern critical school is doubtful about it as well as the rest of the Johannine literature, and the latest theory makes the Apocalypse a Jewish document in a Christianized form (see above, chap. 18, note 1). Compare especially Holtzmann's *Einleitung*, p. 411–413, and Weiss' *Einleitung*, p. 93.

[21] See Bk. VII. chap. 25, where Eusebius quotes a lengthy discussion of the Apocalypse by Dionysius of Alexandria. He also cites opinions favorable to the authenticity of the Apocalypse from Justin (in IV. 18, below), Theophilus (IV. 24), Irenæus (V. 8), and Origen (VI. 25), but such scattered testimonies can hardly be regarded as the fulfillment of the definite promise which he makes in this passage.

[1] This chapter is the only place in which Eusebius attempts to treat the canon systematically, and in it he is speaking purely as an historian, not as a critic. He is endeavoring to give an accurate statement of the general opinion of the orthodox Church of his day in regard to the number and names of its sacred books. He does not, in this passage, apply to the various works any criterion of canonicity further than their acceptance as canonical by the orthodox Church. He simply records the state of the canon; he does not endeavor to form a canon. He has nothing to do, therefore, with the nature and origin of the books which the church accepts. As remarked by Weiss (*Einleitung in das N. T.*, p. 96), the influence of Eusebius in the formation of the canon is very commonly overestimated. He contributed himself very little; his office was to record the usage of the church of his age, not to mould it.

The church whose judgment he takes is, in the main, the church of the Orient, and in that church at this time all the works which we now call canonical (and only those) were already commonly accepted, or were becoming more and more widely accepted as such. From the standpoint, then, of canonicity, Eusebius divided the works which he mentions in this chapter into two classes: the canonical (including the *Homologoumena* and the *Antilegomena*) and the uncanonical (including the νόθοι and the ἀναπλάσματα αἱρετικῶν ἀνδρῶν). But the νόθοι he connects much more closely with the *Homologoumena* and *Antilegomena* than with the heretical works, which are, in fact, separated from all the rest and placed in a class by themselves. What, then, is the relation of the *Homologoumena, Antilegomena,* and νόθοι to each other, as Eusebius classifies them? The crucial point is the relation of the νόθοι to the ἀντιλεγόμενα. Lücke (*Ueber den N. T. Kanon des Eusebius*, p. 11 sq.) identified the two, but such identification is impossible in this passage. The passages which he cites to confirm his view prove only that the word *Antilegomena* is commonly employed by Eusebius in a general sense to include all disputed works, and therefore, of course, the νόθοι also; that is, the term *Antilegomena* is ordinarily used, not as identical with νόθοι, but as inclusive of it. This, however, establishes nothing as to Eusebius' technical use of the words in the present passage, where he is endeavoring to draw close distinctions. Various views have been taken since Lücke's time upon the relation of these terms to each other in this connection; but, to me at least, none of them seem satisfactory, and I have been led to adopt the following simple explanation. The *Antilegomena,* in the narrower sense peculiar to this summary, were works which, in Eusebius' day, were, as he believed, commonly accepted by the Eastern Church as canonical, but which, nevertheless, as he well knew, had not always been thus accepted, and, indeed, were not even then universally accepted as such. The tendency, however, was distinctly in the direction of their ever-wider acceptance. On the other hand, the νόθοι were works which, although they had been used by the Fathers, and were quoted as γραφή by some of them, were, at this time, not acknowledged as canonical. Although perhaps not universally rejected from the canon, yet they were commonly so rejected, and the tendency was distinctly in the direction of their everwider rejection. Whatever their merit, and whatever their antiquity and their claims to authenticity, Eusebius could not place them among the canonical books. The term νόθοι, then, in this passage, must not be taken, as it commonly is, to mean spurious or unauthentic, but to mean uncanonical. It is in this sense, as against the canonical *Homologoumena* and *Antilegomena,* that Eusebius, as I believe, uses it here, and his use of it in this sense is perfectly legitimate. In using it he passes no judgment upon the authenticity of the works referred to; that, in the present case, is not his concern. As an historian he observed tendencies, and judged accordingly. He saw that the authority of the *Antilegomena* was on the increase, that of the νόθοι on the decrease, and already he could draw a sharp distinction between them, as Clement of Alexandria could not do a century before. The distinction drawn has no relation to the authenticity or original authority of the works of the two classes, but only to their canonicity or uncanonicity at the time Eusebius wrote.

This interpretation will help us to understand the peculiar way in which Eusebius treats the Apocalypse, and thus his treatment of it becomes an argument in favor of the interpretation. He puts it, first, among the *Homologoumena* with an εἴγε φανείη, and then among the νόθοι with an εἰ φανείη. No one, so far as I know, has explained why it should be put among the νόθοι as an alternative to the *Homologoumena,* instead of among the *Antilegomena,* which, on the common interpretation of the relation of the classes, might be naturally expected. If the view presented is correct, the reason is clear. The *Antilegomena* were those works which had been disputed, but were becoming more and more widely accepted as canonical. The Apocalypse could not, under any circumstances, fall into this class, for the doubts raised against it in the orthodox Church were of recent date. It occupied, in fact, a peculiar position, for there was no other work which, while accepted as canonical, was doubted in the present more than in the past. Eusebius then must either put it into a special class or put it conditionally into two different classes, as he does. If the doubts should become so widespread as to destroy its canonicity, it would fall naturally into the νόθοι, for then it would hold the same position as the other works of that class. As an historian, Eusebius sees the tendency and undoubtedly has the idea that the Apocalypse may eventually, like the other Christian works of the same class (the Shepherd, the Apocalypse of Peter, etc.), become one of the νόθοι, one of the works which, formerly accepted, is at length commonly denied to be canonical: and so, as an historian, he presents the alternative. The Apocalypse was the only work in regard to which any doubt could exist.

Eusebius' failure to mention explicitly in this passage the Epistle to the Hebrews, has caused considerable misunderstanding. The explanation, if the view presented be adopted, is simple. Eusebius included it, I believe, among the epistles of Paul, and did not especially mention it, simply because there was no dispute about its canonicity. Its Pauline authorship had been widely disputed, as Eusebius informs us elsewhere, and various theories had been proposed to account for it; but its canonicity had not been doubted in the orthodox Church, and therefore doubts as to the authorship of it did not in the least endanger its place among the *Homologoumena,* as used here in a technical sense; and since Eusebius was simply stating the works of each class, not discussing the nature and origin of those works, he could, in perfect fairness, include it in Paul's epistles (where he himself believed it belonged) without entering upon any discussion of it.

Another noticeable omission is that of the Epistle of Clement to the Corinthians. All efforts to find a satisfactory reason for this are fruitless. It should have been placed among the νόθοι with the Epistle of Barnabas, etc., as Eusebius' treatment of it in other passages shows. It must be assumed, with Holtzmann, that the omission of it was nothing more nor less than an oversight.

Eusebius, then, classifies the works mentioned in this chapter upon two principles: first, in relation to canonicity, into the canonical and the uncanonical; and secondly, in relation to character, into the orthodox (*Homologoumena, Antilegomena,* which are canonical, and νόθοι, which are uncanonical), and heterodox (which are not, and never have been, canonical, never have been accepted of use or authority). The *Homologoumena* and *Antilegomena,* then, are both canonical and orthodox, the ἀναπλάσματα αἱρετικῶν ἀνδρῶν are neither canonical nor orthodox, while the νόθοι occupy a peculiar position, being orthodox but not canonical. The lastnamed are much more closely related to the canonical than to the heterodox works, because when the canon was a less concrete and exact thing than it had at length become, they were associated with the other orthodox works as, like them, useful for edification and instruction. With the heretical works they had never been associated, and possessed in common with them only the negative characteristic of non-canonicity. Eusebius naturally connects them closely with the former, and severs them completely from the latter. The only reason for mentioning the latter at all was the fact that they bore the names of apostles, and thus might be supposed, as they often had been — by Christians, as well as by unbelievers — to be sacred books like the rest. The statement of the canon gives Eusebius an opportunity to warn his readers against them.

Upon Eusebius' New Testament Canon, see especially the work of Lücke referred to above, also Westcott's *Canon of the New Testament,* 5th ed., p. 414 sq., Harnack's *Lehre der Zwölf Apostel,* p. 6 sq., Holtzmann's *Einleitung in das N.T.,* p. 154 sq., and Weiss' *Einleitung,* p. 92 sq.

The greater part of the present note was read before the American Society of Church History in December, 1888, and is printed in Vol. I. of that Society's papers, New York, 1889, p. 251 sq.

[2] On Matthew, see the previous chapter, note 5; on Mark, Bk. II. chap. 15, note 4; on Luke, Bk. III. chap. 4, notes 12 and 15; on John, the previous chapter, note 1.

[3] See above, chap. 4, note 14.

[4] See chap. 3, note 16. Eusebius evidently means to include the

order the extant former epistle of John,[5] and likewise the epistle of Peter,[6] must be maintained.[6] After them is to be placed, if it really seem proper, the Apocalypse of John,[7] concerning which we shall give the different opinions at the proper time.[8] These then belong among the accepted writings.[9] Among the 3 disputed writings,[10] which are nevertheless recognized[11] by many, are extant the so-called epistle of James[12] and that of Jude,[13] also the second epistle of Peter,[14] and those that are called the second and third of John,[15] whether they belong to the evangelist or to another person of the same name. Among the rejected 4 writings[16] must be reckoned also the Acts of Paul,[17] and the so-called Shepherd,[18] and the Apocalypse of Peter,[19] and in addition to these the extant epistle of Barnabas,[20] and the so-called

Teachings of the Apostles;[21] and besides, as I said, the Apocalypse of John, if it seem proper, which some, as I said, reject,[22] but which others class with the accepted books.[23] And 5 among these some have placed also the Gospel according to the Hebrews,[24] with which

Nicene Fathers, Vol. I. p. 133 sqq. For the most important literature, see Schaff, *Ch. Hist.* II. p. 671 sqq., and Gebhardt and Harnack's edition, p. xl. sqq.

[21] τῶν ἀποστόλων αἱ λεγόμεναι διδαχαί. *The Teaching of the Twelve Apostles*, Διδαχὴ τῶν δώδεκα ἀποστόλων, a brief document in sixteen chapters, was published in 1884 by Philotheos Bryennios, Metropolitan of Nicomedia, from a MS. discovered by him in the Jerusalem convent in Constantinople in 1873. The discovery threw the whole theological world into a state of excitement, and the books and articles upon the subject from America and from every nation in Europe have appeared by the hundred. No such important find has been made for many years. The light which the little document has thrown upon early Church history is very great, while at the same time the questions which it has opened are numerous and weighty. Although many points in regard to its origin and nature are still undecided, the following general positions may be accepted as practically established. It is composed of two parts, of which the former (chaps. 1–6) is a redaction of an independent moral treatise, probably of Jewish origin, entitled the *Two Ways*, which was known and used in Alexandria, and there formed the basis of other writings (e.g. the Epistle of Barnabas, chaps. 18–21, and the *Ecclesiastical Canons*) which were at first supposed to have been based upon the *Teaching* itself. (Bryennios, Harnack, and others supposed that the *Teaching* was based upon Barnabas, but this view has never been widely accepted.) This (Jewish) *Two Ways* which was in existence certainly before the end of the first century (how much earlier we do not know) was early in the second century (if not before) made a part of a primitive church manual, viz. our present *Teaching of the Twelve Apostles*. The *Two Ways*, both before and at the time of (perhaps after) its incorporation into the *Teaching*, received important additions, partly of a Christian character. The completed *Teaching* dates from Syria, though this is denied by many writers (e.g. by Harnack), who prefer, upon what seem to me insufficient grounds, Egypt as the place of composition. The completed *Teaching* formed the basis of a part of the seventh book of the *Apostolic Constitutions*, which originated in Syria in the fourth century. The most complete and useful edition is that of Schaff (*The Teaching of the Twelve Apostles*, 3d ed., New York, 1889), which contains the Greek text with English translation and a very full discussion of the work itself and of the various questions which are affected by its discovery. Harnack's important edition *Die Lehre der zwölf Apostel* (*Texte und Untersuchungen zur Gesch. der altchrist. Lit.*, II. 1 and 2, 1884) is still the standard German work upon the subject, though it represents many positions in regard to the origin and history of the work which have since been proved incorrect, and which he himself has given up. His article in Herzog, 2d ed., XVII. 656 sqq. and his *Die Apostel-Lehre und die jüdischen Beiden Wege*, 1886, should therefore be compared with his original work. Schaff's book contains a very complete digest of the literature down to the close of 1888. As to the position which the *Teaching* occupied in the canon we know very little, on account of the very sparing use of it made by the early Fathers. Clement of Alexandria cites it once as Scripture (γραφή), but no other writer before the time of Eusebius treats it in the same way, and yet Eusebius' mention of it among the νόθοι shows that it must have enjoyed a wide circulation at some time and have been accepted by at least a portion of the Church as a book worthy to be read in divine service, and thus in a certain sense as a part of the canon. In Eusebius' time, however, its canonicity had been denied (though according to Athanasius *Fest. Ep.* 39, it was still used in catechetical instruction), and he was therefore obliged to relegate it to a position among the νόθοι. Upon Eusebius' use of the plural διδαχαί, see the writer's article in the *Andover Review*, April, 1886, p. 439 sq.

[22] ἀθετοῦσιν. See the previous chapter, note 20.

[23] τοῖς ὁμολογουμένοις. See note 1, above.

[24] This Gospel, probably composed in Hebrew (Aramaic), is no longer extant, but we possess a few fragments of it in Greek and Latin which are collected by Grabe, *Spic.* I. 15–31, and by Hilgenfeld, *N. T. Extra Can. rec.* II. The existing material upon which to base a judgment as to the nature of the lost Gospel and as to its relation to our canonical gospels is very limited. It is certain, however, that it cannot in its original form have been a working over of our canonical Matthew (as many have thought); it contains too many little marks of originality over against our Greek Matthew to admit of such a supposition. That it was, on the other hand, the original of which our Greek Matthew is the translation is also impossible; a comparison of its fragments with our Matthew is sufficient to prove this. That it was the original source from which Matthew and Luke derived their common matter cannot be said. Lipsius (*Dict. of Christ. Biog.* II. 709–712) and Westcott (*Hist. of the Canon*, p. 515 sqq.) give the various quotations which are supposed to have been made from it. How many of them are actually to be traced back to it as their source is not certain. It is possible, but not certain, that Papias had seen it (see chap. 39,

Epistle to the Hebrews among Paul's epistles at this point, for he mentions it nowhere else in this chapter (see above, note 1).

[5] See the previous chapter, note 18.
[6] See chap. 3, note 1.   [6a] κιωτέον.
[7] See the previous chapter, note 20. Upon Eusebius' treatment in this chapter of the canonicity of the Apocalypse, see note 1, above.
[8] Compare the previous chapter, note 21.
[9] ἐν ὁμολογουμένοις.   [15] See the previous chapter,
[10] τῶν ἀντιλεγομένων.   note 19.
[11] γνωρίμων.   [16] ἐν τοῖς νόθοις.
[12] See Bk. II. chap. 23, note 46.   [17] See above, chap. 3, note 20.
[13] See *ibid.* note 47.   [18] *Ibid.* note 23.
[14] See above, chap. 3, note 4.   [19] *Ibid.* note 9.
[20] The author of the so-called Epistle of Barnabas is unknown. No name appears in the epistle itself, and no hints are given which enable us to ascribe it to any known writer. External testimony, without a dissenting voice, ascribes it to Barnabas, the companion of Paul. But this testimony, although unanimous, is neither very strong nor very extensive. The first to use the epistle is Clement of Alexandria, who expressly and frequently ascribes it to Barnabas the companion of Paul. Origen quotes from the epistle twice, calling it the Epistle of Barnabas, but without expressing any judgment as to its authenticity, and without defining its author more closely. Jerome (*de vir. ill.* 6) evidently did not doubt its authenticity, but placed it nevertheless among the Apocrypha, and his opinion prevailed down to the seventeenth century. It is difficult to decide what Eusebius thought in regard to its authorship. His putting it among the νόθοι here does not prove that he considered it unauthentic (see note 1, above); nor, on the other hand, does his classing it among the *Antilegomena* just below prove that he considered it authentic, but non-apostolic, as some have claimed. Although, therefore, the direct external testimony which we have is in favor of the apostolic Barnabas as its author, it is to be noticed that there must have existed a widespread doubt as to its authenticity, during the first three centuries, to have caused its complete rejection from the canon before the time of Eusebius. That this rejection arose from the fact that Barnabas was not himself one of the twelve apostles cannot be. For apostolic authorship was not the sole test of canonicity, and Barnabas stood in close enough relation to the apostles to have secured his work a place in the canon, during the period of its gradual formation, had its authenticity been undoubted. We may therefore set this inference over against the direct external testimony for Barnabas' authorship. When we come to internal testimony, the arguments are conclusive against "the Levite Barnabas" as the author of the epistle. These arguments have been well stated by Donaldson, in his *History of Christian Literature*, I. p. 204 sqq. Milligan, in Smith and Wace's *Dict. of Christ. Biog.*, endeavors to break the force of these arguments, and concludes that the authenticity of the epistle is highly probable; but his positions are far from conclusive, and he may be said to stand almost alone among modern scholars. Especially during the last few years, the verdict against the epistle's authenticity has become practically unanimous. Some have supposed the author to have been an unknown man by the name of Barnabas; but this is pure conjecture. That the author lived in Alexandria is apparently the ruling opinion, and is quite probable. It is certain that the epistle was written between the destruction of Jerusalem (A.D. 70) and the time of Clement of Alexandria; almost certain that it was written before the building of Ælia Capitolina; and probable that it was written between 100 and 120, though dates ranging all the way from the beginning of Vespasian's reign to the end of Hadrian's have been, and are still, defended by able scholars. The epistle is still extant in a corrupt Greek original and in an ancient Latin translation. It is contained in all the editions of the Apostolic Fathers (see especially Gebhardt and Harnack's second edition, 1876, and Hilgenfeld's edition of 1877). An English translation is given in the *Ante-*

those of the Hebrews that have accepted Christ are especially delighted. And all these may be reckoned among the disputed books.[25]

6 But we have nevertheless felt compelled to give a catalogue of these also, distinguishing those works which according to ecclesiastical tradition are true and genuine and commonly accepted,[26] from those others which, although not canonical but disputed,[27] are yet at the same time known to most ecclesiastical writers — we have felt compelled to give this catalogue in order that we might be able to know both these works and those that are cited by the heretics under the name of the apostles, including, for instance, such books as the Gospels of Peter,[28] of Thomas,[29] of Matthias,[30] or of any others besides

them, and the Acts of Andrew[31] and John[32] and the other apostles, which no one belonging to the succession of ecclesiastical writers has deemed worthy of mention in his writings. And further, the character of the style is at 7 variance with apostolic usage, and both the thoughts and the purpose of the things that are related in them are so completely out of accord with true orthodoxy that they clearly show themselves to be the fictions of heretics.[33] Wherefore they are not to be placed even among the rejected[34] writings, but are all of them to be cast aside as absurd and impious.

Let us now proceed with our history.

CHAPTER XXVI.

Menander the Sorcerer.

MENANDER,[1] who succeeded Simon Magus,[2] 1 showed himself in his conduct another in-

note 28), possible also that Ignatius had, but the passage relied on to establish the fact fails to do so (see chap. 36, note 14). It was probably used by Justin (see Westcott, *ibid.* p. 516, and Lipsius, *ibid.* p. 712), undoubtedly by Hegesippus (see below, Bk. IV. chap. 22), and was perhaps known to Pantænus (see below, Bk. V. chap. 10, note 8). Clement of Alexandria (*Strom.* II. 9) and Origen (*in Johan.* II. 6 and often) are the first to bear explicit testimony to the existence of such a gospel. Eusebius also was personally acquainted with it, as may be gathered from his references to it in III. 39 and IV. 22, and from his quotation in (the Syriac version of) his *Theophany*, IV. 13 (Lee's trans. p. 234), and in the Greek *Theophany*, § 22 (Migne, VI. 685). The latter also shows the high respect in which he held the work. Jerome's testimony in regard to it is very important, but it must be kept in mind that the gospel had undergone extensive alterations and additions before his time, and as known to him was very different from the original form (cf. Lipsius, *ibid.* p. 711), and therefore what he predicates of it cannot be applied to the original without limitation. Epiphanius has a good deal to say about it, but he evidently had not himself seen it, and his reports of it are very confused and misleading. The statement of Lipsius, that according to Eusebius the gospel was reckoned by many among the *Homologoumena*, is incorrect; ἐν τούτοις refers rather to the νόθοι among which its earlier acceptance by a large part of the Church, but present uncanonicity, places it by right. Irenæus expressly states that there were but four canonical gospels (*Adv. Hær.* III. 2, 8), so also Tertullian (*Adv. Marc.* IV. 5), while Clement of Alexandria cites the gospel with the same formula which he uses for the Scriptures in general, and evidently looked upon it as, if not quite, at least almost, on a par with the other four Gospels. Origen on the other hand (*in Johan.* II. 6, *Hom. in Jer.* XV. 4, and often) clearly places it upon a footing lower than that of the four canonical Gospels. Upon the use of the gospel by the Ebionites and upon its relation to the Hebrew Gospel of Matthew, see chap. 27, note 8.

The literature upon the Gospel according to the Hebrews is very extensive. Among recent discussions the most important are by Hilgenfeld, in his *Evangelien nach ihrer Entstehung* (1854); in the *Zeitschrift f. wiss. Theol.*, 1863, p. 345 sqq.; in his *N. T. extra Canon. rec.* (2d ed. 1884); and in his *Einleitung z. N. T.* (1875); by Nicholson, *The Gospel according to the Hebrews* (1879); and finally, a very thorough discussion of the subject, which reached me after the composition of the above note, by Handmann, *Das Hebräer-Evangelium* (Gebhardt and Harnack's *Texte und Untersuchungen*, Bd. V. Heft 3, Leipzig, 1888). This work gives the older literature of the subject with great fullness. Still more recently Resch's *Agrapha* (*ibid.* V. 4, Leipzig, 1889) has come to hand. It discusses the Gospel on p. 322 sq.

[25] τῶν ἀντιλεγομένων. [26] ἀνωμολογημένας.

[27] οὐκ ἐνδιαθήκους μὲν, ἀλλὰ καὶ ἀντιλεγομένας. Eusebius, in this clause, refers to the νόθοι, which, of course, while distinguished from the canonical *Antilegomena*, yet are, like them, disputed, and hence belong as truly as they to the more general class of *Antilegomena*. This, of course, explains how, in so many places in his History, he can use the words νόθοι and ἀντιλεγόμενα interchangeably (as e.g. in chap. 31, § 6). In the present passage the νόθοι, as both uncanonical and disputed, are distinguished from the canonical writings, — including both the universally accepted and the disputed, — which are here thrown together without distinction. The point to be emphasized is that he is separating here the uncanonical from the canonical, without regard to the character of the individual writings within the latter class. [28] See chap. 3, note 5.

[29] The Gospel of Thomas is of Gnostic origin and thoroughly Docetic. It was written probably in the second century. The original Gnostic form is no longer extant, but we have fragmentary Catholic recensions of it in both Latin and Greek, from which heretical traits are expunged with more or less care. The gospel contained many very fabulous stories about the childhood of Jesus. It is mentioned frequently by the Fathers from Origen down, but always as an heretical work. The Greek text is given by Tischen-

dorf, p. 36 sqq., and an English translation is contained in the *Ante-Nicene Fathers*, VIII. 395–405. See Lipsius in the *Dict. of Christ. Biog.* II. p. 703–705.

[30] This gospel is mentioned by Origen (*Hom. in Lucam* I.), by Jerome (*Præf. in Matt.*), and by other later writers. The gospel is no longer extant, though some fragments have been preserved by Clement of Alexandria, e.g. in *Strom.* II. 9, *Strom.* III. 4 (quoted below in chap. 30), and *Strom.* VII. 13, which show that it had a high moral tone and emphasized asceticism. We know very little about it, but Lipsius conjectures that it was "identical with the παραδόσεις Ματθίου which were in high esteem in Gnostic circles, and especially among the Basilidæans." See Lipsius, *ibid.* p. 716.

[31] Eusebius so far as we know is the first writer to refer to these Acts. But they are mentioned after him by Epiphanius, Philaster, and Augustine (see Tischendorf's *Acta Apost. Apoc.* p. xl.). The Acts of Andrew (*Acta Andreæ*) were of Gnostic origin and circulated among that sect in numerous editions. The oldest extant portions (both in Greek and somewhat fragmentary) are the *Acts of Andrew and Matthew* (translated in the *Ante-Nicene Fathers*, VIII. 517–525) and the *Acts of Peter and Andrew* (*ibid.* 526–527). The *Acts and Martyrdom of the Holy Apostle Andrew* (*ibid.* 511–516), or the so-called *Epistle of the Presbyters and Deacons of Achaia concerning the Passion of Andrew*, is a later work, still extant in a Catholic recension in both Greek and Latin. The fragments of these three are given by Tischendorf in his *Acta Apost. Apoc.* p. 105 sqq. and 132 sqq., and in his *Apocal. Apoc.* p. 161 sq. See Lipsius in the *Dict. of Christ. Biog.* I. p. 30.

[32] Eusebius is likewise, so far as we know, the first writer to refer to these Acts. But they are afterward mentioned by Epiphanius, Photius, Augustine, Philaster, &c. (see Tischendorf, *ibid.* p. lxxiii.). They are also of Gnostic origin and extant in a few fragments (collected by Thilo, *Fragmenta Actum S. Johannis a Leucio Charino conscriptorum*, Halle, 1847). A Catholic extract very much abridged, but containing clear Gnostic traits, is still extant and is given by Tischendorf, *Acta Apost. Apoc.* p. 266 sq. (translated in the *Ante-Nicene Fathers*, VIII. 560–564).

The last two works mentioned belong to a collection of apocryphal Acts which were commonly ascribed to Leucius, a fictitious character who stands as the legendary author of the whole of this class of Gnostic literature. From the fourth century on, frequent reference is made to various Gnostic Acts whose number must have been enormous. Although no direct references are made to them before the time of Eusebius, yet apparent traces of them are found in Clement of Alexandria, Tertullian, Origen, &c., which make it probable that these writers were acquainted with them, and it may at any rate be assumed as established that many of them date from the third century and some of them even from the second century. See Salmon's article *Leucius* in the *Dict. of Christ. Biog.* III. 703–707, and Lipsius' article in the same work, I. 28.

[33] αἱρετικῶν ἀνδρῶν ἀναπλάσματα. [34] ἐν νόθοις.

[1] Justin, in the passage quoted just below, is the first one to tell us about Menander. According to him, he was a Samaritan and a disciple of Simon Magus, and, like him, deceived many by the practice of magic arts. Irenæus (*Adv. Hær.* I. 23) gives a somewhat fuller account of him, very likely based upon Justin's work against heresies which the latter mentions in his *Apol.* I. 26, and from which Irenæus quotes in IV. 6. 2 (at least he quotes from a *Contra Marcionem*, which was in all probability a part of the same work; see Bk. IV. chap. 11, note 22), and perhaps in V. 26. 2. From this account of Irenæus that of Eusebius is drawn, and no new particulars are

strument of diabolical power,[3] not inferior to the former. He also was a Samaritan and carried his sorceries to no less an extent than his teacher had done, and at the same time reveled in still more marvelous tales than he. For he said that he was himself the Saviour, who

2 had been sent down from invisible æons for the salvation of men;[4] and he taught that no one could gain the mastery over the world-creating angels themselves[5] unless he had first gone through the magical discipline imparted by him and had received baptism from him. Those who were deemed worthy of this would partake even in the present life of perpetual immortality, and would never die, but would remain here forever, and without growing old become immortal.[6] These facts can be easily

3 learned from the works of Irenæus.[7] And Justin, in the passage in which he mentions Simon, gives an account of this man also, in the following words:[8] "And we know that a certain Menander, who was also a Samaritan, from the village of Capparattea,[9] was a disciple of Simon, and that he also, being driven by the demons, came to Antioch[10] and deceived many by his magical art. And he persuaded his followers that they should not die. And there are

4 still some of them that assert this." And it was indeed an artifice of the devil to endeavor, by means of such sorcerers, who assumed the name of Christians, to defame the great mys-

tery of godliness by magic art, and through them to make ridiculous the doctrines of the Church concerning the immortality of the soul and the resurrection of the dead.[11] But they that have chosen these men as their saviours have fallen away from the true hope.

CHAPTER XXVII.

The Heresy of the Ebionites.[1]

THE evil demon, however, being unable   1
to tear certain others from their allegiance

---

added. Tertullian also mentions Menander (*De Anima*, 23, 50) and his resurrection doctrine, but evidently knows only what Irenæus has already told; and so the accounts of all the early Fathers rest wholly upon Justin and Irenæus, and probably ultimately upon Justin alone. See Salmon's article *Menander* in the *Dict. of Christ. Biog.*

[2] Upon Simon Magus, see above, Bk. II. chap. 13, note 3.

[3] "Instrument of diabolical power," is an embellishment of Eusebius' own, quite in keeping with his usual treatment of heretics. It is evident, however, that neither Justin nor Irenæus looked upon Menander with any greater degree of allowance.

[4] Simon (Irenæus, I. 23. 1) taught that he himself was the Supreme Power; but Menander, according to Irenæus (*ibid.* § 5), taught that the Supreme Power continues unknown to all, but that he himself (as Eusebius here says) was sent forth as a saviour for the deliverance of men.

[5] He agreed with Simon in teaching that the world was formed by angels who had taken their origin from the Ennœa of the Supreme Power, and that the magical power which he imparted enabled his followers to overcome these creative angels, as Simon had taught of himself before him.

[6] This baptism (according to Irenæus "into his own name"), and the promise of the resurrection as a result, seem to have been an original addition of Menander's. The exemption from death taught by Menander was evidently understood by Irenæus, Tertullian (*De Anima*, 50), and Eusebius in its physical, literal sense; but the followers of Menander must of course have put a spiritual meaning upon it, or the sect could not have continued in existence for any length of time. It is certain that it was flourishing at the time of Justin; how much longer we do not know. Justin himself does not emphasize the physical element, and he undoubtedly understood that the immortality taught was spiritual simply. Hegesippus (quoted below, in Bk. IV. chap. 22) mentions the Menandrianists, but this does not imply that he was himself acquainted with them, for he draws his information largely from Justin Martyr.

[7] Irenæus, *Adv. Hær.* I. 23. 5. In III. 4. 3 he mentions Menander again, making him the father of all the Gnostics.

[8] Justin, *Apol.* I. 26.

[9] The situation of the village of Capparattea is uncertain. See Harnack's *Quellen-Kritik des Gnosticismus*, p. 84.

[10] Menander's Antiochene activity is reported only by Justin. It is probable, therefore, that Tertullian used Irenæus alone in writing his account of Menander, for it is unlikely that both of them would have omitted the same fact if they drew independently from Justin.

[11] Cyril of Jerusalem (*Cat.* XVIII. 1) says that the denial of the resurrection of the body was a peculiarly Samaritan heresy, and it would seem therefore that the heresy of these Menandrianists was in that direction, i.e. that they taught rather a spiritual immortality and denied a bodily resurrection (as suggested in note 6); evidently, however, this was not Eusebius' idea. He probably looked upon them as discrediting the Christian doctrine of a resurrection by teaching a physical immortality, which of course was soon proved contrary to truth, and which thus, being confounded by the masses with the doctrines of the Christians, brought the latter also into contempt, and threw discredit upon immortality and resurrection of every kind.

[1] The Ebionites were not originally heretics. Their characteristic was the more or less strict insistence upon the observance of the Jewish law; a matter of cultus, therefore, not of theology, separated them from Gentile Christians. Among the early Jewish Christians existed all shades of opinion, in regard to the relation of the law and the Gospel, from the freest recognition of the uncircumcised Gentile Christian to the bitterest insistence upon the necessity for salvation of full observance of the Jewish law by Gentile as well as by Jewish Christians. With the latter Paul himself had to contend, and as time went on, and Christianity spread more and more among the Gentiles, the breach only became wider. In the time of Justin there were two opposite tendencies among such Christians as still observed the Jewish law: some wished to impose it upon all Christians; others confined it to themselves. Upon the latter Justin looks with charity; but the former he condemns as schismatics (see *Dial. c. Trypho.* 47). For Justin the distinguishing mark of such schismatics is not a doctrinal heresy, but an anti-Christian principle of life. But the natural result of these Judaizing tendencies and of the involved hostility to the apostle of the Gentiles was the ever more tenacious clinging to the Jewish idea of the Messiah; and as the Church, in its strife with Gnosticism, laid an ever-increasing stress upon Christology, the difference in this respect between itself and these Jewish Christians became ever more apparent, until finally, left far behind by the Church in its rapid development, they were looked upon as heretics. And so in Irenæus (I. 26. 2) we find a definite heretical sect called Ebionites, whose Christology is like that of Cerinthus and Carpocrates, who reject the apostle Paul, use the Gospel of Matthew only, and still cling to the observance of the Jewish law; but the distinction which Justin draws between the milder and stricter class is no longer drawn: all are classed together in the ranks of heretics, because of their heretical Christology (cf. *ibid.* III. 21. 1; IV. 33. 4; V. 1. 3). In Tertullian and Hippolytus their deviation from the orthodox Christology is still more clearly emphasized, and their relation to the Jewish law drops still further into the background (cf. Hippolytus, *Phil.* VII. 22; X. 18; and Tertullian, *De Carne Christi*, 14, 18, &c.). So Origen is acquainted with the Ebionites as an heretical sect, but, with a more exact knowledge of them than was possessed by Irenæus, who lived far away from their chief centre, he distinguishes two classes; but the distinction is made upon Christological lines, and is very different from that drawn by Justin. This distinction of Origen's between those Ebionites who accepted and those who denied the supernatural birth of Christ is drawn also by Eusebius (see below, § 3). Epiphanius (*Hær.* XXIX. sqq.) is the first to make two distinct heretical sects — the Ebionites and the Nazarenes. It has been the custom of historians to carry this distinction back into apostolic times, and to trace down to the time of Epiphanius the continuous existence of a milder party — the Nazarenes — and of a stricter party — the Ebionites; but this distinction Nitzsch (*Dogmengesch.* p. 37 sqq.) has shown to be entirely groundless. The division which Epiphanius makes is different from that of Justin, as well as from that of Origen and Eusebius; in fact, it is doubtful if he himself had any clear knowledge of a distinction, his reports are so contradictory. The Ebionites known to him were most pronounced heretics; but he had heard of others who were said to be less heretical, and the conclusion that they formed another sect was most natural. Jerome's use of the two words is fluctuating; but it is clear enough that they were not looked upon by him as two distinct sects. The word "Nazarenes" was, in fact, in the beginning a general name given to the Christians of Palestine by the Jews (cf. Acts xxiv. 5), and as such synonymous with "Ebionites." Upon the later syncretistic

to the Christ of God, yet found them susceptible in a different direction, and so brought them over to his own purposes. The ancients quite properly called these men Ebionites, because they held poor and mean opinions concerning

2 Christ.[2] For they considered him a plain and common man, who was justified only because of his superior virtue, and who was the fruit of the intercourse of a man with Mary. In their opinion the observance of the ceremonial law was altogether necessary, on the ground that they could not be saved by faith in Christ

3 alone and by a corresponding life.[3] There were others, however, besides them, that were of the same name,[4] but avoided the strange and absurd beliefs of the former, and did not deny that the Lord was born of a virgin and of the Holy Spirit. But nevertheless, inasmuch as they also refused to acknowledge that he pre-existed,[5] being

God, Word, and Wisdom, they turned aside into the impiety of the former, especially when they, like them, endeavored to observe strictly the bodily worship of the law.[6] These men, 4 moreover, thought that it was necessary to reject all the epistles of the apostle, whom they called an apostate from the law;[7] and they used only the so-called Gospel according to the Hebrews[8] and made small account of the rest. The Sabbath and the rest of the dis- 5 cipline of the Jews they observed just like them, but at the same time, like us, they celebrated the Lord's days as a memorial of the

---

[6] There seems to have been no difference between these two classes in regard to their relation to the law; the distinction made by Justin is no longer noticed.

[7] This is mentioned by Irenæus (I. 26. 2) and by Origen (Cont. Cels. V. 65 and Hom. in Jer. XVIII. 12). It was a general characteristic of the sect of the Ebionites as known to the Fathers, from the time of Origen on, and but a continuation of the enmity to Paul shown by the Judaizers during his lifetime. But their relations to Paul and to the Jewish law fell more and more into the background, as remarked above, as their Christological heresy came into greater prominence over against the developed Christology of the Catholic Church (cf. e.g. the accounts of Tertullian and of Hippolytus with that of Irenæus).

The "these" (οὗτοι δὲ) here would seem to refer only to the second class of Ebionites; but we know from the very nature of the case, as well as from the accounts of others, that this conduct was true as well of the first, and Eusebius, although he may have been referring only to the second, cannot have intended to exclude the first class in making the statement.

[8] Eusebius is the first to tell us that the Ebionites used the Gospel according to the Hebrews. Irenæus (Adv. Hær. I. 26. 2, III. 11. 7) says that they used the Gospel of Matthew, and the fact that he mentions no difference between it and the canonical Matthew shows that, so far as he knew, they were the same. But according to Eusebius, Jerome, and Epiphanius the Gospel according to the Hebrews was used by the Ebionites, and, as seen above (chap. 25, note 18), this Gospel cannot have been identical with the canonical Matthew. Either, therefore, the Gospel used by the Ebionites in the time of Irenæus, and called by him simply the Gospel of Matthew, was something different from the canonical Matthew, or else the Ebionites had given up the Gospel of Matthew for another and a different gospel (for the Gospel of the Hebrews cannot have been an outgrowth of the canonical Matthew, as has been already seen, chap. 25, note 24). The former is much more probable, and the difficulty may be most simply explained by supposing that the Gospel according to the Hebrews is identical with the so-called Hebrew Gospel of Matthew (see chap. 24, note 5), or at least that it passed among the earliest Jewish Christians under Matthew's name, and that Irenæus, who was personally acquainted with the sect, simply hearing that they used a Gospel of Matthew, naturally supposed it to be identical with the canonical Gospel. In the time of Jerome a Hebrew "Gospel according to the Hebrews" was used by the "Nazarenes and Ebionites" as the Gospel of Matthew (cf. in Matt. XII. 13; Contra Pelag. III. 2). Jerome refrains from expressing his own judgment as to its authorship, but that he did not consider it in its existing form identical with the Hebrew Gospel of Matthew is clear from his words in de vir. ill. chap. 3, taken in connection with the fact that he himself translated it into Greek and Latin, as he states in chap. 2. Epiphanius (Hær. XXIX. 9) says that the Nazarenes still preserved the original Hebrew Matthew in full, while the Ebionites (XXX. 13) had a Gospel of Matthew "not complete, but spurious and mutilated"; and elsewhere (XXX. 3) he says that the Ebionites used the Gospel of Matthew and called it the "Gospel according to the Hebrews." It is thus evident that he meant to distinguish the Gospel of the Ebionites from that of the Nazarenes, i.e. the Gospel according to the Hebrews from the original Hebrew Matthew. So, likewise, Eusebius' treatment of the Gospel according to the Hebrews and of the Hebrew Gospel of Matthew clearly indicates that he considered them two different gospels (cf. e.g. his mention of the former in chap. 25 and in Bk. IV. chap. 22, and his mention of the latter in chap. 24, and in Bk. IV. chap. 10). Of course he knew that the former was not identical with the canonical Matthew, and hence, naturally supposing that the Hebrew Matthew agreed with the canonical Matthew, he could not do otherwise than make a distinction between the Gospel according to the Hebrews and the Hebrew Matthew, and he must therefore make the change which he did in Irenæus' statement in mentioning the Gospel used by the Ebionites, as he knew them. Moreover, as we learn from Bk. VI. chap. 17, the Ebionite Symmachus had written against the Gospel of Matthew (of course the canonical Gospel), and this fact would only confirm Eusebius in his opinion that Irenæus was mistaken, and that the Ebionites did not use the Gospel of Matthew.

But none of these facts militate against the assumption that the Gospel of the Hebrews in its original form was identical with the Hebrew Gospel of Matthew, or at least passed originally under his

---

[Ebionism, see Bk. VI. chap. 38, note 1. Upon the general subject] of Ebionism, see especially Nitzsch, ibid., and Harnack, Dogmengeschichte, I. p. 226 sqq.

[2] The word Ebionite comes from the Hebrew אֶבְיוֹן, which signifies "poor." Different explanations more or less fanciful have been given of the reason for the use of the word in this connection. It occurs first in Irenæus (I. 26. 2), but without a definition of its meaning. Origen, who uses the term often, gives different explanations, e.g., in Contra Celsum, II. 1, he says that the Jewish converts received their name from the poverty of the law, "for Ebion signifies poor among the Jews, and those Jews who have received Jesus as Christ are called by the name of Ebionites." In De Prin. IV. 1. 22, and elsewhere, he explains the name as referring to the poverty of their understanding. The explanation given by Eusebius refers to their assertion that Christ was only a common man, born by natural generation, and applied only to the first class of Ebionites, a description of whom follows. For the same name as applied to the second class (but see note 9) who accepted Christ's supernatural birth, he gives a different reason at the end of the chapter, the same which Origen gives for the application of the name to Ebionites in general. The explanation given in this place is so far as we know original with Eusebius (something similar occurs again in Epiphanius, Hær. XXX. 17), and he shows considerable ingenuity in thus treating the name differently in the two cases. The various reasons do not of course account for the existence of the name, for most of them could have become reasons only long after the name was in use. Tertullian (De Præscr. Hær. 33, De Carne Christi, 14, 18, &c.) and Hippolytus (in his Syntagma, — as can be gathered from Pseudo-Tertullian, Adv. Hær. chap. 3, and Epiph. Hær. XXX., — and also in his Phil. chap. 23, where he mentions Ebion incidentally) are the first to tell us of the existence of a certain Ebion from whom the sect derived its name, and Epiphanius and later writers are well acquainted with the man. But Ebion is a myth invented simply for the purpose of explaining the origin of Ebionism. The name Ebionite was probably used in Jerusalem as a designation of the Christians there, either applied to them by their enemies as a term of ridicule on account of their poverty in worldly goods, or, what is more probable, assumed by themselves as a term of honor, — "the poor in spirit," — or (as Epiphanius, XXX. 17, says the Ebionites of his day claimed) on account of their voluntarily taking poverty upon themselves by laying their goods at the feet of the apostles. But, however the name originated, it became soon, as Christianity spread outside of Palestine, the special designation of Jewish Christians as such, and thus when they began to be looked upon as heretical, it became the name of the sect.

[3] ὡς μὴ ἂν διὰ μόνης τῆς εἰς τὸν χριστὸν πίστεως καὶ τοῦ κατ' αὐτὴν βίου σωθησομένοις. The addition of the last clause reveals the difference between the doctrine of Eusebius' time and the doctrine of Paul. Not until the Reformation was Paul understood and the true formula, διὰ μόνης τῆς εἰς τὸν χριστὸν πίστεως, restored.

[4] Eusebius clearly knew of no distinction in name between these two classes of Ebionites such as is commonly made between Nazarenes and Ebionites, — nor did Origen, whom he follows (see note 1, above).

[5] That there were two different views among the Ebionites as to the birth of Christ is stated frequently by Origen (cf. e.g. Contra Cels. V. 61), but there was unanimity in the denial of his pre-existence and essential divinity, and this constituted the essence of the heresy in the eyes of the Fathers from Irenæus on. Irenæus, as remarked above (note 1), knows of no such difference as Eusebius here mentions; and that the denial of the supernatural birth even in the time of Origen was in fact ordinarily attributed to the Ebionites in general, without a distinction of the two classes, is seen by Origen's words in his Hom. in Luc. XVII.

6   resurrection of the Saviour.[9] Wherefore, in consequence of such a course they received the name of Ebionites, which signified the poverty of their understanding. For this is the name by which a poor man is called among the Hebrews.[10]

CHAPTER XXVIII.

Cerinthus the Heresiarch.

1   WE have understood that at this time Cerinthus,[1] the author of another heresy,

made his appearance. Caius, whose words we quoted above,[2] in the Disputation which is ascribed to him, writes as follows concerning this man : " But Cerinthus also, by means   2 of revelations which he pretends were written by a great apostle, brings before us marvelous things which he falsely claims were shown him by angels ; and he says that after the resurrection the kingdom of Christ will be set up on earth, and that the flesh dwelling in Jerusalem will again be subject to desires and pleasures. And being an enemy of the Scriptures of God, he asserts, with the purpose of deceiving men, that there is to be a period of a thousand years [3] for marriage festivals." [4] And Dionysius,[5] who   3 was bishop of the parish of Alexandria in our day, in the second book of his work On the Promises, where he says some things concerning the Apocalypse of John which he draws from tradition, mentions this same man in the following words : [6] " But (they say that)   4 Cerinthus, who founded the sect which was called, after him, the Cerinthian, desiring reputable authority for his fiction, prefixed the name. For the doctrine which he taught was this : that the kingdom of Christ will be an

name among Jewish Christians. For it is by no means certain that the original Hebrew Matthew agreed with the canonical Matthew, and, therefore, lack of resemblance between the Gospel according to the Hebrews and the canonical Matthew is no argument against its identity with the Hebrew Matthew. Moreover, it is quite conceivable that, in the course of time, the original Gospel according to the Hebrews underwent alterations, especially since it was in the hands of a sect which was growing constantly more heretical, and that, therefore, its resemblance to the canonical Matthew may have been even less in the time of Eusebius and Jerome than at the beginning. It is possible that the Gospel of Matthew, which Jerome claims to have seen in the library at Cæsarea (*de vir. ill.* chap. 3), may have been an earlier, and hence less corrupt, copy of the Gospel according to the Hebrews.

Since the writing of this note, Handmann's work on the Gospel according to the Hebrews (*Das Hebräer-Evangelium*, von Rudolf Handmann. Von Gebhardt and Harnack's *Texte und Untersuchungen*, Bd. V. Heft 3) has come into my hands, and I find that he denies that that Gospel is to be in any way identified with the traditional Hebrew Matthew, or that it bore the name of Matthew. The reasons which he gives, however, are practically the same as those referred to in this note, and, as already shown, do not prove that the two were not originally identical. Handmann holds that the Gospel among the Jewish Christians was called simply " the Gospel," or some general name of the kind, and that it received from others the name " Gospel according to the Hebrews," because it was used by them. This may well be, but does not militate at all against the existence of a tradition among the Jewish Christians that Matthew was the author of their only gospel. Handmann makes the Gospel according to the Hebrews a second independent source of the Synoptic Gospels, alongside of the " Ur-Marcus," (a theory which, if accepted, would go far to establish its identity with the Hebrew Matthew), and even goes so far as to suggest that it is to be identified with the λόγια of Papias (cf. the writer's notice of Handmann's book, in the *Presbyterian Review*, July, 1889). For the literature on this Gospel, see chap. 25, note 24. I find that Resch in his *Agrapha* emphasizes the apocryphal character of the Gospel in its original form, and makes it later than and in part dependent upon our Matthew, but I am unable to agree with him.

[9] The question again arises whether Eusebius is referring here to the second class of Ebionites only, and is contrasting their conduct in regard to Sabbath observance with that of the first class, or whether he refers to all Ebionites, and contrasts them with the Jews. The subject remains the same as in the previous sentence; but the persons referred to are contrasted with ἐκεῖνοι, whom they resemble in their observance of the Jewish Sabbath, but from whom they differ in their observance of the Lord's day. The most natural interpretation of the Greek is that which makes the οὗτοι δὲ refer to the second class of Ebionites, and the ἐκεῖνοι to the first; and yet we hear from no one else of two sharply defined classes separated by religious customs, in addition to doctrinal opinions, and it is not likely that they existed. If this interpretation, however, seems necessary, we may conclude that some of them observed the Lord's day, while others did not, and that Eusebius naturally identified the former with the more, and the latter with the less, orthodox class, without any especial information upon the subject. It is easier, too, to explain Eusebius' suggestion of a second derivation for the name of Ebionite, if we assume that he is distinguishing here between the two classes. Having given above a reason for calling the first class by that name, he now gives the reason for calling the second class by the same.

[10] See note 2.

[1] The earliest account which we have of Cerinthus is that of Irenæus (*Adv. Hær.* I. 26. 1; cf. III. 3. 4, quoted at the end of this chapter, and II. 1), according to which Cerinthus, a man educated in the wisdom of the Egyptians, taught that the world was not made by the supreme God, but by a certain power distinct from him. He denied the supernatural birth of Jesus, making him the son of Joseph and Mary, and distinguishing him from Christ, who descended upon him at baptism and left him again at his crucifixion. He was thus Ebionitic in his Christology, but Gnostic in his doctrine of the creation. He claimed no supernatural power for himself as did Simon Magus and Menander, but pretended to angelic revelations, as recorded by Caius in this paragraph. Irenæus (who is followed by

Hippolytus, VII. 21 and X. 17) says nothing of his chiliastic views, but these are mentioned by Caius in the present paragraph, by Dionysius (quoted by Eusebius, VII. 25, below), by Theodoret (*Hær. Fab.* II. 3), and by Augustine (*De Hær.* I. 8), from which accounts we can see that those views were very sensual. The fullest description which we have of Cerinthus and his followers is that of Epiphanius (*Hær.* XXVIII.), who records a great many traditions as to his life (e.g. that he was one of the false apostles who opposed Paul, and one of the circumcision who rebuked Peter for eating with Cornelius, &c.), and also many details as to his system, some of which are quite contradictory. It is clear, however, that he was Jewish in his training and sympathies, while at the same time possessed of Gnostic tendencies. He represents a position of transition from Judaistic Ebionism to Gnosticism, and may be regarded as the earliest Judaizing Gnostic. Of his death tradition tells us nothing, and as to his dates we can say only that he lived about the end of the first century. Irenæus (III. 2. 1) supposed John to have written his gospel and epistle in opposition to Cerinthus. On the other hand, Cerinthus himself was regarded by some as the author of the Apocalypse (see Bk. VII. chap. 25, below), and most absurdly as the author of the Fourth Gospel also (see above, chap. 24, note 1).

[2] See Bk. II. chap. 25, § 7. Upon Caius, see the note given there. The *Disputation* is the same that is quoted in that passage.

[3] Cf. Rev. xx. 4. On chiliasm in the early Church, see below, chap. 39, note 19.

[4] It is a commonly accepted opinion founded upon this passage that Caius rejected the apostolic authorship of the Apocalypse and considered it a work of Cerinthus. But the quotation by no means implies this. Had he believed that Cerinthus wrote the Apocalypse commonly ascribed to John, he would certainly have said so plainly, and Eusebius would just as certainly have quoted his opinion, prejudiced as he was himself against the Apocalypse. Caius simply means that Cerinthus abused and misinterpreted the vision of the Apocalypse for his own sensual purposes. That this is the meaning is plain from the words " being an enemy to the Divine Scriptures," and especially from the fact that in the Johannine Apocalypse itself occur no such sensual visions as Caius mentions here. The sensuality was evidently superimposed by the interpretation of Cerinthus. Cf. Weiss' *N. T. Einleitung*, p. 82.

[5] Upon Dionysius and his writings, see below, Bk. VI. chap. 40, note 1.

[6] The same passage is quoted with its context in Bk. VII. chap. 25, below. The verbs in the portion of the passage quoted here are all in the infinitive, and we see, from Bk. VII. chap. 25, that they depend upon an indefinite λέγουσιν, " they say "; so that Eusebius is quite right here in saying that Dionysius is drawing from tradition in making the remarks which he does. Inasmuch as the verbs are not independent, and the statement is not, therefore, Dionysius' own, I have inserted, at the beginning of the quotation, the words " they say that," which really govern all the verbs of the passage. Dionysius himself rejected the theory of Cerinthus' authorship of the Apocalypse, as may be seen from Bk. VII. chap. 25, § 7.

5   earthly one. And as he was himself devoted
to the pleasures of the body and altogether
sensual in his nature, he dreamed that that kingdom would consist in those things which he
desired, namely, in the delights of the belly and
of sexual passion, that is to say, in eating and
drinking and marrying, and in festivals and sacrifices and the slaying of victims, under the guise
of which he thought he could indulge his appetites with a better grace." These are the
6   words of Dionysius. But Irenæus, in the
first book of his work Against Heresies,[7]
gives some more abominable false doctrines of
the same man, and in the third book relates a
story which deserves to be recorded. He says,
on the authority of Polycarp, that the apostle
John once entered a bath to bathe ; but, learning
that Cerinthus was within, he sprang from the
place and rushed out of the door, for he could
not bear to remain under the same roof with him.
And he advised those that were with him to do
the same, saying, " Let us flee, lest the bath fall ;
for Cerinthus, the enemy of the truth, is within."[8]

CHAPTER XXIX.

Nicolaus and the Sect named after him.

1   AT this time the so-called sect of the
Nicolaitans made its appearance and lasted
for a very short time. Mention is made of it
in the Apocalypse of John.[1] They boasted that

---

[7] Irenæus, *Adv. Hær.* I. 26. 1.
[8] See *ibid.* III. 3. 4. This story is repeated by Eusebius, in Bk.
IV. chap. 14. There is nothing impossible in it. The occurrence
fits well the character of John as a " son of thunder," and shows the
same spirit exhibited by Polycarp in his encounter with Marcion
(see below, Bk. IV. chap. 14). But the story is not very well authenticated, as Irenæus did not himself hear it from Polycarp, but
only from others to whom Polycarp had told it. The unreliability
of such second-hand tradition is illustrated abundantly in the case of
Irenæus himself, who gives some reports, very far from true, upon
the authority of certain presbyters (e.g. that Christ lived fifty years;
II. 22. 5). This same story, with much more fullness of detail, is
repeated by Epiphanius (*Hær.* XXX. 24), but of Ebion (who never
existed), instead of Cerinthus. This shows that the story was a
very common one, while, at the same time, so vague in its details as
to admit of an application to any heretic who suited the purpose.
That somebody met somebody in a bath seems quite probable, and
there is nothing to prevent our accepting the story as it stands in
Irenæus, if we choose to do so. One thing, at least, is certain, —
that Cerinthus is a historical character, who in all probability was,
for at least a part of his life, contemporary with John, and thus
associated with him in tradition, whether or not he ever came into
personal contact with him.
[1] Rev. ii. 6, 15. Salmon, in his article *Nicolaitans*, in the *Dict.
of Christ. Biog.*, states, as I think, quite correctly, that " there
really is no trustworthy evidence of the continuance of a sect so
called after the death of the apostle John "; and in this he is in
agreement with many modern scholars. An examination of extant
accounts of this sect seems to show that nothing more was known of
the Nicolaitans by any of the Fathers than what is told in the Apocalypse. Justin, whose lost work against heretics Irenæus follows in
his description of heresies, seems to have made no mention of the
Nicolaitans, for they are dragged in by Irenæus at the close of the
text, quite out of their chronological place. Irenæus (I. 26. 3; III.
11. 1) seems to have made up his account from the Apocalypse, and
to have been the sole source for later writers upon this subject.
That the sect was licentious is told us by the Apocalypse. That
Nicolas, one of the Seven, was their founder is stated by Irenæus (I.
26. 3), Hippolytus (VII. 24), Pseudo-Tertullian (*Adv. omnes Hær.*
chap. 1), and Epiphanius (*Hær.* 25), the last two undoubtedly
drawing their account from Hippolytus, and he in turn from Irenæus. Jerome and the writers of his time and later accept this view,
believing that Nicolas became licentious and fell into the greatest

---

the author of their sect was Nicolaus, one of the
deacons who, with Stephen, were appointed by
the apostles for the purpose of ministering to the
poor.[2] Clement of Alexandria, in the third book
of his Stromata, relates the following things
concerning him.[3] " They say that he had   2
a beautiful wife, and after the ascension of
the Saviour, being accused by the apostles of
jealousy, he led her into their midst and gave
permission to any one that wished to marry her.
For they say that this was in accord with that
saying of his, that one ought to abuse the flesh.
And those that have followed his heresy, imitat-
ing blindly and foolishly that which was done
and said, commit fornication without shame.
But I understand that Nicolaus had to do   3
with no other woman than her to whom he was
married, and that, so far as his children are concerned, his daughters continued in a state of virginity until old age, and his son remained uncorrupt.
If this is so, when he brought his wife, whom
he jealously loved, into the midst of the apostles, he was evidently renouncing his passion ;
and when he used the expression, ' to abuse the
flesh,' he was inculcating self-control in the face
of those pleasures that are eagerly pursued. For
I suppose that, in accordance with the command
of the Saviour, he did not wish to serve two
masters, pleasure and the Lord.[4] But they   4
say that Matthias also taught in the same
manner that we ought to fight against and abuse
the flesh, and not give way to it for the sake of
pleasure, but strengthen the soul by faith and
knowledge." [5] So much concerning those who
then attempted to pervert the truth, but in less
time than it has taken to tell it it became entirely
extinct.

CHAPTER XXX.

The Apostles that were married.

1   CLEMENT, indeed, whose words we have
just quoted, after the above-mentioned facts
gives a statement, on account of those who rejected marriage, of the apostles that had wives.[1]

---

wickedness. Whether the sect really claimed Nicolas as their
founder, or whether the combination was made by Irenæus in consequence of the identity of his name with the name of a sect mentioned in the Apocalypse, we cannot tell; nor have we any idea, in
the latter case, where the sect got the name which they bore. Clement of Alexandria, in the passage quoted just below, gives us quite
a different account of the character of Nicolas; and as he is a more
reliable writer than the ones above quoted, and as his statement explains excellently the appeal of the sect to Nicolas' authority, without impeaching his character, which certainly his position among
the Seven would lead us to expect was good, and good enough
to warrant permanence, we feel safe in accepting his account as the
true one, and denying that Nicolas himself bore the character which
marked the sect of the Nicolaitans; though the latter may, as Clement says, have arisen from abusing a saying of Nicolas which had
been uttered with a good motive.
[2] See Acts vi.   [3] *Stromata*, III. 4.
[4] Compare Matt. vi. 24.
[5] This teaching was found in the Gospel of Matthias, or the
παραδόσεις Ματθίου, mentioned in chap. 25 (see note 30 on that
chapter).
[1] A chapter intervenes between the quotation given by Eusebius

"Or will they," says he,[2] "reject even the apostles? For Peter[3] and Philip[4] begat children; and Philip also gave his daughters in marriage. And Paul does not hesitate, in one of his epistles, to greet his wife,[5] whom he did not take about with him, that he might not be inconvenienced in his ministry." And since we have mentioned this subject it is not improper to subjoin another account which is given by the same author and which is worth reading. In the seventh book of his Stromata he writes as follows:[6] "They say, accordingly, that when the blessed Peter saw his own wife led out to die, he rejoiced because of her summons and her return home, and called to her very encouragingly and comfortingly, addressing her by name, and saying, 'Oh thou, remember the Lord.' Such was the marriage of the blessed, and their perfect disposition toward those dearest to them." This account being in keeping with the subject in hand, I have related here in its proper place.

CHAPTER XXXI.

The Death of John and Philip.

1   THE time and the manner of the death of Paul and Peter as well as their burial places,

---

just above and the one which follows. In it Clement had referred to two classes of heretics, — without giving their names, — one of which encouraged all sorts of license, while the other taught celibacy. Having in that place refuted the former class, he devotes the chapter from which the following quotation is taken to a refutation of the latter, deducing against them the fact that some of the apostles were married. Clement here, as in his *Quis dives salvetur* (quoted in chap. 23), shows his good common sense which led him to avoid the extreme of asceticism as well as that of license. He was in this an exception to most of the Fathers of his own and subsequent ages, who in their reaction from the licentiousness of the times advised and often encouraged by their own example the most rigid asceticism, and thus laid the foundation for monasticism.

[2] *Strom.* III. 6.
[3] Peter was married, as we know from Matt. viii. 14 (cf. 1 Cor. ix. 5). Tradition also tells us of a daughter, St. Petronilla. She is first called St. Peter's daughter in the Apocryphal *Acts of SS. Nereus and Achilles*, which give a legendary account of her life and death. In the Christian cemetery of Flavia Domitilla was buried an *Aurelia Petronilla filia dulcissima*, and Petronilla being taken as a diminutive of Petrus, she was assumed to have been a daughter of Peter. It is probable that this was the origin of the popular tradition. Petronilla is not, however, a diminutive of Petrus, and it is probable that this woman was one of the Aurelian gens and a relative of Flavia Domitilla. Compare the article *Petronilla* in the *Dict. of Christ. Biog.* Petronilla has played a prominent rôle in art. The immense painting by Guercino in the Palace of the Conservators in Rome attracts the attention of all visitors.
[4] It is probable that Clement here confounds Philip the evangelist with Philip the apostle. See the next chapter, note 6.
Philip the evangelist, according to Acts xxi. 9, had four daughters who were virgins. Clement (assuming that he is speaking of the same Philip) is the only one to tell us that they afterward married, and he tells us nothing about their husbands. Polycrates in the next chapter states that two of them at least remained virgins. If so, Clement's statement can apply at most only to the other two. Whether his report is correct as respects them we cannot tell.
[5] The passage to which Clement here refers and which he quotes in this connection is 1 Cor. ix. 5; but this by no means proves that Paul was married, and 1 Cor. vii. 8 seems to imply the opposite, though the words might be used if he were a widower. The words of Phil. iv. 3 are often quoted as addressed to his wife, but there is no authority for such a reference. Clement is the only Father who reports that Paul was married; many of them expressly deny it; e.g. Tertullian, Hilary, Epiphanius, Jerome, &c. The authority of these later Fathers is of course of little account. But Clement's conclusion is based solely upon exegetical grounds, and therefore is no argument for the truth of the report.
[6] *Strom.* VII. 11. Clement, so far as we know, is the only one to relate this story, but he bases it upon tradition, and although its

---

have been already shown by us.[1] The time   2
of John's death has also been given in a general way,[2] but his burial place is indicated by an epistle of Polycrates[3] (who was bishop of the parish of Ephesus), addressed to Victor,[4] bishop of Rome. In this epistle he mentions him together with the apostle Philip and his daughters in the following words:[5] "For in   3
Asia also great lights have fallen asleep, which shall rise again on the last day, at the coming of the Lord, when he shall come with glory from heaven and shall seek out all the saints. Among these are Philip, one of the twelve apostles,[6] who sleeps in Hierapolis,[7] and his two aged virgin daughters, and another daughter who lived in the Holy Spirit and now rests at Ephesus;[8] and

---

truth cannot be proved, there is nothing intrinsically improbable in it.
[1] See Bk. II. chap. 25, §§ 5 sqq.   [2] See chap. 23, §§ 3, 4.
[3] Upon Polycrates, see Bk. V. chap. 22, note 9.
[4] Upon Victor, see *ibid.* note 1.
[5] This epistle is the only writing of Polycrates which is preserved to us. This passage, with considerably more of the same epistle, is quoted below in Bk. V. chap. 24. From that chapter we see that the epistle was written in connection with the Quarto-deciman controversy, and after saying, "We therefore observe the following genuine day," Polycrates goes on in the words quoted here to mention the "great lights of Asia" as confirming his own practice. (See the notes upon the epistle in Bk. V. chap. 24.) The citation here of this incidental passage from a letter upon a wholly different subject illustrates Eusebius' great diligence in searching out all historical notices which could in any way contribute to his history.
[6] Philip the apostle and Philip the evangelist are here confounded. That they were really two different men is clear enough from Luke's account in the Acts (cf. Acts vi. 2–5, viii. 14–17, and xxi. 8). That it was the evangelist, and not the apostle, that was buried in Hierapolis may be assumed upon the following grounds: (1) The evangelist (according to Acts xxi. 8) had four daughters, who were virgins and prophetesses. Polycrates speaks here of three daughters, at least two of whom were virgins, and Proclus, just below, speaks of four daughters who were prophetesses. (2) Eusebius, just below, expressly identifies the apostle and evangelist, showing that in his time there was no separate tradition of the two men. Lightfoot (*Colossians*, p. 45) maintains that Polycrates is correct, and that it was the apostle, not the evangelist, that was buried in Hierapolis; but the reasons which he gives are trivial and will hardly convince scholars in general. Certainly we need strong grounds to justify the separation of two men so remarkably similar so far as their families are concerned. But the truth is, there is nothing more natural than that later generations should identify the evangelist with the apostle of the same name, and should assume the presence of the latter wherever the former was known to have been. This identification would in itself be a welcome one to the inhabitants of Hierapolis, and hence it would be assumed there more readily than anywhere else. Of course it is not impossible that Philip the apostle also had daughters who were virgins and prophetesses, but it is far more probable that Polycrates (and possibly Clement too; see the previous chapter) confounded him with the evangelist, — as every one may have done for some generations before them. Eusebius at any rate, historian though he was, saw no difficulty in making the identification, and certainly it was just as easy for Polycrates and Clement to do the same. Lightfoot makes something of the fact that Polycrates mentions only three daughters, instead of four. But the latter's words by no means imply that there had not been a fourth daughter (see note 8, below).
[7] Hierapolis was a prominent city in Proconsular Asia, about five miles north of Laodicea, in connection with which city it is mentioned in Col. iv. 13. The ruins of this city are quite extensive, and its site is occupied by a village called Pambouk Kelessi.
[8] The fact that only three of Philip's daughters are mentioned here, when from the Acts we know he had four, shows that the fourth had died elsewhere; and therefore it would have been aside from Polycrates' purpose to mention her, since, as we see from Bk. V. chap. 24, he was citing only those who had lived in Asia (the province), and had agreed as to the date of the Passover. The separate mention of this third daughter by Polycrates has been supposed to arise from the fact that she was married, while the other two remained virgins. This is, however, not at all implied, as the fact that she was buried in a different place would be enough to cause the separate mention of her. Still, inasmuch as Clement (see the preceding chapter) reports that Philip's daughters were married, and inasmuch as Polycrates expressly states that two of them were virgins, it is quite possible that she (as well as the fourth daughter, not mentioned here) may have been a married woman, which would, perhaps, account for her living in Ephesus and being buried there,

moreover John, who was both a witness[9] and a teacher, who reclined upon the bosom of the Lord, and being a priest wore the sacerdotal plate.[10] He also sleeps at Ephesus." [11] So

4 much concerning their death. And in the Dialogue of Caius which we mentioned a little above,[12] Proclus,[13] against whom he directed his disputation, in agreement with what has been quoted,[14] speaks thus concerning the death of Philip and his daughters: "After him [15] there were four prophetesses, the daughters of Philip, at Hierapolis in Asia. Their tomb is there and the tomb of their father." Such is his state-

5 ment. But Luke, in the Acts of the Apostles, mentions the daughters of Philip who were at that time at Cæsarea in Judea with their father, and were honored with the gift of prophecy. His words are as follows : "We came unto Cæsarea ; and entering into the house of Philip the evangelist, who was one of the seven, we

abode with him. Now this man had four daughters, virgins, which did prophesy." [16]

6 We have thus set forth in these pages what has come to our knowledge concerning the apostles themselves and the apostolic age, and concerning the sacred writings which they have left us, as well as concerning those which are disputed, but nevertheless have been publicly used by many in a great number of churches,[17] and moreover, concerning those that are altogether rejected and are out of harmony with apostolic orthodoxy. Having done this, let us now proceed with our history.

CHAPTER XXXII.

Symeon, Bishop of Jerusalem, suffers Martyrdom.

1 IT is reported that after the age of Nero and Domitian, under the emperor whose times we are now recording,[1] a persecution was stirred up against us in certain cities in consequence of a popular uprising.[2] In this persecution we have understood that Symeon, the son of Clopas, who, as we have shown, was the second bishop of the church of Jerusalem,[3] suffered martyr-

2 dom. Hegesippus, whose words we have already quoted in various places,[4] is a witness to this fact also. Speaking of certain heretics[5] he adds that Symeon was accused by them at this time ; and since it was clear that he was a Christian, he was tortured in various ways for many days, and astonished even the judge himself and his attendants in the highest degree, and finally he suffered a death similar to that of our Lord.[6]

3 But there is nothing like hearing the historian himself, who writes as follows : " Certain of these heretics brought accusation against Symeon, the son of Clopas, on the ground that he was a descendant of David[7] and a Christian ;

---

instead of with her father and sister in Hierapolis. It is noticeable that while two of the daughters are expressly called virgins, the third is not.

[9] μάρτυς; see chap. 32, note 15.

[10] The Greek word is πέταλον, which occurs in the LXX. as the technical term for the plate or diadem of the high priest (cf. Ex. xxviii. 36, &c.). What is meant by the word in the present connection is uncertain. Epiphanius (*Hær.* LXXVII. 14) says the same thing of James, the brother of the Lord. But neither James nor John was a Jewish priest, and therefore the words can be taken literally in neither case. Valesius and others have thought that John and James, and perhaps others of the apostles, actually wore something resembling the diadem of the high priest; but this is not at all probable. The words are either to be taken in a purely figurative sense, as meaning that John bore the character of a priest, — i.e. the high priest of Christ as his most beloved disciple, — or, as Hefele suggests, the report is to be regarded as a mythical tradition which arose after the second Jewish war. See Kraus' *Real-Encyclopædie der christlichen Alterthümer,* Band II. p. 212 sq.

[11] Upon John's Ephesian activity and his death there, see Bk. III. chap. 1, note 6.

[12] Bk. II. chap. 25, § 6, and Bk. III. chap. 28, § 1. Upon Caius and his dialogue with Proclus, see the former passage, note 8.

[13] Upon Proclus, a Montanistic leader, see Bk. II. chap. 25, note 12.

[14] The agreement of the two accounts is not perfect, as Polycrates reports that two daughters were buried at Hierapolis and one at Ephesus, while Proclus puts them all four at Hierapolis. But the report of Polycrates deserves our credence rather than that of Proclus, because, in the first place, Polycrates was earlier than Proclus; in the second place, his report is more exact, and it is hard to imagine how, if all four were really buried in one place, the more detailed report of Polycrates could have arisen, while on the other hand it is quite easy to explain the rise of the more general but inexact account of Proclus; for with the general tradition that Philip and his daughters lived and died in Hierapolis needed only to be combined the fact that he had four daughters, and Proclus' version was complete. In the third place, Polycrates' report bears the stamp of truth as contrasted with mere legend, because it accounts for only three daughters, while universal tradition speaks of four.

How Eusebius could have overlooked the contradiction it is more difficult to explain. He can hardly have failed to notice it, but was undoubtedly unable to account for the difference, and probably considered it too small a matter to concern himself about. He was quite prone to accept earlier accounts just as they stood, whether contradictory or not. The fact that they had been recorded was usually enough for him, if they contained no improbable or fabulous stories. He cannot be accused of intentional deception at this point, for he gives the true accounts side by side, so that every reader might judge of the agreement for himself. Upon the confusion of the apostle and evangelist, see above, note 6.

[15] I read μετὰ τοῦτον with the majority of the MSS., with Burton, Routh, Schwegler, Heinichen, &c., instead of μετὰ τοῦτο, which occurs in some MSS. and in Rufinus, and is adopted by Valesius, Crusè, and others. As Burton says, the copyists of Eusebius, not knowing to whom Eusebius here referred, changed τοῦτον to τοῦτο; but if we had the preceding context we should find that Proclus had been referring to some prophetic man such as the Montanists were fond of appealing to in support of their position. Schwegler suggests that it may have been the Quadratus mentioned in chap. 37, but this is a mere guess. As the sentence stands isolated from its connection, τοῦτον is the harder reading, and could therefore have more easily been changed into τοῦτο than the latter into τοῦτον.

[16] Acts xxi. 8, 9. Eusebius clearly enough considers Philip the apostle and Philip the evangelist identical. Upon this identification, see note 6, above.

[17] ἱερῶν γραμμάτων, καὶ τῶν ἀντιλεγομένων μὲν, ὅμως . . . δεδημοσιευμένων. The classification here is not inconsistent with that given in chap. 25, but is less complete than it, inasmuch as here Eusebius draws no distinction between ἀντιλεγόμενα and νόθοι, but uses the former word in its general sense, and includes under it both the particular classes (*Antilegomena* and νόθοι) of chap. 25 (see note 27 on that chapter).

[1] Trajan, who reigned from 98 to 117 A.D.

[2] Upon the state of the Christians under Trajan, see the next chapter, with the notes.   [3] See chap. 11.

[4] Quoted in Bk. II. chap. 23, and in Bk. III. chap. 20, and mentioned in Bk. III. chap. 11. Upon his life and writings, see Bk. IV. chap. 8, note 1.

[5] In the passage quoted in Bk. IV. chap. 22, § 4, Hegesippus speaks of various heretics, and it looks as if the passage quoted there directly preceded the present one in the work of Hegesippus.

[6] That is, by crucifixion, as stated in § 6.

[7] It is noticeable that Symeon was not sought out by the imperial authorities, but was accused to them as a descendant of David and as a Christian. The former accusation shows with what suspicion all members of the Jewish royal family were still viewed, as possible instigators of a revolution (cf. chap. 20, note 2) ; the latter shows that in the eyes of the State Christianity was in itself a crime (see the next chapter, note 6). In the next paragraph it is stated that search was made by the officials for members of the Jewish royal

and thus he suffered martyrdom, at the age of one hundred and twenty years,[8] while Trajan was emperor and Atticus governor."[9]

4   And the same writer says that his accusers also, when search was made for the descendants of David, were arrested as belonging to that family.[10] And it might be reasonably assumed that Symeon was one of those that saw and heard the Lord,[11] judging from the length of his life, and from the fact that the Gospel makes mention of Mary, the wife of Clopas,[12] who was the father of Symeon, as has been already

5   shown.[13] The same historian says that there were also others, descended from one of the so-called brothers of the Saviour, whose name was Judas, who, after they had borne testimony before Domitian, as has been already recorded,[14] in behalf of faith in Christ, lived

6   until the same reign. He writes as follows : " They came, therefore, and took the lead

of every church [14a] as witnesses [15] and as relatives of the Lord. And profound peace being established in every church, they remained until the reign of the Emperor Trajan,[16] and until the above-mentioned Symeon, son of Clopas, an uncle of the Lord, was informed against by the heretics, and was himself in like manner accused for the same cause [17] before the governor Atticus.[18] And after being tortured for many days he suffered martyrdom, and all, including even the proconsul, marveled that, at the age of one hundred and twenty years, he could endure so much. And orders were given that he should be cruci-

7   fied." In addition to these things the same man, while recounting the events of that period, records that the Church up to that time had remained a pure and uncorrupted virgin, since, if there were any that attempted to corrupt the sound norm of the preaching of salvation, they lay until then concealed in obscure darkness. But when the sacred college of

8   apostles had suffered death in various forms, and the generation of those that had been deemed worthy to hear the inspired wisdom with their own ears had passed away, then the league of godless error took its rise as a result of the folly of heretical teachers,[19] who, because none of the apostles was still living, attempted henceforth, with a bold face, to proclaim, in opposition to the preaching of the truth, the ' knowledge which is falsely so-called.'[20]

CHAPTER XXXIII.

Trajan forbids the Christians to be sought after.

1   So great a persecution was at that time opened against us in many places that Plinius Secundus, one of the most noted of governors, being disturbed by the great number of martyrs, communicated with the emperor concerning the multitude of those that were put to death for

---

family. This was quite natural, after the attention of the government had been officially drawn to the family by the arrest of Symeon.

[8] The date of the martyrdom of Symeon is quite uncertain. It has been commonly ascribed (together with the martyrdom of Ignatius) to the year 106 or 107, upon the authority of Eusebius' *Chron.*, which is supposed to connect these events with the ninth or tenth year of Trajan's reign. But an examination of the passage in the *Chron.*, where Eusebius groups together these two events and the persecutions in Bithynia, shows that he did not pretend to know the exact date of any of them, and simply put them together as three similar events known to have occurred during the reign of Trajan (cf. Lightfoot's *Ignatius*, II. p. 447 sqq.). The year of Atticus' proconsulship we unfortunately do not know, although Wieseler, in his *Christen-Verfolgungen der Cæsaren*, p. 126, cites Waddington as his authority for the statement that Herodes Atticus was proconsul of Palestine from 105 to 107; but all that Waddington says (*Fastes des prov. Asiat.*, p. 720) is, that since the proconsul for the years 105 to 107 is not known, and Eusebius puts the death of Symeon in the ninth or tenth year of Trajan, we may assume that this was the date of Atticus' proconsulship. This, of course, furnishes no support for the common opinion. Lightfoot, on account of the fact that Symeon was the son of Clopas, wishes to put the martyrdom earlier in Trajan's reign, and it is probable that it occurred earlier rather than later; more cannot be said. The great age of Symeon and his martyrdom under Trajan are too well authenticated to admit of doubt; at the same time, the figure 120 may well be an exaggeration, as Lightfoot thinks. Renan (*Les Evangiles*, p. 466) considers it very improbable that Symeon could have had so long a life and episcopate, and therefore invents a second Symeon, a great-grandson of Clopas, as fourth bishop of Jerusalem, and makes him the martyr mentioned here. But there is nothing improbable in the survival of a contemporary of Jesus to the time of Trajan, and there is no warrant for rejecting the tradition, which is unanimous in calling Symeon the son of Clopas, and also in emphasizing his great age.

[9] ἐπὶ Τραϊανοῦ καίσαρος καὶ ὑπατικοῦ Ἀττικοῦ. The nouns being without the article, the phrase is to be translated, " while Trajan was emperor, and Atticus governor." In § 6, below, where the article is used, we must translate, " before Atticus the governor" (see Lightfoot's *Ignatius*, I. p. 59).

The word ὑπατικός is an adjective signifying " consular, pertaining to a consul." It " came to be used in the second century especially of provincial governors who had held the consulship, and at a later date of such governors even though they might not have been consuls" (Lightfoot, p. 59, who refers to Marquardt, *Römische Staatsverwaltung*, I. 409).

[10] This is a peculiar statement. Members of the house of David would hardly have ventured to accuse Symeon on the ground that he belonged to that house. The statement is, however, quite indefinite. We are not told what happened to these accusers, nor indeed that they really were of David's line, although the ὡσάν with which Eusebius introduces the charge does not imply any doubt in his own mind, as Lightfoot quite rightly remarks. It is possible that some who were of the line of David may have accused Symeon, not of being a member of that family, but only of being a Christian, and that the report of the occurrence may have become afterward confused.

[11] This is certainly a reasonable supposition, and the unanimous election of Symeon as successor of James at a time when there must have been many living who had seen the Lord, confirms the conclusion.

[12] Mary, the wife of Clopas, is mentioned in John xix. 25.

[13] See above, chap. 11.

[14] See above, chap. 20.   [14a] See p. 389, note.

[15] μάρτυρες. The word is evidently used here in its earlier sense of " witnesses," referring to those who testified to Christ even if they did not seal their testimony with death. This was the original use of the word, and continued very common during the first two centuries, after which it became the technical term for persons actually martyred and was confined to them, while ὁμολογητής, " confessor," gradually came into use as the technical term for those who had borne testimony in the midst of persecution, but had not suffered death. As early as the first century (cf. Acts xxii. 20 and Rev. ii. 13) μάρτυς was used of martyrs, but not as distinguishing them from other witnesses to the truth. See the remarks of Lightfoot, in his edition of Clement of Rome, p. 46.

[16] This part of the quotation has already been given in Eusebius' own words in chap. 20, § 8. See note 5 on that chapter.

[17] ἐπὶ τῷ αὐτῷ λόγῳ, that is, was accused for the same reason that the grandsons of Judas (whom Hegesippus had mentioned just before) were; namely, because he belonged to the line of David. See chap. 20; but compare also the remarks made in note 10, above.

[18] ἐπὶ Ἀττικοῦ τοῦ ὑπατικοῦ. See above, note 9.

[19] On the heretics mentioned by Hegesippus, see Bk. IV. chap. 22.

[20] τὴν ψευδώνυμον γνῶσιν; 1 Tim. vi. 20. A few MSS., followed by Stephanus, Valesius (in his text), Closs, and Cruse, add the words (in substance) : " Such is the statement of Hegesippus. But let us proceed with the course of our history." The majority of the MSS., however, endorsed by Valesius in his notes, and followed by Burton, Heinichen, and most of the editors, omit the words, which are clearly an interpolation.

their faith.[1] At the same time, he informed him in his communication that he had not heard of their doing anything profane or contrary to the laws, — except that they arose at dawn[2] and sang hymns to Christ as a God ; but that they renounced adultery and murder and like crimi-nal offenses, and did all things in accordance with the laws. In reply to this Trajan made the following decree : that the race of Christians should not be sought after, but when found should be punished. On account of this the persecution which had threatened to be a most terrible one was to a certain degree checked, but there were still left plenty of pretexts for those who wished to do us harm. Sometimes the people, sometimes the rulers in various places, would lay plots against us, so that, although no great persecutions took place, local persecutions were nevertheless going on in particular provinces,[3] and many of the faithful endured martyrdom in various forms.

We have taken our account from the Latin Apology of Tertullian which we mentioned above.[4] The translation runs as follows :[5] " And indeed we have found that search for us has been forbidden.[6] For when Plinius Secundus, the governor of a province, had condemned certain Christians and deprived them of their dignity,[7] he was confounded by the multitude, and was uncertain what further course to pursue. He therefore communicated with Trajan the emperor, informing him that, aside from their unwillingness to sacrifice,[8] he had found no impiety in them. And he reported this also, that the Christians arose[9] early in the

---

[1] Plinius Cæcilius Secundus, commonly called " Pliny the younger" to distinguish him from his uncle, Plinius Secundus the elder, was a man of great literary attainments and an intimate friend of the Emperor Trajan. Of his literary remains the most important are his epistles, collected in ten books. The epistle of which Eusebius speaks in this chapter is No. 96 (97), and the reply of Trajan No. 97 (98) of the tenth book. The epistle was written from Bithynia, probably within a year after Pliny became governor there, which was in 110 or 111. It reads as follows: " It is my custom, my Lord, to refer to thee all questions concerning which I am in doubt; for who can better direct my hesitation or instruct my ignorance? I have never been present at judicial examinations of the Christians; therefore I am ignorant how and to what extent it is customary to punish or to search for them. And I have hesitated greatly as to whether any distinction should be made on the ground of age, or whether the weak should be treated in the same way as the strong; whether pardon should be granted to the penitent, or he who has ever been a Christian gain nothing by renouncing it; whether the mere name, if unaccompanied with crimes, or crimes associated with the name, should be punished. Meanwhile, with those who have been brought before me as Christians I have pursued the following course. I have asked them if they were Christians, and if they have confessed, I have asked them a second and third time, threatening them with punishment; if they have persisted, I have commanded them to be led away to punishment. For I did not doubt that whatever that might be which they confessed, at any rate pertinacious and inflexible obstinacy ought to be punished. There have been others afflicted with like insanity who as Roman citizens I have decided should be sent to Rome. In the course of the proceedings, as commonly happens, the crime was extended, and many varieties of cases appeared. An anonymous document was published, containing the names of many persons. Those who denied that they were or had been Christians I thought ought to be released, when they had followed my example in invoking the gods and offering incense and wine to thine image, — which I had for that purpose ordered brought with the images of the gods, — and when they had besides cursed Christ — things which they say that those who are truly Christians cannot be compelled to do. Others, accused by an informer, first said that they were Christians and afterwards denied it, saying that they had indeed been Christians, but had ceased to be, some three years, some several years, and one even twenty years before. All adored thine image and the statues of the gods, and cursed Christ. Moreover, they affirmed that this was the sum of their guilt or error; that they had been accustomed to come together on a fixed day before daylight and to sing responsively a song unto Christ as God; and to bind themselves with an oath, not with a view to the commission of some crime, but, on the contrary, that they would not commit theft, nor robbery, nor adultery, that they would not break faith, nor refuse to restore a deposit when asked for it. When they had done these things, their custom was to separate and to assemble again to partake of a meal, common yet harmless (which is not the characteristic of a nefarious superstition); but this they had ceased to do after my edict, in which according to thy demands I had prohibited fraternities. I therefore considered it the more necessary to examine, even with the use of torture, two female slaves who were called deaconesses (ministræ), in order to ascertain the truth. But I found nothing except a superstition depraved and immoderate ; and therefore, postponing further inquiry, I have turned to thee for advice. For the matter seems to me worth consulting about, especially on account of the number of persons involved. For many of every age and of every rank and of both sexes have been already and will be brought to trial. For the contagion of this superstition has permeated not only the cities, but also the villages and even the country districts. Yet it can apparently be arrested and corrected. At any rate, it is certainly a fact that the temples, which were almost deserted, are now beginning to be frequented, and the sacred rites, which were for a long time interrupted, to be resumed, and fodder for the victims to be sold, for which previously hardly a purchaser was to be found. From which it is easy to gather how great a multitude of men may be reformed if there is given a chance for repentance."

The reply of Trajan — commonly called " Trajan's Rescript " — reads as follows: " Thou hast followed the right course, my Secundus, in treating the cases of those who have been brought before thee as Christians. For no fixed rule can be laid down which shall be applicable to all cases. They are not to be searched for; if they are accused and convicted, they are to be punished; nevertheless, with the proviso that he who denies that he is a Christian, and proves it by his act (re ipsa), — i.e. by making supplication to our gods, — although suspected in regard to the past, may by repentance obtain pardon. Anonymous accusations ought not to be admitted in any proceedings; for they are of most evil precedent, and are not in accord with our age."

[2] ἅμα τῇ ἕῳ διεγειρομένους. See note 9, below.

[3] This is a very good statement of the case. There was nothing approaching a universal persecution, — that is a persecution simultaneously carried on in all parts of the empire, until the time of Decius.

[4] Mentioned in Bk. II. chap. 2. On the translation of Tertullian's Apology employed by Eusebius, see note 9 on that chapter. The present passage is rendered, on the whole, with considerable fidelity ; much more accurately than in the two cases noticed in the previous book. [5] Apol. chap. 2.

[6] The view which Tertullian here takes of Trajan's rescript is that it was, on the whole, favorable, — that the Christians stood after it in a better state in relation to the law than before, — and this interpretation of the edict was adopted by all the early Fathers, and is, as we can see, accepted likewise by Eusebius (and so he entitles this chapter, not " Trajan commands the Christians to be punished, if they persist in their Christianity," but " Trajan forbids the Christians to be sought after," thus implying that the rescript is favorable). But this interpretation is a decided mistake. Trajan's rescript expressly made Christianity a religio illicita, and from that time on it was a crime in the sight of the law to be a Christian; whereas, before that time, the matter had not been finally determined, and it had been left for each ruler to act just as he pleased. Trajan, it is true, advises moderation in the execution of the law; but that does not alter the fact that his rescript is an unfavorable one, which makes the profession of Christianity — what it had not been before — a direct violation of an established law. Compare, further, Bk. IV. chap. 8, note 14.

[7] κατακρίνας χριστιανούς τινας καὶ τῆς ἀξίας ἐκβαλών. The Latin original reads: damnatis quibusdam christianis, quibusdam gradu pulsis. The Greek translator loses entirely the antithesis of quibusdam . . . quibusdam (some he condemned, others he deprived of their dignity). He renders gradu by τῆς ἀξίας, which is quite allowable; but Thelwall, in his English translation in the Ante-Nicene Fathers, renders the second phrase, " and driven some from their steadfastness," in which the other sense of gradus is adopted.

[8] Greek: ἔξω τοῦ μὴ βούλεσθαι αὐτοὺς εἰδωλολατρεῖν. Latin original: præter obstinationem non sacrificandi. The εἰδωλολατρεῖν is quite indefinite, and might refer to any kind of idolatry; but the Latin sacrificandi is definite, referring clearly to the sacrifices which the accused Christians were required to offer in the presence of the governor, if they wished to save their lives. I have, therefore, translated the Greek word in the light of the Latin word which it is employed to reproduce.

[9] Greek: ἀνίστασθαι ἕωθεν. Latin original: cœtus antelucanos. The Latin speaks of " assemblies " (which is justified by the ante lucem convenire of Pliny's epistle), while the Greek (both here and in § 1, above) speaks only of " arising," and thus fails to reproduce the full sense of the original.

morning and sang hymns unto Christ as a God, and for the purpose of preserving their discipline [10] forbade murder, adultery, avarice, robbery, and the like. In reply to this Trajan wrote that the race of Christians should not be sought after, but when found should be punished." Such were the events which took place at that time.

CHAPTER XXXIV.

Evarestus, the Fourth Bishop of the Church of Rome.

IN the third year of the reign of the emperor mentioned above,[1] Clement[2] committed the episcopal government of the church of Rome to Evarestus,[3] and departed this life after he had superintended the teaching of the divine word nine years in all.

CHAPTER XXXV.

Justus, the Third Bishop of Jerusalem.

BUT when Symeon also had died in the manner described,[1] a certain Jew by the name of Justus[2] succeeded to the episcopal throne in Jerusalem. He was one of the many thousands of the circumcision who at that time believed in Christ.

CHAPTER XXXVI.

Ignatius and his Epistles.

1   AT that time Polycarp,[1] a disciple of the apostles, was a man of eminence in Asia, having been entrusted with the episcopate of the church of Smyrna by those who had seen and heard the Lord.

2   And at the same time Papias,[2] bishop of

the parish of Hierapolis,[3] became well known, as did also Ignatius, who was chosen bishop of Antioch, second in succession to Peter, and whose fame is still celebrated by a great many.[4]

gree of accuracy. A notice in the *Chron. Paschale*, which makes him a martyr and connects his death with that of Polycarp, assigning both to the year 164 A.D., has been shown by Lightfoot (*Contemp. Review*, 1875, II. p. 381) to rest upon a confusion of names, and to be, therefore, entirely untrustworthy. We learn, however, from chap. 39, below, that Papias was acquainted with personal followers of the Lord (e.g. with Aristion and the "presbyter John"), and also with the daughters of Philip. He must, therefore, have reached years of maturity before the end of the first century. On the other hand, the five books of his *Expositions* cannot have been written very long before the middle of the second century, for some of the extant fragments seem to show traces of the existence of Gnosticism in a somewhat advanced form at the time he wrote. With these data we shall not be far wrong in saying that he was born in the neighborhood of 70 A.D., and died before the middle of the second century. He was a pronounced chiliast (see chap. 39, note 19), and according to Eusebius, a man of limited understanding (see chap. 39, note 20); but the claim of the Tübingen school that he was an Ebionite is not supported by extant evidence (see Lightfoot, *ibid.* p. 384). On the writings of Papias, see below, chap. 39, note 1.

[3] Four MSS. insert at this point the words ἀνὴρ τὰ πάντα ὅτι μάλιστα λογιώτατος καὶ τῆς γραφῆς εἰδήμων ("a man of the greatest learning in all lines and well versed in the Scriptures"), which are accepted by Heinichen, Closs, and Crusè. The large majority of the best MSS., however, supported by Rufinus, and followed by Valesius (in his notes), Stroth, Laemmer, Burton, and the German translator, Stigloher, omit the words, which are undoubtedly to be regarded as an interpolation, intended perhaps to offset the derogatory words used by Eusebius in respect to Papias in chap. 39, § 13. In discussing the genuineness of these words, critics (among them Heinichen) have concerned themselves too much with the question whether the opinion of Papias expressed here contradicts that expressed in chap. 39, and therefore, whether Eusebius *can* have written these words. Even if it be possible to reconcile the two passages and to show that Papias may have been a learned man, while at the same time he was of "limited judgment," as Eusebius informs us, the fact nevertheless remains that the weight of MS. authority is heavily against the genuineness of the words, and that it is much easier to understand the interpolation than the omission of such an expression in praise of one of the apostolic Fathers, especially when the lack of any commendation here and in chap. 39 must be unpleasantly noticeable.

[4] Eusebius follows what was undoubtedly the oldest tradition in making Evodius the first bishop of Antioch, and Ignatius the second (see above, chap. 22, note 2). Granting the genuineness of the shorter Greek recension of the Ignatian epistles (to be mentioned below), the fact that Ignatius was bishop of the church of Antioch in Syria is established by *Ep. ad Rom.* 9, compared with *ad Smyr.* 11 and *ad Polycarp.* 7. If the genuineness of the epistles be denied, these passages seem to prove at least his connection with the church of Antioch and his influential position in it, for otherwise the forgery of the epistles under his name would be inconceivable.

There are few more prominent figures in early Church history than Ignatius, and yet there are few about whom we have less unquestioned knowledge. He is known in history pre-eminently as a martyr. The greater part of his life is buried in complete obscurity. It is only as a man condemned to death for his profession of Christianity that he comes out into the light, and it is with him in this character and with the martyrdom which followed that tradition has busied itself. There are extant various Acts of the Martyrdom of St. Ignatius which contain detailed accounts of his death, but these belong to the fourth and subsequent centuries, are quite contradictory in their statements, and have been conclusively proved to be utterly unreliable and to furnish no trustworthy information on the subject in hand. From writers before Eusebius we have but four notices of Ignatius (Polycarp's *Ep. ad Phil.* 9, 13; Irenæus' *Adv. Hær.* V. 28. 3, quoted below; Origen, *Prol. in Cant.*, and *Hom. VI. in Luc.*). These furnish us with very little information. If the notice in Polycarp's epistle be genuine (and though it has been widely attacked, there is no good reason to doubt it), it furnishes us with our earliest testimony to the martyrdom of a certain Ignatius and to the existence of epistles written by him. Irenæus does not name Ignatius, but he testifies to the existence of the Epistle to the Romans which bears his name, and to the martyrdom of the author of that epistle. Origen informs us that Ignatius, the author of certain epistles, was second bishop of the church of Antioch and suffered martyrdom at Rome. Eusebius, in the present chapter, is the first one to give us an extended account of Ignatius, and his account contains no information beyond what he might have drawn from the Ignatian epistles themselves as they lay before him, except the statements, already made by Origen, that Ignatius was the second bishop of Antioch and suffered martyrdom at Rome. The former statement must have rested on a tradition, at least in part, independent of the epistles (for they imply only the fact of his Antiochian episcopacy, without specifying the time); the latter might have arisen from the epistles themselves (in which it is clearly stated that the writer is on his way to Rome to suffer martyrdom),

---

[10] Greek: πρὸς τὸ τὴν ἐπιστήμην αὐτῶν διαφυλάσσειν. Latin original: *ad confœderandum disciplinam*. The Greek translation is again somewhat inaccurate. ἐπιστήμη (literally, "experience," "knowledge") expresses certain meanings of the word *disciplina*, but does not strictly reproduce the sense in which the latter word is used in this passage; namely, in the sense of moral discipline. I have again translated the Greek version in the light of its Latin original.

[1] The Emperor Trajan.
[2] On Clement of Rome, see chap. 4, note 19.
[3] In Bk. IV. chap. 1, Eusebius gives eight years as the duration of Evarestus' episcopate; but in his *Chron.* he gives seven. Other catalogues differ widely, both as to the time of his accession and the duration of his episcopate. The truth is, as the monarchical episcopate was not yet existing in Rome, it is useless to attempt to fix his dates, or those of any of the other so-called bishops who lived before the second quarter of the second century.

[1] See above, chap. 32.
[2] Of this Justus we know no more than Eusebius tells us here. Epiphanius (*Hær.* LXVI. 20) calls him Judas.
[1] On Polycarp, see Bk. IV. chap. 14, note 5.
[2] Of the life of Papias, bishop of Hierapolis, we know very little. He is mentioned by Irenæus, *Adv. Hær.* V. 33. 3 and 4, who informs us that he was a companion of Polycarp and a hearer of the apostle John. The latter statement is in all probability incorrect (see chap. 39, note 4); but there is no reason to question the truth of the former. Papias' dates we cannot ascertain with any great de-

3 Report says that he was sent from Syria to Rome, and became food for wild beasts on

for of course it would be natural to assume that his expectation was realized.

The connection in which Eusebius records the martyrdom implies that he believed that it took place in the reign of Trajan, and in his *Chronicle* he gives precise dates for the beginning of his episcopate (the 212th Olympiad, i.e. 69–72 A.D.) and for his martyrdom (the tenth year of Trajan, i.e. 107 A.D.). Subsequent notices of Ignatius are either quite worthless or are based solely upon the epistles themselves or upon the statements of Eusebius. The information, independent of the epistles, which has reached us from the time of Eusebius or earlier, consequently narrows itself down to the report that Ignatius was second bishop of Antioch, and that he was bishop from about 70 to 107 A.D. The former date may be regarded as entirely unreliable. Even were it granted that there could have been a bishop at the head of the Antiochian church at so early a date (and there is no warrant for such a supposition), it would nevertheless be impossible to place any reliance upon the date given by Eusebius, as it is impossible to place any reliance upon the dates given for the so-called bishops of other cities during the first century (see Bk. IV. chap. 1, note 1). But the date of Ignatius' martyrdom given by Eusebius seems at first sight to rest upon a more reliable tradition, and has been accepted by many scholars as correct. Its accuracy, however, has been impugned, especially by Zahn and Lightfoot, who leave the date of Ignatius' death uncertain, claiming simply that he died under Trajan; and by Harnack, who puts his death into the reign of Hadrian. We shall refer to this again further on. Meanwhile, since the information which we have of Ignatius, independent of the Ignatian epistles, is so small in amount, we are obliged to turn to those epistles for our chief knowledge of his life and character.

But at this point a difficulty confronts us. There are extant three different recensions of epistles ascribed to Ignatius. Are any of them genuine, and if so, which? The first, or longer Greek recension, as it is called, consists of fifteen epistles, which were first published in the fifteenth and sixteenth centuries. Of these fifteen, eight are clearly spurious, and seven are at least largely interpolated. The genuineness of the former and the integrity of the latter now find no defenders among scholars. The second, or shorter Greek recension, contains seven of the fifteen epistles of the longer recension, in a much shorter form. Their titles are the same that are given by Eusebius in this chapter. They were first discovered and published in the seventeenth century. The third, or Syriac recension, contains three of these seven epistles (to Polycarp, to the Ephesians, and to the Romans), in a still shorter form, and was discovered in the present century. Since its discovery, opinions have been divided between it and the shorter Greek recension; but the defense of the genuineness of the latter by Zahn and Lightfoot may be regarded as finally settling the matter, and establishing the originality of the shorter Greek recension as over against that represented by the Syriac version. The former, therefore, alone comes into consideration in discussing the genuineness of the Ignatian epistles. Their genuineness is still stoutly denied by some; but the evidence in their favor, external and internal, is too strong to be set aside; and since the appearance of Lightfoot's great work, candid scholars almost unanimously admit that the question is settled, and their genuineness triumphantly established. The great difficulties which have stood in the way of the acceptance of the epistles are, first and chiefly, the highly developed form of church government which they reveal; and secondly, the attacks upon heresy contained in them. Both of these characteristics seem to necessitate a date later than the reign of Trajan, the traditional time of Ignatius' martyrdom. Harnack regards these two difficulties as very serious, if not absolutely fatal to the supposition that the epistles were written during the reign of Trajan; but in a very keen tract, entitled *Die Zeit des Ignatius* (Leipzig, 1878), he has endeavored to show that the common tradition that Ignatius suffered martyrdom under Trajan is worthless, and he therefore brings the martyrdom down into the reign of Hadrian, and thus does away with most of the internal difficulties which beset the acceptance of the epistles. Whether or not Harnack's explanation of Eusebius' chronology of the Antiochian bishops be accepted as correct (and the number of its adherents is not great), he has, at least, shown that the tradition that Ignatius suffered martyrdom under Trajan is not as strong as it has been commonly supposed to be, and that it is possible to question seriously its reliability. Lightfoot, who discusses Harnack's theory at considerable length (II. p. 450–469), rejects it, and maintains that Ignatius died sometime during the reign of Trajan, though, with Zahn and Harnack, he gives up the traditional date of 107 A.D., which is found in the *Chronicle* of Eusebius, and has been very commonly accepted as reliable. Lightfoot, however, remarks that the genuineness of the epistles is much more certain than the chronology of Ignatius, and that, therefore, if it is a question between the rejection of the epistles and the relegation of Ignatius' death to the reign of Hadrian (which he, however, denies), the latter alternative must be chosen without hesitation. A final decision upon this knotty point has not yet been, and perhaps never will be, reached; but Harnack's theory that the epistles were written during the reign of Hadrian deserves even more careful consideration than it has yet received.

Granting the genuineness of the Ignatian epistles, we are still in possession of no great amount of information in regard to his life. We know from them only that he was bishop of the church of Antioch in Syria, and had been condemned to martyrdom, and that he

account of his testimony to Christ.[5] And **4** as he made the journey through Asia under the strictest military surveillance, he fortified the parishes in the various cities where he stopped by oral homilies and exhortations, and warned them above all to be especially on their guard against the heresies that were then beginning to prevail, and exhorted them to hold fast to the tradition of the apostles. Moreover, he thought it necessary to attest that tradition in writing, and to give it a fixed form for the sake of greater security. So when he came to **5** Smyrna, where Polycarp was, he wrote an epistle to the church of Ephesus,[6] in which he

was, at the time of their composition, on his way to Rome to suffer death in the arena. His character and opinions, however, are very clearly exhibited in his writings. To quote from Schaff, "Ignatius stands out in history as the ideal of a Catholic martyr, and as the earliest advocate of the hierarchical principle in both its good and its evil points. As a writer, he is remarkable for originality, freshness, and force of ideas, and for terse, sparkling, and sententious style; but in apostolic simplicity and soundness, he is inferior to Clement and Polycarp, and presents a stronger contrast to the epistles of the New Testament. Clement shows the calmness, dignity, and governmental wisdom of the Roman character. Ignatius glows with the fire and impetuosity of the Greek and Syrian temper which carries him beyond the bounds of sobriety. He was a very uncommon man, and made a powerful impression upon his age. He is the incarnation, as it were, of the three closely connected ideas: the glory of martyrdom, the omnipotence of episcopacy, and the hatred of heresy and schism. Hierarchical pride and humility, Christian charity and churchly exclusiveness, are typically represented in Ignatius."

The literature on Ignatius and the Ignatian controversy is very extensive. The principal editions to be consulted are Cureton's *The Ancient Syriac Version of the Epistles of St. Ignatius to St. Polycarp, the Ephesians, and the Romans*, with English translation and notes (the *editio princeps* of the Syriac version), London and Berlin, 1845; Zahn's *Ignatii et Polycarpi Epistulæ, Martyria fragmenta*, Lips. 1876 (*Patrum Apostolicorum Opera*, ed. Gebhardt, Harnack, and Zahn, Vol. II.); Bishop Lightfoot's *St. Ignatius and St. Polycarp* (*The Apostolic Fathers*, Part II.), London, 1885. This edition (in two volumes) is the most complete and exhaustive edition of Ignatius' epistles which has yet appeared, and contains a very full and able discussion of all questions connected with Ignatius and his writings. It contains the text of the longer Greek recension and of the Syriac version, in addition to that of the seven genuine epistles, and practically supersedes all earlier editions. An English translation of all the epistles of Ignatius (Syriac and Greek, in both recensions) is given in the *Ante-Nicene Fathers* (Am. ed.), Vol. I. pp. 45–126. The principal discussions which it is necessary to refer to here are those of Lightfoot in his edition of the Ignatian epistles just referred to; Zahn's *Ignatius von Antiochien*, Gotha, 1873 (very full and able); Harnack's *Die Zeit des Ignatius*, Leipzig, 1878; and the reviews of Lightfoot's edition contributed by Harnack to the *Expositor*, December, 1885, January and March, 1886. For a more extended list of works on the subject, and for a brief review of the whole matter, see Schaff's *Church History*, Vol. II. p. 651–664.

[5] That Ignatius was on his way from Syria to Rome, under condemnation for his testimony to Christ, and that he was expecting to be cast to the wild beasts upon reaching Rome, appears from many passages of the epistles themselves. Whether the tradition, as Eusebius calls it, that he actually did suffer martyrdom at Rome was independent of the epistles, or simply grew out of the statements made in them, we cannot tell. Whichever is the case, we may regard the tradition as reliable. That he suffered martyrdom somewhere is too well attested to be doubted for a moment; and there exists no tradition in favor of any other city as the place of his martyrdom, except a late one reported by John Malalas, which names Antioch as the place. This is accepted by Volkmar and by the author of *Supernatural Religion*, but its falsity has been conclusively shown by Zahn (see his edition of the Ignatian epistles, p. xii, 343, 381).

[6] The seven genuine epistles of Ignatius (all of which are mentioned by Eusebius in this chapter) fall into two groups, four having been written from one place and three from another. The first four — to the *Ephesians, Magnesians, Trallians,* and *Romans* — were written from Smyrna, while Ignatius was on his way to Rome, as we can learn from notices in the epistles themselves, and as is stated below by Eusebius, who probably took his information from the statements of the epistles, as we take ours. Ephesus, Magnesia, and Tralles lay to the south of Smyrna, on one of the great highways of Asia Minor. But Ignatius was taken by a road which lay further north, passing through Philadelphia and Sardis (see Lightfoot, I. **33** sq.), and thus did not visit the three cities to which he now sends epistles from Smyrna. The four epistles written from Smyrna con-

mentions Onesimus, its pastor ;[7] and another to the church of Magnesia, situated upon the Mæander, in which he makes mention again of a bishop Damas ; and finally one to the church of Tralles, whose bishop, he states, was at that

6 time Polybius. In addition to these he wrote also to the church of Rome, entreating them not to secure his release from martyrdom, and thus rob him of his earnest hope. In confirmation of what has been said it is proper to quote briefly from this epistle. He writes

7 as follows :[8] " From Syria even unto Rome I fight with wild beasts, by land and by sea, by night and by day, being bound amidst ten leopards,[9] that is, a company of soldiers who only become worse when they are well treated. In the midst of their wrongdoings, however, I am more fully learning discipleship, but I

8 am not thereby justified.[10] May I have joy of the beasts that are prepared for me ; and I pray that I may find them ready ; I will even coax them to devour me quickly that they may not treat me as they have some whom they have refused to touch through fear.[11] And if they are unwilling, I will compel them. Forgive me.

9 I know what is expedient for me. Now do I begin to be a disciple. May naught of things visible and things invisible envy me ;[12] that I may attain unto Jesus Christ. Let fire and cross and attacks of wild beasts, let wrenching of bones, cutting of limbs, crushing of the whole body, tortures of the devil, — let all these come upon me if I only I may attain unto Jesus Christ."

10 These things he wrote from the above-mentioned city to the churches referred to. And when he had left Smyrna he wrote again from Troas [13] to the Philadelphians and to the church of Smyrna ; and particularly to Polycarp, who presided over the latter church. And since he knew him well as an apostolic man, he commended to him, like a true and good shepherd, the flock at Antioch, and besought him to care

diligently for it.[14] And the same man, 11 writing to the Smyrnæans, used the following words concerning Christ, taken I know not whence :[15] " But I know and believe that he was in the flesh after the resurrection. And when he came to Peter and his companions he said to them, Take, handle me, and see that I am not an incorporeal spirit.[16] And immediately they touched him and believed." [17] Ire- 12 næus also knew of his martyrdom and mentions his epistles in the following words :[18] " As one of our people said, when he was condemned to the beasts on account of his testimony unto God, I am God's wheat, and by the teeth of wild beasts am I ground, that I may be found pure bread." Polycarp also mentions these 13 letters in the epistle to the Philippians which is ascribed to him.[19] His words are as follows :[20] " I exhort all of you, therefore, to be obedient and to practice all patience such as ye saw with your own eyes not only in the blessed Ignatius and Rufus and Zosimus,[21] but also in others from among yourselves as well as in Paul himself and the rest of the apostles ; being persuaded that all these ran not in vain, but in faith and righteousness, and that they are gone to their rightful place beside the Lord, with whom also they suffered. For they loved not the present world, but him that died for our sakes and was raised by God for us." And afterwards 14 he adds :[22] " You have written to me, both you and Ignatius, that if any one go to Syria he may carry with him the letters from you. And this I will do if I have a suitable opportunity, either I myself or one whom I send to be an ambassador for you also. The epistles 15 of Ignatius which were sent to us by him and the others which we had with us we sent to you as you gave charge. They are appended to this epistle, and from them you will be able

---

tain no indication of the chronological order in which they were written, and whether Eusebius in his enumeration followed the manuscript of the epistles which he used (our present MSS. give an entirely different order, which is not at all chronological and does not even keep the two groups distinct), or whether he exercised his own judgment, we do not know.

[7] Of this Onesimus, and of Damas and Polybius mentioned just below, we know nothing more.

[8] Ignatius, *Ep. ad Rom.* chap. 5.

[9] λεοπάρδοις. This is the earliest use of this word in any extant writing, and an argument has been drawn from this fact against the authenticity of the epistle. For a careful discussion of the matter, see Lightfoot's edition, Vol. II. p. 212.

[10] Compare 1 Cor. iv. 4.

[11] Compare the instances of this mentioned by Eusebius in Bk. V. chap. 1, § 42, and in Bk. VIII. chap. 7.

[12] The translation of this sentence is Lightfoot's, who prefers with Rufinus and the Syriac to read the optative ζηλῶσαι instead of the infinitive ζηλῶσαι, which is found in most of the MSS. and is given by Heinichen and the majority of the other editors. The sense seems to require, as Lightfoot asserts, the optative rather than the infinitive.

[13] That Troas was the place from which Ignatius wrote to the Philadelphians, to the Smyrnæans, and to Polycarp is clear from indications in the epistles themselves. The chronological order in which the three were written is uncertain. He had visited both churches upon his journey to Troas and had seen Polycarp in Smyrna.

[14] See *Ep. ad Polycarp.* chap. 7.

[15] *Ep. ad Smyr.* chap. 3. Jerome, quoting this passage from Ignatius in his *de vir. ill.* 16, refers it to the gospel which had lately been translated by him (according to *de vir. ill.* 3), viz.: the *Gospel of the Nazarenes* (or the *Gospel according to the Hebrews*). In his *Comment. in Isaiam*, Bk. XVIII. introd., Jerome quotes the same passage again, referring it to the same gospel (*Evangelium quod Hebræorum lectitant Nazaræi*). But in Origen *de prin.* præf. 8, the phrase is quoted as taken from the *Teaching of Peter* (" *qui Petri doctrina apellatur* "). Eusebius' various references to the Gospel according to the Hebrews show that he was personally acquainted with it (see above, chap. 25, note 24), and knowing his great thoroughness in going through the books which he had access to, it is impossible to suppose that if this passage quoted from Ignatius were in the Gospel according to the Hebrews he should not have known it. We seem then to be driven to the conclusion that the passage did not originally stand in the Gospel according to the Hebrews, but was later incorporated either from the *Teaching of Peter*, in which Origen found it, or from some common source or oral tradition.

[16] δαιμόνιον ἀσώματον. [17] Compare Luke xxiv. 39.

[18] Irenæus, *Adv. Hær.* V. 28. 4.

[19] On Polycarp's epistle to the Philippians, see Bk. IV. chap. 14, note 16.

[20] Polycarp, *Ep. ad Phil.* chap. 9.

[21] Of these men, Rufus and Zosimus, we know nothing.

[22] Polycarp, *Ep. ad Phil.* chap. 13. The genuineness of this chapter, which bears such strong testimony to the Ignatian epistles, has been questioned by some scholars, but without good grounds. See below, Bk. IV. chap. 14, note 16.

to derive great advantage. For they comprise faith and patience, and every kind of edification that pertaineth to our Lord." So much concerning Ignatius. But he was succeeded by Heros[23] in the episcopate of the church of Antioch.

CHAPTER XXXVII.

The Evangelists that were still Eminent at that Time.

1   AMONG those that were celebrated at that time was Quadratus,[1] who, report says, was renowned along with the daughters of Philip for his prophetical gifts. And there were many others besides these who were known in those days, and who occupied the first place among the successors of the apostles. And they also, being illustrious disciples of such great men, built up the foundations of the churches which had been laid by the apostles in every place, and preached the Gospel more and more widely and scattered the saving seeds of the kingdom of heaven far and near throughout the whole 2   world.[2] For indeed most of the disciples of that time, animated by the divine word with a more ardent love for philosophy,[3] had already fulfilled the command of the Saviour, and had distributed their goods to the needy.[4] Then starting out upon long journeys they performed the office of evangelists, being filled with the desire to preach Christ to those who had not yet heard the word of faith, and to deliver to 3   them the divine Gospels. And when they had only laid the foundations of the faith in foreign places, they appointed others as pastors, and entrusted them with the nurture of those that had recently been brought in, while they themselves went on again to other countries and nations, with the grace and the co-operation of God. For a great many wonderful works were done through them by the power of the divine Spirit, so that at the first hearing whole multitudes of men eagerly embraced the religion of the Creator of the universe. But since 4 it is impossible for us to enumerate the names of all that became shepherds or evangelists in the churches throughout the world in the age immediately succeeding the apostles, we have recorded, as was fitting, the names of those only who have transmitted the apostolic doctrine to us in writings still extant.

CHAPTER XXXVIII.

The Epistle of Clement and the Writings falsely ascribed to him.

THUS Ignatius has done in the epistles 1 which we have mentioned,[1] and Clement in his epistle which is accepted by all, and which he wrote in the name of the church of Rome to the church of Corinth.[2] In this epistle he gives many thoughts drawn from the Epistle to the Hebrews, and also quotes verbally some of its expressions, thus showing most plainly that it is not a recent production. Wherefore it 2 has seemed reasonable to reckon it with the other writings of the apostle. For as Paul had written to the Hebrews in his native tongue, some say that the evangelist Luke, others that this Clement himself, translated the epistle. The 3 latter seems more probable, because the epistle of Clement and that to the Hebrews have a similar character in regard to style, and still further because the thoughts contained in the two works are not very different.[3]

But it must be observed also that there is 4 said to be a second epistle of Clement. But we do not know that this is recognized like the former, for we do not find that the ancients have made any use of it.[4] And certain men 5 have lately brought forward other wordy and

---

[23] According to Eusebius' *Chronicle* Heros became bishop of Antioch in the tenth year of Trajan (107 A.D.), and was succeeded by Cornelius in the twelfth year of Hadrian (128 A.D.). In the *History* he is mentioned only once more (Bk. IV. chap. 20), and no dates are given. The dates found in the *Chronicle* are entirely unreliable (see on the dates of all the early Antiochian bishops, Harnack's *Zeit des Ignatius*). Of Heros himself we have no trustworthy information. His name appears in the later martyrologies, and one of the spurious Ignatian epistles is addressed to him.

[1] This Quadratus had considerable reputation as a prophet, as may be gathered from Eusebius' mention of him here, and also from the reference to him in the anonymous work against the Montanists (see below, Bk. V. chap. 16). We know nothing about this Quadratus except what is told us in these two passages, unless we identify him, as many do, with Quadratus the apologist mentioned below in Bk. IV. chap. 3. This identification is possible, but by no means certain. See Bk. IV. chap. 3, note 2.

[2] This rhetorical flourish arouses the suspicion that Eusebius, although he says there were "many others" that were well known in those days, was unacquainted with the names of such persons as we, too, are unacquainted with them. None will deny that there may have been some men of prominence in the Church at this time, but Eusebius apparently had no more information to impart in regard to them than he gives us in this chapter, and he makes up for his lack of facts in a way which is not at all uncommon.

[3] That is, an ascetic mode of life. See Bk. VI. chap. 3, note 9.

[4] See Matt. xix. 21. Eusebius agrees with nearly all the Fathers, and with the Roman Catholic Church of the past and present, in his misinterpretation of this advice given by Christ to the rich young man.

---

[1] In chap. 36, above.   [2] See above, chap. 16.
[3] On the Epistle to the Hebrews and the various traditions as to its authorship, see above, chap. 3, note 17.
[4] Eusebius is the first one to mention the ascription of a second epistle to Clement, but after the fifth century such an epistle (whether the one to which Eusebius here refers we cannot tell) was in common circulation and was quite widely accepted as genuine. This epistle is still extant, in a mutilated form in the Alexandrian MS., complete in the MS. discovered by Bryennios in Constantinople in 1875. The publication of the complete work proves, what had long been suspected, that it is not an epistle at all, but a homily. It cannot have been written by the author of the first epistle of Clement, nor can it belong to the first century. It was probably written in Rome about the middle of the second century (see Harnack's articles in the *Zeitschrift für Kirchengeschichte*, Vol. I. p. 264–283 and 329–364), and is the oldest extant homily, and as such possesses considerable interest. It has always gone by the name of the Second Epistle of Clement, and hence continues to be so called although the title is a misnomer, for neither is it an epistle, nor is it by Clement. It is published in all the editions of the apostolic Fathers, but only those editions that have appeared since the discovery of the complete homily by Bryennios are now of value. Of these, it is necessary to mention only Gebhardt, Harnack, and Zahn's *Patrum Apost. Opera*, 2d ed., 1876, in which Harnack's prolegomena and notes are especially valuable, and the appendix to Lightfoot's edi-

lengthy writings under his name, containing dia-logues of Peter and Apion.[5] But no mention has been made of these by the ancients; for they do not even preserve the pure stamp of apostolic orthodoxy. The acknowledged writ-ing of Clement is well known. We have spoken also of the works of Ignatius and Polycarp.[6]

CHAPTER XXXIX.

The Writings of Papias.

1   THERE are extant five books of Papias, which bear the title Expositions of Oracles of the Lord.[1] Irenæus makes mention of these

as the only works written by him,[2] in the follow-ing words:[3] "These things are attested by Papias, an ancient man who was a hearer of John and a companion of Polycarp, in his fourth book. For five books have been written by him." These are the words of Irenæus.

But Papias himself in the preface to his   2 discourses by no means declares that he was himself a hearer and eye-witness of the holy apostles, but he shows by the words which he uses that he received the doctrines of the faith from those who were their friends.[4]

He says: "But I shall not hesitate also to   3 put down for you along with my interpreta-

tion of Clement (1877), which contains the full text, notes, and an English translation. English translation also in the *Ante-Nicene Fathers* (Am. ed.), Vol. VII. p. 509 sq. Compare the article by Sal-mon in the *Dict. of Christian Biography* and Harnack's articles in the *Zeitschr. f. Kirchengesch.* referred to above.

[5] There are extant a number of Pseudo-Clementine writings of the third and following centuries, the chief among which purports to contain a record made by Clement of discourses of the apostle Peter, and an account of Clement's family history and of his travels with Peter, constituting, in fact, a sort of didactico-historical ro-mance. This exists now in three forms (the *Homilies, Recogni-tions,* and *Epitome*), all of which are closely related; though whether the first two (the last is simply an abridgment of the first) are drawn from a common original, or whether one of them is the original of the other, is not certain. The works are more or less Ebionitic in character, and play an important part in the history of early Christian literature. For a careful discussion of them, see Salmon's article *Clementine Literature*, in the *Dict. of Christian Biography;* and for the literature of the subject, which is very ex-tensive, see especially Schaff's *Church History*, II. p. 435 sq.

The fourth, fifth, and sixth books of the *Homilies* contain ex-tended conversations purporting to have been held between Clement and Apion, the famous antagonist of the Jews (see Bk. II. chap. 5, note 5). It is quite possible that the "wordy and lengthy writings, con-taining dialogues of Peter and Apion," which Eusebius refers to here may be identical with the *Homilies*, in which case we must suppose Eusebius' language to be somewhat inexact; for the dialogues in the *Homilies* are between Clement and Apion, not between Peter and Apion. It seems more probable, however, when we realize the vast number of works of a similar character which were in circulation during the third and subsequent centuries, that Eusebius refers here to another work, belonging to the same general class, which is now lost. If such a work existed, it may well have formed a basis for the dialogues between Clement and Apion given in the *Homilies*. In the absence of all further evidence of such a work, we must leave the matter quite undecided. It is not necessary here to enumerate the other Pseudo-Clementine works which are still extant. Compare Schaff's *Church History*, II. 648 sq. Clement's name was a favorite one with pseudographers of the early Church, and works of all kinds were published under his name. The most complete collection of these spurious works is found in Migne's *Patr. Græc.* Vols. I. and II.   [6] In chap. 36, above.

[1] λογίων κυριακῶν ἐξηγήσεις. This work is no longer extant, but a number of fragments of it have been preserved by Irenæus, Eusebius, and others, which are published in the various editions of the Apostolic Fathers (see especially Gebhardt, Harnack and Zahn's edition, Vol. I. Appendix), and by Routh in his *Rel. Sacræ,* I. p. 3-16. English translation in the *Ante-Nicene Fathers* (Am. ed.), Vol. I. p. 151 sq. The exact character of the work has been long and sharply disputed. Some contend that it was a record of oral tra-ditions in regard to the Lord which Papias had gathered, together with a commentary upon these traditions, others that it was a com-plete Gospel, others that it was a commentary upon an already ex-isting Gospel or Gospels. The last is the view which accords best with the language of Eusebius, and it is widely accepted, though there is controversy among those who accept it as to whether the Gospel or Gospels which he used are to be identified with either of our canonical Gospels. But upon this question we cannot dwell at this point. Lightfoot, who believes that a written text lay at the base of Papias' work, concludes that the work contained, first, the text; secondly, "the interpretations which explained the text, and which were the main object of the work"; and thirdly, the oral tra-ditions, which "were subordinate to the interpretation" (*Con-temporary Review*, 1875, II. p. 389). This is probably as good a description of the plan of Papias' work as can be given, whatever decision may be reached as to the identity of the text which he used with any one of our Gospels. Lightfoot has adduced strong argu-ments for his view, and has discussed at length various other views which it is not necessary to repeat here. On the significance of the

word λόγια, see below, note 26. As remarked there, λόγια cannot be confined to words or discourses only, and therefore the "oracles" which Papias expounded in his work may well have included, so far as the title is concerned, a complete Gospel or Gospels. In the ab-sence of the work itself, however, we are left entirely to conjecture, though it must be remarked that in the time of Papias at least some of our Gospels were certainly in existence and already widely ac-cepted. It is difficult, therefore, to suppose that if written docu-ments lay at the basis of Papias' work, as we have concluded that they did, that they can have been other than one or more of the commonly accepted Gospels. But see Lightfoot's article already referred to for a discussion of this question. The date of the com-position of Papias' work is now commonly fixed at about the middle of the second century, probably nearer 130 than 150 A.D. The books and articles that have been written upon this work are far too numer-ous to mention. Besides the article by Lightfoot in the *Contem-porary Review*, which has been already referred to, we should mention also Salmon's article in the *Dict. of Christian Biography,* Schleiermacher's essay in the *Studien und Kritiken,* 1832, p. 735 sq.,—the first critical discussion of Papias' testimony in regard to the Gospels of Matthew and Mark, and still valuable,—dissertations by Weiffenbach, 1874 and 1878, and by Leimbach, 1875, with reviews of the last two in various periodicals, notably the articles by Hilgen-feld in his *Zeitschrift für wiss. Theol.* 1875, 1877, 1879. See also p. 389, note, below. On the life of Papias, see above, chap. 36, note 2.

[2] ὡς μόνων αὐτῷ γραφέντων. Irenæus does not expressly say that these were the only works written by Papias. He simply says, "For five books have been written by him" (ἔστι γὰρ αὐτῷ πέντε βιβλία συντεταγμένα). Eusebius' interpretation of Irenæus' words is not, however, at all unnatural, and probably expresses Irenæus' meaning.   [3] Irenæus, *Adv. Hær.* V. 33. 4.

[4] The justice of this criticism, passed by Eusebius upon the state-ment of Irenæus, has been questioned by many, who have held that, in the passage quoted just below from Papias, the same John is meant in both cases. See the note of Schaff in his *Church History,* II. p. 697 sq. A careful exegesis of the passage from Papias quoted by Eusebius seems, however, to lead necessarily to the conclusion which Eusebius draws, that Papias refers to two different persons bearing the same name,—John. In fact, no other conclusion can be reached, unless we accuse Papias of the most stupid and illogical method of writing. Certainly, if he knew of but one John, there is no possible excuse for mentioning him twice in the one passage. On the other hand, if we accept Eusebius' interpretation, we are met by a serious difficulty in the fact that we are obliged to assume that there lived in Asia Minor, early in the second century, a man to whom Papias appeals as possessing exceptional authority, but who is men-tioned by no other Father; who is, in fact, otherwise an entirely un-known personage. And still further, no reader of Papias' work, be-fore the time of Eusebius, gathered from that work, so far as we know, a single hint that the John with whom he was acquainted was any other than the apostle John. These difficulties are so serious that they have led many to deny that Papias meant to refer to a sec-ond John, in spite of his apparently clear reference to such a per-son. Among those who deny this second John's existence are such scholars as Zahn and Salmon. (Compare, for instance, the latter's able article on *Joannes the Presbyter*, in the *Dict. of Christian Biography.*) In reply to their arguments, it may be said that the silence of all other early writers does not necessarily disprove the existence of a second John; for it is quite conceivable that all trace of him should be swallowed up in the reputation of his greater name-sake who lived in the same place. Moreover, it is quite conceivable that Papias, writing for those who were well acquainted with both Johns, may have had no suspicion that any one would confound the presbyter with the apostle, and would imagine that he was referring to the latter when he was speaking of his personal friend John; and therefore he would have no reason for stating expressly that there were two Johns, or for expressly distinguishing the one from the other. It was, then, quite natural that Irenæus, a whole generation later, knowing that Polycarp was a disciple of the apostle John, and finding constant mention of a John in Papias' works, should simply take for granted that the same John was meant; for by his time the lesser John may easily, in the minds of most people, have become

tions [5] whatsoever things I have at any time learned carefully from the elders [6] and carefully remembered, guaranteeing their truth. For I did not, like the multitude, take pleasure in those that speak much, but in those that teach the truth; not in those that relate strange commandments, but in those that deliver [7] the commandments given by the Lord to faith, [8] and 4 springing from the truth itself. If, then, any one came, who had been a follower of the elders, I questioned him in regard to the words of the elders, — what Andrew or what Peter said, or what was said by Philip, or by Thomas, or by James, or by John, or by Matthew, or by any other of the disciples of the Lord, and what things Aristion [9] and the presbyter John, [10] the disciples of the Lord, say. For I did not think that what was to be gotten from the books [11] would profit me as much as what came from the living and abiding voice."

It is worth while observing here that the 5 name John is twice enumerated by him. [12] The first one he mentions in connection with Peter and James and Matthew and the rest of the apostles, clearly meaning the evangelist; but the other John he mentions after an interval, and places him among others outside of the number of the apostles, putting Aristion before him, and he distinctly calls him a presbyter. This shows that the statement of those 6 is true, who say that there were two persons in Asia that bore the same name, and that there were two tombs in Ephesus, each of which, even to the present day, is called John's. [13] It is important to notice this. For it is probable that it was the second, if one is not willing to admit that it was the first that saw the Revelation, which is ascribed by name to John. [14] And Papias, of whom we are now speaking, 7 confesses that he received the words of the apostles from those that followed them, but says that he was himself a hearer of Aristion

lost in the tradition of his greater namesake. In view of these possibilities, it cannot be said that the silence of other Fathers in regard to this John is fatal to his existence; and if this is so, we are hardly justified in doing such violence to Papias' language as is required to identify the two Johns mentioned by him in the passage quoted below. Among those who accept Eusebius' conclusion, that Papias refers to two different persons, are such scholars as Tischendorf, Donaldson, Westcott and Lightfoot. If Eusebius has recovered for us from the ancient history of the Church an otherwise unknown personage, it will not be the only time that he has corrected an error committed by all his predecessors. In this case, as in a number of other cases, I believe Eusebius' wide information, sharp-sightedness, and superiority to the trammels of traditionalism receive triumphant vindication, and we may accept his conclusion that Papias was personally acquainted with a second John, who was familiarly known as "the Presbyter," and thus distinguished from the apostle John, who could be called a presbyter or elder only in the general sense in which all the leading men of his generation were elders (see below, note 6), and could not be designated emphatically as "the presbyter." In regard to the connection of this "presbyter John" with the Apocalypse, see below, note 14. But although Papias distinguishes, as we may conclude, between two Johns in the passage referred to, and elsewhere, according to Eusebius, pronounces himself a hearer of the second John, it does not necessarily follow that Irenæus was mistaken in saying that he was a hearer of the apostle John; for Irenæus may have based his statement upon information received from his teacher, Polycarp, the friend of Papias, and not upon the passage quoted by Eusebius, and hence Papias may have been a hearer of both Johns. At the same time, it must be said that if Papias had been a disciple of the apostle John, he could scarcely have failed to state the fact expressly somewhere in his works; and if he had stated it anywhere, Eusebius could hardly have overlooked it. The conclusion, therefore, seems most probable that Eusebius is right in correcting Irenæus' statement, and that the latter based his report upon a misinterpretation of Papias' own words. In that case, we have no authority for speaking of Papias as a disciple of John the apostle.

[5] This sentence gives strong support to the view that oral traditions did not form the basis of Papias' work, but that the basis consisted of written documents, which he interpreted, and to which he then added the oral traditions which he refers to here. See *Contemporary Review*, 1885, II. p. 388 sq. The words ταῖς ἑρμηνείαις have been translated by some scholars, "the interpretations of them," thus making the book consist only of these oral traditions with interpretations of them. But this translation is not warranted by the Greek, and the *also* at the beginning of the sentence shows that the work must have contained other matter which preceded these oral traditions and to which the "interpretations" belong.

[6] As Lightfoot points out (*Contemp. Rev. ibid.* p. 379 sq.), Papias uses the term "elders" in a general sense to denote the Fathers of the Church in the generations preceding his own. It thus includes both the apostles and their immediate disciples. The term was thus used in a general sense by later Fathers to denote all earlier Fathers of the Church; that is, those leaders of the Church belonging to generations earlier than the writers themselves. The term, therefore, cannot be confined to the apostles alone, nor can it be confined, as some have thought (e.g. Weiffenbach in his *Das Papias Fragment*), to ecclesiastical officers, presbyters in the official sense. Where the word πρεσβύτερος is used in connection with the second John (at the close of this extract from Papias), it is apparently employed in its official sense. At least we cannot otherwise easily understand how it could be used as a peculiar designation of this John, which should distinguish him from the other John. For in the general sense of the word, in which Papias commonly uses it, both Johns were elders. Compare Lightfoot's words in the passage referred to above.

[7] παραγινομένοις, instead of παραγινομένας, agreeing with ἐντολάς. The latter is the common reading, but is not so well supported by manuscript authority, and, as the easier reading, is to be rejected in favor of the former. See the note of Heinichen *in loco*.

[8] That is, "to those that believe, to those that are possessed of faith."

[9] Of this Aristion we know only what we can gather from this mention of him by Papias. [10] See above, note 6.

[11] ἐκ τῶν βιβλίων. These words have been interpreted by many critics as implying that Papias considered the written Gospel accounts, which were extant in his time, of small value, and preferred to them the oral traditions which he picked up from "the elders." But as Lightfoot has shown (*ibid.* p. 390 sq.), this is not the natural interpretation of Papias' words, and makes him practically stultify and contradict himself. He cannot have considered the written documents which he laid at the base of his work as of little value, nor can he have regarded the writings of Matthew and Mark, which he refers to in this chapter as extant in his time, and the latter of which he praises for its accuracy, as inferior to the oral traditions, which came to him at best only at second hand. It is necessary to refer the τῶν βιβλίων, as Lightfoot does, to "interpretations" of the Gospel accounts, which had been made by others, and to which Papias prefers the interpretations or expositions which he has received from the disciples of the apostles. This interpretation of the word alone saves us from difficulties and perhaps from self-stultification. [12] See above, note 4.

[13] The existence of two tombs in Ephesus bearing the name of John is attested also by Dionysius of Alexandria (quoted in Bk. VII. chap. 25, below) and by Jerome (*de vir. ill.* c. 9). The latter, however, says that some regard them both as memorials of the one John, the apostle; and Zahn, in his *Acta Joannis*, p. cliv. sq., endeavors to prove that a church stood outside of the walls of Ephesus, on the spot where John was buried, and another inside of the walls, on the site of the house in which he had resided, and that thus two spots were consecrated to the memory of a single John. The proof which he brings in support of this may not lead many persons to adopt his conclusions, and yet after reading his discussion of the matter one must admit that the existence of two memorials in Ephesus, such as Dionysius, Eusebius, and Jerome refer to, by no means proves that more than one John was buried there.

[14] A similar suggestion had been already made by Dionysius in the passage quoted by Eusebius in Bk. VII. chap. 25, and Eusebius was undoubtedly thinking of it when he wrote these words. The suggestion is a very clever one, and yet it is only a guess, and does not pretend to be more. Dionysius concludes that the Apocalypse must have been written by some person named John, because it testifies to that fact itself; but the style, and other internal indications, lead him to think that it cannot have been written by the author of the fourth Gospel, whom he assumes to be John the apostle. He is therefore led to suppose that the Apocalypse was written by some other John. He does not pretend to say who that John was, but thinks it must have been some John that resided in Asia; and he then adds that there were said to be two tombs in Ephesus bearing the name of John, — evidently implying, though he does not say it, that he is inclined to think that this second John thus commemorated was the author of the Apocalypse. It is plain from this that he had

and the presbyter John. At least he mentions them frequently by name, and gives their traditions in his writings. These things, we hope, have not been uselessly adduced by us.

8 But it is fitting to subjoin to the words of Papias which have been quoted, other passages from his works in which he relates some other wonderful events which he claims to

9 have received from tradition. That Philip the apostle dwelt at Hierapolis with his daughters has been already stated.[15] But it must be noted here that Papias, their contemporary, says that he heard a wonderful tale from the daughters of Philip. For he relates that in his time [16] one rose from the dead. And he tells another wonderful story of Justus, surnamed Barsabbas: that he drank a deadly poison, and yet, by the grace of the Lord, suffered no

10 harm. The Book of Acts records that the holy apostles after the ascension of the Saviour, put forward this Justus, together with Matthias, and prayed that one might be chosen in place of the traitor Judas, to fill up their number. The account is as follows: "And they put forward two, Joseph, called Barsabbas, who was surnamed Justus, and Matthias; and they

11 prayed and said."[17] The same writer gives also other accounts which he says came to him through unwritten tradition, certain strange parables and teachings of the Saviour, and

12 some other more mythical things.[18] To these belong his statement that there will be a period of some thousand years after the resurrection of the dead, and that the kingdom of Christ will be set up in material form on this very earth.[19] I suppose he got these ideas

through a misunderstanding of the apostolic accounts, not perceiving that the things said by them were spoken mystically in figures. For he appears to have been of very limited

13 understanding,[20] as one can see from his discourses. But it was due to him that so many of the Church Fathers after him adopted a like opinion, urging in their own support the antiquity of the man; as for instance Irenæus and any one else that may have proclaimed similar views.[21] Papias gives also in his

14 own work other accounts of the words of the Lord on the authority of Aristion who was mentioned above, and traditions as handed down by the presbyter John; to which we refer those who are fond of learning. But now we must add to the words of his which we have already quoted the tradition which he gives in regard to Mark, the author of the Gospel. It is in the following words: "This also

15 the presbyter [22] said: Mark, having become the interpreter of Peter, wrote down accurately, though not indeed in order, whatsoever he remembered of the things said or done by Christ.[23]

so constantly by chiliasts in support of their views was the reason why Dionysius, Eusebius, and others were anxious to disprove its apostolic authorship. Chief among the chiliasts of the ante-Nicene age were the author of the epistle of Barnabas, Papias, Justin Martyr, Irenæus, and Tertullian; while the principal opponents of the doctrine were Caius, Origen, Dionysius of Alexandria, and Eusebius. After the time of Constantine, chiliasm was more and more widely regarded as a heresy, and received its worst blow from Augustine, who framed in its stead the doctrine, which from his time on was commonly accepted in the Church, that the millennium is the present reign of Christ, which began with his resurrection. See Schaff's *Church History*, II. p. 613 sq., for the history of the doctrine in the ante-Nicene Church and for the literature of the subject.

[20] σφόδρα σμικρὸς τὸν νοῦν. Eusebius' judgment of Papias may have been unfavorably influenced by his hostility to the strong chiliasm of the latter; and yet a perusal of the extant fragments of Papias' writings will lead any one to think that Eusebius was not far wrong in his estimate of the man. On the genuineness of the words in his praise, given by some MSS., in chap. 36, § 2, see note 3 on that chapter.   [21] See above, note 19.

[22] We cannot, in the absence of the context, say with certainty that the presbyter here referred to is the "presbyter John," of whom Papias has so much to say, and who is mentioned in the previous paragraph, and yet this seems quite probable. Compare Weiffenbach's *Die Papias Fragmente über Marcus und Matthaeus*, p. 26 sq.

[23] Papias is the first one to connect the Gospel of Mark with Peter, but the tradition recorded by him was universally accepted by those who came after him (see above, Bk. II. chap. 15, note 4). The relation of this Gospel of Mark to our canonical Gospel has been a very sharply disputed point, but there is no good reason for distinguishing the Gospel referred to here from our second Gospel, which corresponds excellently to the description given by Papias. Compare the remarks of Lightfoot, *ibid.* p. 393 sq. We know from other sources (e.g. Justin Martyr's *Dial.* c. 106) that our second Gospel was in existence in any case before the middle of the second century, and therefore there is no reason to suppose that Papias was thinking of any other Gospel when he spoke of the Gospel written by Mark as the interpreter of Peter. Of course it does not follow from this that it was actually our second Gospel which Mark wrote, and of whose composition Papias here speaks. He may have written a Gospel which afterward formed the basis of our present Gospel, or was one of the sources of the synoptic tradition as a whole; that is, he may have written what is commonly known as the "Ur-Marcus" (see above, Bk. II. chap. 15, note 4). As to that, we cannot decide with absolute certainty, but we may say that Papias certainly understood the tradition which he gives to refer to our Gospel of Mark. The exact significance of the word ἑρμηνευτής as used in this sentence has been much disputed. It seems best to give it its usual significance,—the significance which we attach to the English word "interpreter." See Weiffenbach, *ibid.* p. 37 sq. It may be, supposing the report to be correct, that Peter found it advantageous to have some one more familiar than himself with the language of the people among whom he labored to assist him in his preaching. What language it was for which he needed an interpreter we cannot say. We might think naturally of Latin, but it is

no tradition whatever in favor of this theory, that it was solely an hypothesis arising from critical difficulties standing in the way of the ascription of the book to the apostle John. Eusebius sees in this suggestion a very welcome solution of the difficulties with which he feels the acceptance of the book to be beset, and at once states it as a possibility that this "presbyter John," whom he has discovered in the writings of Papias, may have been the author of the book. But the authenticity of the Apocalypse was too firmly established to be shaken by such critical and theological difficulties as influenced Dionysius, Eusebius, and a few others, and in consequence nothing came of the suggestion made here by Eusebius. In the present century, however, the "presbyter John" has again played an important part among some critics as the possible author of certain of the Johannine writings, though the authenticity of the Apocalypse has (until very recently) been so commonly adopted even by the most negative critics that the "presbyter John" has not figured at all as the author of it; nor indeed is he likely to in the future.

[15] In chap. 31, above. On the confusion of the evangelist with the apostle Philip, see that chapter, note 6.

[16] That is, in the time of Philip.   [17] Acts i. 23.

[18] Compare the extract from Papias given by Irenæus (*Adv. Hær.* V. 32), in which is contained a famous parable in regard to the fertility of the millennium, which is exceedingly materialistic in its nature, and evidently apocryphal. "The days will come when vines shall grow, each having ten thousand branches, and in each branch ten thousand twigs, and in each twig ten thousand shoots, and in every one of the shoots ten thousand grapes, and every grape when pressed will give five and twenty measures of wine," &c.

[19] Chiliasm, or millennarianism,—that is, the belief in a visible reign of Christ on earth for a thousand years before the general judgment,—was very widespread in the early Church. Jewish chiliasm was very common at about the beginning of the Christian era, and is represented in the voluminous apocalyptic literature of that day. Christian chiliasm was an outgrowth of the Jewish, spiritualized it, and fixed it upon the second, instead of the first, coming of Christ. The chief Biblical support for this doctrine is found in Rev. xx. 1-6, and the fact that this book was appealed to

For he neither heard the Lord nor followed him, but afterward, as I said, he followed Peter, who adapted his teaching to the needs of his hearers, but with no intention of giving a connected account of the Lord's discourses,[24] so that Mark committed no error while he thus wrote some things as he remembered them. For he was careful of one thing, not to omit any of the things which he had heard, and not to state any of them falsely." These things are related 16 by Papias concerning Mark. But concerning Matthew he writes as follows: "So then[25] Matthew wrote the oracles in the Hebrew language, and every one interpreted them as he was able."[26] And the same writer uses

testimonies from the first Epistle of John[27] and from that of Peter likewise.[28] And he relates another story of a woman, who was accused of many sins before the Lord, which is contained in the Gospel according to the Hebrews.[29] These things we have thought it necessary to observe in addition to what has been already stated.

assuming that the Gospel of Matthew which Papias was acquainted with was a different Gospel from our own. This, however, does not prove that the λόγια which Matthew wrote (supposing Papias' report to be correct) were identical with, or even of the same nature as our Gospel of Matthew. It is urged by many that the word λόγια could be used only to describe a collection of the words or discourses of the Lord, and hence it is assumed that Matthew wrote a work of this kind, which of course is quite a different thing from our first Gospel. But Lightfoot has shown (*ibid.* p. 399 sq.) that the word λόγια, "oracles," is not necessarily confined to a collection of discourses merely, but that it may be used to describe a work containing also a narrative of events. This being the case, it cannot be said that Matthew's λόγια must necessarily have been something different from our present Gospel. Still our Greek Matthew is certainly not a translation of a Hebrew original, and hence there may be a long step between Matthew's Hebrew λόγια and our Greek Gospel. But if our Greek Matthew was known to Papias, and if it is not a translation of a Hebrew original, then one of two alternatives follows: either he could not accept the Greek Matthew, which was in current use (that is, our canonical Matthew), or else he was not acquainted with the Hebrew Matthew. Of the former alternative we have no hint in the fragments preserved to us, while the latter, from the way in which Papias speaks of these Hebrew λόγια, seems highly probable. It may, therefore, be said to be probable that Papias, the first one that mentions a Hebrew Matthew, speaks not from personal knowledge, but upon the authority of tradition only.

[27] Since the first Epistle of John and the fourth Gospel are indisputably from the same hand (see above, chap. 24, note 18), Papias' testimony to the apostolic authorship of the Epistle, which is what his use of it implies, is indirect testimony to the apostolic authorship of the Gospel also.

[28] On the authenticity of the first Epistle of Peter, see above, chap. 3, note 1.

[29] It is very likely that the story referred to here is identical with the story of the woman taken in adultery, given in some MSS., at the close of the eighth chapter of John's Gospel. The story was clearly not contained in the original Gospel of John, but we do not know from what source it crept into that Gospel, possibly from the Gospel according to the Hebrews, where Eusebius says the story related by Papias was found. It must be noticed that Eusebius does not say that Papias took the story from the Gospel according to the Hebrews, but only that it was contained in that Gospel. We are consequently not justified in claiming this statement of Eusebius as proving that Papias himself was acquainted with the Gospel according to the Hebrews (see above, chap. 25, note 24). He may have taken it thence, or he may, on the other hand, have taken it simply from oral tradition, the source whence he derived so many of his accounts, or, possibly, from the lost original Gospel, the "Ur-Matthaeus."

not impossible that Greek or that both languages were meant; for Peter, although of course possessed of some acquaintance with Greek, might not have been familiar enough with it to preach in it with perfect ease. The words "though not indeed in order" (οὐ μέντοι τάξει) have also caused considerable controversy. But they seem to refer chiefly to a lack of chronological arrangement, perhaps to a lack of logical arrangement also. The implication is that Mark wrote down without regard to order of any kind the words and deeds of Christ which he remembered. Lightfoot and most other critics have supposed that this accusation of a "lack of order" implies the existence of another written Gospel, exhibiting a different order, with which Papias compares it (e.g. with the Gospel of Matthew, as Weiss, Bleck, Holtzmann, and others think; or with John, as Lightfoot, Zahn, Renan, and others suppose). This is a natural supposition, but it is quite possible that Papias in speaking of this lack of order is not thinking at all of another written Gospel, but merely of the order of events which he had received from tradition as the true one.

[24] λόγων, "discourses," or λογίων, "oracles." The two words are about equally supported by MS. authority. The latter is adopted by the majority of the editors; but it is more likely that it arose from λόγων under the influence of the λογίων, which occurred in the title of Papias' work, than that it was changed into λόγων. The matter, however, cannot be decided, and the alternative reading must in either case be allowed to stand. See the notes of Burton and Heinichen, *in loco*.

[25] μὲν οὖν. These words show plainly enough that this sentence in regard to Matthew did not in the work of Papias immediately follow the passage in regard to Mark, quoted above. Both passages are evidently torn out of their context; and the latter apparently stood at the close of a description of the origin of Matthew's Gospel. That this statement in regard to Matthew rests upon the authority of "the presbyter" we are consequently not at liberty to assert.

[26] On the tradition that Matthew wrote a Hebrew gospel, see above, chap. 24, note 5. Our Greek Gospel of Matthew was certainly in existence at the time Papias wrote, for it is quoted in the epistle of Barnabas, which was written not later than the first quarter of the second century. There is, therefore, no reason for

BOOK IV.

CHAPTER I.

The Bishops of Rome and of Alexandria during the Reign of Trajan.[1]

1 ABOUT the twelfth year of the reign of Trajan the above-mentioned bishop of the parish of Alexandria[2] died, and Primus,[3] the fourth in succession from the apostles, was 2 chosen to the office. At that time also Alexander,[4] the fifth in the line of succession from Peter and Paul, received the episcopate at Rome, after Evarestus had held the office eight years.[5]

---

[1] We still have lists of bishops as old as the end of the second century. The most ancient is that of the Roman bishops given by Irenæus (III. 3.3); but this has no dates. The list is probably the official catalogue as it had been handed down to the time of Eleutherus; but it is not authentic, as there was no monarchical episcopate in Rome at the time of Clement, nor even in the time of Hermas. For other churches the oldest lists date from the end of the third century. According to one interpretation of a passage from Hegesippus, quoted in chapter 22, below, Hegesippus drew up a list of Roman bishops down to the time of Anicetus; and Bishop Lightfoot thinks he has discovered this lost catalogue in Epiphanius, *Hær.* XXVII. 6 (see his article in the *Academy* for May 27, 1887). If Lightfoot is right, we have recovered the oldest Papal catalogue; but it is very doubtful whether Hegesippus composed such a catalogue (see note on chap. 22), and even if he did, it is uncertain whether the list which Epiphanius gives is identical with it. See the writer's notice of Lightfoot's article in the *Theologische Literatur-Zeitung*, 1887; No. 18, Col. 435 sqq.

The list of Roman bishops which Eusebius gives is the same as that of Irenæus; but it has dates, while Irenæus' has none. From what source Eusebius took his dates we do not know. His *Chronicle* contains different dates. It is possible that the difference is owing, in part, to defective transcriptions or translations; but it is more probable that Eusebius himself discovered another source, before writing his *History*, which he considered more authentic, and therefore substituted for the one he had used in his *Chronicle*. Lipsius (*Chronologie der römischen Bischöfe*, p. 145) says, "We may assume that the oldest catalogue extended as far as Eleutherus, but rested upon historical knowledge only from Xystus, or, at the farthest, from Alexander down." On the chronology of the Roman bishops in general, see especially the important work of Lipsius just referred to.

[2] Cerdon, mentioned in Bk. III. chap. 21.

[3] The *Chronicle* of Eusebius (Armenian) makes Primus succeed to the bishopric of Alexandria in the eleventh year of Trajan; the version of Jerome, in the ninth. According to chap. 4, below, he held office twelve years. No reliance can be placed upon any of the figures. The Alexandrian church is shrouded in darkness until the latter part of the second century, and all extant traditions in regard to its history before that time are about equally worthless. Of Primus himself we have no authentic knowledge, though he figures somewhat in later tradition. See Smith and Wace's *Dict. of Christian Biography, in loco.*

[4] According to the *Chronicle* of Eusebius (Armenian), Alexander became bishop of Rome in the eighth year of Trajan; according to Jerome's version, in the twelfth year. He is said, in chap. 4, below, to have died in the third year of Hadrian, after holding office ten years. On the reliability of these dates, see note 1, above. Of Alexander's life and character we know nothing.

[5] On Evarestus, see Bk. III. chap. 34, note 3.

CHAPTER II.

The Calamities of the Jews during Trajan's Reign.

THE teaching and the Church of our 1 Saviour flourished greatly and made progress from day to day; but the calamities of the Jews increased, and they underwent a constant succession of evils. In the eighteenth year of Trajan's reign[1] there was another disturbance of the Jews, through which a great multitude of them perished.[2] For in Alexandria and 2 in the rest of Egypt, and also in Cyrene,[3] as if incited by some terrible and factious spirit, they rushed into seditious measures against their fellow-inhabitants, the Greeks. The insurrection increased greatly, and in the following year, while Lupus was governor of all Egypt,[4] it developed into a war of no mean magnitude. In the first attack it happened that they were 3 victorious over the Greeks, who fled to Alexandria and imprisoned and slew the Jews that were in the city. But the Jews of Cyrene, although deprived of their aid, continued to plunder the land of Egypt and to devastate its districts,[5] under the leadership of Lucuas.[6] Against them the emperor sent Marcius Turbo[7] with a foot and naval force and also with a force of cavalry. He carried on the war against them for a 4

---

[1] 115 A.D.

[2] Closs says: "According to Dion Cassius, LXVIII. 32, they slew in Cyrene 220,000 persons with terrible cruelty. At the same time there arose in Cyprus a disturbance of the Jews, who were very numerous in that island. According to Dion, 240,000 of the inhabitants were slain there. Their leader was Artemion." Compare Dion Cassius, *Hist. Rom.* LXVIII. 32, and LXIX. 12 sq. The Jews and the Greeks that dwelt together in different cities were constantly getting into trouble. The Greeks scorned the Jews, and the Jews in return hated the Greeks and stirred up many bloody commotions against them. See Jost's *Geschichte der Israeliten,* chap. III. p. 181 sq. The word "another" in this passage is used apparently with reference to the Jewish war under Vespasian, of which Eusebius has spoken at length in the early part of the third Book.

[3] The Jews were very numerous both in Egypt and in Cyrene, which lay directly west of Egypt. The Jews of Cyrene had a synagogue at Jerusalem, according to Acts vi. 9.

[4] Lupus is, to me at least, an otherwise unknown character.

[5] νόμοι. See Bk. II. chap. 17, note 10.

[6] Lucuas is called by Dion Cassius (LXVIII. 32) Andreas. Münter suggests that he may have borne a double name, a Jewish and a Roman, as did many of the Jews of that time.

[7] Marcius Turbo was one of the most distinguished of the Roman generals under Trajan and Hadrian, and finally became prætorian prefect under Hadrian. See Dion Cassius, LXIX. 18, and Spartian, *Hadr.* 4–9, 15.

long time and fought many battles, and slew many thousands of Jews, not only of those of Cyrene, but also of those who dwelt in Egypt and had come to the assistance of their king 5 Lucuas. But the emperor, fearing that the Jews in Mesopotamia would also make an attack upon the inhabitants of that country, commanded Lucius Quintus[8] to clear the province of them. And he having marched against them slew a great multitude of those that dwelt there; and in consequence of his success he was made governor of Judea by the emperor. These events are recorded also in these very words by the Greek historians that have written accounts of those times.[9]

CHAPTER III.

The Apologists that wrote in Defense of the Faith during the Reign of Adrian.

1   AFTER Trajan had reigned for nineteen and a half years[1] Ælius Adrian became his successor in the empire. To him Quadratus addressed a discourse containing an apology for our religion,[2] because certain wicked men[3] had attempted to trouble the Christians. The work is still in the hands of a great many of the brethren, as also in our own, and furnishes clear proofs of the man's understanding and of his apostolic orthodoxy.[4] He himself re- 2 veals the early date at which he lived in the following words : " But the works of our Saviour were always present,[5] for they were genuine : — those that were healed, and those that were raised from the dead, who were seen not only when they were healed and when they were raised, but were also always present; and not merely while the Saviour was on earth, but also after his death, they were alive for quite a while, so that some of them lived even to our day." [6] Such then was Quadratus.

Aristides also, a believer earnestly de- 3 voted to our religion, left, like Quadratus, an apology for the faith, addressed to Adrian.[7] His work, too, has been preserved even to the present day by a great many persons.

CHAPTER IV.

The Bishops of Rome and of Alexandria under the Same Emperor.[1]

IN the third year of the same reign, Alexander,[2] bishop of Rome, died, after holding office

---

[8] Lucius Quintus was an independent Moorish chief, who served voluntarily in the Roman army and became one of Trajan's favorite generals. He was made governor of Judea by Trajan, and was afterward raised to the consulship. According to Themistius (*Orat.* XVI.), Trajan at one time intended to make him his successor. See Dion Cassius, LXVIII. 8, 22, 30, 32; LXIX. 2; Spartian, *Hadr.* 5, 7, and cf. Valesius' note on this passage.

[9] The language of Eusebius might imply that he had other sources than the Greek writers, but this does not seem to have been the case. He apparently followed Dion Cassius for the most part, but evidently had some other source (the same which Orosius afterward followed), for he differs from Dion in the name of the Jewish leader, calling him Lucuas instead of Andreas. The only extant accounts of these affairs by Greek historians are those of Dion Cassius and Orosius, but there were evidently others in Eusebius' time.

[1] Trajan reigned from Jan. 27, 98, to Aug. 7 or 8, 117.

[2] The importance of Quadratus' Apology in the mind of Eusebius is shown by his beginning the events of Hadrian's reign with it, as well as by the fact that he gives it also in his *Chronicle*, year 2041 of Abraham (124 to 125 A.D.), where he calls Quadratus " *Auditor Apostolorum.* " Eusebius gives few events in his *Chronicle*, and therefore the reference to this is all the more significant. We find no mention of Quadratus and Aristides before Eusebius, and of the Apology of Quadratus we have only the few lines which are given in this chapter. In the *Chronicle* Eusebius says that Quadratus and Aristides addressed apologies to Hadrian during his stay in Athens. One MS. of the *Chronicle* gives the date as 125 A.D. (2141 Abr.), and this is correct; for, according to Dürr (*Die Reisen des Kaisers Hadrian,* Wien, 1881, p. 42 to 44, and 70 to 71), Hadrian was in Athens from the fall of 125 to the summer of 126 and from the spring of 129 to the spring of 130. Eusebius adds in his *Chronicle* (but omits here) that these apologies were the cause of a favorable edict from Hadrian, but this is incorrect. Eusebius (IV. 12) makes a similar statement in regard to the Apology of Justin, making a favorable edict (which has been proved to be unauthentic) of the Emperor Antoninus the result of it. (See Overbeck, *Studien zur Geschichte der alten Kirche,* I. 108 sq., 139.) Quadratus and Aristides are the oldest apologists known to us. Eusebius does not mention them again. This Quadratus must not be confounded with Quadratus, bishop of Athens in the time of Marcus Aurelius, who is mentioned in chap. 23; for the apologist Quadratus who belonged to the time of the apostles can hardly have been a bishop during the reign of Marcus Aurelius. Nor is there any decisive ground to identify him with the prophet mentioned in Bk. III. chap. 37 and Bk. V. chap. 7, for Quadratus was a very common name, and the prophet and the apologist seem to have belonged to different countries (see Harnack, *Ueberlieferung der griech. Apol.* p. 103). Many scholars, however, identify the prophet and the apologist, and it must be said that Eusebius' mention of the prophet in III. 37, and of the apologist in IV. 3, without any qualifying phrases, looks as if one well-known Quadratus were referred to. The matter must remain undecided. Jerome speaks of Quadratus and Aristides once in the *Chronicle,* year 2142, and in *de vir. ill.* chap. 19 and 20. In chap. 19 he identifies Quadratus, the apologist, and Quadratus, the bishop of Athens, but he evidently had no other source than Eusebius (as

was usually the case, so that he can very rarely be accepted as an independent witness), and his statements here are the result simply of a combination of his own. The later scattering traditions in regard to Quadratus and Aristides (chiefly in the Martyrologies) rest probably only upon the accounts of Eusebius and Jerome, and whatever enlargement they offer is untrustworthy. The Apology of Quadratus was perhaps extant at the beginning of the seventh century; see Photius, *Cod.* 162. One later tradition made Quadratus the angel of Philadelphia, addressed in the Apocalypse; another located him in Magnesia (this Otto accepts). Either tradition might be true, but one is worth no more than the other. Compare Harnack, *Die Ueberlieferung der griech. Apol.,* and Otto, *Corpus Apol. Christ.* IX. p. 333 sq.

[3] This phrase is very significant, as showing the idea of Eusebius that the persecutions did not proceed from the emperors themselves, but were the result of the machinations of the enemies of the Christians.

[4] ὀρθοτομία. Compare the use of ὀρθοτομοῦντα in 2 Tim. ii. 15.

[5] The fragment begins τοῦ δὲ σωτῆρος ἡμῶν τὰ ἔργα ἀεὶ παρῆν. The δὲ seems to introduce a contrast, and allows us to assume with some measure of assurance that an exposure of the pretended wonders of heathen magicians, who were numerous at that time, preceded this ocular proof of the genuineness of Christ's miracles.

[6] Quadratus had evidently seen none of these persons himself; he had simply heard of them through others. We have no record elsewhere of the fact that any of those raised by Christ lived to a later age.

[7] Aristides of Athens, a contemporary of Quadratus, is called by Eusebius in his *Chronicle* " a philosopher " (*nostri dogmatis philosophus Atheniensis*). Eusebius does not quote his work, perhaps because he did not himself possess a copy, perhaps because it contained no historical matter suitable to his purpose. He does not mention him again (the Aristides, the friend of Africanus, of Bk. I. chap. 7 and of Bk. VI. chap. 31, lived a century later), and his Apology is quoted by none of the Fathers, so far as is known. Vague and worthless traditions of the Middle Ages still kept his name alive, as in the case of Quadratus, but the Apology itself disappeared long ago, until in 1878 a fragment of an Apology, bearing the name of "Aristides, the Philosopher of Athens," was published by the Mechitarists from a codex of the year 981. It is a fragment of an Armenian translation of the fifth century; and although its genuineness has been denied, it is accepted by most critics, and seems to be an authentic fragment from the age of Hadrian. See especially Harnack, *ibid.* p. 109 sq., and again in Herzog, 2d ed., Supplement Vol. p. 675-681; also Schaff, *Ch. Hist.* II. p. 709.

[1] I.e. the emperor Hadrian.

[2] On Alexander, see above, chap. 1, note 4.

ten years. His successor was Xystus.[3] About the same time Primus, bishop of Alexandria, died in the twelfth year of his episcopate,[4] and was succeeded by Justus.[5]

CHAPTER V.

The Bishops of Jerusalem from the Age of our Saviour to the Period under Consideration.

1   THE chronology of the bishops of Jerusalem I have nowhere found preserved in writing;[1] for tradition says that they were
2   all short lived. But I have learned this much from writings,[2] that until the siege of the Jews, which took place under Adrian,[3] there were fifteen bishops in succession there,[4] all of

whom are said to have been of Hebrew descent, and to have received the knowledge of Christ in purity, so that they were approved by those who were able to judge of such matters, and were deemed worthy of the episcopate. For their whole church consisted then of believing Hebrews who continued from the days of the apostles until the siege which took place at this time; in which siege the Jews, having again rebelled against the Romans, were conquered after severe battles. But since the bishops of 3 the circumcision ceased at this time, it is proper to give here a list of their names from the beginning. The first, then, was James, the so-called brother of the Lord;[5] the second, Symeon;[6] the third, Justus;[7] the fourth, Zacchæus;[8] the fifth, Tobias; the sixth, Benjamin; the seventh, John; the eighth, Matthias; the ninth, Philip; the tenth, Seneca;[9] the eleventh, Justus; the twelfth, Levi; the thirteenth, Ephres;[10] the fourteenth, Joseph;[11] and finally, the fifteenth, Judas. These are the bishops of 4 Jerusalem that lived between the age of the apostles and the time referred to, all of them belonging to the circumcision.

In the twelfth year of the reign of Adrian, 5 Xystus, having completed the tenth year of

---

[3] Known as Sixtus·I. (Sixtus, or Sistus, being the Latin form of the name) in the list of Roman bishops. He was supposed to be the author of a collection of religious and moral maxims, which were widely read in the ancient Church and are mentioned by many of the Fathers. His authorship was disputed by Jerome and others, and the work from that time on was commonly assigned to a heathen author, until recently some voices have again been heard in favor of the authorship of Bishop Sixtus (notably de Lagarde and Ewald). See Schaff's *Church Hist.* II. p. 703 sq.

He is, according to Lipsius, the first Roman bishop whose dates we have any means of ascertaining, and it may be assumed that he was the first one that occupied an episcopal position in Rome; and yet, even in his time, the monarchical episcopate can hardly have been established in its full sense. In the next chapter we are told that he held office ten years; and this figure, which is supported by most of the ancient catalogues, may be accepted as approximately correct. The date of his accession given here by Eusebius cannot, however, be correct; for, as Lipsius has shown (*Chron. de röm. Bischöfe*, p. 183 sq.) he must have died at least as early as 126 A.D. (possibly as early as 124), so that his accession took place not later than 116; that is, before the death of Trajan. Like most of the other early Roman bishops he is celebrated as a martyr in the martyrologies, but the fact of his martyrdom rests upon a very late and worthless tradition.

[4] On Primus, see chap. 1, note 4. Eusebius contradicts his own dates here. For in chap. 1 he says that Alexander of Rome and Primus of Alexandria became bishops at the same time; but according to this chapter, Alexander died at the close of the tenth year of his episcopate, and Primus in the twelfth year of his. Eusebius may have used the word " about " advisedly, to cover considerable ground, and may have grouped the two bishops together simply for convenience' sake. No reliance is to be placed upon the dates in any case.

[5] We know nothing about Justus except that he ruled eleven years, according to the next chapter. If Primus died in the twelfth year of his episcopate, as Eusebius says in this chapter, and entered upon his office in the twelfth year of Trajan, as he says in chapter 1, Justus must have become bishop about 120 A.D., in the third or fourth year of Hadrian. It must be remembered, however, that all of these dates are historically worthless.

[1] In his *Chron.* Eusebius also gives the names of these bishops of Jerusalem, without assigning dates to more than two or three of them. But in Nicephorus Callisti the dates are given. From what source Nicephorus drew we do not know. He is, at any rate, too late to be of any worth as an authority on such a subject. In fact, these men were not regular monarchical bishops, holding office in succession (see note 4), and hence Eusebius is quite excusable for his ignorance in regard to their dates. See Ritschl's *Entstehung der alt-kath. Kirche*, p. 246 sq.

[2] Reuterdahl (*De Fontibus Hist. eccles. Euseb.*, p. 55) conjectures that these "writings" were found in the church of Jerusalem itself, and compares a passage in the *Dem. Evang.* III. 5: "The first bishops that presided there [i.e. at Jerusalem] are said to have been Jews, and their names are preserved by the inhabitants of the country." Had Hegesippus or any other known author been the source of his information, he would probably have mentioned his name.

[3] In 135 A.D. See below, chap. 7.

[4] From Hegesippus (see above, Bk. III. chap. 32) we learn that Symeon, the successor of James, was martyred during Trajan's reign. As was seen in note 6 of the chapter referred to, the martyrdom probably occurred early in that reign. Eusebius, in his *Chron.*, refers the martyrdom and the accession of Justus to the tenth year of Trajan (107 A.D.). This leaves thirteen bishops to be inserted between 107 (or, if this date is not reliable, 98+) and 135 A.D., which is, to say the least, very suspicious. The true explanation appears to be that, after the death of Symeon, the last prominent relative of

Christ, the presbyters took the lead, and that they were afterward made by tradition into successive monarchical bishops. Closs and Gieseler suppose that there were bishops of a number of churches in Palestine at the same time, whom tradition made successive bishops of Jerusalem. But the fact is, that the episcopate is of Greek, not of Jewish, origin, and in the strictly Jewish Christian churches of Palestine no such person as a bishop can have existed. Only after the church there came under the influence of the Gentile church, and lost its prevailingly Jewish character, was it possible for a bishop, in the general sense of the term, to exist there. The Jewish Christians assumed for their church government the form of the Jewish Sanhedrim, though while James and Symeon were alive, they were naturally leaders (according to the common Oriental custom, which exalted the relatives of the founder of a religion). The Jewish character of the Jerusalem congregation was very marked until the destruction of the city under Hadrian (note that all but two of the fifteen bishops have Jewish names), after which all circumcised Jews — Christians as well as unbelievers — were excluded, and a heathen Christian congregation took its place (see the next chapter). According to Stroth, followed by Closs, Stigloher, and Heinichen, the church of Jerusalem remained in Pella after 70 A.D., and was called the church of Jerusalem because it was made up of Christians from Jerusalem. This is possible; but Eusebius evidently did not understand it so (compare, too, his *Dem. Evang.* III. 5), and Epiphanius (*de Mensa et Pond.* chap. 15) says expressly that, after the destruction of the city by Titus, the church returned again to Jerusalem, and there is no good reason to doubt the report.

[5] On James, see above, Bk. II. chap. 1.

[6] On Symeon, see above, Bk. III. chap. 11, note 4.

[7] Of Justus and the following named bishops we know nothing more. Justus is called Judas by Epiphanius, *Hær.* LXVI. 20.

[8] Zacchæus is called Zacharias by Epiphanius. According to Jerome's version of Eusebius' *Chron.* he became bishop in the fifteenth year of Trajan; according to the Armenian version, in the twelfth year. Dates are given by the *Chron.* for this bishop and for Seneca, but no confidence is to be reposed in the dates, nor in those given by Epiphanius and Eutychius. The former, when he gives dates at all, is hopelessly at sea. The latter gives exact dates for every bishop, but quite without the support of ancient tradition.

[9] The name Seneca is Latin, the only Latin name in the list. But there is nothing particularly surprising in a Jew's bearing a Latin name. It was quite common even for native Jews to bear both a Latin, or Greek, and a Hebrew name, and often the former was used to the exclusion of the latter. The name therefore does not disprove Seneca's Hebrew origin.

[10] Ἐφρῆς. Epiphanius calls him Ὀνάβρις. The Armenian version of the *Chron.* calls him Ephrem; Jerome's version, Ephres. Syncellus calls him Ἐφραίμ, which is the Hebrew form of the name.

[11] Ἰωσήφ. He is called Ἰωσίς by Epiphanius, and Joses by Jerome.

his episcopate,[12] was succeeded by Telesphorus,[13] the seventh in succession from the apostles. In the meantime, after the lapse of a year and some months, Eumenes,[14] the sixth in order, succeeded to the leadership of the Alexandrian church, his predecessor having held office eleven years.[15]

CHAPTER VI.

The Last Siege of the Jews under Adrian.

1   As the rebellion of the Jews at this time grew much more serious,[1] Rufus, governor of Judea, after an auxiliary force had been sent him by the emperor, using their madness as a pretext, proceeded against them without mercy, and destroyed indiscriminately thousands of men and women and children, and in accordance with the laws of war reduced their country to a state of complete subjection.

2   The leader of the Jews at this time was a man by the name of Barcocheba[2] (which signifies a star), who possessed the character of a robber and a murderer, but nevertheless, relying upon his name, boasted to them, as if they were slaves, that he possessed wonderful powers; and he pretended that he was a star that had come down to them out of heaven to bring them light in the midst of their misfortunes.

The war raged most fiercely in the eigh-   3 teenth year of Adrian,[3] at the city of Bithara,[4] which was a very secure fortress, situated not far from Jerusalem. When the siege had lasted a long time, and the rebels had been driven to the last extremity by hunger and thirst, and the instigator of the rebellion had suffered his just punishment, the whole nation was prohibited from this time on by a decree, and by the commands of Adrian, from ever going up to the country about Jerusalem. For the emperor gave orders that they should not even see from a distance the land of their fathers. Such is the account of Aristo of Pella.[5]   And   4 thus, when the city had been emptied of the Jewish nation and had suffered the total destruction of its ancient inhabitants, it was colonized by a different race, and the Roman city which subsequently arose changed its name and was called Ælia, in honor of the emperor Ælius Adrian. And as the church there was now com-

---

[12] On Xystus, see chap. 4, note 3.

[13] Telesphorus was a martyr, according to Irenæus, III. 3. 3 (compare below, chap. 10, and Bk. V. chap. 6), and the tradition is too old to be doubted. Eusebius here agrees with Jerome's version of the *Chron.* in putting the date of Telesphorus' accession in the year 128 A.D., but the Armenian version puts it in 124; and Lipsius, with whom Overbeck agrees, puts it between 124 and 126. Since he held office eleven years (according to Eusebius, chap. 10, below, and other ancient catalogues), he must have died, according to Lipsius and Overbeck, between 135 and 137 A.D. (the latter being probably the correct date), and not in the first year of Antoninus Pius (138 A.D., as Eusebius states in chap. 10, below). Tradition says that he fought against Marcion and Valentinus (which is quite possible), and that he was very strict in regard to fasts, sharpening them and increasing their number, which may or may not be true.

[14] We know nothing more about Eumenes. He is said in chap. 11 to have held office thirteen years, and this brings the date of his death into agreement with the date given by the Armenian version of the *Chron.*, which differs by two years from the date given by Jerome.

[15] His predecessor was Justus. See the previous chapter.

[1] The rebellions of the Jews which had broken out in Cyrene and elsewhere during the reign of Trajan only increased the cruelty of the Romans toward them, and in Palestine, as well as elsewhere in the East, their position was growing constantly worse. Already during the reign of Trajan Palestine itself was the scene of many minor disturbances and of much bitter persecution. Hadrian regarded them as a troublesome people, and showed in the beginning of his reign that he was not very favorably disposed toward them. Indeed, it seems that he even went so far as to determine to build upon the site of Jerusalem a purely heathen city. It was at about this time, when all the Jews were longing for the Messiah, that a man appeared (his original name we do not know, but his coins make it probable that it was Simon), claiming to be the Messiah, and promising to free the Jews from the Roman yoke. He took the name Bar-Cochba, "Son of a star," and was enthusiastically supported by Rabbi Akiba and other leading men among the Jews, who believed him to be the promised Messiah. He soon gathered a large force, and war finally broke out between him and Rufus, the governor of Judea, about the year 132. Rufus was not strong enough to put down the rebellion, and Julius Severus, Hadrian's greatest general, was therefore summoned from Britain with a strong force. Bar-Cochba and his followers shut themselves up in Bethar, a strong fortification, and after a long siege the place was taken in 135 A.D., in the fourth year of the war, and Bar-Cochba was put to death. The Romans took severe revenge upon the Jews. Hadrian built upon the site of Jerusalem a new city, which he named Ælia Capitolina, and upon the site of the temple a new temple to the Capitoline Jupiter, and passed a law that no Jew should henceforth enter the place. Under Bar-Cochba the Christians, who refused to join him in his rebellion, were very cruelly treated (cf. Justin Martyr, *Apol.* I. 31, quoted in chap. 8, below). Upon this last war of the Jews, see Dion Cassius, LXIX. 12–14, and compare Jost's *Gesch. der Israeliten*, III. p. 227 sq., and Münter's *Jüdischer Krieg.*

[2] Heb. בוכבא בר, Bar-Cochba, which signifies "Son of a star" (cf. Num. xxiv. 17). After his defeat the Jews gave him the name בר כוזיבא, Bar-Coziba, which means "Son of a lie."

[3] I.e. Aug. 134 to Aug. 135.

[4] Βίθθηρα, Rufinus *Bethara*. The exact situation of this place cannot be determined, although various localities have been suggested by travelers (see Robinson's *Bibl. Researches*, III. p. 267 sqq.). We may conclude at any rate that it was, as Eusebius says, a strongly fortified place, and that it was situated somewhere in Judea.

[5] Whether the whole of the previous account, or only the close of it, was taken by Eusebius from Aristo of Pella, we do not know. Of Aristo of Pella himself we know very little. Eusebius is the first writer to mention him, and he and Maximus Confessor (in his notes on the work *De mystica Theol.* cap. I. p. 17, ed. Corderii) are the only ones to give us any information about him (for the notices in Moses Chorenensis and in the *Chron. Paschale*—the only other places in which Aristo is mentioned—are entirely unreliable). Maximus informs us that Aristo was the author of a *Dialogue of Papiscus and Jason*, a work mentioned by many of the Fathers, but connected by none of them with Aristo. The dialogue, according to Maximus, was known to Clement of Alexandria, and therefore must have been written as early as, or very soon after, the middle of the second century; and the fact that it recorded a dialogue between a Hebrew Christian and an Alexandrian Jew (as we learn from the epistle of Celsus, *De Judaica Incredulitate*, printed with the works of Cyprian, in Hartel's edition, III. p. 119–132) would lead us to expect an early date for the work. There can be found no good reason for doubting the accuracy of Maximus' statement; and if it be accepted, we must conclude that the writer whom Eusebius mentions here was the author of the dialogue referred to. If this be so, it is quite possible that it was from this dialogue that Eusebius drew the account which he here ascribes to Aristo; for such an account might well find a place in a dialogue between two Hebrews. It is possible, of course, that Aristo wrote some other work in which he discussed this subject; but if it had been an historical work, we should expect Eusebius, according to his custom, to give its title. Harnack is quite correct in assuming that Eusebius' silence in regard to the work itself is significant. Doubtless the work did not please him, and hence he neither mentions it, nor gives an account of its author. This is just what we should expect Eusebius' attitude to be toward such a Jewish Christian work (and at the same time, such a 'simple' work, as Origen calls it in *Contra Cels.* IV. 52) as we know the dialogue to have been. There can be of course, left largely to conjecture in this matter; but the above conclusions seem at least reasonable. Compare Harnack's *Ueberlieferung der griech. Apol.*, p. 115 sq.; and for a discussion of the nature of the dialogue (which is no longer extant), see his *Altercatio Simonis Judæi et Theophili Christiani* (*Texte und Untersuchungen*, I. 3), p. 115 sq. (Harnack looks upon this Latin *altercatio* as, in part at least, a free reproduction of the lost dialogue). See, also, the writer's *Dialogue between a Christian and a Jew* ('Αντιβολὴ Παπίσκου καὶ φίλωνος 'Ιουδαίων πρὸς μοναχόν τινα), p. 33.

The town of Pella lay east of the Jordan, in Perea. See Bk. III. chap. 5, note 10, above.

posed of Gentiles, the first one to assume the government of it after the bishops of the circumcision was Marcus.[6]

CHAPTER VII.

The Persons that became at that Time Leaders of Knowledge falsely so-called.[1]

1 As the churches throughout the world were now shining like the most brilliant stars, and faith in our Saviour and Lord Jesus Christ was flourishing among the whole human race,[2] the demon who hates everything that is good, and is always hostile to the truth, and most bitterly opposed to the salvation of man, turned all his arts against the Church.[3] In the beginning he armed himself against it with

2 external persecutions. But now, being shut off from the use of such means,[4] he devised all sorts of plans, and employed other methods in his conflict with the Church, using base and deceitful men as instruments for the ruin of souls and as ministers of destruction. Instigated by him, impostors and deceivers, assuming the name of our religion, brought to the depths of ruin such of the believers as they could win over, and at the same time, by means of the deeds which they practiced, turned away from the path which leads to the word of salvation those

3 who were ignorant of the faith. Accordingly there proceeded from that Menander, whom we have already mentioned as the successor of Simon,[5] a certain serpent-like power, double-tongued and two-headed, which produced the leaders of two different heresies, Saturninus, an Antiochian by birth,[6] and Basilides, an

Alexandrian.[7] The former of these established schools of godless heresy in Syria, the latter in Alexandria. Irenæus states[8] that the 4 false teaching of Saturninus agreed in most respects with that of Menander, but that Basilides, under the pretext of unspeakable mysteries, invented monstrous fables, and carried the fictions of his impious heresy quite beyond bounds. But as there were at that time a 5 great many members of the Church[9] who were fighting for the truth and defending apostolic and ecclesiastical doctrine with uncommon eloquence, so there were some also that furnished posterity through their writings with means of defense against the heresies to which we have referred.[10] Of these there 6 has come down to us a most powerful refutation of Basilides by Agrippa Castor,[11] one of

---

[6] Of this Marcus we know nothing more. Upon the Gentile bishops of Jerusalem, see Bk. V. chap. 12.

[1] ψευδωνύμου γνώσεως. Compare 1 Tim. vi. 20.

[2] This statement is of course an exaggeration. See above, Bk. II. chap. 3, note 1.

[3] These two paragraphs furnish an excellent illustration of Eusebius' dualistic and transcendental conception of history. In his opinion, heresy was not a natural growth from within, but an external evil brought upon the Church by the devil, when he could no longer persecute. According to this conception the Church conquers this external enemy, heresy, and then goes on as before, unaffected by it. In agreement with this is his conception of heretics themselves, whom he, in common with most other Christians of that age, considered without exception wicked and abandoned characters.

[4] Eusebius' belief that persecution had ceased at the time of Hadrian is an illusion (see below, chap. 8, note 14) which falls in with his general conceptions upon this subject — conceptions which ruled among Christian writers until the end of the fourth century.

[5] See Bk. III. chap. 26.

[6] Saturninus is called Saturnilus by Hippolytus, Epiphanius, and Theodoret, and his followers Saturnilians by Hegesippus, quoted in chap. 22, below. Irenæus (*Adv. Hær.* I. 24) and Hippolytus (VII. 16) give accounts of the man and his doctrine which are evidently taken from the same source, probably the lost *Syntagma* of Justin Martyr. Neither of them seems to have had any independent information, nor do any other writers know more about him than was contained in that original source. Irenæus was possibly Eusebius' sole authority, although Irenæus assigns Saturninus only to Syria, while Eusebius makes him a native of Antioch. Hippolytus says that he "spent his time in Antioch of Syria," which may have been the statement of the original, or may have been a mere deduction from a more general statement such as Irenæus gives. In the same way Eusebius may have needed no authority for his still more exact statement.

[7] Basilides was one of the greatest and most famous of the Gnostics. Irenæus (I. 24) and the early *Compendium* of Hippolytus (now lost, but used together with Irenæus' work by Epiphanius in his treatise against heresies) described a form of Basilidianism which was not the original, but a later corruption of the system. On the other hand, Clement of Alexandria surely, and Hippolytus, in the fuller account in his *Philosoph.* (VII. 2 sq.), probably drew their knowledge of the system directly from Basilides' own work, the *Exegetica*, and hence represent the form of doctrine taught by Basilides himself, — a form differing greatly from the later corruptions of it which Irenæus discusses. This system was very profound, and bore in many respects a lofty character. Basilides had apparently few followers (his son Isidore is the only prominent one known to us); and though his system created a great impression at the start, — so much so that his name always remained one of the most famous of Gnostic names, — it had little vitality, and soon died out or was corrupted beyond recognition. He was mentioned of course in all the general works against heresies written by the Fathers, but no one seems to have composed an especial refutation of his system except Agrippa Castor, to whom Eusebius refers. Irenæus informs us that he taught at Alexandria, Hippolytus (VII. 15) mentions simply Egypt, while Epiphanius (XXI. 1) names various Egyptian cities in which he labored, but it is evident that he is only enumerating places in which there were Basilidians in his time. It is not certain whether he is to be identified with the Basilides who is mentioned in the *Acts of Archelaus* as preaching in Persia. For an excellent account of Basilides and his system, see the article by Hort in the *Dict. of Christ. Biog.*; and in addition to the works of Neander, Baur, and Lipsius on Gnosticism in general, see especially Uhlhorn's *Das Basilidianische System*, Göttingen, 1855.

[8] See Irenæus, *Adv. Hær.* I. 24.

[9] ἐκκλησιαστικῶν ἀνδρῶν.

[10] The only one of these — "that furnished posterity with means of defense against heresies" — whom Eusebius mentions is Agrippa Castor, and it is evident that he knew of no others. Moreover, it is more than doubtful whether Agrippa Castor belonged to that time. We do not know when he wrote, but it is hardly possible that the Church had at that period any one capable of answering such a work as the Commentary of Basilides, or any one who would wish to if he could. The activity of the Church was at this early period devoted chiefly if not wholly to the production of apologies for the defense of the Church against the attacks of enemies from the outside, and to the composition of apocalypses. Eusebius in the next chapter mentions Hegesippus as another of these "writers of the time." But the passage which he quotes to prove that Hegesippus wrote then only proves that the events mentioned took place during his lifetime, and not necessarily within forty or fifty years of the time at which he was writing. The fact is, that Hegesippus really wrote about 175 A.D. (later therefore than Justin Martyr), and in chap. 21 of this book Eusebius restores him to his proper chronological place. The general statement made here by Eusebius in regard to the writers against heresy during the reign of Hadrian rest upon his preconceived idea of what must have been the case. If the devil raised up enemies against the truth, the Church must certainly have had at the same time able defenders to meet them. It is a simple example of well-meaning subjective reconstruction. He had the work of Agrippa Castor before him, and undoubtedly believed that he lived at the time stated (which indeed we cannot absolutely deny), and believed, moreover, that other similar writers, whose names he did not know, lived at the same time.

[11] Of Agrippa Castor we know only what Eusebius tells us here. Jerome (*de vir. ill.* chap. 21) adds nothing new, and Theodoret's statement (*Fab.* I. 4), that Agrippa wrote against Basilides' son, Isidore, as well as against Basilides himself, is simply an expansion of Eusebius' account, and does not imply the existence of another

the most renowned writers of that day, which shows the terrible imposture of the man.

7 While exposing his mysteries he says that Basilides wrote twenty-four books upon the Gospel,[12] and that he invented prophets for himself named Barcabbas and Barcoph,[13] and others that had no existence, and that he gave them barbarous names in order to amaze those who marvel at such things; that he taught also that the eating of meat offered to idols and the unguarded renunciation of the faith in times of persecution were matters of indifference;[14] and that he enjoined upon his followers, like

8 Pythagoras, a silence of five years.[15] Other similar things the above-mentioned writer has recorded concerning Basilides, and has

9 ably exposed the error of his heresy. Ire-

næus also writes[16] that Carpocrates was a contemporary of these men, and that he was the father of another heresy, called the heresy of the Gnostics,[17] who did not wish to transmit any longer the magic arts of Simon, as that one[18] had done, in secret, but openly.[19] For they boasted — as of something great — of love potions that were carefully prepared by them, and of certain demons that sent them dreams and lent them their protection, and of other similar agencies; and in accordance with these things they taught that it was necessary for those who wished to enter fully into their mysteries, or rather into their abominations, to practice all the worst kinds of wickedness, on the ground that they could escape the cosmic powers, as they called them, in no other way than by discharging their

---

work. Agrippa's production, of which we do not know even the title, has entirely disappeared.

[12] εἰς τὸ εὐαγγέλιον βιβλία. Clement of Alexandria (*Strom.* IV. 12) quotes from the twenty-third book of the *Exegetica* of Basilides. Origen (*Hom. in Luc.* I.) says that Basilides "had even the audacity to write a *Gospel according to Basilides*," and this remark is repeated by Ambrose (*Exp. in Luc.* I. 1), and seems to be Jerome's authority for the enumeration of a *Gospel of Basilides* among the Apocryphal Gospels in his *Comment in Matt., præf.* We know nothing more about this Gospel, and it is quite possible that Origen mistook the *Exegetica* for a Gospel. We do not know upon what Gospels Basilides wrote his Commentary (or *Exegetica*), but it is hardly probable that he would have expounded his own Gospel even if such a work existed. The passage from the *Exegetica* which Clement quotes looks to me like a part of an exposition of John ix. (although Lipsius, in the *Dict. of Christ. Biog.* II. 715, suggests Luke xxi. 12). Meanwhile, in the *Acta Archelai*, chap. 55 (see *Gallandii Bibl. PP.* III. 608), is a quotation from "the thirteenth book of the treatises (*tractatuum*) of Basilides," which is an exposition of the parable of Dives and Lazarus (Luke xvi.). If this is the same work, it would seem that the *Exegetica* must have included at least Luke and John, possibly Matthew also, for we know that the Gospels of Matthew, Luke, and John were all used by the Basilidians. The respective positions in the work of the expositions of the passages from Luke and John (the former in the thirteenth, the latter in the twenty-third, book) would seem, however, to exclude Matthew, if the books were at all of equal length. If Lipsius were correct in regarding the latter passage as an exposition of Luke xxi. 12, there would be no evidence that the Commentary covered more than a single Gospel.

[13] According to Epiphanius, some of the Ophites appealed to a certain prophet called Barcabbas. What his connection was with the one mentioned here we do not know. Clement of Alexandria (*Strom.* VI. 6) speaks of the *Expositions of the Prophet Parchor* by Isidore, the son of Basilides. This may be another of Basilides' prophets, but is more probably identical with the oft-mentioned Barcoph. In the second book of these *Expositions*, as quoted by Clement, occurs a reference to the prophecy of Cham or Ham. Rienstra (*De Euseb. Hist. Eccles.* p. 29) thinks that Agrippa Castor was mistaken in saying that Basilides mentioned these prophets; but there seems to be no good reason to deny the accuracy of the report, even though we know nothing more about the prophets mentioned. Hort (*Dict. of Christ. Biog.*, article *Barcabbas*) thinks it likely that the prophecies current among the various Gnostic bodies belonged to the apocryphal Zoroastrian literature.

[14] This was not a doctrine of Basilides himself, but of his followers (compare the accounts of Irenæus and Hippolytus). If Agrippa Castor represented Basilides' position thus, as Eusebius says he did (though Eusebius may be only following Irenæus), it is an evidence that he did not live at the early date to which Eusebius assigns him, and this goes to confirm the view stated above, in note 10. Basilides himself taught at least a moderate asceticism, while his followers went off into crude dualism and moral license (see the excellent account of Schaff, *Ch. Hist.* II. 466 sq.).

[15] Exactly what is meant by this "five years of silence" is uncertain. Whether it denoted unquestioning and silent obedience of all commands, as it meant in the case of the Pythagoreans (if, indeed, the traditions in regard to the latter have any basis in fact), or strict secrecy as to the doctrines taught, cannot be decided. The report in regard to the Basilidians, in so far as it has any truth, probably arose on the ground of some such prohibition, which may have been made by some follower of Basilides, if not by the latter himself. A bond of secrecy would lend an air of mystery to the school, which would accord well with the character of its later teachings. But we cannot make Basilides responsible for such proceedings. Agrippa Castor, as reproduced here by Eusebius, is our sole authority for the enjoinment of silence by Basilides.

[16] See Irenæus, *Adv. Hær.* I. 25.

[17] The date of the rise of Gnosticism cannot be fixed. Indeed, all the requisite conditions existed from the beginning. It was the "acute Verweltlichung" (as Harnack calls it) of Christianity, the development of it in connection with the various ethnic philosophies, and it began as soon as Christianity came in contact with the Greek mind. At first it was not heretical, simply because there were no standards by which to try it. There was only the preaching of the Christians; the canon was not yet formed; episcopacy was not yet established; both arose as safeguards against heresy. It was in the time of Hadrian, perhaps, that these speculations began to be regarded as heresies, because they contradicted certain fundamental truths to which the Christians felt that they must cling, such as the unity of God, his graciousness, his goodness, etc.; and therefore the Christians dated Gnosticism from that time. Gnosticism was ostensibly conquered, but victory was achieved only as the Church itself became in a certain sense Gnostic. It followed the course of Gnosticism a century later; that is, it wrote commentaries, systems of doctrine, &c., philosophizing about religious things (cf. Harnack's *Dogmengeschichte*, I. p. 162 sq.). It must be remembered in reading the Fathers' accounts of Gnosticism that they took minor and unimportant details and magnified them, and treated them as the essentials of the system or systems. In this way far greater variety appears to have existed in Gnosticism than was the case. The essential principles were largely the same throughout; the differences were chiefly in regard to details. It is this conduct on the part of the Fathers that gives us such a distorted and often ridiculous view of Gnosticism.

The Carpocratians are the first of whom Irenæus expressly says that they called themselves Gnostics (*adv. Hær.* I. 25, 6), while Hippolytus first speaks of the name as adopted by the Naasseni (V. 1). The Carpocratians are mentioned by Hegesippus (quoted below in chap. 22). The system was more exclusively Greek in its character than any other of the Gnostic systems. The immorality of the sect was proverbial; Tertullian (*de Anima*, c. 35) calls Carpocrates a magician and a fornicator. He taught the superiority of man over the powers of the world, the moral indifference of things in themselves, and hence, whether he himself was immoral or not, his followers carried out his principles to the extreme, and believed that the true Gnostic might and even must have experience of everything, and therefore should practice all sorts of immoralities.

Eusebius is probably right in assigning Carpocrates to this period. The relation of his system to those of Saturninus and Basilides seems to imply that he followed them, but at no great interval. Other sources for a knowledge of Carpocrates and his sect are Irenæus (I. 25 and II. 31-33), Clement of Alexandria (*Strom.* III. 2), Hippolytus (*Phil.* VII. 20), Tertullian (*de Anima*, 23, 35), Pseudo-Tertullian (*adv. omnes Hær.* 3), Epiphanius (*Hær.* 27), and Philaster (c. 35). Of these only Irenæus, Clement of Alexandria, and the earlier treatise of Hippolytus (which lies at the base of Pseudo-Tertullian and Philaster) are independent; and probably, back of Irenæus, lies Justin Martyr's lost *Syntagma;* though it is very likely that Irenæus knew the sect personally, and made additions of his own. Compare Harnack's *Quellenkritik des Gnosticismus*, p. 41 sq.

[18] ἐκεῖνος, referring back to Basilides.

[19] Where Eusebius secured the information that the Carpocratians made the magic rites of Simon public, instead of keeping them secret, as Basilides had done, I cannot tell. None of our existing sources mentions this fact, and whether Eusebius took it from some lost source, or whether it is simply a deduction of his own, I am not certain. In other respects his account agrees closely with that of Irenæus. It is possible that he had seen the lost work of Hippolytus (see below, VI. 22, note 9), and from that had picked up this item which he states as a fact. But the omission of it in Philaster, Pseudo-Tertullian, and Epiphanius are against this supposition. Justin's *Syntagma* Eusebius probably never saw (see below, chap. 11, note 31).

obligations to them all by infamous con-
10   duct. Thus it came to pass that the malignant demon, making use of these ministers,
on the one hand enslaved those that were so
pitiably led astray by them to their own destruction, while on the other hand he furnished to
the unbelieving heathen abundant opportunities
for slandering the divine word, inasmuch as the
reputation of these men brought infamy
11   upon the whole race of Christians. In this
way, therefore, it came to pass that there
was spread abroad in regard to us among the
unbelievers of that age, the infamous and most
absurd suspicion that we practiced unlawful
commerce with mothers and sisters, and
12   enjoyed impious feasts.[20] He did not, however, long succeed in these artifices, as the
truth established itself and in time shone
13   with great brilliancy. For the machinations
of its enemies were refuted by its power
and speedily vanished. One new heresy arose
after another, and the former ones always passed
away, and now at one time, now at another, now
in one way, now in other ways, were lost in ideas
of various kinds and various forms. But the
splendor of the catholic and only true Church,
which is always the same, grew in magnitude
and power, and reflected its piety and simplicity and freedom, and the modesty and purity of
its inspired life and philosophy to every na-
14   tion both of Greeks and of Barbarians. At the
same time the slanderous accusations which
had been brought against the whole Church[21]

also vanished, and there remained our teaching alone, which has prevailed over all, and
which is acknowledged to be superior to all in
dignity and temperance, and in divine and philosophical doctrines. So that none of them now
ventures to affix a base calumny upon our faith,
or any such slander as our ancient enemies
formerly delighted to utter. Nevertheless,   15
in those times the truth again called forth
many champions who fought in its defense against
the godless heresies, refuting them not only with
oral, but also with written arguments.[22]

CHAPTER VIII.

Ecclesiastical Writers.

AMONG these Hegesippus was well   1
known.[1] We have already quoted his
words a number of times,[2] relating events which
happened in the time of the apostles according to his account. He records in five   2
books the true tradition of apostolic doctrine in a most simple style, and he indicates
the time in which he flourished when he writes
as follows concerning those that first set up
idols: " To whom they erected cenotaphs and
temples, as is done to the present day. Among
whom is also Antinoüs,[3] a slave of the Emperor
Adrian, in whose honor are celebrated also the
Antinoian games, which were instituted in our
day. For he [i.e. Adrian] also founded a city
named after Antinoüs,[4] and appointed prophets."

At the same time also Justin, a genuine lover   3
of the true philosophy, was still continuing
to busy himself with Greek literature.[5] He indicates this time in the Apology which he addressed
to Antonine, where he writes as follows: [6] " We
do not think it out of place to mention here
Antinoüs also, who lived in our day, and whom all

---

[20] The chief accusations urged against the early Christians by
their antagonists were atheism, cannibalism, and incest. These
charges were made very early. Justin Martyr (*Apol.* I. 26) mentions them, and Pliny in his epistle to Trajan speaks of the innocent
meals of the Christians, implying that they had been accused of
immorality in connection with them. (Compare, also, Tertullian's
Apol. 7, 8, and *Ad Nationes*, 7.) In fact, suspicions arose among
the heathen as soon as their love feasts became secret. The persecution in Lyons is to be explained only by the belief of the officers
that these and similar accusations were true. The Christians commonly denied all such charges *in toto*, and supported their denial by
urging the absurdity of such conduct; but sometimes, as in the
present case, they endeavored to exonerate themselves by attributing the crimes with which they were charged to heretics. This
course, however, helped them little with the heathen, as the latter
did not distinguish between the various parties of Christians, but
treated them all as one class. The statement of Eusebius in the
present case is noteworthy. He thinks that the crimes were really
committed by heretics, and occasioned the accusations of the heathen,
and he thus admits that the charges were founded upon fact. In
this case he acts toward the heretics in the same way that the heathen acted toward the Christians as a whole. This method of exon-
erating themselves appears as early as Justin Martyr (compare his
Apol. I. 26). Irenæus also (I. 25, 3), whom Eusebius substantially
follows in this passage, and Philaster (c. 57), pursue the same
course.

[21] Eusebius is correct in his statement that such accusations were
no longer made in his day. The Church had, in fact, lived them
down completely. It is noticeable that in the elaborate work of
Celsus against the Christians, no such charges are found. From
Origen (*Contra Cels.* VI. 27), however, we learn that there were
still in his time some who believed these reports about the Christians, though they were no longer made the basis of serious attacks.
Whether Eusebius' synchronization of the cessation of these slanderous stories with the cessation of the heresies of which he has
been talking, is correct, we cannot be certain, as we know neither exactly
when these heresies ran out, nor precisely the time at which the
accusations ceased. At any rate, we cannot fully agree with Eusebius' explanation of the matter. The two things were hardly connected as direct cause and effect, though it cannot be denied that
the actual immoralities of some of these antinomian sects may have
had some effect in confirming these tales, and hence that their ex-

tinction may have had some tendency to hasten the obliteration of
the vile reports.
[22] See above, note 10.
[1] On the life and writings of Hegesippus, see below, chap. 22,
note 1. Eusebius in this passage puts his literary activity too early
(see above, chap. 7, note 10). Jerome follows Eusebius' chronological arrangement in his *de vir ill.*, giving an account of Hegesippus
in chap. 22, between his accounts of Agrippa Castor and Justin
Martyr.
[2] Already quoted in Bk. II. chap. 23, and in Bk. III. chap. 32.
[3] Antinoüs, a native of Bithynia, was a beautiful page of the
Emperor Hadrian, and the object of his extravagant affections. He
was probably drowned in the Nile, in 130 A.D. After his death he
was raised to the rank of the gods, and temples were built for his
worship in many parts of the empire, especially in Egypt. In Athens
too games were instituted in his honor, and games were also celebrated every fifth year at Mantinea, in Arcadia, according to Valesius, who cites Pausanias as his authority.
[4] Hadrian rebuilt the city of Besa in the Thebais, in whose neighborhood Antinoüs was drowned, and called it Antinoöpolis.
[5] On Justin Martyr, see chap. 16, below. We do not know the
date of his conversion, but as it did not take place until mature years,
it is highly probable that he was still a heathen during the greater
part of Hadrian's reign. There is no reason, however, to suppose
that Eusebius is speaking here with more than approximate accuracy. He may not have known any better than we the exact time
of Justin's conversion.
[6] Justin, *Apol.* I. 29.

were driven by fear to worship as a god, although they knew who he was and whence he came."

4   The same writer, speaking of the Jewish war which took place at that time, adds the following :[7] "For in the late Jewish war Barcocheba, the leader of the Jewish rebellion, commanded that Christians alone[8] should be visited with terrible punishments unless they would

5   deny and blaspheme Jesus Christ." And in the same work he shows that his conversion from Greek philosophy to Christianity[9] was not without reason, but that it was the result of deliberation on his part. His words are as follows :[10] "For I myself, while I was delighted with the doctrines of Plato, and heard the Christians slandered, and saw that they were afraid neither of death nor of anything else ordinarily looked upon as terrible, concluded that it was impossible that they could be living in wickedness and pleasure. For what pleasure-loving or intemperate man, or what man that counts it good to feast on human flesh, could welcome death that he might be deprived of his enjoyments, and would not rather strive to continue permanently his present life, and to escape the notice of the rulers, instead of giving him-

6   self up to be put to death?" The same writer, moreover, relates that Adrian having received from Serennius Granianus,[11] a most distinguished governor, a letter[12] in behalf of the Christians, in which he stated that it was not just to slay the Christians without a regular accusation and trial, merely for the sake of gratifying the outcries of the populace, sent a rescript[13] to Minucius Fundanus,[14] proconsul of Asia, com-

manding him to condemn no one without an indictment and a well-grounded accusation.

And he gives a copy of the epistle, preserv-   7 ing the original Latin in which it was written,[15] and prefacing it with the following words :[16] "Although from the epistle of the greatest and most illustrious Emperor Adrian, your father, we have good ground to demand that you order judgment to be given as we have desired, yet we have asked this not because it was ordered by Adrian, but rather because we know that what we ask is just. And we have subjoined the copy of Adrian's epistle that you may know that we are

---

[7] Justin, *Apol.* I. 31.

[8] χριστιανοὺς μόνους. "This ' alone ' is, as Münter remarks, not to be understood as implying that Barcocheba did not treat the Greeks and Romans also with cruelty, but that he persecuted the Christians especially, from religious hate, if he could not compel them to apostatize. Moreover, he handled the Christians so roughly because of their hesitation to take part in the rebellion" (Closs).

[9] ἐπὶ τὴν θεοσέβειαν.

[10] Justin, *Apol.* II. 12. Eusebius here quotes from what is now known as the Second Apology of Justin, but identifies it with the first, from which he has quoted just above. This implies that the two as he knew them formed but one work, and this is confirmed by his quotations in chaps. 16 and 17, below. For a discussion of this matter, see chap. 18, note 3.

[11] The best MSS. of Eusebius write the name Σερέννιος Γρανιανός, but one MS., supported by Syncellus, writes the first word Σερένιος. Rufinus writes "Serenius"; Jerome, in his version of Eusebius' *Chronicle*, followed by Orosius (VII. 13), writes "Serenius Granius," and this, according to Kortholdt (quoted by Heinichen), is shown by an inscription to have been the correct form (see Heinichen's edition, *in loco*). We know no more of this man, except that he was Minucius Fundanus' predecessor as proconsul of Asia, as we learn from the opening sentence of the rescript quoted in the next chapter.

[12] γράμματα. The plural is often used like the Latin *literæ* to denote a single epistle, and we learn from the opening sentence of the rescript itself (if the Greek of Eusebius is to be relied on) that Hadrian replies, not to a number of letters, but to a single one, — an ἐπιστολή, as Eusebius calls it.

[13] ἀντιγράψαι.

[14] This Minucius Fundanus is the same person that is addressed by Pliny, *Ep.* I. 9 (see Mommsen's note in Keil's ed. of Pliny's epistles, p. 419). He is mentioned also by Melito (Eusebius, IV. 26) as proconsul of Asia, and it is there said that Hadrian wrote to him concerning the Christians. The authenticity of this rescript is a disputed point. Keim (*Theol. Jahrbücher*, 1856, p. 387 sqq.) was the first to dispute its genuineness. He has been followed by many scholars, especially Overbeck, who gives a very keen discussion of

the various edicts of the early emperors relating to the Christians in his *Studien zur Gesch. der alten Kirche*, I. p. 93 sqq. The genuineness of the edict, however, has been defended against Keim's attack by Wieseler, Renan, Lightfoot, and others. The whole question hinges upon the interpretation of the rescript. According to Gieseler, Neander, and some others, it is aimed only against tumultuous proceedings, and, far from departing from the principle laid down by Trajan, is an attempt to return to that principle and to substitute orderly judicial processes for popular attacks. If this be the sense of the edict, there is no reason to doubt its genuineness, but the next to the last sentence certainly cannot be interpreted in that way: "if any one therefore brings an accusation, and shows that they have done something contrary to the laws (τι παρὰ τοὺς νόμους) determine thus *according to the heinousness of the crime*" (κατὰ τὴν δύναμιν τοῦ ἁμαρτήματος). These last words are very significant. They certainly imply various crimes of which the prisoners are supposed to be accused. According to the heinousness of these crimes the punishment is to be regulated. In other words, the trial of the Christians was to be for the purpose of ascertaining whether they were guilty of moral or political crimes, not whether they merely professed Christianity; that is, the profession of Christianity, according to this rescript, is not treated as a crime in and of itself. If the edict then be genuine, Hadrian reversed completely Trajan's principle of procedure which was to punish the profession of Christianity in and of itself as a crime. But in the time of Antoninus Pius and Marcus Aurelius the rescript of Trajan is seen still to be in full force. For this and other reasons presented by Keim and Overbeck, I am constrained to class this edict with those of Antoninus Pius and Marcus Aurelius as a forgery. It can hardly have been composed while Hadrian was still alive, but must have been forged before Justin wrote his Apology, for he gives it as a genuine edict, i.e. it must belong to the early part of the reign of Antoninus Pius.

The illusion under which the early Christian writers labored in regard to the relations of the emperors to Christianity is very remarkable. Both Melito and Tertullian state that no emperor had persecuted the Christians except Nero and Domitian. Christian writers throughout the second century talk in fact as if the mode of treatment which they were receiving was something new and strange, and in opposition to the better treatment which previous emperors had accorded the Christians. In doing this, they ignore entirely the actual edicts of the emperors, all of which are now lost, and notice only forged edicts which are favorable to the Christians; when and by whom they were forged we do not know. Thus Tertullian, in addressing Septimius Severus, speaks of the favors which his predecessors had granted the Christians and contrasts their conduct with his; Melito addresses Marcus Aurelius in the same way, and so Justin addresses Antoninus Pius. This method probably arose from a misunderstanding of the original edict of Trajan (cf. Bk. III. chap. 33, note 6), which they all considered favorable, and therefore presupposed a friendly attitude on the part of the emperors toward the Christians, which, not finding in their own age, they naturally transferred to a previous age. This led gradually to the idea — which Lactantius first gives precise expression to — that only the bad emperors persecuted Christianity, while the good ones were favorable to it. But after the empire became Christian, the belief became common that all the heathen emperors had been persecutors, the good as well as the bad; — all the Christian emperors were placed upon one level, and all the heathen on another, the latter being looked upon, like Nero and Domitian, as wicked tyrants. Compare Overbeck, *l.c.*

[15] Our two MSS. of Justin have substituted the Greek translation of Eusebius for the Latin original given by the former. Rufinus, however, in his version of Eusebius' *History*, gives a Latin translation which is very likely the original one. Compare Kimmel's *De Rufino*, p. 175 sq., and Lightfoot's *Ignatius*, I. p. 463 sq., and see Otto's *Corpus Apol.* I. p. 190 sq., where the edict is given, both in the Greek of our MSS. of Justin and in the Latin of Rufinus. Keim (*Aus dem Urchristenthum*, p. 184 sq.) contends that the Latin of Rufinus is not the original, but a translation of Eusebius' Greek. His arguments, however, do not possess any real weight, and the majority of scholars accept Kimmel's view.

[16] Justin, *Apol.* I. 68.

speaking the truth in this matter also. And
8 this is the copy." After these words the
author referred to gives the rescript in
Latin, which we have translated into Greek as
accurately as we could.[17] It reads as follows :

CHAPTER IX.

*The Epistle of Adrian, decreeing that we should
not be punished without a Trial.*

1   " To Minucius Fundanus. I have received
an epistle,[1] written to me by Serennius
Granianus, a most illustrious man, whom you
have succeeded. It does not seem right to me
that the matter should be passed by without
examination, lest the men[2] be harassed and
opportunity be given to the informers for
2 practicing villainy. If, therefore, the inhabitants of the province can clearly sustain
this petition against the Christians so as to give
answer in a court of law, let them pursue this
course alone, but let them not have resort to
men's petitions and outcries. For it is far more
proper, if any one wishes to make an accusation, that you should examine into it.
3   If any one therefore accuses them and
shows that they are doing anything contrary to the laws, do you pass judgment according to the heinousness of the crime.[3] But, by
Hercules ! if any one bring an accusation
through mere calumny, decide in regard to his
criminality,[4] and see to it that you inflict punishment."[5]
Such are the contents of Adrian's rescript.

CHAPTER X.

*The Bishops of Rome and of Alexandria during
the Reign of Antoninus.*

ADRIAN having died after a reign of twenty-
one years,[1] was succeeded in the government of
the Romans by Antoninus, called the Pious.
In the first year of his reign Telesphorus[2] died
in the eleventh year of his episcopate, and Hyginus became bishop of Rome.[3] Irenæus
records that Telesphorus' death was made glorious by martyrdom,[4] and in the same connection he states that in the time of the above-
mentioned Roman bishop Hyginus, Valentinus,
the founder of a sect of his own, and Cerdon,
the author of Marcion's error, were both well
known at Rome.[5] He writes as follows : [6]

CHAPTER XI.

The Heresiarchs of that Age.

" FOR Valentinus came to Rome under   1
Hyginus, flourished under Pius, and remained until Anicetus.[1] Cerdon[2] also, Mar-

---

[17] We cannot judge as to the faithfulness of the Greek translation which follows, because we are not absolutely sure whether
the Latin of Rufinus is its original, or itself a translation of it.
Eusebius and Rufinus, however, agree very well, and if the
Latin of Rufinus is the original of Eusebius' translation, the latter has succeeded much better than the Greek translator of the
Apology of Tertullian referred to in Bk. II. chap. 2, above. We
should expect, however, that much greater pains would be taken
with the translation of a brief official document of this kind than
with such a work as Tertullian's *Apology*, and Eusebius' translation
of the rescript does not by any means prove that he was a fluent
Latin scholar. As remarked above (Bk. II. chap. 2, note 9), he
probably had comparatively little acquaintance with the Latin, but
enough to enable him to translate brief passages for himself in cases
of necessity.
[1] Greek, ἐπιστολήν; Latin, *litteras.*
[2] Greek, οἱ ἄνθρωποι; Latin, *innoxii.*
[3] This is the only really suspicious sentence in the edict. That
Hadrian should desire to protect his Christian subjects as well as
others from tumultuous and illegal proceedings, and from unfounded
accusations, would be of course quite natural, and quite in accord
with the spirit shown by Trajan in his rescript. But in this one
sentence he implies that the Christians are to be condemned only
for actual crimes, and that the mere profession of Christianity is not
in itself a punishable offense. Much, therefore, as we might otherwise be tempted to accept the edict as genuine, — natural as the
style is and the position taken in the other portions of it, — this one
sentence, considered in the light of all that we know of the attitude
of Hadrian's predecessors and successors toward the Christians, and
of all that we can gather of his own views, must, as I believe, condemn it as a forgery.
[4] Compare this sentence with the closing words of the forged
edict of Antoninus Pius quoted by Eusebius in chap. 13. Not only
are the Christians to be released, but their accusers are to be punished. Still there is a difference between the two commands in that
here only an accusation made with the purpose of slander is to be
punished, while there the accuser is to be unconditionally held as
guilty, if actual crimes are not proved against the accused Christian.

The latter command would be subversive of all justice, and brands
itself as a counterfeit on its very face; but in the present case the
injunction to enforce the law forbidding slander against those who
should slanderously accuse the Christians is not inconsistent with
the principles of Trajan and Hadrian, and hence not of itself alone
an evidence of ungenuineness.
[5] Greek, ὅπως ἂν ἐκδικήσειας; Latin, *suppliciis severioribus
vindices.*
[1] Hadrian reigned from Aug. 8, 117, to July 10, 138 A.D.
[2] On Telesphorus, see above, chap. 5, note 13. The date given
here by Eusebius (138–139 A.D.) is probably (as remarked there) at
least a year too late.
[3] We know very little about Hyginus. His dates can be fixed
with tolerable certainty as 137–141, the duration of his episcopate
being four years, as Eusebius states in the next chapter. See Lipsius' *Chron. d. röm. Bischöfe*, p. 169 and 263. The Roman martyrologies make him a martyr, but this means nothing, as the early
bishops of Rome almost without exception are called martyrs by
these documents. The forged decretals ascribe to him the introduction of a number of ecclesiastical rites.
[4] In his *Adv. Hær.* III. 3. 3. The testimony of Irenæus rests
upon Roman tradition at this point, and is undoubtedly reliable.
Telesphorus is the first Roman bishop whom we know to have
suffered martyrdom, although the Roman Catholic Church celebrates
as martyrs all the so-called popes down to the fourth century.
[5] On Valentinus, Cerdon, and Marcion, see the next chapter.
[6] Irenæus, *Adv. Hær.* III. 4. 3.
[1] Valentinus is the best known of the Gnostics. According to
Epiphanius (*Hær.* XXXI. 2) he was born on the coast of Egypt,
and studied Greek literature and science at Alexandria. The same
writer, on the authority of the lost *Syntagma* of Hippolytus, informs
us that he taught in Cyprus, and this must have been before he went
to Rome. The direct statement of Irenæus as to the date of his
activity is confirmed by Tertullian, and perhaps by Clement
of Alexandria, and is not to be doubted. Since Hyginus held office
in all probability from 137–141, and Anicetus from 154 or 155 to 166
or 167, Valentinus must have been in Rome at least thirteen years.
His chronological position between Basilides and Marcion (as given
by Clement of Alexandria, *Strom.* VII. 17) makes it probable that
he came to Rome early in Antoninus' reign, and remained there
during all or the most of that reign, but not longer. Valentinus'
followers divided into two schools, an Oriental and an Italian, and
constituted by far the most numerous and influential Gnostic sect.
His system is the most profound and artistic of the Gnostic systems,
and reveals great depth and power of mind. For an excellent
account of Valentinus and Valentinianism, see Lipsius' article in
the *Dict. of Christ. Biog.* Vol. IV. Valentinus occupies a prominent place in all works on Gnosticism.
[2] Cerdon is best known as the teacher of Marcion. Epiphanius
(*Hær.* XLI.) and Philaster (*Hær.* XLIV.) call him a native of Syria.

cion's[3] predecessor, entered the Church in the time of Hyginus, the ninth[4] bishop, and made confession, and continued in this way, now teaching in secret, now making confession again, and now denounced for corrupt doctrine and withdrawing[5] from the assembly of the brethren." These words are found in the third book of
2　the work Against Heresies. And again in the first book he speaks as follows concerning Cerdon :[6] "A certain Cerdon, who had taken his system from the followers of Simon, and had come to Rome under Hyginus, the ninth in the episcopal succession from the apostles,[7] taught that the God proclaimed by the law and prophets was not the father of our Lord Jesus Christ. For the former was known, but the latter un-

known ; and the former was just, but the latter good.[8] Marcion of Pontus succeeded Cerdon and developed his doctrine, uttering shameless blasphemies." The same Irenæus un-　3 folds with the greatest vigor the unfathomable abyss of Valentinus' errors in regard to matter, and reveals his wickedness, secret and hidden like a serpent lurking in its nest. And　4 in addition to these men he says that there was also another that lived in that age, Marcus by name,[9] who was remarkably skilled in magic arts. And he describes also their unholy initiations and their abominable mysteries in the following words :[10] "For some of them pre-　5 pare a nuptial couch and perform a mystic rite with certain forms of expression addressed to those who are being initiated, and they say that it is a spiritual marriage which is celebrated by them, after the likeness of the marriages above. But others lead them to water, and while they baptize them they repeat the following words : Into the name of the unknown father of the universe, into truth, the mother of all things, into the one that descended upon Jesus.[11] Others repeat Hebrew names[12] in order the better to confound those who are being initiated."

But Hyginus[13] having died at the close　6 of the fourth year of his episcopate, Pius[14]

Epiphanius speaks of a sect of Cerdonians, but there seems never to have been such a sect, and his disciples probably early became followers of Marcion, who joined Cerdon soon after reaching Rome. It is not possible to distinguish his teachings from those of his pupil, Marcion. Hippolytus (X. 15) treats Cerdon and Marcion together, making no attempt to distinguish their doctrines. Irenæus, in the passage quoted, and the lost *Syntagma* of Hippolytus (represented by Pseudo-Tertullian's *Adv. Hær.* and by Epiphanius) distinguish the two, treating Cerdon separately but very briefly. The doctrines of Cerdon, however, given by them, are identical with or at least very similar to the known views of Marcion. If they were really Cerdon's positions before Marcion came to him, then his influence over Marcion was most decided.

[3] On Marcion, see below, note 24.
[4] The Latin text of Irenæus here reads "eighth" instead of "ninth." See below, note 7.
[5] ἐφιστάμενος. This is commonly taken to mean that Cerdon was excommunicated. But as Valesius remarks, the participle is strictly middle, not passive. The distinction, however, cannot be insisted upon in the present case, and therefore we cannot determine decisively whether Cerdon was excluded by the congregation or excluded himself.
[6] Irenæus, *Adv. Hær.* I. 27. 1–2.
[7] Hyginus is here called the ninth bishop, and the reading is confirmed by a passage in Cyprian's epistle to Pompey (*Ep.* LXXIII. 2 in the *Ante-Nicene Fathers*), and also by Epiphanius (*Hær.* LXI. 1). In the passage quoted just above, however, from the third book of Irenæus, although Eusebius calls Hyginus the "ninth," the Latin text of Irenæus makes him the "eighth," and according to Salmon in the *Dict. of Christ. Biog.* : "The MS. evidence is decisive that Irenæus here [in the passage quoted above from III. 4. 3] describes Hyginus as the eighth bishop, and this agrees with the list of Roman bishops given in the preceding chapter (*Adv. Hær.* III. 3. 3), and with the description of Anicetus as the tenth bishop a couple of chapters further on. Lipsius hence infers that Irenæus drew his account of Cerdon from two sources in which Hyginus was differently described, but this inference is very precarious. In the interval between the composition of the first and third books, Irenæus may have been led to alter his way of counting by investigations concerning the succession of the Roman bishops, which he had in the meantime either made himself, or adopted from Hegesippus. As for the numeration 'ninth,' we do not venture to pronounce whether it indicates a list in which Peter was counted first bishop, or one in which Cletus and Anacletus were reckoned as distinct." According to Eusebius' own reckoning up to the present chapter, Hyginus was the eighth, not the ninth, from the apostles, for in chap. 5, above, he calls Telesphorus (Hyginus' predecessor) the seventh, in chap. 1, Alexander (the predecessor of Xystus, who preceded Telesphorus) the fifth, and so on. Why, in the passage quoted at the beginning of this chapter, he should change his reckoning, and call Hyginus the ninth if the original list of Irenæus from which he drew said eighth is difficult to see. It is possible that he made the change under the influence of the "ninth," in the present passage, which certainly stood in the original text. It would be easier to think this if the order in which the passages were quoted were reversed, but it may be that Eusebius had the present quotation in mind when making the first, or that he went back afterward and corrected that to correspond. If he ventured to change the text of Irenæus in that passage, he must have done it in all good faith, assuming a mistake in transcription, where the contradiction was so glaring. It still remains to me inexplicable, however, why he did not change the "ninth" of the second passage to "eighth" instead of the "eighth" of the first passage to "ninth." He would thus have gotten rid of all contradictions, and have remained consistent with himself. I am tempted, in fact, to believe that Eusebius found "ninth" in the original of both passages quoted, and copied just what he found. At the same time, I do not feel disposed in the face of what Lipsius and Salmon say as to the original text of Irenæus to claim that Irenæus himself wrote "ninth" at that point.

[8] Marcion drew this same distinction between the strictly just God of the Old Testament and the good or merciful God of the New, and the distinction was a fundamental one in his system. It is noticeable that Pseudo-Tertullian (*Adv. Omnes Hær.* chap. 6) says that Cerdon taught two Gods, one good, the other cruel (*sævum*) ; the good being the superior God, — the latter, the cruel one, being the creator of the world.
[9] Irenæus gives an account of Marcus and the Marcosians in I. 13–21. He was a Gnostic of the sect of Valentinus. Jerome calls him a Basilidian (*Ep.* LXXV. 3), but he was mistaken. Hippolytus and Epiphanius (*Hær.* 34) copy their accounts from Irenæus, and probably had no direct knowledge of the works of Marcus, or of his sect. Clement of Alexandria, however, knew and used his writings. It is probable that Asia Minor was the scene of his labors. He is spoken of in the present tense by Irenæus, and hence seems to have been alive when he wrote ; that is, in the latter part of the second century. His additions to Valentinianism lay chiefly, perhaps solely, in the introduction of worthless magic rites. He seems to have lowered greatly the tone of the philosophical Gnosticism of Valentinus. See Salmon's article in the *Dict. of Christ. Biog.*
[10] Irenæus, *Adv. Hær.* I. 21. 3.
[11] εἰς τὸν κατελθόντα εἰς τὸν Ἰησοῦν. Taking the Greek simply as it stands, we should naturally put a comma before the second εἰς, and translate " into the one that descended, into Jesus," identifying the " one that descended" with Jesus. But the Gnostics in general taught that Jesus was only a man, upon whom descended one of the æons, or higher spiritual powers, and hence it is plain that in the present case the " one that descended upon [or literally "into"] Jesus " is referred to here as the third person of the baptismal Trinity.
[12] The Greek and Latin texts of Irenæus add at this point widely variant lists of these words, but in both lists the words are quite meaningless.
[13] On Hyginus, see the previous chapter, note 3.
[14] Eusebius states, just below, that Pius held office fifteen years, and in his *Chronicle* he gives the same figure. In that work (Armen. version) he places his accession in the first year of Antoninus Pius, though the version of Jerome assigns it to the fifth year, and with this Eusebius agrees in his *History*, for in the previous chapter he puts the accession of Hyginus in the first year of Antoninus Pius, and here tells us that Hyginus held office four years. Lipsius assigns Pius' episcopate to the years 139–154, as the earliest possible termini ; the years 141–156 as the latest. But since we learn from chapter 14, below, that Polycarp was in Rome during the episcopate of Anicetus, and from other sources (see chapter 15, note 2) that he was martyred in Asia Minor in 155 or 156, we may assume it as certain that Pius cannot have held office as late as 156. The earlier date for his death (154) may therefore be accepted as more probable.

succeeded him in the government of the church of Rome. In Alexandria Marcus [15] was appointed pastor, after Eumenes [16] had filled the office thirteen years in all. And Marcus having died after holding office ten years was succeeded by Celadion [17] in the government of the church of Alexandria. And in Rome Pius died in the fifteenth year of his episcopate, and Anicetus [18] assumed the leadership of the Christians there. Hegesippus records that he himself was in Rome at this time, and that he remained there until the episcopate of Eleutherus.[19]

8   But Justin [20] was especially prominent in those days. In the guise of a philosopher [21] he preached the divine word, and contended for the faith in his writings. He wrote also a work against Marcion,[22] in which he states that the latter was alive at the time he wrote. He speaks as follows : [23] "And there is a certain Marcion [24] of Pontus,[25] who is even now   9

not have been far from the beginning of the second century. He was born in Flavia Neapolis, a Roman town built close by the ruins of the ancient Sychem, in Samaria. He was of heathen parentage, and received a thoroughly Greek education. He became an earnest student of philosophy, and after turning to many different systems in his search for truth, he was at last converted to Christianity, where he found that for which he had been searching; and his whole conception of Christianity shows the influence of the manner in which he accepted it. The date of his conversion is unknown, but it seems (from *Dial.* I. 1) to have taken place at least before the close of the Barcochba war (135 A.D.). He died as a martyr at Rome. The date of his death is difficult to determine, but it probably took place under Marcus Aurelius, in 163+. Upon his death, see below, chap. 16, note 4. Upon Justin, see Semich's *Justin der Märtyrer*, Otto's edition of the Greek Apologists, von Engelhardt's article in Herzog, 2d ed., Holland's article in Smith and Wace's *Dict. of Christ. Biog.*, and finally Schaff's *Ch. Hist.* II. p. 110 sq., where the most important literature is mentioned. Upon his theology, see especially von Engelhardt's masterly monograph, *Das Christenthum Justins des Märtyrers* (Erlangen, 1878). A recent and interesting discussion of Justin's testimony to early Christianity is found in Purves' work on that subject (New York, 1889).

[21] ἐν σχήματι φιλοσόφου. The reference here is to the distinctive cloak or mantle of the Greek philosophers, which was called the *pallium*, and to which Justin refers in his *Dial. c. Trypho*, § 1. The wearing of the mantle was an advantage to the philosophers, inasmuch as it gave them peculiar opportunities to engage in philosophic discourse in the street or market, or other public places, which they could not otherwise so easily have enjoyed. Perhaps it was this fact which led Justin to continue wearing the cloak, and we see from the introduction to his Dialogue that it was the wearing of it which was the immediate occasion of his conversation with Trypho and his friends. Heraclas, the friend of Origen, also continued to wear the philosopher's cloak after his conversion, as we learn from Bk. VI. chap. 19.

[22] This work against Marcion is also mentioned by Irenæus, who quotes from it in his *Adv. Hær.* IV. 16. 2 (see below, chap. 18), and by Photius, *Cod.* 125. The work is lost, and we have only the single brief fragment preserved by Irenæus. It is possible that it formed a part of the larger *Syntagma contra omnes Hæreses*, mentioned by Justin in his *Apol.* I. 26 (see below), and it has been urged in support of this possibility that Irenæus nowhere mentions a work of Justin's *Against all Heresies*, although it is highly probable that he made use of such a work (see Lipsius' *Quellen der ältesten Ketzergesch.* and Harnack's *Zur Quellenkritik des Gnosticismus*). It would seem that Irenæus is referring to this work when he mentions the *Syntagma contra Marcionem*. On the other hand, Photius mentions the work against Marcion and the one against all heresies as two separate works. He does not seem, however, to have had a personal knowledge of them, and is possibly only repeating Eusebius (Harnack says he is certainly doing so, *Ueberlieferung d. griech. Apol.* p. 150; but in view of the fact that he omits two works mentioned by Eusebius, this seems to me somewhat doubtful); and if this is so, no reliance is to be placed upon his report, for it is evident that Eusebius himself knew neither of the two works, and hence the fact that he distinguishes them has no significance. Although, therefore, it cannot be determined whether Justin wrote two separate works against heretics, it is quite probable that he did not.

The conduct of Eusebius in this connection is very peculiar. After mentioning the work against Marcion, he at once gives a quotation in such a way as to convey the impression that the quotation is taken from this work, but it is really taken from the first *Apology*. This makes it very probable that he had not seen this work against Marcion, a conclusion which is confirmed by its omission from the list of Justin's writings given in chap. 18. It is claimed by many that Eusebius practices a little deception here, wishing to convey the impression that he knew a book which he did not know. This is not in accord with his usual conduct (as he seldom hesitates to confess his ignorance of any matter), and his general character for candor and honesty must be taken into account in deciding the case. He does not state directly that the quotation is taken from the work against Marcion, and it is possible that the seeming reference of it to that source was an oversight on his part. But it must be acknowledged, if that be the case, that he was very careless in making the quotation.   [23] Justin, *Apol.* I. 26.

[24] Marcion cannot be called a Gnostic in the strict sense of the term. He was rather an anti-Jewish reformer. He had much in common with the Gnostics, but laid stress upon belief rather than upon knowledge. He developed no complete system as did the other Gnostics, but aimed at a practical reform in the interest of an extreme and perverted Paulinism, considering Paul the only true apostle and rejecting the others as Judaizing teachers. He cut the Gospel away from its historical connections, repudiating the Old

---

The Liberian and Felician Catalogues put Anicetus between Hyginus and Pius; but that is certainly incorrect, for, in support of the order given here by Eusebius, we have the testimony both of Hegesippus, quoted below, in chap. 22, and of Irenæus (III. 3). Pius is commonly regarded as the first monarchical bishop in the strict sense, the so-called bishops before his time having been simply leading presbyters or presbyter bishops of the Roman church (see chap. 11, note 14). According to the Muratorian Fragment and the Liberian Catalogue, Pius was the brother of Hermas, the author of the *Shepherd.* Upon this alleged relationship, see Bk. III. chap. 3, note 23.

[15] Of Marcus we know only what Eusebius tells us here: that he succeeded Eumenes, after the latter had held office thirteen years, and that he continued in office ten years. If Eumenes became bishop in 132 or 133 (see above, chap. 5, note 16), then Marcus must have succeeded him in 145 or 146, and this agrees with the Armenian *Chron.* of Eusebius, which, while it does not mention the accession of Marcus, yet puts the accession of his successor Celadin in the eighteenth year of Antoninus Pius, which would make the beginning of his own episcopate the eighth year of the same ruler. Jerome's version of the *Chron.*, however, puts it in the sixth year. Little reliance is to be placed upon any of the dates of the Alexandrian bishops during the first two centuries.

[16] Of Eumenes, see above, chap. 5, note 14.

[17] Of Celadion we know only what Eusebius tells us here, and in chap. 19, where he gives fourteen years as the duration of his episcopate. As mentioned in the previous note, the Armenian *Chron.* of Eusebius puts his accession in the eighteenth year of Antoninus Pius, i.e. 155 or 156, while the version of Jerome puts it in the sixteenth year.

[18] Anicetus, according to the Armenian *Chron.* of Eusebius, succeeded Pius in the fifteenth year of Antoninus Pius; according to Jerome's version, in the eighteenth year (i.e. 155 or 156), which is more nearly correct. Lipsius puts his accession between 154 and 156 (see note 14, above). According to chap. 19, below, with which both versions of the *Chron.* agree, Anicetus held office eleven years; i.e. until 165 to 167, when he was succeeded by Soter. Irenæus (as quoted by Eusebius in Bk. V. chap. 24) informs us that Polycarp was in Rome in the time of Anicetus, and endeavored to induce him to adopt the Quartodeciman practice of celebrating Easter; but that, while the two remained perfectly friendly to one another, Anicetus would not change the custom of the Roman church (see the notes on the chapter referred to). As stated in note 13, the Liberian and Felician Catalogues incorrectly insert the name of Anicetus between those of Hyginus and Pius.

[19] Eusebius evidently makes a mistake here. That Hegesippus remained so long in Rome (Anicetus ruled from 154-168 (?), and Eleutherus from 177-190) is upon the face of it very improbable. And in this case we can see clearly how Eusebius made his mistake. In chap. 22 he quotes a passage from Hegesippus in regard to his stay in Rome, and it was in all probability this passage from which Eusebius drew his conclusion. But Hegesippus says there that he "remained in Rome until the time of Anicetus," &c. It is probable, therefore, that he returned to the East during Anicetus' episcopacy. He does not express himself as one who had remained in Rome until the reign of Eleutherus; but Eusebius, from a hasty reading, might easily have gathered that idea. According to Hegesippus' account in chap. 22, he must, then, have come to Rome *before* Anicetus, i.e. during the reign of Pius, and this Eusebius does not here contradict, though he is said to do so by Reading, who translates the Greek words, ἐπιδημῆσαι τῇ 'Ρώμῃ, "came to the city" (so, also, Closs, Stigloher, and Crusè). But the words properly mean "to be in Rome," not "to come to Rome," which would require, rather, ἐπιδημῆσαι εἰς τὴν 'Ρώμην, as in § 2, above, where the words are used of Cerdon. Jerome, to be sure (*de vir. ill.* 22), says that Hegesippus came to Rome in the time of Anicetus; but his account rests solely upon Eusebius, whom he mistranslated. The tradition, therefore, that Hegesippus came to Rome in the time of Anicetus has no foundation; he was already there, as he himself informs us, in chap. 22, below. Cf. the note on this passage, in chap. 22.

[20] Eusebius here puts Justin in his proper place, in the time of Antoninus Pius. The date of his birth is unknown, though it can-

still teaching his followers to think that there is some other God greater than the creator. And by the aid of the demons [26] he has persuaded many of every race of men [27] to utter blasphemy, and to deny that the maker of this universe is the father of Christ, and to confess that some other, greater than he, was the creator.[28] And all who followed them are, as we have said,[29] called Christians, just as the name of philosophy is given to philosophers, although they 10 may have no doctrines in common." To this he adds : [30] "And we have also written a work against all the heresies that have existed,[31] which we will give you if you wish to read it."

But this same Justin contended most suc- 11 cessfully against the Greeks, and addressed discourses containing an apology for our faith to the Emperor Antoninus, called Pius, and to the Roman senate.[32] For he lived at Rome. But who and whence he was he shows in his Apology in the following words.[33]

CHAPTER XII.

The Apology of Justin addressed to Antoninus.

"To the Emperor Titus Ælius Adrian Antoninus Pius Cæsar Augustus,[1] and to Verissimus his son,[2] the philosopher, and to Lucius the philosopher,[3] own son of Cæsar and adopted son of Pius, a lover of learning, and to the sacred senate and to the whole Roman people, I, Justin, son of Priscus and grandson of Bacchius,[4] of Flavia Neapolis in Palestine, Syria, present this address and petition in behalf of those men of every nation who are unjustly hated and persecuted, I myself being one of them." And the same emperor having learned also from other brethren in Asia of the injuries of all kinds which they were suffering from the inhabitants of the province, thought it proper to address the following ordinance to the Common Assembly [5] of Asia.

Testament and all of the New except a mutilated Gospel of Luke and the Epistles of Paul, and denying the identity of the God of the Old Testament with the Supreme God, and the identity of Jesus with the promised Jewish Messiah. He magnified the mercy of God in redemption at the expense of creation, which he attributed to the demiurge, and in which he saw nothing good. He was an extreme anti-metaphysician, and the first Biblical critic. He was born in Pontus, was the son of a bishop, went to Rome about 135 A.D., and endeavored to carry out his reforms there, but was unsuccessful, and very soon broke with the Church. He traveled extensively and disseminated his doctrines very widely. The sect existed well on into the Middle Ages, and some of his opinions have never been completely eradicated. In Rome the Gnostic Cerdon exercised great influence over him, and to him are doubtless due many of Marcion's Gnostic traits. The dualism which he held in common with the Gnostics arose rather from practical than speculative considerations; but his followers in the fourth and fifth centuries, when they had lost his practical religious spirit and yet retained his dualism, passed over quite naturally into Manicheeism. He was attacked by Justin, Irenæus, Tertullian, and all the anti-heretical writers of the early Church, and was considered one of the most dangerous of heretics. A complete monograph upon Marcion is still a desideratum, but he is discussed in all the general accounts of Gnosticism; see especially the brief but excellent account by Harnack, *Dogmengeschichte*, I. 197-214.

[25] Pontus was a province in Northeastern Asia Minor, bordering upon the Black Sea.

[26] Justin here agrees with Eusebius in his transcendental theory of heresy, looking upon it not as a natural growth from within, but as an infliction upon the Church from without, through the agency of demons. Indeed, this was the prevailing notion of the early Church.

[27] The extent of Marcion's influence referred to here is very significant. Gnosticism was not intended for common people, and never spread among the masses, but on the contrary was confined to philosophers and speculative thinkers. In this respect, Marcion, whose sect included multitudes of all classes, was distinguished most sharply from them, and it was because of the popularity of his sect that his heresy appeared so dangerous to the early Church.

[28] ἄλλον δέ τινα ὡς, ὄντα μείζονα παρὰ τοῦτον ὁμολογεῖν πεποιηκέναι. The sentence as it thus stands is very difficult to construe, for we are compelled to take the last verb without an object, in the sense of *create*. Our MSS. of Justin Martyr insert after the ὡς ὄντα μείζονα the words τὰ μείζονα, and the sentence then reads, "some other one, greater than he, has done greater works." It is plain that this was the original form of the sentence, and that the harsh construction found in Eusebius is a result of defective transcription. It was very easy for a copyist to drop out the second μείζονα.

[29] Justin refers here to *Apol.* I. 7. He wishes to have it clear that not all that call themselves Christians are really such. From chaps. 26–29, we see that in Justin's time the Christians were accused of great immoralities, and in this same chapter (chap. 26) he is rather inclined to throw the guilt upon heretics, although he does not expressly accuse them of it (" whether they perpetrate these shameful deeds — we know not "). See above, chap. 7, note 20. His mention of philosophers here in his appeal to the philosophical emperors is very shrewd.

[30] *Ibid.* I. 26.

[31] This work is not mentioned by Eusebius in the list of Justin's works which he gives in chap. 18. He had, therefore, undoubtedly never seen it. Irenæus nowhere mentions it under this title, though he seems to have made extensive use of it, and he does mention a work, *Against Marcion*, which is very likely to be identified with the work referred to here (see Harnack's *Zur Quellenkritik des Gnosticismus*). The work, which is now lost, is mentioned by Photius (*Cod.* 125), but he evidently had not seen it, and is simply copying some earlier list, perhaps that of Eusebius. His testimony to the work, therefore, amounts to little. Compare note 22, above.

[32] On Justin's *Apology* and his work *Against the Greeks*, see below, chap. 18, notes 3 and 4. As shown in note 3 of that chapter, he really wrote only one *Apology*.

[33] Justin, *Apol.* I. 1.

[1] On the titles of the Emperor Antoninus Pius, see Otto's notes in his edition of Justin's works (*Corpus Apol. Christianorum*, Vol. I. p. 2 sq.).

[2] That is, Marcus Aurelius, whose original name was Marcus Annius Verus, but who, after his adoption by the Emperor Antoninus Pius, was styled Marcus Ælius Aurelius Verus Cæsar. As a tribute to his sincerity and truthfulness, he was quite commonly called, instead of *Verus, Verissimus.*

[3] The MSS. are divided here between the forms φιλοσόφῳ and φιλοσόφου. If the former reading be adopted, we must translate as we have done, "to Lucius, the philosopher, own son of Cæsar." If the latter reading be followed, we must translate, "to Lucius, own son of Cæsar the philosopher." The MSS. are about equally divided, and the latter reading is adopted by Stephanus, Valesius, Stroth, and Burton. But our MSS. of Justin support the former reading, which is adopted by Schwegler and Heinichen, and which, as the latter remarks, is far more natural than the other reading, for Justin had greater reason for giving the appellation of "philosopher" to a' Cæsar who was still living, even though he may not have been noted for his philosophical tastes, than to a Cæsar who was already dead, and whose character certainly entitled him to the appellation no more than, if as much as, his son. See Heinichen's note *in loco*, and Otto's note. in his edition of Justin's works, Vol. I. p. 3 ff. The Lucius addressed here was Lucius Ceionius Commodus, whose father, bearing the same name, had been adopted as Cæsar by Hadrian. The younger Lucius was adopted as Cæsar along with Marcus by Antoninus Pius, and later became Marcus' colleague in the empire, when he added to his own name the name Verus, which Marcus had formerly borne. He is therefore commonly known in history as Lucius Verus (see the respective articles in Smith's *Dict. of Greek and Roman Biog.*).

[4] Of Justin's father and grandfather we know nothing except their names. On the place of his birth, see above, chap. 11, note 20.

[5] This "Assembly of Asia" (τὸ κοινὸν τῆς Ἀσίας) was one of the regular provincial diets which Augustus had called into being as fixed institutions. It was an annual assembly of the civic deputies of the province, and served as a general organ of the province, especially in bringing the wishes of the people to the knowledge of the governor, and through him to the emperor, and decrees of the emperor were often addressed to it, and legates chosen by it were sent to the emperor whenever occasion required. See Marquardt, *Röm. Staatsverwaltung*, I. p. 366 sq.

CHAPTER XIII.

The Epistle of Antoninus to the Common Assembly of Asia in Regard to our Doctrine.[1]

1   "THE Emperor Cæsar Marcus Aurelius Antoninus Augustus,[2] Armenicus, Pontifex Maximus, for the fifteenth time Tribune, for the third time Consul, to the Common Assem-
2   bly of Asia, Greeting. I know that the gods also take care that such persons do not escape detection. For they would much rather punish those who will not worship them
3   than you would. But you throw them into confusion, and while you accuse them of atheism you only confirm them in the opinion which they hold. It would indeed be more desirable for them, when accused, to appear to die for their God, than to live. Wherefore also they come off victorious when they give up their lives rather than yield obedience to your com-
4   mands. And in regard to the earthquakes which have been and are still taking place,[3] it is not improper to admonish you who lose heart whenever they occur, and nevertheless are accustomed to compare your conduct with
5   theirs.[4] They indeed become the more con-

fident in God, while you, during the whole time, neglect, in apparent ignorance, the other gods and the worship of the Immortal, and oppress and persecute even unto death the Christians who worship him.[5] But in re-
6   gard to these persons, many of the governors of the provinces wrote also to our most divine father, to whom he wrote in reply that they should not trouble these people unless it should appear that they were attempting something affecting the Roman government.[6] And to me also many have sent communications concerning these men, but I have replied to them in the same way that my father did. But if any
7   one still persists in bringing accusations against any of these people as such, the person who is accused shall be acquitted of the charge, even if it appear that he is one of them, but the accuser shall be punished.[7] Published in Ephesus in the Common Assembly of Asia."
To these things Melito,[8] bishop of the
8   church of Sardis, and a man well known at that time, is a witness,[9] as is clear from his words in the Apology which he addressed to the Emperor Verus in behalf of our doctrine.

---

[1] This edict is undoubtedly spurious. It contradicts all that we know in regard to the relation of Christianity to the State during this century, and both the language and the sentiments make it impossible to call it genuine. It is probably a forgery of the second century. It is found in our two (or more properly one, as one is simply a slavish copy of the other) MSS. of Justin; but this is simply accidental, as it does not belong there, but was appended to the edict of Hadrian by some late copyist. The edict is now almost universally acknowledged to be a forgery; compare Overbeck, *Studien zur Gesch. der alt. Kirche*, p. 93 sqq. Wieseler contends for its genuineness, but no good critic follows him.

[2] Eusebius gives this as an edict of Antoninus Pius, and yet its inscription assigns it to Marcus Aurelius. Overbeck concludes that Eusebius was led by internal evidence to assign the rescript to Antoninus Pius, but that he did not venture to change the inscription of the original which lay before him. This seems the only possible explanation, and as Eusebius at any rate was badly confused in regard to the names of the Antonines, the glaring discrepancy may not have meant very much to him. In our MSS. of Justin Martyr, where this edict is appended to the first Apology, the superscription and text are quite different from the form given by Eusebius. The rescript is in fact assigned there by its superscription to Antoninus Pius, instead of to Marcus Aurelius. But if that was its original form, we cannot understand the later change to Marcus Aurelius, for certainly his authorship is precluded on the very face of the document; but it is easier to see how it could have been later assigned to Antoninus Pius under the influence of Eusebius' direct statement. We have no knowledge of the original Latin of this pretended edict. Rufinus evidently did not know it, for he translates the document from the Greek of Eusebius. The text of the edict as given by Eusebius differs considerably at many points from the text found in the MSS. of Justin, and the variations are such as can hardly be explained as due merely to copyists' errors or alterations. At the same time the two texts are plainly not independent of each other, and cannot be looked upon as independent translations of one Latin original. We may perhaps suppose that one text represents the original translation, the other a revision of it. Whether the revision was made by a comparison with the original, and thus more accurately represents it, we cannot tell. If, then, one is a revision of the other, the form given in the MSS. of Justin is evidently the later, for its statements in more places than one are an improvement upon those of the other text in point of clearness and decisiveness. Moreover, as remarked just above, the ascription of the edict to Antoninus Pius must be later than its ascription to Marcus Aurelius.

[3] Numerous earthquakes took place in Asia Minor and in Rhodes during the reign of Antoninus Pius, and these, as well as famines and other occurrences of the kind which were uncomfortably frequent at this time, were always made the signal for renewed attacks upon the Christians, who were held by the people in general responsible for these misfortunes. See Julius Capitolinus' *Vita Antonini Pii*, chap. 9.

[4] This sentence has caused great difficulty. Cruse translates,

"But as to those earthquakes which have taken place and still continue, it is not out of place to admonish you who are cast down whenever these happen, that you compare your own deportment with theirs." Most of the older translators and, among the moderns, Stigloher, have translated in the same way; but the Greek of the last clause will not warrant this construction. The original runs as follows: . . . ὑπομνῆσαι ἀθυμοῦντας μὲν ὅταν περ' ὦσιν, παραβάλλοντας δὲ τὰ ὑμέτερα πρὸς τὰ ἐκείνων. Stroth inserts μή before ἀθυμοῦντας, and translates, "Was die Erdbeben betrifft, die sich ereignet haben, und noch ereignen, halte ich nicht für undienlich euch zu erinnern dass ihr den vorkommenden Fall den Muth nicht sinken lasst, sondern euer Betragen einmal mit jener ihrem vergleicht." The insertion, however, is quite unwarranted and must be rejected. Valesius renders: *Caeterum de terrae motibus, qui vel facti sunt vel etiamnum fiunt, non absurdum videtur vos commonere, qui et animos abjicitis, quoties hujusmodi casus contingunt, et vestra cum illorum institutis comparatis;* which makes excellent sense and might be accepted, were it not for the fact that it fails to bring out adequately the force of μέν and δέ. Heinichen discusses the passage at length (in his edition of Eusebius, Vol. III. pp. 670–674), and translates as follows: *Non alienum videtur vos admonere (corripere) de terrae motibus qui vel fuerunt vel adhuc sunt, vos qui estis quidem animo abjecto, quoties illi eveniunt, nihilo autem minus vestram agendi rationem conferre soletis cum illorum.* Overbeck follows Heinichen in his German translation of the edict (*ibid.* p. 127 sqq.), and the translation of Closs is similar. It seems to be the only rendering which the Greek will properly admit, and I have therefore felt compelled to adopt it, though I should have preferred to interpret as Valesius does, had the original permitted.

[5] An orthodox worshiper of the Roman gods, like Antoninus Pius, can hardly have called the God of the Christians "The Immortal," in distinction from the gods of the Romans.

[6] Among these epistles the writer of this edict undoubtedly meant to include the rescript ostensibly addressed by Hadrian to Minucius Fundanus. See chap. 9, above.

[7] This is the climax of the whole. Not only is the accused to be set free, but the accuser is to be held as guilty! This really goes further than Constantine. See above, chap. 9, note 4.

[8] On Melito and his writings, see chap. 26, note 1.

[9] Eusebius evidently draws this conclusion from the passage from Melito's *Apology*, quoted below, in chap. 26, where Melito refers to edicts of Antoninus Pius; for had Eusebius referred to another passage, he would undoubtedly have quoted it. But according to Melito, the edicts of Antoninus were to prevent any new methods of procedure against the Christians, i.e. tumultuous proceedings in opposition to the custom established by Trajan. The edicts of which he speaks were intended, then, to perpetuate the principles of Trajan, which had been, since his time, the silent law of the empire upon the subject. The edicts cannot have been edicts of toleration (even Melito himself does not regard them so), but edicts against illegal, tumultuous proceedings, and the accusations of informers, and therefore quite in the spirit of Trajan. But as the significance of Trajan's rescript was entirely misunderstood in the early Church (see above, Bk. III. chap. 33, note 6), so it was the

CHAPTER XIV.

The Circumstances related of Polycarp, a Friend of the Apostles.

1　At this time, while Anicetus was at the head of the church of Rome,[1] Irenæus relates that Polycarp, who was still alive, was at Rome,[2] and that he had a conference with Anicetus on a question concerning the

2 day of the paschal feast.[3] And the same writer gives another account of Polycarp which I feel constrained to add to that which has been already related in regard to him. The account is taken from the third book of Irenæus' work Against Heresies, and is as follows:[4]

3　"But Polycarp[5] also was not only instructed by apostles, and acquainted with many that had seen Christ, but was also appointed by apostles in Asia bishop of the church of Smyrna.[6] We too saw him in our early 4 youth; for he lived a long time, and died, when a very old man, a glorious and most illustrious martyr's death,[7] having always taught the things which he had learned from the apostles, which the Church also hands down, and which alone are true.[8] To these things 5 all the Asiatic churches testify, as do also those who, down to the present time, have succeeded Polycarp,[9] who was a much more trustworthy and certain witness of the truth than Valentinus and Marcion and the rest of the heretics.[10] He also was in Rome in the time of Anicetus[11] and caused many to turn away from the above-mentioned heretics to the Church of God, proclaiming that he had received from the apostles this one and only system of truth which has been transmitted by the Church. And there are those that heard from him 6 that John, the disciple of the Lord, going to bathe in Ephesus and seeing Cerinthus within, ran out of the bath-house without bathing, crying, 'Let us flee, lest even the bath fall, because Cerinthus, the enemy of the truth, is within.'[12] And Polycarp himself, when 7 Marcion once met him[13] and said, 'Knowest[14] thou us?' replied, 'I know the first born of Satan.' Such caution did the apostles and their disciples exercise that they might not even converse with any of those who perverted the truth; as Paul also said, 'A man that is a heretic, after the first and second admonition,

---

common opinion that the attitude of the State toward the Church was at bottom friendly to Christianity, and therefore all edicts forbidding the introduction of new methods were regarded as favorable edicts, as in the present case by Eusebius. Again, had Melito known of such a favorable edict as this of Antoninus, he would certainly have called special and particular attention to it. Melito's testimony, therefore, instead of being in favor of the genuineness of this edict, is really against it.

[1] On Anicetus, see above, chap. 11, note 18. He was bishop probably from 154 to 165 A.D.

[2] γένεσθαι ἐπὶ Ῥώμης. It is quite commonly said that Polycarp came to Rome during the episcopate of Anicetus; but our authorities say only that he was in Rome at that time, and do not specify the date at which he arrived there. Neither these words, nor the words of Irenæus in § 5 below (ἐπιδημήσας τῇ Ῥώμῃ), are to be translated "came to Rome," as is often done (e.g. by Crusè, by Roberts and Rambaut, in their translation of Irenæus, and by Salmon, in the *Dict. of Christ. Biog.*), but "was at Rome" (as Closs, Stigloher, Lightfoot, &c., correctly render the words). Inasmuch as Polycarp suffered martyrdom in 155 or 156 A.D. (see below, chap. 15, note 2), he must have left Rome soon after Anticetus' accession (which took place probably in 154); and though of course he may have come thither sometime before that event, still the fact that his stay there is connected with Anicetus' episcopate, and his alone, implies that he went thither either immediately after, or shortly before Anicetus became bishop.

[3] On the paschal controversies of the early Church, see below, Bk. V. chap. 23, note 1. We learn from Bk. V. chap. 24, that though Polycarp and Anicetus did not reach an agreement on the subject, they nevertheless remained good friends, and that Polycarp celebrated the eucharist in Rome at the request of Anicetus.

[4] Irenæus, *Adv. Hær.* III. 3. 4.

[5] Eusebius takes his account of Polycarp solely from Irenæus, and from the epistle of the church of Smyrna, given in the next chapter. He is mentioned by Irenæus again in his *Adv. Hær.* V. 33. 4 (quoted by Eusebius in Bk. III. chap. 39), and in his epistle to Florinus and to Victor. From the epistle to Florinus (quoted below in Bk. V. chap. 20), where quite an account of Polycarp is given, we learn that the latter was Irenæus' teacher. He was one of the most celebrated men of the time, not because of his ability or scholarship, but because he had been a personal friend of some of the disciples of the Lord, and lived to a great age, when few if any were still alive that had known the first generation of Christians. He suffered martyrdom about 155 A.D. (see below, chap. 15, note 2); and as he was at least eighty-six years old at the time of his death (see the next chap., § 20), he must have been born as early as 70 A.D. He was a personal disciple of John the apostle, as we learn from Irenæus' epistle to Florinus, and was acquainted also with others that had seen the Lord. That he was at the head of the church of Smyrna cannot be doubted (cf. Ignatius' epistle to him), but Irenæus' statement that he was appointed bishop of Smyrna by apostles is probably to be looked upon as a combination of his own. He reasoned that bishops were the successors of the apostles; Polycarp was a bishop, and lived in the time of the apostles; and therefore he must have been appointed by them. The only known writing of Polycarp's is his epistle to the Philippians, which is still extant (see below, note 16). His character is plainly revealed in that epistle as well as in the accounts given us by Irenæus and by the church of Smyrna in their epistle. He was a devoutly pious and simple-minded Christian, burning with intense personal love for his Master, and yet not at all fanatical like his contemporary Ignatius. The instances related in this chapter show his intense horror of heretics, of those whom he believed to be corrupting the doctrine of Christ, and yet he does not seem to have had the taste or talent to refute their errors. He simply wished to avoid them as instruments of Satan. He was pre-eminently a man that lived in the past. His epistle is full of reminiscences of New Testament thought and language, and his chief significance to the Christians of the second

century was as a channel of apostolic tradition. He does not compare with Ignatius for vigor and originality of thought, and yet he was one of the most deeply venerated characters of the early Church, his noble piety, his relation to John and other disciples of the Lord, and finally his glorious martyrdom, contributing to make him such. Upon Polycarp, see especially Lightfoot's edition of Ignatius and Polycarp, and the article of Salmon, in Smith and Wace's *Dict. of Christ. Biog.*

[6] The church of Smyrna (situated in Asia Minor) was one of the "seven churches of Asia," and is mentioned in Rev. i. 11; ii. 8–11.

[7] On his age and the date of his death, see chap. 15, note 2. A full account of his martyrdom is given in the epistle of the church of Smyrna, quoted in the next chapter.

[8] Irenæus emphasizes here, as was his wont, the importance of tradition in determining true doctrine. Compare also Eusebius' words in chap. 21.

[9] Of these successors of Polycarp we know nothing.

[10] κακογνωμόνων.　　[11] See above, note 2.

[12] See above, Bk. III. chap. 28, where the same story is related.

[13] Marcion came to Rome about 135 A.D., but how long he remained there we do not know. Polycarp's words show the great abhorrence in which he was held by the Church. He was considered by many the most dangerous of all the heretics, for he propagated his errors and secured many followers among all classes. Marcion's conduct in this case is very significant when compared with that of the Gnostics. He tried everywhere to gain support and to make friends with the Church, that he might introduce his reforms within it; while the genuine Gnostics, on the contrary, held themselves aloof from the Church, in pride and in a feeling of superiority. Polycarp in his Epistle to the Philippians, chap. 7, shows the same severity toward false teachers, and even uses the same expression, "first born of Satan," perhaps referring to Marcion himself; but see below, note 16.

[14] ἐπιγινώσκεις, which is the reading of the great majority of the MSS., and is adopted by Schwegler, Laemmer, Harnack, Lightfoot, and others. Three MSS., supported by Nicephorus, Rufinus, and the Latin version of Irenæus, read ἐπιγινώσκεε, and this is adopted by Valesius, Heinichen, Stroth, Closs, and Crusè.

reject ; knowing that he that is such is subverted, and sinneth, being condemned of himself.'[15]

8   There is also a very powerful epistle of Polycarp written to the Philippians,[16] from which those that wish to do so, and that are concerned for their own salvation, may learn the character of his faith and the preaching of the

9   truth." Such is the account of Irenæus. But Polycarp, in his above-mentioned epistle to the Philippians, which is still extant, has made use of certain testimonies drawn from the First Epistle of Peter.[17]

10   And when Antoninus, called Pius, had completed the twenty-second year of his reign,[18] Marcus Aurelius Verus, his son, who was also called Antoninus, succeeded him, together with his brother Lucius.[19]

CHAPTER XV.

Under Verus,[1] Polycarp with Others suffered Martyrdom at Smyrna.

1   At this time,[2] when the greatest persecutions were exciting Asia, Polycarp ended his life by martyrdom. But I consider it most important that his death, a written account of which is still extant, should be recorded in this history. There is a letter, written in   2 the name of the church over which he himself presided,[3] to the parishes in Pontus,[4] which relates the events that befell him, in the following words : " The church of God which   3 dwelleth at Smyrna to the church of God which dwelleth in Philomelium,[5] and to all the parishes of the holy catholic Church[6] in every place ; mercy and peace and love from God the Father and our Lord Jesus Christ be multiplied. We write[7] unto you, brethren, an account of what happened to those that suffered martyrdom and to the blessed Polycarp, who put an end to the persecution, having, as it were, sealed it

[15] Titus iii. 10, 11.
[16] Polycarp's Epistle to the Philippians is still extant, and is the only work of Polycarp which we have. (The Greek text is given in all editions of the apostolic Fathers, and with especially valuable notes and discussions in Zahn's *Ignatius von Antiochien*, and in Lightfoot's *Ignatius and Polycarp*, II. p. 897 sqq.; an English translation is contained in the same edition, and also in the *Ante-Nicene Fathers*, Vol. I. p. 31-36.) The date of its composition it is very difficult to determine. It must have been written after the death of Ignatius (chap. 9), and yet soon after, as Polycarp does not seem to know all the circumstances attending that event (see chap. 13). Its date therefore depends upon the date of the martyrdom of Ignatius, which is a very difficult question, not yet fully decided. The attack upon false teachers reminds us of Marcion, and contains traits which seem to imply that Polycarp had Marcion in his mind at the time of writing. If this be so, the epistle was written as late as 135 A.D., which puts the date of Ignatius' death much later than the traditional date (on the date of Ignatius' death, see above, Bk. III. chap. 36, note 4). The genuineness of Polycarp's epistle has been sharply disputed — chiefly on account of its testimony to the Ignatian epistles in chap. 13. Others, while acknowledging its genuineness as a whole, have regarded chap. 13 as an interpolation. But the external testimony for its genuineness is very strong, beginning with Irenæus, and the epistle itself is just what we should expect from such a man as Polycarp. There is no good reason therefore to doubt its genuineness nor the genuineness of chap. 13, the rejection of which is quite arbitrary. The genuineness of the whole has been ably defended both by Zahn and by Lightfoot, and may be regarded as definitely established.
[17] Polycarp in his epistle makes constant use of the First Epistle of Peter, with which he was evidently very familiar, though it is remarkable that he nowhere mentions Peter as its author (cf. Bk. III. chap. 3, note 1).
[18] Antoninus Pius reigned from July 2, 138, to March 7, 161.
[19] Both were adopted sons of Antoninus Pius. See above, chap. 12, note 3.
[1] Marcus Aurelius Verus. See below, p. 390, note.
[2] Polycarp's martyrdom occurred in Smyrna, not during the reign of Marcus Aurelius, as Eusebius says, but during the reign of Antoninus Pius, between 154 and 156 (probably in 155). This has been proved by Waddington in his *Mémoire sur la Chronologie de la vie du rheteur Ælius Aristide* (in *Mem. de l'acad. des inscript. et belles lettres*, Tom. XXVI., part II., 1867, p. 232 sq.; see, also, his *Fastes des provinces Asiatiques*, 1872, p. 219 sq.), and the date is now almost universally accepted (for example, by Renan, Ewald, Hilgenfeld, Lightfoot, Harnack, &c.). But the *Chron.* of Eusebius seems to put the martyrdom in the seventh year of Marcus Aurelius (166-167 A.D.), and this is the date given by Jerome and others, who based their chronology upon Eusebius, and was commonly accepted until Waddington proved it false. Lightfoot, however, shows that Eusebius did not mean to assign Polycarp's death to the seventh year of Marcus Aurelius, but that he meant only to place it in the reign of that emperor, and did not pretend to fix the year. How he made the mistake of assigning it to

the wrong emperor we do not know, but knowing Eusebius' common confusion of the various emperors that bore the name of Antonine, we are not surprised at his error at this point. For the best and most recent discussion of this whole subject, see Lightfoot's *Ignatius*, I. p. 629 sq. Since Waddington published his researches, Wieseler (in his *Christenverfolgungen*, 1878, p. 34-87) and Keim (*Aus dem Urchristenthum*, 1878, p. 92-133) have ventured to dispute his conclusions and to advocate the old date (167), but their arguments are worthless, and have been completely refuted by Lightfoot (*ibid.* p. 655 sq.).
[3] I.e. the church of Smyrna. This letter (the greater part of which Eusebius gives in this chapter) is still extant in four Greek MSS., and also in a poor Latin version which is preserved in numerous MSS. The letter has been published a number of times, most recently by Zahn (in Gebhardt, Harnack, and Zahn's *Patrum Ap. opera*, II. p. 132 sq.), and by Lightfoot (in his *Apostolic Fathers*, Part II.; *St. Ignatius and St. Polycarp*, p. 947 sq.). Lightfoot gives the Greek text with full notes and an English translation, and to his edition the reader is referred for fuller particulars on the whole subject.
[4] Pontus was the northeast province of Asia Minor, bordering on the Black Sea. What led Eusebius to suppose that this epistle was addressed to the church in Pontus, we do not know. The letter is addressed to the church in Philomelium, and that city was not in Pontus (according to Lightfoot, *ibid.* II. p. 948). Valesius suggests that we should read πάντα τόπον instead of Πόντον, but the latter reading is confirmed both by Rufinus and by the Syriac as well as by all the Greek MSS. I am inclined to think that Eusebius may have read hastily and erroneously in the heading of the letter Πόντον instead of πάντα τοπον, and, not knowing that Philomelium was not in Pontus, never thought that his reading was incorrect. Such careless mistakes are by no means uncommon, even in these days, and, having once written Pontus, it is easy enough to suppose that nothing would occur to call his attention to his mistake, and of course no copyist would think of making a correction.
[5] Philomelium, according to Lightfoot (*ibid.* p. 947), was an important city in Phrygia Paroreios, not far from Pisidian Antioch.
[6] τῆς ἁγίας καθολικῆς ἐκκλησίας. The phrase " Catholic Church" occurs first in Ignatius' *Ep. ad Smyr.*, chap. 8, and there the word " catholic" evidently has the common and early meaning, " universal" (see Lightfoot's *Ignatius*, I. p. 398 sqq.). In later usage (so in Tertullian, Clement of Alexandria, and the Muratorian Fragment) it has the meaning " orthodox," as opposed to heretical and schismatical bodies. In the present epistle it occurs four times (§§ 3, 15, 39, below, and in a passage not quoted in this chapter), and at least the first three times with the later meaning, and consequently, in all probability, it has the same meaning the fourth time also. (Lightfoot, it is true, contends that it has the earlier meaning, " universal," in the first, second and fourth cases; but in at least the first two that sense of the word produces most decided tautology, and is therefore to be rejected.) The occurrence of the word in the later sense has caused some critics to deny the genuineness of the epistle; but its genuineness is too well established to admit of doubt, and it must be granted that it is by no means impossible that a word which was used at the end of the second century (in Alexandria, in Rome, and in Carthage) with a certain common and early meaning, may have been employed in the same sense a generation earlier. On the other hand it is possible, as suggested by some, that the word " Catholic" itself is an interpolation; for it is just such a word that would most easily slip into a document, through the inadvertency of copyists, at a later time, when the phrase " Catholic Church" had become current. Lightfoot (*ibid.* p. 605 sq.) maintains the genuineness of the word (taking it in its earlier sense) in all but the third instance, where he substitutes ἁγίας upon what seem to me insufficient grounds.
[7] ἐγράψαμεν, the epistolary aorist, referring, not to another epistle, but to the one which follows, the writer putting himself in thought in the position of those who are reading the letter. See Lightfoot's note on Gal. vi. 11, in his Commentary on that epistle.

4 by his martyrdom." After these words, before giving the account of Polycarp, they record the events which befell the rest of the martyrs, and describe the great firmness which they exhibited in the midst of their pains. For they say that the bystanders were struck with amazement when they saw them lacerated with scourges even to the innermost veins and arteries, so that the hidden inward parts of the body, both their bowels and their members, were exposed to view ; and then laid upon sea-shells and certain pointed spits, and subjected to every species of punishment and of torture, and **5** finally thrown as food to wild beasts. And they record that the most noble Germanicus [8] especially distinguished himself, overcoming by the grace of God the fear of bodily death implanted by nature. When indeed the proconsul [9] wished to persuade him, and urged his youth, and besought him, as he was very young and vigorous, to take compassion on himself, he did not hesitate, but eagerly lured the beast toward himself, all but compelling and irritating him, in order that he might the sooner be freed **6** from their unrighteous and lawless life. After his glorious death the whole multitude, marveling at the bravery of the God-beloved martyr and at the fortitude of the whole race of Christians, began to cry out suddenly, "Away with the atheists ; [10] let Polycarp be sought." **7** And when a very great tumult arose in consequence of the cries, a certain Phrygian, Quintus [11] by name, who was newly come from Phrygia, seeing the beasts and the additional tortures, was smitten with cowardice ' and **8** gave up the attainment of salvation. But the above-mentioned epistle shows that he, too hastily and without proper discretion, had rushed forward with others to the tribunal, but when seized had furnished a clear proof to all, that it is not right for such persons rashly and recklessly to expose themselves to danger. Thus did matters turn out in connection with them. **9** But the most admirable Polycarp, when he first heard of these things, continued undisturbed, preserved a quiet and unshaken mind, and determined to remain in the city. But being persuaded by his friends who entreated and exhorted him to retire secretly,

he went out to a farm not far distant from the city and abode there with a few companions, night and day doing nothing but wrestle with the Lord in prayer, beseeching and imploring, and asking peace for the churches throughout the whole world. For this was always his custom. And three days before his **10** arrest, while he was praying, he saw in a vision at night the pillow under his head suddenly seized by fire and consumed ; and upon this awakening he immediately interpreted the vision to those that were present, almost foretelling that which was about to happen, and declaring plainly to those that were with him that it would be necessary for him for Christ's sake to die by fire.

Then, as those who were seeking him **11** pushed the search with vigor, they say that he was again constrained by the solicitude and love of the brethren to go to another farm. Thither his pursuers came after no long time, and seized two of the servants there, and tortured one of them for the purpose of learning from him Polycarp's hiding-place. And coming **12** late in the evening, they found him lying in an upper room, whence he might have gone to another house, but he would not, saying, "The will of God be done." And when **13** he learned that they were present, as the account says, he went down and spoke to them with a very cheerful and gentle countenance, so that those who did not already know the man thought that they beheld a miracle when they observed his advanced age and the gravity and firmness of his bearing, and they marveled that so much effort should be made to capture a man like him.

But he did not hesitate, but immediately **14** gave orders that a table should be spread for them. Then he invited them to partake of a bounteous meal, and asked of them one hour that he might pray undisturbed. And when they had given permission, he stood up and prayed, being full of the grace of the Lord, so that those who were present and heard him praying were amazed, and many of them now repented that such a venerable and godly old man was about to be put to death. In addition to **15** these things the narrative concerning him contains the following account : " But when at length he had brought his prayer to an end, after remembering all that had ever come into contact with him, small and great, famous and obscure, and the whole catholic Church throughout the world, the hour of departure being come, they put him upon an ass and brought him to the city, it being a great Sabbath.[12] And he was met by

---

[8] Of Germanicus we know only what is told us in this epistle.

[9] This proconsul was Statius Quadratus, as we are told in the latter part of this epistle, in a passage which Eusebius does not quote. Upon his dates, see the discussions of the date of Polycarp's martyrdom mentioned in note 2, above.

[10] Compare Justin Martyr's *Apol.* I. 6; Tertullian's *Apol.* 10, &c.; and see chap. 7, note 20, above.

[11] Of Quintus we know only what is told us in this epistle. It is significant that he was a Phrygian, for the Phrygians were proverbially excitable and fanatical, and it was among them that Montanism took its rise. The conduct of Polycarp, who avoided death as long as he could without dishonor, was in great contrast to this; and it is noticeable that the Smyrnæans condemn Quintus' hasty and ill-considered action, and that Eusebius echoes their judgment (see above, p. 8).

[12] Σαββάτου μεγάλου. "The great Sabbath" in the Christian Church, at least from the time of Chrysostom on, was the Saturday between Good-Friday and Easter. But so far as we know, there are no examples of that use of the phrase earlier than Chrysostom's

Herod,[13] the captain of police,[14] and by his father Nicetes, who took him into their carriage, and sitting beside him endeavored to persuade him, saying, 'For what harm is there in saying, Lord Cæsar, and sacrificing and saving your 16 life?' He at first did not answer; but when they persisted, he said, 'I am not going to do what you advise me.' And when they failed to persuade him, they uttered dreadful words, and thrust him down with violence, so that as he descended from the carriage he lacerated his shin. But without turning round, he went on his way promptly and rapidly, as if nothing had happened to him, and was taken to the 17 stadium. But there was such a tumult in the stadium that not many heard a voice from heaven, which came to Polycarp as he was entering the place: 'Be strong, Polycarp, and play the man.'[15] And no one saw the speaker, but many of our people heard the voice. 18 And when he was led forward, there was a great tumult, as they heard that Polycarp was taken. Finally, when he came up, the proconsul asked if he were Polycarp. And when he confessed that he was, he endeavored to persuade him to deny, saying, 'Have regard for thine age,' and other like things, which it is 19 their custom to say: 'Swear by the genius of Cæsar;[16] repent and say, Away with the Atheists.' But Polycarp, looking with dignified countenance upon the whole crowd that was gathered in the stadium, waved his hand to them, and groaned, and raising his eyes toward 20 heaven, said, 'Away with the Atheists.' But when the magistrate pressed him, and said, 'Swear, and I will release thee; revile Christ,' Polycarp said, 'Fourscore and six years[17] have I been serving him, and he hath done me no wrong; how then can I blaspheme my king who saved me?' 21 "But when he again persisted, and said, 'Swear by the genius of Cæsar,' Polycarp replied, 'If thou vainly supposest that I will swear by the genius of Cæsar, as thou sayest,

feigning to be ignorant who I am, hear plainly: I am a Christian. But if thou desirest to learn the doctrine of Christianity, assign a day and hear.' The proconsul said, 'Per- 22 suade the people.' But Polycarp said, 'As for thee, I thought thee worthy of an explanation; for we have been taught to render to princes and authorities ordained by God the honor that is due,[18] so long as it does not injure us;[19] but as for these, I do not esteem them the proper persons to whom to make my defense.'[20] But the proconsul said, 'I have 23 wild beasts; I will throw thee to them unless thou repent.' But he said, 'Call them; for repentance from better to worse is a change we cannot make. But it is a noble thing to turn from wickedness to righteousness.' But 24 he again said to him, 'If thou despisest the wild beasts, I will cause thee to be consumed by fire, unless thou repent.' But Polycarp said, 'Thou threatenest a fire which burneth for an hour, and after a little is quenched; for thou knowest not the fire of the future judgment and of the eternal punishment which is reserved for the impious. But why dost thou delay? Do what thou wilt.' Saying these and 25 other words besides, he was filled with courage and joy, and his face was suffused with grace, so that not only was he not terrified and dismayed by the words that were spoken to him, but, on the contrary, the proconsul was amazed, and sent his herald to proclaim three times in the midst of the stadium: 'Polycarp hath confessed that he is a Christian.' And when 26 this was proclaimed by the herald, the whole multitude, both of Gentiles and of Jews,[21] who dwelt in Smyrna, cried out with ungovernable wrath and with a great shout, 'This is the teacher of Asia, the father of the Christians, the overthrower of our gods, who teacheth many not to sacrifice nor to worship.' When they 27 had said this, they cried out and asked the Asiarch Philip[22] to let a lion loose upon Polycarp. But he said that it was not lawful for

---

time. Lightfoot points out that, in the present instance, it is not "*The* great Sabbath" (τὸ μέγα Σάββατον), but only "*A* great Sabbath"; and therefore, in the present instance, any great Sabbath might be meant,— that is, any Sabbath which coincided with a festival or other marked day in the Jewish calendar. Lightfoot gives strong reasons for assuming that the traditional day of Polycarp's death (Feb. 23) is correct, and that the Sabbath referred to here was a great Sabbath because it coincided with the Feast of Purim (see Lightfoot, *ibid.* I. p. 660 sqq. and 690 sqq.).

[13] Of Herod and Nicetes we know only what is told us in this epistle. The latter was not an uncommon name in Smyrna, as we learn from inscriptions (see Lightfoot, *ibid.* II. p. 958).

[14] εἰρήναρχος (see Lightfoot, *ibid.* p. 955).

[15] Compare Joshua i. 6, 7, 9, and Deut. i. 7, 23.

[16] τὴν Καίσαρος τύχην. This oath was invented under Julius Cæsar, and continued under his successors. The oath was repudiated by the Christians, who regarded the "genius" of the emperor as a false God, and therefore the taking of the oath a species of idolatry. It was consequently employed very commonly by the magistrates as a test in times of persecution (cf. Tertullian, *Apol.* 32; Origen, *Contra Cels.* VIII. 65, and many other passages).

[17] See above, chap. 14, note 5. Whether the eighty-six years are to be reckoned from Polycarp's birth, or from the time of his conversion or baptism, we cannot tell. At the same time, inasmuch as he speaks of serving *Christ*, for eighty-six years, not *God*, I am in-

clined to think that he is reckoning from the time of his conversion or baptism, which may well be if we suppose him to have been baptized in early boyhood.

[18] See Rom. xiii. 1 sq., 1 Pet. ii. 13 sq.

[19] τιμήν . . . τὴν μὴ βλάπτουσαν ἡμᾶς. Compare Pseudo-Ignatius, *ad Antioch.* 11, and *Mart. Ignat. Rom.* 6 (in both of which are found the words ἐν οἷς ἀκίνδυνος ἡ ὑποταγή).

[20] The proconsul made quite a concession here. He would have been glad to have Polycarp quiet the multitude if he could. Polycarp was not reckless and foolish in refusing to make the attempt, for he knew it would fail, and he preferred to retain his dignity and not compromise himself by appearing to ask for mercy.

[21] The Jews appear very frequently as leading spirits in the persecution of Christians. The persecution under Nero was doubtless due to their instigation (see Bk. II. chap. 25, note 4). Compare also Tertullian, *Scorp.* 10, and Eusebius, *H. E.* V. 16. That the Jews were numerous in Smyrna has been shown by Lightfoot, *ibid.* p. 966.

[22] "The Asiarch was the head of the Commune Asiæ, the confederation of the principal cities of the Roman province of Asia. As such, he was the 'chief priest' of Asia, and president of the games" (Lightfoot, *ibid.* p. 967; on p. 987 ff. of the same volume, Lightfoot discusses the Asiarchate at considerable length). The Asiarch Philip mentioned here was a Trallian, as we learn from a statement toward the close of the epistle, which Eusebius does not quote:

him, since he had closed the games. Then they thought fit to cry out with one accord that
28 Polycarp should be burned alive. For it was necessary that the vision should be fulfilled which had been shown him concerning his pillow, when he saw it burning while he was praying, and turned and said prophetically to the faithful that were with him, ' I must
29 needs be burned alive.' These things were done with great speed,—more quickly than they were said, — the crowds immediately collecting from the workshops and baths timber and fagots, the Jews being especially zeal-
30 ous in the work, as is their wont. But when the pile was ready, taking off all his upper garments, and loosing his girdle, he attempted also to remove his shoes, although he had never before done this, because of the effort which each of the faithful always made to touch his skin first ; for he had been treated with all honor on account of his virtuous life even before his
31 gray hairs came. Forthwith then the materials prepared for the pile were placed about him ; and as they were also about to nail him to the stake,[23] he said, ' Leave me thus ; for he who hath given me strength to endure the fire, will also grant me strength to remain in the fire unmoved without being secured by you with nails.' So they did not nail him, but bound
32 him. And he, with his hands behind him, and bound like a noble ram taken from a great flock, an acceptable burnt-offering unto
33 God omnipotent, said, ' Father of thy beloved and blessed Son[24] Jesus Christ, through whom we have received the knowledge of thee, the God of angels and of powers and of the whole creation and of the entire race of the righteous who live in thy presence, I bless thee that thou hast deemed me worthy of this day and hour, that I might receive a portion in the number of the martyrs, in the cup of Christ, unto resurrection of eternal life,[25] both of soul and of body, in the immortality of the Holy Spirit.
34 Among these may I be received before thee this day, in a rich and acceptable sacrifice, as thou, the faithful and true God, hast beforehand prepared and revealed, and
35 hast fulfilled. Wherefore I praise thee also for everything ; I bless thee, I glorify thee, through the eternal high priest, Jesus Christ, thy beloved Son, through whom, with him, in the Holy Spirit, be glory unto thee, both now
36 and for the ages to come, Amen.' When he had offered up his Amen and had finished his prayer, the firemen lighted the fire ;

and as a great flame blazed out, we, to whom it was given to. see, saw a wonder, and we were preserved that we might relate what happened to the others. For the fire presented 37 the appearance of a vault, like the sail of a vessel filled by the wind, and made a wall about the body of the martyr,[26] and it was in the midst not like flesh burning, but like gold and silver refined in a furnace. For we perceived such a fragrant odor, as of the fumes of frankincense or of some other precious spices. So 38 at length the lawless men, when they saw that the body could not be consumed by the fire, commanded an executioner[27] to approach and pierce him with the sword. And 39 when he had done this there came forth a quantity of blood[28] so that it extinguished the fire ; and the whole crowd marveled that there should be such a difference between the unbelievers and the elect, of whom this man also was one, the most wonderful teacher in our times, apostolic and prophetic, who was bishop of the catholic Church[29] in Smyrna. For every word which came from his mouth was accomplished and will be accomplished. But the 40 jealous and envious Evil One, the adversary of the race of the righteous, when he saw the greatness of his martyrdom, and his blameless life from the beginning, and when he saw him crowned with the crown of immortality and bearing off an incontestable prize, took care that not even his body should be taken away by us, although many desired to do it and to have communion with his holy flesh. Accord- 41 ingly certain ones secretly suggested to Nicetes, the father of Herod and brother of Alce,[30] that he should plead with the magistrate

---

[26] It is not necessary to dispute the truthfulness of the report in this and the next sentences on the ground that the events recorded are miraculous in their nature, and therefore cannot have happened. Natural causes may easily have produced some such phenomena as the writers describe, and which they of course regarded as miraculous. Lightfoot refers to a number of similar cases, Vol. I. p. 598 ff. Compare also Harnack in the *Zeitschrift für Kirchengesch.* II. p. 291 ff.
[27] Κομφέκτορα. It was the common business of the *Confectores* to dispatch such wild beasts as had not been killed outright during the combat in the arena. See Lightfoot, p. 974.
[28] Before the words " a quantity of blood " are found in all the Greek MSS. of the epistle the words περιστερὰ καί, " a dove and." It seems probable that these words did not belong to the original text, but that they were, as many critics believe, an unintentional corruption of some other phrase, or that they were, as Lightfoot thinks, a deliberate interpolation by a late editor (see Lightfoot, II. 974 ff. and I. 627 ff.). No argument, therefore, against the honesty of Eusebius can be drawn from his omission of the words.
[29] See above, note 6. That the word καθολικῆς is used here in the later sense of " orthodox," as opposed to heretical and schismatical bodies, can be questioned by no one. Lightfoot, however, reads at this point ἁγίας instead of καθολικῆς in his edition of the epistle. It is true that he has some MS. support, but the MSS. and versions of Eusebius are unanimous in favor of the latter word, and Lightfoot's grounds for making the change seem to be quite insufficient. If any change is to be made, the word should be dropped out entirely, as suggested by the note already referred to.
[30] All, or nearly all, the MSS. of Eusebius read Δάλκης, and that reading is adopted by Stephanus, Valesius (in his text), Schwegler, Laemmer, Heinichen, and Crusè. On the other hand, the MSS. of the epistle itself all support the form Ἀλκης (or Ἀλκῆς, Ἑλκεις, as it appears respectively in two MSS.), and Lightfoot accepts this unhesitatingly as the original form of the word, and it is adopted by many editors of Eusebius (Valesius, in his notes, Stroth, Zimmer-

---

Lightfoot identifies him with a person named in various Trallian inscriptions.
[23] The Greek reads simply προσηλοῦν αὐτόν.
[24] παιδός not υἱοῦ. παις commonly conveys the meaning of servant rather than son, although in this passage it is evidently used in the latter sense. Its use in connection with Christ was in later times dropped as Arianistic in its tendency.　[25] Compare John v. 29.

not to give up his body, 'lest,' it was said, 'they should abandon the crucified One and begin to worship this man.'[31] They said these things at the suggestion and impulse of the Jews, who also watched as we were about to take it from the fire, not knowing that we shall never be able either to forsake Christ, who suffered for the salvation of the whole world of those that 42 are saved, or to worship any other. For we worship him who is the Son of God, but the martyrs, as disciples and imitators of the Lord, we love as they deserve on account of their matchless affection for their own king and teacher. May we also be made partakers 43 and fellow-disciples with them. The centurion, therefore, when he saw the contentiousness exhibited by the Jews, placed him in the midst and burned him, as was their custom. And so we afterwards gathered up his bones, which were more valuable than precious stones and more to be esteemed than gold, and 44 laid them in a suitable place. There the Lord will permit us to come together as we are able, in gladness and joy to celebrate the birthday of his martyrdom,[32] for the commemoration of those who have already fought and for the training and preparation of those who 45 shall hereafter do the same. Such are the events that befell the blessed Polycarp, who suffered martyrdom in Smyrna with the eleven[33]

from Philadelphia. This one man is remembered more than the others by all, so that even by the heathen he is talked about in every place."

Of such an end was the admirable and 46 apostolic Polycarp deemed worthy, as recorded by the brethren of the church of Smyrna in their epistle which we have mentioned. In the same volume[34] concerning him are subjoined also other martyrdoms which took place in the same city, Smyrna, about the same period of time with Polycarp's martyrdom. Among them also Metrodorus, who appears to have been a proselyte of the Marcionitic sect, suffered death by fire. A celebrated martyr of those times was 47 a certain man named Pionius. Those who desire to know his several confessions, and the boldness of his speech, and his apologies in behalf of the faith before the people and the rulers, and his instructive addresses, and, moreover, his greetings to those who had yielded to temptation in the persecution, and the words of encouragement which he addressed to the brethren who came to visit him in prison, and the tortures which he endured in addition, and besides these the sufferings and the nailings, and his firmness on the pile, and his death after all the extraordinary trials,[35] — those we refer to that epistle which has been given in the Martyrdoms of the Ancients,[36] collected by us, and which contains a very full account of him. And there are also records extant of others 48 that suffered martyrdom in Pergamus, a city

---

mann, Burton, and Closs). Dalce is an otherwise unknown name, while Alce, though rare, is a good Greek name, and is once connected with Smyrna in an inscription. Moreover, we learn from Ignatius, *ad Smyr.* 13, and *ad Polyc.* VIII., that Alce was a well-known Christian in Smyrna at the time Ignatius wrote his epistles. The use of the name at this point shows that its possessor was or had been a prominent character in the church of Smyrna, and the identification of the two seems to me beyond all reasonable doubt (see, also, Lightfoot, I. 353; II. 325 and 978). That Eusebius, however, wrote Alce is not so certain. In fact, in view of the external testimony, it might be regarded as quite as likely that he, by a mistake, wrote Dalce, as that some copyist afterwards committed the error. Still, the name Alce must have been to Eusebius, with his remarkable memory, familiar from Ignatius' epistles, and hence his mistaking it for another word seems a little strange. But whether Eusebius himself wrote Dalce or Alce, believing the latter to be the correct form, the form which he should have written, I have ventured to adopt it in my translation.

[31] This shows that the martyrs were highly venerated even at this early date, as was indeed most natural, and as is acknowledged by the writers themselves just below. But it does not show that the Christians already worshiped or venerated their relics as they did in later centuries. The heathen, in their own paganism, might easily conclude from the Christians' tender care of and reverence for the martyrs' relics that they also worshiped them.

[32] This is, so far as I am aware, the earliest notice of the annual celebration of the day of a martyr's death, a practice which early became so common in the Church. The next reference to the custom is in Tertullian's *de Corona*, 3 (cf. also *Scorp.* 15). So natural a practice, however, and one which was soon afterward universal, need not surprise us at this early date (see Ducange, *Natalis*, and Bingham, *Ant.* XIII. 9. 5, XX. 7. 2).

[33] The majority of the MSS. read δώδεκα τοῦ ἐν Σμύρνῃ μαρτυρήσαντος, which, however, is quite ungrammatical as it stands in the sentence, and cannot be accepted. Heinichen reads δώδεκα τὸν ἐν κ.τ.λ., changing the genitive of the majority of the MSS. to an accusative, but like them, as also like Rufinus, making twelve martyrs besides Polycarp. But the MSS. of the epistle itself read δωδέκατος ἐν Σμ. μαρτυρήσας, thus making only eleven martyrs in addition to Polycarp, and it cannot be doubted that this idiomatic Greek construction is the original. In view of that fact, I am constrained to read with Valesius, Schwegler, and Zahn (in his note on this passage in his edition of the epistle), δωδέκατον ἐν Σμ. μαρτυρήσαντα, translating literally, "suffered martyrdom with those from Philadelphia, the twelfth"; or, as I have rendered it freely in the text, "suffered martyrdom with the eleven from Philadelphia." It is, of course, possible that Eusebius himself substituted the δώδεκα for

the δωδέκατος, but the variations and inconsistencies in the MSS. at this point make it more probable that the change crept in later, and that Eusebius agreed with his original in making Polycarp the twelfth martyr, not the thirteenth. Of these eleven only Germanicus is mentioned in this epistle, and who the others were we do not know. They cannot have been persons of prominence, or Polycarp's martyrdom would not so completely have overshadowed theirs.

[34] γραφῇ. These other accounts were not given in the epistle of the Smyrnæans, but were doubtless appended to that epistle in the MS. which Eusebius used. The accounts referred to are not found in any of our MSS. of the epistle, but there is published in Ruinart's *Acta Martyrum Sincera*, p. 188 sq., a narrative in Latin of the martyrdom of a certain Pionius and of a certain Marcionist Metrodorus, as well as of others, which appears to be substantially the same as the document which Eusebius knew in the original Greek, and which he refers to here. The account bears all the marks of genuineness, and may be regarded as trustworthy, at least in the main points. But Eusebius has fallen into a serious chronological blunder in making these other martyrs contemporaries of Polycarp. We learn from a notice in the document given by Ruinart that Pionius, Metrodorus, and the others were put to death during the persecution of Decius, in 250 A.D., and this date is confirmed by external evidence. The document which Eusebius used may not have contained the distinct chronological notice which is now found in it, or Eusebius may have overlooked it, and finding the narrative given in his MS. in close connection with the account of Polycarp's martyrdom, he may have jumped hastily to the conclusion that both accounts relate to the same period of time. Or, as Lightfoot suggests, in the heading of the document there may have stood the words ἡ αὐτὴ περίοδος τοῦ χρόνου (a peculiar phrase, which Eusebius repeats) indicating (as the words might indicate) that the events took place at the same season of the year, while Eusebius interpreted them to mean the same period of time. Upon these *Acts*, and upon Metrodorus and Pionius, see Lightfoot, I. p. 622 sqq. The *Life of Polycarp*, which purports to have been written by Pionius, is manifestly spurious and entirely untrustworthy, and belongs to the latter part of the fourth century. The true Pionius, therefore, who suffered under Decius, and the Pseudo-Pionius who wrote that *Life* are to be sharply distinguished (see Lightfoot, I. p. 626 sqq.).

[35] This is an excellent summary of Pionius' sufferings, as recorded in the extant *Acts* referred to in the previous note.

[36] This is the *Collection of Ancient Martyrdoms*, which is no longer extant, but which is referred to by Eusebius more than once in his *History*. For particulars in regard to it, see above, p. 30 sq.

of Asia, — of Carpus and Papylus, and a woman named Agathonice, who, after many and illustrious testimonies, gloriously ended their lives.[37]

CHAPTER XVI.

Justin the Philosopher preaches the Word of Christ in Rome and suffers Martyrdom.

1　ABOUT this time[1] Justin, who was mentioned by us just above,[2] after he had addressed a second work in behalf of our doctrines to the rulers already named,[3] was crowned with divine martyrdom,[4] in consequence of a plot laid against him by Crescens,[5] a philosopher who emulated the life and manners of the Cynics, whose name he bore. After Justin had frequently refuted him in public discussions he won by his martyrdom the prize of victory, dying in behalf of the truth which he preached. And he himself, a man most learned in the **2** truth, in his Apology already referred to[6] clearly predicts how this was about to happen to him, although it had not yet occurred. His words are as follows:[7] " I, too,[8] there- **3** fore, expect to be plotted against and put in the stocks[9] by some one of those whom I have named, or perhaps by Crescens, that unphilosophical and vainglorious man. For the man is not worthy to be called a philosopher who publicly bears witness against those concerning whom he knows nothing, declaring, for the sake of captivating and pleasing the multitude, that the Christians are atheistical and impious.[10] Doing this he errs greatly. For if he assails **4** us without having read the teachings of Christ, he is thoroughly depraved, and is much worse than the illiterate, who often guard against discussing and bearing false witness about matters which they do not understand. And if he has read them and does not understand the majesty that is in them, or, understanding it, does these things in order that he may not be suspected of being an adherent, he is far more base and totally depraved, being enslaved to vulgar applause and irrational fear. For I **5** would have you know that when I proposed certain questions of the sort and asked him in regard to them, I learned and proved that he indeed knows nothing. And to show that I speak the truth I am ready, if these disputations have not been reported to you, to discuss the questions again in your presence. And this indeed would be an act worthy of an emperor. But if my questions and his **6**

---

[37] A detailed account of the martyrdoms of Carpus, Papylus, and Agathonice is extant in numerous MSS., and has been published more than once. It has, however, long been recognized as spurious and entirely untrustworthy. But in 1881 Aubè published in the *Revue Archæologique* (Dec., p. 348 sq.) a shorter form of the Acts of these martyrs, which he had discovered in a Greek MS. in the Paris Library. There is no reason to doubt that these Acts are genuine and, in the main, quite trustworthy. The longer Acts assign the death of these martyrs to the reign of Decius, and they have always been regarded as suffering during that persecution. Aubè, in publishing his newly discovered document, still accepted the old date; but Zahn, upon the basis of the document which he had also seen, remarked in his *Tatian's Diatessaron* (p. 279) that Eusebius was correct in assigning these martyrdoms to the reign of Marcus Aurelius, and Lightfoot (I. p. 625) stated his belief that they are to be assigned either to that reign or to the reign of Septimius Severus. In 1888 Harnack (*Texte und Unters.* III. 4) published a new edition of the Acts from the same MS. which Aubè had used, accompanying the text with valuable notes and with a careful discussion of the age of the document. He has proved beyond all doubt that these martyrs were put to death during the reign of Marcus Aurelius, and that the shorter document which we have contains a genuine account related by an eye-witness. These are evidently the Acts which Eusebius had before him. In the spurious account Carpus is called a bishop, and Papylus a deacon. But in the shorter account they are simply Christians, and Papylus informs the judge that he is a citizen of Thyatira.

Eusebius apparently did not include the account of these martyrs in his collection of Ancient Martyrdoms, and Harnack concludes from that that he found in it something that did not please him, viz. the fanaticism of Agathonice, who rashly and needlessly rushes to martyrdom, and the approval of her conduct expressed by the author of the Acts. We are reminded of the conduct of the Phrygian Quintus mentioned in the epistle of the Smyrnæans but in that epistle such conduct is condemned.

[1] That is, during the reign of Marcus Aurelius and Lucius Verus, 161-169 A.D. Inasmuch as Eusebius is certainly in error in ascribing the death of Polycarp, recorded in the previous chapter, to the reign of Marcus Aurelius (see note 2 on that chapter), the fact that he here connects Justin's death with that reign furnishes no evidence that it really occurred then; but we have other good reasons for supposing that it did (see below, note 4).

[2] In chap. 11.

[3] Marcus Aurelius and Lucius Verus, whom he mentioned at the close of chap. 14, and the events of whose reign he is now ostensibly recording. But in regard to this supposed second apology addressed to them, see chap. 18, note 3.

[4] That Justin died a martyr's death is the universal tradition of antiquity, which is crystallized in his name. Irenæus (*Adv. Hær.* I. 28. 1) is the first to mention it, but does so casually, as a fact well known. The only account of his martyrdom which we have is contained in the *Acta Martyrii Justini Philosophi* (Galland. I. 707 sq.), which, although belonging to a later age (probably the third century), yet bear every evidence of containing a comparatively truthful account of Justin's death. According to these Acts, Justin, with six companions, was brought before Rusticus, prefect of Rome, and by him condemned to death, upon his refusal to sacrifice to the gods. The date of his martyrdom is very difficult to determine. There are two lines of tradition, one of which puts his death under Antoninus Pius, the other under Marcus Aurelius. The latter has the most in its favor; and if we are to accept the report of the *Acta Justini* (which can be doubted least of all at this point), his death took place under Rusticus, who, as we know, became prefect of Rome in 163. Upon the date of Justin's death, see especially Holland, in Smith and Wace, III. p. 562 sq.

[5] Of this cynic philosopher Crescens we know only what is told us by Justin and Tatian, and they paint his character in the blackest colors. Doubtless there was sufficient ground for their accusations; but we must remember that we have his portrait only from the pen of his bitterest enemies. In the *Acta* Crescens is not mentioned in

connection with the death of Justin, — an omission which is hardly to be explained, except upon the supposition of historical truthfulness. Eusebius' report here seems to rest solely upon the testimony of Tatian (see §§ 8 and 9, below), but the passage of Tatian which he cites does not prove his point; it simply proves that Crescens plotted against Justin; whether his plotting was successful is not stated, and the contrary seems rather to be implied (see note 13, below).

[6] Harnack thinks that Eusebius at this point wishes to convey the false impression that he quotes from the second apology, whereas he really quotes from what was to him the first, as can be seen from chap. 17. But such conduct upon the part of Eusebius would be quite inexplicable (at the beginning of the very next chapter, e.g., he refers to this same apology as the first), and it is far better to refer the words ἐν τῇ δεδηλωμένῃ Ἀπολογίᾳ to chap. 13 sq., where the apology is quoted repeatedly.

[7] Justin, *Apol.* II. 3.

[8] κἀγὼ οὖν. In the previous chapter (quoted by Eusebius in the next chapter) Justin has been speaking of the martyrdom of various Christians, and now goes on to express his expectation that he, too, will soon suffer death.

[9] ξύλῳ ἐντιναγῆναι. Compare Acts xvii. 24, and see Otto's note on this passage, in his edition of Justin's *Apology* (*Corpus Apol. Christ.* I. p. 204). He says: ξύλον *erat truncus foramina habens, quibus pedes captivorum immitebantur, ut securius in carcere servarentur aut tormentis vexarentur* (" a ξύλον was a block, with holes in which the feet of captives were put, in order that they might be kept more securely in prison, or might be afflicted with tortures ").

[10] This accusation was very commonly made against the Christians in the second century. See above, chap. 7, note 20.

answers have been made known to you, it is obvious to you that he knows nothing about our affairs ; or if he knows, but does not dare to speak because of those who hear him, he shows himself to be, as I have already said,[11] not a philosopher, but a vainglorious man, who indeed does not even regard that most admirable saying of Socrates." [12] These are the words of Justin.

7   And that he met his death as he had predicted that he would, in consequence of the machinations of Crescens, is stated by Tatian,[13] a man who early in life lectured upon

[11] In § 3, above.

[12] This saying of Socrates is given by Justin as follows: ἀλλ' οὔτι γὲ πρὸ τῆς ἀληθείας τιμητέος ἀνήρ, "a man must not be honored before the truth" (from Plato's *Republic*, Bk. X.). It is hard to say why Eusebius should have omitted it. Perhaps it was so well known that he did not think it necessary to repeat it, taking for granted that the connection would suggest the same to every reader, or it is possible that the omission is the fault of a copyist, not of Eusebius himself.

[13] On Tatian and his writings, see below, chap. 29.

Eusebius has been accused by Dembowski, Zahn, Harnack, and others of practicing deception at this point. The passage from Tatian's *Oratio ad Græcos*, which Eusebius appeals to for testimony in regard to Justin's death, and which he quotes just below, is not given by him exactly as it stands in the extant text of the *Oratio*. In the latter we read, " He who taught that death should be despised was himself so greatly in fear of it, that he endeavored to inflict death as if it were an evil upon Justin, *and indeed on me also*, because when preaching he had proved that the philosophers were gluttons and impostors." The difference between the two texts consists in the substitution of the word μεγάλῳ for the words καὶ ἐμὲ ὡς; and it is claimed that this alteration was intentionally made by Eusebius. As the text stands in Tatian, the passage is far from proving that Justin's death was caused by the machinations of Crescens, for Tatian puts himself on a level with Justin as the object of these machinations, and of course since they did not succeed in his case, there is no reason to suppose that they succeeded in Justin's case. It is claimed, therefore, that Justin, realizing this, struck out the καὶ ἐμὲ ὡς in order to permit the reader to gather from the passage that Tatian meant to imply that the plots of Crescens were successful, and resulted in Justin's death. Before accepting this conclusion, however, it may be well to realize exactly what is involved in it. The change does not consist merely in the omission of the words καὶ ἐμὲ ὡς, but in the substitution for them of the word μεγάλῳ. It cannot, therefore, be said that Eusebius only omitted some words, satisfying his conscience that there was no great harm in that; whoever made the change, if he did it intentionally, directly falsified the text, and substituted the other word for the sake of covering up his alteration; that is, he committed an act of deceit of the worst kind, and deliberately took steps to conceal his act. Certainly such conduct is not in accord with Eusebius' general character, so far as we can ascertain it from his writings. Even Zahn and Harnack, who accuse him of intentional deception here, yet speak of his general conscientiousness, and treat this alteration as one which Eusebius allowed himself to make while, at the same time, his " conscientiousness did not permit him even this time to change truth completely into untruth." But if he could allow himself to make so deliberate an alteration, and then cover the change by inserting another word, there is little cause to speak of " conscientiousness " in connection with the matter; if he could do that, his conscience would certainly permit him to make any false quotations, however great, so long as he thought he could escape detection. But few would care to accuse Eusebius of possessing such a character. Certainly if he possessed it, we should find clearer traces of it than we do in his *History*, where we have the opportunity to control a large portion of his statements on an immense variety of subjects. Moreover, for such a grave act of deception as Eusebius is supposed to have committed, some adequate ground must have existed. But what ground was there? The only motive suggested is that he desired to appear to possess specific knowledge about the manner of Justin's death, when in fact he did not possess it. It is not maintained that he had any larger motive, such as reconciling apparent contradictions in sacred records, or shedding an added luster upon the Christian religion, for neither of these purposes has any relation to the statement in regard to Crescens' connection with Justin's death. Solely then for the sake of producing the impression that he knew more about Justin's death than he did, he must have made the change. But certainly when we realize how frequently Eusebius directly avows his ignorance on points far more important (to his mind) than this (e.g., the dates of the Jerusalem bishops, which he might so easily have invented), and when we consider how sober his history is in comparison with the accounts of the majority of his contemporaries, both Pagan and Christian, how few fables he introduces, how seldom he embellishes the narratives which he finds related in his sources with imaginary

the sciences of the Greeks and won no little fame in them, and who has left a great many

figments of his own brain, — when, in fact, no such instances can be found elsewhere, although, writing in the age he did, and for the public for whom he did, he might have invented so many stories without fear of detection, as his successors during the ancient and middle ages were seldom loath to do, — when all this is taken into consideration, we should hesitate long before we accuse Eusebius of such deceptive conduct as is implied in the intentional alteration of Tatian's account at this point. It has been quite the custom to accuse Eusebius of intentional deviations from the truth here and there, but it must be remembered that he was either honest or dishonest, and if he ever deliberately and intentionally deviated from the truth, his general character for truthfulness is gone, unless the deviation were only in some exceptional case, where the pressure to misrepresentation was unusually strong, under which circumstances his reputation for veracity in general might not be seriously impaired. But the present instance is not such an one, and if he was false here on so little provocation, why should we think his character such as to guarantee truthfulness in any place where falsehood might be more desirable?

The fact is, however, that the grounds upon which the accusation against Eusebius is based are very slender. Nothing but the strongest evidence should lead us to conclude that such a writer as he practiced such wilful deception for reasons absolutely trivial. But when we realize how little is known of the actual state of the text of Tatian's *Oratio* at the time Eusebius wrote, we must acknowledge that to base an accusation on a difference between the text of the *History* and the extant MSS. of the *Oratio* is at least a little hasty. An examination of the latest critical edition of Tatian's *Oratio* (that of Schwartz, in Gebhardt, and Harnack's *Texte und Untersuch.* IV. 1) shows us that in a number of instances the testimony of the MSS. of Eusebius is accepted over against that of the few extant MSS. of Tatian. The MS. of Tatian which Eusebius used was therefore admittedly different at a number of points from all our existing MSS. of Tatian. It is consequently not at all impossible that the MS. which he used read μεγάλῳ instead of καὶ ἐμὲ ὡς. It happens, indeed, to be a fact that our three MSS. of Tatian all present variations at this very point (one reads καὶ ἐμὲ ὡς, another, καὶ ἐμὲ οἷον, another, καὶ ἐμὲ οὖς), showing that the archetype, whatever it was, either offered difficulties to the copyists, or else was partially illegible, and hence required conjectural emendations or additions. It will be noticed that the closing verb of this sentence is in the singular, so that the mention of both Justin and Tatian in the beginning of the sentence may well have seemed to some copyist quite incongruous, and it is not difficult to suppose that under such circumstances, the text at this point being in any case obscure or mutilated, such a copyist permitted himself to make an alteration which was very clever and at the same time did away with all the trouble. Textual critics will certainly find no difficulty in such an assumption. The MSS. of Tatian are undoubtedly nearer the original form at this point than those of Eusebius, but we have no good grounds for supposing that Eusebius did not follow the MS. which lay before him.

The question as to Eusebius' interpretation of the passage as he found it is quite a different one. It contains no direct statement that Justin met his death in consequence of the plots of Crescens; and finding no mention of such a fact in the Acts of Martyrdom of Justin, we may dismiss it as unhistorical and refuse to accept Eusebius' interpretation of Tatian's words. To say, however, that Eusebius intentionally misinterpreted those words is quite unwarranted. He found in Justin's work an expressed expectation that he would meet his death in this way, and he found in Tatian's work the direct statement that Crescens did plot Justin's death as the latter had predicted he would. There was nothing more natural than to conclude that Tatian meant to imply that Crescens had succeeded, for why did he otherwise mention the matter at all, Eusebius might well say, looking at the matter from his point of view, as an historian interested at that moment in the fact of Justin's death. He does undoubtedly show carelessness and lack of penetration in interpreting the passage as he does; but if he had been aware of the defect in the evidence he presents, and had yet wished deceitfully to assert the fact as a fact, he would certainly have omitted the passage altogether, or he would have bolstered it up with the statement that other writers confirmed his conclusion, — a statement which only a thoroughly and genuinely honest man would have scrupled to make. Finally, to return to the original charge of falsification of the sources, if he realized that the text of Tatian, with the καὶ ἐμὲ ὡς, did not establish Justin's death at the instigation of Crescens, he must have realized at the same time that his altered text, while it might imply it, certainly did not absolutely prove it, and hence he would not have left his conclusion, which he stated as a demonstrated fact, to rest upon so slender a basis, when he might so easily have adduced any number of oral traditions in confirmation of it. If he were dishonest enough to alter the text, he would not have hesitated to state in general terms that the fact is " *also* supported by tradition." We conclude, finally, that he read the passage as we now find it in the MSS. of his *History*, and that his interpretation of the passage, while false, was not intentionally so.

The attacks upon Eusebius which have been already referred to are to be found in Dembowski's *Quellen der christlichen Apologetik*, I. p. 60; Zahn's *Tatian's Diatessaron*, p. 275 sq., and Harnack's *Ueberlieferung der griech. Apologeten*, p. 141 sq. Semisch (*Justin der Märtyrer*, I. 53) takes for granted that Eusebius fol-

monuments of himself in his writings. He records this fact in his work against the Greeks, where he writes as follows :[14] " And that most admirable Justin declared with truth that the aforesaid persons were like robbers."

8　Then, after making some remarks about the philosophers, he continues as follows :[15] " Crescens, indeed, who made his nest in the great city, surpassed all in his unnatural lust, and was wholly devoted to the love of money.

9　And he who taught that death should be despised, was himself so greatly in fear of it that he endeavored to inflict death, as if it were a great evil, upon Justin, because the latter, when preaching the truth, had proved that the philosophers were gluttons and impostors." And such was the cause of Justin's martyrdom.

CHAPTER XVII.

The Martyrs whom Justin mentions in his Own Work.

1　THE same man, before his conflict, mentions in his first Apology[1] others that suffered martyrdom before him, and most fittingly records the following events. He writes thus :[2]

2　" A certain woman lived with a dissolute husband ; she herself, too, having formerly been of the same character. But when she came to the knowledge of the teachings of Christ, she became temperate, and endeavored to persuade her husband likewise to be temperate, repeating the teachings, and declaring the punishment in eternal fire which shall come upon those who do not live temperately

3　and conformably to right reason. But he, continuing in the same excesses, alienated his wife by his conduct. For she finally, thinking it wrong to live as a wife with a man who, contrary to the law of nature and right, sought every possible means of pleasure, desired

4　to be divorced from him. And when she was earnestly entreated by her friends, who counseled her still to remain with him, on the ground that her husband might some time give hope of amendment, she did violence to

5　herself and remained. But when her husband had gone to Alexandria, and was reported to be conducting himself still worse, she

— in order that she might not, by continuing in wedlock, and by sharing his board and bed, become a partaker in his lawlessness and impiety — gave him what we[3] call a bill of divorce and left him. But her noble and 6 excellent husband, — instead of rejoicing, as he ought to have done, that she had given up those actions which she had formerly recklessly committed with the servants and hirelings, when she delighted in drunkenness and in every vice, and that she desired him likewise to give them up, — when she had gone from him contrary to his wish, brought an accusation concerning her, declaring that she was a Christian. And 7 she petitioned you, the emperor, that she might be permitted first to set her affairs in order, and afterwards, after the settlement of her affairs, to make her defense against the accusation. And this you granted. But 8 he who had once been her husband, being no longer able to prosecute her, directed his attacks against a certain Ptolemæus,[4] who had been her teacher in the doctrines of Christianity, and whom Urbicius[5] had punished. Against him he proceeded in the following manner :

" He persuaded a centurion who was his 9 friend to cast Ptolemæus into prison, and to take him and ask him this only : whether he were a Christian ? And when Ptolemæus, who was a lover of truth, and not of a deceitful and false disposition, confessed that he was a Christian, the centurion bound him and punished him for a long time in the prison. And finally, 10 when the man was brought before Urbicius he was likewise asked this question only : whether he were a Christian ? And again, conscious of the benefits which he enjoyed through the teaching of Christ, he confessed his schooling in divine virtue. For whoever 11 denies that he is a Christian, either denies because he despises Christianity, or he avoids confession because he is conscious that he is unworthy and an alien to it ; neither of which is the case with the true Christian. And when 12 Urbicius commanded that he be led away to punishment, a certain Lucius,[6] who was also a Christian, seeing judgment so unjustly passed,

---

lowed the text of Tatian which lay before him, but does not attempt to prove it.

[14] Tatian, *Oratio ad Græcos*, c. 18. It is quite probable that Tatian is here appealing, not to a written work of Justin's, but to a statement which he had himself heard him make. See Harnack's *Ueberlieferung der griech. Apologeten*, p. 130. Harnack is undoubtedly correct in maintaining that Tatian's *Oratio* is quite independent of Justin's *Apology* and other writings.

[15] *Ibid.* chap. 19.

[1] Eusebius in this chapter quotes what we now know as Justin's second Apology, calling it his first. It is plain that the two were but one to him. See chap. 18, note 3.

[2] Justin, *Apol.* II. 2.

[3] Our authorities are divided between ἡμῖν and ὑμῖν, but I have followed Heinichen in adopting the former, which has much stronger MS. support, and which is in itself at least as natural as the latter.

[4] Of this Ptolemæus we know only what is told us here. Tillemont, Ruinart, and others have fixed the date of his martyrdom as 166, or thereabouts. But inasmuch as the second Apology is now commonly regarded as an appendix to, or as a part of, the first, and was at any rate written during the reign of Antoninus Pius, the martyrdom of Ptolemæus must have taken place considerably earlier than the date indicated, in fact in all probability as early as 152 (at about which time the *Apology* was probably written). We learn from the opening of the second *Apology* that the martyrdoms which are recorded in the second chapter, and the account of which Eusebius here quotes, happened very shortly before the composition of the *Apology* (χθὲς δὲ καὶ πρώην, " yesterday and the day before ").

[5] Ὀυρβίκιος, as all the MSS. of Eusebius give the name. In Justin, the form Ὀυρβίκος occurs, which is a direct transcription of the Latin *Urbicus*.

[6] Of this Lucius we know only what is told us here.

said to Urbicius, 'Why have you punished this man who is not an adulterer, nor a fornicator, nor a murderer, por a thief, nor a robber, nor has been convicted of committing any crime at all, but has confessed that he bears the name of Christian? You do not judge, O Urbicius, in a manner befitting the Emperor Pius, or the philosophical son[7] of Cæsar, or the sacred

13 senate.' And without making any other reply, he said to Lucius, 'Thou also seemest to me to be such an one.' And when Lucius said, 'Certainly,' he again commanded that he too should be led away to punishment. But he professed his thanks, for he was liberated, he added, from such wicked rulers and was going to the good Father and King, God. And still a third having come forward was condemned to be punished."

14 To this, Justin fittingly and consistently adds the words which we quoted above,[8] saying, "I, too, therefore expect to be plotted against by some one of those whom I have named," &c.[9]

CHAPTER XVIII.

The Works of Justin which have come down to us.

1 THIS writer has left us a great many monuments of a mind educated and practiced in divine things, which are replete with profitable matter of every kind. To them we shall refer the studious, noting as we proceed those

2 that have come to our knowledge.[1] There is a certain discourse[2] of his in defense of our doctrine addressed to Antoninus surnamed the Pious, and to his sons, and to the Roman senate. Another work contains his second Apology[3] in behalf of our faith, which he of-

fered to him who was the successor of the emperor mentioned and who bore the same name, Antoninus Verus, the one whose times we are now recording. Also another work

3 against the Greeks,[4] in which he discourses at length upon most of the questions at issue between us and the Greek philosophers, and discusses the nature of demons. It is not necessary for me to add any of these things here. And still another work of his against the

4 Greeks has come down to us, to which he gave the title Refutation. And besides these another, On the Sovereignty of God,[5] which he establishes not only from our Scriptures, but also from the books of the Greeks. Still

5 further, a work entitled Psaltes,[6] and another disputation On the Soul, in which, after propounding various questions concerning the problem under discussion, he gives the opinions of the Greek philosophers, promising to refute it, and to present his own view in another work. He composed also a dialogue against

6 the Jews,[7] which he held in the city of Ephesus with Trypho, a most distinguished man among the Hebrews of that day. In it he shows how the divine grace urged him on to the doctrine of the faith, and with what earnestness he had formerly pursued philosophical studies, and how ardent a search he had made for the truth.[8] And he records of the

7 Jews in the same work, that they were plotting against the teaching of Christ, asserting the

---

[7] Marcus Aurelius. See above, chap. 12, note 2.
[8] In chap. 16, § 3.
[9] Justin, *Apol.* II. 3. These words, in Justin's *Apology*, follow immediately the long account quoted just above.
[1] Eusebius apparently cites here only the works which he had himself seen, which accounts for his omission of the work against Marcion mentioned above, in chap. 11.
[2] This *Apology* is the genuine work of Justin, and is still extant in two late and very faulty MSS., in which it is divided into two, and the parts are commonly known as Justin's First and Second Apologies, though they were originally one. The best edition of the original is that of Otto in his *Corpus Apologetarum Christianorum ;* English translation in the *Ante-Nicene Fathers*, Vol. I. p. 163 ff. Eusebius, in his *Chronicle*, places the date of its composition as 141, but most critics are now agreed in putting it ten or more years later; it must, however, have been written before the death of Antoninus Pius (161). See Schaff, *Ch. Hist.* II. p. 716.
[3] Eusebius here, as in chap. 16 above, ascribes to Justin a second Apology, from which, however, he nowhere quotes. From Eusebius the tradition has come down through history that Justin wrote two apologies, and the tradition seems to be confirmed by the existing MSS. of Justin, which give two. But Eusebius' two cannot have corresponded to the present two; for, from chap. 8, §§ 16 and 17, it is plain, too, from internal evidence (as is now very generally admitted ; Wieseler's arguments against this, in his *Christenverfolgungen,* p. 104 ff., are not sound), that the two were originally one, our second forming simply a supplement to the first. What, then, has become of the second Apology mentioned by Eusebius? There is much difference of opinion upon this point. But the explanation

given by Harnack (p. 171 ff.) seems the most probable one. According to his theory, the Apology of Athenagoras (of whom none of the Fathers, except Methodius and Philip of Side, seem to have had any knowledge) was attributed to Justin by a copyist of the third century, — who altered the address so as to throw it into Justin's time, — and as such it came into the hands of Eusebius, who mentions it among the works of Justin. That he does not quote from it may be due to the fact that it contained nothing suited to his purpose, or it is possible that he had some suspicions about it; the last, however, is not probable, as he nowhere hints at them. That some uncertainty, however, seemed to hang about the work is evident. The erasure of the name of Athenagoras and the substitution of Justin's name accounts for the almost total disappearance of the former from history. This Apology and his treatise on the resurrection first appear again under his name in the eleventh century, and exist now in seventeen MSS. (see Schaff, II. 731). The traditional second Apology of Justin having thus after the eleventh century disappeared, his one genuine Apology was divided by later copyists, so that we still have apparently two separate apologies.
[4] This and the following were possibly genuine works of Justin; but, as they are no longer extant, it is impossible to speak with certainty. The two extant works, *Discourse to the Greeks (Oratio ad Græcos)* and *Hortatory Address to the Greeks (Cohortatio ad Græcos)*, which are translated in the *Ante-Nicene Fathers*, I. p. 271-289, are to be regarded as the productions of later writers, and are not to be identified with the two mentioned here (although Otto defends them both, and Semisch defends the latter).
[5] We have no reason to think that this work was not genuine, but it is no longer extant, and therefore certainty in the matter is impossible. It is not to be identified with the extant work upon the same subject (translated in the *Ante-Nicene Fathers*, I. p. 290-293), which is the production of a later writer.
[6] This work and the following have entirely disappeared, but were genuine productions of Justin, for all that we know to the contrary.
[7] This is a genuine work of Justin, and is still extant (translated in the *Ante-Nicene Fathers*, I. p. 194-270). Its exact date is uncertain, but it was written after the *Apology* (to which it refers in chap. 120), and during the reign of Antoninus Pius (137-161). Of Trypho, whom Eusebius characterizes as "a most distinguished man among the Hebrews," we know nothing beyond what we can gather from the dialogue itself.
[8] See *Dial.* chap. 2 sq.

same things against Trypho : " Not only did you not repent of the wickedness which you had committed, but you selected at that time chosen men, and you sent them out from Jerusalem through all the land, to announce that the godless heresy of the Christians had made its appearance, and to accuse them of those things which all that are ignorant of us say against us, so that you become the causes not only of your own injustice, but also of all other men's." [9]

8 He writes also that even down to his time prophetic gifts shone in the Church.[10] And he mentions the Apocalypse of John, saying distinctly that it was the apostle's.[11] He also refers to certain prophetic declarations, and accuses Trypho on the ground that the Jews had cut them out of the Scripture.[12] A great many other works of his are still in the hands of many

9 of the brethren.[13] And the discourses of the man were thought so worthy of study even by the ancients, that Irenæus quotes his words : for instance, in the fourth book of his work Against Heresies, where he writes as follows : [14] " And Justin well says in his work against Marcion, that he would not have believed the Lord himself if he had preached another God besides the Creator " ; and again in the fifth book of the same work he says : [15] " And Justin well said that before the coming of the Lord Satan never dared to blaspheme God,[16] because he did not yet know his condemnation."

10 These things I have deemed it necessary to say for the sake of stimulating the studious to peruse his works with diligence. So much concerning him.

CHAPTER XIX.

The Rulers of the Churches of Rome and Alexandria during the Reign of Verus.

IN the eighth year of the above-mentioned reign [1] Soter [2] succeeded Anicetus [3] as bishop of the church of Rome, after the latter had held office eleven years in all. But when Celadion [4] had presided over the church of Alexandria for fourteen years he was succeeded by Agrippinus.[5]

CHAPTER XX.

The Rulers of the Church of Antioch.

AT that time also in the church of Antioch, Theophilus [1] was well known as the sixth from the apostles. For Cornelius,[2] who succeeded Hero,[3] was the fourth, and after him Eros,[4] the fifth in order, had held the office of bishop.

CHAPTER XXI.

The Ecclesiastical Writers that flourished in Those Days.

AT that time there flourished in the Church Hegesippus, whom we know from what has gone before,[1] and Dionysius,[2] bishop of Corinth, and another bishop, Pinytus of Crete,[3] and besides

have been reading on the Lord's day an epistle written to them by Soter. It was during his episcopate that Montanus labored in Asia Minor, and the anonymous author of the work called *Prædestinatus* (written in the middle of the fifth century) states that Soter wrote a treatise against him which was answered by Tertullian, but there seems to be no foundation for the tradition. Two spurious epistles and several decretals have been falsely ascribed to him.
[3] On Anicetus, see above, chap. 11, note 18.
[4] On Celadion, see above, chap. 11, note 17.
[5] Of Agrippinus we know only what Eusebius tells us here and in Bk. V. chap. 9, where he says that he held office twelve years. Jerome's version of the *Chron.* agrees as to the duration of his episcopate, but puts his accession in the sixth year of Marcus Aurelius. In the Armenian version a curious mistake occurs in connection with his name. Under the ninth year of Marcus Aurelius are found the words, *Romanorum ecclesiæ XII. episcopus constitutus est Agrippinus annis IX.*, and then Eleutherus (under the thirteenth year of the same ruler) is made the thirteenth bishop, while Victor, his successor, is not numbered, and Zephyrinus, the successor of the latter, is made number fourteen. It is of course plain enough that the transcriber by an oversight read *Romanorum ecclesiæ* instead of *Alexandrinæ ecclesiæ*, and then having given Soter just above as the eleventh bishop, he felt compelled to make Agrippinus the twelfth, and hence reversed the two numbers, nine and twelve, given in connection with Agrippinus, and made him the twelfth bishop, ruling nine years, instead of the ninth bishop, ruling twelve years. He then found himself obliged to make Eleutherus the thirteenth, but brought the list back into proper shape again by omitting to number Victor as the fourteenth. It is hard to understand how a copyist could commit such a flagrant error and not discover it when he found himself subsequently led into difficulty by it. It simply shows with what carelessness the work of translation or of transcription was done. As a result of the mistake no ninth bishop of Alexandria is mentioned, though the proper interval of twelve years remains between the death of Celadion and the accession of Julian.
[1] On Theophilus and his writings, see chap. 24.
[2] Of the life and character of Cornelius and Eros we know nothing. The *Chron.* of Eusebius puts the accession of Cornelius into the twelfth year of Trajan (128 A.D.), and the accession of his successor Eros into the fifth year of Antoninus Pius (142). These dates, however, are quite unreliable, and we have no means of correcting them (see Harnack's *Zeit des Ignatius*, p. 12 sqq.). Theophilus, the successor of Eros, we have reason to think became bishop about the middle of Marcus Aurelius' reign, and hence the *Chron.*, which puts his accession into the ninth year of that reign, (169 A.D.) cannot be far out of the way. This gives us the approximate date for the death of Eros.
[3] On Hero, see above, Bk. III. chap. 36, note 23.
[4] On Eros, see note 2.
[1] On Hegesippus' life and writings, see the next chapter. He has been already mentioned in Bk. II. chap. 23; Bk. III. chaps. 11, 16, 20, 32; and Bk. IV. chap. 8.
[2] On the life and writings of Dionysius, see below, chap. 23.
[3] On Pinytus, see below, chap. 23, note 14.

---

[9] *ibid.* chap. 17.
[10] *ibid.* chap. 82.
[11] *ibid.* chap. 81.
[12] *ibid.* chap. 71.
[13] Of the many extant and non-extant works attributed to Justin by tradition, all, or the most of them (except the seven mentioned by Eusebius, and the work *Against Marcion*, quoted by Irenæus, — see just below, — and the *Syntagma Contra omnes Hær.*), are the productions of later writers.
[14] Irenæus, *Adv. Hær.* IV. 6. 2.
[15] Irenæus, V. 26. 2. Irenæus does not name the work which he quotes here, and the quotation occurs in none of Justin's extant works, but the context and the sense of the quotation itself seem to point to the same work, *Against Marcion.*
[16] Epiphanius expresses the same thought in his *Hær.* XXXIX. 9.
[1] The reign of Marcus Aurelius and Lucius Verus mentioned at the end of chap. 14.
[2] As was remarked in chap. 11, note 18, Anicetus held office until 165 or 167, i.e. possibly until the seventh year of Marcus Aurelius. The date therefore given here for the accession of Soter is at least a year out of the way. The Armenian *Chron.* puts his accession in the 236th Olympiad, i.e. the fourth to the seventh year of this reign, while the version of Jerome puts it in the ninth year. From Bk. V. chap. 1 we learn that he held office eight years, and this is the figure given by both versions of the *Chron.* In chap. 23 Eusebius quotes from a letter of Dionysius, bishop of Corinth, addressed to Soter, in which he remarks that the Corinthian church

these, Philip,[4] and Apolinarius,[5] and Melito,[6] and Musanus,[7] and Modestus,[8] and finally, Irenæus.[9]

[4] On Philip, see below, chap. 25.
[5] On Apolinarius, see below, chap. 27.
[6] On Melito, see chap. 26.
[7] On Musanus, see chap. 28.
[8] On Modestus, see chap. 25.
[9] Irenæus was born in Asia Minor, probably between the years 120 and 130. There is great uncertainty as to the date of his birth, some bringing it down almost to the middle of the second century, while Dodwell carried it back to the year 97 or 98. But these extremes are wild; and a careful examination of all the sources which can throw any light on the subject leads to the conclusion adopted by Lipsius, and stated above. In Asia Minor he was a pupil of Polycarp (cf. the fragment of Irenæus' letter to Florinus, quoted by Eusebius, Bk. V. chap. 20). The Moscow MS. of the *Martyrium Polycarpi* states that Irenæus was in Rome at the time of Polycarp's martyrdom (155 or 156 A.D.), and appeals for its authority to a statement in Irenæus' own writings, which does not exist in any extant work, but may have been taken from an authentic work now lost (cf. Gebhardt, in the *Zeitschrift für die hist. Theologie*, 1875, p. 362 sqq.). But whatever truth there may be in the report, we find him, at the time of the great persecution of Lyons and Vienne (described in the next book, chap. 1), a presbyter of the church at Lyons, and carrying a letter from the confessors of that church to the bishop Eleutherus of Rome (see Bk. V. chap. 4). After the death of Pothinus, which took place in 177 (see Bk. V. *præf.* note 3, and chap. 1, § 29), Irenæus became bishop of Lyons, according to Bk. V. chap. 5. The exact date of his accession we do not know; but as Pothinus died during the persecution, and Irenæus was still a presbyter after the close of the persecution in which he met his death, he cannot have succeeded immediately. Since Irenæus, however, was, according to Eusebius, Pothinus' next successor, no great length of time can have elapsed between the death of the latter and the accession of the former. At the time of the paschal controversy, while Victor was bishop of Rome, Irenæus was still bishop (according to Bk. V. chap. 23). This was toward the close of the second century. His death is ordinarily put in the year 202 or 203, on the assumption that he suffered martyrdom under Septimius Severus. Jerome is the first to call him a martyr, and that not in his *de vir. ill.*, but in his *Comment. in Esaiam* (chap. 64), which was written some years later. It is quite possible that he confounded the Irenæus in question with another of the same name, who met his death in the persecution of Diocletian. Gregory of Tours first gives us a detailed account of the martyrdom, and in the Middle Ages Irenæus always figured as a martyr. But all this has no weight at all, when measured against the silence of Tertullian, Hippolytus, Eusebius, and all the earlier Fathers. Their silence must be accepted as conclusive evidence that he was not a martyr; and if he was not, there is no reason for assigning his death to the year 202 or 203. As we have no trace of him, however, subsequent to the time of the paschal controversy, it is probable that he died, at the latest, soon after the beginning of the third century.

Irenæus was the most important of the polemical writers of antiquity, and his works formed a storehouse from which all subsequent heresiographers drew. He is quoted very frequently by Eusebius as an authority for events which happened during the second century, and is treated by him with the most profound respect as one of the greatest writers of the early Church. Jerome devotes an unusually long chapter of his *de vir. ill.* to him (chap. 35), but tells us nothing that is not found in Eusebius' *History*. His greatest work, and the only one now extant, is his Ἐλεγχος καὶ ἀνατροπὴ τῆς ψευδωνύμου γνώσεως, which is commonly cited under the brief title πρὸς Αἱρέσεις, or *Adversus Hæreses* ("Against Heresies"). It consists of five books, and is extant only in a very ancient and literal Latin translation; though the numerous extracts made from it by later writers have preserved for us the original Greek of nearly the whole of the first book and many fragments of the others. There are also extant numerous fragments of an ancient Syriac version of the work. It was written — or at least the third book was — while Eleutherus was bishop of Rome, i.e. between 174 and 189 (see Bk. III. chap. 3, § 3, of the work itself). We are not able to fix the date of its composition more exactly. The author's primary object was to refute Valentinianism (cf. Bk. I. *præf.*, and Bk. III. *præf.*), but in connection with that subject he takes occasion to say considerable about other related heresies. The sources of this great work have been carefully discussed by Lipsius, in his *Quellenkritik des Epiphanios*, and in his *Quellen der ältesten Ketzergeschichte*, and by Harnack in his *Quellenkritik der Geschichte des Gnosticismus* (see also the article by Lipsius mentioned below). Of the other works of Irenæus, many of which Eusebius refers to, only fragments or bare titles have been preserved. Whether he ever carried out his intention (stated in *Adv. Hær.* I. 27. 4, and III. 12. 12) of writing a special work against Marcion, we cannot tell. Eusebius mentions this intention in Bk. V. chap. 20; and in Bk. IV. chap. 25 he classes Irenæus among the authors who had written against Marcion. But we hear nothing of the existence of the work from Irenæus' successors, and it is possible that Eusebius is thinking in chap. 25 only of the great work *Adv. Hær.* For a notice of Irenæus' epistle *On Schism*, addressed to Blastus, and the one *On Sovereignty*, addressed to Florinus, see Bk. V. chap. 20, notes 2 and 3; and on his treatise *On the Ogdoad*, see the same chapter, note 4. On his epistle to Victor in regard to the paschal dispute,

From them has come down to us in writing, the sound and orthodox faith received from apostolic tradition.[10]

CHAPTER XXII.

Hegesippus and the Events which he mentions.

HEGESIPPUS in the five books of Memoirs[1] **1** which have come down to us has left a most complete record of his own views. In them he states that on a journey to Rome he met a great many bishops, and that he received the same doctrine from all. It is fitting to hear what he says after making some remarks about the epistle of Clement to the Corinthians. His words are as follows: "And the church **2** of Corinth continued in the true faith until Primus[2] was bishop in Corinth. I conversed with them on my way to Rome, and abode with the Corinthians many days, during which we were mutually refreshed in the true doctrine. And when I had come to Rome I remained **3** there until Anicetus,[3] whose deacon was

see below, Bk. V. chap. 24, note 13. Other epistles upon the same subject are referred to by Eusebius at the close of the same chapter (see note 21 on that chapter). In Bk. V. chap. 26, Eusebius mentions four other works of Irenæus (see notes on that chapter). In addition to the works referred to by Eusebius, there are extant a number of fragments which purport to be from other works of Irenæus. Some of them are undoubtedly genuine, others not. Upon these fragments and the works to which they belong, see Harvey's edition of Irenæus' works, II. p. 431 sq., and Lipsius in the *Dict. of Christ. Biog.* article *Irenæus*, p. 265 sqq.

The best edition of Irenæus' works is that of Harvey (Cambridge, 1857, in 2 vols.). In connection with this edition, see Loof's important article on *Irenæushandschriften*, in *Kirchengeschichtliche Studien*, p. 1–93 (Leipzig, 1888). The literature on Irenæus is very extensive (for a valuable list, see Schaff's *Ch. Hist.* II. 746), but a full and complete biography is greatly to be desired. Lipsius' article, referred to just above, is especially valuable.

[10] ὧν καὶ εἰς ἡμᾶς τῆς ἀποστολικῆς παραδόσεως, ἡ τῆς ὑγιοῦς πίστεως ἔγγραφος κατῆλθεν ὀρθοδοξία.   Compare chap. 14, § 4.

[1] The five books of Hegesippus, ὑπομνήματα or *Memoirs*, are unfortunately lost; but a few fragments are preserved by Eusebius, and one by Photius, which have been collected by Routh, *Rel. Sac.* I. 205–219, and by Grabe, *Spicilegium*, II. 203–214. This work has procured for him from some sources the title of the "Father of Church History," but the title is misplaced, for the work appears to have been nothing more than a collection of reminiscences covering the apostolic and post-apostolic ages, and drawn partly from written, partly from oral sources, and in part from his own observation, and quite without chronological order and historical completeness. We know of no other works of his. Of Hegesippus himself we know very little. He apparently wrote his work during the episcopate of Eleutherus (175–189 A.D.), for he does not name his successor. How old he was at that time we do not know; but he was very likely a man past middle life, and hence was probably born early in the second century. With this, his own statement in the passage quoted by Eusebius, in chap. 8, that the deification of Antinoüs took place in his own day is quite consistent. The words of Jerome (*de vir. ill.* 22), who calls him a *vicinus apostolicorum temporum*, are too indefinite to give us any light, even if they rest upon any authority, as they probably do not. The journey which is mentioned in this chapter shows that his home must have been somewhere in the East, and there is no reason to doubt that he was a Hebrew Christian (see below, note 16).

[2] Of this Primus we know only what Hegesippus tells us here. We do not know the exact date of his episcopate, but it must have been at least in part synchronous with the episcopate of Pius of Rome (see chap. 11, note 14), for it was while Hegesippus was on his way to Rome that he saw Primus; and since he remained in Rome until the accession of Anicetus, he must have arrived there while Pius, Anicetus' predecessor, was bishop, for having gone to Rome on a visit, he can hardly have remained there a number of years.

[3] The interpretation of this sentence is greatly disputed. The Greek reads in all the MSS. γενόμενος δὲ ἐν Ῥώμῃ διαδοχὴν ἐποιησάμην μέχρις Ἀνικήτου, and this reading is confirmed by the Syriac

Eleutherus. And Anicetus was succeeded by Soter, and he by Eleutherus. In every succession, and in every city that is held which is preached by the law and the prophets and the Lord."

4 The same author also describes the beginnings of the heresies which arose in his time, in the following words : "And after James the Just had suffered martyrdom, as the Lord had also on the same account, Symeon, the son of the Lord's uncle, Clopas,[4] was appointed the next bishop. All proposed him as second bishop because he was a cousin of the Lord.

"Therefore,[4a] they called the Church a virgin, for it was not yet corrupted by vain discourses. But Thebuthis,[5] because he was not made bishop, began to corrupt it. He also was sprung from the seven sects[6] among the people, like Simon,[7] from whom came the Simonians, and Cleobius,[8] from whom came the Cleobians, and Dositheus,[9] from whom came the Dositheans, and Gorthæus,[10] from whom came the Goratheni, and Masbotheus,[11] from whom came the Masbothæans. From them sprang the Menandrianists,[12] and Marcionists,[13] and Carpocratians, and Valentinians, and Basilidians, and Saturnilians. Each introduced privately and separately his own peculiar opinion. From them came false Christs, false prophets, false apostles, who divided the unity of the Church by corrupt doctrines uttered against God and against his Christ." The same writer also records the 6 ancient heresies which arose among the Jews, in the following words : "There were, moreover, various opinions in the circumcision, among the children of Israel. The following were those that were opposed to the tribe of Judah and the Christ : Essenes, Galileans, Hemerobap-

---

version (according to Lightfoot). If these words be accepted as authentic, the only possible rendering seems to be the one which has been adopted by many scholars: "Being in Rome, I composed a catalogue of bishops down to Anicetus." This rendering is adopted also by Lightfoot, who holds that the list of Hegesippus is reproduced by Epiphanius in his *Panarium* XXVII. 6 (see his essay in *The Academy*, May 27, 1887, where this theory is broached, and compare the writer's notice of it in Harnack's *Theol. Lit. Zeitung* 1887, No. 18). But against this rendering it must be said, first, that it is very difficult to translate the words διαδοχὴν ἐποιησάμην, "I composed a catalogue of bishops," for διαδοχή nowhere else, so far as I am aware, means "catalogue," and nowhere else does the expression διαδοχὴν ποιεῖσθαι occur. Just below, the same word signifies "succession," and this is its common meaning. Certainly, if Hegesippus wished to say that he had composed a catalogue of bishops, he could not have expressed himself more obscurely. In the second place, if Hegesippus had really composed a catalogue of bishops and referred to it here, how does it happen that Eusebius, who is so concerned to ascertain the succession of bishops in all the leading sees nowhere refers to that catalogue, and nowhere even refers to it. He does give Irenæus' catalogue of the Roman bishops in Bk. V. chap. 6, but gives no hint there that he knows anything of a similar list composed by Hegesippus. In fact, it is very difficult to think that Hegesippus, in this passage, can have meant to say that he had composed a catalogue of bishops, and it is practically impossible to believe that Eusebius can have understood him to mean that. But the words διαδοχὴν ἐποιησάμην, if they can be made to mean anything at all, can certainly be made to mean nothing else than the composition of a catalogue, and hence it seems necessary to make some correction in the text. It is significant that Rufinus at this point reads *permansi ibi*, which shows that he at least did not understand Hegesippus to be speaking of a list of bishops. Rufinus' rendering gives us a hint of what must have stood in the original from which he drew, and so Savilius, upon the margin of his MS., substituted for διαδοχὴν the word διατριβήν, probably simply as a conjecture, but possibly upon the authority of some other MS. now lost. He has been followed by some editors, including Heinichen, who prints the word διατριβήν in the text. Val. retains διαδοχὴν in his text, but accepts διατριβήν as the true reading, and so translates. This reading is now very widely adopted; and it, or some other word with the same meaning, in all probability stood in the original text. In my notice of Lightfoot's article, I suggested the word διαγωγήν, which, while not so common as διατριβήν, is yet used with ποιεῖσθαι in the same sense, and its very uncommonness would account more easily for the change to the much commoner διαδοχὴν, which is epigraphically so like it.

The word μέχρι is incorrectly translated *apud* by Valesius, who reads, *mansi apud Anicetum*. He is followed by Crusè, who translates "I made my stay with Anicetus"; but μέχρι can mean only "until." Hegesippus therefore, according to his own statement, came to Rome before the accession of Anicetus and remained there until the latter became bishop. See chap. 11, note 19, for the relation of this statement to that of Eusebius.

For particulars in regard to Anicetus, see chap. 11, note 18; on Soter, see chap. 19, note 2, and on Eleutherus, Bk. V. Preface, note 2.

[4] See Bk. III. chap. 11, note 4. [4a] Διὰ τοῦτο. Valesius proposes to read μέχρι τούτου, which certainly makes better sense and which finds some support in the statement made by Eusebius in Bk. III. chap. 32, § 7. But all the MSS. have διὰ τοῦτο, and, as Stroth remarks, the illogical use of "therefore" at this point need not greatly surprise us in view of the general looseness of Hegesippus' style. The phrase is perhaps used proleptically, with a reference to what follows.

[5] Of Thebuthis we know only what is told us here. The statement that he became a heretic because he was not chosen bishop has about as much foundation as most reports of the kind. It was quite common for the Fathers to trace back the origin of schisms to this cause (compare e.g. Tertullian's *Adv. Val.* 4, and *De Bapt.* 17).

[6] The seven sects are mentioned by Hegesippus just below. Harnack maintains that Hegesippus in his treatment of heresies used two sources, one of them being the lost *Syntagma* of Justin (see his *Quellenkritik des Gnosticismus*, p. 37 sqq.). Lipsius, who in his *Quellen der Ketzergesch.* combats many of Harnack's positions, thinks it possible that Hegesippus *may* have had Justin's *Syntagma* before him.

[7] Simon Magus (see Bk. II. chap. 13, note 3).

[8] Cleobius is occasionally mentioned as a heretic by ecclesiastical writers, but none of them seems to know anything more about him than is told here by Hegesippus (see the article *Cleobius* in the *Dict. of Christ. Biog.*).

[9] Trustworthy information in regard to Dositheus is very scanty, but it is probable that he was one of the numerous Samaritan false messiahs, and lived at about the time of, or possibly before, Christ. "It seems likely that the Dositheans were a Jewish or Samaritan ascetic sect, something akin to the Essenes, existing from before our Lord's time, and that the stories connecting their founder with Simon Magus and with John the Baptist [see the *Clementine Recognitions*, II. 8 and *Homilies*, II. 24], may be dismissed as merely mythical" (Salmon, in the *Dict. of Christ. Biog.* art. *Dositheus*).

[10] Epiphanius and Theodoret also mention the Goratheni, but apparently knew no more about them than Hegesippus tells us here, Epiphanius classing them among the Samaritans, and Theodoret deriving them from Simon Magus.

[11] The name Masbotheus is supported by no MS. authority, but is given by Rufinus and by Nicephorus, and is adopted by most editors. The majority of the MSS. read simply Μασβωθαῖοι or Μασβώθεοι. Just below, Hegesippus gives the Masbotheans as one of the seven Jewish sects, while here he says they were derived from them. This contradiction Harnack explains by Hegesippus' use of two different sources, an unknown oral or written one, and Justin's *Syntagma*. The list of heresies given here he maintains stood in Justin's *Syntagma*, but the derivation of them from the seven Jewish sects cannot have been Justin's work, nor can the list of the seven sects have been made by Justin, for he gives quite a different list in his *Dialogue*, chap. 80. Lipsius, p. 25, thinks the repetition of the "Masbotheans" is more easily explained as a mere oversight or accident. The *Apostolic Const.* VI. 6 name the Masbotheans among Jewish sects, describing them as follows: "The Basmotheans, who deny providence, and say that the world is ruled by spontaneous motion, and take away the immortality of the soul." From what source this description was taken we do not know, and cannot decide as to its reliability. Salmon (in the *Dict. of Christ. Biog.*) remarks that "our real knowledge is limited to the occurrence of the name in Hegesippus, and there is no reason to think that any of those who have undertaken to explain it knew any more about the matter than ourselves."

[12] On Menander and the Menandrianists, see Bk. II. chap. 26; on the Carpocratians, chap. 7, note 17; on the Valentinians, see chap. 11, note 1; on the Basilidæans, chap. 7, note 7; on the Saturnilians, chap. 7, note 6.

[13] There is some dispute about this word. The Greek is Μαρκιανισταί, which Harnack regards as equivalent to Μαρκιωνισταί, or "followers of Marcion," but which Lipsius takes to mean "followers of Marcus." The latter is clearly epigraphically more correct, but the reasons for reading in this place Marcionites, or followers of Marcion, are strong enough to outweigh all other considerations (see Harnack, p. 31 ff. and Lipsius, p. 29 ff.).

tists, Masbothæans, Samaritans, Sadducees, Pharisees." [14]

7   And he wrote of many other matters, which we have in part already mentioned, introducing the accounts in their appropriate places. And from the Syriac Gospel according to the Hebrews he quotes some passages in the Hebrew tongue,[15] showing that he was a convert from the Hebrews,[16] and he mentions other matters as taken from the unwritten tradition of the 8 Jews. And not only he, but also Irenæus and the whole company of the ancients, called the Proverbs of Solomon All-virtuous Wisdom.[17] And when speaking of the books called Apocrypha, he records that some of them were composed in his day by certain heretics. But let us now pass on to another.

[14] These are the seven Jewish heresies mentioned above by Hegesippus. Justin (*Dial.* chap. 80) and Epiphanius (*Anaceph.*) also name seven Jewish sects, but they are not the same as those mentioned here (those of Justin: Sadducees, Genistæ, Meristæ, Galileans, Hellenianians, Pharisees, Baptists). Epiphanius (Vol. I. p. 230, Dindorf's ed.,— Samaritan sects 4: Gorothenes, Σεβουαῖοι, Essenes, Dositheans; Jewish 7: Scribes, Pharisees, Sadducees, Hemerobaptists, Ὀσσαῖοι, Nazarenes, Herodians). See Jess, in the *Zeitschr. für hist. Theol.* 1865, p. 45 sq.

[15] The exact meaning of this sentence is very difficult to determine. The Greek reads: ἔκ τε τοῦ καθ᾽ Ἑβραίους εὐαγγελίου καὶ τοῦ Συριακοῦ καὶ ἰδίως ἐκ τῆς Ἑβραΐδος διαλέκτου τινὰ τίθησιν. It is grammatically necessary to supply εὐαγγελίου after Συριακοῦ, and this gives us a Syriac gospel in addition to the Hebrew. Some have concluded that Tatian's *Diatessaron* is meant by it, but this will not do; for, as Handmann remarks, the fact that Hegesippus quotes from the work or works referred to is cited as evidence that he was a Hebrew. Hilgenfeld supposes that the *Chaldæo syroque scriptum evangelium secundum Hebræos*, which Jerome mentions, is referred to, and that the first-named εὐαγγέλιον καθ᾽ Ἑβραίους is a Greek translation, while the τὸ Συριακόν represents the original; so that Hegesippus is said to have used both the original and the translation. Eusebius, however, could not have made the discovery that he used both, unless the original and the translation differed in their contents, of which we have no hint, and which in itself is quite improbable. As the Greek reads, however, there is no other explanation possible, unless the τὸ Συριακὸν εὐαγγέλιον be taken to represent some other unknown Hebrew gospel, in which case the following clause refers to the citations from both of the gospels. That such a gospel existed, however, and was referred to by Eusebius so casually, as if it were a well-known work, is not conceivable. The only resource left, sp far as the writer can discover, is to amend the text, with Eichhorn, Nicholson, and Handmann, by striking out the first καί. The τοῦ Συριακοῦ then becomes a description of the εὐαγγέλιον καθ᾽ Ἑβραίους, " The Syriac Gospel according to the Hebrews." By the Syriac we are to understand, of course, the vulgar dialect, which had before the time of Christ taken the place of the Hebrew, and which is ordinarily called Aramaic. Eusebius then, on this interpretation, first qualifies the Gospel of the Hebrews more exactly, and then adds that Hegesippus quotes from the Hebrew original of it (ἐκ τῆς Ἑβραΐδος διαλέκτου), and not from a translation; e.g. from the Greek translation, which we know existed early. There is, to be sure, no MS. authority for the alteration of the text, and yet the sense of the passage seems to demand it, and I have consequently omitted the καί in my translation. Upon the interpretation of the passage, see Handmann's *Hebräer-Evangelium*, p. 32 ff., and upon the Gospel according to the Hebrews, see above, Bk. III. chap. 25, note 24, and chap. 27, note 8.

[16] Eusebius had abundant opportunity to learn from Hegesippus' works whether or not he was a Hebrew Christian, and hence we cannot doubt that his conclusion in regard to Hegesippus' nationality (whether based merely upon the premises given here, or partly upon other facts unknown to us) is correct. His nationality explains the fact that he deduces the Christian heresies from Jewish, and not, like other writers, from heathen roots. There is, however, no reason, with Baur and others, to suppose that Hegesippus was a Judaizer. In fact, Eusebius' respectful treatment of him is in itself conclusive proof that his writings cannot have revealed heretical notions.

[17] This phrase (πανάρετος σοφία) was very frequently employed among the Fathers as a title of the Book of Proverbs. Clement of Rome (1 Cor. lvii.) is, so far as I know, the first so to use it. The word πανάρετος is applied also to the apocryphal Wisdom of Solomon, by Epiphanius (*de mens. et pond.* § 4) and others. Among the Fathers the Book of Sirach, the Solomonic Apocrypha, and the Book of Proverbs all bore the common title σοφία, " Wisdom," which well defines the character of each of them; and this simple title is commoner than the compound phrase which occurs in this pas-

CHAPTER XXIII.

Dionysius, Bishop of Corinth, and the Epistles which he wrote.[1]

AND first we must speak of Dionysius, 1 who was appointed bishop of the church in Corinth, and communicated freely of his inspired labors not only to his own people, but also to those in foreign lands, and rendered the greatest service to all in the catholic epistles which he wrote to the churches. Among these is 2 the one addressed to the Lacedæmonians,[2] containing instruction in the orthodox faith and an admonition to peace and unity ; the one also addressed to the Athenians, exciting them to faith and to the life prescribed by the Gospel, which he accuses them of esteeming lightly, as if they had almost apostatized from the faith since the martyrdom of their ruler Publius,[3] which had taken place during the persecutions of those days. He mentions Quadratus[4] also, stating that he was appointed 3 their bishop after the martyrdom of Publius, and testifying that through his zeal they were brought together again and their faith revived. He records, moreover, that Dionysius the Areopagite,[5]

sage (cf. e.g. Justin Martyr's *Dial.* c. 129, and Melito, quoted by Eusebius in chap. 26, below). For further particulars, see especially Lightfoot's edition of the epistles of Clement of Rome, p. 164.

[1] Eusebius speaks, in this chapter, of seven Catholic epistles, and of one addressed to an individual. None of these epistles are now extant, though Eusebius here, and in Bk. II. chap. 25, gives us four brief but interesting fragments from the Epistle to the Romans. We know of the other epistles only what Eusebius tells us in this chapter. That Dionysius was held in high esteem as a writer of epistles to the churches is clear, not only from Eusebius' statement, but also from the fact that heretics thought it worth while to circulate interpolated and mutilated copies of them, as stated below. The fact that he wrote epistles to churches so widely scattered shows that he possessed an extended reputation.

Of Dionysius himself (who is, without foundation, called a martyr by the Greek Church, and a confessor by the Latin Church) we know only what we are told by Eusebius, for Jerome (*de vir. ill.* 27) adds nothing to the account given in this chapter. In his *Chron.* Eusebius mentions Dionysius in connection with the eleventh year of Marcus Aurelius. According to Eusebius' statement in this same chapter, Dionysius' Epistle to the Romans was addressed to the bishop Soter, and as Eusebius had the epistle before him, there is no reason for doubting his report. Soter was bishop from about 167 to 175 (see above, chap. 19, note 4), and therefore the statements of the *Chron.* and the *History* are in accord. When Dionysius died we do not know, but he was no longer living in 199, for Bacchylus was bishop of Corinth at that time (see Bk. V. chap. 22). It is commonly said that Dionysius was the immediate successor of Primus, bishop of Corinth. This may be true, but we have no ground for the assumption. We know only that Primus' episcopate was synchronous, at least in part, with that of Pius of Rome (see the previous chapter, note 2), who was bishop from about 139 or 141 to 154 or 156, and that Dionysius' episcopate was synchronous at least in part with that of Soter of Rome (about 167 to 175).

[2] This is, so far as I am aware, the earliest mention of a church at Lacedæmon or Sparta. The bishop of Sparta is mentioned in the synodical letter of the province of Hellas to the emperor Leo (457–477 A.D.), and also still later in the Acts of the Sixth and Eighth General Synods, according to Wiltsch's *Geography and Statistics of the Church* (London ed. p. 134 and 466).

[3] Of this Publius we know only what Eusebius tells us here. What particular persecution is referred to we cannot tell, but Publius' martyrdom seems to have occurred in the reign of Antoninus Pius or Marcus Aurelius; for he was the immediate predecessor of Quadratus, who was apparently bishop at the time Dionysius was writing.

[4] We know nothing more about this Quadratus, for he is to be distinguished from the prophet and from the apologist (see chap. 3, note 2). Eusebius' words seem to imply that he was bishop at the time Dionysius was writing.

[5] On Dionysius the Areopagite, see Bk. III. chap. 4, note 20.

who was converted to the faith by the apostle Paul, according to the statement in the Acts of the Apostles,[6] first obtained the episcopate

4 of the church at Athens. And there is extant another epistle of his addressed to the Nicomedians,[7] in which he attacks the heresy of Marcion, and stands fast by the canon of

5 the truth. Writing also to the church that is in Gortyna,[8] together with the other parishes in Crete, he commends their bishop Philip,[9] because of the many acts of fortitude which are testified to as performed by the church under him, and he warns them to be on their guard against the aberrations of the heretics.

6 And writing to the church that is in Amastris,[10] together with those in Pontus, he refers to Bacchylides[11] and Elpistus, as having urged him to write, and he adds explanations of passages of the divine Scriptures, and mentions their bishop Palmas[12] by name. He gives them much advice also in regard to marriage and chastity, and commands them to receive those who come back again after any fall, whether it be

7 delinquency or heresy.[13] Among these is inserted also another epistle addressed to the Cnosians,[14] in which he exhorts Pinytus, bishop of

the parish, not to lay upon the brethren a grievous and compulsory burden in regard to chastity, but to have regard to the weakness of the mul-

8 titude. Pinytus, replying to this epistle, admires and commends Dionysius, but exhorts him in turn to impart some time more solid food, and to feed the people under him, when he wrote again, with more advanced teaching, that they might not be fed continually on these milky doctrines and imperceptibly grow old under a training calculated for children. In this epistle also Pinytus' orthodoxy in the faith and his care for the welfare of those placed under him, his learning and his comprehension of divine things, are revealed as in a most perfect image.

9 There is extant also another epistle written by Dionysius to the Romans, and addressed to Soter,[15] who was bishop at that time. We cannot do better than to subjoin some passages from this epistle, in which he commends the practice of the Romans which has been retained down to the persecution in our own days. His

10 words are as follows : " For from the beginning it has been your practice to do good to all the brethren in various ways, and to send contributions to many churches in every city. Thus relieving the want of the needy, and making provision for the brethren in the mines by the gifts which you have sent from the beginning, you Romans keep up the hereditary customs of the Romans, which your blessed bishop Soter has not only maintained, but also added to, furnishing an abundance of supplies to the saints, and encouraging the brethren from abroad with blessed words, as a loving father his chil-

11 dren." In this same epistle he makes mention also of Clement's epistle to the Corinthians,[16] showing that it had been the custom from the beginning to read it in the church. His words are as follows : " To-day we have passed the Lord's holy day, in which we have read your epistle. From it, whenever we read it, we shall always be able to draw advice, as also from the former epistle, which was written

12 to us through Clement." The same writer also speaks as follows concerning his own epistles, alleging that they had been mutilated : " As the brethren desired me to write epistles, I wrote. And these epistles the apostles of the devil have filled with tares, cutting out some things and adding others.[17] For them a woe is reserved.[18] It is, therefore, not to be wondered

---

[6] See Acts xvii. 34.

[7] The extent of Dionysius' influence is shown by his writing an epistle to so distant a church as that of Nicomedia in Bithynia, and also to the churches of Pontus (see below). The fact that he considers it necessary to attack Marcionism in this epistle to the Nicomedians is an indication of the wide and rapid spread of that sect, — which indeed is known to us from many sources.

[8] Gortyna was an important city in Crete, which was early the seat of a bishop. Tradition, indeed, makes Titus the first bishop of the church there.

[9] Of this Philip, bishop of Gortyna, and a contemporary of Dionysius, we know only what Eusebius tells us here and in chap. 25.

[10] Amastris was a city of Pontus, which is here mentioned for the first time as the seat of a Christian church. Its bishop is referred to frequently in the Acts of Councils during the next few centuries (see also note 12, below).

[11] This Bacchylides is perhaps identical with the Bacchylus who was afterward bishop of Corinth (Bk. V. chap. 22). Elpistus is an otherwise unknown personage.

[12] This Palmas, bishop of Amastris in Pontus, presided as senior bishop over a council of the bishops of Pontus held toward the close of the century on the paschal question (see Bk. V. chap. 23). Nothing more is known of him.

[13] It is quite likely, as Salmon suggests (in the Dict. of Christ. Biog.), that Dionysius, who wrote against Marcion in this epistle to the Nicomedians, also had Marcionism in view in writing on life and discipline to the churches of Pontus and Crete. It was probably in consequence of reaction against their strict discipline that he advocated the readmission to the Church of excommunicated offenders, in this anticipating the later practice of the Roman church, which was introduced by Callixtus and soon afterward became general, though not without bitter opposition from many quarters. Harnack (Dogmengeschichte, p. 332, note 4) throws doubt upon the correctness of this report of Eusebius: but such doubt is unwarranted, for Eusebius had Dionysius' epistle before him, and the position which he represents him as taking is quite in accord with the mildness which he recommends to Pinytus, and is therefore just what we should expect. The fact that Callixtus' principle is looked upon by Tertullian and Hippolytus as an innovation does not militate at all against the possibility that Dionysius in Corinth, or other individuals in other minor churches, held the same principles some time before.

[14] Cnossus, or Cnosus, was the capital city of Crete. This epistle is no longer extant, nor do we know anything about Pinytus himself except what is told us here and in chap. 21, above, where he is mentioned among the ecclesiastical writers of the day. Jerome (de vir. ill. 28) only repeats what Eusebius says, and Rufinus, in stating that Pinytus was convinced by the epistle of Dionysius and changed his course, seems simply to have misunderstood what Eusebius says about his admiration for and praise of Dionysius. It is evident from the tone of his reply that Pinytus was not led by Dionysius' epistle to agree with him.

[15] On Soter, see chap. 19, note 2.
This practice of the Roman church combined with other causes to secure it that position of influence and prominence which resulted in the primacy of its bishop, and finally in the papacy. The position of the Roman church, as well as its prosperity and numerical strength, gave it early a feeling that it was called upon in an especial way to exercise oversight and to care for weaker sister churches, and thus its own good offices helped to promote its influence and its power.

[16] On Clement's Epistle to the Corinthians, see Bk. III. chap. 16.

[17] See above, note 1.

[18] Compare Rev. xxii. 18.

at if some have attempted to adulterate the Lord's writings also,[19] since they have formed designs even against writings which are of less account." [20]

There is extant, in addition to these, another epistle of Dionysius, written to Chrysophora,[21] a most faithful sister. In it he writes what is suitable, and imparts to her also the proper spiritual food. So much concerning Dionysius.

CHAPTER XXIV.

Theophilus Bishop of Antioch.

1   OF Theophilus,[1] whom we have mentioned as bishop of the church of Antioch,[2]

three elementary works addressed to Autolycus are extant ; also another writing entitled Against the Heresy of Hermogenes,[3] in which he makes use of testimonies from the Apocalypse of John, and finally certain other catechetical books.[4] And as the heretics, no less then than at   2 other times, were like tares, destroying the pure harvest of apostolic teaching, the pastors of the churches everywhere hastened to restrain them as wild beasts from the fold of Christ, at one time by admonitions and exhortations to the brethren, at another time by contending more openly against them in oral discussions and refutations, and again by correcting their opinions with most accurate proofs in written works. And that Theophilus also, with   3 the others, contended against them, is manifest from a certain discourse of no common merit written by him against Marcion.[5] This work too, with the others of which we have spoken, has been preserved to the present day.

Maximinus,[6] the seventh from the apostles, succeeded him as bishop of the church of Antioch.

---

[19] A probable, though not exclusive, reference to Marcion, for he was by no means the only one of that age that interpolated and mutilated the works of the apostles to fit his theories. Apostolic works — true and false — circulated in great numbers, and were made the basis for the speculations and moral requirements of many of the heretical schools of the second century.   [20] οὐ τοιαύταις.

[21] Chrysophora is an otherwise unknown person.

[1] Eusebius is the only early writer of the early centuries to mention Theophilus and his writings. Among the Latin Fathers, Lactantius and Gennadius refer to his work, *ad Autolycum ;* and Jerome devotes chap. 25 of his *de vir. ill.* to him. Beyond this there is no direct mention of Theophilus, or of his works, during the early centuries (except that of Malalas, which will be referred to below). Eusebius here calls Theophilus bishop of Antioch, and in chap. 20 makes him the sixth bishop, as does also Jerome in his *de vir. ill.* chap. 25. But in his epistle, *ad Algas.* (Migne, *Ep.* 121), Jerome calls him the seventh bishop of Antioch, beginning his reckoning with the apostle Peter. Eusebius, in his *Chron.,* puts the accession of Theophilus into the ninth year of Marcus Aurelius (169); and this may be at least approximately correct. The accession of his successor Maximus is put into the seventeenth year (177); but this date is at least four years too early, for his work, *ad Autolycum,* quotes from a work in which the death of Marcus Aurelius (who died in 180) was mentioned, and hence cannot have been written before 181 or 182. We know that his successor, Maximus, became bishop sometime between 189 and 192, and hence Theophilus died between 181 and that time. We have only Eusebius' words (Jerome simply repeats Eusebius' statement) for the fact that Theophilus was bishop of Antioch (his extant works do not mention the fact, nor do those who quote from his writings), but there is no good ground for doubting the truth of the report. We know nothing more about his life.

In addition to the works mentioned in this chapter, Jerome (*de vir. ill.*) refers to Commentaries upon the Gospel and the book of Proverbs, in the following words: *Legi sub nomine ejus in Evangelium et in Proverbia Salomonis Commentarios qui mihi cum superiorum voluminum elegantia et phrasi non videntur congruere.* The commentary upon the Gospel is referred to by Jerome again in the preface to his own commentary on Matthew; and in his epistle, *ad Algasiam,* he speaks of a harmony of the four Gospels, by Theophilus (*qui quatuor Evangelistarum in unum opus dicta compingens*), which may have been identical with the commentary, or may have formed a basis for it. This commentary is mentioned by none of the Fathers before or after Jerome; and Jerome himself expresses doubts as to its genuineness, or at least he does not think that its style compares with that of the other works ascribed to Theophilus. Whether the commentary was genuine or not we have no means of deciding, for it is no longer extant. There is in existence a Latin commentary on the Gospels in four books, which bears the name of Theophilus, and is published in Otto's *Corpus Apol.* Vol. VIII. p. 278-324. This was universally regarded as a spurious work until Zahn, in 1883 (in his *Forschungen zur Gesch. des N. T. Canons,* Theil II.) made an elaborate effort to prove it a genuine work of Theophilus of Antioch. Harnack, however, in his *Texte und Unters.* I. 4, p. 97-175, has shown conclusively that Zahn is mistaken, and that the extant commentary is nothing better than a Post-Nicene compilation from the works of various Latin Fathers. Zahn, in his reply to Harnack (*Forschungen,* Theil III. Beilage 3), still maintains that the Commentary is a genuine work of Theophilus, with large interpolations, but there is no adequate ground for such a theory; and it has found few, if any, supporters. We must conclude, then, that if Theophilus did write such a commentary, it is no longer extant.

The three books addressed to Autolycus (a heathen friend otherwise unknown to us) are still extant in three Mediæval MSS. and have been frequently published both in the original and in translation. The best edition of the original is that of Otto (*Corp. Apol.* Vol. VIII.); English translation by Dods, in the *Ante-Nicene Fathers,* Vol. II. p. 85-121. The work is an apology, designed to exhibit

the falsehood of idolatry and the truth of Christianity. The author was a learned writer, well acquainted with Greek philosophy; and his literary style is of a high order. He acknowledges no good in the Greek philosophers, except what they have taken from the Old Testament writers. The genuineness of the work has been attacked, but without sufficient reason.

From Book II. chap. 30 of his *ad Autol.* we learn that Theophilus had written also a work *On History.* No such work is extant, nor is it mentioned by Eusebius or any other Father. Malalas, however, cites a number of times "The chronologist Theophilus," and it is possible that he used this lost historical work. It is possible, on the other hand, that he refers to some other unknown Theophilus (see Harnack, *Texte und Unters.* I. 1, p. 291).

[2] In chap. 20, above.

[3] This work against Hermogenes is no longer extant. Harnack (p. 294 ff.) gives strong grounds for supposing that it was the common source from which Tertullian, in his work *ad Hermogenem,* Hippolytus, in his *Phil.* VIII. 10 and X. 24, and Clement of Alexandria, in his *Proph. Selections,* 56, all drew. If this be true, as seems probable, the Hermogenes attacked by these various writers is one man, and his chief heresy, as we learn from Tertullian and Hippolytus, was that God did not create the world out of nothing, but only formed it out of matter which, like himself, was eternally existent.

[4] These catechetical works (τινα κατηχητικὰ βιβλία), which were extant in the time of Eusebius, are now lost. They are mentioned by none of the Fathers except Jerome, who speaks of *alii breves elegantesque tractatus ad ædificationem Ecclesiæ pertinentes* as extant in his time. We know nothing more of their nature than is thus told us by Jerome.

[5] This work, which is also now lost, is mentioned by no other Father except Jerome, who puts it first in his list of Theophilus' writings, but does not characterize it in any way, though he says it was extant in his time. Irenæus, in four passages of his great work, exhibits striking parallels to Bk. II. chap. 25 of Theophilus' *ad Autol.,* which have led to the assumption that he knew the latter work. Harnack, however, on account of the shortness of time which elapsed between the composition of the *ad Autol.* and Irenæus' work, and also on account of the nature of the resemblances between the parallel passages, thinks it improbable that Irenæus used the *ad Autol.,* and concludes that he was acquainted rather with Theophilus' work against Marcion, a conclusion which accords best with the facts known to us.

[6] Here, and in Bk. V. chap. 19, § 1, Eusebius gives this bishop's name as Maximinus. In the *Chron.* we find Μάξιμος, and in Jerome's version Maximus, though one MS. of the latter gives Maximinus. According to the *Chron.* he became bishop in 177, and was succeeded by Serapion in 190. As remarked in note 1, above, the former date is incorrect, for Theophilus must have lived at least as late as 181 or 182. We cannot reach certainty in regard to the date either of his accession or of his death; but if Eusebius' statement (in Bk. V. chap. 19), that Serapion was bishop while Commodus was still emperor, is to be believed (see further, Bk. V. chap. 19, note 1), Maximinus must have died at least as early as 192, which gives us for his episcopate some part of the period from 181 to 192. We know no particulars in regard to the life of Maximinus.

CHAPTER XXV.

Philip and Modestus.

PHILIP who, as we learn from the words of Dionysius,[1] was bishop of the parish of Gortyna, likewise wrote a most elaborate work against Marcion,[2] as did also Irenæus[3] and Modestus.[4] The last named has exposed the error of the man more clearly than the rest to the view of all. There are a number of others also whose works are still preserved by a great many of the brethren.

CHAPTER XXVI.

Melito and the Circumstances which he records.

1   IN those days also Melito,[1] bishop of the parish in Sardis, and Apolinarius,[2] bishop

---

[1] See above, chap. 23, § 5.

[2] Philip's work against Marcion which Eusebius mentions here is no longer extant, and, so far as the writer knows, is mentioned by no other Father except Jerome (*de vir. ill.* 30), who tells us only what Eusebius records here, using, however, the adjective *præclarum* for Eusebius' σπουδαιότατον.

[3] On Irenæus, see above, chap. 21, note 9.

[4] Modestus, also, is a writer known to us only from Eusebius (here, and in chap. 21) and from Jerome (*de vir. ill.* 32). According to the latter, the work against Marcion was still extant in his day, but he gives us no description of it. He adds, however, that a number of spurious works ascribed to Modestus were in circulation at that time (*Feruntur sub nomine ejus et alia syntagmata, sed ab eruditis quasi ψευδόγραφα repudiantur*). Neither these nor the genuine works are now extant, so far as we know.

[1] The first extant notice of Melito, bishop of Sardis, is found in the letter addressed by Polycrates to Bishop Victor of Rome (c. 190–202 A.D.) in support of the Quartodeciman practice of the Asia Minor churches. A fragment of this letter is given by Eusebius in Bk. V. chap. 24, and from it we learn that Melito also favored the Quartodeciman practice, that he was a man whose walk and conversation were altogether under the influence of the Holy Spirit, and that he was buried at Sardis. Polycrates in this fragment calls Melito a eunuch. Whether the word is to be understood in its literal sense or is to be taken as meaning simply that Melito lived in "virgin continence" is disputed. In favor of the latter interpretation may be urged the fact that the Greek word and its Latin equivalent were very commonly used by the Fathers in this figurative sense, e.g. by Athenagoras, by Tertullian, by Clement of Alexandria, by Cassianus (whose work on continence bore the title περὶ ἐγκρατείας, ἢ περὶ εὐνουχίας), by Jerome, Epiphanius, Chrysostom, Theodoret, Gregory Nazianzen, &c. (see Smith and Wace's *Dict. of Christ. Biog.*, article *Melito*, and Suicer's *Thesaurus*). On the other hand, such continence cannot have been a rare thing in Asia Minor in the time of Polycrates, and the fact that Melito is called specifically "the eunuch" looks peculiar if nothing more than that is meant by it. The case of Origen, who made himself a eunuch for the sake of preserving his chastity, at once occurs to us in this connection (see Renan, *L'église chrét.* p. 436, and compare Justin Martyr's *Apol.* I. 29). The canonical rule that no such eunuch could hold clerical office came later, and hence the fact that Melito was a bishop cannot be urged against the literal interpretation of the word here. Polycrates' meaning hardly admits of an absolute decision, but at least it cannot be looked upon as it is by most historians as certain that he uses the word here in its figurative sense.

Polycrates says nothing of the fact that Melito was a writer, but we learn from this chapter (§ 4), and from Bk. VI. chap. 13, that Clement of Alexandria, in a lost work, mentioned his writings and even wrote a work in reply to one of his (see below, note 23). According to the present chapter he was a very prolific writer, and that he was a man of marked talent is clear from Jerome's words in his *de vir. ill.* chap. 24 (where he refers to Tertullian's lost work, *de Ecstasi*): *Hujus* [i.e. *Melitonis*] *elegans et declamatorium ingenium Tertullianus in septem libris, quos scripsit adversus ecclesiam pro Montano, cavillatur, dicens eum a plerisque nostrorum prophetam putari.* In spite of the fact that Tertullian satirized Melito's talent, he nevertheless was greatly influenced by his writings and owed much to them (see the points of contact between the two men given by Harnack, p. 250 sqq.). The statement that he was regarded by many as a prophet accords well with Polycrates' description of him referred to above. The indications all point to the fact that Melito was decidedly ascetic in his tendencies, and that he had a great deal in common with the spirit which gave

---

of Hierapolis, enjoyed great distinction. Each of them on his own part addressed apologies in behalf of the faith to the above-mentioned emperor[3] of the Romans who was reigning at that time. The following works of these   2 writers have come to our knowledge. Of Melito,[4] the two books On the Passover,[5] and

---

rise to Montanism and even made Tertullian a Montanist, and yet at the same time he opposed Montanism, and is therefore spoken of slightingly by Tertullian. His position, so similar to that of the Montanists, was not in favor with the orthodox theologians of the third century, and this helps to explain why, although he was such a prolific and talented writer, and although he remained orthodox, he nevertheless passed almost entirely out of the memory of the Church of the third and following centuries. To this is to be added the fact that Melito was a chiliast; and the teachings of the Montanists brought such disrepute upon chiliasm that the Fathers of the third and following centuries did not show much fondness for those who held or had held these views. Very few notices of Melito's works are found among the Fathers, and none of those works is to-day extant. Eusebius is the first to give us an idea of the number and variety of his writings, and he does little more than mention the titles, a fact to be explained only by his lack of sympathy with Melito's views.

The time at which Melito lived is indicated with sufficient exactness by the fact that he wrote his *Apology* during the reign of Marcus Aurelius, but after the death of his brother Lucius, i.e. after 169 (see below, note 21); and that when Polycrates wrote his epistle to Victor of Rome, he had been dead already some years. It is possible (as held by Piper, Otto, and others) that his *Apology* was his last work, for Eusebius mentions it last in his list. At the same time, it is quite as possible that Eusebius enumerates Melito's works simply in the order in which he found them arranged in the library of Cæsarea, where he had perhaps seen them. Of the dates of his episcopacy, and of his predecessors and successors in the see of Sardis, we know nothing.

In addition to the works mentioned in this chapter by Eusebius, who does not pretend to give a full list, we find in Anastasius Sinaita's *Hodegos seu dux viæ c. aceph.* fragments from two other works entitled εἰς τὸ πάθος and περὶ σαρκώσεως χριστοῦ (the latter directed against Marcion), which cannot be identified with any mentioned by Eusebius (see Harnack, I. 1, p. 254). The *Codex Nitriacus Musei Britannici* 12,156 contains four fragments ascribed to Melito, of which the first belongs undoubtedly to his genuine work περὶ ψυχῆς καὶ σώματος, which is mentioned in this chapter by Eusebius. The second purports to be taken from a work, περὶ σταυροῦ, of which we hear nowhere else, and which may or may not have been by Melito. The third fragment bears the title *Melitonis episcopi de fide*, and might be looked upon as an extract from the work περὶ πίστεως, mentioned by Eusebius (as Otto regards it); but the same fragment is four times ascribed to Irenæus by other early authorities, and an analysis of these authorities shows that the tradition in favor of Irenæus is stronger than that in favor of Melito, and so Harnack mentions a work, περὶ πίστεως, which is ascribed by Maximus Confessor to Irenæus, and from which the quotation may have been taken (see Harnack, *ibid.* p. 266 ff.). The fourth fragment was taken in all probability from Melito's work, περὶ πάθους, mentioned by Anastasius. An Apology in Syriac, bearing the name of Melito, is extant in another of the Nitrian MSS. in the British Museum (No. 14,658), and has been published with an English translation by Cureton, in his *Spic. Syr.* (p. 41–51). It has been proved, however, that this Apology (which we have entire) was not written by Melito, but probably by an inhabitant of Syria, in the latter part of the second, or early part of the third century, — whether originally in the Greek or Syriac language is uncertain (see Harnack, p. 261 ff., and Smith and Wace, Vol. III. p. 895). In addition to the genuine writings, there must be mentioned also some spurious works which are still extant. Two Latin works of the early Middle Ages, entitled *de transitu Mariæ* and *de passione S. Joannis Evangelistæ*, and also a *Catena* of the latter Middle Ages on the Apocalypse, and a *Clavis Scripturæ* of the Carlovingian period (see below, note 18) bear in some MSS. the name of Melito. This fact shows that Melito's name was not entirely forgotten in the Occidental Church of the Middle Ages, though little exact knowledge of him seems to have existed.

On Melito and his writings, see Piper's article in the *Theol. Studien und Kritiken*, 1838, p. 54–154; Salmon's article in Smith and Wace, and especially Harnack's *Texte und Unters.* I. 1, p. 240–278. The extant fragments of Melito's writings are given in Routh's *Rel. Sac.* I. 111–153, and in Otto's *Corp. Apol.* IX. 374–478, and an English translation in the *Ante-Nicene Fathers*, Vol. VIII. p. 750–762.   [2] On Apolinarius and his writings, see chap. 27.

[3] Marcus Aurelius.

[4] The following list of Melito's works is at many points very uncertain, owing to the various readings of the MSS. and versions. We have as authorities for the text, the Greek MSS. of Eusebius, the *History* of Nicephorus, the translation of Rufinus, chap. 24 of Jerome's *de vir. ill.*, and the Syriac version of this passage of Eusebius' *History*, which has been printed by Cureton, in his *Spic. Syr.* p. 56 ff.

[5] The quotation from this work given by Eusebius in § 7, per-

one On the Conduct of Life and the Prophets,[6] the discourse On the Church,[7] and one On the Lord's Day,[8] still further one On the Faith of Man,[9] and one On his Creation,[10] another also On the Obedience of Faith, and one On the Senses ;[11] besides these the work On the Soul and Body,[12] and that On Baptism,[13] and the one

On Truth,[14] and On the Creation and Generation of Christ ;[15] his discourse also On Prophecy,[16] and that On Hospitality ;[17] still further, The Key,[18] and the books On the Devil and the Apocalypse of John,[19] and the work On the Corporeality of God,[20] and finally the book ad-

---

haps enables us to fix approximately the date at which it was written. Rufinus reads Sergius Paulus, instead of Servilius Paulus, which is found in all the Greek MSS. Sergius Paulus is known to have had his second consulship in 168, and it is inferred by Waddington that he was proconsul about 164 to 166 (see *Fastes des provinces Asiatiques*, chap. 2, § 148). No Servilius Paulus is known in connection with the province of Asia, and hence it seems probable that Rufinus is correct; and if so, the work on the Passover was written early in the sixties. The fragment which Eusebius gives in this chapter is the only part of his work that is extant. It was undoubtedly in favor of the Quartodeciman practice, for Polycrates, who was a decided Quartodeciman, cites Melito in support of his position.

[6] The exact reading at this point is disputed. I read, with a number of MSS., τὸ περὶ πολιτείας καὶ προφητῶν, making but one work, *On the Conduct of Life and the Prophets*. Many MSS., followed by Valesius, Heinichen, and Burton, read τὰ instead of τό, thus making either two works (one *On the Conduct of Life*, and the other *On the Prophets*), or one work containing more than one book. Rufinus translates *de optima conversatione liber unus, sed et de prophetis*, and the Syriac repeats the preposition, as if it read καὶ περὶ πολιτείας καὶ περὶ προφητῶν. It is not quite certain whether Rufinus and the Syriac thought of two works in translating thus, or of only one. Jerome translates, *de vita prophetarum librum unum*, and in accordance with this translation Otto proposes to read τῶν προφητῶν instead of καὶ προφητῶν. But this is supported by no MS. authority, and cannot be accepted. No fragments of this work are extant.

[7] ὁ περὶ ἐκκλησίας. Jerome, *de ecclesia librum unum*.

[8] ὁ περὶ κυριακῆς λόγος. Jerome, *de Die Dominica librum unum*.

[9] Valésius, Otto, Heinichen, and other editors, following the majority of the MSS., read περὶ φύσεως ἀνθρώπου, *On the Nature of Man*. Four important MSS., however, read περὶ πίστεως ἀνθρώπου, and this reading is confirmed both by Rufinus and by the Syriac; whether by Jerome also, as claimed by Harnack, is uncertain, for he omits both this work and the one *On the Obedience of Faith*, given just below, and mentions a *de fide librum unum*, which does not occur in Eusebius' list, and which may have arisen through mistake from either of the titles given by Eusebius, or, as seems more probable, may have been derived from the title of the work mentioned below, *On the Creation and Generation of Christ*, as remarked in note 15. If this supposition be correct, Jerome omits all reference to this work περὶ πίστεως ἀνθρώπων. The text of Jerome is unfortunately very corrupt at this point. In the present passage πίστεως is better supported by tradition than φύσεως, and at the same time is the more difficult reading, and hence I have adopted it as more probably representing the original.

[10] ὁ περὶ πλάσεως. Jerome, *de plasmate librum unum*.

[11] All the Greek MSS. combine these two titles into one, reading ὁ περὶ ὑπακοῆς πίστεως αἰσθητηρίων: "On the subjection (or *obedience*) of the senses to faith." This reading is adopted by Valesius, Heinichen, Otto, and others; but Nicephorus reads ὁ περὶ ὑπακοῆς πίστεως, καὶ ὁ περὶ αἰσθητηρίων, and Rufinus translates, *de obedientia fidei, de sensibus*, both of them making two works, as I have done in the text. Jerome leaves the first part untranslated, and reads only *de sensibus*, while the Syriac reproduces only the words ὁ περὶ ὑπακοῆς (or ἀκοῆς) πίστεως, omitting the second clause. Christophorsonus, Stroth, Zimmermann, Burton, and Harnack consequently read ὁ περὶ ὑπακοῆς πίστεως, ὁ περὶ αἰσθητηρίων, concluding that the words ὁ περὶ after πίστεως have fallen out of the Greek text. I have adopted this reading in my translation.

[12] A serious difficulty arises in connection with this title from the fact that most of the Greek MSS. read ὁ περὶ ψυχῆς καὶ σώματος ἢ νοός, while the Syriac, Rufinus, and Jerome omit the ἢ νοός entirely. Nicephorus and two of the Greek MSS. meanwhile read ἣν ἐν οἷς, which is evidently simply a corruption of ἢ νοός, so that the Greek MSS. are unanimous for this reading. Otto, Crusè, and Salmon read καὶ νοός, but there is no authority for καὶ instead of ἢ, and the change cannot be admitted. The explanation which Otto gives (p. 376) of the change of ἢ to καὶ will not hold, as Harnack shows on p. 247, note 346. It seems to me certain that the words ἢ νοός did not stand in the original, but that the word νοός (either alone or preceded by ἢ or καὶ) was written upon the margin by some scribe, perhaps as an alternative to ψυχῆς, perhaps as an addition in the interest of trichotomy, and was later inserted in the text after ψυχῆς and σώματος, under the impression that it was an alternative title of the book. My reasons for this opinion are the agreement of the versions in the omission of νοός, the impossibility of explaining the ἢ before νοός in the original text, the fact that in the Greek MSS., in Rufinus, and in the Syriac, the words καὶ περὶ ψυχῆς καὶ σώματος are repeated further down in the list, — a repetition which Harnack thinks was made inadvertently by Eusebius himself, and which in omitting νοός confirms the omission of it in the present case, — and

finally, a fact which seems to me decisive, but which has apparently hitherto escaped notice, that the νοός follows instead of precedes the σώματος, and thus breaks the logical order, which would certainly have been preserved in the title of a book.

[13] ὁ περὶ λουτροῦ; Jerome, *de baptismate*.

[14] Apolinarius (according to chap. 27) also wrote a work *On Truth*, and the place which it holds in that list, between an apologetical work addressed to the Greeks and one addressed to the Jews, makes it probable that it too bore an apologetic character, being perhaps devoted to showing that Christianity is pre-eminently the truth. Melito's work on the same subject very likely bore a similar character, as suggested by Salmon.

[15] Six MSS., with Nicephorus, read κτίσεως, "creation," but five MSS., with the Syriac and Rufinus, and possibly Jerome, read πίστεως. The latter reading therefore has the strongest external testimony in its favor, but must be rejected (with Stroth, Otto, Heinichen, Harnack, etc.) as evidently a dogmatic correction of the fourth century, when there was an objection to the use of the word κτίσις in connection with Christ. Rufinus divides the one work *On the Creation and Generation of Christ* into two, — *On Faith* and *On the Generation of Christ and his prophecy*, connecting the second with the next-mentioned work. Jerome omits the first clause entirely at this point, and translates simply *de generatione Christi librum unum*. The *de fide*, however, which he inserts earlier in his list, where there is no corresponding word in the Greek, may be the title which he omits here (see above, note 9), displaced, as the title *de sensibus* is also displaced. If this be true, he becomes with Rufinus and the Syriac a witness to the reading πίστεως instead of κτίσεως, and like Rufinus divides the one work of Eusebius into two.

[16] All the Greek MSS. read καὶ λόγος αὐτοῦ περὶ προφητείας, which can rightly mean only "his work on Prophecy"; but Jerome translates *de prophetia sua librum unum*, and Rufinus *de prophetia ejus*, while the Syriac reads as if there stood in the Greek περὶ λόγου τῆς προφητείας αὐτοῦ. All three therefore connect the αὐτοῦ with the προφητείας instead of with the λόγος, which of course is much more natural, since the αὐτοῦ with the λόγος seems quite unnecessary at this point. The translation of the Syriac, Rufinus, and Jerome, however, would require περὶ προφητείας αὐτοῦ or περὶ τῆς αὐτοῦ προφητείας, and there is no sign that the αὐτοῦ originally stood in such connection with the προφητείας. We must, therefore, reject the rendering of these three versions as incorrect.

[17] περὶ φιλοξενίας. After this title a few of the MSS., with Rufinus and the Syriac, add the words καὶ περὶ ψυχῆς καὶ σώματος, a repetition of a title already given (see above, note 12).

[18] ἡ κλείς; Jerome, *et alium librum qui Clavis inscribitur*. The word is omitted in the Syriac version. The nature of this work we have no means of determining. It is possible that it was a key to the interpretation of the Scriptures, designed to guide the reader in the study especially of the figures of the prophecies (cf. Otto, p. 401) and of the Apocalypse. Piper is right, however, in saying that it cannot have been intended to supply the allegorical meaning of Scripture words, like the extant Latin *Clavis* of Pseudo-Melito, mentioned just below; for Melito, who like Tertullian taught the corporeality of God, must have been very literal — not allegorical — in his interpretation of Scripture. A Latin work bearing the title *Melitonis Clavis Sanctæ Scripturæ* was mentioned by Labbe in 1653 as contained in the library of Clermont College, and after years of search was recovered and published by Pitra in his *Spicileg. Solesm.* Vols. II. and III. He regarded the work as a translation, though with interpolations, of the genuine κλείς of Melito, but this hypothesis has been completely disproved (see the article by Steitz in the *Studien und Kritiken*, 1857, p. 184 sqq.), and the work has been shown to be nothing more than a mediæval dictionary of allegorical interpolations of Scripture, compiled from the Latin Fathers. There is, therefore, no trace extant of Melito's *Key*.

[19] All the Greek MSS. read καὶ τὰ περὶ τοῦ διαβόλου, καὶ τῆς ἀποκαλύψεως Ἰωάννου, making but one work, with two or more books, upon the general subject, *The Devil and the Apocalypse of John*. The Syriac apparently agrees with the Greek in this respect (see Harnack, p. 248, note 350); but Jerome and Rufinus make two works, the latter reading *de diabolo librum unum, de Apocalypsi Joannis librum unum*. Origen, *in Psalm. III.* (ed. Lommatzsch, XI. p. 411), says that Melito treated Absalom as a type of the devil warring against the kingdom of Christ. It has been conjectured that the reference may be to this work of Melito's, and that reference is an argument for the supposition that Melito treated the devil and the Apocalypse in one work (cf. Harnack, p. 248, and Smith and Wace, p. 898).

[20] ὁ περὶ ἐνσωμάτου θεοῦ. Jerome does not translate this phrase, but simply gives the Greek. Rufinus renders *de deo corpore induto*, thus understanding it to refer to the incarnation of God, and the Syriac agrees with this rendering. But as Harnack rightly remarks, we should expect, if this were the author's meaning, the words περὶ ἐνσωματώσεως θεοῦ, or rather λόγου. Moreover, Origen

3 dressed to Antoninus.[21] In the books On the Passover he indicates the time at which he wrote, beginning with these words : " While Servilius Paulus was proconsul of Asia, at the time when Sagaris suffered martyrdom, there arose in Laodicea a great strife concerning the Passover, which fell according to rule in those

4 days ; and these were written." [22] And Clement of Alexandria refers to this work in his own discourse On the Passover,[23]

(*Selecta in Gen.* I. 26; Lommatzsch, VIII. p. 49) enumerates Melito among those who taught the corporeality of God, and says that he had written a work περὶ τοῦ ἐνσώματον εἶναι τὸν θεόν. It is possible, of course, that he may not have seen Melito's work, and that he may have misunderstood its title and have mistaken a work on the incarnation for one on the corporeality of God; but this is not at all likely. Either he had read the book, and knew it to be upon the subject he states, or else he knew from other sources that Melito believed in the corporeality of God, and hence had no doubt that this work was upon that subject. There is no reason in any case for doubting the accuracy of Origen's statement, and for hesitating to conclude that the work mentioned by Eusebius was upon the corporeality of God. The close relationship existing between Melito and Tertullian has already been referred to, and this fact furnishes confirmation for the belief that Melito held God to be corporeal, for we know Tertullian's views on that subject. Gennadius (*de eccles. dogmat.* chap. 4) classes Melito and Tertullian together, as both teaching a corporeality in the Godhead. What was the source of his statement, and how much dependence is to be put upon it, we cannot say, but it is at least a corroboration of the conclusion already reached. We conclude then that Rufinus and the Syriac were mistaken in their rendering, and that this work discussed the corporeality, not the incarnation, of God.

[21] ἐπὶ πᾶσι καὶ τὸ πρὸς Ἀντωνῖνον βιβλίδιον. βιβλίδιον (*libellus*) was the technical name for a petition addressed to the emperor, and does not imply that the work was a brief one, as Piper supposes. The *Apology* is mentioned also in chap. 13, above, and at the beginning of this chapter. Jerome puts it first in his list, with the words: *Melito Asianus, Sardensis episcopus, librum imperatori M. Antonini Vero, qui Frontonis oratoris discipulus fuit, pro christiano dogmate dedit.* This *Apology* is no longer extant, and we have only the fragments which Eusebius gives in this chapter. As remarked in note 1, above, the extant Syriac *Apology* is not a work of Melito's. The *Apology* is mentioned in Jerome's version of the *Chron.*, and is assigned to the tenth year of Marcus Aurelius, 120 A.D. The notice is omitted in the Armenian, which, however, assigns to the eleventh year of Marcus Aurelius the *Apology* of Apolinarius, which is connected with that of Melito in the *Ch. Hist.* Moreover, a notice of the *Apology* is given by Syncellus in connection with the tenth year of Marcus Aurelius, and also by the *Chron. Pasch.;* so that it is not improbable that Eusebius himself mentioned it in his *Chron.*, and that its omission in the Armenian is a mistake (as Harnack thinks likely). But though the notice may thus have been made by Eusebius himself, we are nevertheless not at liberty to accept the date given as conclusive. We learn from the quotations given by Eusebius that the work was addressed to the emperor after the death of Lucius Verus, i.e. after the year 169. Whether before or after the association of Commodus with his father in the imperial power, which took place in 176, is uncertain; but I am inclined to think that the words quoted in § 7, below, point to a prospective rather than to a present association of Commodus in the empire, and that therefore the work was written between 169 and 176. It must be admitted, however, that we can say with certainty only that the work was written between 169 and 180. Some would put the work at the beginning of those persecutions which raged in 177, and there is much to be said for this. But the dates of the local and minor persecutions, which were so frequent during this period, are so uncertain that little can be based upon the fact that we know of persecutions in certain parts of the empire in 177. Piper, Otto, and others conclude from the fact that the *Apology* is mentioned last by Eusebius that it was Melito's latest work; but that, though not at all unlikely, does not necessarily follow (see above, note 1).

[22] A Sagaris, bishop and martyr, and probably the same man, is mentioned by Polycrates in his epistle to Victor (Euseb. V. 24) as buried in Laodicea. This is all we know of him. The date of his martyrdom, and of the composition of the work *On the Passover*, depends upon the date of the proconsulship of Servilius (or Sergius) Paulus (see above, note 5). The words ἐμπέσοντος κατὰ καιρόν have unnecessarily caused Salmon considerable trouble. The words κατὰ καιρόν mean no more than " properly, regularly, according to appointment or rule," and do not render ἐκείναις ταῖς ἡμέραις superfluous, as he thinks. The clause καὶ ἐγράφη ταῦτα (" and these were written ") expresses result, — it was in consequence of the passover strife that Melito wrote this work.

[23] This work of Clement's, *On the Passover*, which he says he wrote on occasion of Melito's work, was clearly written in reply to and therefore against the work of Melito, not as a supplement to it, as Hefele supposes (*Conciliengesch.* I. 299). The work of Clement (which is mentioned by Eusebius, VI. 13, in his list of Clement's

---

which, he says, he wrote on occasion of Melito's work. But in his book addressed 5 to the emperor he records that the following events happened to us under him : " For, what never before happened,[24] the race of the pious is now suffering persecution, being driven about in Asia by new decrees. For the shameless informers and coveters of the property of others, taking occasion from the decrees, openly carry on robbery night and day, despoiling those who are guilty of no wrong." And a little further on he says : " If these things are done by thy command, well and good. For a just ruler will never take unjust measures ; and we indeed gladly accept the honor of such a death. But 6 this request alone we present to thee, that thou wouldst thyself first examine the authors of such strife, and justly judge whether they be worthy of death and punishment, or of safety and quiet. But if, on the other hand, this counsel and this new decree, which is not fit to be executed even against barbarian enemies, be not from thee, much more do we beseech thee not to leave us exposed to such lawless plundering by the populace."

Again he adds the following : [25] " For our 7 philosophy formerly flourished among the Barbarians ; but having sprung up among the nations under thy rule, during the great reign of thy ancestor Augustus, it became to thine empire especially a blessing of auspicious omen. For from that time the power of the Romans has grown in greatness and splendor. To this power thou hast succeeded, as the desired possessor,[26] and such shalt thou continue with thy son, if thou guardest the philosophy which grew up with the empire and which came into existence with Augustus ; that philosophy which thy ancestors also honored along with the other religions. And a most convincing proof that our 8 doctrine flourished for the good of an empire happily begun, is this — that there has no evil happened since Augustus' reign, but that, on the contrary, all things have been splendid and glorious, in accordance with the prayers of all. Nero and Domitian, alone, per- 9 suaded by certain calumniators, have wished to slander our doctrine, and from them it has come to pass that the falsehood [26a] has been

---

writings) is no longer extant, but some brief fragments of it have been preserved (see Bk. VI. chap. 13, note 8).

[24] This statement of Melito's is a very remarkable one. See chap. 8, note 14.

[25] The resemblance between this extract from Melito's *Apology* and the fifth chapter of Tertullian's *Apology* is close enough to be striking, and too close to be accidental. Tertullian's chapter is quite different from this, so far as its arrangement and language are concerned, but the same thought underlies both: That the emperors in general have protected Christianity; only Nero and Domitian, the most wicked of them, have persecuted it; and that Christianity has been a blessing to the reigns of all the better emperors. We cannot doubt that Tertullian was acquainted with Melito's *Apology*, as well as with others of his works.   [26] εὐκταῖος.

[26a] The reference here seems to be to the common belief that the Christians were responsible for all the evils which at any time happened, such as earthquakes, floods, famines, etc.

10 handed down, in consequence of an unreasonable practice which prevails of bringing slanderous accusations against the Christians.[27] But thy pious fathers corrected their ignorance, having frequently rebuked in writing[28] many who dared to attempt new measures against them. Among them thy grandfather Adrian appears to have written to many others, and also to Fundanus,[29] the proconsul and governor of Asia. And thy father, when thou also wast ruling with him, wrote to the cities, forbidding them to take any new measures against us; among the rest to the Larissæans, to the Thessalonians, to the Athenians, and 11 to all the Greeks.[30] And as for thee,— since thy opinions respecting the Christians[31] are the same as theirs, and indeed much more benevolent and philosophic,— we are the more persuaded that thou wilt do all that we ask of thee." These words are found in the above-mentioned work.

12 But in the Extracts[32] made by him the same writer gives at the beginning of the introduction a catalogue of the acknowledged books of the Old Testament, which it is necessary to quote at this point. He writes as follows: 13 "Melito to his brother Onesimus,[33] greeting: Since thou hast often, in thy zeal for the word, expressed a wish to have extracts made from the Law and the Prophets concerning the Saviour, and concerning our entire faith, and hast also desired to have an accurate statement of the ancient book, as regards their number and their order, I have endeavored to perform the task, knowing thy zeal for the faith, and thy desire to gain information in regard to the word, and knowing that thou, in thy yearning after God, esteemest these things above all else, strug-14 gling to attain eternal salvation. Accord-

ingly when I went East and came to the place where these things were preached and done, I learned accurately the books of the Old Testament, and send them to thee as written below. Their names are as follows: Of Moses, five books: Genesis, Exodus, Numbers, Leviticus,[34] Deuteronomy; Jesus Nave, Judges, Ruth; of Kings, four books; of Chronicles, two; the Psalms of David,[35] the Proverbs of Solomon, Wisdom also,[36] Ecclesiastes, Song of Songs, Job; of Prophets, Isaiah, Jeremiah; of the twelve prophets, one book[37]; Daniel, Ezekiel, Esdras.[38] From which also I have made the extracts, dividing them into six books." Such are the words of Melito.

CHAPTER XXVII.

Apolinarius, Bishop of the Church of Hierapolis.

A NUMBER of works of Apolinarius[1] have been preserved by many, and the following have

[34] Some MSS., with Rufinus, place Leviticus before Numbers, but the best MSS., followed by Heinichen, Burton, and others, give the opposite order.
[35] ψαλμῶν Δαβίδ. Literally, "of the Psalms of David" [one book].
[36] ἡ καὶ Σοφία: i.e. the Book of Proverbs (see above, p. 200).
[37] Literally, "in one book" (τῶν δώδεκα ἐν μονοβίβλῳ).
[38] Ἐσδρας: the Greek form of the Hebrew name עֶזְרָא, Ezra. Melito refers here to the canonical Book of Ezra, which, among the Jews, commonly included our Ezra and Nehemiah (see Bk. III. chap. 10, note 1).
[1] The first extant notice of Apolinarius is that of Serapion, bishop of Antioch from about 192 to 209 (see Harnack, *Zeit des Ignatius*, p. 46), in the epistle quoted by Eusebius in V. 19. We learn from this notice that Apolinarius was already dead when Serapion wrote (he calls him "most blessed bishop"; μακαριώτατος), and that he had been a skillful opponent of Montanism. His name is not mentioned again, so far as we know, by any Father of the second or third century. Jerome (*de vir. ill.* 26) simply repeats the account of Eusebius, but in his *Epist. ad Magnum*, c. 4 (Migne, I. 607), he enumerates Apolinarius among those Christian writers who were acquainted with heathen literature, and made use of it in the refutation of heresies. Photius (*Cod.* 14) praises his literary style in high terms. Socrates (*H. E.* III. 7) names Apolinarius with Irenæus, Clement of Alexandria, and Serapion as holding that the incarnate Christ had a human soul (ἔμψυχον τὸν ἐνανθρωπήσαντα). Jerome, in his *de vir. ill.* chap. 18, mentions an Apolinarius in connection with Irenæus as a chiliast. But in his *Comment. in Ezech.* Bk. XI. chap. 36, he speaks of Irenæus as the first, and Apolinarius as the last, of the Greek Millenarians, which shows that some other Apolinarius is meant in that place, and therefore without doubt in the former passage also; and in another place (*Prooem. in lib. XVIII. Comm. in Esaiam*) he says that Apolinarius replied to Dionysius of Alexandria on the subject of the Millenium, and we are therefore led to conclude that Apolinarius, bishop of Laodicea (of the fourth century), is meant (see Routh, *Rel. Sac.* I. 174). Of the bishops of Hierapolis, besides Apolinarius, we know only Papias and Abircius Marcellus (of whom we have a Martyrdom, belonging to the second century; see Pitra, *Spic. Solesm.* III. 533), who, if he be identical with the Abircius Marcellus of Eusebius, Bk. V. chap. 16 (as Harnack conjectures) must have been bishop after, not before Apolinarius (see note 6 on Bk. V. chap. 16). It is impossible to determine the exact date of Apolinarius' episcopate, or of his death. As we see from Serapion's notice of him, he must have been dead at least before 202. And if Abircius Marcellus was bishop after him, and also bishop in the second century, Apolinarius must have died some years before the year 200, and thus about the same time as Melito. The fact that he is mentioned so commonly in connection with Melito, sometimes before and sometimes after him, confirms this conclusion. The *Chron.* mentions him as flourishing in the tenth (Syncellus and Jerome), or the eleventh (Armenian) year of Marcus Aurelius. His Apology was addressed, as we learn from Eusebius, to Marcus Aurelius; and the fact that only the one emperor is mentioned may perhaps be taken (as some have taken it) as a sign that it was written while Marcus Aurelius was sole emperor (i.e. between 169 and 176). In Bk. V. chap. 5, Eusebius speaks of the story of the thundering legion as recorded by Apolinarius, and it has been thought (e.g. by Salmon, in the *Dict. of Christ. Biog.*) that this circumstance was

[27] ἀφ' ὧν καὶ τὸ τῆς συκοφαντίας ἀλόγῳ συνηθείᾳ περὶ τοὺς τοιούτους ῥυῆναι συμβέβηκε ψεῦδος. The sentence is a difficult one and has been interpreted in various ways, but the translation given in the text seems to me best to express the writer's meaning.
[28] ἐγγράφως: i.e. in edicts or rescripts.
[29] This epistle to Fundanus is given in chap. 9, above. Upon its genuineness, see chap. 8, note 14.
[30] On these epistles of Antoninus Pius, see chap. 13, note 9. These ordinances to the Larissæans, Thessalonians, Athenians, and all the Greeks, are no longer extant. What their character must have been is explained in the note just referred to.
[31] περὶ τούτων.
[32] ἐν δὴ ταῖς γραφείσαις αὐτῷ ἐκλογαῖς. Jerome speaks of this work as Ἐκλογῶν, *libros sex*. There are no fragments of it extant except the single one from the preface given here by Eusebius. The nature of the work is clear from the words of Melito himself. It was a collection of testimonies to Christ and to Christianity, drawn from the Old Testament law and prophets. It must, therefore, have resembled closely such works as Cyprian's *Testimonia*, and the *Testimonia* of Pseudo-Gregory, and other anti-Jewish works, in which the appeal was made to the Old Testament—the common ground accepted by both parties—for proof of the truth of Christianity. Although the *Eclogæ* of Melito were not anti-Jewish in their design, their character leads us to classify them with the general class of anti-Jewish works whose distinguishing mark is the use of Old Testament prophecy in defense of Christianity (cf. the writer's article on *Christian Polemics against the Jews*, in the *Pres. Review*, July, 1888, and also the writer's *Dialogue between a Christian and a Jew*, entitled Ἀντιβολὴ Παπίσκου καὶ Φίλωνος (New York, 1889).
On the canon which Melito gives, see Bk. III. chap. 10, note 1.
[33] This Onesimus is an otherwise unknown person.

reached us: the Discourse addressed to the above-mentioned emperor,[2] five books Against the Greeks,[3] On Truth, a first and second book,[4] and those which he subsequently wrote against the heresy of the Phrygians,[5] which not long afterwards came out with its innovations,[6] but at that time was, as it were, in its incipiency, since Montanus, with his false prophetesses, was then laying the foundations of his error.

CHAPTER XXVIII.

Musanus and his Writings.

AND as for Musanus,[1] whom we have mentione among the foregoing writers, a certain very elegant discourse is extant, which was written by him against some brethren that had gone over to the heresy of the so-called Encratites,[2] which had recently sprung up, and which introduced a strange and pernicious error. It is said that Tatian was the author of this false doctrine.

CHAPTER XXIX.

The Heresy of Tatian.[1]

HE is the one whose words we quoted 1 a little above[2] in regard to that admirable

---

recorded in the *Apology*, which cannot then have been written before the year 174. Harnack, however, remarks that this venturesome report can hardly have stood in a work addressed to the emperor himself. But that seems to assume that the story was not fully believed by Apolinarius, which can hardly have been the case. The truth is, the matter cannot be decided; and no more exact date can be given for the *Apology*. Eusebius, in the present chapter, informs us that he has seen four works by Apolinarius, but says that there were many others extant in his day. In addition to the ones mentioned by Eusebius, we know of a work of his, *On the Passover* (περὶ τοῦ πάσχα), which is mentioned in the *Chron. Paschale*, and two brief fragments of which are preserved by it. These fragments have caused a discussion as to whether Apolinarius was a Quartodeciman or not. The language of the first fragment would seem to show clearly that he was opposed to the Quartodecimans, and this explains the fact that he is never cited by the later Quartodecimans as a witness for their opinions. The tone of the work, however, as gathered from the fragments, shows that it must have been written before the controversy had assumed the bitter tone which it took when Victor became bishop of Rome; i.e. it was written, probably, in the seventies (see, also, Bk. V. chap. 23, note 1). Photius (*Cod.* 14) mentions three apologetic works by Apolinarius known to him: πρὸς Ἕλληνας, περὶ εὐσεβείας, and περὶ ἀληθείας. The first and last are mentioned by Eusebius, but the second is a work otherwise unknown to us. There is no reason to suppose, as some have done, that the περὶ εὐσεβείας does not designate a separate work (cf. e.g., Donaldson, *Hist. of Christ. Lit. and Doctrine*, III. 243), for Eusebius expressly says that he mentions only a part of Apolinarius' writings. Theodoret (*Hær. Fab.* I. 21) mentions Apolinarius, together with Musanus and Clement, as having written against the Severians (see chap. 29, below). But, as Harnack justly remarks (p. 235), the most we can conclude from this is, that Apolinarius, in his Anti-Montanistic work, had mentioned the Severians with disapproval. Five MSS. of Eusebius, and the *Church Hist.* of Nicephorus, mention just after the work *On Truth*, a work *Against the Jews*, in two books (καὶ πρὸς Ἰουδαίους πρῶτον καὶ δεύτερον). The words are found in many of our editions, but are omitted by the majority of the best Greek MSS., and also by Rufinus and Jerome, and therefore must be regarded as an interpolation; and so they are viewed by Heinichen, Laemmer, Otto, Harnack, and others. Harnack suggests that they were inserted under the influence of Bk. V. chap. 17, § 5, where the works of Miltiades are given. We thus have knowledge of six, and only six, distinct works of Apolinarius, though, since no writer has pretended to give a complete list, it is quite probable that he wrote many others.

[2] On the approximate date of this Apology, see the previous note. No fragments of the work are now extant, unless the account of the thundering legion mentioned by Eusebius in Bk. V. chap. 5 belong to it (see the previous note). Jerome speaks of the work as an *insigne volumen pro fide Christianorum*, and in chap. 26, § 1, Eusebius speaks of it as λόγος ὑπὲρ τῆς πίστεως. This has given rise to the idea that the περὶ εὐσεβείας mentioned by Photius may be identical with this Apology (see the previous note). But such an important work would certainly not have been mentioned with such an ambiguous title by Photius. We may conclude, in fact, that Photius had not seen the Apology. The *Chron. Paschale* mentions the Apology in connection with those of "Melito and many others," as addressed to the Emperor Marcus Aurelius.

[3] No fragments of this work are known to us. Nicephorus (*H. E.* IV. 11) says that it was in the form of a dialogue, and it is quite possible that he speaks in this case from personal knowledge, for the work was still extant in the time of Photius, who mentions it in *Cod.* 14 (see Harnack, p. 236).

[4] No fragments of this work are extant, and its nature is unknown to us. It may have resembled the work of Melito upon the same subject (see the previous chapter). The work is mentioned by Photius as one of three, which he had himself seen.

[5] Eusebius states here that the works against the Montanists were written later than the other works mentioned. Where he got this information we do not know; it is possible, as Harnack suggests, that he saw from the writings themselves that Marcus Aurelius was no longer alive when they were composed. Eusebius speaks very highly of these Anti-Montanistic works, and in Bk. V. chap. 16, § 1, he speaks of Apolinarius as a "powerful weapon and antagonist" of the Montanists. And yet it is a remarkable fact that he does not take his account of the Montanists from the works of Apolinarius, but from later writings. This fact can be explained only as Harnack explains it by supposing that Apolinarius was not decided and clear enough in his opposition to the sect. The writer from whom Eusebius quotes is certainly strong enough in his denunciations to suit Eusebius or any one else. Eusebius' statement, that the Montanistic movement was only beginning at the time Apolinarius wrote against it (i.e. according to him between 175 and 180), is far from the truth (see on this subject, Bk. V. chap. 16, note 12). How many of these works Apolinarius wrote, and whether they were books, or merely letters, we do not know. Eusebius says

simply καὶ ἃ μετὰ ταῦτα συνέγραψε. Serapion (in Eusebius, Bk. V. chap. 19) calls them γράμματα, which Jerome (*de vir. ill.* chap. 41) translates *litteras*. These γράμματα are taken as "letters" by Valesius, Stroth, Danz, and Salmon; but Otto contends that the word γράμματα, in the usage of Eusebius (cf. Eusebius, V. 28. 4), properly means "writings" or "books" (*scripta* or *libri*), not "letters," and so the word is translated by Closs. The word itself is not absolutely decisive, but it is more natural to translate it "writings," and the circumstances of the case seem to favor that rather than the rendering "letters." I have therefore translated it thus in Bk. VI. chap. 19. On the life and writings of Apolinarius, see especially Salmon's article in the *Dict. of Christ. Biog.* and Harnack's *Texte und Untersuch.* I. 1, 232–239. The few extant fragments of his works are published by Routh (I. 151–174), and by Otto (IX. 479–495); English translation in the *Ante-Nicene Fathers*, VIII. 772.   [6] καινοτομηθείσης.

[1] Of this Musanus, we know only what Eusebius tells us here, for Jerome (*de vir. ill.* 31) and Theodoret (*Hær. Fab.* I. 21) simply repeat the account of Eusebius. It is clear from Eusebius' language, that he had not himself seen this work of Musanus; he had simply heard of it. Here, and in chap. 21, Eusebius assigns the activity of Musanus to the reign of Marcus Aurelius, making him a contemporary of Melito, Apolinarius, Irenæus, &c. But in the *Chron.* he is put much later. The Armenian version, under the year of Abr. 2220 (the eleventh year of Septimius), has the entry *Musanus noster scriptor cognoscebatur*. Jerome, under the same year (2220 of Abr., but twelfth year of Severus) has *Musanus nostræ filosofiæ scriptor agnoscitur*; while Syncellus, under the year of Abr. 2231 (fourth year of Caracalla) has Μουσιανὸς ἐκκλησιαστικὸς συγγραφεὺς ἐγνωρίζετο. All of them, therefore, speak of Musanus (or Musianus) as a writer, but do not specify any of his works. The dates in the *Chron.* (whichever be taken as original) and in the *History* are not mutually exclusive; at the same time it is clear that Eusebius was not working upon the same information in the two cases. We have no means of testing the correctness of either statement.

[2] On Tatian and the Encratites, see the next chapter.

[1] From his *Oratio* (chap. 42) we learn that Tatian was born in Assyria, and that he was early educated in Greek philosophy, from which we may conclude that he was of Greek parentage, — a conclusion confirmed by the general tone of the *Oratio* (cf. Harnack, *Ueberlieferung der Griech. Apol.* p. 199 sq., who refutes Zahn's opinion that Tatian was a Syrian by race). We learn from his *Oratio* also that he was converted to Christianity in mature life (cf. chap. 29 sq.). From the passage quoted in the present chapter from Irenæus, we learn that Tatian, after the death of Justin (whose disciple he was; see also chap. 16, above), fell into heresy, and the general fact is confirmed by Tertullian, Hippolytus, Clement of Alexandria, Origen, and others. Beyond these meager notices we have little information in regard to Tatian's life. Rhodo (quoted in Bk. V. below) mentions him, and "confesses" that he was a pupil of Tatian's in Rome, perhaps implying that this was after Tatian had left the Catholic Church (though inasmuch as the word "confesses" is Eusebius', not Rhodo's, we can hardly lay the stress that Harnack does upon its use in this connection). Epi-

man, Justin, and whom we stated to have been a disciple of the martyr. Irenæus declares this in the first book of his work Against Heresies, where he writes as follows concerning both 2 him and his heresy: [3] "Those who are called Encratites,[4] and who sprung from

Saturninus[5] and Marcion, preached celibacy, setting aside the original arrangement of God and tacitly censuring him who made male and female for the propagation of the human race. They introduced also abstinence from the things called by them animate,[6] thus showing ingratitude to the God who made all things. And they deny the salvation of the first man.[7] But 3 this has been only recently discovered by them, a certain Tatian being the first to introduce this blasphemy. He was a hearer of Justin, and expressed no such opinion while he was with him, but after the martyrdom of the latter he left the Church, and becoming exalted with the thought of being a teacher, and puffed up with the idea that he was superior to others, he established a peculiar type of doctrine of his own, inventing certain invisible æons like the followers of Valentinus,[8] while, like Marcion and Saturninus, he pronounced marriage to be corruption and fornication. His argument against the salvation of Adam, however, he devised for

---

phanius gives quite an account of Tatian in his *Hær.* XLVI. 1, but as usual he falls into grave errors (especially in his chronology). The only trustworthy information that can be gathered from him is that Tatian, after becoming a Christian, returned to Mesopotamia and taught for a while there (see Harnack, *ibid.* p. 208 sq.). We learn from his *Oratio* that he was already in middle life at the time when he wrote it, i.e. about 152 A.D. (see note 13, below), and as a consequence it is commonly assumed that he cannot have been born much later than 110 A.D. Eusebius in his *Chron.* (XII. year of Marcus Aurelius, 172 A.D.) says, *Tatianus hæreticus agnoscitur, a quo Encratitæ.* There is no reason to doubt that this represents with reasonable accuracy the date of Tatian's break with the Catholic Church. We know at any rate that it did not take place until after Justin's death (165 A.D.). In possession of these various facts in regard to Tatian, his life has been constructed in various ways by historians, but Harnack seems to have come nearest to the truth in his account of him on p. 212 sq. He holds that he was converted about 150, but soon afterward left for the Orient, and while there wrote his *Oratio ad Græcos;* that afterward he returned to Rome, and was an honored teacher in the Church for some time, but finally becoming heretical, broke with the Church about the year 172. The arguments which Harnack urges over against Zahn (who maintains that he was but once in Rome, and that he became a heretic in the Orient and spent the remainder of his life there) seem fully to establish his main positions. Of this, too, all traces have perished. Of the date, place, and circumstances of Tatian's death, we know nothing.

Eusebius informs us in this chapter that Tatian left "a great many writings," but he mentions the titles of only two, the *Address to the Greeks* and the *Diatessaron* (see below, notes 11 and 13). He seems, however, in § 6, to refer to another work on the Pauline Epistles, — a work of which we have no trace anywhere else, though we learn from Jerome's preface to his Commentary on Titus that Tatian rejected some of Paul's epistles, as Marcion did, but unlike Marcion accepted the epistle to Titus. We know the titles of some other works written by Tatian. He himself, in his *Oratio* 15, mentions a work which he had written *On Animals.* The work is no longer extant, nor do we know anything about it. Rhodo (as we are told by Eusebius in Bk. V. chap. 13) mentioned a book of *Problems* which Tatian had written. Of this, too, all traces have perished. Clement of Alexandria (*Strom.* III. 12) mentions an heretical work of Tatian's, entitled περὶ τοῦ κατὰ τὸν σωτῆρα καταρτισμοῦ, *On Perfection according to the Saviour,* which has likewise perished. Clement (as also Origen) was evidently acquainted with still other heretical works, especially one on Genesis (see below, note 7), but he mentions the title only of the one referred to. Rufinus (*H. E.* VI. 11) says that Tatian composed a *Chronicon,* which we hear about from no other writer. Malalas calls Tatian a chronographer, but he is evidently thinking of the chronological passages in his *Oratio,* and in the absence of all trustworthy testimony we must reject Rufinus' notice as a mistake. In his *Oratio,* chap. 40, Tatian speaks of a work *Against those who have discoursed on Divine Things,* in which he intends to show "what the learned among the Greeks have said concerning our polity and the history of our laws, and how many and what kind of men have written of these things." Whether he ever wrote the work or not we do not know; we find no other notice of it. Upon Tatian, see especially Zahn's *Tatian's Diatessaron* and Harnack's *Ueberlieferung,* &c., p. 196; also Donaldson's *Hist. of Christ. Lit. and Doct.* II. p. 3 sqq., and J. M. Fuller's article in the *Dict. of Christ. Biog.*

[2] In chap. 16.   [3] Irenæus, *Adv. Hær.* I. 28. 1.

[4] Ἐγκρατεῖς, a word meaning "temperate" or "continent." These Encratites were heretics who abstained from flesh, from wine, and from marriage, not temporarily but permanently, and because of a belief in the essential impurity of those things. They are mentioned also by Hippolytus (*Phil.* VIII. 13), who calls them ἐγκρατῖται; by Clement of Alexandria (*Pæd.* II. 2, *Strom.* I. 15, &c.), who calls them ἐγκρατηταί; by Epiphanius (*Hær.* 47), who agrees with Hippolytus in the form of the name, and by others. The Encratites whom Irenæus describes seem to have constituted a distinct sect, anti-Jewish and Gnostic in its character. As described by Hippolytus they appear to have been mainly orthodox in doctrine but heretical in their manner of life, and we may perhaps gather the same thing from Clement's references to them. It is evident, therefore, that Irenæus and the others are not referring to the same men. So Theodoret, *Hær. Fab.* I. 21, speaks of the Severian Encratites; but the Severians, as we learn from this chapter of Eusebius and from Epiphanius (*Hær.* XLV.), were Ebionitic and anti-Pauline in their tendencies — the exact opposites, therefore, of the Encratites referred to by Irenæus. That there was a distinct sect of Encratites of the character described by Irenæus cannot be denied, but we must certainly conclude that the word was used very commonly in a wider sense to denote men of various schools who taught excessive and heretical abstinence. Of course the later writers may have supposed that they all belonged to one compact sect, but it is certain that they did not. As to the particular sect which Irenæus describes, the statement made by Eusebius at the close of the preceding chap-

ter is incorrect, if we are to accept Irenæus' account. For the passage quoted in this chapter states that they sprung from Marcion and Saturninus, evidently implying that they were not founded by Tatian, but that he found them already in existence when he became heretical. It is not surprising, however, that his name should become connected with them as their founder — for he was the best-known man among them. That the Encratites as such (whether a single sect or a general tendency) should be opposed by the Fathers, even by those of ascetic tendencies, was natural. It was not always easy to distinguish between orthodox and heretical asceticism, and yet there was felt to be a difference. The fundamental distinction was held by the Church — whenever it came to self-consciousness on the subject — to lie in the fact that the heretics pronounced the things from which they abstained essentially evil in themselves, thus holding a radical dualism, while the orthodox abstained only as a matter of discipline. The distinction, it is true, was not always preserved, but it was this essentially dualistic principle of the Encratites which the early Fathers combated; it is noticeable, however, that they do not expend as much vigor in combating it as in refuting errors in doctrine. In fact, they seem themselves to have been somewhat in doubt as to the proper attitude to take toward these extreme ascetics.

[5] On Saturninus and on Marcion, see chap. 7, note 6, and 11, note 15. On their asceticism, see especially Irenæus, *Adv. Hær.* I. 24.

[6] τῶν λεγομένων ἐμψύχων: i.e. animal food in general.

[7] Cf. Irenæus, *Adv. Hær.* III. 23, where this opinion of Tatian's is refuted at considerable length. The opinion seems a little peculiar, but was a not unnatural consequence of Tatian's strong dualism, and of his doctrine of a conditional immortality for those who have been reunited with the Holy Spirit, who took his departure at the time of the fall (cf. especially his *Oratio,* chap. 15). That Adam, who, by his fall, brought about this separation, which has been of such direful consequence to the race, should be saved, was naturally to Tatian a very repugnant thought. He seems, moreover, to have based his opinion, as Donaldson remarks, upon exegetical grounds, interpreting the passage in regard to Adam (1 Cor. xv. 22) as meaning that Adam is and remains the principle of death, and as such, of course, cannot himself enjoy life (see Irenæus, *ibid.*). This is quite in accord with the distinction between the psychical and physical man which he draws in his *Oratio.* It is quite possible that he was moved in part also by the same motive which led Marcion to deny the salvation of Abraham and the other patriarchs (see Irenæus, *Adv. Hær.* I. 27 and IV. 8), namely, the opposition between the God of the Old Testament and the Christ of the New Testament, which led him to assert that those who depended on the former were lost. We learn from Clement (*Strom.* III. 12) and from Origen (*de Orat.* chap. 24) that among Tatian's heretical works was one in which he discussed the early chapters of Genesis, and perhaps it was in this work that he developed his peculiar views in regard to Adam.

[8] On Valentinus, see chap. 11, note 1. That Tatian was Gnostic in many of his tendencies is plain enough, not only from these words of Irenæus, but also from the notices of him in other writers (cf. especially Hippolytus, *Phil.* VIII. 9). To what extent he carried his Gnosticism, however, and exactly in what it consisted, we cannot tell. He can hardly have been a pronounced follower of Valentinus and a zealous defender of the doctrine of Æons, or we should find him connected more prominently with that school. He was, in fact, a decided eclectic, and a follower of no one school, and doubtless this subject, like many others, occupied but a subordinate place in his speculations.

himself." Irenæus at that time wrote thus.
4 But a little later a certain man named
Severus[9] put new strength into the aforesaid heresy, and thus brought it about that those
who took their origin from it were called,
5 after him, Severians. They, indeed, use
the Law and Prophets and Gospels, but
interpret in their own way the utterances of the
Sacred Scriptures. And they abuse Paul the
apostle and reject his epistles, and do not
6 accept even the Acts of the Apostles. But
their original founder, Tatian, formed a
certain combination and collection of the Gospels, I know not how,[10] to which he gave the
title *Diatessaron*,[11] and which is still in the

hands of some. But they say that he ventured
to paraphrase certain words of the apostle,[12] in order to improve their style. He   7
has left a great many writings. Of these
the one most in use among many persons is his
celebrated Address to the Greeks,[13] which also
appears to be the best and most useful of all his
works. In it he deals with the most ancient
times, and shows that Moses and the Hebrew
prophets were older than all the celebrated men
among the Greeks.[14] So much in regard to
these men.

CHAPTER XXX.

Bardesanes the Syrian and his Extant Works.

In the same reign, as heresies were   1
abounding in the region between the riv-
ers,[1] a certain Bardesanes,[2] a most able man and a

---

[9] That the Severians, whoever they were, were Encratites in the wide sense, that is, strict abstainers from flesh, wine, and marriage, cannot be denied (compare with this description of Eusebius that of Epiphanius in *Hær.* XLV., also Theodoret's *Hær. Fab.* I. 21, who says that Apolinarius wrote against the Severian Encratites, — a sign that the Severians and the Encratites were in some way connected in tradition even though Theodoret's statement may be unreliable). But that they were connected with Tatian and the Encratitic sect to which he belonged, as Eusebius states, is quite out of the question. Tatian was a decided Paulinist (almost as much so as Marcion himself). He cannot, therefore, have had anything to do with this Ebionitic, anti-Pauline sect, known as the Severians. Whether there was ever such a person as Severus, or whether the name arose later to explain the name of the sect (possibly taken from the Latin *severus*, "severe," as Salmon suggests), as the name Ebion was invented to explain the term Ebionites, we do not know. We are ignorant also of the source from which Eusebius took his description of the Severians, as we do not find them mentioned in any of the earlier anti-heretical works. Eusebius must have heard, as Epiphanius did, that they were extreme ascetics, and this must have led him, in the absence of specific information as to their exact position, to join them with Tatian and the Encratites, — a connection which can be justified on no other ground.

[10] οὐκ οἶδ᾽ ὅπως. Eusebius clearly means to imply in these words that he was not acquainted with the *Diatessaron*. Lightfoot, it is true, endeavors to show that these words may mean simply disapproval of the work, and not ignorance in regard to it. But his interpretation is an unnatural one, and has been accepted by few scholars.

[11] τὸ διὰ τεσσάρων. Eusebius is the first one to mention this *Diatessaron*, and he had evidently not seen it himself. After him it is not referred to again until the time of Epiphanius, who in his *Hær.* XLVI. 1 incorrectly identifies it with the Gospel according to the Hebrews, evidently knowing it only by hearsay. Theodoret (*Hær. Fab.* I. 20) informs us that he found a great many copies of it in circulation in his diocese, and that, finding that it omitted the account of our Lord's birth, he replaced it by the four Gospels, fearing the mischief which must result from the use of such a mutilated Gospel. In the *Doctrine of Addai* (ed. Syr. and Engl. by G. Phillips, 1876), which belongs to the third century, a Diatessaron is mentioned which is without doubt to be identified with the one under consideration (see Zahn I. p. 90 sq.). Meanwhile we learn from the preface to Dionysius bar Salibi's Commentary on Mark (see Assemani, *Bibl. Or.* I. 57), that Ephraem wrote a commentary upon the *Diatessaron* of Tatian (*Tatianus Justini Philosophi ac Martyris Discipulus, ex quatuor Evangeliis unum digessit, quod Diatessaron nuncupavit. Hunc librum Sanctus Ephraem commentariis illustravit*). Ephraem's commentary still exists in an Armenian version (published at Venice in 1836, and in Latin in 1876 by Mœsinger). There exists also a Latin Harmony of the Gospels, which is without doubt a substantial reproduction of Tatian's *Diatessaron*, and which was known to Victor of Capua (of the sixth century). From these sources Zahn has attempted to reconstruct the text of the *Diatessaron*, and prints the reconstructed text, with a critical commentary, in his *Tatian's Diatessaron*. Zahn maintains that the original work was written in Syriac, and he is followed by Lightfoot, Hilgenfeld, Fuller, and others; but Harnack has given very strong reasons for supposing that it was composed by Tatian in Greek, and that the Syriac which Ephraem used was a translation of that original, not the original itself. Both Zahn and Harnack agree, as do most other scholars, that the work was written before Tatian became a heretic, and with no heretical intent. Inasmuch as he later became a heretic, however, his work was looked upon with suspicion, and of course in later days, when so much stress was laid (as e.g. by Irenæus) upon the fourfold Gospel, Christians would be naturally distrustful of a single Gospel proposed as a substitute for them. It is not surprising, therefore, that the work failed to find acceptance in the Church at large. For further particulars, see especially Zahn's monograph, which is the most complete and exhaustive discussion of the whole subject. See also Harnack's

Ueberlieferung der Griech. Apologeten, p. 213 ff., Fuller's article referred to in note 1, the article by Lightfoot in the *Contemporary Review* for May, 1877, and those by Wace in the *Expositor* for 1881 and 1882.

[12] i.e. of Paul, who was quite commonly called simply ὁ ἀπόστολος. This seems to imply that Tatian wrote a work on Paul's epistles (see note 1, above).

[13] λόγος ὁ πρὸς Ἕλληνας: *Oratio ad Græcos*. This work is still extant, and is one of the most interesting of the early apologies. The standpoint of the author is quite different from that of Justin, for he treats Greek philosophy with the greatest contempt, and finds nothing good in it. As remarked in note 1, above, the *Oratio* was probably written after Tatian had left Rome for the first time, but not long after his conversion. We may follow Harnack (p. 196) in fixing upon 152 to 153 as an approximate date. The work is printed with a Latin translation and commentary in Otto's *Corp. Apol.* Vol. VI. The best critical edition is that of Schwartz, in v. Gebhardt and Harnack's *Texte und Untersuchungen*, IV. 1 (Leipzig, 1888), though it contains only the Greek text. An English translation is given in the *Ante-Nicene Fathers*, Vol. II. p. 59–83.

[14] Tatian devotes a number of chapters to this subject (XXXI., XXXV.–XLI.). Eusebius mentions him, with Clement, Africanus, Josephus, and Justus, in the preface to his *Chron.* (Schöne, II. p. 4), as a witness to the antiquity of Moses, and it is probable that Julius Africanus drew from him in the composition of his chronological work (cf. Harnack, *ibid.* p. 224). Clement of Alexandria likewise made large use of his chronological results (see especially his *Strom.* I. 21), and Origen refers to them in his *Contra Cels.* I. 16. It was largely on account of these chapters on the antiquity of Moses that Tatian's *Oratio* was held in such high esteem, while his other works disappeared.

[1] i.e. Mesopotamia: ἐπὶ τῆς μέσης τῶν ποταμῶν.

[2] Bardesanes or Bardaisan (Greek, Βαρδησάνης), a distinguished Syrian scholar, poet, and theologian, who lived at the court of the king of Edessa, is commonly classed among the Gnostics, but, as Hort shows, without sufficient reason. Our reports in regard to him are very conflicting. Epiphanius and Barhebræus relate that he was at first a distinguished Christian teacher, but afterward became corrupted by the doctrines of Valentinus. Eusebius on the other hand says that he was originally a Valentinian, but afterward left that sect and directed his attacks against it. Moses of Chorene gives a similar account. To Hippolytus he appeared as a member of the Eastern school of Valentinians, while to Ephraem the Syrian he seemed in general one of the most pernicious of heretics, who nevertheless pretended to be orthodox, veiling his errors in ambiguous language, and thus carrying away many of the faithful. According to Hort, who has given the subject very careful study, " there is no reason to suppose that Bardesanes rejected the ordinary faith of the Christians as founded on the Gospels and the writings of the apostles, except on isolated points. The more startling peculiarities of which we hear belong for the most part to an outer region of speculation, which it may easily have seemed possible to combine with Christianity, more especially with the undeveloped Christianity of Syria in the third century. The local color is everywhere prominent. In passing over to the new faith Bardaisan could not shake off the ancient glamour of the stars, or abjure the Semitic love of clothing thoughts in mythological forms." This statement explains clearly enough the reputation for heresy which Bardesanes enjoyed in subsequent generations. There is no reason to think that he taught a system of æons like the Gnostics, but he does seem to have leaned toward docetism, and also to have denied the proper resurrection of the body. Ephraem accuses him of teaching Polytheism, in effect if not in words, but this charge seems to have

most skillful disputant in the Syriac tongue, having composed dialogues against Marcion's followers and against certain others who were authors of various opinions, committed them to writing in his own language, together with many

other works. His pupils,[3] of whom he had very many (for he was a powerful defender of the faith), translated these productions from the Syriac into Greek. Among them there is also his most able dialogue On Fate,[4] addressed to Antoninus, and other works which they say he wrote on occasion of the persecution which arose at that time.[5] 2

He indeed was at first a follower of Valentinus,[6] but afterward, having rejected his teaching and having refuted most of his fictions, he fancied that he had come over to the more correct opinion. Nevertheless he did not entirely wash off the filth of the old heresy.[7] 3

About this time also Soter,[8] bishop of the church of Rome, departed this life.

---

arisen from a misunderstanding of his mythological forms; he apparently maintained always the supremacy of the one Christian God. There is nothing in his theology itself to imply Valentinian influence, but the traditions to that effect are too strong to be entirely set aside. It is not improbable that he may, as Eusebius says, have been a Valentinian for a time, and afterward, upon entering the orthodox church, have retained some of the views which he gained under their influence. This would explain the conflicting reports of his theology. It is not necessary to say more about his beliefs. Hort's article in Smith and Wace's *Dict. of Christ. Biog.* contains an excellent discussion of the subject, and the student is referred to that.

The followers of Bardesanes seem to have emphasized those points in which he differed with the Church at large, and thus to have departed further from catholic orthodoxy. Undoubtedly Ephraem (who is our most important authority for a knowledge of Bardesanes) knows him only through his followers, who were very numerous throughout the East in the fourth century, and hence passes a harsher judgment upon him than he might otherwise have done. Ephraem makes the uprooting of the "pernicious heresy" one of his foremost duties.

Eusebius in this chapter, followed by Jerome (*de vir. ill.* chap. 33), Epiphanius, Theodoret, and others, assigns the activity of Bardesanes to the reign of Marcus Aurelius (so also in the *Chron.*). But Hort says that according to the Chronicle of Edessa (Assemani, *Bibl. Or.* I. 389) he was born July 11, 155, and according to Barhebræus (*Chron. Eccl.* ed. Abbeloos and Lamy, p. 49) he died in 223 at the age of sixty-eight, which confirms the date of his birth given by the Chronicle of Edessa. These dates are accepted as correct by Hilgenfeld and Hort, and the error committed by Eusebius and those who followed him is explained by their confusion of the later with the earlier Antonines, a confusion which was very common among the Fathers.

His writings, as stated by Eusebius, Epiphanius, Theodoret, and others, were very numerous, and were translated (at least many of them) into Greek. The dialogues against the Marcionists and other heretics are mentioned also by Theodoret (*Hær. Fab.* I. 22) and by Barhebræus. Epiphanius (who apparently had some independent knowledge of the man and his followers) mentions (*Hær.* LVI.) an Apology " in which he resisted Apollonius, the companion of Antoninus, when urged to deny that he was a Christian." This was probably one of the many works which Eusebius says he wrote on occasion of the persecution which arose at the time.

The *Dialogue on Fate* is said by Eusebius, followed by Rufinus and Jerome, to have been addressed to Antoninus. Epiphanius says that in this work he " copiously refuted Avidas the astronomer," and it is quite possible that Eusebius' statement rests upon a confusion of the names Avidas and Antoninus, for it is difficult to conceive that the work can have been addressed to an emperor, and in any case it cannot have been addressed to Marcus Aurelius, whom Eusebius here means. This *Dialogue on Fate* is identified either

wholly or in part with a work entitled *Book of the Laws of Countries*, which is still extant in the original Syriac, and has been published with an English translation by Cureton in his *Spicileg. Syr.* A fragment of this work is given in Eusebius' *Præp. Evang.* VI. 9–10, and, until the discovery of the Syriac text of the entire work, this was all that we had of it. This is undoubtedly the work referred to by Eusebius, Epiphanius, and other Fathers, but it is no less certain that it was not written by Bardesanes himself. As Hort remarks, " the natural impulse to confuse the author with the chief interlocutor in an anonymous dialogue will sufficiently explain the early ascription of the Dialogue to Bardaisan himself by the Greek Fathers." It was undoubtedly written by one of Bardesanes' disciples, probably soon after his death, and it is quite likely that it does not depart widely from the spirit of Bardesanes' teaching. Upon Bardesanes, see, in addition to Hort's article, the monograph of Merx, *Bardesanes von Edessa* (Halle, 1863), and that of Hilgenfeld, *Bardesanes, der Letzte Gnostiker* (Leipz. 1864).

[3] γνώριμοι.   [4] See note 2.

[5] Hort conjectures that Caracalla, who spent the winter of 216 in Edessa, and threw the Prince Bar-Manu into captivity, may have allied himself with a party which was discontented with the rule of that prince, and which instituted a heathen reaction, and that this was the occasion of the persecution referred to here, in which Bardesanes proved his firmness in the faith as recorded by Epiphanius.

[6] See note 2.

[7] It is undoubtedly quite true, as remarked in note 2, that Bardesanes, after leaving Valentinianism, still retained views acquired under its influence, and that these colored all his subsequent thinking. This fact may have been manifest to Eusebius, who had evidently read many of Bardesanes' works, and who speaks here as if from personal knowledge.

[8] On Soter, see chap. 19, note 2.

BOOK V.

INTRODUCTION.

1   Soter,[1] bishop of the church of Rome, died after an episcopate of eight years, and was succeeded by Eleutherus,[2] the twelfth from the apostles. In the seventeenth year of the Emperor Antoninus Verus,[3] the persecution of our people was rekindled more fiercely in certain districts on account of an insurrection of the masses in the cities ; and judging by the number in a single nation, myriads suffered martyrdom throughout the world. A record of this was written for posterity, and in truth it is 2   worthy of perpetual remembrance. A full

account, containing the most reliable information on the subject, is given in our Collection of Martyrdoms,[4] which constitutes a narrative instructive as well as historical. I will repeat here such portions of this account as may be needful for the present purpose.

Other writers of history record the victo-   3 ries of war and trophies won from enemies, the skill of generals, and the manly bravery of soldiers, defiled with blood and with innumerable slaughters for the sake of children and country and other possessions. But our   4 narrative of the government of God[5] will record in ineffaceable letters the most peaceful wars waged in behalf of the peace of the soul, and will tell of men doing brave deeds for truth rather than country, and for piety rather than dearest friends. It will hand down to imperishable remembrance the discipline and the much-tried fortitude of the athletes of religion, the trophies won from demons, the victories over invisible enemies, and the crowns placed upon all their heads.

CHAPTER I.

The Number of those who fought for Religion in Gaul under Verus and the Nature of their Conflicts.

The country in which the arena was pre-   1 pared for them was Gaul, of which Lyons and Vienne[1] are the principal and most celebrated cities. The Rhone passes through both of them, flowing in a broad stream through the entire re-

---

[1] On Soter, see above, Bk. IV. chap. 19, note 2.
[2] Eusebius in his *Chronicle* gives the date of Eleutherus' accession as the seventeenth year of Marcus Aurelius (177 A.D.), and puts his death into the reign of Pertinax (192), while in chap. 22 of the present book he places his death in the tenth year of Commodus (189). Most of our authorities agree in assigning fifteen years to his episcopate, and this may be accepted as undoubtedly correct. Most of them, moreover, agree with chap. 22 of this book, in assigning his death to the tenth. year of Commodus, and this too may be accepted as accurate. But with these two data we are obliged to push his accession back into the year 174 (or 175), which is accepted by Lipsius (see his *Chron. der röm. Bischöfe*, p. 184 sq.). We must therefore suppose that he became bishop some two years before the outbreak of the persecution referred to just below, in the fourteenth or fifteenth year of Marcus Aurelius. In the Armenian version of the *Chron.* Eleutherus is called the thirteenth bishop of Rome (see above, Bk. IV. chap. 19, note 5), but this is a mistake, as pointed out in the note referred to. Eleutherus is mentioned in Bk. IV. chap. 11, in connection with Hegesippus, and also in Bk. IV. chap. 22, by Hegesippus himself. He is chiefly interesting because of his connection with Irenæus and the Gallican martyrs (see chap. 4, below), and his relation to the Montanistic controversy (see chap. 3). Bede, in his *Hist. Eccles.*, chap. 4, connects Eleutherus with the origin of British Christianity, but the tradition is quite groundless. One of the decretals and a spurious epistle are falsely ascribed to him.
[3] i.e., the seventeenth year of the reign of Marcus Aurelius, A.D. 177 (upon Eusebius' confusion of Marcus Aurelius with Lucius Verus, see below, p. 390, note). In the *Chron.* the persecution at Lyons and Vienne is associated with the seventh year of Marcus Aurelius (167), and consequently some (e.g. Blondellus, Stroth, and Jachmann), have maintained that the notice in the present passage is incorrect, and Jachmann has attacked Eusebius very severely for the supposed error. The truth is, however, that the notice in the *Chron.* (in the Armenian, which represents the original form more closely than Jenner's version does) is not placed opposite the seventh year of Marcus Aurelius (as the notices in the *Chron.* commonly are), but is placed after it, and grouped with the notice of Polycarp's martyrdom, which occurred, not in 167, but in 155 or 156 (see above, Bk. IV. chap. 15, note 2). It would seem, as remarked by Lightfoot (*Ignatius*, I. p. 630), that Eusebius simply connected together the martyrdoms which he supposed occurred about this time, without intending to imply that they all took place in the same year. Similar groupings of kindred events which occurred at various times during the reign of an emperor are quite common in the *Chron.* (cf. the notices of martyrdoms under Trajan and of apologies and rescripts under Hadrian). Over against the distinct statement of the history, therefore, in the present instance, the notice in the *Chron.* is of no weight. Moreover, it is clear from the present passage that Eusebius had strong grounds for putting the persecution into the time of Eleutherus, and the letter sent by the confessors to Eleutherus (as recorded below in chap. 4) gives us also good reason for putting the persecution into the time of his episcopate. But Eleutherus cannot have become bishop before 174 (see Lipsius' *Chron. der röm. Bischöfe*, p. 184 sq., and note 2, above). There is no reason, therefore, for doubting the date given here by Eusebius.

[4] All the MSS. read μαρτύρων, but I have followed Valesius (in his notes) and Heinichen in reading μαρτυρίων, which is supported by the version of Rufinus (*de singulorum martyriis*), and which is the word used by Eusebius in all his other references to the work (Bk. IV. chap. 15 and Bk. V. chaps. 4 and 21), and is in fact the proper word to be employed after συναγωγή, " collection." We speak correctly of a "collection of martyrdoms," not of a "collection of martyrs," and I cannot believe that Eusebius, in referring to a work of his own, used the wrong word in the present case. Upon the work itself, see the Prolegomena, p. 30, of this volume.
[5] τοῦ κατὰ θεὸν πολιτεύματος, with the majority of the MSS. supported by Rufinus. Some MSS., followed by Stroth, Burton, and Schwegler, read καθ' ἡμᾶς instead of κατὰ θεὸν (see Heinichen's note *in loco*). Christophorsonus translates *divinam vivendi rationem*, which is approved by Heinichen. But the contrast drawn seems to be rather between earthly kingdoms, or governments, and the kingdom, or government, of God; and I have, therefore, preferred to give πολίτευμα its ordinary meaning, as is done by Valesius (*divinæ reipublicæ*), Stroth (*Republik Gottes*), and Closs (*Staates Gottes*).
[1] Λούγδουνος καὶ Βίεννα, the ancient Lugdunum and Vienna, the modern Lyons and Vienne in southeastern France.

2 gion. The most celebrated churches in that country sent an account of the witnesses[2] to the churches in Asia and Phrygia, relating in the following manner what was done among them. I will give their own words.[3]

3 "The servants of Christ residing at Vienne and Lyons, in Gaul, to the brethren throughout Asia and Phrygia, who hold the same faith and hope of redemption, peace and grace and glory from God the Father and Christ Jesus our Lord."

4 Then, having related some other matters, they begin their account in this manner:

"The greatness of the tribulation in this region, and the fury of the heathen against the saints, and the sufferings of the blessed witnesses, we cannot recount accurately, nor indeed **5** could they possibly be recorded. For with all his might the adversary fell upon us, giving us a foretaste of his unbridled activity at his future coming. He endeavored in every

manner to practice and exercise his servants against the servants of God, not only shutting us out from houses and baths and markets, but forbidding any of us to be seen in any place whatever. But the grace of God led **6** the conflict against him, and delivered the weak, and set them as firm pillars, able through patience to endure all the wrath of the Evil One. And they joined battle with him, undergoing all kinds of shame and injury; and regarding their great sufferings as little, they hastened to Christ, manifesting truly that 'the sufferings of this present time are not worthy to be compared with the glory which shall be revealed to us-ward.'[4] First of all, they endured nobly **7** the injuries heaped upon them by the populace; clamors and blows and draggings and robberies and stonings and imprisonments,[5] and all things which an infuriated mob delight in inflicting on enemies and adversaries. Then, **8** being taken to the forum by the chiliarch[6] and the authorities of the city, they were examined in the presence of the whole multitude, and having confessed, they were imprisoned until the arrival of the governor. When, **9** afterwards, they were brought before him, and he treated us with the utmost cruelty, Vettius Epagathus,[7] one of the brethren, and a man filled with love for God and his neighbor, interfered. His life was so consistent that, although young, he had attained a reputation equal to that of the elder Zacharias: for he 'walked in all the commandments and ordinances of the Lord blameless,'[8] and was untir-

[2] μαρτύρων. This word is used in this and the following chapters of all those that suffered in the persecution, whether they lost their lives or not, and therefore in a broader sense than our word "martyr." In order, therefore, to avoid all ambiguity I have translated the word in every case "witness," its original significance. Upon the use of the words μάρτυρ and μάρτυς in the early Church, see Bk. III. chap. 32, note 15.

[3] The fragments of this epistle, preserved by Eusebius in this and the next chapter, are printed with a commentary by Routh, in his *Rel. Sacræ.* I. p. 285 sq., and an English translation is given in the *Ante-Nicene Fathers*, VIII. p. 778 sq. There can be no doubt as to the early date and reliability of the epistle. It bears no traces of a later age, and contains little of the marvelous, which entered so largely into the spurious martyrologies of a later day. Its genuineness is in fact questioned by no one so far as I am aware. It is one of the most beautiful works of the kind which we have, and well deserves the place in his *History* which Eusebius has accorded it. We may assume that we have the greater part of the epistle in so far as it related to the martyrdoms. Ado, in his *Mart.*, asserts that forty-eight suffered martyrdom, and even gives a list of their names. It is possible that he gained his information from the epistle itself, as given in its complete form in Eusebius' *Collection of Martyrdoms;* but I am inclined to think rather that Eusebius has mentioned if not all, at least the majority of the martyrs referred to in the epistle, and that therefore Ado's list is largely imaginary. Eusebius' statement, that a "multitude" suffered signifies nothing, for μυρία was a very indefinite word, and might be used of a dozen or fifteen as easily as of forty-eight. To speak of the persecution as "wholesale," so that it was not safe for any Christian to appear out of doors (Lightfoot, *Ignatius*, Vol. I. p. 499), is rather overstating the case. The persecution must, of course, whatever its extent, appear terrible to the Christians of the region; but a critical examination of the epistle itself will hardly justify the extravagant statements which are commonly made in regard to the magnitude and severity of the persecution. It may have been worse than any single persecution that had preceded it, but sinks into insignificance when compared with those which took place under Decius and Diocletian.

It is interesting to notice that this epistle was especially addressed to the Christians of Asia and Phrygia. We know that Southern Gaul contained a great many Asia Minor people, and that the intercourse between the two districts was very close. Irenæus, and other prominent Christians of Gaul, in the second and following centuries, were either natives of Asia Minor, or had pursued their studies there; and so the Church of the country always bore a peculiarly Greek character, and was for some centuries in sympathy and in constant communication with the Eastern Church. Witness, for instance, the rise and spread of semi-Pelagianism there in the fifth century,—a simple reproduction in its main features of the anthropology of the Eastern Church. Doubtless, at the time this epistle was written, there were many Christians in Lyons and Vienne, who had friends and relations in the East, and hence it was very natural that an epistle should be sent to what might be called, in a sense, the mother churches. Valesius expressed the opinion that Irenæus was the author of this epistle; and he has been followed by many other scholars. It is possible that he was, but there are no grounds upon which to base the opinion, except the fact that Irenæus lived in Lyons, and was, or afterward became, a writer. On the other hand, it is significant that no tradition has connected the letter with Irenæus' name, and that even Eusebius has no thought of such a connection. In fact, Valesius' opinion seems to me in the highest degree improbable.

[4] Rom. viii. 18.

[5] Of course official imprisonment cannot be referred to here. It may be that the mob did actually shut Christians up in one or another place, or it may mean simply that their treatment was such that the Christians were obliged to avoid places of public resort and were perhaps even compelled to remain somewhat closely at home, and were thus in a sense "imprisoned."

[6] χιλιαρχής, strictly the commander of a thousand men, but commonly used also to translate the Latin *Tribunus militum.*

[7] Of the various witnesses mentioned in this chapter (Vettius Epagathus, Sanctus, Attalus, Blandina, Biblias, Pothinus, Maturus, Alexander, Ponticus) we know only what this epistle tells us. The question has arisen whether Vettius Epagathus really was a martyr. Renan (*Marc Aurèle*, p. 307) thinks that he was not even arrested, but that the words " taken into the number of martyrs " (§ 10, below) imply simply that he enjoyed all the merit of martyrdom without actually undergoing any suffering. He bases his opinion upon the fact that Vettius is not mentioned again among the martyrs whose sufferings are recorded, and also upon the use of the words, " He was *and is* a true disciple " (§ 10, below). It is quite possible, however, that Vettius, who is said to have been a man of high station, was simply beheaded as a Roman citizen, and therefore there was no reason for giving a description of his death; and still further the words, " taken into the order of witnesses," and also the words used in § 10, " being well pleased to lay down his life," while they do not prove that he suffered martyrdom, yet seem very strongly to imply that he did, and the quotation from the Apocalypse in the same paragraph would seem to indicate that he was dead, not alive, at the time the epistle was written. On the whole, it may be regarded as probable, though not certain, that Vettius was one of the martyrs. Valesius refers to Gregory of Tours (*H. E.* chaps. 29, 31) as mentioning a certain senator who was " of the lineage of Vettius Epagathus, who suffered for the name of Christ at Lyons." Gregory's authority is not very great, and he may in this case have known no more about the death of Vettius than is told in the fragment which we still possess, so that his statement can hardly be urged as proof that Vettius did suffer martyrdom. But it may be used as indicating that the latter was of a noble family, a fact which is confirmed in § 10, below, where he is spoken of as a man of distinction.

[8] Luke i. 6.

ing in every good work for his neighbor, zealous for God and fervent in spirit. Such being his character, he could not endure the unreasonable judgment against us, but was filled with indignation, and asked to be permitted to testify in behalf of his brethren, that there is among

10 us nothing ungodly or impious. But those about the judgment seat cried out against him, for he was a man of distinction; and the governor refused to grant his just request, and merely asked if he also were a Christian. And he, confessing this with a loud voice, was himself taken into the order [9] of the witnesses, being called the Advocate of the Christians, but having the Advocate [10] in himself, the Spirit [11] more abundantly than Zacharias.[12] He showed this by the fullness of his love, being well pleased even to lay down his life [13] in defense of the brethren. For he was and is a true disciple of Christ, 'following the Lamb whithersoever he goeth.' [14]

11 "Then the others were divided,[15] and the proto-witnesses were manifestly ready, and finished their confession with all eagerness. But some appeared unprepared and untrained, weak as yet, and unable to endure so great a conflict. About ten of these proved abortions,[16] causing us great grief and sorrow beyond measure, and impairing the zeal of the others who had not yet been seized, but who, though suffering all kinds of affliction, continued constantly with the witnesses and did not forsake

12 them. Then all of us feared greatly on account of uncertainty as to their confession; not because we dreaded the sufferings to be endured, but because we looked to the end, and were afraid that some of them might fall

13 away. But those who were worthy were seized day by day, filling up their number, so that all the zealous persons, and those through whom especially our affairs had been established, were collected together out of the two

14 churches. And some of our heathen ser-

vants also were seized, as the governor had commanded that all of us should be examined publicly. These, being ensnared by Satan, and fearing for themselves the tortures which they beheld the saints endure,[17] and being also urged on by the soldiers, accused us falsely of Thyestean banquets and Œdipodean intercourse,[18] and of deeds which are not only unlawful for us to speak of or to think, but which we cannot believe were ever done by men. When 15 these accusations were reported, all the people raged like wild beasts against us, so that even if any had before been moderate on account of friendship, they were now exceedingly furious and gnashed their teeth against us. And that which was spoken by our Lord was fulfilled: 'The time will come when whosoever killeth you will think that he doeth God service.' [19] Then finally the holy witnesses endured 16 sufferings beyond description, Satan striving earnestly that some of the slanders might be uttered by them also.[20]

"But the whole wrath of the populace, and 17 governor, and soldiers was aroused exceedingly against Sanctus, the deacon from Vienne,[21] and Maturus, a late convert, yet a noble combatant, and against Attalus, a native of Pergamos,[22] where he had always been a pillar and foundation, and Blandina, through whom Christ showed that things which appear mean and obscure and despicable to men are with God of great glory,[23] through love toward him manifested in power, and not boasting in appearance. For while we all trembled, and her earthly 18 mistress, who was herself also one of the witnesses, feared that on account of the weakness of her body, she would be unable to make bold confession, Blandina was filled with such

---

[9] κλῆρον, employed in the sense of "order," "class," "category." Upon the significance of the word κλῆρος in early Christian literature, see Ritschl's exhaustive discussion in his *Entstehung der altkatholischen Kirche*, 2d ed., p. 388 sq.

[10] παράκλητον; cf. John xiv. 16.

[11] πνεῦμα is omitted by three important MSS., followed by Laemmer and Heinichen. Burton retains the word in his text, but rejects it in a note. They are possibly correct, but I have preferred to follow the majority of the codices, thinking it quite natural that Eusebius should introduce the πνεῦμα in connection with Zacharias, who is said to have been filled with the "Spirit," not with the "Advocate," and thinking the omission of the word by a copyist, to whom it might seem quite superfluous after παράκλητον, much easier than its insertion.

[12] See Luke i. 67.   [13] Compare John xv. 13.

[14] Rev. xiv. 4.

[15] διεκρίνοντο. Valesius finds in this word a figure taken from the athletic combats; for before the contests began the combatants were examined, and those found eligible were admitted (εἰσκρίνεσθαι), while the others were rejected (ἐκκρίνεσθαι).

[16] ἐξέτρωσαν, with Stroth, Zimmermann, Schwegler, Burton, and Heinichen. ἐξέπεσον has perhaps a little stronger MS. support, and was read by Rufinus, but the former word, as Valesius remarks, being more unusual than the latter, could much more easily be changed into the latter by a copyist than the latter into the former.

[17] Gieseler (*Ecclesiastical History*, Harper's edition, I. p. 127) speaks of this as a violation of the ancient law that slaves could not be compelled to testify against their masters; but it is to be noticed that it is not said in the present case that they were called upon to testify against their masters, but only that through fear of what might come upon them they yielded to the solicitation of the soldiers and uttered falsehoods against their masters. It is not implied therefore that any illegal methods were employed in this respect by the officials in connection with the trials.

[18] i.e. of cannibalism and incest; for according to classic legend Thyestes had unwittingly eaten his own sons served to him at a banquet by an enemy, and Œdipus had unknowingly married his own mother. Upon the terrible accusations brought against the Christians by their heathen enemies, see above, Bk. IV. chap. 7, note 20.

[20] καὶ δι' ἐκείνων ῥηθῆναί τι τῶν βλασφήμων. The word βλασφήμων evidently refers here to the slanderous reports against the Christians such as had been uttered by those mentioned just above. This is made clear, as Valesius remarks, by the καὶ δι' ἐκείνων, "by them *also*."

[21] Valesius maintains that Sanctus was a deacon of the church of Lyons, and that the words ἀπὸ Βιέννης signify only that he was a native of Vienne, but it is certainly more natural to understand the words as implying that he was a deacon of the church of Vienne, and it is not at all difficult to account for his presence in Lyons and his martyrdom there. Indeed, it is evident that the church of Vienne was peculiarly involved in the persecution as well as that of Lyons. Cf. § 13, above.

[22] Pergamos in Asia Minor (mentioned in Rev. ii. 12, and the seat of a Christian church for a number of centuries) is apparently meant here. As already remarked, the connection between the inhabitants of Gaul and of Asia Minor was very close.

[23] Cf. 1 Cor. i. 27, 28.

power as to be delivered and raised above those who were torturing her by turns from morning till evening in every manner, so that they acknowledged that they were conquered, and could do nothing more to her. And they were astonished at her endurance, as her entire body was mangled and broken; and they testified that one of these forms of torture was sufficient to destroy life, not to speak of so

19 many and so great sufferings. But the blessed woman, like a noble athlete, renewed her strength in her confession; and her comfort and recreation and relief from the pain of her sufferings was in exclaiming, 'I am a Christian, and there is nothing vile done by us.'

20 "But Sanctus also endured marvelously and superhumanly [24] all the outrages which he suffered. While the wicked men hoped, by the continuance and severity of his tortures to wring something from him which he ought not to say, he girded himself against them with such firmness that he would not even tell his name, or the nation or city to which he belonged, or whether he was bond or free, but answered in the Roman tongue to all their questions, 'I am a Christian.' He confessed this instead of name and city and race and everything besides, and the people

21 heard from him no other word. There arose therefore on the part of the governor and his tormentors a great desire to conquer him; but having nothing more that they could do to him, they finally fastened red-hot brazen plates to the most tender parts of his body.

22 And these indeed were burned, but he continued unbending and unyielding, firm in his confession, and refreshed and strengthened by the heavenly fountain of the water of life,

23 flowing from the bowels of Christ. And his body was a witness of his sufferings, being one complete wound and bruise, drawn out of shape, and altogether unlike a human form. Christ, suffering in him, manifested his glory, delivering him from his adversary, and making him an ensample for the others, showing that nothing is fearful where the love of the Father is, and nothing painful where there

24 is the glory of Christ. For when the wicked men tortured him a second time after some days, supposing that with his body swollen and inflamed to such a degree that he could not bear the touch of a hand, if they should again apply the same instruments, they would overcome him, or at least by his death under his sufferings others would be made afraid, not only did not this occur, but, contrary to all human expectation, his body arose and stood erect in the midst of the subsequent torments, and resumed its original appearance and the use of its limbs,

so that, through the grace of Christ, these second sufferings became to him, not torture, but healing.

"But the devil, thinking that he had al- 25 ready consumed Biblias, who was one of those who had denied Christ, desiring to increase her condemnation through the utterance of blasphemy,[25] brought her again to the torture, to compel her, as already feeble and weak, to report impious things concerning us. But 26 she recovered herself under the suffering, and as if awaking from a deep sleep, and reminded by the present anguish of the eternal punishment in hell, she contradicted the blasphemers. 'How,' she said, 'could those eat children who do not think it lawful to taste the blood even of irrational animals?' And thenceforward she confessed herself a Christian, and was given a place in the order of the witnesses.

"But as the tyrannical tortures were 27 made by Christ of none effect through the patience of the blessed, the devil invented other contrivances, — confinement in the dark and most loathsome parts of the prison, stretching of the feet to the fifth hole in the stocks,[26] and the other outrages which his servants are accustomed to inflict upon the prisoners when furious and filled with the devil. A great many were suffocated in prison, being chosen by the Lord for this manner of death, that he might manifest in them his glory. For some, 28 though they had been tortured so cruelly that it seemed impossible that they could live, even with the most careful nursing, yet, destitute of human attention, remained in the prison, being strengthened by the Lord, and invigorated both in body and soul; and they exhorted and encouraged the rest. But such as were young, and arrested recently, so that their bodies had not become accustomed to torture, were unable to endure the severity of their confinement, and died in prison.

"The blessed Pothinus, who had been 29 entrusted with the bishopric of Lyons, was dragged to the judgment seat. He was more than ninety years of age, and very infirm, scarcely indeed able to breathe because of physical weakness; but he was strengthened by spiritual zeal through his earnest desire for martyrdom. Though his body was worn out by old age and disease, his life was preserved that Christ might triumph in it. When he was brought by the soldiers to 30 the tribunal, accompanied by the civil magistrates and a multitude who shouted against him in every manner as if he were Christ himself, he bore noble witness. Being asked 31

---

[24] ὑπὲρ πάντα ἄνθρωπον.

[25] Blasphemy against Christianity, not against God or Christ; that is, slanders against the Christians (cf. § 14, above), as is indicated by the words that follow (so Valesius also).
[26] See Bk. IV. chap. 16, note 9.

by the governor, Who was the God of the Christians, he replied, ' If thou art worthy, thou shalt know.' Then he was dragged away harshly, and received blows of every kind. Those near him struck him with their hands and feet, regardless of his age ; and those at a distance hurled at him whatever they could seize ; all of them thinking that they would be guilty of great wickedness and impiety if any possible abuse were omitted. For thus they thought to avenge their own deities. Scarcely able to breathe, he was cast into prison and died after two days.

32   " Then a certain great dispensation of God occurred, and the compassion of Jesus appeared beyond measure,[27] in a manner rarely seen among the brotherhood, but not beyond the power of Christ. For those who 33 had recanted at their first arrest were imprisoned with the others, and endured terrible sufferings, so that their denial was of no profit to them even for the present. But those who confessed what they were were imprisoned as Christians, no other accusation being brought against them. But the first were treated afterwards as murderers and defiled, and were punished twice as severely as the others. 34 For the joy of martyrdom, and the hope of the promises, and love for Christ, and the Spirit of the Father supported the latter ; but their consciences so greatly distressed the former that they were easily distinguishable from all the rest by their very countenances when they 35 were led forth. For the first went out rejoicing, glory and grace being blended in their faces, so that even their bonds seemed like beautiful ornaments, as those of a bride adorned with variegated golden fringes ; and they were perfumed with the sweet savor of Christ,[28] so that some supposed they had been anointed with earthly ointment. But the others were downcast and humble and dejected and filled with every kind of disgrace, and they were reproached by the heathen as ignoble and weak, bearing the accusation of murderers, and having lost the one honorable and glorious and life-giving Name. The rest, beholding this, were strengthened, and when apprehended, they confessed without hesitation, paying no attention to the persuasions of the devil."

36   After certain other words they continue : " After these things, finally, their martyrdoms were divided into every form.[29] For plaiting a crown of various colors and of all kinds of flowers, they presented it to the Father. It was proper

therefore that the noble athletes, having endured a manifold strife, and conquered grandly, should receive the crown, great and incorruptible.

" Maturus, therefore, and Sanctus and 37 Blandina and Attalus were led to the amphitheater to be exposed to the wild beasts, and to give to the heathen public a spectacle of cruelty, a day for fighting with wild beasts being specially appointed on account of our people. Both Maturus and Sanctus passed again 38 through every torment in the amphitheater, as if they had suffered nothing before, or rather, as if, having already conquered their antagonist in many contests,[30] they were now striving for the crown itself. They endured again the customary running of the gauntlet[31] and the violence of the wild beasts, and everything which the furious people called for or desired, and at last, the iron chair in which their bodies being roasted, tormented them with the fumes. And not with this did the 39 persecutors cease, but were yet more mad against them, determined to overcome their patience. But even thus they did not hear a word from Sanctus except the confession which he had uttered from the beginning. These, 40 then, after their life had continued for a long time through the great conflict, were at last sacrificed, having been made throughout that day a spectacle to the world, in place of the usual variety of combats.

" But Blandina was suspended on a stake, 41 and exposed to be devoured by the wild beasts who should attack her.[32] And because she appeared as if hanging on a cross, and because of her earnest prayers, she inspired the combatants with great zeal. For they looked on her in her conflict, and beheld with their outward eyes, in the form of their sister, him who was crucified for them, that he might persuade those who believe on him, that every one who suffers for the glory of Christ has fellowship always with the living God. As 42 none of the wild beasts at that time touched her, she was taken down from the stake, and cast again into prison. She was preserved thus for another contest, that, being victorious in more conflicts, she might make the punishment of the crooked serpent irrevocable ;[33] and, though small and weak and despised, yet clothed with Christ the mighty and conquering Athlete, she

---

[27] The compassion of Jesus appeared not in the fact that those who denied suffered such terrible punishments, but that the difference between their misery in their sufferings and the joy of the faithful in theirs became a means of strength and encouragement to the other Christians. Compare the note of Heinichen (III. p. 180).

[28] Cf. 2 Cor. ii. 15. Cf. also Bk. IV. chap. 15, § 37, above.

[29] μετὰ ταῦτα δὴ λοιπὸν εἰς πᾶν εἶδος διῃρεῖτο τὰ μαρτύρια τῆς ἐξόδου αὐτῶν.

[30] διὰ πλειόνων κλήρων ; undoubtedly a reference to the athletic combats (see Valesius' note *in loco*).

[31] τὰς διεξόδους τῶν μαστίγων τὰς ἐκεῖσε εἰθισμένας. It was the custom to compel the bestiarii before fighting with wild beasts to run the gauntlet. Compare Shorting's and Valesius' notes *in loco*, and Tertullian's *ad Nationes*, 18, and *ad Martyras*, 5, to which the latter refers.

[32] Among the Romans crucifixion was the mode of punishment commonly inflicted upon slaves and the worst criminals. Roman citizens were exempt from this indignity. See Lipsius' *De Cruce* and the various commentaries upon the Gospel narratives of the crucifixion of Christ.

[33] Compare Isa. xxvii. 1, which is possibly referred to here.

might arouse the zeal of the brethren, and, having overcome the adversary many times might receive, through her conflict, the crown incorruptible.

43   "But Attalus was called for loudly by the people, because he was a person of distinction. He entered the contest readily on account of a good conscience and his genuine practice in Christian discipline, and as he had always been a witness for the truth among

44   us. He was led around the amphitheater, a tablet being carried before him on which was written in the Roman language 'This is Attalus the Christian,' and the people were filled with indignation against him. But when the governor learned that he was a Roman, he commanded him to be taken back with the rest of those who were in prison concerning whom he had written to Cæsar, and whose answer he was awaiting.

45   "But the intervening time was not wasted nor fruitless to them; for by their patience the measureless compassion of Christ was manifested. For through their continued life the dead were made alive, and the witnesses showed favor to those who had failed to witness. And the virgin mother had much joy in receiving alive those whom she had brought forth as

46   dead.[34] For through their influence many who had denied were restored, and re-begotten, and rekindled with life, and learned to confess. And being made alive and strengthened, they went to the judgment seat to be again interrogated by the governor; God, who desires not the death of the sinner,[35] but mercifully invites to repentance, treating them

47   with kindness. For Cæsar commanded that they should be put to death,[36] but that any who might deny should be set free. Therefore, at the beginning of the public festival[37] which took place there, and which was attended by crowds of men from all nations, the governor brought the blessed ones to the judgment seat, to make of them a show and spectacle for the multitude. Wherefore also he examined them again, and beheaded those who appeared to possess Roman citizenship, but he sent the others to the wild beasts.

48   "And Christ was glorified greatly in those who had formerly denied him, for, contrary to the expectation of the heathen, they confessed. For they were examined by themselves,

as about to be set free; but confessing, they were added to the order of the witnesses. But some continued without, who had never possessed a trace of faith, nor any apprehension of the wedding garment,[38] nor an understanding of the fear of God; but, as sons of perdition, they blasphemed the Way through their apostasy. But all the others were added to the   49 Church. While these were being examined, a certain Alexander, a Phrygian by birth, and physician by profession, who had resided in Gaul for many years, and was well known to all on account of his love to God and boldness of speech (for he was not without a share of apostolic grace), standing before the judgment seat, and by signs encouraging them to confess, appeared to those standing by as if in travail. But the people being enraged be-   50 cause those who formerly denied now confessed, cried out against Alexander as if he were the cause of this. Then the governor summoned him and inquired who he was. And when he answered that he was a Christian, being very angry he condemned him to the wild beasts. And on the next day he entered along with Attalus. For to please the people, the governor had ordered Attalus again to the wild beasts. And they were tortured in   51 the amphitheater with all the instruments contrived for that purpose, and having endured a very great conflict, were at last sacrificed. Alexander neither groaned nor murmured in any manner, but communed in his heart with God. But when Attalus was placed in   52 the iron seat, and the fumes arose from his burning body, he said to the people in the Roman language: 'Lo! this which ye do is devouring men; but we do not devour men; nor do any other wicked thing.' And being asked, what name God has, he replied, 'God has not a name as man has.'

"After all these, on the last day of the   53 contests, Blandina was again brought in, with Ponticus, a boy about fifteen years old. They had been brought every day to witness the sufferings of the others, and had been pressed to swear by the idols. But because they remained steadfast and despised them, the multitude became furious, so that they had no compassion for the youth of the boy nor respect for the sex of the woman. Therefore they exposed them   54 to all the terrible sufferings and took them through the entire round of torture, repeatedly urging them to swear, but being unable to effect this; for Ponticus, encouraged by his sister so that even the heathen could see that she was confirming and strengthening him, having nobly endured every torture, gave up the ghost.

---

34 ὡς νεκροὺς ἐξέτρωσε. Compare § 11, above.
35 Ezek. xxxiii. 11.
36 ἀποτυμπανισθῆναι. The word means literally "beaten to death," but it is plain that it is used in a general sense here, from the fact that some were beheaded and some sent to the wild beasts, as we are told just below.
37 Renan (Marc Aurèle, p. 329) identifies this with the meeting of the general assembly of the Gallic nations, which took place annually in the month of August for the celebration of the worship of Augustus, and was attended with imposing ceremonies, games, contests, &c. The identification is not at all improbable.

38 Cf. Matt. xxii. 11.

55 But the blessed Blandina, last of all, having, as a noble mother, encouraged her children and sent them before her victorious to the King, endured herself all their conflicts and hastened after them, glad and rejoicing in her departure as if called to a marriage supper, rather than

56 cast to wild beasts. And, after the scourging, after the wild beasts, after the roasting seat,[39] she was finally enclosed in a net, and thrown before a bull. And having been tossed about by the animal, but feeling none of the things which were happening to her, on account of her hope and firm hold upon what had been entrusted to her, and her communion with Christ, she also was sacrificed. And the heathen themselves confessed that never among them had a woman endured so many and such terrible tortures.

57 "But not even thus was their madness and cruelty toward the saints satisfied. For, incited by the Wild Beast, wild and barbarous tribes were not easily appeased, and their violence found another peculiar opportunity in

58 the dead bodies.[40] For, through their lack of manly reason, the fact that they had been conquered did not put them to shame, but rather the more enkindled their wrath as that of a wild beast, and aroused alike the hatred of governor and people to treat us unjustly; that the Scripture might be fulfilled: 'He that is lawless, let him be lawless still, and he that is righteous,

59 let him be righteous still.'[41] For they cast to the dogs those who had died of suffocation in the prison, carefully guarding them by night and day, lest any one should be buried by us. And they exposed the remains left by the wild beasts and by fire, mangled and charred, and placed the heads of the others by their bodies, and guarded them in like manner from burial by a watch of soldiers for many days.

60 And some raged and gnashed their teeth against them, desiring to execute more severe vengeance upon them; but others laughed and mocked at them, magnifying their own idols, and imputed to them the punishment of the Christians. Even the more reasonable, and those who had seemed to sympathize somewhat, reproached them often, saying, 'Where is their God, and what has their religion, which they have chosen rather than life, profited them?'

61 So various was their conduct toward us; but we were in deep affliction because we could not bury the bodies. For neither did night avail us for this purpose, nor did money persuade, nor entreaty move to compassion; but they kept watch in every way, as if the prevention of the burial would be of some great advantage to them."

In addition, they say after other things:

"The bodies of the martyrs, having thus 62 in every manner been exhibited and exposed for six days, were afterward burned and reduced to ashes, and swept into the Rhone by the wicked men, so that no trace of them might appear on the earth. And this 63 they did, as if able to conquer God, and prevent their new birth; 'that,' as they said, 'they may have no hope of a resurrection,[42] through trust in which they bring to us this foreign and new religion, and despise terrible things, and are ready even to go to death with joy. Now let us see if they will rise again, and if their God is able to help them, and to deliver them out of our hands.'"

CHAPTER II.

The Martyrs, beloved of God, kindly ministered unto those who fell in the Persecution.

SUCH things happened to the churches 1 of Christ under the above-mentioned emperor,[1] from which we may reasonably conjecture the occurrences in the other provinces. It is proper to add other selections from the same letter, in which the moderation and compassion of these witnesses is recorded in the following words:

"They were also so zealous in their imi- 2 tation of Christ, — 'who, being in the form of God, counted it not a prize to be on an equality with God,'[2] — that, though they had attained such honor, and had borne witness, not once or twice, but many times, — having been brought back to prison from the wild beasts, covered with burns and scars and wounds, — yet they did not proclaim themselves witnesses, nor did they suffer us to address them by this name. If any one of us, in letter or conversation, spoke of them as witnesses, they rebuked him

---

[39] τήγανον: literally, "frying-pan," by which, however, is evidently meant the instrument of torture spoken of already more than once in this chapter as an iron seat or chair.

[40] The Christians were very solicitous about the bodies of the martyrs, and were especially anxious to give them decent burial, and to preserve the memory of their graves as places of peculiar religious interest and sanctity. They sometimes went even to the length of bribing the officials to give them the dead bodies (cf. § 61, below).

[41] Rev. xxii. 11. The citation of the Apocalypse at this date as Scripture (ἵνα ἡ γραφὴ πληρωθῇ) is noteworthy.

[42] These words show us how much emphasis the Christians of that day must have laid upon the resurrection of the body (an emphasis which is abundantly evident from other sources), and in what a sensuous and material way they must have taught the doctrine, or at least how unguarded their teaching must have been, which could lead the heathen to think that they could in the slightest impede the resurrection by such methods as they pursued. The Christians, in so far as they laid so much emphasis as they did upon the material side of the doctrine, and were so solicitous about the burial of their brethren, undoubtedly were in large part responsible for this gross misunderstanding on the part of the heathen.

[1] Namely, Antoninus Verus (in reality Marcus Aurelius, but wrongly distinguished by Eusebius from him), mentioned above in the Introduction. Upon Eusebius' separation of Marcus Aurelius and Antoninus Verus, see below, p. 390, note.

[2] Phil. ii. 6.

3   sharply. For they conceded cheerfully the appellation of Witness to Christ 'the faithful and true Witness,'[3] and 'firstborn of the dead,'[4] and prince of the life of God;[5] and they reminded us of the witnesses who had already departed, and said, 'They are already witnesses whom Christ has deemed worthy to be taken up in their confession, having sealed their testimony by their departure; but we are lowly and humble confessors.'[6] And they besought the brethren with tears that earnest prayers should be offered that they might be made perfect.[7]

4   They showed in their deeds the power of 'testimony,' manifesting great boldness toward all the brethren, and they made plain their nobility through patience and fearlessness and courage, but they refused the title of Witnesses as distinguishing them from their brethren,[8] being filled with the fear of God."

5   A little further on they say: "They humbled themselves under the mighty hand, by which they are now greatly exalted.[9] They defended all,[10] but accused none. They absolved all, but bound none.[11] And they prayed for those who had inflicted cruelties upon them, even as Stephen, the perfect witness, 'Lord, lay not this sin to their charge.'[12] But if he prayed for those who stoned him, how much more for the brethren!"

6   And again after mentioning other matters, they say:

"For, through the genuineness of their love, their greatest contest with him was that the Beast, being choked, might cast out alive those whom he supposed he had swallowed. For they did not boast over the fallen, but helped them in their need with those things in which they themselves abounded, having the compassion of a mother, and shedding many tears

7   on their account before the Father. They asked for life, and he gave it to them, and they shared it with their neighbors. Victorious over everything, they departed to God. Having

always loved peace, and having commended peace to us,[13] they went in peace to God, leaving no sorrow to their mother, nor division or strife to the brethren, but joy and peace and concord and love."

This record of the affection of those   8
blessed ones toward the brethren that had fallen may be profitably added on account of the inhuman and unmerciful disposition of those who, after these events, acted unsparingly toward the members of Christ.[14]

CHAPTER III.

The Vision which appeared in a Dream to the Witness Attalus.

THE same letter of the above-mentioned   1
witnesses contains another account worthy of remembrance. No one will object to our bringing it to the knowledge of our readers. It runs as follows: "For a certain Alci-   2
biades,[1] who was one of them, led a very austere life, partaking of nothing whatever but bread and water. When he endeavored to continue this same sort of life in prison, it was revealed to Attalus after his first conflict in the amphitheater that Alcibiades was not doing well in refusing the creatures of God and placing a stumbling-block before others. And Alci-   3
biades obeyed, and partook of all things without restraint, giving thanks to God. For they were not deprived of the grace of God, but the Holy Ghost was their counselor." Let this suffice for these matters.

The followers of Montanus,[2] Alcibiades[3]   4
and Theodotus[4] in Phrygia were now first giving wide circulation to their assumption in regard to prophecy, — for the many other miracles

---

[3] Rev. iii. 14.   [4] Rev. i. 5.
[5] ἀρχηγῷ τῆς ζωῆς τοῦ θεοῦ. Cf. Rev. iii. 14.
[6] ὁμολόγοι. The regular technical term for "confessor," which later came into general use, was ὁμολογητής.
[7] τελειωθῆναι; i.e. be made perfect by martyrdom. For this use of τελειόω, see below, Bk. VI. chap. 3, § 13, and chap. 5, § 1; also Bk. VII. chap. 15, § 5, and see Suicer's *Thesaurus, s.v.*
[8] πρὸς τοὺς ἀδελφούς.   [9] Compare 1 Pet. v. 6.
[10] πᾶσι μὲν ἀπολογοῦντο. Rufinus translates *placabant omnes;* Musculus, *omnibus rationem fidei suæ reddebant;* Valesius, *omnium defensionem suscipiebant,* though he maintains in a note that the rendering of Musculus, or the translation *omnibus se excusabant,* is more correct. It is true that πᾶσι ἀπολογοῦντο ought strictly to mean "apologized *to* all" rather than "*for* all," the latter being commonly expressed by the use of ὑπέρ with the genitive (see the lexicons *s.v.* ἀπολογέομαι). At the same time, though it may not be possible to produce any other examples of the use of the dative, instead of ὑπέρ with the genitive, after ἀπολογοῦμαι, it is clear from the context that it must be accepted in the present case.
[11] The question of the readmission of the lapsed had not yet become a burning one. The conduct of the martyrs here in absolving (ἔλυον) those who had shown weakness under persecution is similar to that which caused so much dispute in the Church during and after the persecution of Decius. See below, Bk. VI. chap. 43, note 1.
[12] Acts vii. 60.

[13] ἡμῖν, which is found in four important MSS. and in Nicephorus, and is supported by Rufinus and adopted by Stephanus, Stroth, Burton, and Zimmermann. The majority of the MSS., followed by all the other editors, including Heinichen, read ἀεί.
[14] Eusebius refers here to the Novatians, who were so severe in their treatment of the lapsed, and who in his day were spread very widely and formed an aggressive and compact organization (see below, Bk. VI. chap. 43, note 1).
[1] Of this Alcibiades we know only what is told us in this connection. Doubtless Eusebius found this extract very much to his taste, for we know that he was not inclined to asceticism. The enthusiastic spirit of the Lyons Christians comes out strongly in the extract, and considerable light is thrown by it upon the state of the Church there. Imprisoned confessors were never permitted to suffer for want of food and the other comforts of life so long as their brethren were allowed access to them. Compare e.g. Lucian's *Peregrinus Proteus.*
[2] On Montanus and the Montanists, see below, chap. 16 sq.
[3] Of this Montanist Alcibiades we know nothing. He is, of course, to be distinguished from the confessor mentioned just above. The majority of the editors of Eusebius substitute his name for that of Miltiades in chap. 16, below, but the MSS. all read Μιλτιάδην, and the emendation is unwarranted (see chap. 16, note 7). Salmon suggests that we should read Miltiades instead of Alcibiades in the present passage, supposing that the latter may have crept in through a copyist's error, under the influence of the name Alcibiades mentioned just above. Such an error is possible, but not probable (see chap. 16, note 7).
[4] Of the Montanist Theodotus we know only what is told us here and in chap. 16, below (see that chapter, note 25).

that, through the gift of God, were still wrought in the different churches caused their prophesying to be readily credited by many, — and as dissension arose concerning them, the brethren in Gaul set forth their own prudent and most orthodox judgment in the matter, and published also several epistles from the witnesses that had been put to death among them. These they sent, while they were still in prison, to the brethren throughout Asia and Phrygia, and also to Eleutherus,[5] who was then bishop of Rome, negotiating for the peace of the churches.[6]

CHAPTER IV.

Irenæus commended by the Witnesses in a Letter.

1   THE same witnesses also recommended Irenæus,[1] who was already at that time a presbyter of the parish of Lyons, to the above-mentioned bishop of Rome, saying many favorable things in regard to him, as the following extract shows :

2   "We pray, father Eleutherus, that you may rejoice in God in all things and always. We have requested our brother and comrade Irenæus to carry this letter to you, and we ask you to hold him in esteem, as zealous for the covenant of Christ. For if we thought that office could confer righteousness upon any one, we should commend him among the first as a presbyter of the church, which is his position."

3   Why should we transcribe the catalogue

of the witnesses given in the letter already mentioned, of whom some were beheaded, others cast to the wild beasts, and others fell asleep in prison, or give the number of confessors[2] still surviving at that time? For whoever desires can readily find the full account by consulting the letter itself, which, as I have said, is recorded in our Collection of Martyrdoms.[3] Such were the events which happened under Antoninus.[4]

CHAPTER V.

God sent Rain from Heaven for Marcus Aurelius Cæsar in Answer to the Prayers of our People.

IT is reported[1] that Marcus Aurelius   1 Cæsar, brother of Antoninus,[2] being about to engage in battle with the Germans and Sarmatians, was in great trouble on account of his army suffering from thirst.[3] But the soldiers of the so-called Melitene legion,[4] through

---

[5] On Eleutherus, see above, Bk. V. Introd. note 2.

[6] It is commonly assumed that the Gallic martyrs favored the Montanists and exhorted Eleutherus to be mild in his judgment of them, and to preserve the peace of the Church by permitting them to remain within it and enjoy fellowship with other Christians. But Salmon (in the *Dict. of Christian Biog.* III. p. 937) has shown, in my opinion conclusively, that the Gallic confessors took the opposite side, and exhorted Eleutherus to confirm the Eastern Church in its condemnation of the Montanists, representing to him that he would threaten the peace of the Church by refusing to recognize the justice of the decision of the bishops of the East and by setting himself in opposition to them. Certainly, with their close connection with Asia Minor, we should expect the Gallic Christians to be early informed of the state of affairs in the East, and it is not difficult to think that they may have formed the same opinion in regard to the new prophecy which the majority of their brethren there had formed. The decisive argument for Salmon's opinion is the fact that Eusebius calls the letter of the Lyons confessors to Eleutherus "pious and most orthodox." Certainly, looking upon Montanism as one of the most execrable of heresies and as the work of Satan himself (cf. his words in chap. 16, below), it is very difficult to suppose that he can have spoken of a letter written expressly in favor of the Montanists in any such terms of respect. Salmon says: "It is monstrous to imagine that Eusebius, thinking thus of Montanism, could praise as pious or orthodox the opinion of men who, ignorant of Satan's devices, should take the devil's work for God's. The way in which we ourselves read the history is that *the Montanists had appealed to Rome ;* that the Church party solicited the good offices of their countrymen settled in Gaul, who wrote to Eleutherus representing the disturbance to the peace of the churches (a phrase probably preserved by Eusebius from the letter itself) which would ensue if the Roman Church should approve what the Church on the spot had condemned. . . . To avert, then, the possibility of a calamity of a breach between the Eastern and Western churches, the Gallic churches, it would appear, not only wrote, but sent Irenæus to Rome at the end of 177 or the beginning of 178. The hypothesis here made relieves us from the necessity of supposing this πρεσβεία to have been unsuccessful, while it fully accounts for the necessity of sending it."

[1] On Irenæus, see above, Bk. IV. chap. 21, note 9.

[2] ὁμολογητῶν. Eusebius here uses the common technical term for confessors; i.e. for those who had been faithful and had suffered in persecution, but had not lost their lives. In the epistle of the churches of Lyons and Vienne, the word ὁμόλογοι is used to denote the same persons (see above, chap. 2, note 6).

[3] Cf. § 2 of the Introduction to this book (Bk. V.). On Eusebius' *Collection of Martyrdoms*, see above, p. 30.

[4] i.e. Antoninus Verus, whom Eusebius expressly distinguishes from Marcus Aurelius at the beginning of the next chapter. See below, p. 390, note.

[1] The expression λόγος ἔχει, employed here by Eusebius, is ordinarily used by him to denote that the account which he subjoins rests simply upon verbal testimony. But in the present instance he has written authority, which he mentions below. He seems, therefore, in the indefinite phrase λόγος ἔχει, to express doubts which he himself feels as to the trustworthiness of the account which he is about to give. The story was widely known in his time, and the Christians' version of it undoubtedly accepted by the Christians themselves with little misgiving, and yet he is too well informed upon this subject to be ignorant of the fact that the common version rests upon a rather slender foundation. He may have known of the coins and monuments upon which the emperor had commemorated his own view of the matter, — at any rate he was familiar with the fact that all the heathen historians contradicted the claims of the Christians, and hence he could not but consider it a questionable matter. At the same time, the Christian version of the story was supported by strong names and was widely accepted, and he, as a good Christian, of course wished to accept it, if possible, and to report it for the edification of posterity.

[2] τούτου δὲ ἀδελφόν: the τούτου the τούτου referring to the Antoninus mentioned at the close of the previous chapter. Upon Eusebius' confusion of the successors of Antoninus Pius, see below, p. 390, note.

[3] It is an historical fact that, in 174 A.D., the Roman army in Hungary was relieved from a very dangerous predicament by the sudden occurrence of a thunder-storm, which quenched their thirst and frightened the barbarians, and thus gave the Romans the victory. By heathen writers this event (quite naturally considered miraculous) was held to have taken place in answer to prayer, but by no means in answer to the prayers of the Christians. Dion Cassius (LXXI. 8) ascribes the supposed miracle to the conjurations of the Egyptian magician Arnuphis; Capitolinus (*Vita Marc. Aurelii*, chap. 24, and *Vita Heliogabali*, chap. 9), to the prayer of Marcus Aurelius. The emperor himself expresses his view upon a coin which represents Jupiter as hurling lightning against the barbarians (see Eckhel. *Numism.* III. 61).

As early as the time of Marcus Aurelius himself the Christians ascribed the merit of the supposed miracle to their own prayers (e.g. Apolinarius, mentioned just below), and this became the common belief among them (cf. Tertullian, *Apol.* chap. 5, quoted just below, and *ad Scap.* chap. 4, and the forged edict of Marcus Aurelius, appended to Justin Martyr's first Apology). It is probable that the whole legion prayed for deliverance to their respective deities, and thus quite naturally each party claimed the victory for its particular gods. That there were some Christians in the army of Marcus Aurelius there is, of course, no reason to doubt, but that a legion at that time was wholly composed of Christians, as Eusebius implies, is inconceivable.

[4] This legion was called the Melitene from the place where it was

the faith which has given strength from that time to the present, when they were drawn up before the enemy, kneeled on the ground, as is our custom in prayer,[5] and engaged in sup-

2 plications to God. This was indeed a strange sight to the enemy, but it is reported[6] that a stranger thing immediately followed. The lightning drove the enemy to flight and destruction, but a shower refreshed the army of those who had called on God, all of whom had been on the point of perishing with thirst.

3 This story is related by non-Christian writers who have been pleased to treat the times referred to, and it has also been recorded by our own people.[7] By those historians who were strangers to the faith, the marvel is mentioned, but it is not acknowledged as an answer to our prayers. But by our own people, as friends of the truth, the occurrence is related in a simple and artless manner.

4 Among these is Apolinarius,[8] who says that from that time the legion through whose prayers the wonder took place received from the emperor a title appropriate to the event, being called in the language of the Romans

5 the Thundering Legion. Tertullian is a

trustworthy witness of these things. In the Apology for the Faith, which he addressed to the Roman Senate, and which work we have already mentioned,[9] he confirms the history with greater and stronger proofs. He **6** writes[10] that there are still extant letters[11] of the most intelligent Emperor Marcus in which he testifies that his army, being on the point of perishing with thirst in Germany, was saved by the prayers of the Christians. And he says also that this emperor threatened death[12] to those who brought accusation against us. He adds further:[13] **7**

"What kind of laws are those which impious, unjust, and cruel persons use against us alone? which Vespasian, though he had conquered the Jews, did not regard;[14] which Trajan partially annulled, forbidding Christians to be sought after;[15] which neither Adrian,[16] though inquisitive in all matters, nor he who was called Pius[17] sanctioned." But let any one treat these things as he chooses;[18] we must pass on to what followed.

Pothinus having died with the other mar- **8** tyrs in Gaul at ninety years of age,[19] Irenæus succeeded him in the episcopate of the church at Lyons.[20] We have learned that, in his youth, he was a hearer of Polycarp.[21] In the **9** third book of his work Against Heresies he has inserted a list of the bishops of Rome, bringing it down as far as Eleutherus (whose times we are now considering), under whom he composed his work. He writes as follows:[22]

---

regularly stationed,—Melitene, a city in Eastern Cappadocia, or Armenia.

[5] Kneeling was the common posture of offering prayer in the early Church, but the standing posture was by no means uncommon, especially in the offering of thanksgiving. Upon Sunday and during the whole period from Easter to Pentecost all prayers were regularly offered in a standing position, as a symbolical expression of joy (cf. Tertullian, *de Corona*, chap. 3; *de Oratione*, chap. 23, &c.). The practice, however, was not universal, and was therefore decreed by the Nicene Council in its twentieth canon (Hefele, *Concilien-gesch.* I. 430). See Kraus' *Real-Encyclopädie der Christlichen Alterthümer*, Bd. I. p. 557 sqq.

[6] λόγος ἔχει. See above, note 1.

[7] Dion Cassius and Capitolinus record the occurrence (as mentioned above, note 2). It is recorded also by other writers after Eusebius' time, such as Claudian and Zonaras. None of them, however, attribute the occurrence to the prayers of the Christians, but all claim it for the heathen gods. The only pre-Eusebian *Christian* accounts of this event still extant are those contained in the forged edict of Marcus Aurelius and in the *Apology* of Tertullian, quoted just below (cf. also his *de Orat.* 29). Cyprian also probably refers to the same event in his *Tractat. ad Demetriadem*, 20. Eusebius, in referring to Apolinarius and Tertullian, very likely mentions all the accounts with which he was acquainted. Gregory Nyssa, Jerome, and other later Christian writers refer to the event.

[8] i.e. Claudius Apolinarius, bishop of Hierapolis. Upon him and his writings, see above, Bk. IV. chap. 27, note 1. This reference is in all probability to the *Apology* of Apolinarius, as this is the only work known to us which would have been likely to contain an account of such an event. The fact that in the reign of the very emperor under whom the occurrence took place, and in an Apology addressed to him, the Christians could be indicated as the source of the miracle, shows the firmness of their belief among the Christians themselves, and also proves that they must have been so numerous in the army as to justify them in setting up a counter-claim over against the heathen soldiers.

Apolinarius is very far from the truth in his statement as to the name of the legion. From Dion Cassius, LV. 23, it would seem that the legion bore this name even in the time of Augustus; but if this be uncertain, at any rate it bore it as early as the time of Nero (as we learn from an inscription in its eleventh year, *Corp. Ins. Lat.* III. 30). Neander thinks it improbable that Apolinarius, a contemporary who lived in the neighborhood of the legion's winter quarters, could have committed such a mistake. He prefers to think that the error is Eusebius', and resulted from a too rapid perusal of the passage in Apolinarius, where there must have stood some such words as, " Now the emperor could with right call the legion the Thundering Legion." His opinion is at least plausible. Tertullian certainly knew nothing of the naming of the legion at this time, or if he had heard the report, rejected it.

[9] In Bk. II. chap. 2, § 4, and Bk. III. chap. 33, § 3 (quoted also in Bk. III. chap. 20, § 9).

[10] *Apol.* chap. 5.

[11] A pretended epistle of Marcus Aurelius, addressed to the Senate, in which he describes the miraculous deliverance of his army through the prayers of the Christians, is still extant, and stands at the close of Justin Martyr's first Apology. It is manifestly the work of a Christian, and no one now thinks of accepting it as genuine. It is in all probability the same epistle to which Tertullian refers, and therefore must have been forged before the end of the second century, although its exact date cannot be determined. See Overbeck, *Studien zur Gesch. d. alten Kirche*, I.

[12] The epistle says that the accuser is to be burned alive (ζῶντα καίεσθαι). Tertullian simply says that he is to be punished with a " condemnation of greater severity" (*damnatione et quidem tetriore*). Eusebius therefore expresses himself more definitely than Tertullian, though it is very likely that the poor Greek translation which he used had already made of *damnatio tetrior* the simpler and more telling expression, θάνατος.

[13] *Apol. ibid.*

[14] See Bk. III. chap. 12, note 1.

[15] Upon Trajan's rescript, and the universal misunderstanding of it in the early Church, see above, Bk. III. chap. 33 (notes).

[16] Upon Hadrian's treatment of the Christians, see above, Bk. IV. chap. 9.

[17] Upon Antoninus Pius' relation to them, see above, Bk. IV. chap. 13.

[18] Whether Eusebius refers in this remark only to the report of Tertullian, or to the entire account of the miracle, we do not know. The remark certainly has reference at least to the words of Tertullian. Eusebius had apparently not himself seen the epistle of Marcus Aurelius; for in the first place, he does not cite it; secondly, he does not rest his account upon it, but upon Apolinarius and Tertullian; and thirdly, in his *Chron.* both the Armenian and Greek say, " *it is said* that there are epistles of Marcus Aurelius extant," while Jerome says directly, " *there are* letters extant."

[19] See above, chap. 1, § 29.

[20] Upon Irenæus, see Bk. IV. chap. 21, note 9.

[21] Cf. *Adv. Hær.* II. 3. 4, &c., and Eusebius, chap. 20, below.

[22] *Adv. Hær.* III. 3. 3.

CHAPTER VI.

Catalogue of the Bishops of Rome.

1   "THE blessed apostles[1] having founded and established the church, entrusted the office of the episcopate to Linus.[2] Paul speaks of this Linus in his Epistles to Timothy.[3]

2   Anencletus[4] succeeded him, and after Anencletus, in the third place from the apostles, Clement[5] received the episcopate. He had seen and conversed with the blessed apostles,[6] and their preaching was still sounding in his ears, and their tradition was still before his eyes. Nor was he alone in this, for many who had been taught by the apostles yet survived.

3   In the times of Clement, a serious dissension having arisen among the brethren in Corinth,[7] the church of Rome sent a most suitable letter to the Corinthians,[8] reconciling them in peace, renewing their faith, and proclaiming[9] the doctrine lately received from the apostles." [10]

4   A little farther on he says : [11]

"Evarestus[12] succeeded Clement, and Alexander,[13] Evarestus. Then Xystus,[14] the sixth from the apostles, was appointed. After him Telesphorus,[15] who suffered martyrdom gloriously ; then Hyginus ; [16] then Pius ; [17] and after him Anicetus ; [18] Soter[19] succeeded Anicetus ; and now, in the twelfth place from the apostles, Eleutherus[20] holds the office of bishop.

5   In the same order and succession[21] the

tradition in the Church and the preaching of the truth has descended from the apostles unto us."

CHAPTER VII.

Even down to those Times Miracles were performed by the Faithful.

1   THESE things Irenæus, in agreement with the accounts already given by us,[1] records in the work which comprises five books, and to which he gave the title Refutation and Overthrow of the Knowledge Falsely So-called.[2] In the second book of the same treatise he shows that manifestations of divine and miraculous power continued to his time in some of the churches. He says : [3]

2   "But so far do they come short of raising the dead, as the Lord raised them, and the apostles through prayer. And oftentimes in the brotherhood, when, on account of some necessity, our entire Church has besought with fasting and much supplication, the spirit of the dead has returned,[4] and the man has been restored through the prayers of the saints."

3   And again, after other remarks, he says : [5]

---

[1] Namely, Peter and Paul; but neither of them founded the Roman church. See above, Bk. II. chap. 25, note 17.

[2] On Linus, see above, Bk. III. chap. 2, note 1; and for the succession of the early Roman bishops, see the same note.

[3] 2 Tim. iv. 21.

[4] On Anencletus, see above, Bk. III. chap. 13, note 3.

[5] On Clement, see above, Bk. III. chap. 4, note 19.

[6] Although the identification of this Clement with the one mentioned in Phil. iv. 3 is more than doubtful, yet there is no reason to doubt that, living as he did in the first century at Rome, he was personally acquainted at least with the apostles Peter and Paul.

[7] See the Epistle of Clement itself, especially chaps. 1 and 3.

[8] Upon the epistle, see above, Bk. III. chap. 16, note 1.

[9] ἀνεοῦσα τὴν πίστιν αὐτῶν καὶ ἣν νεωστὶ ἀπὸ τῶν ἀποστόλων παράδοσιν εἰλήφει. The last word being in the singular, the tradition must be that received by the Roman, not by the Corinthian church (as it is commonly understood), and hence it is necessary to supply some word which shall govern παράδοσιν, for it is at least very harsh to say that the Roman church, in its epistle to the Corinthians "renewed" the faith which *it* had received. The truth is, that both in Rufinus and in Irenæus an extra participle is found (in the former *exprimens*, in the latter *annuntians*), and Stroth has in consequence ventured to insert the word καταγγέλουσα in his text. I have likewise, for the sake of the sense, inserted the word *proclaiming*, not thereby intending to imply, however, the belief that καταγγέλουσα stood in the original text of Eusebius.

[10] It is interesting to notice how strictly Eusebius carries out his principle of taking historical matter wherever he can find it, but of omitting all doctrinal statements and discussions. The few sentences which follow in Irenæus are of a doctrinal nature, and in the form of a brief polemic against Gnosticism.

[11] *Ibid.*

[12] Upon Evarestus, see above, Bk. III. chap. 34, note 3.

[13] Upon Alexander, see Bk. IV. chap. 1, note 4.

[14] Upon Xystus, see IV. 4, note 3.

[15] Upon Telesphorus, see IV. 5, note 13.

[16] Upon Hyginus, see IV. 10, note 3.

[17] Upon Pius, see IV. 11, note 14.

[18] Upon Anicetus, see IV. 11, note 18.

[19] Upon Soter, see IV. 19, note 2.

[20] Upon Eleutherus, see Introd. to this book, note 2.

[21] διαδοχῇ, which is confirmed by the ancient Latin version of

Irenæus (*successione*), and which is adopted by Zimmermann, Heinichen, and Valesius (in his notes). All the MSS. of Eusebius, followed by the majority of the editors, read διδαχῇ, which, however, makes no sense in this place, and can hardly have been the original reading (see Heinichen's note *in loco*).

[1] In the various passages referred to in the notes on the previous chapter.

[2] ἐλέγχου καὶ ἀνατροπῆς τῆς ψευδωνύμου γνώσεως (cf. 1 Tim. vi. 20). This work of Irenæus, which is commonly known under its Latin title, *Adversus Hæreses (Against Heresies)*, is still extant in a barbarous Latin version, of which we possess three MSS. The original Greek is lost, though a great part of the first book can be recovered by means of extensive quotations made from it by Hippolytus and Epiphanius. The work is directed against the various Gnostic systems, among which that of Valentinus is chiefly attacked. The first book is devoted to a statement of their doctrines, the second to a refutation of them, and the remaining three to a presentation of the true doctrines of Christianity as opposed to the false positions of the Gnostics. The best edition of the original is that of Harvey: *S. Irenæi libros quinque adv. Hæreses.*, Cambr. 1857, 2 vols.; English translation in the *Ante-Nicene Fathers*, I. p. 309 ff. For the literature of the subject, see Schaff, II. p. 746 ff. On Irenæus himself, see Book IV. chap. 21, note 9.

[3] *Adv. Hær.* II. 31. 2. The sentence as it stands in Eusebius is incomplete. Irenæus is refuting the pretended miracles of Simon and Carpocrates. The passage runs as follows: "So far are they [i.e. Simon and Carpocrates] from being able to raise the dead as the Lord raised them and as the apostles did by means of prayer, and as has been frequently done in the brotherhood on account of some necessity — the entire Church in that locality entreating with much fasting and prayer [so that] the spirit of the dead man has returned, and he has been bestowed in answer to the prayer of the saints — that they do not even believe this can possibly be done, [and hold] that the resurrection from the dead is simply an acquaintance with that truth which they proclaim."

This resurrection of the dead recorded by Irenæus is very difficult to explain, as he is a truth-loving man, and we can hardly conceive of his uttering a direct falsehood. Even Augustine, "the iron man of truth," records such miracles, and so the early centuries are full of accounts of them. The Protestant method of drawing a line between the apostolic and post-apostolic ages in this matter of miracles is arbitrary, and based upon dogmatic, not historical grounds. The truth is, that no one can fix the point of time at which miracles ceased; at the same time, it is easy to appreciate the difference between the apostolic age and the third, fourth, and following centuries in this regard. That they did cease at an early date in the history of the Church is clear enough. Upon post-apostolic miracles, see Schaff, *Ch. Hist.* II. p. 116 ff., J. H. Newman's *Two Essays on Biblical and Eccles. Miracles*, and J. B. Mozley's Bampton lectures *On Miracles.*

[4] See the previous note.   [5] *Adv. Hær.* II. 32. 4.

" If they will say that even the Lord did these things in mere appearance, we will refer them to the prophetic writings, and show from them that all things were beforehand spoken of him in this manner, and were strictly fulfilled ; and that he alone is the Son of God. Wherefore his true disciples, receiving grace from him, perform such works in his Name for the benefit of other men, as each has received the gift from

4   him. For some of them drive out demons effectually and truly, so that those who have been cleansed from evil spirits frequently believe and unite with the Church. Others have a foreknowledge of future events, and visions, and prophetic revelations. Still others heal the sick by the laying on of hands, and restore them to health. And, as we have said, even dead persons have been raised, and remained with

5   us many years. But why should we say more? It is not possible to recount the number of gifts which the Church, throughout all the world, has received from God in the name of Jesus Christ, who was crucified under Pontius Pilate, and exercises every day for the benefit of the heathen, never deceiving any nor doing it for money. For as she has received freely from God, freely also does she minister."[6]

6   And in another place the same author writes :[7]

" As also we hear that many brethren in the Church possess prophetic gifts, and speak, through the Spirit, with all kinds of tongues, and bring to light the secret things of men for their good, and declare the mysteries of God."

So much in regard to the fact that various gifts remained among those who were worthy even until that time.

CHAPTER VIII.

The Statements of Irenæus in regard to the Divine Scriptures.

1   SINCE, in the beginning of this work,[1] we promised to give, when needful, the words of the ancient presbyters and writers of the Church, in which they have declared those traditions which came down to them concerning the canonical books, and since Irenæus was one of them, we will now give his words and, first, what he says of the sacred Gospels :[2]

2   " Matthew published his Gospel among the Hebrews in their own language,[3] while Peter and Paul were preaching and founding the church in Rome.[4] After their de-   3 parture Mark, the disciple and interpreter of Peter, also transmitted to us in writing those things which Peter had preached ;[5] and Luke, the attendant of Paul, recorded in a book the Gospel which Paul had declared.[6] After-   4 wards John, the disciple of the Lord, who also reclined on his bosom, published his Gospel, while staying at Ephesus in Asia."[7]

He states these things in the third book   5 of his above-mentioned work. In the fifth book he speaks as follows concerning the Apocalypse of John, and the number of the name of Antichrist :[8]

" As these things are so, and this number is found in all the approved and ancient copies,[9] and those who saw John face to face confirm it, and reason teaches us that the number of the name of the beast, according to the mode of calculation among the Greeks, appears in its letters. . . ."[10]

And farther on he says concerning the   6 same :[11]

" We are not bold enough to speak confidently of the name of Antichrist. For if it were necessary that his name should be declared clearly at the present time, it would have been announced by him who saw the revelation. For it was seen, not long ago, but almost in our generation, toward the end of the reign of Domitian."[12]

He states these things concerning the   7 Apocalypse[13] in the work referred to. He also mentions the first Epistle of John,[14] taking

---

[6] Cf. Matt. x. 8.   [7] *Adv. Hær.* V. 6. 1.

[1] Eusebius is apparently thinking of the preface to his work contained in Bk. I. chap. 1, but there he makes no such promise as he refers to here. He speaks only of his general purpose to mention those men who preached the divine word either orally or in writing. In Bk. III. chap. 3, however, he distinctly promises to do what he here speaks of doing, and perhaps remembered only that he had made such a promise without recalling where he had made it.

[2] *Adv. Hær.* III. 1. 1.

[3] See above, Bk. III. chap. 24, note 5. Irenæus, in this chapter traces the four Gospels back to the apostles themselves, but he is unable to say that Matthew translated his Gospel into Greek, which is of course bad for his theory, as the Matthew Gospel which the Church of his time had was in Greek, not in Hebrew. He puts the Hebrew Gospel, however, upon a par with the three Greek ones, and thus, although he does not say it directly, endeavors to convey the impression that the apostolicity of the Hebrew Matthew is a guarantee for the Greek Matthew also. Of Papias' statement, " Each one translated the Hebrew Gospel of Matthew as he was able," he could of course make no use even if he was acquainted with it. Whether his account was dependent upon Papias' or not we cannot tell.   [4] See above, Bk. II. chap. 25, note 17.

[5] See above, Bk. II. chap. 15, note 4.

[6] See above, Bk. III. chap. 4, note 15.

[7] See above, Bk. III. chap. 24, note 1.

[8] Irenæus, *Adv. Hær.* V. 30. 1.

[9] Rev. xiii. 18. Already in Irenæus' time there was a variation in the copies of the Apocalypse. This is interesting as showing the existence of old copies of the Apocalypse even in his time, and also as showing how early works became corrupted in the course of transmission. We learn from his words, too, that textual criticism had already begun.

[10] The sentence as Eusebius quotes it here is incomplete; he repeats only so much of it as suits his purpose. Irenæus completes his sentence, after a few more dependent clauses, by saying, " I do not know how it is that some have erred, following the ordinary mode of speech, and have vitiated the middle number in the name," &c. This shows that even in Irenæus' time there was as much controversy about the interpretation of the Apocalypse as there has always been, and that at that day exegetes were as a rule in no better position than we are. Irenæus refers in this sentence to the fact that the Greek numerals were indicated by the letters of the alphabet : Alpha, " one," Beta, " two." &c.

[11] i.e. concerning the Beast or Antichrist. Irenæus, *Adv. Hær.* V. 30. 3; quoted also in Bk. III. chap. 18, above.

[12] See above, Bk. III. chap. 18, note 1.

[13] Upon the Apocalypse, see Bk. III. chap. 24, note 20.

[14] In *Adv. Hær.* III. 16. 5, 8. Irenæus also quotes from the

many proofs from it, and likewise the first Epistle of Peter.[15] And he not only knows, but also receives, The Shepherd,[16] writing as follows : [17]

"Well did the Scripture[18] speak, saying,[19] 'First of all believe that God is one, who has created and completed all things,'" &c.

8 And he uses almost the precise words of the Wisdom of Solomon, saying : [20] "The vision of God produces immortality, but immortality renders us near to God." He mentions also the memoirs[21] of a certain apostolic presbyter,[22] whose name he passes by in silence, and gives his expositions of the sacred

9 Scriptures. And he refers to Justin the Martyr,[23] and to Ignatius,[24] using testimonies also from their writings. Moreover, he promises to refute Marcion from his own writings, in a special work.[25]

10 Concerning the translation of the inspired[26] Scriptures by the Seventy, hear the very words which he writes : [27]

"God in truth became man, and the Lord himself saved us, giving the sign of the virgin ;

but not as some say, who now venture to translate the Scripture, 'Behold, a young woman shall conceive and bring forth a son,'[28] as Theodotion of Ephesus and Aquila of Pontus,[29] both of them Jewish proselytes, interpreted ; following whom, the Ebionites say[30] that he was begotten by Joseph."

Shortly after he adds : 11

"For before the Romans had established their empire, while the Macedonians were still holding Asia, Ptolemy, the son of Lagus,[31] being desirous of adorning the library which he had founded in Alexandria with the meritorious writings of all men, requested the people of Jerusalem to have their Scriptures translated into the Greek language. But, as they were 12 then subject to the Macedonians, they sent to Ptolemy seventy elders, who were the most skilled among them in the Scriptures and in both languages. Thus God accomplished his purpose.[32] But wishing to try them individ- 13

---

second Epistle of John, without distinguishing it from the first, in III. 16. 8, and I. 16. 3. Upon John's epistles, see Bk. III. chap. 24, notes 18 and 19.

[15] In *Adv. Hær.* IV. 9. 2. In IV. 16. 5 and V. 7. 2 he quotes from the first Epistle of Peter, with the formula " Peter says." He is the first one to connect the epistle with Peter. See above, Bk. III. chap. 4, note 1.

[16] i.e. the *Shepherd* of Hermas ; see above, Bk. III. chap. 3, note 23.

[17] *Adv. Hær.* IV. 20. 2.

[18] ἡ γραφή, the regular word used in quoting Scripture. Many of the Fathers of the second and third centuries used this word in referring to Clement, Hermas, Barnabas, and other works of the kind (compare especially Clement of Alexandria's use of the word).

[19] The *Shepherd* of Hermas, II. 1.

[20] *Adv. Hær.* IV. 38. 3. Irenæus in this passage quotes freely from the apocryphal Book of Wisdom, VI. 19, without mentioning the source of his quotation, and indeed without in any way indicating the fact that he is quoting.

[21] ἀπομνημονευμάτων. Written memoirs are hardly referred to here, but rather oral comments, expositions, or accounts of the interpretations of the apostles and others of the first generation of Christians.

[22] *Adv. Hær.* IV. 27. 1, where Irenæus mentions a "certain presbyter who had heard it from those who had seen the apostles," &c. Who this presbyter was cannot be determined. Polycarp, Papias, and others have been suggested, but we have no grounds upon which to base a decision, though we may perhaps safely conclude that so prominent a man as Polycarp would hardly have been referred to in such an indefinite way ; and Papias seems ruled out by the fact that the presbyter is here not made a hearer of the apostles themselves, while in V. 33. 4 Papias is expressly stated to have been a hearer of John, — undoubtedly in Irenæus' mind the evangelist John (see above, Bk. III. chap. 39, note 4). Other anonymous authorities under the titles, "One superior to us," "One before us," &c., are quoted by Irenæus in *Præf.* § 2, I. 13. 3, III. 17. 4, etc. See Routh, *Rel. Sacræ*, I. 45–68.

[23] In *Adv. Hær.* IV. 6. 2, where he mentions Justin Martyr and quotes from his work *Against Marcion* (see Eusebius, Bk. IV. chap. 18), and also in *Adv. Hær.* V. 26. 2, where he mentions him again by name and quotes from some unknown work (but see above, *ibid.* note 15).

[24] Irenæus nowhere mentions Ignatius by name, but in V. 28. 4 he quotes from his epistle to the Romans, chap. 4, under the formula, "A certain one of our people said, when he was condemned to the wild beasts." It is interesting to note how diligently Eusebius had read the works of Irenæus, and extracted from them all that could contribute to his *History*.

Upon Ignatius, see above, III. 36.

[25] *Adv. Hær.* I. 27. 4, III. 12. 12. This promise was apparently never fulfilled, as we hear nothing of the work from any of Irenæus' successors. But in Bk. IV. chap. 25 Eusebius speaks of Irenæus as one of those who had written against Marcion, whether in this referring to his special work promised here, or only to his general work *Adv. Hær.*, we cannot tell.

[26] θεοπνεύστων.   [27] *Adv. Hær.* III. 21. 1.

[28] Isa. vii. 14. The original Hebrew has עַלְמָה, which means simply a "young woman," not distinctively a "virgin." The LXX, followed by Matt. i. 23, wrongly translated by παρθένος, "virgin" (cf. Toy's *Quotations in the New Testament*, p. 1 sqq., and the various commentaries on Matthew). Theodotion and Aquila translated the Hebrew word by νεᾶνις, which is the correct rendering, in spite of what Irenæus says. The complete dependence of the Fathers upon the LXX, and their consequent errors as to the meaning of the original, are well illustrated in this case (cf. also Justin's *Dial.* chap. 71).

[29] This is the earliest direct reference to the translations of Aquila and Theodotion, though Hermas used the version of the latter, as pointed out by Hort (see above, Bk. III. chap. 3, note 23). Upon the two versions, see Bk. VI. chap. 16, notes 3 and 5.

[30] Upon the Ebionites and their doctrines, see Bk. III. chap. 27.

[31] Ptolemy, the son of Lagus, or Ptolemy Soter (the Preserver), was king of Egypt from 323–285 (283) B.C.

The following story in regard to the origin of the LXX is first told in a spurious letter (probably dating from the first century B.C.), which professes to have been written by Aristeas, a high officer at the court of Ptolemy Philadelphus (285[283]–247 B.C.). This epistle puts the origin of the LXX in the reign of the latter monarch instead of in that of his father, Ptolemy Soter, and is followed in this by Philo, Josephus, Tertullian, and most of the other ancient writers (Justin Martyr calls the king simply Ptolemy, while Clement of Alex. says that some connect the event with the one monarch, others with the other). The account given in the letter (which is printed by Gallandius, *Bibl. Patr.* II. 771, as well as in many other editions) is repeated over and over again, with greater or less variations, by early Jewish and Christian writers (e.g. by Philo, *Vit. Mos.* 2 ; by Josephus, *Ant.* XII. 2 ; by Justin Martyr, *Apol.* I. 31 ; by Clement of Alexandria, *Strom.* I. 22 ; by Tertullian, *Apol.* 18, and others ; see the article *Aristeas* in Smith's *Dict. of Greek and Roman Biog.*). It gives the number of the elders as seventy-two, — six from each tribe. That this marvelous tale is a fiction is clear enough, but whether it is based upon a groundwork of fact is disputed (see Schürer, *Gesch. der Juden im Zeitalter Jesu Christi*, II. p. 697 sqq.). It is at any rate certain that the Pentateuch (the original account applies only to the Pentateuch, but later it was extended to the entire Old Testament) was translated into Greek in Alexandria as early as the third century B.C. ; whether under Ptolemy Philadelphus, and at his desire, we cannot tell. The translation of the remainder of the Old Testament followed during the second century B.C., the books being translated at various times by unknown authors, but all or most of them probably in Egypt (see Schürer, *ibid.*). It was, of course, to the interest of the Christians to maintain the miraculous origin of the LXX, for otherwise they would have to yield to the attacks of the Jews, who often taunted them with having only a translation of the Scriptures. Accepting the miraculous origin of the LXX, the Christians, on the other hand, could accuse the Jews of falsifying their Hebrew copies wherever they differed from the LXX, making the latter the only authoritative standard (cf. Justin Martyr's *Dial.* chap. 71, and many other passages in the work). Upon the attitude of the Christians, and the earlier and later attitude of the Jews toward the LXX, see below, Bk. VI. chap. 16, note 8.

[32] ποιήσαντος τοῦ θεοῦ ὅπερ ἠβούλετο. This is quite different from the text of Irenæus, which reads *facturos hoc quod ipse voluisset* (implying that the original Greek was ποιήσοντας τοῦτο ὅπερ

ually, as he feared lest, by taking counsel together, they might conceal the truth of the Scriptures by their interpretation, he separated them from one another, and commanded all of them to write the same translation.[33] He
14 did this for all the books. But when they came together in the presence of Ptolemy, and compared their several translations, God was glorified, and the Scriptures were recognized as truly divine. For all of them had rendered the same things in the same words and with the same names from beginning to end, so that the heathen perceived that the Scriptures had been translated by the inspiration [34] of God.
15 And this was nothing wonderful for God to do, who, in the captivity of the people under Nebuchadnezzar, when the Scriptures had been destroyed, and the Jews had returned to their own country after seventy years, afterwards, in the time of Artaxerxes, king of the Persians, inspired Ezra the priest, of the tribe of Levi, to relate all the words of the former prophets, and to restore to the people the legislation of Moses." [35]

Such are the words of Irenæus.

CHAPTER IX.

The Bishops under Commodus.

AFTER Antoninus[1] had been emperor for nine-teen years, Commodus received the government.[2] In his first year Julian[3] became bishop of the Alexandrian churches, after Agrippinus[4] had held the office for twelve years.

ἠβούλετο), "to carry out what he [viz. Ptolemy] had desired." Heinichen modifies the text of Eusebius somewhat, substituting ποιήσοντας τὰ for ποιήσαντος τοῦ, but there can be little doubt that Eusebius originally wrote the sentence in the form given at the beginning of this note. That Irenæus wrote it in that form, however, is uncertain, though, in view of the fact that Clement of Alex. (*Strom.* I. 22) confirms the reading of Eusebius (reading θεοῦ γὰρ ἦν βούλημα), I am inclined to think that the text of Eusebius represents the original more closely than the text of the Latin translation of Irenæus does. Most of the editors, however, both of Eusebius and of Irenæus, take the other view (cf. Harvey's note in his edition of Irenæus, Vol. II. p. 113).

[33] τὴν αὐτὴν ἑρμηνειαν γράφειν, as the majority of the MSS., followed by Burton and most other editors, read. Stroth, Zimmermann, and Heinichen, on the authority of Rufinus and of the Latin version of Irenæus, read, τὴν αὐτὴν ἑρμηνεύειν γραφήν.

[34] κατ᾽ ἐπίπνοιαν.

[35] This tradition, which was commonly accepted until the time of the Reformation, dates from the first Christian century, for it is found in the fourth book of Ezra (xiv. 44). It is there said that Ezra was inspired to dictate to five men, during forty days, ninety-four books, of which twenty-four (the canonical books) were to be published. The tradition is repeated quite frequently by the Fathers, but that Ezra formed the Old Testament canon is impossible, for some of the books were not written until after his day. The truth is, it was a gradual growth and was not completed until the second century B.C. See above, Bk. III. chap. 10, note 1.

[1] i.e. Marcus Aurelius. See below, p. 390, note.

[2] March 17, 180 A.D.

[3] Of this Julian we know nothing except what is told us by Eusebius here and in chap. 22, below, where he is said to have held office ten years. In the *Chron.* he is also said to have been bishop for ten years, but his accession is put in the nineteenth year of Marcus Aurelius (by Jerome), or in the second year of Commodus (by the Armenian version).

[4] Upon Agrippinus, see above, Bk. IV. chap. 19, note 5.

CHAPTER X.

Pantænus the Philosopher.

ABOUT that time, Pantænus,[1] a man highly   1
distinguished for his learning, had charge of the school of the faithful in Alexandria.[2] A school of sacred learning, which continues to our day, was established there in ancient times,[3]

---

[1] Pantænus is the first teacher of the Alexandrian school that is known to us, and even his life is involved in obscurity. His chief significance for us lies in the fact that he was the teacher of Clement, with whom the Alexandrian school first steps out into the full light of history, and makes itself felt as a power in Christendom. Another prominent pupil of Pantænus was Alexander, bishop of Jerusalem (see below, Bk. VI. chap. 14). Pantænus was originally a Stoic philosopher, and must have discussed philosophy in his school in connection with theology, for Origen appeals to him as his example in this respect (see below, Bk. VI. chap. 19). His abilities are testified to by Clement (in his *Hypotyposes ;* see the next chapter, § 4), who speaks of him always in terms of the deepest respect and affection. Of his birth and death we know nothing. Clement, *Strom.* I. 1, calls him a "Sicilian bee," which may, perhaps, have reference to his birthplace. The statement of Philip of Side, that he was an Athenian, is worthless. We do not know when he began his work in Alexandria, nor when he finished it. But from Bk. VI. chap. 6 we learn that Clement had succeeded Pantænus, and was in charge of the school in the time of Septimius Severus. This probably means not merely that Pantænus had left Egypt, but that he was already dead; and if that be the case, the statement of Jerome (*de vir. ill.* 36), that Pantænus was in charge of the school during the reigns of Septimius Severus and Caracalla, is erroneous (Jerome himself expressly says, in *ibid.* chap. 38, that Clement succeeded Pantænus upon the death of the latter). Jerome's statement, however, that Pantænus was sent to India by Demetrius, bishop of Alexandria, is not necessarily in conflict with the indefinite account of Eusebius, who gives no dates. What authority Jerome has for his account we do not know. If his statement be correct, the journey must have taken place after 190; and thus after, or in the midst of, his Alexandrian activity. Eusebius apparently accepted the latter opinion, though his statement at the end of this chapter is dark, and evidently implies that he was very uncertain in regard to the matter. His whole account rests simply on hearsay, and therefore too much weight must not be laid upon its accuracy. After Clement comes upon the scene (which was at least some years before the outbreak of the persecution of Severus, 200 A.D. — when he left the city) we hear nothing more of Pantænus. Some have put his journey to India in this later period; but this is contrary to the report of Eusebius, and there is no authority for the opinion. Photius (*Cod.* 118) records a tradition that Pantænus had himself heard some of the apostles; but this is impossible, and is asserted by no one else. According to Jerome, numerous commentaries of Pantænus were extant in his time. Eusebius, at the close of this chapter, speaks of his expounding the Scriptures "both orally and in writing," but he does not enumerate his works, and apparently had never seen them. No traces of them are now extant, unless some brief reminiscences of his teaching, which we have, are supposed to be drawn from his works, and not merely from his lectures or conversations (see Routh, *Rel. Sac.* I. p. 375-383).

[2] The origin of this school of the faithful, or "catechetical school," in Alexandria is involved in obscurity. Philip of Side names Athenagoras as the founder of the school, but his account is full of inconsistencies and contradictions, and deserves no credence. The school first comes out into the light of history at this time with Pantænus at its head, and plays a prominent part in Church history under Clement, Origen, Heraclas, Dionysius, Didymus, &c., until the end of the fourth century, when it sinks out of sight in the midst of the dissensions of the Alexandrian church, and its end like its beginning is involved in obscurity. It probably owed its origin to no particular individual, but arose naturally as an outgrowth from the practice which flourished in the early Church of instructing catechumens in the elements of Christianity before admitting them to baptism. In such a philosophical metropolis as Alexandria, a school, though intended only for catechumens, would very naturally soon assume a learned character, and it had already in the time of Pantænus at least become a regular theological school for the preparation especially of teachers and preachers. It exercised a great influence upon theological science, and numbered among its pupils many celebrated theologians and bishops. See the article by Redepenning in Herzog, 2d ed. I. 290-292, and Schaff's *Ch. Hist.* II. 777-781, where the literature of the subject is given.

[3] Jerome (*de vir. ill.* c. 36) states that there had always been ecclesiastical teachers in Alexandria from the time of Mark. He is evidently, however, giving no independent tradition, but merely draws his conclusion from the words of Eusebius, who simply says "from ancient times." The date of the origin of the school is in fact entirely unknown, though there is nothing improbable in the statement of Jerome that ecclesiastical teachers were always there. It must, however, have been some years before a school could be developed or the need of it be felt.

and as we have been informed,[4] was managed by men of great ability and zeal for divine things. Among these it is reported[5] that Pantænus was at that time especially conspicuous, as he had been educated in the philo-
2 sophical system of those called Stoics. They say that he displayed such zeal for the divine Word, that he was appointed as a herald of the Gospel of Christ to the nations in the East, and was sent as far as India.[6] For indeed[7] there were still many evangelists of the Word who sought earnestly to use their inspired zeal, after the examples of the apostles, for the increase and building up of the Divine Word.
3 Pantænus was one of these, and is said to have gone to India. It is reported that among persons there who knew of Christ, he found the Gospel according to Matthew, which had anticipated his own arrival. For Bartholomew,[8] one of the apostles, had preached to them, and left with them the writing of Matthew in the Hebrew language,[9] which they had preserved till that time.
4 After many good deeds, Pantænus finally became the head of the school at Alexandria,[10] and expounded the treasures of divine doctrine both orally and in writing.[11]

---

[4] παρειλήφαμεν.   [5] λόγος ἔχει.
[6] Jerome (de vir. ill. 36) says that he was sent to India by the bishop Demetrius at the request of the Indians themselves, — a statement more exact than that of Eusebius, whether resting upon tradition merely, or upon more accurate information, or whether it is simply a combination of Jerome's, we do not know. It is at any rate not at all improbable (see above, note 1). A little farther on Eusebius indicates that Pantænus preached in the same country in which the apostle Bartholomew had done missionary work. But according to Lipsius (Dict. of Christ. Biog. I. p. 22) Bartholomew's traditional field of labor was the region of the Bosphorus. He follows Gutschmid therefore in claiming that the Indians here are confounded with the Sindians, over whom the Bosphorian kings of the house of Polemo ruled. Jerome (Ep. ad Magnum; Migne, Ep. 70) evidently regards the India where Pantænus preached as India proper (Pantænus Stoicæ sectæ philosophus, ob præcipue eruditionis gloriam, a Demetrio Alexandriæ episcopo missus est in Indiam, ut Christum apud Brachmanas, et illius gentis philosophos prædicaret). Whether the original tradition was that Pantænus went to India, and his connection with Bartholomew (who was wrongly supposed to have preached to the Indians) was a later combination, or whether, on the other hand, the tradition that he preached in Bartholomew's field of labor was the original and the mission to India a later combination, we cannot tell. It is probable that Eusebius meant India proper, as Jerome certainly did, but both of them may have been mistaken.
[7] ἦσαν γὰρ, ἦσαν εἰσέτι. Eusebius seems to think it a remarkable fact that there should still have been preaching evangelists. Evidently they were no longer common in his day. It is interesting to notice that he calls them "evangelists." In earlier times they were called "apostles" (e.g. in the Didache), but the latter had long before Eusebius' time become a narrower, technical term.
[8] See note 6.
[9] If the truth of this account be accepted, Pantænus is a witness to the existence of a Hebrew Matthew. See above, Bk. III. chap. 24, note 5. It has been assumed by some that this Gospel was the Gospel according to the Hebrews (see Bk. III. chap. 25, note 24). This is possible; but even if Pantænus really did find a Hebrew Gospel of Matthew as Eusebius says (and which, according to Jerome, de vir. ill. 36, he brought back to Alexandria with him), we have no grounds upon which to base a conclusion as to its nature, or its relation to our Greek Matthew.
[10] Eusebius apparently puts the journey of Pantænus in the middle of his Alexandrian activity, and makes him return again and teach there until his death. Jerome also agrees in putting the journey in the middle and not at the beginning or close of his Alexandrian activity. It must be confessed, however, that Eusebius' language is very vague, and of such a nature as perhaps to imply that he really had no idea when the mission took place.
[11] See above, note 1.

CHAPTER XI.

Clement of Alexandria.

AT this time Clement,[1] being trained with   1
him[2] in the divine Scriptures at Alexandria, became well known. He had the same name as the one who anciently was at the head of the Roman church, and who was a disciple of the apostles.[3] In his Hypotyposes[4] he   2
speaks of Pantænus by name as his teacher. It seems to me that he alludes to the same person also in the first book of his Stromata, when, referring to the more conspicuous of the successors of the apostles whom he had met,[5] he says:[6]

"This work[7] is not a writing artfully   3
constructed for display; but my notes are stored up for old age, as a remedy against forgetfulness; an image without art, and a rough sketch of those powerful and animated words which it was my privilege to hear, as well as of blessed and truly remarkable men. Of   4
these the one — the Ionian[8] — was in

---

[1] Of the place and time of Titus Flavius Clement's birth we have no certain knowledge, though it is probable that he was an Athenian by training at least, if not by birth, and he must have been born about the middle of the second century. He received a very extensive education, and became a Christian in adult years, after he had tried various systems of philosophy, much as Justin Martyr had. He had a great thirst for knowledge, and names six different teachers under whom he studied Christianity (see below, § 4). Finally he became a pupil of Pantænus in Alexandria, whom he afterward succeeded as the head of the catechetical school there. It is at this time (about 190 A.D.) that he comes out clearly into the light of history, and to this period (190–202) belongs his greatest literary activity. He was at the head of the school probably until 202, when the persecution of Severus having broken out, he left Alexandria, and we have no notice that he ever returned. That he did not leave Alexandria dishonorably, through fear, may be gathered from his presence with Alexander during his imprisonment, and from the letters of the latter (see below, Bk. VI. chaps. 11 and 14, and cf. Bk. VI. chap. 6, notes). This is the last notice that we have of him (A.D. 212); and of the place and time of his death we know nothing, though he cannot have lived many years after this. He was never a bishop, but was a presbyter of the Alexandrian church, and was in ancient times commemorated as a saint, but his name was dropped from the roll by Clement VIII. on account of suspected heterodoxy. He lived in an age of transition, and his great importance lies in the fact that he completed the bond between Hellenism and Christianity, and as a follower of the apologists established Christianity as a philosophy, and yet not as they had done in an apologetic sense. He was the teacher of Origen, and the real father of Greek theology. He published no system, as did Origen; his works were rather desultory and fragmentary, but full of wide and varied learning, and exhibit a truly broad and catholic spirit. Upon his works, see Bk. VI. chap. 13. Upon Clement, see especially Westcott's article in Smith and Wace, I. 559–567, and Schaff, II. 781–785, where the literature is given with considerable fullness. For an able and popular presentation of his theology, see Allen's Continuity of Christian Thought, p. 38–70.
[2] συνασκούμενος.
[3] Upon Clement of Rome and his relation to the apostles, see Bk. III. chap. 4, note 19.
[4] On Clement's Hypotyposes, see Bk. VI. chap. 13, note 3. The passage in which he mentions Pantænus by name has not been preserved. Eusebius repeats the same statement in Bk. VI. chap. 13, § 1.
[5] τοὺς ἐμφανεστέρους ἧς κατείληφεν ἀποστολικῆς διαδοχῆς ἐπισημαινόμενος. Rufinus reads apostolicæ prædicationis instead of successionis. And so Christophorsonus and Valesius adopt διαδαχῆς instead of διαδοχῆς, and translate doctrinæ. But διαδοχῆς is too well supported by MS. authority to be rejected; and though the use of the abstract "succession," instead of the concrete "successors," seems harsh, it is employed elsewhere in the same sense by Eusebius (see Bk. I. chap. 1, § 1).
[6] Strom. I. 1.   [7] i.e. his Stromata.
[8] This is hardly a proper name, although many have so considered it, for Clement gives no other proper name in this connection, and it is much more natural to translate "the Ionian."

Greece, the other in Magna Græcia;[9] the one of them was from Cœle-Syria,[10] the other from Egypt. There were others in the East, one of them an Assyrian,[11] the other a Hebrew in Palestine.[12] But when I met with the last,[13] — in ability truly he was first, — having hunted him out in his concealment in Egypt, I found rest. These men, preserving the true tradition of the blessed doctrine, directly from the holy apostles, Peter and James and John and Paul, the son receiving it from the father (but few were like the fathers), have come by God's will even to us to deposit those ancestral and apostolic seeds."[14]

CHAPTER XII.

The Bishops in Jerusalem.

1 AT this time Narcissus[1] was the bishop of the church at Jerusalem, and he is cele-

brated by many to this day. He was the fifteenth in succession from the siege of the Jews under Adrian. We have shown that from that time first the church in Jerusalem was composed of Gentiles, after those of the circumcision, and that Marcus was the first Gentile bishop that presided over them.[2] After him the 2 succession in the episcopate was: first Cassianus; after him Publius; then Maximus;[3] following them Julian; then Gaius;[4] after him Symmachus and another Gaius, and again another Julian; after these Capito[5] and Valens and Dolichianus; and after all of them Narcissus, the thirtieth in regular succession from the apostles.

Various conjectures have been made as to who these teachers were, but none are more than mere guesses. Philip of Side tells us that Athenagoras was a teacher of Clement, but, as we have seen, no confidence can be placed in his statement. It has been conjectured also that Melito may be the person referred to as "the Ionian," for Clement mentions his works, and wrote a book on the paschal question in reply to Melito's work on the same subject (see above, Bk. IV. chap. 26, note 23). This too, however, is mere conjecture.
[9] The lower part of the peninsula of Italy was called Magna Græcia, because it contained so many Greek colonies.
[10] Cœle-Syria was the valley lying between the eastern and western ranges of Lebanon.
[11] This has been conjectured to be Tatian. But in the first place, Clement, in *Strom.* III. 12, calls Tatian a Syrian instead of an Assyrian (the terms are indeed often used interchangeably, but we should nevertheless hardly expect Clement to call his own teacher in one place a Syrian, in another an Assyrian). And again, in II. 12, he speaks very harshly of Tatian, and could hardly have referred to him in this place in such terms of respect and affection.
[12] Various conjectures have been made as to the identity of this teacher, — for instance, Theophilus of Cæsarea (who, however, was never called a Hebrew, according to Valesius), and Theodotus (so Valesius).
[13] Pantænus. There can be no doubt as to his identity, for Clement says that he remained with him and sought no further. Eusebius omits a sentence here in which Clement calls Pantænus the "Sicilian bee," from which it is generally concluded that he was a native of Sicily (see the previous chapter, note 1).
[14] This entire passage is very important, as showing not only the extensiveness of Clement's own acquaintance with Christians, but also the close intercourse of Christians in general, both East and West. Clement's statement in regard to the directness with which he received apostolic tradition is not definite, and he by no means asserts that his teachers were hearers of the apostles (which in itself would not be impossible, but Clement would certainly have spoken more clearly had it been a fact), nor indeed that they were hearers of disciples of the apostles. But among so many teachers, so widely scattered, he could hardly have failed to meet with some who had at least known those who had known the apostles. In any case he considers his teachers very near the apostles as regards the accuracy of their traditions.
The passage is also interesting, as showing the uniformity of doctrine in different parts of Christendom, according to Clement's view, though this does not prove much, as Clement himself was so liberal and so much of an eclectic. It is also interesting, as showing how much weight Clement laid upon tradition, how completely he rested upon it for the truth, although at the same time he was so free and broad in his speculation.
[1] The date of Narcissus' accession to the see of Jerusalem is not known to us. The *Chron.* affords us no assistance; for although it connects him among other bishops with the first (Armen.) or third (Jerome) year of Severus, it does not pretend to give the date of accession, and in one place says expressly that the dates of the Jerusalem bishops are not known (*non potuimus discernere tempora singulorum*). But from chap. 22 we learn that he was already bishop in the tenth year of Commodus (189 A.D.); from chap. 23, that he was one of those that presided at a Palestinian council, called in the time of Bishop Victor, of Rome, to discuss the paschal question (see

chap. 23, § 2); from Bk. VI. chap. 8, that he was alive at the time of the persecution of Severus (202 sq.); and from the fragment of one of Alexander's epistles given in Bk. VI. chap. 11, that he was still alive in his 116th year, sometime after 212 A.D. (see Bk. VI. chap. 11, note 1). Epiphanius (*Hær.* LXVI. 20) reports that he lived until the reign of Alexander Severus (222 A.D.), and this in itself would not be impossible; for the epistle of Alexander referred to might have been written as late as 222. But Epiphanius is a writer of no authority; and the fact is, that in connection with Origen's visit in Palestine, in 216 (see Bk. VI. chap. 19), Alexander is mentioned as bishop of Jerusalem; and Narcissus is not referred to. We must, therefore, conclude that Narcissus was dead before 216. We learn from Bk. VI. chap. 9 that Narcissus had the reputation of being a great miracle-worker, and he was a man of such great piety and sanctity as to excite the hatred of a number of evil-doers, who conspired against him to blacken his character. In consequence of this he left Jerusalem, and disappeared entirely from the haunts of men, so that it became necessary to appoint another bishop in his place. Afterward, his slanderers having suffered the curses imprecated upon themselves in their oaths against him, Narcissus returned, and was again made bishop, and was given an assistant, Alexander (see Bk. VI. chaps. 10 and 11). A late tradition makes Narcissus a martyr (see Nicephorus, *H. E.* IV. 19), but there is no authority for the report.
[2] Upon the so-called bishops of Jerusalem down to the destruction of the city under Hadrian, see Bk. IV. chap. 5. Upon the destruction of Jerusalem under Hadrian, and the founding of the Gentile Church in Ælia Capitolina, and upon Marcus the first Gentile bishop, see Bk. IV. chap. 6.
The list given here by Eusebius purports to contain fifteen names, Marcus being the sixteenth, and Narcissus being the thirtieth; but only thirteen names are given. In the *Chron.*, however, and in Epiphanius (*Hær.* LXVI. 20) the list is complete, a second Maximus and a Valentinus being inserted, as 26th and 27th, between Capito and Valens. The omission here is undoubtedly due simply to the mistake of some scribe. The *Chron.* puts the accession of Cassianus into the 23d year of Antoninus Pius (160 A.D.), and the accession of the second Maximus into the sixth year of Commodus (185 A.D.), but it is said in the *Chron.* itself that the dates of the various bishops are not known, and hence no reliance can be placed upon these figures. Epiphanius puts the accession of the first Gaius into the tenth year of Antoninus Pius, which is thirteen years earlier than the date of the *Chron.* for the fourth Pius preceding. He also puts the death of the second Gaius in the eighth year of Marcus Aurelius (168 A.D.), and the death of the second Maximus in the sixteenth year of the same reign, thus showing a variation from the *Chron.* of more than nine years. The episcopate of Dolichianus is brought down by him to the reign of Commodus (180 A.D.). As shown in note 1, however, the date given by him for Narcissus is quite wrong, and there is no reason for bestowing any greater credence upon his other dates. Syncellus assigns five years to Cassianus, five to Publius, four to Maximus, two to Julian, three to the first Gaius, two to Symmachus, three to the second Gaius, four to the second Julian, two to an Elias who is not named by our other authorities, four to Capito, four to the second Maximus, five to Antoninus, three to Valens, four to Narcissus the first time, and ten the second time. His list, however, is considerably confused, — Dolichianus being thrown after Narcissus with an episcopate of twelve years, — and at any rate no reliance can be placed upon the figures given. We must conclude that we have no means of ascertaining the dates of these various bishops until we reach Narcissus. We know nothing about any of them (Narcissus excepted) beyond the fact that they were bishops.
[3] Called Maximinus by the Armenian *Chron.*, but all our other authorities call him Maximus.
[4] The name is given Γάϊος in this chapter, and by Syncellus; but Jerome and the Armenian give Gaianus, and Epiphanius Γαϊανός. All the authorities agree upon the name of the next Gaius (who is, however, omitted by Rufinus).
[5] Eusebius has Καπίτων, so also Epiphanius, with whom Jerome agrees, writing *Capito*. The Armenian, however, has Apion, and Syncellus says Ἀπίων, οἱ δὲ Καπίτων.

CHAPTER XIII.

Rhodo and his Account of the Dissension of Marcion.

1   At this time Rhodo,[1] a native of Asia, who had been instructed, as he himself states, by Tatian, with whom we have already become acquainted,[2] having written several books, published among the rest one against the heresy of Marcion.[3]   He says that this heresy was divided in his time into various opinions;[4] and while describing those who occasioned the division, he refutes accurately the falsehoods devised

2   by each of them.   But hear what he writes :[5]

"Therefore also they disagree among themselves, maintaining an inconsistent opinion.[6]   For Apelles,[7] one of the herd, priding

himself on his manner of life[8] and his age, acknowledges one principle,[9] but says that the prophecies[10] are from an opposing spirit, being led to this view by the responses of a maiden by name Philumene,[11] who was possessed by a

---

[1] We know nothing of Rhodo except what is contained in this chapter.   Jerome gives a very brief account of him in his *de vir. ill.* 37, but it rests solely upon this chapter, with the single addition of the statement that Rhodo wrote a work *Against the Phrygians.* It is plain enough, however, that he had for his account no independent source, and that he in this statement simply attributed to Rhodo the work quoted by Eusebius as an anonymous work in chap. 16.   Jerome permits himself such unwarranted combinations very frequently, and we need not be at all surprised at it.   With him a guess is often as good as knowledge, and in this case he doubtless considered his guess a very shrewd one.   There is no warrant for supposing that he himself saw the work mentioned by Eusebius, and thus learned its authorship.   What Eusebius did not learn from it he certainly could not, and his whole account betrays the most slavish and complete dependence upon Eusebius as his only source.   In chap. 39 Jerome mentions Rhodo again as referring, in a book which he wrote against Montanus, Prisca, and Maximilla, to Miltiades, who also wrote against the same heretics.   This report is plainly enough taken directly from Eusebius, chap. 17, where Eusebius quotes from the same anonymous work.   Jerome's utterly baseless combination is very interesting, and significant of his general method.
   Rhodo's works are no longer extant, and the only fragments we have are those preserved by Eusebius in this chapter.

[2] See Bk. IV. chap. 29.

[3] Upon Marcion and Marcionism, see Bk. IV. chap. 11, note 22.

[4] It is noticeable that Rhodo says γνώμας, *opinions*, not *parties.* Although the different Marcionites held various theoretical beliefs, which gave rise to different schools, yet they did not split up into sects, but remained one church, and retained the one general name of Marcionites, and it is| by this general name alone that they are always referred to by the Fathers.   The fact that they could hold such variant beliefs (e.g. one, two, or three principles; see below, note 9) without splitting up into sects, shows that doctrines were but a side issue with them, and that the religious spirit was the matter upon which they laid the chief emphasis.   This shows the fundamental difference between Marcion and the Gnostics.

[5] These fragments of Rhodo are collected and discussed by Routh in his *Rel. Sacræ,* I. 437–446.

[6] The Fathers entirely misunderstood Marcion, and mistook the significance of his movement.   They regarded it, like Gnosticism in general, solely as a speculative system, and entirely overlooked its practical aim.   The speculative and theological was not the chief thing with Marcion, but it is the only thing which receives any attention from his opponents.   His positions, all of which were held only with a practical interest, were not treated by him in a speculative manner, nor were they handled logically and systematically. As a consequence, many contradictions occur in them.   These contradictions were felt by his followers, who laid more and more emphasis upon the speculative over against the practical; and hence, as Rhodo reports, they fell into disagreement, and, in their effort to remove the inconsistencies, formed various schools, differing among themselves according to the element upon which the greatest weight was laid.   There is thus some justification for the conduct of the Fathers, who naturally carried back and attributed to Marcion the principles of his followers.   But it is our duty to distinguish the man from his followers, and to recognize his greatness in spite of their littleness.   Not all of them, however, fell completely away from his practical religious spirit.   Apelles, as we shall see below, was in many respects a worthy follower of his master.

[7] Apelles was the greatest and most famous of Marcion's disciples.   Tertullian wrote a special work against him, which is unfortunately lost, but from his own quotations, and from those of Pseudo-Tertullian and Hippolytus, it can be in part restored (cf. Harnack's *De Apellis Gnosis Monarchia,* p. 11 sqq.).   As he was an old man (see § 5, below) when Rhodo conversed with him,

he must have been born early in the second century.   We know nothing definite either as to his birth or death.   The picture which we have of him in this chapter is a very pleasing one.   He was a man evidently of deep religious spirit and moral life, who laid weight upon "trust in the crucified Christ" (see § 5, below), and upon holiness in life in distinction from doctrinal beliefs; a man who was thus thoroughly Marcionitic in his principles, although he differed so widely with Marcion in some of his doctrinal positions that he was said to have founded a new sect (so Origen, *Hom. in Gen.* II. 2).   The slightest difference, however, between his teaching and Marcion's would have been sufficient to make him the founder of a separate Gnostic sect in the eyes of the Fathers, and therefore this statement must be taken with allowance (see note 4, above).   The account which Hippolytus (*Phil.* X. 16) gives of the doctrinal positions of Apelles is somewhat different from that of Rhodo, but ambiguous and less exact.   The scandal in regard to him, reported by Tertullian in his *De Præscriptione,* 30, is quite in accord with Tertullian's usual conduct towards heretics, and may be set aside as not having the slightest foundation in fact, and as absolutely contradicting what we know of Apelles from this report of his contemporary, Rhodo.   His moral character was certainly above reproach, and the same may be said of his master, Marcion.   Upon Apelles, see especially Harnack's *De Apellis Gnosis Monarchia,* Lips. 1874.

[8] The participle (σεμνυνόμενος) carries with it the implication that Apelles' character was affected or assumed.   The implication, however, does not lessen the value of Rhodo's testimony to his character.   He could not deny its purity, though he insinuated that it was not sincere.

[9] This means that Apelles accepted only one God, and made the creator but an angel who was completely under the power of the Supreme God.   Marcion, on the contrary, held, as said below, two principles, teaching that the world-creator was himself a God, eternal, uncreated, and independent of the good God of the Christians.   It is true that Marcion represented the world-creator as limited in power and knowledge, and taught that the Christian God would finally be supreme, and the world-creator become subject to him; but this, while it involves Marcion in self-contradiction as soon as the matter is looked at theoretically, yet does not relieve him from the charge of actual dualism.   His followers were more consistent, and either accepted one principle, subordinating the world-creator completely to the good God, as did Apelles, or else carried out Marcion's dualism to its logical result and asserted the continued independence of the Old Testament God and the world-creator, who was thus very early identified with Satan and made the enemy of the Christian God.   (Marcion's world-creator was not the bad God, but the righteous in distinction from the good God.)   Still others held three principles: the good God of the Christians, the righteous God or world-creator, and the bad God, Satan.   The varying doctrines of these schools explain the discrepant and often contradictory reports of the Fathers in regard to the doctrines of Marcion.   Apelles' doctrine was a decided advance upon that of Marcion, as he rejected the dualism of the latter, which was the destructive element in his system, and thus approached the Church, whose foundation must be *one* God who rules the world for good.   His position is very significant, as remarked by Harnack, because it shows that one could hold Marcion's fundamental principle without becoming a dualist.

[10] i.e. the Old Testament prophecies.   Apelles in his *Syllogisms* (see above, note 28) exhibited the supposed contradictions of the Old Testament in syllogistic form, tracing them to two adverse angels, of whom the one spoke falsely, contradicting the truth spoken by the other.   Marcion, on the other hand (in his *Antitheses*), referred all things to the same God, the world-creator, and from the contradictions of the book endeavored to show his vacillating and inconsistent character.   He, however, accepted the Old Testament as in the main a trustworthy book, but referred the prophecies to the Jewish Messiah in distinction from the Christ of the New Testament.   But Apelles, looking upon two adverse angels as the authors of the book, regarded it as in great part false.   Marcion and Apelles were one, however, in looking upon it as an anti-Christian book.

[11] This virgin, Philumene, is connected with Apelles in all the reports which we have of him (e.g. in Hippolytus, Tertullian, Jerome, &c.), and is reported to have been looked upon by Apelles as a prophetess who received revelations from an angel, and who worked miracles.   Tertullian, *De Præscriptione,* 6, evidently accepts these miracles as facts, but attributes them to the agency of a demon.   They all unite in considering her influence the cause of Apelles' heretical opinions.   Tertullian (*ibid.* 30, &c.) calls her a prostitute, but the silence of Rhodo and Hippolytus is sufficient refutation of such a charge, and it may be rejected as a baseless slander, like the report of Apelles' immorality mentioned in note 7. There is nothing strange in the fact that Apelles should follow the prophecies of a virgin, and the Fathers who mention it evidently do not consider it as anything peculiar or reprehensible in itself.   It was very common in the early Church to appeal to the relatives of virgins and widows.   Cf. e.g. the virgin daughters of Philip who

3   demon. But others, among whom are Potitus
    and Basilicus,[12] hold to two principles,[13] as
4   does the mariner[14] Marcion himself.   These
following the wolf[15] of Pontus, and, like him,
unable to fathom the division of things, became
reckless, and without giving any proof asserted
two principles.   Others, again, drifting into a
worse error, consider that there are not only
two, but three natures.[16]   Of these, Syneros[17] is
    the leader and chief, as those who defend
5   his teaching[18] say."   The same author writes
    that he engaged in conversation with Apelles.
He speaks as follows:
    "For the old man Apelles, when conversing
with us,[19] was refuted in many things which he
spoke falsely; whence also he said that it was
not at all necessary to examine one's doctrine,[20]
but that each one should continue to hold what
he believed.   For he asserted that those who
trusted in the Crucified would be saved, if only
they were found doing good works.[21]   But as we

have said before, his opinion concerning God
was the most obscure of all.   For he spoke of
one principle, as also our doctrine does."
    Then, after stating fully his own opinion,   6
he adds:
    "When I said to him, Tell me how you know
this or how can you assert that there is one principle, he replied that the prophecies refuted themselves, because they have said nothing true;[22]
for they are inconsistent, and false, and self-con-
tradictory.   But how there is one principle he
said that he did not know, but that he was
thus persuaded.   As I then adjured him to   7
speak the truth, he swore that he did so
when he said that he did not know how there is
one unbegotten God, but that he believed it.
Thereupon I laughed and reproved him because,
though calling himself a teacher, he knew not how
to confirm what he taught."[23]
    In the same work, addressing Callistio,[24] the   8
same writer acknowledges that he had been
instructed at Rome by Tatian.[25]   And he says
that a book of Problems[26] had been prepared by
Tatian, in which he promised to explain the ob-

---

prophesied (Acts xxi. 9; Eusebius, III. 31), also the *Eccles. Canons*,
chap. 21, where it is directed that three widows shall be appointed,
of whom two shall give themselves to prayer, waiting for revelations
in regard to any question which may arise in the Church, and the
third shall devote herself to nursing the sick. Tertullian also appeals for proof of the materiality of the soul to a vision enjoyed by
a Christian sister (*de Anima*, 9). So Montanus had his prophetesses Priscilla and Maximilla (see the next chapter).

[12] Of these two men we know only what is told us here. They
are not mentioned elsewhere.

[13] See note 9.

[14] ὁ ναύτης. This word is omitted by many MSS., but is found
in the best ones and in Rufinus, and is accepted by most of the editors of Eusebius. Tertullian calls Marcion a ship-master (*Adv.
Marc.* III. 6, and IV. 9, &c.) and a pilot (*ibid.* I. 18), and makes
many plays upon his profession (e.g. *ibid.* V. 1), and there is no
reason to take the word in a figurative sense (as has been done) and
suppose that he is called a mariner simply because of his nationality. We know that he traveled extensively, and that he was a
rich man (for he gave 200,000 sesterces at one time to the church of
Rome, which was a large sum for those days; see Tertullian, *de
Præscript.* 30). There is, therefore, no reason to doubt that he was
a "ship-master," as Tertullian calls him.

[15] It was the custom of the Fathers to call the heretics hard
names, and Marcion received his full share of them from his opponents, especially from Tertullian. He is compared to a wolf by
Justin also, *Apol.* I. 58, on account of his "carrying away" so
many "lambs" from the truth.

[16] See note 9.

[17] Of Syneros we know only what is told us here. He is not
mentioned elsewhere. Had the Marcionites split into various sects,
these leaders must have been well known among the Fathers, and
their names must have been frequently referred to. As it was, they
all remained Marcionites, in spite of their differences of opinion (see
above, note 4).

[18] διδασκάλιον, which is the reading of the majority of the MSS.,
and is adopted by Heinichen. Burton and Schwegler read διδασκα-
λείον, on the authority of two MSS.

[19] Apelles was evidently like Marcion in his desire to keep within the Church as much as possible, and to associate with Church
people. He had no esoteric doctrines to conceal from the multitude,
and in this he shows the great difference between himself and the
Gnostics. Marcion did not leave the Church until he was obliged
to, and he founded his own church only under compulsion, upon being driven out of the Catholic community.

[20] τὸν λόγον.

[21] This is a truly Christian sentiment, and Apelles should be
honored for the expression of it. It reveals clearly the religious
character of Marcionism in distinction from the speculative and theological character of the Gnostics, and indeed of many of the Fathers.
With Marcion and Apelles we are in a world of sensitive moral principle and of deep religious feeling like that in which Paul and Augustine lived, but few others in the early Church. Rhodo, in spite of
his orthodoxy, shows himself the real Gnostic over against the sincere believer, though the latter was in the eyes of the Church a
"blasphemous heretic." Apelles' noble words do honor to the
movement — however heretical it was — which in that barren age of
theology could give them birth.
The latter clause, taken as it stands, would seem to indicate an
elevation of good works to the level of faith; but though it is pos-

sible that Apelles may have intended to express himself thus, it is
more probable, when we remember the emphasis which Marcion laid
upon Paul's doctrine of salvation by the grace of God alone, that he
meant to do no more than emphasize good works as a natural result
of true faith, as we do to-day. The apparent co-ordination of the
two may perhaps lie simply in Rhodo's reproduction of Apelles'
words. He, at least, did not comprehend Paul's grand doctrine of
Christian liberty, nor did any of his orthodox contemporaries. The
difference between the common conception of Christ's relation to the
law, and the conception of Paul as grasped by Marcion and perhaps
by Apelles, is well illustrated by a passage in Tertullian, in which
he expresses astonishment that the Marcionites do not sin freely, so
long as they do not expect to be punished, and exclaims (to his own
dishonor), "I would sin without scruple, if I believed as you do."

[22] Rhodo had probably brought forward against Apelles proof
from prophecy which led to the discussion of the Old Testament
prophecies in general. Although Apelles had rejected Marcion's
dualism, and accepted the "one principle," he still rejected the Old
Testament. This is quite peculiar, and yet perfectly comprehen-
sible; for while Marcion was indeed the only one of that age that
understood Paul, yet as Harnack well says, even he misunderstood
him; and neither himself nor his followers were able to rise to Paul's
noble conception of the Old Testament law as a "schoolmaster to
bring us to Christ," and thus a part of the good God's general plan
of salvation. It took, perhaps, a born Jew, as Paul was, to reach
that high conception of the law in those days. To Marcion and his
followers the law seemed to stand in irreconcilable conflict with the
Gospel, — Jewish law on the one side, Gospel liberty on the other, —
they could not reconcile them; they must, therefore, reject the
former as from another being, and not from the God of the Gospel.
There was in that age no historical interpretation of the Old Testament. It must either be interpreted allegorically, and made a completely Christian book, or else it must be rejected as opposed to
Christianity. Marcion and his followers, in their conception of law
and Gospel as necessarily opposed, could follow only the latter
course. Marcion, in his rejection of the Old Testament, proceeded
simply upon dogmatic presumptions. Apelles, although his rejection of it undoubtedly originated in the same presumptions, yet subjected it to a criticism which satisfied him of the correctness of his
position, and gave him a fair basis of attack. His procedure was,
therefore, more truly historical than that of Marcion, and anticipated modern methods of higher criticism.

[23] A true Gnostic sentiment, over against which the pious
"agnosticism" of Apelles is not altogether unrefreshing. The
Church did not fully conquer Gnosticism, — Gnosticism in some
degree conquered the Church, and the anti-Gnostics, like Apelles,
were called heretics. It was the vicious error of Gnosticism that it
looked upon Christianity as knowledge, that it completely identified
the two, and our existing systems of theology, some of them, testify
to the fact that there are still Gnostics among us.

[24] Of this Callistio we know nothing; but, as has been remarked
by another, he must have been a well-known man, or Eusebius
would probably have said "a certain Callistio" (see Salmon's
article in Smith and Wace).

[25] Upon Tatian, see Bk. IV. chap. 29, note 1.

[26] Upon this work (προβλημάτων βιβλίον), see *ibid.*

scure and hidden parts of the divine Scriptures. Rhodo himself promises to give in a work of his own solutions of Tatian's problems.[27] There is also extant a Commentary of his on the Hexæmeron.[28]

9　　But this Apelles wrote many things, in an impious manner, of the law of Moses, blaspheming the divine words in many of his works, being, as it seemed, very zealous for their refutation and overthrow.[29]

So much concerning these.

CHAPTER XIV.

The False Prophets of the Phrygians.

THE enemy of God's Church, who is emphatically a hater of good and a lover of evil, and leaves untried no manner of craft against men, was again active in causing strange heresies to spring up against the Church.[1] For some persons, like venomous reptiles, crawled over Asia and Phrygia, boasting that Montanus was the Paraclete, and that the women that followed him, Priscilla and Maximilla, were prophetesses of Montanus.[2]

CHAPTER XV.

The Schism of Blastus at Rome.[1]

OTHERS, of whom Florinus[2] was chief, flourished at Rome. He fell from the presbyterate of the Church, and Blastus was involved in a similar fall. They also drew away many of the Church to their opinion, each striving to introduce his own innovations in respect to the truth.

---

[27] Whether Rhodo fulfilled this promise we do not know. The work is mentioned by no one else, and Eusebius evidently had no knowledge of its existence, or he would have said so.
[28] εἰς τὴν ἐξαήμερον ὑπόμνημα. This work of Rhodo's, on the Hexæmeron (or six days' work), is mentioned by no one else, and no fragments of it are known to us. For a notice of other works on the same subject, see below, Bk. VI. chap. 22, note 3.
[29] Hippolytus (X. 16) also mentions works of Apelles against the law and the prophets. We know of but one work of his, viz. the Syllogisms, which was devoted to the criticism of the Old Testament, and in which he worked out the antitheses of Marcion in a syllogistic form. The work is cited only by Origen (in Gen. II. 2) and by Ambrose (De Parad. V. 28), and they have preserved but a few brief fragments. It must have been an extensive work, as Ambrose quotes from the 38th book. From these fragments we can see that Apelles' criticism of the Old Testament was very keen and sagacious. For the difference between himself and Marcion in the treatment of the Old Testament, see above, note 9. The words of Eusebius, " as it seemed," show that he had not himself seen the book, as might indeed be gathered from his general account of Apelles, for which he depended solely upon secondary sources.
[1] Cf. Bk. IV. chap. 7, note 3.
[2] On Montanus and the Montanists, see chap. 16.
[1] The separation of chaps. 14 and 15 is unfortunate. They are closely connected (οἱ μὲν in chap. 14 and οἱ δὲ in chap. 15), and constitute together a general introduction to the following chapters, Montanism being treated in chaps. 16 to 19, and the schism of Florinus and Blastus in chap. 20.
[2] On Florinus and Blastus, see chap. 20.

CHAPTER XVI.

The Circumstances related of Montanus and his False Prophets.[1]

AGAINST the so-called Phrygian[2] heresy,　1 the power which always contends for the

---

[1] Montanism must not be looked upon as a heresy in the ordinary sense of the term. The movement lay in the sphere of life and discipline rather than in that of theology. Its fundamental proposition was the continuance of divine revelation which was begun under the old Dispensation, was carried on in the time of Christ and his apostles, and reached its highest development under the dispensation of the Paraclete, which opened with the activity of Montanus. This Montanus was a Phrygian, who, in the latter part of the second century, began to fall into states of ecstasy and to have visions, and believed himself a divinely inspired prophet, through whom the promised Paraclete spoke, and with whom therefore the dispensation of that Paraclete began. Two noble ladies (Priscilla and Maximilla) attached themselves to Montanus, and had visions and prophesied in the same way. These constituted the three original prophets of the sect, and all that they taught was claimed to be of binding authority on all. They were quite orthodox, accepted fully the doctrinal teachings of the Catholic Church, and did not pretend to alter in any way the revelation given by Christ and his apostles. But they claimed that some things had not been revealed by them, because at that early stage the Church was not able to bear them; but that such additional revelations were now given, because the fullness of time had come which was to precede the second coming of Christ. These revelations had to do not at all with theology, but wholly with matters of life and discipline. They taught a rigid asceticism over against the growing worldliness of the Church, severe discipline over against its laxer methods, and finally the universal priesthood of believers (even female), and their right to perform all the functions of church officers, over against the growing sacerdotalism of the Church. They were thus in a sense reformers, or perhaps reactionaries is a better term, who wished to bring back, or to preserve against corruption, the original principles and methods of the Church. They aimed at a puritanic reaction against worldliness, and a democratic reaction against growing aristocracy in the Church. They insisted that ministers were made by God alone, by the direct endowment of his Spirit in distinction from human ordination. They looked upon their prophets — supernaturally called and endowed by the Spirit — as supreme in the Church. They claimed that all gross offenders should be excommunicated, and that neither they nor the lax should ever be re-admitted to the Church. They encouraged celibacy, increased the number and severity of fasts, eschewed worldly amusements, &c. This rigid asceticism was enjoined by the revelation of the Spirit through their prophets, and was promoted by their belief in the speedy coming of Christ to set up his kingdom on earth, which was likewise prophesied. They were thus pre-Millenarians or Chiliasts.
　The movement spread rapidly in Asia Minor and in North Africa, and for a time in Rome itself. It appealed very powerfully to the sterner moralists, stricter disciplinarians, and more deeply pious minds among the Christians. All the puritanically inclined schisms of this period attracted many of the better class of Christians, and this one had the additional advantage of claiming the authority of divine revelation for its strict principles. The greatest convert was Tertullian, who, in 201 or 202, attracted by the asceticism and disciplinary rigor of the sect, attached himself to it, and remained until his death its most powerful advocate. He seems to have stood at the head of a separatist congregation of Montanists in Carthage, and yet never to have been excommunicated by the Catholic Church. Montanism made so much stir in Asia Minor that synods were called before the end of the second century to consider the matter, and finally, though not without hesitation, the whole movement was officially condemned. Later, the condemnation was ratified in Rome and also in North Africa, and Montanism gradually degenerated, and finally, after two or three centuries, entirely disappeared.
　But although it failed and passed away, Montanism had a marked influence on the development of the Church. In the first place, it aroused a general distrust of prophecy, and the result was that the Church soon came to the conviction that prophecy had entirely ceased. In the second place, the Church was led to see the necessity of emphasizing the historical Christ and historical Christianity over against the Montanistic claims of a constantly developing revelation, and thus to put great emphasis upon the Scripture canon. In the third place, the Church had to lay increased stress upon the organization — upon its appointed and ordained officers — over against the claims of irregular prophets who might at any time arise as organs of the Spirit. The development of Christianity into a religion of the book and of the organization was thus greatly advanced, and the line began to be sharply drawn between the age of the apostles, in which there had been direct supernatural revelations, and the later age, in which such revelations had disappeared. We are, undoubtedly, to date from this time that exalted conception of the glory of the apostolic age, and of its absolute separation from all subsequent ages, which marks so strongly the Church of succeeding centuries, and which led men to

truth raised up a strong and invincible weapon, Apolinarius of Hierapolis, whom we have mentioned before,[3] and with him many other men of ability, by whom abundant material for our 2 history has been left. A certain one of these, in the beginning of his work against them,[4] first intimates that he had contended 3 with them in oral controversies. He commences his work in this manner :[5]

" Having for a very long and sufficient time, O beloved Avircius Marcellus,[6] been urged by you to write a treatise against the heresy of those who are called after Miltiades,[7] I have hesitated

endeavor to gain apostolic authority for every advance in the constitution, in the customs, and in the doctrine of the Church. There had been little of this feeling before, but now it became universal, and it explains the great number of pseudo-apostolic works of the third and following centuries. In the fourth place, the Chiliastic ideas of Montanism produced a reaction in the Church which caused the final rejection of all grossly physical Premillenarian beliefs which up to this time had been very common. For further particulars in regard to Montanism, see the notes on this and the following chapters.

Our chief sources for a knowledge of Montanism are to be found in the writings of Tertullian. See, also, Epiphanius, *Hær.* XLVIII. and XLIX., and Jerome's Epistle to Marcella (Migne, *Ep.* 41). The fragments from the anonymous anti-Montanistic writer quoted by Eusebius in this and the following chapter, and the fragments of Apollonius' work, quoted in chap. 18, are of the greatest importance. It is to be regretted that Eusebius has preserved for us no fragments of the anti-Montanistic writings of Apolinarius and Melito, who might have given us still earlier and more trustworthy accounts of the sect. It is probable that their works were not decided enough in their opposition to Montanism to suit Eusebius, who, therefore, chose to take his account from somewhat later, but certainly bitter enough antagonists. The works of the Montanists themselves (except those of Tertullian) have entirely perished, but a few "Oracles," or prophetic utterances, of Montanus, Priscilla, and Maximilla, have been preserved by Tertullian and other writers, and are printed by Bonwetsch, p. 197–200. The literature upon Montanism is very extensive. We may mention here C. W. F. Walch's *Ketzerhistorie,* I. p. 611–666, A. Schwegler's *Der Montanismus und die christliche Kirche des zweiten Jahrh.* (Tübingen, 1841), and especially G. N. Bonwetzsch's *Die Geschichte des Montanismus* (Erlangen, 1881), which is the best work on the subject, and indispensable to the student. Compare, also, Schaff's *Ch. Hist.* II. p. 415 sq., where the literature is given with great fullness, Salmon's article in the *Dict. of Christ. Biog.,* and especially Harnack's *Dogmengeschichte,* I. p. 319 sq.

[2] τὴν λεγομένην κατὰ Φρύγας αἵρεσιν. The heresy of Montanus was commonly called the Phrygian heresy because it took its rise in Phrygia. The Latins, by a solecism, called it the Cataphrygian heresy. Its followers received other names also, e.g. Priscillianists (from the prophetess Priscilla), and Pepuziani (from Pepuza, their headquarters). They called themselves πνευματικοί (spiritual), and the adherents of the Church ψυχικοί (carnal).

[3] In Bk. IV. chaps. 21, 26 and 27, and in Bk. V. chap. 5. See especially Bk. IV. chap. 27, note 1.

[4] The author of this work is unknown. Jerome (*de vir. ill.* 37) ascribes it to Rhodo (but see above, chap. 13, note 1). It is sometimes ascribed to Asterius Urbanus, mentioned by Eusebius in § 17 below, but he was certainly not its author (see below, note 27). Upon the date of the work, see below, note 32.

[5] The fragments of this anonymous work are given by Routh, *Rel. Sac.* Vol. II. p. 183 sqq., and in English in the *Ante-Nicene Fathers,* Vol. VII. p. 335 sqq.

[6] Ἀουίρκιε, as most of the MSS. read. Others have Ἀνίρκιε or Ἀβίρκιε; Nicephorus, Ἀβέρκιε. The name is quite commonly written Abercius in English, and the person mentioned here is identified by many scholars (among them Lightfoot) with Abercius, a prominent bishop of Hieropolis (not Hierapolis, as was formerly supposed). A spurious *Life of S. Abercius* is given by Simeon Metaphrastes (in Migne's *Patr. Gr.* CXV. 1211 sq.), which, although of a decidedly legendary character, rests upon a groundwork of fact as proved by the discovery, in recent years, of an epitaph from Abercius' tomb. This Abercius was bishop in the time of Marcus Aurelius, and therefore must have held office at least twelve or fifteen years (on the date of this anonymous treatise, see below, note 32), or, if the date given by the spurious Acts for Abercius' visit to Rome be accepted (163 A.D.), at least thirty years. On Abercius and Avercius, see the exhaustive note of Lightfoot, in his *Apostolic Fathers,* Part II. (*Ignatius and Polycarp*), Vol. I. p. 477–485.

[7] εἰς τὴν τῶν κατὰ Μιλτιάδην λεγομένων αἵρεσιν. The occurrence of the name Miltiades, in this connection, is very puzzling, for we nowhere else hear of a Montanist Miltiades, while the man referred to here must have held a very prominent place among them. It is true that it is commonly supposed that the Muratorian Canon

till the present time, not through lack of ability to refute the falsehood or bear testimony for the truth, but from fear and apprehension that I might seem to some to be making additions to the doctrines or precepts of the Gospel of the New Testament, which it is impossible for one who has chosen to live according to the Gospel, either to increase or to diminish. But 4 being recently in Ancyra[8] in Galatia, I found the church there[9] greatly agitated by this novelty, not prophecy, as they call it, but rather false prophecy, as will be shown. Therefore, to the best of our ability, with the Lord's help, we disputed in the church many days concerning these and other matters separately brought forward by them, so that the church rejoiced and was strengthened in the truth, and those of the opposite side were for the time confounded, and the adversaries were grieved. The 5 presbyters in the place, our fellow-presbyter Zoticus[10] of Otrous also being present, requested us to leave a record of what had been said against the opposers of the truth. We did not do this, but we promised to write it out as soon as the Lord permitted us, and to send it to them speedily."

refers to some heretic Miltiades, but since Harnack's discussion of the matter (see especially his *Texte und Untersuchungen,* I. 1, p. 216, note) it is more than doubtful whether a Miltiades is mentioned at all in that document. In any case the prominent position given him here is surprising, and, as a consequence, Valesius (in his notes), Stroth, Zimmermann, Schwegler, Laemmer, and Heinichen substitute Ἀλκιβιάδην (who is mentioned in chap. 3 as a prominent Montanist) for Μιλτιάδην. The MSS., however, are unanimous in reading Μιλτιάδην; and it is impossible to see how, if Ἀλκιβιάδην had originally stood in the text, Μιλτιάδην could have been substituted for it. It is not impossible that instead of Alcibiades in chap. 3 we should read, as Salmon suggests, Miltiades. The occurrence of the name Alcibiades in the previous sentence might explain its substitution for Miltiades immediately afterward. It is at least easier to account for that change than for the change of Alcibiades to Miltiades in the present chapter. Were Salmon's suggestion accepted, the difficulty in this case would be obviated, for we should then have a Montanist Miltiades of sufficient prominence to justify the naming of the sect after him in some quarters. The suggestion, however, rests upon mere conjecture, and it is safer to retain the reading of our MSS. in both cases. Until we get more light from some quarter we must be content to let the matter rest, leaving the reason for the use of Miltiades' name in this connection unexplained. There is, of course, nothing strange in the existence of a Montanist named Miltiades; it is only the great prominence given him here which puzzles us. Upon the ecclesiastical writer, Miltiades, and Eusebius' confusion of him with Alcibiades, see chap. 17, note 1.

[8] Ancyra was the metropolis and one of the three principal cities of Galatia. Quite an important town, Angora, now occupies its site.

[9] κατὰ τόπον, which is the reading of two of the MSS. and Nicephorus, and is adopted by Burton and Heinichen. The phrase seems harsh, but occurs again in the next paragraph. The majority of the MSS. read κατὰ Πόντον, which is adopted by Valesius, Schwegler, Laemmer, and Crusè. It is grammatically the easier reading, but the reference to Pontus is unnatural in this connection, and in view of the occurrence of the same phrase, κατὰ τόπον, in the next paragraph, it seems best to read thus in the present case as well.

[10] Of this Zoticus we know only what is told us here. He is to be distinguished, of course, from Zoticus of Comana, mentioned in § 17, below, and in chap. 18, § 13.

Otrous (or Otrys, as it is sometimes written) was a small Phrygian town about two miles from Hieropolis (see W. H. Ramsay's paper, entitled *Trois Villes Phrygiennes,* in the *Bulletin de Correspondance Hellenique,* Juillet, 1882). Its bishop was present at the Council of Chalcedon, and also at the second Council of Nicæa (see Wiltsch's *Geography and Statistics of the Church*). We may gather from this passage that the anonymous author of this anti-Montanistic work was a presbyter (he calls Zoticus συμπρεσβύτερος), but we have no hint of his own city, though the fact that Avircius Marcellus, to whom the work was addressed, was from

6   Having said this with other things, in the beginning of his work, he proceeds to state the cause of the above-mentioned heresy as follows :

"Their opposition and their recent heresy which has separated them from the Church
7   arose on the following account. There is said to be a certain village called Ardabau in that part of Mysia, which borders upon Phrygia.[11] There first, they say, when Gratus was proconsul of Asia,[12] a recent convert, Montanus by name, through his unquenchable desire for leadership,[13] gave the adversary opportunity against him. And he became beside himself, and being suddenly in a sort of frenzy and ecstasy, he raved, and began to babble and utter strange things, prophesying in a manner contrary to the constant custom of the Church handed down by tradition from the be-
8   ginning.[14] Some of those who heard his spurious utterances at that time were indignant, and they rebuked him as one that was possessed, and that was under the control of a demon, and was led by a deceitful spirit, and was distracting the multitude ; and they forbade him to talk, remembering the distinction [15] drawn by the Lord and his warning to guard watchfully against the coming of false prophets.[16] But others imagining themselves possessed of the Holy Spirit and of a prophetic gift,[17] were elated and not a little puffed up ; and forgetting the distinction of the Lord, they challenged the mad and insidious and seducing spirit, and were cheated and deceived by him. In consequence of this, he could no longer be held in check, so as to keep silence. Thus by artifice, or   9 rather by such a system of wicked craft, the devil, devising destruction for the disobedient, and being unworthily honored by them, secretly excited and inflamed their understandings which had already become estranged from the true faith. And he stirred up besides two women,[18] and filled them with the false spirit, so that they talked wildly and unreasonably and strangely, like the person already mentioned.[19] And the spirit pronounced them blessed as they rejoiced and gloried in him, and puffed them up by the magnitude of his promises. But sometimes he rebuked them openly in a wise and

[11] Hieropolis (see note 6), and that the anonymous companion Zoticus was from Otrous, would lead us to look in that neighborhood for the home of our author, though hardly to either of those towns (the mention of the name of the town in connection with Zoticus' name would seem to shut out the latter, and the opening sentences of the treatise would seem to exclude the former).

[11] ἐν τῇ κατὰ τὴν Φρυγίαν Μυσίᾳ. It is not said here that Montanus was born in Ardabau, but it is natural to conclude that he was, and so that village is commonly given as his birthplace. As we learn from this passage, Ardabau was not in Phrygia, as is often said, but in Mysia. The boundary line between the two districts was a very indefinite one, however, and the two were often confounded by the ancients themselves; but we cannot doubt in the present instance that the very exact statement of the anonymous writer is correct. Of the village of Ardabau itself we know nothing.

[12] The exact date of the rise of Montanism cannot be determined. The reports which we have of the movement vary greatly in their chronology. We have no means of fixing the date of the proconsulship of the Gratus referred to here, and thus the most exact and reliable statement which we have does not help us. In his *Chron.* Eusebius fixes the rise of the movement in the year 172, and it is possible that this statement was based upon a knowledge of the time of Gratus' proconsulship. If so, it possesses considerable weight. The first notice we have of a knowledge of the movement in the West is in connection with the martyrs of Lyons, who in the year 177 (see Introd. to this book, note 3) were solicited to use their influence with the bishop of Rome in favor of the Montanists (see above, chap. 3, note 6). This goes to confirm the approximate accuracy of the date given by Eusebius, for we should expect that the movement cannot have attracted public notice in the East very many years before it was heard of in Gaul, the home of many Christians from Asia Minor. Epiphanius (*Hær.* XLVIII.) gives the nineteenth year of Antoninus Pius (156–157) as the date of its beginning, but Epiphanius' figures are very confused and contradictory, and little reliance can be placed upon them in this connection. At the same time Montanus must have begun his prophesying some years before his teaching spread over Asia Minor and began to agitate the churches and alarm the bishops, and therefore it is probable that Montanism had a beginning some years before the date given by Eusebius; in fact, it is not impossible that Montanus may have begun his work before the end of the reign of Antoninus Pius.

[13] Ambition was almost universally looked upon by the Church Fathers as the occasion of the various heresies and schisms. Novatian, Donatus, and many others were accused of it by their orthodox opponents. That heretics or schismatics could be actuated by high and noble motives was to them inconceivable. We are thus furnished another illustration of their utter misconception of the nature of heresy so often referred to in these notes.

[14] The fault found by the Church with Montanus' prophecy was rather because of its form than because of its substance. It was admitted that the prophecies contained much that was true, but the soberer sense of the Church at large objected decidedly to the frenzied ecstasy in which they were delivered. That a change had come over the Church in this respect since the apostolic age is perfectly clear. In Paul's time the speaking with tongues, which involved a similar kind of ecstasy, was very common; so, too, at the time the *Didache* was written the prophets spoke in an ecstasy (ἐν πνεύματι, which can mean nothing else; cf. Harnack's edition, p. 122 sq.). But the early enthusiasm of the Church had largely passed away by the middle of the second century; and though there were still prophets (Justin, for instance, and even Clement of Alexandria knew of them), they were not in general characterized by the same ecstatic and frenzied utterance that

marked their predecessors. To say that there were none such at this time would be rash; but it is plain that they had become so decidedly the exception that the revival by the Montanists of the old method on a large scale and in its extremest form could appear to the Church at large only a decided innovation. Prophecy in itself was nothing strange to them, but prophecy in this form they were not accustomed to, and did not realize that it was but a revival of the ancient form (cf. the words of our author, who is evidently quite ignorant of that form). That they should be shocked at it is not to be wondered at, and that they should, in that age, when all such manifestations were looked upon as supernatural in their origin, regard these prophets as under the influence of Satan, is no more surprising. There was no other alternative in their minds. Either the prophecies were from God or from Satan; not their content mainly, but the manner in which they were delivered aroused the suspicion of the bishops and other leaders of the Church. Add to that the fact that these prophets claimed supremacy over the constituted Church authorities, claimed that the Church must be guided by the revelations vouchsafed to women and apparently half-crazy enthusiasts and fanatics, and it will be seen at once that there was nothing left for the leaders of the Church but to condemn the movement, and pronounce its prophecy a fraud and a work of the Evil One. That all prophecy should, as a consequence, fall into discredit was natural. Clement (*Strom.* I. 17) gives the speaking in an ecstasy as one of the marks of a false prophet, — Montanism had evidently brought the Church to distinct consciousness on that point, — while Origen, some decades later, is no longer acquainted with prophets, and denies that they existed even in the time of Celsus (see *Contra Cels.* VII. 11).

[15] i.e. between true and false prophets.   [16] Cf. Matt. vii. 15.

[17] ὡς ἁγίῳ πνεύματι καὶ προφητικῷ χαρίσματι.

[18] Maximilla and Priscilla, or Prisca (mentioned in chap. 14). They were married women, who left their husbands to become disciples of Montanus, were given the rank of virgins in his church, and with him were the greatest prophets of the sect. They were regarded with the most profound reverence by all Montanists, who in many quarters were called after the name of the latter, Priscillianists. It was a characteristic of the Montanists that they insisted upon the religious equality of men and women; that they accorded just as high honor to the women as to the men, and listened to their prophecies with the same reverence. The human person was but an instrument of the Spirit, according to their view, and hence a woman might be chosen by the Spirit as his instrument just as well as a man, the ignorant just as well as the learned. Tertullian, for instance, cites, in support of his doctrine of the materiality of the soul, a vision seen by one of the female members of his church, whom he believed to be in the habit of receiving revelations from God (*de anima*, 9).   [19] i.e. Montanus.

faithful manner, that he might seem to be a reprover. But those of the Phrygians that were deceived were few in number.

"And the arrogant spirit taught them to revile the entire universal Church under heaven, because the spirit of false prophecy received neither honor from it nor entrance into it.

10 For the faithful in Asia met often in many places throughout Asia to consider this matter,[20] and examined the novel utterances and pronounced them profane, and rejected the heresy, and thus these persons were expelled from the Church and debarred from communion."

11 Having related these things at the outset, and continued the refutation of their delusion through his entire work, in the second book he speaks as follows of their end :

12 "Since, therefore, they called us slayers of the prophets [21] because we did not receive their loquacious prophets, who, they say, are those that the Lord promised to send to the people,[22] let them answer as in God's presence : Who is there, O friends, of these who began to talk, from Montanus and the women down, that was persecuted by the Jews, or slain by lawless men? None. Or has any of them been seized and crucified for the Name? Truly not. Or has one of these women ever been scourged in the synagogues of the Jews, or stoned? No ;

13 never anywhere.[23] But by another kind of death Montanus and Maximilla are said to have died. For the report is that, incited by the spirit of frenzy, they both hung themselves ;[24] not at the same time, but at the time which common report gives for the death of each. And thus they died, and ended their lives like the traitor Judas. So also, as gen-

14 eral report says, that remarkable person, the first steward,[25] as it were, of their so-called prophecy, one Theodotus — who, as if at sometime taken up and received into heaven, fell into trances, and entrusted himself to the deceitful spirit — was pitched like a quoit, and died miserably.[26] They say that these things hap-

15 pened in this manner. But as we did not see them, O friend, we do not pretend to know. Perhaps in such a manner, perhaps not, Montanus and Theodotus and the above-mentioned woman died."

He says again in the same book that the

16 holy bishops of that time attempted to refute the spirit in Maximilla, but were prevented by others who plainly co-operated with the spirit. He writes as follows :

17 "And let not the spirit, in the same work of Asterius Urbanus,[27] say through Maximilla, 'I am driven away from the sheep like a wolf.[28] I am not a wolf. I am word and spirit and power.' But let him show clearly and prove the power in the spirit. And by the spirit let him compel those to confess him who were then present for the purpose of proving and reasoning with the talkative spirit, — those eminent men

---

[20] That synods should early be held to consider the subject of Montanism is not at all surprising. Doubtless our author is quite correct in asserting that many such met during these years. They were probably all of them small, and only local in their character. We do not know the places or the dates of any of these synods, although the *Libellus Synodicus* states that one was held at Hierapolis under Apolinarius, with twenty-six bishops in attendance, and another at Anchialus under Sotas, with twelve bishops present. The authority for these synods is too late to be of much weight, and the report is just such as we should expect to have arisen upon the basis of the account of Montanism given in this chapter. It is possible, therefore, that synods were held in those two cities, but more than that cannot be said. Upon these synods, see Hefele (*Conciliengesch.* I. p. 83 sq.), who accepts the report of the *Libellus Synodicus* as trustworthy.

[21] Cf. the complaint of Maximilla, quoted in § 17, below. The words are employed, of course, only in the figurative sense to indicate the hostility of the Church toward the Montanists. The Church, of course, had at that time no power to put heretics to death, even if it had wished to do so. The first instance of the punishment of heresy by death occurred in 385, when the Spanish bishop Priscillian and six companions were executed at Trèves.

[22] Cf. Matt. xxiii. 34.

[23] There is a flat contradiction between this passage and § 21, below, where it is admitted by this same author that the Montanists have had their martyrs. The sweeping statements here, considered in the light of the admission made in the other passage, furnish us with a criterion of the trustworthiness and honesty of the reports of our anonymous author. It is plain that, in his hostility to Montanism, he has no regard whatever for the truth; that his aim is to paint the heretics as black as possible, even if he is obliged to misrepresent the facts. We might, from the general tone of the fragment which Eusebius has preserved, imagine this to be so: the present passage proves it. We know, indeed, that the Montanists had many martyrs, and that their principles were such as to lead them to martyrdom, even when the Catholics avoided it (cf. Tertullian's *De fuga in persecutione*).

[24] Whether this story is an invention of our author's, or whether it was already in circulation, as he says, we cannot tell. Its utter

worthlessness needs no demonstration. Even our anonymous author does not venture to call it certain.

[25] ἐπίτροπος : a steward, or administrator of funds. The existence of such an officer shows that the Montanists formed a compact organization at an early date, and that much stress was laid upon it (cf. chap. 18, § 2). According to Jerome (*Ep. ad Marcellam*; Migne, *Ep.* XLI. 3) the Montanists at Pepuza had three classes of officers: first, Patriarchs; second, Cenonæ; third, Bishops (*Habent enim primos de Pepusa Phrygiæ Patriarchas: secundos, quos appellant Cenonas: atque ita in tertium, id est, pene ultimum locum Episcopi devolvuntur*). The peculiar word *Cenonas* occurs nowhere else, so far as I am aware, but its meaning is plain enough. Whether it is merely a reproduction of the Greek οἰκόνομοι (" administrators "), or whether it is a Latin word connected with *cœna*, in either case the officers designated by it were economic officers, and thus performed the same class of duties as this ἐπίτροπος, Theodotus. The reliability of Jerome's report is confirmed by its agreement in this point with the account of the Anonymous. Of Theodotus himself (to be distinguished, of course, from the two Theodoti mentioned in chap. 28) we know only what is told us in this chapter and in chap. 3, above. It is plain that he was a prominent man among the early Montanists.

[26] The reference here seems to be to a death like that recorded by a common tradition of Simon Magus, who by the help of demons undertook to fly up to heaven, but when in mid air fell and was killed. Whether the report in regard to Theodotus was in any way connected with the tradition of Simon's death we cannot tell, though our author can hardly have thought of it, or he would certainly have likened Theodotus' fate to that of the arch-heretic Simon, as he likened the fate of Montanus and Maximilla to that of Judas. Whatever the exact form of death referred to, there is of course no more confidence to be placed in this report than in the preceding one.

[27] Of this Asterius Urbanus we know only what we can gather from this reference to him. Valesius, Tillemont, and others supposed that the words ἐν τῷ αὐτῷ λόγῳ τῷ κατὰ 'Αστέριον Οὐρβανόν were a scholium written on the margin of his copy by Eusebius himself or some ancient commentator to indicate the authorship of the anonymous work from which the fragments in this chapter are taken (and so in the *Ante-Nicene Fathers*, Vol. VII., these fragments are given as from the work of Asterius Urbanus). But Eusebius himself evidently did not know the author, and it is at any rate much easier to suppose the words a part of the text, and the work of Asterius a work which our anonymous author has been discussing, and from which he quotes the words of Maximilla, just below. Accepting this most natural interpretation of the words, we learn that Asterius Urbanus was a Montanist who had written a work in defense of that sect.

[28] Cf. note 21, above.

and bishops, Zoticus,[29] from the village Comana, and Julian,[30] from Apamea, whose mouths the followers of Themiso[31] muzzled, refusing to permit the false and seductive spirit to be refuted by them."

18   Again in the same work, after saying other things in refutation of the false prophecies of Maximilla, he indicates the time when he wrote these accounts, and mentions her predictions in which she prophesied wars and anarchy. Their falsehood he censures in the following manner :

19   "And has not this been shown clearly to be false? For it is to-day more than thirteen years since the woman died, and there has been neither a partial nor general war in the world ; but rather, through the mercy of God, continued peace even to the Christians."[32] These things are taken from the second book.

20   I will add also short extracts from the third book, in which he speaks thus against their boasts that many of them had suffered martyrdom :

"When therefore they are at a loss, being refuted in all that they say, they try to take refuge in their martyrs, alleging that they have many martyrs, and that this is sure evidence of the power of the so-called prophetic spirit that is with them. But this, as it appears, is en-

21   tirely fallacious.[33] For some of the heresies have a great many martyrs ; but surely we shall not on that account agree with them or

confess that they hold the truth. And first, indeed, those called Marcionites, from the heresy of Marcion, say that they have a multitude of martyrs for Christ ; yet they do not confess Christ himself in truth."

A little farther on he continues :   22

"When those called to martyrdom from the Church for the truth of the faith have met with any of the so-called martyrs of the Phrygian heresy, they have separated from them, and died without any fellowship with them,[34] because they did not wish to give their assent to the spirit of Montanus and the women. And that this is true and took place in our own time in Apamea on the Mæander,[35] among those who suffered martyrdom with Gaius and Alexander of Eumenia, is well known."

CHAPTER XVII.

Miltiades and his Works.

In this work he mentions a writer, Miltiades,[1] stating that he also wrote a certain   1

---

[29] Of this Bishop Zoticus we know only what is told us here and in chap. 18, § 13. On the proposed identification of Zoticus and Sotas, bishop of Anchialus, see chap. 19, note 10.

Comana (Κομάνης, according to most of the MSS. and editors; Κουμάνης, according to a few of the MSS. followed by Laemmer and Heinichen) was a village of Pamphylia, and is to be distinguished from Comana in Pontus and from Comana in Cappadocia (Armenia), both of which were populous and important cities.

[30] Of this Julian we know nothing more. His city was Apamea Cibotus or Ciboti, which, according to Wiltsch, was a small town on Mount Signia in Pisidia, to be distinguished from the important Phrygian Apamea Cibotus on the Mæander. Whether Wiltsch has good grounds for this distinction I am unable to say. It would certainly seem natural to think in the present case of Apamea on the Mæander, inasmuch as it is spoken of without any qualifying phrase, as if there could be no doubt about its identity.

[31] Themiso is mentioned again in chap. 18 as a confessor, and as the author of a catholic epistle. It is plain that he was a prominent man among the Montanists in the time of our anonymous author, that is, after the death of Montanus himself; and it is quite likely that he was, as Salmon suggests, the head of the sect.

[32] This gives us a clear indication of the date of the composition of this anonymous work. The thirteen years must fall either before the wars which began in the reign of Septimius Severus, or after their completion. The earliest possible date in the latter case is 232, and this is certainly much too late for the composition of this work, which speaks of Montanism more than once as a recent thing, and which it seems clear from other indications belongs rather to the earlier period of the movement. If we put its composition before those wars, we cannot place it later than 192, the close of the reign of Commodus. This would push the date of Maximilla's death back to 179, which, though it seems rather early, is not at all impossible. The period from 179 to 192 might very well be called a time of peace by the Christians ; for no serious wars occurred during that interval, and we know that the Christians were left comparatively undisturbed throughout the reign of Commodus.

[33] Our author tacitly admits in this paragraph, what he has denied in § 12, above, that the Montanists had martyrs among their number; and having admitted it, he endeavors to explain away its force. In the previous paragraph he had claimed that the lack of martyrs among them proved that they were heretics; here he claims that the existence of such martyrs does not in any way argue for their orthodoxy. The inconsistency is glaringly apparent (cf. the remarks made in note 23, above).

[34] This shows the bitterness of the hostility of the Catholics toward the Montanists. That even when suffering together for the one Lord they could not recognize these brethren seems very sad, and it is not to be wondered at that the Montanists felt themselves badly used, and looked upon the Catholics as " slayers of the prophets," &c. More uncompromising enmity than this we can hardly imagine. That the Catholics, however, were sincere in their treatment of the Montanists, we cannot doubt. It is clear that they firmly believed that association with them meant association with the devil, and hence the deeper their devotion to Christ, the deeper must be their abhorrence of these instruments of Satan. Compare, for instance, Polycarp's words to Marcion, quoted in Bk. IV. chap. 14, above. The attitude of these Catholic martyrs is but of a piece with that of nearly all the orthodox Fathers toward heresy. It only shows itself here in its extremest form.

[35] Apamea Cibotus in Eastern Phrygia, a large and important commercial center. Of the two martyrs, Gaius and Alexander, we know only what is told us here. They were apparently both of them from Eumenia, a Phrygian town lying a short distance north of Apamea. We have no means of fixing the date of the martyrdoms referred to here, but it seems natural to assign them to the reign of Marcus Aurelius, after Montanism had become somewhat widespread, and when martyrdoms were a common thing both in the East and West. Thraseas, bishop of Eumenia, is referred to as a martyr by Polycrates in chap. 24, but he can hardly have suffered with the ones referred to here, or his name would have been mentioned instead of the more obscure names of Gaius and Alexander.

[1] This Miltiades is known to us from three sources: from the present chapter, from the Roman work quoted by Eusebius in chap. 28, and from Tertullian (*adv. Val.* chap. 5). Jerome also mentions him in two places (*de vir. ill.* 39 and *Ep. ad Magnum ;* Migne's ed. *Ep.* 70, § 3), but it is evident that he derived his knowledge solely from Eusebius. That Miltiades was widely known at the end of the second century is clear from the notices of him by an Asiatic, a Roman, and a Carthaginian writer. The position in which he is mentioned by Tertullian and by the anonymous Roman writer would seem to indicate that he flourished during the reign of Marcus Aurelius. His *Apology* was addressed to the emperors, as we learn from § 5, below, by which might be meant either Marcus Aurelius and Lucius Verus (161–169), or Marcus Aurelius and Commodus (177–180). Jerome states that he flourished during the reign of Commodus (*Floruit autem M. Antonini Commodi temporibus ;* Vallarsi adds a *que* after *Commodi*, thus making him flourish in the times of M. Antoninus *and* Commodus, but there is no authority for such an addition. It is quite possible that he was still alive in the time of Commodus (though Jerome's statement is of no weight, for it rests upon no independent authority), but he must at any rate have written his *Apology* before the death of Marcus Aurelius. The only works of Miltiades named by our authorities are the anti-Montanistic work referred to here, and the three mentioned by Eusebius at the close of this chapter (two books *Against the Greeks*, two books *Against the Jews*, and an *Apology*). Tertullian speaks of him as an anti-Gnostic writer, so that it is clear that he must have written another work not mentioned by Eusebius, and it was perhaps that work that won for him the commendation of the

book against the above-mentioned heresy. After quoting some of their words, he adds :

" Having found these things in a certain work of theirs in opposition to the work of the brother Alcibiades,[2] in which he shows that a prophet ought not to speak in ecstasy,[3] I made an abridgment."

2 A little further on in the same work he gives a list of those who prophesied under the new covenant, among whom he enumerates a certain Ammia[4] and Quadratus,[5] saying :

" But the false prophet falls into an ecstasy, in which he is without shame or fear. Beginning with purposed ignorance, he passes on, as has been stated, to involuntary madness of soul. They cannot show that one of the old or 3 one of the new prophets was thus carried away in spirit. Neither can they boast of Agabus,[6] or Judas,[7] or Silas,[8] or the daughters of Philip,[9] or Ammia in Philadelphia, or Quadratus, or any others not belonging to them."

And again after a little he says : " For if 4 after Quadratus and Ammia in Philadelphia, as they assert, the women with Montanus received the prophetic gift, let them show who among them received it from Montanus and the women. For the apostle thought it necessary that the prophetic gift should continue in all the Church until the final coming. But they cannot show it, though this is the fourteenth year since the death of Maximilla." [10]

He writes thus. But the Miltiades to 5 whom he refers has left other monuments of his own zeal for the Divine Scriptures,[11] in the discourses which he composed against the Greeks and against the Jews,[12] answering each of them separately in two books.[13] And in addition he addresses an apology to the earthly rulers,[14] in behalf of the philosophy which he embraced.

---

anonymous writer quoted in chap. 28, who ranks him with Justin, Tatian, Irenæus, Melito, and Clement as one who had asserted the divinity of Christ. Eusebius appears to have seen the three works which he mentions at the close of this chapter, but he does not quote from them, and no fragments of any of Miltiades' writings have been preserved to us; he seems indeed to have passed early out of the memory of the Church.

A very perplexing question is his relation to Montanism. According to Eusebius, he was the author of an anti-Montanistic work, but this report is beset with serious difficulties. The extract which Eusebius quotes just below as his authority has " Alcibiades," not " Miltiades," according to the unanimous testimony of the MSS. and versions. It is very difficult to understand how Miltiades, if it stood originally in the text, could have been changed to Alcibiades. Nevertheless, most editors have thought it necessary to make the change in the present case, and most historians (including even Harnack) accept the alteration, and regard Miltiades as the author of a lost anti-Montanistic work. I confess that, imperative as this change at first sight seems to be, I am unable to believe that we are justified in making it. I should be inclined to think rather that Eusebius had misread his authority and that, finding Miltiades referred to in the immediate context (perhaps the Montanist Miltiades mentioned in chap. 16), he had, in a hasty perusal of the work, overlooked the less familiar name Alcibiades, and had confounded Miltiades with the author of the anti-Montanistic work referred to here by our Anonymous. He would then naturally identify him at once with the Miltiades known to him through other works. If we suppose, as Salmon suggests, that Eusebius did not copy his own extracts, but employed a scribe to do that work (as we should expect so busy a man to do), it may well be that he simply marked this extract in regard to the anti-Montanistic work without noticing his blunder, and that the scribe, copying the sentence just as it stood, correctly wrote Alcibiades instead of Miltiades. In confirmation of the supposition that Eusebius was mistaken in making Miltiades the author of an anti-Montanistic work may be urged the fact that Tertullian speaks of Miltiades with respect, and ranks him with the greatest Fathers of the second century. It is true that the term by which he describes him (ecclesiarum sophista) may not (as Harnack maintains) imply as much praise as is given to Proculus in the same connection; nevertheless Tertullian does treat Miltiades with respect, and does accord him a high position among ecclesiastical writers. But it is certainly difficult to suppose that Tertullian can thus have honored a man who was known to have written against Montanism. Still further, it must be noticed that Eusebius himself had not seen Miltiades' anti-Montanistic work; he knew it only from the supposed mention of it in this anonymous work from which he was quoting. Certainly it is not, on the whole, difficult to suppose him mistaken and our MSS. and versions correct. I therefore prefer to retain the traditional reading Alcibiades, and have so translated. Of the Alcibiades who wrote the anti-Montanistic treatise referred to, we know nothing. Upon Miltiades, see especially Harnack's Texte und Untersuchungen, I. 1, p. 278 sqq., Otto's Corpus Apol. Christ. IX. 364 sqq., and Salmon's article in the Dict. of Christ. Biog. III. 916.

[2] 'Aλκιβιάδου, with all the MSS. and versions, followed by Valesius (in his text), by Burton, Laemmer, and Crusè; Nicephorus, followed by Valesius in his notes, and by all the other editors, and by the translations of Stroth, Closs, and Stigloher, read Μιλτιάδου. See the previous note.

[3] This was the first work, so far as we know, to denounce the practice of prophesying in ecstasy. The practice, which had doubtless fallen almost wholly into disuse, was brought into decided disrepute on account of the excesses of the Montanists, and the position taken by this Alcibiades became very soon the position of the whole Church (see the previous chapter, note 14).

[4] Of this prophetess Ammia of Philadelphia we know only what we can gather from this chapter. She would seem to have lived early in the second century, possibly in the latter part of the first, and to have been a prophetess of considerable prominence. That the Montanists had good ground for appealing to her, as well as to the other prophets mentioned as their models, cannot be denied. These early prophets were doubtless in their enthusiasm far more like the Montanistic prophets than like those whom the Church of the latter part of the second century alone wished to recognize.

[5] This Quadratus is to be identified with the Quadratus men-

tioned in Bk. III. chap. 37, and was evidently a man of prominence in the East. He seems to have been a contemporary of Ammia, or to have belonged at any rate to the succession of the earliest prophets. He is to be distinguished from the bishop of Athens, mentioned in Bk. IV. chap. 23, and also in all probability from the apologist, mentioned in Bk. IV. chap. 3. Cf. Harnack, Texte und Unters. I. 1. p. 102 and 104; and see Bk. III. chap. 37, note 1, above.

[6] On Agabus, see Acts xi. 28, xxi. 10.

[7] On Judas, see Acts xv. 22, 27, 32.

[8] On Silas, see Acts xv.–xviii. passim ; also 2 Cor. i. 19, 1 Thess. i. 1, 2 Thess. i. 1, and 1 Pet. v. 12, where Silvanus (who is probably the same man) is mentioned.

[9] On the daughters of Philip, see Acts xxi. 9; also Bk. III. chap. 31, note 8, above.

[10] On the date of Maximilla's death, see the previous chapter, note 32. To what utterance of " the apostle " (ὁ ἀπόστολος, which commonly means Paul) our author is referring, I am not able to discover. I can find nothing in his writings, nor indeed in the New Testament, which would seem to have suggested the idea which he here attributes to the apostle. The argument is a little obscure, but the writer apparently means to prove that the Montanists are not a part of the true Church, because the gift of prophecy is a mark of that Church, and the Montanists no longer possess that gift. This seems a strange accusation to bring against the Montanists, — we might expect them to use such an argument against the Catholics. In fact, we know that the accusation is not true, at least not entirely so; for we know that there were Montanistic prophetesses in Tertullian's church in Carthage later than this time, and also that there was still a prophetess at the time Apollonius wrote (see chap. 18, § 6), which was some years later than this (see chap. 18, note 3).

[11] περὶ τὰ θεῖα λόγια. These words are used to indicate the Scriptures in Bk. VI. chap. 23, § 2, IX. 9. 7, X. 4. 28, and in the Martyrs of Palestine, XI. 2.

[12] ἐν τε οἷς πρὸς Ἕλληνας συνέταξε λόγοις, καὶ τοῖς πρὸς Ἰουδαίους. Eusebius is the only one to mention these works, and no fragments of either of them are now extant. See above, note 1.

[13] ἐκατέρᾳ ἰδίως ὑποθέσει ἐν δυσὶν ὑπαντήσας συγγράμμασιν.

[14] Or, " to the rulers of the world " (πρὸς τοὺς κοσμικοὺς ἄρχοντας). Valesius supposed these words to refer to the provincial governors, but it is far more natural to refer them to the reigning emperors, both on account of the form of the phrase itself and also because of the fact that it was customary with all the apologists to address their apologies to the emperors themselves. In regard to the particular emperors addressed, see above, note 1.

CHAPTER XVIII.

The Manner in which Apollonius refuted the Phrygians, and the Persons[1] whom he mentions.

1 As the so-called Phrygian heresy[2] was still flourishing in Phrygia in his time, Apollonius[3] also, an ecclesiastical writer, undertook its refutation, and wrote a special work against it, correcting in detail the false prophecies current among them and reproving the life of the founders of the heresy. But hear his own words respecting Montanus :

2 " His actions and his teaching show who this new teacher is. This is he who taught the dissolution of marriage ;[4] who made laws for fasting ;[5] who named Pepuza and Tymion,[6] small towns in Phrygia, Jerusalem, wishing to gather people to them from all directions ; who appointed collectors of money ;[7] who contrived the receiving of gifts under the name of offerings ; who provided salaries for those who preached his doctrine, that its teaching might prevail through gluttony." [8]

He writes thus concerning Montanus ; 3 and a little farther on he writes as follows concerning his prophetesses : " We show that these first prophetesses themselves, as soon as they were filled with the Spirit, abandoned their husbands. How falsely therefore they speak who call Prisca a virgin." [9]

Afterwards he says : " Does not all Scrip- 4 ture seem to you to forbid a prophet to receive gifts and money ? [10] When therefore I see the prophetess receiving gold and silver and costly garments, how can I avoid reproving her ? "

And again a little farther on he speaks 5 thus concerning one of their confessors :

" So also Themiso,[11] who was clothed with plausible covetousness, could not endure the sign of confession, but threw aside bonds for an abundance of possessions. Yet, though he should have been humble on this account, he dared to boast as a martyr, and in imitation of the apostle, he wrote a certain catholic[12] epistle,

---

[1] Or *events* (τίνων).

[2] On the name, see chap. 16, note 2.

[3] Of this Apollonius we know little more than what Eusebius tells us in this chapter. The author of *Prædestinatus* (in the fifth century) calls him bishop of Ephesus, but his authority is of no weight. Jerome devotes chap. 40 of his *de vir. ill.* to Apollonius, but it is clear that he derives his knowledge almost exclusively from Eusebius. He adds the notice, however, that Tertullian replied to Apollonius' work in the seventh book of his own work, *de Ecstasi* (now lost). The character of Apollonius' work may be gathered from the fragments preserved by Eusebius in this chapter. It was of the same nature as the work of the anonymous writer quoted in chap. 16, very bitter in tone and not over-scrupulous in its statements. Apollonius states (see in § 12, below) that he wrote the work forty years after the rise of Montanism. If we accepted the Eusebian date for its beginning (172), this would bring us down to 212, but (as remarked above, in chap. 16, note 12) Montanism had probably begun in a quiet way sometime before this, and so Apollonius' forty years are perhaps to be reckoned from a somewhat earlier date. His mention of " the prophetess " as still living (in § 6, below) might lead us to think that Maximilla was still alive when he wrote ; but when the anonymous wrote she was already dead, and the reasons for assigning the latter to a date as early as 192 are too strong to be set aside. We must therefore suppose Apollonius to be referring to some other prophetess well known in his time. That there were many such prophetesses in the early part of the third century is clear from the works of Tertullian. Jerome (*ibid.*) states that an account of the death of Montanus and his prophetesses by hanging was contained in Apollonius' work, but it has been justly suspected that he is confusing the work of the anonymous, quoted in chap. 16, above, with the work of Apollonius, quoted in this chapter. The fragments of Apollonius' work, preserved by Eusebius, are given, with a commentary, in Routh's *Rel. Sac.* I. p. 467 sq., and an English translation in the *Ante-Nicene Fathers*, VIII. p. 775 sq.

[4] We are not to gather from this that the Montanists forbade marriage. They were, to be sure, decidedly ascetic in their tendencies, and they did teach the unlawfulness of second marriages,—which had long been looked upon with disfavor in many quarters, but whose lawfulness the Church had never denied,—and magnified the blessedness of the single state; but beyond this they did not go, so far as we are able to judge. Our chief sources for the Montanistic view of marriage are Tertullian's works *ad Uxorem, de Pudicit., de Monogamia, de Exhort. ad castitat.*, and Epiphanius' *Hær.* XLVIII. 9.

[5] One great point of dispute between the Montanists and the Catholics was the subject of fasts (cf. Hippolytus, VIII. 12, X. 21, who makes it almost the only ground of complaint against the Montanists). The Montanist prophetesses ordained two new fasts of a week each in addition to the annual paschal fast of the Church; and the regulations for these two weeks were made very severe. Still further they extended the duration of the regular weekly (Wednesday and Friday) fasts, making them cover the whole instead of only a part of the day. The Catholics very strenuously opposed these ordinances, not because they were opposed to fasting (many of them indulged extensively in the practice), but because they objected to the imposition of such extra fasts as binding upon the Church. They were satisfied with the traditional customs in this matter, and did not care to have heavier burdens imposed upon the Christians in general than their fathers had borne. Our principal sources for a knowledge of the dispute between the Montanists and Catholics on this subject are Tertullian's *de Jejuniis*; Epiphanius, *Hær.* XLVIII. 8; Jerome, *Ep. ad Marcellam* (Migne, *Ep.* XLI. 3), *Comment. in Matt.* c. 9, vers. 15; and Theodoret, *Hær. Fab.* III. 2.

[6] Pepuza was an obscure town in the western part of Phrygia; Tymion, otherwise unknown, was probably situated in the same neighborhood. Pepuza was early made, and long continued, the chief center—the Jerusalem—of the sect, and even gave its name to the sect in many quarters. Harnack has rightly emphasized the significance of this statement of Apollonius, and has called attention to the fact that Montanus' original idea must have been the gathering of the chosen people from all the world into one region, that they might form one fold, and freed from all the political and social relations in which they had hitherto lived might await the coming of the Lord, who would speedily descend, and set up his kingdom in this new Jerusalem. Only after this idea had been proved impracticable did Montanism adapt itself to circumstances and proceed to establish itself in the midst of society as it existed in the outside world. That Montanus built upon the Gospel of John, and especially upon chaps. x. and xvii., in this original attempt of his, is perfectly plain (cf. Harnack's *Dogmengeschichte*, I. p. 319 and 323. With this passage from Apollonius, compare also Epiphanius, *Hær.* XLVIII. 14 and XLIX. 1, and Jerome *Ep. ad Marcellam*).

[7] This appointment of economic officers and the formation of a compact organization were a part of the one general plan, referred to in the previous note, and must have marked the earliest years of the sect. Later, when it was endeavoring to adapt itself to the catholic Church, and to compromise matters in such a way as still to secure recognition from the Church, this organization must have been looked upon as a matter of less importance, and indeed probably never went far beyond the confines of Phrygia. That it continued long in that region, however, is clear from Jerome's words in his Epistle to Marcella already referred to. Compare also chap 16, note 25.

[8] There can be little doubt that the Church teachers and other officers were still supported by voluntary contributions, and hence Apollonius was really scandalized at what he considered making merchandise of spiritual things (cf. the *Didache*, chaps. XI. and XII.; but even in the *Didache* we find already a sort of stated salary provided for the prophets; cf. chap. XII.). For him to conclude, however, from the practice instituted by the Montanists in accordance with their other provisions for the formation of a compact organization, that they were avaricious and gluttonous, is quite unjustifiable, just as much so as if our salaried clergy to-day should be accused, as a class, of such sins.

[9] See chap. 16, note 18. [10] See note 8.

[11] On Themiso, see chap. 16, note 31.

[12] καθολικὴν ἐπιστολήν. Catholic in the sense in which the word is used of the epistles of James, Peter, John, and Jude; that is, general, addressed to no particular church. The epistle is no longer extant. Its " blasphemy " against the Lord and his apostles lay undoubtedly in its statement of the fundamental doctrine of the Montanists, that the age of revelation had not ceased, but that through the promised Paraclete revelations were still given, which supplemented or superseded those granted the apostles by Christ.

to instruct those whose faith was better than his own, contending for words of empty sound, and blaspheming against the Lord and the apostles and the holy Church."

6   And again concerning others of those honored among them as martyrs, he writes as follows :

"Not to speak of many, let the prophetess herself tell us of Alexander,[13] who called himself a martyr, with whom she is in the habit of banqueting, and who is worshiped[13a] by many. We need not mention his robberies and other daring deeds for which he was punished, but the

7   archives[14] contain them. Which of these forgives the sins of the other? Does the prophet the robberies of the martyr, or the martyr the covetousness of the prophet? For although the Lord said, 'Provide neither gold, nor silver, neither two coats,'[15] these men, in complete opposition, transgress in respect to the possession of the forbidden things. For we will show that those whom they call prophets and martyrs gather their gain not only from rich men, but also from the poor, and orphans,

8   and widows. But if they are confident, let them stand up and discuss these matters, that if convicted they may hereafter cease transgressing. For the fruits of the prophet must be tried ; 'for the tree is known by its fruit.'[16]

9   But that those who wish may know concerning Alexander, he was tried by Æmilius Frontinus,[17] proconsul at Ephesus ; not on account of the Name,[18] but for the robberies which he had committed, being already an apostate.[19] Afterwards, having falsely declared for the name of the Lord, he was released, having deceived the faithful that were there.[20] And his

own parish, from which he came, did not receive him, because he was a robber.[21] Those who wish to learn about him have the public records[22] of Asia. And yet the prophet with whom he spent many years knows nothing about him![23] Exposing him, through him we ex- 10 pose also the pretense[24] of the prophet. We could show the same thing of many others. But if they are confident, let them endure the test."

Again, in another part of his work he 11 speaks as follows of the prophets of whom they boast :

"If they deny that their prophets have received gifts, let them acknowledge this : that if they are convicted of receiving them, they are not prophets. And we will bring a multitude of proofs of this. But it is necessary that all the fruits of a prophet should be examined. Tell me, does a prophet dye his hair?[25] Does a prophet stain his eyelids?[26] Does a prophet delight in adornment? Does a prophet play with tables and dice? Does a prophet lend on usury? Let them confess whether these things are lawful or not ; but I will show that they have been done by them."[27]

This same Apollonius states in the same 12 work that, at the time of his writing, it was the fortieth year since Montanus had begun his pretended prophecy.[28] And he says 13 also that Zoticus, who was mentioned by the former writer,[29] when Maximilla was pretending to prophesy in Pepuza, resisted her and endeavored to refute the spirit that was working in her ; but was prevented by those who agreed with her. He mentions also a certain Thraseas[30] among the martyrs of that time.

He speaks, moreover, of a tradition that the Saviour commanded his apostles not to depart from Jerusalem for twelve years.[31] He uses testimonies also from the Revelation of John,[32] and

---

[13] This fragment gives us our only information in regard to this Alexander. That there may be some truth in the story told by Apollonius cannot be denied. It is possible that Alexander was a bad man, and that the Montanists had been deceived in him, as often happens in all religious bodies. Such a thing might much more easily happen after the sect had been for a number of years in a flourishing condition than in its earlier years; and the exactness of the account, and the challenge to disprove it, would seem to lend it some weight. At the same time Apollonius is clearly as unprincipled and dishonest a writer as the anonymous, and hence little reliance can be placed upon any of his reports to the discredit of the Montanists. If the anonymous made so many accusations out of whole cloth, Apollonius may have done the same in the present instance; and the fact that many still "worshiped" him would seem to show that Apollonius' accusations, if they possessed any foundation, were at any rate not proven.
[13a] A very common accusation brought against various sects. Upon the significance of it, see Harnack, Dogmengeschichte, I. p. 82, note 2.
[14] ὀπισθόδομος, originally the back chamber of the old temple of Athenæ on the Acropolis at Athens, where the public treasure was kept. It then came to be used of the inner chamber of any temple where the public treasure was kept, and in the present instance is used of the apartment which contained the public records or archives. Just below, Apollonius uses the phrase δημόσιον ἀρχεῖον, in referring to the same thing.
[15] Matt. x. 9, 10.   [16] Matt. xii. 33.
[17] We know, unfortunately, nothing about this proconsul, and hence have no means of fixing the date of this occurrence.
[18] i.e. of Christ.
[19] παραβάτης.
[20] εἶτα ἐπιψευσάμενος τῷ ὀνόματι τοῦ κυρίου ἀπολέλυται πλανήσας τοὺς ἐκεῖ πιστούς. The meaning seems to be that while in prison he pretended to be a Christian, and thus obtained the favor of the brethren, who procured his release by using their influence with the judge.

[21] We have no means of controlling the truth of this statement.
[22] δημόσιον ἀρχεῖον.
[23] ὃν ὁ προφήτης συνὼν πολλοῖς ἔτεσιν ἀγνοεῖ, as is read by all the MSS., followed by the majority of the editors. Heinichen reads ᾧ ὁ προφήτης συνὼν πολλοῖς ἔτεσιν ἀγνοεῖ, but the emendation is quite unnecessary. The ἀγνοεῖ implies ignorance of the man's true character; although with him so many years, he knows nothing about him, is ignorant of his true character ! The sentence is evidently ironical.   [24] τὴν ὑπόστασιν.
[25] βάπτεται.   [26] στιβίζεται.
[27] Knowing what we do of the asceticism and the severe morality of the Montanists, we can look upon the implications of this passage as nothing better than baseless slanders. That there might have been an individual here and there whose conduct justified this attack cannot be denied, but to bring such accusations against the Montanists in general was both unwarranted and absurd, and Apollonius cannot but have been aware of the fact. His language is rather that of a bully or braggadocio who knows the untruthfulness of his statements, than of a man conscious of his own honesty and of the reliability of his account.
[28] On the date of Apollonius' work, see above, note 3.
[29] See chap. 16, § 17.
[30] This Thraseas is undoubtedly to be identified with Thraseas, "bishop and martyr of Eumenia," mentioned by Polycrates, as quoted in chap. 24, below. We know no more about him than is told us there.
[31] Clement (Strom. VI. 5) records the same tradition, quoting it from the Preaching of Peter, upon which work, see Bk. III. chap. 3, note 8, above.
[32] Compare Eusebius' promise in Bk. III. chap. 24, § 18, and see note 21 on that chapter.

he relates that a dead man had, through the Divine power, been raised by John himself in Ephesus.[33] He also adds other things by which he fully and abundantly exposes the error of the heresy of which we have been speaking. These are the matters recorded by Apollonius.

CHAPTER XIX.

Serapion on the Heresy of the Phrygians.

1   SERAPION,[1] who, as report says, succeeded Maximinus[2] at that time as bishop of the church of Antioch, mentions the works of Apolinarius[3] against the above-mentioned heresy. And he alludes to him in a private letter to Caricus and Pontius,[4] in which he himself exposes the same heresy, and adds the following words:[5]

2   " That you may see that the doings of this lying band of the new prophecy, so called, are an abomination to all the brother-

hood throughout the world, I have sent you writings[6] of the most blessed Claudius Apolinarius, bishop of Hierapolis in Asia."

In the same letter of Serapion the signa-   3 tures of several bishops are found,[7] one of whom subscribes himself as follows :

" I, Aurelius Cyrenius, a witness,[8] pray for your health."

And another in this manner :

" Ælius Publius Julius,[9] bishop of Debeltum, a colony of Thrace. As God liveth in the heavens, the blessed Sotas in Anchialus desired to cast the demon out of Priscilla, but the hypocrites did not permit him."[10]

And the autograph signatures of many   4 other bishops who agreed with them are contained in the same letter.

So much for these persons.

CHAPTER XX.

The Writings of Irenæus against the Schismatics at Rome.

IRENÆUS[1] wrote several letters against   1 those who were disturbing the sound ordinance of the Church at Rome. One of them was to Blastus On Schism ;[2] another to Florinus

---

[33] No one else, so far as I am aware, records this tradition, but it is of a piece with many others in regard to John which were afloat in the early Church.

[1] Both versions of the *Chron.* agree in putting the accession of Serapion into the eleventh year of Commodus (190 A.D.), and that of his successor Asclepiades into the first year of Caracalla, which would give Serapion an episcopate of twenty-one years (Syncellus says twenty-five years, although giving the same dates of accession for both bishops that the other versions give). Serapion was a well-known person, and it is not too much to think that the dates given by the *Chron.* in connection with him may be more reliable than most of its dates. The truth is, that from the present chapter we learn that he was already bishop before the end of Commodus' reign, i.e. before the end of 192 A.D. Were the statement of Eutychius,— that Demetrius of Alexandria wrote at the same time to Maximus of Antioch and Victor of Rome,— to be relied upon, we could fix his accession between 189 and 192 (see Harnack's *Zeit des Ignatius*, p. 45). But the truth is little weight can be attached to his report. While we cannot therefore reach certainty in the matter, there is no reason for doubting the approximate accuracy of the date given by the *Chron.* As to the time of his death, we can fix the date of Asclepiades' accession approximately in the year 211 (see Bk. VI. chap. 11, note 6), and from the fragment of Alexander's epistle to the Antiochenes, quoted in that chapter, it seems probable that there had been a vacancy in the see of Antioch for some time. But from the mention of Serapion's epistles to Domninus (Bk. VI. chap. 12) we may gather that he lived until after the great persecution of the Edessene church, as we learn from Zahn's *Doctrina Addai* (*Gött. Gel. Anz.* 1877, St. 6, p. 173, 179, according to Harnack's *Zeit des Ignatius*, p. 46 sqq.).

[2] On Maximinus, see Bk. IV. chap. 24, note 6.

[3] See Bk. IV. chap. 27, note 1.

[4] Caricus and Pontius (called Ponticus in this passage by most of the MSS. of Eusebius, but Pontius by one of the best of them, by Nicephorus, Jerome, and Eusebius himself in Bk. VI. chap. 12, which authorities are followed by Stroth, Burton, Schwegler, and Heinichen) are called in Bk. VI. chap. 12, ἐκκλησιαστικοὺς ἀνδρὰς. They are otherwise unknown personages. In that chapter the plural article τά is used of the writing, or writings, addressed to Caricus and Pontius, implying that ὑπομνήματα is to be supplied. This seems to imply more than one writing, but it is not necessary to conclude that more than the single epistle mentioned here is meant, for the plural ὑπομνήματα was often used in a sort of collective sense to signify a collection of notes, memoranda, &c.

[5] This fragment is given by Routh, *Rel. Sacræ*, and, in English, in the *Ante-Nicene Fathers*, VIII. p. 775.

[6] See Bk. IV. chap. 27, note 5.

[7] Valesius justly remarks that Eusebius does not say that these bishops signed Serapion's epistle, but only that their signatures or notes (ὑποσημειώσεις) were contained in the epistle. He thinks it is by no means probable that a bishop of Thrace (the nationality of the other bishops we do not know) should have signed this epistle of Serapion's, and he therefore concludes that Serapion simply copies from another epistle sent originally from Thrace. This is possible; but at the end of the chapter Eusebius says that other bishops put in their signatures or notes with their own hands (αὐτόγραφοι σημειώσεις), which precludes the idea that Serapion simply copies their testimony from another source, and if they signed thus it is possible that the Thracian bishop did likewise. It may be that Serapion took pains to compose a semi-official communication which should have the endorsement of as many anti-Montanistic bishops as possible, and that, in order to secure their signatures he sent it about from one to the other before forwarding it to Caricus and Pontius.

[8] Of this Aurelius Cyrenius we know nothing. It is possible that he means to call himself simply a witness (μαρτύς) to the facts recorded by Serapion in his epistle, but more probable that he uses the word to indicate that he has "witnessed for Christ" under persecution.

[9] Ælius Publius Julius is also an otherwise unknown personage. Debeltum and Anchialus were towns of Thrace, on the western shore of the Black Sea.

[10] Lightfoot (*Ignatius*, II. 111) suggests that this Sotas (Σωτᾶς) may be identical with the Zoticus (Ζωτικός) mentioned in the preceding chapter, the interchange of the initial Σ and Z being very common. But we learn from chap. 16 that Zoticus was bishop of Comana, so that he can hardly be identified with Sotas, bishop of Anchialus.

[1] On Irenæus, see Bk. IV. chap. 21, note 9.

[2] Eusebius, in chap. 15, informs us that both Blastus and Florinus drew many away from the church of Rome by their heretical innovations. He does not tell us either there or here the nature of the opinions which Blastus held, but from Pseudo-Tertullian's *Adv. omnes Hær.* chap. 8, we learn that Blastus was a Quartodeciman. ("In addition to all these, there is likewise Blastus, who would latently introduce Judaism. For he says the passover is not to be kept otherwise than according to the law of Moses, on the fourteenth of the month.") From Pacianus' *Epistola ad Sympronian. de catholico nomine*, chap. 2, we learn that he was a Montanist ; and since the Montanists of Asia Minor were, like the other Christians of that region, Quartodecimans, it is not surprising that Blastus should be at the same time a Montanist and a Quartodeciman. Florinus, as will be shown in the next note, taught his heresies while Victor was bishop of Rome (189-198 or 199) ; and since Eusebius connects Blastus so closely with him, we may conclude that Blastus flourished at about the same time. Irenæus' epistle to Blastus, *On Schism*, is no longer extant. A Syriac fragment of an epistle of Irenæus, addressed to " an Alexandrian," on the paschal

On Monarchy,[3] or That God is not the Author of Evil. For Florinus seemed to be defending this opinion. And because he was being drawn away by the error of Valentinus, Irenæus wrote his work On the Ogdoad,[4] in which he shows

that he himself had been acquainted with the first successors of the apostles.[5] At the close of the treatise we have found a most beautiful note which we are constrained to insert in this work.[6] It runs as follows : 2

"I adjure thee who mayest copy this book, by our Lord Jesus Christ, and by his glorious advent when he comes to judge the living and the dead, to compare what thou shalt write, and correct it carefully by this manuscript, and also to write this adjuration, and place it in the copy."

These things may be profitably read in his work, and related by us, that we may have those ancient and truly holy men as the best example of painstaking carefulness. 3

In the letter to Florinus, of which we have spoken,[7] Irenæus mentions again his intimacy with Polycarp, saying : 4

"These doctrines, O Florinus, to speak mildly, are not of sound judgment. These doctrines disagree with the Church, and drive into the greatest impiety those who accept them. These doctrines, not even the heretics outside of the Church, have ever dared to publish. These doctrines, the presbyters who were before us, and who were companions of the apostles, did not deliver to thee.

"For when I was a boy, I saw thee in lower Asia with Polycarp, moving in splendor in the royal court,[8] and endeavoring to gain his approbation. I remember the events of that time more clearly than those of recent years. For what boys learn, growing with their mind, becomes joined with it ; so that I am able to describe the very place in which the blessed Polycarp sat as he discoursed, and his goings out and his comings in, and the man- 5 6

---

question (Fragment 27 in Harvey's edition) is possibly a part of this lost epistle. If the one referred to in this fragment be Blastus, he was an Alexandrian, and in that case must have adopted the Quartodeciman position under the influence of the Asiatic Montanists, for the paschal calendar of the Alexandrian church was the same as that of Rome (see the *Dict. of Christ. Biog.* III. p. 264). If Blastus was a Montanist, as stated by Pacianus, his heresy was quite different from that of Florinus (who was a Gnostic) ; and the fact that they were leaders of different heresies is confirmed by the words of Eusebius in chap. 15, above : " Each one striving to introduce *his own* innovations in respect to the truth." Whether Blastus, like Florinus, was a presbyter, and like him was deposed from his office, we do not know, but the words of Eusebius in chap. 15 seem to favor this supposition.

[3] Florinus, as we learn from chap. 15, was for a time a presbyter of the Roman Church, but lost his office on account of heresy. From the fragment of this epistle of Irenæus to Florinus quoted by Eusebius just below, we learn that Florinus was somewhat older than Irenæus, but like him a disciple of Polycarp. The title of this epistle shows that Florinus was already a Gnostic, or at least inclined toward Gnostic views. Eusebius evidently had no direct knowledge of the opinions of Florinus on the origin of evil, for he says that he *appeared* to maintain (ἐδόκει προασπίζειν) the opinion that God was the author of evil. Eusebius' conclusion is accepted by most ancient and modern writers, but it is suggested by Salmon (*Dict. of Christ. Biog.* II. 544) that Eusebius was perhaps mistaken, " for, since the characteristic of dualism is not to make God the author of evil, but to clear him from the charge by ascribing evil to an independent origin, the title would lead us to think that the letter was directed, not against one who had himself held God to be the author of evil, but against one who had charged the doctrine of a single first principle with necessarily leading to this conclusion. And we should have supposed that the object of Irenæus was to show that it was possible to assert God to be the sole origin and ruler of the universe, without holding evil to be his work." Since Eusebius had seen the epistle of Irenæus to Florinus, it is difficult to understand how he can have misconceived Florinus' position. At the same time, he does not state it with positiveness ; and the fact that Florinus, if not already, certainly was soon afterward a Valentinian, and hence a dualist, makes Salmon's supposition very plausible. Florinus is not mentioned in Irenæus' great work against heresies, nor by Tertullian, Pseudo-Tertullian, Hippolytus, or Epiphanius. It is probable, therefore, that he was not named in Hippolytus' earlier work, nor in the lectures of Irenæus which formed the groundwork (see Salmon, *l.c.*). The silence of Irenæus is easily explained by supposing Florinus' fall into heresy to have taken place after the composition of his lectures against heresies and of his great work ; and the silence of the later writers is probably due to the fact that Irenæus' work makes no mention of him, and that, whatever his influence may have been during his lifetime, it did not last, and hence his name attracted no particular attention after his death.

It has been maintained by some (e.g. Lightfoot, in the *Contemporary Review*, 1875, p. 834) that this epistle to Florinus was one of the earliest of Irenæus' writings but Lipsius (*Dict. of Christ. Biog.* III. 263) has given other and satisfactory reasons for thinking that Florinus' heresy, and therefore Irenæus' epistle and his work *On the Ogdoad*, belonged to the time of Victor, and hence were later than the work *Against Heresies*. A Syriac fragment of an epistle concerning Florinus, addressed by Irenæus to Victor (Harvey's edition, Fragm. 28), is extant, and supports Lipsius' conclusion. It would seem that Irenæus, subsequent to the writing of his great work, learning that Florinus was holding heretical opinions on the origin of evil, addressed him the epistle mentioned in this chapter. That afterward, Florinus having embraced Valentinianism, and having written " an abominable book " (as the fragment just referred to says), Irenæus wrote his work *On the Ogdoad*, and subsequently addressed his epistle to Victor, calling upon him to take decisive measures against Florinus, now seen to be a regular heretic. What was the result of Irenæus' epistles and book we do not know ; we hear nothing more about the matter, nor do we know anything more about Florinus (for Augustine's mention of Florinus as the founder of a sect of Floriniani is a mistake ; see Salmon, *l.c.*).

[4] This treatise, *On the Ogdoad*, is no longer extant, though it is probable that we have a few fragments of it (see Harvey, I. clxvi.). The importance which Irenæus attached to this work is seen from the solemn adjuration with which he closed it. It must have been largely identical in substance with the portions of his *Adv. Hær.* which deal with the æons of the Valentinians. It may have been little more than an enlargement of those portions of the earlier work. The Ogdoad (Greek, ὀγδόας, a word signifying primarily a thing in eight parts) occupied a prominent place in the speculations of the Gnostics. Valentinus taught eight primary æons, in four pairs, as the root and origin of the other æons and of all beings. These eight he called the first or primary Ogdoad ; and hence a work upon the Ogdoad, written against a Valentinian, must, of course, be a general discussion of the Valentinian doctrine of the æons. The word Og-

doad was not used by all the Gnostics in the same sense. It was commonly employed to denote the supercelestial region which lay above the seven planetary spheres (or Hebdomad), and hence above the control of the seven angels who severally presided over these spheres. In the Valentinian system a higher sphere, the Pleroma, the abode of the æons, was added, and the supercelestial sphere, the Ogdoad of the other systems, was commonly called the Mesotes, or middle region. For further particulars in regard to the Ogdoad, see Salmon's articles *Hebdomad* and *Ogdoad* in the *Dict. of Christ. Biog.*

[5] Literally, " in which he shows that he himself had seized upon (κατειληφέναι) the first succession (διαδοχήν) of the apostles." In order to emphasize the fact that he was teaching true doctrine, he pointed out, as he did so often elsewhere, the circumstance that he was personally acquainted with disciples of the apostles.

[6] It was not at all uncommon for copyists, both by accident and by design, to make changes, often serious, in copying books. We have an instance of intentional alterations mentioned in Bk. IV. chap. 23. It is not at all strange, therefore, that such an adjuration should be attached to a work which its author considered especially liable to corruption, or whose accurate transcription he regarded as peculiarly important. Compare the warning given in Rev. xxii. 18, 19. The fragments from Irenæus' works preserved in this chapter are translated in the *Ante-Nicene Fathers*, I. p. 568 sq.

[7] The epistle *On Monarchy* mentioned at the beginning of this chapter.

[8] ἐν τῇ βασιλικῇ αὐλῇ. This expression is a little puzzling, as the word βασιλική implies the imperial court, and could not properly be used of the provincial court of the proconsul. No sojourn of an emperor in Asia Minor is known which will meet the chronology of the case ; and hence Lightfoot (*Contemporary Review*, May, 1875, p. 834) has offered the plausible suggestion that the words may have been loosely employed to denote the court of Titus Aurelius Fulvus, who was proconsul of Asia about 136 A.D., and afterward became the emperor Antoninus Pius.

ner of his life, and his physical appearance, and his discourses to the people, and the accounts which he gave of his intercourse with John and with the others who had seen the Lord. And as he remembered their words, and what he heard from them concerning the Lord, and concerning his miracles and his teaching, having received them from eyewitnesses of the 'Word of life,'[9] Polycarp related all things in harmony with the Scriptures. These things 7 being told me by the mercy of God, I listened to them attentively, noting them down, not on paper, but in my heart. And continually, through God's grace, I recall them faithfully. And I am able to bear witness before God that if that blessed and apostolic presbyter had heard any such thing, he would have cried out, and stopped his ears, and as was his custom, would have exclaimed, O good God, unto what times hast thou spared me that I should endure these things? And he would have fled from the place where, sitting or standing, he had heard 8 such words.[10] And this can be shown plainly from the letters[11] which he sent, either to the neighboring churches for their confirmation, or to some of the brethren, admonishing and exhorting them."

Thus far Irenæus.

CHAPTER XXI.

How Apollonius suffered Martyrdom at Rome.

1   ABOUT the same time, in the reign of Commodus, our condition became more favorable, and through the grace of God the churches throughout the entire world enjoyed peace,[1] and the word of salvation was leading every soul from every race of man to the devout worship of the God of the universe. So that now at Rome many who were highly distinguished for wealth and family turned with all their household and relatives unto their salvation.

2   But the demon who hates what is good, being malignant in his nature, could not endure this, but prepared himself again for conflict, contriving many devices against us. And he brought to the judgment seat Apollonius,[2] of

the city of Rome, a man renowned among the faithful for learning and philosophy, having stirred up one of his servants, who was well fitted for such a purpose, to accuse him.[3] But this wretched man made the charge 3 unseasonably, because by a royal decree it was unlawful that informers of such things should live. And his legs were broken immediately, Perennius the judge having pronounced this sentence upon him.[4] But the 4 martyr, highly beloved of God, being ear-

defended himself before the Senate; and this possibility might seem to be strengthened by the fact that Eusebius does not call him a senator here, as we should expect him to do if he knew him to be one. On the other hand, it is highly probable (as shown in the next note) that Jerome had read the fuller account of Apollonius' martyrdom included by Eusebius in his *Collection of Martyrdoms*, and hence it seems likely that that account contained the statement that Apollonius was a senator. Jerome makes Apollonius the author of an *insigne volumen*, which he read in the Senate in defense of his faith; but there seems to be no foundation for such a report. It is apparently the result simply of a misunderstanding of the words of Eusebius, who states that Apollonius delivered before the Senate a most eloquent defense of the faith, but does not imply that he wrote an apology. The words that Eusebius uses at the close of this chapter imply rather that the defense made by Apollonius was recorded after its delivery, and that it is this report of it which can be read in his *Collection of Martyrdoms*.

[3] Jerome, followed by Sophronius, reports that the accusation against Apollonius was brought by a slave. Jerome gives the slave's name as Severus (*a servo Severo proditus*); while Sophronius makes Severus the name of the judge (παρὰ τοῦ δούλου παρὰ Σεβήρῳ προδοθεὶς χριστιανὸς εἶναι). The latter is impossible, however, as the name of the judge was Perennius according to Eusebius. Vallarsi states that some MSS. of Jerome read *sub Commodo principe ac Severo proditus*, and supposes that *ac Severo* is a corruption for the words *a servo* (which he thinks may have stood alone in the original text), and that some student, perceiving the error, wrote upon the margin of his copy the words *a servo*, and that subsequently the note crept into the text, while the word *Severo* was still retained, thus producing our present reading *a servo Severo*. This is an ingenious suggestion, but the fact is overlooked that Sophronius undoubtedly read in the original translated by him the words *a servo Severo*, for we can explain his rendering only by supposing that he read thus, but understood the word *Severo* as the dative of the indirect object after *proditus*, instead of the ablative in apposition with *servo*. In the face of Sophronius' testimony to the original form of the text, no alteration of the common reading can be accepted. As to the source of Jerome's *Severus*, since there is nothing in the present chapter of Eusebius to suggest such an addition, and no reason can be imagined for the independent insertion of the name, the only legitimate conclusion seems to be, that the name occurred in the account of Apollonius' martyrdom referred to by Eusebius just below, and that Jerome took it thence. If this be so, then that martyrology must have been the authority also for Jerome's statement that Apollonius was accused by a slave; and hence the statement may be accepted as true, and not as the result of a misinterpretation of the reference of Eusebius' words (ἕνα γέ τινα τῶν εἰς ταῦτα ἐπιτηδείων αὐτῷ), as supposed by some. Since it is thus almost certain that Jerome had himself examined the fuller account of Apollonius' martyrdom referred to by Eusebius, a favorable light is thrown back upon his report that Apollonius was a senator, and it becomes probable that he obtained this statement from the same source (see the previous note).

[4] M. de Mandajors, in his *Histoire de l'Acad. des Inscript.* tom. 18, p. 226 (according to Gieseler's *Ch. Hist.*, Harper's edition, I. p. 127), "thinks that the slave was put to death as the betrayer of his master, according to an old law renewed by Trajan; but that the occurrence had been misunderstood by the Christians, and had given rise to the tradition, which is found in Tertullian and in the *Edictum ad Comm. Asiæ*, that an emperor at this period had decreed the punishment of death for denouncing a Christian." Such a law against the denunciation of masters by slaves was passed under Nerva; but Gieseler remarks that, in accordance with the principles of the laws upon this subject, "either Apollonius only, or his slave only, could have been put to death, but in no case both. Jerome does not say either that Severus was the slave of Apollonius, or that he was executed; and since Eusebius grounds this execution expressly on a suppositious law, it may have belonged only to the Oriental tradition which may have adduced this instance in support of the alleged law." It is possible that Gieseler is right in this conclusion; but it is also quite possible that Eusebius' statement that the slave was executed is correct. The ground of the execution was, of course, not, as Eusebius thinks, the fact that he brought an accusation against a Christian, but, as remarked by de Mandajors, the fact that, being a slave, he betrayed his master. Had the informant been executed because he brought an accusation against a Christian, the subsequent execution of the latter would be inexplicable. But

---

[9] 1 John i. 1.

[10] This would have been quite like Polycarp, who appears to have had a special horror of heretics. Compare his words to Marcion, quoted above, in Bk. IV. chap. 14. He seems to have inherited this horror from John the apostle, if Irenæus' account is to be believed; see *Adv. Hær.* III. 3, 4, quoted by Eusebius in Bk. III. chap. 28, and in Bk. IV. chap. 14.

[11] We know of only one epistle by Polycarp, that to the Philippians, which is still extant. Upon his life and epistle, see Bk. IV. chap. 14, notes 5 and 16.

[1] Marcia, concubine of Commodus, and possessed of great influence over him, favored the Christians (according to Dion Cassius, LXII. 4), and as a consequence they enjoyed comparative peace during his reign.

[2] Jerome (*de vir. ill.* chap. 42, and *Epist. ad Magnum*, 4) calls Apollonius a Roman senator. It is possible that this is only a natural conclusion drawn by Jerome from Eusebius' statement that he

nestly entreated and requested by the judge to give an account of himself before the Senate, made in the presence of all an eloquent defense of the faith for which he was witnessing. And as if by decree of the Senate he was put to death by decapitation; an ancient law requiring that those who were brought to the judgment seat and refused to recant should not be liber-
5   ated.[5] Whoever desires to know his arguments before the judge and his answers to the questions of Perennius, and his entire defense before the Senate will find them in the records of the ancient martyrdoms which we have collected.[6]

CHAPTER XXII.

The Bishops that were well known at this Time.

IN the tenth year of the reign of Commodus, Victor[1] succeeded Eleutherus,[2] the latter having

held the episcopate for thirteen years. In the same year, after Julian[3] had completed his tenth year, Demetrius[4] received the charge of the parishes at Alexandria. At this time the above-mentioned Serapion,[5] the eighth from the apostles, was still well known as bishop of the church at Antioch. Theophilus[6] presided at Cæsarea in Palestine; and Narcissus,[7] whom we have mentioned before, still had charge of the church at Jerusalem. Bacchylus[8] at the same time was bishop of Corinth in Greece, and Polycrates[9] of

the part of Eusebius of a trustworthy tradition that he died in the tenth year of Commodus, which, since he incorrectly put his accession into the seventeenth year of Marcus Aurelius (or Antoninus Verus, as he calls him), made it necessary for him to draw the false conclusion that he held office only thirteen years.

[3] On Julian, bishop of Alexandria, see chap. 9, note 2.
[4] The date of the accession of Demetrius, the eleventh bishop of Alexandria, as given here and in the *Chron.*, was 189 A.D. According to Bk. VI. chap. 26, below, confirmed by the *Chron.*, he held office forty-three years. There is no reason for doubting the approximate accuracy of these dates. Demetrius is known to us chiefly because of his relations to Origen, which were at first friendly, but finally became hostile. He seems to have been a man of great energy, renowned as an administrator rather than as a literary character. He was greatly interested in the catechetical school at Alexandria, but does not seem to have taught in it, and he left no writings, so far as we know. His relations with Origen will come up frequently in the Sixth Book, where he is mentioned a number of times (see especially chap. 8, note 4).
[5] On Serapion, bishop of Antioch, see above, chap. 19.
[6] Theophilus, bishop of Cæsarea, has gained prominence chiefly on account of his connection with the paschal controversy. He presided with Narcissus over the council mentioned in the next chapter, which was called to consider the paschal question, and in conjunction with the other bishops present composed an epistle, which was still extant in Eusebius' time (according to the next chapter), and of which he gives a fragment in chap. 25. Jerome, in his *de vir. ill.* c. 43, speaks very highly of this epistle (*synodicam valde utilem composuit epistolam*); but it seems to have been no longer extant in his time, for in mentioning it and the epistle of Bacchylus of Corinth and others in his *Chron.*, he says that the memory of them still endured (*quarum memoria ad nos usque perdurat*). The dates of Theophilus' accession to office and of his death are not known to us.
[7] On Narcissus, see above, chap. 12.
[8] This Bacchylus is possibly identical with the Bacchylides who is mentioned in Bk. IV. chap. 23 as one of those who had urged Dionysius, bishop of Corinth, to write a certain epistle. Bacchylus also is prominent solely on account of his connection with the paschal controversy. According to the next chapter, he was himself the author of an epistle on the subject, which he wrote, according to Jerome (*de vir. ill.* c. 44), in the name of all the bishops of Achaia (*ex omnium qui in Achaia erant episcoporum persona*). But the words of Eusebius seem to imply that the epistle was an individual, not a synodical one, for he does not say, "an epistle of those in," &c., as he does in every other case. We must conclude, therefore, that Jerome, who had not seen the epistle, was mistaken in making it a synodical letter. Jerome characterizes it as an elegant composition (*elegantem librum*); but, like the epistle of Theophilus, mentioned in the preceding note, it seems not to have been extant in Jerome's time. The dates of Bacchylus' accession to office and of his death are not known to us.
[9] Polycrates, bishop of Ephesus, is one of the most noted men connected with the paschal controversy, for the reason that he was the leader of the bishops of the province of Asia, in which province alone the Quartodeciman practice was uniformly observed. He was thus the leading opponent of Bishop Victor of Rome. His relation to the paschal controversy is brought out more fully in chap. 24. The dates of Polycrates' accession to office and of his death are not known to us; though, of course, with Theophilus, Narcissus, Bacchylus, and the other bishops concerned in the paschal controversy, he flourished during the reign of Septimius Severus, while Victor was bishop of Rome. The only writing of Polycrates of which we know is his epistle to Victor, a portion of which is quoted by Eusebius, in Bk. III. chap. 31, and a still larger portion in chap. 24 of this book.
Jerome, in his *de vir. ill.* c. 45, speaks in terms of the highest praise of Polycrates, and quotes from Eusebius the larger fragment, given in chap. 24, adding, *Hæc propterea posui, ut ingenium et auctoritatem viri ex parvo opusculo demonstrarem.* The fact that he quotes only the passages given by Eusebius would be enough to show that he quoted from Eusebius, and not directly from Polycrates, even were it not plain from the statement in his *Chron.*, referred to in note 6, that Polycrates' epistle was, so far as Jerome knew, no longer extant. Polycrates himself informs us, in the second fragment given in chap. 24, that he wrote his epistle with the consent and approval of all the bishops present at the council sum-

it is conceivable that the prefect Perennius may have sentenced the informant to death, in accordance with the old law mentioned by de Mandajors, and that then, Apollonius being a senator, he may have requested him to appear before that body, and make his defense to them, in order that he might pass judgment upon him in accordance with the decision of the Senate. It is quite conceivable that, the emperor being inclined to favor the Christians, Perennius may not have cared to pass judgment against Apollonius until he had learned the opinion of the Senate on the matter (cf. what Neander has to say on the subject, in his *Ch. Hist.*). As remarked by Valesius, the Senate was not a judicial court, and hence could not itself sentence Apollonius; but it could, of course, communicate to the prefect its opinion, and he could then pass judgment accordingly. It is significant that the Greek reads ὡσὰν ἀπὸ δόγματος συγκλήτου, inserting the particle ὡσάν, "as if"; i.e. "*as if* by decree of the Senate."
[5] Valesius thinks the reference here is to Pliny's rescript to Trajan (see above, Bk. III. chap. 33). This is possible, though the language of Eusebius seems to imply a more general reference to all kinds of cases, not simply to the cases of Christians.
[6] On Eusebius' great *Collection of Martyrdoms*, which is now lost, see above, p. 30.
[1] The dates assigned to Victor's episcopate by the ancient authorities vary greatly. Eusebius here puts his accession in the tenth year of Commodus (i.e. 189 A.D.), and this is accepted by Lipsius as the correct date. Jerome's version of the *Chron.* puts his accession in the reign of Pertinax, or the first year of Septimius Severus (i.e. 193), while the Armenian version puts it in the seventh year of Commodus (186). Eusebius, in his *History*, does not state directly the duration of his episcopate, but in chap. 28 he says that Zephyrinus succeeded him about the ninth year of Severus, i.e. according to his erroneous reckoning (see Bk. VI. chap. 21, note 3) about 200, which would give Victor an episcopate of about eleven years. Jerome, in his version of the *Chron.* and in his *de vir. ill.*, assigns him ten years; the Armenian version of the *Chron.* twelve years. The Liberian Catalogue makes his episcopate something over nine years long; the Felician Catalogue something over ten. Lipsius, considering Victor in connection with his successors, concludes that he held office between nine and ten years, and therefore gives as his dates 189-198 or 199 (see p. 172 sq.). According to an anonymous writer quoted in chap. 28, Victor excommunicated Theodotus of Byzantium for teaching that Christ was a mere man. He is best known, however, on account of his action in connection with the great Quartodeciman controversy (see chap. 24). Jerome, in his version of the *Chron.*, says of him *cujus mediocria de religione extant volumina*, and in his *de vir. ill.* chap. 34, he tells us that he wrote upon the passover, and also some other works (*super quæstione Paschæ, et alia quædam scribens opuscula*). Harnack believes that he has discovered one of these works (all of which have been supposed lost) in the Pseudo-Cyprianic *de Aleatoribus*. In his *Texte und Unters.* Bd. V. Heft 1, he has discussed the subject in a very learned and ingenious manner. The theory has much to commend it, but there are difficulties in its way which have not yet been removed; and I am inclined to think it a product of the first half of the third century, rather than of the last quarter of the second (see the writer's review of Harnack's discussion in the *Presbyterian Review*, Jan., 1889, p. 143 sqq.).
[2] On Eleutherus, see the Introduction to this book, note 2. As remarked there, Eleutherus, according to the testimony of most of our sources, held office fifteen years. The "thirteen years" of this chapter are therefore an error, clearly caused by the possession on

the parish of Ephesus. And besides these a multitude of others, as is likely, were then prominent. But we have given the names of those alone, the soundness of whose faith has come down to us in writing.

CHAPTER XXIII.

The Question then agitated concerning the Passover.

1 A QUESTION of no small importance arose at that time. For the parishes of all Asia, as from an older tradition, held that the fourteenth day of the moon, on which day the Jews were commanded to sacrifice the lamb, should be observed as the feast of the Saviour's passover.[1] It was

therefore necessary to end their fast on that day, whatever day of the week it should happen to be. But it was not the custom of the churches in the rest of the world to end it at this time, as they observed the practice which, from apostolic tradition, has prevailed to the present time, of terminating the fast on no other day than on that of the resurrection of our Saviour.

Synods and assemblies of bishops were **2** held on this account,[2] and all, with one consent, through mutual correspondence drew up an ecclesiastical decree, that the mystery of the resurrection of the Lord should be celebrated on no other but the Lord's day, and that we should observe the close of the paschal fast on this day only. There is still extant a writing of those who were then assembled in Palestine, over whom Theophilus,[3] bishop of Cæsarea, and Narcissus, bishop of Jerusalem, presided. And there is also another writing extant of those who were assembled at Rome to consider the same question, which bears the name of Bishop Victor;[4] also of the bishops in

moned by him to discuss the paschal question. The fact that both Eusebius and Jerome praise Polycrates so highly, and testify to his orthodoxy, shows how completely the paschal question had been buried before their time, and how little the Quartodeciman practice was feared.

[1] The great question of dispute between the church of Asia Minor and the rest of Christendom was whether the paschal communion should be celebrated on the fourteenth of Nisan, or on the Sunday of the resurrection festival, without regard to Jewish chronology. The Christians of Asia Minor, appealing to the example of the apostles, John and Philip, and to the uniform practice of the Church, celebrated the Christian passover always on the fourteenth of Nisan, whatever day of the week that might be, by a solemn fast, and closed the day with the communion in commemoration of the last paschal supper of Christ. The Roman church, on the other hand, followed by all the rest of Christendom, celebrated the death of Christ always on Friday, and his resurrection on the Sunday following the first full moon after the vernal equinox, and continued their paschal fast until the latter day. It thus happened that the fast of the Asiatic Christians, terminating, as it did, with the fourteenth of Nisan, often closed some days before the fast of the other churches, and the lack of uniformity occasioned great scandal. As Schaff says: " The gist of the paschal controversy was, whether the Jewish paschal day (be it a Friday or not) or the Christian Sunday should control the idea and time of the entire festival." The former practice emphasized Christ's death; the latter his resurrection. The first discussion of the question took place between Polycarp and Anicetus, bishop of Rome, when the former was on a visit to that city, between 150 and 155. Irenæus gives an account of this, which is quoted by Eusebius in chap. 25. Polycarp clung to the Asiatic practice of observing the 14th of Nisan, but could not persuade Anicetus to do the same, nor could Anicetus persuade him not to observe that day. They nevertheless communed together in Rome, and separated in peace. About 170 A.D. the controversy broke out again in Laodicea, the chief disputants being Melito of Sardis and Apolinarius of Hierapolis (see above, Bk. IV. chap. 26, note 1, and chap. 27, note 1). In this controversy Melito advocated the traditional Asiatic custom of observing the fourteenth day, while Apolinarius opposed it. To distinguish two parties of Quartodecimans, — a Judaizing and a more orthodox, — as must be done if Apolinarius is regarded, as he is by many, as a Quartodeciman, is, as Schaff shows, entirely unwarranted. We know only of the one party, and Apolinarius did not belong to it. The third stage of the controversy, which took place while Victor was bishop of Rome, in the last decade of the second century, was much more bitter and important. The leaders of the two sides were Polycrates, bishop of Ephesus, and Victor, bishop of Rome, — the latter an overbearing man, who believed that he, as Bishop of Rome, had a right to demand of all other churches conformity to the practices of his own church. The controversy came to an open rupture between the churches of Asia and that of Rome, but other churches did not sympathize with the severe measures of Victor, and the breach was gradually healed, — just how and when we do not know; but the Roman practice gradually prevailed over the Asiatic, and finally, at the Council of Nicæa (325), was declared binding upon the whole Church, while the old Asiatic practice was condemned. This decision was acquiesced in by the bishops of Asia, as well as by the rest of the world, and only scattered churches continued to cling to the practice of the earlier Asiatics, and they were branded as heretics, and called Quartodecimanians (from *quarta decima*), a name which we carry back and apply to all who observed the fourteenth day, even those of the second and third centuries. This brief summary will enable us better to understand the accounts of Eusebius, who is our chief authority on the subject. The paschal controversy has had an important bearing upon the question of the authenticity of the fourth Gospel, the Tübingen critics having drawn from this controversy one of their strongest arguments against its genuineness. This subject

cannot be discussed here, but the reader is referred, for a brief statement of the case, to Schaff's *Ch. Hist.* II. 219. The Johannine controversy has given rise to an extensive literature on these paschal disputes. Among the most important works are Hilgenfeld's *Der Paschastreit der alten Kirche nach seiner Bedeutung fur die Kirchengesch. u. s. w.;* and Schürer's *Die Paschastreitigkeiten des zweiten Jahrhunderts,* in the *Zeitschrift für hist. Theologie,* 1870, p. 182–284, — the latter perhaps the ablest extended discussion of the subject extant. The reader is also referred to the article *Easter,* in Smith's *Dict. of Christ. Ant.;* to Hefele's *Conciliengesch.* I. p. 86–101; and especially to the chapter on the paschal controversies in Schaff's *Ch. Hist.* Vol. II. p. 209–220. This chapter of Schaff's is the clearest, and, in the opinion of the writer, by far the most satisfactory, brief statement of the whole subject which we have.

[2] Although other synods are mentioned by the *Libellus synodicus* (of the ninth century), the only ones which we have good reason for accepting are those mentioned by Eusebius in this chapter and the next; viz. one in Palestine, presided over by Narcissus, and another at Cæsarea, presided over by Theophilus, but the report is too late to be of authority); one in Pontus, under the presidency of Palmas; one in Gaul, under Irenæus; one in Osrhoëne in Mesopotamia; and one in Asia Minor, under Polycrates. Hefele (*Conciliengesch.* I. p. 101) adds one in Rome under Victor; and although Eusebius does not distinctly mention such a synod, we are undoubtedly to conclude that the epistle written by Victor was a synodical epistle, and hence Hefele is, in all probability, correct in assuming that some kind of a synod, whether municipal or provincial, took place there at this time (see note 4). From the words of Eusebius, at the close of the chapter, we may gather that still other synods than those mentioned by him were held on this subject. The date of all of these councils is commonly given as 198 A.D., but there is no particular authority for that year. Jerome's version of the *Chron.* assigns the composition of the various epistles to the fourth year of Septimius Severus (196–197); but it is clear that he is giving only an approximate date. We can say only that the synods took place sometime during Victor's episcopate. All the councils, as we learn from this chapter, except the one under Polycrates in Asia Minor, decided against the Quartodeciman practice. Athanasius however (*de Syn.* c. 5), speaks of Christians of Syria, Cilicia, and Mesopotamia as celebrating the paschal feast on the fourteenth day; and Jerome (*de vir. ill.* c. 35) says that many bishops of Asia *and of the Orient* kept up this observance. It is possible that the practice was from the beginning more widely spread than Eusebius supposed, or, what is more probable, that the words of Athanasius and Jerome refer to individual churches and bishops, whose observance of the fourteenth day was not general enough to invalidate what Eusebius says of the common consent of the whole Church, outside of Asia Minor, against the Quartodeciman practice, and that this individual observance, not being officially recognized by any synod, did not seem to him to require mention.

[3] On Theophilus and Narcissus, see the preceding chapter, notes 6 and 7.

[4] ἐπίσκοπον βίκτορα δηλοῦσα. This and the following epistles are no longer extant, nor have we any fragments of them. They seem to have disappeared, even before Jerome's time; at least, he speaks only of the memory of them as remaining to his day (see

Pontus over whom Palmas,[5] as the oldest, presided; and of the parishes in Gaul of which Irenæus was bishop, and of those in

3   Osrhoëne[6] and the cities there ; and a personal letter of Bacchylus,[7] bishop of the church at Corinth, and of a great many others, who uttered the same opinion and judgment, and cast the same vote. And that which has been given above was their unanimous decision.[8]

CHAPTER XXIV.

The Disagreement in Asia.

1   But the bishops of Asia, led by Polycrates, decided to hold to the old custom handed down to them.[1] He himself, in a letter which he addressed to Victor and the church of Rome, set forth in the following words the tradition which had come down to him :[2]

2   "We observe the exact day ; neither adding, nor taking away. For in Asia also great lights have fallen asleep, which shall rise again on the day of the Lord's coming, when he shall come with glory from heaven, and shall seek out all the saints. Among these are Philip, one of the twelve apostles, who fell asleep in Hierapolis ; and his two aged virgin daughters, and another daughter, who lived in the Holy Spirit and

3   now rests at Ephesus ; and, moreover, John, who was both a witness and a teacher, who reclined upon the bosom of the Lord, and, being a priest, wore the sacerdotal plate. And Polycarp[3] in

4   Smyrna, who was a bishop and martyr ; and Thraseas,[4] bishop and martyr from Eumenia,

who fell asleep in Smyrna.   Why need I   5 mention the bishop and martyr Sagaris[5] who fell asleep in Laodicea, or the blessed Papirius,[6] or Melito,[7] the Eunuch who lived altogether in the Holy Spirit, and who lies in Sardis, awaiting the episcopate from heaven, when he shall rise from the dead? All these observed the   6 fourteenth day of the passover according to the Gospel, deviating in no respect, but following the rule of faith.[8]   And I also, Polycrates, the least of you all, do according to the tradition of my relatives, some of whom I have closely followed. For seven of my relatives were bishops ; and I am the eighth. And my relatives always observed the day when the people[9] put away the leaven. I, therefore, brethren,   7 who have lived sixty-five years in the Lord, and have met with the brethren throughout the world, and have gone through every Holy Scripture, am not affrighted by terrifying words. For those greater than I have said 'We ought to obey God rather than man.'"[10]   He then   8 writes of all the bishops who were present with him and thought as he did.   His words are as follows :

"I could mention the bishops who were present, whom I summoned at your desire ;[11] whose names, should I write them, would constitute a great multitude. And they, beholding my littleness, gave their consent to the letter, knowing that I did not bear my gray hairs in vain, but had always governed my life by the Lord Jesus."

Thereupon Victor, who presided over the   9 church at Rome, immediately attempted to cut off from the common unity the parishes of all Asia, with the churches that agreed with them, as heterodox ; and he wrote letters and declared all the brethren there wholly excommuni-

---

chap. 22, note 6). Heinichen is certainly wrong in making this epistle an individual letter from Victor alone, for Eusebius expressly says that the epistle was from "those at Rome" (τῶν ἐπὶ 'Ρώμης), which seems to imply a council, as in the other cases. The grammatical construction naturally leads us to supply with the τῶν the word used with it in the previous sentence, συγκεκροτημένων, — "those who were assembled." Valesius, Hefele, and others are, therefore, quite justified in assuming that, according to Eusebius, a synod met at Rome, also, at this time.

[5] Palmas, bishop of Amastris, in Pontus, mentioned by Dionysius, in Bk. IV. chap. 23, above.

[6] Osrhoëne was a region of country in northwestern Mesopotamia.

[7] This epistle of Bacchylus is distinguished from the preceding ones by the fact that it is not a synodical or collective epistle, but the independent production of one man, if Eusebius' report is correct (see the preceding chapter, note 8). The epistles "of many others," mentioned in the next sentence, may have been of the same kind.

[8] Namely, against the observance of the fourteenth day.

[1] For a general account of the paschal controversy, see the preceding chapter, note 1. On Polycrates, see chap. 22, note 9.

[2] A part of this passage from Polycrates' epistle is quoted in Bk. III. chap. 31. The extract above begins with the second sentence of the fragment ("For in Asia great lights," &c.), and extends to the report of John's burial at Ephesus. For comments upon this portion of the fragment, see the notes given there.

[3] On Polycarp, see Bk. IV. chap. 14, note 5.

[4] This Thraseas, said by Polycrates to have been bishop of Eumenia (a city in the southern part of Phrygia), was mentioned also by Apollonius in his work against the Montanists (according to Eusebius, chap. 18, § 13, of this book). He is called by Polycrates a martyr, and by Eusebius, in reference to Apollonius' mention of him, "one of the martyrs of that time." There is no reason to doubt that he was a martyr, in the full sense, as Polycarp was ; but upon the more general use of the word μάρτυς as, e.g., in connection with John just above, see Bk. III. chap. 32, note 15. We know nothing more about this bishop Thraseas.

[5] On Sagaris, see above, Bk. IV. chap. 26, note 22.

[6] Polycrates does not call Papirius a bishop or a martyr, and we know nothing about him. Simeon Metaphrastes, upon whose reports little reliance can be placed, in his life of Polycarp (according to Valesius), makes Papirius a successor of Polycarp, as bishop of Smyrna.

[7] On Melito, see Bk. IV. chap. 26, note 1.

[8] A careful exegesis of the passages in John's Gospel, which are supposed by some to contradict the synoptic account, and to put Christ's death on the fourteenth day of Nisan instead of on the fifteenth, shows that John agrees with the Synoptists in putting the passover meal on the fourteenth and the death of Christ on the fifteenth (see Schaff's Ch. Hist. Vol I. p. 133 ff., and the authorities referred to by him). The Asiatic churches, in observing the fourteenth of Nisan, were commemorating the last passover feast and the death of the paschal Lamb. Their practice did not imply that they believed that Christ died on the fourteenth (as can be seen from fragments of Apolinarius' work quoted in the Chron. Paschale, and referred to above ; see, also, Schaff, Vol. II. p. 214). They were in full agreement with all four Gospels in putting his death on the fifteenth. But the paschal controversy did not hinge on the day of the month on which Christ died, — in regard to which there was no widespread disagreement, — but on the question as to whether a particular day of the week or of the month was to be celebrated.

[9] i.e. the Jews. The passover feast among the Jews took place on the evening of the fourteenth of Nisan, and was eaten with unleavened bread (Ex. xii. 6 et passim). It was on the fourteenth of Nisan, therefore, that the Jews "threw away" the leaven, and until the evening of the twenty-first, when the seven days' feast of unleavened bread closed, they used no leaven.

[10] Acts v. 29.

[11] According to this, the Asiatic Council was summoned at the request of Victor of Rome, and in all probability this was the case with all the councils referred to in the last chapter.

10 cate.[12] But this did not please all the bishops. And they besought him to consider
the things of peace, and of neighborly unity and
love. Words of theirs are extant, sharply
11 rebuking Victor. Among them was Irenæus,
who, sending letters in the name of the
brethren in Gaul over whom he presided, maintained that the mystery of the resurrection of
the Lord should be observed only on the Lord's
day. He fittingly admonishes Victor that he
should not cut off whole churches of God which
observed the tradition of an ancient custom,
and after many other words he proceeds as
follows : [13]
12   " For the controversy is not only concerning the day, but also concerning the very
manner of the fast. For some think that they
should fast one day, others two, yet others more ;
some, moreover, count their day as consist-
13 ing of forty hours day and night.[14] And this
variety in its observance has not originated
in our time ; but long before in that of our ancestors.[15] It is likely that they did not hold to
strict accuracy, and thus formed a custom for
their posterity according to their own simplicity
and peculiar mode. Yet all of these lived none
the less in peace, and we also live in peace with
one another ; and the disagreement in regard to
the fast confirms the agreement in the faith."

He adds to this the following account, 14
which I may properly insert :

" Among these were the presbyters before Soter, who presided over the church which thou now
rulest. We mean Anicetus, and Pius, and Hyginus, and Telesphorus, and Xystus. They neither
observed it [16] themselves, nor did they permit
those after them to do so. And yet though not
observing it, they were none the less at peace
with those who came to them from the parishes
in which it was observed ; although this observance was more opposed to those who did
not observe it.[17] But none were ever cast 15
out on account of this form ; but the presbyters before thee who did not observe it, sent
the eucharist to those of other parishes who
observed it.[18] And when the blessed Poly- 16
carp was at Rome [19] in the time of Anicetus,

---

[12] There has been considerable discussion as to whether Victor actually excommunicated the Asiatic churches or only threatened to do so. Socrates (*H. E.* V. 22) says directly that he excommunicated them, but many have thought that Eusebius does not say it. For my part, I cannot understand that Eusebius' words mean anything else than that he did actually cut off communion with them. The Greek reads ἀκοινωνήτους πάντας ἄρδην τοὺς ἐκεῖσε ἀνακηρύττων ἀδελφούς. This seems to me decisive.

[13] This epistle is no longer extant, but in addition to the fragments given in this chapter by Eusebius, a few other extracts from it are found in other writers; thus, in the Pseudo-Justinian *Quæstiones et responsa ad orthodoxos* occurs a quotation from Irenæus' work *On Easter* (περὶ τοῦ πάσχα), which is doubtless to be identified with this epistle to Victor (ed. Harvey, *Græc. fragm.* 7; Eng. translation in *Ante-Nicene Fathers*, I. p. 569). Maximus of Turin, also, in his *Sermo VII. de Eleemos.,* gives a brief quotation from " The epistle to Victor " (Harvey, *Græc. fragm.* 5, trans. *ibid.*). It is possible that some other unnamed fragments given by Harvey are from this epistle. From Eusebius' words we learn that Irenæus agreed with Victor as to the proper time of keeping the feast, and yet he did not agree with him in his desire to excommunicate those who followed the other practice.

[14] The punctuation of this sentence is a disputed matter. Some editors omit the semicolon after the words " yet others more," translating, " For some think that they should fast one day, others two, yet others more, and some forty; and they count the hours of the day and night together as their day." The sense is thus materially changed, but the Greek seems to necessitate rather the punctuation which I have followed in my translation, and so that punctuation is adopted by Valesius, Zimmermann, Burton, Schwegler, Laemmer, Heinichen, Closs, Crusè, and others. We should expect, moreover, that the forty hours' fast should be mentioned in this connection by Irenæus, as we learn from Tertullian that it was very common; whereas we have no other trace of the forty days' fast at so early a date (cf. the next note).

[15] The fast preceding the celebration of the paschal supper, which has grown gradually into our Lent of forty days preceding Easter, is, we are told here by Irenæus, much older than his day. It is thus carried back at least close to apostolic times, and there is no reason to think that it was not observed about as soon as the celebration of the paschal supper itself was established. Tertullian also mentions the fast, which continued, according to him (*de Jejunio,* chap. 2), during the period " in which the bridegroom was taken away," i.e. in which Jesus was under the power of death.

We learn from this passage of Irenæus' epistle that the duration of the fast varied greatly. From Socrates (*H. E.* V. 22) and Sozomen (*H. E.* VII. 19) we learn that the variation was as great in their time. Some fasted three, some six, some seven weeks, and so on. Socrates (*l.c.*) informs us that the fast, whatever its duration, was always called τεσσαρακοστή (*quadrigesima*). He does not know why this is, but says that various reasons are given by others. The time between Jesus' death and his resurrection was very early computed as forty hours in length, — from noon of Friday to four o'clock Sunday morning. This may have lain at the basis of the number forty, which was so persistently used to designate the fast, for Tertullian tells us that the fast was intended to cover the period during which Jesus was dead. It is this idea which undoubtedly underlay the fast of forty hours which Irenæus mentions. The fasts

of Moses, of Elijah, and of Jesus in the desert would also of course have great influence in determining the length of this, the most important fast of the year. Already before the end of the third century the fast had extended itself in many quarters to cover a number of weeks, and in the time of Eusebius the forty days' fast had already become a common thing (see his *de Pasch.* chap. 5), and even Origen refers to it (*Hom. in Lev.* X. 2). The present duration of the fast — forty days exclusive of Sundays — was fixed in the seventh or eighth century. Cf. Sinker's article on Lent in Smith's *Dict. of Christ. Ant.* and Krieg's article, *Feste,* in Kraus' *Encyclop. der Christ. Alterthümer,* I. p. 489.

[16] i.e. the fourteenth day.

[17] The Greek reads: καί τοι μᾶλλον ἐναντίον ἦν τὸ τηρεῖν τοῖς μὴ τηροῦσι. The meaning is, that the observance of the fourteenth day by these strangers in Rome itself, among those who did not observe that day, would be noticeable and more distasteful than the mere report that the day was observed in Asia could be. If Victor's predecessor, therefore, allowed such persons to observe that day even in Rome, how much more should he allow the Asiatics to observe it in their own land.

[18] Valesius, followed by others, interprets this sentence as meaning that the presbyters of Rome sent the eucharist to other parishes where the paschal festival was observed on the fourteenth of the month. The council of Laodicea (Can. 14) forbade the sending of the eucharist to other parishes, which shows that the custom must have been widespread before the end of the fourth century, and it is therefore quite possible that the bishops of Rome, even as early as the time of Irenæus, pursued the same practice. But in regard to the statement made here by Irenæus, it must be said that, so far as we are able to ascertain, only the churches of Asia Minor observed the fourteenth day at that early date, and it is difficult to imagine that the presbyters of Rome before Victor's time had been in the habit of sending the eucharist all the way from Rome to Asia Minor. Moreover, this is the only passage in which we have notice, before the fourth century, of the existence of the general practice condemned by the council of Laodicea. The Greek reads οἱ πρὸ σοῦ πρεσβύτεροι τοῖς ἀπὸ τῶν παροικιῶν τηροῦσιν ἔπεμπον εὐχαριστίαν. These words taken by themselves can as well, if not better, be understood of persons (whether presbyters or others is not in any case distinctly stated) who had come to Rome from other parishes, and who continued to observe the fourteenth day. This transmission of the eucharist to communicants who were kept away from the service by illness or other adequate cause was a very old custom, being mentioned by Justin Martyr in his *Apol.* I. 65. It is true that it is difficult to understand why Irenæus should speak in the present case of sending the eucharist to those persons who observed the fourteenth day, instead of merely mentioning the fact that the Roman church communed with them, In the face of the difficulties on both sides it must be admitted that neither of the interpretations mentioned can be insisted upon. On the practice of sending the eucharistic bread to persons not present at the service, or to other parishes, see the article *Eulogia,* in Smith's *Dict. of Christ. Ant.*

[19] ἐπιδημήσαντος τῇ Ῥώμῃ. Upon the significance of this phrase, see Bk. IV. chap. 11, note 19. On the date of Polycarp's visit to Rome, see *ibid.,* chap. 14, note 2. In his *Adv. Hær.,* where he mentions this visit (as quoted in chap. 14), Irenæus does

and they disagreed a little about certain other things, they immediately made peace with one another, not caring to quarrel over this matter. For neither could Anicetus persuade Polycarp not to observe what he had always observed with John the disciple of our Lord, and the other apostles with whom he had associated ; neither could Polycarp persuade Anicetus to observe it, as he said that he ought to follow the customs of the presbyters that had preceded him.

17   But though matters were in this shape, they communed together, and Anicetus conceded the administration of the eucharist in the church to Polycarp, manifestly as a mark of respect.[20]   And they parted from each other in peace, both those who observed, and those who did not, maintaining the peace of the whole church."

18   Thus Irenæus, who truly was well named,[21] became a peacemaker in this matter, exhorting and negotiating in this way in behalf of the peace of the churches. And he conferred by letter about this mooted question, not only with Victor, but also with most of the other rulers of the churches.[22]

CHAPTER XXV.

How All came to an Agreement respecting the Passover.

THOSE in Palestine whom we have recently mentioned, Narcissus and Theophilus,[1] and with them Cassius,[2] bishop of the church of Tyre, and Clarus of the church of Ptolemais, and those who met with them,[3] having stated many things respecting the tradition concerning the passover which had come to them in succession from the apostles, at the close of their writing add these words : [4]

"Endeavor to send copies of our letter to every church, that we may not furnish occasion to those who easily deceive their souls. We show you indeed that also in Alexandria they keep it on the same day that we do. For letters are carried from us to them and from them to us, so that in the same manner and at the same time we keep the sacred day."[5]

CHAPTER XXVI.

The Elegant Works of Irenæus which have come down to us.

BESIDES the works and letters of Irenæus which we have mentioned,[1] a certain book of his On Knowledge, written against the Greeks,[2] very concise and remarkably forcible, is extant ; and another, which he dedicated to a brother Marcian, In Demonstration of the Apostolic Preaching ; [3] and a volume containing various Dissertations,[4] in which he mentions the Epistle to the Hebrews and the so-called Wisdom of Solomon, making

---

not speak of the affair of the passover which he refers to here. The omission, however, has no significance, as he is discussing Gnosticism there, and refers to Polycarp's visit to Rome only because his attitude toward Marcion was revealed in connection with it.

[20] The meaning of this passage has been disputed. The Greek reads: καὶ ἐν τῇ ἐκκλησίᾳ παρεχώρησεν ὁ Ἀνίκητος τὴν εὐχαριστίαν τῷ Πολυκάρπῳ κατ᾽ ἐντροπὴν δηλονότι. Valesius understands Irenæus' meaning to be that Anicetus invited Polycarp to administer the eucharist in Rome ; and this is the common interpretation of the passage. Heinichen objects, however, that παρεχώρησεν τὴν εὐχαριστίαν cannot refer to the administration of the sacrament, and hence concludes that Irenæus means simply to say that Anicetus permitted Polycarp to partake of the eucharist in his church, thereby proclaiming publicly their fraternal fellowship, in spite of their differences on the paschal question. The common interpretation, however, seems to the writer better than Heinichen's ; for if the latter be adopted, the sentence in question says no more than the one which precedes it, — "they communed with each other" (ἐκοινώνησαν ἑαυτοῖς). And moreover, as Valesius remarks, Anicetus would in that case have shown Polycarp no more honor than any other Christian pilgrim who might happen to be in Rome. Irenæus seems to intend to say that Anicetus showed Polycarp especial honor, and that in spite of their difference of opinion on the paschal question. But simply to have allowed Polycarp to partake of the eucharist in the church would certainly have been no honor, and, on the other hand, not to invite him to assist in the administration of the sacrament might have seemed a sign of disrespect, and have emphasized their differences. The old interpretation, therefore, must be followed, and so far as the Greek is concerned, there is no difficulty about the construction. In the παρεχώρησεν resides the idea of "yielding," "giving place to" ; and so Anicetus yielded to Polycarp the eucharist, or gave place to him in the matter of the eucharist. This in fact brings out the force of the παρεχώρησεν better than Heinichen's interpretation.

[21] The Greek form of the name is Εἰρηναῖος, from εἰρήνη, which means "peace."

[22] None of these epistles are extant ; it is possible that some of the fragments commonly assigned to Irenæus' epistle to Victor may belong to one or more of them (see the *Dict. of Christ. Biog.* III. p. 265). We do not know to what bishops or churches these epistles were sent. Jerome does not mention them.

[1] In chaps. 22 and 23. For particulars in regard to them, see chap. 22, notes 6 and 7.

[2] Cassius and Clarus are otherwise unknown men.

[3] i.e. in the Palestinian council mentioned in chap. 23. Upon this and the other councils held at the same period, see chap. 23, note 2.

[4] This fragment is given, with annotations, by Routh, *Rel. Sac.* II. p. 3 sq. English translation in the *Ante-Nicene Fathers,* VIII. p. 774.

[5] These epistles, like all the rest written at this time on the paschal question, are now lost (see chap. 23, note 4).

[1] For a general summary of the works of Irenæus mentioned by Eusebius, see Bk. IV. chap. 21, note 9.

[2] πρὸς Ἕλληνας λόγος . . . περὶ ἐπιστήμης. Jerome (*de vir. ill.* 35) makes two works out of this : one *Against the Gentiles,* and another *On Knowledge (et contra Gentes volumen breve, et de disciplina aliud).* Harvey (I. p. clxvi.) states that one of the Syriac fragments of Irenæus' works mentions the work of Eusebius *On Knowledge,* and specifies that it was directed against the Valentinians. In that case it would be necessary to make two separate works, as Jerome does, and so Harvey thinks that the text of Eusebius must be amended by the insertion of an ἄλλος τε. Unfortunately, Harvey did not name the Syriac fragment which contains the statement referred to, and it is not to be found among those collected in his edition (Venables, in Smith and Wace, states that he could find no such fragment, and I have also searched in vain for it). Evidently some blunder has been committed, and it looks as if Harvey's statement were unverifiable. Meanwhile, Jerome's testimony alone is certainly not enough to warrant an emendation of the text in opposition to all the MSS. and versions. We must therefore conclude, with our present light, that the treatise περὶ ἐπιστήμης was directed against the Greeks, as Eusebius says. The work has entirely perished, with the possible exception of a single brief fragment (the first of the Pfaffian fragments ; *Gr. Frag.* XXXV. in Harvey's edition), which Harvey refers to it.

[3] εἰς ἐπίδειξιν τοῦ ἀποστολικοῦ κηρύγματος. This work, too, has perished, though possibly a few of the fragments published by Harvey are to be referred to it (see Harvey, I. p. clxvii.). Harvey conjectures that the work discussed the articles of the early Rule of faith, which is quite possible. Of the "brother Marcian" to whom it was addressed, we know nothing.

[4] βιβλίον τι διαλέξεων διαφόρων. This work (no longer extant) was probably, as Harvey remarks, "a collection of sermons and expositions of various texts and passages of Scripture." To it are undoubtedly to be referred a great many of the fragments in which passages of Scripture are discussed (see Harvey, I. p. clxvii.).

quotations from them. These are the works of Irenæus which have come to our knowledge.

Commodus having ended his reign after thirteen years, Severus became emperor in less than six months after his death, Pertinax having reigned during the intervening time.[5]

CHAPTER XXVII.

The Works of Others that flourished at that Time.

NUMEROUS memorials of the faithful zeal of the ancient ecclesiastical men of that time are still preserved by many. Of these we would note particularly the writings of Heraclitus[1] On the Apostle, and those of Maximus on the question so much discussed among heretics, the Origin of Evil, and on the Creation of Matter.[2] Also those of Candidus on the Hexæmeron,[3] and

of Apion[4] on the same subject; likewise of Sextus[5] on the Resurrection, and another treatise of Arabianus,[6] and writings of a multitude of others, in regard to whom, because we have no data, it is impossible to state in our work when they lived, or to give any account of their history.[7] And works of many others have come

---

[5] Commodus was strangled on the 31st of December, 192, and Pertinax, who immediately succeeded him, was murdered, on March 28, 193, by the Prætorian guard, which then sold the imperial power to Didius Julianus, who, at the approach of Septimius Severus, who had been proclaimed emperor by the Pannonian legions, was declared a public enemy by the Senate, and beheaded after a reign of only sixty-six days.

[1] This Heraclitus is mentioned only by Eusebius and by Jerome (*de vir. ill.* chap. 46), who, in his description of him and in the five following chapters (on Maximus, Candidus, Apion, Sextus, and Arabianus), does nothing more than repeat the words of Eusebius in this chapter. The work which Eusebius calls τὰ Ἡρακλείτου εἰς τὸν ἀπόστολον is called by Jerome *in apostolum Commentarios*. The word ἀπόστολος was quite commonly used among the Fathers to denote the epistles of Paul (see Suicer's *Thesaurus*), and hence Eusebius seems here to refer to commentaries (the plural article τὰ is used) on the Pauline epistles. These commentaries are no longer extant, and we know nothing of their nature.

[2] The Greek reads καὶ τὰ Μαξίμου περὶ τοῦ πολυθρυλήτου παρὰ τοῖς αἱρεσιώταις ζητήματος, τοῦ πόθεν ἡ κακία, καὶ περὶ τοῦ γενητὴν ὑπάρχειν τὴν ὕλην. The plural τὰ (*sc.* ὑπομνήματα) might lead us to suppose Eusebius refers here to separate works, were it not for the fact that in his *Præp. Evang.* VII. 22 is found a long extract from a work of Maximus *On Matter* (περὶ τῆς ὕλης) in which the subject of the origin of evil is discussed in connection with the origin and nature of matter. In that age one could hardly discuss the origin of evil without at the same time discussing matter, to which the origin of evil was referred by the great majority of the ancients. We are to suppose, then, that the work of Maximus bore the double title given by Eusebius in this chapter. Jerome in his *de vir. ill.* chap. 47, says: *Maximus . . . famosam quæstionem insigni volumine ventilavit, unde malum, et quod materia a Deo facta sit.* As remarked above, a long extract, which has been taken from this work, is given by Eusebius in his *Præp. Evang.* It appears from this extract that the work was written in the form of a dialogue between three speakers, — two inquirers, and one orthodox Christian. The same fragment of Maximus' work is found also in the twenty-fourth chapter of the *Philocalia* of Origen, and is said by the editors, Gregory and Basil, to have been copied by them from Eusebius' work. The *Dialogue on Free Will*, ascribed to Methodius (of the early part of the fourth century), made large use of this work of Maximus; and the same is to be said of the Pseudo-Origenistic *Dialogue against the Marcionites*, though according to Routh (*Rel. Sac.* II. p. 79) the latter drew his quotations from Methodius and not directly from Maximus. The work of Methodius undoubtedly contains much more of Maximus' work than is given here by Eusebius; but it is difficult to ascertain what is his own and what belongs to Maximus, and Routh, in publishing the fragments of Maximus' work (*ibid.* p. 87–107), gives only the extract quoted by Eusebius. In his *Præp. Evang.* Eusebius speaks of Maximus as τῆς χριστοῦ διατριβῆς οὐκ ἄσημος ἀνήρ, but we know no more about him than has been already indicated. Gallandius suggests that he may be identical with Maximus, the twenty-sixth bishop of Jerusalem (see above, chap. 12), who it is quite probable, lived about this time (cf. Eusebius' *Chron.*, year of Abr. 2202). But Eusebius, neither in this chapter nor in his *Præp. Evang.*, calls Maximus a bishop, and it seems proper to conclude that he at least did not know that he was a bishop; and hence Gallandius' conjecture, which rests only upon agreement in a very common name, must be pronounced quite baseless.

[3] εἰς τὴν ἑξαήμερον (*sc.* κοσμοποιΐαν or δημιουργίαν). The adjective ἑξαήμερος was commonly used in this way, with the feminine

article, implying a noun understood, and referring to the six days' work of creation (see Suicer's *Thesaurus*). The subject was quite a favorite one with the Fathers. Hippolytus, Basil, Gregory of Nyssa, Ambrose, and others wrote upon it, as did also the Apion mentioned in the next sentence. The work of Candidus is no longer extant, nor do we know anything more about it and its author than Eusebius tells us here. The plural τὰ occurs again, and Jerome supplies *tractatus*. Whether the word fitly describes the work, or works, or whether they were rather of the nature of homilies, like Basil's, we do not know. Sophronius, in translating Jerome, puts ὁμιλίας for *tractatus*, but this of course is of no authority.

[4] Apion's work is mentioned also by Jerome (*de vir. ill.* chap. 4), but nothing is added to the statement of Eusebius. We know nothing more about him or his work.

[5] Sextus also is mentioned by Jerome, in his *de vir. ill.* chap. 50, but we know nothing about him or his work, except what Eusebius tells us here.

[6] Nothing more is known of this Arabianus, and Eusebius does not even tell us the name of his work. His silence is difficult to explain. We can hardly imagine that the title was intentionally omitted; for had there been a reason for such a course, there must have been as much reason for omitting the writer's name also. It does not seem probable that he had never known the title of the book, for he was not in the habit of mentioning works which he had not seen, except with the formula λόγος ἔχει, or something of the kind, to indicate that he makes his statement only on the authority of others. It is possible that he had seen this, with the other works mentioned (perhaps all bound in one volume), at sometime in the past, but that the title of Arabianus' work had escaped him, and hence he simply mentioned the work along with the others, without considering the title a matter of great importance. He speaks of but a single work, — ἄλλη τις ὑπόθεσις, — but Jerome (chap. 51) mentions *quædam opuscula ad christianum dogma pertinentia*. His description is not specific enough to lead us to think that he had personal knowledge of Arabianus' writings. It must rather be concluded that he allowed himself some license, and that, not satisfied to speak of a writer without naming his works, and, at the same time, knowing nothing definite about him, he simply calls them, in the most general terms, *ad christianum dogma pertinentia*; for if they were Christian works, he was pretty safe in concluding that they had to do, in some way at least, with Christian doctrine. The substitution of the plural for the singular (*quædam opuscula* for τις ὑπόθεσις) can hardly have been an accident. It is, perhaps, safe to say, knowing Jerome's methods, that he permitted himself to make the change in order to conceal his own ignorance of the writings of Arabianus; for to mention a single book, and say no more about it than that it had to do with Christian doctrine, would be a betrayal of entire ignorance in regard to it; but to sum up a number of writings under the general head *ad christianum dogma pertinentia*, instead of giving all the titles in detail, would be, of course, quite consistent with an exact acquaintance with all of them. If our supposition be correct, we have simply another instance of Jerome's common sin, and an instance which, in this case, reveals a sharp contrast between his character and that of Eusebius, who never hesitated to confess his ignorance.

[7] Eusebius does not imply, in this sentence, that he is not acquainted with these works to which he refers. As the words are commonly translated, we might imagine that he was not familiar with them, for all the translators make him speak of not being able to draw any extracts from them for his own history. Thus Valesius: *nec narrationem ullam libris nostris intexere possumus;* Stroth: "noch etwas darauserzählen kann"; Closs: "noch etwas daraus anführen können"; Crusè: "we can neither insert the time nor any extracts in our History." The Greek of the whole sentence reads, ὧν διὰ τὸ μηδεμίαν ἔχειν ἀφορμὴν οὐχ οἷόν τε οὔτε τοὺς χρόνους παραδοῦναι γραφῇ, οὐθ᾿ ἱστορίας μνήμην ὑποσημήνασθαι, which seems to mean simply that their works contain no information which enables him to give the dates of the authors, or to recount anything about their lives; that is, they contain no personal allusions. This is quite different from saying that he was not acquainted with the works; in fact, had he not been quite familiar with them, he could not have made such a broad statement. He seems to have searched them for personal notices, and to have failed in the search. Whether these words of Eusebius apply to all the works already mentioned, or only to the μυρίων ἄλλων just referred to, cannot be certainly determined. The latter seems most natural; but even if the reference be only to those last mentioned, there is every reason to think that the words are just as true of the writings of Heraclitus, Maximus, and the others, for he tells us nothing about their lives, nor the time in which they lived, but introduces them in the most general terms, as "ancient ecclesiastical men." There seems, therefore, no good reason for connecting these writers with the reign of Commodus, rather than with any other reign of the late second or of the third century.

down to us whose names we are unable to give, orthodox and ecclesiastical, as their interpretations of the Divine Scriptures show, but unknown to us, because their names are not stated in their writings.[8]

CHAPTER XXVIII.

Those who first advanced the Heresy of Artemon; their Manner of Life, and how they dared to corrupt the Sacred Scriptures.

1   IN a laborious work by one of these writers against the heresy of Artemon,[1]

It must be noticed that Eusebius does not say that " these men lived at this time"; he simply mentions them in this connection because it is a convenient place, and perhaps because there were indications which led him to think they could not have lived early in the second or late in the third century. It is quite possible, as suggested in the previous note, that the works of the writers whose names are mentioned in this chapter were collected in a single volume, and that thus Eusebius was led to class them all together, although the subjects of their works were by no means the same, and their dates may have been widely different.

[8] Eusebius mentioned first those works whose authors' names were known to him, but now adds that he is acquainted with many other writings which bear the name of no author. He claims, however, that the works testify to their authors' orthodoxy, and he seems to imply, by this statement, that he has convinced himself of their orthodoxy by a personal examination of them.

[1] This anonymous work against the heresy of Artemon is no longer extant, and the only fragments of it which we have are those preserved by Eusebius in this chapter. Theodoret (*Hær. Fab.* II. 5) mentions the work, and says that it was directed against the heresies of Theodotus and Artemon, and that it bore the name *Little Labyrinth*. It is plain, from the fragments which Eusebius gives, that it was written in Rome some little time before the middle of the third century, probably not far from 230 or 240 A.D. The work is commonly ascribed to Hippolytus, in favor of which may be urged both the time and the place of its composition as well as some internal resemblance between it and the *Philosophumena*. On the other hand, Photius (*Cod.* 48) ascribes to Caius of Rome a work against Artemon, which may well be identical with the anonymous work quoted in the present chapter. It is therefore contended by some (e.g. by Salmon) that Caius was the author of the work. It must be noted, however, that in the same connection Photius ascribes another work to Caius which we know to have been written by Hippolytus, and hence his testimony is rather in favor of Hippolytus than Caius as the author of the work. On the other hand, several objections have been urged by Salmon against the Hippolytine authorship, which, while not decisive, yet make it extremely doubtful. In view of these facts, we must conclude that it is possible, but very improbable, that Hippolytus wrote the work; that it is not impossible, though we are quite without evidence for the supposition, that Caius wrote it; that it is more likely that a work which even to Eusebius was anonymous, was written by an unknown man, who must remain unknown to us also. The extant fragments of the work are given, with notes, by Routh in his *Rel. Sac.*, and an English translation in the *Ante-Nicene Fathers*, Vol. V. p. 601 sq., among the works of Caius. Although the work is said by Eusebius to have been directed against the heresy of Artemon, he has preserved only extracts relating to the Theodoti and their heresy. They are described also by Hippolytus, both in his lost *Syntagma* (as we can learn from Pseudo-Tertullian, Epiphanius, and Philaster) and in his *Philosophumena* (VII. 23–24, and X. 19). Other ancient writers that mention him know only what our anonymous author or Hippolytus reports. It seems that the older Theodotus, a native of Byzantium, came to Rome in the time of Eleutherus or Victor, and taught a species of adoptionism, which reminds us somewhat of the Asia Minor Alogi, in whose circle he may have been trained. Hippolytus informs us that he was orthodox in his theology and cosmology, but that he was heretical in his Christology. He did not deny Christ's birth from a virgin (as the Ebionites had done), but he did deny his divinity, teaching that he was a mere man (ψιλὸς ἄνθρωπος), upon whom the Holy Spirit descended at the time of his baptism, in consequence of which he became the Christ, received power to fulfill his special mission, and by his righteousness was raised above all other men. The descent of the Holy Spirit, however, although raising him to a very exalted position, did not make him divine; some of Theodotus' followers denying that he ever acquired divinity, others believing that he acquired it by his resurrection. Theodotus was excommunicated by Victor on account of his heretical Christology, but gained a number of followers, and after his excommunication founded a schismatical sect, which had a bishop Natalius, to whom a regular salary was paid (see below, § 10), and which continued under the leadership of another Theodotus, a banker, and a certain Asclepiodotus,

---

which Paul of Samosata[2] attempted to revive again in our day, there is an account appropriate to the history which we are now examining.

For he criticises, as a late innovation, the 2 above-mentioned heresy which teaches that the Saviour was a mere man, because they were attempting to magnify it as ancient.[3] Having given in his work many other arguments in refutation of their blasphemous falsehood, he adds the following words:

"For they say that all the early teachers 3 and the apostles received and taught what they now declare, and that the truth of the Gospel was preserved until the times of Victor, who was the thirteenth bishop of Rome from Peter,[4] but that from his successor, Zephyrinus,[5] the truth had been corrupted. And what 4 they say might be plausible, if first of all

---

both of them disciples of the first Theodotus, during the episcopate of Zephyrinus, but seems soon to have disappeared, and to have exerted comparatively little influence during its brief existence. Theodotus, the banker, appears to have agreed substantially with the older Theodotus, but to have indulged himself in speculations concerning Melchizedek, pronouncing him to be a heavenly power still higher than Christ. Epiphanius makes the second Theodotus the founder of a second party, and gives his school the name of Melchizedekians, which appears in later works on heresy, but there is no reason to suppose that there were two separate parties.

A few years later another attempt was made in Rome to revive the old adoptionist Christology (essentially the same as that represented by Hermas early in the second century), by a certain Artemon, against whom the *Little Labyrinth*, quoted in this chapter, was directed. It is common to connect Artemon and his followers with the Theodotians; but, as Harnack remarks, it is plain that they did not look upon themselves as the followers of the Theodoti (see below, note 15). We cannot tell, however, in what respect their Christology differed from that of the latter, for we know very little about them. They at any rate agreed with the Theodotians in denying the divinity of Christ. From the epistle of the synod of Antioch (quoted below, in Bk. VII. chap. 30) we learn that Artemon was still living in the year 268, or thereabouts. He seems, however, to have accomplished little in Rome, and to have dropped into comparative obscurity some time before this; at least, we hear nothing of him during all these years. In the controversy with Paul of Samosata he was called the father of the latter (see below, Bk. VII. chap. 30, §   ), and thus acquired considerable celebrity in the East, where his name became permanently connected with that of Paul as one of the leading heretics. Whether Paul really learned his Christology from Artemon we do not know, but that it closely resembled that of the latter there can be no doubt. He really reproduced the old adoptionist Christology of Hermas (as both the Theodotians and Artemon had done), but modified it under the influence partly of Origen's teachings, partly of the Aristotelian method. For further particulars in regard to the Theodoti and Artemon, see the remaining notes on this chapter. For an admirable discussion of the whole subject, see Harnack's *Dogmengeschichte*, I. p. 573 sq. On the *Little Labyrinth*, see especially the *Dict. of Christian Biog.* III. p. 98.

[2] On Paul of Samosata, see below, Bk. VII. chap. 27, note 4.

[3] The Artemonites were certainly correct in maintaining that the adoptionism which they held was, at least in its essential principles, an ancient thing, and their opponents were wrong in trying to deny it. It is the Christology which Hermas represents, and early in the second century it was undoubtedly a widespread popular belief. No one thought of questioning the orthodoxy of Hermas. The Christology of the Theodotians and of Artemon was an innovation, however, in so far as it attempted to formulate in scientific terms and to treat philosophically what had hitherto been only a popular belief. So soon as the logical conclusions were drawn, and its consequences to the divinity of the Son were perceived, it began to be felt as heresy, but not until then.

[4] On Victor, see above, chap. 22, note 1. Victor is the thirteenth bishop if Cletus and Anencletus be reckoned as one, otherwise the fourteenth. This is used by Salmon as an argument against the Hippolytine authorship of the *Little Labyrinth*, for Hippolytus reckoned Cletus and Anencletus as two bishops, and therefore made Victor the fourteenth (see above, Bk. III. chap. 13, note 3).

[5] The dates of Zephyrinus' episcopate are to be gained by reckoning backward from that of Callistus, which is shown in Bk. VI. chap. 21, note 3, to have begun in the year 217. A comparison of the various sources shows that Zephyrinus was bishop eighteen or nineteen years, which brings us back to the year 198 or 199 as the date of his accession. Eusebius says "about the ninth year of the reign

the Divine Scriptures did not contradict them. And there are writings of certain brethren older than the times of Victor, which they wrote in behalf of the truth against the heathen, and against the heresies which existed in their day. I refer to Justin[6] and Miltiades[7] and Tatian[8] and Clement[9] and many others, in all of whose 5 works Christ is spoken of as God.[10] For who does not know the works of Irenæus[11] and of Melito[12] and of others which teach that Christ is God and man?[13] And how many psalms and hymns,[14] written by the faithful brethren from the beginning, celebrate Christ the Word of God, speaking of him as 6 Divine. How then since the opinion held by the Church has been preached for so many years, can its preaching have been delayed as they affirm, until the times of Victor? And

how is it that they are not ashamed to speak thus falsely of Victor, knowing well that he cut off from communion Theodotus, the cobbler,[15] the leader and father of this God-denying apostasy, and the first to declare that Christ is mere man? For if Victor agreed with their opinions, as their slander affirms, how came he to cast out Theodotus, the inventor of this heresy?"

So much in regard to Victor. His bish- 7 opric lasted ten years, and Zephyrinus was appointed his successor about the ninth year of the reign of Severus.[16] The author of the above-mentioned book, concerning the founder of this heresy, narrates another event which occurred in the time of Zephyrinus, using these words:

"I will remind many of the brethren of 8 a fact which took place in our time, which, had it happened in Sodom, might, I think, have proved a warning to them. There was a certain confessor, Natalius,[17] not long ago, but in our own day. This man was deceived at 9 one time by Asclepiodotus[18] and another Theodotus,[19] a money-changer. Both of them were disciples of Theodotus, the cobbler, who, as I have said, was the first person excommunicated by Victor, bishop at that time, on account of this sentiment, or rather senselessness.[20] Natalius was persuaded by them to allow 10 himself to be chosen bishop of this heresy with a salary, to be paid by them, of one hundred and fifty denarii a month.[21] When 11 he had thus connected himself with them, he was warned oftentimes by the Lord through visions. For the compassionate God and our Lord Jesus Christ was not willing that a witness of his own sufferings, being cast out of the Church, should perish. But as he paid little 12 regard to the visions, because he was en-

---

of Severus," which according to the correct reckoning would be the year 201, but according to his erroneous reckoning of the dates of the emperors' reigns (see the note already referred to) gives the year 200, so that the agreement is reasonably close (see Lipsius' *Chron. der röm. Bischöfe*, p. 172 sq., and see above, Bk. V. chap. 22, note 1). In Bk. IX. of his great work Hippolytus gives quite an account of Zephyrinus and his successor, Callistus. The former is described as ignorant and illiterate, a taker of bribes, an uninformed and shamefully corrupt man, &c. How much of this is true and how much is due to prejudice, we cannot tell. But it seems at least to be a fact that Zephyrinus was completely under the influence of Callistus, as Hippolytus states. We learn from the latter that Zephyrinus at least countenanced the heresy of Patripassianism (at the opposite extreme from that of the Theodotians and Artemon), if he did not directly teach it.

[6] On Justin Martyr, see Bk. IV. chap. 11, note 20.
[7] On Miltiades, see above, chap. 17, note 1.
[8] On Tatian, see Bk. III. chap. 29. The fact that Tatian is here spoken of with respect is urged by Salmon as an argument against the Hippolytine authorship of this work, for Hippolytus devotes two chapters of his *Philosophumena* (VIII. 9, X. 14) to the heresy of Tatian.
[9] On Clement of Alexandria, see above, chap. 11, note 1.
[10] θεολογεῖται ὁ χριστός. Our author is quite correct in making this statement. The apologists are agreed in their acceptance of the Logos Christology of which they are the earliest patristic exponents, and in the time of Clement of Alexandria it had become, as yet in an undeveloped form, the commonly accepted doctrine of the orthodox Church.
[11] On Irenæus, see Bk. IV. chap. 21, note 9.
[12] On Melito, see Bk. IV. chap. 26, note 1.
[13] Irenæus' utterances on this subject were epoch-making in the history of doctrine. No one before him had emphasized so energetically and brought out so clearly the God-manhood of Christ. His great significance in Christology is the emphasis which he laid upon the unity of God and man in Christ, — a unity in which the integrity both of the divine and of the human was preserved. Our author is also doubtless correct in saying that Melito called Christ God and man. If the two fragments from the *Discourse on the Soul and Body*, and from the *Discourse on the Cross* (printed from the Syriac by Cureton, in his *Spic. Syr.* p. 52 sq.), be genuine, as is quite probable (see above, Bk. IV. chap. 26, note 1), we have clear indications that Melito taught both the humanity and the deity of Christ ("when He was become incarnate through the womb of the Virgin, and was born man." "Inasmuch as He was man, He needed food; still, inasmuch as He was God, He ceased not to feed the universe").
[14] This passage is sometimes interpreted as indicating that hymns written by the Christians themselves were sung in the church of Rome at this time. But this is by no means implied. So far as we are able to gather from our sources, nothing, except the Psalms and New Testament hymns (such as the "Gloria in Excelsis," the "Magnificat," the "Nunc Dimittis," &c.), was as a rule, sung in public worship before the fourth century (the practice which had sprung up in the church of Antioch seems to have been exceptional; see Kraus, p. 673). Before the end of that century, however, the practice of singing other hymns in the service of the Church had become common, both in the East and West. On the other hand, the private use of hymns among the Christians began very early. We need refer here only to Pliny's epistle to Trajan (translated above, in Bk. III. chap. 33, note 1); Clement of Alexandria, *Strom.* VII. 7; Tertullian, *ad Uxor.* II. 8; Origen, *Contra Cels.* VIII. 67; the epistle of Dionysius quoted below, in Bk. VII. chap. 24, &c. Compare the article *Hymnen* in Kraus' *Real-Encyclopädie der Christl. Alterthümer*, and the article *Hymns* in Smith and Cheetham's *Dict. of Christ. Antiquities*.

[15] τὸν σκυτέα: "cobbler," or "worker in leather." On Theodotus, see above, note 1. As Harnack remarks, the Artemonites must have known that Victor had excommunicated Theodotus, and therefore, if they regarded themselves as his followers, it would have been impossible to claim that all the Roman bishops, including Victor, held their opinions. When to this is added the apparent effort of our author to identify the Artemonites with the Theodotians, it becomes clear that they must themselves have denied their connection with them, though in what points they differed with them, we do not know (see above, note 1; and cf. Harnack's *Dogmengesch.* I. p. 583).   [16] See above, note 5.
[17] Of Natalius, we know only what is told us in this passage. The suggestion of Valesius that he might be identified with Cæcilius Natalis, the heathen who is represented as converted by Octavius, in the *Octavius* of Minucius Felix, is quite baseless.
[18] Ἀσκληπιοδότου, according to all the MSS. except one, which reads Ἀσκληπιάδου, and with which Nicephorus and Theodoret agree. He is undoubtedly the same man that is referred to in § 17, below, where all the MSS. unite in reading Ἀσκληπιάδου. Of this man we know only what is told us in this chapter. Theodoret (*Hær. Fab.* II. 5) mentions him, but adds nothing new, while Hippolytus in his *Philosophumena*, and apparently in his lost *Syntagma*, passes him by without notice.
[19] On this second Theodotus, a money-changer or banker (τραπεζίτης), who is distinguished from the first Theodotus by both our sources (Hippolytus and the *Little Labyrinth* quoted here), see above, note 1.
[20] The Greek contains a play of words at this point: ἐπὶ ταύτῃ τῇ φρονήσει, μᾶλλον δὲ ἀφροσύνῃ.
[21] This is the earliest instance we have of a salaried clergyman. The practice of paying salaries was followed also by the Montanists, and brought great reproach upon them (see above, chap. 18, note 8). A Roman denarius was equal to about seventeen cents, so that Natalius' monthly salary was a little over twenty-five dollars.

snared by the first position among them and by that shameful covetousness which destroys a great many, he was scourged by holy angels, and punished severely through the entire night.[22] Thereupon having risen in the morning, he put on sackcloth and covered himself with ashes, and with great haste and tears he fell down before Zephyrinus, the bishop, rolling at the feet not only of the clergy, but also of the laity; and he moved with his tears the compassionate Church of the merciful Christ. And though he used much supplication, and showed the welts of the stripes which he had received, yet scarcely was he taken back into communion."

13   We will add from the same writer some other extracts concerning them, which run as follows:[23]

"They have treated the Divine Scriptures recklessly and without fear. They have set aside the rule of ancient faith; and Christ they have not known. They do not endeavor to learn what the Divine Scriptures declare, but strive laboriously after any form of syllogism which may be devised to sustain their impiety. And if any one brings before them a passage of Divine Scripture, they see whether a conjunctive or disjunctive form of syllogism can be

14   made from it. And as being of the earth and speaking of the earth, and as ignorant of him who cometh from above, they forsake the holy writings of God to devote themselves to geometry.[24]   Euclid is laboriously measured[25] by some of them; and Aristotle and Theophrastus are admired; and Galen, perhaps, by

15   some is even worshiped. But that those

who use the arts of unbelievers for their heretical opinions and adulterate the simple faith of the Divine Scriptures by the craft of the godless, are far from the faith, what need is there to say? Therefore they have laid their hands boldly upon the Divine Scriptures, alleging that they have corrected them.   That   16 I am not speaking falsely of them in this matter, whoever wishes may learn. For if any one will collect their respective copies, and compare them one with another, he will find that they differ greatly. Those of As-   17 clepiades,[26] for example, do not agree with those of Theodotus. And many of these can be obtained, because their disciples have assiduously written the corrections, as they call them, that is the corruptions,[27] of each of them. Again, those of Hermophilus[28] do not agree with these, and those of Apollonides[29] are not consistent with themselves. For you can compare those prepared by them at an earlier date with those which they corrupted later, and you will find them widely different. But   18 how daring this offense is, it is not likely that they themselves are ignorant. For either they do not believe that the Divine Scriptures were spoken by the Holy Spirit, and thus are unbelievers, or else they think themselves wiser than the Holy Spirit, and in that case what else are they than demoniacs? For they cannot deny the commission of the crime, since the copies have been written by their own hands. For they did not receive such Scriptures from their instructors, nor can they produce any copies from which they were transcribed. But some of them have not thought it   19 worth while to corrupt them, but simply deny the law and the prophets,[30] and thus through their lawless and impious teaching under pretense of grace, have sunk to the lowest depths of perdition."

Let this suffice for these things.

---

[22] It is not necessary to doubt the truth of this report, if we substitute " muscular Christians " for " holy angels." As Stroth dryly remarks: "Eben kein löblich Geschäft für die heiligen Engel; es werden aber ohne zweifel Engel mit guten starken Knochen und Nerven gewesen sein."

[23] The information which is given us here in regard to the methods of the Theodotians is very interesting. What is said in regard to their philosophical principles makes it evident that they used the grammatical and critical mode of exegesis as opposed to the prevalent allegorical mode. Nothing could seem more irreverent and irreligious to the Church of that age than such a method of interpretation, the method which we now recognize as the only true one. They were, moreover, textual critics. They may have been rash in their methods, but it is not necessary to suppose them dishonest in their purposes. They seem to have looked upon the Scriptures as inspired as truly as their opponents did, but they believed that radical criticism was needed if the true reading of the originals was to be reached, while their opponents were shocked at anything of the kind. That textual criticism was necessary, even at that early day, is clear enough from the words of Irenæus (quoted in chap. 20, above), and from the words of Dionysius (quoted in Bk. IV. chap. 23), as well as from many other sources. Finally, these men seem to have offended their opponents by the use of dialectical methods in their treatment of theology. This is very significant at that early date. It is indeed the earliest instance known to us of that method which seemed entirely irreligious to the author of the *Little Labyrinth*, but which less than a century later prevailed in the Antiochian school, and for a large part of the Middle Ages ruled the whole Church.

[24] The author makes a play here upon the word *earth*, which cannot be reproduced in a translation. γεωμετρίαν (literally, " *earth*-measure ") ἐπιτηδεύουσιν, ὡσὰν ἐκ τῆς γῆς ὄντες καὶ ἐκ τῆς γῆς λαλοῦντες.

[25] Ἐυκλείδης ... γεωμετρεῖται: literally, *Euclid is geometrized.*

[26] All the MSS. read Ἀσκληπιάδου, which is adopted by most of the editors. Rufinus and Nicephorus, however, followed by a few editors, among them Heinichen, read Ἀσκληπιοδότου (see above, note 18).

[27] κατωρθωμένα, τουτέστιν ἠφανισμένα.

[28] Of this Hermophilus we know nothing more.

[29] Ἀπολλωνίδου, which is the reading of one ancient MS., of Rufinus, Theodoret, and Nicephorus, and which is adopted by Stroth, Burton, Heinichen, and Closs. The majority of the MSS. read Ἀπολλωνίου, while a few read Ἀπολλωνιάδου.

[30] These persons can hardly have rejected the Law and the Prophets utterly,—at least, no hint is given us that they maintained a fundamental difference between the God of the Old and the God of the New Testament, as Marcion did,—nor would such wholesale rejection be natural for critics such as they were. It is more likely that they simply, as many of the Gnostics did, emphasized the merely relative authority of the Old Testament, and that they applied historical criticism to it, distinguishing between its various parts in the matter of authority. Such action is just what we should expect from members of a critical school like that of Theodotus, and such criticism in its extremest form would naturally seem to an orthodox Catholic the same as throwing over the whole book. Cf. Harnack, *Dogmengeschichte*, p. 579 and p. 488 sqq.

BOOK VI.

CHAPTER I.

The Persecution under Severus.

WHEN Severus began to persecute the churches,[1] glorious testimonies were given everywhere by the athletes of religion. This was especially the case in Alexandria, to which city, as to a most prominent theater, athletes of God were brought from Egypt and all Thebais according to their merit, and won crowns from God through their great patience under many tortures and every mode of death. Among these was Leonides, who was called the father of Origen,[2] and who was beheaded while his son was still young. How remarkable the predilection of this son was for the Divine Word, in consequence of his father's instruction, it will not be amiss to state briefly, as his fame has been very greatly celebrated by many.

CHAPTER II.

The Training of Origen from Childhood.[1]

MANY things might be said in attempt- 1
ing to describe the life of the man while in school; but this subject alone would require a separate treatise. Nevertheless, for the present, abridging most things, we shall state a few facts concerning him as briefly as possible, gathering them from certain letters, and from the statement of persons still living who were acquainted with him. What they report of 2
Origen seems to me worthy of mention, even, so to speak, from his swathing-bands.

It was the tenth year of the reign of Severus,

---

[1] During the early years of the reign of Septimius Severus the Christians enjoyed comparative peace, and Severus himself showed them considerable favor. Early in the third century a change set in, and in 202 the emperor issued an edict forbidding conversions to Christianity and to Judaism (Spartianus, *in Severo*, c. 16; cf. Tillemont, *Hist. des Emp.* III. p. 58). The cause of this radical change of conduct we do not know, but it is possible that the excesses of the Montanists produced a reaction in the emperor's mind against the Christians, or that the rapidity with which Christianity was spreading caused him to fear that the old Roman institutions would be overturned, and hence produced a reaction against it. Why the Jews, too, should have been attacked, it is hard to say, — possibly because of a new attempt on their part to throw off the Roman yoke (see Spartianus, *in Severo*, c. 16); or perhaps there underlay the whole movement a reaction in the emperor's mind toward the old Roman paganism (he was always superstitious), and Judaism and Christianity being looked upon as alike opposed to it, were alike to be held in check. The edict was aimed, not against those already Christians, but only against new converts, the idea being to prevent the further spread of Christianity. But the change in the emperor's attitude, thus published abroad, at once intensified all the elements which were hostile to Christianity; and the popular disfavor, which continued widespread and was continually venting itself in local persecutions, now allowed itself freer rein, and the result was that severe persecutions broke out, which were confined, however, almost wholly to Egypt and North Africa. Our principal authorities for these persecutions (which went on intermittently during the rest of Severus' reign) are the first twelve chapters of this book of Eusebius' *History*, and a number of Tertullian's works, especially his *De corona milites, Ad Scap.*, and *De fuga in persecutione.*

[2] We know very little about Origen's father. The fame of the son overshadowed that of the father, even though the latter was a martyr. The phrase used in this passage to describe him has caused some trouble. Λεωνίδης ὁ λεγόμενος Ὠριγένους πατήρ. Taken in its usual sense, the expression means "said to be the father of Origen," or the "so-called father of Origen," both of which appear strange, for there can have been no doubt as to his identity. It seems better, with Westcott, to understand that Eusebius means that Origen's fame had so eclipsed his father's that the latter was distinguished as "Leonides, the father of Origen," and hence says here, "Leonides, who was known as the father of Origen." The name Leonides is Greek, and that he was of Greek nationality is further confirmed by the words of Porphyry (quoted in chap. 19, below), who calls Origen "a Greek, and educated in Greek literature." Porphyry may simply have concluded from his knowledge of Greek letters that he was a Greek by birth, and hence his statement taken alone has little weight; but taken in conjunction with Leonides' name, makes it probable that the latter was at least of Greek descent; whether a native of Greece or not we do not know. A late tradition makes him a bishop, but there is no foundation for such a report. From the next chapter we learn that Leonides' martyrdom took place in the tenth year of Severus (201-202 A.D.), which is stated also by the *Chron.*

[1] This sixth book of Eusebius' *History* is our chief source for a knowledge of Origen's life. His own writings give us little information of a personal nature; but Eusebius was in a position to learn a great deal about him. He had the advantage of personal converse with surviving friends of Origen, as he tells us in this connection; he had also a large collection of Origen's epistles (he had himself made a collection of more than one hundred of them, as he tells us in chap. 36); and he had access besides to official documents, and to works of Origen's contemporaries which contained references to him (see chap. 33). As a result, he was in a position to write a full and accurate account of his life, and in fact, in connection with Pamphilus, he did write a *Defense of Origen* in six books, which contained both an exposition of his theology with a refutation of charges brought against him, and a full account of his life. Of this work only the first book is extant, and that in the translation of Rufinus. It deals solely with theological matters. It is greatly to be regretted that the remaining books are lost, for they must have contained much of the greatest interest in connection with Origen's life, especially that period of it about which we are most poorly informed, his residence in Cæsarea after his retirement from Alexandria (see chap. 23). In the present book Eusebius gives numerous details of Origen's life, frequently referring to the *Defense* for fuller particulars. His account is very desultory, being interspersed with numerous notices of other men and events, introduced apparently without any method, though undoubtedly the design was to preserve in general the chronological order. There is no part of Eusebius' work which reveals more clearly the viciousness of the purely chronological method, breaking up as it does the account of a single person or movement into numerous detached pieces, and thus utterly destroying all historical continuity. It may be well, therefore, to sum up in brief outline the chief events of Origen's life, most of which are scattered through the following pages. This summary will be found on p. 391 sq. In addition to the notices contained in this book, we have a few additional details from the *Defense*, which have been preserved by Jerome, Rufinus, and Photius, none of whom seem to have had much, if any, independent knowledge of Origen's life. Epiphanius (*Hær.* LXIII. and LXIV.) relates some anecdotes of doubtful credibility. The *Panegyric* of Gregory Thaumaturgus is valuable as a description of Origen's method of teaching, and of the wonderful influence which he possessed over his pupils. (For outline of Origen's life, see below, p. 391 sq.)

while Lætus[2] was governor of Alexandria and the rest of Egypt, and Demetrius[3] had lately received the episcopate of the parishes

3   there, as successor of Julian.[4]   As the flame of persecution had been kindled greatly,[5] and multitudes had gained the crown of martyrdom, such desire for martyrdom seized the soul of Origen, although yet a boy, that he went close to danger, springing forward and rush-

4   ing to the conflict in his eagerness.   And truly the termination of his life had been very near had not the divine and heavenly Providence, for the benefit of many, prevented his desire through the agency of his mother.

5   For, at first, entreating him, she begged him to have compassion on her motherly feelings toward him; but finding, that when he had learned that his father had been seized and imprisoned, he was set the more resolutely, and completely carried away with his zeal for martyrdom, she hid all his clothing, and

6   thus compelled him to remain at home.   But, as there was nothing else that he could do, and his zeal beyond his age would not suffer him to be quiet, he sent to his father an encouraging letter on martyrdom,[6] in which he exhorted him, saying, "Take heed not to change your mind on our account."

This may be recorded as the first evidence of Origen's youthful wisdom and of his genuine

7   love for piety.   For even then he had stored up no small resources in the words of the faith, having been trained in the Divine Scriptures from childhood.   And he had not studied them with indifference, for his father, besides giving him the usual liberal education,[7] had made them a matter of no sec-

8   ondary importance.   First of all, before inducting him into the Greek sciences, he drilled him in sacred studies, requiring

9   him to learn and recite every day.   Nor was this irksome to the boy, but he was eager and diligent in these studies.   And he was not satisfied with learning what was simple and obvious in the sacred words, but sought for something more, and even at that age

busied himself with deeper speculations.   So that he puzzled his father with inquiries for the true meaning of the inspired Scriptures.

And his father rebuked him seemingly to 10 his face, telling him not to search beyond his age, or further than the manifest meaning. But by himself he rejoiced greatly and thanked God, the author of all good, that he had deemed him worthy to be the father of such a child.

And they say that often, standing by the 11 boy when asleep, he uncovered his breast as if the Divine Spirit were enshrined within it, and kissed it reverently; considering himself blessed in his goodly offspring.

These and other things like them are related of Origen when a boy.   But when 12 his father ended his life in martyrdom, he was left with his mother and six younger brothers when he was not quite seventeen years old.[8]   And the property of his father being 13 confiscated to the royal treasury, he and his family were in want of the necessaries of life. But he was deemed worthy of Divine care. And he found welcome and rest with a woman of great wealth, and distinguished in her manner of life and in other respects.   She was treating with great honor a famous heretic then in Alexandria;[9] who, however, was born in Antioch.   He was with her as an adopted son, and she treated him with the greatest kindness. But although Origen was under the neces- 14 sity of associating with him, he neverthe-less gave from this time on strong evidences of his orthodoxy in the faith.   For when on ac-count of the apparent skill in argument[10] of Paul, — for this was the man's name, — a great multitude came to him, not only of heretics but also of our people, Origen could never be in-duced to join with him in prayer;[11] for he held, although a boy, the rule of the Church,[12] and abominated, as he somewhere expresses it, heretical teachings.[13]   Having been instructed in the sciences of the Greeks by his father, he

[2] This Lætus is to be distinguished from Q. Æmilius Lætus, prætorian prefect under Commodus, who was put to death by the Emperor Didius Julianus, in 193; and from Julius Lætus, minister of Severus, who was executed in 199 (see Dion Cassius, Bk. LXXIII. chap. 16, and LXXV. chap. 10; cf. Tillemont, *Hist. des emp.* III. p. 21, 55, and 58).   The dates of Lætus' rule in Egypt are unknown to us.

[3] On the dates of Demetrius' episcopacy, see Bk. V. chap. 22, note 4.

[4] On Julian, see Bk. V. chap. 9, note 2.

[5] On the persecution, see more particularly chap. 1, note 1.

[6] This epistle, which was apparently extant in the time of Eusebius, and may have been contained in the collection made by him (see chap. 36), is now lost, and we possess only this sentence from it.

[7] τῇ τῶν ἐγκυκλίων παιδείᾳ.   According to Liddell and Scott, ἐγκ. παιδεία in later Greek meant "*the circle of those arts and sciences* which every free-born youth in Greece was obliged to go through before applying to any professional studies; *school learning*, as opposed to the business of life."   So Valesius says that the Greeks understood by ἐγκ. μαθήματα the branches in which the youth were instructed; i.e. mathematics, grammar, and rhetoric, philosophy not being included (see Valesius' note *in loco*).

[8] On the date of Origen's birth, see note 1.

[9] Of this Antiochene heretic Paul we know only what Eusebius tells us here.   His patroness seems to have been a Christian, and in good standing in the Alexandrian church, or Origen would hardly have made his home with her.

[10] διὰ τὸ δοκοῦν ἱκανὸν ἐν λόγῳ.

[11] Redepenning (p. 189) refers to Origen's *In Matt. Comment. Series*, sec. 89, where it is said, *melius est cum nullo orare, quam cum malis orare.*

[12] φυλάττων ἐξέτι παιδὸς κανόνα [two MSS. κανόνας] ἐκκλησίας. Compare the words of the *Apostolic Constitutions*, VIII. 34: "Let not one of the faithful pray with a catechumen, no, not in the house; for it is not reasonable that he who is admitted should be polluted with one not admitted.   Let not one of the godly pray with an heretic, no, not in the house.   For 'what fellowship hath light with darkness?'"   Compare also the *Apostolic Canons*, 11, 12, and 45. The last reads: "Let a bishop, or presbyter, or deacon, who only prays with heretics, be suspended; but if he also permit them to perform any part of the office of a clergyman, let him be deprived." Hefele (*Conciliengsch*. I. p. 815) considers this canon only a "consistent application of apostolic principles to particular cases, — an application which was made from the first century on, and therefore very old."

[13] Redepenning (p. 190) refers to the remarks of Origen upon the nature and destructiveness of heresy collected by Pamphilus (*Fragm. Apol. Pamph.* Opp. Origen, IV. 694 [ed. Delarue]).

devoted himself after his death more assiduously and exclusively to the study of literature, so that he obtained considerable preparation in philology[14] and was able not long after the death of his father, by devoting himself to that subject, to earn a compensation amply sufficient for his needs at his age.[15]

CHAPTER III.

While still very Young, he taught diligently the Word of Christ.

1   But while he was lecturing in the school, as he tells us himself, and there was no one at Alexandria to give instruction in the faith, as all were driven away by the threat of persecution, some of the heathen came to him to
2   hear the word of God. The first of them, he says, was Plutarch,[1] who after living well, was honored with divine martyrdom. The second was Heraclas,[2] a brother of Plutarch; who after he too had given with him abundant evidence of a philosophic and ascetic life, was esteemed worthy to succeed Demetrius in the bishopric of Alexandria.

He was in his eighteenth year when he   3 took charge of the catechetical school.[3] He was prominent also at this time, during the persecution under Aquila,[4] the governor of Alexandria, when his name became celebrated among the leaders in the faith, through the kindness and goodwill which he manifested toward all the holy martyrs, whether known to him or strangers. For not only was he with them   4 while in bonds, and until their final condemnation, but when the holy martyrs were led to death, he was very bold and went with them into danger. So that as he acted bravely, and with great boldness saluted the martyrs with a kiss, oftentimes the heathen multitude round about them became infuriated, and were on the point of rushing upon him. But through   5 the helping hand of God, he escaped absolutely and marvelously. And this same divine and heavenly power, again and again, it is impossible to say how often, on account of his great zeal and boldness for the words of Christ, guarded him when thus endangered.[5] So great was the enmity of the unbelievers toward him, on account of the multitude that were instructed by him in the sacred faith, that they placed bands of soldiers around the house where he abode. Thus day by day the persecution burned   6 against him, so that the whole city could no longer contain him; but he removed from house to house and was driven in every direction because of the multitude who attended upon the divine instruction which he gave. For his life also exhibited right and admirable conduct according to the practice of genuine philosophy. For they say that his manner of life was   7 as his doctrine, and his doctrine as his life.[6] Therefore, by the divine Power working with him he aroused a great many to his own zeal.

But when he saw yet more coming to him   8 for instruction, and the catechetical school

---

[14] ἐπὶ τὰ γραμματικά.   [15] See below, p. 392.
[1] Of this Plutarch we know only what Eusebius tells us here, and in chap. 4, where he says that he was the first of Origen' pupils to suffer martyrdom. (On the date of the persecution in which he suffered, see note 4).
[2] Heraclas, brother of Plutarch, proved himself so good a pupil that, when Origen later found the work of teaching too great for him to manage alone, he made him his assistant, and committed the elementary instruction to him (chap. 15). From chap. 19 we learn that he was for years a diligent student of Greek philosophy (chap. 15 implies his proficiency in it), and that he even went so far as to wear the philosopher's cloak all the time, although he was a presbyter in the Alexandrian church. His reputation for learning became so great, as we learn from chap. 31, that Julius Africanus came to Alexandria to see him. In 231, when Origen took his departure from Alexandria, he left the catechetical school in the charge of Heraclas (chap. 26), and in 231 or 232, upon the death of Demetrius (see Bk. V. chap. 22, note 4), Heraclas became the latter's successor as bishop of Alexandria (chaps. 26 and 29), and was succeeded in the presidency of the catechetical school by Dionysius (chap. 29). According to chap. 35 he was bishop for sixteen years and with this both versions of the *Chron.* agree, though Jerome puts his accession two years too early — into the ninth year of Alexander Severus instead of the eleventh — while giving at the same time, quite inconsistently, the proper date for his death. Heraclas' later relations to Origen are not quite clear. He was evidently, in earlier years, one of his best friends, and there is no adequate ground for the assumption, which is quite common, that he was one of those who united with Bishop Demetrius in condemning him. It is true, no attempt seems to have been made after he became bishop to reverse the sentence against Origen, and to invite him back to Alexandria; but this does not prove that Heraclas did not remain friendly to him; for even when Dionysius (who kept up his relations with Origen, as we know from chap. 46) became bishop (A.D. 248), no such attempt seems to have been made, although Origen was still alive and at the height of his power. The fact that the greater part of the clergy of Alexandria and Egypt were unfavorable to Origen, as shown by their condemnation of him, does not imply that Heraclas could not have been elected unless he too showed hostility to Origen; for Dionysius, who we know was not hostile, was appointed at that time head of the catechetical school, and sixteen years later bishop. It is true that Heraclas may not have sympathized with all of Origen's views, and may have thought some of them heretical (his strict judgment of heretics is seen from Bk. VII. chap. 7), but many even of the best of Origen's friends and followers did likewise, so that among his most devoted adherents were some of the most orthodox Fathers of the Church (e.g. the two Gregories and Basil). That Heraclas did not agree with Origen in all his opinions (if he did not, he may not have cared to *press* his return to Alexandria) does not prove therefore that he took part in the condemnatory action of the synod, and that he was himself in later life hostile to Origen.

[3] See below, p. 392.
[4] It is not clear from Eusebius' language whether Aquila was successor of Lætus as viceroy of Egypt (as Redepenning assumes apparently quite without misgiving), or simply governor of Alexandria. He calls Lætus (in chap. 2) governor of Alexandria and of all Egypt, while Aquila is called simply governor of Alexandria. If this difference were insisted on as marking a real distinction, then Aquila would have to be regarded as the chief officer of Alexandria only, and hence subordinate in dignity to the viceroy of Egypt. The term used to describe his position (ἡγούμενον) is not, however, the technical one for the chief officer of Alexandria (see Mommsen, *Provinces of the Roman Empire;* Scribner's ed., II. p. 267 ff.), and hence his position cannot be decided with certainty. In any case, whether he succeeded Lætus, or was his subordinate, the dates of his accession to and retirement from office are unknown, and hence the time at which the persecutions mentioned took place cannot be determined with exactness. We simply know that they occurred after 203 (for Origen had already taken charge of the catechetical school, and some of his pupils perished in the persecutions) and before 211, the date of Severus' death.
[5] How it happened that Origen escaped the persecution, when, according to Eusebius, he exposed himself so continually, and was so hated by the heathen populace, we cannot tell. Eusebius ascribes it solely to the grace of God here, and in chap. 4.
[6] οἷος ὁ λόγος τοῖος ὁ βίος was a Greek proverb. Compare the words of Seneca, in *Ep.* 114 *ad Lucilium,* "Apud Graecos in proverbium cessit *talis hominibus fuit oratio, qualis vita*" (quoted by Redepenning, p. 196).

had been entrusted to him alone by Demetrius, who presided over the church, he considered the teaching of grammatical science inconsistent with training in divine subjects,[7] and forthwith he gave up his grammatical school as unprofitable

9   and a hindrance to sacred learning. Then, with becoming consideration, that he might not need aid from others, he disposed of whatever valuable books of ancient literature he possessed, being satisfied with receiving from the purchaser four oboli a day.[8] For many years he lived philosophically[9] in this manner, putting away all the incentives of youthful desires. Through the entire day he endured no small amount of discipline ; and for the greater part of the night he gave himself to the study of the Divine Scriptures. He restrained himself as much as possible by a most philosophic life ; sometimes by the discipline of fasting, again by limited time for sleep. And in his zeal he never lay upon a

10 bed, but upon the ground. Most of all, he thought that the words of the Saviour in the Gospel should be observed, in which he exhorts not to have two coats nor to use shoes,[10] nor to occupy oneself with cares for the future.[11]

11 With a zeal beyond his age he continued in cold and nakedness ; and, going to the very extreme of poverty, he greatly astonished those about him. And indeed he grieved many of his friends who desired to share their possessions with him, on account of the wearisome toil which they saw him enduring in the teach-

12 ing of divine things. But he did not relax his perseverance. He is said to have walked

for a number of years never wearing a shoe, and, for a great many years, to have abstained from the use of wine, and of all other things beyond his necessary food ; so that he was in danger of breaking down and destroying his constitution.[12]

By giving such evidences of a philosophic 13 life to those who saw him, he aroused many of his pupils to similar zeal ; so that prominent men even of the unbelieving heathen and men that followed learning and philosophy were led to his instruction. Some of them having received from him into the depth of their souls faith in the Divine Word, became prominent in the persecution then prevailing ; and some of them were seized and suffered martydom.

CHAPTER IV.

The Pupils of Origen that became Martyrs.

THE first of these was Plutarch, who was 1 mentioned just above.[1] As he was led to death, the man of whom we are speaking being with him at the end of his life, came near being slain by his fellow-citizens, as if he were the cause of his death. But the providence of God preserved him at this time also. After 2 Plutarch, the second martyr among the pupils of Origen was Serenus,[2] who gave through fire a proof of the faith which he had received. The third martyr from the same 3 school was Heraclides,[3] and after him the fourth was Hero.[4] The former of these was as yet a catechumen, and the latter had but recently been baptized. Both of them were beheaded. After them, the fifth from the same school proclaimed as an athlete of piety was another Serenus, who, it is reported, was beheaded, after a long endurance of tortures. And of women, Herais[5] died while yet a catechumen, receiving baptism by fire, as Origen himself somewhere says.

---

[7] This does not mean that he considered the study of grammar and literature injurious to the Christian, or detrimental to his theological studies. His opinion on that subject is clear enough from all his writings and from his conduct as pictured in chaps. 18 and 19. Nor does it on the other hand imply, as Crusè supposes, that up to this time he had been teaching secular branches *exclusively ;* but it means simply that the demands upon him for instruction in the faith were so great, now that the catechetical school had been officially entrusted to him by Demetrius, that he felt that he could no longer continue to teach secular literature as he had been doing, but must give up that part of his work, and devote himself exclusively to instruction in sacred things.

[8] The obolus was a small Greek coin, equivalent to about three and a half cents of our money. Four oboli a day could have been sufficient, even in that age, only for the barest necessities of life. But with his ascetic tendencies, these were all that Origen wished.

[9] It was very common from the fourth century on (the writer knows of no instances earlier than Eusebius) to call an ascetic mode of life "philosophical," or "the life of a philosopher" (see § 2 of this chapter, and compare Chrysostom's works, where the word occurs very frequently in this sense). Origen, in his ascetic practices, was quite in accord with the prevailing Christian sentiment of his own and subsequent centuries, which looked upon bodily discipline of an ascetic kind, not indeed as required, but as commended by Christ. The growing sentiment had its roots partly in the prevailing ideas of contemporary philosophy, which instinctively emphasized strongly the dualism of spirit and matter, and the necessity of subduing the latter to the former, and partly in the increasing moral corruptness of society, which caused those who wished to lead holy lives to feel that only by eschewing the things of sense could the soul attain purity. Under pressure from without and within, it became very easy to misinterpret various sayings of Christ, and thus to find in the Gospels ringing exhortations to a life of the most rigid asceticism. Clement of Alexandria was almost the only one of the great Christian writers after the middle of the second century who distinguished between the true and the false in this matter. Compare his admirable tract, *Quis dives salvetur,* and contrast the position taken there with the foolish extreme pursued by Origen, as recorded in this chapter.

[10] See Matt. x. 10.   [11] See Matt. vi. 34.

[12] Greek: θώραξ, properly "chest." Rufinus and Christophorsonus translate *stomachum,* and Valesius approves; but there is no authority for such a use of the term θώραξ, so far as I can ascertain. The proper Greek term for stomach is στόμαχος, which is uniformly employed by Galen and other medical writers.

[1] See the previous chapter, § 2. The martyrdom of these disciples of Origen took place under Aquila, and hence the date depends on the date of his rule, which cannot be fixed with exactness, as remarked in note 4 on the previous chapter.

[2] These two persons named Serenus, the first of whom was burned, the second beheaded, are known to us only from this chapter.

[3] Of this Heraclides, we know only what is told us in this chapter. He, with the other martyrs mentioned in this connection, is commemorated in the mediæval martyrologies, but our authentic information is limited to what Eusebius tells us here.

[4] Our authentic information of Hero is likewise limited to this account of Eusebius.

[5] Herais likewise is known to us from this chapter alone. It is interesting to note that Origen's pupils were not confined to the male sex. His association with female catechumens, which his office of instructor entailed upon him, formed one reason for the act of self-mutilation which he committed (see chap. 8, § 2).

CHAPTER V.

Potamiæna.[1]

1   BASILIDES[2] may be counted the seventh of these. He led to martyrdom the celebrated Potamiæna, who is still famous among the people of the country for the many things which she endured for the preservation of her chastity and virginity. For she was blooming in the perfection of her mind and her physical graces. Having suffered much for the faith of Christ, finally after tortures dreadful and terrible to speak of, she with her mother, Mar-

2   cella,[3] was put to death by fire. They say that the judge, Aquila by name, having inflicted severe tortures upon her entire body, at last threatened to hand her over to the gladiators for bodily abuse. After a little consideration, being asked for her decision, she made a reply which was regarded as impious.

3   Thereupon she received sentence immediately, and Basilides, one of the officers of the army, led her to death. But as the people attempted to annoy and insult her with abusive words, he drove back her insulters, showing her much pity and kindness. And perceiving the man's sympathy for her, she exhorted him to be of good courage, for she would supplicate her Lord for him after her departure, and he would soon receive a reward for the kindness he

4   had shown her. Having said this, she nobly sustained the issue, burning pitch being poured little by little, over various parts of her body, from the sole of her feet to the crown of her head. Such was the conflict endured by this famous maiden.

5   Not long after this Basilides, being asked by his fellow-soldiers to swear for a certain reason, declared that it was not lawful for him to swear at all, for he was a Christian, and he confessed this openly. At first they thought that he was jesting, but when he continued to affirm it, he was led to the judge, and, acknowledging his conviction before him, he was im-

prisoned. But the brethren in God com-   6 ing to him and inquiring the reason of this sudden and remarkable resolution, he is reported to have said that Potamiæna, for three days after her martyrdom, stood beside him by night and placed a crown on his head, and said that she had besought the Lord for him and had obtained what she asked, and that soon she would take him with her. Thereupon the brethren gave him the seal[4] of the Lord; and on the next day, after giving glorious testimony for the Lord, he was beheaded. And many others   7 in Alexandria are recorded to have accepted speedily the word of Christ in those times. For Potamiæna appeared to them in their dreams and exhorted them. But let this suffice in regard to this matter.

CHAPTER VI.

Clement of Alexandria.

CLEMENT[1] having succeeded Pantænus,[2] had charge at that time of the catechetical instruction in Alexandria, so that Origen also, while still a boy,[3] was one of his pupils. In the first

---

[4] The word σφραγίς, " seal," was very commonly used by the Fathers to signify baptism (see Suicer's *Thesaurus*).

[1] This chapter has no connection with the preceding, and its insertion at this point has no good ground, for Clement has been already handled in the fifth book; and if Eusebius wished to refer to him again in connection with Origen, he should have done so in chap. 3, where Origen's appointment as head of the catechetical school is mentioned. (Redepenning, however, approves the present order; vol. I. p. 431 sqq.) Rufinus felt the inconsistency, and hence inserted chaps. 6 and 7 in the middle of chap. 3, where the account of Origen's appointment by Demetrius is given. Valesius considers the occurrence of this mention of Clement at this point a sign that Eusebius did not give his work a final revision. Chap. 13 is inserted in the same abrupt way, quite out of harmony with the context. Upon the life of Clement of Alexandria, see Bk. V. chap. 11, note 1. The catechetical school was vacant, as we learn from chap. 2, in the year 203, and was then taken in charge by Origen, so that the " that time " referred to by Eusebius in this sentence must be carried back to the events related in the previous chapters. The cause of Clement's leaving the school was probably the persecution begun by Severus in 202 (" all were driven away by the threatening aspect of persecution," according to chap. 3, § 1); for since Origen was one of his pupils he can hardly have left long before that time. That it was not unworthy cowardice which led Clement to take his departure is clear enough from the words of Alexander in chaps. 11 and 14, from the high reputation which he continued to enjoy throughout the Church, and from his own utterances on the subject of martyrdom scattered through his works.

[2] On Pantænus, see Bk. V. chap. 10, note 2.

[3] Stephanus, Stroth, Burton, Schwegler, Laemmer, and Heinichen, following two important MSS. and the translation of Rufinus, omit the words παῖδα ὄντα " while a boy." But the words are found in all the other codices (the chief witnesses of two of the three great families of MSS. being for them) and in Nicephorus. The manuscript authority is therefore overwhelmingly in favor of the words, and they are adopted by Valesius, Zimmermann, and Crusè. Rufinus is a strong witness against the words, but, as Redepenning justly remarks, having inserted this chapter, as he did, in the midst of the description of Origen's early years (see note 1), the words παῖδα ὄντα would be quite superfluous and even out of place, and hence he would naturally omit them. So far as the probabilities of the insertion or omission of the words in the present passage are concerned, it seems to me more natural to suppose that a copyist, finding the words at this late stage in the account of Origen's life, would be inclined to omit them, than that, not finding them there he should, upon historical grounds (which he could have reached only after some reflection), think that they ought to be inserted. The latter would be not only a more difficult but also a much graver step than the former. There seems, then, to be no good warrant for omitting these words. We learn from chap. 3 that he took charge of the catechetical school when he was in his eighteenth year, within a year therefore after the death of his father. And we learn that

---

[1] Potamiæna, one of the most celebrated of the martyrs that suffered under Severus, is made by Rufinus a disciple of Origen, but Eusebius does not say that she was, and indeed, in making Basilides the seventh of Origen's disciples to suffer, he evidently excludes Potamiæna from the number. Quite a full account of her martyrdom is given by Palladius in his *Historia Lausiaca*, chap. 3 (Migne's *Patr. Gr.* XXXIV. 1014), which contains some characteristic details not mentioned by Eusebius. It appears from that account that she was a slave, and that her master, not being able to induce her to yield to his passion, accused her before the judge as a Christian, bribing him, if possible, to break her resolution by tortures, and then return her to him, or, if that was not possible, to put her to death as a Christian. We cannot judge as to the exact truth of this and other details related by Palladius, but his history (which was written early in the fifth century) is, in the main at least, reliable, except where it deals with miracles and prodigies (cf. the article on *Palladius of Helenopolis*, in the *Dict. of Christ. Biog.*).

[2] Basilides is clearly reckoned here among the disciples of Origen. The correctness of Eusebius' statement has been doubted, but there is no ground for such doubt, for there is no reason to suppose that all of Origen's pupils became converted under his instruction.

[3] Of Marcella, we know only that she was the mother of the more celebrated Potamiæna, and suffered martyrdom by fire.

book of the work called Stromata, which Clement wrote, he gives a chronological table,[4] bringing events down to the death of Commodus. So it is evident that that work was written during the reign of Severus, whose times we are now recording.

CHAPTER VII.

The Writer, Judas.[1]

At this time another writer, Judas, discoursing about the seventy weeks in Daniel, brings down the chronology to the tenth year of the reign of Severus. He thought that the coming of Antichrist, which was much talked about, was then near.[2] So greatly did the agitation caused by the persecution of our people at this time disturb the minds of many.

CHAPTER VIII.

Origen's Daring Deed.

1   At this time while Origen was conducting catechetical instruction at Alexandria, a deed was done by him which evidenced an immature and youthful mind, but at the same time gave the highest proof of faith and conti-

nence.[1] For he took the words, "There   2 are eunuchs who have made themselves eunuchs for the kingdom of heaven's sake,"[2] in too literal and extreme a sense. And in order to fulfill the Saviour's word, and at the same time to take away from the unbelievers all opportunity for scandal, — for, although young, he met for the study of divine things with women as well as men, — he carried out in action the word of the Saviour. He thought that this would not be known by many of his acquaintances. But it was impossible for him, though desiring to do so, to keep such an action secret.

When Demetrius, who presided over that   3 parish, at last learned of this, he admired greatly the daring nature of the act, and as he perceived his zeal and the genuineness of his faith, he immediately exhorted him to courage, and urged him the more to continue his work of catechetical instruction. Such was he at   4 that time. But soon afterward, seeing that he was prospering, and becoming great and distinguished among all men, the same Demetrius, overcome by human weakness, wrote of his deed

---

before he took charge of the school, all who had given instruction there had been driven away by the persecution. Clement, therefore, must have left before Origen's eighteenth year, and hence the latter must have studied with him before the persecution had broken up the school, and in all probability before the death of Leonides. In any case, therefore, he was still a boy when under Clement, and even if we omit the words — "while a boy" — here, we shall not be warranted in putting his student days into the period of his maturity, as some would do. Upon this subject, see Redepenning, I. p. 431 sqq., who adduces still other arguments for the position taken in this note which it is not necessary to repeat here.

[4] In *Stromata*, Bk. I. chap. 21. On this and the other works of Clement, see chap. 13.

[1] The mention of the writer Judas at this point seems, at first sight, as illogical as the reference to Clement in the preceding chapter. But it does not violate chronology as that did; and hence, if the account of Origen's life was to be broken anywhere for such an insertion, there was perhaps no better place. We cannot conclude, therefore, that Eusebius, had he revised his work, would have changed the position of this chapter, as Valesius suggests (see the previous chapter, note 1).

Jerome (*de vir. ill.* c. 52) repeats Eusebius' notice of Judas, but adds nothing to it, and we know no more about him. Since he believed that the appearance of Antichrist was at hand, he must have written before the persecutions had given place again to peace, and hence not long after 202, the date to which he extended his chronology. Whether the work mentioned by Eusebius was a commentary or a work on chronology is not clear. It was possibly an historical demonstration of the truth of Daniel's prophecies, and an interpretation of those yet unfulfilled, in which case it combined history and exegesis.

[2] It was the common belief in the Church, from the time of the apostles until the time of Constantine, that the second coming of Christ would very speedily take place. This belief was especially pronounced among the Montanists, Montanus having proclaimed that the *parousia* would occur before his death, and even having gone so far as to attempt to collect all the faithful (Montanists) in one place in Phrygia, where they were to await that event and where the new Jerusalem was to be set up (see above, Bk. V. chap. 18, note 6). There is nothing surprising in Judas' idea that this severe persecution must be the beginning of the end, for all through the earlier centuries of the Church (and even to some extent in later centuries) there were never wanting those who interpreted similar catastrophes in the same way; although after the third century the belief that the end was at hand grew constantly weaker.

[1] This act of Origen's has been greatly discussed, and some have even gone so far as to believe that he never committed the act, but that the report of it arose from a misunderstanding of certain figurative expressions used by him (so, e.g., Boehringer, Schnitzer, and Baur). There is no reason, however, to doubt the report, for which we have unimpeachable testimony, and which is in itself not at all surprising (see the arguments of Redepenning, I. p. 444 sqq.). The act was contrary to the civil law (see Suetonius, *Domitian*, c. 7; and cf. Justin Martyr, *Apol.* I. 29), and yet was a very common one; the existence of the law itself would alone prove what we know from many sources to have been the fact. Nor was Origen alone among the Christians (cf. e.g. Origen, *In Matt.*, XV. 1, the passage of Justin Martyr referred to above, and also the first canon of the Council of Nicæa, the very existence of which proves the necessity of it). It was natural that Christians, seeking purity of life, and strongly ascetic in their tendencies, should be influenced by the actions of those about them, who sought thus to be freed from the domination of the passions, and should interpret certain passages of the Bible as commending the act. Knowing it to be so common, and knowing Origen's character, as revealed to us in chap. 3, above (to say nothing of his own writings), we can hardly be surprised that he performed the act. His chief motive was undoubtedly the same as that which actuated him in all his ascetic practices, the attainment of higher holiness through the subjugation of his passions, and the desire to sacrifice everything fleshly for the sake of Christ. Of course this could not have led him to perform the act he did, unless he had entirely misunderstood, as Eusebius says he did, the words of Christ quoted below. But he was by no means the only one to misunderstand them (see Suicer's *Thesaurus*, I. 1255 sq.). Eusebius says that the requirements of his position also had something to do with his resolve. He was obliged to teach both men and women, and both day and night (as we learn from § 7), and Eusebius thinks he would naturally desire to avoid scandal. At the same time, this motive can hardly have weighed very heavily, if at all, with him; for had his giving instruction in this way been in danger of causing serious scandal, other easier methods of avoiding such scandal might have been devised, and undoubtedly would have been, by the bishop. And the fact is, he seems to have wished to conceal the act, which is inconsistent with the idea that he performed it for the sake of avoiding scandal. It is quite likely that his intimate association with women may have had considerable to do with his resolve, because he may have found that such association aroused his unsubdued passions, and therefore felt that they must be eradicated, if he was to go about his duties with a pure and single heart. That he afterward repented his youthful act, and judged the words of Christ more wisely, is clear from what he says in his *Comment. in Matt.* XV. 1. And yet he never outgrew his false notions of the superior virtue of an ascetic life. His act seems to have caused a reaction in his mind which led him into doubt and despondency for a time; for Demetrius found it necessary to exhort him to cherish confidence, and to urge him to continue his work of instruction. Eusebius, while not approving Origen's act, yet evidently admired him the more for the boldness and for the spirit of self-sacrifice shown in its performance.

[2] Matt. xix. 12.

as most foolish to the bishops throughout the world. But the bishops of Cesarea and Jerusalem, who were especially notable and distinguished among the bishops of Palestine, considering Origen worthy in the highest degree of the 5 honor, ordained him a presbyter.[3] Thereupon his fame increased greatly, and his name became renowned everywhere, and he obtained no small reputation for virtue and wisdom. But Demetrius, having nothing else that he could say against him, save this deed of his boyhood, accused him bitterly,[4] and dared to include with him in these accusations those who had raised him to the presbyterate. 6 These things, however, took place a little later. But at this time Origen continued fearlessly the instruction in divine things at Alexandria by day and night to all who came to him; devoting his entire leisure without cessation to divine studies and to his pupils. 7 Severus, having held the government for eighteen years, was succeeded by his son, Antoninus.[5] Among those who had endured courageously the persecution of that time, and had been preserved by the Providence of God through the conflicts of confession, was Alexander, of whom we have spoken already[6] as bishop of the church in Jerusalem. On account of his pre-eminence in the confession of Christ he was thought worthy of that bishopric, while Narcissus,[7] his predecessor, was still living.

CHAPTER IX.

The Miracles of Narcissus.

THE citizens of that parish mention many 1 other miracles of Narcissus, on the tradition of the brethren who succeeded him; among which they relate the following wonder as performed by him. They say that the oil 2 once failed while the deacons were watching through the night at the great paschal vigil. Thereupon the whole multitude being dismayed, Narcissus directed those who attended to the lights, to draw water and bring it to him. This being immediately done he prayed 3 over the water, and with firm faith in the Lord, commanded them to pour it into the lamps. And when they had done so, contrary to all expectation by a wonderful and divine power, the nature of the water was changed into that of oil. A small portion of it has been preserved even to our day by many of the brethren there as a memento of the wonder.[1]

They tell many other things worthy to be 4 noted of the life of this man, among which is this. Certain base men being unable to endure the strength and firmness of his life, and fearing punishment for the many evil deeds of which they were conscious, sought by plotting to anticipate him, and circulated a terrible slander against him. And to persuade 5 those who heard of it, they confirmed their accusations with oaths: one invoked upon himself destruction by fire; another the wasting of his body by a foul disease; the third the loss of

---

[3] See chap. 23.
[4] On the relations existing between Demetrius and Origen, see below, p. 394.
[5] Septimius Severus died on February 4, 211, after a reign of a little more than seventeen years and eight months, and was succeeded by his two sons, Marcus Aurelius Severus Antoninus Bassianus (commonly known by his nickname Caracalla, which, however, was never used in official documents or inscriptions), and Lucius, or Publius, Septimius Geta. Eusebius mentions here only the former, giving him his official name, Antoninus.
[6] Eusebius makes a slip here, as this is the first time he has mentioned Alexander in his *Church History*. He was very likely under the impression that he had mentioned him just above, where he referred to the bishops of Cæsarea and Jerusalem. He does refer to him in his *Chron.*, putting his appointment as assistant bishop into the second year of Caracalla (*Armen.* fourth year), and calling him the thirty-fifth bishop of Jerusalem (*Armen.* thirty-sixth). In Bk. V. chap. 12 of the *History* (also in the *Chron.*) we are told that Narcissus was the thirtieth bishop of Jerusalem. The number thirty-five for Alexander (the number thirty-six of the *Armen.* is a mistake, and is set right in connection with Alexander's successor, who is also called the thirty-sixth) is made out by counting the three bishops mentioned in chap. 10, and then reckoning the second episcopate of Narcissus (see the same chapter) as the thirty-fourth. We learn from chap. 14 that Alexander was an early friend of Origen's, and a fellow-pupil in the school of Clement. We know him next as bishop of some church in Cappadocia (chap. 11; see note 2 on that chapter), whence he was called to be assistant bishop of Jerusalem (see the same chapter). From this passage, compared with chap. 11, we learn that Alexander was imprisoned during the persecutions, and the *Chron.* gives the year of his "confession" as 203 A.D. But from chap. 11 we learn that he wrote while still in prison to the church of Antioch on occasion of the appointment of Asclepiades to the episcopate there. According to the *Chron.* Asclepiades did not become bishop until 211; and though this may not be the exact date, yet it cannot be far out of the way (see chap. 11, note 6); and hence, if Alexander was a confessor in 203, he must have remained in prison a number of years, or else have undergone a second persecution. It is probable either that the date 203 is quite wrong, or else that he suffered a second time toward the close of Severus' reign; for the persecution, so far as we know, was not so continuous during that reign as to keep one man confined for eight years. Our knowledge of the persecutions in Asia Minor at this time is very limited, but they do not seem to have been of great severity or of long duration. The date of Alexander's episcopate in Cappadocia it is impossible to determine, though as he was a fellow-pupil of Origen's in Alexandria, it cannot have begun much, if any, before 202. The date of his translation to the see of Jerusalem is likewise uncertain. The *Chron.* gives the second year of Caracalla (*Armen.* fourth). The connection in which Eusebius mentions it in chap. 11 makes it look as if it took place before Asclepiades' accession to the see of Antioch; but this is hardly possible, for it was his firmness under persecution which elevated him to the see of Jerusalem (according to this passage), and it is apparently that persecution which he is enduring when Asclepiades becomes bishop. We find no reason, then, for correcting the date of his translation to Jerusalem given by the *Chron.* At any rate, he was bishop of Jerusalem when Origen visited Palestine in 216 (see chap. 19, § 17). In 231 he assisted at the ordination of Origen (see chap. 23, note 6), and finally perished in prison during the Decian persecution (see chaps. 39 and 46). His friendship for Origen was warm and steadfast (cf., besides the other passages referred to, chap. 27). The latter compromises the loveliness and gentleness of his character in his first *Homily on 1 Samuel*, § 1. He collected a valuable library in Jerusalem, which Eusebius made use of in the composition of his *History* (see chap. 20). This act shows the literary tastes of the man. Of his epistles only the five fragments preserved by Eusebius (chaps. 11, 14, and 19) are now extant. Jerome (*de vir. ill.* 62) says that other epistles were extant in his day; and he relates, on the authority of an epistle written *pro Origene contra Demetrium*, that Alexander had ordained Origen *juxta testimonium Demetri*. This epistle is not mentioned by Eusebius, but in spite of Jerome's usual dependence upon the latter, there is no good reason to doubt the truth of his statement in this case (see below, p. 396).
[7] On Narcissus, see the next three chapters, and also Bk. V. chap. 12, note 1.
[1] This miracle is related by Eusebius upon the testimony, not of documents, but of those who had shown him the oil, which was preserved in Jerusalem down to that time; οἱ τῆς παροικίας πολῖται . . . ἱστοροῦσι, he says. His travels had evidently not taught him to disbelieve every wonderful tale that was told him.

his eyes. But though they swore in this manner, they could not affect the mind of the believers ; because the continence and virtuous life of Narcissus were well known to all.

6   But he could not in any wise endure the wickedness of these men ; and as he had followed a philosophic[2] life for a long time, he fled from the whole body of the Church, and hid himself in desert and secret places, and

7   remained there many years.[3] But the great eye of judgment was not unmoved by these things, but soon looked down upon these impious men, and brought on them the curses with which they had bound themselves. The residence of the first, from nothing but a little spark falling upon it, was entirely consumed by night, and he perished with all his family. The second was speedily covered with the disease which he had imprecated upon himself, from the

8   sole of his feet to his head. But the third, perceiving what had happened to the others, and fearing the inevitable judgment of God, the ruler of all, confessed publicly what they had plotted together. And in his repentance he became so wasted by his great lamentations, and continued weeping to such an extent, that both his eyes were destroyed. Such were the punishments which these men received for their falsehood.

CHAPTER X.

The Bishops of Jerusalem.

NARCISSUS having departed, and no one knowing where he was, those presiding over the neighboring churches thought it best to ordain another bishop. His name was Dius.[1] He presided but a short time, and Germanio succeeded him. He was followed by Gordius,[2] in whose time Narcissus appeared again, as if raised from the dead.[3] And immediately the brethren besought him to take the episcopate, as all admired him the more on account of his retirement and philosophy, and especially because of the punishment with which God had avenged him.

---

[2] See above, chap. 3, note 9.
[3] The date of Narcissus' retirement we have no means of ascertaining.
[1] Of these three bishops, Dius, Germanio, and Gordius, we know nothing more than is told us here. Syncellus assigns eight years to Dius, four to Germanio, and five to Sardianus, whom he names instead of Gordius. Epiphanius reports that Dius was bishop until Severus (193 A.D.), and Gordius until Antonine (i.e. Caracalla, 211 A.D.). But no reliance is to be placed upon these figures or dates, as remarked above, Bk. V. chap. 12, note 2.
[2] Eusebius and Epiphanius give Γόρδιος, and Jerome, Gordius; but the Armenian has Gordianus, and Syncellus, Σαρδιανός. What became of Gordius when Narcissus reappeared we do not know. He must have died very speedily, or some compromise would have been made, as it seems, which would have rendered the appointment of Alexander as assistant bishop unnecessary.
[3] Literally, " as if from a resurrection " (ὥσπερ ἐξ ἀναβιώσεως).

CHAPTER XI.

Alexander.

BUT as on account of his great age Narcissus was no longer able to perform his official duties,[1] the Providence of God called to the office with him, by a revelation given him in a night vision, the above-mentioned Alexander, who was then bishop of another parish.[2]

---

[1] The extreme age of Narcissus at this time is evident from the fact that Alexander, writing before the year 216 (see note 4), says that Narcissus is already in his 116th year. The translation of Alexander to Jerusalem must have taken place about 212 (see chap. 8, note 6), and hence Narcissus was now more than 110 years old. The appointment of Alexander as Narcissus' assistant involved two acts which were even at that time not common, and which were later forbidden by canon; first the translation of a bishop from one see to another, and secondly the appointment of an assistant bishop, which made two bishops in one city. The *Apost. Canons* (No. 14) ordain that " a bishop ought not to leave his own parish and leap to another, although the multitude should compel him, unless there be some good reason forcing him to do this, as that he can contribute much greater profit to the people of the new parish by the word of piety; but this is not to be settled by himself, but by the judgment of many bishops and very great supplication." It has been disputed whether this canon is older or younger than the fifteenth canon of Nicæa, which forbids unconditionally the practice of translation from one see to another. Whichever may be the older, it is certain that even the Council of Nicæa considered its own canon as liable to exceptions in certain cases, for it translated Eustathius from Berœa to Antioch (see Sozomen, *H. E.* I. 2). The truth is, the rule was established — whether before or for the first time at the Council of Nicæa — chiefly in order to guard against the ambition of aspiring men who might wish to go from a smaller to a greater parish, and to prevent, as the Nicene Canon says, the many disorders and quarrels which the custom of translation caused; and a rule formed on such grounds of expediency was of course liable to exception whenever the good of the Church seemed to demand it, and therefore, whether the fourteenth Apostolic Canon is more ancient than the Nicene Council or not, it certainly embodies a principle which must long have been in force, and which we find in fact acted upon in the present case; for the translation of Alexander takes place " with the common consent of the bishops of the neighboring churches," or, as Jerome puts it, *cunctis in Palestina episcopis in unum congregatis*, which is quite in accord with the provision of the Apostolic Canons. There were some in the early Church who thought it absolutely unlawful under any circumstances for a bishop to be translated (cf. Jerome's *Ep. ad Oceanum*; Migne, *Ep.* 69, § 5), but this was not the common view, as Bingham (*Antiq.* VI. 4. 6) well observes, and instances of translation from one see to another were during all these centuries common (cf. e.g. Socrates, *H. E.* VII. 36), although always of course exceptional, and considered lawful only when made for good and sufficient reasons. To say, therefore, with Valesius that these Palestinian bishops violated a rule of the Church in translating Alexander is too strong. They were evidently unconscious of anything uncanonical, or even irregular in their action, though it is clear that they regarded the step as too important to be taken without the approval of all the bishops of the neighborhood. In regard to assistant bishops, Valesius correctly remarks that this is the first instance of the kind known to us, but it is by no means the only one, for the following centuries furnish numerous examples; e.g. Theotecnus and Anatolius in Cæsarea (see below, Bk. VII. chap. 32), Maximus and Macarius in Jerusalem (see Sozomen, *H. E.* II. 20); and so in Africa Valerius of Hippo had Augustine as his coadjutor (Possidius, *Vita. Aug.* chap. 8; see Bingham's *Antiq.* II. 13. 4 for other instances and for a discussion of the whole subject). The principle was in force from as early as the third century (see Cyprian to Cornelius, *Ep.* 40, *al.* 44 and to Antonianus, *Ep.* 51, *al.* 55) that there should be only one bishop in a city, and we see from the works of various Fathers that this rule was universally accepted at an early date. The eighth canon of Nicæa refers to this principle in passing as if it were already firmly established, and the council evidently did not think it necessary to promulgate a special canon on the subject. Because of this principle, Augustine hesitated to allow himself to be ordained assistant bishop of Hippo; and although his scruples were overcome at the time, he afterward, upon learning of the Nicene Canon, considered the practice of having a coadjutor illegal and refused to ordain one for himself. But, as the instances referred to above and many others show, not all the Church interpreted the principle as rigidly as Augustine did, and hence under certain circumstances exceptions were made to the rule, and were looked upon throughout the Church as quite lawful. The existence of two bishops in one city as a matter of compromise, for the sake of healing a schism, formed one common exception to the general principle (see Bingham, II. 13. 2), and the appointment of coadjutors, as in the present case, formed another.
[2] Of what city in Cappadocia Alexander was bishop we are not told by Eusebius, nor by our other ancient authorities. Valesius

2   Thereupon, as by Divine direction, he journeyed from the land of Cappadocia, where he first held the episcopate, to Jerusalem, in consequence of a vow and for the sake of information in regard to its places.[3] They received him there with great cordiality, and would not permit him to return, because of another revelation seen by them at night, which uttered the clearest message to the most zealous among them. For it made known that if they would go outside the gates, they would receive the bishop foreordained for them by God. And having done this, with the unanimous consent of the bishops of the neighboring churches,

3   they constrained him to remain. Alexander, himself, in private letters to the Antinoites,[4] which are still preserved among us, mentions the joint episcopate of Narcissus and himself, writing in these words at the end of the epistle :

4   " Narcissus salutes you, who held the episcopate here before me, and is now associated with me in prayers, being one hundred and sixteen years of age ; and he exhorts you, as I do, to be of one mind."

These things took place in this manner. But, on the death of Serapion,[5] Asclepiades,[6] who had been himself distinguished among the confessors [7] during the persecution, succeeded to the episcopate of the church at Antioch. Alexander alludes to his appointment, writing thus to the church at Antioch :

5   "Alexander, a servant and prisoner of Jesus Christ, to the blessed church of Antioch, greeting in the Lord. The Lord hath made my bonds during the time of my imprisonment light and easy, since I learned that, by the Divine Providence, Asclepiades, who in regard to the true faith is eminently qualified, has undertaken the bishopric of your holy church at Antioch."

6   He indicates that he sent this epistle by Clement,[8] writing toward its close as follows :

" My honored brethren,[9] I have sent this letter to you by Clement, the blessed presbyter, a man virtuous and approved, whom ye yourselves also know and will recognize. Being here, in the providence and oversight of the Master, he has strengthened and built up the Church of the Lord."

CHAPTER XII.

Serapion and his Extant Works.

1   It is probable that others have preserved other memorials of Serapion's [1] literary industry,[2] but there have reached us only those addressed to a certain Domninus, who, in the time of persecution, fell away from faith in Christ to the Jewish will-worship ;[3] and those addressed

---

(note on this passage) and Tillemont (*Hist. eccles.* III. p. 415) give Flaviopolis or Flaviadis as the name of the city (upon the authority of Basilicon, *Jur. Græco-Rom.* Tom. I. p. 295, according to Tillemont). But Flaviopolis was a city of Cilicia, and hence Tillemont conjectures that it had once been taken from Cappadocia and attached to Cilicia, and that its inhabitants retained the memory of Alexander, their early bishop. The report seems to rest upon a very slender foundation; but not having access to the authority cited, I am unable to form an opinion as to the worth of the tradition.

[3] εὐχῆς καὶ τῶν τόπων ἱστορίας ἕνεκεν.

[4] Ἀντινόεια (Antinoë or Antinoöpolis) was a city of Egypt founded by Hadrian in honor of Antinous (see Bk. IV. chap. 8, note 3). This is the first mention of a church there, but its bishops were present at more than one council in later centuries (see Wiltsch's *Geography and Statistics*, p. 59, 196, 473). This letter must have been written between 212, at about which time Alexander became Narcissus' coadjutor (see chap. 8, note 6), and 216, when Origen visited Palestine (see chap. 19, note 23). For at the time of that visit Alexander is said to have been bishop of Jerusalem, and no mention is made of Narcissus, who must therefore have been already dead (see Bk. V. chap. 12, note 1). The fragments of Alexander's epistles quoted in this chapter are given in Routh's *Rel. Sacræ*, II. p. 161 sq., and in English in the *Ante-Nicene Fathers*, VI. p. 154.

[5] On Serapion, see Bk. V. chap. 19, note 1.

[6] The *Chron.* puts the accession of Asclepiades in the first year of Caracalla (211 A.D.). Harnack (*Zeit des Ignatius*, p. 47) believes that this notice rests upon better knowledge than the notices of most of the Antiochian bishops, because in this case the author departs from the artificial scheme which he follows in the main. But Harnack contends that the date is not quite correct, because Alexander, who suffered under Severus, was still in prison when Asclepiades became bishop, and therefore the latter's accession must be put back into Severus' reign. He would fix, therefore, upon about 209 as the date of it, rightly perceiving that there is good reason for thinking the *Chron.* at least nearly correct in its report, and that in any case his accession cannot be carried back much beyond that, because it is quite probable (from the congratulations which Alexander extends to the church of Antioch) that there had been a vacancy in that church for some time after the death of Serapion (a thing not at all unnatural in the midst of the persecutions of the time), while Serapion was still alive as late as 203 (see Bk. V. chap. 19, note 1). But it seems to me that there is no good ground for making any alteration in the date given by the *Chron.*, for we know that at the very end of Severus' reign the persecution broke out again with considerable severity, and that it continued, at least in Africa, for some time after Caracalla's accession (see Tertullian's *ad Scap.*). The general amnesty issued by Caracalla after the murder of his brother Geta in 212 (see Dion Cassius, LXXVII. 3) seems first to have put a definitive end to the persecutions. There is therefore no ground for confining Alexander's imprisonment to the reign of Severus. It may well have run

---

into the time of Caracalla, and hence it is quite possible that Asclepiades did not become bishop until after the latter became emperor, so that it is not necessary to correct the date of the *Chron.* It is impossible to determine with certainty the length of Asclepiades' episcopate (see chap. 21, note 6). Of Asclepiades himself we know no more than is told us in this chapter. He seems to have been a man of most excellent character, to judge from Alexander's epistle. That epistle, of course, was written immediately after Asclepiades' appointment.

[7] Literally " confessions " (ὁμολογίαις).

[8] On Clement of Alexandria, see above, Bk. V. chap. 11.

[9] κύριοί μου ἀδελφοί.

[1] On Serapion, see Bk. V. chap. 19, note 1.

[2] The Greek reads: τοῦ δὲ Σαραπίωνος τῆς περὶ λόγους ἀσκήσεως καὶ ἄλλα μὲν εἰκὸς σώζεσθαι παρ' ἑτέροις ὑπομνήματα.

[3] Of this Domninus we know only what is told us here. It is suggested by Daniell (in the *Dict. of Christ. Biog.* IV. 630) that this shows that the prohibition uttered by Severus against the Jews " must have been soon relaxed, if it ever was enforced." But in regard to this it must be said, in the first place, that Severus' decree was not levelled against the Jews, but only against conversion to Judaism, — against the *fieri*, not the *esse, Judæos*. The object of the edict was not to disturb the Jews in the exercise of their national faith, but to prevent their proselyting among the non-Jewish residents of the empire. If Domninus, therefore, fell from Christianity into Judaism on account of the persecution, it seems highly probable that he was simply a converted Jew, who gave up now, in order to avoid persecution, his new faith, and again practised the religion of his fathers. Nothing, therefore, can be concluded from Domninus' case as to the strictness with which Severus' law was carried out, even if we suppose Domninus to have fallen from Christianity into Judaism. But it must be remarked, in the second place, that it is by no means certain that Eusebius means to say that Domninus fell into Judaism, or became a Jew. He is said to have fallen into " Jewish will-worship " (ἐκπεπτωκότα ἐπὶ τὴν Ἰουδαϊκὴν ἐθελοθρησκείαν). The word ἐθελοθρησκεία occurs for the first time in Col. ii. 23, and means there an " arbitrary, self-imposed worship " (Ellicott), or a worship which one " affects " (Cremer). The word is used there in connection with the Oriental theosophic and Judaistic errors which were creeping into the churches of Asia Minor at the time the epistle was written, and it is quite possible that the word may be used in the present case in reference to the same class of errors. We know that these theosophizing and Judaizing tenden-

to Pontius and Caricus,[4] ecclesiastical men,
2   and other letters to different persons, and
still another work composed by him on the
so-called Gospel of Peter.[5] He wrote this last
to refute the falsehoods which that Gospel contained, on account of some in the parish of
Rhossus[6] who had been led astray by it into
heterodox notions. It may be well to give some
brief extracts from his work, showing his opinion
of the book. He writes as follows :
3   "For we, brethren, receive both Peter
and the other apostles as Christ ; but we
reject intelligently the writings falsely ascribed
to them, knowing that such were not handed
4   down to us. When I visited you I supposed
that all of you held the true faith, and as I
had not read the Gospel which they put forward under the name of Peter, I said, 'If this
is the only thing which occasions dispute among
you, let it be read.' But now having learned,
from what has been told me, that their mind
was involved in some heresy, I will hasten to
come to you again. Therefore, brethren,
5   expect me shortly. But you will learn,
brethren, from what has been written to you,
that we perceived the nature of the heresy
of Marcianus,[7] and that, not understanding
what he was saying, he contradicted himself.
6   For having obtained this Gospel from others
who had studied it diligently, namely, from
the successors of those who first used it, whom
we call Docetæ[8] (for most of their opinions are

connected with the teaching of that school[9]),
we have been able to read it through, and we
find many things in accordance with the true
doctrine of the Saviour, but some things added
to that doctrine, which we have pointed out for
you farther on."

So much in regard to Serapion.

CHAPTER XIII.

The Writings of Clement.[1]

ALL the eight Stromata of Clement are   1
preserved among us, and have been given by

δοκέω, "to seem or appear." The belief is as old as the first century (cf. 1 John iv. 2; 2 John 7), and was a favorite one with most
of the Gnostic sects. The name *Docetæ*, however, as a general appellation for all those holding this opinion, seems to have been used
first by Theodoret (*Ep.* 82). But the term was employed to designate a particular sect before the end of the second century; thus
Clement of Alexandria speaks of them in *Strom.* VII. 17, and Hippolytus (*Phil.* VIII. 8. 4, and X. 12; *Ante-Nicene Fathers*, Amer.
ed.), and it is evidently this particular sect to which Serapion refers
here. An examination of Hippolytus' account shows that these
Docetæ did not hold what we call Docetic ideas of Christ's body; in
fact, Hippolytus says expressly that they taught that Christ was born,
and had a true body from the Virgin (see *Phil.* VIII. 3). How the
sect came to adopt the name of *Docetæ* we cannot tell. They seem
to have disappeared entirely before the fourth century, for no mention
of.them is found in Epiphanius and other later heresiologists. As was
remarked above, Theodoret uses the term in a general sense and not
as the appellation of a particular sect, and this became the common
usage, and is still. Whether there was anything in the teaching of
the sect to suggest the belief that Christ had only an apparent body,
and thus to lead to the use of their specific name for all who held
that view, or whether the general use of the name *Docetæ* arose
quite independently of their sect name, we do not know. The latter
seems more probable. The *Docetæ* referred to by Hippolytus being
a purely Gnostic sect with a belief in the reality of Christ's body,
we have no reason to conclude that the "Gospel of Peter" contained
what we call Docetic teaching. The description which Serapion
gives of the gospel fits quite well a work containing some such
Gnostic speculations as Hippolytus describes, and thus adding to the
Gospel narrative rather than denying the truth of it in any part.
He could hardly have spoken as he did of a work which denied the
reality of Christ's body. See, on the general subject, Salmon's articles *Docetæ* and *Docetism* in the *Dict. of Christ. Biog.*
   [9] The interpretation of these last two clauses is beset with difficulty.
The Greek reads τουτέστι παρὰ τῶν διαδόχων τῶν καταρξαμένων
αὐτοῦ, οὓς Δοκητὰς καλοῦμεν, (τὰ γὰρ φρονήματα τὰ πλείονα ἐκείνων ἐστὶ τῆς διδασκαλίας), κ.τ.λ. The words τῶν καταρξαμένων
αὐτοῦ are usually translated "who preceded him," or "who led the
way before him"; but the phrase hardly seems to admit of this interpretation, and moreover the αὐτοῦ seems to refer not to Marcianus, whose name occurs some lines back, but to the gospel which
has just been mentioned. There is a difficulty also in regard to the
reference of the ἐκείνων, which is commonly connected with the
words τῆς διδασκαλίας, but which seems to belong rather with the
φρονήματα and to refer to the διαδοχῶν τῶν καταρξαμένων. It thus
seems necessary to define the τῆς διδασκαλίας more closely, and we
therefore venture, with Closs, to insert the words "of that school,"
referring to the *Docetæ* just mentioned.
   [1] On the life of Clement, see Bk. V. chap. 11, note 1. He was a
very prolific writer, as we can gather from the list of works mentioned in this chapter. The list is repeated by Jerome (*de vir. ill.*
c. 38) and by Photius (*Cod.* 109-111), the former of whom merely
copies from Eusebius, with some mistakes, while the latter copies
from Jerome, as is clear from the similar variations in the titles given
by the last two from those given by Eusebius, and also by the
omission in both their lists of one work named by Eusebius (see
below, note 10). Eusebius names ten works in this chapter. In
addition to these there are extant two quotations from a work of
Clement entitled περὶ προνοίας. There are also extant two fragments of a work περὶ ψυχῆς. In the *Instructor*, Bk. II. chap. 10,
Clement refers to a work *On Continence* (ὁ περὶ ἐγκρατείας) as already written by himself, and there is no reason to doubt that this
was a separate work, for the third book of the *Stromata* (to which
Fabricius thinks he refers), which treats of the same subject, was
not yet written. The work is no longer extant. In the *Instructor*,
Bk. III. chap. 8, Clement speaks of a work which he had written *On
Marriage* (ὁ γαμικὸς λόγος). It has been thought possible that he
may have referred here to his discussion of the same subject in Bk.
II. chap. 10 of the same work (see the Bishop of Lincoln's work on
Clement, p. 7), but it seems more probable that he referred to a sep-

---

.cies continued to exert considerable influence in Asia Minor and
Syria during the early centuries, and that the Ebionites and the El-
cesaites were not the only ones affected by them (see Harnack, *Dogmengesch.* I. 218 sq.). The lapse of any one into Ebionism, or into
a Judaizing Gnosticism, or similar form of heresy — a lapse which
cannot have been at all uncommon among the fanatical Phrygians
and other peoples of that section — might well be called a lapse into
"Jewish will-worship." We do not know where Domninus lived,
but it is not improbable that Asia Minor was his home, and that he
may have fallen under the influence of Montanism as well as of Ebionism and Judaizing Gnosticism. I suggest the possibility that his
lapse was into heresy rather than into Judaism pure and simple, for
the reason that it is easier, on that ground, to explain the fact that
Serapion addressed a work to him. He is known to us only as an
opponent of heresy, and it may be that Domninus' lapse gave him
an opportunity to attack the heretical notions of these Ebionites, or
other Judaizing heretics, as he had attacked the Montanists. It
seems to the writer, also, that it is thus easier to explain the complex
phrase used, which seems to imply something different from Judaism pure and simple.
   [4] See Bk. V. chap. 19, note 4.
   [5] On the so-called "Gospel of Peter," see Bk. III. chap. 3,
note 7.
   [6] Rhossus, or Rhosus, was a city of Syria, lying on the Gulf of
Issus, a little to the northwest of Antioch.
   [7] This Marcianus is an otherwise unknown personage, unless
we are to identify him, as Salmon suggests is possible, with Marcion. The suggestion is attractive, and the reference to *Docetæ*
gives it a show of probability. But there are serious objections to
be urged against it. In the first place, the form of the name, Μαρκι-
ανός instead of Μαρκίων. The two names are by no means identical.
Still, according to Harnack, we have more than once Μαρκιανοί and
Μαρκιανισταί for Μαρκιωνισταί (see his *Quellenkritik d. Gesch. d.
Gnosticismus*, p. 31 sqq.). But again, how can Marcion have
used, or his name been in any way connected with, a Gospel of
Peter? Finally, the impression left by this passage is that "Marcianus" was a man still living, or at any rate alive shortly before
Serapion wrote, for the latter seems only recently to have learned
what his doctrines were. He certainly cannot have been so ignorant of the teachings of the great "heresiarch" Marcion. We must,
in fact, regard the identification as improbable.
   [8] By Docetism we understand the doctrine that Christ had no
true body, but only an apparent one. The word is derived from

him the following title : "Titus Flavius Clement's Stromata of Gnostic Notes on the True Philosophy."[2] The books entitled Hypotyposes[3] are of the same number. In them he mentions Pantænus[4] by name as his teacher, and gives his opinions and traditions. Besides these there is his Hortatory Discourse addressed to the Greeks ;[5] three books of a work entitled the Instructor ;[6] another with the title What Rich Man is Saved?[7] the work on the Passover ;[8] discussions on Fasting and on Evil Speaking ;[9] the Hortatory Discourse on Patience, or To Those Recently Baptized ;[10] and the one bearing the title Ecclesiastical Canon, or Against the Judaizers,[11] which he dedicated

---

arate work now lost. Potter, p. 1022, gives a fragment which is possibly from this work.

In addition to these works, referred to as already written, Clement promises to write on *First Principles* (περὶ ἀρχῶν; *Strom.* III. 3, IV. 1, 13, V. 14, *et al.*); on *Prophecy* (*Strom.* I. 24, IV. 13, V. 13); on *Angels* (*Strom.* VI. 13); on the *Origin of the World* (*Strom.* VI. 18),—perhaps a part of the proposed work on *First Principles*, and perhaps to be identified with the commentary on Genesis, referred to below by Eusebius (see note 28),—*Against Heresies* (*Strom.* IV. 13), on the *Resurrection* (*Instructor*, I. 6, II. 10). It is quite possible that Clement regarded his promises as fulfilled by the discussions which he gives in various parts of the *Stromata* themselves, or that he gave up his original purpose.

[2] Clement's three principal works, the *Exhortation to the Greeks* (see below, note 5), the *Instructor* (note 6), and the *Stromata*, form a connected series of works, related to one another (as Schaff says) very much as apologetics, ethics, and dogmatics. The three works were composed in the order named. The *Stromata* (Στρωματεῖς) or *Miscellanies* (said by Eusebius in this passage to bear the title τῶν κατὰ τὴν ἀληθῆ φιλοσοφίαν γνωστικῶν ὑπομνημάτων στρωματεῖς) are said by Eusebius and by Photius (*Cod.* 109) to consist of eight books. Only seven are now extant, although there exists a fragment purporting to be a part of the eighth book, but which is in reality a portion of a treatise on logic, while in the time of Photius some reckoned the tract *Quis dives salvetur* as the eighth book (Photius, *Cod.* 111). There thus exists no uniform tradition as to the character of the lost book, and the suggestion of Westcott seems plausible, that at an early date the logical introduction to the *Hypotyposes* was separated from the remainder of the work, and added to some MSS. of the *Stromata* as an eighth book. If this be true, the *Stromata* consisted originally of only seven books, and hence we now have the whole work (with the exception of a fragment lost at the beginning). The name Στρωματεῖς, "patchwork," sufficiently indicates the character of the work. It is without methodical arrangement, containing a heterogeneous mixture of science, philosophy, poetry, and theology, and yet is animated by one idea throughout,—that Christianity satisfies the highest intellectual desires of man,—and hence the work is intended in some sense as a guide to the deeper knowledge of Christianity, the knowledge to be sought after by the "true Gnostic." It is full of rich thoughts mingled with worthless crudities, and, like nearly all of Clement's works, abounds in wide and varied learning, not always fully digested. The date at which the work was composed may be gathered from a passage in Bk. I. chap. 21, where a list of the Roman emperors is closed with a mention of Commodus, the exact length of whose reign is given, showing that he was already dead, but also showing apparently that his successor was still living. This would lead us to put the composition at least of the first book in the first quarter of the year 193. It might of course be said that Pertinax and Didius Julianus are omitted in this list because of the brevity of their reigns, and this is possible, since in his own list he gives the reigns of the emperors simply by years, omitting Otho and Vitellius. The other list which he quotes, however, gives every emperor, with the number of years, months, and even days of each reign, so that there is no reason, at least in that list, for the omission of Pertinax and Didius Julianus. It seems probable that, under the influence of that exact list, and of the recentness of the reigns of the two emperors named, Clement can hardly have omitted them if they had already ruled. We can say with absolute certainty, however, only that the work was written after 192. Clement left Alexandria in 202, or before, and this, as well as the rest of his works, was written in all probability before that time at the latest.

The standard edition of Clement's works is that of Potter, Oxford, 1715, in two vols. (reprinted in Migne's *Patr. Gr.*, Vols. VIII. and IX.). Complete English translation in the *Ante-Nicene Fathers*, Amer. ed., Vol. II. On his writings, see especially Westcott's article in the *Dict. of Christ. Biog.* and for the literature on the subject, Schaff's *Ch. Hist.* II. 781.

[3] The *Hypotyposes* (ὑποτυπώσεις), or *Outlines* (Eusebius calls them οἱ ἐπιγεγραμμένοι ὑποτυπώσεων αὐτοῦ λόγοι), are no longer extant, though fragments have been preserved. The work (which was in eight books, according to this passage) is referred to by Eusebius, in Bk. I. chap. 12 (the fifth book), in Bk. I. chap. 1 (the sixth and seventh books), in Bk. II. chaps. 9 and 23 (the seventh book), chap. 15 (the sixth book), in Bk. V. chap. 11, and in Bk. VI. chap. 14 (the book not specified). Most of these extracts are of a historical character, but have to do (most of them, not all) with the apostolic age, or the New Testament. We are told in chap. 14 that the work contained abridged accounts of all the Scriptures, but Photius (*Cod.* 109) says that it seems to have dealt only with Genesis, Exodus, the Psalms, Ecclesiastes, the epistles of Paul, and the Catholic epistles (ὁ δὲ ὅλος σκοπὸς ὡσανεὶ ἑρμηνεῖαι τυγχάνουσι τῆς Γενέσεως κ.τ.λ.). Besides the detached quotations there are extant three series of extracts which are supposed to have been taken from the *Hypotyposes*. These are *The Summaries from Theodotus*, *The Prophetic Selections*, and the *Outlines on the Catholic Epistles*. On these fragments, which are very corrupt and desultory, see Westcott in the *Dict. of Christ. Biog.* They discuss all sorts of doctrines, and contain the interpretations of the most various schools, and it is not always clearly stated whether Clement himself adopts the opinion given, or whether he is simply quoting from another for the purpose of refuting him. Photius condemns parts of the *Hypotyposes* severely, but it seems, from these extracts which we have, that he may have read the work, full as it was of the heretical opinions of other men and schools, without distinguishing Clement's own opinions from those of others, and that thus he may carelessly have attributed to him all the wild notions which he mentions. These extracts as well as the various references of Eusebius show that the work, like most of the others which Clement wrote, covered a great deal of ground, and included discussions of a great many collateral subjects. It does not seem, in fact, to have been much more systematic than the *Instructor* or even the *Stromata*. It seems to have been intended as a part of the great series, of which the *Exhortation, Instructor,* and *Stromata* were the first three. If so, it followed them. We have no means of ascertaining its date more exactly.

[4] On Pantænus, see above, Bk. V. chap. 10, note 1.

[5] The *Exhortation to the Greeks* (ὁ λόγος προτρεπτικὸς πρὸς Ἕλληνας), the first of the series of three works mentioned in note 2, is still extant in its entirety. It is called by Jerome (*de vir. ill.* chap. 38) *Adversus Gentes, liber unus*, but, as Westcott remarks, it was addressed not to the Gentiles in general, but to the Greeks, as its title and its contents alike indicate. The general aim of the book is to "prove the superiority of Christianity to the religions and philosophies of heathendom," and thus to lead the unbeliever to accept it. It is full of Greek mythology and speculation, and exhibits, as Schaff says, almost a waste of learning. It was written before the *Instructor*, as we learn from a reference to it in the latter (chap. 1). It is stated above (Bk. V. chap. 28, § 4), by the anonymous writer against the Artemonites, that Clement wrote (at least some of his works) before the time of Victor of Rome (i.e. before 192 A. D.), and hence Westcott concludes that this work was written about 190, which cannot be far out of the way.

[6] The *Instructor* (ὁ παιδαγωγός, or, as Eusebius calls it here, τρεῖς τε οἱ τοῦ ἐπιγεγραμμένου παιδαγωγοῦ), is likewise extant, in three books. The work is chiefly of a moral and practical character, designed to furnish the new convert with rules for the proper conduct of his life over against the prevailing immoralities of the heathen. Its date is approximately fixed by the fact that it was written after the *Exhortation* to which it refers, and before the *Stromata*, which refers to it (see *Strom.* VI. 1).

[7] The *Quis Dives Salvetur ?* as it is called (τίς ὁ σωζόμενος πλούσιος), is a brief tract, discussing the words of Christ in Mark x. 17 sqq. It is still extant, and contains the beautiful story of John and the robber, quoted by Eusebius in Bk. III. chap. 23. It is an eloquent and able work; and when compared with the prevailing notions of the Church of his day, its teaching is remarkably wise and temperate. It is moderately ascetic, but goes to no extremes, and in this furnishes a pleasing contrast to the writings of most of the Fathers of Clement's time.

[8] τὸ περὶ τοῦ πάσχα σύγγραμμα. This work is no longer extant, nor had Photius seen it, although he reports that he had heard of it. Two fragments of it are found in the *Chronicon Paschale*, and are given by Potter. The work was composed, according to § 9, below, at the instigation of friends, who urged him to commit to writing the traditions which he had received from the ancient presbyters. From Bk. IV. chap. 26, we learn that it was written in reply to Melito's work on the same subject (see notes 5 and 23 on that chapter); and hence we may conclude that it was undertaken at the solicitation of friends who desired to see the arguments presented by Melito, as a representative of the Quartodeciman practice, refuted. The date of the work we have no means of ascertaining, for Melito's work was written early in the sixties (see *ibid.*).

[9] διαλέξεις περὶ νηστείας καὶ περὶ καταλαλιᾶς. Photius knew both these works by report (the second under the title περὶ κακολογίας), but had not seen them. Jerome calls the first *de jejunio disceptatio*, the second *de obtrectatione liber unus*. Neither of them is now extant; but fragments of the second have been preserved, and are given by Potter.

[10] ὁ προτρεπτικὸς εἰς ὑπομονὴν ἢ πρὸς τοὺς νεωστὶ βεβαπτισμένους. This work is mentioned neither by Jerome nor by Photius, nor has any vestige of it been preserved, so far as we know.

[11] ὁ ἐπιγεγραμμένος κανὼν ἐκκλησιαστικὸς, ἢ πρὸς τοὺς Ἰουδαΐζοντας. Jerome: *de canonibus ecclesiasticis, et adversum eos, qui Judæorum sequuntur errorum.* Photius mentions the work, calling it περὶ κανόνων ἐκκλησιαστικῶν, but he had not himself seen

to Alexander, the bishop mentioned above.

4   In the Stromata, he has not only treated extensively [12] of the Divine Scripture, but he also quotes from the Greek writers whenever anything that they have said seems to him profitable. He elucidates the opinions of many, both

5   Greeks and barbarians. He also refutes the false doctrines of the heresiarchs, and besides this, reviews a large portion of history, giving us specimens of very various learning ; with all the rest he mingles the views of philosophers. It is likely that on this account he gave his work the appropriate title of Stromata.[13]

6   He makes use also in these works of testimonies from the disputed Scriptures,[14] the so-called Wisdom of Solomon,[15] and of Jesus, the son of Sirach, and the Epistle to the Hebrews,[16] and those of Barnabas,[17] and Clement [18]

and Jude.[19]   He mentions also Tatian's [20]   7 Discourse to the Greeks, and speaks of Cassianus [21] as the author of a chronological work. He refers to the Jewish authors Philo,[22] Aristobulus,[23] Josephus,[24] Demetrius,[25] and Eupolemus,[26] as showing, all of them, in their works, that Moses and the Jewish race existed before the earliest origin of the Greeks. These   8 books abound also in much other learning. In the first of them [27] the author speaks of him-

---

[18] On the Epistle of Clement, see Bk. III. chap. 16, note 1.
[19] On the Epistle of Jude, see Bk. II. chap. 23, note .
[20] On Tatian and his works, see Bk. IV. chap. 29, note 1.
[21] This Cassianus is mentioned twice by Clement: once in *Strom.* I. 21, where Clement engages in a chronological study for the purpose of showing that the wisdom of the Hebrews is older than that of the Greeks, and refers to Cassian's *Exegetica* and Tatian's *Address to the Greeks* as containing discussions of the same subject; again in *Strom.* III. 13 sqq., where he is said to have been the founder of the sect of the *Docetæ*, and to have written a work, *De continentia* or *De castitate* (περὶ ἐγκρατείας ἢ περὶ εὐνουχίας), in which he condemned marriage. Here, too, he is associated with Tatian. He seems from these references to have been, like Tatian, an apologist for Christianity, and also like him to have gone off into an extreme asceticism, which the Church pronounced heretical (see Bk. IV. chap. 29, note 4). Whether he was personally connected with Tatian, or is mentioned with him by Clement simply because his views were similar, we do not know, nor can we fix the date at which he lived. Neither of his works referred to by Clement is now extant. Jerome (*de vir. ill.* chap. 38) mentions the work which Eusebius speaks of here, but says that he had not been able to find a copy of it. It is called by Clement, in the passage referred to here by Eusebius, Ἐξηγητικοί, and so Eusebius calls it in his *Præf. Evang.* X. 12, where he quotes from Clement.   But here he speaks of it as a χρονογραφία, and Jerome transcribes the word without translating it. We can gather from Clement's words (*Strom.* I. 21) that the work of Cassianus dealt largely with chronology, and hence Eusebius' reference to it under the name χρονογραφία is quite legitimate.
[22] On Philo and his works, see Bk. II. chaps. 4, 5, 17 and 18.
[23] The Aristobulus referred to here was an Alexandrian Jew and Peripatetic philosopher (see the passages in Clement and Eusebius referred to below), who lived in the second century B.C., and was the author of *Commentaries upon the Mosaic Law*, the chief object of which was to prove that Greek philosophy was borrowed from the books of Moses (see Clement, *Strom.* V. 14, who refers only to Peripatetic philosophy, which is too narrow). The work is referred to by Clement of Alexandria (in his *Stromata*, I. 15; V. 14; VI. 3, &c.), by Eusebius (in his *Præp. Evang.* VII. 14; VIII. 9, 10; XIII. 12, &c.), by Anatolius (as quoted by Eusebius below, in Bk. VII. chap. 32), and by other Fathers.   The work is no longer extant, but Eusebius gives two considerable fragments of it in his *Præp. Evang.* VIII. 10, and XIII. 12. See Schürer's *Gesch. d. jüdischen Volkes im Zeitalter Jesu*, II. p. 760 sq.   Schürer maintains the authenticity of the work against the attacks of many modern critics.
[24] On Josephus and his works, see Bk. III. chap. 9.
[25] Demetrius was a Grecian Jew, who wrote, toward the close of the third century B.C., a *History of Israel*, based upon the Scripture records, and with especial reference to chronology. Demetrius is mentioned by Josephus (who, however, wrongly makes him a heathen; *contra Apionem*, I. 23), by Clement of Alexandria, and by Eusebius.   His work is no longer extant, but fragments of it are preserved by Clement (*Strom.* I. 21) and by Eusebius (*Præp. Evang.* IX. 21 and 29).   See Schürer (*Præp. Evang.* IX. 17, 26, 30–34, and probably 39).   See Schürer, *ibid.* p. 730 sq.
[26] Eupolymus was also a Jewish historian, who wrote about the middle of the second century B.C., and is possibly to be identified with the Eupolymus mentioned in 1. Macc. viii. 17.   He wrote a *History of the Jews*, which is referred to under various titles by those that mention it, and which has consequently been resolved into three separate works by many scholars, but without warrant, as Schürer has shown.   The work, like that of Aristobulus, was clearly designed to show the dependence of Greek philosophy upon Hebrew wisdom (see Clement's *Strom.* I. 23).   It is no longer extant, but fragments have been preserved by Clement of Alexandria (*Strom.* I. 21, which gives us data for reckoning the time at which Eupolymus wrote, and I. 23) and by Eusebius (*Præp. Evang.* IX. 17, 26, 30–34, and probably 39).   See Schürer, *ibid.* p. 732 sq.
[27] Eusebius is apparently still referring to Clement's *Stromata*. In saying that Clement ὦν ἐν τῷ πρώτῳ περὶ ἑαυτοῦ δηλοῖ ὡς ἔγγιστα τῆς τῶν ἀποστόλων γενομένου διαδοχῆς, he was perhaps thinking of the passage in *Strom.* I. 1, where Clement says, " They [i.e. his teachers], preserving the tradition of the blessed doctrine, derived directly from the holy apostles, Peter, James, John, and Paul, the sons receiving it from the fathers (but few were like the fathers), came by God's will to us also to deposit those ancestral and apostolic seeds."   Clement in this passage does not mean to assert that his teachers were immediate disciples of the apostles, but only that they received the traditions of the apostles in direct descent from

---

it.   It is no longer extant, but a few fragments have been preserved, and are given by Potter.
    Danz (*De Eusebio*, p. 90) refers to Clement's *Stromata*, lib. VI. p. 803, ed. Potter, where he says that " the ecclesiastical canon is the agreement or disagreement of the law and the prophets with the testament given at the coming of Christ."   Danz concludes accordingly that in this work Clement wished to show to those who believed that the teaching of the law and the prophets was not only different from, but superior to the teachings of the Christian faith, — that is, to the Judaizers, — that the writers of the Old and New Testaments were in full harmony.   This might do, were it not for the fact that the work is directed not against Jews, but against Judaizers, i.e. Judaizing Christians.   A work to prove the Old and New Testament in harmony with each other could hardly have been addressed to such persons, ho must have believed them in harmony before they became Christians.   The truth is, the phrase κανὼν ἐκκλησιαστικός is used by the Fathers with a great variety of meanings, and the fact that Clement used it in one sense in one of his works by no means proves that he always used it in the same sense. It is more probable that the work was devoted to a discussion of certain practices or modes of living in which the Judaizers differed from the rest of the Church Catholic, perhaps in respect to feasts (might a reference to the Quartodeciman practice have been perhaps included?), fasts and other ascetic practices, observance of the Jewish Sabbaths, &c.   This use of the word in the sense of *regula* was very common (see Suicer's *Thesaurus*).   The work was dedicated, according to Eusebius, to the bishop Alexander, mentioned above in chap. 8 and elsewhere.   This is sufficient evidence that it was written considerably later than the three great works already referred to. Alexander was a student of Clement's; and since he was likewise a fellow-pupil of Origen's (see chap. 8, note 6), his student days under Clement must have extended at least nearly to the time when Clement left Alexandria (i.e. in or before 202 A.D.).   But Clement of course cannot have dedicated a work to him while he was still his pupil, and in fact we shall be safe in saying that Alexander must have gained some prominence before Clement would be led to dedicate a work to him.   We think naturally of the period which Clement spent with him while he was in prison and before he became bishop of Jerusalem (see chap. 11).   It is quite possible that Clement's residence in Cappadocia with Alexander had given him such an acquaintance with Judaizing heresies and practices that he felt constrained to write against them, and at the same time had given him such an affection for Alexander that he dedicated his work to him.
[12] Literally, " made a spreading" (κατάστρωσιν πεποίηται). Eusebius here plays upon the title of the work (Στρωματεῖς).
[13] See note 2.
[14] ἀντιλεγομένων γραφῶν.   On the *Antilegomena*, see Bk. III. chap. 25, note 1.
[15] The Wisdom of Solomon and the Wisdom of Sirach were two Old Testament apocryphal books.   The Church of the first three centuries made, on the whole, no essential difference between the books of the Hebrew canon and the Apocrypha. We find the Fathers, almost without exception, quoting from both indiscriminately.   It is true that catalogues were made by Melito, Origen, Athanasius, and others, which separated the Apocrypha from the books of the Hebrew canon; but this represented theory simply, not practice, and did not prevent even themselves from using both classes as Scripture.   Augustine went so far as to obliterate completely all distinction between the two, in theory as well as in practice.   The only one of the early Fathers to make a decided stand against the Apocrypha was Jerome; but he was not able to change the common view, and the Church continued (as the Catholic Church continues still) to use them all (with a few minor exceptions) as Holy Scripture.
[16] On the Epistle to the Hebrews, see Bk. III. chap. 3, note 17.
[17] On the Epistle of Barnabas, see Bk. III. chap. 25, note 20.

self as next after the successors of the apostles. In them he promises also to write a com-
9 mentary on Genesis.[28] In his book on the Passover[29] he acknowledges that he had been urged by his friends to commit to writing, for posterity, the traditions which he had heard from the ancient presbyters; and in the same work he mentions Melito and Irenæus, and certain others, and gives extracts from their writings.

CHAPTER XIV.

The Scriptures mentioned by him.

1 To sum up briefly, he has given in the Hypotyposes[1] abridged accounts of all canonical Scripture, not omitting the disputed books,[2] — I refer to Jude and the other Catholic epistles, and Barnabas[3] and the so-
2 called Apocalypse of Peter.[4] He says that the Epistle to the Hebrews[5] is the work of Paul, and that it was written to the Hebrews in the Hebrew language; but that Luke translated it carefully and published it for the Greeks, and hence the same style of expression is found
3 in this epistle and in the Acts. But he says that the words, Paul the Apostle, were probably not prefixed, because, in sending it to the Hebrews, who were prejudiced and suspicious of him, he wisely did not wish to repel them at the very beginning by giving his name.
4 Farther on he says: "But now, as the blessed presbyter said, since the Lord being the apostle of the Almighty, was sent to the Hebrews, Paul, as sent to the Gentiles, on account of his modesty did not subscribe himself an apostle of the Hebrews, through respect for the Lord, and because being a herald and apostle of the Gentiles he wrote to the Hebrews out of his superabundance."
5 Again, in the same books, Clement gives the tradition of the earliest presbyters, as to the order of the Gospels, in the following manner: The Gospels containing the gene-
6 alogies, he says, were written first. The

Gospel according to Mark[6] had this occasion. As Peter had preached the Word publicly at Rome, and declared the Gospel by the Spirit, many who were present requested that Mark, who had followed him for a long time and remembered his sayings, should write them out. And having composed the Gospel he gave
7 it to those who had requested it. When Peter learned of this, he neither directly forbade nor encouraged it. But, last of all, John, perceiving that the external[7] facts had been made plain in the Gospel, being urged by his friends, and inspired by the Spirit, composed a spiritual Gospel.[8] This is the account of Clement.
8 Again the above-mentioned Alexander,[9] in a certain letter to Origen, refers to Clement, and at the same time to Pantænus, as being among his familiar acquaintances. He writes as follows:

"For this, as thou knowest, was the will of God, that the ancestral friendship existing between us should remain unshaken; nay,
9 rather should be warmer and stronger. For we know well those blessed fathers who have trodden the way before us, with whom we shall soon be;[10] Pantænus, the truly blessed man and master, and the holy Clement, my master and benefactor, and if there is any other like them, through whom I became acquainted with thee, the best in everything, my master and brother."[11]

So much for these matters. But Adaman-
10 tius,[12] — for this also was a name of Origen, — when Zephyrinus[13] was bishop of Rome, visited

---

their immediate disciples. Eusebius' words are a little ambiguous, but they seem to imply that he thought that Clement was a pupil of immediate disciples of the apostles, which Clement does not assert in this passage, and can hardly have asserted in any passage, for he was in all probability born too late to converse with those who had seen any of the apostles.

[28] In his *Stromata* (VI. 18) Clement refers to a work on the origin of the world, which was probably to form a part of his work *On Principles*. This is perhaps the reference of which Eusebius is thinking when he says that Clement in the *Stromata* promises εἰς τὴν Γένεσιν ὑπομνηματιεῖσθειν. If so, Eusebius' words, which imply that Clement promised to write a commentary on Genesis, are misleading.

[29] On this work, see note 8.

[1] See the previous chapter, note 3.

[2] On the *Antilegomena* of Eusebius, and on the New Testament canon in general, see Bk. III. chap. 25, note 1.

[3] On the Epistle of Barnabas, see Bk. III. chap. 25, note 20.

[4] On the Apocalypse of Peter, see Bk. III. chap. 3, note 9.

[5] On the Epistle to the Hebrews, see above, Bk. III. chap. 3, note 17.

[6] On the composition of the Gospel of Mark, see Bk. II. chap. 15, note 4, and with this statement of Clement as to Peter's attitude toward its composition, compare the words of Eusebius in § 2 of that chapter, and see the note upon the passage (note 5).

[7] τὰ σωματικά.   [8] See Bk. III. chap. 24, note 7.

[9] Mentioned already in chaps. 8 and 11.

[10] We see from this sentence that at the time of the writing of this epistle both Pantænus and Clement were dead. The latter was still alive when Alexander wrote to the Antiochenes (see chap. 11), i.e. about the year 211 (see note 5 on that chapter). How much longer he lived we cannot tell. The epistle referred to here must of course have been written at any rate subsequent to the year 211, and hence while Alexander was bishop of Jerusalem. The expression " with whom we shall soon be " (πρὸς οὓς μετ' ὀλίγον ἐσόμεθα) seems to imply that the epistle was written when Alexander and Origen were advanced in life, but this cannot be pressed.

[11] It is from this passage that we gather that Alexander was a student of Clement's and a fellow-pupil of Origen's (see chap. 8, note 6, and chap. 2, note 1). The epistle does not state this directly, but the conclusion seems sufficiently obvious.

[12] The name Adamantius ('Αδαμάντιος from ἀδάμας unconquerable, hence *hard, adamantine*) is said by Jerome (*Ep. ad Paulam*, § 3; Migne's ed. *Ep.* XXXIII.) to have been given him on account of his untiring industry, by Photius (*Cod.* 118) on account of the invincible force of his arguments, and by Epiphanius (*Hær.* LXIV. 74) to have been vainly adopted by himself. But Eusebius' simple statement at this point looks rather as if *Adamantius* was a second name which belonged to Origen from the beginning, and had no reference to his character. We know that two names were very common in that age. This opinion is adopted by Tillemont, Redepenning, Westcott, and others, although many still hold the opposite view. Another name, *Chalcenterus*, given to him by Jerome in the epistle already referred to, was undoubtedly, as we can see from the context, applied to him by Jerome, because of his resemblance to Didymus of Alexandria (who bore that surname) in his immense industry as an author.

[13] On Zephyrinus, bishop of Rome, see Bk. V. chap. 28, note 5. He was bishop from about 198, or 199, to 217. This gives considerable range for the date of Origen's visit to Rome, which we have no means of fixing with exactness. There is no reason for supposing

Rome, "desiring," as he himself somewhere says, "to see the most ancient church of Rome."

11 After a short stay there he returned to Alexandria. And he performed the duties of catechetical instruction there with great zeal; Demetrius, who was bishop there at that time, urging and even entreating. him to work diligently for the benefit of the brethren.[14]

CHAPTER XV.

Heraclas.[1]

But when he saw that he had not time for the deeper study of divine things, and for the investigation and interpretation of the Sacred Scriptures, and also for the instruction of those who came to him, — for coming, one after another, from morning till evening to be taught by him, they scarcely gave him time to breathe, — he divided the multitude. And from those whom he knew well, he selected Heraclas, who was a zealous student of divine things, and in other respects a very learned man, not ignorant of philosophy, and made him his associate in the work of instruction. He entrusted to him the elementary training of beginners, but reserved for himself the teaching of those who were farther advanced.

CHAPTER XVI.

Origen's Earnest Study of the Divine Scriptures.

1 So earnest and assiduous was Origen's research into the divine words that he learned the Hebrew language,[1] and procured as his own the original Hebrew Scriptures which were in the hands of the Jews. He investigated also the works of other translators of the Sacred Scriptures besides the Seventy.[2] And in addi-

tion to the well-known translations of Aquila,[3] Symmachus,[4] and Theodotion,[5] he discovered certain others which had been concealed from remote times, — in what out-of-the-way corners I know not, — and by his search he brought them to light.[6] Since he did not 2

[3] Aquila is first mentioned by Irenæus (Adv. Hær. III. 21. 1, quoted by Eusebius, Bk. V. chap. 8, above), who calls him a Jewish proselyte of Pontus; Epiphanius says of Sinope in Pontus. Tradition is uniform that he was a Jewish proselyte, and that he lived in the time of Hadrian, or in the early part of the second century according to Rabbinic tradition. He produced a Greek translation of the Old Testament, which was very slavish in its adherence to the original, sacrificing the Greek idiom to the Hebrew without mercy, and even violating the grammatical structure of the former for the sake of reproducing the exact form of the latter. Because of its faithfulness to the original, it was highly prized by the Rabbinic authorities, and became more popular among the Jews in general than the LXX. (On the causes of the waning popularity of the latter, see note 8, below.) Neither Aquila's version, nor the two following, are now extant; but numerous fragments have been preserved by those Fathers who saw and used Origen's Hexapla.

[4] Symmachus is said by Eusebius, in the next chapter, to have been an Ebionite; and Jerome agrees with him (Comment. in Hab., lib. II. c. 3), though the testimony of the latter is weakened by the fact that he wrongly makes Theodotion also an Ebionite (see next note). It has been claimed that Symmachus was a Jew, not a Christian; but Eusebius' direct statement is too strong to be set aside, and is corroborated by certain indications in the version itself, e.g. in Dan. ix. 26, where the word χριστός, which Aquila avoids, is used. The composition of his version is assigned by Epiphanius and the Chron. paschale to the reign of Septimius Severus (193–211); and although not much reliance is to be placed upon their statements, still they must be about right in this case, for that Symmachus' version is younger than Irenæus is rendered highly probable by the latter's omission of it where he refers to those of Theodotion and Aquila; and, on the other hand, it must of course have been composed before Origen began his Hexapla. Symmachus' version is distinguished from Aquila's by the purity of its Greek and its freedom from Hebraisms. The author's effort was not slavishly to reproduce the original, but to make an elegant and idiomatic Greek translation, and in this he succeeded very well, being excellently versed in both languages, though he sometimes sacrificed the exact sense of the Hebrew, and occasionally altered it under the influence of dogmatic prepossessions. The version is spoken very highly of by Jerome, and was used freely by him in the composition of the Vulgate. For further particulars in regard to Symmachus' version, see the Dict. of Christ. Biog. III. p. 19 sq.

[5] It has been disputed whether Theodotion was a Jew or a Christian. Jerome (de vir. ill. 54, and elsewhere) calls him an Ebionite; in his Ep. ad Augustin. c. 19 (Migne's ed. 112), a Jew; while in the preface to his commentary on Daniel he says that some called him an Ebionite, qui altero genere Judæus est. Irenæus (Adv. Hær. III. 21. 1) and Epiphanius (de mens. et pond. 17) say that he was a Jewish proselyte, which is probably true. The reports in regard to his nationality are conflicting. The time at which he lived is disputed. The Chron. paschale assigns him to the reign of Commodus, and Epiphanius may also be urged in support of that date, though he commits a serious blunder in making a second Commodus, and is thus led into great confusion. But Theodotion, as well as Aquila, is mentioned by Irenæus, and hence must be pushed back well into the second century. It has been discovered, too, that Hermas used his version (see Hort's article in the Johns Hopkins University Circular, December, 1884), which obliges us to throw it back still further, and Schürer has adduced some very strong reasons for believing it older than Aquila's version (see Schürer's Gesch. d. Juden im Zeitalter Jesu, II. p. 709). Theodotion's version, like Aquila's, was intended to reproduce the Hebrew more exactly than the LXX did. It is based upon the LXX, however, which it corrects by the Hebrew, and therefore resembles the former much more closely than Theodotion's does. We have no notices of the use of this version by the Jews. Aquila's version (supposing it younger than Theodotion's) seems to have superseded it entirely. Theodotion's translation of Daniel, however, was accepted by the Christians, instead of the LXX Daniel, and replacing the latter in all the MSS. of the LXX, has been preserved entire. Aside from this we have only such fragments as have been preserved by the Fathers that saw and used the Hexapla. It will be seen that the order in which Eusebius mentions the three versions here is not chronological. He simply follows the order in which they stand in Origen's Hexapla (see below, note 8). Epiphanius is led by that order to make Theodotion's version later than the other, which is quite a mistake, as has been seen.

For further particulars in regard to the versions of Aquila and Theodotion, and for the literature of the subject, see Schürer, ibid. p. 704 sq.

[6] We know very little about these anonymous Greek versions of the Old Testament. Eusebius' words (" which had been concealed from remote times," τὸν πάλαι λανθανούσας χρόνον) would lead us to think them older than the versions of Aquila, Theodotion, and Symmachus. One of them, Eusebius tells us, was found at Nicopo-

that Eusebius is incorrect in putting it among the events occurring during Caracalla's reign (211–217). On the other hand, it must have taken place before the year 216, for in that year Origen went to Palestine (see chap. 19, note 23) and remained there some time. Whether Origen's visit was undertaken simply from the desire to see the church of Rome, as Eusebius says, or in connection with matters of business, we cannot tell.

[14] On Demetrius' relations to Origen, see chap. 8, note 4.

[1] On Heraclas, see chap. 3, note 2.

[1] Origen's study of the Hebrew, which, according to Jerome (de vir. ill. chap. 54), was "contrary to the custom of his day and race," is not at all surprising. He felt that he needed some knowledge of it as a basis for his study of the Scriptures to which he had devoted himself, and also as a means of comparing the Hebrew and Greek texts of the Old Testament, a labor which he regarded as very important for polemical purposes. As to his familiarity with the Hebrew it is now universally conceded that it was by no means so great as has formerly been supposed. He seems to have learned only about enough to enable him to identify the Hebrew which corresponded with the Greek texts which he used, and even in this he often makes mistakes. He sometimes confesses openly his lack of critical and independent knowledge of the Hebrew (e.g. Hom. in Num. XIV. 1; XVI. 4). He often makes blunders which seem absurd, and yet in many cases he shows considerable knowledge in regard to peculiar forms and idioms. His Hebrew learning was clearly fragmentary, and acquired from various sources. Cf. Redepenning, I. p. 365 sq.

[2] On the LXX, see Bk. V. chap. 8, note 31.

know the authors, he simply stated that he had found this one in Nicopolis near Actium [7] and that one in some other place. In the Hexapla [8] of the Psalms, after the four prominent translations, he adds not only a fifth, but also a sixth and seventh.[9] He states of one of these that he found it in a jar in Jericho in the time of Antoninus, the son of Severus. Having collected all of these, he divided them into sections, and placed them opposite each other, with the Hebrew text itself. He thus left us the copies of the so-called Hexapla. He arranged also separately an edition of Aquila and Symmachus and Theodotion with the Septuagint, in the Tetrapla.[10]

---

lis near Actium, another in a jar at Jericho, but where the third was discovered he did not know. Jerome (in his *Prologus in expos. Cant. Cant. sec. Originem ;* Origen's works, ed. Lommatzsch, XIV. 235) reports that the "fifth edition" (*quinta editio*) was found *in Actio litore ;* but Epiphanius, who seems to be speaking with more exact knowledge than Jerome, says that the "fifth" was discovered at Jericho and the "sixth" in Nicopolis, near Actium (*De mens. et pond.* 18). Jerome calls the authors of the "fifth" and "sixth" *Judaïcos translatores,* which according to his own usage might mean either Jews or Jewish Christians (see Redepenning, p. 165), and at any rate the author of the "sixth" was a Christian, as is clear from his rendering of Heb. iii. 13: ἐξῆλθες τοῦ σῶσαι τὸν λαὸν σου διὰ Ἰησοῦ τοῦ χριστοῦ. The "fifth" is quoted by Origen on the Psalms, Proverbs, Song of Songs, minor prophets, Kings, &c.; the "sixth," on the Psalms, Song of Songs, and Habakkuk, according to Field, the latest editor of the *Hexapla.* Whether these versions were fragmentary, or were used only in these particular passages for special reasons, we do not know. Of the "seventh" no clear traces can be discovered, but it must have been used for the Psalms at any rate, as we see from this chapter. As to the time when these versions were found, we are doubtless to assign the discovery of the one at Nicopolis near Actium to the visit made by Origen to Greece in 231 (see below, p. 396). Epiphanius, who in the present case seems to be speaking with more customary accuracy, puts its discovery into the time of the emperor Alexander (222-235). The other one, which Epiphanius calls the "fifth," was found, according to him, in the seventh year of Caracalla's reign (217) "in jars at Jericho." We know that at this time Origen was in Palestine (see chap. 19, note 23), and hence Epiphanius' report may well be correct. If it is, he has good reason for calling the latter the "fifth," and the former the "sixth." The place and time of the discovery of the "seventh" are alike unknown. For further particulars in regard to these versions, see the prolegomena to Field's edition of the *Hexapla,* the article *Hexapla* in the *Dict. of Christ. Biog.,* and Redepenning, II. 164 sq.

[7] Nicopolis near Actium, so designated to distinguish it from a number of other cities bearing the same name, was a city of Epirus, lying on the northern shore of the Ambracian gulf, opposite the promontory of Actium.

[8] Origen's *Hexapla* (τὰ ἑξαπλᾶ, τὸ ἑξαπλοῦν, τὸ ἑξασέλιδον, the first form being used by Eusebius in this chapter) was a polyglot Old Testament containing the Hebrew text, a transliteration of it in Greek letters (important because the Hebrew text was unpointed), the versions of Aquila, of Symmachus, of the LXX, and of Theodotion, arranged in six columns in the order named, with the addition in certain places of a fifth, sixth, and even seventh Greek version (see Jerome's description of it, in his Commentary on Titus, chap. 3, ver. 9). The parts which contained these latter versions were sometimes called *Octapla* (they seem never to have borne the name *nonapla*). The order of the columns was determined by the fact that Aquila's version most closely resembled the Hebrew, and hence was put next to it, followed by Symmachus' version, which was based directly upon the Hebrew, but was not so closely conformed to it; while Theodotion's version, which was based not upon the Hebrew, but upon the LXX, naturally followed the latter. Origen's object in undertaking this great work was not scientific, but polemic; it was not for the sake of securing a correct Hebrew text, but for the purpose of furnishing adequate means for the reconstruction of the original text of the LXX, which in his day was exceedingly corrupt. It was Origen's belief, and he was not alone in his opinion (cf. Justin Martyr's *Dial. with Trypho,* chap. 71), that the Hebrew Old Testament had been seriously altered by the Jews, and that the LXX (an inspired translation, as it was commonly held to be by the Christians) alone represented the true form of Scripture. For two centuries before and more than a century after Christ the LXX stood in high repute among the Jews, even in Palestine, and outside of Palestine had almost completely taken the place of the original Hebrew. Under the influence of its universal use among the Jews the Christians adopted it, and looked upon it as inspired Scripture just as truly as if it had been in the original tongue. Early in the second century (as Schürer points out) various causes were at work to lessen its reputation among the Jews. Chief among these were first, the growing conservative reaction against all non-Hebraic culture, which found its culmination in the Rabbinic schools of the second century; and second, the ever-increasing hostility to Christianity. The latter cause tended to bring the LXX into disfavor with the Jews, because it was universally employed by the Christians, and was cited in favor of Christian doctrines in many cases where it differed from the Hebrew text, which furnished less support to the particular doctrine defended. It was under the influence of this reaction against the LXX, which undoubtedly began even before the second century, that the various versions already mentioned took their rise. Aquila especially aimed to keep the Hebrew text as pure as possible, while making it accessible to the Greek-speaking Jews, who had hitherto been obliged to rely upon the LXX. It will be seen that the Christians and the Jews, who originally accepted the same Scriptures, would gradually draw apart, the one party still holding to the LXX, the other going back to the original; and the natural consequence of this was that the Jews taunted the

Christians with using only a translation which did not agree with the original, and therefore was of no authority, while the Christians, on the other hand, accused the Jews of falsifying their Scriptures, which should agree with the more pure and accurate LXX. Under these circumstances, Origen conceived the idea that it would be of great advantage to the Christians, in their polemics against the Jews, to know more accurately than they did the true form of the LXX text, and the extent and nature of its variations from the Hebrew. As the matter stood everything was indefinite, for no one knew to exactly what extent the two differed, and no one knew, in the face of the numerous variant texts, the precise form of the LXX itself (cf. Redepenning, II. p. 156 sq.). The Hebrew text given by Origen seems to have been the vulgar text, and to have differed little from that in use to-day. With the LXX it was different. Here Origen made a special effort to ascertain the most correct text, and did not content himself with giving simply one of the numerous texts extant, for he well knew that all were more or less corrupt. But his method was not to throw out of the text all passages not well supported by the various witnesses, but rather to enrich the text from all available sources, thus making it as full as possible. Wherever, therefore, the Hebrew contained a passage omitted in the LXX, he inserted in the latter the translation of the passage, taken from one of the other versions, marking the addition with " obeli "; and wherever, on the other hand, the fullest LXX text which he had contained more than the Hebrew and the other versions combined, he allowed the redundant passage to stand, but marked it with asterisks. The *Hexapla* as a whole seems never to have been reproduced, but the LXX text as contained in the fifth column was multiplied many times, especially under the direction of Pamphilus and Eusebius (who had the original MS. at Cæsarea), and this recension came into common use. It will be seen that Origen's process must have wrought great confusion in the text of the LXX ; for future copyists, in reproducing the text given by Origen, would be prone to neglect the critical signs, and give the whole as the correct form of the LXX; and critical editors to-day find it very difficult to reach even the form of the LXX text used by Origen. The *Hexapla* is no longer extant. When the Cæsarean MS. of it perished we do not know. Jerome saw it, and made large use of it, but after his time we have no further trace of it, and it probably perished with the rest of the Cæsarean library before the end of the seventh century, perhaps considerably earlier. Numerous editions have been published of the fragments of the *Hexapla,* taken from the works of the Fathers, from Scholia in MSS. of the LXX, and from a Syriac version of the Hexaplar LXX, which is still in large part extant. The best edition is that of Field, in two vols., Oxford, 1875. His prolegomena contain the fullest and most accurate information in regard to the *Hexapla.* Comp. also Taylor's article in the *Dict. of Christ. Biog.,* and Redepenning, II. p. 156 sq. Origen seems to have commenced his great work in Alexandria. This is implied by the account of Eusebius, and is stated directly by Epiphanius (*Hær.* LXIV. 3), who says that this was the first work which he undertook at the solicitation of Ambrose (see chap. 18). We may accept this as in itself quite probable, for there could be no better foundation for his exegetical labors than just such a piece of critical work, and the numerous scribes furnished him by Ambrose (see chap. 18) may well have devoted themselves largely to this very work, as Redepenning remarks. But the work was by no means completed at once. The time of his discovery of the other versions of the Old Testament (see above, note 6) in itself shows that he continued his labor upon the great edition for many years (the late discovery of these versions may perhaps explain the fact that he did not use them in connection with all the books of the Old Testament?) ; and Epiphanius (*de mens. et pond.* 18) says that he was engaged upon it for twenty-eight years, and completed it at Tyre. This is quite likely, and will explain the fact that the MS. of the work remained in the Cæsarean library. Field, however, maintains that our sources do not permit us to fix the time or place either of the commencement or of the completion of the work with any degree of accuracy (see p. xlviii. sq.).

[9] Valesius remarks that there is an inconsistency here, and that it should be said "not only a fifth and sixth, but also a seventh." All the MSS. and versions, however, support the reading of the text, and we must therefore suppose the inconsistency (if there is one, which is doubtful) to be Eusebius' own, not that of a scribe.

[10] Greek: ἐν τοῖς τετραπλοῖς ἐπικατασκευάσας. The last word indicates that the *Tetrapla* was prepared after, not before, the *Hexapla* (cf. Valesius *in hoc loco*), and Redepenning (p. 175 sq.) gives other satisfactory reasons for this conclusion. The design seems to have been simply to furnish a convenient abridgment of

CHAPTER XVII.

The Translator Symmachus.[1]

As to these translators it should be stated that Symmachus was an Ebionite. But the heresy of the Ebionites, as it is called, asserts that Christ was the son of Joseph and Mary, considering him a mere man, and insists strongly on keeping the law in a Jewish manner, as we have seen already in this history.[2] Commentaries of Symmachus are still extant in which he appears to support this heresy by attacking the Gospel of Matthew.[3] Origen states that he obtained these and other commentaries of Symmachus on the Scriptures from a certain Juliana,[4] who, he says, received the books by inheritance from Symmachus himself.

CHAPTER XVIII.

Ambrose.

1 ABOUT this time Ambrose,[1] who held the heresy of Valentinus,[2] was convinced by

the larger work, fitted for those who did not read Hebrew; that is, for the great majority of Christians, even scholars.

[1] On Symmachus, see the previous chapter, note 4.

[2] In Bk. III. chap. 27. For a discussion of Ebionism, see the notes on that chapter.

[3] On the attitude of the Ebionites toward the Canonical Gospel of Matthew (to which, of course, Eusebius here refers), see *ibid.* note 8. All traces of this work and of Symmachus' " other interpretations of Scripture " (ἄλλων εἰς τὰς γραφὰς ἑρμηνειῶν), mentioned just below, have vanished. We must not include Symmachus' translation of the Old Testament in these other works (as has been done by Huet and others), for there is no hint either in this passage or in that of Palladius (see next note) of a reference to that version, which was, like those of Aquila and Theodotion, well known in Origen's time (see the previous chapter).

[4] This Juliana is known to us only from this passage and from Palladius, *Hist. Laus.* 147. Palladius reports, on the authority of an entry written by Origen himself, which he says he found in an ancient book (ἐν παλαιοτάτῳ βιβλίῳ στιχηρῷ), that Juliana was a virgin of Cæsarea in Cappadocia, and that she gave refuge to Origen in the time of some persecution. If this account is to be relied upon, Origen's sojourn in the lady's house is doubtless to be assigned, with Huet, to the persecution of Maximinus (235–238; see below, chap. 28, note 2). It must be confessed, however, that in the face of the absolute silence of Eusebius and others, the story has a suspicious look.

[1] Of the early life of Ambrose, the friend of Origen, we know nothing. We learn from Origen's *Exhortatio ad Martyr.* c. 14, and Jerome's *de vir. ill.* c. 56, that he was of a wealthy and noble family (cf. chap. 23 of this book), and from the *Exhort. ad Mart.* c. 36, that he probably held some high official position. Eusebius says here that he was for some time a Valentinian, Jerome that he was a Marcionite, others give still different reports. However that was, the authorities all agree that he was converted to the orthodox faith by Origen, and that he remained devoted to him for the rest of his life. From chap. 23 we learn that he urged Origen to undertake the composition of commentaries on the Scriptures, and that he furnished ample pecuniary means for the prosecution of the work. He was also himself a diligent student, as we gather from that chapter (cf. also Jerome, *de vir. ill.* c. 56). From chap. 28 we learn that he was a confessor in the persecution of Maximinus (Jerome calls him also a deacon), and it seems to have been in Cæsarea or its neighborhood that he suffered, whither he had gone undoubtedly on account of his affection for Origen, who was at that time there (cf. the *Exhort.* c. 41). He is mentioned for the last time in the dedication and conclusion of Origen's *Contra Celsum*, which was written between 246 and 250 (see chap. 36, below). Jerome (*l.c.*) states that he died before Origen, so that he cannot have lived long after this. He left no writings, except some epistles which are no longer extant. Jerome, however, in his *Ep. ad Marcellam*, § 1 (Migne's ed., *Ep.* 43), attributes to Ambrose an epistle, a fragment of which is extant under the name of Origen (to whom it doubtless belongs) and which is printed in Lommatzsch's edition of Origen's works, Vol. XVII. p. 5. Origen speaks of him frequently as a man of education and of liter-

Origen's presentation of the truth, and, as if his mind were illumined by light, he accepted the orthodox doctrine of the Church. Many 2 others also, drawn by the fame of Origen's learning, which resounded everywhere, came to him to make trial of his skill in sacred literature. And a great many heretics, and not a few of the most distinguished philosophers, studied under him diligently, receiving instruction from him not only in divine things, but also in secular philosophy. For when he perceived 3 that any persons had superior intelligence he instructed them also in philosophic branches — in geometry, arithmetic, and other preparatory studies — and then advanced to the systems[3] of the philosophers and explained their writings. And he made observations and comments upon each of them, so that he became celebrated as a great philosopher even among the Greeks themselves. And he 4 instructed many of the less learned in the common school branches,[4] saying that these would be no small help to them in the study and understanding of the Divine Scriptures. On this account he considered it especially necessary for himself to be skilled in secular and philosophical learning.[5]

CHAPTER XIX.

Circumstances related of Origen.

THE Greek philosophers of his age are 1 witnesses to his proficiency in these subjects. We find frequent mention of him in their writings. Sometimes they dedicated their own works to him; again, they submitted their labors to him as a teacher for his judgment. Why 2 need we say these things when even Porphyry,[1] who lived in Sicily in our own times and

ary tastes and devoted to the study of the Scriptures, and Jerome says of him *non inelegantis ingenii fuit, sicut ejus ad Originem epistolæ indicio sunt* (*l.c.*). The affection which Origen felt for him is evinced by many notices in his works and by the fact that he dedicated to him the *Exhortatio ad Martyr.*, on the occasion of his suffering under Maximinus. It was also at Ambrose's solicitation that he wrote his great work against Celsus, which he likewise dedicated to him.

[2] On Valentinus, see above, Bk. IV. chap. 11, note 1.

[3] Greek, αἱρέσεις.

[4] ἐγκύκλια γράμματα; "the circle of those arts and sciences which every free-born youth in Greece was obliged to go through before applying to any professional studies" (Liddell and Scott, defining ἐγκ. παιδεία).

[5] On Origen's education, see p. 392, below.

[1] Porphyry, one of the most distinguished of the Neo-Platonists, disciple, biographer, and expounder of Plotinus, was born in 232 or 233 in the Orient (perhaps at Tyre), and at the age of thirty went to Rome, where he came into connection with Plotinus, and spent a large part of his life. He was a man of wide and varied learning; and though not an original thinker, he was a clear and vigorous writer and expounder of the philosophy of Plotinus. It may be well, at this point, to say a word about that remarkable school or system of philosophy, of which Plotinus was the greatest master and Porphyry the chief expounder. Neo-Platonism was the most prominent phenomenon of the age in the philosophic world. The object of the Neo-Platonists was both speculative and practical: on the one side to elaborate an eclectic system of philosophy which should reconcile Platonism and Aristotelianism, and at the same time do justice to elements of truth in other schools of thought; on the other

wrote books against us, attempting to traduce the Divine Scriptures by them, mentions those who have interpreted them; and being unable in any way to find a base accusation against the doctrines, for lack of arguments turns to reviling and calumniating their interpreters, attempting especially to slander Origen, whom he says he
3 knew in his youth. But truly, without knowing it, he commends the man; telling the

truth about him in some cases where he could not do otherwise; but uttering falsehoods where he thinks he will not be detected. Sometimes he accuses him as a Christian; again he describes his proficiency in philosophic learning. But hear his own words:

"Some persons, desiring to find a solu-   4
tion of the baseness of the Jewish Scriptures rather than abandon them, have had recourse to explanations inconsistent and incongruous with the words written, which explanations, instead of supplying a defense of the foreigners, contain rather approval and praise of themselves. For they boast that the plain words of Moses are enigmas, and regard them as oracles full of hidden mysteries; and having bewildered the mental judgment by folly, they make their explanations." Farther on he says:

"As an example of this absurdity take a   5
man whom I met when I was young, and who was then greatly celebrated and still is, on account of the writings which he has left. I refer to Origen, who is highly honored by the teachers of these doctrines. For this man,   6
having been a hearer of Ammonius,[2] who had attained the greatest proficiency in philosophy of any in our day, derived much benefit from his teacher in the knowledge of the sciences; but as to the correct choice of life, he pursued a course opposite to his. For   7
Ammonius, being a Christian, and brought up by Christian parents, when he gave himself to study and to philosophy straightway conformed to the life required by the laws. But Origen, having been educated as a Greek in Greek literature, went over to the barbarian recklessness.[3] And carrying over the learning

---

side, to revivify and strengthen the old paganism by idealizing and purifying it for the sake of the philosophers, and at the same time by giving it a firmer philosophic basis than it had hitherto possessed. Neo-Platonism, taken as a whole, has therefore both a philosophic and a religious motive. It may be defined in the briefest terms, in its philosophic aspect, as an eclectic revival of Greek metaphysics (especially Platonic-Aristotelian), modified by the influence of Oriental philosophy and of Christianity; in its religious aspect, as an attempt to restore and regenerate paganism by means of philosophy. In its earlier and better days, the philosophic element greatly predominated, — in fact, the religious element may be said to have been, in large part, a later growth; but gradually the latter came more and more into the foreground, until, under Jamblichus (d. 330 A.D.), the chief master of the Syrian school, Neo-Platonism degenerated into a system of religious mysteries, in which theurgic practices played a prominent part. Under Proclus (d. 485), the great master of the Athenian school, the philosophic element was again emphasized; but Aristotelianism now gained the predominance, and the system became a sort of scholastic art, and gradually degenerated into pure formalism, until it finally lost all influence. The extent of the influence which Christianity exerted upon Neo-Platonism is a greatly disputed point. We shall, perhaps, come nearest the truth if we say that its influence was in the main not direct, but that it was nevertheless real, inasmuch as it had introduced problems up to that time undiscussed, with which Neo-Platonism busied itself; in fact, it may almost be said that Neo-Platonism was at first little more than (Aristotelian-) Platonism busying itself with the new problems of salvation and redemption which Christianity had thrown into the world of thought. It was un-Christian at first (it became under Porphyry and later Neo-Platonists anti-Christian), because it solved these problems in a way different from the Christian way. This will explain the fact that all through, whether in the more strictly philosophic system of Plotinus, or in the more markedly religious and theurgic system of Jamblichus, there ran a vein of mysticism, the conception of an intimate union with the supreme God as the highest state to which man can attain. Porphyry, with whom we are at present concerned, was eminently practical in his thinking. The end of philosophy with him was not knowledge, but holiness, the salvation of the soul. He recommended a moderate asceticism as a chief means of freeing the soul from the bonds of matter, and thus permitting it to rise to union with God. At the same time, he did not advise the neglect of the customary religious rites of Paganism, which might aid in the elevation of the spirit of man toward the deity. It was with Porphyry that Neo-Platonism first came into direct conflict with Christianity, and its enmity against the latter goes far to explain the increasing emphasis which he and the Neo-Platonists who followed him laid upon religious rites and practices. Its philosophy, its solution of the great problems of the age, was essentially and radically different from that of Christianity; and although at first they might run alongside one another as independent schools, without much thought of conflict, it was inevitable that in time the rivalry, and then the active hostility, should come. Neo-Platonism, like Christianity, had a solution of the great problem of living to offer to the world, — in an age of unexampled corruption, when thoughtful men were all seeking for a solution, — and each was essentially exclusive of the other. The attack, therefore, could not be long delayed. Porphyry seems to have begun it in his famous work in fifteen books, now lost, which was answered in extenso by Methodius of Tyre, Eusebius, and Apolinarius of Laodicea. The answers, too, have perished; but from extant fragments we are able to see that Porphyry's attack was very learned and able. He endeavored to point out the inconsistencies in the sacred narrative, in order to discredit its divine origin. At the same time, he treated Christ with the greatest respect, and ranked him very high as a sage (though only human), and found much that was good in his teaching. Augustine (De consensu Evang. I. 15) says that the Neo-Platonists praised Christ, but railed at his disciples (cf. Eusebius' words in this chapter). Porphyry was a very prolific writer; but only a few of his works are now extant, chief among them the ἀφορμαὶ πρὸς τὰ νοητά, or Sententiæ, a brief but comprehensive exposition of his philosophic system. We learn from this chapter that he had met Origen when very young (he was but about twenty when Origen died); where, we do not know. He lived to be at least sixty-eight years old (see his Vita Plot. 23), and Suidas says that he died under Diocletian, i.e. before 305 A.D.

On Porphyry and Neo-Platonism in general, see the great works of Vacherot (Hist. critique de l'École d'Alexandrie) and Simon (Hist. de l'École d'Alexandrie); also Zeller's Philosophie der Griechen, and especially Erdmann's History of Philosophy (Engl. trans., London, 1889).

---

[2] Of the life of Ammonius Saccas, the "father of Neo-Platonism," very little is known. He is said by Suidas (s. v. Origenes) and by Ammianus Marcellinus to have been a porter in his youth and to have gained his second name from his occupation. That he was of Christian parents and afterward embraced paganism is stated in this passage by Porphyry, though Eusebius (§ 10, below) and Jerome assert that he remained a Christian. From all that we know of the teachings of Ammonius Saccas as reported to us by Plotinus and other Neo-Platonists, we cannot imagine him to have remained a Christian. The only solution of the difficulty then is to suppose Eusebius (whom Jerome follows) to have confounded him with a Christian of the same name who wrote the works which Eusebius mentions (see note 16). Ammonius was an Alexandrian by birth and residence, and died in 243. His teaching was of a lofty and noble character, to judge from Plotinus' descriptions, and as a teacher he was wonderfully fascinating. He numbered among his pupils Herennius, Longinus, the pagan Origen, and Plotinus. The Christian Origen also studied under him for a time, according to this passage. He wrote nothing (according to the Vita Plot. c. 20), and hence we have to rely solely upon the reports of his disciples and successors for our knowledge of his system. It is difficult in the absence of all direct testimony to ascertain his teaching with exactness. Plotinus claims to give only what he learned from Ammonius, but it is evident, from his disagreement in many points with others of Ammonius' disciples, that the system taught by him was largely modified by his own thinking. It is clear that Ammonius, who undoubtedly took much from his great master, Numenius, endeavored to reconcile Plato and Aristotle, thus laying the basis for the speculative eclecticism of Neo-Platonism, while at the same time there must have been already in his teaching the same religious and mystical element which was present to some extent in all his disciples, and which played so large a part in Neo-Platonism.

[3] τὸ βάρβαρον τόλμημα. Porphyry means to say that Origen was originally a heathen, and was afterward converted to Christianity; but this is refuted by the universal tradition of antiquity, and is clearly a mistake, as Eusebius (who calls it a "falsehood")

which he had obtained, he hawked it about, in his life conducting himself as a Christian and contrary to the laws, but in his opinions of material things and of the Deity being like a Greek, and mingling Grecian teachings with foreign fables.[4]

8 For he was continually studying Plato, and he busied himself with the writings of Numenius[5] and Cronius,[6] Apollophanes,[7] Longinus,[8] Moderatus,[9] and Nicomachus,[10] and those famous among the Pythagoreans. And he used the books of Chæremon[11] the Stoic, and of Cornutus.[12]

Becoming acquainted through them with the figurative interpretation of the Grecian mysteries, he applied it to the Jewish Scriptures."[13]

9 These things are said by Porphyry in the third book of his work against the Christians.[14] He speaks truly of the industry and learning of the man, but plainly utters a falsehood (for what will not an opposer of Christians do?) when he says that he went over from the Greeks,[15] and that Ammonius fell from a life of piety into heathen customs. For the 10 doctrine of Christ was taught to Origen by his parents, as we have shown above. And Ammonius held the divine philosophy unshaken and

---

remarks below. Porphyry's supposition, in the absence of definite knowledge, is not at all surprising, for Origen's attainments in secular learning were such as apparently only a pagan youth could or would have acquired.

[4] On Origen's Greek culture, see p. 392, and also his own words quoted below in § 12 sq.

[5] Numenius was a philosopher of Syria, who lived about the middle of the second century, and who exerted great influence over Plotinus and others of the Neo-Platonists. He was, perhaps, the earliest of the Orientalizing Greek philosophers whose thinking was affected by the influence of Christian ideas, and as such occupies an important place in the development of philosophy, which prepared the way for Neo-Platonism. His object seems to have been to reconcile Pythagoras and Plato by tracing the doctrines of the latter back to the former, and also to exhibit their agreement with Jewish and other Oriental forms of thought. It is significant that he was called by the Church Fathers a Pythagorean, and that he himself called Plato a Greek-speaking Moses (cf. Erdmann's Hist. of Phil. I. p. 236). He was a prolific writer, but only fragments of his works are extant. Numerous extracts from the chief of them (περὶ τἀγαθοῦ) have been preserved by Eusebius in his Præp. Evang. (see Heinichen's ed. Index I.).

[6] Of Cronius, a celebrated Pythagorean philosopher, apparently a contemporary of Numenius, and closely related to him in his thinking, we know very little. A brief account of him is given by Porphyry in his Vita Plot. 20.

[7] The Apollophanes referred to here was a Stoic philosopher of Antioch who lived in the third century B.C., and was a disciple of Ariston of Chios. None of his writings are extant.

[8] Longinus was a celebrated philosopher and rhetorician of Athens, who was born about 213 and died in 273 A.D. He traveled widely in his youth, and was for a time a pupil of Ammonius Saccas at Alexandria; but he remained a genuine Platonist, and seems not to have been influenced by the eclecticism of the Neo-Platonists. He was a man of marked ability, of the broadest culture, and a thorough master of Greek style. Of his numerous writings we possess a large part of one beautiful work entitled περὶ ὕψους (often published), and fragments of some others (e.g. in Eusebius' Præp. Evang. XV. 21). Longinus was the teacher of Porphyry before the latter went to Rome to study under Plotinus.

Porphyry has made a mistake in classing Longinus with those other philosophers whose works Origen studied. He was a younger contemporary of Origen, and cannot even have studied with Ammonius until after Origen had left Alexandria. It is possible, of course, that Origen in later life read some of his works; but Porphyry evidently means that the works of all the philosophers, Longinus among them, had an influence upon Origen's intellectual development. Heinichen reads Ἀλβίνου instead of Λογγίνου in his text, on the assumption that Porphyry cannot possibly have written Λογγίνου; but the latter word has the support of all the MSS. and versions, and there is no warrant for making the change. We must simply conclude that Porphyry, who, of course, is not pretending to give an exact list of all the philosophical works which Origen had read, classes Longinus, the celebrated philosopher, along with the rest, as one whose works such a student of Greek philosophy as Origen must have read, without thinking of the serious anachronism involved.

[9] Moderatus was a distinguished Pythagorean philosopher of the first century after Christ, whose works (no longer extant) were not without influence over some of the Neo-Platonists.

[10] Nicomachus was a Pythagorean of the first (or second?) century after Christ, who gained great fame as a mathematician and exerted considerable influence upon European studies in the fifteenth century. Two of his works, one on arithmetic and the other on music, are extant, and have been published.

[11] Chæremon was a Stoic philosopher and historian of Alexandria who lived during the first century after Christ. He was for a time librarian at the Serapeum in Alexandria, and afterward went to Rome to become a tutor of Nero. His chief writings were a history of Egypt, a work on Hieroglyphics, and another on Comets (mentioned by Origen in his Contra Cels. I. 59). He also wrote on grammatical subjects. His works, with the exception of a fragment of the first, are no longer extant. Cf. Eusebius' Præf. Evang. V. 10, and Suidas, s.v. Ὠριγένης.

[12] Cornutus, a distinguished Stoic philosopher, lived and taught in Rome during the reign of Nero, and numbered among his pupils

and friends the poet Persius. Most of his numerous works have perished, but one on the Nature of the Gods is still extant in a mutilated form (see Gall's Opuscula). See Suidas (s.v. Κορνοῦτος) and Dion Cassius, XLII. 29.

[13] Origen was not the first to interpret the Scriptures allegorically. The method began among the Alexandrian Jews some time before the Christian era, the effort being made to reconcile the Mosaic revelation with Greek philosophy, and to find in the former the teachings of the latter. This effort appears in many of the apocryphal books, but the great exponent of the method was the Alexandrian Philo. It was natural that the early Christians, especially in Alexandria, should be influenced by this already existing method of interpretation, which enabled them to make of the Old Testament a Christian book, and to find in it all the teachings of the Gospel. Undoubtedly the Old Testament owes partly to this principle of interpretation its adoption by the Christian Church. Had it been looked upon as the Jewish Scriptures only, containing Jewish national history, and in large part Jewish national prophecy, it could never have retained its hold upon the early Church, which was so bitterly hostile to all that savored of Judaism. The early Gentile Christians were taught from the beginning by Jewish Christians who could not do otherwise than look upon their national Scriptures as divine, that those Scriptures contained prophecies of Jesus Christ, and hence those Gentile Christians accepted them as divine. But it must be remembered that they could of course have no meaning to these Gentile Christians except as they did prophesy of Christian things or contain Christian teaching. They could not be content to find Christian prophecy in one part and only Jewish history or Jewish prophecy in another part. It must all be Christian if it was to have any meaning to them. In this emergency the allegorical method of interpretation, already practiced upon the Old Testament by the Alexandrian Jews, came to their assistance and was eagerly adopted. The so-called epistle of Barnabas is an early and most significant instance of its use. With Clement of Alexandria the matter first took scientific shape. He taught that two senses are everywhere to be assumed; that the verbal sense is only for babes in the faith, and that the allegorical sense alone leads to true spiritual knowledge. With Origen allegorical interpretation reached its height. He taught a threefold sense of Scripture, corresponding to body, soul, and spirit. Many voices were raised against his interpretation, but they were directed against his particular explanations of the meaning of passages, seldom against his method. In the early centuries Alexandria remained the chief center of this kind of exegesis, while Antioch became in the fifth century the seat of a school of exegetes who emphasized rather the grammatical and historical interpretation of Scripture over against the extremes of the Alexandrian teachers. And yet even they were not entirely free from the vicious methods of the age, and, moreover, errors of various kinds crept in to lessen their influence, and the allegorical method finally prevailed almost universally; and it has not even yet fully lost its hold. This method of Scripture interpretation has, as Porphyry says, its analogy in the methods of the Greek philosophers during the centuries immediately preceding the Christian era. It became early the custom for philosophers, scandalized by the licentious stories of their gods, to interpret the current myths allegorically and refer them to the processes of nature. Homer and others of the ancient poets were thus made by these later philosophers to teach philosophies of nature of which they had never dreamed. With the Neo-Platonists this method reached its highest perfection, and while the Christian teachers were allegorizing the Old Testament Scriptures, these philosophers were transforming the popular myths into records of the profoundest physical and spiritual processes. Porphyry saw that the method of pagans and Christians was the same in this respect, and he may be correct in assigning some influence to these writings in the shaping of Origen's thinking, but the latter was an allegorist before he studied the philosophers to whom Porphyry refers (cf. chap. 2, § 9, above), and would have been an allegorist had he never studied them. Allegory was in that age in the atmosphere of the Church as well as of the philosophical school.

[14] On this great work of Porphyry, see note 1.

[15] See note 3.

unadulterated to the end of his life.[16] His works yet extant show this, as he is celebrated among many for the writings which he has left. For example, the work entitled The Harmony of Moses and Jesus, and such others as are in

11 the possession of the learned. These things are sufficient to evince the slander of the false accuser, and also the proficiency of Origen in Grecian learning. He defends his diligence in this direction against some who blamed him for it, in a certain epistle,[17] where he writes as follows:

12 "When I devoted myself to the word, and the fame of my proficiency went abroad, and when heretics and persons conversant with Grecian learning, and particularly with philosophy, came to me, it seemed necessary that I should examine the doctrines of the heretics, and what the philosophers say concerning

13 the truth. And in this we have followed Pantænus,[18] who benefited many before our time by his thorough preparation in such things, and also Heraclas,[19] who is now a member of the presbytery of Alexandria. I found him with the teacher of philosophic learning, with whom he had already continued five years before I began to hear lectures on those subjects.[20]

14 And though he had formerly worn the common dress, he laid it aside and assumed and still wears the philosopher's garment;[21] and he continues the earnest investigation of Greek works."

He says these things in defending himself for his study of Grecian literature. About 15 this time, while he was still at Alexandria, a soldier came and delivered a letter from the governor of Arabia[22] to Demetrius, bishop of the parish, and to the prefect of Egypt who was in office at that time, requesting that they would with all speed send Origen to him for an interview. Being sent by them, he went to Arabia. And having in a short time accomplished the object of his visit, he returned to Alexandria. But sometime after a considerable 16 war broke out in the city,[23] and he departed from Alexandria. And thinking that it would be unsafe for him to remain in Egypt, he went to Palestine and abode in Cæsarea. While there the bishops of the church in that country[24] requested him to preach and expound the Scriptures publicly, although he had not yet been ordained as presbyter.[25] This is evi- 17

---

[16] This is certainly a mistake on Eusebius' part (see above, note 2), in which he is followed by Jerome (de vir. ill. c. 55). Against the identification of the Christian Ammonius, whose works are mentioned by Eusebius and Jerome, with Ammonius Saccas, may be urged first the fact that the teaching of Ammonius Saccas, as known to us from Porphyry's Vita Plotini and from other Neo-Platonic sources, is not such as could have emanated from a Christian; and, in the second place, the fact that the Christian Ammonius, according to Eusebius, was the author of more than one important work, while Longinus (as quoted by Porphyry in the Vita Plot. c. 20) says explicitly that Ammonius Saccas wrote nothing. It is clear from Eusebius' words that his sole reason for supposing that Ammonius Saccas remained a Christian is the existence of the writings to which he refers; and it is quite natural that he and others should erroneously attribute the works of an unknown Christian of Alexandria, named Ammonius, to the celebrated Alexandrian philosopher of the same name, especially since it was known that the latter had been a Christian in his youth, and that he had been Origen's teacher in his mature years. We know nothing about the life of the Christian Ammonius, unless he be identified with the presbyter Ammonius of Alexandria, who is said by Eusebius to have perished in the persecution of Diocletian. The identification is possible; but even if it be accepted, we are helped very little, for is only the death, not the life, of the presbyter Ammonius with which Eusebius acquaints us. Ammonius' writings, whoever he may have been, were well known in the Church. Eusebius mentions here his work On the Harmony of Moses and Jesus (περὶ τῆς Μωϋσέως καὶ Ἰησοῦ συμφωνίας), and in an epistle addressed to Carpianus (see above, p. 38 sq.) speaks of a Diatessaron or Harmony of the Four Gospels (τὸ διὰ τεσσάρων εὐαγγέλιον), composed by Ammonius. Jerome mentions both these works (de vir. ill. 55), the latter under the title Evangelici Canones. He refers to these Canones again in his preface to the Four Gospels (Migne's ed., Vol. X. 528); and so does Victor of Capua. The former work is no longer extant, nor have we any trace of it. But there is extant a Latin translation of a Diatessaron which was made by Victor of Capua, and which was formerly, and is still, by many scholars supposed to be a version of this work of Ammonius. By others it is thought to be a translation of Tatian's Diatessaron. For further particulars, see above, Bk. IV. chap. 29, note 11.
[17] The names of the persons to whom this epistle was addressed we do not know, nor can we ascertain the exact time when it was composed, though it must have been written before Heraclas became bishop of Alexandria, and indeed, we may assume, while Origen was in Alexandria, and still engaged in the study which he defends in the epistle, i.e., if Eusebius is correct in the order of events, before 216 A.D. (see note 23).
[18] On Pantænus, see Bk. V. chap. 10, note 1.
[19] On Heraclas, see chap. 3, note 2.
[20] ἐκείνων τῶν λόγων.

[21] See above, Bk. IV. chap. 11, note 21.
[22] The words used to designate the official who sent for Origen (ὁ τῆς Ἀραβίας ἡγούμενος) lead us to think him a Roman, and governor of the Roman province of Arabia, which was formed by the Emperor Trajan in the year 106, and which comprised only the northern part of the peninsula. We know no particulars of this visit of Origen to that province, but that he was remembered and held in honor by the people is proved by chaps. 33 and 37, which record that he was summoned thither twice to assist in settling doctrinal difficulties.
[23] In the sixth year of his reign (216 A.D.) Caracalla visited Alexandria, and improved the occasion to take bloody vengeance upon the inhabitants of the city, from whom had emanated a number of satirical and cutting comments upon the murder of his brother Geta. He instituted a horrible butchery, in which young and old, guilty and innocent, perished, and in which scholars were objects of especial fury. (See Herodian, IV. 8, 9, and Dion Cassius, LXXVII. 22-24, and cf. Tillemont, Hist. des Emp. III. p. 115 sq.) This was undoubtedly the occasion, referred to here, which caused Origen to flee from the city and retire to Palestine.
[24] οἱ τῇδε ἐπίσκοποι. The τῇδε must refer to Palestine, not to Cæsarea, for "bishops" are spoken of, not "bishop."
[25] In the apostolic age, and the generations immediately succeeding, it was the privilege of every Christian to take part in the public meetings of the Church in the way of teaching or prophesying, the only condition being the consciousness of guidance by the Spirit (see 1 Cor. xiii.). We cannot call this teaching and prophesying preaching in our sense of the term. The services seem rather to have resembled our "open prayer-meetings." Gradually, as the services became more formal and stereotyped, a stated address by the "president" (as Justin calls him) became a regular part of the service (see Justin's Apol. I. 67), and we may assume that the liberty of teaching or prophesying in the public meetings did not now belong to all the members as it had in the beginning. The sermon, in our sense of the word, seems to have been a slow growth, but a direct development from this exhortation of the president mentioned by Justin. The confinement of the speaking (or preaching) to a single individual, — the leader, — which we see in Justin, is what we find in subsequent generations quite generally established. It becomes, in time, the prerogative of the bishop to preach, and this prerogative he confers upon his presbyters also (not universally, but in most cases), while deacons and laymen are almost everywhere excluded from the right. We see from the present chapter, however, that the custom was not the same in all parts of the Church in the time of Origen. The principle had evidently before this become firmly established in Alexandria that only bishops and presbyters should preach. But in Palestine no such rule was recognized as binding. At the same time, it is clear enough that it was exceptional even there for laymen to preach (in the presence of their bishops), for Alexander in his epistle, instead of saying that laymen preach everywhere and of right, cites particular instances of their preaching, and says that where they are qualified they are especially requested by the bishops to use their gifts; so that the theory that the prerogative belonged of right to the bishop existed there just as truly as in Alexandria. Origen of course knew that he was acting contrary to the custom (if not the canon) of his own church in thus preaching publicly, and yet undoubtedly he took it for granted that he was perfectly right in doing what these bishops requested him to

dent from what Alexander,[26] bishop of Jerusalem and Theoctistus [27] of Cæsarea, wrote to Demetrius [28] in regard to the matter, defending themselves thus :

" He has stated in his letter that such a thing was never heard of before, neither has hitherto taken place, that laymen should preach in the presence of bishops. I know not how he comes to 18 say what is plainly untrue. For whenever persons able to instruct the brethren are found, they are exhorted by the holy bishops to preach to the people. Thus in Laranda, Euelpis by Neon ; and in Iconium, Paulinus by Celsus ; and in Synada, Theodorus by Atticus, our blessed brethren.[29] And probably this has been done in other places unknown to us."

He was honored in this manner while yet a young man, not only by his countrymen, but 19 also by foreign bishops.[30] But Demetrius sent for him by letter, and urged him through members and deacons of the church to return to Alexandria. So he returned and resumed his accustomed duties.

CHAPTER XX.

The Extant Works of the Writers of that Age.

1   THERE flourished many learned men in the Church at that time, whose letters to each other have been preserved and are easily accessible. They have been kept until our time in the library at Ælia,[1] which was established by Alexander, who at that time presided over that church. We have been able to gather from that library material for our present work. Among these Beryllus [2] has left us, besides 2 letters and treatises, various elegant works. He was bishop of Bostra in Arabia. Likewise also Hippolytus,[3] who presided over another church, has left writings. There has reached 3 us also a dialogue of Caius,[4] a very learned man, which was held at Rome under Zephyrinus,[5] with Proclus, who contended for the Phrygian heresy. In this he curbs the rashness and boldness of his opponents in setting forth new Scriptures. He mentions only thirteen epistles of the holy apostle, not counting that to the Hebrews [6] with the others. And unto our day there are some among the Romans who do not consider this a work of the apostle.

CHAPTER XXI.

The Bishops that were well known at that Time.

AFTER Antoninus [1] had reigned seven years 1 and six months, Macrinus succeeded him. He held the government but a year, and was succeeded by another Antoninus. During his first year the Roman bishop, Zephyrinus,[2] having held his office for eighteen years, died, and Callistus [3] received the episcopate. He continued for five years, and was succeeded by 2

---

do in their own dioceses. They were supreme in their own churches, and he knew of nothing, apparently, which should hinder him from doing what they approved of, while in those churches. Demetrius, however, thought otherwise, and considered the public preaching of an unordained man irregular, in any place and at any time. Whether jealousy of Origen's growing power had anything to do with his action it is difficult to say with certainty. He seems to have treated Origen in a perfectly friendly way after his return; and yet it is possible that the difference of opinion on this point, and the reproof given by Demetrius, may not have been wholly without influence upon their subsequent relations, which became in the end so painful (see chap. 8, note 4).

[26] On Alexander, see chap. 8, note 6.

[27] Theoctistus, bishop of Cæsarea, seems to have been one of the most influential bishops of the East in his day, and played a prominent part in the controversy which arose in regard to Novatus, as we learn from chap. 46 of this book and from chap. 5 of the next. He was also a firm friend of Origen's for many years (see chap. 27), probably until the latter's death. We do not know the dates of his accession and of his death, but we find him already bishop in the year 216, and still bishop at the time of the episcopate of Stephen of Rome (254–257; see Bk. VII. chap. 5), but already succeeded by Domnus, when Xystus was bishop of Rome ((257–258; see Bk. VII. chap. 14). We must, therefore, put his death between 255 and 258.

[28] Eusebius is apparently mistaken in stating that this epistle was addressed to Demetrius, for the latter is spoken of throughout the epistle in the third person. It seems probable that Eusebius has made a slip and said " to Demetrius" when he meant to say " concerning Demetrius."

[29] Of the persons mentioned here by the Palestinian bishops in support of their conduct, Neon, bishop of Laranda in Lycaonia, Celsus, bishop of Iconium, and Atticus, bishop of Synada in Phrygia, together with the laymen Euelpis, Paulinus, and Theodore, we know only the names.

[30] οὐ πρὸς μόνων τῶν συνήθων, ἀλλὰ καὶ τῶν ἐπὶ ξένης ἐπισκόπων. συνήθων seems here to have the sense of " countrymen" or (bishops) " of his own country" over against the ἐπὶ ξένης, rather than the meaning "friends" or "acquaintances," which is more common.

[1] Ælia, the city built by Hadrian upon the site of Jerusalem (see Bk. IV. chap. 6). We do not know the subsequent history of this

---

library of Alexander, but it had already been in existence nearly a hundred years when Eusebius examined it.

[2] On Beryllus, bishop of Bostra in Arabia, see chap. 33.

[3] On Hippolytus, see chap. 22.

[4] On Caius and his discussion with Proclus, see Bk. II. chap. 25, notes 7 and 8.

[5] Zephyrinus was bishop of Rome from 198 or 199 to 217. See Bk. V. chap. 28, note 5.

[6] On the Epistle to the Hebrews and the opinions of the early Church in regard to its authorship, see Bk. III. chap. 3, note 17.

[1] i.e. Caracalla, who was slain on the 8th of April, 217. Four days later, Marcus Opilius Macrinus, prefect of the prætorians, was proclaimed emperor. After a reign of fourteen months, he was defeated and succeeded by Varius Avitus Bassianus, a cousin of Caracalla, and priest of the Phœnician Sun-god, from which fact is derived the name by which he is commonly known, — Elagabalus, or Heliogabalus. Upon his accession to the imperial power, he took the name Marcus Aurelius Antoninus, which became his official designation.

[2] On Zephyrinus, see Bk. V. chap. 28, note 5.

[3] As shown in the next note, a comparison of our best sources leads us to the year 222 as the date of the accession of Urban, and consequently of the death of Callistus. A careful comparison of the various sources, which differ in regard to the years of the several episcopates of Victor, Zephyrinus, and Callistus, but agree as to the sum of the three, leads to the result that Callistus was bishop for five years, and therefore his accession is to be put into the year 217, and the reign of Macrinus (see Lipsius, *Chron. d. röm. Bischöfe*, p. 171 sq.). This agrees, so far as the years of our era are concerned, with the statement of Eusebius in this chapter; but he wrongly puts Callistus' accession into the first year of Alexander, which is a result of an error of a year in his reckoning of the dates of the emperors, which runs back to Pertinax (see Lipsius, p. 7 sq.). He does not assign Callistus' accession to the first year of Heliogabalus because of a tradition connecting the two, but simply because his reckoning of the lengths of the various episcopates, given in the source used by him, led him to the year 217 for Callistus' accession, and this, according to his erroneous table of the reigns of the emperors, was the first year of Heliogabalus. We thus see that Eusebius is in real, though not in apparent, agreement with the Liberian catalogue in regard to the date of Callistus' accession, which may, therefore, be accepted as certain.

Nothing was known about the character and life of Callistus until the discovery of Hippolytus' *Philosophumena*, or *Refutation of*

Urbanus.[4] After this, Alexander became Roman emperor, Antoninus having reigned but four years.[5] At this time Philetus[6] also succeeded Asclepiades[7] in the church of Antioch.

3   The mother of the emperor, Mammæa[8]

by name, was a most pious woman, if there ever was one, and of religious life. When the fame of Origen had extended everywhere and had come even to her ears, she desired greatly to see the man, and above all things to make trial of his celebrated understanding of divine things. Staying for a time in Anti-   4 och, she sent for him with a military escort. Having remained with her a while and shown her many things which were for the glory of the Lord and of the excellence of the divine teaching, he hastened back to his accustomed work.

CHAPTER XXII.

The Works of Hippolytus which have reached us.

At that time Hippolytus,[1] besides many   1 other treatises, wrote a work on the pass-

---

All Heresies (see the next chapter, note 1). In Bk. IX. of that work is given a detailed description of him, from the pen of a very bitter opponent. At the same time, it can hardly be doubted that at least the groundwork of the account is true. According to Hippolytus, he was a slave; a dishonest banker, who was punished for his dishonesty; the author of a riot in a Jewish synagogue, who was sent as a criminal to the mines; finally, after various other adventures, the right-hand man of the bishop Zephyrinus, and after his death, his successor. According to Hippolytus, he was a Patripassian, and he introduced much laxer methods of church discipline than had hitherto been in vogue; so lax as greatly to scandalize Hippolytus, who was a very rigid disciplinarian. Whatever truth there may be in this highly sensational account (and we cannot doubt that it is greatly overdrawn), it is at least certain that Callistus took the liberal view of Christian morals and church discipline, over against the stricter view represented by Hippolytus and his party. It was, perhaps, owing to his popularity on this account that, after the death of Zephyrinus, he secured the episcopacy of Rome, for which Hippolytus was also a candidate. The latter tells us also that Zephyrinus "set him over the cemetery,"—a most interesting notice, as the largest catacomb in Rome bears the name of St. Callistus, and may be the very one of which Zephyrinus made him the superintendent.

[4] Lipsius, in his *Chron. d. röm. Bischöfe*, p. 170 sq., shows that the only fixed point for a calculation of the dates of Urban and the three bishops preceding him, is the banishment by the Emperor Maximinu of Pontianus to Sardinia, which took place, according to the Liberian catalogue, while Severus and Quintinus were consuls; that is, in the year 235. The duration of Pontianus' episcopate is shown by a comparison of the best sources to have been a little over five years (see chap. 23, note 3). This brings us to the year 230 as the date of Urban's death. According to chap. 23, Urban was bishop eight years, and with this the Liberian catalogue agrees, so that this figure is far better supported than the figure nine given by the *Chron.* Accepting eight years as the duration of Urban's episcopate, we are brought back to 222 as the date of his accession, which agrees with Eusebius' statement in this chapter (see the previous note). There are extant *Acta S. Urbani*, which are accepted as genuine by the Bollandists, and assigned to the second century, but they cannot have been written before the fifth, and are historically quite worthless. For a good discussion of his supposed connection with St. Cecilia, which has played such an important part in ecclesiastical legend, see the article *Urbanus* in the *Dict. of Christ. Biog.* We have no certain knowledge of his life and character.

[5] Elagabalus was slain in March, 222, after a reign of three years and nine months, and was succeeded by his cousin, Alexianus Bassianus, who assumed the names Marcus Aurelius Alexander Severus, by the last two of which he is commonly known.

[6] Philetus, according to the *Chron.* (Armenian), became bishop in the sixth year of Caracalla (216), and was succeeded by Zebinus in the sixth year of Alexander Severus (227). Jerome puts his accession into the reign of Macrinus (217–218), and the accession of Zebinus into the seventh year of Alexander (228). The accession of Zebinus must have taken place at least as early as 231 (see chap. 23, note 4), and there remains therefore no reason to doubt the approximate accuracy of the latter dates. If the dates given for Philetus' accession (216–218) are approximately correct, we must understand the words "at this time" of the present chapter, to refer back to the reign of Macrinus, or the accession of Alexander Severus, mentioned at the beginning of this chapter. This does not seem natural, but we cannot say it is impossible. Knowing the unreliability of the dates given in the *Chron.*, we are compelled to leave the matter undecided. He is called by the *Armen.* Philip, by Syncellus Φίλητος ἢ Φίλιππος. The latter assigns him an episcopate of eight years, which agrees with none of the figures given by the two versions of the *Chronicle* or by the *History*. We know nothing about the person or the life of Philetus.

[7] On Asclepiades, see chap. 11, note 6.

[8] Julia Mamæa or Mammæa (Eusebius, Μαμμαία) was the niece of Septimius Severus' wife Julia Domna, the aunt of the Emperor Elagabalus, and the mother of the Emperor Alexander Severus, by the Syrian Gessius Marcianus. She accompanied Elagabalus to Rome, and had strength of character enough to protect her son from the jealousy of the latter, and to keep him comparatively pure from the vice and debauchery of the court. During the reign of her son she exerted great influence, which was in the main highly beneficial; but her pride and avarice finally proved fatal, both to her son and to herself. Her character seems to have been in the main pure and elevated; and she was apparently inclined to the same sort of religious syncretism which led her son to adopt many Christian principles of action, and to put the busts of Abraham and of Christ, with those of Orpheus, Apollonius of Tyana, and the best of the Roman emperors, in his private chapel (see Lampridius, *Vita Sev.* c. 29, 43). Eusebius calls Mammæa θεοσεβεστάτη and εὐλαβής, and Jerome calls her a *religiosa femina* (*de vir. ill.* c. 54); but there is no evidence that she was a Christian. The date of Origen's interview with her has been greatly disputed. Huet and Redepenning,

accepting the order of events recorded in this chapter as chronological, put the interview in the early years of Alexander Severus, Redepenning assuming an otherwise unrecorded visit of Mammæa to Antioch, Huet connecting her visit there with the Persian expedition of Alexander. Huet assumes, upon the authority of Jerome's *Chron.*, that the Persian expedition took place in the early part of Alexander's reign; but this is against all other ancient authorities, and must be incorrect (see Tillemont, *Mem.* III. 763 sq.). The only occasions known to us, on which Mammæa can have been in Antioch, were this expedition of her son (between 230 and 233) and the visit of her nephew Elagabalus to Antioch, after his victory over Macrinus in 218. At both these times Origen was quite probably in Cæsarea (see chap. 19, note 23, and p. 392, below), whence it is more natural to suppose him summoned than from Alexandria. If we put the interview in 218, we must suppose (as Tillemont suggests) that Eusebius is led by his mention of Alexander to give this account of his mother, and that he does not intend to imply that the interview took place after Alexander's accession. There is nothing at all improbable in this. In fact, it seems more likely that he would mention the interview in connection with Alexander than in connection with Elagabalus, in spite of chronology. On the other hand, it is not impossible that the interview took place subsequently to the year 231, for Origen's fame was certainly by that time much greater in Syria than fifteen years previous. At the same time, to accept this date disarranges seriously the chronological order of the account of Eusebius, for in chap. 24 we are told of those works which Origen wrote while yet in Alexandria; that is, before 231. Moreover, there is not the same reason for inserting this account of Mammæa at this point, if it occurred later in Alexander's reign, that there is if it occurred in the reign of Elagabalus. We shall, therefore, do best to accept the earlier date with Tillemont, Westcott, and others.

[1] Hippolytus (mentioned above in chap. 20) was one of the most learned men and celebrated writers of his age, and yet his personal history is involved in the deepest obscurity. The earliest mention of him is by Eusebius in this passage and in chap. 20, above. But Eusebius tells us there only that he was a bishop of "some other church" (ἑτέρας που ἐκκλησίας), and Jerome (*de vir. ill.* c. 61) says that he was a bishop of some church whose name he did not know (*Hippolytus, cujusdam Ecclesiæ episcopus, nomen quippe urbis scire non potui*). In the East, from the fourth century on, Hippolytus was commonly called bishop of Rome, but the Western tradition makes him simply a presbyter. The late tradition that he was bishop of Portus Romanus is quite worthless. We learn from his *Philosophumena*, or *Refutation of Heresies*, that he was active in Rome in the time of Zephyrinus and Callistus; but what is significant is the fact that he never recognizes Callistus as bishop of Rome, but always treats him as the head of a school opposed to the orthodox Church. This has given scholars the clue for reconciling the conflicting traditions about his position and his church. It seems probable that he was a presbyter of the church of Rome, and was at the head of a party which did not recognize Callistus as lawful bishop, but set Hippolytus up as opposition bishop. This explains why Hippolytus calls himself a bishop, and at the same time recognizes neither Callistus nor any one else as bishop of Rome. The Western Church therefore preserved the tradition of Hippolytus only as a presbyter, while in the Orient, where Hippolytus was known only through his works, the tradition that he was a bishop (a fact directly stated in those works; see the preface to his *Philosophumena*) always prevailed; and since he was known to have resided in Rome, that city was made by tradition his see. The schism, which has left no trace in the writings either of the Western or Eastern Church, cannot have been a serious one. Doubtless Callistus had the sup-

over.[2] He gives in this a chronological table, and presents a certain paschal canon of sixteen years, bringing the time down to the first

2   year of the Emperor Alexander. Of his other writings the following have reached us: On the Hexæmeron,[3] On the Works after the Hexæmeron,[4] Against Marcion,[5] On the Song of Songs,[6] On Portions of Ezekiel,[7] On the Passover,[8] Against All the Heresies;[9] and you can find many other works preserved by many.

---

port of by far the larger part of the Church, and the opposition of Hippolytus never amounted to more than talk, and was never strong enough to enlist, or perhaps even attempt to enlist, the support of foreign bishops. Callistus and the body of the Church could afford to leave it unnoticed; and after Callistus' death Hippolytus undoubtedly returned to the Church and was gladly received, and the memory of his brief schism entirely effaced, while the knowledge of his orthodoxy, and of his great services to the Church as a theologian and a writer, kept his name in high repute with subsequent generations. A Latin translation of a Chronicle written by Hippolytus is extant, and the last event recorded in it is the death of the Emperor Alexander, which took place early in the year 235. The Liberian catalogue, in an entry which Lipsius (*Chron. d. röm. Bischöfe*, p. 194) pronounces critically indisputable, records that, in the year 235, the bishop Pontianus and the presbyter Hippolytus were transported as exiles to the island of Sardinia. There is little doubt that this is the Hippolytus with whom we are concerned, and it is highly probable that both he and Pontianus died in the mines there, and thus gained the title of martyrs; for not only is the account of Hippolytus' martyrdom given by Prudentius in the fifth century not reliable, but also in the *depositio martyrum* of the Liberian catalogue the bodies of Pontianus and Hippolytus are said to have been buried in Rome on the same day; and it is therefore natural to think that Hippolytus' body was brought from Sardinia, as we know Pontianus' was.

The character of Hippolytus, as revealed to us in the *Philosophumena*, is that of a strictly, even rigidly, moral man, of a puritanic disposition, who believed in drawing the reins very tight, and allowing to the members of the Christian Church no license. He was in this directly opposed to Callistus, who was a lax disciplinarian, and favored the readmission to the Church even of the worst offenders upon evidence of repentance and suitable penance (see the previous chapter, note 3). We are reminded greatly of Tertullian and of Novatian in studying Hippolytus' character. He was, moreover, strictly orthodox and bitterly opposed to what he considered the patripassianism of Zephyrinus and of Callistus. He must be admired as a thoroughly independent, sternly moral, and rigidly orthodox man; while at the same time it must be recognized that he was irascible, bitter, and in some respects narrow and bigoted. He is known to have been a very prolific writer, composing all his works in Greek. Eusebius mentions but eight works in this chapter, but says that many others were extant in his day. Jerome, who in the present instance has other sources of information than Eusebius' History, mentions some nineteen works (*de vir. ill.* c. 61), including all of those named by Eusebius, except the commentary on portions of Ezekiel and the work on the Events which followed the Hexæmeron (but see note 4, below). In the year 1551 a statue representing a venerable man sitting in a chair, and with an inscription upon it enumerating the writings of the person commemorated, was found near the church of San Lorenzo, just outside of Rome. The statue, though it bears no name, has been shown to be that of Hippolytus; and with the help of the list given upon it (which contains some thirteen works), together with some extant fragments of writings which seem to have been composed by him, the titles known to us have been increased to about forty, the greater part of which are entirely lost. We cannot discuss these works here. For the most complete list of Hippolytus' writings the reader is referred to Caspari's *Taufsymbol und Glaubensregel*, III. 377 sq., or to the more accessible article by Salmon in the *Dict. of Christ. Biog.* In 1842 was discovered the greater part of a work in ten books directed against heresies, the first book of which had been long before published by the Benedictines among Origen's works with the title of *Philosophumena*. This discovery caused great discussion, but it has been proved to the complete satisfaction of almost every scholar that it is a work of Hippolytus (cf., among other discussions, Döllinger's *Hippolytus und Callistus*, translated by Plummer, and the article in the *Dict. of Christ. Biog.* already referred to). The work was published at Oxford in 1851 by Miller (who, however, wrongly ascribed it to Origen), and at Göttingen, in 1859, by Duncker and Schneidewin. It is given also by Migne; and an English translation is found in the *Ante-Nicene Fathers* (Amer. ed.), Vol. V., under the title the *Refutation of All Heresies*.

[2] This chronological work on the passover, which contained a cycle for the purpose of determining the date of the festival, is mentioned also by Jerome, and is given in the list on the statue, on which the cycle itself is also engraved. Jerome says that this work was the occasion of Eusebius' work upon the same subject in which a nineteen-year cycle was substituted for that of Hippolytus. The latter was a sixteen-year cycle, and was formed by putting together two of the eight-year cycles of the Greek astronomers, — according to whose calculation the full moon fell on the same day of the month once in eight years, — in order to exhibit also the day of the week on which it fell; for he noticed that after sixteen years the full moon moved one day backward (if on Saturday at the beginning of the cycle, it fell on Friday after the sixteen years were past). He therefore put together seven sixteen-year cycles, assuming that after they had passed the full moon would return again to the same

day of the week, as well as month. This cycle is astronomically incorrect, the fact being that after sixteen years the full moon falls not on the same day of the week, but three days later. Hippolytus, however, was not aware of this, and published his cycle in perfect good faith. The work referred to seems to have contained an explanation of the cycle, together with a computation by means of it of the dates of the Old and New Testament passovers. It is no longer extant, but the cycle itself, which was the chief thing, is preserved on the statue, evidently in the form in which it was drawn up by Hippolytus himself.

[3] This treatise on the Hexæmeron, or six days' work, is mentioned also by Jerome, but is not in the list on the statue. It is no longer extant; but according to Jerome (*Ep. ad Pammachium et Oceanum*, c. 7; Migne's ed. *Ep.* 84), was used by Ambrose in the composition of his own work upon the same subject, which is still preserved (cf. also Bk. V. chap. 27, note 3, above).

[4] Greek, εἰς τὰ μετὰ τὴν ἑξαήμερον. This work is not given in the list on the statue. It is mentioned in some of the MSS. of Jerome under the form *et post Hexæmeron*; but the best MSS. omit these words, and substitute for them *et in Exodum*, a work which is not mentioned by any other authority. Jerome mentions also a commentary *in Genesim*, which we hear of from no other source, and which may be identical with this work mentioned by Eusebius. If the two be identical (which is quite possible), the nature of the work is plain enough. Otherwise we are left wholly to conjecture. No fragments of the work have been identified.

[5] This work is mentioned also by Jerome, but is not in the list on the statue. The last work, however, mentioned in that list bears the title περὶ τἀγαθοῦ καὶ πόθεν τὸ κακόν, which, it has been conjectured, may be identical with Eusebius and Jerome's *Contra Marcionem*. No fragments are extant.

[6] Eusebius has simply τὸ ᾆσμα (*The Song*), which is the title given to the book in the LXX. This commentary on the Song of Songs is mentioned also by Jerome, but is not in the statue list. Four fragments of it are given by Lagarde, in his edition of the works of Hippolytus.

[7] This commentary on portions of Ezekiel is mentioned by no one else. A supposed fragment of it is given by Lagarde, *Anal. Syr.*, p. 90.

[8] Jerome agrees with Eusebius in mentioning a work *On the Passover*, in addition to the chronological one already referred to. The list on the statue, however, mentions but one work on the passover, and that the one containing the paschal cycle. Fragments are extant of Hippolytus' work *On the Passover*, — one from his ἐξήγησις εἰς τὸ πάσχα (see Lagarde's edition of Hippolytus, p. 213), and another from "the first book of the treatise on the holy paschal feast" (τοῦ περὶ τοῦ ἁγίου πάσχα συγγράμματος, Lagarde, p. 92). These fragments are of a dogmatic character, and can hardly have occurred in the chronological work, except in a separate section or book; but the last is taken from "the first book" of the treatise, and hence we are safe in concluding that Eusebius and Jerome are correct in enumerating two separate works upon the same subject, — the one chronological, the other dogmatic, or polemical.

[9] This work, *Against All the Heresies*, is mentioned by both Eusebius (πρὸς ἁπάσας τὰς αἱρέσεις) and Jerome (*adv. omnes hæreses*), but is not given in the list on the statue. Quite a full account of it is given from personal knowledge by Photius (*Cod.* 121), who calls it a small book (βιβλιδάριον) directed against thirty-two heresies, beginning with the Dositheans and ending with Noetus, and says that it purported to be an abstract of lectures delivered by Irenæus. The work is no longer extant (it must not be confounded with the *Philosophumena*, or *Refutatio*, mentioned in note 1), but it has been in part restored by Lipsius (in his *Quellenkritik des Epiphanius*) from the anti-heretical works of Pseudo-Tertullian, Epiphanius, and Philaster. There is in existence also a fragment of considerable length, bearing in the MS. the title *Homily of Hippolytus against the Heresy of one Noetus*. It is apparently not a homily, but the conclusion of a treatise against a number of heresies. It was suggested by Fabricius (who first published the original Greek) that it constituted the closing chapter of the work against the thirty-two heresies. The chief objection to this is that if this fragment forms but one of thirty-two chapters, the entire work can hardly have been called a "little book" by Photius. Lipsius suggests that the little book of which Photius speaks was not the complete work of Hippolytus, but only an abbreviated summary of its contents, and this is quite possible. At any rate it seems probable, in spite of the objections which have been urged by some critics, that this constituted a part of the larger work, and hence we have one chapter of that work preserved. The work seems to have been composed in Rome and during the episcopate of Victor (as Lipsius holds), or, as is more probable, in the early part of the episcopate of Zephyrinus (as is maintained by Harnack). This conclusion is drawn from the dates of the heretics mentioned in the work, some of whom were as late as Victor, but none of them later than the early years of Zephyrinus. It must, too, have been composed some years before the *Philosophumena*, which (in the preface) refers to a work against heresies, written by its author "a long time before"

CHAPTER XXIII.

Origen's Zeal and his Elevation to the Presbyterate.

1   At that time Origen began his commentaries on the Divine Scriptures, being urged thereto by Ambrose,[1] who employed innumerable incentives, not only exhorting him by word,

2   but also furnishing abundant means. For he dictated to more than seven amanuenses, who relieved each other at appointed times. And he employed no fewer copyists, besides girls who were skilled in elegant writing. For all these Ambrose furnished the necessary expense in abundance, manifesting himself an inexpressible earnestness in diligence and zeal for the divine oracles, by which he especially pressed him on to the preparation of his commentaries.

3   While these things were in progress, Urbanus,[2] who had been for eight years bishop of the Roman church, was succeeded by Pontianus,[3] and Zebinus[4] succeeded Philetus[5] in

4   Antioch. At this time Origen was sent to Greece on account of a pressing necessity

in connection with ecclesiastical affairs,[6] and went through Palestine, and was ordained as presbyter in Cæsarea by the bishops of that country. The matters that were agitated concerning him on this account, and the decisions on these matters by those who presided over the churches, besides the other works concerning the divine word which he published while in his prime, demand a separate treatise. We have written of them to some extent in the second book of the Defense which we have composed in his behalf.[7]

CHAPTER XXIV.

The Commentaries which he prepared at Alexandria.

1   It may be well to add that in the sixth book of his exposition of the Gospel of John[1] he states that he prepared the first five while in Alexandria. Of his work on the entire Gospel only twenty-two volumes have come down to us. In the ninth of those on

2   Genesis,[2] of which there are twelve in all, he

⟨πάλαι⟩. Upon this work and its relation to the lost *Syntagma* of Justin Martyr, which Lipsius supposes it to have made use of, see his work already referred to and also his *Quellen der ältesten Ketzergeschichte* together with Harnack's *Quellenkritik der Gesch. des Gnosticismus*, and his article in the *Zeitschrift für historische Theologie*, 1874, p. 143–226.

[1] On Ambrose and his relation to Origen, see chap. 18, note 1.

[2] On Urbanus, bishop of Rome, see chap. 21, note 4.

[3] For the dates of the first group of Roman bishops, from Peter to Urbanus, the best source we have is Eusebius' *Church History;* but for the second group, from Pontianus to Liberius, the notices of the *History* are very unreliable, while the Liberian catalogue rests upon very trustworthy data (see Lipsius, *Chron. d. röm. Bischöfe*, p. 39 and p. 142 sq.). We must therefore turn to the latter for the most accurate information in regard to the remaining Roman bishops mentioned by Eusebius, although an occasional mistake in the catalogue must be corrected by our other sources, as Lipsius points out. The notice of Eusebius at this point would throw the accession of Pontianus into the year 231, but this is a year too late, as seen in chap. 21, note 4. According to chap. 29, he was bishop six years, and was succeeded by Anteros at about the same time that Gordian became emperor; that is, in 238. But this is wide of the truth. The Liberian catalogue, which is supported by the best of the other sources, gives a little over five years for his episcopate, and puts his banishment to Sardinia, with which his episcopate ended, on the 28th of September, 235. According to the Felician catalogue, which may be trusted at this point, he was brought to Rome and buried there during the episcopate of Fabian, which began in 236 (see also the preceding chapter, note 1). We know nothing about the life and character of Pontianus.

[4] The notices of the *Chronicle* in connection with Zebinus are especially unreliable. The *Armen.* puts his accession into the sixth (227), Jerome into the seventh year of Alexander (228). Jerome makes no attempt to fix the date of his death, while the *Armen.* puts it in the first year of Gallus (251–252). Syncellus assigns him but six years. In the midst of such confusion we are obliged to rely solely upon the *History*. The only reliable data we have are Origen's ordination to the priesthood, which took place in 231 (see below, p. 392) and apparently, according to this chapter, while Zebinus was bishop of Antioch. If Eusebius is correct in this synchronization, Zebinus became bishop before 231, and therefore the statements of the *Chron.* as to his accession may be approximately correct. As to the time of his death, we know that his successor, Babylas, died in the Decian persecution (see chap. 39), and hence Zebinus must have died some years before that. In chap. 29, Eusebius puts his death in the reign of Gordian (238–244), and this may be accepted as at least approximately correct, for we have reason to think that Babylas was already bishop in the time of Philip (see chap. 29, note 8). This proves the utter incorrectness of the notice of the *Armen.* We know nothing about the person and life of Zebinus. Harnack concludes from his name that he was a Syrian by birth. Most of the MSS. of Eusebius give his name as Ζεβῖνος; one MS. and Nicephorus, as Ζέβενος; Syncellus as Ζέβεννος; Rufinus, Jerome, and the *Armen.* as Zebennus.

[5] On Philetus, see chap. 21, note 6.

[6] See the note on p. 395, below.

[7] Eusebius refers here to the Defense of Origen, composed by himself and Pamphilus, which is unfortunately now lost (see above, chap. 2, note 1, and the Prolegomena, p. 36 sq.).

[1] Origen's commentary upon the Gospel of John was the "first fruits of his labors at Alexandria," as he informs us in Tom. I. § 4. It must have been commenced, therefore, soon after he formed the connection with Ambrose mentioned in the previous chapter, and that it was one of the fruits of this connection is proved by the way in which Ambrose is addressed in the commentary itself (Tom. I. § 3). The date at which the work was begun cannot be determined; but if Eusebius follows the chronological order of events, it cannot have been before 218 (see chap. 21, note 8). Eusebius speaks as if Origen had expounded the entire Gospel (τῆς δ' εἰς τὸ πᾶν εὐαγγέλιον αὐτὸ δὲ τοῦτο πραγματείας), but Jerome, in his catalogue of Origen's works given in his epistle to Paula (in a fragmentary form in Migne's ed., *Ep.* 33, complete in the *Zeitschrift für Hist. Theol.* 1851, p. 75 sq.), reports that the commentary consisted of thirty-two books and some notes (cf. his prologue to his translation of Origen's homilies on Luke, Migne's ed., VII. 219), and Rufinus likewise (*Apol.* II. 22) speaks of thirty-two books only. But in the thirty-second book, which is still extant, Origen discusses the thirteenth chapter of John, and does not promise to continue the commentary, as he does at the close of some of the other books. We may therefore conclude that Eusebius' rather indefinite statement (which was probably not based upon personal knowledge, for he says that he had seen only twenty-two books), is incorrect, and that the commentary extended no further than the thirteenth chapter. We learn from the preface to the sixth book that the first five were composed while the author was still in Alexandria, the remaining books after his removal to Cæsarea, and at least part of them after the persecution of Maximus (235–238), to which reference was made in the twenty-second book, according to Eusebius, chap. 28, below. There are still extant Books I., II., VI., X., XIII., XX., XXVIII., XXXII., small fragments of IV. and V., and the greater part of XIX. (printed in Lommatzsch's ed., Vols. I. and II.). The production of this commentary marked an epoch in the history of theological thought, and it remains in many respects the most important of Origen's exegetical works. It is full of original and suggestive thought, and reveals Origen's genius perhaps in the clearest and best light, though the exegesis is everywhere marred by the allegorizing method and by neglect of the grammatical and historical sense.

[2] Of the commentary on Genesis, only some fragments from the first and third books are extant, together with some *extracts* (ἐκλογαί), and seventeen homilies (nearly complete) in the Latin translation of Rufinus (see Lommatzsch's ed., Vol. VIII.). Eight of the books, Eusebius tells us, were written in Alexandria, and they must, of course, have been begun after the commencement of the commentary on John. Jerome (according to Rufinus, *Apol.* II. 20) gave the number of the book as thirteen (though in his catalogue mentioned in the previous note, he speaks of fourteen), and said that the thirteenth discussed Gen. iv. 15; and in his *Contra Cels.* VI. 49 Origen speaks of his work upon Genesis "from the beginning

states that not only the preceding eight had been composed at Alexandria, but also those on the first twenty-five Psalms[3] and on Lamentations.[4] Of these last five volumes have reached us. In them he mentions also his books On the Resurrection,[5] of which there are two. He wrote also the books De Principiis[6] before leaving Alexandria; and the discourses entitled Stromata,[7] ten in number, he composed in the same city during the reign of Alexander, as the notes by his own hand preceding the volumes indicate.

3

---

of the book up to " V. 1. We may therefore conclude that the commentary covered only the early chapters of Genesis. The homilies, however, discuss brief passages taken from various parts of the book.

[3] Origen's writings on the Psalms comprised a complete commentary (cf. Jerome's *Ep. ad Augustinum*, § 20; Migne's ed.; *Ep.* 112), brief notes (" quod *Enchiridion* ille vocabat," see Migne's edition of Jerome's works, Vol. VIII. 821, and compare the entire *Breviarium in Psalmos* which follows, and which doubtless contains much of Origen's work; see Smith and Wace, IV. p. 108) and homilies. Of these there are still extant numerous fragments in Greek, and nine complete homilies in the Latin version of Rufinus (printed by Lommatzsch in Vols. XI.–XIII.). The catalogue of Jerome mentions forty-six books of notes on the Psalms and 118 homilies. The commentary on the 26th and following Psalms seem to have been written after leaving Alexandria (to judge from Eusebius' statement here).

[4] There are extant some extracts (ἐκλογαί) of Origen's expositions of the book of Lamentations, which are printed by Lommatzsch, XIII. 167–218. They are probably from the commentary which Eusebius tells us was written before Origen left Alexandria, and five books of which were extant in his time. The catalogue of Jerome also mentions five books.

[5] Jerome (in the catalogue and in the passage quoted by Rufinus, *Apol.* II. 20) mentions two books and two dialogues on the Resurrection (*De Resurrectione libros duos. Et alios de Resurrectione dialogos duos*). Whether the dialogues formed an independent work we do not know. We hear of them from no other source. The work was bitterly attacked by Methodius, but there are no traces of heresy in the extant fragments.

[6] Of Origen's *De Principiis* (περὶ ἀρχῶν), which was written before he left Alexandria, there are still extant some fragments in Greek, together with brief portions of a translation by Jerome (in his epistle to Avitus; Migne's ed.; *Ep.* 124), and a complete but greatly altered translation by Rufinus. The latter, together with the extant fragments, is printed by Lommatzsch, Vol. XXI.; and also separately by Redepenning (Lips. 1836); Engl. trans. by Crombie, in the *Ante-Nicene Fathers*. The work is the most important of all Origen's writings, and from it we gather our fullest knowledge as to his opinions, philosophical and theological; though unfortunately Rufinus' alterations have made it doubtful in many cases what Origen's original meaning was. The work constitutes the first attempt to form a system of Christian doctrine. It contains a great many peculiar, often startling errors, and was the chief source of the attacks made upon Origen for heterodoxy; and yet the author's object was only to set forth the doctrines accepted by the Church, and to show how they could be systematized by the aid of Scripture or of reason. He did not intend to bring forward doctrines inconsistent with the received faith of the Church. The work consists of four books. To quote from Westcott: " The composition is not strictly methodical. Digressions and repetitions interfere with the symmetry of the plan. But to speak generally, the first book deals with God and creation (religious statics); the second and third books with creation and providence, with man and redemption (religious dynamics); and the fourth book with Holy Scripture."

Intellectually the work is of a very high order, abounding in deep and original thought as well as in grand and lofty sentiments.

[7] In his catalogue, Jerome gives among the commentaries on the Old Testament the simple title *Stromatum*, without any description of the work. But in his *Ep. ad Magnum*, § 4 (Migne's ed., *Ep.* 70), he says that Origen wrote ten books of *Stromata* in imitation of Clement's work, and in it compared the opinions of Christians and philosophers, and confirmed the dogmas of Christianity by appeals to Plato and other Greek philosophers (*Hunc imitatus Origines, decem scripsit Stromateas, Christianorum et philosophorum inter se sententias comparans: et omnia nostræ religionis dogmata de Platone et Aristotele, Numenio, Cornutoque confirmans*). Only three brief fragments of a Latin translation of the work are now extant (printed in Lommatzsch's ed., XVII. 69–78). These fragments are sufficient to show us that the work was exegetical as well as doctrinal, and discussed topics of various kinds in the light of Scripture as well as in the light of philosophy.

CHAPTER XXV.

His Review of the Canonical Scriptures.

WHEN expounding the first Psalm,[1] he gives a catalogue of the sacred Scriptures of the Old Testament[2] as follows:

" It should be stated that the canonical books, as the Hebrews have handed them down, are twenty-two; corresponding with the number of their letters." Farther on he says:

" The twenty-two books of the Hebrews are the following: That which is called by us Genesis, but by the Hebrews, from the beginning of the book, Bresith,[3] which means, ' In the beginning'; Exodus, Welesmoth,[3a] that is, ' These are the names'; Leviticus, Wikra, 'And he called'; Numbers, Ammesphekodeim; Deuteronomy, Eleaddebareim, 'These are the words'; Jesus, the son of Nave, Josoue ben Noun; Judges and Ruth, among them in one book, Saphateim; the First and Second of Kings, among them one, Samouel, that is, ' The called of God'; the Third and Fourth of Kings in one, Wammelch David, that is, ' The kingdom of David'; of the Chronicles, the First and Second in one, Dabreïamein, that is, ' Records of days'; Esdras,[4] First and Second in one, Ezra, that is, 'An assistant'; the book of Psalms, Spharthelleim; the Proverbs of Solomon, Meloth; Ecclesiastes, Koelth; the Song of Songs (not, as some suppose, Songs of Songs), Sir Hassirim; Isaiah, Jessia; Jeremiah, with Lamentations and the epistle in one, Jeremia; Daniel, Daniel; Ezekiel, Jezekiel; Job, Job; Esther, Esther. And besides these there are the Maccabees, which are entitled Sarbeth Sabanaiel.[5] He gives these in the above-mentioned work.

1

2

[1] On Origen's commentary on Psalms, see the previous chapter, note 3. The first fragment given here by Eusebius is found also in the *Philocalia*, chap. 3, where it forms part of a somewhat longer extract. The second fragment is extant only in this chapter of Eusebius' History.

[2] On the Hebrew canon of the Old Testament, see Bk. III. chap. 10, note 1. Upon Origen's omission of the twelve minor prophets and the insertion of the apocryphal epistle of Jeremiah, see the same note.

[3] I have reproduced Origen's Greek transliteration of this and the following Hebrew words letter by letter. It will be seen by a comparison of the words with the Hebrew titles of the books, as we now have them, that Origen's pronunciation of Hebrew, even after making all due allowance for a difference in the pronunciation of the Greek and for changes in the Hebrew text, must have been, in many respects, quite different from ours.

[3a] Οὐελεσμώθ. I represent the diphthong οὐ at the beginning of a word by " w."

[4] The first and second books of Esdras here referred to are not the apocryphal books known by that name, but Ezra and Nehemiah, which in the Hebrew canon formed but one book, as Origen says here, but which in the LXX were separated (see above, Bk. III. chap. 10, note 4). Esdras is simply the form which the word Ezra assumes in Greek.

[5] Whether this sentence closed Origen's discussion of the Hebrew canon, or whether he went on to mention the other apocryphal books, we cannot tell. The latter seems intrinsically much more probable, for it is difficult to understand the insertion of the Maccabees in this connection, and the omission of all the others; for the Maccabees, as is clear from the words ἔξω δὲ τούτων ἐστὶ τὰ Μακκαβαϊκά, are not reckoned by Origen among the twenty-two books as a part of the Hebrew canon. At the same time, it is hardly conceivable that Eusebius should have broken off thus, in the midst of a passage, without any explanation; though it is, of course, not impossible that he gives only the first sentence of the new paragraph on the books of

3   In his first book on Matthew's Gospel,[6] maintaining the Canon of the Church, he testifies that he knows only four Gospels, writing as follows :

4   " Among the four Gospels,[7] which are the only indisputable ones in the Church of God under heaven, I have learned by tradition that the first was written by Matthew, who was once a publican, but afterwards an apostle of Jesus Christ, and it was prepared for the converts from Judaism, and published in the Hebrew

5   language.[8] The second is by Mark, who composed it according to the instructions of Peter,[9] who in his Catholic epistle acknowledges him as a son, saying, 'The church that is at Babylon elected together with you, saluteth

6   you, and so doth Marcus, my son.'[10] And the third by Luke, the Gospel commended by Paul,[11] and composed for Gentile converts. Last of all that by John." [12]

7   In the fifth book of his Expositions of John's Gospel, he speaks thus concerning the epistles of the apostles : [13]

"But he who was 'made sufficient to be a minister of the New Testament, not of the letter, but of the Spirit,'[14] that is, Paul, who 'fully preached the Gospel from Jerusalem and round about even unto Illyricum,'[15] did not write to all the churches which he had instructed ; and to those to which he wrote he sent but

8   few lines.[16] And Peter, on whom the Church of Christ is built, 'against which the gates of hell shall not prevail,'[17] has left one acknowledged epistle ; perhaps also a second, but this

is doubtful.[18] Why need we speak of him   9
who reclined upon the bosom of Jesus,[19] John, who has left us one Gospel,[20] though he confessed that he might write so many that the world could not contain them?[21] And he wrote also the Apocalypse, but was commanded to keep silence and not to write the words of the seven thunders.[22] He has left also   10
an epistle of very few lines ; perhaps also a second and third ; but not all consider them genuine, and together they do not contain a hundred lines."

In addition he makes the following state-   11
ments in regard to the Epistle to the Hebrews[23] in his Homilies upon it :

"That the verbal style of the epistle entitled 'To the Hebrews,' is not rude like the language of the apostle, who acknowledged himself 'rude in speech,'[24] that is, in expression ; but that its diction is purer Greek, any one who has the power to discern differences of phraseology will acknowledge. Moreover, that the thoughts of   12
the epistle are admirable, and not inferior to the acknowledged apostolic writings, any one who carefully examines the apostolic text[25] will admit."   Farther on he adds :   13

"If I gave my opinion, I should say that the thoughts are those of the apostle, but the diction and phraseology are those of some one who remembered the apostolic teachings, and wrote down at his leisure what had been said by his teacher. Therefore if any church holds that this epistle is by Paul, let it be commended for this. For not without reason have the ancients handed it down as Paul's. But who wrote   14
the epistle, in truth, God knows. The statement of some who have gone before us is that Clement, bishop of the Romans, wrote the epistle, and of others that Luke, the author of the Gospel and the Acts, wrote it." But let this suffice on these matters.

---

the LXX, in order to show that the discussion of the Hebrew canon closes, and a new subject is introduced at this point. But, however that may be, it must be regarded as certain that Origen did not reckon the books of the Maccabees as a part of the Hebrew canon, and on the other hand, that he did reckon those books, as well as others (if not all) of the books given in the LXX, as inspired Scripture. This latter fact is proved by his use of these books indiscriminately with those of the Hebrew canon as sources for dogmatic proof texts, and also by his express citation of at least some of them as Scripture (cf. on this subject, Redepenning, p. 235 sq.). We must conclude, therefore, that Origen did not adopt the Hebrew canon as his own, but that he states it as clearly as he does in this place, in order to bring concretely before the minds of his readers the difference between the canon of the Jews and the canon of the Christians, who looked upon the LXX as the more authoritative form of the Old Testament. Perhaps he had in view the same purpose that led him to compare the Hebrew text and the LXX in his *Hexapla* (see chap. 16, note 8).

[6] On Origen's Commentary on Matthew, see chap. 36, note 4. The fragment given here by Eusebius is all that is extant of the first book of the commentary.

[7] Compare Origen's *Hom. I. in Lucam: Ecclesia quatuor habet evangelia, hæresea plurima* ; and *multi conati sunt scribere, sed et multi conati sunt ordinare: quatuor tantum evangelia sunt probata*, &c. Compare also Irenæus, *Adv. Hær.* III. 11, 8, where the attempt is made to show that it is impossible for the Gospels to be either more or fewer in number than four; and the Muratorian Fragment where the four Gospels are named, but the number four is not represented as in itself the necessary number; also Tertullian's *Adv. Marc.* IV. 2, and elsewhere.

[8] See Bk. III. chap. 24, note 5.

[9] See Bk. II. chap. 15, note 4.   [10] 1 Pet. v. 13.

[11] See Bk. III. chap. 4, notes 12 and 15. Origen refers here to 2 Cor. viii. 18, where, however, it is clear that the reference is not to any specific Gospel any more than in the passages referred to above, III. 4, note 15.   [12] See Bk. III. chap. 24.

[13] This fragment from the fifth book of Origen's Commentary on John is extant only in this chapter. The context is not preserved.

[14] 2 Cor. iii. 6.   [16] See Bk. III. chap. 24, note 2.

[15] Rom. xv. 19.   [17] Matt. xvi. 18.

---

[18] On the first and second Epistles of Peter, see Bk. III. chap. 3, notes 1 and 4.   [19] See John xiii. 23.

[20] On John's Gospel, see Bk. III. chap. 24, note 1; on the Apocalypse, note 20; and on the epistles, notes 18 and 19 of the same chapter.

[21] See John xxi. 25.

[22] See Rev. x. 4.

[23] Upon the Epistle to the Hebrews, and Origen's treatment of it, see Bk. III. chap. 3, note 17. The two extracts given here by Eusebius are the only fragments of Origen's Homilies on the Epistle to the Hebrews now extant. Four brief Latin fragments of his commentary upon that epistle are preserved in the first book of Pamphilus' *Defense of Origen*, and are printed by Lommatzsch in Vol. V. p. 297 sq. The commentaries (or "books," as they are called) are mentioned only in that *Defense*. The catalogue of Jerome speaks only of "eighteen homilies." We know nothing about the extent or the date of composition of these homilies and commentaries.   [24] 2 Cor. xi. 6.

[25] προσέχων, τῇ ἀναγνώσει τῇ ἀποστολικῇ, ἀνάγνωσις meant originally the act of reading, then also that which is read. It thus came to be used (like ἀνάγνωσμα) of the pericope or text or section of the Scripture read in church, and in the plural to designate the church lectionaries, or service books. In the present case it is used evidently in a wider sense of the text of Paul's writings as a whole. This use of the two words to indicate, not simply the selection read in church, but the text of a book or books as a whole, was not at all uncommon, as may be seen from the examples given by Suicer, although he does not mention this wider signification among the uses of the word. See his *Thesaurus, s.v.*

CHAPTER XXVI.

Heraclas becomes Bishop of Alexandria.

IT was in the tenth year of the above-mentioned reign that Origen removed from Alexandria to Cæsarea,[1] leaving the charge of the catechetical school in that city to Heraclas. Not long afterward Demetrius, bishop of the church of Alexandria, died, having held the office for forty-three full years,[2] and Heraclas succeeded him. At this time Firmilianus,[3] bishop of Cæsarea in Cappadocia, was conspicuous.

CHAPTER XXVII.

How the Bishops regarded Origen.

HE was so earnestly affected toward Origen, that he urged him to come to that country for the benefit of the churches, and moreover he visited him in Judea, remaining with him for some time, for the sake of improvement in divine things. And Alexander,[1] bishop of Jerusalem, and Theoctistus,[2] bishop of Cæsarea, attended on him constantly,[3] as their only teacher, and allowed[4] him to expound the Divine Scriptures, and to perform the other duties pertaining to ecclesiastical discourse.[5]

CHAPTER XXVIII.

The Persecution under Maximinus.

THE Roman emperor, Alexander, having finished his reign in thirteen years, was succeeded by Maximinus Cæsar.[1] On account of his hatred toward the household of Alexander,[2] which contained many believers, he began a persecution, commanding that only the rulers of the churches should be put to death, as responsible for the Gospel teaching. Thereupon Origen composed his work On Martyrdom,[3] and dedicated it to Ambrose and Protoctetus,[4] a presbyter of the parish of Cæsarea, because in the persecution there had come upon them both unusual hardships, in which it is reported that they were eminent in confession during the reign of Maximinus, which lasted but three years. Origen has noted this as the time of the persecution in the twenty-second book of his Commentaries on John, and in several epistles.[5]

CHAPTER XXIX.

Fabianus, who was wonderfully designated Bishop of Rome by God.

GORDIANUS succeeded Maximinus as Roman emperor;[1] and Pontianus,[2] who had

---

[1] The tenth year of Alexander Severus, 231 A.D. On Origen's departure from Alexandria at this time, see below, p. 396. On Heraclas, see chap. 3, note 2.

[2] On the episcopacy of Demetrius, see Bk. V. chap. 22, note 4. Forty-three years, beginning with 189 A.D., bring us down to 232 as the date of his death, and this agrees excellently with the statements of this chapter.

[3] Firmilian, bishop of Cæsarea, the capital of Cappadocia (to be distinguished from Cæsarea in Palestine), was one of the most famous prelates of his day in the Eastern Church. He was a friend of Origen, as we learn from the next chapter, and took part in a council called on account of the schism of Novatian (see chap. 46), and also in councils called to consider the case of Paul of Samosata (see Bk. VII. chaps. 28 and 30). He was one of the bishops whom Stephen excommunicated because they rebaptized heretics (see Bk. VII. chap. 2, note 3, and chap. 5, note 4), and he wrote an epistle upon this subject to Cyprian, which is extant in a Latin translation made by Cyprian himself (Ep. 74, al. 75, in the collection of Cyprian's epistles. See Dict. of Christ. Biog. I. 751, note). Basil (de Spiritu Sancto, 29) refers to works (λόγοι) left by Firmilian, but none of them are extant except the single epistle mentioned, nor do we hear from any other source that he was a writer. Jerome does not mention him in his De vir. ill. The exact date of his accession is unknown to us, as it very likely was to Eusebius also. He was a bishop already in the tenth year of Alexander (231 A.D.), or very soon afterward, and from Bk. VII. chap. 30, we learn that he died at Tarsus on his way to Antioch to attend a council which had been summoned to deal with Paul of Samosata. This synod was held about 265 A.D. (not in 272 as is commonly supposed; see Bk. VII. chap. 29, note 1), and it is at this time, therefore, that we must put the death of Firmilian; so that he was bishop of Cæsarea at least some thirty-four years.

[1] On Alexander, bishop of Jerusalem, see chap. 8, note 6.

[2] On Theoctistus, bishop of Cæsarea in Palestine, see chap. 19, note 27.

[3] A number of MSS., followed by Heinichen and some others, insert at this point ὡς ἔπος εἰπεῖν (" so to speak ").

[4] The presbyter derived his authority to preach and teach only from the bishop, and hence these bishops extended to Origen, whom they had ordained a presbyter, full liberty to preach and teach within their dioceses.

[5] τὰ λοιπὰ τοῦ ἐκκλησιαστικοῦ λόγου.

[1] Alexander Severus was murdered early in the year 235, and was succeeded at once by his commanding general, the Thracian Maximinus, or Caius Julius Verus Maximinus, as he called himself.

[2] The reference here is not to the immediate family of Alexander, but to the court as a whole, his family in the widest sense, including court officials, servants, &c. The favor which Alexander had shown to the Christians (see chap. 21, note 8) is clearly seen in the fact that there were so many Christians at court, as Eusebius informs us here. This persecution was at first directed, Eusebius tells us, solely against the heads of the churches (τοὺς τῶν ἐκκλησιῶν ἄρχοντας), i.e. the bishops; and we might imagine only those bishops who had stood nearest Alexander and had been most favored by him to be meant (Pontianus and Hippolytus of Rome were exiled, for instance, at the very beginning of Maximinus, as he called himself; see chap. 22, note 1); for Maximinus' hostility to the Christians seems to have been caused, not by religious motives, but by mere hatred of his predecessor, and of every cause to which he had shown favor. But the persecution was not confined to such persons, as we learn from this chapter, which tells us of the sufferings of Ambrose and Protoctetus, neither of whom was a bishop. It seems probable that most of the persecuting was not the result of positive efforts on the part of Maximinus, but rather of the superstitious hatred of the common people, whose fears had been recently aroused by earthquakes and who always attributed such calamities to the existence of the Christians. Of course under Maximinus they had free rein, and could persecute whenever they or the provincial authorities felt inclined (cf. Firmilian's epistle to Cyprian, and Origen's Exhort. ad Mart.). Eusebius tells us nothing of Origen's whereabouts at this time; but in Palladius' Hist. Laus. 147, it is said that Origen was given refuge by Juliana in Cæsarea in Cappadocia during some persecution, undoubtedly this one, if the report is true (see chap. 17, note 4).

[3] This work on martyrdom (εἰς μαρτύριον προτρεπτικὸς λόγος, Exhortatio ad Martyrium) is still extant, and is printed by Lommatzsch in Vol. XX., p. 231-316. It is a most beautiful and inspiring exhortation.

[4] On Ambrose, see chap. 18, note 1. Protoctetus, a presbyter of the church of Cæsarea (apparently Palestinian Cæsarea), is known to us only from this passage.

[5] On Origen's Commentary on John's Gospel, see chap. 24, note 1. No fragments of the twenty-second book are extant, nor any of the epistles in which reference is made to this persecution.

[1] Gordianus the younger, grandson of Gordianus I., and nephew (or son?) of Gordianus II., became emperor after the murder of Balbinus and Pupienus, in July, 238, at the age of fifteen years, and reigned until early in the year 244, when he was murdered by

been bishop of the church at Rome for six years, was succeeded by Anteros.[3] After he had held the office for a month, Fabianus[4] succeeded

2 him. They say[5] that Fabianus having come, after the death of Anteros, with others from the country, was staying at Rome, and that while there he was chosen to the office through a most wonderful manifestation of divine and

3 heavenly grace. For when all the brethren had assembled to select by vote him who should succeed to the episcopate of the church, several renowned and honorable men were in the minds of many, but Fabianus, although present, was in the mind of none. But they relate that suddenly a dove flying down lighted on his head, resembling the descent of the Holy Spirit on the Saviour in the form of a dove.

4 Thereupon all the people, as if moved by one Divine Spirit, with all eagerness and unanimity cried out that he was worthy, and without delay they took him and placed him upon the episcopal seat.[6]

5 About that time Zebinus,[7] bishop of Antioch died, and Babylas[8] succeeded him.

And in Alexandria Heraclas,[9] having received the episcopal office after Demetrius,[10] was succeeded in the charge of the catechetical school by Dionysius,[11] who had also been one of Origen's pupils.

CHAPTER XXX.

The Pupils of Origen.

WHILE Origen was carrying on his customary duties in Cæsarea, many pupils came to him not only from the vicinity, but also from other countries. Among these Theodorus, the same that was distinguished among the bishops of our day under the name of Gregory,[1] and his brother

---

the soldiers and succeeded by Philip. He is made by Eusebius (both here and in the *Chron.*) the direct successor of Maximinus, simply because only two or three months elapsed between the death of the latter and his own accession.

[2] On Pontianus, see chap. 23, note 3.

[3] Both here and in the *Chron.* the accession of Anteros is synchronized with the accession of Gordianus, but as seen in chap. 23, note 3, Pontianus was succeeded by Anteros in the first year of Maximinus, i.e. in 235, — three years earlier, therefore, than the date given by Eusebius. All the authorities agree in assigning only one month and a few days to the episcopate of Anteros, and this is to be accepted as correct. Of the life and character of Anteros we know nothing.

[4] Greek Φαβιανός, though some MSS. read Φλαβιανός. The Armenian and Hieronymian *Chron.* call him Fabianus; the Liberian catalogue, Fabius; Eutychius and the Alex. cat., Flabianus. According to chap. 39, he suffered martyrdom in the persecution of Decius (250-251). Both versions of the *Chron.* assign thirteen years to his episcopate, and this agrees fairly well with the notices here and in chap. 39 (accession in 238 and death in 250 or 251). But, as already seen, Eusebius is quite wrong in the dates which he gives for the accession of these three bishops, and the statements of the Liberian catalogue are to be accepted, which put Fabian's accession in January, 236, and his death in January, 250, after an episcopate of fourteen years and ten days. The martyrdom of Fabian rests upon good authority (cf. chap. 39, and Jerome's *de vir. ill.* chap. 54, and especially Cyprian's *Epistles*, 3, *al.* 9, and 30). From these epistles we learn that he was a man of ability and virtue. He stands out more clearly in the light of history than most of the early Roman bishops, but tradition has handed down a great many unfounded stories in regard to him (see the article in the *Dict. of Christ. Biog.*).

[5] φασί. Eusebius is our only authority for the following story. Rufinus (VI. 21) tells a similar tale in connection with Zephyrinus.

[6] τὸν θρόνον τῆς ἐπισκοπῆς.

[7] On Zebinus, see chap. 23, note 4.

[8] Babylas occupies an illustrious place in the list of ancient martyrs (cf. Tillemont, *Mem.* III. 400-409). Chrysostom devoted a festal oration to his memory (*In sanctum Babylam contra Julianum et contra Gentiles*); while Jerome, Epiphanius, Sozomen, Theodoret, and others make honorable mention of him. There are extant the *Acta Babylæ* (spurious), which, however, confound him with a martyr who suffered under Numerian. The legends in regard to Babylas and to the miracles performed by his bones are very numerous (see Tillemont, *l.c.*). He is identified by Chrysostom and others with the bishop mentioned by Eusebius in chap. 34, and there is no good reason to doubt the identification (see Harnack, *Zeit des Ignatius*, p. 48). The fact of his martyrdom under Decius (see chap. 39) is too well attested to admit of doubt; though upon the manner of it, not all the traditions are agreed, Eusebius reporting that he died in prison, Chrysostom that he died by violence. The account of Eusebius seems the most reliable. The date of his accession is unknown, but there is no reason to doubt that it took place during the reign of Gordian (238-244), as Eusebius here seems to imply; though it is true that he connects it closely with the death of Demetrius, which certainly took place not later than 232 (see

above, Bk. V. chap. 22, note 4). There is no warrant for carrying the accession of Babylas back so far as that.

[9] On Heraclas, see chap. 3, note 2.

[10] On the episcopate of Demetrius, see Bk. V. chap. 22, note 4.

[11] On Dionysius, see chap. 40, note 1.

[1] Our sources for a knowledge of the life of Gregory, who is known as Gregory Thaumaturgus ("wonder-worker"), are numerous, but not all of them reliable. He is mentioned by Eusebius here and in Bk. VII. chaps. 14 and 28, and a brief account of his life and writings is given by Jerome (*de vir. ill.* chap. 65), who adds some particulars not mentioned by Eusebius. There is also extant Gregory's *Panegyrical Oration* in praise of Origen, which contains an outline of the earlier years of his life. Gregory of Nyssa about a century later wrote a life of Gregory Thaumaturgus, which is still extant, but which is full of marvelous stories, and contains little that is trustworthy. Gregory's fame was very great among his contemporaries and succeeding generations, and many of the Fathers have left brief accounts of him, or references to him which it is not necessary to mention here. He was a native of Neo-Cæsarea in Pontus (according to Gregory Nyssa), the same city of which he was afterward bishop, was of wealthy parentage, and began the study of law when quite young (see his own *Orat. Paneg.* chap. 5). Coming to Cæsarea, in Palestine, on his way to Berytus, where he and his brother Athenodorus were to attend a school of law, he met Origen, and was so attracted by him that he and his brother remained in Cæsarea five years (according to Eusebius and Jerome) and studied logic, physics, mathematics, ethics, Greek philosophy, and theology with him (see his *Orat.*). At the end of this time the brothers returned to Pontus, and afterwards were made bishops, Gregory of Neo-Cæsarea, his native city; Athenodorus of some unknown city (Eusebius here and in VII. 14 and 28 says only that they were both bishops of churches in Pontus). Of the remarkable events connected with the ordination of Gregory, which are told by Gregory of Nyssa, it is not necessary to speak here. He was a prominent scholar and writer, and a man universally beloved and respected for his deep piety and his commanding ability, but his fame rested chiefly upon the reports of his miracle-working, which were widespread. The prodigies told of him are numerous and marvelous. Eusebius is silent about this side of his career (whether because of ignorance or incredulity we cannot tell, but the latter seems most probable), but Jerome refers to his fame as a miracle-worker, Gregory of Nyssa's *Vita*, is full of it, and Basil and other later writers dwell upon it. What the foundation for all these traditions was we do not know. He was a famous missionary, and seems to have been remarkably successful in converting the pagans of his diocese, which was almost wholly heathen when he became bishop. This great missionary success may have given rise to the tales of supernatural power, some cause above the ordinary being assumed by the common people as necessary to account for such results. Miracles and other supernatural phenomena were quite commonly assumed in those days as causes of conversions — especially if the conversions themselves were in any way remarkable (cf. e.g. the close of the anonymous *Dialogue with Herbanus, a Jew*). Not only the miracles, but also many other events reported in Gregory of Nyssa's *Vita*, must be regarded as unfounded; e.g. the account of a long period of study in Alexandria of which our more reliable sources contain no trace. The veneration in which Gregory held Origen is clear enough from his panegyric, and the great regard which Origen cherished for Gregory is revealed in his epistle to the latter, written soon after Gregory's arrival in Neo-Cæsarea, and still preserved in the *Philocalia*, chap. 13. The works of Gregory known to us are his *Panegyrical Oration* in praise of Origen, delivered in the presence of the latter and of a great multitude before Gregory's departure from Cæsarea, and still extant; a paraphrase of the book of Ecclesiastes, mentioned by Jerome (*l.c.*), and likewise extant; several epistles referred to by Jerome (*l.c.*), only one of which, his so-called *Canonical Epistle*, addressed to an anonymous bishop of Pontus, is still preserved; and finally a trinitarian creed, or confession of faith,

Athenodorus,[2] we know to have been especially celebrated. Finding them deeply interested in Greek and Roman learning, he infused into them a love of philosophy, and led them to exchange their old zeal for the study of divinity. Remaining with him five years, they made such progress in divine things, that although they were still young, both of them were honored with a bishopric in the churches of Pontus.

CHAPTER XXXI.

Africanus.

1   AT this time also Africanus,[1] the writer of the books entitled Cesti, was well known.

There is extant an epistle of his to Origen, expressing ·doubts[2]·of the story of Susannah in Daniel, as being spurious and fictitious. Origen answered this very fully. Other 2 works of the same Africanus which have reached us are his five books on Chronology, a work accurately and laboriously prepared. He says in this that he went to Alexandria on account of the great fame of Heraclas,[3] who excelled especially in philosophic studies and other Greek learning, and whose appointment to the bishopric of the church there we have

---

which is given by Gregory of Nyssa in his *Vita*, and whose genuineness has been warmly disputed (e.g. by Lardner, Works, II. p. 634 sq.); but since Caspari's defense of it in his *Gesch. d. Taufsymbols und der Glaubensregel*, its authenticity may be regarded as established. These four writings, together with some works falsely ascribed to Gregory, are translated in *The Ante-Nicene Fathers*, Am. ed., Vol. VI. p. 1–80. Original Greek in Migne's *Patr. Gr.* X. 983–1343. See also Ryssel's *Gregorius Thaumaturgus. Sein Leben und seine Schriften;* Leipzig, 1880. Ryssel gives (p. 65–79) a German translation of two hitherto unknown Syriac writings of Gregory, one on the equality of Father, Son, and Spirit, and the other on the possibility and impassibility of God. Gregory's dates cannot be fixed with exactness; but as he cannot have seen Origen in Cæsarea until after 231, and was very young when he met him there, he must have been born as late as the second decade of the third century. As he was with Origen at least five years, he can hardly have taken his farewell of him until after the persecution of Maximinus (i.e. after 238), for we cannot suppose that he pronounced his panegyrical oration during that persecution. He speaks in the first chapter of that oration of not having delivered an oration for eight years, and this is commonly supposed to imply that it was eight years since he had begun to study with Origen, in which case the oration must be put as late as 239, and it must be assumed, if Eusebius' five years are accepted as accurate, that he was absent for some three years during that period (perhaps while the persecution was going on). But the eight years cannot be pressed in this connection, for it is quite possible that they may have been reckoned from an earlier time, perhaps from the time when he began the study of law, which was before he met Origen (see *Panegyr.* chaps. 1 and 5). If we were to suppose the order followed by Eusebius strictly chronological, we should have to put Gregory's acquaintance with Origen into the reign of Gordian (238–244). The truth is, the matter cannot be decided. He is said by Gregory of Nyssa to have retired into concealment during the persecution of Decius, and to have returned to his charge again after its close. He was present with his brother Athenodorus at one of the councils called to consider the case of Paul of Samosata (see Bk. VII. chap. 28), but was not present at the final one at which Paul was condemned (see *ibid.* chaps. 29 and 30, and note 2 on the latter chapter). This one was held about 265 (see *ibid.* chap. 29, note 1), and hence it is likely that Gregory was dead before that date.

[2] Athenodorus is known to us only as the brother of Gregory and bishop of some church or churches in Pontus (see Bk. VII. chaps. 14 and 28).

[1] Julius Africanus (as he is called by Jerome) was one of the most learned men of the Ante-Nicene age. Not much is known of his life, though he seems to have resided, at least for a time, in Emmaus, a town of Palestine, something over twenty miles from Jerusalem (not the Emmaus of Luke xxiv. 13, which was but seven or eight miles from the city), for we hear in the *Chron.*, and in Jerome's *de vir. ill.* c. 63, of his going on an embassy to the Emperor Heliogabalus, and securing the rebuilding of the ruined city Emmaus under the name of Nicopolis, which it henceforth bore. He does not appear to have been a clergyman, or at any rate not a bishop; for he is spoken of as such by no early authority, and he is addressed by Origen in an extant epistle, which must have been written toward the close of his life, simply as "brother." His dates cannot be fixed with any exactness. He must have been already a prominent man when he went on an embassy to the emperor (between 218 and 222). He must have been considerably older than Origen, for in his epistle to him he calls him "son," and that although Origen was at the time beyond middle life himself. Unless Eusebius is mistaken, he was still alive and active in the time of Gordian (238–244). But if he was enough older than Origen to address him as "son," he can hardly have lived much beyond that reign. He seems to have been a Christian philosopher and scholar rather than an ecclesiastic, and took no such part in the church affairs of the time as to leave mention of his name in the accounts of the synods of his day. He was

quite a traveler, as we learn from his own writings, and had the well-deserved reputation of being one of the greatest scholars of the age. Eusebius mentions four works left by him, the *Cesti*, the *Chronicon*, and the epistles to Origen and to Aristides. Jerome (*l.c.*) mentions only the last three, but Photius (*Cod.* 34) refers to all four. The *Cesti* (κεστοί, "embroidered girdles") seems to have derived its name from the miscellaneous character of its contents, which included notes on geography, the art of war, medicine, agriculture, &c. It is said by Syncellus to have been composed of nine books: Photius mentions fourteen, Suidas twenty-four. It is no longer extant, but numerous scattered fragments have been preserved. Its authenticity has been doubted, chiefly because of its purely secular character, and the nature of some of the notes, which do not seem worthy of the clear-headed and at the same time Christian scholar. But the external evidence, which is not unsupported by the internal, is too strong to be set aside, and we must conclude that the work is genuine. The extant fragments of it are given in various works on mathematics, agriculture, etc. (see Richardson's *Bibliographical Synopsis*, p. 68). The epistle of Africanus to Origen is the only one of his writings preserved in a complete form. It seems that Origen, in a discussion with a certain Bassus (see Origen's epistle to Africanus, § 2), at which Africanus was present, had quoted from that part of the Book of Daniel which contains the apocryphal story of Susannah. Africanus afterward wrote a brief epistle to Origen, in which he contended that the story is not authentic, urging among other arguments differences in style between it and the rest of the book, and the fact that the story is not found in Hebrew, and that certain phrases show that it was composed originally in Greek. Origen replied at considerable length, maintaining the authenticity of the passage, and thereby showing himself inferior to Africanus in critical judgment. Origen's reply was written from Nicomedia (see § 1), where he was staying with Ambrose (see § 15). It seems probable that this visit to Nicomedia was made on his way to or from his second visit to Athens (see next chapter, note 4). Africanus' greatest work, and the one which brought him most fame, was his *Chronicon*, in five books. The work is no longer extant, but considerable fragments of it have been preserved (e.g. in Eusebius' *Præp. Evang.* X. 10, and *Dem. Evang.* VIII., and especially in the *Chronographia* of Syncellus), and the *Chronicon* of Eusebius which is really based upon it, so that we are enabled to gain a very fair idea of its original form. As described by Photius, it was concise, but omitted nothing worthy of mention, beginning with the creation and coming down to the reign of Macrinus. It actually extended to the fourth year of Heliogabalus (221), as we see from a quotation made by Syncellus. The work seems to have been caused by the common desire of the Christians (exhibited by Tatian, Clement of Alexander, and others) to prove in their defense of Christianity the antiquity of the Jewish religion, and thus take away the accusation of novelty brought against Christianity by its opponents. Africanus apparently aimed to produce a universal chronicle and history which should exhibit the synchronism of events in the history of the leading nations of the world, and thus furnish solid ground for Christian apologists to build upon. It was the first attempt of the kind, and became the foundation of Christian chronicles for many centuries. The time at which it was written is determined with sufficient accuracy by the date at which the chronological table closes. Salmon (in the *Dict. of Christ. Biog.*) remarks that it must have been completed early in the year 221, for it did not contain the names of the victors in the Olympic games of the 250th Olympiad, which took place in that year (as we learn from the list of victors copied by Eusebius from Africanus). It is said by Eusebius, just below, that Africanus reports in this work that he had visited Alexandria on account of the great celebrity of Heraclas. This is very surprising, for we should hardly have expected Heraclas' fame to have attracted such a man to Alexandria until after Origen had left, and he had himself become the head of the school. On the fourth writing mentioned by Eusebius, the epistle to Aristides, see above, Bk. I. chap. 7, note 2. The fragments of Africanus' works, with the exception of the *Cesti*, have been printed, with copious and valuable notes, by Routh, *Rel. Sac.* II. 221–509; English translation in the *Ante-Nicene Fathers*, Am. ed., VI. 125–140.

[2] ἀπορούντος. A very mild way of putting his complete rejection of the story!

[3] On Heraclas, see chap. 3, note 2.

3　already mentioned. There is extant also another epistle from the same Africanus to Aristides on the supposed discrepancy between Matthew and Luke in the Genealogies of Christ. In this he shows clearly the agreement of the evangelists, from an account which had come down to him, which we have already given in its proper place in the first book of this work.[4]

CHAPTER XXXII.

The Commentaries which Origen composed in Cæsarea in Palestine.

1　ABOUT this time Origen prepared his Commentaries on Isaiah[1] and on Ezekiel.[2] Of the former there have come down to us thirty books, as far as the third part of Isaiah, to the vision of the beasts in the desert ;[3] on Ezekiel twenty-five books, which are all that he 2　wrote on the whole prophet. Being at that time in Athens,[4] he finished his work on Ezekiel and commenced his Commentaries on the Song of Songs,[5] which he carried forward to the fifth book. After his return to Cæsarea,

he completed these also, ten books in number. But why should we give in this history 3 an accurate catalogue of the man's works, which would require a separate treatise ?[6] we have furnished this also in our narrative of the life of Pamphilus,[7] a holy martyr of our own time. After showing how great the diligence of Pamphilus was in divine things, we give in that a catalogue of the library which he collected of the works of Origen and of other ecclesiastical writers. Whoever desires may learn readily from this which of Origen's works have reached us. But we must proceed now with our history.

CHAPTER XXXIII.

The Error of Beryllus.

BERYLLUS,[1] whom we mentioned recently 1 as bishop of Bostra in Arabia, turned aside from the ecclesiastical standard[2] and attempted to introduce ideas foreign to the faith. He dared to assert that our Saviour and Lord did not pre-exist in a distinct form of being of his own[3] before his abode among men, and that he does not possess a divinity of his own,[4] but only that of the Father dwelling in him. Many bishops carried on investi- 2 gations and discussions with him on this matter, and Origen having been invited with the others, went down at first for a conference with him to ascertain his real opinion. But when he understood his views, and perceived that they were erroneous, having persuaded him by argument, and convinced him by demonstration, he brought him back to the true doctrine, and re-

---

[4] In Bk. I. chap. 7.

[1] "About this time" refers us still to the reign of Gordian (238–244). Eusebius mentions only the commentaries on Isaiah, but Jerome refers also to homilies and notes. The thirty books which were extant in Eusebius' time extended to XXX. 6, as we are informed here. Whether the commentary originally went beyond this point we do not know. There are extant only two brief Latin fragments from the first and eighth books of the commentary, and nine homilies (the last incomplete) in a Latin version by Jerome; printed by Lommatzsch, XIII. 235–301.

[2] Eusebius records that Origen wrote twenty-five books of a commentary on Ezekiel. The form of expression would seem to imply that these did not cover the whole of Ezekiel, but a fragment of the twentieth book, extant in the eleventh chapter of the *Philocalia*, deals with the thirty-fourth chapter of the prophecy, so that the twenty-five books must have covered at any rate most of the ground. The catalogue of Jerome mentions twenty-nine books and twelve homilies, but the former number must be a mistake, for Eusebius' explicit statement that Origen wrote but twenty-five books can hardly be doubted. There are extant only the Greek fragment of the twentieth book referred to above, fourteen homilies in the Latin version of Jerome, and a few extracts; all printed by Lommatzsch, XIV. 1–232.

[3] i.e. to Isa. xxx. 6, where the LXX reads ἡ ὅρασις τῶν τετραπόδων τῶν ἐν τῇ ἐρήμῳ, which are the exact words used by Eusebius. Our English versions, both the authorized and revised, read, "The burden of the beasts of the South." The Hebrew will bear either rendering.

[4] The cause of this second visit to Athens we do not know, nor the date of it; although if Eusebius is to be relied upon, it took place during the reign of Gordian (238–244). He must have remained some time in Athens and have had leisure for study, for he finished his commentary on Ezekiel and wrote five books of his commentary on Canticles. This visit to Athens is to be distinguished from the one referred to in chap. 23, because it is probable that Origen found the Nicopolis copy of the Old Testament (mentioned in chap. 16) on the occasion of a visit to Achaia, and this visit is apparently too late, for he seems to have finished his *Hexapla* before this time; and still further, the epistle in which he refers to spurious accounts of his disputation at Athens (see Jerome's *Apol. adv. Ruf.* II. 18), complains also of Demetrius and of his own excommunication, which, as Redepenning remarks, points to a date soon after that excommunication took place, and not a number of years later, when Demetrius had been long dead.

[5] From the seventh chapter of the *Philocalia* we learn that Origen, in his youth, wrote a small book (μικρὸς τόμος) upon Canticles, of which a single brief fragment is preserved in that chapter. The catalogue of Jerome mentions ten books, two books written early, and two homilies. Eusebius mentions only the commentary, of which, he says, five books were written in Athens, and five more in Cæsarea. The prologue and four books are extant in a Latin translation by Rufinus, and two homilies in a translation by Jerome; besides these, some Greek extracts made by Procopius, — all printed by Lommatzsch, XIV. 233; XV. 108.

[6] ἰδίας δεόμενον σχολῆς.

[7] On Pamphilus, see Bk. VII. chap. 32, note 40. On Eusebius' Life of Pamphilus, see the Prolegomena, p. 28, above.

[1] Beryllus, bishop of Bostra in Arabia (mentioned above, in chap. 20), is chiefly noted on account of the heresy into which he fell, and from which Origen won him back, by convincing him of his error. According to chap. 20, he was a learned and cultured man, and Jerome (*de vir. ill.* c. 60) says of him, *gloriose rexisset ecclesiam*. We do not know his dates, but we may gather from this chapter that the synod which was called on his account convened during the reign of Gordian (238–244), and apparently toward the close of the reign. Our sources for a knowledge of the heresy of Beryllus are very meager. We have only the brief passage in this chapter; a fragment of Origen's commentary on Titus (Lommatzsch, V. 287), which undoubtedly refers to Beryllus' error, though he is not mentioned by name; and finally, a single sentence in Jerome's *de vir. ill.* c. 60 (*Christum ante incarnationem regat*), which, however, is apparently no more than his own interpretation of Eusebius' words. Our sources have been interpreted very differently, some holding Beryllus to have been a Patripassian, others classing him with the Artemonites (see above, Bk. V. chap. 28). He was, at any rate, a Monarchian, and his position, not to enter here into details, seems to have been that our Lord did not pre-exist as an independent being; but that, with the incarnation, he, who had previously been identified with the πατρικὴ θεότης, became a distinct being, possessed of an independent existence (see Dorner's *Person of Christ*, Div. I. Vol. II. p. 35 sq., Edinburgh edition). According to this chapter and chap. 20, Beryllus was the author of numerous treatises and epistles, which were extant in Eusebius' time. According to Jerome (*l.c.*), he wrote, *varia opuscula et maxime epistolas, in quibus Origeni gratias agit.* Jerome reports, also, that there were extant in his time epistles of Origen, addressed to Beryllus, and a dialogue between Origen and Beryllus. All traces of these epistles and other works have perished.

[2] τὸν ἐκκλησιαστικὸν κανόνα: i.e. the rule of faith.

[3] μὴ προϋφεστάναι κατ' ἰδίαν οὐσίας περιγραφήν.

[4] θεότητα ἰδίαν.

stored him to his former sound opinion.

3   There are still extant writings of Beryllus and of the synod held on his account, which contain the questions put to him by Origen, and the discussions which were carried on in his parish, as well as all the things done at that time.

4   The elder brethren among us[5] have handed down many other facts respecting Origen which I think proper to omit, as not pertaining to this work. But whatever it has seemed necessary to record about him can be found in the Apology in his behalf written by us and Pamphilus, the holy martyr of our day. We prepared this carefully and did the work jointly on account of faultfinders.[6]

CHAPTER XXXIV.

Philip Cæsar.

GORDIANUS had been Roman emperor for six years when Philip, with his son Philip, succeeded him.[1] It is reported that he, being a Christian, desired, on the day of the last paschal vigil, to share with the multitude in the prayers of the Church,[2] but that he was not permitted to enter, by him who then presided,[3] until he had made

confession and had numbered himself among those who were reckoned as transgressors and who occupied the place of penance.[4] For if he had not done this, he would never have been received by him, on account of the many crimes which he had committed. It is said that he obeyed readily, manifesting in his conduct a genuine and pious fear of God.

CHAPTER XXXV.

Dionysius succeeds Heraclas in the Episcopate.

IN the third year of this emperor, Heraclas[1] died, having held his office for sixteen years, and Dionysius[2] received the episcopate of the churches of Alexandria.

CHAPTER XXXVI.

Other Works of Origen.

AT this time, as the faith extended and our   1 doctrine was proclaimed boldly before all,[1] Origen, being, as they say, over sixty years old,[2] and having gained great facility by his long practice, very properly permitted his public discourses to be taken down by stenographers, a thing which he had never before allowed. He   2 also at this time composed a work of eight books in answer to that entitled True Discourse, which had been written against us by Celsus[3]

---

[5] τῶν καθ᾽ ἡμᾶς οἱ πρεσβύτεροι. It seems necessary here to take the word πρεσβύτερος in an unofficial sense, which is, to say the least, exceptional at this late date.

[6] On this Defense of Origen, written jointly by Pamphilus and Eusebius, see above, p. 36.

[1] The younger Gordian reigned from the summer of 238 until early in the year 244, when he was murdered by the soldiers, and succeeded by his prætorian prefect, Philip of Arabia, who took the name Marcus Julius Philippus, and reigned until 249, when he was conquered and succeeded by Decius. His son Philip, who was seven years old at the time of his father's accession, was immediately proclaimed Cæsar and afterward given the title of Augustus. He bore the name Marcus Julius Philippus Severus, and was slain at the time of his father's death.

[2] There has been much dispute as to Philip's relation to Christianity. Eusebius is the first one known to us to represent him as a Christian, and he gives the report only upon the authority of oral tradition (τοῦτον κατέχει λόγος χριστιανὸν ὄντα). Jerome (de vir. ill. 54) states explicitly that Philip was the first Christian emperor (qui primus de regibus Romanis christianus fuit), and this became common tradition in the Church. At the same time it must be noticed that Eusebius does not himself state that Philip was a Christian, — he simply records a tradition to that effect; and in his Vita Const. I. 3 he calls Constantine the first Christian emperor. Little reliance can be placed upon Jerome's explicit statement, for he seems only to be repeating as certain what Eusebius reported as possible. The only things known to us which can or could have been urged in support of the alleged fact that Philip was a Christian are his act recorded in this chapter and the letter written to him by Origen, as recorded in chap. 36. Moreover, it happens to be the fact that no heathen writer hints that he was a Christian, and we know that he celebrated games in Rome with pagan rites and great pomp. It seems, on the whole, probable that Philip showed himself favorable to Christianity, and perhaps superstitiously desired to gain the favor of the Christians' God, and hence went through some such process as Eusebius describes in this chapter, looking upon it merely as a sort of sacrifice to be offered to this God as he would offer other sacrifices to other gods. It is quite conceivable that he may have done this much, and this would be quite enough to start the report, after his death, that he had been a Christian secretly, if not openly; and from this to the tradition that he was unconditionally the first Christian emperor is but a step. Some ground for the common tradition must be assumed, but our sources do not warrant us in believing more than has been thus suggested as possible. For a full discussion of the question, see Tillemont, Hist. des Emp. III. p. 494 sq.

[3] Chrysostom (De St. Bab. c. Gentes, Tom. I.) and Leontius of Antioch (quoted in the Chron. pasch.) identify the bishop referred to here with Babylas, bishop of Antioch (see above, chap. 29, note 8). Eusebius' silence as to the name of the bishop looks as if he were ignorant on the matter, but there is nothing inherently improb-

able in the identification, which may therefore be looked upon as very likely correct.

[4] That is, the place assigned to penitents: μετανοίας χώραν. Christians who had committed flagrant transgressions were excluded from communion and required to go through a course of penance, more or less severe according to their offense, before they could be received again into the Church. In some cases they were excluded entirely from the services for a certain length of time; in other cases they were allowed to attend a part of the services, but in no case could they partake of the communion. In the fourth century a regular system of discipline grew up, and the penitents (pænitentes) were divided into various classes, — mourners, hearers, and kneelers; the first of whom were excluded entirely from the church, while the last two were admitted during a part of the service. The statement in the present case is of the most general character. Whether the place which he was obliged to take was without or within the church is not indicated. Upon the whole subject of ancient church discipline, see Bingham's Antiquities, Bk. XVI., and the article Penitence in Smith's Dict. of Christian Antiq.

[1] On Heraclas, see chap. 3, note 2. The third year of Philip's reign extended from the summer of 246 to the summer of 247, so that if Heraclas became bishop in 232, he cannot have held office fully sixteen years. The agreement, however, is so close as to occasion no difficulty.   [2] On Dionysius, see chap. 40, note 1.

[1] τοῦ καθ᾽ ἡμᾶς παρὰ πᾶσι λόγου.

[2] Since Origen was born in the year 185 or 186, this must have been as late as 245. Most if not all of the homilies of Origen, which are now preserved, were probably delivered after this time, and reported, as Eusebius says, by stenographers. The increasing boldness of the Christians referred to here was apparently due to their uncommonly comfortable condition under Philip.

[3] Of the personal history of Celsus, the first great literary opponent of Christianity, we know nothing with certainty, nor did Origen know any more. He had heard that there were two persons of the same name, the one living in the time of Nero, the other, whom he identifies with his opponent, in the time of Hadrian and later, and both of them Epicurean philosophers (see contra Cels. I. 8). The work of Celsus, however, was clearly the work, not of an Epicurean, but of a Platonist, or at least of an eclectic philosopher, with a strong leaning toward Platonism. The author wrote about the middle of the second century, probably in the reign of Marcus Aurelius (Keim fixes the date of the work at 178 A.D.). The True Discourse (ἀληθὴς λόγος) is no longer extant, but it can be reconstructed in great part from Origen's reply to it. It is seen to have been one of

the Epicurean, and the twenty-five books on the Gospel of Matthew,[4] besides those on the Twelve Prophets, of which we have found only twenty-five.[5] There is extant also an epistle[6] of his to the Emperor Philip, and another to Severa his wife, with several others to different persons. We have arranged in distinct books to the number of one hundred, so that they might be no longer scattered, as many of these as we have been able to collect,[7] which have been preserved here and there by different persons. He wrote also to Fabianus,[8] bishop of Rome, and to many other rulers of the churches concerning his orthodoxy. You have examples of these in the eighth book of the Apology[9] which we have written in his behalf.

CHAPTER XXXVII.

The Dissension of the Arabians.[1]

ABOUT the same time others arose in Arabia, putting forward a doctrine foreign to the truth. They said that during the present time the human soul dies and perishes with the body, but that at the time of the resurrection they will be renewed together. And at that time also a synod of considerable size assembled, and Origen, being again invited thither, spoke publicly on the question with such effect that the opinions of those who had formerly fallen were changed.

---

the ablest and most philosophical attacks of ancient times, and to have anticipated a great many arguments urged against Christianity by modern unbelievers. Celsus was well acquainted with Christianity in its various forms and with its literature, and he set himself to work with all his learning and skill to compose a complete refutation of the whole thing. He writes apparently less from a religious than from a political motive. He was an ardent patriot, and considered paganism essential to the life of the State, and Christianity its necessary antagonist. He undertakes first to show that Christianity is historically untenable, and then that it is false from the standpoint of philosophy and ethics. It is noticeable that it is not his desire to exterminate Christianity completely, but to make peace with it; to induce the Christians to give up their claim to possess the only true religion, and, with all their high ethics and lofty ideals, to join hands with the upholders of the ancient religion in elevating the religious ideas of the people, and thus benefiting the state. When we look at his work in this light (and much misunderstanding has been caused by a failure to do this), we must admire his ability, and respect his motives. He was, however, by no means free from the superstitions and prejudices of his age. The most important book upon the work of Celsus is Keim's *Celsus' Wahres Wort*, Zürich, 1873, which reconstructs, from Origen's reply, Celsus' work, and translates and explains it. Origen's reply is philosophical and in parts very able, but it must be acknowledged that in many places he does not succeed in answering his opponent. His honesty, however, must be admired in letting his adversary always speak for himself. He attempts to answer every argument urged by Celsus, and gives the argument usually in Celsus' own words. The result is that the work is quite desultory in its treatment, and often weighted with unimportant details and tiresome repetitions. At the same time, it is full of rich and suggestive thought, well worthy of Origen's genius, and shows a deep appreciation of the true spiritual nature of Christianity. The entire work of eight books is extant in the original Greek, and is printed in all editions of Origen's works (Lommatzsch, Vol. XX. p. 1–226), and is translated in the *Ante-Nicene Fathers*, Am. ed. Vol. IV. 395–669. It was one of Origen's latest works, as we are told here by Eusebius, and was composed (as we learn from its preface) at the urgent request of Ambrose, to whom also it was dedicated.

[4] The commentary on Matthew was written toward the close of Origen's life, as Eusebius informs us here, a fact which is confirmed by references in the work itself to many of his earlier commentaries. There are extant a single fragment from the first book (quoted in chap. 25, above), one from the second book (quoted in the *Philocalia*, chap. 6), and Books X.–XVII. entire in the original Greek, covering Matt. xiii. 36–xxii. 33. There are also extant numerous notes, which may have been taken, some of them from the commentary, and others from the homilies; and a Latin version of the commentary covering Matt. xvi. 13–xxvii. (See Lommatzsch, Vols. III.-V.). The catalogue of Jerome mentions twenty-five books and twenty-five homilies, and in the preface to his commentary on Matthew, Jerome states that he had read the twenty-five books, but elsewhere (in the prologue to his translation of Origen's homilies on Luke; Migne, VII. 219) he speaks of thirty-six (or twenty-six) books of the commentary, but this is doubtless a mistake (and so Vallarsi reads *viginti quinque* in the text). There is no reason to think that Origen wrote more than twenty-five books, which must have covered the whole Gospel (to judge from the portions extant). The books which are preserved contain much that is interesting and suggestive.

[5] Jerome also mentions twenty-five books upon the twelve prophets (*in duodecim Prophetas viginti quinque ἐξηγήσεων Origenis volumina*), of which he had found a copy in the library of Cæsarea, transcribed by the hand of Pamphilus (*de vir. ill.* 75). The catalogue of Jerome enumerates two books on Hosea, two on Joel, six on Amos, one on Jonah, two on Micah, two on Nahum, three on Habakkuk, two on Zephaniah, one on Haggai, two on Zechariah, two on Malachi; but in the preface to his commentary on Malachi, Jerome mentions three books on that prophecy. Of all these books only one fragment of the commentary on Hosea is extant, being preserved in the *Philocalia*, c. 8.

[6] These epistles to Philip and his wife Severa are no longer extant, nor can we form an accurate idea of their contents. We are reminded of Origen's interview with Mammæa, the mother of Alexander Severus, mentioned in chap. 21. Whether he wrote in response to a request from Philip is uncertain, but is not likely in view of the silence of Eusebius. It is possible that the favor shown by the emperor and his wife had led Origen to believe that they might be won for the faith, and there is nothing surprising in his addressing epistles to them with this idea. On Philip's relations to Christianity, see chap. 34, note 2.

[7] This collection of Origen's epistles made by Eusebius is no longer extant. The catalogue of Jerome mentions "eleven books of letters in all; two books in defense of his works." Only two epistles are preserved entire, — the one to Julius Africanus (see chap. 31, note 1); the other to Gregory Thaumaturgus, written, apparently, soon after the departure of the latter from Cæsarea (see chap. 30, note 1), for Gregory was, at the time it was written, still undecided as to the profession which he should follow. In addition to these two complete epistles, there are extant a sentence from a letter to his father (quoted in chap. 2); also a fragment of an epistle to some unknown person, describing the great zeal of his friend Ambrose (see chap. 18, note 1. The fragment is preserved by Suidas *s. v.* Ὠριγένης); also a fragment defending his study of heathen philosophy (quoted in chap. 19, above); and two fragments in Latin, from a letter addressed to some Alexandrian friends, complaining of the alterations made by certain persons in the reports of disputations which he had held with them (see chap. 32, note 4. The one fragment is preserved by Jerome, in his *Apol. adv. Ruf.* II. 18; the other by Rufinus, in his apology for Origen). Of his epistles to Fabian and others no trace remains.

[8] On Fabian, see chap. 29, note 4. We do not know when this letter to Fabian was written; but it cannot have been written in consequence of Origen's condemnation by the Alexandrian synods called by Demetrius, for they were held in 231 or 232, and Fabian did not become bishop until 236. There must have been some later cause, — perhaps a condemnation by a later synod of Alexandria, perhaps only the prevalence of a report that Origen was heterodox, which was causing serious suspicions in Rome and elsewhere. We know that the controversies which raged so fiercely about his memory began even before his death.

[9] On this *Defense*, see above, p. 36.

[1] The exact nature of the heresy which is here described by Eusebius is somewhat difficult to determine. It is disputed whether these heretics are to be reckoned with the θνητοπσυχῖται (whom John of Damascus mentions in his *de Hæres.* c. 90, and to whom Augustine refers, under the name of *Arabici*, in his *de Hæres.* c. 83), that is, those who taught the death of the soul with the body, or with the ὑπνοψυχῖται, who taught that the soul slept between the death and the resurrection of the body. Redepenning, in a very thorough discussion of the matter (II. 105 sq.), concludes that the heresy to which Eusebius refers grew up under Jewish influence, which was very strong in Arabia, and that it did not teach the death (as Eusebius asserts), but only the slumber of the soul. He reckons them therefore with the second, not the first, class mentioned. But it seems to me that Redepenning is almost hypercritical in maintaining that it is impossible that they can have taught that the soul died and afterward was raised again; for it is no more impossible that they should have taught it than that Eusebius and others should have supposed that they did. In fact, there does not seem to be adequate ground for correcting Eusebius' statement, which describes heretics who must distinctly be classed with the θνητοπσυχῖται mentioned later by John of Damascus. We do not know the date at which the synod referred to in this chapter was held. We only know that it was subsequent to the one which dealt with Beryllus, and therefore it must have been toward the close of Philip's reign.

CHAPTER XXXVIII.

The Heresy of the Elkesites.

ANOTHER error also arose at this time, called the heresy of the Elkesites,[1] which was extinguished in the very beginning. Origen speaks of it in this manner in a public homily on the eighty-second Psalm:[2]

"A certain man[3] came just now, puffed up greatly with his own ability, proclaiming that godless and impious opinion which has appeared lately in the churches, styled 'of the Elkesites.' I will show you what evil things that opinion teaches, that you may not be carried away by it. It rejects certain parts of every scripture. Again it uses portions of the Old Testament and the Gospel, but rejects the apostle[4] altogether. It says that to deny Christ is an indifferent matter, and that he who understands will, under necessity, deny with his mouth, but not in his heart. They produce a certain book which they say fell from heaven. They hold that whoever hears and believes[5] this shall receive remission of sins, another remission than that which Jesus Christ has given."

Such is the account of these persons.

CHAPTER XXXIX.

The Persecution under Decius, and the Sufferings of Origen.

AFTER a reign of seven years Philip was   1
succeeded by Decius.[1] On account of his hatred of Philip, he commenced a persecution of the churches, in which Fabianus[2] suffered martyrdom at Rome, and Cornelius succeeded him in the episcopate.[3] In Pales-   2
tine, Alexander,[4] bishop of the church of Jerusalem, was brought again on Christ's account

---

[1] The Elkesites ('Ελκεσαιταί) were not a distinct sect, but "a school scattered among all parties of the Judæo-Christian Church." They are described by Hippolytus (*Phil.* IX. 8–12) and by Epiphanius (in chap. 19 among the Essenes, in 30 among the Ebionites, and in 53 among the Sampsæans). We learn from Hippolytus that, in the time of Callistus or soon afterward, a certain Alcibiades, a native of Apamea in Syria, brought to Rome a book bearing the name of *Elkesai* ('Ηλχασαί), which purported to contain a revelation, made in the time of Trajan, by the Son of God and the Holy Spirit in the form of angels, and teaching the forgiveness of all sins, even the grossest, by means of belief in the doctrines of the book and baptism performed with certain peculiar rites. The controversy in regard to the forgiveness of gross sins committed after baptism was raging high at this time in Rome, and Hippolytus, who took the strict side, naturally opposed this new system of indulgence with the greatest vigor. Among other doctrines taught in the book, was the lawfulness of denying the faith in time of persecution, as told us by Origen in this chapter, and by Epiphanius in chap. 19. The book was strongly Ebionitic in its teaching, and bore striking resemblances to the Clementine *Homilies* and *Recognitions.* Its exact relation to those writings has been disputed; but Uhlhorn (*Homilien und Recognitionen des Clemens Romanus*) has shown conclusively that it is older than the latter, and that it represents a type of Ebionitic Christianity less modified than the latter by the influence of Christianity. In agreement with the Ebionites, the Elkesites (as all those were called who accepted the teachings of the book, to whatever party they might belong) taught that Christ was a created being; and they also repudiated sacrifices, which compelled them to reject certain portions of the Old Testament (cf. Origen's statement just below). They likewise refused recognition to the apostle Paul, and ordained the observance of the Jewish law; but they went beyond the Clementines in teaching the necessity of circumcision and the repetition of baptism as a means to the forgiveness of sins. The origin of the name *Elkesai* has also been disputed. Hippolytus says it was the name of the man who was claimed to have received the revelation, and Epiphanius calls Elkesai a false prophet; but some critics have thought them mistaken, and have supposed that Elkesai must have been the name of the book, or of the angel that gave the revelation. It is more probable, however, as Salmon concludes, that it was the name of a man whom the book represented as receiving the revelation, but that the man was only an imaginary person, and not the real founder of the school, as Epiphanius supposed. The book cannot well be put back of the beginning of the third century, when it first began to be heard of in the Catholic Church. It claimed to have been for a century in secret circulation, but the claim is quite unfounded. Eusebius speaks of the heresy as extinguished in the very beginning, and it seems, in fact, to have played no prominent part in history; and yet it apparently lingered on for a long time in the East, for we hear of a sect in Arabia, as late as the tenth century, who counted El-Chasaiach as their founder (see Salmon's article, p. 98). See the work of Uhlhorn already mentioned; also Ritschl's *Entstehung d. alt-Katholischen Kirche*, p. 234 sq. (Ritschl holds that the Clementines are older than the book of Elkesai), and Hilgenfeld's *Nov. Test. extra Can. rec.* III. 153, where the extant fragments of the book are collected. See also Salmon's article in the *Dict. of Christ. Biog.* II. p. 95 sq.

[2] On Origen's writings on the Psalms, see chap. 24, note 3. This fragment is the only portion of his homily on the eighty-second Psalm extant.

[3] Alciabades, according to Hippolytus (see above, note 1).

[4] The apostle Paul (see note 1).

[5] Origen does not mention the baptism of the Elkesites, which is described at length by Hippolytus. It seems that both belief in the teachings of the book and baptism were necessary. It may be that in Origen's opinion the receiving of the book itself involved the peculiar baptism which it taught, and that, therefore, he thought it unnecessary to mention the latter.

[1] Philip was defeated and slain near Verona, on June 17, 249, by the Pannonian legions who had compelled Decius, the envoy sent by Philip to quell a mutiny among them, to accept the title of Augustus. Philip's death made Decius emperor; and he reigned for a little over two years, when he perished in a campaign against the Goths. The cause given by Eusebius for the terrible persecution of Decius is quite incorrect. The emperor, who before his elevation was one of the most highly respected senators, seems to have been a man of noble character and of high aims. He was a thoroughgoing patriot and a staunch believer in the religion and laws of Rome. He saw the terrible state of corruption and decay into which the empire had fallen; and he made up his mind that it could be arrested only by restoring the ancient Roman customs, and by strengthening the ancient religion. He therefore revived the old censorship, hoping that the moral and social habits of the people might be improved under its influence; and he endeavored to exterminate the Christians, believing that thus the ancient purity of the state religion might be restored. It was no low motive of personal revenge or of caprice which prompted the persecution. We must recognize the fact that Decius was one of the best and noblest of the Roman emperors, and that he persecuted as a patriot and a believer in the religion of his fathers. He was the first one that aimed at the complete extermination of the Christians. He went systematically to work to put the religion out of existence; and the persecution was consequently both universal and of terrible severity, far more terrible than any that had preceded it. The edicts published by Decius early in the year 250 are no longer extant; but we can gather from the notices, especially of Cyprian and Dionysius, that the effort was first made to induce Christians throughout the empire to deny their faith and return to the religion of the state, and only when large numbers of them remained obstinate did the persecution itself begin.

[2] On Fabianus, bishop of Rome, see chap. 29, note 4.

[3] After the martyrdom of Fabianus the church of Rome was without a bishop for about fourteen months. The bishopric of that church was naturally under Decius a place of the greatest danger. Cornelius became bishop in 251, probably in March, while Decius was away from the city. After the emperor's death, which took place in the following winter, Gallus renewed the persecution, and Cornelius with a large part of the church fled to Città Vecchia, where he died in the summer of 253, according to Lipsius (the Liberian catalogue says 252, which is the commonly accepted date, but is clearly incorrect, as Lipsius has shown). Both versions of the *Chron.* are greatly confused at this point, and their statements are very faulty (Jerome's version assigning a reign of only fifteen months to Decius and two years and four months to Gallus). Eusebius, in Bk. VII. chap. 2, says that Cornelius held office "about three years," which is reasonably accurate, for he was actually bishop nearly two years and a half. It was during the episcopate of Cornelius that the Novatian schism took place (see chap. 43). Eight epistles from Cyprian to Cornelius are extant, and two from Cornelius to Cyprian. In chap. 43 Eusebius makes extended quotations from an epistle written by Cornelius to Fabius of Antioch, and mentions still others which are not preserved. In chap. 46 he refers to one against Novatian addressed to Dionysius of Alexandria, which is likewise lost.

[4] On Alexander, bishop of Jerusalem, see chap. 8, note 6.

before the governor's judgment seat in Cæsarea, and having acquitted himself nobly in a second confession was cast into prison, crowned 3 with the hoary locks of venerable age. And after his honorable and illustrious confession at the tribunal of the governor, he fell asleep in prison, and Mazabanes[5] became his suc- 4 cessor in the bishopric of Jerusalem. Baby- las[6] in Antioch, having like Alexander passed away in prison after hi confession, was succeeded by Fabius[7] in the episcopate of that church. 5 But how many and how great things came upon Origen in the persecution, and what was their final result, — as the demon of evil marshaled all his forces, and fought against the man with his utmost craft and power, assaulting him beyond all others against whom he con- tended at that time, — and what and how many things he endured for the word of Christ, bonds and bodily tortures and torments under the iron collar and in the dungeon; and how for many days with his feet stretched four spaces in the stooks[8] he bore patiently the threats of fire and whatever other things were inflicted by his enemies; and how his sufferings terminated, as his judge strove eagerly with all his might not to end his life; and what words he left after these things, full of comfort to those needing aid, a great many of his epistles show with truth and accuracy.[9]

---

[5] The time of Mazabanes' accession is fixed approximately by the fact that Alexander's death took place in the persecution of Decius. His death is put by Eusebius (Bk. VII. chap. 14) in the reign of Gallienus (260–268), and with this the notice in the *Chron.* agrees, which assigns it to the year 265. Since his successor, Hy- menæus, was present at the council of Antioch, in which the case of Paul of Samosata was considered (see below, Bk. VII. chaps. 29 and 30), it will not do to put Mazabanes' death later than 265.

[6] On Babylas, see chap. 29, note 8.

[7] Eusebius gives the name of this bishop as Βάβιος, Jerome as Fabianus, and Syncellus as Φλαβιανός. The time of his accession is fixed by the death of Babylas in the persecution of Decius. He was bishop of Antioch while Cornelius was bishop of Rome, as we learn from the latter's epistle to him, quoted in chap. 43, below. From an epistle written by Dionysius of Alexandria to Cornelius of Rome (referred to in chap. 46), we learn that Fabius died while the latter was still bishop, i.e. before the summer of 253 (see note 3, above). The *Chron. pasch.* assigns three years to the episcopate of Fabius; and though we cannot place much reliance upon the fig- ure, yet it leads us to think that he must have been bishop for some time, — at least more than a year, — and so we are inclined to put his death as late as possible. The *Chron.* puts the accession of his successor Demetrianus in the year 254, which is too late, at least for the death of Fabius. We may conclude that the latter died prob- ably in the year 253, or not long before. Harnack decides for the time between the fall of 252 and the spring of 253. Fabius, as we learn from the epistles addressed to him by Cornelius and Dionysius (see chaps. 43 and 44), was inclined to indorse Novatian and the rigoristic discipline favored by him. We know nothing more of the life or character of Fabius.

[8] τοὺς πόδας ὑπὸ τέσσαρα τοῦ κολαστηρίου ξύλον παρατηθεὶς διαστήματα. Otto, in his edition of Justin's *Apology* (*Corp. Apol. Christ.* I. p. 204), says: ξύλον erat truncus foramina habens, quibus pedes captivorum immitebantur, ut securius in carcere servarentur aut tormentis vexarentur ("a ξύλον was a block, with holes in which the feet of captives were put, in order that they might be kept more securely in prison, or might be afflicted with tortures"). The farther apart the feet were stretched, the greater of course was the torture. Four spaces seems to have been the out- side limit. Compare Bk. VIII. chap. 10, § 8.

[9] A tradition arose in later centuries that Origen died in the per- secution of Decius (see Photius, *Cod.* 118); but this is certainly an error, for Eusebius cannot have been mistaken when he cites Ori- gen's own letters as describing his sufferings during the persecution. The epistles referred to here are no longer extant. On Origen's epistles in general, see chap. 36, note 7.

CHAPTER XL.

The Events which happened to Dionysius.[1]

I SHALL quote from the epistle of Dionysius 1 to Germanus[2] an account of what befell the former. Speaking of himself, he writes as follows :

---

[1] Dionysius the Great (Eusebius in the preface to Bk. VII. calls him ὁ μέγας Ἀλεξανδρέων ἐπίσκοπος) was born toward the close of the second century (he was an aged man, between 260 and 265, as we learn from Bk. VII. chap 27), studied under Origen, and succeeded Heraclas as principal of the catechetical school in Alexan- dria (see above, chap. 29) in the year 231 or 232 (see chap. 3, note 2). In the third year of Philip's reign (246–247) he succeeded Heraclas as bishop of Alexandria, according to chap. 35, above. Whether he continued to preside over the catechetical school after he became bishop we do not know. Dittrich (p. 4 sq.) gives reasons for think- ing that he did, which render it at least probable. He was still living when the earlier synods, in which the case of Paul of Samosata was considered, were held (i.e. between 260 and 264; see Bk. VII. chap. 27, note 4), but he was dead before the last one met, i.e. before 265 A.D. (see Bk. VII. chap. 29, note 1). Dionysius is one of the most prominent, and at the same time pleasing, figures of his age. He seems to have been interested less in speculative than in practi- cal questions, and yet he wrote an important work *On Nature*, which shows that he possessed philosophical ability, and one of his epistles contains a discussion of the authorship of the Apocalypse, which is unsurpassed in the early centuries as an example of keen and yet judicious and well-balanced literary criticism (see Bk. VII. chap. 25). His intellectual abilities must, therefore, not be under- rated, but it is as a practical theologian that he is best known. He took an active part in all the controversies of his time; in the Nova- tian difficulty in which the re-admission of the lapsed was the burning question; in the controversy as to the re-baptism of heretics; and in the case of Paul of Samosata. In all he played a prominent part, and in all he seems to have acted with great wisdom and moderation (see chaps. 44 sq., Bk. VII. chaps. 5, 7 sq., chap. 27). He was taken prisoner during the persecution of Decius, but made his escape (see the present chapter). In the persecution of Valerian he was ban- ished (see Bk. VII. chap. 11), but returned to Alexandria after the accession of Gallienus (see Bk. VII. chap. 21). His conduct during the persecutions exposed him to adverse criticism, and he defended himself warmly against the accusations of a bishop Germanus, in an epistle, portions of which are quoted in this chapter and in Bk. VII. chap. 11. The writings of Dionysius were chiefly in the form of epistles, written for some practical purpose. Of such epistles he wrote a great many, and numerous fragments are extant, pre- served chiefly by Eusebius. Being called forth by particular cir- cumstances, they contain much information in regard to contempo- rary events, and are thus an important historical source, as Eusebius wisely perceived. Such epistles are quoted, or mentioned, in chaps. 41, 44, 45, and 46 of this book, and in Bk. VII. chaps. 1, 2, 4, 5, 6, 7, 9, 10, 11, 20, 21, 22, 23, 26. For particulars in regard to them, see the notes on those chapters. In addition to his epistles a work, *On Promises*, is referred to by Eusebius in Bk. VII. chap. 28, and in Bk. VII. chaps. 24 and 25, where extracts from it are quoted (see Bk. VII. chap. 24, note 1); also a commentary on the beginning of Ecclesiastes in Bk. VII. chap. 26, and in the same chapter a work in four books against Sabellius, addressed to Dionysius, bishop of Rome, in which he defends himself against the charge of tritheism, brought by some Sabellian adversaries. He was able to clear him- self of all suspicion of heresy in the matter, though it is quite clear that he had carried the subordinationism of Origen to a dangerous extreme. The attack upon him led him to be more careful in his statements, some of which were such as in part to justify the suspi- cions of his adversaries. Athanasius defended his orthodoxy in a special work, *De Sententiis Dionysii*, and there can be no doubt that Dionysius was honestly concerned to preserve the divinity of the Son; but as in the case of Eusebius of Cæsarea, and of all those who were called upon to face Sabellianism, his tendency was to lay an over-emphasis upon the subordination of the Son (see above, p. 11 sq.). For further particulars in regard to this work, see the chapter referred to, note 4. Upon Dionysius' views of the Trinity, see Dittrich, p. 91 sq. Besides the writings referred to, or quoted by Eusebius, there should be mentioned an important canonical epistle addressed to Basilides, in which the exact time of the expiration of the lenten fast is the chief subject of discussion (still extant, and printed by Pitra, Routh, and others, and translated in the *Ante- Nicene Fathers;* sc. Dittrich, p. 46 sq.). There are yet a few other fragments of Dionysius' writings, extant in various MSS., which it is not necessary to mention here. See Dittrich, p. 130. The most complete collection of the extant fragments of his writings is that of Migne, *Patr. Gr.* X. 1233 sq., to which must be added Pitra's *Spic. Solesm.* I. 15 sq. English translation in the *Ante- Nicene Fathers*, VI. p. 87–120. The most complete work upon Dionysius is the monograph of Dittrich, *Dionysius der Grosse*, Freiburg, i. Br. 1867.

[2] This Germanus, as we learn from Bk. VII. chap. 11, was a bishop of some see, unknown to us, who had accused Dionysius of cowardice in the face of persecution. In the present instance Dionysius undertakes to refute his calumnies, by recounting accu-

" I speak before God, and he knows that I do not lie. I did not flee on my own impulse
2 nor without divine direction. But even before this, at the very hour when the Decian persecution was commanded, Sabinus[3] sent a frumentarius[4] to search for me, and I remained at home four days awaiting his arrival. But he went about examining all places, — roads, rivers, and fields, — where he thought I might be concealed or on the way. But he was smitten with blindness, and did not find the house,[5] for he did not suppose, that being pursued,
3 I would remain at home. And after the fourth day God commanded me to depart, and made a way for me in a wonderful manner; and I and my attendants[6] and many of the brethren went away together. And that this occurred through the providence of God was made manifest by what followed, in which
4 perhaps we were useful to some." Farther on he relates in this manner what happened to him after his flight :

" For about sunset, having been seized with those that were with me, I was taken by the soldiers to Taposiris,[7] but in the providence of God, Timothy[8] was not present and was not

captured. But coming later, he found the house deserted and guarded by soldiers, and ourselves reduced to slavery."[9] After a little 5 he says :

" And what was the manner of his admirable management? for the truth shall be told. One of the country people met Timothy fleeing and disturbed, and inquired the cause of his haste. And he told him the truth. And 6 when the man heard it (he was on his way to a marriage feast, for it was customary to spend the entire night in such gatherings), he entered and announced it to those at the table. And they, as if on a preconcerted signal, arose with one impulse, and rushed out quickly and came and burst in upon us with a shout. Immediately the soldiers who were guarding us fled, and they came to us lying as we were upon the bare couches. But I, God knows, thought 7 at first that they were robbers who had come for spoil and plunder. So I remained upon the bed on which I was, clothed only in a linen garment, and offered them the rest of my clothing which was lying beside me. But they directed me to rise and come away quickly. Then I understood why they were come, 8 and I cried out, beseeching and entreating them to depart and leave us alone. And I requested them, if they desired to benefit me in any way, to anticipate those who were carrying me off, and cut off my head themselves. And when I had cried out in this manner, as my companions and partners in everything know, they raised me by force. But I threw myself on my back on the ground ; and they seized me by the hands and feet and dragged me away. And the witnesses of all these occurrences 9 followed : Gaius, Faustus, Peter, and Paul.[10] But they who had seized me carried me out of the village hastily, and placing me on an ass without a saddle, bore me away."[11]

Dionysius relates these things respecting himself.

rately his conduct during the persecutions. It must be remembered that the letter is a defense against accusations actually made, or we shall misunderstand it, and misinterpret Dionysius' motives in dwelling at such length upon the details of his own sufferings. The epistle, a part of which is quoted in this chapter, and a part in Bk. VII. chap. 11, was written, as we learn from the latter chapter, § 18, while the persecution of Valerian was still in progress, and recounts his experiences during the persecutions of Decius and of Valerian. The fragment quoted in the present chapter is devoted to the persecution of Decius, the other fragment to the persecution of Valerian. The letter is said to have been written πρὸς Γερμανόν. This might be translated either *to* or *against Germanus*. Analogy would lead us to think the former translation correct, for all the epistles mentioned are said to have been written πρός one or another person, and it is natural, of course, to expect the name of the person addressed to be given. I have therefore translated the word thus, as is done in all the versions. At the same time it must be noticed that Germanus is spoken of in the epistle (especially in § 18 sq. of the other chapter) not as if he were the person addressed, but as if he were the person complained of to others; and, moreover, a letter of defense sent to him alone would probably have little effect, and would fail to put an end to the calumnies which must have found many ready ears. It seems, in fact, quite probable that the epistle was rather a public than a private one, and that while it was nominally addressed to Germanus, it was yet intended for a larger public, and was written with that public in view. This will explain the peculiar manner in which Germanus is referred to. Certainly it is hard to think he would have been thus mentioned in a personal letter.

[3] Sabinus, an otherwise unknown personage, seems to have been prefect of Egypt at this time, as Æmilianus was during the persecution of Valerian, according to Bk. VII. chap. 11.

[4] One of the *frumentarii milites*, or military commissaries, who were employed for various kinds of business, and under the emperors especially as detectives or secret spies.

[5] μὴ εὑρίσκων. It is not meant that the frumentarius could not find the house, but that he did not think to go to the house at all, through an error of judgment (" being smitten with blindness "), supposing that Dionysius would certainly be elsewhere.

[6] οἱ παῖδες. This is taken by many scholars to mean " children," and the conclusion is drawn by them that Dionysius was a married man. Dittrich translates it " pupils," supposing that Dionysius was still at the head of the catechetical school, and that some of his scholars lived with him, as was quite common. Others translate " servants," or " domestics." I have used the indefinite word " attendants " simply, because the παῖδες may well have included children, scholars, servants, and others who made up his family and constituted, any or all of them, his attendants. As shown in note 8, the word at any rate cannot be confined in the present case to servants.

[7] Strabo (Bk. XVII. chap. 1) mentions a small town called Taposiris, situated in the neighborhood of Alexandria.

[8] We know nothing about this Timothy, except that Dionysius addressed to him his work *On Nature*, as reported by Eusebius in

VII. 26. He is there called Τιμώθεος ὁ παῖς. Dionysius can hardly have addressed a book to one of his servants, and hence we may conclude that Timothy was either Dionysius' son (as Westcott holds) or scholar (as Dittrich believes). It is reasonable to think him one of the παῖδες, with others of whom Dionysius was arrested, as recorded just above. It is in that case of course necessary to give the word as used there some other, or at least some broader sense than " servants."

[9] Greek ἐξηνδραποδισμένους, meaning literally " reduced to slavery." The context, however, does not seem to justify such a rendering, for the reference is apparently only to the fact that they were captured. Their capture, had they not been released, would have resulted probably in death rather than in slavery.

[10] These four men are known to us only as companions of Dionysius during the persecution of Decius, as recorded here and in Bk. VII. chap. 11. From that chapter, § 23, we learn that Caius and Peter were alone with Dionysius in a desert place in Libya, after being carried away by the rescuing party mentioned here. From § 3 of the same chapter we learn that Faustus was a deacon, and that he was with Dionysius also during the persecution of Valerian, and from § 26 that he suffered martyrdom at a great age in the Diocletian persecution. See also Bk. VIII. chap. 13, note 11.

[11] As we learn from Bk. VII. chap. 11, § 23, this rescuing party carried Dionysius to a desert place in Libya, where he was left with only two companions until the persecution ceased.

CHAPTER XLI.

The Martyrs in Alexandria.

1　THE same writer, in an epistle to Fabius,[1] bishop of Antioch, relates as follows the sufferings of the martyrs in Alexandria under Decius :

"The persecution among us did not begin with the royal decree, but preceded it an entire year.[2] The prophet and author of evils[3] to this city, whoever he was, previously moved and aroused against us the masses of the heathen, rekindling among them the superstition of

2　their country. And being thus excited by him and finding full opportunity for any wickedness, they considered this the only pious service of their demons, that they should slay us.

"They seized first an old man named Met-　3 ras,[4] and commanded him to utter impious words. But as he would not obey, they beat him with clubs, and tore his face and eyes with sharp sticks, and dragged him out of the city and stoned him. Then they carried to their　4 idol temple a faithful woman, named Quinta, that they might force her to worship. And as she turned away in detestation, they bound her feet and dragged her through the entire city over the stone-paved streets, and dashed her against the millstones, and at the same time scourged her ; then, taking her to the same place, they stoned her to death. Then all　5 with one impulse rushed to the homes of the pious, and they dragged forth whomsoever any one knew as a neighbor, and despoiled and plundered them. They took for themselves the more valuable property ; but the poorer articles and those made of wood they scattered about and burned in the streets, so that the city appeared as if taken by an enemy. But the　6 brethren withdrew and went away, and 'took joyfully the spoiling of their goods,'[5] like those to whom Paul bore witness. I know of no one unless possibly some one who fell into their hands, who, up to this time, denied the Lord. Then they seized also that most admirable virgin, Apollonia, an old woman,　7 and, smiting her on the jaws, broke out all her teeth. And they made a fire outside the city and threatened to burn her alive if she would not join with them in their impious cries. And she, supplicating a little, was released, when she leaped eagerly into the fire and was consumed. Then they seized Serapion in his　8 own house, and tortured him with harsh cruelties, and having broken all his limbs, they threw him headlong from an upper story. And there was no street, nor public road, nor lane open to us, by night or day ; for always and everywhere, all of them cried out that if any one would not repeat their impious words, he should immediately be dragged away and burned. And mat-　9 ters continued thus for a considerable time. But a sedition and civil war came upon the wretched people and turned their cruelty toward us against one another.[6] So we breathed for a little while as they ceased from their rage against us. But presently the change from that milder reign was announced to us,[7] and great fear

---

[1] I read Φάβιον with the majority of the MSS., and with Valesius, Stroth, Burton, Closs, and Crusè, preferring to adopt the same spelling here that is used in the other passages in which the same bishop is mentioned. A number of MSS. read Φαβιανόν, which is supported by Rufinus, and adopted by Schwegler, Laemmer, and Heinichen. On Fabius, bishop of Antioch, see chap. 39, note 7. The time of his episcopate stated in that note fixes the date of this epistle within narrow limits, viz. between 25b and the spring of 253. The whole tone of the letter and the discussion of the readmission of the lapsed would lead us to think that the epistle was written after the close of the persecution, but in § 20, Dioscorus is said to be still among them, waiting for "a longer and more severe conflict," which seems to imply that the persecution, if not raging at the time, was at least expected to break out again soon. This would lead us to think of the closing months of Decius' reign, i.e. late in the year 251, and this date finds confirmation in the consideration that the epistle (as we learn from chap. 44) was written after the breaking out of the Novatian schism, and apparently after the election of Novatian as opposition bishop, for Fabius can hardly have sided with him against his bishop, so long as he was only a presbyter. Doubtless Novatian's official letter, announcing his election, had influenced Fabius. But Novatian was elected bishop in 251, probably in the summer or early fall; at least, some months after Cornelius' accession, which took place in February, 251. It seems, from chap. 44, that Fabius was inclined to side with Novatian, and to favor his rigoristic principles. This epistle was written (as we learn from chap. 42, § 6) with the express purpose of leading him to change his position and to adopt more lenient principles in his treatment of the lapsed. It is with this end in view that Dionysius details at such length in this chapter the sufferings of the martyrs. He wishes to impress upon Fabius their piety and steadfastness, in order to beget greater respect for their opinions. Having done this, he states that they who best understood the temptations to which the persecuted were exposed, had received the lapsed, when repentant, into fellowship as before (see chap. 42, note 6). Dionysius' own position in the matter comes out very clearly in this epistle. He was in full sympathy with the milder treatment of the lapsed advocated in Rome and in Carthage by Cornelius and Cyprian.

[2] The edict of Decius was published early in the year 250, and therefore the persecution in Alexandria began, according to Dionysius, began in 249, while Philip was still emperor. Although the latter showed the Christians favor, yet it is not at all surprising that this local persecution should break out during his reign. The peace which the Christians were enjoying naturally fostered the growth of the Church, and the more patriotic and pious of the heathen citizens of the empire must necessarily have felt great solicitude at its constant increase, and the same spirit which led Decius to persecute would lead many such persons to desire to persecute when the opportunity offered itself; and the closing months of Philip's reign were so troubled with rebellions and revolutions that he had little time, and perhaps less inclination, to interfere in such a minor matter as a local persecution of Christians. The common people of Alexandria were of an excitable and riotous disposition, and it was always easy there to stir up a tumult at short notice and upon slight pretexts.

[3] ὁ κακῶν τῇ πόλει ταύτῃ μάντις καὶ ποιητής. The last word is rendered "poet" by most translators, and the rendering is quite possible; but it is difficult to understand why Dionysius should speak of this person's being a poet, which could have no possible connection with the matter in hand. It seems better to take ποιητής in its common sense of "maker," or "author," and to suppose Dionysius to be thinking of this man, not simply as the prophet of evils to the city, but also as their author, in that he "moved and aroused against us the masses of the heathen."

[4] Of the various martyrs and confessors mentioned in this chapter, we know only what is told us by Dionysius in this epistle.

[5] Heb. x. 34. Upon the authorship of the Epistle to the Hebrews, see Bk. III. chap. 3, note 17; and upon Eusebius' opinion in the matter, see Bk. III. chap. 25, note 1.

[6] We know that the closing months of Philip's reign were troubled with seditions in various quarters; but Dionysius is our only authority for this particular one, unless it be connected, as some think, with the revolt which Zosimus describes as aroused in the Orient by the bad government of Philip's brother, who was governor there, and by excessive taxation (see Tillemont, *Hist. des Emp.* III. p. 272).

[7] This refers to the death of Philip and the accession of Decius. The hostile edicts of the latter seem not to have been published un-

10 of what was threatened seized us. For the decree arrived, almost like unto that most terrible time foretold by our Lord, which if it were possible would offend even the elect.[8]

11 All truly were affrighted. And many of the more eminent in their fear came forward immediately;[9] others who were in the public service were drawn on by their official duties;[10] others were urged on by their acquaintances. And as their names were called they approached the impure and impious sacrifices. Some of them were pale and trembled as if they were not about to sacrifice, but to be themselves sacrifices and offerings to the idols; so that they were jeered at by the multitude who stood around, as it was plain to every one that they were afraid either to die or to sacrifice.

12 But some advanced to the altars more readily, declaring boldly that they had never been Christians. Of these the prediction of our Lord is most true that they shall 'hardly'[11] be saved. Of the rest some followed the one, others the other of these classes, some fled

13 and some were seized. And of the latter some continued faithful until bonds and imprisonment, and some who had even been imprisoned for many days yet abjured the faith before they were brought to trial. Others having for a time endured great tortures finally re-

14 tracted. But the firm and blessed pillars of the Lord being strengthened by him, and having received vigor and might suitable and appropriate to the strong faith which they possessed, became admirable witnesses of his

15 kingdom. The first of these was Julian, a man who suffered so much with the gout that he was unable to stand or walk. They brought him forward with two others who carried him.

One of these immediately denied. But the other, whose name was Cronion, and whose surname was Eunus, and the old man Julian himself, both of them having confessed the Lord, were carried on camels through the entire city, which, as you know, is a very large one, and in this elevated position were beaten and finally burned in a fierce fire,[12] surrounded by all the populace.

But a soldier, named Besas, who stood by 16 them as they were led away rebuked those who insulted them. And they cried out against him, and this most manly warrior of God was arraigned, and having done nobly in the great contest for piety, was beheaded. A 17 certain other one, a Libyan by birth, but in name and blessedness a true Macar,[13] was strongly urged by the judge to recant; but as he would not yield he was burned alive. After them Epimachus and Alexander, having remained in bonds for a long time, and endured countless agonies from scrapers[14] and scourges, were also consumed in a fierce fire.[15] And with them 18 there were four women. Ammonarium, a holy virgin, the judge tortured relentlessly and excessively, because she declared from the first that she would utter none of those things which he commanded; and having kept her promise truly, she was dragged away. The others were Mercuria, a very remarkable old woman, and Dionysia, the mother of many children, who did not love her own children above the Lord.[16] As the governor was ashamed of torturing thus ineffectually, and being always defeated by women, they were put to death by the sword, without the trial of tortures. For the champion, Ammonarium, endured these in behalf of all.

The Egyptians, Heron and Ater and Isi- 19 dorus, and with them Dioscorus,[17] a boy about fifteen years old, were delivered up. At first the judge attempted to deceive the lad by fair words, as if he could be brought over easily, and then to force him by tortures, as one who would readily yield. But Dioscorus was neither persuaded nor constrained. As the 20

til some months after his accession, i.e. early in 250. But his hostility to Christianity might have been known from the start, and it might have been understood that he would persecute as soon as he had attended to the other more important matters connected with his accession.

[8] Matt. xxiv. 24. Eusebius reads σκανδαλίσαι; Matthew, πλανᾶσθαι or πλανῆσαι.

[9] i.e. to sacrifice.

[10] οἱ δὲ δημοσιεύοντες ὑπὸ τῶν πράξεων ἤγοντο. Every officer of the government under the imperial regimen was obliged to sacrifice to the Gods upon taking office, and also to sacrifice at stated times during his term of office, and upon special occasions, or in connection with the performance of important official duties. He might thus be called upon in his official capacity frequently to offer sacrifices, and a failure to perform this part of his duties was looked upon as sacrilege and punished as a crime against the state. Christian officials, therefore, were always in danger of suffering for their religion unless they were allowed, as a special favor, to omit the sacrifices, as was often the case under those emperors who were more favorably inclined toward Christianity. A private citizen was never obliged to sacrifice except in times of persecution, when he might be ordered to do so as a test. But an official could not carry out fully all the duties of his position without sacrificing. This is one reason why many of the Christians avoided public office, and thus drew upon themselves the accusation of a lack of patriotism (cf. Origen, Contra Cels. VI. 5 sq., and Tertullian's Apol. c. 42); and it is also one reason why such Christians as happened to be in office were always the first to suffer under a hostile emperor.

[11] Cf. Matt. xix. 23. This sentence shows that Dionysius did not consider it impossible even for those to be saved who denied Christ before enduring any suffering at all. He was clearly willing to leave a possibility of salvation even to the worst offenders, and in this agreed perfectly with Cornelius, Cyprian, and the body of the Roman and Carthaginian churches.

[12] ἀσβέστῳ πυρί.

[13] The Greek word μάκαρ means "blessed."

[14] ξυστῆρας. "The instrument of torture here mentioned was an iron scraper, calculated to wound and tear the flesh as it passed over it" (Cruse).

[15] πυρὶ ἀσβέστῳ.

[16] Rufinus adds at this point the words et alia Ammonaria ("and another Ammonaria"). Valesius therefore conjectures that the words καὶ Ἀμμονάριον ἕτερα must have stood in the original text, and he is followed by Stroth and Heinichen. The MSS., however, are unanimous in their omission of the words, and the second sentence below, which speaks of only a single Ammonarium, as if there were no other, certainly argues against their insertion. It is possible that Rufinus, finding only three women mentioned after Dionysius had referred to four, ventured to insert the "other" Ammonaria.

[17] It has been suggested (by Birks in the Dict. of Christ. Biog.) that this Dioscorus may be identical with the presbyter of the same name mentioned in Bk. VII. chap. 11, § 24. But this is quite impossible, for Dioscorus, as we learn from this passage, was but fifteen years old at the time of the Decian persecution, and Dionysius is still speaking of the same persecution when he mentions the presbyter Dioscorus in the chapter referred to (see note 31 on that chapter).

others remained firm, he scourged them cruelly and then delivered them to the fire. But admiring the manner in which Dioscorus had distinguished himself publicly, and his wise answers to his persuasions, he dismissed him, saying that on account of his youth he would give him time for repentance. And this most godly Dioscorus is among us now, awaiting a longer conflict and more severe contest.

21 But a certain Nemesion, who also was an Egyptian, was accused as an associate of robbers; but when he had cleared himself before the centurion of this charge most foreign to the truth, he was informed against as a Christian, and taken in bonds before the governor. And the most unrighteous magistrate inflicted on him tortures and scourgings double those which he executed on the robbers, and then burned him between the robbers, thus honoring the blessed man by the likeness to Christ.

22 A band of soldiers, Ammon and Zeno and Ptolemy and Ingenes, and with them an old man, Theophilus, were standing close together before the tribunal. And as a certain person who was being tried as a Christian, seemed inclined to deny, they standing by gnashed their teeth, and made signs with their faces and stretched out their hands, and

23 gestured with their bodies. And when the attention of all was turned to them, before any one else could seize them, they rushed up to the tribunal saying that they were Christians, so that the governor and his council were affrighted. And those who were on trial appeared most courageous in prospect of their sufferings, while their judges trembled. And they went exultingly from the tribunal rejoicing in their testimony; [18] God himself having caused them to triumph gloriously."

CHAPTER XLII.

Others of whom Dionysius gives an Account.

1 "MANY others, in cities and villages, were torn asunder by the heathen, of whom I will mention one as an illustration. Ischyrion [1] was employed as a steward by one of the rulers. His employer commanded him to sacrifice, and on his refusal insulted him, and as he remained firm, abused him. And as he still held out he seized a long staff and thrust it through his bowels [2] and slew him.

"Why need I speak of the multitude that 2 wandered in the deserts and mountains, and perished by hunger, and thirst, and cold, and sickness, and robbers, and wild beasts? Those of them who survived are witnesses of their election and victory. But I will 3 relate one occurrence as an example. Chæremon, [3] who was very old, was bishop of the city called Nilus. He fled with his wife [4] to the Arabian mountain [5] and did not return. And though the brethren searched diligently they could not find either them or their bodies. And many who fled to the same 4 Arabian mountain were carried into slavery by the barbarian Saracens. Some of them were ransomed with difficulty and at a large price; others have not been to the present time. I have related these things, my brother, not without an object, but that you may understand how many and great distresses came upon us. Those indeed will understand them the best who have had the largest experience of them."

A little further on he adds: "These 5 divine martyrs among us, who now are seated with Christ, and are sharers in his kingdom, partakers of his judgment and judges with him, received some of the brethren who had fallen away and become chargeable with the guilt of sacrificing. When they perceived that their conversion and repentance were sufficient to be acceptable with him who by no means desires the death of the sinner, but his repentance, having proved them they received them back and brought them together, and met with them and had fellowship with them in prayers and feasts. [6] What counsel then, 6

---

[18] μαρτυρία. It is difficult to ascertain from Dionysius' language whether these five soldiers suffered martyrdom or whether they were released. The language admits either interpretation, and some have supposed that the magistrate was so alarmed at what he feared might be a general defection among the troops that he dismissed these men without punishing them. At the same time it seems as if Dionysius would have stated this directly if it were a fact. There is nothing in the narrative to imply that their fate was different from that of the others; and moreover, it hardly seems probable that the defection of five soldiers should so terrify the judge as to cause him to cease executing the imperial decree, and of course if he did not execute it in the case of the soldiers, he could hardly do it in the case of others.

[1] Ischyrion is known to us only from this passage.

[2] ἐντέρων καὶ σπλάγχνων.

[3] Of the bishop Chæremon of Nilus we know only what is told us here. The city Nilus or Nilopolis was situated on an island in the Nile, in middle Egypt, some distance south of Memphis.

[4] τῇ συμβίῳ ἑαυτοῦ. The word σύμβιος, which means a "companion" or "partner," can signify nothing else than "wife" as used here in the feminine.

[5] τὸ Ἀράβιον ὄρος. The name Arabicus mons, τὸ Ἀράβιον οὖρος, was given by Herodotus to the range of mountains which separated that part of Arabia lying west of the Arabian Gulf from the Nile valley (see Smith's Dict. of Greek and Rom. Geography).

[6] εἰσεδέξαντο καὶ συνήγαγον καὶ συνέστησαν καὶ προσευχῶν αὐτοῖς καὶ ἑστιάσεων ἐκοινώνησαν. It will be observed that nothing is said here about joining with these persons in celebrating the eucharist, or about admitting them to that service, and hence Valesius is quite right in distinguishing the kind of communion spoken of here from official communion in the church, around the Lord's table. Dionysius does not imply that these confessors had the power given them to receive the lapsed back again into the Church, and to dispense the eucharist to them. That was the prerogative of the bishop, and evidently Dionysius has no thought of its being otherwise. The communion of which he speaks was private fellowship merely, and implied a recognition on the part of these confessors that the persons in question had truly repented of their sin, and could be recommended for readmission into the Church. As we see from chap. 44, § 2, the recommendation of these persons or of the people in general was quite necessary, before the bishop would consent to absolve the fallen person and receive him back into the Church. And Dionysius' words in this passage show that he felt that the judgment of these confessors in regard to the fitness of the lapsed for readmission ought to be received with consideration, and have influence upon the final decision. Dionysius thus shows great respect to the

brethren, do you give us concerning such persons? What should we do? Shall we have the same judgment and rule as theirs, and observe their decision and charity, and show mercy to those whom they pitied? Or, shall we declare their decision unrighteous, and set ourselves as judges of their opinion, and grieve mercy and overturn order?"[7] These words Dionysius very properly added when making mention of those who had been weak in the time of persecution.

CHAPTER XLIII.

Novatus,[1] his Manner of Life and his Heresy.

1   AFTER this, Novatus, a presbyter of the church at Rome, being lifted up with arro-

gance against these persons, as if there was no longer for them a hope of salvation, not even if they should do all things pertaining to a genuine and pure conversion, became leader of the heresy of those who, in the pride of their imagination, call themselves Cathari.[2] There- 2 upon a very large synod assembled at Rome,[3] of bishops in number sixty, and a great many more presbyters and deacons; while the pastors of the remaining provinces deliberated in their places privately concerning what ought to be done. A decree was confirmed by all, that Novatus and those who joined with him, and those who adopted his brother-hating and inhuman opinion, should be considered by the church as strangers; but that they should heal such of the brethren as had fallen into misfortune,[4] and should minister to them with the medicines of repentance.

There have reached us epistles[5] of Cor- 3 nelius, bishop of Rome, to Fabius, of the church at Antioch, which show what was done at the synod at Rome, and what seemed best to all those in Italy and Africa and the regions thereabout.[6] Also other epistles, written in the

---

confessors, but does not accord them the privileges which they claimed in some places (as we learn from Tertullian's *de Pudicitia*, 22, and from a number of Cyprian's *Epistles*) of themselves absolving the lapsed and readmitting them to church communion. In this he showed again his agreement with Cyprian and with the principles finally adopted in the Roman and Carthaginian churches (cf. e.g. Cyprian's *Epistles*, 9 sq., *al.* 15; see also Dittrich, p. 51 sq.).

[7] The object of the letter is clearly revealed in these sentences (see chap. 41, note 1).

[1] Eusebius, and the Greeks in general, write the name Ναυάτος (though in Bk. VII. chap. 8, below, Dionysius writes Ναυατιάνος). Socrates has the form Ναυάτος, which appears also in some MSS. of Eusebius. Cyprian and the Latins write the name Novatianus. Lardner, in a note on chap. 47 of his *Credibility*, argues with great force for the correctness of the name Novatus, while Heinichen and others maintain that Novatianus is the right form. The name *Novatiani*, Ναυατιανοί, which was given to his followers, is urged with some reason by Lardner as an argument for the shorter form of the name. But even if his opinion is correct, the name Novatian is too long established to be displaced, and serves to distinguish him from the Carthaginian presbyter Novatus. The schism of Novatian was only one of the outcrops of the old strife between lax and strict discipline in the Church, the strife which had shown itself in connection with Montanism and also between Callistus and Hippolytus (see above, chap. 21, note 3). But in the present case the immediate cause of the trouble was the treatment of the lapsed. The terrible Decian persecution had naturally caused many to deny the faith, but afterward, when the stress was past, they repented and desired to be readmitted to the Church. The question became a very serious one, and opinions were divided, some advocating their acceptance after certain prescribed penances, others their continued exclusion. The matter caused a great deal of discussion, especially in Rome and Carthage. The trouble came to a head in Rome, when Cornelius, who belonged to the lax party, was chosen bishop in the year 251, after the see had been vacant for more than a year. The stricter party at once aroused to action and chose Novatian, the leader of the party, opposition bishop. He had been made a presbyter by the bishop Fabian, and occupied a very prominent position in the Roman Church. He seems originally to have held less rigid notions in regard to the treatment of the lapsed, but before the end of the persecution he became very decided in his opposition to their absolution and restoration. His position, as well as his ability and piety, made him the natural leader of the party and the rival candidate for the bishopric. He does not, however, seem to have desired to accept consecration as an opposition bishop, but his party insisted. He immediately sent the usual letters announcing the fact to the bishops of the principal sees, to Carthage, Alexandria, and Rome. Cyprian at once refused to recognize his appointment. Dionysius wrote to him advising him to withdraw (see his epistle, quoted in chap. 45). But Fabius of Antioch was inclined to take his side (see chap. 44, § 1). Novatian was excommunicated by the council mentioned just below, and then founded an independent church, baptizing all who came over to his side. We know nothing of his subsequent career (according to the tradition of his followers, and also Socrates, *H. E.* IV. 28, he suffered martyrdom under Valerian), but his sect spread throughout the East and West, and continued in existence until the sixth century. Novatian was not at all heretical in doctrine. His work upon the Trinity is both able and orthodox. His character was austere and of unblemished purity (the account given by Cornelius below is a gross misrepresentation, from the pen of an enemy), and his talents were of a high order. But the tendency of the Church was toward a more merciful treatment of the lapsed and of other sinners, and the stricter methods advocated by him fell more and more into disfavor. Novatian was quite a prolific writer. According to Jerome, *de vir. ill.* chap. 10, he wrote *de Pascha, de Sabbato, de Circumcisione, de Sacerdote, de Oratione, de Cibis*

Judaicis, de Instantia, de Attalo Multaque alia, et de Trinitate grande Volumen. The *de Cibis Judaicis* and the *de Trinitate* are still extant. The best edition of his works is that of Jackson (London, 1728). An English translation is given in the *Ante-Nicene Fathers*, V. 611-650. Novatian was the author also of one of the epistles of the Roman clergy to Cyprian (*Ep.* 30). Our contemporaneous sources for a knowledge of Novatian and his schism are the epistles of Cyprian (some ten of them), and the epistles of Dionysius and Cornelius, quoted by Eusebius in this chapter and in chaps. 44 and 45.

[2] καθαροί, "pure."

[3] This council is undoubtedly identical with the one mentioned in Cyprian's epistle to Antonianus (*Ep.* 51, § 6; *al.* 55). It was held, according to Cyprian, soon after the Carthaginian synod, in which the treatment of the *lapsi* was first discussed, and accepted the decisions of that council. The Carthaginian synod met in the spring of 251 (see Hefele, *Conciliengesch.* I. p. 112). The Roman synod must, therefore, have been held before the end of the same year; Hefele thinks about October (*ibid.* p. 114). Cornelius would not, of course, have waited long before procuring the official condemnation of the opposition bishop. We know nothing more about the constitution of the council than is told us here. It was, of course, only a local synod. The pastors of the remaining provinces were the other Italian bishops who could not be present at the council. Cornelius solicits their opinion, in order that the decree passed by the council may represent as large a number of bishops as possible.

[4] τοὺς δὲ τῇ συμφορᾷ περιπεπτωκότας. The Carthaginian synod had decided that no offenses are beyond the regular power of the Church to remit.

[5] Jerome (*de vir. ill.* chap. 66) gives the singular instead of the plural (*epistolam ad Fabium*); so also Rufinus; but there is no reason for doubting the integrity of the Greek text of Eusebius, which runs, ἦλθον δ' οὖν εἰς ἡμᾶς ἐπιστολαὶ Κορνηλίου. Valesius, although translating *epistolæ Cornelii*, yet follows Jerome and Rufinus in believing that only one epistle is meant here. Neither Rufinus nor, apparently, Jerome knew anything about the epistle, except what they read in Eusebius, and therefore it is more probable that Eusebius was correct in using the plural than that they were correct in using the singular. It is easy to understand the change of Eusebius' indefinite plural into their definite singular. They were evidently written in Greek; for in speaking of Cyprian's epistles immediately afterward, Eusebius especially mentions the fact that they were written in Latin. The epistle from which Eusebius quotes just below was also written in Greek, for Eusebius would otherwise, as is his custom, have mentioned the fact that he gives only a translation of it. This has been pointed out by Valesius; but, as Routh remarks, we can certainly go further, and say that the other epistle mentioned by Eusebius must have been in Greek, too, since it was written by the same Cornelius, and addressed to the same Fabius. These epistles are no longer extant.

[6] Eusebius says, τὰ περὶ τῆς Ῥωμαίων συνόδου καὶ τὰ δόξαντα πᾶσι τοῖς κατὰ τὴν Ἰταλίαν κ.τ.λ., which Jerome has transformed or compressed into *de Synodo Romana, Italica, Africana*, another instance of the careless way in which his *de vir. ill.* was composed.

Latin language, of Cyprian and those with him in Africa,[7] which show that they agreed as to the necessity of succoring those who had been tempted, and of cutting off from the Catholic Church the leader of the heresy and all 4 that joined with him. Another epistle of Cornelius, concerning the resolutions of the synod, is attached to these; and yet others,[8] on the conduct of Novatus, from which it is proper for us to make selections, that any one who 5 sees this work may know about him. Cornelius informs Fabius what sort of a man Novatus was, in the following words:

"But that you may know that a long time ago this remarkable man desired the episcopate, but kept this ambitious desire to himself and concealed it, — using as a cloak for his rebellion those confessors who had adhered to him from the beginning, — I desire to speak. 6 Maximus,[9] one of our presbyters, and Urbanus,[10] who twice gained the highest honor by confession, with Sidonius,[11] and Celerinus,[12] a man who by the grace of God most heroically endured all kinds of torture, and by the strength of his faith overcame the weakness of the flesh, and mightily conquered the adversary, — these men found him out and detected his craft and duplicity, his perjuries and falsehoods, his unsociability and cruel friendship. And they returned to the holy church and proclaimed in the presence of many, both bishops and presbyters and a large number of the laity, all his craft and wickedness, which for a long time he had concealed. And this they did with lamentations and repentance, because through the persuasions of the crafty and malicious beast they had left the church for the time." A little farther on he says:

"How remarkable, beloved brother, the 7 change and transformation which we have seen take place in him in a short time. For this most illustrious man, who bound himself with terrible oaths in nowise to seek the bishopric,[13] sudden-

---

[7] These epistles from Cyprian and the African bishops Jerome transforms into a single epistle from Cornelius to Fabius, *de Novatiano, et de his qui lapsi sunt.* At least, it seems impossible to explain this epistle mentioned by Jerome in any other way. Knowing the slovenly way in which he put his work together, it is not surprising that he should attribute these epistles to the same person who wrote the ones mentioned just before and after. Since the first epistles mentioned are said to have been addressed to Fabius and also the last one, from which Eusebius quotes, it is reasonable to conclude that all mentioned in this connection were addressed to him; and it would of course be quite natural for Cyprian, too, to write to Fabius (who was known to be inclined to favor Novatian), in order to confirm the account of Cornelius, and to announce that he agreed with the latter in regard to the treatment of the lapsed. No epistle, however, of Cyprian or other African bishops to Fabius are extant, though the same subject is discussed in many epistles of Cyprian addressed to the people.

[8] Rufinus mentions only two epistles of Cornelius in this connection, apparently confounding this one on the deeds of the Novatians with the one mentioned just before on the Decrees of the Council. Jerome, on the other hand, making Cornelius, as already mentioned, the author of the epistles of Cyprian and the African bishops, assigns four epistles to Cornelius. None of the epistles mentioned in this section are extant, except the long fragment of the last one quoted just below. As mentioned in the next chapter, Fabius inclined to take the side of Novatian over against the laxer party; and it was on this account that Cornelius wrote him so many epistles (compare also the epistle of Dionysius of Alexandria, quoted in chaps. 41 and 42, and see note 1 on the former chapter), and endeavored to blacken the character of Novatian as he does in the passages quoted.

[9] This Maximus was a presbyter, and one of a party of Roman confessors who played a prominent part in the controversy about the lapsed. He and his companions were imprisoned at the very beginning of the Decian persecution (Cyprian, *Ep.* 24; *al.* 28), i.e. early in the year 250, and while in prison they adopted rigoristic views and wrote to some Carthaginian confessors, urging strict methods in dealing with the lapsed (see Cyprian, *Ep.* 22; *al.* 27). Early in the year 251, after eleven months in prison, the presbyter Moses, the leading spirit of the party, died, and Maximus became the chief one among them. Moses before his death, in spite of his rigoristic principles, refused to commune with Novatian and his five presbyters (as we learn from § 20 of this chapter), apparently because he saw that his insistence upon strict discipline was tending toward schism, and that such discipline could not be maintained without sacrificing the Church. But Maximus and those mentioned with him here, together with some others (see Cyprian, *Ep.* 45; *al.* 49), became even stricter than at first, and finally went over to the party of Novatian (which took its rise after the election of Cornelius in 251), but were at length reconciled to Cornelius and the rest of the Church, and received back with rejoicing (see Cyprian, *Ep.* 43, 45, 46, 49, 50; *al.* 46, 49, 51, 53, 54). The notices of Maximus and Urbanus in Cyprian's epistles, which with the epistle of Cornelius constitute our only source for a knowledge of their lives, do not mention a second confession made by these two men, so that we cannot tell when it took place, but it must of course have been during the persecution of Decius.

[10] Urbanus was a confessor only, not a presbyter or deacon, as we learn from the notices of him in Cyprian's epistles, in connection with the party referred to in the previous note.

[11] Sidonius likewise was a confessor simply, and is mentioned with the others in the epistles of Cornelius and Cyprian.

[12] Celerinus was also one of this party of Roman confessors (as we learn from Cyprian, *Ep.* 15, *al.* 87), who, upon his release from prison, went to Carthage, and was there ordained a reader by Cyprian (*Ep.* 33, *al.* 39). His release from prison and departure for Carthage took place before the release of the others and before the death of Moses (as we learn from *Ep.* 15), that is, before the end of the year 250. He was still in Rome, however, at Easter of that year, as we learn from his epistle to Lucian, mentioned below. He came of a family of martyrs (*Ep.* 33), and was himself one of the most celebrated confessors of his time. There is extant an epistle written by him to Lucian, the Carthaginian confessor (Cyprian, *Ep.* 21), in which he begs absolution for his sisters, who had denied the faith. The epistle (as we learn from its own statements) was written at Easter time and in the year 250, for there was no bishop of Rome at the time of its composition. As we learn from this passage, Celerinus went over with these other Roman confessors to the party of Novatian, and returned with them to the Church. He is, however, mentioned neither by Cyprian nor by Cornelius (in his epistle to Cyprian) in connection with the schism of these confessors. This is very remarkable, especially since Celerinus was quite a prominent character. It is possible that he was in Carthage the greater part of the time, and did not return to Rome until shortly before the confessors returned to the Church. He might then have thrown in his lot with them, and have returned with them to the orthodox church; and yet, not having been mentioned by Cornelius' earlier epistle to Cyprian, announcing the schismatic position of the confessors, he was omitted also in the later letters announcing their return (which in fact only mentions the three leaders), and in Cyprian's reply, which of course would only mention those of whom he had been told in Cornelius' first epistle. Of the subsequent career of Celerinus and of these other confessors we know nothing.

[13] There is no reason to doubt, as Cornelius does, Novatian's sincerity in declaring that he did not seek the office of bishop. Both Cornelius and Cyprian make his ambition and his jealousy of Cornelius, the successful candidate, the cause of his schism. But such an accusation was made against every schismatic, even when there was not a shadow of support for it, and there is no reason to suppose it nearer the truth in this than in other cases. In fact, his own protestation, as recorded here by Cornelius, and as testified to by Dionysius in chap. 45, as well as the character of the man as revealed in his life previous to his episcopal ordination (as certified to even by his enemies), and in his writings, are entirely opposed to the supposition that he sought the episcopal office and that his schism was a result of his defeat. We shall do much better to reject entirely this exceedingly hostile and slanderous account of his enemy Cornelius, and to accept his own account of the matter as reported by Dionysius in chap. 25. He was the natural head of the rigoristic party, made such by his commanding ability, his deep piety, and his ascetic principles of living; and when Cornelius, the head of the lax party, was made bishop (in March, 251), the strict party revolted, and it could not be otherwise than that Novatian should be elected bishop, and that even if reluctant he should feel compelled to accept the office in order to assert the principles which he believed vital, and to prevent the complete ruin of the Church. Cornelius gives a sad story of his ordination to the episcopate. But one thing is certain, he had with him for some time a large portion of the best people in the Roman church, among them Maximus and others of the most influential confessors, who seem at length to have returned

8 ly appears a bishop as if thrown among us by some machine.[14] For this dogmatist, this defender of the doctrine of the Church,[15] attempting to grasp and seize the episcopate, which had not been given him from above, chose two of his companions who had given up their own salvation. And he sent them to a small and insignificant corner of Italy, that there by some counterfeit argument he might deceive three bishops, who were rustic and very simple men. And they asserted positively and strongly that it was necessary that they should come quickly to Rome, in order that all the dissension which had arisen there might be appeased through their mediation, jointly with other 9 bishops. When they had come, being, as we have stated, very simple in the craft and artifice of the wicked, they were shut up with certain selected men like himself. And by the tenth hour, when they had become drunk and sick, he compelled them by force to confer on him the episcopate through a counterfeit and vain imposition of hands. Because it had not come to him, he avenged himself by craft 10 and treachery. One of these bishops shortly after came back to the church, lamenting and confessing his transgression. And we communed with him as with a layman, all the people present interceding for him. And we ordained successors of the other bishops, and sent 11 them to the places where they were. This avenger of the Gospel[16] then did not know that there should be one bishop in a catholic church;[17] yet he was not ignorant (for how

could he be?) that in it there were forty-six presbyters, seven[18] deacons, seven sub-deacons,[19] forty-two acolyths,[20] fifty-two exorcists,[21] readers,[22] and janitors,[23] and over fifteen hundred widows and persons in distress, all of whom the grace and kindness of the Master nourish. But 12 not even this great multitude, so necessary in the church, nor those who, through God's providence, were rich and full, together with the very many, even innumerable people, could turn him from such desperation and presumption and recall him to the Church." Again, 13 farther on, he adds these words:

"Permit us to say further: On account of what works or conduct had he the assurance to contend for the episcopate? Was it that he had been brought up in the Church from the beginning, and had endured many conflicts in her behalf, and had passed through many and great dangers for religion? Truly this is not the fact. But Satan, who entered and dwelt in 14 him for a long time, became the occasion of his believing. Being delivered by the exorcists, he fell into a severe sickness; and as he seemed about to die, he received baptism by affusion,

opinion of Christendom, or otherwise Cyprian could not have appealed to universal custom as he does in discussing the matter. I mean simply that the principle had never before been brought to such a test as to require its formal enunciation and public recognition by the clergy and the Church at large. The emergency which now arose compelled such formal statement of it; and the Council of Nicæa made it canon law (cf. Bingham's *Antiquities*, I. p. 160 sq.).

[18] The limitation of the deacons to seven in number was due to the fact that the appointment of the Seven by the apostles (Acts vi.) was commonly looked upon as the institution of the office of the diaconate. But upon this matter, see above, Bk. II. chap. 1, note 2 *a*. The practice of limiting the number of the deacons to seven was quite a common one, and was enacted as a law in the fifteenth canon of the Council of Neo-Cæsarea (held early in the third century). The practice, however, was by no means universal, as we are informed by Sozomen (*H. E.* VII. 19). Indeed, at least in Alexandria and in Constantinople, their number was much greater (see Bingham's *Ant.* I. p. 286).

[19] The sub-deacons (the highest of the inferior orders of the clergy) are first mentioned in this epistle of Cornelius and in various epistles of Cyprian. At what time they arose we cannot tell, but they seem to have appeared in the East later than in the West, at least the first references we have to them in the Orient are in the fourth century, e.g. in the *Apost. Const.* VIII. 21. They acted as deacons' assistants, preparing the sacred vessels for use at the altar, attended the doors during communion service, and were often employed by the bishops for the conveyance of letters or messages to distant churches. See Bingham's *Ant.* Bk. III. chap. 2.

[20] The Acolyths (ἀκόλουθοι), another of the inferior orders of the clergy, are likewise first mentioned here and in Cyprian's epistles. They seem to have been of much later institution in the East, for we first hear of them there in the time of Justinian (Justin. *Novel.* 59). Their duties seem to have been to attend to the lights of the church and to procure the wine for communion service. See Bingham, *ibid.* chap. 3.

[21] The Exorcists likewise constituted one of the inferior orders of the clergy; but although we find exorcism very frequently referred to by the Fathers of the second century, there seems to have been no such office until the third century, the present being the earliest distinct reference to it. In the fourth century we find the office in all parts of the Church East and West. Their duty was to take charge of those supposed to be possessed of an evil spirit; to pray with them, care for them, and exorcise the demon when possible. See Bingham, *ibid.* chap. 4.

[22] The Readers, or Lectors (Greek, ἀναγνῶσται; Latin, *Lectores*), constituted still another of the inferior orders, and were already a distinct office in the time of Tertullian (cf. *de Præscrip.* chap. 41). From the third century on the order seems to have been universal. Their duty was to read the Scriptures in the public services of the sanctuary. See Bingham, *ibid.* chap. 5.

[23] The Janitors, or Doorkeepers (Greek, πυλωροί or θυρωροί; Latin, *ostiarii* or *janitores*), are first mentioned in this passage. In the fourth century, however, we find them frequently referred to. Their office seems to have been about the same as that of the modern janitor or sexton. See Bingham, *ibid.* chap. 6.

to the Church only because they saw that the schism was injuring it. Certainly if Novatian had been a self-seeker, as Cornelius describes him, and if his ordination had been of such a nature as Cornelius reports, he could never have had the support of so many earnest and prominent men. It is doubtless true, as Cornelius states, that Novatian was ordained by three Italian bishops, very likely bishops of rural and comparatively insignificant sees, and it is quite possible that one of them, as he also records, afterwards repented of his act as schismatic, and returned to the Church and received absolution. But all this does not imply that these three bishops were deceived by false pretenses on the part of Novatian, or that they were intoxicated when they performed the service. This, in fact, may be looked upon as baseless calumny. Novatus, the Carthaginian agitator who had caused Cyprian so much trouble, took a prominent part in the Novatian schism, though to make him the author of it, as Cyprian does, is undoubtedly incorrect (see Lardner, *Works*, III. p. 94 sq.; London ed. 1829). It was perhaps he (as reported by Eulogius, according to Photius, *Cod.* 182, and by Theodoret, *Hær. Fab.* III. 5) that found these three bishops to ordain Novatian. It is not at all improbable, when so many prominent men in the Roman church favored the stricter principles and supported Novatian, that bishops could be found in Italy who held the same principles and would be glad to ordain Novatian as bishop of Rome.

[14] μάγγανον.

[15] As Closs remarks, these words are evidently an allusion to Novatian's work, *de Trinitate*.

[16] ἐκδικητὴς τοῦ εὐαγγελίου. Possibly another sarcastic reference to Novatian's work in defense of the doctrine of the Church; possibly only an allusion to the fact that he prided himself on his orthodoxy.

[17] The principle, that there should be only one bishop in a city, was not clearly enunciated and forcibly emphasized until the third century. Cyprian's writings are full of it (cf. his treatise *On the Unity of the Church*), and in connection with this Novatian schism, which showed so plainly the disintegrating effects of a division of the church under two bishops, the principle was established so firmly as never again to be questioned. I do not mean to assert here that the principle so clearly and conclusively established at this time was a new principle. We find it enunciated even by Ignatius at the beginning of the second century, and it was the common

on the bed where he lay;[24] if indeed we
15　can say that such a one did receive it. And
when he was healed of his sickness he did
not receive the other things which it is necessary
to have according to the canon of the ⸱Church,
even the being sealed by the bishop.[25] And as
he did not receive this,[26] how could he re-
16　ceive the Holy Spirit?" Shortly after he
says again:

"In the time of persecution, through cowardice and love of life, he denied that he was a
presbyter. For when he was requested and entreated by the deacons to come out of the
chamber in which he had imprisoned himself,
and give aid to the brethren as far as was lawful
and possible for a presbyter to assist those of
the brethren who were in danger and needed
help, he paid so little respect to the entreaties of
the deacons that he went away and departed in
anger. For he said that he no longer desired
to be a presbyter, as he was an admirer
17　of another philosophy."[27] Passing by a few
things, he adds the following:

"For this illustrious man forsook the Church
of God, in which, when he believed, he was
judged worthy of the presbyterate through the
favor of the bishop who ordained him to the
presbyterial office. This had been resisted by
all the clergy and many of the laity; because it
was unlawful that one who had been affused on
his bed on account of sickness as he had been
should enter into any clerical office;[28] but the
bishop requested that he might be permitted
to ordain this one only." He adds to these　18
yet another, the worst of all the man's offenses, as follows:

"For when he has made the offerings, and
distributed a part to each man, as he gives it he
compels the wretched man to swear in place of
the blessing. Holding his hands in both of his
own, he will not release him until he has sworn
in this manner (for I will give his own words):
'Swear to me by the body and blood of our
Lord Jesus Christ that you will never forsake me and turn to Cornelius.' And the　19
unhappy man does not taste until he has
called down imprecations on himself; and instead of saying Amen, as he takes the bread,
he says, I will never return to Cornelius."
Farther on he says again:　　　　　　20

"But know that he has now been made
bare and desolate; as the brethren leave him
every day and return to the church. Moses[29]

---

[24] There is no reason to doubt that Novatian received clinical
baptism, as here stated by Cornelius. This does not imply, as is
commonly supposed, that he was of heathen parentage, for many
Christians postponed baptism as long as possible, in order not to
sacrifice baptismal grace by sins committed after baptism. We do
not know whether his parents were heathen or Christians. Upon
the objection to Novatian's ordination, based upon his irregular
baptism, see below, § 17.

[25] τοῦ τε σφραγισθῆναι ὑπὸ τοῦ ἐπισκόπου. σφραγισθῆναι here
means confirmation or consignation (as it was commonly called
among the Latins); that is, the imposition of the hands of the
bishop which regularly followed baptism, immediately if the bishop
were on the ground, in other cases at as early a date as possible.
The imposition of hands was for the purpose of conveying the Holy
Spirit, who should supply the newly baptized Christian with the
necessary grace to fit him for the Christian life. Confirmation was
thus looked upon as completing the baptism and as a necessary pre-
condition of receiving the eucharist. At the same time, if a person
died after baptism, before it was possible to receive imposition of
hands, the baptism was not regarded as rendered invalid by the omission, for in the baptism itself the full remission of sins was supposed
to be granted. The confirmation was not necessary for such remission, but was necessary for the bestowal of the requisite sustaining
grace for the Christian life. Cornelius in the present paragraph does
not intend to imply that regenerating grace was not given in Novatian's baptism. He means simply that the Holy Spirit was not given
in that full measure in which it was given by the laying on of hands,
and which was necessary for growth in grace and Christian living.
The baptism was looked on in ordinary cases as in a sense negative,
— effecting the washing away of sin, the laying on of hands as positive, confirming the gift of the Spirit. The former, therefore, was
sufficient to save the man who died immediately thereafter; the
latter was necessary to sustain the man who still remained in the
world. Compare with these words of Cornelius Tertullian's de
Baptism. chap. 6. The earliest extant canon on this subject is the
thirty-eighth of the synod of Elvira (306 A.D.), which decrees that
a sick person may in case of necessity be baptized by a layman, but
that he is afterward, if he recovers, to be taken to the bishop that
the baptism may be perfected by the laying on of hands. The
seventy-seventh canon decrees the same thing for those baptized by
deacons, but expressly declares that if the baptized person die before
the imposition of hands, he is to be regarded as saved in virtue of the
faith which he confessed in his baptism. It is not necessary to give
other references in connection with this matter. For further particulars, see Bingham, ibid. Bk. XII.

On the signification of the verb σφραγίζω, see Suicer's Thesaurus. We can hardly believe that Novatian failed to receive imposition of hands from the bishop, for it is inconceivable that the latter
would have omitted what was regarded as such an important pre-
requisite to church communion in the case of one whom he ordained
to the presbyterate. Novatian may not have received confirmation
immediately after his recovery, but he must have received it before
his ordination. As seen in § 17, it is not the omission of confirmation that causes the objections on the part of the clergy, but the
clinical baptism.

[26] The majority of the MSS., followed by Schwegler, Laemmer,
and Heinichen, read τούτων. But some of the best MSS., followed
by all the other editors, read τούτου.

[27] This is certainly a calumny. It is possible, as Neander suggests, that Novatian, although a presbyter, withdrew somewhat
from active duty and lived the life of an ascetic, and that it is this
to which Cornelius refers in speaking of his admiration for "another
philosophy." But however that may be, Cornelius' interpretation
of his conduct as cowardly or unworthy is quite false. See above,
note 1.

[28] Clinic baptism (so-called from κλίνη, "a bed.") was ordinarily
looked upon in the early Church, in which immersion was the common mode of baptism, as permanently debarring a person from the
presbyterate, and by many persons it was denied that such baptism
was baptism at all. The latter opinion, however, the Church refused to sustain (cf. Cyprian, Ep. 75; al. 19). The twelfth canon
of the Council of Neo-Cæsarea (held early in the fourth century)
says, "If any man is baptized only in time of sickness, he shall not
be ordained a presbyter; because his faith was not voluntary, but
as it were of constraint; except his subsequent faith and diligence
recommend him, or else the scarcity of men make it necessary to
ordain him." It is clear that this canon meant to apply only to
persons whose baptism was delayed by their own fault. It was
common for catechumens to postpone the rite as long as possible in
order not to forfeit baptismal grace by their post-baptismal sins,
and it was to discourage this practice that such canons as this of
Neo-Cæsarea were passed. Even this canon, however, provided
for exceptional cases, and the fact that Novatian was ordained in
spite of his irregular baptism is a proof that he must have been an
exceptionally pious and zealous man.

[29] On Moses (or Moyses, as he is called by Cyprian), see note 9,
above.

Lipsius (Chron. der röm. Bischöfe, p. 202, note) maintains
that Cornelius is referring, at this point, not to Novatian, but to
Novatus, the Carthaginian presbyter, and that Eusebius has confounded the two men. He bases this opinion upon the mention of
the five presbyters, whom he identifies with those who, with Novatus, separated from the Carthaginian church in connection with the
schism of Felicissimus (see Cyprian, Ep. 39; al. 43), and also upon
the fact that Moses died before the election of Novatian as opposition bishop. In regard to the first point, it must be noticed that, in
an epistle to Cyprian upon the schism of Novatian (Cyprian, Ep. 47;
al. 50), Cornelius mentions five presbyters (including Novatus) as
connected with Novatian in his schism. Certainly it is most natural
to refer Cornelius' words in this paragraph to the same five men.
Indeed, to speak of Novatus and the five presbyters with him would
be very peculiar, for Novatus himself was one of the five, and therefore there were but four with him. As to the second point, it may
simply be said that Moses might well have refused to commune with
Novatian, before the election of the latter, seeing that his position

also, the blessed martyr, who lately suffered among us a glorious and admirable martyrdom, while he was yet alive, beholding his boldness and folly, refused to commune with him and with the five presbyters who with him had separated themselves from the church."

21   At the close of his letter he gives a list of the bishops who had come to Rome and condemned the silliness of Novatus, with their names and the parish over which each of 22 them presided. He mentions also those who did not come to Rome, but who expressed by letters their agreement with the vote of these bishops, giving their names and the cities from which they severally sent them.[30] Cornelius wrote these things to Fabius, bishop of Antioch.

CHAPTER XLIV.

Dionysius' Account of Serapion.

1   To this same Fabius, who seemed to lean somewhat toward this schism,[1] Dionysius of Alexandria also wrote an epistle.[2] He writes in this many other things concerning repentance, and relates the conflicts of those who had lately suffered martyrdom at Alexandria. After the other account he mentions a certain wonderful fact, which deserves a place in this work. It is as follows:

2   " I will give thee this one example which occurred among us. There was with us a certain Serapion,[3] an aged believer who had lived for a long time blamelessly, but had fallen in the trial. He besought often, but no one gave heed to him, because he had sacrificed. But he became sick, and for three successive days continued speechless and senseless.

3   Having recovered somewhat on the fourth day he sent for his daughter's son, and said, 'How long do you detain me, my child? I beseech you, make haste, and absolve me speedily. Call one of the presbyters to me.' And when he had said this, he became again speechless. And the boy ran to the presbyter. But it was night and he was sick, and there-

4   fore unable to come. But as I had commanded that persons at the point of death, if they requested it, and especially if they had asked for it previously, should receive remission,

that they might depart with a good hope, he gave the boy a small portion of the eucharist, telling him to soak[4] it and let the drops fall into the old man's mouth.[5] The boy re- 5 turned with it, and as he drew near, before he entered, Serapion again arousing, said, 'Thou art come, my child, and the presbyter could not come; but do quickly what he directed, and let me depart.' Then the boy soaked it and dropped it into his mouth. And when he had swallowed a little, immediately he gave up the ghost. Is it not evident that he was 6 preserved and his life continued till he was absolved, and, his sin having been blotted out, he could be acknowledged[6] for the many good deeds which he had done?"

Dionysius relates these things.

CHAPTER XLV.

An Epistle of Dionysius to Novatus.

BUT let us see how the same man addressed Novatus[1] when he was disturbing the Roman brotherhood. As he pretended that some of the brethren were the occasion of his apostasy and schism, as if he had been forced by them to proceed as he had,[2] observe the manner in which he writes to him:

"Dionysius to his brother Novatus, greeting. If, as thou sayest, thou hast been led on unwillingly, thou wilt prove this if thou retirest willingly. For it were better to suffer everything, rather than divide the Church of God. Even martyrdom for the sake of preventing division would not be less glorious than for refusing to worship idols. Nay, to me it seems greater. For in the one case a man suffers martyrdom

---

[4] ἀποβρέξαι. This is translated by Crusè and by Salmond (in the *Ante-Nicene Fathers*, VI. p. 101) " soak (or steep) in water"; but the liquid is not specified in the text, and it has consequently been thought by others that the bread was dipped in the wine, as was commonly done in the celebration of the eucharist in the Eastern Church (see Bingham's *Ant.* Bk. XV.). But it must be noticed that the bread was soaked not by the presbyter but by the boy, and that too after his return home, where there can have been no consecrated wine for eucharistic use, and there is no hint that wine was given him for the purpose by the presbyter. It therefore seems probable that the bread was soaked simply in water, and that the soaking was only in order that the old man, in his enfeebled state, might be able to receive the element in a liquid instead of in a solid form.
[5] κατὰ τοῦ στόματος ἐπιστάξαι.
[6] ὁμολογηθῆναι. The meaning is apparently " acknowledged or confessed by Christ," and Valesius is doubtless correct in remarking that Dionysius was alluding to the words of Matt. x. 32.
[1] This epistle to Novatian was doubtless written in reply to a letter from him announcing his election to the episcopate of Rome, for we know that Novatian sent such letters, as was customary, to all the prominent bishops of the Church. Dionysius' epistle, therefore, must have been written soon after the election of Novatian, which took place in the year 251. We have only the fragment quoted in this chapter.
[2] Novatian may well have been urged against his will to permit himself to be made opposition bishop; but of course, once having taken the step, so long as he believed in the justice of the cause for which he was contending, he could not turn back, but must maintain his position with vigor and firmness. This, of course, would lead his enemies to believe that he had himself sought the position, as Dionysius evidently believed that he had.

---

would inevitably lead to schism. There remains, therefore, no reason for supposing Eusebius mistaken, and for referring these words to Novatus of Carthage, instead of Novatian of Rome.
[30] These lists of the bishops present at the council, and of those who expressed their agreement with the decision of the synod, are no longer extant.
[1] See above, chap. 39, note 7.
[2] This epistle, as we may gather from the description of its contents in the next sentence, is without doubt the same from which Eusebius has quoted at such length in chaps. 41 and 42. Upon the date and purpose of it, see chap. 41, note 1. We possess only the fragments quoted by Eusebius in these three chapters.
[3] Of this Serapion we know only what is told us in this chapter.

for the sake of his own soul; in the other case in behalf of the entire Church. And now if thou canst persuade or induce the brethren to come to unanimity, thy righteousness will be greater than thine error, and this will not be counted, but that will be praised. But if thou canst not prevail with the disobedient, at least save thine own soul. I pray that thou mayst fare well, maintaining peace in the Lord."

This he wrote to Novatus.

CHAPTER XLVI.

Other Epistles of Dionysius.

1   He wrote also an epistle to the brethren in Egypt on Repentance.[1] In this he sets forth what seemed proper to him in regard to those who had fallen, and he describes the

2   classes of transgressions. There is extant also a private letter on Repentance, which he wrote to Conon,[2] bishop of the parish of Hermopolis, and another of an admonitory[3] character, to his flock at Alexandria. Among them also is the one written to Origen on Martyrdom[4] and to the brethren at Laodicea,[5] of whom Thelymidres was bishop. He likewise sent one on Repentance to the brethren in Armenia,[6] of

3   whom Merozanes was bishop. Besides all these, he wrote to Cornelius of Rome, when he had received from him an epistle against

Novatus.[7] He states in this that he had been invited by Helenus,[8] bishop of Tarsus, in Cilicia, and the others who were with him, Firmilianus,[9] bishop in Cappadocia, and Theoctistus,[10] of Palestine, to meet them at the synod in Antioch, where some persons were endeavoring to establish the schism of Novatus. Besides this

4   he writes that he had been informed that Fabius[11] had fallen asleep, and that Demetrianus[12] had been appointed his successor in the episcopate of Antioch. He writes also in these words concerning the bishop of Jerusalem: "For the blessed Alexander[13] having been confined in prison, passed away happily." In addi-

5   tion to this there is extant also a certain other diaconal epistle of Dionysius, sent to those in Rome through Hippolytus.[14] And he wrote

---

[1] This epistle on the subject of repentance or penance, which was the burning one just at this time in connection with the lapsed, was doubtless written at about the same time with those to Fabius and Novatian, already referred to. No fragments of it have been preserved.

[2] This work (πρὸς Κόνωνα ἰδία τις περὶ μετανοίας γραφή), which was probably written at about this same time, is mentioned also by Jerome (*de vir. ill.* 69). Eusebius preserves no extract from it, but extended fragments have been preserved in various MSS., and have been published by Pitra (*Spic. Solesm.* I. p. 15 sq.), though it is questionable whether all that he gives are genuine. The translation of Dionysius' works in the *Ante-Nicene Fathers* omits all of these fragments, though they are interesting and valuable. For further particulars, see Dittrich, p. 62. The general character of the letter must have been the same as that of the preceding.

[3] ἐπιστρεπτική; literally, "calculated to turn." Musculus and Christophorsonus translate *hortatoria ;* Valesius, *objurgatoria ;* Stroth and Closs, "Ermahnungsschrift"; Crusè, "epistle of reproof." The word does not necessarily carry the idea of reproof with it, but it is natural to suppose in the present case that it was written while Dionysius was absent from Alexandria, during the persecution of Decius, and if so, may well have contained an admonition to steadfastness, and at the same time, possibly, an argument against rigoristic measures which some of the people may have been advocating in reference to the lapsed. At least, the connection in which Eusebius mentions it might lead us to think that it had something to do with that question, though, as the epistle is no longer extant, we can reach no certainty in the matter.

[4] This epistle was doubtless written while Origen was suffering imprisonment in the persecution of Decius (see above, chap. 39, and below, p. 394), and was for the purpose of comforting and encouraging him (cf. Origen's own work on martyrdom, referred to in chap. 28, above). The epistle is no longer extant. Numerous fragments are given by Gallandi, Migne, and others, which they assign to this work; but Dittrich has shown (p. 35 sq.) that they are to be ascribed to some one else, perhaps to another Dionysius who lived much later than the great bishop.

[5] This epistle to the Laodiceans, which is no longer extant, very likely dealt, like so many of the others, with the question of discipline. Of Thelymidres, bishop of Laodicea, we know nothing.

[6] We know no more about this epistle to the Armenians than is told us here. The character of the letter must have been similar to the two upon the same subject mentioned above. Of the bishop Merozanes nothing is known.

[7] On Cornelius, see above, chap. 39, note 3. His epistle to Dionysius is no longer extant. Dionysius' epistle to him is likewise lost, and is known to us only from what Eusebius tells us here. It was written after the death of Fabius of Antioch (see below, § 4), and therefore probably in 253 (see above, chap. 39, note 7). It has been questioned whether this synod of Antioch to which, according to Eusebius, Dionysius referred, was really held, or only projected. The *Libellus Synodicus* records it as an actual synod, but its authority is of no weight. On the other hand, Eusebius' words seem plainly to indicate that he believed that the council was really held, for he speaks of it as "*the* synod at Antioch"; had he thought of it only as projected, he could hardly have referred to it in such definite terms. In spite, therefore, of the doubts of Dittrich, Hefele, and others, I am inclined to believe that Eusebius supposed that the synod had actually been held in Antioch. Whether the epistle of Dionysius warranted him in drawing that conclusion is another question, which cannot be decided. I look upon it, however, as probable that, had the synod been simply projected and failed to convene, some indication of that fact would have been given by Dionysius, and would have caused a modification of Eusebius' statement.

[8] Helenus, bishop of Tarsus, played a prominent part in the controversy concerning the re-baptism of heretics, maintaining, like most of the Oriental bishops, the necessity of re-baptizing them (see below, Bk. VII. chap. 5), and also in the controversy which arose about Paul of Samosata (see Bk. VII. chaps. 28 and 30). From the latter chapter we should gather that he presided at the final council in Antioch, which passed condemnation upon Paul, Firmilian, who seems to have presided at the previous councils, having died on his way to the last one. Of Helenus' dates we know only what we can gather from the facts here stated. He must have been bishop as early as 252; and he cannot have died until after 265 (on the date of the Antiochian synod at which Paul was condemned, see Bk. VII. chap. 29, note 1).

[9] On Firmilian, see above, chap. 26, note 3.

[10] On Theoctistus, see above, chap. 19, note 27.

[11] On Fabius, bishop of Antioch, see above, chap. 39, note 7.

[12] Demetrianus, the successor of Fabius, and predecessor of Paul in the bishopric of Antioch, is mentioned also in Bk. VII. chaps. 5, 14, 27, and 30. The date of his accession is uncertain; but as Fabius died probably in 253 (possibly in 252), we can fix approximately the beginning of his episcopate. In Bk. VII. chaps. 5 and 14, he is said to have survived Gallienus' edict of toleration (260 A.D.); but as Harnack has shown (*Zeit des Ignatius*, p. 51), this notice is quite unreliable, as are also the notices in the *Chronicle*. We can only say that his successor, Paul, became bishop between the years 257 and 260.

[13] On Alexander, bishop of Jerusalem, see above, chap. 8, note 6.

[14] The interpretation of this sentence is very difficult. The Greek runs ἐξῆς ταύτῃ καὶ ἑτέρα τις ἐπιστολὴ τοῖς ἐν Ῥώμῃ τοῦ Διονυσίου φέρεται διακονικὴ διὰ Ἱππολύτου. The φέρεται, according to the usage of Eusebius, must mean "is extant," and some participle (e.g. "written" or "sent") must then be supplied before διὰ Ἱππολύτου. Whether Eusebius means that the letter was written by Hippolytus or was carried by him to Rome cannot be determined. The latter is more probable, and is the commonly accepted interpretation. That Eusebius should name a messenger in this particular case and in no other seems peculiar, unless it be supposed that Hippolytus was so prominent a character as to merit especial mention. Who he was we do not know, for chronology will not permit us (as was formerly done by some scholars) to identify him with the great writer of the Roman church (see above, chaps. 20 and 22), and no other Hippolytus of prominence is known to us. In view of Eusebius' mention of the name at this point, I am inclined, however, to think that he, knowing so little about the Roman Hippolytus, fancied that this was the same man. If he did, he had good reason to mention him. The word "diaconal" (διακονικὴ) in this sentence has caused much

another to them on Peace, and likewise on Repentance ; [15] and yet another to the confessors

there who still held to the opinion of Novatus.[16]
He sent two more to the same persons after
they had returned to the Church. And he communicated with many others by letters, which
he has left behind him as a benefit in various
ways to those who now diligently study his
writings.[17]

---

dispute. Rufinus translates *epistola de ministeriis ;* Valesius,
epistola de officio diaconi, that is, " concerning the office (or duties)
of the diaconate," and it seems out of the question to understand
the word in any other way. Why Dionysius should address an epistle
on this subject to the Roman church it is impossible to say. Magistris supposed that it was called " diaconal " because it was to be
read in church by a deacon, and concluded that it was an exhortation to peace, since it was customary for the deacons to offer the
εἰρηνικά, or prayers for peace. The supposition is attractive, for it
is natural to think that this epistle, like the others, discussed the
Novatian schism and contained an exhortation to peace. But we
cannot without further evidence adopt Magistris' explanation, nor
indeed can we assume that a diaconal epistle as such (whether the
word is a technical one or not, and though it might seem such we
have no other trace of such a use of it) had to do with the unity
or peace of the Church. We must, in fact, leave the matter quite
undetermined. Compare Dittrich, *ibid.* p. 55.

[15] Of these two epistles to the Romans we know only the titles,
as given here by Eusebius.

[16] On these confessors, and their return to the Church, see above,
chap. 43, note 9. Dionysius' epistles to them are known to us only
from Eusebius' reference to them in this passage.

[17] Besides the epistles mentioned by Eusebius in this and the
previous chapter we know at least the titles of a number of others.
In Bk. VII. many are referred to, and extracts from some are quoted
by Eusebius. See especially Bk. VII. chap. 26, where another partial list of them is given. Eusebius does not pretend to mention all
of Dionysius' epistles; indeed, he states that he wrote many besides
those mentioned. For further particulars in regard to all the epistles
known to us, see Dittrich's monograph.

BOOK VII.

INTRODUCTION.

IN this seventh book of the Church History, the great bishop of Alexandria, Dionysius,[1] shall again assist us by his own words; relating the several affairs of his time in the epistles which he has left. I will begin with them.

CHAPTER I.

The Wickedness of Decius and Gallus.

WHEN Decius had reigned not quite two years,[1] he was slain with his children, and Gallus succeeded him. At this time Origen died, being sixty-nine years of age.[2] Dionysius, writing to Hermammon,[3] speaks as follows of Gallus:[4]

"Gallus neither recognized the wickedness of Decius, nor considered what had destroyed him; but stumbled on the same stone, though it lay before his eyes. For when his reign was prosperous and affairs were proceeding according to his mind, he attacked the holy men who were interceding with God for his peace and welfare. Therefore with them he persecuted also their prayers in his behalf." So much concerning him.

---

[1] On Dionysius, see especially Bk. VI. chap. 40, note 1.

[1] Decius reigned about thirty months, from the summer of 249 until almost the close of the year 251 (see Tillemont, *Hist. des Emp.* III. p. 285). His son Herennius Etruscus was slain with his father in a battle fought against the Goths in Thrace; another son, Hostilianus, was associated in the purple with Decius' successor, Gallus, but died soon afterwards, probably by the plague, which was at that time raging; possibly, as was suspected, by the treachery of Gallus. There has been some controversy as to whether Hostilianus was a son, or only a nephew, or a son-in-law of Decius. Eusebius in speaking of more than one son becomes an independent witness to the former alternative, and there is really little reason to doubt it, for Zosimus' statements are explicit (see Zosimus, I. 25, and cf. Tillemont, *ibid.* p. 506). Two other sons are mentioned in one inscription, but its genuineness is doubtful. Eusebius, however, may be urged as a witness that he had more than two (cf. Tillemont, *ibid.*).

[2] ἑνὸς δέοντα τῆς ζωῆς ἑβδομήκοντα ἀποπλήσας ἔτη τελευτᾷ. Upon the date of Origen's birth and upon his life in general, see above, Bk. VI. chap. 2, note 1, and below, p. 391 sq.

[3] Of this Hermammon we know nothing. The words of Eusebius at the close of chap. 22, below, lead us to think that he was probably a bishop of some church in Egypt. Fragments of the epistle addressed to him are preserved in this chapter and in chapters 10 and 23, below. It is possible that Dionysius wrote more than one epistle to Hermammon and that the fragments which we have are from different letters. This, however, is not probable, for Eusebius gives no hint that he is quoting from more than one epistle, and, moreover, the three extracts which we have correspond excellently with one another, seeming to be drawn from a single epistle which contained a description of the conduct of successive emperors toward the Christians. The date of the epistle is given at the close of chap. 23; namely, the ninth year of the Emperor Gallienus (i.e. August, 261–August, 262), reckoning from the time of his association with his father Valerian in the purple.

[4] Gallus succeeded Decius toward the close of the year 251 and reigned until the summer of 253 (some with less ground say

CHAPTER II.

The Bishops of Rome in those Times.

CORNELIUS,[1] having held the episcopate in the city of Rome about three years, was succeeded by Lucius.[2] He died in less than eight months, and transmitted his office to Stephen.[3] Diony-

---

254), when he was slain, with his son, by his own soldiers. His persecution of the Christians (under him, for instance, Cornelius, bishop of Rome, was banished, see above, Bk. VI. chap. 39, note 3), seems to have been less the result of a deeply rooted religious conviction and a fixed political principle (such as Decius possessed) than of the terrible plague which had begun during the reign of Decius and was ravaging the empire during the early part of Gallus' reign (see Tillemont's *Hist. des Emp.* III. p. 288). He persecuted, therefore, not so much as a matter of principle as because he desired either to appease the populace or to propitiate the Gods, whom he superstitiously believed, as the people did, to be the authors of the terrible scourge.

[1] On Cornelius, see Bk. VI. chap. 39, note 3.

[2] Eusebius makes Cornelius' episcopate a year too long (see Bk. VI. chap. 39, note 3), and hence puts the accession of Julius too late. Jerome puts him in the second year of Gallus (see the same note) and gives the duration of his episcopate as eight months, agreeing with Eusebius in the present passage. The Armenian *Chron.* puts Lucius in the seventh year of Philip, and assigns only two months to his episcopate. But it is far out of the way, as also in regard to Cornelius. The Liberian catalogue assigns three years and eight months to Lucius' episcopate, putting his death in 255; but Lipsius has shown conclusively that this must be incorrect, and concludes that he held office eight months, from June, 253, to March, 254. He was banished while bishop of Rome, but returned very soon, and died in a short time, probably a natural death. The strife in regard to the lapsed, begun while Cornelius was bishop, continued under him, and he followed the liberal policy of his predecessor. One letter of Cyprian addressed to him is extant (*Ep.* 57; *al.* 61).

[3] Lipsius puts the accession of Stephen on the twelfth of May, 254, and his death on the second of August, 257, assigning him an episcopate of three years, two months and twenty-one days. The dates given by the chief authorities vary greatly. The Liberian catalogue gives four years, two months and twenty-one days, which Lipsius corrects simply by reading three instead of four years, for the latter figure is impossible (see chap. 5, note 5). Eusebius, in chap. 5, tells us that Stephen held office two years. Jerome's version of the *Chron.* says three years, but puts his accession in the second year of Gallus, which is inconsistent with his own statement that Cornelius became bishop in the first year of Gallus. The Armenian *Chron.* agrees with Eusebius' statement in chap. 5, below, in assigning two years to the episcopate of Stephen, but puts his accession in the seventh year of Philip, which, like his notices of Cornelius and Lucius is far out of the way.

The discussion in regard to the lapsed still continued under Stephen. But the chief controversy of the time was in regard to the re-baptism of heretics, which caused a severe rupture between the churches of Rome and Carthage. Stephen held, in accordance with ancient usage and the uniform custom of the Roman church (though under Callistus heretics were re-baptized according to Hippolytus, *Phil.* IX. 7), that baptism, even by heretics and schismatics, is valid; and that one so baptized is not to be re-baptized upon entering the orthodox church, but is to be received by the imposition of hands. Cyprian, on the other hand, supported by the whole of the Asiatic and African church, maintained the invalidity of such baptism and the necessity of re-baptism. The controversy became very sharp, and seems to have resulted in Stephen's hurling an excommunication against the Asiatic and African churches. Compare the epistle of Firmilian to Cyprian (*Ep.* 75), and that of Dionysius, quoted by Eusebius in chap. 5, below. Stephen appears to have been a man of very dictatorial and overbearing temper, if our authorities are to be relied upon, and seems to have made overweening claims in regard to Rome's prerogatives; to have been the first in fact to assume that the bishop of Rome had the right of exercising control over the whole Church (see especially the epistle of Firmilian to Cyprian; Cyprian's *Epistles*, No. 74, *al.* 75). It must be remembered, however, that we know Stephen only through

sius wrote to him the first of his letters on baptism,[4] as no small controversy had arisen as to whether those who had turned from any heresy should be purified by baptism. For the ancient custom prevailed in regard to such, that they should receive only the laying on of hands with prayers.[5]

CHAPTER III.

Cyprian, and the Bishops with him, first taught that it was necessary to purify by Baptism those converted from Heresy.

FIRST of all, Cyprian, pastor of the parish of Carthage,[1] maintained that they should not be received except they had been purified from their error by baptism. But Stephen considering it unnecessary to add any innovation contrary to the tradition which had been held from the beginning, was very indignant at this.[2]

CHAPTER IV.

The Epistles which Dionysius wrote on this Subject.

DIONYSIUS, therefore, having communicated with him extensively on this question by letter,[1] finally showed him that since the persecution had abated,[2] the churches everywhere had rejected the novelty of Novatus, and were at peace among themselves. He writes as follows:

CHAPTER V.

The Peace following the Persecution.

"BUT know now, my brethren, that all 1 the churches throughout the East and beyond, which formerly were divided, have become united. And all the bishops everywhere are of one mind, and rejoice greatly in the peace which has come beyond expectation. Thus Demetrianus in Antioch,[1] Theoctistus in Cæsarea, Mazabanes in Ælia, Marinus in Tyre (Alexander having fallen asleep),[2] Heliodorus in Laodicea (Thelymidres being dead), Helenus in Tarsus, and all the churches of Cilicia, Firmilianus, and all Cappadocia. I have named only the more illustrious bishops, that I may not make my epistle too long and my words too burdensome. And all Syria, and Arabia to which 2 you send help when needed,[3] and whither you have just written,[4] Mesopotamia, Pontus, Bithynia, and in short all everywhere are rejoicing and glorifying God for the unanimity and brotherly love." Thus far Dionysius.

But Stephen, having filled his office two 3 years, was succeeded by Xystus.[5] Diony-

---

the accounts of his opponents. It had been the practice in the churches of Asia for a long time before Cyprian to re-baptize heretics and schismatics (cf. the epistle of Firmilian to Cyprian, and the epistle of Dionysius, quoted by Eusebius in chap. 5, below), and the custom prevailed also in Africa, though it seems to have been a newer thing there. Cyprian, in his epistle to Jubaianus (*Ep.* 72, *al.* 73), does not trace it back beyond Agrippinus, bishop of Carthage, under whom the practice was sanctioned by a council (186–187 or 215–217 A.D.). Under Cyprian himself the practice was confirmed by a council at Carthage, in 255 A.D. The more liberal view of the Roman church, however, in time prevailed and was confirmed with some limitations by the Council of Arles, in 314. Stephen figures in tradition as a martyr, but there is no reason to think that he was one, for the Church was enjoying comparative peace at the time of his death. Two epistles are extant, addressed to him by Cyprian (Nos. 66 and 71, *al.* 68 and 72). A number of Cyprian's epistles refer to Stephen.
[4] Six epistles by Dionysius on the subject of baptism are mentioned by Eusebius (see below, chap. 5, note 6). It is clear that Dionysius, so far as Eusebius knew, wrote but one to Stephen on this subject, for he calls the one which he wrote to Xystus the second (in chap. 5). Dionysius' own opinion on the subject of re-baptism is plain enough from Eusebius' words in this chapter, and also from Dionysius' own words in chap. 5, below. He sided with the entire Eastern and African church in refusing to admit the validity of heretical baptism, and in requiring a convert from the heretics to be "washed and cleansed from the filth of the old and impure leaven" (see chap. 5, § 5).   [5] See note 3.
[1] From 247 or 248 to 258, when he suffered martyrdom.
[2] See the previous chapter, note 3.
[1] διὰ γραμμάτων, which might mean "letters," but in the present case must refer apparently to a single letter, the plural, γράμματα, like the Latin *litterae*, was very commonly used to denote a single epistle), for in chap. 2 Eusebius says that Dionysius' first epistle on baptism was addressed to Stephen, and in chap. 5 informs us that his second was addressed to Xystus. The epistle mentioned here must be the one referred to in chap. 2 and must have been devoted chiefly to the question of the re-baptism of heretics or schismatics (περὶ τούτου referring evidently to the subject spoken of in the previous chapter). But Eusebius quite irrelevantly quotes from the epistle a passage not upon the subject in hand, but upon an entirely different one, viz. upon the peace which had been established in the Eastern churches, after the disturbances caused by the schism of Novatian (see Bk. VI. chap. 43 sq.). That the peace spoken of in this epistle cannot mean, as Baronius held, that the Eastern churches had come over to Stephen's opinion in regard to the subject of baptism is clear enough from the fact that Dionysius wrote another epistle to Stephen's successor (see the next chapter)

in which he still defended the practice of re-baptism. In fact, the passage quoted by Eusebius from Dionysius' epistle to Stephen has no reference to the subject of baptism.
[2] The persecution referred to is that of Decius.
[1] On Demetrianus, Thelymidres, and Helenus, see Bk. VI. chap. 46. On Theoctistus, see *ibid.* chap. 19, note 27; on Firmilian, *ibid.* chap. 26, note 3; on Mazabanes, *ibid.* chap. 39, note 5.
[2] This clause (κοιμηθέντος Ἀλεξάνδρου) is placed by Rufinus, followed by Stroth, Zimmermann, Valesius (in his notes), Closs, and Crusè, immediately after the words "Mazabanes in Ælia." But all the MSS. followed by all the other editors give the clause in the position which it occupies above in my translation. It is natural, of course, to think of the famous Alexander of Jerusalem as referred to here (Bk. VI. chap. 8, note 6), but it is difficult to see how, if he were referred to, the words could stand in the position which they occupy in the text. It is not impossible, however, to assume simple carelessness on Dionysius' part to explain the peculiar order, and thus hold that Alexander of Jerusalem is here referred to. Nor is it, on the other hand, impossible (though certainly difficult) to suppose that Dionysius is referring to a bishop of Tyre named Alexander, whom we hear of from no other source.
[3] The church of Rome had been from an early date very liberal in assisting the needy in every quarter. See the epistle of Dionysius of Corinth to Soter, bishop of Rome, quoted above in Bk. IV. chap. 23.
[4] Dionysius speaks just below (§ 6) of epistles or an epistle of Stephen upon the subject of baptism, in which he had announced that he would no longer commune with the Oriental bishops, who held to the custom of baptizing heretics. And it is this epistle which must have stirred up the rage of Firmilian, which shows itself in his epistle to Cyprian, already mentioned. The epistle of Stephen referred to here, however, cannot be identical with that one, or Dionysius would not speak of it in such a pleasant tone. It very likely had something to do with the heresy of Novatian, about which Dionysius is writing. It is no longer extant, and we know only what Dionysius tells us about it in this passage.
[5] Known as Sixtus II. in the list of Roman bishops. On Sixtus I. see above, Bk. IV. chap. 4, note 3. That Xystus (or Sixtus) was martyred under Valerian we are told not only by the Liberian catalogue, but also by Cyprian, in an epistle written shortly before his own death, in 258 (Ep. No. 81, *al.* 80), in which he gives a detailed account of it. There is no reason to doubt the date given by the Liberian catalogue (Aug. 6, 258); for the epistle of Cyprian shows that it must have taken place just about that time, Valerian having sent a very severe rescript to the Senate in the summer of 258. This fixed point for the martyrdom of Xystus enables

sius wrote him a second epistle on baptism,[6] in which he shows him at the same time the opinion and judgment of Stephen and the other bishops, and speaks in this manner of

4　Stephen : " He therefore had written previously concerning Helenus and Firmilianus, and all those in Cilicia and Cappadocia and Galatia and the neighboring nations, saying that he would not commune with them for this same cause ; namely, that they re-baptized heretics. But consider the importance of the

5　matter. For truly in the largest synods of the bishops, as I learn, decrees have been passed on this subject, that those coming over from heresies should be instructed, and then should be washed[7] and cleansed from the filth of the old and impure leaven. And I wrote entreating him concerning all these things." Further on he says :

6　" I wrote also, at first in few words, recently in many, to our beloved fellow-presbyters, Dionysius[8] and Philemon,[9] who formerly had held the same opinion as Stephen, and had written to me on the same matters." So much in regard to the above-mentioned controversy.

CHAPTER VI.

The Heresy of Sabellius.

HE refers also in the same letter to the heretical teachings of Sabellius,[1] which were in his time becoming prominent, and says :

" For concerning the doctrine now agitated in Ptolemais of Pentapolis, — which is impious and marked by great blasphemy against the Almighty God, the Father, and our Lord Jesus Christ, and contains much unbelief respecting his Only Begotten Son and the first-born of every creature, the Word which became man, and a want of perception of the Holy Spirit, — as there came to me communications from both sides and brethren discussing the matter, I wrote certain letters treating the subject as instructively as, by the help of God, I was able.[2] Of these I send[3] thee copies."

CHAPTER VII.

The Abominable Error of the Heretics ; the Divine Vision of Dionysius ; and the Ecclesiastical Canon which he received.

IN the third epistle on baptism which　1 this same Dionysius wrote to Philemon,[1] the Roman presbyter, he relates the following :

" But I examined the works and traditions of the heretics, defiling my mind for a little time with their abominable opinions, but receiving this benefit from them, that I refuted them by myself, and detested them all the more. And when a certain brother among the　2 presbyters restrained me, fearing that I should be carried away with the filth of their wickedness (for it would defile my soul), — in which also, as I perceived, he spoke the truth,

us to rectify all the dates of the bishops of this period (cf. Lipsius, *l.c.*). As to the duration of his episcopate, the ancient authorities differ greatly. The Liberian catalogue assigns to it two years eleven months and six days, but this is impossible, as can be gathered from Cyprian's epistle. Lipsius retains the months and days (twelve or six days), rejecting the two years as an interpolation, and thus putting his accession on Aug. 24 (or 31), 257. According to Eusebius, chap. 27, and the Armenian *Chron.*, he held office eleven years, which is quite impossible, and which, as Lipsius remarks, is due to the eleven months which stood in the original source from which the notice was taken, and which appears in the Liberian catalogue. Jerome's version of the *Chron.* ascribes eight years to his episcopate, but this, too, is quite impossible, and the date given for his accession (the first year of Valerian) is inconsistent with the notice which he gives in regard to Stephen. Xystus upheld the Roman practice of accepting heretics and schismatics without re-baptism, but he seems to have adopted a more conciliatory tone toward those who held the opposite view than his predecessor Stephen had done (cf Pontius' *Vita Cypriani*, chap. 14).
　[6] The first of Dionysius' epistles on baptism was written to Stephen of Rome, as we learn from chap. 2, above. Four others are mentioned by Eusebius, addressed respectively to Philemon, a Roman presbyter (chap. 7, § 1), to Dionysius of Rome (*ibid.* § 6), to Xystus of Rome (chap. 9, § 1), and to Xystus and the church of Rome (*ibid.* § 6).
　[7] ἀπολούσασθαι.
　[8] Dionysius afterward became Xystus' successor as bishop of Rome. See below, chap. 27, note 2.
　[9] Of this Philemon we know only that he was a presbyter of Rome at this time (see below, chap. 7, § 1). A fragment from Dionysius' epistle to him on the subject of baptism is quoted in that chapter.
　[1] Of the life of Sabellius we know very little. He was at the head of the Monarchian (modalistic) party in Rome during the episcopate of Zephyrinus (198–217), and was there perhaps even earlier. He is, and was already in the fourth century, commonly called a native of Africa, but the first one directly to state this is Basil, and the opinion seems to rest upon the fact that his views were especially popular in Pentapolis as early as the middle of the third century, as Dionysius says here. Hippolytus in speaking of him does not mention his birthplace, which causes Stokes to incline

to the opinion that he was a native of Rome. The matter, in fact, cannot be decided. We are told by Hippolytus that Callistus led Sabellius into heresy, but that after he became pope he excommunicated him in order to gain a reputation for orthodoxy. Of the later life of Sabellius we know nothing. His writings are no longer extant, though there are apparently quotations from some of them in Epiphanius, *Hær.* 62, and Athanasius, *Contra Arian. Oratio* 4.
　In the third century those Monarchians (modalists) who were known as Patripassians in the West were called Sabellians in the East. In the fourth and fifth centuries the Fathers used the term Sabellianism in a general sense for various forms of Monarchianism, all of which, however, tended in the one direction, viz. toward the denial of any personal distinction in the Godhead, and hence the identification of Father and Son. And so we characterize every teaching which tends that way as Sabellianistic, although this form of Monarchianism is really much older than Sabellius. See Harnack's article on Monarchianism in Herzog, 2d ed. (abridged translation in Schaff-Herzog), and Stokes' article on Sabellius and Sabellianism in the *Dict. of Christ. Biog.*, both of which give the literature, and Schaff's *Ch. Hist.* II. p. 580 sqq., which gives the sources in full. Neander's account deserves especial notice. Upon Eusebius' attitude toward Sabellianism, see above, p. 13 sq.
　[2] ἐπέστειλά τινα ὡς ἐδυνήθην, παρασχόντος τοῦ θεοῦ, διδασκαλικώτερον ὑφηγούμενος, ὧν τὰ ἀντίγραφα ἐπεμψά σοι. Of these letters no fragments are extant. They are not to be confounded with the four books against Sabellius, addressed to Dionysius of Rome, and mentioned in chap. 26, below. It is possible, as Dittrich suggests, that they included the letters on the same subject to Ammon, Telesphorus, Euphranor, and others which Eusebius mentions in that chapter. Upon Dionysius' attitude toward Sabellianism, see above, Bk. VI. chap. 46, note 1.
　[3] ἐπεμψα. The epistolary aorist as used here does not refer to a past time, but to the time of the writing of the letter, which is past when the person to whom the letter is sent reads the words. The same word (ἐπεμψα) is used in this sense in Acts xxiii. 30, 2 Cor. ix. 3, Eph. vi. 22, Col. iv. 8. Cf. the remarks of Bishop Lightfoot in his Commentary on Galatians, VI. 11.
　[1] Of this Philemon we know no more than we can gather from this chapter. Upon Dionysius' position on the re-baptism of heretics, see above, chap. 2, note 4, and upon his other epistles on that subject, see chap. 5, note 6.

— a vision sent from God came and strengthened me. And the word which came to

3 me commanded me, saying distinctly, 'Read everything which thou canst take in hand,[2] for thou art able to correct and prove all; and this has been to thee from the beginning the cause of thy faith.' I received the vision as agreeing with the apostolic word, which says to them that are stronger, 'Be skillful money-changers.'"[3]

4 Then after saying some things concerning all the heresies he adds: "I received this rule and ordinance from our blessed father,[4] Heraclas.[5] For those who came over from heresies, although they had apostatized from the Church, — or rather had not apostatized, but seemed to meet with them, yet were charged with resorting to some false teacher, — when he had expelled them from the Church he did not receive them back, though they entreated for it, until they had publicly reported all things which they had heard from their adversaries; but then he received them without requiring of them another baptism.[6] For they had formerly received the Holy Spirit from him."

Again, after treating the question thor- 5 oughly, he adds: "I have learned also that this[7] is not a novel practice introduced in Africa alone, but that even long ago in the times of the bishops before us this opinion has been adopted in the most populous churches, and in synods of the brethren in Iconium and Synnada,[8] and by many others. To overturn their counsels and throw them into strife and contention, I cannot endure. For it is said,[9] 'Thou shalt not remove thy neighbor's landmark, which thy fathers have set.'"[10]

His fourth epistle on baptism[11] was writ- 6 ten to Dionysius[12] of Rome, who was then a presbyter, but not long after received the episcopate of that church. It is evident from what is stated of him by Dionysius of Alexandria, that he also was a learned and admirable man. Among other things he writes to him as follows concerning Novatus:

CHAPTER VIII.

The Heterodoxy of Novatus.

"For with good reason do we feel hatred toward Novatian,[1] who has sundered the Church and drawn some of the brethren into impiety and blasphemy, and has introduced impious teaching concerning God, and has calumniated our most compassionate Lord Jesus Christ as unmerciful. And besides all this he rejects the

---

[2] Dionysius, in following this vision, was but showing himself a genuine disciple of his master Origen, and exhibiting the true spirit of the earlier Alexandrian school.

[3] ὡς ἀποστολικῇ φωνῇ συντρέχον . . . γίνεσθε δόκιμοι τραπεζῖται. This saying, sometimes in the brief form given here, sometimes as part of a longer sentence (e.g. in Clement of Alex. *Strom.* I. 28, γίνεσθε δὲ δόκιμοι τραπεζῖται, τὰ μὲν ἀποδοκιμάζοντες, τὸ δὲ καλὸν κατέχοντες), appears very frequently in the writings of the Fathers. In some cases it is cited (in connection with 1 Thess. v. 21, 22) on the authority of Paul (in the present case as an "apostolic word"), in other cases on the authority of "Scripture" (ἡ γραφή, or γέγραπται, or θεῖος λόγος), in still more cases as an utterance of Christ himself. There can be little doubt that Christ really did utter these words, and that the words used by Paul in 1 Thess. v. 21, 22, were likewise spoken by Christ in the same connection. We may, in fact, with considerable confidence recognize in these words part of a genuine extra-canonical saying of Christ, which was widely current in the early Church. We are to explain the words then not as so many have done, as merely based upon the words of Christ, reported in Matt. xxv. 12 sq., or upon the words of Paul already referred to, but as an actual utterance of the Master. Moreover, we may, since Resch's careful discussion of the whole subject of the *Agrapha* (or extra-canonical sayings of Christ), with considerable confidence assume that these words were handed down to post-apostolic times not in an apocryphal gospel, nor by mere oral tradition, but in the original Hebrew Matthew, of which Papias and many others tell us, and which is probably to be looked upon as a pre-canonical gospel, *with* the "Ur-Marcus" the main source of our present gospels of Matthew and Luke, and *through* the "Ur-Marcus" one of the sources of our present Gospel of Mark. Looked upon in this light these words quoted by Dionysius become of great interest to us. They (or a part of the same saying) are quoted more frequently by the Fathers than any other of the *Agrapha* (Resch, on p. 116 sq. gives 69 instances). Their interpretation, in connection with the words of Paul in 1 Thess. v. 21, 22, has been very satisfactorily discussed by Hänsel in the *Studien und Kritiken*, 1836, p. 170 sq. They undoubtedly mean that we are to test and to distinguish between the true and the false, the good and the bad, as a skillful money-changer distinguishes good and bad coins. For a full discussion of this utterance, and for an exhibition of the many other patristic passages in which it occurs, see the magnificent work of Alfred Resch, *Agrapha: Aussercanonische Evangelienfragmente*, in Gebhardt and Harnack's *Texte und Untersuchungen*, Bd. V. Heft 4, Leipzig, 1889; the most complete and satisfactory discussion of the whole subject of the Agrapha which we have.

[4] πάπα. According to Suicer (*Thesaurus*) all bishops in the Occident as late as the fifth century were called *Papæ* as a mark of honor, and though the term by that time had begun to be used in a distinctive sense of the bishop of Rome, the older usage continued in parts of the West outside of Italy, until Gregory VII. (A.D. 1075) forbade the use of the name for any other than the pope. In the East the word was used for a long time as the especial title of the bishops of Alexandria and of Rome (see Suicer's *Thesaurus* and Gieseler's *Church Hist.* Harper's edition, I. p. 499).

[5] On Heraclas, see Bk. VI. chap. 3, note 2.

[6] Compare Cyprian's epistle to Quintus concerning the baptism of heretics (*Ep.* 70, *al.* 71). Cyprian there takes the position stated here, that those who have been baptized in the Church and have afterward gone over to heresy and then returned again to the Church are not to be re-baptized, but to be received with the laying on of hands only. This of course does not at all invalidate the position of Cyprian and the others who re-baptized heretics, for they baptized heretics not because they had been heretics, but because they had not received true baptism, nor indeed any baptism at all, which it was impossible, in their view, for a heretic to give. They therefore repudiated (as Cyprian does in the epistle referred to) the term re-baptism, denying that they *re*-baptized anybody.

[7] Namely the re-baptism (or, as they would say, the *baptism*) of those who had received baptism only at the hands of heretics standing without the communion of the Church.

[8] Iconium was the principal city of Lycaonia, and Synnada a city of Phrygia. The synod of Iconium referred to here is mentioned also by Firmilian in his epistle to Cyprian, §§ 7 and 19 (*Cypriani Ep.* 74, *al.* 75). From that epistle we learn that the synod was attended by bishops from Phrygia, Cilicia, Galatia, and other countries, and that heretical baptism was entirely rejected by it. Moreover, we learn that Firmilian himself was present at the synod, and that it was held a considerable time before the writing of his epistle. This leads us to place the synod between 230 (on Firmilian's dates, see above, Bk. VI. chap. 26, note 3) and 240 or 250. Since it took place a considerable time before Firmilian wrote, it can hardly have been held much later than 240. Of the synod of Synnada, we know nothing. It very likely took place about the same time. See Hefele's *Conciliengesch.* I. p. 107 sq. Dionysius was undoubtedly correct in appealing to ancient custom for the practice which he supported (see above, chap. 2, note 3).

[9] φησί, i.e. "The Scripture saith."

[10] Deut. xix. 14.

[11] On Dionysius' other epistles on baptism, see above, chap. 5, note 6.

[12] On Dionysius of Rome, see below, chap. 27, note 2.

[1] The majority of the MSS. have Νοουατιανῷ, a few Ναυατιανῷ. This is the only place in which the name Novatian occurs in Eusebius' *History*, and here it is used not by Eusebius himself but by Dionysius. Eusebius, in referring to the same man, always calls him Novatus (see above, Bk. VI. chap. 43, note 1). Upon Novatian and his schism, see the same note.

holy baptism,[2] and overturns the faith and confession which precede it,[3] and entirely banishes from them the Holy Ghost, if indeed there was any hope that he would remain or return to them."[4]

CHAPTER IX.

The Ungodly Baptism of the Heretics.

1   His fifth epistle[1] was written to Xystus,[2] bishop of Rome. In this, after saying

---

[2] λουτρόν. That Novatian re-baptized all those who came over to him from the Church is stated by Cyprian in his epistle to Jubaianus, § 2 (No. 72, al. 73). His principle was similar to that which later actuated the Donatists, namely, that baptism is valid only when performed by priests of true and approved Christian character. Denying, then, that those who defiled themselves and did despite to God's holy Church by communing with the lapsed were true Christians, he could not do otherwise than reject their baptism as quite invalid.

[3] It was the custom from a very early period to cause the candidate for baptism to go through a certain course of training of greater or less length, and to require him to assent to a formulated statement of belief before the administration of the sacred rite. Thus we learn from the *Didache* that even as early as the very beginning of the second century the custom of pre-baptismal training was already in vogue, and we know that by the third century the system of catechetical instruction was a highly developed thing, extending commonly over two to three years. Candidates for baptism were then known as catechumens. So far as a baptismal creed or confession of faith is concerned, Caspari (see his great work, *Studien zur Gesch. des Taufsymbols*) has shown that such a creed was in use in the Roman church before the middle of the second century, and that it formed the basis of what we know as the Apostles' Creed, which in the form in which we have it is a later development. Inasmuch as Novatian, so far as we can learn, was perfectly orthodox on matters of faith, he would not have cared to make any alteration in such a creed as the present Apostles' Creed. Exactly what Dionysius means in the present case is not certain. It is possible that he is simply speaking in general terms, assuming that if Novatian does not accept the Church baptism, he must overturn and pervert with it the instruction which had preceded; or it may be that he is thinking of that form of confession to which the candidate was required to give his assent, according to Cyprian, *Ep.* 69 (al. 70): *credis in vitam æternam et remissionem peccatorum per sanctam ecclesiam?* "Dost thou believe in eternal life and remission of sins through the holy Church?" The latter is the view of Valesius, who is followed by all others that have discussed the passage so far as I am aware. Of course Novatian could not put the last clause of this question to his converts, and hence Dionysius may have been thinking of this omission in using the words he does. At the same time I confess myself unable to agree with others in interpreting him thus. In the first place, it is, to say the least, very doubtful whether the question quoted above from Cyprian formed an article in the baptismal confession of the Church in general. It does not appear in the Apostles' Creed, and can therefore hardly have formed a part of the earlier Roman formula which underlay that. And so far as I am aware there are no traces of the use of such an article in the church of Alexandria. In the second place, Dionysius' language seems to me too general to admit of such a particular application. Had he been thinking of one especial article of the confession, as omitted or altered by Novatian, he would, in my opinion, have given some indication of it. I am, therefore, inclined to take his words in the most general sense, suggested as possible just above.

[4] These last clauses are, according to Valesius, fraught with difficulty. He interprets the αὐτῶν ("entirely banished from *them*") as referring to the *lapsi*, and interpreted thus I find the passage not simply difficult, as he does, but incomprehensible. But I confess myself again unable to accept his interpretation. To me the αὐτῶν seems not to refer to the *lapsi*, to whom there has been no direct reference in this fragment quoted by Eusebius, but rather to Novatian's baptism, to whom reference is made in the previous sentence, and who are evidently in the mind of the writer in referring to Novatian's baptism in the first clause of the present sentence. It seems to me that Dionysius means simply to say that in rejecting the baptism of the Church, and the "faith and confession which precede it," Novatian necessarily drove away from his converts the Holy Spirit, who works in and through right confession and true baptism. The meaning of the words "if, indeed, there was any hope," &c., thus becomes very clear; Dionysius does not believe, of course, that the Holy Spirit would remain with those who should leave the Church to go with Novatian, but even if he should remain, he would be driven entirely away from them when they blasphemed him and denied his work, by rejecting the true baptism and submitting to another baptism without the Church.

[1] i.e. his fifth epistle on the subject of baptism (see above, chap.

---

much against the heretics, he relates a certain occurrence of his time as follows:

"For truly, brother, I am in need of counsel, and I ask thy judgment concerning a certain matter which has come to me, fearing that I may be in error. For one of the breth- **2** ren that assemble, who has long been considered a believer, and who, before my ordination, and, I think before the appointment of the blessed Heraclas,[3] was a member of the congregation, was present with those who were recently baptized. And when he heard the questions and answers,[4] he came to me weeping, and bewailing himself; and falling at my feet he acknowledged and protested that the baptism with which he had been baptized among the heretics was not of this character, nor in any respect like this, because it was full of impiety and blasphemy.[5] And he said that **3** his soul was now pierced with sorrow, and that he had not confidence to lift his eyes to God, because he had set out from those impious words and deeds. And on this account he besought that he might receive this most perfect purification, and reception and grace. But I did not dare to do this; and said **4** that his long communion was sufficient for this. For I should not dare to renew from the beginning one who had heard the giving of thanks and joined in repeating the Amen; who had stood by the table and had stretched forth his hands to receive the blessed food; and who had received it, and partaken for a long while of the body and blood of our Lord Jesus Christ. But I exhorted him to be of good courage, and to approach the partaking of the saints with firm faith and good hope. But he does not **5** cease lamenting, and he shudders to approach the table, and scarcely, though entreated, does he dare to be present at the prayers."[6]

5, note 6). The sixth, likewise addressed to Xystus, is mentioned below in § 6.

[2] On Xystus II. of Rome, see chap 5, note 5.

[3] On Heraclas, see above, Bk. VI. chap. 3, note 2.

[4] See the previous chapter, note 3.

[5] The reference here, of course, is not to the Novatians, because this old man, who had been a regular attendant upon the orthodox Church since the time of Heraclas, if not before, had been baptized by the heretics long before Novatian arose. The epistle seems to contain no reference to Novatian; at least, the fragment which we have is dealing with an entirely different subject.

[6] Dittrich finds in this epistle an evidence that Dionysius was not fully convinced of the advisability of re-baptizing converts from heretical bodies, that he wavered in fact between the Eastern and the Roman practices, but I am unable to see that the epistle implies anything of the kind. It is not that he doubts the necessity of re-baptism in ordinary cases, — he is not discussing that subject at all, — the question is, does long communion itself take the place of baptism; does not a man, unwittingly baptized, gain through such communion the grace from the Spirit which is ordinarily conveyed in baptism, and might not the rite of baptism at so late a date be an insult to the Spirit, who might have been working through the sacrament of the eucharist during all these years? It is this question which Dionysius desires to have Xystus assist him in answering — a question which has nothing to do, in Dionysius' mind, with the validity or non-validity of heretical baptism, for it will be noticed that he does not base his refusal to baptize the man upon the fact that he has already been baptized, partially, or imperfectly, or in any other way, but solely upon the fact that he has for so long been partaking of the eucharist.

6   Besides these there is also extant another epistle of the same man on baptism, addressed by him and his parish to Xystus and the church at Rome. In this he considers the question then agitated with extended argument. And there is extant yet another after these, addressed to Dionysius of Rome,[7] concerning Lucian.[8] So much with reference to these.

CHAPTER X.

Valerian and the Persecution under him.

1   GALLUS and the other rulers,[1] having held the government less than two years, were overthrown, and Valerian, with his son Gallienus, received the empire. The circum-
2   stances which Dionysius relates of him we may learn from his epistle to Hermammon,[2] in which he gives the following account:

"And in like manner it is revealed to John; 'For there was given to him,' he says, 'a mouth speaking great things and blasphemy; and there was given unto him authority and forty and
3   two months.'[3] It is wonderful that both of these things occurred under Valerian; and it is the more remarkable in this case when we consider his previous conduct, for he had been mild and friendly toward the men of God, for none of the emperors before him had treated them so kindly and favorably; and not even those who were said openly to be Christians[4] received them with such manifest hospitality and friendliness as he did at the beginning of his reign. For his entire house was filled with
4   pious persons and was a church of God. But the teacher and ruler of the synagogue of the Magi from Egypt[5] persuaded him to

change his course, urging him to slay and persecute pure and holy men[6] because they opposed and hindered the corrupt and abominable incantations. For there are and there were men who, being present and being seen, though they only breathed and spoke, were able to scatter the counsels of the sinful demons. And he induced him to practice initiations and abominable sorceries and to offer unacceptable sacrifices; to slay innumerable children and to sacrifice the offspring of unhappy fathers; to divide the bowels of new-born babes and to mutilate and cut to pieces the creatures of God, as if by such practices they could attain happiness."

He adds to this the following: "Splendid   5
indeed were the thank-offerings which Macrianus brought them[7] for the empire which was the object of his hopes. He is said to have been formerly the emperor's general finance minister[8]; yet he did nothing praiseworthy or of general benefit,[9] but fell under the pro-

---

[7] On Dionysius of Rome, see chap. 27, note 2.

[8] So many Lucians of this time are known to us that we cannot speak with certainty as to the identity of the one referred to here. But it may perhaps be suggested that the well-known Carthaginian Confessor is meant, who caused Cyprian so much trouble by granting letters of pardon indiscriminately to the lapsed, in defiance of regular custom and of Cyprian's authority (see *Cypriani Ep.* 16, 17, 20, 21, 22; *al.* 23, 26, 21, 22, 27). If this be the Lucian referred to, the epistle must have discussed the *lapsi*, and the conditions upon which they were to be received again into the Church. That the epistle did not, like the one mentioned just before, have to do with the subject of baptism, seems clear from the fact that it is not numbered among the epistles on that subject, as six others are.

[1] οἱ ἀμφὶ τὸν Γάλλον. Eusebius is undoubtedly referring to Gallus, Volusian, his son and co-regent, and Æmilian, his enemy and successor. Gallus himself, with his son Volusian, whom he made Cæsar and co-regent, reigned from the latter part of the year 251 to about the middle of the year 253, when the empire was usurped by Æmilian, and he and his son were slain. Æmilian was recognized by the senate as the legal emperor, but within four months Valerian, Gallus' leading general,—who had already been proclaimed emperor by his legions,—revenged the murder of Gallus and came to the throne. Valerian reigned until 260, when his son Gallienus, who had been associated with him in the government from the beginning, succeeded him and reigned until 268.

[2] Upon this epistle, see above, chap. 1, note 3.

[3] Rev. xiii. 5.

[4] Philip was the only emperor before this time that was openly said to have been a Christian (see above, Bk. VI. chap. 34, note 2). Alexander Severus was very favorable to the Christians, and Eusebius may have been thinking of him also in this connection.

[5] viz. Macrianus, one of the ablest of Valerian's generals, who had acquired great influence over him and had been raised by him

to the highest position in the army and made his chief counselor. Dionysius is the only one to tell us that he was the chief of the Egyptian magicians. Gibbon doubts the statement, but Macrianus may well have been an Egyptian by birth and devoted, as so many of the Egyptians were, to arts of magic, and have gained power over Valerian in this way which he could have gained in no other. It is not necessary of course to understand Dionysius' words as implying that Macrianus was officially at the head of the body of Egyptian magicians, but simply that he was the greatest, or one of the greatest, of them. He figures in our other sources simply as a military and political character, but it was natural for Dionysius to emphasize his addiction to magic, though he could hardly have done it had Macrianus' practices in this respect not been commonly known.

[6] The persecution which the Christians suffered under Valerian was more terrible than any other except that of Diocletian. Numerous calamities took place during his reign. The barbarians were constantly invading and ravaging the borders of the empire, and on the east the Persians did great damage. Still worse was the terrible plague which had begun in the reign of Decius and raged for about fifteen years. All these calamities aroused the religious fears of the emperor. Dionysius tells us that he was induced by Macrianus to have recourse to human sacrifices and other similar means of penetrating the events of the future, and when these rites failed, the presence of Christians — irreligious men hated by the gods — in the imperial family was urged as the reason for the failure, and thus the hostility of the emperor was aroused against all Christians. As a consequence an edict was published in 257 requiring all persons to conform at least outwardly to the religion of Rome on the penalty of exile. And at the same time the Christians were prohibited from holding religious services, upon pain of death. In 258 followed a rescript of terrible severity. Only the clergy and the higher ranks of the laity were attacked, but they were sentenced to death if they refused to repent, and the clergy, apparently, whether they repented or not. The persecution continued until Valerian's captivity, which took place probably late in 260. The dates during this period are very uncertain, but Dionysius' statement that the persecution continued forty-two months is probably not far out of the way; from late in the year 257 to the year 261, when it was brought to an end by Gallienus. In Egypt and the Orient the persecution seems to have continued a few months longer than elsewhere (see chap. 13, note 3). The martyrs were very numerous during the Valerian persecution, especially in Rome and Africa. The most noted were Cyprian and Xystus II. On the details of the persecution, see Tillemont, *H. E.* IV. p. 1 sq.

[7] i.e. the evil spirits. As Valesius remarks, the meaning is that since the evil spirits had promised him power, he showed his gratitude to them by inducing the Emperor Valerian to persecute the Christians.

[8] ἐπὶ τῶν καθόλου λόγων. The phrase is equivalent to the Latin *Rationalis* or *Procurator summæ rei*, an official who had charge of the imperial finances, and who might be called either treasurer or finance minister. The position which Macrianus held seems to have been the highest civil position in the empire (cf. Valesius' note *ad locum*). Gibbon calls him Prætorian Prefect, and since he was the most famous of Valerian's generals, he doubtless held that position also, though I am not aware that any of our sources state that he did.

[9] The Greek contains a play upon the words καθόλου and λόγος in this sentence. It reads ὃς πρότερον μὲν ἐπὶ τῶν καθόλου λόγων λεγόμενος εἶναι βασιλέως, οὐδὲν εὔλογον οὐδὲ καθολικὸν ἐφρόνησεν. The play upon the word καθόλου continues in the next sentence,

6   phetic saying, 'Woe unto those who prophesy from their own heart and do not consider the general good.'[10] For he did not perceive the general Providence, nor did he look for the judgment of Him who is before all, and through all, and over all. Wherefore he became an enemy of his Catholic[11] Church, and alienated and estranged himself from the compassion of God, and fled as far as possible from his salvation. In this he showed the truth of his own name."[12]

7   And again, farther on he says : " For Valerian, being instigated to such acts by this man, was given over to insults and reproaches, according to what was said by Isaiah : 'They have chosen their own ways and their abominations in which their soul delighted ; I also will choose their delusions and will render unto

8   them their sins.'[13] But this man[14] madly desired the kingdom though unworthy of it, and being unable to put the royal garment on his crippled body, set forward his two sons to bear their father's sins.[15] For concerning them the declaration which God spoke was plain, 'Visiting the iniquities of the fathers upon the children unto the third and fourth genera-

9   tion of them that hate me.'[16] For heaping on the heads of his sons his own evil desires, in which he had met with success,[17] he wiped off upon them his own wickedness and hatred toward God."

Dionysius relates these things concerning Valerian.

---

where the Greek runs τὸ καθόλου μὴ βλέπουσιν, and in the following, where it reads οὐ γὰρ συνῆκε τὴν καθόλου πρόνοιαν. Again in the next sentence the adjective καθολική occurs: "his *universal* Church."   [10] Ezek. xiii. 3.
[11] καθολικῆς, "catholic" in the sense of "general" or "universal," the play upon the word still continuing.
[12] Μακριανός. The Greek word μακράν means "far," "at a distance."
[13] Isa. lxvi. 3, 4.   [14] i.e. Macrianus.
[15] Valerian reposed complete confidence in Macrianus and followed his advice in the conduct of the wars against the Persians. The result was that by Macrianus' "weak or wicked counsels the imperial army was betrayed into a situation where valor and military skill were equally unavailing." (Gibbon.) Dionysius, in chap. 23, below, directly states that Macrianus betrayed Valerian, and this is the view of the case commonly taken. Valerian fell into the hands of the Persians (late in 260 A.D.), and Macrianus was proclaimed emperor by his troops, and on account of his lameness (as both Dionysius and Zonaras put it) or his age, associated with him his two sons, Quietus and Macrianus. After some months he left his son Quietus in charge of Syria, and designing to make himself master of the Occident, marched with his son Macrianus against Gallienus, but was met in Illyrium by the Pretender Aureolus (262) and defeated, and both himself and son slain. His son Quietus meanwhile was besieged in Edessa by the Pretender Odenathus and slain. Cf. Tillemont's *Histoire des Empereurs*, III. p. 333 sq. and p. 340 sq.   [16] Ex. xx. 5.
[17] ηὐτύχει. Three MSS., followed by Stephanus, Valesius, Burton, Stroth (and by the translators Closs, Crusè, and Salmond in the *Ante-Nicene Fathers*, VI. p. 107), read ἠτύχει, "failed" ("in whose gratification he failed"). ηὐτύχει, however, is supported by overwhelming MS. authority, and is adopted by Schwegler and Heinichen, and approved by Valesius in his notes. It seems at first sight the harder reading, and is, therefore, in itself to be preferred to the easier reading, ἠτύχει. Although it seems harder, it is really fully in accord with what has preceded. Macrianus had not made himself emperor (if Dionysius is to be believed), but he had succeeded fully in his desires, in that he had raised his sons to the purple. If he had acquired such power as to be able to do that, he must have given them the position, because he preferred to govern in that way; and if that be so, he could hardly be said to have failed in his desires.

CHAPTER XI.

The Events which happened at this Time to Dionysius and those in Egypt.

BUT as regards the persecution which   1
prevailed so fiercely in his reign, and the sufferings which Dionysius with others endured on account of piety toward the God of the universe, his own words shall show, which he wrote in answer to Germanus,[1] a contemporary bishop who was endeavoring to slander him. His statement is as follows :

"Truly I am in danger of falling into   2
great folly and stupidity through being forced to relate the wonderful providence of God toward us. But since it is said[2] that 'it is good to keep close the secret of a king, but it is honorable to reveal the works of God,'[3] I will join issue with the violence of Germanus. I went not alone to Æmilianus;[4] but my   3
fellow-presbyter, Maximus,[5] and the deacons Faustus,[6] Eusebius,[7] and Chæremon,[8] and a brother who was present from Rome, went with me. But Æmilianus did not at   4
first say to me : 'Hold no assemblies;'[9] for this was superfluous to him, and the last thing to one who was seeking to accomplish the first. For he was not concerned about our assembling, but that we ourselves should not be Christians. And he commanded me to give this up; supposing if I turned from it, the others also would follow me. But I an-   5
swered him, neither unsuitably nor in many

---

[1] On Germanus, and Dionysius' epistle to him, see above, Bk. VI. chap. 40, note 2.
[2] Literally "it says" (φησί), a common formula in quoting from Scripture.
[3] Tob. xii. 7.
[4] This Æmilianus, prefect of Egypt, under whom the persecution was carried on in Alexandria during Valerian's reign, later, during the reign of Gallienus, was induced (or compelled) by the troops of Alexandria to revolt against Gallienus, and assume the purple himself. He was defeated, however, by Theodotus, Gallienus' general, and was put to death in prison, in what year we do not know. Cf. Tillemont's *Hist. des Emp.* III. p. 342 sq.
[5] Maximus is mentioned a number of times in this chapter in connection with the persecution. After the death of Dionysius he succeeded him as bishop of Alexandria, and as such is referred to below, in chaps. 28, 30, and 32. For the dates of his episcopate, see chap. 28, note 10.
[6] On Faustus, see above, Bk. VI. chap. 40, note 10.
[7] In regard to this deacon Eusebius, who later became bishop of Laodicea, see chap. 32, note 12.
[8] Chæremon is mentioned three times in the present chapter, but we have no other reliable information in regard to him.
[9] We may gather from § 11, below, that Germanus had accused Dionysius of neglecting to hold the customary assemblies, and of seeking safety by flight. Valesius, in his report *ad locum*, remarks, "Dionysius was accused by Germanus of neglecting to hold the assemblies of the brethren before the beginning of the persecution, and of providing for his own safety by flight. For as often as persecution arose the bishops were accustomed first to convene the people, that they might exhort them to hold fast to their faith in Christ. Then they baptized infants and catechumens, that they might not depart this life without baptism, and they gave the eucharist to the faithful, because they did not know how long the persecution might last." Valesius refers for confirmation of his statements to an epistle sent to Pope Hormisdas, by Germanus and others, in regard to Dorotheus, bishop of Thessalonica (circa A.D. 519). I have not been able to verify the reference. The custom mentioned by Valesius is certainly a most natural one, and therefore Valesius' statements are very likely quite true, though there seems to be little direct testimony upon which to rest them.

words : 'We must obey God rather than men.'[10] And I testified openly that I worshiped the one only God, and no other ; and that I would not turn from this nor would I ever cease to be a Christian. Thereupon he commanded us to go to a village near the desert, called Cephro.[11]

6　But listen to the very words which were spoken on both sides, as they were recorded :

"Dionysius, Faustus, Maximus, Marcellus,[12] and Chæremon being arraigned, Æmilianus the prefect said : 'I have reasoned verbally with you concerning the clemency which our rulers

7　have shown to you ; for they have given you the opportunity to save yourselves, if you will turn to that which is according to nature, and worship the gods that preserve their empire, and forget those that are contrary to nature.[13] What then do you say to this? For I do not think that you will be ungrateful for their kindness, since they would turn you to

8　a better course.' Dionysius replied : ' Not all people worship all gods ; but each one those whom he approves. We therefore reverence and worship the one God, the Maker of all ; who hath given the empire to the divinely favored and august Valerian and Gallienus ; and we pray to him continually for their em-

9　pire, that it may remain unshaken.' Æmilianus, the prefect, said to them : ' But who forbids you to worship him, if he is a god, together with those who are gods by nature. For ye have been commanded to reverence the gods, and the gods whom all know.' Dionysius

10　answered : 'We worship no other.' Æmilianus, the prefect, said to them : ' I see that you are at once ungrateful, and insensible to the kindness of our sovereigns. Wherefore ye shall not remain in this city. But ye shall be sent into the regions of Libya, to a place called Cephro. For I have chosen this place at the command of our sovereigns, and it shall by no means be permitted you or any others, either to hold assemblies, or to enter into the so-

11　called cemeteries.[14] But if any one shall be seen without the place which I have commanded, or be found in any assembly, he will bring peril on himself. For suitable punishment shall not fail. Go, therefore where ye have been ordered.'

"And he hastened me away, though I was sick, not granting even a day's respite. What opportunity then did I have, either to hold assemblies, or not to hold them? "[15]

Farther on he says : "But through the 12 help of the Lord we did not give up the open assembly. But I called together the more diligently those who were in the city, as if I were with them ; being, so to speak,[16] 'absent in body but present in spirit.'[17] But in Cephro a large church gathered with us of the brethren that followed us from the city, and those that joined us from Egypt ; and there 'God opened unto us a door for the Word.'[18] At 13 first we were persecuted and stoned ; but afterwards not a few of the heathen forsook the idols and turned to God. For until this time they had not heard the Word, since it was then first sown by us. And as if God had 14 brought us to them for this purpose, when we had performed this ministry he transferred us to another place. For Æmilianus, as it appeared, desired to transport us to rougher and more Libyan-like places ;[19] so he commanded them to assemble from all quarters in Mareotis,[20] and assigned to them different villages throughout the country. But he ordered us to be placed nearer the highway that we might be seized first.[21] For evidently he arranged and prepared matters so that whenever he wished to seize us he could take all of us without difficulty. When 15 I was first ordered to go to Cephro I did not know where the place was, and had scarcely ever heard the name ; yet I went readily and cheerfully. But when I was told that I was to remove to the district of Colluthion,[22] those

hence Æmilian speaks of them as the " so-called (καλούμενα) cemeteries."　[15] See above, note 9.

[16] ὡς εἰπεῖν, a reading approved by Valesius in his notes, and adopted by Schwegler and Heinichen. This and the readings ὡς εἶπεν, "as he said" (adopted by Stroth, Zimmermann, and Laemmer), and ὡς εἶπον, "as I said" (adopted by Stephanus, Valesius in his text, and Burton), are about equally supported by MS. authority, while some MSS. read ὡς εἶπεν ὁ ἀπόστολος, "as the apostle said." It is impossible to decide with any degree of assurance between the first three readings.

[17] 1 Cor. v. 3.　[18] Col. iv. 3.

[19] Λιβυκωτέρους τόπους. Libya was an indefinite term among the ancients for that part of Africa which included the Great Desert and all the unexplored country lying west and south of it. Almost nothing was known about the country, and the desert and the regions beyond were peopled by the fancy with all sorts of terrible monsters, and were looked upon as the theater of the most dire forces, natural and supernatural. As a consequence, the term " Libyan" became a synonym for all that was most disagreeable and dreadful in nature.

[20] Mareotis, or Mareia, or Maria, was one of the land districts into which Egypt was divided. A lake, a town situated on the shore of the lake, and the district in which they lay, all bore the same name. The district Mareotis lay just south of Alexandria, but did not include it, for Alexandria and Ptolemais formed an independent sphere of administration sharply separated from the thirty-six land districts of the country. Cf. Bk. II. chap. 17, notes 10 and 12, above. Mommsen (Roman Provinces, Scribner's ed. Vol. II. p. 255) remarks that these land districts, like the cities, became the basis of episcopal dioceses. This we should expect to be the case, but I am not aware that we can prove it to have been regularly so, at any rate not during the earlier centuries. Cf. Wiltsch's Geography and Statistics of the Church, London ed., I. p. 192 sq.

[21] ἡμᾶς δὲ μᾶλλον ἐν ὁδῷ καὶ πρώτους καταληφθησομένους ἔταξεν.

[22] τὰ Κολλουθίωνος (sc. μέρη), i.e. the parts or regions of Colluthion. Of Colluthion, so far as I am aware, nothing is known. It

[10] Acts v. 29.

[11] We learn from § 10, below, that Cephro was in Libya. Beyond this nothing is known of the place so far as I am aware.

[12] This Marcellus, the only one not mentioned in § 3, above, is an otherwise unknown person.

[13] τῶν παρὰ φύσιν. That the τῶν refers to "gods" (viz. the gods of the Christians, Æmilianus thinking of them as plural) seems clear, both on account of the θεοὺς just preceding, and also in view of the fact that in § 9 we have the phrase τῶν κατὰ φύσιν θεῶν. A contrast, therefore, is drawn in the present case between the gods of the heathen and those of the Christians.

[14] κοιμητήρια; literally, " sleeping-places." The word was used only in this sense in classic Greek; but the Christians, looking upon death only as a sleep, early applied the name to their burial places;

who were present know how I was affected.
16 For here I will accuse myself. At first I was grieved and greatly disturbed; for though these places were better known and more familiar to us, yet the country was said to be destitute of brethren and of men of character, and to be exposed to the annoyances of travelers and
17 incursions of robbers. But I was comforted when the brethren reminded me that it was nearer the city, and that while Cephro afforded us much intercourse with the brethren from Egypt, so that we were able to extend the Church more widely, as this place was nearer the city we should enjoy more frequently the sight of those who were truly beloved and most closely related and dearest to us. For they would come and remain, and special meetings[23] could be held, as in the more remote suburbs. And thus it turned out."

After other matters he writes again as follows of the things which happened to him:
18 "Germanus indeed boasts of many confessions. He can speak forsooth of many adversities which he himself has endured. But is he able to reckon up as many as we can, of sentences, confiscations, proscriptions, plundering of goods, loss of dignities, contempt of worldly glory, disregard for the flatteries of governors and of councilors, and patient endurance of the threats of opponents, of outcries, of perils and persecutions, and wandering and distress, and all kinds of tribulation, such as came upon me under Decius and Sabinus,[24] and such as continue even now under Æmilianus? But where has Germanus been seen? And what
19 account is there of him? But I turn from this great folly into which I am falling on account of Germanus. And for the same reason I desist from giving to the brethren who know it an account of everything which took place."
20 The same writer also in the epistle to Domitius and Didymus[25] mentions some

particulars of the persecution as follows: "As our people are many and unknown to you, it would be superfluous to give their names; but understand that men and women, young and old, maidens and matrons, soldiers and civilians, of every race and age, some by scourging and fire, others by the sword, have conquered in the strife and received their crowns. But
21 in the case of some a very long time was not sufficient to make them appear acceptable to the Lord; as, indeed, it seems also in my own case, that sufficient time has not yet elapsed. Wherefore he has retained me for the time which he knows to be fitting, saying, 'In an acceptable time have I heard thee, and in a day of salvation have I helped thee.'[26] For as you
22 have inquired of our affairs and desire us to tell you how we are situated, you have heard fully that when we — that is, myself and Gaius and Faustus and Peter and Paul[27] — were led away as prisoners by a centurion and magistrates, with their soldiers and servants, certain persons from Mareotis came and dragged us away by force, as we were unwilling to follow them.[28] But
23 now I and Gaius and Peter are alone, deprived of the other brethren, and shut up in a desert and dry place in Libya, three days' journey from Paraetonium."[29]

He says farther on: "The presbyters,
24 Maximus,[30] Dioscorus,[31] Demetrius, and Lucius[32] concealed themselves in the city, and visited the brethren secretly; for Faustinus and Aquila,[33] who are more prominent in the world, are wandering in Egypt. But the deacons, Faustus, Eusebius, and Chæremon,[34] have survived those who died in the pestilence. Eusebius is one whom God has strengthened and endowed from the first to fulfill energetically the ministrations for the imprisoned confessors, and to attend to the dangerous task of preparing for burial the bodies of the perfected and blessed martyrs. For as I have said be- 25

seems to have been a town, possibly a section of country in the district of Mareotis. Nicephorus spells the word with a single *l*, which Valesius contends is more correct because the word is derived from Colutho, which was not an uncommon name in Egypt (see Valesius' note *ad locum*).
23 κατὰ μέρος συναγωγαί, literally, "partial meetings." It is plain enough from this that persons living in the suburbs were allowed to hold special services in their homes or elsewhere, and were not compelled always to attend the city church, which might be a number of miles distant. It seems to me doubtful whether this passage is sufficient to warrant Valesius' conclusion, that in the time of Dionysius there was but one church in Alexandria, where the brethren met for worship. It may have been so, but the words do not appear to indicate, as Valesius thinks they do, that matters were in a different state then from that which existed in the time of Athanasius, who, in his *Apology to Constantius*, § 14 sq., expressly speaks of a number of church buildings in Alexandria.
24 Sabinus has been already mentioned in Bk. VI. chap. 40, § 2, from which passage we may gather that he held the same position under Decius which Æmilianus held under Valerian (see note 3 on the chapter referred to).
25 We learn from chap. 20, below, that this epistle to Domitius and Didymus was one of Dionysius' regular festal epistles (for there is no ground for assuming that a different epistle is referred to in that chapter). Domitius and Didymus are otherwise unknown personages. Eusebius evidently (as we can see both from this chapter and from chapter 20) supposes this epistle to refer to the persecution,

of which Dionysius has been speaking in that portion of his epistle to Germanus quoted in this chapter; namely, to the persecution of Valerian. But he is clearly mistaken in this supposition; for, as we can see from a comparison of § 22, below, with Bk. VI. chap. 40, § 6 sq., Dionysius is referring in this epistle to the same persecution to which he referred in that chapter; namely, to the persecution of Decius. But the present epistle was written (as we learn from § 23) while this same persecution was still going on, and, therefore, some years before the time of Valerian's persecution, and before the writing of the epistle to Germanus (see Bk. VI. chap. 40, note 2), with which Eusebius here associates it. Cf. Valesius' note *ad locum* and Dittrich's *Dionysius der Grosse*, p. 40 sq.
26 Isa. xlix. 8.
27 See above, Bk. VI. chap. 40, note 10.
28 See *ibid.* § 6 sq.
29 Paraetonium was an important town and harbor on the Mediterranean, about 150 miles west of Alexandria. A day's journey among the ancients commonly denoted about 180 to 200 stadia (22 to 25 miles), so that Dionysius' retreat must have lain some 60 to 70 miles from Paraetonium, probably to the south of it.
30 On Maximus, see above, note 5.
31 Of Dioscorus we know only what is told us here. He is not to be identified with the lad mentioned in Bk. VI. chap. 41, § 19 (see note 17 on that chapter).
32 Of Demetrius and Lucius we know only what is recorded here.
33 Faustinus and Aquila are known to us only from this passage.
34 On these three deacons, see above, notes 6–8.

fore, unto the present time the governor continues to put to death in a cruel manner those who are brought to trial. And he destroys some with tortures, and wastes others away with imprisonment and bonds; and he suffers no one to go near them, and investigates whether any one does so. Nevertheless God gives relief to the afflicted through the zeal and persistence of the brethren."

26 Thus far Dionysius. But it should be known that Eusebius, whom he calls a deacon, shortly afterward became bishop of the church of Laodicea in Syria;[35] and Maximus, of whom he speaks as being then a presbyter, succeeded Dionysius himself as bishop of Alexandria.[36] But the Faustus who was with him, and who at that time was distinguished for his confession, was preserved until the persecution in our day,[37] when being very old and full of days, he closed his life by martyrdom, being beheaded. But such are the things which happened at that time [38] to Dionysius.

CHAPTER XII.

The Martyrs in Cæsarea in Palestine.

DURING the above-mentioned persecution under Valerian, three men in Cæsarea in Palestine, being conspicuous in their confession of Christ, were adorned with divine martyrdom, becoming food for wild beasts. One of them was called Priscus, another Malchus, and the name of the third was Alexander.[1] They say that these men, who lived in the country, acted at first in a cowardly manner, as if they were careless and thoughtless. For when the opportunity was given to those who longed for the prize with heavenly desire, they treated it lightly, lest they should seize the crown of martyrdom prematurely. But having deliberated on the matter, they hastened to Cæsarea, and went before the judge and met the end we have mentioned. They relate that besides these, in the same persecution and the same city, a certain woman endured a similar conflict. But it is reported that she belonged to the sect of Marcion.[2]

CHAPTER XIII.

The Peace under Gallienus.

SHORTLY after this Valerian was reduced 1 to slavery by the barbarians,[1] and his son having become sole ruler, conducted the government more prudently. He immediately restrained the persecution against us by public proclamations,[2] and directed the bishops to perform in freedom their customary duties, in a rescript [3] which ran as follows:

"The Emperor Cæsar Publius Licinius 2 Gallienus, Pius, Felix, Augustus,[4] to Dionysius, Pinnas, Demetrius,[5] and the other bishops. I have ordered the bounty of my gift to be declared through all the world, that they may depart from the places of religious worship.[6] And for this purpose you may use this copy of my rescript, that no one may molest you. And this which you are now enabled lawfully to do, has already for a long time been conceded by me.[7] Therefore Aurelius Cyrenius,[8] who is the chief administrator of affairs,[9] will observe this ordinance which I have given."

[1] Valerian was taken captive by Sapor, king of Persia, probably late in the year 260 (the date is somewhat uncertain) and died in captivity. His son Gallienus, already associated with him in the empire, became sole emperor when his father fell into the Persians' hands.
[2] Eusebius has not preserved the text of these edicts (προγράμματα, which were public proclamations, and thus differed from the rescripts, which were private instructions), but the rescript to the bishops which he quotes shows that they did more than simply put a stop to the persecution,—that they in fact made Christianity a *religio licita*, and that for the first time. The right of the Christians as a body (the *corpus Christianorum*) to hold property is recognized in this rescript, and this involves the legal recognition of that body. Moreover, the rescript is addressed to the "bishops," which implies a recognition of the organization of the Church. See the article of Görres, *Die Toleranzedicte des Kaisers Gallienus*, in the *Jahrb. für prot. Theol.*, 1877, p. 606 sq.
[3] ἀντιγραφή: the technical term for an epistle containing private instructions, in distinction from an edict or public proclamation. This rescript was addressed to the bishops of the province of Egypt (including Dionysius of Alexandria). It was evidently issued some time after the publication of the edicts themselves. Its exact date is uncertain, but it was probably written immediately after the fall of the usurper Macrianus (i.e. in 261 or early in 262), during the time of whose usurpation the benefits of Gallienus' edicts of toleration could of course not have been felt in Egypt and the Orient.
[4] Εὐσεβής, Εὐτυχής, Σεβαστός.
[5] Of Pinnas and Demetrius we know nothing. The identification of Demetrius with the presbyter mentioned in chap. 11, § 24, might be suggested as possible. There is nothing to prevent such an identification, nor, on the other hand, is there anything to be urged in its favor beyond mere agreement in a name which was not uncommon in Egypt.
[6] ὅπως ἀπὸ τῶν τόπων τῶν θρησκευσίμων ἀποχωρήσωσι. This is commonly taken to mean that the ",Christians may come forth from their religious retreats," which, however, does not seem to be the sense of the original. I prefer to read, with Closs, "that the heathen may depart from the Christians' places of worship," from those, namely, which they had taken possession of during the persecution.
[7] The reference is doubtless to the edicts, referred to above, which he had issued immediately after his accession, but which had not been sooner put in force in Egypt because of the usurper Macrianus (see above, note 3).
[8] So far as I am aware, this man is known to us only from this passage.
[9] ὁ τοῦ μεγίστου πράγματος προστατεύων. Heinichen, following Valesius, identifies this office with the ὁ ἐπὶ τῶν καθόλου λόγων (mentioned in chap. 10, § 5), with the ὁ τῶν καθόλου λόγων ἔπαρχος (mentioned in Bk. IX. chap. 11, § 4), &c. For the nature of that office, see chap. 10, note 8. The phrase used in this passage seems to suggest the identification, and yet I am inclined to think, inasmuch as the rescript has to do specifically with the Church in Egypt, that Aurelius Cyrenius was not (as Macrianus was under Valerian) the emperor's general finance minister, in charge of the

[35] See below, chap. 32, § 5.
[36] See chap. 28, note 8.
[37] That is, until the persecution of Diocletian, A.D. 303 sq.
[38] That is, according to Eusebius, in the time of Valerian, but only the events related in the first part of the chapter took place at that time; those recorded in the epistle to Domitius and Didymus in the time of Decius. See above, note 25.
[1] Of these three men we know only what is told us in this chapter.
[2] Marcionitic martyrs are mentioned by Eusebius in Bk. IV. chap. 15, and in *Martyrs of Pal.* chap. 10. In *H. E.* V. 16, it is stated that the Marcionites as well as the Montanists had many martyrs, but that the orthodox Christians did not acknowledge them as Christians, and would not recognize them even when they were martyred together. Of course they were all alike Christians in the eyes of the state, and hence all alike subject to persecution.

3   I have given this in a translation from the Latin, that it may be more readily understood. Another decree of his is extant addressed to other bishops, permitting them to take possession again of the so-called cemeteries.[10]

CHAPTER XIV.

The Bishops that flourished at that Time.

AT that time Xystus[1] was still presiding over the church of Rome, and Demetrianus,[2] successor of Fabius,[3] over the church of Antioch, and Firmilianus[4] over that of Cæsarea in Cappadocia ; and besides these, Gregory[5] and his brother Athenodorus,[6] friends of Origen, were presiding over the churches in Pontus ; and Theoctistus[7] of Cæsarea in Palestine having died, Domnus[8] received the episcopate there. He held it but a short time, and Theotecnus,[9] our contemporary, succeeded him. He also was a member of Origen's school. But in Jerusalem, after the death of Mazabanes,[10] Hymenæus,[11] who has been celebrated among us for a great many years, succeeded to his seat.

CHAPTER XV.

The Martyrdom of Marinus at Cæsarea.

AT this time, when the peace of the   1
churches had been everywhere[1] restored, Marinus in Cæsarea in Palestine, who was honored for his military deeds, and illustrious by virtue of family and wealth, was beheaded for his testimony to Christ, on the following account. The vine-branch[2] is a certain   2
mark of honor among the Romans, and those who obtain it become, they say, centurions. A place being vacated, the order of succession called Marinus to this position. But when he was about to receive the honor, another person came before the tribunal and claimed that it was not legal, according to the ancient laws, for him to receive the Roman dignity, as he was a Christian and did not sacrifice to the emperors ; but that the office belonged rather to him. Thereupon the judge, whose name was   3
Achæus,[3] being disturbed, first asked what opinion Marinus held. And when he perceived that he continually confessed himself a Christian, he gave him three hours for reflection. When he came out from the tribunal, Theo-   4
tecnus,[4] the bishop there, took him aside and conversed with him, and taking his hand led him into the church. And standing with him within, in the sanctuary, he raised his cloak a little, and pointed to the sword that hung by his side ; and at the same time he placed before him the Scripture of the divine Gospels, and told him to choose which of the two he wished. And without hesitation he reached forth his right hand, and took the divine Scripture. " Hold fast then," says Theotecnus to him, " hold fast to God, and strengthened by him mayest thou obtain what thou hast chosen, and go in peace." Immediately on his return the   5
herald cried out calling him to the tribunal, for the appointed time was already completed. And standing before the tribunal, and manifesting greater zeal for the faith, immediately, as he was, he was led away and finished his course by death.

affairs of the empire, but simply the supreme finance minister or administrator of Egypt (cf. Mommsen's *Provinces of the Roman Empire*, Scribner's ed., II. p. 268).
    [10] The use of their cemeteries, both as places of burial and as meeting-places for religious worship, had been denied to the Christians by Valerian. On the origin of the word κοιμητήρια, see chap. 11, note 14.
    [1] On Xystus II., see chap. 5, note 5.
    [2] On Demetrianus, see Bk. VI. chap. 46, note 12.
    [3] On Fabius, see Bk. VI. chap. 39, note 7.
    [4] On Firmilianus, see Bk. VI. chap. 26, note 3.
    [5] Gregory Thaumaturgus, bishop of Neo-Cæsarea in Pontus from about 233–270 (?). Upon Gregory, see Bk. VI. chap. 30, note 1.
    [6] On Athenodorus, see *ibid*. note 2.
    [7] On Theoctistus, see Bk. VI. chap. 19, note 27.
    [8] Of the life and character of Domnus we know nothing. So far as I am aware he is mentioned only here. His dates are uncertain, but his predecessor, Theoctistus, was still bishop in the time of Stephen of Rome (254–257; see above, Bk. VI. chap. 19, note 27), while he himself became bishop before the death of Xystus of Rome, as we may gather from this chapter, i.e. before August, 258 (see chap. 5, note 5), so that between these dates his accession must be placed. Eusebius' words in this passage will hardly admit an episcopate of more than one or two years; possibly he was bishop but a few months.
    [9] The dates of Theotecnus are likewise uncertain. Eusebius in Bk. VII. chap. 32, says that he was acquainted with Pamphilus during the episcopate of Agapius (the successor of Theotecnus), implying that he first made his acquaintance then. It is therefore likely that Agapius became bishop some years before the persecution of Diocletian, for otherwise we hardly allow enough time for the acquaintance of Pamphilus and Eusebius who did so much work together, and apparently were friends for so long a time. Pamphilus himself suffered martyrdom in 309 A.D. Theotecnus was quite a prominent man and was present at the two Antiochian synods mentioned in chaps. 27 and 30, which were convened to consider the heresy of Paul of Samosata.
    [10] On Mazabanes, see Bk. VI. chap. 39, note 5.
    [11] According to the *Chron*. of Eusebius, Hymenæus was bishop of Jerusalem from 265–298. It is expressly stated in the *Chron.* that the dates of the earlier Jerusalem bishops are not known (see Bk. V. chap. 12, note 1) ; but with the dates of the bishops of the latter part of the third century Eusebius can hardly have been unacquainted, and that Hymenæus was bishop at any rate as early as 265 is proved by chaps. 27 and 30 (see the note on Mazabanes referred to just above). The dates given in the *Chron.* may therefore be accepted as at least approximately correct.

    [1] The martyrdom of Marinus after the promulgation of Gallienus' edict of toleration and after peace had been, as Eusebius remarks, everywhere restored to the churches, has caused historians some difficulty. It is maintained, however, by Tillemont and others, and with especial force by Görres in the *Jahrbücher für prot. Theol.*, 1877, p. 620 sq., that the martyrdom of Marinus took place while the usurper Macrianus, who was exceedingly hostile to the Christians, was still in power in the East, and at a time, therefore, when the edicts of Gallienus could have no force there. This of course explains the difficulty completely. The martyrdom then must have taken place toward the beginning of Gallienus' reign, for Macrianus was slain as early as 262. Of the martyr Marinus we know only what Eusebius tells us here.
    [2] τὸ κλῆμα. The centurion received as a badge of office a vine-branch or vine-switch, which was called by the Romans *Vitis*.
    [3] Achæus is an otherwise unknown person. That he was governor of Palestine, as Valesius asserts, is apparently a pure assumption, for the term used of him (δικαστής) is quite indefinite.
    [4] On Theotecnus, see above, chap. 14, note 9.

CHAPTER XVI.

Story in Regard to Astyrius.

ASTYRIUS[1] also is commemorated on account of his pious boldness in connection with this affair. He was a Roman of senatorial rank, and in favor with the emperors, and well known to all on account of his noble birth and wealth. Being present at the martyr's death, he took his body away on his shoulder, and arraying him in a splendid and costly garment, prepared him for the grave in a magnificent manner, and gave him fitting burial.[2] The friends of this man that remain to our day, relate many other facts concerning him.

CHAPTER XVII.

The Signs at Paneas of the Great Might of our Saviour.

AMONG these is also the following wonder. At Cæsarea Philippi, which the Phœnicians call Paneas,[1] springs are shown at the foot of the Mountain Panius, out of which the Jordan flows. They say that on a certain feast day, a victim was thrown in,[2] and that through the power of the demon it marvelously disappeared and that which happened was a famous wonder to those who were present. Astyrius was once there when these things were done, and seeing the multitude astonished at the affair, he pitied their delusion ; and looking up to heaven he supplicated the God over all through Christ, that he would rebuke the demon who deceived the people, and bring the men's delusion to an end. And they say that when he had prayed thus, immediately the sacrifice floated on the surface of the fountain. And thus the miracle departed ; and no wonder was ever afterward performed at the place.

CHAPTER XVIII.

The Statue which the Woman with an Issue of Blood erected.[1]

SINCE I have mentioned this city I do   1 not think it proper to omit an account which is worthy of record for posterity. For they say that the woman with an issue of blood, who, as we learn from the sacred Gospel,[2] received from our Saviour deliverance from her affliction, came from this place, and that her house is shown in the city, and that remarkable memorials of the kindness of the Saviour to her remain there. For there stands upon   2 an elevated stone, by the gates of her house, a brazen image of a woman kneeling, with her hands stretched out, as if she were praying. Opposite this is another upright image of a man, made of the same material, clothed decently in a double cloak, and extending his hand toward the woman. At his feet, beside the statue itself,[3] is a certain strange plant, which climbs up to the hem of the brazen cloak, and is a remedy for all kinds of diseases. They say that this statue is an image of   3 Jesus. It has remained to our day, so that we ourselves also saw it when we were staying in the city. Nor is it strange that those   4 of the Gentiles who, of old, were benefited by our Saviour, should have done such things, since we have learned also that the likenesses of his apostles Paul and Peter, and of Christ himself, are preserved in paintings,[4] the ancients being accustomed, as it is likely, according to a habit of the Gentiles, to pay this kind of honor indiscriminately to those regarded by them as deliverers.

---

[1] This account of the statue erected by the woman with the issue of blood is repeated by many later writers, and Sozomen (*H. E.* V. 21) and Philostorgius (*H. E.* VII. 3) inform us that it was destroyed by the Emperor Julian. Gieseler remarks (*Eccles. Hist.*, Harper's ed. I. p. 70), "Judging by the analogy of many coins, the memorial had been erected in honor of an emperor (probably Hadrian), and falsely interpreted by the Christians, perhaps on account of a σωτῆρι or θεῷ appearing in the inscription." There can be no doubt of Eusebius' honesty in the matter, but no less doubt that the statue commemorated something quite different from that which Christian tradition claimed. Upon this whole chapter, see Heinichen's Excursus, in Vol. III. p. 698 sq.
[2] See Matt. ix. 20 sq.
[3] οὗ παρὰ τοῖς ποσὶν ἐπὶ τῆς στήλης αὐτῆς. This is commonly translated "at his feet, *upon the pedestal*;" but, as Heinichen remarks, in the excursus referred to just above, the plant can hardly have grown *upon* the pedestal, and what is more, we have no warrant for translating στήλη "pedestal." Paulus, in his commentary on Matthew *in loco*, maintains that Eusebius is speaking only of a representation upon the base of the statue, not of an actual plant. But this interpretation, as Heinichen shows, is quite unwarranted. For the use of ἐπὶ in the sense of "near" or "beside," we have numerous examples (see the instances given by Heinichen, and also Liddell and Scott's Greek Lexicon, *s.v.*).
[4] Eusebius himself, as we learn from his letter to the Empress Constantia Augusta (see above, p. 44), did not approve of the use of images or representations of Christ, on the ground that it tended to idolatry. In consequence of this disapproval he fell into great disrepute in the later image-worshiping Church, his epistle being cited by the iconoclasts at the second Council of Nicæa, in 787, and his orthodoxy being in consequence fiercely attacked by the defenders of image-worship, who dominated the council, and won the day.

---

[1] We know nothing more about this Astyrius than is recorded here. Rufinus, in his *H. E.* VII. 13, tells us that he suffered martyrdom at about this time; but Eusebius says nothing of the kind, and it is therefore not at all probable that Rufinus is correct. He probably concluded, from Eusebius' account of him, that he also suffered martyrdom.
[2] Burton and Crusè close the chapter at this point, throwing the next sentence into chap. 17. Such a transposition, however, is unnecessary, and I have preferred to follow Valesius, Heinichen, Schwegler, and other editors, in dividing as above.
[1] Cæsarea Philippi (to be distinguished from Cæsarea, the chief city of Palestine, mentioned in previous chapters) was originally called Paneas by the Greeks, — a name which it retained even after the name Cæsarea Philippi had been given it by Philip the Tetrarch, who enlarged and beautified it. The place, which is now a small village, is called Banias by the Arabs. It lies at the base of Mt. Hermon, and is noted for one of the principal sources of the Jordan, which issues from springs beneath the rocks of Mt. Hermon at this point. The spot is said to be remarkably beautiful. See Robinson's *Biblical Researches in Palestine*, Vol. III. p. 409 sq.
[2] Valesius remarks that the heathen were accustomed to throw victims into their sacred wells and fountains, and that therefore Publicola asks Augustine, in Epistle 153, whether one ought to drink from a fountain or well whither a portion of sacrifice had been sent.

CHAPTER XIX.

The Episcopal Chair of James.

THE chair of James, who first received the episcopate of the church at Jerusalem from the Saviour himself[1] and the apostles, and who, as the divine records show,[2] was called a brother of Christ, has been preserved until now,[3] the brethren who have followed him in succession there exhibiting clearly to all the reverence which both those of old times and those of our own day maintained and do maintain for holy men on account of their piety. So much as to this matter.

CHAPTER XX.

The Festal Epistles of Dionysius, in which he also gives a Paschal Canon.

DIONYSIUS, besides his epistles already mentioned,[1] wrote at that time[2] also his extant Festal Epistles,[3] in which he uses words of panegyric respecting the passover feast. He addressed one of these to Flavius,[4] and another

to Domitius and Didymus,[5] in which he sets forth a canon of eight years,[6] maintaining that it is not proper to observe the paschal feast until after the vernal equinox. Besides these he sent another epistle to his fellow-presbyters in Alexandria, as well as various others to different persons while the persecution was still prevailing.[7]

CHAPTER XXI.

The Occurrences at Alexandria.

PEACE had but just been restored when   1
he returned to Alexandria ;[1] but as sedition and war broke out again, rendering it impossible for him to oversee all the brethren, separated in different places by the insurrection, at the feast of the passover, as if he were still an exile from Alexandria, he addressed them again by letter.[2] And in another festal epistle   2
written later to Hierax,[3] a bishop in Egypt, he mentions the sedition then prevailing in Alexandria, as follows :

"What wonder is it that it is difficult for me to communicate by letters with those who live far away, when it is beyond my power even to reason with myself, or to take counsel for my own life? Truly I need to send letters   3
to those who are as my own bowels,[4] dwelling in one home, and brethren of one soul, and citizens of the same church ; but how to send them I cannot tell. For it would be easier for one to go, not only beyond the limits of the province, but even from the East to the West, than from Alexandria to Alexandria itself.

---

[1] That James was appointed bishop of Jerusalem by Christ himself was an old and wide-spread tradition. Compare, e.g., the Clementine *Recognitions*, Bk. I. chap. 43, the *Apostolic Constitutions*, Bk. VIII. chap. 35, and Chrysostom's *Homily XXXVIII. on First Corinthians.* See Valesius' note *ad locum ;* and on the universal tradition that James was bishop of Jerusalem, see above, Bk. II. chap. 1, note 11.

[2] See Gal. i. 19. On the actual relationship of "James, the Brother of the Lord" to Christ, see Bk. I. chap. 12, note 14.

[3] There can be no doubt that a chair (θρόνος), said to be the episcopal seat of James, the first bishop of Jerusalem, was shown in that church in the time of Eusebius, but there can be no less doubt that it was not genuine. Even had James been bishop of Jerusalem, and possessed a regular episcopal chair, or throne (a very violent supposition, which involves a most glaring anachronism), it was quite out of the question that it should have been preserved from destruction at the fall of the city in 70 A.D. As Stroth drily remarks: "Man hatte auch wohl nichts wichtigeres zu retten, als einen Stuhl!" The beginning of that veneration of relics which later took such strong hold on the Church, and which still flourishes within the Greek and Roman communions is clearly seen in this case recorded by Eusebius. At the same time, we can hardly say that that superstitious veneration with which we are acquainted appeared in this case. There seems to be nothing more than the customary respect for an article of old and time-honored associations which is seen everywhere and in all ages (cf. Heinichen's Excursus on this passage, Vol. III. p. 208 sq.). Cruse has unaccountably rendered θρόνος in this passage as if it referred to the see of Jerusalem, not to the chair of the bishop. It is plain enough that such an interpretation is quite unwarranted.

[1] Upon Dionysius of Alexandria, see Bk. VI. chap. 40, note 1, and see that note for references to the various passages in which Eusebius mentions or quotes from his epistles.

[2] Eusebius supposes all of these epistles to have been written in the time of Valerian or Gallienus; but he is mistaken, at least so far as the epistle to Domitius and Didymus is concerned (see above, chap. 11, note 25), and possibly in regard to some of the others also.

[3] τὰς φερομένας ἑορταστικάς. It was the custom for the bishops of Alexandria to write every year before Easter a sort of epistle, or homily, and in it to announce the time of the festival. These writings thus received the name Festal or Festival Epistles or Homilies (see Suicer's *Thesaurus s.v. ἑορταστικός,* and Valesius' note *ad locum*). This is apparently the earliest mention of such epistles. Others are referred to by Eusebius in chaps. 21 and 22, as written by Dionysius to various persons. Undoubtedly all the Alexandrian bishops during these centuries wrote such epistles, but none are extant, so far as I am aware, except a number by Athanasius (extant only in a Syriac version, published in Syriac and English by Cureton in 1846 and 1848), a few by Theophilus (extant only in Latin), and thirty by Cyril (published in Migne's *Patr. Gr.* LXXVII. 391 sq.).

[4] Of this Flavius we know nothing. The epistle addressed to him is no longer extant.

[5] On Domitius and Didymus, and the epistle addressed to them, see above, chap. 11, note 25. Eusebius quotes from the epistle in that chapter.

[6] That is, an eight-year cycle for the purpose of determining the time of the full moon. Hippolytus had employed the old eight-year cycle, but had, as he thought, improved it by combining two in a single sixteen-year cycle (see above, Bk. VI. chap. 22), as was done also by the author of the so-called Cyprianic Chronicle at the middle of the third century. The more accurate nineteen-year Metonic cycle (already in use among the Greeks in the fifth century B.C.) had not come into general use in the Church until later than this time. The Nicene Council sanctioned it and gave it wide currency, but it had apparently not yet come into use in the Church. In fact, the first Christian to make use of it for the computation of Easter, so far as we know, was Anatolius of Alexandria, later bishop of Laodicea (see below, chap. 32, § 14). It was soon adopted in the Alexandrian church, and already in the time of Athanasius had become the basis of all Easter calculations, as we can gather from Athanasius' Festal Epistles. From about the time of the Nicene Council on, Alexandria was commonly looked to for the reckoning of the date of Easter, and although an older and less accurate cycle remained in use in the West for a long time, the nineteen-year cycle gradually won its way everywhere. See Ideler's great work on chronology, and cf. Hefele's *Conciliengesch.* 2d ed. I. p. 332, and Lightfoot in the *Dict. of Christ. Biog.* II. p. 313 sq.

[7] These various epistles are no longer extant, nor do we know the names of the persons to whom they were addressed. At least a part of them, if not all, were very likely written during the Valerian persecution, as Eusebius states, for the fact that he made a mistake in connection with the epistle to Domitius and Didymus does not prove that he was in error in regard to all the others as well.

[1] This was after the fall of the usurper Macrianus, probably late in the year 261 or early in 262 (see above, chap. 13, note 3).

[2] This epistle written by Dionysius during the civil war to his scattered flock is no longer extant.

[3] Of this Hierax we know no more than is told us here.

[4] cf. Philemon, vers. 12.

4 For the very heart of the city is more intricate and impassable than that great and trackless desert which Israel traversed for two generations. And our smooth and waveless harbors have become like the sea, divided and walled up, through which Israel drove and in whose highway the Egyptians were overwhelmed.

For often from the slaughters there committed they appear like the Red Sea. And 5 the river which flows by the city has sometimes seemed drier than the waterless desert, and more parched than that in which Israel, as they passed through it, so suffered for thirst, that they cried out against Moses, and the water flowed for them from the steep rock,[5] 6 through him who alone doeth wonders. Again it has overflowed so greatly as to flood all the surrounding country, and the roads and the fields; threatening to bring back the deluge of water that occurred in the days of Noah. And it flows along, polluted always with blood and slaughter and drownings, as it became for Pharaoh through the agency of Moses, when he 7 changed it into blood, and it stank.[6] And what other water could purify the water which purifies everything? How could the ocean, so great and impassable for men, if poured into it, cleanse this bitter sea? Or how could the great river which flowed out of Eden, if it poured the four heads into which it is divided into the one of Geon,[7] wash away this pollu- 8 tion? Or when can the air poisoned by these noxious exhalations become pure? For such vapors arise from the earth, and winds from the sea, and breezes from the river, and mists from the harbors, that the dews are, as it were, discharges from dead bodies putrefy- 9 ing in all the elements around us. Yet men wonder and cannot understand whence these continuous pestilences; whence these severe sicknesses; whence these deadly diseases of all kinds; whence this various and vast human destruction; why this great city no longer contains as many inhabitants, from tender infants to those most advanced in life, as it formerly contained of those whom it called hearty old men. But the men from forty to seventy years of age were then so much more numerous that their number cannot now be filled out, even when those from fourteen to eighty years are enrolled and registered for the public allow- 10 ance of food. And the youngest in appearance have become, as it were, of equal age with those who formerly were the oldest. But though they see the race of men thus constantly

diminishing and wasting away, and though their complete destruction is increasing and advancing, they do not tremble."

CHAPTER XXII.

The Pestilence which came upon them.

AFTER these events a pestilential disease 1 followed the war, and at the approach of the feast he wrote again to the brethren, describing the sufferings consequent upon this calamity.[1]

"To other men[2] the present might not 2 seem to be a suitable time for a festival. Nor indeed is this or any other time suitable for them; neither sorrowful times, nor even such as might be thought especially cheerful.[3] Now, indeed, everything is tears and every one is mourning, and wailings resound daily through the city because of the multitude of the dead and dying. For as it was written of 3 the firstborn of the Egyptians, so now 'there has arisen a great cry, for there is not a house where there is not one dead.'[4] And would that this were all![5] For many terrible things 4 have happened already. First, they drove us out; and when alone, and persecuted, and put to death by all, even then we kept the feast. And every place of affliction was to us a place of festival: field, desert, ship, inn, prison; but the perfected martyrs kept the most joyous festival of all, feasting in heaven. After these 5 things war and famine followed, which we endured in common with the heathen. But we bore alone those things with which they afflicted us, and at the same time we experienced also the effects of what they inflicted upon and suffered from one another; and again, we rejoiced in the peace of Christ, which he gave to us alone.

"But after both we and they had enjoyed 6 a very brief season of rest this pestilence assailed us; to them more dreadful than any dread, and more intolerable than any other calamity; and, as one of their own writers has said, the only thing which prevails over all hope.

---

[5] ἐκ πέτρας ἀκροτόμου. The adjective is an addition of Dionysius' own. The LXX of Ex. xvii. 6 has only πέτρα, " rock."
[6] ἐποζέσας; the same word which is used in the LXX of Ex. vii. 21.
[7] Γηὼν; LXX (Gen. ii. 13), Γεὼν; Heb. גִּיחוֹן; A. V. and R. V., Gihon.

[1] This letter seems to have been written shortly before Easter of the year 263; for the festal epistle to Hierax, quoted in the last chapter, was written while the war was still in progress (i.e. in 262), this one after its close. It does not seem to have been a regular festal epistle so-called, for in § 11, below, we are told that Dionysius wrote a regular festal letter (ἑορταστικὴν γραφήν) to the brethren in Egypt, and that apparently in connection with this same Easter of the year 263.
[2] i.e. to the heathen.
[3] i.e. there is no time when heathen can fitly rejoice.
[4] Ex. xii. 30.
[5] καὶ ὀφελόν γε, with the majority of the MSS., followed by Valesius, Schwegler, and Heinichen. Stroth, Burton, and Zimmermann, upon the authority of two MSS., read καὶ ὀφελόν γε εἰς (" and would that there were but one!"), a reading which Valesius approves in his notes. The weight of MS. authority, however, is with the former, and it alone justifies the γάρ of the following sentence.

But to us this was not so, but no less than the other things was it an exercise and probation. For it did not keep aloof even from us, but the heathen it assailed more severely."

7 Farther on he adds:

"The most of our brethren were unsparing in their exceeding love and brotherly kindness. They held fast to each other and visited the sick fearlessly, and ministered to them continually, serving them in Christ. And they died with them most joyfully, taking the affliction of others, and drawing the sickness from their neighbors to themselves and willingly receiving their pains. And many who cared for the sick and gave strength to others died themselves, having transferred to themselves their death. And the popular saying which always seems a mere expression of courtesy, they then made real in action, taking their departure as the others' ' offscouring.' [6]

8 " Truly the best of our brethren departed from life in this manner, including some presbyters and deacons and those of the people who had the highest reputation; so that this form of death, through the great piety and strong faith it exhibited, seemed to lack
9 nothing of martyrdom. And they took the bodies of the saints in their open hands and in their bosoms, and closed their eyes and their mouths; and they bore them away on their shoulders and laid them out; and they clung to them and embraced them; and they prepared them suitably with washings and garments. And after a little they received like treatment themselves, for the survivors were continually following those who had gone before them.
10 " But with the heathen everything was quite otherwise. They deserted those who began to be sick, and fled from their dearest friends. And they cast them out into the streets when they were half dead, and left the dead like refuse, unburied. They shunned any participation or fellowship with death; which yet, with all their precautions, it was not easy for them to escape."
11 After this epistle, when peace had been restored to the city, he wrote another festal letter [7] to the brethren in Egypt, and again several others besides this. And there is also

a certain one extant On the Sabbath, [8] and another On Exercise. Moreover, he wrote 12 again an epistle to Hermammon [9] and the brethren in Egypt, describing at length the wickedness of Decius and his successors, and mentioning the peace under Gallienus.

CHAPTER XXIII.

The Reign of Gallienus.

But there is nothing like hearing his own 1 words, which are as follows:

"Then he, [1] having betrayed one of the emperors that preceded him, and made war on the other, [2] perished with his whole family speedily and utterly. But Gallienus was proclaimed and universally acknowledged at once an old emperor and a new, being before them and continuing after them. For according to 2 the word spoken by the prophet Isaiah, ' Behold the things from the beginning have come to pass, and new things shall now arise.' [3] For as a cloud passing over the sun's rays and obscuring them for a little time hides it and appears in its place; but when the cloud has passed by or is dissipated, the sun which had risen before appears again; so Macrianus who put himself forward and approached the existing empire of Gallienus, is not, since he never was. But the other is just as he was. And 3 his kingdom, as if it had cast aside old age, and had been purified from the former wickedness, now blossoms out more vigorously, and is seen and heard farther, and extends in all directions." [4]

He then indicates the time at which he 4 wrote this in the following words:

"It occurs to me again to review the days of the imperial years. For I perceive that those most impious men, though they have been famous, yet in a short time have become nameless. But the holier and more godly prince, [5] having

<hr />

[6] περίψημα; cf. 1 Cor. iv. 13. Valesius suggests that this may have been a humble and complimentary form of salutation among the Alexandrians: ἐγὼ εἰμὶ περίψημά σου (cf. our words, "Your humble servant"); or, as he thinks more probable, that the expression had come to be habitually applied to the Christians by the heathen. The former interpretation seems to me the only possible one in view of the words immediately preceding: "which always seems a mere expression of courtesy." Certainly these words rule out the second interpretation suggested by Valesius.
[7] The connection into which this festal epistle is brought with the letter just quoted would seem to indicate that it was written not a whole year, but very soon after that one. We may, therefore, look upon it as Dionysius' festal epistle of the year 263 (see above, note 1). Neither this nor the " several others " spoken of just below is now extant.

[8] This and the next epistle are no longer extant, and we know neither the time of their composition nor the persons to whom they were addressed.
[9] On Hermammon and the epistle addressed to him, see above, chap. 1, note 3. An extract from this same epistle is given in that chapter and also in chap. 10.
[1] i.e. Macrianus; see above, chap. 10, note 5.
[2] He is supposed to have betrayed Valerian into the hands of the Persians, or at least, by his treachery, to have brought about the result which took place, and after Valerian's capture he made war upon Gallienus, the latter's son and successor. See the note referred to just above.
[3] Isa. xlii. 9.
[4] Dionysius is evidently somewhat dazzled and blinded by the favor shown by Gallienus to the Christians. For we know from the profane historians of this period that the reign of Gallienus was one of the darkest in all the history of the Roman Empire, on account of the numerous disasters which came upon the empire, and the internal disturbances and calamities it was called upon to endure.
[5] Gallienus is known to us as one of the most abandoned and profligate of emperors, though he was not without ability and courage which he displayed occasionally. Dionysius' words at this point are not surprising, for the public benefits conferred by Gallienus upon the Christians would far outweigh his private vices in

passed the seventh year, is now completing the ninth,[6] in which we shall keep the feast."

CHAPTER XXIV.

Nepos and his Schism.[1]

1   BESIDES all these the two books on the Promises[2] were prepared by him. The oc-

the minds of those who had suffered from the persecutions of his predecessors.

[6] The peculiar form of reckoning employed here (the mention of the seventh and then the ninth year) has caused considerable perplexity. Stroth thinks that "Dionysius speaks here of the time when Gallienus actually ruled in Egypt. For Macrianus had ruled there for a year, and during that time the authority of Gallienus in that country had been interrupted." The view of Pearson, however, seems to me better. He remarks: "Whoever expressed himself thus, that one after his seven years was passing his ninth year? This *septennium* (ἑπταετηρίς) must designate something peculiar and different from the time following. It is therefore the septennium of imperial power which he had held along with his father. In the eighth year of that empire [the father, Valerian, being in captivity in Persia], Macrianus possessed himself of the imperial honor especially in Egypt. After his assumption of the purple, however, Gallienus had still much authority in Egypt. At length in the ninth year of Gallienus, i.e. in 261, Macrianus, the father and the two sons being slain, the sovereignty of Gallienus was recognized also among the Egyptians." "The ninth year of Gallienus, moreover, began about midsummer of this year; and the time at which this letter was written by Dionysius, as Eusebius observes, may be gathered from that, and falls consequently before the Paschal season of 262 A.D." See also chap. 1, note 3, above.

[1] Of this Egyptian bishop, Nepos, we know only what is told us in this chapter. Upon chiliasm in the early Church, see above, Bk. III. chap. 39, note 19. It is interesting to note, that although chiliasm had long lost its hold wherever the philosophical theology of the third century had made itself felt, it still continued to maintain its sway in other parts of the Church, especially in outlying districts in the East, which were largely isolated from the great centers of thought, and in the greater part of the West. By such Christians it was looked upon, in fact, as the very kernel of Christianity,—they lived as most Christians of the second century had, in the constant hope of a speedy return of Christ to reign in power upon the earth. The gradual exclusion of this remnant of early Christian belief involved the same kind of consequences as the disappearance of the belief in the continued possession by the Church of the spirit of prophecy (see Bk. V. chap. 16, note 1), and marks another step in the progress of the Church from the peculiarly enthusiastic spirit of the first and second, to the more formal spirit of the third and following centuries. Compare the remarks of Harnack in his *Dogmengeschichte*, I. p. 484 sq. It seems, from § 6, below, that Dionysius had engaged in an oral discussion of the doctrines taught in the book of Nepos, which had prevailed for a long time in Arsinoë, where the disputation was held. The best spirit was exhibited by both parties in the discussion, and the result was a decided victory for Dionysius. He was evidently afraid, however, that the book of Nepos, which was widely circulated, would still continue to do damage, and therefore he undertook to refute it in a work of his own, entitled *On the Promises* (see the next note). His work, like his disputation, undoubtedly had considerable effect, but chiliasm still prevailed in some of the outlying districts of Egypt for a number of generations.

[2] περὶ ἐπαγγελιῶν. This work, as we learn from § 3, below, contained in the first book Dionysius' own views on the subject under dispute, in the second a detailed discussion of the Apocalypse upon which Nepos based his chiliastic opinions. The work is no longer extant, though Eusebius gives extracts from the second book in this and in the next chapter, and three brief fragments have been preserved in a Vatican MS., and are published in the various editions of Dionysius' works. The Eusebian extracts are translated in the *Ante-Nicene Fathers*, Vol. VI. p. 81–84. We have no means of ascertaining the date of Dionysius' work. Hefele (*Conciliengesch.* I. p. 134), Dittrich (p. 69), and others, put the disputation at Arsinoë, in 254 or 255, and the composition of the work of Dionysius of course soon thereafter; but we have no authority for fixing the date of the disputation with such exactness, and must be content to leave it quite undetermined, though it is not improbable that it took place, as Dittrich maintains, between the persecutions of Decius and Valerian. In the preface to the eighteenth book of his commentary on Isaiah, Jerome speaks of a work of Dionysius, *On the Promises* (evidently referring to this same work), directed against Irenæus. In his *de vir. ill.* 69, however, he follows Eusebius in stating that the work was written against Nepos. There can be no doubt on this score, and Jerome's statement in his commentary seems to be a direct error. It is possible, however, that Irenæus, as the most illustrious representative of chiliastic views, may have been mentioned, and his positions refuted in the work, and thus Jerome have had some justification for his report.

casion of these was Nepos, a bishop in Egypt, who taught that the promises to the holy men in the Divine Scriptures should be understood in a more Jewish manner, and that there would be a certain millennium of bodily luxury upon this earth. As he thought that he   2 could establish his private opinion by the Revelation of John, he wrote a book on this subject, entitled Refutation of Allegorists.[3] Dionysius opposes this in his books on the   3 Promises. In the first he gives his own opinion of the dogma; and in the second he treats of the Revelation of John, and mentioning Nepos at the beginning, writes of him in this manner :

"But since they bring forward a certain   4 work of Nepos, on which they rely confidently, as if it proved beyond dispute that there will be a reign of Christ upon earth, I confess that[4] in many other respects I approve and love Nepos, for his faith and industry and diligence in the Scriptures, and for his extensive psalmody,[5] with which many of the brethren are still delighted ; and I hold him in the more reverence because he has gone to rest before us. But the truth should be loved and honored most of all. And while we should praise and approve ungrudgingly what is said aright, we ought to examine and correct what does not seem to have been written soundly. Were he pres-   5 ent to state his opinion orally, mere unwritten discussion, persuading and reconciling those who are opposed by question and answer, would be sufficient. But as some think his work very plausible, and as certain teachers regard the law and prophets as of no consequence, and do not follow the Gospels, and treat lightly the apostolic epistles, while they make promises[6] as to the teaching of this work as if it were some great hidden mystery, and do not permit our simpler brethren to have any sublime and lofty thoughts concerning the glorious and truly divine appearing of our Lord, and our resurrection from the dead, and our being gathered together unto him, and made like him, but on the contrary lead them to hope for small and mortal things in the kingdom of God, and for things such as exist now, — since this is the case, it is necessary that we should dispute with our brother

[3] Evidently directed against Origen and other allegorical interpreters like him, who avoided the materialistic conceptions deduced by so many from the Apocalypse, by spiritualizing and allegorizing its language. This work of Nepos has entirely perished.

[4] The words "I confess that" are not in the original, but the insertion of some clause of the kind is necessary to complete the sentence.

[5] On early Christian hymnody, see above, Bk. V. chap. 28, note 14.

[6] "i.e. *dire ante promittunt quam tradunt*. The metaphor is taken from the mysteries of the Greeks, who were wont to promise great and marvelous discoveries to the initiated, and then kept them on the rack by daily expectation in order to confirm their judgment and reverence by suspense of knowledge, as Tertullian says in his book *Against the Valentinians* [chap. 1]." Valesius.

Nepos as if he were present." Farther on he says :

6   "When I was in the district of Arsinoë,[7] where, as you know, this doctrine has prevailed for a long time, so that schisms and apostasies of entire churches have resulted, I called together the presbyters and teachers of the brethren in the villages, — such brethren as wished being also present, — and I exhorted them to make a public examination of this
7   question. Accordingly when they brought me this book, as if it were a weapon and fortress impregnable, sitting with them from morning till evening for three successive days, I endeavored to correct what was written in
8   it. And I rejoiced over the constancy, sincerity, docility, and intelligence of the brethren, as we considered in order and with moderation the questions and the difficulties and the points of agreement. And we abstained from defending in every manner and contentiously the opinions which we had once held, unless they appeared to be correct. Nor did we evade objections, but we endeavored as far as possible to hold to and confirm the things which lay before us, and if the reason given satisfied us, we were not ashamed to change our opinions and agree with others ; but on the contrary, conscientiously and sincerely, and with hearts laid open before God, we accepted whatever was established by the proofs and
9   teachings of the Holy Scriptures. And finally the author and mover of this teaching, who was called Coracion,[8] in the hearing of all the brethren that were present, acknowledged and testified to us that he would no longer hold this opinion, nor discuss it, nor mention nor teach it, as he was fully convinced by the arguments against it. And some of the other brethren expressed their gratification at the conference, and at the spirit of conciliation and harmony which all had manifested."

CHAPTER XXV.

The Apocalypse of John.[1]

1   AFTERWARD he speaks in this manner of the Apocalypse of John.

"Some before us have set aside and rejected the book altogether, criticising it chapter by chapter, and pronouncing it without sense or argument, and maintaining that the title is
2   fraudulent. For they say that it is not the work of John, nor is it a revelation, because it is covered thickly and densely by a vail of obscurity. And they affirm that none of the apostles, and none of the saints, nor any one in the Church is its author, but that Cerinthus, who founded the sect which was called after him the Cerinthian, desiring reputable authority for his fiction, prefixed the name. For the doc-   3 trine which he taught was this : that the kingdom of Christ will be an earthly one. And as he was himself devoted to the pleasures of the body and altogether sensual in his nature, he dreamed that that kingdom would consist in those things which he desired, namely, in the delights of the belly and of sexual passion ; that is to say, in eating and drinking and marrying, and in festivals and sacrifices and the slaying of victims, under the guise of which he thought he could indulge his appetites with a better grace.[2]

"But I could not venture to reject the   4 book, as many brethren hold it in high esteem. But I suppose that it is beyond my comprehension, and that there is a certain concealed and more wonderful meaning in every part. For if I do not understand I suspect that a deeper sense lies beneath the words. I do not measure and judge them by my   5 own reason, but leaving the more to faith I regard them as too high for me to grasp. And I do not reject what I cannot comprehend, but rather wonder because I do not understand it."

After this he examines the entire Book   6 of Revelation, and having proved that it is impossible to understand it according to the literal sense, proceeds as follows :

"Having finished all the prophecy, so to speak, the prophet pronounces those blessed who shall observe it, and also himself. For he says, 'Blessed is he that keepeth the words of the prophecy of this book, and I, John, who saw and heard these things.'[3] There-   7 fore that he was called John, and that this book is the work of one John, I do not deny. And I agree also that it is the work of a holy and inspired man. But I cannot readily admit that he was the apostle, the son of Zebedee, the brother of James, by whom the Gospel of John and the Catholic Epistle[4] were written. For I judge from the character of both,   8 and the forms of expression, and the entire execution of the book,[5] that it is not his. For

---

7   ἐν τῷ Ἀρσινοείτῃ. The Arsinoite nome or district (on the nomes of Egypt, see above, Bk. II. chap. 17, note 10) was situated on the western bank of the Nile, between the river and Lake Mœris, southwest of Memphis.
8   Of this Coracion, we know only what is told us here.
1   Upon the Apocalypse in the early Church, and especially upon Dionysius' treatment of it, see above, Bk. III. chap. 24, note 20.

2   A portion of this extract (§§ 2 and 3) has been already quoted by Eusebius in Bk. III. chap. 28.
3   Rev. xxii. 7, 8. Dionysius punctuates this passage peculiarly, and thus interprets it quite differently from all our versions of the Book of Revelation. The Greek text as given by him agrees with our received text of the Apocalypse; but the words κἀγὼ Ἰωάννης ὁ ἀκούων καὶ βλέπων ταῦτα, which Dionysius connects with the preceding, should form an independent sentence: " And I, John, am he that heard and saw these things."
4   On the Gospel and Epistle, see Bk. III. chap. 24, notes 1 and 18.
5   τῆς τοῦ βιβλίου διεξαγωγῆς λεγομένης. Valesius considers διεξαγωγή equivalent to dispositionem or οἰκονομίαν, " for διεξ-

the evangelist nowhere gives his name, or proclaims himself, either in the Gospel or
9　Epistle." Farther on he adds:
"But John never speaks as if referring to himself, or as if referring to another person.[6] But the author of the Apocalypse introduces himself at the very beginning: 'The Revelation of Jesus Christ, which he gave him to show unto his servants quickly; and he sent and signified it by his angel unto his servant John, who bare witness of the word of God and of his testimony, even of all things that he saw.'[7]
10　Then he writes also an epistle: 'John to the seven churches which are in Asia, grace be with you, and peace.'[8] But the evangelist did not prefix his name even to the Catholic Epistle; but without introduction he begins with the mystery of the divine revelation itself: 'That which was from the beginning, which we have heard, which we have seen with our eyes.'[9] For because of such a revelation the Lord also blessed Peter, saying, 'Blessed art thou, Simon Bar-Jonah, for flesh and blood hath not revealed it unto thee, but my heavenly
11　Father.'[10] But neither in the reputed second or third epistle of John, though they are very short, does the name John appear; but there is written the anonymous phrase, 'the elder.'[11] But this author did not consider it sufficient to give his name once and to proceed with his work; but he takes it up again: 'I, John, who also am your brother and companion in tribulation, and in the kingdom and in the patience of Jesus Christ, was in the isle that is called Patmos for the Word of God and the testimony of Jesus.'[12] And toward the close he speaks thus: 'Blessed is he that keepeth the words of the prophecy of this book, and I, John, who saw and heard these things.'[13]
12　"But that he who wrote these things was called John must be believed, as he says it; but who he was does not appear. For he did not say, as often in the Gospel, that he was the beloved disciple of the Lord,[14] or the one who lay on his breast,[15] or the brother of James, or the eyewitness and hearer of the Lord.
13　For he would have spoken of these things

if he had wished to show himself plainly. But he says none of them; but speaks of himself as our brother and companion, and a witness of Jesus, and blessed because he had seen and heard the revelations. But I am　14 of the opinion that there were many with the same name as the apostle John, who, on account of their love for him, and because they admired and emulated him, and desired to be loved by the Lord as he was, took to themselves the same surname, as many of the children of the faithful are called Paul or Peter. For　15 example, there is also another John, surnamed Mark, mentioned in the Acts of the Apostles,[16] whom Barnabas and Paul took with them; of whom also it is said, 'And they had also John as their attendant.'[17] But that it is he who wrote this, I would not say. For it is not written that he went with them into Asia, but, 'Now when Paul and his company set sail from Paphos, they came to Perga in Pamphylia; and John departing from them returned to Jerusalem.'[18] But I think that he was some　16 other one of those in Asia; as they say that there are two monuments in Ephesus, each bearing the name of John.[19]
"And from the ideas, and from the words　17 and their arrangement, it may be reasonably conjectured that this one is different from that one.[20] For the Gospel and Epistle　18 agree with each other and begin in the same manner. The one says, 'In the beginning was the Word';[21] the other, 'That which was from the beginning.'[22] The one: 'And the Word was made flesh and dwelt among us, and we beheld his glory, the glory as of the only begotten of the Father';[23] the other says the same things slightly altered: 'Which we have heard, which we have seen with our eyes; which we have looked upon and our hands have handled of the Word of life,—and the life was manifested.'[24] For he introduces these things　19 at the beginning, maintaining them, as is evident from what follows, in opposition to those who said that the Lord had not come in the flesh. Wherefore also he carefully adds, 'And we have seen and bear witness, and declare unto you the eternal life which was with the Father and was manifested unto us. That which we have seen and heard declare we unto you also.'[25] He holds to this and does not　20 digress from his subject, but discusses every-

---

ἀγωγείν is the same as διοικείν, as Suidas says." He translates *ex libelli totius ductu ac dispositione*, remarking that the words may be interpreted also as *formam et rationem scribendi, seu characterem.* The phrase evidently means the "general disposition" or "form" of the work. Closs translates "aus ihrer ganzen Ausführung"; Salmond, "the whole disposition and execution of the book"; Crusè, "the execution of the whole book."

[6] i.e. never speaks of himself in the first person, as "I, John"; nor in the third person, as e.g. "his servant, John."

[7] Rev. i. 1, 2.
[8] Rev. i. 4.
[9] 1 John i. 1.
[10] Matt. xvi. 17.
[11] See 2 John, ver. 1, and 3 John, ver. 1.
[12] Rev. i. 9.
[13] Rev. xxii. 7, 8. See above, note 3.
[14] See John xiii. 23, xix. 26, xx. 2, xxi. 7, 20.
[15] See John xiii. 23, 25. These words, οὐδὲ τὸν ἀναπεσόντα ἐπὶ τὸ στῆθος αὐτοῦ, are wanting in Heinichen's edition; but as they are found in all the other editions and versions, and Heinichen gives no reason for their omission, it is clear that they have been omitted inadvertently.

[16] In Acts xii. 12, 25, xiii. 5, 13, xv. 37. On Mark and the second Gospel, see above, Bk. II. chap. 15, note 4.
[17] Acts xiii. 5.
[18] Acts xiii. 13.
[19] See above, Bk. III. chap. 39, note 13; and on the "presbyter John," mentioned by Papias, see also note 4 on the same chapter, and on his relation to the Apocalypse, the same chapter, note 14.
[20] i.e. the writer of the Apocalypse is different from the writer of the Gospel and Epistles.
[21] John i. 1.
[22] 1 John i. 1.
[23] John i. 14.
[24] 1 John i. 1, 2.
[25] 1 John i. 2, 3.

thing under the same heads and names; some of which we will briefly mention. Any one who examines carefully will find the phrases, 'the life,' 'the light,' 'turning from darkness,' frequently occurring in both; also continually, 'truth,' 'grace,' 'joy,' 'the flesh and blood of the Lord,' 'the judgment,' 'the forgiveness of sins,' 'the love of God toward us,' the 'commandment that we love one another,' that we should 'keep all the commandments'; the 'conviction of the world, of the Devil, of Antichrist,' the 'promise of the Holy Spirit,' the 'adoption of God,' the 'faith continually required of us,' 'the Father and the Son,' occur everywhere. In fact, it is plainly to be seen that one and the same character marks the Gospel and the Epistle throughout. But the Apocalypse is different from these writings and foreign to them; not touching, nor in the least bordering upon them; almost, so to speak, without even a syllable in common with them. Nay more, the Epistle — for I pass by the Gospel — does not mention nor does it contain any intimation of the Apocalypse, nor does the Apocalypse of the Epistle. But Paul, in his epistles, gives some indication of his revelations,[26] though he has not written them out by themselves.

"Moreover, it can also be shown that the diction of the Gospel and Epistle differs from that of the Apocalypse. For they were written not only without error as regards the Greek language, but also with elegance in their expression, in their reasonings, and in their entire structure. They are far indeed from betraying any barbarism or solecism, or any vulgarism whatever. For the writer had, as it seems, both the requisites of discourse, — that is, the gift of knowledge and the gift of expression, — as the Lord had bestowed them both upon him. I do not deny that the other writer saw a revelation and received knowledge and prophecy. I perceive, however, that his dialect and language are not accurate Greek, but that he uses barbarous idioms, and, in some places, solecisms. It is unnecessary to point these out here, for I would not have any one think that I have said these things in a spirit of ridicule, for I have said what I have only with the purpose of showing clearly the difference between the writings."

21

22

23

24

25

26

27

CHAPTER XXVI.

The Epistles of Dionysius.

1   BESIDES these, many other epistles of Dionysius are extant, as those against Sabel-

lius,[1] addressed to Ammon,[2] bishop of the church of Bernice, and one to Telesphorus,[3] and one to Euphranor, and again another to Ammon and Euporus. He wrote also four other books on the same subject, which he addressed to his namesake Dionysius, in Rome.[4] Besides these many of his epistles are with us, and large books written in epistolary form, as those on Nature,[5] addressed to the young man Timothy, and one on Temptations,[6] which he also dedicated to Euphranor. Moreover, in a letter to Basilides,[7] bishop of the parishes in Pentapolis, he says that he had written an exposition of the beginning of Ecclesiastes.[8] And he has left us also various letters

2

3

[1] On Sabellius, and on Dionysius' attitude toward Sabellianism, see above, chap. 6, note 1.

[2] The works addressed to Ammon, Telesphorus, Euphranor, and Euporus, are no longer extant, nor do we know anything about them (but see chap. 6, note 2, above). It is possible that it was in these epistles that Dionysius laid himself open in his zeal against the Sabellians to the charge of tritheism, which aroused complaints against him, and resulted in his being obliged to defend himself in his work addressed to Dionysius of Rome. If so, these letters must have been written before that work, though perhaps not long before. Of Ammon himself we know nothing. There were a number of cities in North Africa, called Berenice (the form Bernice is exceptional), but, according to Wiltsch, Berenice, a city of Libya Pentapolis, or Cyrenaica, is meant in the present case. This city (whose original name was Hesperides) lay on the Mediterranean some six hundred miles west of Alexandria.

[3] Of Telesphorus, Euphranor, and Euporus, we know nothing.

[4] On these books addressed to Dionysius of Rome, see below, p. 397.

[5] οἱ περὶ φύσεως. The date and immediate occasion of this work cannot be determined. The supposition of Dittrich, that it was written before Dionysius became bishop, while he had more leisure than afterward for philosophical study, has much in its favor. The young man, Timothy, to whom it was addressed, is perhaps to be identified with the one mentioned in Bk. VI. chap. 40, § 4. That it was a work of considerable extent, embracing more than one book, is indicated by Eusebius in this passage. A long extract from it is given by Eusebius in his *Præp. Evang.* XIV. 23–27 (printed with commentary by Routh, *Rel. Sac.* IV. p. 393 sq.; translated in the *Ante-Nicene Fathers,* Vol. VI. p. 84–91), and a few fragments are still preserved in a Vatican codex, and have been published by Simon de Magistris, in his edition of Dionysius' works (Rome, 1796), p. 44 sq. (cf. also Routh, IV. p. 418, 419). In the extract quoted by Eusebius, Dionysius deals solely with the atomic theory of Democritus and Epicurus. This subject may have occupied the greater part of the work, but evidently, as Dittrich remarks (*Dionysius der Grosse,* p. 12), the doctrines of other physicists were also dealt with (cf. the words with which Eusebius introduces his extracts; *Præp. Evang.* XIV. 22. 10: "I will subjoin from the books [of Dionysius] On *Nature* a few of the things urged against Epicurus." The translation in the *Ante-Nicene Fathers,* Vol. VI. p. 84, note 7, which implies that the work was written "against the Epicureans" is not correct). φύσις seems to have been taken by Dionysius in the sense of the "Universe" (compare, for instance, the words of Cicero, *De nat. deorum,* II., to which Dittrich refers: *Sunt autem, qui naturæ nomine rerum universitatem intelligunt*), and to have been devoted to a refutation of the doctrines of various heathen philosophers in regard to the origin of the universe. For a fuller discussion of the work, see Dittrich, *ibid.* p. 12 sq.

[6] This work on Temptations (περὶ πειρασμῶν) is no longer extant, nor do we know anything about the time or occasion of its composition. Dittrich strangely omits all reference to it. Of Euphranor, as remarked in note 3, we know nothing.

[7] Of this Basilides we know only what Eusebius tells us here, that he was bishop of the "parishes in Pentapolis" (or Cyrenaica, a district, and under the Romans a province, lying west of Egypt, along the Mediterranean Sea), which would seem to imply that he was metropolitan of that district (cf. Routh, *Rel. Sac.* III. p. 235). A canonical epistle addressed to him by Dionysius is still extant (see above, Bk. VI. chap. 40, note 1). Eusebius tells us that Dionysius addressed "various epistles" to him, but no others are known to us.

[8] It is possible that this work also, like that On *Nature*, was written, as Dittrich thinks, before Dionysius became bishop. Eusebius evidently had not seen the commentary himself, for he speaks only of Dionysius' reference to it. A few fragments, supposed to be parts of this commentary, were published in the appendix to the fourteenth volume of Galland's *Bibliotheca Patrum Veterum*, after the latter's death, and were afterward reprinted in De Magistris' edition of Dionysius' works, p. 1 sq. (English translation in the *Ante-Nicene Fathers*, VI. p. 111–114). The fragments, or at least

[26] See 2 Cor. xii. 1 sq., Gal. ii. 2.

addressed to this same person. Thus much Dionysius.

But our account of these matters being now completed, permit us to show to posterity the character of our own age.[9]

CHAPTER XXVII.

Paul of Samosata, and the Heresy introduced by him at Antioch.

1   AFTER Xystus had presided over the church of Rome for eleven years,[1] Dionysius,[2] namesake of him of Alexandria, succeeded him. About the same time Demetrianus[3] died in Antioch, and Paul of Samosata[4] received

that episcopate. As he held, contrary to   2 the teaching of the Church, low and degraded views of Christ, namely, that in his nature he was a common man, Dionysius of Alexandria was entreated to come to the synod.[5] But being unable to come on account of age and physical weakness, he gave his opinion on the subject under consideration by letter.[6] But all the other pastors of the churches from all directions, made haste to assemble at Antioch, as against a despoiler of the flock of Christ.

CHAPTER XXVIII.

The Illustrious Bishops of that Time.

OF these, the most eminent were Firmilianus,[1] bishop of Cæsarea in Cappadocia;   1 the brothers Gregory[2] and Athenodorus, pastors of the churches in Pontus; Helenus[3] of the parish of Tarsus, and Nicomas[4] of Iconium; moreover, Hymenæus,[5] of the church of Jerusalem, and Theotecnus[6] of the neighboring church of Cæsarea; and besides these Maximus,[7] who presided in a distinguished manner over the brethren in Bostra. If any should count them up he could not fail to note a great many others, besides presbyters and deacons, who were at that time assembled for the same cause in the above-mentioned city.[8] But

---

a part of them, are ascribed to Dionysius in the codex in which they are found, and are very likely genuine, though we cannot speak with certainty. For fuller particulars, see Dittrich, p. 22 sq.

[9] τὴν καθ᾽ ἡμᾶς γενεάν. This seems to indicate that the events recorded by Eusebius from this point on took place during his own lifetime. See above, p. 4.

[1] Xystus II. was bishop only eleven months, not eleven years. See chap. 5, note 5. Eusebius' chronology of the Roman bishops of this time is in inextricable confusion.

[2] After the martyrdom of Xystus II. the bishopric of Rome remained vacant for nearly a year on account of the severe persecution of Valerian. Dionysius became bishop on the 22d of July, 259, according to the Liberian catalogue. Lipsius accepts this as the correct date. Jerome's version of the *Chron.* gives the twelfth year of "Valerian and Gallienus" (i.e. 265–266) which is wide of the mark. The Armenian *Chron.* gives the eighth year of the same reign. As to the duration of his episcopate, authorities vary considerably. Eusebius (chap. 30, § 23, below) and Jerome's version of the *Chron.* say nine years; the Armenian *Chron.*, twelve; the Liberian catalogue, eight. Lipsius shows that nine is the correct figure, and that five months and two days are to be read instead of the two months and four days of the Liberian catalogue. According to Lipsius, then, he was bishop until Dec. 27, 268. Dionysius of Alexandria addressed to Dionysius of Rome, while the latter was still a presbyter, one of his epistles on baptism (see above, chap. 7, § 6, where the latter is called by Eusebius a "learned and capable man"). Another epistle of the same writer addressed to him is mentioned in chap. 9, § 6. Dionysius of Alexandria's four books against the Sabellians were likewise addressed to him (see chap. 26, above, and Bk. VI. chap. 40, note 1). Gallienus' edict of toleration was promulgated while Dionysius was bishop (see chap. 13, note 3).

[3] On Demetrianus, see Bk. VI. chap. 46, note 12.

[4] Paul of Samosata was one of the most famous heretics of the early Church. He was bishop of Antioch and at the same time viceroy of Zenobia, Queen of Palmyra. Both versions of Eusebius' *Chron.* put the date of his accession to the see of Antioch in the seventh year of Valerian and Gallienus, the year of Abr. 2277 (2278), i.e. in A.D. 259 (260); and Jerome's version puts his deposition in the year of Abr. 2283, i.e. A.D. 265. These dates, however, are not to be relied upon. Harnack (*Zeit des Ignatius*, p. 51) shows that he became bishop between 257 and 260. Our chief knowledge of his character and career is derived from the encyclical letter written by the members of the council which condemned him, and quoted in part by Eusebius in chap. 30, below. This, as will be seen, paints his character in very black colors. It may be somewhat overdrawn, for it was written by his enemies; at the same time, such an official communication can hardly have falsified the facts to any great extent. We may rely then upon its general truthfulness. Paul reproduced the heresy of Artemon (see above, Bk. V. chap. 28), teaching that Christ was a mere man, though he was filled with divine power, and that from his birth, not merely from his baptism, as the Ebionites had held. He admitted, too, the generation by the Holy Spirit. "He denied the personality of the Logos and of the Holy Spirit, and considered them merely powers of God, like reason and mind in man; but granted that the Logos dwelt in Christ in a larger measure than in any former messenger of God, and taught, like the Socinians in later times, a gradual elevation of Christ, determined by his own moral development, to divine dignity. He admitted that Christ remained free from sin, conquered the sin of our forefathers, and then became the Saviour of the race" (Schaff). At various Antiochian synods (the exact number of them we do not know), efforts were made to procure his condemnation, but they were not successful. Finally one of the synods condemned and excommunicated him, and Domnus was appointed bishop in his place. The date of this synod is ordinarily fixed at 268 or 269, but it cannot have occurred in 269, and probably occurred rather than 268 (see below, chap. 30, note 1). Since Paul was in favor with Zenobia, his deposition could not be effected until 272, when Aurelian conquered her. Being appealed to by the Church, Aurelian left the decision between the claims of Paul and

Domnus to the bishops of Rome and Italy, who decided at once for Domnus, and Paul was therefore deposed and driven out in disgrace.

Our sources for a knowledge of Paul and his heresy are the letter quoted in chap. 30; a number of fragments from the acts of the council, given by Routh, *Rel. Sac.* III. 287 sq.; and scattered notices in the Fathers of the fourth century, especially Athanasius, Hilary, Gregory of Nyssa, &c. Cf. also Jerome's *de vir. ill.* 71, and Epiphanius' *Hær.* 65. See Harnack's article *Monarchianismus*, in Herzog, second ed. (abbreviated in Schaff-Herzog); also Smith and Wace's *Dict. of Christ. Biog.*, art. *Paulus of Samosata.*

[5] This synod to which Dionysius was invited was not the last one, at which Paul was condemned, but one of the earlier ones, at which his case was considered. It is not probable that the synod was called especially to consider his case, but that at two or more of the regular annual synods of Antioch the subject was discussed without result, until finally condemnation was procured (cf. Harnack, *ibid.* p. 52, and Lipsius, *ibid.* p. 228). Dionysius mentions the fact that he was invited to attend this synod in an epistle addressed to Cornelius, according to Eusebius, Bk. VI. chap. 46.

[6] Jerome, *de vir. ill.* 69, tells us that Dionysius wrote a few days before his death, but that is only an inference drawn from Eusebius' statement. This epistle of Dionysius is no longer extant, although a copy of it was originally appended to the encyclical of the Antiochian synod (as we learn from chap. 30, § 4), and hence must have been extant in the time of Eusebius, and also of Jerome. An epistle purporting to have been written by Dionysius to Paul of Samosata is given by Labbe, *Concil.* I. 850–893, but it is not authentic.

[1] On Firmilianus, see Bk. VI. chap. 26, note 3.

[2] Gregory Thaumaturgus. On him and his brother, Athenodorus, see Bk. VI. chap. 30, notes 1 and 2.

[3] On Helenus, see Bk. VI. chap. 46, note 8. He presided at the final council which deposed Paul of Samosata, according to the *Libellus Synodicus* (see Labbe, *Concilia,* I. 893, 901), and this is confirmed by the fact that in the encyclical epistle written by this synod his name stands first (see chap. 30).

[4] Of Nicomas, bishop of Iconium in Lycaonia, we know nothing. An earlier bishop of the same city, named Celsus, is mentioned in Book VI. chap. 19, above.

[5] On Hymenæus, see chap. 14, note 11.

[6] On Theotecnus, see chap. 14, note 9.

[7] Of Maximus, bishop of Bostra, in Arabia, we know nothing. On Beryllus, an earlier and more celebrated bishop of the same city, see above, Bk. VI. chap. 33.

[8] i.e. Antioch.

2 these were the most illustrious. When all of these assembled at different times and frequently to consider these matters, the arguments and questions were discussed at every meeting; the adherents of the Samosatian endeavoring to cover and conceal his heterodoxy, and the others striving zealously to lay bare and make manifest his heresy and blasphemy against Christ.

3 Meanwhile, Dionysius died in the twelfth year of the reign of Gallienus,[9] having held the episcopate of Alexandria for seventeen

4 years, and Maximus [10] succeeded him. Gallienus after a reign of fifteen years [11] was succeeded by Claudius,[12] who in two years delivered the government to Aurelian.

CHAPTER XXIX.

Paul, having been refuted by Malchion, a Presbyter from the Sophists, was excommunicated.

1 DURING his reign a final synod [1] composed of a great many bishops was held, and the leader of heresy [2] in Antioch was detected, and his false doctrine clearly shown before all, and he was excommunicated from the Catholic

2 Church under heaven.[3] Malchion especially drew him out of his hiding-place and refuted

him. He was a man ·learned in other respects, and principal of the sophist school of Grecian learning in Antioch; yet on account of the superior nobility of his faith in Christ he had been made a presbyter of that parish. This man, having conducted a discussion with him, which was taken down by stenographers and which we know is still extant, was alone able to detect the man who dissembled and deceived the others.

CHAPTER XXX.

The Epistle of the Bishops against Paul.

1 THE pastors who had assembled about this matter, prepared by common consent an epistle addressed to Dionysius,[1] bishop of Rome, and Maximus [2] of Alexandria, and sent it to all the provinces. In this they make manifest to all their own zeal and the perverse error of Paul, and the arguments and discussions which they had with him, and show the entire life and conduct of the man. It may be well to put on record at the present time the following extracts from their writing:

2 "To Dionysius and Maximus, and to all our fellow-ministers throughout the world, bishops, presbyters, and deacons, and to the whole Catholic Church under heaven,[3] Helenus,[4] Hymenæus, Theophilus, Theotecnus, Maximus, Proclus, Nicomas, Ælianus, Paul, Bolanus, Protogenes, Hierax, Eutychius, Theodorus,[5] Malchion, and Lucius, and all the others who dwell with us in the neighboring cities and nations, bishops, presbyters, and deacons, and the churches of God, greeting to the beloved brethren in the Lord." A little farther on

3 they proceed thus: " We sent for and called many of the bishops from a distance to relieve us from this deadly doctrine; as Dionysius of Alexandria [6] and Firmilianus [7] of Cappadocia,

---

[9] In both versions of the *Chron.* the death of Dionysius is put in the eleventh year of Gallienus, i.e. August, 263, to August, 264, and this, or the date given here by Eusebius (the twelfth year, August, 264, to August, 265) is undoubtedly correct. Upon the dates of his accession and death, see Bk. VI. chap. 40, note 1.

[10] Maximus had been a presbyter while Dionysius was bishop of Alexandria, and had shared with him the hardships of the Decian and Valerian persecutions (see above, chap. 11). In chap. 32, he is said to have held office eighteen years, and with this both versions of the *Chron.* agree, and there is no reason to doubt the accuracy of the report.

[11] Eusebius here, as in his *Chron.*, reckons the reign of Gallienus as beginning with the date of his association with his father in the supreme power; i.e. August, 253.

[12] Claudius became emperor in March, 268, and died of an epidemic in Sirmium some time in the year 270, when he was succeeded by Aurelian, whom he had himself appointed his successor just before his death. It is, perhaps, with this in mind that Eusebius uses the somewhat peculiar phrase, μεταδίδωσι τὴν ἡγεμονίαν.

[1] Eusebius puts this council in the reign of Aurelian (270–275), and in chap. 32 makes it subsequent to the siege of the Brucheium, which, according to his *Chron.*, took place in 272. The epistle written at this council (and given in the next chapter) is addressed to Maximus, bishop of Alexandria, and Dionysius, bishop of Rome, so that the latter must have been alive in 272, if the council was held as late as that. The council is ordinarily, however, assigned to the year 269, and Dionysius' death to December of the same year; but Lipsius has shown (*ibid.* p. 226 ff.) that the synod which Eusebius mentions here was held in all probability as early as 265 (but not earlier than 264, because Dionysius of Alexandria was not succeeded by Maximus until that year), certainly not later than 268, and hence it is not necessary to extend the episcopate of Dionysius of Rome beyond 268, the date which he has shown to be most probable (see chap. 27, note 2). Eusebius then is entirely mistaken in putting the council into the reign of Aurelian.

[2] i.e. Paul of Samosata.

[3] Malchion gained such fame from his controversy with Paul that an account of him is given by Jerome in his *de vir. ill.* 71. He tells us, however, nothing new about him, except that he was the author of an epistle to the bishops of Alexandria and Rome, referring probably to the encyclical letter given in the next chapter. We do not know upon what authority he bases this statement; in fact, knowing the character of his work, we shall probably be safe in assuming that the statement is no more than a guess on his part. There is nothing improbable in the report, but we must remember that Jerome is our only authority for it, and he is in such a case very poor authority (nevertheless, in Fremantle's article, *Malchion,*

in the *Dict. of Christ. Biog.*, the report is repeated as a fact). Both Eusebius and Jerome tell us that the report of his discussion with Paul was extant in their day, and a few fragments of it have been preserved, and are given by Leontius (*de Sectis*, III. p. 504, according to Fremantle).

[3] τῆς ὑπὸ τὸν οὐρανὸν καθολικῆς ἐκκλησίας, i.e. "from the *entire* Catholic Church." The phrase is usually strengthened by a πᾶς, as in the next chapter, § 2. On the use of the phrase, "Catholic Church," see Bk. IV. chap. 15, note 6.

[1] On Dionysius of Rome, see chap. 27, note 2.

[2] On Maximus of Alexandria, see chap. 28, note 10.

[3] This phrase differs from that used in the previous chapter by the addition of πᾶς.

[4] On Helenus, see Bk. VI. chap. 46, note 8. On Hymenæus and Theotecnus, see above, chap. 14, notes 11 and 9. Hierax is possibly the bishop addressed by Dionysius in the epistle quoted in chap. 21. Malchion is mentioned in the preceding chapter; Maximus of Bostra and Nicomas of Iconium, in chap. 28, as distinguished bishops. Of the others we know nothing.

[5] It has been suggested that Theodorus may be Gregory Thaumaturgus, who was also known by that name (see Bk. VI. chap. 30); but this is extremely improbable, for everywhere else in referring to him as bishop, Eusebius calls him Gregory, and in chap. 31 speaks of him as one of the most celebrated bishops, and puts him near the head of the list. Here Theodorus is placed near the end of the list, and no prominence is given him. There is in fact no reason to identify the two. The name Theodorus was a very common one.

[6] See chap. 27.

[7] On Firmilianus, see Bk. VI. chap. 26, note 3.

those blessed men. The first of these not considering the author of this delusion worthy to be addressed, sent a letter to Antioch,[8] not written to him, but to the entire parish, of which
4   we give a copy below.   But Firmilianus came twice[9] and condemned his innovations, as we who were present know and testify, and many others understand. But as he promised to change his opinions, he believed him and hoped that without any reproach to the Word what was necessary would be done.   So he delayed the matter, being deceived by him who denied even his own God and Lord,[10] and had not kept the faith which he formerly held.
5   And now Firmilianus was again on his way to Antioch, and had come as far as Tarsus, because he had learned by experience his God-denying wickedness. But while we, having come together, were calling for him and awaiting his arrival, he died."[11]
6   After other things they describe as follows the manner of life which he[12] led : "Whereas he has departed from the rule of faith,[12a] and has turned aside after base and spurious teachings, it is not necessary, — since he is without, — that we should pass judgment upon his practices : as for instance in that al-
7   though formerly destitute and poor, and having received no wealth from his fathers, nor made anything by trade or business, he now possesses abundant wealth through his iniquities and sacrilegious acts, and through those things which he extorts from the brethren,[13] depriving the injured of their rights and promising to assist them for reward, yet deceiving them, and plundering those who in their trouble are ready to give that they may obtain reconciliation with their oppressors,
8   'supposing that gain is godliness';[14] — or in that he is haughty, and is puffed up,

and assumes worldly dignities, preferring to be called ducenarius[15] rather than bishop ; and struts in the market-places, reading letters and reciting them as he walks in public, attended by a body-guard, with a multitude preceding and following him, so that the faith is envied and hated on account of his pride and haughtiness of heart ; — or in that he practices   9 chicanery in ecclesiastical assemblies, contrives to glorify himself, and deceive with appearances, and astonish the minds of the simple, preparing for himself a tribunal and lofty throne,[16] — not like a disciple of Christ, — and possessing a 'secretum,'[17] — like the rulers of the world, — and so calling it, and striking his thigh with his hand, and stamping on the tribunal with his feet ; — or in that he rebukes and insults those who do not applaud, and shake their handkerchiefs as in the theaters, and shout and leap about like the men and women that are stationed around him, and hear him in this unbecoming manner, but who listen reverently and orderly as in the house of God ; — or in that he violently and coarsely assails in public the expounders of the Word that have departed this life, and magnifies himself, not as a bishop, but as a sophist and juggler, and stops the   10 psalms to our Lord Jesus Christ, as being the modern productions of modern men, and trains women to sing psalms to himself in the midst of the church on the great day of the passover, which any one might shudder to hear, and persuades the bishops and presbyters of the neighboring districts and cities who fawn

---

[8] On this epistle, see chap. 27, note 6. As we see from this passage, the epistle of Dionysius was addressed not to Paul himself, but to the council, and hence could not be identified with the epistle given by Labbe, even were the latter authentic.

[9] It is plain from this passage that the case of Paul of Samosata had been discussed in at least two Antiochian synods before the one which deposed him, and not only in one as has been claimed. The passage shows, too, the way in which Paul escaped condemnation so long.   Not merely on account of his influential position, as some have said, but also because he promised that he would give up his heresy and conform his teaching to the orthodox faith.   The language would seem to imply that Firmilian had presided at the synod or synods, which are referred to here; and this is assumed by most writers.   On Firmilian, see Bk. VI. chap. 26, note 3.

[10] The words "and Lord" are wanting in some good MSS. as well as in Rufinus, and are consequently omitted by Schwegler and Heinichen.   But I have preferred to follow the majority of the MSS. and all the other editors in retaining the words which are really necessary to the sense; for it is not meant that Paul denied God, but that he denied his God and Lord Jesus Christ; namely, by rejecting his essential deity.

[11] On the date of Firmilian's death, see Bk. VI. chap. 26, note 3, above.

[12] i.e. Paul of Samosata.   [12a] τοῦ κανόνος.

[13] I follow Heinichen in reading ὧν ἔτι ἐκσείει τοὺς ἀδελφούς, which is supported by five important MSS. (cf. Heinichen's note in loco).   The majority of the editors read ὧν αἰτεῖ καὶ σείει κ.τ.λ., which, however, is not so well supported by MS. authority.   Laemmer, on the authority of a single codex, reads ὧν ἔτι καὶ σείει, and still other variations occur in some MSS.

[14] 1 Tim. vi. 5.

[15] Paul was the " Procurator Ducenarius " of Zenobia, the queen of Palmyra, an official so-called because his salary was 200 sestertia. "The Ducenarius was an imperial procurator, so-called from his salary of 200 sesteria, or 1600 pounds a year.   Some critics suppose that the bishop of Antioch had actually obtained such an office from Zenobia" (Gibbon).   There seems to be no reason to doubt that Paul held such a position under Zenobia, which appears to be the implication of the words here, and so he is commonly spoken of as a high official, even as "Viceroy" of Zenobia.   We know from Athanasius (Hist. Ar. § 71, Oxf. ed: Chap. VIII. § 10), that he was a great favorite with Zenobia, and that to her he owed the privilege of retaining his bishopric after she had deposed him.   This friendship shown toward him by Zenobia, who was of the strictest manners, is much in his favor, and almost tempts us to doubt the terrible character given him in this epistle by the members of the synod.   There must have been some palliating circumstances in the case.   He can hardly have been as unqualifiedly bad as this letter paints him.

[16] Valesius says, " The Fathers do not here condemn Paul because he had a throne; . . . but because he erected a tribunal for himself in the church and placed upon that a high throne.   Rufinus, therefore, translates this passage correctly: In ecclesia vero tribunal sibi multo altius quam fuerat exstrui, et thronum in excelsioribus collocari jubet.   Bishops did sit on a seat a little higher than the rest of the presbyters, but they did not have a tribunal."   This has been frequently quoted, and is on the whole a true statement of facts.   But the Greek is βῆμα μὲν καὶ θρόνον ὑψηλόν, and Rufinus is certainly wrong in putting his multo altius with the tribunal.   The emphasis, as the Greek reads, is upon the βῆμα as such, not upon the height of it, while the θρόνος is condemned because of its height.   The translation of Rufinus shows what was the custom in his day.   He could not understand that a βῆμα should be objected to as such.

[17] Greek σήκρητον, for the Latin secretum, which was the name of the place where the civil magistrates and higher judges sat to decide cases, and which was raised and enclosed with railings and curtains in order to separate it from the people.   In the present case it means of course a sort of cabinet which Paul had at the side of the tribunal, in which he could hold private conferences, and whose resemblance to the secretum of a civil magistrate he delighted to emphasize.

upon him, to advance the same ideas in
11　their discourses to the people. For to anticipate something of what we shall presently
write, he is unwilling to acknowledge that the
Son of God has come down from heaven. And
this is not a mere assertion, but it is abundantly
proved from the records which we have sent
you; and not least where he says 'Jesus Christ
is from below.'[18]　But those singing to him and
extolling him among the people say that their
impious teacher has come down an angel from
heaven.[19]　And he does not forbid such things;
but the arrogant man is even present when
12　they are uttered. And there are the women,
the 'subintroductæ,'[19a] as the people of Antioch call them, belonging to him and to the
presbyters and deacons that are with him. Although he knows and has convicted these men,
yet he connives at this and their other incurable
sins, in order that they may be bound to him, and
through fear for themselves may not dare to accuse him for his wicked words and deeds.[20]　But he
has also made them rich; on which account he is
loved and admired by those who covet such
13　things. We know, beloved, that the bishop
and all the clergy should be an example to
the people of all good works. And we are not
ignorant how many have fallen or incurred suspicion, through the women whom they have thus
brought in. So that even if we should allow
that he commits no sinful act, yet he ought to
avoid the suspicion which arises from such a
thing, lest he scandalize some one, or lead
14　others to imitate him. For how can he reprove or admonish another not to be too
familiar with women, — lest he fall, as it is written,[21] — when he has himself sent one away already, and now has two with him, blooming and

beautiful, and takes them with him wherever he
goes, and at the same time lives in luxury
and surfeiting? Because of these things all　15
mourn and lament by themselves; but they
so fear his tyranny and power, that they
dare not accuse him. But as we have said,　16
while one might call the man to account
for this conduct, if he held the Catholic doctrine and was numbered with us,[22] since he has
scorned the mystery and struts about in the
abominable heresy of Artemas[23] (for why should
we not mention his father?), we think it unnecessary to demand of him an explanation of
these things."

Afterwards, at the close of the epistle,　17
they add these words:

"Therefore we have been compelled to excommunicate him, since he sets himself against
God, and refuses to obey; and to appoint in
his place another bishop for the Catholic Church.
By divine direction, as we believe, we have appointed Domnus,[24] who is adorned with all the
qualities becoming in a bishop, and who is a
son of the blessed Demetrianus,[25] who formerly
presided in a distinguished manner over the
same parish. We have informed you of this that
you may write to him, and may receive letters of
communion[26] from him. But let this man write
to Artemas; and let those who think as Artemas
does, communicate with him."[27]

---

[18] Ἰησοῦν χριστὸν κάτωθεν. Compare, by way of contrast, the words of John iii. 31: "He that cometh from above is above all" (ὁ ἄνωθεν ἐρχόμενος ἐπάνω πάντων ἐστίν). The words quoted in the epistle can hardly have been used by Paul himself. They are rather to be regarded as a logical inference from his positions stated by the writers of the epistle in order to bring out the blasphemous nature of his views when contrasted with the statement in John, which was doubtless in their minds while they wrote.

[19] The account seems to me without doubt overdrawn at this point. It was such a common thing, from the time of Herod Agrippa down, to accuse a man who was noted for his arrogance of encouraging the people to call him an angel descended from heaven, that we should almost be surprised if the accusation were omitted here. We have no reason to think, in spite of the report of these good Fathers, that Paul's presumption went to such a blasphemous and at the same time absurd length.

[19a] σύνεισακτοι. On these Subintroductæ, see Smith and Cheetham's Dict. of Christ. Antiq., s.v.

[20] It is quite probable that Paul had given some ground for the suspicions which the worthy bishops breathe here, but that is very far from saying that he was actually guilty of immorality. In fact, just below (§ 13), they show that these are nothing more than sus-picions. Exactly what position the two women held who are men-tioned in § 14 it is difficult to say, but Paul must of course have given some plausible reason for their presence, and this is implied in § 16, where the writers say that were he orthodox, they would in-quire his reasons for this conduct, but since he is a heretic, it is not worth while to investigate the matter. As remarked above, while the direct statements of the epistle can in the main hardly be doubted, we must nevertheless remember that the prejudices of the writers would lead them to paint the life of Paul as black as circum-stances could possibly warrant, and unfounded suspicions might therefore easily be taken as equivalent to proved charges.

[21] cf. Ecclesiasticus xxv.

[22] We get a glimpse here of the relative importance of orthodoxy and morality in the minds of these Fathers. Had Paul been ortho-dox, they would have asked him to explain his course, and would have endeavored to persuade him to reform his conduct; but since he was a heretic, it was not worth while. It is noticeable that he is not condemned because he is immoral, but because he is heretical. The implication is that he might have been even worse than he was in his morals and yet no decisive steps have been taken against him, had he not deviated from the orthodox faith. The Fathers, in fact, by their letters, put themselves in a sad dilemma. Either Paul was not as wicked as they try to make him out, or else they were shame-fully indifferent to the moral character of their bishops, and even of the incumbents of their most prominent sees.

[23] On Artemas, or Artemon, see Bk. V. chap. 28, note 1. Paul's heresy was a reproduction of his, as remarked above, chap. 27, note 4.

[24] The action of this council in appointing Domnus was entirely irregular, as the choice of the bishop devolved upon the clergy and the people of the diocese. But the synod was afraid that Paul's influence would be great enough to secure his re-election, and hence they took this summary means of disposing of him. But it was only after the accession of Aurelian that Paul was actually removed from his bish-opric and Domnus was enabled to enter upon his office (see chap. 27, note 4). The exact date of Domnus' appointment is uncertain, as already shown (see the note just referred to); so also the date of his death. Both versions of the Chron. put his accession in the year of Abr. 2283 (A.D. 265), and Jerome's version puts the acces-sion of his successor, Timæus, in the year of Abr. 2288 (A.D. 270), while the Armenian omits the notice entirely. We can place no reliance whatever upon these dates; the date of Domnus' death is certainly at least two years too early (see the note already re-ferred to).

[25] On Demetrianus, the predecessor of Paul in the episcopate of Antioch, see Bk. VI. chap. 46, note 12.

[26] τὰ κοινωνικὰ γράμματα. Valesius says: "The Latins call them literas communicatorias, and the use of them is very ancient in the Church. They were also called formatæ (cf. Augustine Epistle 163). These writers were of two kinds: the one given to the clergy and laity when they were going to travel, in order that they might be admitted to communion by foreign bishops; while the other kind were sent by bishops to other bishops to declare their communion with them, and were in turn received from other bish-ops. Of the latter the synod speaks here. They were usually sent by new bishops soon after their ordination." Valesius refers to Augustine (ibid.), to Cyprian's epistle to Cornelius (Ep. 41, al. 45), and to the synodical epistle of the Council of Sardica.

[27] This is a very keen bit of sarcasm. As Harnack remarks, the mention of Artemas in this way proves (or at least renders it very

18   As Paul had fallen from the episcopate, as well as from the orthodox faith, Domnus, as has been said, became bishop of the
19 church at Antioch. But as Paul refused to surrender the church building, the Emperor Aurelian was petitioned; and he decided the matter most equitably, ordering the building to be given to those to whom the bishops of Italy and of the city of Rome should adjudge it.[28] Thus this man was driven out of the church, with extreme disgrace, by the worldly power.
20   Such was Aurelian's treatment of us at that time; but in the course of his reign he changed his mind in regard to us, and was moved by certain advisers to institute a persecution against us.[29] And there was great talk about
21 this on every side. But as he was about to do it, and was, so to speak, in the very act of signing the decrees against us, the divine judgment came upon him and restrained him at the very verge [30] of his undertaking, showing in a manner that all could see clearly, that the rulers of this world can never find an opportunity against the churches of Christ, except the hand that defends them permits it, in divine and heavenly judgment, for the sake of discipline and correction, at such times as it sees best.
22   After a reign of six years,[31] Aurelian was succeeded by Probus. He reigned for the same number of years, and Carus, with his sons, Carinus and Numerianus, succeeded him. After they had reigned less than three years the government devolved on Diocletian, and those associated with him.[32] Under them took place

the persecution of our time, and the destruction of the churches connected with it. Shortly before this, Dionysius,[33] bishop of 23 Rome, after holding office for nine years, died, and was succeeded by Felix.[34]

CHAPTER XXXI.

The Perversive Heresy of the Manicheans which began at this Time.

AT this time, the madman,[1] named from 1 his demoniacal heresy, armed himself in the perversion of his reason, as the devil, Satan,

---

probable) that he was still alive at this time, in which case his activity in Rome must be put somewhat later than the commonly accepted dates, viz. the episcopate of Zephyrinus (202–217).
[28] See chap. 27, note 4. The bishop of Rome to whose judgment Aurelian appealed was Felix, mentioned below.
[29] Aurelian, according to tradition, was the author of the ninth of the " ten great persecutions " against the Church. But the report is a mistake. Eusebius apparently is the ultimate source to which the report is to be referred, but he says expressly that he died before he was able to begin his intended persecution, and more than that, that he was even prevented from signing the decree, so that it is not proper to speak even of an hostile edict of Aurelian (as many do who reject the actual persecution). It is true that in Lactantius' *De mort. persecutorum*, chap. 6, it is said that Aurelian actually issued edicts against the Christians, but that he died before they had found their way to the most distant provinces. It seems probable, however, that Eusebius' account is nearest the truth, and that the reports that Aurelian actually signed the edicts as well as that he commenced the persecution are both developments from the original and more correct version of the affair which Eusebius gives. There is no reason to doubt the account of Eusebius. Aurelian's conduct in the case of Paul does not imply any special friendliness on his part toward the Church. The Christians had secured legal recognition under Gallienus; and it was a simple act of common justice to put the valuable property of the Church in Antioch into the hands of the rightful owners whoever they might be. His act does imply, however, that he cannot have been in the beginning actively hostile to the Church, for in that case he would simply have driven Paul out, and confiscated the property.
[30] μονονουχὶ ἐξ ἀγκώνων τῆς ἐγχειρήσεως αὐτὸν ἐπιδεσμοῦσα.
[31] Aurelian reigned from 270 to 275, and was succeeded by Tacitus, who ruled only six months, and he in turn by Probus (276 to 282), who was followed by Carus and his sons Carinus and Numerian, and they in turn by Diocletian in 284. Eusebius here omits Tacitus, although he mentions him in his *Chron.*, and assigns six months to his reign, and five years and six months to the reign of Aurelian.
[32] Diocletian associated Maximian with himself in the government in 286, and sent him to command the West with the title of Augustus. In 293 he appointed Constantius Chlorus and Galerius as Cæsars, giving to the former the government of Gaul and Britain,

to the latter that of the provinces between the Adriatic and the Euxine, while Maximian held Africa and Italy, and Diocletian himself retained the provinces of Asia. He issued an edict, opening his famous persecution against the Christians, of which Eusebius gives an account in the next book, on Feb. 23, 303.
[33] On Dionysius, bishop of Rome, see chap. 27, note 2.
[34] According to the Liberian catalogue, Felix became bishop on the fifth of January, 269, and held office five years eleven months and twenty-five days, until the thirtieth of December, 274, and these dates Lipsius accepts as correct. Eusebius, in chap. 32, gives five years as the duration of his episcopate, and with this Jerome's version of the *Chron.* agrees, while the Armenian gives nineteen years, which is absolutely inconsistent with its own notices, and must be of course a copyist's mistake. Jerome puts the accession of Felix in the first year of Probus, which is wide of the mark, and the Armenian in the first year of Aurelian, which is not so far out of the way.
Felix addressed a letter, in regard to Paul of Samosata, to Maximus and the clergy of Antioch, of which fragments have been preserved in the Apology of Cyril of Alexandria, and in the Acts of the Council of Ephesus (given by Mansi, *Conc.* I. 1114). The report of his martyrdom is probably a mistake, and has resulted from confusing him with Felix II., who was bishop of Rome in the fourth century.
[1] The name Manes, or Mani, is not of Greek, but of Persian or Semitic origin. It has not yet been satisfactorily explained. The Greek form is Μάνης or Μανιχαῖος; the Latin form, *Manes* or *Manichæus*. In this place Eusebius instead of giving him his true name makes a play upon it, calling him ὁ μανεὶς τὰς φρένας, " the madman." This does not imply that Eusebius supposed his name was originally Greek. He perhaps — as others of the Fathers did — regarded it as a sign of divine providence that the Persian name chosen by himself (Mani was not his original name) should when reproduced in Greek bear such a significant meaning. See Stroth's note on this passage.
Eusebius' brief account is the first authentic description we have of Manes and Manichæism. It is difficult to get at the exact truth in regard to the life of Manes himself. We have it reported in two conflicting forms, an Oriental and an Occidental. The former, however, — though our sources for it are much later than for the latter — is undoubtedly the more reliable of the two. The differences between the two accounts cannot be discussed here. We know that Mani was a well-educated Persian philosopher of the third century (according to Kessler, 205–276 A.D.; according to the Oriental source used by Beausobre, about 240–276), who attempted to supersede Zoroastrianism, the old religion of Persia, by a syncretistic system made up of elements taken from Parsism, Buddhism, and Christianity. He was at first well received by the Persian king, Sapor I., but aroused the hatred of the Magian priests, and was compelled to flee from the country. Returning after some time, he gained a large following, but was put to death by King Varanes I. about 276 A.D. His sect spread rapidly throughout Christendom, and in spite of repeated persecutions flourished for many centuries. The mysteriousness of its doctrine, its compact organization, its apparent solution of the terrible problem of evil, and its show of ascetic holiness combined to make it very attractive to thoughtful minds, as, e.g. to Augustine. The fundamental principle of the system is a radical dualism between good and evil, light and darkness. This dualism runs through its morals as well as through its theology, and the result is a rigid asceticism. Christianity furnished some ideas, but its influence is chiefly seen in the organization of the sect, which had apostles, bishops, presbyters, deacons, and traveling missionaries. Manichæism cannot be called a heresy, — it was rather an independent religion as Mohammedanism was. The system cannot be further discussed here. The chief works upon the subject are Beausobre's *Hist. Crit. de Manichée et du Manichéisme*, Amst. 1734 and 1739, 2 vols.; Baur's *Das Manichäische Religionssystem*, Tüb. 1831; Flügel's *Mani, Seine Lehre und seine Schriften, aus den Fihrist des Abû Jakub an-Nadûn*, Leipzig, 1882: and two works by Kessler (Leipzig, 1876 and 1882). See also the discussions of the system in the various Church histories, and especially the respective articles by Stokes and Kessler in Smith and Wace's *Dict. of Christ. Biog.* and in Herzog.

who himself fights against God, put him forward to the destruction of many. He was a barbarian in life, both in word and deed; and in his nature demoniacal and insane. In consequence of this he sought to pose as Christ, and being puffed up in his madness, he proclaimed himself the Paraclete and the very Holy Spirit;[2] and afterwards, like Christ, he chose twelve disciples as partners of his new doctrine. And he patched together false and godless doctrines collected from a multitude of long-extinct impieties, and swept them, like a deadly poison, from Persia to our part of the world. From him the impious name of the Manicheans is still prevalent among many. Such was the foundation of this "knowledge falsely so-called,"[3] which sprang up in those times.

CHAPTER XXXII.

The Distinguished Ecclesiastics[1] *of our Day, and which of them survived until the Destruction of the Churches.*

1 At this time, Felix,[2] having presided over the church of Rome for five years, was succeeded by Eutychianus,[3] but he in less than ten months left the position to Caius,[4] who lived in our day. He held it about fifteen years, and was in turn succeeded by Marcellinus,[5] who was

overtaken by the persecution. About the same time Timæus[6] received the episcopate of Antioch after Domnus,[7] and Cyril,[8] who lived in our day, succeeded him. In his time we became acquainted with Dorotheus,[9] a man of learning among those of his day, who was honored with the office of presbyter in Antioch. He was a lover of the beautiful in divine things, and devoted himself to the Hebrew language, so that he read the Hebrew Scriptures with facility.[10] He belonged to those who were especially liberal, and was not unacquainted with Grecian propædeutics.[11] Besides this he was a eunuch,[12] having been so from his very birth. On this account, as if it were a miracle, the emperor[13] took him into his family, and honored him by placing him over the purple dye-works at Tyre. We have heard him expound the Scriptures wisely in the Church. After Cyril, Tyrannus[14] re-

[2] Beausobre maintains that Mani did not pretend to be the Paraclete, but merely a man, the messenger of the Paraclete. The Fathers generally, however, agree with Eusebius in asserting that his claims were of the very highest sort. The point cannot be satisfactorily settled.

[3] See 1 Tim. vi. 20.   [1] ἐκκλησιαστικῶν ἀνδρῶν.

[2] On Felix, see chap. 30, note 34.

[3] Jerome's version of the *Chron.* agrees with this passage in assigning eight months to the episcopate of Eutychianus, while the Armenian gives him only two months. The Liberian catalogue, however, gives eight years eleven months and three days; and Lipsius accepts these figures as correct, putting his accession on the fifth of January, 275, and his death on the eighth of December, 283. Jerome puts his accession in the fifth year of Probus, which is wide of the mark, the Armenian in the second year, which is also too late by about two years. Lipsius explains the eight months of the *Church History* and the *Chron.* as a lapse, in their original source, of years to months. The present error makes up in part for the error in chap. 27, where Xystus is given eleven years instead of eleven months. Eutychianus was not a martyr, but was buried, according to the Liberian catalogue, in the Catacombs of St. Calixtus, a statement which has been confirmed by the discovery of a stone bearing his name.

[4] According to the Liberian catalogue, Caius became bishop on the 17th of December, 283, and held office for twelve years four months and six (or seven) days, i.e. until April 22, 296, and these dates are accepted by Lipsius as correct. Both versions of the *Chron.* agree with the *History* in assigning fifteen years to Caius' episcopate, but this error is of a piece with the others which abound in this period. The report of his martyrdom is fabulous.

[5] According to the Liberian catalogue, Marcellinus became bishop on the 30th of June, 296, and held office for eight years three months and twenty-five days, i.e. until the 25th of October, 304, and these dates Lipsius accepts as correct, although there is considerable uncertainty as to the exact date of his death. Jerome's version of the *Chron.* puts his accession in the twelfth year of Diocletian, which is not far out of the way, but does not give the duration of his episcopate, nor does Eusebius in his *History*. The Armenian *Chron.* does not mention Marcellinus at all. Tradition, although denied by many of the Fathers, says that he proved wanting in the Diocletian persecution, and this seems to have been a fact. It is also said that he afterward repented and suffered martyrdom, but that is only an invention. The expression of Eusebius in this connection is ambiguous; he simply says he was "overtaken by the persecution," which might mean martyrdom, or might mean simply arrest. The eleven bishops that preceded him from Pontianus to

Caius were buried in the Catacombs of St. Calixtus, but he was buried in those of Priscilla.

[6] Of Timæus we know nothing, nor can we fix his dates. The *Chron.* puts his accession in the year of Abr. 2288 (270 A.D.), and the accession of his successor, Cyril, in 2297 (279 A.D.), but the former at least is certainly far too early. Harnack (*Zeit des Ignatius*, p. 53) concludes that Cyril must have been bishop as early as 280, and hence neither Domnus nor Timæus can have held office a great while.

[7] On Domnus, see chap. 30, note 24.

[8] According to Jerome's *Chron.*, Cyril became bishop in the year of Abr. 2297, or fourth year of Probus (279-280 A.D.); and Harnack accepts this as at least approximately correct. The same authority puts the accession of his successor, Tyrannus, in the eighteenth year of Diocletian (301-302 A.D.), and just below Eusebius says that the destruction of the churches (in Diocletian's persecution) took place under Tyrannus, not under Cyril. But the *Passio sanctorum quattuor coronatorum* (see Mason's *Persecution of Diocletian*, p. 259-271) contains a reference to him which assumes that he was condemned to the mines, and died there after three years. The condemnation, if a fact, must have taken place after the second edict of Diocletian (303 A.D.), and his death therefore in 306. There is no other authority for this report, but Harnack considers it in the highest degree probable, and the indirect way in which Cyril is mentioned certainly argues for its truth. Neither Eusebius nor Jerome, however, seems to have known anything about it, and this is very hard to explain. The matter must, in fact, be left undecided. See Harnack, *Zeit des Ignatius*, p. 53 sq.

[9] This Dorotheus and his contemporary, Lucian (mentioned below, in Bk. VIII. chap. 13), are the earliest representatives of the sound critical method of Biblical exegesis, for which the theological school at Antioch was distinguished, over against the school of Alexandria, in which the allegorical method was practiced. From Bk. VIII. chap. 6 we learn that Dorotheus suffered martyrdom by hanging early in the Diocletian persecution, so that it must have been from this emperor, and not from Constantine, that he received his appointment mentioned just below. Diocletian, before he began to persecute, had a number of Christian officials in his household, and treated them with considerable favor.

[10] As Closs remarks, the knowledge of Hebrew was by no means a common thing among the early teachers of the Church; and therefore Dorotheus is praised for his acquaintance with it.

[11] προπαιδείας τῆς καθ' Ἕλληνας. Compare Bk. VI. chap. 18, § 3.

[12] According to the first canon of the Council of Nicæa (see Hefele, *Conciliengeschichte*, I. p. 376), persons who made themselves eunuchs were not to be allowed to become clergymen, nor to remain clergymen if already such. But this prohibition was made to apply to persons who were made eunuchs by physicians or by their persecutors; and the latter part of the canon confines the prohibition expressly to those who have purposely performed the act upon themselves, and hence nothing would have stood in the way of the advancement of one born a eunuch as Dorotheus was, even had he lived after the Council of Nicæa, and still less previous to that time. Closs (followed by Heinichen) is therefore hardly correct in regarding the fact that Dorotheus held office as an exception to the established order of things.

[13] i.e. Diocletian.

[14] According to Jerome's *Chron.* Tyrannus became bishop in the eighteenth year of Diocletian (301-302). If the account of Cyril's death accepted by Harnack be taken as correct, this date is at least a year too early. If Cyril was sent to the mines in 303 and died in 306, Tyrannus may have become bishop in 303, or not until

ceived the episcopate of the parish of Antioch. In his time occurred the destruction of the churches.

5   Eusebius,[15] who had come from the city of Alexandria, ruled the parishes of Laodicea after Socrates.[16] The occasion of his removal thither was the affair of Paul. He went on this account to Syria, and was restrained from returning home by those there who were zealous in divine things. Among our contemporaries he was a beautiful example of religion, as is readily seen from the words of Diony-

6   sius which we have quoted.[17] Anatolius[18] was appointed his successor; one good man, as they say, following another. He also was an Alexandrian by birth. In learning and skill in Greek philosophy, such as arithmetic and geometry, astronomy, and dialectics in general, as well as in the theory of physics, he stood first among the ablest men of our time, and he was also at the head in rhetorical science. It is reported that for this reason he was requested by the citizens of Alexandria to establish there a school of Aristotelian philosophy.[19]

7   They relate of him many other eminent deeds during the siege of the Pyrucheium[20]

in Alexandria, on account of which he was especially honored by all those in high office; but I will give the following only as an example. They say that bread had failed the besieged,   8 so that it was more difficult to withstand the famine than the enemy outside; but he being present provided for them in this manner. As the other part of the city was allied with the Roman army, and therefore was not under siege, Anatolius sent for Eusebius, — for he was still there before his transfer to Syria, and was among those who were not besieged, and possessed, moreover, a great reputation and a renowned name which had reached even the Roman general, — and he informed him of those who were perishing in the siege from famine. When he learned this he requested   9 the Roman commander as the greatest possible favor, to grant safety to deserters from the enemy. Having obtained his request, he communicated it to Anatolius. As soon as he received the message he convened the senate of Alexandria, and at first proposed that all should come to a reconciliation with the Romans. But when he perceived that they were angered by this advice, he said, " But I do not think you will oppose me, if I counsel you to send the supernumeraries and those who are in nowise useful to us, as old women and children and old men, outside the gates, to go wherever they may please. For why should we retain for no purpose these who must at any rate soon die? and why should we destroy with hunger those who are crippled and maimed in body, when we ought to provide only for men and youth, and to distribute the necessary bread among those who are needed for the garrison of the city?" With such arguments he persuaded the as-   10 sembly, and rising first he gave his vote that the entire multitude, whether of men or women, who were not needful for the army, should depart from the city, because if they remained and unnecessarily continued in the city, there would be for them no hope of safety, but they would perish with famine. As all the others in the   11 senate agreed to this, he saved almost all the besieged. He provided that first, those belonging to the church, and afterwards, of the others in the city, those of every age should escape, not only the classes included in the decree, but, under cover of these, a multitude of others, secretly clothed in women's garments; and through his management they went out of the gates by night and escaped to the Roman camp.

306. According to Theodoret, H. E. I. 3, his successor, Vitalis, is said to have become bishop "after peace had been restored to the Church," which seems to imply, though it is not directly said, that Tyrannus himself lived until that time (i.e. until 311). We know nothing certainly either about his character or the dates of his episcopate.

[15] This Eusebius, who is mentioned with praise by Dionysius of Alexandria, in the epistle quoted in chap. 11, above, was a deacon in the church of Alexandria, who distinguished himself by his good offices during the persecution of Valerian (A.D. 257), as recorded in that epistle, and also during the revolt and siege of Alexandria after the death of Valerian (in 262), as recorded in this chapter. From the account given here we see that he attended the first, or at least one of the earlier councils of Antioch in which the case of Paul was discussed (undoubtedly as the representative of Dionysius, whose age prevented his attending the first one, as mentioned in chap. 27), and the Laodiceans, becoming acquainted with him there, compelled him to accept the bishopric of their church, at that time vacant. As we see from the account of Anatolius' appointment farther on in this chapter, he died before the meeting of the council which condemned Paul. We know in regard to him only what is told us in these two chapters. The name Eusebius was a very common one in the early Church. The Dict. of Christ. Biog. mentions 137 persons of that name belonging to the first eight centuries.

[16] Of this Socrates we know nothing.

[17] In chap. 11, above.

[18] Anatolius we are told here was a man of great distinction both for his learning and for his practical common sense. It is not said that he held any ecclesiastical office in Alexandria, but farther on in the chapter we are told that he left that city after the close of the siege, as Eusebius had done, and that he was ordained assistant bishop by Theotecnus, bishop of Cæsarea, and was the latter's colleague in that church for a short time. When on his way to (possibly on his return from) the synod of Antioch, which passed condemnation upon Paul (and at which Theotecnus was also present), he passed through Laodicea and was prevailed upon to accept the bishopric of that city, Eusebius, his old friend, being deceased. The way in which Laodicea got its two bishops is thus somewhat remarkable. The character of Anatolius is clear from the account which follows. Jerome mentions him in his de vir. ill. chap. 73, and in his Ep. ad Magnum (Migne, No. 70), but adds nothing to Eusebius' account. Upon his writings, one of which is quoted in this chapter, see below, notes 21 and 32.

[19] τῆς Ἀριστοτέλους διαδοχῆς τὴν διατριβήν: "A school of the Aristotelian succession," or "order."

[20] The Pyrucheium (the MSS. of Eusebius vary considerably in their spelling, but I have adopted that form which seems best supported) or Brucheium (as it is called by other ancient writers and as it is more generally known) was one of the three districts of Alexandria and was inhabited by the royal family and by the Greeks. It was the finest and most beautiful quarter of the city, and contained, besides the royal palaces, many magnificent public buildings. Comprising, as it did, the citadel as well, it was besieged a number

of times, and it is uncertain which siege is meant in the present case. It seems to me most likely that we are to think of the time of the revolt of Æmilian (see above, chap. 11, note 4), in 260 A.D., when the Romans under Theodotus besieged and finally (just how soon we cannot tell, but the city seems to have been at peace again at least in 264) took the Brucheium. Valesius and others think of a later siege under Claudius, but that seems to me too late (see Tillemont, Hist. des Emp. III. p. 345 sq.).

There Eusebius, like a father and physician, received all of them, wasted away through the long siege, and restored them by every kind

12 of prudence and care.   The church of Laodicea was honored by two such pastors in succession, who, in the providence of God, came after the aforesaid war from Alexandria to that city.

13 Anatolius did not write very many works; but in such as have come down to us we can discern his eloquence and erudition. In these he states particularly his opinions on the passover. It seems important to give here the following extracts from them.[21]

From the Paschal Canons of Anatolius.

14 " There is then in the first year the new moon of the first month, which is the beginning of every cycle of nineteen years,[21a] on the twenty-sixth day of the Egyptian Phamenoth;[22] but according to the months of the Macedonians, the twenty-second day of Dystrus,[23] or, as the Romans would say, the eleventh before

15 the Kalends of April.   On the said twenty-sixth of Phamenoth, the sun is found not only entered on the first segment,[24] but already passing through the fourth day in it.   They are accustomed to call this segment the first dodecatomorion,[25] and the equinox, and the beginning of months, and the head of the cycle, and the starting-point of the planetary circuit.   But they call the one preceding this the last of months, and the twelfth segment, and the final dodecatomorion, and the end of the planetary circuit. Wherefore we maintain that those who place the first month in it, and determine by it the fourteenth of the passover, commit no slight

16 or common blunder.   And this is not an opinion of our own; but it was known to the Jews of old, even before Christ, and was carefully observed by them.   This may be learned from what is said by Philo, Josephus,

and Musæus;[26] and not only by them, but also by those yet more ancient, the two Agathobuli,[27] surnamed 'Masters,' and the famous Aristobulus,[28] who was chosen among the seventy interpreters of the sacred and divine Hebrew Scriptures[29] by Ptolemy Philadelphus and his father, and who also dedicated his exegetical books on the law of Moses to the same kings. These

17 writers, explaining questions in regard to the Exodus, say that all alike should sacrifice the passover offerings after the vernal equinox, in the middle of the first month.   But this occurs while the sun is passing through the first segment of the solar, or as some of them have styled it, the zodiacal circle.   Aristobulus adds that it is necessary for the feast of the passover, that not only the sun should pass through the equinoctial segment, but the moon also. For as there are two equinoctial segments,

18 the vernal and the autumnal, directly opposite each other, and as the day of the passover was appointed on the fourteenth of the month, beginning with the evening, the moon will hold a position diametrically opposite the sun, as may be seen in full moons; and the sun will be in the segment of the vernal equinox, and of necessity the moon in that of the autumnal. I know that many other things have been

19 said by them, some of them probable, and some approaching absolute demonstration, by which they endeavor to prove that it is altogether necessary to keep the passover and the feast of unleavened bread after the equinox. But I refrain from demanding this sort of demonstration for matters from which the veil of the Mosaic law has been removed, so that now at

[26] So far as I am aware, Musæus is known to us only from this reference of Anatolius.

[27] Who the two Agathobuli were we do not know. In the *Chron.* of Eusebius a philosopher Agathobulus is mentioned under the third year of Hadrian in connection with Plutarch, Sextus, and Œnomaus. Valesius therefore suspects that Anatolius is in error in putting the Agathobuli earlier than Philo and Josephus. I must confess, however, that the connection in which Eusebius mentions Agathobulus in his *Chron.* makes it seem to me very improbable that he can be referring to either of the Agathobuli whom Anatolius mentions, and that it is much more likely that the latter were two closely related Jewish writers (perhaps father and son), who lived, as Anatolius says, before the time of Philo.

[28] Aristobulus was a well-known Hellenistic philosopher of Alexandria, who lived in the time of Ptolemy Philometor in the second century B.C. He was thoroughly acquainted with Greek philosophy, and was in many respects the forerunner of Philo. Anatolius' statement that he wrote in the time of Ptolemy Philadelphus, and consequently his report that he was one of the seventy translators of the Septuagint (on the legend as to its composition, see Bk. V. chap. 8, note 31) must be looked upon as certainly an error (see Clement Alex. *Strom.* I. 22, Eusebius' *Præp. Evang.* IX. 6, and XIII. 12, and his *Chron.*, year of Abr. 1841). He is mentioned often by Clement of Alexandria, by Origen (*Contra Cels.* IV. 51), and by Eusebius, who in his *Præp. Evang.* (VII. 14 and VIII. 10) gives two fragments of his work (or works) *On the Mosaic Law.* It is doubtless to the same work that Anatolius refers in the present passage. No other fragments of his writings are extant. See especially Schürer, *Gesch. der Juden im Zeitalter Jesu Christi*, II. p. 760 sq. See also Bk. VI. chap. 23, note 13, above.

[29] On the origin of the LXX, see above, Bk. V. chap. 8, note 31. The mythical character of the common legend in regard to its composition is referred to in that note, and that the LXX (or at least that part of it which comprises the law) was already in existence before the time of Aristobulus is clear from the latter's words, quoted by Eusebius, *Præp. Evang.* XIII. 12, 1–2 (Heinichen's ed.).

[21] Anatolius' work on the passover is still extant in a Latin translation supposed to be the work of Rufinus (though this is uncertain), and which was first published by Ægidius Bucherius in his *Doctrina Temporum*, Antwerp, 1634. Ideler (*Chron.* II. 230) claims that this supposed translation of Anatolius is a work of the seventh century. But there are the best of reasons for supposing it an early translation of Anatolius' genuine work (see Zahn, *Forschungen zur Gesch. des N. T. Kanons*, III. p. 177-196). The Latin version is given with the other extant fragments of Anatolius' works in Migne's *Pat. Gr.* X. 209-222, 231-236, and an English translation of the *Paschal Canons* in the *Ante-Nicene Fathers*, VI. p. 146-151. Upon this work of Anatolius, see especially the works of Ideler and Zahn referred to just above.

[21a] Anatolius was, so far as we know, the first Christian to employ the old Metonic nineteen-year cycle for the determination of Easter (see above, chap. 20, note 6).

[22] Phamenoth was the seventh month of the Alexandrian year, which was introduced in the reign of Augustus (B.C. 25) and began on the 29th of August. The month Phamenoth, therefore, began on the 25th of February, and the 26th of the month corresponded to the 22d of our March.

[23] Dystrus was the seventh month of the Macedonian year, and corresponded exactly with our March, so that the 22d of Dystrus was the 22d of March, which according to the Roman method of reckoning was the eleventh day before the Kalends of April.

[24] i.e. the first of the twelve signs of the Zodiac. On Anatolius' method of calculation, see Ideler, *ibid.*

[25] δωδεκατημόριον: " twelfth-part."

length with uncovered face we continually behold as in a glass Christ and the teachings and sufferings of Christ.[30] But that with the Hebrews the first month was near the equinox, the teachings also of the Book of Enoch show." [31]

20 The same writer has also left the Institutes of Arithmetic, in ten books,[32] and other evidences of his experience and proficiency

21 in divine things. Theotecnus,[33] bishop of Cæsarea in Palestine, first ordained him as bishop, designing to make him his successor in his own parish after his death. And for a short time both of them presided over the same church.[34] But the synod which was held to consider Paul's case [35] called him to Antioch, and as he passed through the city of Laodicea, Eusebius being dead, he was detained by

22 the brethren there. And after Anatolius had departed this life, the last bishop of that parish before the persecution was Stephen,[36] who was admired by many for his knowledge of philosophy and other Greek learning. But he was not equally devoted to the divine faith, as the progress of the persecution manifested ; for it showed that he was a cowardly and unmanly dissembler rather than a true philoso-

23 pher. But this did not seriously injure the church, for Theodotus [37] restored their af-

fairs, being straightway made bishop of that parish by God himself, the Saviour of all. He justified by his deeds both his lordly name [38] and his office of bishop. For he excelled in the medical art for bodies, and in the healing art for souls. Nor did any other man equal him in kindness, sincerity, sympathy, and zeal in helping such as needed his aid. He was also greatly devoted to divine learning. Such an one was he.

In Cæsarea in Palestine, Agapius [39] suc- 24 ceeded Theotecnus, who had most zealously performed the duties of his episcopate. Him too we know to have labored diligently, and to have manifested most genuine providence in his oversight of the people, particularly caring for all the poor with liberal hand. In his 25 time we became acquainted with Pamphilus,[40] that most eloquent man, of truly philosophical life, who was esteemed worthy of the office of presbyter in that parish. It would be no small matter to show what sort of a man he was and whence he came. But we have de-

---

[30] Cf. 2 Cor. iii. 18.

[31] The Book of Enoch is one of the so-called Old Testament Pseudepigrapha, which was widely used in the ancient Church, and is quoted in the Epistle of Jude, 14 sq. The work disappeared after about the fifth century, and was supposed to have perished (with the exception of a few fragments) until in 1773 it was discovered entire in an Ethiopic Bible, and in 1838 was published in Ethiopic by Lawrence, who in 1821 had already translated it into English. Dillmann also published the Ethiopic text in 1851, and in 1853 a German translation with commentary. Dillmann's edition of the original entirely supersedes that of Lawrence, and his translation and commentary still form the standard work upon the subject. More recently it has been re-translated into English and discussed by George H. Schodde: *The Book of Enoch, translated, with Introduction and Notes*, Andover, 1882. The literature on the book of Enoch is very extensive. See especially Schodde's work, the German translation of Dillmann, Schürer's *Gesch. der Juden*, II. p. 616 sq., and Lipsius' article, *Enoch, Apocryphal Book of*, in the *Dict. of Christ. Biog.*

The teachings of the book to which Anatolius refers are found in the seventy-second chapter (Schodde's ed. p. 179 sq.), which contains a detailed description of the course of the sun during the various months of the year.

[32] Ἀριθμητικὰς εἰσαγωγάς. A few fragments of this work are given in the *Theologumena Arithmeticæ* (Paris, 1543), p. 9, 16, 24, 34, 56, 64 (according to Fabricius), and by Fabricius in his *Bibl. Gr.* II. 275-277 (ed. Harles, III. 462 sq.).

[33] On Theotecnus, see chap. 14, note 9.

[34] On the custom of appointing assistant bishops, see Bk. VI. chap. 11, note 1.

[35] Eusebius doubtless refers here to the final council at which Paul was condemned, and which has been already mentioned in chaps. 29 and 30 (on its date, see chap. 29, note 1). That it is this particular council to which he refers is implied in the way in which it is spoken of, — as if referring to the well-known synod, of which so much has been said, — and still further by the fact that Eusebius, who had attended the first one (see above, § 5), and had then become bishop of Laodicea, was already dead.

[36] Of Stephen, bishop of Laodicea, we know only what Eusebius tells us in this passage.

[37] Theodotus, of whom Eusebius speaks in such high terms in this passage, was bishop of Laodicea for a great many years, and played a prominent part in the Arian controversy, being one of the most zealous supporters of the Arian cause (see Theodoret, *H. E.* I. 5 and V. 7, and Athanasius *de Synodis Arim. et Selenc.* I. 17). He was present at the Council of Nicæa (Labbe, *Concil.* II. 51), and took part in the council which deposed Eustathius of Antioch in 330 (according to Theodoret, *H. E.* I. 21, whose account, though unreliable, is very likely correct so far as its list of bishops is concerned; on the council, see also p. 21, above). He was already

dead in the year 341; for his successor, George, was present at the Council of Antioch (*In Encæniis*), which was held in that year (see Sozomen, *H. E.* III. 5, and cf. Hefele, *Conciliengesch.* I. p. 502 sq.). We have no information that he was present at the Council of Tyre, in 335 (as is incorrectly stated by Labbe, who confounds Theodore of Heraclea with Theodotus; see Theodoret, *H. E.* I. 28). It is, therefore, possible that he was at that time, though his absence of course does not prove it. According to Socrates, *H. E.* II. 46, and Sozomen, *H. E.* VI. 25, Theodotus had trouble with the two Apolinarii, father and son, who resided at Antioch. We do not know the date of the younger Apolinarius' birth (the approximate date, 335, given in the article in the *Dict. of Christ. Biog.* is a gross error), but we can hardly put it much earlier than 320, and therefore as he was a reader in the church, according to Socrates (Sozomen calls him only a youth) in the time of Theodotus, it seems best to put the death of the latter as late as possible, perhaps well on toward 340. The date of his accession is unknown to us; but as Eusebius says that he became bishop straightway after the fall of Stephen, we cannot well put his accession later than 311; so that he held office in all probability some thirty years. Venables' article on Theodotus, in the *Dict. of Christ. Biog.* is a tissue of errors, caused by identifying Theodotus with Theodore of Heraclea (an error committed by Labbe before him) and with another Theodotus, present at the Council of Seleucia, in 359 (Athanasius, *ibid.* I. 12; cf. Hefele, *Conciliengesch.* I. p. 713).

[38] Θεόδοτος: "God-given."

[39] Of Agapius we know only what Eusebius tells us in this passage. He was the immediate predecessor of Eusebius in the church of Cæsarea, and probably survived the persecution, but not for many years (see above, p. 10 sq.). Eusebius speaks of him in the past tense, so that he was clearly already dead at the time this part of the History was written (i.e. probably in 313; see above, p. 45).

[40] Pamphilus, a presbyter of Cæsarea, was Eusebius' teacher and most intimate friend, and after his death Eusebius showed his affection and respect for him by adopting his name, styling himself Eusebius Pamphili. He pursued his studies in Alexandria (according to Photius, under Pierius, more probably under Achillas, the head of the catechetical school there; see below, notes 42 and 53), and conceived an unbounded admiration for Origen, the great light of that school, which he never lost. Pamphilus is chiefly celebrated for the library which he collected at Cæsarea and to which Eusebius owes a large part of the materials of his history. Jerome also made extensive use of it. It was especially rich in copies of the Scripture, of commentaries upon it, and of Origen's works (see above, p. 38). He wrote very little, devoting himself chiefly to the study of Scripture, and to the transcription of MSS. of it and of the works of Origen. During the last two years of his life, however, while in prison, he wrote with the assistance of Eusebius a *Defense of Origen* in five books, to which Eusebius afterward added a sixth (see above, p. 36 sq.). During the persecution under Maximinus, he was thrown into prison by Urbanus, prefect of Cæsarea, in 307, and after remaining two years in close confinement, cheered by the companionship of Eusebius, he was put to death by Firmilian, the successor of Urbanus, in 309, as recorded below, in the *Martyrs of Palestine*, chap. 11 (see above, p. 9). The *Life of Pamphilus* which Eusebius wrote is no longer extant (see above, p. 38). On Pamphilus, see Jerome, *de vir. ill.* chap. 75, and Photius, *Cod.* 118. See also the present volume, p. 5-9 *passim*.

scribed, in our special work concerning him,[41] all the particulars of his life, and of the school which he established, and the trials which he endured in many confessions during the persecution, and the crown of martyrdom with which he was finally honored. But of all that were there he was indeed the most admirable.

26 Among those nearest our times, we have known Pierius,[42] of the presbyters in Alexandria, and Meletius,[43] bishop of the 27 churches in Pontus, — rarest of men. The first was distinguished for his life of extreme poverty and his philosophic learning, and was exceedingly diligent in the contemplation and exposition of divine things, and in public discourses in the church. Meletius, whom the learned called the "honey of Attica,"[44] was a man whom every one would describe as most accomplished in all kinds of learning; and it

would be impossible to admire sufficiently his rhetorical skill. It might be said that he possessed this by nature; but who could surpass the excellence of his great experience and erudition in other respects? For in all 28 branches of knowledge had you undertaken to try him even once, you would have said that he was the most skillful and learned. Moreover, the virtues of his life were not less remarkable. We observed him well in the time of the persecution, when for seven full years he was escaping from its fury in the regions of Palestine.

Zambdas[45] received the episcopate of the 29 church of Jerusalem after the bishop Hymenæus, whom we mentioned a little above.[46] He died in a short time, and Hermon,[47] the last before the persecution in our day, succeeded to the apostolic chair, which has been preserved there until the present time.[48] In 30 Alexandria, Maximus,[49] who, after the death of Dionysius,[50] had been bishop for eighteen years, was succeeded by Theonas.[51] In his time Achillas,[52] who had been appointed a pres-

---

[41] On Eusebius' *Life of Pamphilus*, see above, p. 28 sq.

[42] According to Jerome (*de vir. ill.* 76) Pierius was a presbyter and a teacher in Alexandria under the emperors Carus and Diocletian, while Theonas was bishop there (see note 51, below), on account of the elegance of his writings was called "the younger Origen," was skilled, moreover, in dialectics and rhetoric, lived an ascetic life, and passed his later years, after the persecution, in Rome. According to Photius, *Cod.* 118, he was at the head of the catechetical school of Alexandria, was the teacher of Pamphilus, and finally suffered martyrdom. Photius may be correct in the former statements. The last statement is at variance with Jerome's distinct report, which in the present instance at least is to be decidedly preferred to that of Photius. The first statement also is subject to grave doubt, for according to Eusebius (§ 30, below), Achillas, who was made presbyter at the same time as Pierius, and who lived until after the persecution (when he became bishop), was principal of the school. Eusebius' statement must be accepted as correct, and in that case it is difficult to believe the report of Photius, both on account of Eusebius' silence in regard to Pierius' connection with the school, and also because if Pierius was principal of the school, he must apparently have given it up while he was still in Alexandria, or must have left the city earlier than Jerome says. It is more probable that Photius' report is false and rests upon a combination of the accounts of Eusebius and Jerome. If both the first and third statements of Photius are incorrect, little faith can be placed on the second, which may be true, or which may be simply a combination of the known fact that Pamphilus studied in Alexandria with the supposed fact that Pierius was the principal of the catechetical school while he was there. It is quite as probable that Pamphilus studied with Achillas. Jerome tells us that a number of works (*tractatuum*) by Pierius were extant in his day, among them a long homily on Hosea (cf. also Jerome's *Comment. in Osee, prologus*). In his second epistle to Pammachius (Migne, No. 49) Jerome refers also to Pierius' commentary on First Corinthians, and quotes from it the words, "In saying this Paul openly preaches celibacy." Photius, *Cod.* 119, mentions a work in twelve books, whose title he does not name, but in which he tells us Pierius had uttered some dangerous sentiments in regard to the Spirit, pronouncing him inferior to the Father and the Son. This work contained, according to Photius, a book on Luke's Gospel, and another on the passover, and on Hosea. Pierius' writings are no longer extant. The passages from Jerome's epistle to Pammachius and from Photius, *Cod.* 119, are given, with notes, by Routh, *Rel. Sac.* 2d ed. III. 429 sq., and an English translation in the *Ante-Nicene Fathers*, VI. p. 157. Pierius was evidently a "younger Origen" in his theology as well as in his literary character, as we can gather from Photius' account of him (cf. Harnack's *Dogmengesch.* I. p. 640).

[43] A Meletius, bishop of Sabastopolis, is mentioned by Philostorgius (*H. E.* I. 8) as in attendance upon the Council of Nicæa, and it is commonly assumed that this is the same one referred to here by Eusebius. But Eusebius' words seem to me to imply clearly that the Meletius of whom he speaks was already dead at the time he wrote; and, therefore, if we suppose that Philostorgius is referring to the same man, we must conclude that he was mistaken in his statement, possibly confounding him with the later Meletius of Sebaste, afterwards of Antioch. Our Meletius is, however, doubtless to be identified with the orthodox Meletius mentioned in terms of praise by Athanasius, in his *Ep. ad Episc. Æg.* § 8, and by Basil in his *De Spir. Sanct.* chap. 29, § 74. It is suggested by Stroth that Eusebius was a pupil of Meletius during the time that the latter was in Palestine, but this is not implied in Eusebius' words (see above, p. 5).

[44] τὸ μέλι τῆς Ἀττικῆς, in allusion to Meletius' name.

[45] The majority of the MSS. and editors read Ζάμβδας. A few MSS. followed by Laemmer read Ζαβαδᾶς, and a few others with Rufinus, both versions of the *Chron.* and Nicephorus Ζάβδας. We know nothing about this bishop, except what is told us here and in the *Chron.*, where he is called the thirty-eighth bishop (Jerome calls him the thirty-seventh, but incorrectly according to his own list), and is said to have entered upon his office in the fifteenth year of Diocletian (Armen. fourteenth), i.e. in 298. Hermon succeeded him three years later, according to Jerome; two years later, according to the Armenian version.

[46] In chap. 14. See note 11 on that chapter.

[47] According to Jerome's version of the *Chron.*, Hermon became bishop in the eighteenth year of Diocletian, A.D. 301; according to the Armenian, in the sixteenth year. The accession of his successor Macharius is put by Jerome in the eighth year of Constantine, A.D. 312. Eusebius' words seem to imply that Hermon was still bishop at the time he was writing, though it is not certain that he means to say that. Jerome's date may be incorrect, but is probably not far out of the way. Of Hermon himself we know nothing more.

[48] See above, chap. 19.

[49] On Maximus, see chap. 28, note 10.

[50] On Dionysius the Great, see especially Bk. VI. chap. 40, note 1.

[51] According to Jerome's *Chron.*, Theonas became bishop in the sixth year of Probus (281 A.D.); according to the Armenian, in the first year of Numerian and Carinus, i.e. a year later. Both agree with the *History* in assigning nineteen years to his episcopate. An interesting and admirable epistle is extant addressed to Lucian, the chief chamberlain of the emperor, and containing advice in regard to the duties of his position, which is commonly and without doubt correctly ascribed to Theonas. The name of the emperor is not given, but all of the circumstances point to Diocletian, who had a number of Christians in influential positions in his household during the earlier years of his reign. The epistle, which is in Latin (according to some a translation of a Greek original), is given by Routh, *Rel. Sac.* III. 439-445, and an English translation is contained in the *Ante-Nicene Fathers*, VI. p. 158-161.

[52] The character given to Achillas by Eusebius is confirmed by Athanasius, who calls him "the great Achillas" (in his *Epistle to the Bishops of Egypt*, § 23). He succeeded Peter as bishop of Alexandria (Epiphanius makes him the successor of Alexander, but wrongly, for the testimony of Athanasius, to say nothing of Jerome, Socrates, and other writers, is decisive on this point; see Athanasius' *Apology against the Arians*, §§ 11 and 59, and *Epist. to the Bishops of Egypt*, § 23), but our authorities differ as to the date of his accession and the length of his episcopate. Eusebius, in this chapter, § 31, puts the death of Peter in the ninth year of the persecution (311-312), and with this Jerome agrees in his *Chron.*, and there can be no doubt as to the correctness of the report. But afterwards, quite inconsistently (unless it be supposed that Achillas became bishop before Peter's death, which, in the face of Eusebius' silence on the subject, is very improbable), Jerome puts the accession of Achillas into the fifth year of Constantine, A.D. 309. Jerome commits another error in putting the accession of his successor, Alexander, in the sixteenth year of Constantine (A.D. 320); for Alexander's

byter in Alexandria at the same time with Pierius, became celebrated. He was placed over the school of the sacred faith,[53] and exhibited fruits of philosophy most rare and inferior to none, and conduct genuinely evangelical. After Theonas had held the office for nineteen years, Peter[54] received the episcopate in Alexandria, and was very eminent among them for twelve entire years. Of these he governed the church less than three years before the persecution, and for the remainder of his life he subjected himself to a more rigid discipline and cared in no secret manner for the general interest of the churches. On this account he was beheaded in the ninth year of the persecution, and was adorned with the crown of martyrdom.

Having written out in these books the account of the successions from the birth of our Saviour to the destruction of the places of worship, — a period of three hundred and five years,[55] — permit me to pass on to the contests of those who, in our day, have heroically fought for religion, and to leave in writing, for the information of posterity, the extent and the magnitude of those conflicts.

---

controversy with Arius (see above, p. 11 sq.) can hardly have broken out later than 318 or 319, and it would appear that Alexander had been bishop already some time when that took place. Theodoret (*H. E.* I. 2) states that Achillas ruled the church but a short time, and with him agrees Epiphanius (*Hær.* LXIX. 11), who says that he held office but three months. The casual way in which Achillas is spoken of in all our sources, most of which mention him only in passing from Peter to Alexander, would seem to confirm Theodoret's report, and Alexander's accession may, therefore, be put not long after 311.

[53] τῆς ἱερᾶς πίστεως τὸ διδασκαλεῖον. Eusebius refers here to the famous catechetical school of Alexandria (upon which, see above, Bk. V. chap. 10, note 2). The appointment of Achillas to the principalship of this school would seem to exclude Pierius, who is said by Photius to have been at the head of it (see above, note 42).

[54] Peter is mentioned again in Bk. VIII. chap. 13, and in Bk. IX. chap. 6, and both times in the highest terms. In the latter passage his death is said to have taken place by order of Maximinus, quite unexpectedly and without any reason. This was in the ninth year of the persecution, as we learn from the present passage (i.e. Feb. 311 to Feb. 312, or according to Eusebius' own reckoning, Mar. or Apr. 311 to Mar. or Apr. 312; see below Bk. VII. chap. 2, note o), and evidently after the publication of the toleration edict of Galerius, when the Christians were not looking for any further molestation

(see below, Bk. VIII. chap. 14, note 2). According to this passage, Peter was bishop less than three years before the outbreak of the persecution, and hence he cannot have become bishop before the spring of 300. On the other hand since he died as early as the spring of 312, and was bishop twelve years he must have become bishop not later than the spring of 300, and he must have died not long before the spring of 312, and even then, if Eusebius' other statements are exact, it is impossible to make his episcopate fully twelve years in length. The date thus obtained for his accession is in accord with the dates given for the episcopate of his predecessor Theonas (see above, note 51). Jerome puts his accession in the nineteenth year of Diocletian (A.D. 302), but this is at variance with his own figures in connection with Theonas, and is plainly incorrect.

Fourteen *Canons*, containing detailed directions in regard to the lapsed were drawn up by Peter in 306 (see the opening sentence of the first canon), and are still extant. They are published in all collections of canons and also in numerous other works. See especially Routh's *Rel. Sac.* IV. p. 23 sq. An English translation is given in the *Ante-Nicene Fathers*, VI. p. 269–278. Brief fragments of other works — *On the Passover*, *On the Godhead*, *On the Advent of the Saviour*, *On the Soul*, and the beginning of an epistle addressed to the Alexandrians — are given by Routh, *ibid.* p. 45 sq. These fragments, together with a few others of doubtful origin, given by Gallandius and Mai, are translated in the *Ante-Nicene Fathers*, *ibid.* p. 280–283. In the same volume (p. 261–268) are given *The Genuine Acts of Peter*, containing an account of his life and martyrdom. These, however, are spurious and historically quite worthless.

Peter seems, to judge from the extant fragments, to have been in the main an Origenist, but to have departed in some important respects from the teachings of Origen, especially on the subject of anthropology (cf. Harnack's *Dogmengesch.* I. p. 644). The famous Meletian schism took its rise during the episcopate of Peter (see Athanasius, *Apology against the Arians*, § 59).

[55] Diocletian's edict decreeing the demolition of the churches was published in February, 303. See Bk. VIII. chap. 2, note 3.

BOOK VIII.

INTRODUCTION.

As we have described in seven books the events from the time of the apostles,[1] we think it proper in this eighth book to record for the information of posterity a few of the most important occurrences of our own times, which are worthy of permanent record. Our account will begin at this point.

CHAPTER I.

The Events which preceded the Persecution in our Times.

1　It is beyond our ability to describe in a suitable manner the extent and nature of the glory and freedom with which the word of piety toward the God of the universe, proclaimed to the world through Christ, was honored among all men, both Greeks and barbarians, be-
2　fore the persecution in our day. The favor shown our people by the rulers might be adduced as evidence; as they committed to them the government of provinces,[1] and on account of the great friendship which they entertained toward their doctrine, released them
3　from anxiety in regard to sacrificing. Why need I speak of those in the royal palaces, and of the rulers over all, who allowed the members of their households, wives[2] and children and servants, to speak openly before them for the Divine word and life, and suffered them almost to boast of the freedom of their faith? Indeed they esteemed them highly, and
4　preferred them to their fellow-servants. Such an one was that Dorotheus,[3] the most de-

voted and faithful to them of all, and on this account especially honored by them among those who held the most honorable offices and governments. With him was the celebrated Gorgonius,[4] and as many as had been esteemed worthy of the same distinction on account of the word of God. And one could see the　5 rulers in every church accorded the greatest favor[5] by all officers and governors.

But how can any one describe those vast assemblies, and the multitude that crowded together in every city, and the famous gatherings in the houses of prayer; on whose account not being satisfied with the ancient buildings they erected from the foundation large churches in all the cities? No envy　6 hindered the progress of these affairs which advanced gradually, and grew and increased day by day. Nor could any evil demon slander them or hinder them through human counsels, so long as the divine and heavenly hand watched over and guarded his own people as worthy.

But when on account of the abundant　7 freedom, we fell into laxity and sloth, and envied and reviled each other, and were almost, as it were, taking up arms against one another, rulers assailing rulers with words like spears, and people forming parties against people, and monstrous hypocrisy and dissimulation rising to the greatest height of wickedness, the divine judgment with forbearance, as is its pleasure, while the multitudes yet continued to assemble, gently and moderately harassed the episcopacy. This persecution began with the brethren　8 in the army. But as if without sensibility, we were not eager to make the Deity favorable and propitious; and some, like atheists, thought that our affairs were unheeded and ungoverned; and thus we added one wickedness to another.

---

[1] Literally, "the succession of the apostles" (τὴν τῶν ἀποστόλων διαδοχήν).

[1] τὰς τῶν ἐθνῶν ἡγεμονίας.

[2] γαμεταῖς. Prisca, the wife, and Valeria, the daughter, of Diocletian, and the wife of Galerius, were very friendly to the Christians, and indeed there can be little doubt that they were themselves Christians, or at least catechumens, though they kept the fact secret and sacrificed to the gods (Lactantius, *De mort. pers.* 15) when all of Diocletian's household were required to do so, after the second conflagration in the palace (see Mason's *Persecution of Diocletian*, p. 40, 121 sq.). It is probable in the present case that Eusebius is thinking not simply of the wives of Diocletian and Galerius, but also of all the women and children connected in any way with the imperial household.

[3] Of this Dorotheus we know only what is told us here and in chap. 6, below, where it is reported that he was put to death by strangling. It might be thought at first sight that he is to be identified with the Dorotheus mentioned above in Bk. VII. chap. 32, for both lived at the same time, and the fact that the Dorotheus mentioned there was a eunuch would fit him for a prominent station in

the emperor's household. At the same time it is said by Eusebius to have been made superintendent of the purple dye house at Tyre, and nothing is said either as to his connection with the household of the emperor or as to his martyrdom; nor is the Dorotheus mentioned in this chapter said to have been a presbyter. In fact, inasmuch as Eusebius gives no hint of the identity of the two men, we must conclude that they were different persons in spite of the similarity of their circumstances.

[4] Of Gorgonius, who is mentioned also in chap. 6, we know only that he was one of the imperial household, and that he was strangled, in company with Dorotheus and others, in consequence of the fires in the Nicomedian palace. See chap. 6, note 3.

[5] ἀποδοχῆς. A few MSS., followed by Stephanus, Valesius, Stroth, Burton, and most translators, add the words καὶ θεραπείας καὶ δεξιώσεως οὐ τῆς τυχούσης, but the weight of MS. authority is against them, and they are omitted by the majority of editors.

And those esteemed our shepherds, casting aside the bond of piety, were excited to conflicts with one another, and did nothing else than heap up strifes and threats and jealousy and enmity and hatred toward each other, like tyrants eagerly endeavoring to assert their power. Then, truly, according to the word of Jeremiah, "The Lord in his wrath darkened the daughter of Zion, and cast down the glory of Israel from heaven to earth, and remembered not his footstool in the day of his anger. The Lord also overwhelmed all the beautiful things of Israel, and threw down all his strongholds." [6]

9   And according to what was foretold in the Psalms: "He has made void the covenant of his servant, and profaned his sanctuary to the earth, — in the destruction of the churches, — and has thrown down all his strongholds, and has made his fortresses cowardice. All that pass by have plundered the multitude of the people; and he has become besides a reproach to his neighbors. For he has exalted the right hand of his enemies, and has turned back the help of his sword, and has not taken his part in the war. But he has deprived him of purification, and has cast his throne to the ground. He has shortened the days of his time, and besides all, has poured out shame upon him." [7]

CHAPTER II.

The Destruction of the Churches.

1   ALL these things were fulfilled in us, when we saw with our own eyes the houses of prayer thrown down to the very foundations, and the Divine and Sacred Scriptures committed to the flames in the midst of the market-places, and the shepherds of the churches basely hidden here and there, and some of them captured ignominiously, and mocked by their enemies. When also, according to another prophetic word, "Contempt was poured out upon rulers, and he caused them to wander in an untrodden and pathless way." [1]

2   But it is not our place to describe the sad misfortunes which finally came upon them, as we do not think it proper, moreover, to record their divisions and unnatural conduct to each other before the persecution. Wherefore we have decided to relate nothing concerning them except the things in which we can vindicate the Divine judgment. Hence we

3   shall not mention those who were shaken by the persecution, nor those who in everything pertaining to salvation were shipwrecked, and by their own will were sunk in the depths of the

flood. But we shall introduce into this history in general only those events which may be useful first to ourselves and afterwards to posterity. [2] Let us therefore proceed to describe briefly the sacred conflicts of the witnesses of the Divine Word.

It was in the nineteenth year of the reign   4 of Diocletian, [3] in the month Dystrus, [4] called March by the Romans, when the feast of the Saviour's passion was near at hand, [5] that royal edicts were published everywhere, commanding that the churches be leveled to the ground and the Scriptures be destroyed by fire, and ordering that those who held places of honor be degraded, and that the household servants, if they persisted in the profession of Christianity, be deprived of freedom. [6]

---

[2] Gibbon uses this passage as the basis for his severe attack upon the honesty of Eusebius (*Decline and Fall*, chap. 16), but he has certainly done our author injustice (cf. the remarks made on p. 49, above).

[3] Diocletian began to reign Sept. 17, 284, and therefore his nineteenth year extended from Sept. 17, 302, to Sept. 16, 303. Eusebius is in agreement with all our authorities in assigning this year for the beginning of the persecution, and is certainly correct. In regard to the month, however, he is not so accurate. Lactantius, who was in Nicomedia at the time of the beginning of the persecution, and certainly much better informed than Eusebius in regard to the details, states distinctly (in his *De mort. pers.* chap. 12) that the festival of the god Terminus, the seventh day before the Kalends of March (i.e. Feb. 23), was chosen by the emperors for the opening of the persecution, and there is no reason for doubting his exact statement. At the beginning of the *Martyrs of Palestine* (p. 342, below) the month Xanthicus (April) is given as the date, but this is still further out of the way. It was probably March or even April before the edicts were published in many parts of the empire, and Eusebius may have been misled by that fact, not knowing the exact date of their publication in Nicomedia itself. We learn from Lactantius that on February 23d the great church of Nicomedia, together with the copies of Scripture found in it, was destroyed by order of the emperors, but that the edict of which Eusebius speaks just below was not issued until the following day. For a discussion of the causes which led to the persecution of Diocletian see below, p. 397.

[4] Δύστρος, the seventh month of the Macedonian year, corresponding to our March. See the table on p. 403, below.

[5] Valesius (*ad locum*) states, on the authority of Scaliger and Petavius, that Easter fell on April 18th in the year 303. I have not attempted to verify the statement.

[6] This is the famous First Edict of Diocletian, which is no longer extant, and the terms of which therefore have to be gathered from the accounts of Eusebius and Lactantius. The interpretation of the edict has caused a vast deal of trouble. It is discussed very fully by Mason in his important work, *The Persecution of Diocletian*, p. 105 sq. and p. 343 sq. As he remarks, Lactantius simply describes the edict in a general way, while Eusebius gives an accurate statement of its substance, even reproducing its language in part. The first provision (that the churches be leveled to the ground) is simply a carrying out of the old principle, that it was unlawful for the Christians to hold assemblies, under a new form. The second provision, directed against the sacred books, was entirely new, and was a very shrewd move, revealing at the same time an appreciation on the part of the authors of the persecution of the important part which the Scriptures occupied in the Christian Church. The third provision, as Mason has pointed out, is a substantial reproduction of a part of the edict of Valerian, and was evidently consciously based upon that edict. (Upon the variations from the earlier edict, see Mason, p. 115 sq.) It is noticeable that not torture nor death is decreed, but only civil degradation. This degradation, as can be seen from a comparison with the description of Lactantius (*ibid.* chap. 13) and with the edict of Valerian (given in Cyprian's Epistle to Successus, Ep. No. 81, *al.* 80), consisted, in the case of those who held public office (τιμῆς ἐπειλημμένους), in the loss of rank and also of citizenship; that is, they fell through two grades, as is pointed out by Mason. In the interpretation of the fourth provision, however, Mason does not seem to me to have been so successful. The last clause runs τοὺς δὲ ἐν οἰκετίαις, εἰ ἐπιμένοιεν τῇ τοῦ χριστιανισμοῦ προθέσει ἐλευθερίας στερεῖσθαι. The difficult point is the interpretation of the τοὺς ἐν οἰκετίαις. The words usually mean "household slaves" and are commonly so translated in this passage. But, as Valesius remarks, there is certainly no sense then in depriving them of freedom (ἐλευθερία) which they do not possess. Valesius consequently translates *plebeii*, "common people," and Mason argues at length for a similar interpretation (p. 344 sq.), looking upon these persons as common people, or individuals in private life, as contrasted with the officials

---

[6] Lam. ii. 1, 2.   [7] Ps. lxxxix. 39–45.
[1] Ps. cvii. 40.

5   Such was the first edict against us. But not long after, other decrees were issued, commanding that all the rulers of the churches in every place be first thrown into prison,[7] and

mentioned in the previous clause. The only objection, but in my opinion a fatal objection, to this attractive interpretation is that it gives the phrase οἱ ἐν οἰκετίαις a wider meaning than can legitimately be applied to it. Mason remarks: "The word οἰκετία means, and is here a translation of, *familia ;* οἱ ἐν οἰκετίαις means *ii qui in familiis sunt,* — not graceful Latin certainly, but plainly signifying 'those who live in private households.' Now in private households there lived not *only* slaves, thank goodness, but free men too, both as masters and as servants; therefore in the phrase τοὺς ἐν οἰκετίαις itself there is nothing which forbids the paraphrase 'private persons.'" But I submit that, to use so clumsy a phrase, so unnecessary a circumlocution, to designate simply private people in general — οἱ πολλοί — would be the height of absurdity. The interpretation of Stroth (which is approved by Heinichen) seems to me much more satisfactory. He remarks: "Das Edict war zunächst nur gegen zwei Klassen von Leuten gerichtet, einmal gegen die, welche in kaiserlichen Ämtern standen, und dann gegen die freien oder freigelassenen Christen, welche bei den Kaisern oder ihren Hofleuten und Statthaltern in Diensten standen, und zu ihrem Hausgesinde gehörten." This seems to me more satisfactory, both on verbal and historical grounds. The words οἱ ἐν οἰκετίαις certainly cannot, in the present case, mean "household slaves," but they can mean servants, attendants, or other persons at court, or in the households of provincial officials, who did not hold rank as officials, but at the same time were freemen born, or freedmen, and thus in a different condition from slaves. Such persons would naturally be reduced to slavery if degraded at all, and it is easier to think of their reduction to slavery than of that of the entire mass of Christians not in public office. Still further, this proposition finds support in the edict of Valerian, in which this class of people is especially mentioned. And finally, it is, in my opinion, much more natural to suppose that this edict (whose purpose I shall discuss on p. 399) was confined to persons who were in some way connected with official life, — either as chiefs or assistants or servants, — and therefore in a position peculiarly fitted for the formation of plots against the government, than that it was directed against Christians indiscriminately. The grouping together of the two classes seems to me very natural; and the omission of any specific reference to bishops and other church officers, who are mentioned in the second edict, is thus fully explained, as it cannot be adequately explained, in my opinion, on any other ground.

[7] As we learn from chap. 6, § 8, the edict commanding the church officers to be seized and thrown into prison followed popular uprisings in Melitene and Syria, and if Eusebius is correct, was caused by those outbreaks. Evidently the Christians were held in some way responsible for those rebellious outbursts (possibly they were a direct consequence of the first edict), and the natural result of them must have been to make Diocletian realize, as he had not realized before, that the existence of such a society as the Christian Church within the empire — demanding as it did supreme allegiance from its members — was a menace to the state. It was therefore not strange that what began as a purely political thing, as an attempt to break up a supposed treasonable plot formed by certain Christian officials, should speedily develop into a religious persecution. The first step in such a persecution would naturally be the seizure of all church officers (see below, p. 397 sq.).

The decrees of which Eusebius speaks in this paragraph are evidently to be identified with the one mentioned in chap. 6, § 8. This being so, it is clear that Eusebius' account can lay no claims to chronological order. This must be remembered, or we shall fall into repeated difficulties in reading this eighth book. We are obliged to arrange the order of events for ourselves, for his account is quite desultory, and devoid both of logical and chronological sequence. The decrees or writings (γράμματα) mentioned in this paragraph constituted really but one edict (cf. chap. 6, § 8), which is known to us as the Second Edict of Diocletian. Its date cannot be determined with exactness, for, as Mason remarks, it may have been issued at any time between February and November; but it was probably published not many months after the first, inasmuch as it was a result of disturbances which arose in consequence of the first. Mason is inclined to place it in March, within a month after the issue of the first, but that seems to me a little too early. In issuing the edict Diocletian followed the example of Valerian in part, and yet only in part; for instead of commanding that the church officers be slain, he commanded only that they be seized. He evidently believed that he could accomplish his purpose best by getting the leading men of the church into his hands and holding them as hostages, while denying them the glory of martyrdom (cf. Mason, p. 132 sq.). The persons affected by the edict, according to Eusebius, were "all the rulers of the churches" (τοὺς τῶν ἐκκλησιῶν προεδρους πάντας; cf. also *Mart. Pal.* Introd., § 2). In chap. 6, § 8, he says τοὺς πανταχόσε τῶν ἐκκλησιῶν προεστῶτας. These words would seem to imply that only the bishops were intended, but we learn from Lactantius (*De mort. pers.* 15) that presbyters and other officers (*presbyteri ac ministri*) were included, and this is confirmed, as Mason remarks (p. 133, note), by the sequel. We must therefore take the words used by Eusebius in the general sense of "church officers." According to Lactantius, their families suffered with them (*cum omnibus suis deducebantur*), but Eusebius says nothing of that.

afterwards by every artifice be compelled to sacrifice.[8]

CHAPTER III.

The Nature of the Conflicts endured in the Persecution.

THEN truly a great many rulers of the   1 churches eagerly endured terrible sufferings, and furnished examples of noble conflicts. But a multitude of others,[1] benumbed in spirit by fear, were easily weakened at the first onset. Of the rest each one endured different forms of torture.[2] The body of one was scourged with rods. Another was punished with insupportable rackings and scrapings, in which some suffered a miserable death. Others passed   2 through different conflicts. Thus one, while those around pressed him on by force and dragged him to the abominable and impure sacrifices, was dismissed as if he had sacrificed, though he had not.[3] Another, though he had not approached at all, nor touched any polluted

[8] We learn from Lactantius (*l.c.*) that the officers of the church, under the terms of the second edict, were thrown into prison without any option being given them in the matter of sacrificing. They were not asked to sacrifice, but were imprisoned unconditionally. This was so far in agreement with Valerian's edict, which had decreed the instant death of all church officers without the option of sacrificing. But as Eusebius tells us here, they were afterwards called upon to sacrifice, and as he tells us in the first paragraph of the next chapter, multitudes yielded, and that of course meant their release, as indeed we are directly told in chap. 6, § 10. We may gather from the present passage and from the other passages referred to, taken in connection with the second chapter of the *Martyrs of Palestine*, that this decree, ordaining their release on condition of sacrificing, was issued on the occasion of Diocletian's Vicennalia, which were celebrated in December, 303, on the twentieth anniversary of the death of Carus, which Diocletian reckoned as the beginning of his reign, though he was not in reality emperor until the following September. A considerable time, therefore, elapsed between the edict ordaining the imprisonment of church officers and the edict commanding their release upon condition of sacrificing. This latter is commonly known as Diocletian's Third Edict, and is usually spoken of as still harsher than any that preceded it. It is true that it did result in the torture of a great many, — for those who did not sacrifice readily were to be compelled to do so, if possible, — but their death was not aimed at. If they would not sacrifice, they were simply to remain in prison, as before. Those who did die at this time seem to have died under torture that was intended, not to kill them, but to bring about their release. As Mason shows, then, this third edict was of the nature of an amnesty; was rather a step toward toleration than a sharpening of the persecution. The prisons were to be emptied, as was customary on such great occasions, and the church officers were to be permitted to return to their homes, on condition that they should sacrifice. Inasmuch as they had not been allowed to leave prison on any condition before, this was clearly a mark of favor (see Mason, p. 206 sq.). Many were released even without sacrificing, and in their desire to empty the prisons, the governors devised various expedients for freeing at least a part of those who would not yield (cf. the instances mentioned in the next chapter). At the same time, some governors got rid of their prisoners by putting them to death, sometimes simply by increasing the severity of the tortures intended to try them, sometimes as a penalty for rash or daring words uttered by the prisoners, which were interpreted as treasonable, and which, perhaps, the officials had employed their ingenuity, when necessary, to elicit. Thus many might suffer death, under various legal pretenses, although the terms of the edict did not legally permit death to be inflicted as a punishment for Christianity. The death penalty was not decreed until the issue of the Fourth Edict (see below, *Mart. Pal.* chap. 3, note 2).

[1] μυρίοι δ' ἄλλοι. See the previous chapter, note 8.
[2] i.e. those who, when freedom was offered them on condition of sacrificing, refused to accept it at that price. It was desirous that the prisons which had for so long been filled with these Christian prisoners (see chap. 6, § 9) should, if possible, be cleared; and this doubtless combined with the desire to break the stubbornness of the prisoners to promote the use of torture at this time.
[3] See the previous chapter, note 8.

thing, when others said that he had sacrificed, went away, bearing the accusation in silence. Another being taken up half dead, was cast aside as if already dead, and again a certain 3 one lying upon the ground was dragged a long distance by his feet and counted among those who had sacrificed. One cried out and with a loud voice testified his rejection of the sacrifice; another shouted that he was a Christian, being resplendent in the confession of the saving Name. Another protested that he had not sacrificed and never would. But they were struck in the mouth and silenced by a large band of soldiers who were drawn 4 up for this purpose; and they were smitten on the face and cheeks and driven away by force; so important did the enemies of piety regard it, by any means, to seem to have accomplished their purpose. But these things did not avail them against the holy martyrs; for an accurate description of whom, what word of ours could suffice?

CHAPTER IV.

The Famous Martyrs of God, who filled Every Place with their Memory and won Various Crowns in behalf of Religion.

1   FOR we might tell of many who showed admirable zeal for the religion of the God of the universe, not only from the beginning of the general persecution, but long before 2 that time, while yet peace prevailed. For though he who had received power was seemingly aroused now as from a deep sleep, yet from the time after Decius and Valerian, he had been plotting secretly and without notice against the churches. He did not wage war against all of us at once, but made trial at first only of those in the army. For he supposed that the others could be taken easily if he should first attack and subdue these. Thereupon many of the soldiers were seen most cheerfully embracing private life, so that they might not deny their piety toward the Creator of 3 the universe. For when the commander,[1] whoever he was,[2] began to persecute the sol-

diers, separating into tribes and purging those who were enrolled in the army, giving them the choice either by obeying to receive the honor which belonged to them, or on the other hand to be deprived of it if they disobeyed the command, a great many soldiers of Christ's kingdom, without hesitation, instantly preferred the confession of him to the seeming glory and prosperity which they were enjoying. And 4 one and another of them occasionally received in exchange, for their pious constancy,[3] not only the loss of position, but death. But as yet the instigator of this plot proceeded with moderation, and ventured so far as blood only in some instances; for the multitude of believers, as it is likely, made him afraid, and deterred him from waging war at once against all. But when he made the attack more boldly, 5 it is impossible to relate how many and what sort of martyrs of God could be seen, among the inhabitants of all the cities and countries.[4]

CHAPTER V.

Those in Nicomedia.[1]

IMMEDIATELY on the publication of the 1 decree against the churches in Nicomedia,[2] a certain man, not obscure but very highly honored with distinguished temporal dignities, moved with zeal toward God, and incited with ardent faith, seized the edict as it was posted openly and publicly, and tore it to pieces as a profane and impious thing;[3] and this was done

---

1 στρατοπεδάρχης.
2 In the *Chron.* we are told of a commander by name Veturius, who is doubtless to be identified with the one referred to here. Why Eusebius does not give his name in the History, we do not know. There seems to be contempt in the phrase, "whoever he was," and it may be that he did not consider him worth naming. In Jerome's version of the *Chron.* (sixteenth year of Diocletian) we read: *Veturius magister militiæ Christianos milites persequitur, paulatim ex illo jam tempore persecutione adversum nos incipiente;* in the Armenian (fourteenth year): *Veturius magister militiæ eos qui in exercitu Christiani erant, clanculum opprimebat atque ex hoc inde tempore ubique locorum persecutio se extendit.* Evidently the occurrence took place a few years before the outbreak of the regular persecution, but the exact date cannot be determined. It is probable, moreover, from the way in which Eusebius refers to the man in the History that he was a comparatively insignificant commander, who took the course he did on his own responsibility.

At least, there is no reason to connect the act with Diocletian and to suppose it ordered by him. All that we know of his relation to the Christians forbids such a supposition. There may have been some particular occasion for such a move in the present instance, which evidently affected only a small part of the army, and resulted in only a few deaths (see the next paragraph). Perhaps some insubordination was discovered among the Christian soldiers, which led the commander to be suspicious of all of them, and hence to put the test to them, — which was always in order, — to prove their loyalty. It is plain that he did not intend to put any of them to death, but only to dismiss such as refused to evince their loyalty by offering the customary sacrifices. Some of the Christian soldiers, however, were not content with simple dismission, but in their eagerness to evince their Christianity said and did things which it was impossible for any commander to overlook (cf. the instances given by Mason, p. 41 sq.). It was such soldiers as these that suffered death; and they of course were executed, not because they were Christians, but because they were insubordinate. Their death was brought on themselves by their foolish fanaticism; and they have no claim to be honored as martyrs, although Eusebius evidently regarded them as such.
3 We should rather say "for their rash and unjustifiable fanaticism."
4 In this sentence reference is made to the general persecution, which did not begin until some time after the events recorded in the previous paragraphs.
1 Nicomedia, the capital city of Bithynia, became Diocletian's chief place of residence, and was made by him the Eastern capital of the empire.
2 The great church of Nicomedia was destroyed on Feb. 23, 303, and the First Edict was published on the following day (see above, chap. 2, note 3).
3 Lactantius relates this account in his *De mort. pers.* chap. 13, and expresses disapproval of the act, while admiring the spirit of the man. He, too, is silent in regard to the name of the man, though, living as he did in Nicomedia, he can hardly have been ignorant of it. We may perhaps imagine that he did not care to perpetuate the name of a man whom he considered to have acted rashly and illegally. The old martyrologies give the man's

while two of the sovereigns were in the same city, — the oldest of all, and the one who held the fourth place in the government after him.[4]

2　But this man, first in that place, after distinguishing himself in such a manner suffered those things which were likely to follow such daring, and kept his spirit cheerful and undisturbed till death.

CHAPTER VI.

Those in the Palace.

1　THIS period produced divine and illustrious martyrs, above all whose praises have ever been sung and who have been celebrated for courage, whether among Greeks or barbarians, in the person of Dorotheus [1] and the servants that were with him in the palace. Although they received the highest honors from their masters, and were treated by them as their own children, they esteemed reproaches and trials for religion, and the many forms of death that were invented against them, as, in truth, greater riches than the glory and luxury of this life.

We will describe the manner in which one of them ended his life, and leave our readers to infer from his case the sufferings of the others.

2　A certain man was brought forward in the above-mentioned city, before the rulers of whom we have spoken.[2] He was then commanded to sacrifice, but as he refused, he was ordered to be stripped and raised on high and beaten with rods over his entire body, until, being conquered, he should, even against

3　his will, do what was commanded. But as he was unmoved by these sufferings, and his bones were already appearing, they mixed vinegar with salt and poured it upon the mangled parts of his body. As he scorned these agonies, a gridiron and fire were brought forward. And the remnants of his body, like flesh intended for eating, were placed on the fire, not at once, lest he should expire instantly, but a little at a time. And those who placed him on the pyre were not permitted to desist until, after such sufferings, he should assent to the

4　things commanded. But he held his purpose firmly, and victoriously gave up his

life while the tortures were still going on. Such was the martyrdom of one of the servants of the palace, who was indeed well worthy of his name, for he was called Peter.[3] The martyr-　5 doms of the rest, though they were not inferior to his, we will pass by for the sake of brevity, recording only that Dorotheus and Gorgonius,[4] with many others of the royal household, after varied sufferings, ended their lives by strangling, and bore away the trophies of God-given victory.

At this time Anthimus,[5] who then pre-　6 sided over the church in Nicomedia, was beheaded for his testimony to Christ. A great multitude of martyrs were added to him, a conflagration having broken out in those very days in the palace at Nicomedia, I know not how, which through a false suspicion was laid to our

---

[3] πέτρος, "a rock." It is clear from the account of Lactantius (chap. 15) that this man, and the others mentioned in this connection, suffered after the second conflagration in the palace and in consequence of it (see below, p. 400). The two conflagrations led Diocletian to resort to torture in order to ascertain the guilty parties, or to obtain information in regard to the plots of the Christians. Examination by torture was the common mode of procedure under such circumstances, and hence implies no unusual cruelty in the present case. The death even of these men, therefore, cannot be looked upon as due to persecution. Their offense was purely a civil one. They were suspected of being implicated in a treasonable plot, and of twice setting fire to the palace. Their refusal to sacrifice under such circumstances, and thus evince their loyalty at so critical a time, was naturally looked upon as practically a confession of guilt, — at any rate as insubordination on a most grave occasion, and as such fitly punishable by death. Compare Pliny's epistle to Trajan, in which he expresses the opinion that "pertinacious and inflexible obstinacy" ought at any rate to be punished, whatever might be thought of Christianity as such (see above, Bk. III. chap. 33, note 1); and at such a time as this Diocletian must have felt that the first duty of all his subjects was to place their loyalty beyond suspicion by doing readily that which was demanded. His impatience with the Christians must have been increasing under all these provocations, and thus the regular persecution was becoming ever more imminent.

[4] Gorgonius has been already mentioned in chap. 1, above. See note 4 on that chapter.

[5] In a fragment preserved by the *Chron. Paschale*, and purporting to be a part of an epistle written from prison, shortly before his death, by the presbyter Lucian of Antioch to the church of that city, Anthimus, bishop of Nicomedia, is mentioned as having just suffered martyrdom (see Routh's *Rel. Sac.* IV. p. 5). Lucian, however, was imprisoned and put to death during the persecution of Maximinus (A.D. 311 or 312). See below, Bk. IX. chap. 6, and Jerome's *de vir. ill.* chap. 77. It would seem, therefore, if the fragment given in the *Chron. Paschale* be genuine, and there seems no good reason to doubt it, that Anthimus suffered martyrdom not under Diocletian, but under Maximinus, in 311 or 312. In that case Eusebius is mistaken in putting his death at this early date, in connection with the members of the imperial household. Indeed, we see no reason for his execution at this time, and should find it difficult to explain if we were to accept it. In the time of Maximinus, however, it is perfectly natural, and of a piece with the execution of Peter of Alexandria and other notable prelates. Eusebius, as we have already seen, pays no attention to chronology in this Eighth Book, and hence there is no great weight to be placed upon his mention of the death of Anthimus at this particular place. Mason (p. 324) says that Hunziker (p. 281) has conclusively shown Eusebius' mistake at this point. I have not seen Hunziker, and therefore cannot judge of the validity of his arguments, but, on the grounds already stated, have no hesitation in expressing my agreement with his conclusion. Of Anthimus himself, we know nothing beyond what has been already intimated. In chap. 13, § 1, below, he is mentioned again, but nothing additional is told us in regard to him.

Having observed Eusebius' mistake in regard to Anthimus, we realize that there is no reason to consider him any more accurate in respect to the other martyrdoms referred to in this paragraph. In fact, it is clear enough that, in so far as his account is not merely rhetorical, it relates to events that took place not at this early date, but during a later time, after the regular religious persecution had begun. No such "multitude" suffered in consequence of the conflagration as Eusebius thinks. The martyrdoms of which he has heard belong rather to the time after the Fourth Edict (see below, *Mart. Pal.* chap. 3, note 2), or possibly to the still later time when Maximinus was at Nicomedia, and was in the midst of his bloody career of persecution.

---

name as John. That he deserved death is clear enough. He was not a martyr to the faith, but a criminal, who was justly executed for treasonable conduct. The first edict contemplated no violence to the persons of the Christians. If they suffered death, it was solely in consequence of their own rashness, as in the present case. It is clear that such an incident as this would anger Diocletian and increase his suspicions of Christians as a class, and thus tend to precipitate a regular persecution. It must have seemed to the authorities that the man would hardly commit such a foolhardy act unless he was conscious of the support of a large body of the populace, and so the belief in the wide extension of the plot which had caused the movement on the part of the emperors must have been confirmed. See below, p. 398 sq.　　　　[4] i.e. Diocletian and Galerius.

[1] On Dorotheus, see above, chap. 1, note 3.

[2] i.e. in Nicomedia, before Diocletian and Galerius.

people.[6] Entire families of the pious in that place were put to death in masses at the royal command, some by the sword, and others by fire. It is reported that with a certain divine and indescribable eagerness men and women rushed into the fire. And the executioners bound a large number of others and put them on boats [7] and threw them into the depths of

7   the sea. And those who had been esteemed their masters considered it necessary to dig up the bodies of the imperial servants, who had been committed to the earth with suitable burial, and cast them into the sea, lest any, as they thought, regarding them as gods, might worship them lying in their sepulchers.[8]

Such things occurred in Nicomedia at the

8   beginning of the persecution.[9] But not long after, as persons in the country called Melitene,[10] and others throughout Syria,[11] at-

tempted to usurp the government, a royal edict directed that the rulers of the churches everywhere [12] should be thrown into prison and bonds. What was to be seen after this   9 exceeds all description. A vast multitude were imprisoned in every place; and the prisons everywhere, which had long before been prepared for murderers and robbers of graves, were filled with bishops, presbyters and deacons, readers and exorcists,[13] so that room was no longer left in them for those condemned for crimes. And as other decrees followed   10 the first, directing that those in prison if they would sacrifice should be permitted to depart in freedom, but that those who refused should be harassed with many tortures,[14] how could any one, again, number the multitude of martyrs in every province,[15] and especially of those in Africa, and Mauritania, and Thebais, and Egypt? From this last country many went into other cities and provinces, and became illustrious through martyrdom.

CHAPTER VII.

The Egyptians in Phœnicia.

THOSE of them that were conspicuous in   1 Palestine we know, as also those that were at Tyre in Phœnicia.[1] Who that saw them was

---

[6] Eusebius does not accuse Galerius of being the author of the conflagration, as Lactantius does. In fact, he seems to have known very little about the matter. He mentions only one fire, whereas Lactantius distinctly tells us there were two, fifteen days apart (chap. 14). Eusebius evidently has only the very vaguest information in regard to the progress of affairs at Nicomedia, and has no knowledge of the actual order and connection of events. In regard to the effects of the fire upon Diocletian's attitude toward the Christians, see above, note 3, and below, p. 400. Constantine (*Orat. ad Sanct. Coet.* XXV. 2) many years afterwards referred to the fire as caused by lightning, which is clearly only a makeshift, for, as Burckhardt remarks, there could have been no doubt in that case how the fire originated. And, moreover, such an explanation at best could account for only one of the fires. The fact that Constantine feels it necessary to invent such an explanation gives the occurrence a still more suspicious look, and one not altogether favorable to the Christians. In fact, it must be acknowledged that the case against them is pretty strong.

[7] Literally, "The executioners, having bound a large number of others on boats, threw them into the depths of the sea" (δήσαντες δὲ οἱ δήμιοι ἄλλο τι πλῆθος ἐπὶ σκάφαις, τοῖς θαλαττίοις ἐναπέρριπτον βυθοῖς). The construction is evidently a pregnant one, for it cannot be supposed that boats and all were thrown into the depths of the sea. They seem to have bound the prisoners, and carried them out to sea on boats, and then thrown them overboard. Compare the *Passion of St. Theodotus* (Mason, p. 362), where we are told that the "President then bade them hang stones about their necks, and embark them on a small shallop and row them out to a spot where the lake was deeper; and so they were cast into the water at the distance of four or five hundred feet from the shore." Crusè translates, "binding another number upon planks," but σκάφη will hardly bear that meaning; and even if it could, we should scarcely expect men to be bound to *planks* if the desire was to "cast them into the depths of the sea." Lactantius (chap. 15), in speaking of these same general occurrences, says, "Servants, having millstones tied about their necks, were cast into the sea."

Closs remarks that drowning was looked upon in ancient times as the most disgraceful punishment, because it implied that the criminals were not worthy to receive burial.

[8] Compare Bk. IV. chap. 15, § 41, above, and Lactantius, *Div. Inst.* V. 11. That in the present case the suspicion that the Christians would worship the remains of these so-called martyrs was not founded merely upon knowledge of the conduct of Christians in general in relation to the relics of their martyrs, but upon actual experience of their conduct in connection with these particular martyrs, is shown by the fact that the emperor first buried them, and afterward had them dug up. Evidently Christians showed them such honor, and collected in such numbers about their tombs, that he believed it was necessary to take some such step in order to prevent the growth of a spirit of rebellion, which was constantly fostered by such demonstrations. Compare the remarks of Mason on p. 135.

[9] Part of the events mentioned in this chapter occurred at the beginning; others, a considerable time later. See note 5, above.

[10] Melitene was the name of a district and a city in Eastern Cappadocia. Upon the outbreak there we know only what can be gathered from this passage, although Mason (p. 126 sq.) connects it with a rebellion, of which an account is given in Simeon Metaphrastes. It is possible that the account of the Metaphrast is authentic, and that the uprising referred to here is to be identified with it, but more than that cannot be said. There can be no doubt that the outbreak was one of the causes of the promulgation of the Second Edict, in which case of course it is clear that the Christians, whether rightly or wrongly, were held responsible for it. See above, chap. 2, note 7.

[11] Valesius identifies this usurpation in Syria with that of Eugenius in Antioch, of which we are told by Libanius (in his *Oratio ad Theodosium post reconciliationem*, and in his *Oratio ad Theod. de seditione Antioch.*, according to Valesius). The latter was but a small affair, involving only a band of some five hundred soldiers, who compelled their commander Eugenius, to assume the purple, but were entirely destroyed by the people of the city within twenty-four hours. See the note of Valesius *ad locum*, Tillemont's *Hist. des Emp.* IX. 73 sq., and Mason, p. 124 sq. This rebellion took place in the time of Diocletian, but there is no reason for connecting it with the uprising mentioned here by Eusebius. The words of Eusebius would seem to imply that he was thinking, not of a single rebellion, but of a number which took place in various parts of Syria. In that case, the Antiochian affair may have been one of them.

[12] τοὺς πανταχόσε τῶν ἐκκλησιῶν προεστῶτας. Upon this second edict, see above, chap. 2, note 7.

[13] It is evident enough from this clause alone that the word προεστῶτας, "rulers," is to be taken in a broad sense. See the note just referred to.

[14] The Third Edict of Diocletian. Eusebius evidently looks upon the edict as a sharpening of the persecution, but is mistaken in his view. The idea was not that those who refused to sacrifice should be punished by torture for not sacrificing, but that torture should be applied in order to induce them to sacrifice, and thus render it possible to release them. The end sought was their release, not their punishment. Upon the date and interpretation of this edict, see chap. 2, note 8.

[15] Eusebius is probably again in error, as so often in this book, in connecting a "multitude of martyrs in every province" with this Third Edict. Wholesale persecution and persecution as such—aimed directly at the destruction of all Christians—did not begin until the issue of the Fourth Edict (see below, *Mart. Pal.* chap. 3, note 2). These numerous martyrdoms referred to here doubtless belong to the period after the issue of that edict, although in Africa and Mauritania, which were under Maximian, considerable blood was probably shed even before that time. For it was possible, of course, for a cruel and irresponsible ruler like Maximian to fix the death penalty for refusal to deliver up the Christian books, or for other acts of obstinacy which the Christian would quite commonly commit. These cases, however, must be looked upon as exceptional at this stage of affairs, and certainly rare.

[1] From the *Martyrs of Palestine*, chap. 8 sq. (more fully in the Syriac; Cureton's English translation, p. 26 sq.), we learn that in the sixth and following years of the persecution, many Egyptian Christians were sent to Palestine to labor in the mines there, and that they underwent the severest tortures in that country. No men-

not astonished at the numberless stripes, and at the firmness which these truly wonderful athletes of religion exhibited under them? and at their contest, immediately after the scourging, with bloodthirsty wild beasts, as they were cast before leopards and different kinds of bears and wild boars and bulls goaded with fire and red-hot iron? and at the marvelous endurance of these noble men in the face of all sorts of wild beasts?

2   We were present ourselves when these things occurred, and have put on record the divine power of our martyred Saviour Jesus Christ, which was present and manifested itself mightily in the martyrs. For a long time the man-devouring beasts did not dare to touch or draw near the bodies of those dear to God, but rushed upon the others who from the outside irritated and urged them on. And they would not in the least touch the holy athletes, as they stood alone and naked and shook their hands at them to draw them toward themselves, — for they were commanded to do this. But whenever they rushed at them, they were restrained as if by some diviner power and retreated
3   again. This continued for a long time, and occasioned no little wonder to the spectators. And as the first wild beast did nothing, a second and a third were let loose
4   against one and the same martyr. One could not but be astonished at the invincible firmness of these holy men, and the enduring and immovable constancy of those whose bodies were young. You could have seen a youth not twenty years of age standing unbound and stretching out his hands in the form of a cross, with unterrified and untrembling mind, engaged earnestly in prayer to God, and not in the least going back or retreating from the place where he stood, while bears and leopards, breathing rage and death, almost touched his flesh. And yet their mouths were restrained, I know not how, by a divine and incomprehensible power, and they ran back again to their place. Such an one was he.
5   Again you might have seen others, for they were five in all, cast before a wild bull, who tossed into the air with his horns those who approached from the outside, and mangled them, leaving them to be taken up half dead; but when he rushed with rage and threatening upon the holy martyrs, who were standing alone, he was unable to come near them; but though he stamped with his feet, and pushed in all

directions with his horns, and breathed rage and threatening on account of the irritation of the burning irons, he was, nevertheless, held back by the sacred Providence. And as he in nowise harmed them, they let loose other wild beasts upon them. Finally, after these 6 terrible and various attacks upon them, they were all slain with the sword; and instead of being buried in the earth they were committed to the waves of the sea.

CHAPTER VIII.

Those in Egypt.[1]

SUCH was the conflict of those Egyptians 1 who contended nobly for religion in Tyre. But we must admire those also who suffered martyrdom in their native land; where thousands of men, women, and children, despising the present life for the sake of the teaching of our Saviour, endured various deaths. Some of them, after scrapings and rackings 2 and severest scourgings, and numberless other kinds of tortures, terrible even to hear of, were committed to the flames; some were drowned in the sea; some offered their heads bravely to those who cut them off; some died under their tortures, and others perished with hunger. And yet others were crucified; some according to the method commonly employed for malefactors; others yet more cruelly, being nailed to the cross with their heads downward, and being kept alive until they perished on the cross with hunger.

CHAPTER IX.

Those in Thebais.[1]

IT would be impossible to describe the 1 outrages and tortures which the martyrs in Thebais endured. They were scraped over the entire body with shells instead of hooks until they died. Women were bound by one foot and raised aloft in the air by machines, and with their bodies altogether bare and uncovered, presented to all beholders this most shameful, cruel, and inhuman spectacle. Others being 2 bound to the branches and trunks of trees perished. For they drew the stoutest branches

---

tion is made of such persons in the *Martyrs of Palestine* previous to the sixth year. Those in Tyre to whom Eusebius refers very likely suffered during the same period; not under Diocletian, but under Maximinus, when the persecution was at its height. Since in his *Martyrs of Palestine* Eusebius confines himself to those who suffered in that country (or were natives of it), he has nothing to say about those referred to in this chapter, who seem, from the opening of the next chapter, to have suffered, all of them, in Tyre.

[1] No part of Christendom suffered more severely during these years than the territory of the tyrant Maximinus, who became a Cæsar in 305, and who ruled in Egypt and Syria.

[1] Thebais, or the territory of Thebes, was one of the three great divisions of Egypt, lying between lower Egypt on the north and Æthiopia on the south. From § 4, below, we learn that Eusebius was himself an eye-witness of at least some of the martyrdoms to which he refers in the present chapter. Reasons have been given on p. 10, above, for supposing that he did not visit Egypt until the later years of the persecution, indeed not until toward the very end of it; and it is therefore to this period that the events described in this chapter are to be ascribed.

together with machines, and bound the limbs of the martyrs to them; and then, allowing the branches to assume their natural position, they tore asunder instantly the limbs of those
3   for whom they contrived this. All these things were done, not for a few days or a short time, but for a long series of years. Sometimes more than ten, at other times above twenty were put to death. Again not less than thirty, then about sixty, and yet again a hundred men with young children and women, were slain in one day, being condemned to various and diverse torments.
4   We, also, being on the spot ourselves, have observed large crowds in one day; some suffering decapitation, others torture by fire; so that the murderous sword was blunted, and becoming weak, was broken, and the very executioners grew weary and relieved each
5   other. And we beheld the most wonderful ardor, and the truly divine energy and zeal of those who believed in the Christ of God. For as soon as sentence was pronounced against the first, one after another rushed to the judgment seat, and confessed themselves Christians. And regarding with indifference the terrible things and the multiform tortures, they declared themselves boldly and undauntedly for the religion of the God of the universe. And they received the final sentence of death with joy and laughter and cheerfulness; so that they sang and offered up hymns and thanksgivings to the God of the universe till their very last breath.
6   These indeed were wonderful; but yet more wonderful were those who, being distinguished for wealth, noble birth, and honor, and for learning and philosophy, held everything secondary to the true religion and to faith
7   in our Saviour and Lord Jesus Christ. Such an one was Philoromus, who held a high office under the imperial government at Alexandria,[2] and who administered justice every day, attended by a military guard corresponding to his rank and Roman dignity. Such also was Phileas,[3] bishop of the church of Thmuis, a man

eminent on account of his patriotism and the services rendered by him to his country, and also on account of his philosophical learning. These persons, although a multitude of   8 relatives and other friends besought them, and many in high position, and even the judge himself entreated them, that they would have compassion on themselves and show mercy to their children and wives, yet were not in the least induced by these things to choose the love of life, and to despise the ordinances of our Saviour concerning confession and denial. But with manly and philosophic minds, or rather with pious and God-loving souls, they persevered against all the threats and insults of the judge; and both of them were beheaded.

CHAPTER X.

The Writings of Phileas the Martyr describing the Occurrences at Alexandria.

SINCE we have mentioned Phileas as having a high reputation for secular learning, let him be his own witness in the following extract, in which he shows us who he was, and at the same time describes more accurately than we can the martyrdoms which occurred in his time at Alexandria:[1]
"Having before them all these examples   2 and models and noble tokens which are given us in the Divine and Sacred Scriptures, the blessed martyrs who were with us did not hesitate, but directing the eye of the soul in sincerity toward the God over all, and having their mind set upon death for religion, they adhered firmly to their calling. For they understood that our Lord Jesus Christ had become man on our account, that he might cut off all sin and furnish us with the means of entrance into eter-

---

[2] ἀρχήν τινα οὐ τὴν τυχοῦσαν τῆς κατ' Ἀλεξάνδρειαν βασιλικῆς διοικήσεως ἐγκεχειρισμένος. Valesius says that Philoromus was the *Rationalis, seu procurator summarum Ægypti*, i.e. the general finance minister of Egypt (see above, Bk. VII. chap. 10, note 8). But the truth is, that the use of the τινα implies that Eusebius is not intending to state the particular office which he held, but simply to indicate that he held some high office, and this is all that we can claim for Philoromus. We know no more of him than is told us here, though *Acts of St. Phileas and St. Philoromus* are extant, which contain an account of his martyrdom, and are printed by the Bollandists and by Ruinart (interesting extracts given by Tillemont, *H. E.* V. p. 486 sq., and by Mason, p. 290 sq.). Tillemont (*ibid.* p. 777) and others defend their genuineness, but Lardner doubts it (*Credibility*, chap. 60). I have examined only the extracts printed by Tillemont and Mason, and am not prepared to express an opinion in the matter.
[3] Phileas, bishop of Thmuis (an important town in lower Egypt, situated between the Tanite and Mendeaian branches of the Nile), occupies an important place among the Diocletian martyrs. The extant *Acts* of his martyrdom have been referred to in the previous note. He is mentioned again by Eusebius in chaps. 10 and 13, and

in the former a considerable part of his epistle to the people of his diocese is quoted. Jerome mentions him in his *de vir. ill.* chap. 78, where he says: *elegantissimum librum de martyrum laude composuit, et disputatione actorum habita adversum judicem, qui eum sacrificare cogebat, pro Christo capite truncatur.* The book referred to by Jerome seems to be identical with the epistle quoted by Eusebius in the next chapter, for we have no record of another work on this subject written by him. There is extant, however, the Latin version of an epistle purporting to have been written by the imprisoned bishops Hesychius, Pachymius, Theodorus, and Phileas, to Meletius, author of the Meletian schism. There seems to be nothing in the epistle to disprove its genuineness, and it is accepted by Routh and others. The authorship of the epistle is commonly ascribed to Phileas, both because he is known to us as a writer, and also because his name stands last in the opening of the epistle. Eusebius says nothing of such an epistle (though the names of all four of the bishops are mentioned in chap. 13, below). Jerome's silence in regard to it signifies nothing, for he only follows Eusebius. This epistle, and also the fragment of the one quoted in the next chapter by Eusebius, are given by Routh, *Rel. Sac.* IV. p. 87 sq., and an English translation in the *Ante-Nicene Fathers,* VI. p. 161 sq.
Phileas' learning is praised very highly by Eusebius and Jerome, and his scholarly character is emphasized in his *Acts.* The date of his death cannot be determined with exactness, but we may be confident that it did not, at any rate, take place before 306, and very likely not before 307. The epistle quoted in the next chapter was written shortly before his martyrdom, as we learn from § 11 of that chapter.
[1] On this epistle, see the previous chapter, note 3.

nal life. For 'he counted it not a prize to be on an equality with God, but emptied himself, taking the form of a servant; and being found in fashion as a man, he humbled himself unto
3   death, even the death of the cross.'[2] Wherefore also being zealous for the greater gifts, the Christ-bearing martyrs endured all trials and all kinds of contrivances for torture; not once only, but some also a second time. And although the guards vied with each other in threatening them in all sorts of ways, not in words only, but in actions, they did not give up their resolution; because 'perfect love casteth out fear.'[3]
4   "What words could describe their courage and manliness under every torture? For as liberty to abuse them was given to all that wished, some beat them with clubs, others with rods, others with scourges, yet others with
5   thongs, and others with ropes. And the spectacle of the outrages was varied and exhibited great malignity. For some, with their hands bound behind them, were suspended on the stocks, and every member stretched by certain machines. Then the torturers, as commanded, lacerated with instruments[4] their entire bodies; not only their sides, as in the case of murderers, but also their stomachs and knees and cheeks. Others were raised aloft, suspended from the porch by one hand, and endured the most terrible suffering of all, through the distension of their joints and limbs. Others were bound face to face to pillars, not resting on their feet, but with the weight of their bodies bearing on their bonds and drawing them tightly.
6   And they endured this, not merely as long as the governor talked with them or was at leisure, but through almost the entire day. For when he passed on to others, he left officers under his authority to watch the first, and observe if any of them, overcome by the tortures, appeared to yield. And he commanded to cast them into chains without mercy, and afterwards when they were at the last gasp to throw them
7   to the ground and drag them away. For he said that they were not to have the least concern for us, but were to think and act as if we no longer existed, our enemies having invented this second mode of torture in addition to the stripes.
8   "Some, also, after these outrages, were placed on the stocks, and had both their feet stretched over the four[5] holes, so that they

were compelled to lie on their backs on the stocks, being unable to keep themselves up on account of the fresh wounds with which their entire bodies were covered as a result of the scourging. Others were thrown on the ground and lay there under the accumulated infliction of tortures, exhibiting to the spectators a more terrible manifestation of severity, as they bore on their bodies the marks of the various and diverse punishments which had been invented.
As this went on, some died under the tortures, shaming the adversary by their con- **9** stancy. Others half dead were shut up in prison, and suffering with their agonies, they died in a few days; but the rest, recovering under the care which they received, gained confidence by time and their long detention in prison. When therefore they were ordered to choose **10** whether they would be released from molestation by touching the polluted sacrifice, and would receive from them the accursed freedom, or refusing to sacrifice, should be condemned to death, they did not hesitate, but went to death cheerfully. For they knew what had been declared before by the Sacred Scriptures. For it is said,[6] 'He that sacrificeth to other gods shall be utterly destroyed,'[7] and, 'Thou shalt have no other gods before me.'"[8]
Such are the words of the truly philosoph- **11** ical and God-loving martyr, which, before the final sentence, while yet in prison, he addressed to the brethren in his parish, showing them his own circumstances, and at the same time exhorting them to hold fast, even after his approaching death, to the religion of Christ. But why need we dwell upon these things, **12** and continue to add fresh instances of the conflicts of the divine martyrs throughout the world, especially since they were dealt with no longer by common law, but attacked like enemies of war?

CHAPTER XI.

Those in Phrygia.

A SMALL town[1] of Phrygia, inhabited **1** solely by Christians, was completely sur-

---

good MSS., and is adopted by all the other editors and translators, and seems necessary in the present case. Upon the instrument referred to here, see above, Bk. IV. chap. 16, note 9. It would seem that "four holes" constituted in ordinary cases the extreme limit. But in two cases (Bk. V. chap. 1, § 27, and *Mart. Pal.* chap. 2) we are told of a "fifth hole." It is possible that the instruments varied in respect to the number of the holes, for the way in which the "four" is used here and elsewhere seems to indicate that the extreme of torture is thought of.
[6] φησί: "He says," or "the Scripture saith."
[7] Ex. xxii. 20.   [8] Ex. xx. 3.
[1] I read πολίχνην with the majority of MSS. and editors. A number of MSS. read πόλιν, which is supported by Rufinus (*urbem quandam*) and Nicephorus, and is adopted by Laemmer and Heinichen; but it would certainly be more natural for a copyist to exaggerate than to understate his original.
[2] Lactantius (*Div. inst.* V. 11), in speaking of persecutions in general, says, "Some were swift to slaughter, as an individual in

---

[2] Phil. ii. 6–8.   [3] 1 John iv. 18.
[4] τοῖς ἀμυντηρίοις. The word ἀμυντήριον means literally a weapon of defense, but the word seems to indicate in the present case some kind of a sharp instrument with claws or hooks. Rufinus translates *ungulæ*, the technical term for an instrument of torture of the kind just described. Valesius remarks, however, that these ἀμυντήρια seem to have been something more than *ungulæ*, for Hesychius interprets ἀμυντήριον as ξίφος δίστομον, i.e. a "two-edged sword."
[5] The majority of the MSS., followed by Laemmer and Heinichen, omit τεσσάρων, "four." The word, however, is found in a few

rounded by soldiers while the men were in it. Throwing fire into it, they consumed them with the women and children while they were calling upon Christ. This they did because all the inhabitants of the city, and the curator himself, and the governor, with all who held office, and the entire populace, confessed themselves Christians, and would not in the least obey those who commanded them to worship idols.

2   There was another man of Roman dignity named Adauctus,[2] of a noble Italian family, who had advanced through every honor under the emperors, so that he had blamelessly filled even the general offices of magistrate, as they call it, and of finance minister.[3] Besides all this he excelled in deeds of piety and in the confession of the Christ of God, and was adorned with the diadem of martyrdom. He endured the conflict for religion while still holding the office of finance minister.

CHAPTER XII.

Many Others, both Men and Women, who suffered in Various Ways.

1   WHY need we mention the rest by name, or number the multitude of the men, or picture the various sufferings of the admirable martyrs of Christ? Some of them were slain with the axe, as in Arabia. The limbs of some were

broken, as in Cappadocia. Some, raised on high by the feet, with their heads down, while a gentle fire burned beneath them, were suffocated by the smoke which arose from the burning wood, as was done in Mesopotamia. Others were mutilated by cutting off their noses and ears and hands, and cutting to pieces the other members and parts of their bodies, as in Alexandria.[1] Why need we revive the recol-   2 lection of those in Antioch who were roasted on grates, not so as to kill them, but so as to subject them to a lingering punishment? Or of others who preferred to thrust their right hand into the fire rather than touch the impious sacrifice? Some, shrinking from the trial, rather than be taken and fall into the hands of their enemies, threw themselves from lofty houses, considering death preferable to the cruelty of the impious.

A certain holy person, — in soul admira-   3 ble for virtue, in body a woman, — who was illustrious beyond all in Antioch for wealth and family and reputation, had brought up in the principles of religion her two daughters, who were now in the freshness and bloom of life. Since great envy was excited on their account, every means was used to find them in their concealment; and when it was ascertained that they were away, they were summoned deceitfully to Antioch. Thus they were caught in the nets of the soldiers. When the woman saw herself and her daughters thus helpless, and knew the things terrible to speak of that men would do to them, — and the most unbearable of all terrible things, the threatened violation of their chastity,[2] — she exhorted herself and the maidens that they ought not to submit even to hear of this. For, she said, that to surrender their souls to the slavery of demons was worse than all deaths and destruction; and she set before them the only deliverance from all these things, — escape to Christ. They then   4 listened to her advice. And after arranging their garments suitably, they went aside from the middle of the road, having requested of the guards a little time for retirement, and cast themselves into a river which was flowing

---

Phrygia who burnt an entire people, together with their place of meeting (*universum populum cum ipso pariter conventiculo*)." This apparently refers to the same incident which Eusebius records in this chapter. Gibbon contends that not the city, but only the church with the people in it was burned; and so Fletcher, the translator of Lactantius in the *Ante-Nicene Fathers*, understands the passage (" who burnt a whole assembly of people, together with their place of meeting "). Mason, on the other hand, contends that the population of the entire city is meant. The Latin would seem, however, to support Gibbon's interpretation rather than Mason's; but in view of the account in Eusebius, the latter has perhaps most in its favor. If the two passages be interpreted differently, we can hardly determine which is the true version of the incident. Mason has "no hesitation" in referring this episode to the period immediately following the First Edict of Diocletian, at the time when the rebellions in Melitene and Syria were taking place. It may have occurred at that time, but I should myself have *considerable* hesitation in referring it definitely to any particular period of the persecution. If Eusebius' statement at the close of this paragraph could be relied upon, we should be obliged to put the event after the issue of the fourth edict, for not until that time were Christians in general called upon to offer sacrifices. But the statement may be merely a conclusion of Eusebius' own; and since he does not draw a clear distinction between the various steps in the persecution, little weight can be laid upon it.

[2] Rufinus connects this man with the town of Phrygia just referred to, and makes him one of the victims of that catastrophe. But Eusebius does not intimate any such connection, and indeed seems to separate him from the inhabitants of that city by the special mention of him as a martyr. Moreover, the official titles given to him are hardly such as we should expect the citizen of an insignificant Phrygian town to bear. He is said, in fact, to have held the highest imperial — not merely municipal — offices. We know nothing more about the man than is told us here; nor do we know when and where he suffered.

[3] τὰς καθόλου διοικήσεις τῆς παρ' αὐτοῖς καλουμένης μαγιστρότητος τε καὶ καθολικότητος. The second office (καθολικότης) is apparently to be identified with that mentioned in Bk. VII. chap. 10, § 5 (see note 8 on that chapter). We can hardly believe, however, that Adauctus (of whom we hear nowhere else) can have held so high a position as is meant there, and therefore are forced to conclude that he was but one of a number of such finance ministers, and had the administration of the funds only of a particular district in his hands.

[1] The barbarous mutilation of the Christians which is spoken of here and farther on in the chapter, began, as we learn from the *Martyrs of Palestine*, in the sixth year of the persecution (A.D. 308). The tyrant Maximin seems to have become alarmed at the number of deaths which the persecution was causing, and to have hit upon this atrocious expedient as a no less effectual means of punishment. It was practiced apparently throughout Maximin's dominions; we are told of numbers who were treated in this way, both in Egypt and Palestine (see *Mart. Pal.* chap. 8 sq.).

[2] This abominable treatment of female Christians formed a feature of the persecutions both of Maximian and Maximin, who were alike monsters of licentiousness. It was entirely foreign to all the principles of Diocletian's government, and could never have been allowed by him. It began apparently in Italy under Maximian, after the publication by him of the Fourth Edict (see *Mart. Pal.* chap. 3, note 2), and was continued in the East by Maximin, when he came into power. We have a great many instances given of this kind of treatment, and in many cases, as in the present, suicide relieved the victims of the proposed indignity.

5   by. Thus they destroyed themselves.[3] But there were two other virgins in the same city of Antioch who served God in all things, and were true sisters, illustrious in family and distinguished in life, young and blooming, serious in mind, pious in deportment, and admirable for zeal. As if the earth could not bear such excellence, the worshipers of demons commanded to cast them into the sea. And this was done to them.

6   In Pontus, others endured sufferings horrible to hear. Their fingers were pierced with sharp reeds under their nails. Melted lead, bubbling and boiling with the heat, was poured down the backs of others, and they were roasted in the most sensitive parts of the

7   body. Others endured on their bowels and privy members shameful and inhuman and unmentionable torments, which the noble and law-observing judges, to show their severity, devised, as more honorable manifestations of wisdom. And new tortures were continually invented, as if they were endeavoring, by surpassing one another, to gain

8   prizes in a contest. But at the close of these calamities, when finally they could contrive no greater cruelties, and were weary of putting to death, and were filled and satiated with the shedding of blood, they turned to what they considered merciful and humane treatment, so that they seemed to be no longer devis-

9   ing terrible things against us. For they said that it was not fitting that the cities should be polluted with the blood of their own people, or that the government of their rulers, which was kind and mild toward all, should be defamed through excessive cruelty; but that rather the beneficence of the humane and royal authority should be extended to all, and we should no longer be put to death. For the infliction of this punishment upon us should be stopped in consequence of the human-

10   ity of the rulers. Therefore it was commanded that our eyes should be put out, and that we should be maimed in one of our limbs. For such things were humane in their sight, and the lightest of punishments for us. So that now on account of this kindly treatment accorded us by the impious, it was impossible to tell the incalculable number of those whose right eyes had first been cut out with the sword, and then had been cauterized with fire; or who had been disabled in the left foot by burning the joints, and afterward condemned to the provincial copper mines, not so much for service as for distress and hardship. Besides all these, others encountered other trials, which it is impossible to recount; for their manly endurance surpasses all description. In

11   these conflicts the noble martyrs of Christ shone illustrious over the entire world, and everywhere astonished those who beheld their manliness; and the evidences of the truly divine and unspeakable power of our Saviour were made manifest through them. To mention each by name would be a long task, if not indeed impossible.

CHAPTER XIII.

The Bishops of the Church that evinced by their Blood the Genuineness of the Religion which they preached.

1   As for the rulers of the Church that suffered martyrdom in the principal cities, the first martyr of the kingdom of Christ whom we shall mention among the monuments of the pious is Anthimus,[1] bishop of the city of Nicomedia, who was beheaded. Among the martyrs

2   at Antioch was Lucian,[2] a presbyter of that parish, whose entire life was most excellent. At Nicomedia, in the presence of the emperor, he proclaimed the heavenly kingdom of Christ, first in an oral defense, and afterwards by deeds as well. Of the martyrs in Phœnicia

3   the most distinguished were those devoted pastors of the spiritual flocks of Christ: Tyrannion,[3] bishop of the church of Tyre; Zenobius, a presbyter of the church at Sidon; and Silvanus,[4] bishop of the churches about Emesa.

---

[3] Eusebius evidently approved of these women's suicide, and it must be confessed that they had great provocation. The views of the early Church on the subject of suicide were in ordinary cases very decided. They condemned it unhesitatingly as a crime, and thus made a decided advance upon the position held by many eminent Pagans of that age, especially among the Stoics. In two cases, however, their opinion of suicide was somewhat uncertain. There existed in many quarters a feeling of admiration for those who voluntarily rushed to martyrdom and needlessly sacrificed their lives. The wiser and steadier minds, however, condemned this practice unhesitatingly (cf. p. 8, above). The second case in connection with which the opinions of the Fathers were divided, was that which meets us in the present passage. The majority of them evidently not only justified but commended suicide in such an extremity. The first Father distinctly to condemn the practice was Augustine (*De civ. Dei.* I. 22–27). He takes strong ground on the subject, and while admiring the bravery and chastity of the many famous women that had rescued themselves by taking their own lives, he denounces their act as sinful under all circumstances, maintaining that suicide is never anything else than a crime against the law of God. The view of Augustine has very generally prevailed since his time. Cf. Lecky's *History of European Morals*, 3d edition (Appleton, New York), Vol. II. p. 43 sq.

[1] On Anthimus, see above, chap. 6, note 5.

[2] On Lucian of Antioch, see below, Bk. IX. chap. 6, note 4.

[3] Of Tyrannion and Zenobius, we know only what is told us here and in the next paragraph. All of the martyrs of whom Eusebius tells us in this and the following books are commemorated in the Martyrologies, and accounts of the passions of many of them are given in various Acts, usually of doubtful authority. I shall not attempt to mention such documents in my notes, nor to give references to the Martyrologies, unless there be some special reason for it in connection with a case of particular interest. Wherever we have farther information in regard to any of these martyrs, in Eusebius himself or other early Fathers, I shall endeavor to give the needed references, passing other names by unnoticed. Tillemont (*H. E.* V.) contains accounts of all these men, and all the necessary references to the Martyrologies, the Bollandist Acts, etc. To his work the curious reader is referred.

[4] Silvanus is mentioned again in Bk. IX. chap. 6, and from that passage we learn that he was a very old man at the time of his death, and that he had been bishop forty years. It is, moreover, directly stated in that passage that Silvanus suffered martyrdom at

4   The last of these, with others, was made food for wild beasts at Emesa, and was thus received into the ranks of martyrs. The other two glorified the word of God at Antioch through patience unto death. The bishop[5] was thrown into the depths of the sea. But Zenobius, who was a very skillful physician, died through severe tortures which were applied to his sides.

5   Of the martyrs in Palestine, Silvanus,[6] bishop of the churches about Gaza, was beheaded with thirty-nine others at the copper mines of Phæno.[7] There also the Egyptian bishops, Peleus and Nilus,[8] with others, suffered

6   death by fire. Among these we must mention Pamphilus, a presbyter, who was the great glory of the parish of Cæsarea, and among the men of our time most admirable. The virtue of his manly deeds we have recorded

7   in the proper place.[9] Of those who suffered death illustriously at Alexandria and throughout Egypt and Thebais, Peter,[10] bishop of Alexandria, one of the most excellent teachers of the religion of Christ, should first be mentioned; and of the presbyters with him Faustus,[11] Dius and Ammonius, perfect martyrs of Christ; also Phileas,[12] Hesychius,[13] Pachymius and Theodorus, bishops of Egyptian churches, and besides them many other distinguished persons who are commemorated by the parishes of their country and region.

It is not for us to describe the conflicts of those who suffered for the divine religion throughout the entire world, and to relate accurately what happened to each of them. This would be the proper work of those who were eye-witnesses of the events. I will describe for posterity in another work[14] those which I myself witnessed. But in the present book[15] I will   8
add to what I have given the revocation issued by our persecutors, and those events that occurred at the beginning of the persecution, which will be most profitable to such as shall read them.

What words could sufficiently describe the   9
greatness and abundance of the prosperity of the Roman government before the war against us, while the rulers were friendly and peaceable toward us? Then those who were highest in the government, and had held the position ten or twenty years, passed their time in tranquil peace, in festivals and public games and most joyful pleasures and cheer. While   10
thus their authority was growing uninterruptedly, and increasing day by day, suddenly they changed their peaceful attitude toward us, and began an implacable war. But the second year of this movement was not yet past, when a

the same period with Peter of Alexandria, namely, in the year 312 or thereabouts. This being the date also of Lucian's martyrdom, mentioned just above, we may assume it as probable that all mentioned in this chapter suffered about the same time.

[5] i.e. Tyrannion.

[6] Silvanus, bishop of Gaza, is mentioned also in *Mart. Pal.* chaps. 7 and 13. From the former chapter we learn that he became a confessor at Phæno in the fifth year of the persecution (A.D. 307), while still a presbyter; from the latter, that he suffered martyrdom in the seventh year, at the very close of the persecution in Palestine, and that he had been eminent in his confessions from the beginning of the persecution.

[7] Phæno was a village of Arabia Petræa, between Petra and Zoar, and contained celebrated copper mines, which were worked by condemned criminals.

[8] Peleus and Nilus are mentioned in *Mart. Pal.* chap. 13, from which passage we learn that they, like Silvanus, died in the seventh year of the persecution. An anonymous presbyter, and a man named Patermuthius, are named there as perishing with them in the flames.

[9] On Pamphilus, see above, Bk. VII. chap. 32, note 40. Eusebius refers here to his *Life of Pamphilus* (see above, p. 28).

[10] On Peter of Alexandria, see above, Bk. VII. chap. 32, note 54.

[11] Faustus is probably to be identified with the deacon of the same name, mentioned above in Bk. VI. chap. 40 and in Bk. VII. chap. 11. At any rate, we learn from the latter chapter that the Faustus mentioned there lived to a great age, and died in the persecution of Diocletian, so that nothing stands in the way of identifying the two, though in the absence of all positive testimony, the identification cannot be insisted upon. Of Dius and Ammonius we know nothing.

[12] On Phileas, see above, chap. 9, note 3.

[13] A Latin version of an epistle purporting to have been written by these four bishops is still extant (see above, chap. 9, note 3). We know nothing more about the last three named here. It has been customary to identify this Hesychius with the reviser of the text of the LXX and the Gospels which was widely current in Egypt in the time of Jerome, and was known as the Hesychian recension (see Jerome, *Præf. in Paralipom.*, *Apol. adv. Ruf.* II. 27, *Præf. in quattuor Evangelia*; and cf. *Comment. in Isaiam*, LVIII. 11). We know little about this text; but Jerome speaks of it slightingly, as does also the Decretal of Gelasius, VI. § 15 (according to Westcott's *Hist. of the Canon*, 5th ed. p. 392, note 5). The identification of the two men is quite possible, for the recension referred to belonged no doubt to this period; but no positive arguments beyond agreement in name and country can be urged in support of it. Fabricius proposed to identify our Hesychius with the author of the famous Greek Lexicon, which is still extant. But this identification is now commonly rejected; and the author of the lexicon is regarded as a pagan, who lived in Alexandria during the latter part of the fourth century. See Smith's *Dict. of Greek and Roman Biography* and Smith and Wace's *Dict. of Christ. Biog. s.v.*

[14] Eusebius refers here to his *Martyrs of Palestine.* See above, p. 29 sq.

[15] κατὰ τὸν παρόντα λόγον. Eusebius seems to refer here to the eighth book of his *History;* for he uses λόγος frequently in referring to the separate books of his work, but nowhere else, so far as I am aware, in referring to the work as a whole. This would seem to indicate that he was thinking at this time of writing only eight books, and of bringing his *History* to an end with the toleration edict of Galerius, which he gives in chap. 17, below. Might it be supposed that the present passage was written immediately after the publication of the edict of Galerius, and before the renewal of the persecution by Maximin? If that were so, we might assume that after the close of that persecution, in consequence of the victory of Constantine and Licinius, the historian felt it necessary to add yet a ninth book to his work, not contemplated at the time he was writing his eighth; as he seems still later, after the victory of Constantine over Licinius, to have found it necessary to add a tenth book, in order that his work might cover the entire period of persecution and include the final triumph of the Church. His motive, indeed, in adding the tenth book seems not to have been to bring the history down to the latest date possible, for he made no additions during his later years, in spite of the interesting and exciting events which took place after 325 A.D., but to bring it down to the final triumph of Church over its pagan enemies. Had there been another persecution and another toleration edict between 325 and 338, we can hardly doubt that Eusebius would have added an account of it to his *History.* In view of these considerations, it is possible that some time may have elapsed between the composition of the eighth and ninth books, as well as between the composition of the ninth and tenth.

It must be admitted, however, that a serious objection to this supposition lies in the fact that in chaps. 15 and 16, below, the tenth year of the persecution is spoken of, and in the latter chapter the author is undoubtedly thinking of the Edict of Milan, which was issued in 312, after the renewal of Maximin's persecution described in Book IX. I am, nevertheless, inclined to think that Eusebius, when he wrote the present passage, was expecting to close his work with the present book, and that the necessity for another book made itself manifest before he finished the present one. I base my belief the words in chaps. 15 and 16 are a later insertion. I do not regard this as probable, but knowing the changes that were made in the ninth book in a second edition of the *History*, it must be admitted that such changes in the eighth book are not impossible (see above, p. 30 and 45). At the same time I prefer the former alternative, that the necessity for another book became manifest before he finished the present one. A slight confirmation of the theory that the ninth book was a later addition, necessitated by the persecution of Maximin's later years, may be found in the appendix to the eighth book which is found in many MSS. See below, p.   , note 1.

revolution took place in the entire govern-
11 ment and overturned all things. For a
severe sickness came upon the chief of
those of whom we have spoken, by which his
understanding was distracted ; and with him
who was honored with the second rank, he retired into private life.[16] Scarcely had he done
this when the entire empire was divided ; a
thing which is not recorded as having ever
12 occurred before.[17] Not long after, the Emperor Constantius, who through his entire
life was most kindly and favorably disposed
toward his subjects, and most friendly to the Divine Word, ended his life in the common course
of nature, and left his own son, Constantine, as
emperor and Augustus in his stead.[18] He was

the first that was ranked by them among the
gods, and received after death every honor which
one could pay to an emperor.[19] He was
the kindest and mildest of emperors, and   13
the only one of those of our day that passed
all the time of his government in a manner
worthy of his office. Moreover, he conducted
himself toward all most favorably and beneficently. He took not the smallest part in the
war against us, but preserved the pious that were
under him unharmed and unabused. He neither
threw down the church buildings,[20] nor did he
devise anything else against us. The end of his
life was honorable and thrice blessed. He alone
at death left his empire happily and gloriously
to his own son as his successor, — one who was
in all respects most prudent and pious.
His son Constantine entered on the govern-   14
ment at once, being proclaimed supreme
emperor and Augustus by the soldiers, and long
before by God himself, the King of all. He
showed himself an emulator of his father's piety
toward our doctrine. Such an one was he.

But after this, Licinius was declared emperor
and Augustus by a common vote of the
rulers.[21] These things grieved Maximinus   15
greatly, for until that time he had been
entitled by all only Cæsar. He therefore, being
exceedingly imperious, seized the dignity for
himself, and became Augustus, being made such
by himself.[22] In the mean time he whom we

[16] The abdication of Diocletian and Maximian, the two Augusti, took place on May 1, 305, and therefore a little more, not a little less, than two years after the publication of Diocletian's First Edict. The causes of the abdication have been given variously by different writers, and our original authorities are themselves in no better agreement. I do not propose to enter here into a discussion of the subject, but am convinced that Burckhardt, Mason, and others are correct in looking upon the abdication, not as the result of a sudden resolve, but as a part of Diocletian's great plan, and as such long resolved upon and regarded as one of the fundamental requirements of his system to be regularly observed by his successors, as well as by himself. The abdication of Diocletian and Maximian raised the Cæsars Constantius and Galerius to the rank of Augusti, and two new Cæsars, Maximinus Daza in the East, and Severus in the West, were appointed to succeed them. Diocletian himself retired to Dalmatia, his native province, where he passed the remainder of his life in rural pursuits, until his death in 313.

[17] Eusebius is correct in saying that the empire had never been divided up to this time. For it had always been ruled as one whole, even when the imperial power was shared by two or more princes. And even the system of Diocletian was not meant to divide the empire into two or more independent parts. The plan was simply to vest the supreme power in two heads, who should be given lieu-tenants to assist them in the government, but who should jointly represent the unity of the whole while severally administering their respective territories. Imperial acts to be valid had to be joint, not individual acts, and had to bear the name of both Augusti, while the Cæsars were looked upon only as the lieutenants and representatives of their respective superiors. Finally, in the last analysis, there was theoretically but the one supreme head, the first Augustus. While Diocletian was emperor, the theoretical unity was a practical thing. So long as his strong hand was on the helm, Maximian, the other Augustus, did not venture to do anything in opposition to his wishes, and thus the great system worked smoothly. But with Diocletian's abdication, everything was changed. Theoretically Constantius was the first Augustus, but Galerius, not Constantius, had had the nam-ing of the Cæsars; and there was no intention on Galerius' part to acknowledge in any way his inferiority to Constantius. In fact, being in the East, whence the government had been carried on for twenty years, it was natural that he should be entirely independent of Constantius, and that thus, as Eusebius says, a genuine division of the empire, not theoretical but practical, should be the result. The principle remained the same; but West and East seemed now to stand, not under one great emperor, but under two equal and independent heads.

[18] Constantius Chlorus died at York, in Britain, July 25, 306. According to the system of Diocletian, the Cæsar Severus should regularly have succeeded to his place, and a new Cæsar should have been appointed to succeed Severus. But Constantine, the oldest son of Constantius, who was with his father at the time of his death, was at once proclaimed his successor, and hailed as Augustus by the army. This was by no means to Galerius' taste, for he had far other plans in mind; but he was not in a position to dispute Con-stantine's claims, and so made the best of the situation by recogniz-ing Constantine not as Augustus, but as second Cæsar, while he raised Severus to the rank of Augustus, and made his own Cæsar Maximin first Cæsar. Constantine was thus theoretically subject to Severus, but the subjection was only a fiction, for he was practically independent in his own district from that time on.

Our sources are unanimous in giving Constantius an amiable and pious character, unusually free from bigotry and cruelty. Although he was obliged to show some respect to the persecuting edicts of his superiors, Diocletian and Maximian, he seems to have been averse to persecution, and to have gone no further than was necessary in that direction, destroying some churches, but apparently subjecting none of the Christians to bodily injury. We have no hint, however, that he was a Christian, or that his generous treatment of the Chris-tians was the result in any way of a belief in their religion. It was simply the result of his natural tolerance and humanity, combined,

doubtless, with a conviction that there was nothing essentially vicious or dangerous in Christianity.

[19] Not the first of Roman emperors to be so honored, but the first of the four rulers who were at that time at the head of the empire. It had been the custom from the beginning to decree divine honors to the Roman emperors upon their decease, unless their characters or their reigns had been such as to leave universal hatred behind them, in which case such honors were often denied them, and their memory publicly and officially execrated, and all their public monuments destroyed. The ascription of such honors to Constantius, therefore, does not in itself imply that he was supe-rior to the other three rulers, nor indeed superior to the emperors in general, but only that he was not a monster, as some had been. The last emperor to receive such divine honors was Diocletian himself, with whose death the old pagan régime came finally to an end.

[20] This is a mistake; for though Constantius seems to have pro-ceeded as mildly as possible, he did destroy churches, as we are directly informed by Lactantius (de Mort. pers. 15), and as we can learn from extant Acts and other sources (see Mason, p. 146 sq.). Eusebius, perhaps, knew nothing about the matter, and simply drew a conclusion from the known character of Constantius and his gen-eral tolerance toward the Christians.

[21] The steps which led to the appointment of Licinius are omitted by Eusebius. Maxentius, son of the old Augustus Max-imian, spurred on by the success of Constantine's move in Britain, attempted to follow his example in Italy. He won the support of a considerable portion of the army and of the Roman people, and in October of the same year (306) was proclaimed emperor by soldiers and people. Severus, who marched against the usurper, was de-feated and slain, and Galerius, who endeavored to revenge his fallen colleague, was obliged to retreat without accomplishing any-thing. This left Italy and Africa in the hands of an independent ruler, who was recognized by none of the others. Toward the end of the year 307, Licinius, an old friend and comrade-in-arms of Galerius, was appointed Augustus to succeed Severus, whose death had occurred a number of months before, but whose place had not yet been filled. The appointment of Licinius took place at Carnuntum on the Danube, where Galerius, Diocletian, and Max-imian met for consultation. Inasmuch as Italy and Africa were still in the hands of Maxentius, Licinius was given the Illyrian provinces with the rank of second Augustus, and was thus nomi-nally ruler of the entire West.

[22] Early in 308 Maximinus, the first Cæsar, who was naturally incensed at the promotion of a new man, Licinius, to a position above himself, was hailed as Augustus by his troops, and at once notified

have mentioned as having resumed his dignity after his abdication, being detected in conspiring against the life of Constantine, perished by a most shameful death.[23] He was the first whose decrees and statues and public monuments were destroyed because of his wickedness and impiety.[24]

CHAPTER XIV.

The Character of the Enemies of Religion.

1   MAXENTIUS his son, who obtained the government at Rome,[1] at first feigned our faith,

Galerius of the fact. The latter could not afford to quarrel with Maximinus, and therefore bestowed upon him the full dignity of an Augustus, as upon Constantine also at the same time. There were thus four independent Augusti (to say nothing of the emperor Maxentius), and the system of Diocletian was a thing of the past.
[23] The reference is to the Augustus Maximian. After his abdication he retired to Lucania, but in the following year was induced by his son, Maxentius, to leave his retirement, and join him in wresting Italy and Africa from Severus. It was due in large measure to his military skill and to the prestige of his name that Severus was vanquished and Galerius repulsed. After his victories Maximian went to Gaul, to see Constantine and form an alliance with him. He bestowed upon him the title of Augustus and the hand of his daughter Fausta, and endeavored to induce him to join him in a campaign against Galerius. This, however, Constantine refused to do; and Maximian finally returned to Rome, where he found his son Maxentius entrenched in the affections of the soldiers and the people, and bent upon ruling for himself. After a bitter quarrel with him, in which he attempted, but failed, to wrest the purple from him, he left the city, attended the congress of Carnuntum, and acquiesced in the appointment of Licinius as second Augustus, which of course involved the formal renunciation of his own claims and those of his son. He then betook himself again to Constantine, but during the latter's temporary absence treacherously had himself proclaimed Augustus by some of the troops. He was, however, easily overpowered by Constantine, but was forgiven and granted his liberty again. About two years later, unable to resist the desire to reign, he made an attempt upon Constantine's life with the hope of once more securing the power for himself, but was detected and allowed to choose the manner of his own death, and in February, 310, strangled himself. The general facts just stated are well made out, but there is some uncertainty as to the exact order of events, in regard to which our sources are at variance. Compare especially the works of Hunziker, Burckhardt, and Mason, and the respective articles in Smith's *Dict. of Greek and Roman Biog.*
Eusebius' memory plays him false in this passage; for he has not mentioned, as he states, Maximian's resumption of the imperial dignity after his abdication. A few important MSS., followed by Heinichen, omit the entire clause, "whom we have mentioned as having resumed his dignity after his abdication." But the words are found in the majority of the MSS. and in Rufinus, and are accepted by all the other editors. There can, in fact, be no doubt that Eusebius wrote the words, and that the omission of them in some codices is due to the fact that some scribe or scribes perceived his slip, and consequently omitted the clause.
[24] Valesius understands by this (as in § 12, above), the first of the four emperors. But we find in Lactantius (*ibid.* chap. 42) the distinct statement that Diocletian (whose statues were thrown down in Rome with those of Maximian, to which they were joined, Janus-fashion) was the first emperor that had ever suffered such an indignity, and there is no hint in the text that Eusebius means any less than that in making his statement, though we know that it is incorrect.
[1] See the previous chapter, note 21.
The character which Eusebius gives to Maxentius in this chapter is borne out by all our sources, both heathen and Christian, and seems not to be greatly overdrawn. It has been sometimes disputed whether he persecuted the Christians, but there is no ground to suppose that he did, though they, in common with all his subjects, had to suffer from his oppression, and therefore hated him as deeply as the others did. His failure to persecute the Christians as such, and his restoration to them of the rights which they had enjoyed before the beginning of the great persecution, can hardly be looked upon as a result of a love or respect for our religion. It was doubtless in part due to hostility to Galerius, but chiefly to political considerations. He apparently saw what Constantine later saw and profited by, — that it would be for his profit, and would tend to strengthen his government, to gain the friendship of that large body of his subjects which had been so violently handled under the reign of his father. And, no doubt, the universal toleration which he offered was one of the great sources of his strength at the beginning of his reign. Upon his final defeat by Constantine, and his death, see below, Bk. IX. chap. 9.

in complaisance and flattery toward the Roman people. On this account he commanded his subjects to cease persecuting the Christians, pretending to religion that he might appear merciful and mild beyond his predecessors. But he did not prove in his deeds 2 to be such a person as was hoped, but ran into all wickedness and abstained from no impurity or licentiousness, committing adulteries and indulging in all kinds of corruption. For having separated wives from their lawful consorts, he abused them and sent them back most dishonorably to their husbands. And he not only practiced this against the obscure and unknown, but he insulted especially the most prominent and distinguished members of the Roman senate. All his subjects, people and rulers, 3 honored and obscure, were worn out by grievous oppression. Neither, although they kept quiet, and bore the bitter servitude, was there any relief from the murderous cruelty of the tyrant. Once, on a small pretense, he gave the people to be slaughtered by his guards ; and a great multitude of the Roman populace were slain in the midst of the city, with the spears and arms, not of Scythians and barbarians, but of their own fellow-citizens. It would be 4 impossible to recount the number of senators who were put to death for the sake of their wealth ; multitudes being slain on various pretenses. To crown all his wickedness, 5 the tyrant resorted to magic. And in his divinations he cut open pregnant women, and again inspected the bowels of newborn infants. He slaughtered lions, and performed various execrable acts to invoke demons and avert war. For his only hope was that, by these means, victory would be secured to him. It is impossible to tell the ways in 6 which this tyrant at Rome oppressed his subjects, so that they were reduced to such an extreme dearth of the necessities of life as has never been known, according to our contemporaries, either at Rome or elsewhere.

But Maximinus, the tyrant in the East, 7 having secretly formed a friendly alliance with the Roman tyrant as with a brother in wickedness, sought to conceal it for a long time. But being at last detected, he suffered merited punishment.[2] It was wonderful 8

[2] On the alliance of Maximinus with Maxentius, his war with Licinius, and his death, see below, Bk. IX. chaps. 9 and 10. Upon his accession to the Cæsarship and usurpation of the title of Augustus, see above, chap. 13, notes 16 and 22.
Maximinus Daza was a nephew of Galerius, who owed his advancement, not to his own merits, but solely to the favor of his uncle, but who, nevertheless, after acquiring power, was by no means the tool Galerius had expected him to be. Eusebius seems not to have exaggerated his wickedness in the least. He was the most abandoned and vicious of the numerous rulers of the time, and was utterly without redeeming qualities, so far as we can ascertain. Under him the Christians suffered more severely than under any of his colleagues, and even after the toleration edict and death of Galerius (A.D. 311), he continued the persecution for more than a year. His territory comprised Egypt and Syria, and consequently the

how akin he was in wickedness to the tyrant at Rome, or rather how far he surpassed him in it. For the chief of sorcerers and magicians were honored by him with the highest rank. Becoming exceedingly timid and superstitious, he valued greatly the error of idols and demons. Indeed, without soothsayers and oracles he did not venture to move even a 9 finger,[3] so to speak. Therefore he persecuted us more violently and incessantly than his predecessors. He ordered temples to be erected in every city, and the sacred groves which had been destroyed through lapse of time to be speedily restored. He appointed idol priests in every place and city ; and he set over them in every province, as high priest, some political official who had especially distinguished himself in every kind of service, giving him a band of soldiers and a body-guard. And to all jugglers, as if they were pious and beloved of the gods, he granted governments and the greatest 10 privileges. From this time on he distressed and harassed, not one city or country, but all the provinces under his authority, by extreme exactions of gold and silver and goods, and most grievous prosecutions and various fines. He took away from the wealthy the property which they had inherited from their ancestors, and bestowed vast riches and large sums of 11 money on the flatterers about him. And he went to such an excess of folly· and drunkenness that his mind was deranged and crazed in his carousals ; and he gave commands when intoxicated of which he repented afterward when sober. He suffered no one to surpass him in debauchery and profligacy, but made himself an instructor in wickedness to those about him, both rulers and subjects. He urged on the army to live wantonly in every kind of revelry and intemperance, and encouraged the governors and generals to abuse their subjects with rapacity and covetousness, almost 12 as if they were rulers with him. Why need we relate the licentious, shameless deeds of the man, or enumerate the multitude with whom he committed adultery ? For he could not pass through a city without continually corrupting women and ravishing vir- 13 gins. And in this he succeeded with all excèpt the Christians. For as they despised death, they cared nothing for his power. For the men endured fire and sword and crucifixion and wild beasts and the depths of the sea,

and cutting off of limbs, and burnings, and pricking and digging out of eyes, and mutilations of the entire body, and besides these, hunger and mines and bonds. In all they showed patience in behalf of religion rather than transfer to idols the reverence due to God. And the 14 women were not less manly than the men in behalf of the teaching of the Divine Word, as they endured conflicts with the men, and bore away equal prizes of virtue. And when they were dragged away for corrupt purposes, they surrendered their lives to death rather than their bodies to impurity.[4]

One only of those who were seized for 15 adulterous purposes by the tyrant, a most distinguished and illustrious Christian woman in Alexandria, conquered the passionate and intemperate soul of Maximinus by most heroic firmness. Honorable on account of wealth and family and education, she esteemed all of these inferior to chastity. He urged her many times, but although she was ready to die, he could not put her to death, for his desire was stronger than his anger. He therefore punished her 16 with exile, and took away all her property. Many others, unable even to listen to the threats of violation from the heathen rulers, endured every form of tortures, and rackings, and deadly punishment.

These indeed should be admired. But far the most admirable was that woman at Rome, who was truly the most noble and modest of all, whom the tyrant Maxentius, fully resembling Maximinus in his actions, endeavored to abuse. For when she learned that those 17 who served the tyrant in such matters were at the house (she also was a Christian), and that her husband, although a prefect of Rome, would suffer them to take and lead her away, having requested a little time for adorning her body, she entered her chamber, and being alone, stabbed herself with a sword. Dying immediately, she left her corpse to those who had come for her. And by her deeds, more powerfully than by any words, she has shown to all men now and hereafter that the virtue which prevails among Christians is the only invincible and indestructible possession.[5]

Such was the career of wickedness which 18 was carried forward at one and the same time by the two tyrants who held the East and the West. Who is there that would hesitate, after careful examination, to pronounce the persecution against us the cause of such evils? Especially since this extreme confusion of affairs did not cease until the Christians had obtained liberty.

---

greater part of the martyrdoms recorded by Eusebius in his *Martyrs of Palestine* took place under him. (See that work, for the details.) Upon the so-called Fifth Edict, which was issued by him in 308, see *Mart. Pal.* chap. 9, note 1. Upon his treatment of the Christians after the death of Galerius, and upon his final toleration edict, see Bk. IX. chap. 2 sq. and chap. 9 sq.
  [3] Literally, " a finger-nail " (ὄνυχος).

[4] Compare chap. 12, note 3, above.
  [5] *Ibid.*

CHAPTER XV.

The Events which happened to the Heathen.[1]

1   DURING the entire ten years[2] of the persecution, they were constantly plotting and warring against one another.[3] For the sea could not be navigated, nor could men sail from any port without being exposed to all kinds of outrages; being stretched on the rack and lacerated in their sides, that it might be ascertained through various tortures, whether they came from the enemy; and finally being subjected 2 to punishment by the cross or by fire. And besides these things shields and breastplates were preparing, and darts and spears and other warlike accoutrements were making ready, and galleys and naval armor were collecting in every place. And no one expected anything else than to be attacked by enemies any day. In addition to this, famine and pestilence came upon them, in regard to which we shall relate what is necessary in the proper place.[4]

CHAPTER XVI.

The Change of Affairs for the Better.

1   SUCH was the state of affairs during the entire persecution. But in the tenth year, through the grace of God, it ceased altogether, having begun to decrease after the eighth year.[1] For when the divine and heavenly grace showed us favorable and propitious oversight, then truly our rulers, and the very persons[2] by whom the war against us had been earnestly prosecuted, most remarkably changed their minds, and issued a revocation, and quenched the great fire of persecution which had been kindled, by merciful proclamations and ordinances concerning us. But this was not due to any 2 human agency; nor was it the result, as one might say, of the compassion or philanthropy of our rulers; — far from it, for daily from the beginning until that time they were devising more and more severe measures against us, and continually inventing outrages by a greater variety of instruments; — but it was manifestly due to the oversight of Divine Providence, on the one hand becoming reconciled to his people, and on the other, attacking him[3] who instigated these evils, and showing anger toward him as the author of the cruelties of the entire persecution. For though it was necessary that 3 these things should take place, according to the divine judgment, yet the Word saith, "Woe to him through whom the offense cometh."[4] Therefore punishment from God came upon him, beginning with his flesh, and proceeding to his soul.[5] For an abscess 4 suddenly appeared in the midst of the secret parts of his body, and from it a deeply perforated sore, which spread irresistibly into his inmost bowels. An indescribable multitude of worms sprang from them, and a deathly odor arose, as the entire bulk of his body had, through his gluttony, been changed, before his sickness, into an excessive mass of soft fat, which became putrid, and thus presented an awful and intolerable sight to those who came near. Some of the physicians, being wholly 5 unable to endure the exceeding offensiveness of the odor, were slain; others, as the entire mass had swollen and passed beyond hope of restoration, and they were unable to render any help, were put to death without mercy.

---

[1] τοῖς ἐκτός.

[2] Diocletian's First Edict was issued on Feb. 24, 303; and the persecution was brought to a final end by Constantine and Licinius' edict of toleration, which was issued at Milan late in the year 312 (see below, Bk. IX. chap. 9, note 17). The persecution may therefore be said to have lasted altogether ten years; although of course there were many cessations during that period, and in the West it really came to an end with the usurpation of Maxentius in 306, and in the East (except in Maximin's dominions) with the edict of Galerius in 311.

[3] This passage is largely rhetorical. It is true that enough plotting and warring went on after the usurpation of Maxentius in 306, and after the death of Galerius in 311, to justify pretty strong statements. Gibbon, for instance, says: "The abdication of Diocletian and Maximian was succeeded by eighteen years of discord and confusion. The empire was afflicted by five civil wars; and the remainder of the time was not so much a state of tranquillity as a suspension of arms between several hostile monarchs, who, viewing each other with an eye of fear and hatred, strove to increase their respective forces at the expense of their subjects" (chap. xiv.). At the same time, during the four years between 307 and 311, though there was not the harmony which had existed under Diocletian, and though the interests of the West and East were in the main hostile, yet the empire was practically at peace, barring the persecution of the Christians.

[4] See below, Bk. IX. chap. 8.

[1] The edict of Milan, issued by Constantine and Licinius toward the close of the year 312 (upon the date, see Mason, p. 333, note) put an end to the persecution in its tenth year, though complete toleration was not proclaimed by Maximin until the following spring. Very soon after the close of the eighth year, in April, 311, Galerius issued his edict of toleration, which is given in the next chapter. It is, therefore, to the publication of this edict that Eusebius refers when he says that the persecution had begun to decrease after the eighth year. Maximin yielded reluctant and partial consent to this edict for a few months, but before the end of the year he began to persecute again; and during the year 312 the Christians suffered severely in his dominions (see Bk. IX. chap. 2 sq.).

[2] The plural here seems a little peculiar, for the edict was issued only in the name of Galerius, Constantine, and Licinius, not in the name of Maximin. We have no record of Licinius as a persecutor before this time, and Eusebius' words of praise in the ninth book would seem to imply that he had not shown himself at all hostile to the Church. And in fact Licinius seems ruled out by § 2, below, where "they" are spoken of as having "from the beginning devised more and more severe measures against us." And yet, since Constantine did not persecute, we must suppose either that Licinius is included in Eusebius' plural, or what is perhaps more probable, that Eusebius thinks of the edict as proceeding from all four emperors though bearing the names of only three of them. It is true that the latter is rather a violent supposition in view of Eusebius' own words in the first chapter of Bk. IX. I confess that I find no satisfactory explanation of the apparent inconsistency.

[3] i.e. Galerius.

[4] Matt. xviii. 7.

[5] Galerius seems to have been smitten with the terrible disease, which Eusebius here refers to, and which is described by Lactantius at considerable length (De mort. pers. chap. 33) and with many imaginative touches (e.g. the stench of his disease pervades "not only the palace, but even the whole city"!), before the end of the year 310, and his death took place in May of the following year.

CHAPTER XVII.

The Revocation of the Rulers.

1   WRESTLING with so many evils, he thought
of the cruelties which he had committed
against the pious. Turning, therefore, his thoughts
toward himself, he first openly confessed to the
God of the universe, and then summoning his
attendants, he commanded that without delay
they should stop the persecution of the Christians, and should by law and royal decree, urge
them forward to build their churches and to
perform their customary worship, offering prayers
in behalf of the emperor.   Immediately the
2   deed followed the word.   The imperial decrees were published in the cities, containing the revocation of the acts against us in the
following form :
3   "The Emperor Cæsar Galerius Valerius
Maximinus, Invictus, Augustus, Pontifex
Maximus, conqueror of the Germans, conqueror
of the Egyptians, conqueror of the Thebans,
five times conqueror of the Sarmatians, conqueror of the Persians, twice conqueror of the
Carpathians, six times conqueror of the Armenians, conqueror of the Medes, conqueror of
the Adiabeni, Tribune of the people the twentieth time, Emperor the nineteenth time, Consul
the eighth time, Father of his country, Pro-
4   consul ; and the Emperor Cæsar Flavius
Valerius Constantinus, Pius, Felix, Invictus,
Augustus, Pontifex Maximus, Tribune of the
people, Emperor the fifth time, Consul,
5   Father of his country, Proconsul ; and the
Emperor Cæsar Valerius Licinius, Pius,
Felix, Invictus, Augustus, Pontifex Maximus,
Tribune of the people the fourth time, Emperor
the third time, Consul, Father of his country,
Proconsul ; to the people of their provinces,
greeting :[1]
6   "Among the other things which we have
ordained for the public advantage and profit, we formerly wished to restore everything to

conformity with the ancient laws and public discipline [2] of the Romans, and to provide that the
Christians also, who have forsaken the religion
of their ancestors,[3] should return to a good

[2] τὴν δημοσίαν ἐπιστήμην. Latin: *publicam disciplinam*.
[3] τῶν γονέων τῶν ἑαυτῶν τὴν αἵρεσιν. Latin: *parentum su-
orum sectam.* There has been some discussion as to whether
Galerius here refers to primitive Christianity or to paganism, but the
almost unanimous opinion of scholars (so far as I am aware) is that
he means the former (cf. among others, Mason, p. 298 sq.). I confess myself, however, unable, after careful study of the document, to
accept this interpretation. Not that I think it impossible that Galerius should pretend that the cause of the persecution had been the
departure of the Christians from primitive Christianity, and its object the reform of the Church, because, although that was certainly
not his object, he may nevertheless, when conquered, have wished
to make it appear so to the Christians at least (see Mason, p. 302 sq.).
My reason for not accepting the interpretation is that I cannot see
that the language of the edict warrants it; and certainly, inasmuch
as it is not what we should *a priori* expect Galerius to say, we are
hardly justified in adopting it except upon very clear grounds.
But in my opinion such grounds do not exist, and in fact the interpretation seems to me to do violence to at least a part of the decree.
In the present sentence it is certainly not *necessarily* implied that
the ancestors of the Christians held a different religion from the ancestors of the heathen; in fact, it seems on the face of it more natural
to suppose that Galerius is referring to the earlier ancestors of both
Christians and heathen, who were alike pagans. This is confirmed
by the last clause of the sentence: *ad bonas mentes redirent* (εἰς
ἀγαθὴν πρόθεσιν ἐπανέλθοιεν), which in the mouth of Galerius, and
indeed of any heathen, would naturally mean " return to the worship
of our gods." This in itself, however, proves nothing, for Galerius
may, as is claimed, have used the words hypocritically; but in the
next sentence, which is looked upon as the main support of the interpretation which I am combating, it is not said that they have
deserted *their* ancient institutions in distinction from the institutions of the rest of the world, but *illa veterum instituta* (a term
which he could hardly employ in this unqualified way to indicate the
originators of Christianity without gross and gratuitous insult to his
heathen subjects) *quæ forsitan primum parentes eorumdem con-
stituerant,* " those institutions of the ancients which *perchance*
their own fathers had first established" (the Greek is not quite accurate, omitting the demonstrative, and reading πρότερον for *primum*). There can hardly have been a " perchance" about the fact
that the Christians' ancestors had first established Christian institutions, whatever they were — certainly Galerius would never have
thought of implying that his ancestors, or the ancestors of his brother-
pagans, had established them. His aim seems to be to suggest, as
food for reflection, not only that the ancestors of the Christians had
certainly, with the ancestors of the heathen, originally observed
pagan institutions, but that perhaps they had themselves been the
very ones to establish those institutions, which would make the guilt
of the Christians in departing from them all the worse. In the
next clause, the reference to the Christians as making laws for
themselves and assembling in various places may as easily be a
rebuke to the Christians for their separation from their heathen
fellow-citizens in matters of life and worship as a rebuke to them
for their departure from the original unity of the Christian Church.
Again, in the next sentence the " institutions of the ancients" (*veterum instituta*) are referred to in the most general way, without
any such qualification as could possibly lead the Christians or any
one else to think that the institutions of the Christian religion were
meant. Conformity to " the ancient laws and public discipline of
the Romans" is announced in the beginning of the edict as the
object which Galerius had in view. Could he admit, even for the
sake of propitiating his Christian subjects, that those laws and that
discipline were Christian? *Veterum instituta* in fact could mean
to the reader nothing else, as thus absolutely used, than the institutions of the old Romans.
    Still further it is to be noticed that in § 9 Galerius does not say
"*but although* many persevere in their purpose . . . *nevertheless,*
in consideration of our philanthropy, we have determined that we
ought to extend our indulgence," &c., but rather "*and since* (*atque cum*) many persevere in their purpose," &c. The significance
of this has apparently been hitherto quite overlooked. Does he
mean to say that he feels that he ought to extend indulgence just
because they do exactly what they did before — worship neither the
gods of the heathen nor the God of the Christians? I can hardly
think so. He seems to me to say rather, " Since many, in spite of
my severe measures, still persevere in their purpose (*in proposito
perseverarent*) and refuse to worship our gods, while at the same
time they cease under the pressure to worship their own God as
they have been accustomed to do, I have decided to permit them to
return to their own worship, thinking it better that they worship the
God of the Christians than that they worship no God; provided in
worshiping him they do nothing contrary to discipline (*contra
disciplinam*), i.e. contrary to Roman law." Thus interpreted, the
entire edict seems to me consistent and at the same time perfectly
natural. It is intended to propitiate the Christians and to have them
pray for the good of the emperor to their own God, rather than refuse to pray for him altogether. It is not an acknowledgment even
to the Christians that their God is the supreme and only true God,
but it is an acknowledgment that their God is probably better than

---

[1] This edict was issued in April, 311 (see the previous chapter,
note 1). There has been considerable discussion as to the reason
for the omission of Maximin's name from the heading of the edict.
The simplest explanation is that he did not wish to have his name
appear in a document which was utterly distasteful to him and which
he never fully sanctioned, as we learn from Bk. IX. chaps. 1 and 2,
below. It is possible, as Mason suggests, that in the copies of the
edict which were designed for other parts of the empire than his
own the names of all four emperors appeared. Eusebius gives a
Greek translation of the edict. The original Latin is found in Lactantius' *De mort. pers.* chap. 34. The translation in the present
case is in the main accurate though somewhat free. The edict is
an acknowledgment of defeat on Galerius' part, and was undoubtedly caused in large part by a superstitious desire, brought on by his
sickness, to propitiate the God of the Christians whom he had been
unable to conquer. And yet, in my opinion, it is not as Mason calls
it, " one of the most bizarre state documents ever penned," " couched
in language treacherous, contradictory, and sown with the most virulent hatred"; neither does it " lay the blame upon the Christians
because they had *forsaken Christ*," nor aim to " dupe and outwit
the angry Christ, by pretending to be not a persecutor, but a reformer." As will be seen from note 3, below, I interpret the document in quite another way, and regard it as a not inconsistent
statement of the whole matter from Galerius' own point of view.

7 disposition. For in some way such arrogance had seized them and such stupidity had overtaken them, that they did not follow the ancient institutions which possibly their own ancestors had formerly established, but made for themselves laws according to their own purpose, as each one desired, and observed them, and thus assembled as separate congrega-

8 tions in various places. When we had issued this decree that they should return to the institutions established by the ancients,[4] a great many[5] submitted under danger, but a great many being harassed endured all kinds of death.[6]

9 And since many continue in the same folly,[7] and we perceive that they neither offer to the heavenly gods the worship which is due, nor pay regard to the God of the Christians, in consideration of our philanthropy and our invariable custom, by which we are wont to extend pardon to all, we have determined that we ought most cheerfully to extend our indulgence in this matter also ; that they may again be Christians, and may rebuild the conventicles in which they were accustomed to assemble,[8] on condition that nothing be done by them contrary to discipline.[9] In another letter we shall indicate to the mag-

10 istrates what they have to observe. Wherefore, on account of this indulgence of ours, they ought to supplicate their God for our safety, and that of the people, and their own, that the public welfare may be preserved in every place,[10] and that they may live securely in their several homes."

Such is the tenor of this edict, translated, 11 as well as possible, from the Roman tongue into the Greek.[11] It is time to consider what took place after these events.

That which follows is found in Some Copies in the Eighth Book.[1]

THE author of the edict very shortly after 1 this confession was released from his pains and died. He is reported to have been the original author of the misery of the persecution, having endeavored, long before the movement of the other emperors, to turn from the faith the Christians in the army, and first of all those in his own house, degrading some from the military rank, and abusing others most shamefully, and threatening still others with death, and finally inciting his partners in the empire to the general persecution. It is not proper to pass over the death of these emperors in silence. As four of them held the supreme author- 2 ity, those who were advanced in age and honor, after the persecution had continued not quite two years, abdicated the government, as we have already stated,[2] and passed the remainder of their lives in a common and private station. The end of their lives 3 was as follows. He who was first in honor and age perished through a long and most grievous physical infirmity.[3] He who held the second place ended his life by strangling,[4] suffering

---

no god, and that the empire will be better off if they become loyal, peaceable, prayerful citizens again (even if their prayers are not directed to the highest gods), than if they continue disaffected and disloyal and serve and worship no superior being. That the edict becomes, when thus interpreted, much more dignified and much more worthy of an emperor cannot be denied; and, little respect as we may have for Galerius, we should not accuse him of playing the hypocrite and the fool in this matter, except on better grounds than are offered by the extant text of this edict.

[4] ἐπὶ τὰ ὑπὸ τῶν ἀρχαίων καταστάθεντα. Latin: *ad veterum instituta.*

[5] πλείστοι. Latin: *multi.*

[6] παντοίους θανάτους ὑπέφερον. Latin: *deturbati sunt.*

[7] τῇ αὐτῇ ἀπονοίᾳ διαμενόντων. Latin: *in proposito perseverarent.*

[8] τοὺς οἴκους, ἐν οἷς συνήγοντο, συνθῶσιν. Latin: *conventicula sua componant.*

[9] *contra disciplinam,* i.e. " against the discipline or laws of the Romans." Galerius does not tell us just what this indefinite phrase is meant to cover, and the letter to the magistrates, in which he doubtless explained himself and laid down the conditions, is unfortunately lost. The edict of Milan, as Mason conclusively shows, refers to this edict of Galerius and to these accompanying conditions; and from that edict some light is thrown upon the nature of these conditions imposed by Galerius. It has been conjectured that in Galerius' edict, Christianity was forbidden to all but certain classes: " that if a man chose to declare himself a Christian, he would incur no danger, but might no longer take his seat as a decurion in his native town, or the like"; that Galerius had endeavored to make money out of the transaction whereby Christians received their church property back again; that proselytizing was forbidden; that possibly the toleration of Christianity was made a matter of local option, and that any town or district by a majority vote could prohibit its exercise within its own limits (see Mason, p. 330 sq.). These conjectures are plausible, though of course precarious.

[10] The Greek reads, in all our MSS., κατὰ πάντα τρόπον, " in every manner." The Latin original, however, reads *undique versum.* In view of that fact, I feel confident that the Greek translator must have written τόπον instead of τρόπον. If, therefore, that translator was Eusebius, we must suppose that the change to τρόπον is due to the error of some scribe. If, on the other hand, Eusebius simply copied the Greek translation from some one else, he may

himself have carelessly written τρόπον. In either case, however, τόπον must have been the original translation, and I have therefore substituted it for τρόπον, and have rendered accordingly. I find that Crusè has done likewise, whether for the same reason I do not know.

[11] Eusebius does not say whether the translating was done by himself or by some one else. The epistle of Hadrian to Minucius Fundanus, quoted in Bk. IV. chap. 9, above, was translated by himself, as he directly informs us (see *ibid.* chap. 8, note 17). This might lead us to suppose him the translator in the present case; but, on the other hand, in that case he directly says that the translation was his work, in the present he does not. It is possible that Greek copies of the edict were in common circulation, and that Eusebius used one of them. At the same time, the words " translated as well as possible" (κατὰ τὸ δυνατόν) would seem to indicate that Eusebius had supervised the present translation, if he had not made it himself. Upon his knowledge of Latin, see the note just referred to.

[1] The words of this title, together with the section which follows, are found in the majority of our MSS. at the close of the eighth book, and are given by all the editors. The existence of the passage would seem to imply that the work in only eight books came into the hands of some scribe, who added the appendix to make the work more complete. (Cf. chap. 13, note 15, above.) Whoever he was, he was not venturesome in his additions, for, except the notice of Diocletian's death and the statement of the manner of the death of Maximinus, he adds nothing that has not been already said in substance by Eusebius himself. The appendix must have been added in any case as late as 313, for Diocletian died in that year.

[2] See above, chap. 13, § 11.

[3] Diocletian died in 313, at the age of sixty-seven. The final ruin of all his great plans for the permanent prosperity of the empire, the terrible misfortunes of his daughter, and the indignities heaped upon him by Maximin, Licinius, and Constantine, wore him out and at length drove the spirit from the shattered body. According to Lactantius (*De mort. pers.* 42), "having been treated in the most contumelious manner, and compelled to abhor life, he became incapable of receiving nourishment, and, worn out with anguish of mind, expired."

[4] Upon the death of Maximian, see above, chap. 13, note 23.

thus according to a certain demoniacal prediction, on account of his many daring crimes.

4   Of those after them, the last,[5] of whom we have spoken as the originator of the entire persecution, suffered such things as we have related.   But he who preceded him, the most merciful and kindly emperor Constantius,[6] passed all the time of his government in a manner worthy of his office.[6]   Moreover, he conducted himself towards all most favorably and beneficently.   He took not the smallest part in the war against us, and preserved the pious that were under him unharmed and unabused.   Neither did he throw down the church buildings, nor devise anything else against us.   The end of his life was happy and thrice blessed.   He alone at death left his empire happily and gloriously to his own son[7] as his successor, one who was in all respects most prudent and pious.   He entered on the government at once, being proclaimed supreme emperor and Augustus by the soldiers ; and he showed himself an em   5 ulator of his father's piety toward our doctrine.

Such were the deaths of the four of whom we have written, which took place at different times.   Of these, moreover, only the one   6 referred to a little above by us,[8] with those who afterward shared in the government, finally[9] published openly to all the above-mentioned confession, in the written edict which he issued.

---

[5] ὁ μὲν ὕστατος, i.e. Galerius, who was the second Cæsar and therefore the last, or lowest, of the four rulers. Upon his illness and death, see chap. 16, above.

[6] Constantius was first Cæsar, and thus held third rank in the government. The following passage in regard to him is found also in chap. 13, §§ 12-14, above.

[7] i.e. Constantine.

[8] i.e. Galerius.

[9] I read λοιπόν which is found in some MSS. and is adopted by Stephanus and Burton. Valesius, Schwegler, Laemmer and Heinichen follow other MSS. in reading λιπών, and this is adopted by Stroth, Closs and Crusè in their translations.   The last, however, makes it govern "the above-mentioned confession," which is quite ungrammatical, while Stroth and Closs (apparently approved by Heinichen) take it to mean "still alive" or "still remaining" (" Der unter diesen allein noch Ueberlebende"; " Der unter diesen noch allein uebrige"), a meaning which belongs to the middle but not properly to the active voice of λείπω.   The latter translation, moreover, makes the writer involve himself in a mistake, for Diocletian did not die until nearly two years after the publication of Galerius' edict.   In view of these considerations I feel compelled to adopt the reading λοιπόν which is nearly, if not quite, as well supported by MS. authority as λιπών.

MARTYRS OF PALESTINE.[1]

The Following also we found in a Certain Copy in the Eighth Book.[2]

IT was in the nineteenth year of the reign of Diocletian, in the month Xanthicus,[3] which is called April by the Romans, about the time of the feast of our Saviour's passion, while Flavianus[4] was governor of the province of Palestine, that letters were published every-where, commanding that the churches be leveled to the ground and the Scriptures be destroyed by fire, and ordering that those who held places of honor be degraded, and that the household servants, if they persisted in the profession of Christianity, be deprived of freedom.

Such was the force of the first edict against us. But not long after other letters were issued, commanding that all the bishops of the churches everywhere be first thrown into prison, and afterward, by every artifice, be compelled to sacrifice.

CHAPTER I.

THE first of the martyrs of Palestine was   1 Procopius,[1] who, before he had received the trial of imprisonment, immediately on his first appearance before the governor's tribunal, having been ordered to sacrifice to the so-called gods, declared that he knew only one to whom it was proper to sacrifice, as he himself wills. But when he was commanded to offer libations to the four emperors, having quoted a sentence which displeased them, he was immediately beheaded. The quotation was from the poet:

---

[1] On this work, see above, p. 29 sq. As remarked there, the shorter form of the work, the translation of which follows, is found in most, but not all, of the MSS. of Eusebius' *Church History*, in some of them at the close of the tenth book, in one of them in the middle of Bk. VIII. chap. 13, in the majority of them between Bks. VIII. and IX. It is found neither in the Syriac version of the *History*, nor in Rufinus. Musculus omits it in his Latin version, but a translation of it is given both by Christophorsonus and Valesius. The Germans Stroth and Closs omit it; but Stigloher gives it at the close of his translation of the *History*. The English translators insert it at the close of the eighth book. The work is undoubtedly genuine, in this, its shorter, as well as in its longer form, but was in all probability attached to the *History*, not by Eusebius himself, but by some copyist, and therefore is not strictly entitled to a place in a translation of the *History*. At the same time it has seemed best in the present case to include it and to follow the majority of the editors in inserting it at this point. In all the MSS. except one the work begins abruptly without a title, introduced only by the words καὶ ταῦτα ἐν τινι ἀντιγράφῳ ἐν τῷ ὀγδόῳ τόμῳ εὕρομεν: "The following also we found in a certain copy in the eighth book." In the Codex Castellanus, however, according to Reading (in his edition of Valesius, Vol. I. p. 796, col. 2), the following title is inserted immediately after the words just quoted: Εὐσεβίου συγγραμμα περὶ τῶν κατ᾽ αὐτὸν μαρτυρησάντων ἐν τῷ ὀκταετεῖ Διοκλητιανοῦ καὶ ἐφεξῆς Γαλερίου τοῦ Μαξιμίνου διωγμῷ. Heinichen consequently prints the first part of this title (Εὐσεβίου . . . μαρτυρησάντων) at the head of the work in his edition, and is followed by Burton and Migne. This title, however, can hardly be looked upon as original, and I have preferred to employ rather the name by which the work is described at its close, where we read Εὐσεβίου τοῦ Παμφίλου περὶ τῶν ἐν Παλαιστίνῃ μαρτυρησάντων τέλος. This agrees with the title of the Syriac version, and must represent very closely the original title; and so the work is commonly known in English as the *Martyrs of Palestine*, in Latin *de Martyribus Palestinæ*. The work is much more systematic than the eighth book of the *Church History;* in fact, it is excellently arranged, and takes up the persecution year by year in chronological order. The ground covered, however, is very limited, and we can consequently gather from the work little idea of the state of the Church at large during these years. All the martyrs mentioned in the following pages are commemorated in the various martyrologies under particular days, but in regard to most of them we know only what Eusebius tells us. I shall not attempt to give references to the martyrologies. Further details gleaned from them and from various Acts of martyrdom may be found in Ruinart, Tillemont, &c. I shall endeavor to give full particulars in regard to the few martyrs about whom we have any reliable information beyond that given in the present work, but shall pass over the others without mention.

[2] The *Martyrs of Palestine*, in all the MSS. that contain it, is introduced with these words. The passage which follows, down to the beginning of Chap. I., is a transcript, with a few slight variations, of Bk. VIII. chap. 2, §§ 4 and 5. For notes upon it, see that chapter.

[3] The month Xanthicus was the eighth month of the Macedonian year, and corresponded to our April (see the table on p. 403, below). In Bk. VIII. chap. 2, Eusebius puts the beginning of the prosecution in the seventh month, Dystrus. But the persecution really began, or at least the first edict was issued, and the destruction of the churches in Nicomedia took place, in February. See Bk. VIII. chap. 2, note 3.

[4] Flavianus is not mentioned in Bk. VIII. chap. 2. In the Syriac version he is named as the judge by whom Procopius was condemned (Cureton, p. 4). Nothing further is known of him, so far as I am aware.

[1] The account of Procopius was somewhat fuller in the longer recension of the *Martyrs of Palestine*, as can be seen from the Syriac version (English translation in Cureton, p. 3 sq.). There exists also a Latin translation of the Acts of St. Procopius, which was evidently made from that longer recension, and which is printed by Valesius and also by Cureton (p. 50 sq.), and in English by Crusè *in loco*. We are told by the Syriac version that his family was from Baishan. According to the Latin, he was a native of Ælia (Jerusalem), but resided in Scythopolis (the Greek name of Baishan). With the Latin agrees the Syriac version of these Acts, which is published by Assemani in his *Acta SS. Martt. Orient. et Occident.* ed. 1748, Part II. p. 169 sq. (see Cureton, p. 52). We learn from the longer account that he was a lector, interpreter, and exorcist in the church, and that he was exceedingly ascetic in his manner of life. It is clear from this paragraph that Procopius was put to death, not because he was a Christian, but because he uttered words apparently treasonable in their import. To call him a Christian martyr is therefore a misuse of terms. We cannot be sure whether Procopius was arrested under the terms of the first or under the terms of the second edict. If in consequence of the first, it may be that he was suspected of complicity in the plot which Diocletian was endeavoring to crush out, or that he had interfered with the imperial officers when they undertook to execute the decree for the destruction of the church buildings. The fact that he was commanded by the governor to sacrifice would lead us to think of the first, rather than of the second edict (see above, Bk. VIII. chap. 6, note 3, and chap. 2, note 8). Still, it must be admitted that very likely many irregularities occurred in the methods by which the decrees were executed in the province, and the command to sacrifice can, therefore, not be claimed as proving that he was not arrested under the terms of the second edict; and in fact, the mention of imprisonment as the punishment which he had to expect would lead us to think of the second edict as at least the immediate occasion of his arrest. In any case, there is no reason to suppose that his arrest would have resulted in his death had he not been rash in his speech.

"The rule of many is not good; let there be one ruler and one king."[2]

2   It was the seventh[3] day of the month Desius,[4] the seventh before the ides of June,[5] as the Romans reckon, and the fourth day of the week, when this first example was given at Cæsarea in Palestine.

3   Afterwards,[6] in the same city, many rulers of the country churches readily endured terrible sufferings, and furnished to the beholders an example of noble conflicts. But others, benumbed in spirit by terror, were easily weakened at the first onset. Of the rest, each one endured different forms of torture, as scourgings without number, and rackings, and tearings of their sides, and insupportable fetters, by which

4   the hands of some were dislocated. Yet they endured what came upon them, as in accordance with the inscrutable purposes of God. For the hands of one were seized, and he was led to the altar, while they thrust into his right hand the polluted and abominable offering, and he was dismissed as if he had sacrificed. Another had not even touched it, yet when others said that he had sacrificed, he went away in silence. Another, being taken up half dead, was cast aside as if already dead, and released from his bonds, and counted among the sacrificers. When another cried out, and testified that he would not obey, he was struck in the mouth, and silenced by a large band of those who were drawn up for this purpose, and driven away by force, even though he had not sacrificed. Of such consequence did they consider it, to seem by any means to have accomplished their purpose.

5.   Therefore, of all this number, the only ones who were honored with the crown of the holy martyrs were Alphæus and Zacchæus.[7] After stripes and scrapings and severe bonds and additional tortures and various other trials, and after having their feet stretched for a night and day over four holes in the stocks,[8] on the seventeenth day of the month Dius,[9] — that is, according to the Romans, the fifteenth before the Kalends of December, — having confessed one only God and Christ Jesus as king,[10] as if they had uttered some blasphemy, they were beheaded like the former martyr.

CHAPTER II.

WHAT occurred to Romanus on the same   1 day[1] at Antioch, is also worthy of record. For he was a native of Palestine, a deacon and exorcist in the parish of Cæsarea; and being present at the destruction of the churches, he beheld many men, with women and children, going up in crowds to the idols, and sacrificing.[2] But, through his great zeal for religion, he could not endure the sight, and rebuked them with a loud voice. Being arrested for his boldness, he proved a most noble witness of the   2 truth, if there ever was one. For when the judge informed him that he was to die by fire,[3]

[7] We learn from the Syriac version that Zacchæus was a deacon of the church of Gadara, and that Alphæus belonged to a noble family of the city of Eleutheropolis, and was a reader and exorcist in the church of Cæsarea.
[8] See above, Bk. IV. chap. 16, note 9.
[9] The month Dius was the third month of the Macedonian year, and corresponded with our November (see below, p. 403).
[10] μόνον ἕνα Θεὸν καὶ χριστὸν βασιλέα Ἰησοῦν ὁμολογήσαντες. Βασιλεύς was the technical term for emperor, and it is plain enough from this passage that these two men, like Procopius, were beheaded because they were regarded as guilty of treason, not because of their religious faith. The instances given in this chapter are very significant, for they reveal the nature of the persecution during its earlier months, and throw a clear light back upon the motives which had led Diocletian to take the step against the Christians which he did.
[1] We learn from the Syriac version that the death of Romanus occurred on the same day as that of Alphæus and Zacchæus. His arrest, therefore, must have taken place some time before, according to § 4, below. In fact, we see from the present paragraph that his arrest took place in connection with the destruction of the churches; that is, at the time of the execution of the first edict in Antioch. We should naturally think that the edict would be speedily published in so important a city, and hence can hardly suppose the arrest of Romanus to have occurred later than the spring of 303. He therefore lay in prison a number of months (according to § 4, below, a "very long time," πλεῖστον χρόνον). Mason is clearly in error in putting his arrest in November, and his death at the time of the vicennalia, in December. It is evident from the Syriac version that the order for the release of prisoners, to which the so-called third edict was appended, preceded the vicennalia by some weeks, although issued in view of the great anniversary which was so near at hand. It is quite possible that the decree was sent out some weeks beforehand, in order that time might be given to induce the Christians to sacrifice, and thus enjoy release at the same time with the others.
[2] There is no implication here that these persons were not commanded, or even asked, to sacrifice. They seem, in their dread of what might come upon them, when they saw the churches demolished, to have hastened of their own accord to sacrifice to the idols, and thus disarm all possible suspicion.
[3] As Mason remarks, to punish Romanus with death for dissuading the Christians from sacrificing was entirely illegal, as no imperial edict requiring them to sacrifice had yet been issued, and therefore no law was broken in exhorting them not to do so. At the same time, that he should be arrested as a church officer was, under the terms of the second edict, legal, and, in fact, necessary; and that the judge should incline to be very severe in the present case, with the emperor so near at hand, was quite natural. That death, however, was not yet made the penalty of Christian confession is plain enough from the fact that, when the emperor was appealed to, as we learn from the Syriac version, he remanded Romanus to prison, thus

[2]   οὐκ ἀγαθὸν πολυκοιρανίη εἷς κοίρανος ἔστω, εἷς βασιλεύς.
The sentence is from Homer's Iliad, Bk. II. vers. 204 and 205. It was a sort of proverb, like many of Homer's sayings, and was frequently quoted. As a consequence the use of it by Procopius does not prove at all his acquaintance with Homer or Greek literature in general.
[3] The majority of the MSS. read "eighth," which according to Eusebius' customary mode of reckoning the Macedonian months is incorrect. For, as Valesius remarks, he always synchronizes the Macedonian with the Roman months, as was commonly done in his time. But the seventh before the Ides of June is not the eighth, but the seventh of June (or Desius). In fact, a few good MSS. read "seventh" instead of "eighth," and I have followed Burton, Schwegler, and Heinichen in adopting that reading.
[4] Desius was the tenth month of the Macedonian year, and corresponded to our June (see the table on p. 403, below).
[5] On the Roman method of reckoning the days of the month, see below, p. 402.
[6] We may gather from § 5, below, that the sufferings to which Eusebius refers in such general terms in this and the following paragraphs took place late in the year 303. In fact, from the Syriac version of the longer recension (Cureton, p. 4) we learn that the tortures inflicted upon Alphæus and Zacchæus were, in consequence of the third edict, issued at the approach of the emperor's vicennalia, and intended rather as a step toward amnesty than as a sharpening of the persecution (see above, Bk. VIII. chap. 2, note 8). This leads us to conclude that all the tortures mentioned in these paragraphs had the same occasion, and this explains the eagerness of the judges to set the prisoners free, even if they had not sacrificed, so long as they might be made to appear to have done so, and thus the law not be openly violated. Alphæus and Zacchæus alone suffered death, as we are told in § 5, and they evidently on purely political grounds (see note 10).

he received the sentence with cheerful countenance and most ready mind, and was led away. When he was bound to the stake, and the wood piled up around him, as they were awaiting the arrival of the emperor before lighting the fire, he cried, "Where is the fire for me?"

3 Having said this, he was summoned again before the emperor,[4] and subjected to the unusual torture of having his tongue cut out. But he endured this with fortitude and showed to all by his deeds that the Divine Power is present with those who endure any hardship whatever for the sake of religion, lightening their sufferings and strengthening their zeal. When he learned of this strange mode of punishment, the noble man was not terrified, but put out his tongue readily, and offered it with the greatest alacrity to those who cut it off.

4 After this punishment he was thrown into prison, and suffered there for a very long time. At last the twentieth anniversary of the emperor being near,[5] when, according to an established gracious custom, liberty was proclaimed everywhere to all who were in bonds, he alone had both his feet stretched over five holes in the stocks,[6] and while he lay there was strangled, and was thus honored with mar-

5 tyrdom, as he desired. Although he was outside of his country, yet, as he was a native of Palestine, it is proper to count him among the Palestinian martyrs. These things occurred in this manner during the first year, when the persecution was directed only against the rulers of the Church.

CHAPTER III.

1 IN the course of the second year, the persecution against us increased greatly. And at that time Urbanus[1] being governor of the province, imperial edicts were first issued to him, commanding by a general decree that all

the people should sacrifice at once in the different cities, and offer libations to the idols.[2]

In Gaza, a city of Palestine, Timotheus endured countless tortures, and afterwards was subjected to a slow and moderate fire. Having given, by his patience in all his sufferings, most genuine evidence of sincerest piety toward the Deity, he bore away the crown of the victorious athletes of religion. At the same time Agapius[3] and our contemporary, Thecla,[4] having exhibited most noble constancy, were condemned as food for the wild beasts.

But who that beheld these things would 2 not have admired, or if they heard of them by report, would not have been astonished? For when the heathen everywhere were holding a festival and the customary shows, it was noised abroad that besides the other entertainments, the public combat of those who had lately been condemned to wild beasts would also

---

[2] This is the famous fourth edict of Diocletian, which was issued in the year 304. It marks a stupendous change of method; in fact, Christianity as such is made, for the first time since the toleration edict of Gallienus, a *religio illicita*, whose profession is punishable by death. The general persecution, in the full sense, begins with the publication of this edict. Hitherto persecution had been directed only against supposed political offenders and church officers. The edict is a complete stultification of Diocletian's principles as revealed in the first three edicts, and shows a lamentable lack of the wisdom which had dictated those measures. Mason has performed an immense service in proving (to my opinion conclusively) that this brutal edict, senseless in its very severity, was not issued by Diocletian, but by Maximian, while Diocletian was quite incapacitated by illness for the performance of any public duties. Mason's arguments cannot be reproduced here; they are given at length on p. 212 sq. of his work. He remarks at the close of the discussion: " Diocletian, though he might have wished Christianity safely abolished, feared the growing power of the Church, and dared not persecute (till he was forced), lest he should rouse her from her passivity. But this Fourth Edict was nothing more nor less than a loud alarum to muster the army of the Church: as the centurions called over their lists, it taught her the statistics of her numbers, down to the last child: it proved to her that her troops could endure all the hardships of the campaign: it ranged her generals in the exact order of merit. Diocletian, by an exquisite refinement of thought, while he did not neglect the salutary fear which strong penalties might inspire in the Christians, knew well enough that though he might torture every believer in the world into sacrificing, yet Christianity was not killed: he knew that men were Christians again afterwards as well as before: could he have seen deeper yet, he would have known that the utter humiliation of a fall before men and angels converted many a hard and worldly prelate into a broken-hearted saint: and so he rested his hopes, not merely on the punishment of individuals, but on his three great measures for crushing the corporate life, — the destruction of the churches, the Scriptures, and the clergy. But this Fourth Edict evidently returns with crass dullness and brutal complacency to the thought that if half the church were racked till they poured the libations, and the other half burned or butchered, Paganism would reign alone forever more, and that the means were as eminently desirable as the end. Lastly, Diocletian had anxiously avoided all that could rouse fanatic zeal. The first result of the Fourth Edict was to rouse it." According to the *Passio S. Sabini*, which Mason accepts as in the main reliable, and which forms the strongest support for his theory, the edict was published in April, 304. Diocletian, meanwhile, as we know from Lactantius (*de Mort. pers.* 17) did not recover sufficiently to take any part in the government until early in the year 305, so that Maximian and Galerius had matters all their own way during the entire year, and could persecute as severely as they chose. As a result, the Christians, both east and west, suffered greatly during this period.

[3] Agapius, as we learn from chap. 6, below, survived his contest with the wild beasts at this time, and was thrown into prison, where he remained until the fourth year of the persecution, when he was again brought into the arena in the presence of the tyrant Maximinus, and was finally thrown into the sea.

[4] ἡ καθ' ἡμᾶς Θέκλα. Thecla seems to be thus designated to distinguish her from her more famous namesake, whom tradition connected with Paul, and who has played so large a part in romantic legend (see the *Acts of Paul and Thecla* in the *Ante-Nicene Fathers*, VIII. 487 sq., and the *Dict. of Christ. Biog., s.v.*). She is referred to again in chap. 6, below, but we are not told whether she actually suffered or not.

---

inflicting upon him the legal punishment, according to the terms of the second edict. Upon the case of Romanus, see Mason, p. 188 sq.

[4] Valesius assumes that this was Galerius, and Mason does the same. In the Syriac version, however, he is directly called Diocletian; but on the other hand, in the Syriac acts published by Assemani (according to Cureton, p. 55), he is called " Maximinus the son-in-law of Diocletian"; i.e. Galerius, who was known as Maximianus (of which Maximinus, in the present case, is evidently only a variant form). The emperor's conduct in the present case is much more in accord with Galerius' character, as known to us, than with the character of Diocletian; and moreover, it is easier to suppose that the name of Maximinus was later changed into that of Diocletian, by whose name the whole persecution was known, than that the greater name was changed into the less. I am therefore convinced that the reference in the present case is to Galerius, not to Diocletian.

[5] See above, Bk. VIII. chap. 2, note 8.

[6] See above, Bk. IV. chap. 16, note 9, and Bk. VIII. chap. 10, note 5.

[1] Of Urbanus, governor of Palestine, we know only what is told us in the present work (he is mentioned in this passage and in chaps. 4, 7, and 8, below) and in the Syriac version. From the latter we learn that he succeeded Flavianus in the second year of the persecution (304), and that he was deposed by Maximinus in the fifth year (see also chap. 8, § 7, below), and miserably executed.

3   take place. As this report increased and spread in all directions, six young men, namely, Timolaus, a native of Pontus, Dionysius from Tripolis in Phœnicia, Romulus, a sub-deacon of the parish of Diospolis,[5] Pæsis and Alexander, both Egyptians, and another Alexander from Gaza, having first bound their own hands, went in haste to Urbanus, who was about to open the exhibition, evidencing great zeal for martyrdom. They confessed that they were Christians, and by their ambition for all terrible things, showed that those who glory in the religion of the God of the universe do not cower before the attacks of wild beasts.

4   Immediately, after creating no ordinary astonishment in the governor and those who were with him, they were cast into prison. After a few days two others were added to them. One of them, named Agapius,[6] had in former confessions endured dreadful torments of various kinds. The other, who had supplied them with the necessaries of life, was called Dionysius. All of these eight were beheaded on one day at Cæsarea, on the twenty-fourth day of the month Dystrus,[7] which is the ninth before the

5   Kalends of April. Meanwhile, a change in the emperors occurred, and the first of them all in dignity, and the second retired into private life,[8] and public affairs began to be troubled.

6   Shortly after the Roman government became divided against itself, and a cruel war arose among them.[9] And this division, with the troubles which grew out of it, was not settled until peace toward us had been established

7   throughout the entire Roman Empire. For when this peace arose for all, as the daylight after the darkest and most gloomy night, the public affairs of the Roman government were re-established, and became happy and peaceful, and the ancestral good-will toward each other was revived. But we will relate these things more fully at the proper time. Now let us return to the regular course of events.

CHAPTER IV.

1   MAXIMINUS CÆSAR[1] having come at that time into the government, as if to manifest

to all the evidences of his inborn enmity against God, and of his impiety, armed himself for persecution against us more vigorously than his predecessors. In consequence, no little   2 confusion arose among all, and they scattered here and there, endeavoring in some way to escape the danger; and there was great commotion everywhere.

But what words would suffice for a suitable description of the Divine love and boldness, in confessing God, of the blessed and truly innocent lamb, — I refer to the martyr Apphianus,[2] — who presented in the sight of all, before the gates of Cæsarea, a wonderful example of piety toward the only God? He was at   3 that time not twenty years old. He had first spent a long time at Berytus,[3] for the sake of a secular Grecian education, as he belonged to a very wealthy family. It is wonderful to relate how, in such a city, he was superior to youthful passions, and clung to virtue, uncorrupted neither by his bodily vigor nor his young companions; living discreetly, soberly and piously, in accordance with his profession of the Christian doctrine and the life of his teachers.

If it is needful to mention his native   4 country, and give honor to it as producing this noble athlete of piety, we will do so with pleasure. The young man came from   5 Pagæ,[4] — if any one is acquainted with the place, — a city in Lycia of no mean importance. After his return from his course of study in Berytus, though his father held the first place in his country, he could not bear to live with him and his relatives, as it did not please them to live according to the rules of religion. Therefore, as if he were led by the Divine Spirit, and in accordance with a natural, or rather an inspired and true philosophy, regarding this preferable to what is considered the glory of life, and despising bodily comforts, he secretly left his family. And because of his faith and hope in God, paying no attention to his daily needs, he was led by the Divine Spirit to the city of Cæsarea, where was prepared for him the crown of martyrdom for piety. Abiding with us there,   6 and conferring with us in the Divine Scriptures diligently for a short time, and fitting himself zealously by suitable exercises, he exhibited such an end as would astonish any one should it be seen again. Who, that hears   7 of it, would not justly admire his courage, boldness, constancy, and even more than these

---

5 A city of Palestine, lying northwest of Jerusalem, and identical with the Lydda of Acts ix. 32 sq. For many centuries the seat of a bishop, and still prominent in the time of the crusades. The persons referred to in this paragraph are to be distinguished from others of the same names mentioned elsewhere.

6 To be distinguished from the Agapius mentioned earlier in the chapter, as is clear from the date of his death, given in this paragraph.

7 Dystrus was the seventh month of the Macedonian year, corresponding to our March. See the table on p. 403, below.

8 Diocletian and Maximian abdicated on May 1, 305. See above, Bk. VIII. chap. 13, note 16.

9 When Maxentius usurped the purple in Rome, in the year 306. See above, Bk. VIII. chap. 13, note 21.

1 On Maximinus and his attitude toward the Christians, see above, Bk. VIII. chap. 14, note 2. He was made a Cæsar at the

time of the abdication of Diocletian and Maximian, May 1, 305, and Egypt and Syria were placed under his supervision.

2 Apphianus is called, in the Syriac version, Epiphanius. We know him only from this account of Eusebius. For some remarks upon his martyrdom, see above, p. 8 sq.

3 The modern Beirût. A celebrated school of literature and law flourished there for a number of centuries.

4 The MSS., according to Valesius, are somewhat at variance in the spelling of this name, and the place is perhaps to be identified with Araxa, a city of some importance in northwestern Lycia.

the daring deed itself, which evidenced a zeal for religion and a spirit truly superhuman?

8   For in the second attack upon us under Maximinus, in the third year of the persecution, edicts of the tyrant were issued for the first time, commanding that the rulers of the cities should diligently and speedily see to it that all the people offered sacrifices.[5] Throughout the city of Cæsarea, by command of the governor, the heralds were summoning men, women, and children to the temples of the idols, and besides this, the chiliarchs were calling out each one by name from a roll, and an immense crowd of the wicked were rushing together from all quarters. Then this youth fearlessly, while no one was aware of his intentions, eluded both us who lived in the house with him and the whole band of soldiers that surrounded the governor, and rushed up to Urbanus as he was offering libations, and fearlessly seizing him by the right hand, straightway put a stop to his sacrificing, and skillfully and persuasively, with a certain divine inspiration, exhorted him to abandon his delusion, because it was not well to forsake the one and only true God, and

9   sacrifice to idols and demons. It is probable that this was done by the youth through a divine power which led him forward, and which all but cried aloud in his act, that Christians, who were truly such, were so far from abandoning the religion of the God of the universe which they had once espoused, that they were not only superior to threats and the punishments which followed, but yet bolder to speak with noble and untrammeled tongue, and, if possible, to summon even their persecutors to turn from their ignorance and acknowledge the only true God.

10   Thereupon, he of whom we are speaking, and that instantly, as might have been expected after so bold a deed, was torn by the governor and those who were with him as if by wild beasts. And having endured manfully innumerable blows over his entire body, he

11   was straightway cast into prison. There he was stretched by the tormentor with both his feet in the stocks for a night and a day; and the next day he was brought before the judge. As they endeavored to force him to surrender, he exhibited all constancy under suffering and terrible tortures. His sides were torn, not once or twice, but many times, to the bones and the very bowels; and he received so many blows on his face and neck that those who for a long time had been well acquainted with him could

12   not recognize his swollen face. But as he would not yield under this treatment, the torturers, as commanded, covered his feet with linen cloths soaked in oil and set them on fire. No word can describe the agonies which the blessed one endured from this. For the fire consumed his flesh and penetrated to his bones, so that the humors of his body were melted and oozed out and dropped down like wax. But as

13   he was not subdued by this, his adversaries being defeated and unable to comprehend his superhuman constancy, cast him again into prison. A third time he was brought before the judge; and having witnessed the same profession, being half dead, he was finally thrown into the depths of the sea.

But what happened immediately after

14   this will scarcely be believed by those who did not see it. Although we realize this, yet we must record the event, of which to speak plainly, all the inhabitants of Cæsarea were witnesses. For truly there was no age but beheld this marvelous sight. For as soon as

15   they had cast this truly sacred and thrice-blessed youth into the fathomless depths of the sea, an uncommon commotion and disturbance agitated the sea and all the shore about it, so that the land and the entire city were shaken by it. And at the same time with this wonderful and sudden perturbation, the sea threw out before the gates of the city the body of the divine martyr, as if unable to endure it.[6]

Such was the death of the wonderful Apphianus. It occurred on the second day of the month Xanthicus,[7] which is the fourth day before the Nones of April, on the day of preparation.[8]

---

[5] This was simply a republication in its fullness of Maximian's fourth edict, which was referred to in chap. 3 (see note 2 on that chapter). Eusebius does not mean to say that this was the first time that such an edict was published, but that this was the first edict of Maximinus, the newly appointed Cæsar.

[6] It is perhaps not necessary to doubt that an earthquake took place at this particular time. Nor is it surprising that under the circumstances the Christians saw a miracle in a natural phenomenon.

[7] Xanthicus was the eighth month of the Macedonian year, and corresponded to our April (see table on p. 403, below). The martyrdom of Apphianus must have taken place in 306, not 305; for according to the direct testimony of Lactantius (de Mort. pers. chap. 19; the statement is unaccountably omitted in the English translation given in the Ante-Nicene Fathers), Maximinus did not become Cæsar until May 1, 305; while, according to the present chapter, Apphianus suffered martyrdom after Maximinus had been raised to that position. Eusebius himself puts the abdication of the old emperors and the appointment of the new Cæsars early in April or late in March (see above, chap. 3, § 5, and the Syriac version of the Martyrs, p. 12), and with him agree other early authorities. But it is more difficult to doubt the accuracy of Lactantius' dates than to suppose the others mistaken, and hence May 1st is commonly accepted by historians as the day of abdication. About the year there can be no question; for Lactantius' account of Diocletian's movements during the previous year exhibits a very exact knowledge of the course of events, and its accuracy cannot be doubted. (For a fuller discussion of the date of the abdication, see Tillemont's Hist. des Emp., 2d ed., IV. p. 609.) But even if it were admitted that the abdication took place four or five weeks earlier (according to Eusebius' own statement, it did not at any rate occur before the twenty-fourth of March: see chap. 3, above, and the Syriac version, p. 12), it would be impossible to put Apphianus' death on the second of April, for this would not give time for all that must intervene between the day of his appointment and the republication and execution of the persecuting edicts. In fact, it is plain enough from the present chapter that Apphianus did not suffer until some time after the accession of Maximinus, and therefore not until the following year. Eusebius, as can be seen from the first paragraph of this work on the martyrs, reckoned the beginning of the persecution in Palestine not with the issue of the first edict in Nicomedia on Feb. 24, 303, but with the month of April of that same year. Apphianus' death therefore took place at

CHAPTER V.

1   ABOUT the same time, in the city of Tyre, a youth named Ulpianus,[1] after dreadful tortures and most severe scourgings, was enclosed in a raw oxhide, with a dog and with one of those poisonous reptiles, an asp, and cast into the sea. Wherefore I think that we may properly mention him in connection with the martyrdom of Apphianus.

2   Shortly afterwards, Ædesius,[2] a brother of Apphianus, not only in God, but also in the flesh, being a son of the same earthly father, endured sufferings like his, after very many confessions and protracted tortures in bonds, and after he had been sentenced by the governor to the mines in Palestine. He conducted himself through them all in a truly philosophic manner; for he was more highly educated than his brother, and had prosecuted 3 philosophic studies. Finally in the city of Alexandria, when he beheld the judge, who was trying the Christians, offending beyond all bounds, now insulting holy men in various ways, and again consigning women of greatest modesty and even religious virgins to procurers for shameful treatment, he acted like his brother. For as these things seemed insufferable, he went forward with bold resolve, and with his words and deeds overwhelmed the judge with shame and disgrace. After suffering in consequence many forms of torture, he endured a death similar to his brother's, being cast into the sea. But these things, as I have said, happened to him in this way a little later.

CHAPTER VI.

1   IN the fourth year of the persecution against us, on the twelfth day before the Kalends of December, which is the twentieth day of the month Dius,[1] on the day before the Sabbath,[2] while the tyrant Maximinus was pres-

ent and giving magnificent shows in honor of his birthday, the following event, truly worthy of record, occurred in the city of Cæsarea. As it was an ancient custom to furnish the 2 spectators more splendid shows when the emperors more present than at other times, — new and foreign spectacles taking the place of the customary amusements, such as animals brought from India or Ethiopia or other places, or men who could astonish the beholders with skillful bodily exercises, — it was necessary at this time, as the emperor was giving the exhibition, to add to the shows something more wonderful. And what should this be? A witness of our doctrine was brought into 3 the midst and endured the contest for the true and only religion. This was Agapius, who, as we have stated a little above,[3] was, with Thecla, the second to be thrown to the wild beasts for food. He had also, three times and more, marched with malefactors from the prison to the arena; and every time, after threats from the judge, whether in compassion or in hope that he might change his mind, had been reserved for other conflicts. But the emperor being present, he was brought out at this time, as if he had been appropriately reserved for this occasion, until the very word of the Saviour should be fulfilled in him, which through divine knowledge he declared to his disciples, that they should be brought before kings on account of their testimony unto him.[4] He was taken 4 into the midst of the arena with a certain malefactor who they said was charged with the murder of his master. But this murderer of his master, when he had been cast 5 to the wild beasts, was deemed worthy of compassion and humanity, almost like Barabbas in the time of our Saviour. And the whole theater resounded with shouts and cries of approval, because the murderer was humanely saved by the emperor, and deemed worthy of honor and freedom. But the athlete of religion 6 was first summoned by the tyrant and promised liberty if he would deny his profession. But he testified with a loud voice that, not for any fault, but for the religion of the Creator of the universe, he would readily and with pleasure endure whatever might be inflicted upon him. Having said this, he joined the deed 7 to the word, and rushed to meet a bear which had been let loose against him, surrendering himself most cheerfully to be devoured by him. After this, as he still breathed, he was cast into prison. And living yet one day, stones

the very close of the third year of the persecution, according to this reckoning.

[8] i.e. Friday, the old Jewish term being still retained and widely used, although with the change of the Sabbath from the seventh to the first day of the week it had entirely lost its meaning. Upon the prevalence of the word among the Fathers as a designation of Friday, see Suicer's *Thesaurus*, s.v. παρασκευή and νηστεία. The day of Christ's crucifixion was called μεγάλη παρασκευή, the "great preparation."

[1] The martyrdom of Ulpian is omitted in the Syriac version. It was apparently a later addition, made when the abridgment of the longer version was produced; and this perhaps accounts for the brevity of the notice and the words of explanation with which the mention of him is concluded.

[2] Called Alosis in the Syriac version.

[1] The month Dius was the third month of the Macedonian year, and corresponded to our November (see table on p. 403, below).

[2] προσαββάτου ἡμέρᾳ, i.e. on Friday, προσάββατος being sometimes used among the Jews as a designation of that day, which was more commonly called παρασκευή (cf. Mark xv. 42). Whether it was widely used in the Christian Church of Eusebius' day I am unable to say (Suicer does not give the word); but the use of it here shows that it was familiar at least in Palestine. It is said in Kraus' *Real-Encyclop. d. christ. Alterth.* s.v. *Wochentage*, to occur in a

decree of Constantine, quoted in Eusebius' *Vita Const.* IV. 18; but the text is doubtful, and at best, the use of it there proves no more as to the prevalence of the word than its use in the present case, for Eusebius simply gives, in his own language, the substance of Constantine's edict.

[3] See above, chap. 3, § 1.   [4] Cf. Matt. x. 18.

were bound to his feet, and he was drowned in the depths of the sea. Such was the martyrdom of Agapius.

CHAPTER VII.

1　Again, in Cæsarea, when the persecution had continued to the fifth year, on the second day of the month Xanthicus,[1] which is the fourth before the Nones of April, on the very Lord's day of our Saviour's resurrection,[2] Theodosia, a virgin from Tyre, a faithful and sedate maiden, not yet eighteen years of age, went up to certain prisoners who were confessing the kingdom of Christ and sitting before the judgment seat, and saluted them, and, as is probable, besought them to remember her when they 2　came before the Lord. Thereupon, as if she had committed a profane and impious act, the soldiers seized her and led her to the governor. And he immediately, like a madman and a wild beast in his anger, tortured her with dreadful and most terrible torments in her sides and breasts, even to the very bones. And as she still breathed, and withal stood with a joyful and beaming countenance, he ordered her thrown into the waves of the sea. Then passing from her to the other confessors, he condemned all of them to the copper mines in Phæno in Palestine. 3　Afterwards on the fifth of the month Dius,[3] on the Nones of November according to the Romans, in the same city, Silvanus[4] (who at that time was a presbyter and confessor, but who shortly after was honored with the episcopate and died a martyr), and those with him, men who had shown the noblest firmness in behalf of religion, were condemned by him to labor in the same copper mines, command

being first given that their ankles be disabled with hot irons. At the same time he 4 delivered to the flames a man who was illustrious through numerous other confessions. This was Domninus, who was well known to all in Palestine for his exceeding fearlessness.[5] After this the same judge, who was a cruel contriver of suffering, and an inventor of devices against the doctrine of Christ, planned against the pious punishments that had never been heard of. He condemned three to single pugilistic combat. He delivered to be devoured by wild beasts Auxentius, a grave and holy old man. Others who were in mature life he made eunuchs, and condemned them to the same mines. Yet others, after severe tortures, he cast into prison.

Among these was my dearest friend Pamphilus,[6] who was by reason of every virtue the most illustrious of the martyrs in our time. Urbanus first tested him in rhetorical phi- 5 losophy and learning; and afterwards endeavored to compel him to sacrifice. But as he saw that he refused and in nowise regarded his threats, being exceedingly angry, he ordered him to be tormented with severest tortures. And when the brutal man, after he had 6 almost satiated himself with these tortures by continuous and prolonged scrapings in his sides, was yet covered with shame before all, he put him also with the confessors in prison.

But what recompense for his cruelty to 7 the saints, he who thus abused the martyrs of Christ, shall receive from the Divine judgment, may be easily determined from the preludes to it, in which immediately, and not long after his daring cruelties against Pamphilus, while he yet held the government, the Divine judgment came upon him. For thus suddenly, he who but yesterday was judging on the lofty tribunal, guarded by a band of soldiers, and ruling over the whole nation of Palestine, the associate and dearest friend and table companion of the tyrant himself, was stripped in one night, and overwhelmed with disgrace and shame before those who had formerly admired him as if he were himself an emperor; and he appeared cowardly and unmanly, uttering womanish cries and supplications to all the people whom he had ruled. And Maximinus himself, in reliance upon whose favor Urbanus was formerly so arrogantly insolent, as if he loved him exceedingly for his deeds against us, was set as a harsh and most severe judge in this same Cæsarea to pronounce sentence of death against him, for the great disgrace of the crimes of which he was convicted. Let us say this in passing. A suit- 8 able time may come when we shall have leisure to relate the end and the fate of those impious

---

[1] i.e. April 2, 307. Eusebius is inconsistent with himself in this case. In chap. 3, above, he states that Apphianus suffered on April 2, in the third year of the persecution. But as shown in the note on that passage, Apphianus suffered in April, 306, and therefore, in that case, Eusebius reckons the first year of the persecution as beginning after the second of April. But in the present case he reckons it as beginning before the second of April, and the latter date as falling early in a new year of the persecution. That the martyrdom recorded in the present case actually took place in 307, and not in 308, as it must have done if Eusebius were consistent with himself, is proved, first, by the fact that, in entering upon this new chapter, he says, "the persecution having continued to the fifth year," implying thereby that the event which he is about to relate took place at the beginning, not at the end, of the fifth year; and secondly, by the fact that later on, in this same chapter, while still relating the events of the fifth year, he recounts martyrdoms as taking place in the month of November (Dius). This is conclusive, for November of the fifth year can be only November, 307, and hence the April mentioned in the present paragraph can be only April of the same year. Evidently Eusebius did not reckon the beginning of the persecution in Palestine from a fixed day, but rather from the month Xanthicus (April). As a consequence, the inconsistency into which he has fallen is not very strange; the second day of April might easily be reckoned either as one of the closing days of a year, or as the beginning of the ensuing year. In the present case, he evidently forgot that he had previously used the former reckoning.

[2] i.e. on Easter Sunday. In the Syriac version, the events recorded in the present chapter are put on a Sunday; but that it was Easter is not stated.

[3] i.e. November fifth.

[4] On Silvanus, who afterward became bishop of Gaza, see above, Bk. VIII. chap. 13.

[5] Or "frankness"; literally, "freedom" (ἐλευθερία).

[6] On Pamphilus, see above, Bk. VII. chap. 32, note 40.

men who especially fought against us,[7] both of Maximinus himself and those with him.

CHAPTER VIII.

1   Up to the sixth year the storm had been incessantly raging against us. Before this time there had been a very large number of confessors of religion in the so-called Porphyry quarry in Thebais, which gets its name from the stone found there. Of these, one hundred men, lacking three, together with women and infants, were sent to the governor of Palestine. When they confessed the God of the universe and Christ, Firmilianus,[1] who had been sent there as governor in the place of Urbanus, directed, in accordance with the imperial command, that they should be maimed by burning the sinews of the ankles of their left feet, and that their right eyes with the eyelids and pupils should first be cut out, and then destroyed by hot irons to the very roots. And he then sent them to the mines in the province to endure hardships with severe toil and suffering.

2   But it was not sufficient that these only who suffered such miseries should be deprived of their eyes, but those natives of Palestine also, who were mentioned just above as condemned to pugilistic combat, since they would neither receive food from the royal storehouse nor undergo the necessary preparatory exercises. Having been brought on this account not only before the overseers, but also
3   before Maximinus himself, and having manifested the noblest persistence in confession by the endurance of hunger and stripes, they received like punishment with those whom we have mentioned, and with them other con-
4   fessors in the city of Cæsarea. Immediately afterwards others who were gathered to hear the Scriptures read, were seized in Gaza, and some endured the same sufferings in the feet and eyes; but others were afflicted with yet greater torments and with most terrible
5   tortures in the sides. One of these, in body a woman, but in understanding a man, would not endure the threat of fornication, and spoke directly against the tyrant who entrusted the government to such cruel judges. She was first scourged and then raised aloft on the

stake, and her sides lacerated. As those   6
appointed for this purpose applied the tortures incessantly and severely at the command of the judge, another, with mind fixed, like the former, on virginity as her aim, — a woman who was altogether mean in form and contemptible in appearance, but, on the other hand, strong in soul, and endowed with an understanding superior to her body, — being unable to bear the merciless and cruel and inhuman deeds, with a boldness beyond that of the combatants famed among the Greeks, cried out to the judge from the midst of the crowd : " And how long will you thus cruelly torture my sister ? " But he was greatly enraged, and ordered the woman to be immediately seized. There-   7
upon she was brought forward and having called herself by the august name of the Saviour, she was first urged by words to sacrifice, and as she refused she was dragged by force to the altar. But her sister continued to maintain her former zeal, and with intrepid and resolute foot kicked the altar, and overturned it with the fire that was on it. There-   8
upon the judge, enraged like a wild beast, inflicted on her such tortures in her sides as he never had on any one before, striving almost to glut himself with her raw flesh. But when his madness was satiated, he bound them both together, this one and her whom she called sister, and condemned them to death by fire. It is said that the first of these was from the country of Gaza ; the other, by name Valentina, was of Cæsarea, and was well known to many.

But how can I describe as it deserves the   9
martyrdom which followed, with which the thrice-blessed Paul was honored. He was condemned to death at the same time with them, under one sentence. At the time of his martyrdom, as the executioner was about to cut off his head, he requested a brief respite. This being granted, he first, in a clear and   10
distinct voice, supplicated God in behalf of his fellow-Christians,[2] praying for their pardon, and that freedom might soon be restored to them. Then he asked for the conversion of the Jews to God through Christ ; and proceeding in order he requested the same things for the Samaritans, and besought that those Gentiles, who were in error and were ignorant of God, might come to a knowledge of him, and adopt the true religion. Nor did he leave neglected the mixed multitude who were standing around. After all these, oh ! great   11
and unspeakable forbearance ! he entreated the God of the universe for the judge who had condemned him to death, and for the highest

---

[7] The death of Maximinus is related in Bk. IX. chap. 10. Nothing further is said in regard to Urbanus; but the fate of his successor Firmilianus is recorded in chap. 11, below. It is quite possible that Eusebius, in the present case, is referring to a more detailed statement of the fates of the various persecutors, which was to form the second part of the present work; and it is possible, still further, that the appendix printed at the close of the eighth book is a fragment of this second part, as suggested by Lightfoot (see above, p. 29).

[1] Of Firmilianus, the successor of Urbanus, we know only what is told us here and in chaps. 9 and 11, below. In the latter chapter, § 31, his execution is recorded.

[2] ὁμοεθνῶν.

rulers, and also for the one who was about to behead him, in his hearing and that of all present, beseeching that their sin toward him

12 should not be reckoned against them. Having prayed for these things with a loud voice, and having, as one who was dying unjustly, moved almost all to compassion and tears, of his own accord he made himself ready, and submitted his bare neck to the stroke of the sword, and was adorned with divine martyrdom. This took place on the twenty-fifth day of the month Panemus,[3] which is the eighth before the Kalends of August.

13 Such was the end of these persons. But not long after, one hundred and thirty admirable athletes of the confession of Christ, from the land of Egypt, endured, in Egypt itself, at the command of Maximinus the same afflictions in their eyes and feet with the former persons, and were sent to the above-mentioned mines in Palestine. But some of them were condemned to the mines in Cilicia.

CHAPTER IX.

1 AFTER such noble acts of the distinguished martyrs of Christ, the flame of persecution lessened, and was quenched, as it were, by their sacred blood, and relief and liberty were granted to those who, for Christ's sake, were laboring in the mines of Thebais, and for a little time we were beginning to breath pure air. But by some new impulse, I know not what, he who held the power to persecute was

2 again aroused against the Christians. Immediately letters from Maximinus against us were published everywhere in every province.[1] The governors and the military prefect[2] urged by

---

[3] i.e. July 25 (A.D. 308). See the table on p. 403, below.
[1] This is the so-called Fifth Edict, and was issued (according to the *Passio S. Theodori*) by Galerius and Maximinus, but was evidently inspired by Maximinus himself. Mason speaks of it as follows: " It would be inaccurate to say that this Fifth Edict (if so we may call it) was worse than any of the foregoing. But there is in it a thin bitterness, a venomous spitefulness, which may be noticed as characteristic of all the later part of the persecution. This spitefulness is due to two main facts. The first was that Paganism was becoming conscious of defeat; the Church had not yielded a single point. The second fact was that the Church had no longer to deal with the sensible, statesmanlike hostility of Diocletian, — not even with the bluff bloodiness of Maximian. Galerius himself was now, except in name, no longer persecutor-in-chief. He was content to follow the lead of a man who was in all ways even worse than himself. Galerius was indeed an Evil Beast; his nephew was more like the Crooked Serpent. The artful sour spirit of Maximin employed itself to invent, not larger measures of solid policy against his feared and hated foes, but petty tricks to annoy and sting them." For a fuller discussion of the edict, see Mason, p. 284 sq. It must have been published in the autumn of the year 308, for the martyrdom of Paul, recorded in the previous chapter, took place in July of that year, and some little time seems to have elapsed between that event and the present. On the other hand, the martyrdoms mentioned below, in § 5, took place in November of this same year, so that we can fix the date of the edict within narrow limits.
[2] ὁ τοῦ τῶν στρατοπέδων ἄρχειν ἐπιτεταγμένος. Many regard this officer as the prætorian prefect. But we should naturally expect so high an official to be mentioned before the governors (ἡγεμόνες). It seems probable, in fact, that the commander in charge of the military forces of Palestine, or possibly of Syria, is referred to in the present case. See Valesius' note, *ad locum*.

---

edicts and letters and public ordinances the magistrates and generals and notaries[3] in all the cities to carry out the imperial decree, which ordered that the altars of the idols should with all speed be rebuilt; and that all men, women, and children, even infants at the breast, should sacrifice and offer oblations; and that with diligence and care they should cause them to taste of the execrable offerings; and that the things for sale in the market should be polluted with libations from the sacrifices; and that guards should be stationed before the baths in order to defile with the abominable sacrifices those who went to wash in them. When these 3 orders were being carried out, our people, as was natural, were at the beginning greatly distressed in mind; and even the unbelieving heathen blamed the severity and the exceeding absurdity of what was done. For these things appeared to them extreme and burdensome.

As the heaviest storm impended over all in every quarter, the divine power of our Saviour again infused such boldness into his athletes,[4] that without being drawn on or dragged forward by any one, they spurned the threats. Three of the faithful joining together, rushed 4 on the governor as he was sacrificing to the idols, and cried out to him to cease from his delusion, there being no other God than the Maker and Creator of the universe. When he asked who they were, they confessed boldly that they were Christians. Thereupon Firmilianus, being greatly enraged, sentenced 5 them to capital punishment without inflicting tortures upon them. The name of the eldest of these was Antoninus; of the next, Zebinas, who was a native of Eleutheropolis; and of the third, Germanus. This took place on the thirteenth of the month Dius, the Ides of November.[5]

There was associated with them on the 6 same day Ennathas, a woman from Scythopolis, who was adorned with the chaplet of virginity. She did not indeed do as they had done, but was dragged by force and brought before the judge. She endured scourgings 7 and cruel insults, which Maxys, a tribune of a neighboring district, without the knowledge of the superior authority, dared to inflict upon her. He was a man worse than his name,[6] sanguinary in other respects, exceedingly harsh, and altogether cruel, and censured by all who knew him. This man stripped the blessed woman of

---

[3] Or "town clerks," ταβουλάριοι.
[4] Literally, " *its* athletes" (αὐτῆς), the antecedent of the pronoun being " the divine power."
[5] i.e. Nov. 13, 308.
[6] Μάξυς is not a Greek word. Ruinart, *Acta Martt.*, p. 327, remarks, *An a Syris repetenda, apud quos mochos est pulicanus a casas increpare?* But the derivation is, to say the least, very doubtful. Cureton throws no light on the matter. The word in the Syriac version seems to be simply a reproduction of the form found in the Greek original.

all her clothing, so that she was covered only from her loins to her feet and the rest of her body was bare. And he led her through the entire city of Cæsarea, and regarded it as a great thing to beat her with thongs while she was dragged

8 through all the market-places. After such treatment she manifested the noblest constancy at the judgment seat of the governor himself; and the judge condemned her to be burned alive. He also carried his rage against the pious to a most inhuman length and transgressed the laws of nature, not being ashamed even to deny burial to the lifeless bodies of the sacred

9 men. Thus he ordered the dead to be exposed in the open air as food for wild beasts and to be watched carefully by night and day. For many days a large number of men attended to this savage and barbarous decree. And they looked out from their post of observation, as if it were a matter worthy of care, to see that the dead bodies should not be stolen. And wild beasts and dogs and birds of prey scattered the human limbs here and there, and the whole city was strewed with the entrails and bones of

10 men, so that nothing had ever appeared more dreadful and horrible, even to those who formerly hated us; though they bewailed not so much the calamity of those against whom these things were done, as the outrage against themselves and the common nature of man.

11 For there was to be seen near the gates a spectacle beyond all description and tragic recital; for not only was human flesh devoured in one place, but it was scattered in every place; so that some said that limbs and masses of flesh and parts of entrails were to be seen even within the gates.

12 After these things had continued for many days, a wonderful event occurred. The air was clear and bright and the appearance of the sky most serene. When suddenly throughout the city from the pillars which supported the public porches many drops fell like tears; and the market places and streets, though there was no mist in the air, were moistened with sprinkled water, whence I know not. Then immediately it was reported everywhere that the earth, unable to endure the abomination of these things, had shed tears in a mysterious manner; and that as a rebuke to the relentless and unfeeling nature of men, stones and lifeless wood had wept for what had happened. I know well that this account may perhaps appear idle and fabulous to those who come after us, but not to those to whom the truth was confirmed at the time.[7]

---

[7] This is a glaring instance of uncritical credulity on Eusebius' part, and yet even Crusè can say: " Perhaps some might smile at the supposed credulity of our author, but the *miracle* in this account was not greater than the *malignity*, and if man can perform miracles of vice, we can scarcely wonder if Providence should present, at least, miracles of admonition." Cureton more sensibly re-

CHAPTER X.

On the fourteenth day of the following 1 month Appellæus,[1] the nineteenth before the Kalends of January, certain persons from Egypt were again seized by those who examined people passing the gates. They had been sent to minister to the confessors in Cilicia. They received the same sentence as those whom they had gone to help, being mutilated in their eyes and feet. Three of them exhibited in Ascalon, where they were imprisoned, marvelous bravery in the endurance of various kinds of martyrdom. One of them named Ares was condemned to the flames, and the others, called Probus[2] and Elias, were beheaded.

On the eleventh day of the month Audy- 2 næus,[3] which is the third before the Ides of January, in the same city of Cæsarea, Peter an ascetic, also called Apselamus,[4] from the village of Anea,[5] on the borders of Eleutheropolis, like purest gold, gave noble proof by fire of his faith in the Christ of God. Though the judge and those around him besought him many times to have compassion on himself, and to spare his own youth and bloom, he disregarded them, preferring hope in the God of the universe to all things, even to life itself. A certain Asclepius, supposed to be[6] a bishop of the sect of Marcion, possessed as he thought with zeal for religion, but " not according to knowledge,"[7] ended his life on one and the same funeral pyre. These things took place in this manner.

CHAPTER XI.

It is time to describe the great and cele- 1 brated spectacle of Pamphilus,[1] a man thrice dear to me, and of those who finished their course with him. They were twelve in all; being counted worthy of apostolic grace and number. Of these the leader and the only one 2 honored with the position of presbyter at Cæsarea, was Pamphilus; a man who through

---

marks: " This, which doubtless was produced by natural causes, seemed miraculous to Eusebius, more especially if he looked upon it as fulfilling a prophecy of our Lord — Luke xix. 40: ' I tell you, that if these should hold their peace, the stones would immediately cry out.' See also Hab. ii. 11."
[1] i.e. Dec. 14, 308 (see the tables on p. 403, below).
[2] The majority of the codices read Πρόμος, but as Valesius remarks, such a proper name is quite unknown in Greek, and the form probably arose from a confusion of β and μ, which in ancient MSS. were written alike. Two of our existing codices read Πρόβος, and this has been adopted by Zimmermann and Heinichen, whom I have followed in the text.
[3] i.e. Jan. 11, 309.
[4] In the Syriac version " Absalom."
[5] Of this village we know nothing, but Eleutheropolis (originally Bethozabris) was an important place lying some forty miles southwest of Jerusalem.
[6] εἶναι δοκῶν. Eusebius did not wish to admit that he was a bishop in a true sense.   [7] Rom. x. 2.
[1] On Pamphilus, see above, Bk. VII. chap. 32, note 40.

his entire life was celebrated for every virtue, for renouncing and despising the world, for sharing his possessions with the needy, for contempt of earthly hopes, and for philosophic deportment and exercise. He especially excelled all in our time in most sincere devotion to the Divine Scriptures and indefatigable industry in
3   whatever he undertook, and in his helpfulness to his relatives and associates. In a separate treatise on his life,[2] consisting of three books, we have already described the excellence of his virtue. Referring to this work those who delight in such things and desire to know them, let us now consider the martyrs in order.
4   Second after Pamphilus, Vales, who was honored for his venerable gray hair, entered the contest. He was a deacon from Ælia,[3] an old man of gravest appearance, and versed in the Divine Scriptures, if any one ever was. He had so laid up the memory of them in his heart that he did not need to look at the books if he undertook to repeat any passage of Scripture.
5   The third was Paul from the city of Jamna,[4] who was known among them as most zealous and fervent in spirit. Previous to his martyrdom, he had endured the conflict of confession by cauterization.

After these persons had continued in prison for two entire years, the occasion of their martyrdom was a second arrival of Egyptian
6   brethren who suffered with them. They had accompanied the confessors in Cilicia to the mines there and were returning to their homes. At the entrance of the gates of Cæsarea, the guards, who were men of barbarous character, questioned them as to who they were and whence they came. They kept back nothing of the truth, and were seized as malefactors taken in the very act. They were five
7   in number. When brought before the tyrant, being very bold in his presence, they were immediately thrown into prison. On the next day, which was the nineteenth of the month Peritius,[5] according to the Roman reckoning the fourteenth before the Kalends of March, they were brought, according to command, before the judge, with Pamphilus and his associates whom we have mentioned. First, by all kinds of torture, through the invention of strange and various machines, he tested the invincible constancy

of the Egyptians. Having practised these   8
cruelties upon the leader[5a] of all, he asked him first who he was. He heard in reply the name of some prophet instead of his proper name. For it was their custom, in place of the names of idols given them by their fathers, if they had such, to take other names; so that you would hear them calling themselves Elijah or Jeremiah or Isaiah or Samuel or Daniel, thus showing themselves inwardly true Jews, and the genuine Israel of God, not only in deeds, but in the names which they bore. When Firmilianus had heard some such name from the martyr, and did not understand the force of the word, he asked next the name of his country. But   9
he gave a second answer similar to the former, saying that Jerusalem was his country, meaning that of which Paul says, "Jerusalem which is above is free, which is our mother,"[6] and, "Ye are come unto Mount Sion, and unto the city of the living God, the heavenly Jerusalem."[7] This was what he meant; but   10
the judge thinking only of the earth, sought diligently to discover what that city was, and in what part of the world it was situated. And therefore he applied tortures that the truth might be acknowledged. But the man, with his hands twisted behind his back, and his feet crushed by strange machines, asserted firmly that he had spoken the truth. And being   11
questioned again repeatedly what and where the city was of which he spoke, he said that it was the country of the pious alone, for no others should have a place in it, and that it lay toward the far East and the rising sun.
He philosophized about these things ac-   12
cording to his own understanding, and was in nowise turned from them by the tortures with which he was afflicted on every side. And as if he were without flesh or body he seemed insensible of his sufferings. But the judge being perplexed, was impatient, thinking that the Christians were about to establish a city somewhere, inimical and hostile to the Romans. And he inquired much about this, and investigated where that country toward the East was located. But when he had for a long   13
time lacerated the young man with scourgings, and punished him with all sorts of torments, he perceived that his persistence in what he had said could not be changed, and passed against him sentence of death. Such a scene was exhibited by what was done to this man. And having inflicted similar tortures on the others, he sent them away in the same manner.
Then being wearied and perceiving that   14

---

2 On Eusebius' *Life of Pamphilus*, see above, p. 28 sq.
3 i.e. Jerusalem.
4 τῆς Ἰαμνιτῶν πόλεως. Jamna, or Jamnia, was a town of Judea, lying west of Jerusalem, near the sea.
5 i.e. Feb. 19 (see the table on p. 403, below). We learn from chap. 7, §§ 3-5, that Pamphilus was thrown into prison in the fifth year of the persecution and as late as November of that year, i.e. between November, 307, and April, 308. Since he had lain two whole years in prison (according to § 5, above), the date referred to in the present passage must be February of the year 310. The martyrdom of Pamphilus is commonly, for aught I know to the contrary, uniformly put in the year 309, as the seventh year of the persecution is nearly synchronous with that year. But that the common date is a mistake is plain enough from the present chapter.

5a προήγορος, literally "advocate," or "defender."
6 Gal. iv. 26.
7 Heb. xii. 22. Upon Eusebius' view of the authorship of the Epistle to the Hebrews, see above, Bk. III. chap. 25, note 1.

he punished the men in vain, having satiated his desire, he proceeded against Pamphilus and his companions. And having learned that already under former tortures they had manifested an unchangeable zeal for the faith, he asked them if they would now obey. And receiving from every one of them only this one answer, as their last word of confession in martyrdom, he inflicted on them punishment similar to the others.

15 When this had been done, a young man, one of the household servants of Pamphilus, who had been educated in the noble life and instruction of such a man, learning the sentence passed upon his master, cried out from the midst of the crowd asking that their bodies

16 might be buried. Thereupon the judge, not a man, but a wild beast, or if anything more savage than a wild beast, giving no consideration to the young man's age, asked him only the same question. When he learned that he confessed himself a Christian, as if he had been wounded by a dart, swelling with rage, he ordered the tormentors to use their utmost

17 power against him. And when he saw that he refused to sacrifice as commanded, he ordered them to scrape him continually to his very bones and to the inmost recesses of his bowels, not as if he were human flesh but as if he were stones or wood or any lifeless thing. But after long persistence he saw that this was in vain, as the man was speechless and insensible and almost lifeless, his body being worn out

18 by the tortures. But being inflexibly merciless and inhuman, he ordered him to be committed straightway, as he was, to a slow fire. And before the death of his earthly master, though he had entered later on the conflict, he received release from the body, while those who had been zealous about the others were yet

19 delaying. One could then see Porphyry,[8] like one who had come off victorious in every conflict, his body covered with dust, but his countenance cheerful, after such sufferings, with courageous and exulting mind, advancing to death. And as if truly filled with the Divine Spirit, covered only with his philosophic robe thrown about him as a cloak, soberly and intelligently he directed his friends as to what he wished, and beckoned to them, preserving still a cheerful countenance even at the stake. But when the fire was kindled at some distance around him in a circle, having inhaled the flame into his mouth, he continued most nobly in silence from that time till his death, after the single word which he uttered when the flame first touched him, and he cried out for the help of Jesus the Son of God. Such was the contest of Porphyry.

20 His death was reported to Pamphilus by a messenger, Seleucus. He was one of the confessors from the army. As the bearer of such a message, he was forthwith deemed worthy of a similar lot. For as soon as he related the death of Porphyry, and had saluted one of the martyrs with a kiss, some of the soldiers seized him and led him to the governor. And he, as if he would hasten him on to be a companion of the former on the way to heaven, commanded that he be put to death immediately. This man was from Cappado-

21 cia, and belonged to the select band of soldiers, and had obtained no small honor in those things which are esteemed among the Romans. For in stature and bodily strength, and size and vigor, he far excelled his fellow-soldiers, so that his appearance was matter of common talk, and his whole form was admired on account of

22 its size and symmetrical proportions. At the beginning of the persecution he was prominent in the conflicts of confession, through his patience under scourging. After he left the army he set himself to imitate zealously the religious ascetics, and as if he were their father and guardian he showed himself a bishop and patron of destitute orphans and defenceless widows and of those who were distressed with penury or sickness. It is likely that on this account he was deemed worthy of an extraordinary call to martyrdom by God, who rejoices in such things more than in the smoke and

23 blood of sacrifices. He was the tenth athlete among those whom we have mentioned as meeting their end on one and the same day. On this day, as was fitting, the chief gate was opened, and a ready way of entrance into the kingdom of heaven was given to the martyr Pamphilus and to the others with him.

24 In the footsteps of Seleucus came Theodulus, a grave and pious old man, who belonged to the governor's household, and had been honored by Firmilianus himself more than all the others in his house on account of his age, and because he was a father of the third generation, and also on account of the kindness and most faithful conscientiousness which he had manifested toward him.[9] As he pursued the course of Seleucus when brought before his master, the latter was more angry at him than at those who had preceded him, and condemned him to endure the martyrdom of the Saviour on the cross.[10] As there lacked yet one to fill

25 up the number of the twelve martyrs of

---

[8] The reference is still to the same slave of Pamphilus whose tortures Eusebius has just been describing, as we learn from the Syriac version, where the slave's name is given at the beginning of the account.

[9] I read περὶ αὐτὸν with Zimmermann, Heinichen, Burton, and Migne. The MSS. all have περὶ αὐτοὺς, which can hardly have stood in the original.

[10] The common mode of punishment inflicted on slaves.

whom we have spoken, Julian came to complete it. He had just arrived from abroad, and had not yet entered the gate of the city, when having learned about the martyrs while still on the way, he rushed at once, just as he was, to see them. When he beheld the tabernacles of the saints prone on the ground, being filled with joy, he embraced and kissed them all.

26 The ministers of slaughter straightway seized him as he was doing this and led him to Firmilianus. Acting as was his custom, he condemned him to a slow fire. Thereupon Julian, leaping and exulting, in a loud voice gave thanks to the Lord who had judged him worthy of such things, and was honored with the crown

27 of martyrdom. He was a Cappadocian by birth, and in his manner of life he was most circumspect, faithful and sincere, zealous in all other respects, and animated by the Holy Spirit himself.

Such was the company which was thought worthy to enter into martyrdom with Pam-

28 philus. By the command of the impious governor their sacred and truly holy bodies were kept as food for the wild beasts for four days and as many nights. But since, strange to say, through the providential care of God, nothing approached them, — neither beast of prey, nor bird, nor dog, — they were taken up uninjured, and after suitable preparation were buried in the customary manner.

29 When the report of what had been done to these men was spread in all directions, Adrianus and Eubulus, having come from the so-called country of Manganaea [11] to Caesarea, to see the remaining confessors, were also asked at the gate the reason for their coming; and having acknowledged the truth, were brought to Firmilianus. But he, as was his custom, without delay inflicted many tortures in their sides, and condemned them to be devoured by wild

30 beasts. After two days, on the fifth of the month Dystrus,[12] the third before the Nones of March, which was regarded as the birthday of the tutelary divinity of Caesarea,[13] Adrianus was thrown to a lion, and afterwards slain with the sword. But Eubulus, two days later, on the Nones of March, that is, on the seventh of the month Dystrus, when the judge had earnestly entreated him to enjoy by sacrificing that which was considered freedom among them, preferring a glorious death for religion to transitory life, was made like the other an offer-

ing to wild beasts, and as the last of the martyrs in Caesarea, sealed the list of athletes.

It is proper also to relate here, how in a 31 short time the heavenly Providence came upon the impious rulers, together with the tyrants themselves. For that very Firmilianus, who had thus abused the martyrs of Christ, after suffering with the others the severest punishment, was put to death by the sword.

Such were the martyrdoms which took place at Caesarea during the entire period of the persecution.

CHAPTER XII.

I think it best to pass by all the other events which occurred in the meantime: such as those which happened to the bishops of the churches, when instead of shepherds of the rational[1] flocks of Christ, over which they presided in an unlawful manner, the divine judgment, considering them worthy of such a charge, made them keepers of camels,[2] an irrational beast[3] and very crooked in the structure of its body, or condemned them to have the care of the imperial horses; — and I pass by also the insults and disgraces and tortures they endured from the imperial overseers and rulers on account of the sacred vessels and treasures of the Church; and besides these the lust of power on the part of many, the disorderly and unlawful ordinations, and the schisms among the confessors themselves; also the novelties which were zealously devised against the remnants of the Church by the new and factious members, who added innovation after innovation and forced them in unsparingly among the calamities of the persecution, heaping misfortune upon misfortune. I judge it more suitable to shun and avoid the account of these things, as I said at the beginning.[4] But such things as are sober and praiseworthy, according to the sacred word, — "and if there be any virtue and praise,"[5] — I consider it most proper to tell and to record, and to present to believing hearers in the history of the admirable martyrs. And after this I think it best to crown the entire work with an account of the peace which has appeared unto us from heaven.

CHAPTER XIII.

The seventh year of our conflict was 1 completed; and the hostile measures which

[11] Of the so-called country of Μαγγαναία I know nothing. The Syriac version reads Batanea, which was a district of country lying to the northeast of Palestine, and it may be that Manganea was another name for the same region.
[12] i.e. March 5, 310.
[13] It was the universal custom in ancient times for a city to have its special tutelary divinity, to which it looked for protection and to which it paid especial honor. The name of the Caesarean deity is unknown to us.

[1] λογικῶν.
[2] "It was a punishment among the Romans that freemen should be condemned to take care of the emperor's horses or camels, and to perform other personal offices of that kind" (Valesius). For fuller particulars, see Valesius' note ad locum. In the Acts of St. Marcellus (who was bishop of Rome) we are told that he was set by Maximian to groom his horses in a church which the emperor had turned into a stable.   [3] ἀλόγου ζώου.
[4] Cf. Bk. VIII. chap. 2, §§ 2 and 3, and the note on that passage.
[5] Phil. iv. 8.

had continued into the eighth year were gradually and quietly becoming less severe. A large number of confessors were collected at the copper mines in Palestine, and were acting with considerable boldness, so far as even to build places of worship. But the ruler of the province, a cruel and wicked man, as his acts against the martyrs showed, having come there and learned the state of affairs, communicated it to the emperor, writing in accusation what-
2 ever he thought best. Thereupon, being appointed superintendent of the mines, he divided the band of confessors as if by a royal decree, and sent some to dwell in Cyprus and others in Lebanon, and he scattered others in different parts of Palestine and ordered
3 them to labor in various works. And, selecting the four who seemed to him to be the leaders, he sent them to the commander of the armies in that section. These were Peleus and Nilus,[1] Egyptian bishops, also a presbyter,[2] and Patermuthius, who was well known among them all for his zeal toward all. The commander of the army demanded of them a denial of religion, and not obtaining this, he condemned them to death by fire.
4 There were others there who had been allotted to dwell in a separate place by themselves, — such of the confessors as on account of age or mutilations, or for other bodily infirmities, had been released from service. Silvanus,[3] a bishop from Gaza, presided over them, and set a worthy and genuine ex-
5 ample of Christianity. This man having from the first day of the persecution, and throughout its entire continuance, been eminent for his confessions in all sorts of conflicts, had been kept all that time that he might, so to speak, set the final seal upon the whole con-
6 flict in Palestine. There were with him many from Egypt, among whom was John, who surpassed all in our time in the excellence of his memory. He had formerly been deprived of his sight. Nevertheless, on account of his eminence in confession he had with the others suffered the destruction of his foot by cauterization. And although his sight had been destroyed he was subjected to the same burning with fire, the executioners aiming after everything that was merciless and pitiless and cruel and in-
7 human. Since he was such a man, one would not be so much astonished at his habits and his philosophic life, nor would he seem so wonderful for them, as for the strength of his memory. For he had written whole books

of the Divine Scriptures, "not in tables of stone"[4] as the divine apostle says, neither on skins of animals, nor on paper which moths and time destroy, but truly "in fleshy tables of the heart,"[5] in a transparent soul and most pure eye of the mind, so that whenever he wished he could repeat, as if from a treasury of words, any portion of the Scripture, whether in the law, or the prophets, or the historical books, or the gospels, or the writings of the apostles.
8 I confess that I was astonished when I first saw the man as he was standing in the midst of a large congregation and repeating portions of the Divine Scripture. While I only heard his voice, I thought that, according to the custom in the meetings, he was reading. But when I came near and perceived what he was doing, and observed all the others standing around him with sound eyes while he was using only the eyes of his mind, and yet was speaking naturally like some prophet, and far excelling those who were sound in body, it was impossible for me not to glorify God and wonder. And I seemed to see in these deeds evident and strong confirmation of the fact that true manhood consists not in excellence of bodily appearance, but in the soul and understanding alone. For he, with his body mutilated, manifested the superior excellence of the power that was within him.
9 But as to those whom we have mentioned as abiding in a separate place, and attending to their customary duties in fasting and prayer and other exercises, God himself saw fit to give them a salutary issue by extending his right hand in answer to them. The bitter foe, as they were armed against him zealously through their prayers to God, could no longer endure them, and determined to slay and destroy them from off the earth because they troubled him. And God permitted him to accomplish
10 this, that he might not be restrained from the wickedness he desired, and that at the same time they might receive the prizes of their manifold conflicts. Therefore at the command of the most accursed Maximinus, forty, lacking one,[6] were beheaded in one day.
11 These martyrdoms were accomplished in Palestine during eight complete years; and of this description was the persecution in our time. Beginning with the demolition of the churches, it increased greatly as the rulers rose up from time to time against us. In these assaults the multiform and various conflicts of those who wrestled in behalf of religion produced an innumerable multitude of martyrs in every province, — in the regions extending from Libya and throughout all Egypt, and Syria, and

---

[1] On Peleus and Nilus, see above, Bk. VIII. chap. 13, note 8. Peleus is called Paul in the Syriac version.
[2] The name of this man is given as Elias in the Syriac version; but both he and Patermuthius are called laymen.
[3] On Silvanus, bishop of Gaza, see above, Bk. VIII. chap. 13, note 6.

[4] 2 Cor. iii. 3.   [5] Ibid.
[6] The Syriac version says forty.

from the East round about to the district of Illyricum.

12   But the countries beyond these, all Italy and Sicily and Gaul, and the regions toward the setting sun, in Spain, Mauritania, and Africa, suffered the war of persecution during less than two years,[7] and were deemed worthy of a speedier divine visitation and peace; the heavenly Providence sparing the singleness of purpose

13   and faith of those men. For what had never before been recorded in the annals of the Roman government, first took place in our day, contrary to all expectation; for during the persecution in our time the empire was divided into two parts.[8] The brethren dwelling in the part of which we have just spoken enjoyed peace; but those in the other part endured trials without number. But when the divine 14 grace kindly and compassionately manifested its care for us too, then truly our rulers also, those very ones through whom the wars against us had been formerly carried on, changed their minds in a most wonderful manner, and published a recantation;[9] and by favorable edicts and mild decrees concerning us, extinguished the conflagration against us. This recantation also must be recorded.[10]

---

[7] On the cessation of the persecution in the West at the accession of Maxentius, see Bk. VIII. chap. 14, note 1.

[8] On the division of the empire to which Eusebius here refers, see above, Bk. VIII. chap. 13, note 17.

[9] i.e. the toleration edict of Galerius, published in the spring of 311. See above, Bk. VIII. chap. 17, note 1.

[10] It would seem that the edict was originally appended to this shorter recension of the martyrs (the longer recension is complete in its present form, and contains no hint of such an addition). Very likely it was dropped with the second half of the work (see above, p. 29) as unnecessary, when the first half was inserted in the *History*. The edict is given in full in Bk. VIII. chap. 17, above.

[11] περὶ τῶν ἐν Παλαιστίνῃ μαρτυρησάντων τέλος. On the title of the work, see above, p. 342, note 1.

THE END OF THE BOOK OF EUSEBIUS PAMPHILI CONCERNING THOSE WHO SUFFERED MARTYRDOM IN PALESTINE.[11]

BOOK IX.

CHAPTER I.

The Pretended Relaxation.

1 THE imperial edict of recantation, which has been quoted above,[1] was posted in all parts of Asia and in the adjoining provinces. After this had been done, Maximinus, the tyrant in the East, — a most impious man, if there ever was one, and most hostile to the religion of the God of the universe, — being by no means satisfied with its contents,[2] instead of sending the above-quoted decree to the governors under him, **2** gave them verbal commands to relax the war against us. For since he could not in any other way oppose the decision of his superiors, keeping the law which had been already issued secret, and taking care that it might not be made known in the district under him, he gave an unwritten order to his governors that they should relax the persecution against us. They communicated the com- **3** mand to each other in writing. Sabinus,[3] at least, who was honored with the highest official rank among them, communicated the will of the emperor to the provincial governors in a Latin epistle, the translation of which is as follows:

4 " With continuous and most devoted earnestness their Majesties, our most divine masters, the emperors,[4] formerly directed the minds of all men to follow the holy and correct course of life, that those also who seemed to live in a manner foreign to that of the Romans, should render the worship due to the immortal gods. But the obstinacy and most unconquerable determination of some went so far that they could neither be turned back from their purpose by the just reason of the command, nor be intimidated by the impending punishment. **5** Since therefore it has come to pass that by such conduct many have brought themselves into danger, their Majesties, our most powerful masters, the emperors, in the exalted nobility of piety, esteeming it foreign to their Majesties' purpose to bring men into so great danger for such a cause, have commanded their devoted servant, myself, to write to thy wisdom,[5] that if any Christian be found engaging in the worship of his own people, thou shouldst abstain from molesting and endangering him, and shouldst not suppose it necessary to punish any one on this pretext. For it has been proved by the experience of so long a time that they can in no way be persuaded to abandon such obstinate conduct. Therefore it should be **6** thy care to write to the curators[6] and magistrates and district overseers[7] of every city, that they may know that it is not necessary for them to give further attention to this matter."[8] Thereupon the rulers of the prov- **7**

---

[1] The toleration edict of Galerius, given in Bk. VIII. chap. 17.

[2] For the reason of Maximin's failure to join with the other emperors in the issue of this edict, see Bk. VIII. chap. 17, note 1.

[3] Of Sabinus we know only what is told us here. He seems to have been Maximin's prime minister, or prætorian prefect (τῷ τῶν ἐξοχωτάτων ἐπάρχων ἀξιώματι τετιμημένος, Eusebius says of him). He is mentioned again in chap. 9, where an epistle of Maximin addressed to him is quoted.

[4] Literally, " the divinity of our most divine masters, the emperors." The style throughout the epistle is of an equally stilted character.

[5] Literally, " have commanded my devotedness to write to thy wisdom." It is clear that the communication was dictated, or at least directly inspired, by Maximin himself.

[6] τοὺς λογιστάς, commonly used to translate the Latin *curatores urbium*.

[7] τοὺς στρατηγοὺς (the common designation for the chief magistrates of cities in the eastern part of the empire) καὶ τοὺς πραιποσίτους τοῦ πάγου.

[8] The MSS. all read γράμματος, but Valesius conjectures that πράγματος is the true reading, and his conjecture is supported by Nicephorus, who has φροντίδα περὶ χριστιανῶν ποιεῖσθαι. Stroth follows Valesius, and I have done the same. Heinichen remarks: " *Sed non necessaria, credo, est hæc emendatio, immo eadem fere exsistet sententia per γράμματος, hoc modo : ut scient sibi non licere operam dare sc. ut facile intelligitur persequendis Christianis, ultra hoc scriptum, id est, magis quam hoc scripto est designatum.*" Closs interprets in the same way, translating: " dass sie sich nicht weiter, als in diesem Schreiben befohlen ist, mit den Christen zu befassen haben." The Greek, however, does not seem to me to admit of this interpretation (it reads ἵνα γνῶεν, περαιτέρω αὐτοῖς τούτου τοῦ γράμματος φροντίδα ποιεῖσθαι μὴ προσήκειν), and there seems to be no other alternative than to change the word γράμματος to πράγματος, or at least give it the meaning of πράγματος, as Mason does, without emending the text (though I am not aware that γράμμα can legitimately be rendered in any such way). I am inclined to think that the word *negotium* stood in the original, and that it was translated by the word πρᾶγμα. Had *epistola* or *litteræ* been used, referring to the present document, — and it could not well refer to anything else, — we should expect Eusebius to translate by ἐπιστολή, for he calls the document an ἐπιστολή in § 3, above. On the other hand, if *scriptura*, or any other similar word, had been used and translated γράμμα by Eusebius, we should have expected him to call the document a γράμμα, not an ἐπιστολή in § 3.

The general drift of the letter cannot be mistaken. As Mason paraphrases it: " In other words, Christianity strictly is still illicit, though in particular cases not to be punished as severely as heretofore; and the emperor, though forced for the present not to *require* you to persecute, will expect you not to relax your exertions more than can be helped." Mason justly emphasizes in the same connection the use of the words μὴ προσήκειν in the last clause, which do not mean *non licere* (" it is not permitted ") as Valesius, followed by many others, render them, but " it is not necessary," " they need not." It is plain that Maximin made his concessions very unwillingly and only because compelled to; and it is clear that he suppressed the edict of Galerius, and substituted general and not wholly unambiguous directions of his own, in order that as little as possible might be done for the Christians, and that he might be left free for a future time when he should find himself in a more independent position; he evidently did not care to compromise and hamper himself by officially sanctioning the full and explicit toleration accorded in the edict of Galerius. For a fuller discussion of Maximin's attitude in the matter, see Mason, p. 309 sq. As he

inces, thinking that the purpose of the things
which were written was truly made known to
them, declared the imperial will to the curators and magistrates and prefects of the various
districts[9] in writing. But they did not limit
themselves to writing, but sought more quickly to
accomplish the supposed will of the emperor in
deeds also. Those whom they had imprisoned
on account of their confession of the Deity, they
set at liberty, and they released those of them
who had been sent to the mines for punishment;
for they erroneously supposed that this was
8   the true will of the emperor. And when
these things had thus been done, immediately, like a light shining forth in a dark night,
one could see in every city congregations gathered and assemblies thronged, and meetings held
according to their custom. And every one of
the unbelieving heathen was not a little astonished at these things, wondering at so marvelous
a transformation, and exclaiming that the God
of the Christians was great and alone true.
9   And some of our people, who had faithfully and bravely sustained the conflict of
persecution, again became frank and bold toward
all; but as many as had been diseased in the
faith and had been shaken in their souls by the
tempest, strove eagerly for healing, beseeching
and imploring the strong to stretch out to them
a saving hand, and supplicating God to be
10   merciful unto them. Then also the noble
athletes of religion who had been set free
from their sufferings in the mines returned to
their own homes. Happily and joyfully they
passed through every city, full of unspeakable
pleasure and of a boldness which cannot
11   be expressed in words. Great crowds of
men pursued their journey along the highways and through the market-places, praising
God with hymns and psalms. And you might
have seen those who a little while before had
been driven in bonds from their native countries
under a most cruel sentence, returning with
bright and joyful faces to their own firesides;
so that even they who had formerly thirsted for
our blood, when they saw the unexpected wonder, congratulated us on what had taken place.

CHAPTER II.

The Subsequent Reverse.

1   But the tyrant who, as we have said,
ruled over the districts of the Orient, a

thorough hater of the good and an enemy of
every virtuous person, as he was, could no longer
bear this; and indeed he did not permit matters
to go on in this way quite six months.[1] Devising all possible means of destroying the peace,
he first attempted to restrain us, under a pretext,[2] from meeting in the cemeteries.
Then through the agency of some wicked   2
men he sent an embassy to himself against
us,[3] inciting the citizens of Antioch to ask from
him as a very great favor that he would by no
means permit any of the Christians to dwell in
their country; and others were secretly induced
to do the same thing. The author of all this in
Antioch was Theotecnus,[4] a violent and wicked
man, who was an impostor, and whose character
was foreign to his name.[5] He appears to have
been the curator[6] of the city.

---

[1] The Edict of Galerius was issued in April, 311 (see Lactantius, de Mort. pers. 35, and Bk. VIII. chap. 17, note 1, above), so that Maximin's change of policy, recorded in this chapter, must have begun in October, or thereabouts. Valesius supposes that the death of Galerius was the cause of Maximin's return to persecuting meas- ures. But Galerius died, not some months after the issue of the edict, as Valesius, and others after him, assert, but within a few days after it, as is directly stated by Lactantius (ibid.), whose ac- curacy in this case there is no reason to question. Another mis- statement made by Valesius in the same connection, and repeated by Heinichen, Crusè, and others, is that Maximin became Augustus only after the death of Galerius. The truth is, he was recognized as an Augustus in 308 (see Lactantius, ibid. chap. 32; and Bk. VIII. chap. 13, note 22, above). The cause of the renewal of the persecu- tion seems to have been simply impatience at the exultation of the Church and at the wonderful recuperative power revealed the moment the pressure was taken off. That it was not renewed sooner was doubtless due to the more important matters which engaged the attention of Maximinus immediately after the death of Galerius, in connection with the division of the Eastern Empire between himself and Licinius (see Lactantius, ibid. chap. 36). It would seem from the passage just referred to, that as soon as these matters were satis- factorily adjusted, Maximin turned his attention again to the Chris- tians, and began to curtail their liberty.
[2] Very likely under the pretext that night gatherings at the tombs of the martyrs, with the excitement and enthusiasm neces- sarily engendered under such circumstances, were of immoral ten- dency. Naturally, the honor shown by the Christians to their fellows who had been put to death at the command of the state was looked upon as an insult to the authorities, and could not but be very distasteful to them. They imagined that such meetings would only tend to foster discontent and disloyalty on the part of those who en- gaged in them, and consequently they were always suspicious of them.
[3] The same account is given by Lactantius, ibid. chap. 36 ("First of all he took away the toleration and general protection granted by Galerius to the Christians, and, for this end, he secretly procured addresses for the different cities, requesting that no Chris- tian church might be built within their walls; and thus he meant to make that which was his own choice appear as if extorted from him by importunity"). It is possible that the account is correct, but it is more probable that the embassies were genuine, and were voluntarily sent to the emperor, while he was on a tour through his dominions, by the pagan population of some of the cities who knew the emperor's own position in the matter, and desired to conciliate him and secure favors from him. Of course such deputations would delight him greatly; and what one city did, others would feel compelled to do also, in order not to seem behindhand in religious zeal and in order not to run the risk of offending the emperor, who since the death of Galerius was of course a more absolute master than before. Cf. Mason, p. 313 sq.
[4] Theotecnus, according to the Passion of St. Theodotus (trans- lated in Mason, p. 354 sq.) an apostate from Christianity, was for some time chief magistrate of Galatia, where he indulged in the most terrible cruelties against the Christians. Beyond the account given in the Passion referred to we know in regard to Theotecnus only what is told us by Eusebius in the present book, in which he is fre- quently mentioned. His hatred of the Christians knew no bounds. He seems, moreover, to have been something of a philosopher and literary man (Mason calls him a Neo-Platonist, and makes him the author of the anti-Christian Acta Pilati; but see below, chap. 5, note 1). He was executed by command of Licinius, after the death of Maximinus (see below, chap. 11).
[5] Θεότεκνος, "child of God."
[6] The λογισταί, or curatores urbium, were the chief finance officers of municipalities. See Valesius' note on Bk. VIII. chap. 11.

remarks, it is " almost a wonder that the judges interpreted Maxi- min's document in a sense so favorable to the brotherhood as they really did. Though no effectual security was given against the re- currence of the late atrocities, the Persecution of Diocletian was at an end, even in the East. The subordinate officers issued and posted local mandates, which conceded more than they were bidden to concede."   [9] τοῖς κατ' ἀγροὺς ἐπιτεταγμένοις.

CHAPTER III.

The Newly Erected Statue at Antioch.

AFTER this man had carried on all kinds of war against us and had caused our people to be diligently hunted up in their retreats, as if they were unholy thieves, and had devised every sort of slander and accusation against us, and become the cause of death to vast numbers, he finally erected a statue of Jupiter Philius[1] with certain juggleries and magic rites. And after inventing unholy forms of initiation and ill-omened mysteries in connection with it, and abominable means of purification,[2] he exhibited his jugglery, by oracles which he pretended to utter, even to the emperor; and through a flattery which was pleasing to the ruler he aroused the demon against the Christians and said that the god had given command to expel the Christians as his enemies beyond the confines of the city and the neighboring districts.

CHAPTER IV.

The Memorials against us.[1]

1   THE fact that this man, who took the lead in this matter, had succeeded in his purpose was an incitement to all the other officials in the cities under the same government to prepare a similar memorial.[2] And the governors of the provinces perceiving that this was agreeable to the emperor suggested to their subjects that they should do the same.
2   And as the tyrant by a rescript declared himself well pleased with their measures,[3] persecution was kindled anew against us. Priests for the images were then appointed in the cities, and besides them high priests by Maximinus himself.[4] The latter were taken from among those who were most distinguished in public life and had gained celebrity in all the offices which they had filled; and who were imbued, moreover, with great zeal for the service of those whom they worshiped. Indeed, the extraordinary 3 superstition of the emperor, to speak in brief, led all his subjects, both rulers and private citizens, for the sake of gratifying him, to do everything against us, supposing that they could best show their gratitude to him for the benefits which they had received from him, by plotting murder against us and exhibiting toward us any new signs of malignity.

CHAPTER V.

The Forged Acts.

HAVING therefore forged Acts of Pilate[1] 1 and our Saviour full of every kind of blasphemy against Christ, they sent them with the emperor's approval to the whole of the empire subject to him, with written commands that they should be openly posted to the view of all in every place, both in country and city, and that the schoolmasters should give them to their scholars, instead of their customary lessons, to be studied and learned by heart. While 2 these things were taking place, another military commander, whom the Romans call Dux,[2] seized some infamous women in the market-place at Damascus in Phœnicia,[3] and by threatening to inflict tortures upon them compelled them to make a written declaration that

---

a positive aggressive power over against Christianity by giving it a regular organization and placing the entire institution in the hands of honorable and able men, whose business it should be to increase its stability and power in every way and in all quarters. We are compelled to admire the wisdom of Maximin's plan. No persecutor before him had ever seen the need of thus replacing the Christian Church by another institution as great and as splendid as itself. The effort, like that of Julian a half-century later, must remain memorable in the annals of the conflict of paganism with Christianity.

[1] These Acts are no longer extant, but their character can be gathered from this chapter. They undoubtedly contained the worst calumnies against Christ's moral and religious character. They cannot have been very skillful forgeries, for Eusebius in Bk. I. chap. 9, above, points out a palpable chronological blunder which stamped them as fictitious on their very face. And yet they doubtless answered every purpose; for few of the heathen would be in a position to detect such an error, and perhaps fewer still would care to expose it if they discovered it. These Acts are of course to be distinguished from the numerous *Acta Pilati* which proceeded from Christian sources (see above, Bk. II. chap. 2, note 1). The way in which these Acts were employed was diabolical in its very shrewdness. Certainly there was no more effectual way of checking the spread of Christianity than systematically and persistently to train up the youth of the empire to look with contempt and disgust upon the founder of Christianity, the Christian's Saviour and Lord. Incalculable mischief must inevitably have been produced had Maximin's reign lasted for a number of years. As it was, we can imagine the horror of the Christians at this new and sacrilegious artifice of the enemy. Mason assigns "the crowning, damning honor of this masterstroke" to Theotecnus, but I am unable to find any proof that he was the author of the documents. It is, of course, not impossible nor improbable that he was; but had Eusebius known him to be the author, he would certainly have informed us. As it is, his statement is entirely indefinite, and the Acts are not brought into any connection with Theotecnus.

[2] The commandant of the Roman garrison in Damascus.

[3] Damascus, from the time of Hadrian (according to Spruner-Menke), or of Severus (according to Mommsen), was the capital of the newly formed province of Syria-Phœnice, or Syro-Phœnicia.

---

[1] Jupiter Philius, the god of friendship or good-will, was widely honored in the East. He seems to have been the tutelary divinity of Antioch, and, according to Valesius, a temple of his at Antioch is mentioned by the emperor Julian and by Libanius.

[2] "The ceremonies of the Gentiles, used in the erection and consecration of images to their gods, were various. Jupiter Ctesius was consecrated with one sort of rites, Herceus with another, and Philius with a third sort" (Valesius). For farther particulars, see his note *ad locum*.

   [1] περὶ τῶν καθ' ἡμῶν ψηφισμάτων.
   [2] ψηφόν.   [3] ψηφίσμασι.

[4] Lactantius (*ibid.* chap. 36) says: "In compliance with those addresses he [Maximinus] introduced a new mode of government in things respecting religion, and for each city he created a high priest, chosen from among the persons of most distinction. The office of those men was to make daily sacrifices to all their gods, and, with the aid of the former priests, to prevent the Christians from erecting churches, or from worshiping God, either publicly or in private; and he authorized them to compel the Christians to sacrifice to idols and, on their refusal, to bring them before the civil magistrate; and, as if this had not been enough, in every province he established a superintendent priest, one of chief eminence in the state; and he commanded that all those priests newly instituted should appear in white habits, that being the most honorable distinction of dress." Maximin perceived the power that existed in the Catholic Church with its wonderful organization, and conceived the stupendous idea of rejuvenating paganism by creating a pagan Catholic Church. The Roman religion should cease to be the loose, unorganized, chaotic thing it had always been, and should be made

they had once been Christians and that they were acquainted with their impious deeds, — that in their very churches they committed licentious acts; and they uttered as many other slanders against our religion as he wished them to. Having taken down their words in writing, he communicated them to the emperor, who commanded that these documents also should be published in every place and city.

CHAPTER VI.

Those who suffered Martyrdom at this Time.

1　Not long afterward, however, this military commander became his own murderer and paid the penalty for his wickedness. But we were obliged again to endure exile and severe persecutions, and the governors in every province were once more terribly stirred up against us; so that even some of those illustrious in the Divine Word were seized and had sentence of death pronounced upon them without mercy. Three of them in the city of Emesa[1] in Phœnicia, having confessed that they were Christians, were thrown as food to the wild beasts. Among them was a bishop Silvanus,[2] a very old man, who had filled his
2　office full forty years. At about the same time Peter[3] also, who presided most illustriously over the parishes in Alexandria, a divine example of a bishop on account of the excellence of his life and his study of the sacred Scriptures, being seized for no cause and quite unexpectedly, was, as if by command of Maximinus, immediately and without explanation, beheaded. With him also many other bish-
3　ops of Egypt suffered the same fate. And Lucian,[4] a presbyter of the parish at Antioch, and a most excellent man in every respect, temperate in life and famed for his learning in sacred things, was brought to the city of Nicomedia, where at that time the emperor hap-

pened to be staying, and after delivering before the ruler an apology for the doctrine which he professed, was committed to prison and put to death. Such trials were brought　4 upon us in a brief time by Maximinus, the enemy of virtue, so that this persecution which was stirred up against us seemed far more cruel than the former.

CHAPTER VII.

The Decree against us which was engraved on Pillars.

The memorials against us[1] and copies of　1 the imperial edicts issued in reply to them were engraved and set up on brazen pillars in the midst of the cities,[2] — a course which had never been followed elsewhere. The children in the schools had daily in their mouths the names of Jesus and Pilate, and the Acts which had been forged in wanton insolence.[3] It appears to me necessary to insert here　2 this document of Maximinus which was posted on pillars, in order that there may be made manifest at the same time the boastful and haughty arrogance of the God-hating man, and the sleepless evil-hating divine vengeance upon the impious, which followed close upon him, and under whose pressure he not long afterward took the opposite course in respect to us and confirmed it by written laws.[4]

The rescript is in the following words:

Copy of a translation of the rescript of Maximinus in answer to the memorials against us, taken from the pillar in Tyre.

"Now at length the feeble power of the　3 human mind has become able to shake off and to scatter every dark mist of error, which before this besieged the senses of men, who were more miserable than impious, and enveloped them in dark and destructive ignorance; and to perceive that it is governed and estab-

---

[1] Emesa was an important city in Northern Phœnicia, the birthplace of the Emperor Elagabalus, and chiefly famous for its great temple of the Sun.
[2] On Silvanus, bishop of Emesa, see above, Bk. VIII. chap. 13, note 4.
[3] On Peter, bishop of Alexandria, see above, Bk. VII. chap. 32, note 54. According to that chapter he suffered in the ninth year of the persecution; that is, at least as early as April, 312.
[4] The presbyter Lucian, who is mentioned also in Bk. VIII. chap. 13, above, was one of the greatest scholars of the early Church, and with Dorotheus (see above, Bk. VII. chap. 32, note 9) at the head of the famous theological school at Antioch. He produced a revised version of the LXX, which enjoyed a wide circulation (see Jerome's *de vir. ill.* 77, and Westcott's *Hist. of the N. T. Canon*, p. 392 sq.); and also wrote some books on Faith (see Jerome, *ibid.*), some epistles (see *ibid.*, and Suidas, *s.v.*), and a commentary on Job, of which a Latin fragment has been preserved and is given by Routh, *Rel. Sacræ*, IV. p. 7–10. His works have perished, with the exception of a brief fragment of an epistle, the fragment from his commentary on Job just referred to, and a part of his defense before Maximinus (referred to in the present chapter) which is preserved by Rufinus, *H. E.* IX. 6, and is probably genuine (cf. Westcott, *ibid.* p. 393). These extant fragments are given, with annotations, by Routh, *ibid.* p. 5 sq. Lucian's chief historical significance lies in his relation to Arianism. On this subject, see above, p. 11 sq.

[1] See above, chaps. 2 and 4.
[2] These decrees must have been published in this way in June, 312, or thereabouts; for in chap. 10, § 12, we learn that they were thus made public a little less than a year before the final edict of toleration, which was apparently issued in May, 313.
[3] See chap. 5.
[4] οὐκ εἰς μακρὸν τἀναντία περὶ ἡμῶν ἐβουλεύσατό τε καὶ δι' ἐγγράφων νόμων ἐδογμάτισε. Crusè translates, "So that he did not long devise hostilities and form decrees against us." It is true that the phrase οὐκ εἰς μακρόν may in general bear the meaning "not for long," as well as "not long afterward"; but an examination of the numerous passages in which the words are used by Eusebius (e.g. I. 11. 1; I. 13. 4; II. 6. 5; II. 7; III. 5. 7; IV. 7. 12; VII. 13. 1) will show that, with a single exception, he uniformly employs them in the sense of "not long afterward." The single exception occurs in Bk. IV. chap. 7, § 12, where the phrase is clearly used with the other meaning — "not for long." In view of this preponderance of instances for the former use of the phrase in this single work, it seems best in the present case — the only doubtful one, so far as I am aware — to follow Valesius, Stroth, and Closs in translating "not long afterward," which is in full accord with the context, and more in harmony than the other reading with the structure of this particular sentence.

4 lished by the beneficent providence of the immortal gods. It passes belief how grateful, how pleasing and how agreeable it is to us, that you have given a most decided proof of your pious resolution ; for even before this it was known to every one how much regard and reverence you were paying to the immortal gods, exhibiting not a faith of bare and empty words, but continued and wonderful exam-

5 ples of illustrious deeds. Wherefore your city may justly be called a seat and dwelling of the immortal gods. At least, it appears by many signs that it flourishes because of the pres-

6 ence of the celestial gods. Behold, therefore, your city, regardless of all private advantages, and omitting its former petitions in its own behalf, when it perceived that the adherents of that execrable vanity were again beginning to spread, and to start the greatest conflagration, — like a neglected and extinguished funeral pile when its brands are rekindled, — immediately resorted to our piety as to a metropolis of all religiousness, asking some remedy

7 and aid. It is evident that the gods have given you this saving mind on account of your faith and piety.

"Accordingly that supreme and mightiest Jove, who presides over your illustrious city, who preserves your ancestral gods, your wives and children, your hearths and homes from every destructive pest, has infused into your souls this wholesome resolve ; showing and proving how excellent and glorious and salutary it is to observe with the becoming reverence the worship and sacred rites of the immortal gods.

8 For who can be found so ignorant or so devoid of all understanding as not to perceive that it is due to the kindly care of the gods that the earth does not refuse the seed sown in it, nor disappoint the hope of the husbandmen with vain expectation ; that impious war is not inevitably fixed upon earth, and wasted bodies dragged down to death under the influence of a corrupted atmosphere ; that the sea is not swollen and raised on high by blasts of intemperate winds ; that unexpected hurricanes do not burst forth and stir up the destructive tempest ; moreover, that the earth, the nourisher and mother of all, is not shaken from its lowest depths with a terrible tremor, and that the mountains upon it do not sink into the opening chasms. No one is ignorant that all these, and evils still worse than these, have oftentimes happened hitherto.

9 And all these misfortunes have taken place on account of the destructive error of the empty vanity of those impious men, when it prevailed in their souls, and, we may almost say, weighed down the whole world with shame."

10 After other words he adds : " Let them look at the standing crops already flourishing with waving heads in the broad fields, and at the meadows glittering with plants and flowers, in response to abundant rains and the restored mildness and softness of the atmosphere.

11 Finally, let all rejoice that the might of the most powerful and terrible Mars has been propitiated by our piety, our sacrifices, and our veneration ; and let them on this account enjoy firm and tranquil peace and quiet ; and let as many as have wholly abandoned that blind error and delusion and have returned to a right and sound mind rejoice the more, as those who have been rescued from an unexpected storm or severe disease and are to reap the fruits of pleasure for the rest of their life.

12 But if they still persist in their execrable vanity, let them, as you have desired, be driven far away from your city and territory, that thus, in accordance with your praiseworthy zeal in this matter, your city, being freed from every pollution and impiety, may, according to its native disposition, attend to the sacred rites of the immortal gods with becoming reverence.

13 But that ye may know how acceptable to us your request respecting this matter has been, and how ready our mind is to confer benefits voluntarily, without memorials and petitions, we permit your devotion to ask whatever great gift ye may desire in return for this your pious disposition.

14 And now ask that this may be done and that ye may receive it ; for ye shall obtain it without delay. This, being granted to your city, shall furnish for all time an evidence of reverent piety toward the immortal gods, and of the fact that you have obtained from our benevolence merited prizes for this choice of yours ; and it shall be shown to your children and children's children."

15 This was published against us in all the provinces, depriving us of every hope of good, at least from men ; so that, according to that divine utterance, " If it were possible, even the elect would have stumbled "[5] at these things.

16 And now indeed, when the hope of most of us was almost extinct, suddenly while those who were to execute against us the above decree had in some places scarcely finished their journey, God, the defender of his own Church, exhibited his heavenly interposition in our behalf, well-nigh stopping the tyrant's boasting against us.

CHAPTER VIII.

The Misfortunes which happened in Connection with these Things, in Famine, Pestilence, and War.

1 THE customary rains and showers of the winter season ceased to fall in their wonted

[5] Matt. xxiv. 24.

abundance upon the earth and an unexpected famine made its appearance, and in addition to this a pestilence, and another severe disease consisting of an ulcer, which on account of its fiery appearance was appropriately called a carbuncle.[1] This, spreading over the whole body, greatly endangered the lives of those who suffered from it ; but as it chiefly attacked the eyes, it deprived multitudes of men, women, 2 and children of their sight. In addition to this the tyrant was compelled to go to war with the Armenians, who had been from ancient times friends and allies of the Romans. As they were also Christians [2] and zealous in their piety toward the Deity, the enemy of God had attempted to compel them to sacrifice to idols and demons, and had thus made friends 3 foes, and allies enemies. All these things suddenly took place at one and the same time, and refuted the tyrant's empty vaunt against the Deity. For he had boasted that, because of his zeal for idols and his hostility against us, neither famine nor pestilence nor war had happened in his time.[3] These things, therefore, coming upon him at once and together, furnished a prelude also of his own 4 destruction. He himself with his forces was defeated in the war with the Armenians, and the rest of the inhabitants of the cities under him were terribly afflicted with famine and pestilence, so that one measure of wheat was sold for twenty-five hundred Attic 5 drachms.[4] Those who died in the cities were innumerable, and those who died in the country and villages were still more. So that the tax lists which formerly included a great rural population were almost entirely wiped out ; nearly all being speedily destroyed by famine and pestilence. Some, therefore, de- 6 sired to dispose of their most precious things to those who were better supplied, in return for the smallest morsel of food, and others, selling their possessions little by little, fell into the last extremity of want. Some, chewing wisps of hay and recklessly eating noxious herbs, undermined and ruined their constitutions. And some of the high-born 7 women in the cities, driven by want to shameful extremities, went forth into the market-places to beg, giving evidence of their former liberal culture by the modesty of their appearance and the decency of their apparel. Some, wasted away like ghosts and at the 8 very point of death, stumbled and tottered here and there, and too weak to stand fell down in the middle of the streets ; lying stretched out at full length they begged that a small morsel of food might be given them, and with their last gasp they cried out Hunger ! having strength only for this most painful cry. But others, who seemed to be better sup- 9 plied, astonished at the multitude of the beggars, after giving away large quantities, finally became hard and relentless, expecting that they themselves also would soon suffer the same calamities as those who begged. So that in the midst of the market-places and lanes, dead and naked bodies lay unburied for many days, presenting the most lamentable spectacle to those who beheld them. Some 10 also became food for dogs, on which account the survivors began to kill the dogs, lest they should become mad and should go to devouring men.

But still worse was the pestilence which 11 consumed entire houses and families, and especially those whom the famine was not able to destroy because of their abundance of food. Thus men of wealth, rulers and governors and multitudes in office, as if left by the famine on purpose for the pestilence, suffered swift and speedy death. Every place therefore was full of lamentation ; in every lane and market-place and street there was nothing else to be seen or heard than tears, with the customary instruments and the voices of the mourners.[5] In 12 this way death, waging war with these two weapons, pestilence and famine, destroyed whole families in a short time, so that one could see two or three dead bodies carried out at once. Such were the rewards of the boast- 13 ing of Maximinus and of the measures of the cities against us.

Then did the evidences of the universal zeal and piety of the Christians become manifest to all the heathen. For they alone in the 14 midst of such ills showed their sympathy

---

[1] ἄνθραξ: "a carbuncle, malignant pustule (acc. to some, small-pox)." Liddell and Scott. Eusebius is the only writer to tell us of this famine and pestilence during Maximin's reign, though Lactantius (De Mort. pers. 37) does refer in a single sentence to a famine, without giving us any particulars in regard to it, or informing us of its severity or extent.

[2] We do not know when Christianity was first preached in Armenia, but late in the third century Gregory, "the Illuminator," an Armenian of royal blood who had received a Christian training in Cappadocia, returned as a missionary to his native land, which was mainly heathen, and at the beginning of the fourth century succeeded in converting the king, Tiridates III., and a large number of the nobles and people, and Christianity was established as the state religion (see the articles Armenia and Gregory, the Illuminator, in the Dict. of Christ. Biog.).

The Armenians had been friends of the Romans for many generations and allies in their wars with the Persians on many occasions. The present war is mentioned, so far as I know, only by Eusebius. According to § 4, below, it ended in a defeat for Maximinus. It cannot have been a war of great consequence. It was very likely little more than a temporary misunderstanding, resulting perhaps in a few skirmishes between troops on the border, and speedily settled by a treaty of some kind or another. Maximinus at any rate could not afford to quarrel long with his Eastern neighbors, in view of the struggle with Licinius which he knew must come in time. Whether the Armenians or the Romans were the aggressors in this affair, Eusebius does not tell us. It is very probable, as Mason suggests, that Maximinus tried to put down Christianity in Lesser Armenia, which was a Roman province and therefore under his sway, and that their brethren in the kingdom of Armenia took up arms against Rome to avenge their kindred and their faith.

[3] See the previous chapter, § 8.

[4] An Attic drachm was a silver coin, worth about eighteen or nineteen cents.

[5] αὐλῶν τε καὶ κτύπων.

and humanity by their deeds. Every day some continued caring for and burying the dead, for there were multitudes who had no one to care for them; others collected in one place those who were afflicted by the famine, throughout the entire city, and gave bread to them all; so that the thing became noised abroad among all men, and they glorified the God of the Christians; and, convinced by the facts themselves, confessed that they alone were truly pious and
15 religious. After these things were thus done,
God, the great and celestial defender of the Christians, having revealed in the events which have been described his anger and indignation at all men for the great evils which they had brought upon us, restored to us the bright and gracious sunlight of his providence in our behalf; so that in the deepest darkness a light of peace shone most wonderfully upon us from him, and made it manifest to all that God himself has always been the ruler of our affairs. From time to time indeed he chastens his people and corrects them by his visitations, but again after sufficient chastisement he shows mercy and favor to those who hope in him.

CHAPTER IX.

The Victory of the God-Beloved Emperors.[1]

1 THUS when Constantine, whom we have already mentioned[1a] as an emperor, born of an emperor, a pious son of a most pious and prudent father, and Licinius, second to him,[2]— two God-beloved emperors, honored alike for their intelligence and their piety, — being stirred up against the two most impious tyrants by God, the absolute Ruler and Saviour of all, engaged in formal war against them, with God as their ally, Maxentius[3] was defeated at Rome by Constantine in a remarkable manner, and the tyrant of the East[4] did not long survive him, but met a most shameful death at the hand of Licinius, who had not yet become insane.[5] Con- 2
stantine, who was the superior both in dignity and imperial rank,[6] first took compassion upon those who were oppressed at Rome, and having invoked in prayer the God of heaven, and his Word, and Jesus Christ himself, the Saviour of all, as his aid, advanced with his whole army,[7] proposing to restore to the Romans
their ancestral liberty. But Maxentius, put- 3
ting confidence rather in the arts of sorcery than in the devotion of his subjects, did not dare to go forth beyond the gates of the city, but fortified every place and district and town which was enslaved by him, in the neighborhood of Rome and in all Italy, with an immense multitude of troops and with innumerable bands of soldiers. But the emperor, relying upon the assistance of God, attacked the first, second, and third army of the tyrant, and conquered them all; and having advanced through the greater part of Italy, was already very near Rome.
Then, that he might not be compelled to 4
wage war with the Romans for the sake of the tyrant, God himself drew the latter, as if bound in chains, some distance without the gates, and confirmed those threats against the impious which had been anciently inscribed in sacred books, — disbelieved, indeed, by most as a myth, but believed by the faithful, — confirmed them, in a word, by the deed itself to all, both believers and unbelievers, that saw the wonder
with their eyes. Thus, as in the time of 5
Moses himself and of the ancient God-beloved race of Hebrews, "he cast Pharaoh's chariots and host into the sea, and overwhelmed his chosen charioteers in the Red Sea, and covered them with the flood,"[8] in the same way Maxentius also with his soldiers and body-guards "went down into the depths like a stone,"[9] when he fled before the power of God which was with Constantine, and passed through the river which lay in his way, over which he had formed a

[1] All the MSS., followed by Valesius and Crusè, give this as the title of the next chapter, and give as the title of this chapter the one which I have placed at the head of chapter 10. It is plain enough from the contents of the two chapters that the titles have in some way become transposed in the MSS., and so they are restored to their proper position by the majority of the editors, whom I have followed.

[1a] See above, Bk. VIII. chap. 13.

[2] On Licinius, see *ibid.* note 21. Constantine and Licinius were both Augusti, and thus nominally of equal rank. Nevertheless, both in the edict of Galerius, quoted in Bk. VIII. chap. 17, and in the edict of Milan, given in full in the *De Mort. pers.* chap. 48, Constantine's name precedes that of Licinius, showing that he was regarded as in some sense the latter's senior, and thus confirming Eusebius' statement, the truth of which Closs unnecessarily denies. It seems a little peculiar that Constantine should thus be recognized as Licinius' senior, especially in the edict of Galerius; for although it is true that he had been a Cæsar some time before Licinius had been admitted to the imperial college, yet, on the other hand, Licinius was made Augustus by Galerius before Constantine was, and enjoyed his confidence and favor much more fully than the latter.

[3] On Maxentius, see above, Bk. VIII. chap. 14, note 1.

[4] i.e. Maximinus. For an account of his defeat by Licinius and his death, see below, chap. 10.

[5] *οὔπω μανέντος τότε.* This refers to Licinius' hostility to the Christians, which made its appearance some years later, and resulted in a persecution (see below, Bk. X. chap. 8). The clause, if a part of the original, obliges us to suppose that the ninth book was composed after Licinius had begun to persecute, but there are strong reasons for thinking that the first nine books were completed before 314 (see above, p. 45); indeed, we cannot explain Eusebius' eulogistic words in speaking of Licinius here and elsewhere in this book on any other ground. It seems necessary, therefore, to regard this clause and the similar clause in § 12, below, as later insertions, made possibly at the time of the addition of the tenth book (see p. 45).

[6] See above, note 2.

[7] Constantine's battle with Maxentius, described in this chapter, took place on the sixth anniversary of the latter's accession, Oct. 27, 312 (see Lactantius, *De Mort. pers.* 44 and 46). For particulars respecting Constantine himself and his campaign against Maxentius, see Dr. Richardson's prolegomena to his translation of the *Life of Constantine*, p. 416. sq. of this volume.

[8] Ex. xv. 4, 5. The phrase translated "charioteers" is *ἀναβάτας τριστάτας*, which is employed in the LXX to translate the Hebrew שָׁלִשָׁיו. The word שָׁלִישׁ, which means literally a "third," and hence a "third man" (Greek *τριστάτης*), is used, according to Gesenius, to denote a chariot warrior, who was so called because "three always stood upon one chariot, one of whom fought, while the second protected him with the shield, and the third drove."

[9] Ex. xv. 5.

bridge with boats, and thus prepared the
6 means of his own destruction. In regard
to him one might say, " he digged a pit and
opened it and fell into the hole which he had
made ; his labor shall turn upon his own head,
and his unrighteousness shall fall upon his
7 own crown." [10] Thus, then, the bridge over
the river being broken, the passageway settled down, and immediately the boats with the
men disappeared in the depths, and that most
impious one himself first of all, then the shield-
bearers who were with him, as the divine oracles
foretold, " sank like lead in the mighty
8 waters " ; [11] so that those who obtained the
victory from God, if not in words, at least
in deeds, like Moses, the great servant of God,
and those who were with him, fittingly sang as
they had sung against the impious tyrant of old,
saying, " Let us sing unto the Lord, for he hath
gloriously glorified himself ; horse and rider
hath he thrown into the sea ; a helper and a
protector hath he become for my salvation ; " [12]
and " Who is like unto thee, O Lord ; among the
gods, who is like unto thee ? glorious in holiness, [13] marvelous in glory, doing wonders." [14]
9 These and the like praises Constantine, by
his very deeds, sang to God, the universal
Ruler, and Author of his victory, as he entered
Rome in triumph. Immediately all the members of the senate and the other most celebrated
men, with the whole Roman people, together
with children and women, received him as their
deliverer, their saviour, and their benefactor,
with shining eyes and with their whole souls,
with shouts of gladness and unbounded joy.
10 But he, as one possessed of inborn piety
toward God, did not exult in the shouts, nor
was he elated by the praises ; but perceiving
that his aid was from God, he immediately commanded that a trophy of the Saviour's passion
be put in the hand of his own statue. And when
he had placed it, with the saving sign of the
cross in its right hand, in the most public place
in Rome, he commanded that the following inscription should be engraved upon it in the
11 Roman tongue : " By this salutary sign, the
true proof of bravery, I have saved and
freed your city from the yoke of the tyrant ;
and moreover, having set at liberty both the
senate and the people of Rome, I have restored
them to their ancient distinction and splen-

dor." [15] And after this both Constantine 12
himself and with him the Emperor Licinius,
who had not yet been seized by that madness
into which he later fell, [16] praising God as the
author of all their blessings, with one will and
mind drew up a full and most complete decree
in behalf of the Christians, [17] and sent an account
of the wonderful things done for them by God,
and of the victory over the tyrant, together with
a copy of the decree itself, to Maximinus, who
still ruled over the nations of the East and
pretended friendship toward them. But he, 13
like a tyrant, was greatly pained by what he
learned ; but not wishing to seem to yield to others,
nor, on the other hand, to suppress that which
was commanded, for fear of those who enjoined
it, as if on his own authority, he addressed, under
compulsion, to the governors under him this
first communication in behalf of the Christians, [18]
falsely inventing things against himself which had
never been done by him.

Copy of a translation of the epistle of the tyrant Maximinus.

"Jovius Maximinus Augustus to Sabinus. [19] I
am confident that it is manifest both to thy firmness and to all men that our masters Diocletian
and Maximianus, our fathers, when they saw
almost all men abandoning the worship of
the gods and attaching themselves to the 14
party of the Christians, rightly decreed that
all who gave up the worship of those same
immortal gods should be recalled by open chastisement and punishment to the worship of
the gods. But when I first came to the 15

---

[10] Psa. vii. 15, 16.   [11] Ex. xv. 10.
[12] *Ibid.* verse 1. Eusebius, in this and the next passage, follows
the LXX, which differs considerably from the Hebrew.
[13] The LXX, followed by Eusebius, reads δεδοξασμένος ἐν ἁγίοις
to translate the Hebrew נֶאְדָּר בַּקֹּדֶשׁ. It seems probable, both
from the Hebrew original and from the use of the plural δόξαις in
the next clause, that the LXX translator used the plural ἁγίοις, not
to denote " saints," as Closs renders (" durch die Heiligen "), which
would in strictness require the article, but " holiness." I have
therefore ventured to render the word thus in the text, although
quite conscious that the translation does not accurately reproduce
the Greek phrase as it stands.   [14] Ex. xv. 11.

[15] Upon Constantine's conversion, see Dr. Richardson's prolegomena, p. 431, below. On the famous tale of the flaming cross, with
its inscription τούτῳ νίκα, related in the *Life of Constantine*, I. 28,
see his note on that passage, p. 490, below.
[16] See above, note 5.
[17] This is the famous edict of Milan, which was issued late in the
year 312, and which is given in the Latin original in Lactantius' *De
Mort. pers.* 48, and in a Greek translation in Eusebius' *History*,
Bk. X. chap. 5, below. For a discussion of its date and significance,
see the notes upon that chapter.
[18] This epistle or rescript (Eusebius calls it here a γράμμα, just below an ἐπιστολή) of Maximin's was written before the end of the year
312, as can be seen from the fact that in § 17, below, his visit to Nicomedia is spoken of as having taken place in the previous year. But that
visit, as we learn from the *De Mort. pers.* chap. 36, occurred in 311
(cf. chap. 2, note 1, above). It must therefore have been issued immediately upon the receipt of the edict of Constantine and Licinius.
As Mason remarks, his reasons for writing this epistle can hardly
have been fear of Constantine and Licinius, as Eusebius states, for
he was bent upon war against them, and attacked Licinius at the
earliest possible moment. He cannot have cared, therefore, to take
any special pains to conciliate them. He was probably moved by a
desire to conciliate, just at this crisis, the numerous and influential
body of his subjects whom he had persecuted, in order that he might
not have to contend with disaffection and disloyalty within his own
dominions during his impending conflict with Licinius. The document itself is a most peculiar one, full of false statements and contradictions. Mason well says: " In this curious letter Maximin
contradicts himself often enough to make his Christian subjects
dizzy. First he justifies bloody persecution, then plumes himself
upon having stopped it, next apologizes for having set it again on foot,
then denies that it was going on, and lastly orders it to cease. We
cannot wonder at what Eusebius relates, that the people whose
wrongs the letter applauded and forbade, neither built church nor
held meeting in public on the strength of it; they did not know
where to have it."
[19] On Sabinus, see above, chap. 1, note 3.

East under favorable auspices and learned that in some places a great many men who were able to render public service had been banished by the judges for the above-mentioned cause, I gave command to each of the judges that henceforth none of them should treat the provincials with severity, but that they should rather recall them to the worship of the gods by flattery 16 and exhortations.[20] Then when, in accordance with my command, these orders were obeyed by the judges, it came to pass that none of those who lived in the districts of the East were banished or insulted, but that they were rather brought back to the worship of the gods by the fact that no severity was employed 17 toward them. But afterwards, when I went up last year [21] under good auspices to Nicomedia and sojourned there, citizens of the same city came to me with the images of the gods, earnestly entreating that such a people should by no means be permitted to dwell in their 18 country.[22] But when I learned that many men of the same religion dwelt in those regions, I replied that I gladly thanked them for their request, but that I perceived that it was not proffered by all, and that if, therefore, there were any that persevered in the same superstition, each one had the privilege of doing as he pleased, even if he wished to recognize the 19 worship of the gods.[23] Nevertheless, I considered it necessary to give a friendly answer to the inhabitants of Nicomedia and to the other cities which had so earnestly presented to me the same petition, namely, that no Christians should dwell in their cities, — both because this same course had been pursued by all the ancient emperors, and also because it was pleasing to the gods, through whom all men and the government of the state itself endure, — and to confirm the request which they presented in 20 behalf of the worship of their deity. Therefore, although before this time, special letters have been sent to thy devotedness, and commands have likewise been given that no harsh measures should be taken against those provincials who desire to follow such a course, but that they should be treated mildly and moderately, — nevertheless, in order that they may

not suffer insults or extortions [24] from the beneficiaries,[25] or from any others, I have thought meet to remind thy firmness in this epistle [26] also that thou shouldst lead our provincials rather by flatteries and exhortations to recognize the care of the gods. Hence, if any one 21 of his own choice should decide to adopt the worship of the gods, it is fitting that he should be welcomed, but if any should wish to follow their own religion, do thou leave it in their power. Wherefore it behooves thy 22 devotedness to observe that which is committed to thee, and to see that power is given to no one to oppress our provincials with insults and extortions,[27] since, as already written, it is fitting to recall our provincials to the worship of the gods rather by exhortations and flatteries. But, in order that this command of ours may come to the knowledge of all our provincials, it is incumbent upon thee to proclaim that which has been enjoined, in an edict issued by thyself."

Since he was forced to do this by necessity and did not give the command by his 23 own will, he was not regarded by any one as sincere or trustworthy, because he had already shown his unstable and deceitful disposition after his former similar concession. None 24 of our people, therefore, ventured to hold meetings or even to appear in public, because his communication did not cover this, but only commanded to guard against doing us any injury, and did not give orders that we should hold meetings or build churches or perform any of our customary acts. And yet Constan- 25 tine and Licinius, the advocates of peace and piety, had written him to permit this, and had granted it to all their subjects by edicts and ordinances.[28] But this most impious man did not choose to yield in this matter until, being driven by the divine judgment, he was at last compelled to do it against his will.

---

[20] Nothing could be farther from the truth than this and the following statement.

[21] That is, after the death of Galerius in the year 311. "Maximinus, on receiving this news (i.e. of the death of Galerius), hasted with relays of horses from the East that he might seize the provinces, and, while Licinius delayed, might arrogate to himself the Chalcedonian straits. On his entry into Bithynia, with the view of acquiring immediate popularity, he abolished the tax to the great joy of all. Dissension arose between the two emperors, and almost war. They stood on the opposite shores with their armies. But peace and friendship were established under certain conditions; a treaty was concluded on the narrow sea, and they joined hands" (Lactantius, De mort. pers. 36). See above, chap. 2, note 1.

[22] On these embassies, see ibid. note 3.

[23] There is no sign of such consideration in Maximin's rescript, quoted in chap. 7, above. The sentences which follow are quite

contradictory. Certainly no one could gain from them any idea as to what the emperor had done in the matter.

[24] σεισμούς, literally, "shakings," or "shocks." The word is doubtless used to translate the Latin concussio, which in legal language meant the extortion of money by threats or other similar means. The words concussio, concussor, concutit, are used very frequently by Tertullian in this sense; e.g. in his De fuga in persecutione, chap. 12, ad Scap. chaps. 4 and 5, Apol. chap. 7. See especially Oehler's note on the word in his edition of Tertullian's works, I. p. 484.

[25] βενεφικιαλίων, a simple reproduction of the Latin beneficiarii. These beneficiarii were "free or privileged soldiers, who through the favor of their commander were exempt from menial offices" (Andrews' Lexicon). We are nowhere told, so far as I am aware, that these beneficiarii were especially active in thus practicing extortions upon the Christians; but we can gather from Tertullian's words in the various passages referred to that the Christians had to suffer particularly from the soldiers in this respect, and doubtless from the beneficiarii most of all; for they possessed more leisure than the common soldiers, and at the same time greater opportunity, because of their more intimate relations with the authorities, of bringing the Christians into difficulty by entering accusations against them.

[26] τοῖς γράμμασι. On the use of the plural in speaking of a single epistle, see above, Bk. IV. chap. 8, note 12.

[27] See note 24.

[28] See above, note 17, and below, Bk. X. chap. 5.

CHAPTER X.

The Overthrow of the Tyrants and the Words which they uttered before their Death.[1]

1   THE circumstances which drove him to this course were the following. Being no longer able to sustain the magnitude of the government which had been undeservedly committed to him, in consequence of his want of prudence and imperial understanding, he managed affairs in a base manner, and with his mind unreasonably exalted in all things with boastful pride, even toward his colleagues in the empire who were in every respect his superiors, in birth, in training, in education, in worth and intelligence, and, greatest of all, in temperance and piety toward the true God, he began to venture to act audaciously and to arrogate 2 to himself the first rank.[2] Becoming mad in his folly, he broke the treaties which he had made with Licinius[3] and undertook an implacable war. Then in a brief time he threw all things into confusion, and stirred up every city, and having collected his entire force, comprising an immense number of soldiers, he went forth to battle with him, elated by his hopes in demons, whom he supposed to be gods, and 3 by the number of his soldiers. And when he joined battle[4] he was deprived of the oversight of God, and the victory was given to Licinius,[5] who was then ruling, by the one 4 and only God of all. First, the army in which he trusted was destroyed, and as all his guards abandoned him and left him alone, and fled to the victor, he secretly divested himself as quickly as possible of the imperial garments, which did not fitly belong to him, and in a cowardly and ignoble and unmanly way mingled with the crowd, and then fled, concealing himself in fields and villages.[6] But though he was so careful for his safety, he scarcely escaped the hands of his enemies, revealing by his deeds

that the divine oracles are faithful and true, in which it is said, "A king is not saved by 5 a great force, and a giant shall not be saved by the greatness of his strength ; a horse is a vain thing for safety, nor shall he be delivered by the greatness of his power. Behold, the eyes of the Lord are upon them that fear him, upon them that hope in his mercy, to deliver their souls from death."[7] Thus the ty- 6 rant, covered with shame, went to his own country. And first, in frantic rage, he slew many priests and prophets of the gods whom he had formerly admired, and whose oracles had incited him to undertake the war, as sorcerers and impostors, and besides all as betrayers of his safety. Then having given glory to the God of the Christians and enacted a most full and complete ordinance in behalf of their liberty,[8] he was immediately seized with a mortal disease, and no respite being granted him, departed this life.[9] The law enacted by him was as follows :

Copy of the edict of the tyrant in behalf of 7 *the Christians, translated from the Roman tongue.*

" The Emperor Cæsar Caius Valerius Maximinus, Germanicus, Sarmaticus, Pius, Felix, Invictus, Augustus. We believe it manifest that no one is ignorant, but that every man who looks back over the past knows and is conscious that in every way we care continually for the good of our provincials, and wish to furnish them with those things which are of especial advantage to all, and for the common benefit and profit, and whatever contributes to the public welfare and is agreeable to the views of each. When, 8 therefore, before this, it became clear to our mind that under pretext of the command of our parents, the most divine Diocletian and Maximianus, which enjoined that the meetings of the

---

[1] On the transposition of the titles of chaps. 9 and 10, see the previous chapter, note 1.

[2] That Maximin should arrogate to himself, as Eusebius says, the highest rank is not very surprising, when we realize that that position, in so far as any difference in rank between the different rulers was acknowledged, belonged to him by right, inasmuch as he was Constantine's senior (having been first Cæsar when the latter was only second), while Constantine (see above, chap. 9, note 2) was regarded as the senior of Licinius.

[3] The treaty made in 311, just after the death of Galerius (see *De mort. pers.* 36).

[4] This battle between Licinius and Maximin was fought on April 30, 313, at Adrianople, in Thrace. For a more detailed but somewhat imaginative account of the battle, see *De mort. pers.* chap. 45 sq. Lactantius is considerate enough to accord Licinius the honor of a divine vision, that he may not be behind his imperial colleague Constantine; and he is pious enough to ascribe the victory wholly to the divine aid vouchsafed in response to the prayers of Licinius and his soldiers.

[5] The word Licinius is omitted by Laemmer and Heinichen, but without sufficient warrant, for it is found in nearly all the MSS.

[6] Lactantius (*ibid.* chap. 47) informs us that Maximin's flight was so rapid that he reached Nicomedia, which was 160 miles from Adrianople, on the evening of the day following the battle. As Gibbon remarks, " The incredible speed which Maximin exerted in his flight is much more celebrated than his prowess in battle."

[7] Ps. xxxiii. 16–19.

[8] The final toleration edict of Maximin must have been issued very soon after his defeat, and its occasion is plain enough. If he were to oppose Licinius successfully, he must secure the loyalty of all his subjects, and this could be done only by granting the Christians full toleration. He could see plainly enough that Licinius' religious policy was a success in securing the allegiance of his subjects, and he found himself compelled in self-defense to pursue a similar course, distasteful as it was to him. · There is no sign that he had any other motive in taking this step. Religious considerations seem to have had nothing to do with it; he was doubtless as much of a pagan as ever. The edict itself is composed in an admirable vein. As Mason remarks, " Maximin made the concession with so much dignity and grace, that it is impossible to help wishing that his language were truer." As in the previous decree, he indulges his passion for lying without restraint; but, unlike that one, the present edict is straightforward and consistent throughout, and grants the Christians full liberty in the most unequivocal terms.

[9] Maximin's death took place at Tarsus (according to *De mort. pers.* chap. 49), and apparently within a few weeks after his defeat at Adrianople and the publication of his edict of toleration. The reports of his death are somewhat conflicting. Zosimus and the epitomist of Victor say merely that he died a natural death; Lactantius tells us that he took poison; while Eusebius in § 14 sq. gives us a horrible account of his last sickness which, according to him, was marked, to say the least, with some rather remarkable symptoms. Mason facetiously remarks that Eusebius seems to be thinking of a spontaneous combustion. It was quite the fashion in the early Church to tell dreadful tales in connection with the deaths

Christians should be abolished, many extortions[10] and spoliations had been practiced by officials; and that those evils were continually increasing, to the detriment of our provincials, toward whom we are especially anxious to exercise proper care, and that their possessions were in consequence perishing, letters were sent last year[11] to the governors of each province, in which we decreed that, if any one wished to follow such a practice or to observe this same religion, he should be permitted without hindrance to pursue his purpose and should be impeded and prevented by no one, and that all should have liberty to do without any fear or suspi-

9 cion that which each preferred. But even now we cannot help perceiving that some of the judges have mistaken our commands, and have given our people reason to doubt the meaning of our ordinances, and have caused them to proceed too reluctantly to the observance of those religious rites which are pleasing to

10 them. In order, therefore, that in the future every suspicion of fearful doubt may be taken away, we have commanded that this decree be published, so that it may be clear to all that whoever wishes to embrace this sect and religion is permitted to do so by virtue of this grant of ours; and that each one, as he wishes or as is pleasing to him, is permitted to practice this religion which he has chosen to observe according to his custom. It is also granted them to

11 build Lord's houses. But that this grant of ours may be the greater, we have thought good to decree also that if any houses and lands before this time rightfully belonged to the Christians, and by the command of our parents fell into the treasury, or were confiscated by any city, — whether they have been sold or presented to any one as a gift, — that all these should be restored to their original possessors, the Christians, in order that in this also every one may have knowledge of our piety and care."

12 These are the words of the tyrant which were published not quite a year after the decrees against the Christians engraved by him on pillars.[12] And by him to whom a little before we seemed impious wretches and atheists and destroyers of all life, so that we were not permitted to dwell in any city nor even in country or desert, — by him decrees and ordinances were issued in behalf of the Christians, and they

who recently had been destroyed by fire and sword, by wild beasts and birds of prey, in the presence of the tyrant himself, and had suffered every species of torture and punishment, and most miserable deaths as atheists and impious wretches, were now acknowledged by him as possessors of religion and were permitted to build churches; and the tyrant himself bore witness and confessed that they had some rights. And having made such confessions, 13 as if he had received some benefit on account of them, he suffered perhaps less than he ought to have suffered, and being smitten by a sudden scourge of God, he perished in the second campaign of the war. But his end 14 was not like that of military chieftains who, while fighting bravely in battle for virtue and friends, often boldly encounter a glorious death; for like an impious enemy of God, while his army was still drawn up in the field, remaining at home and concealing himself, he suffered the punishment which he deserved. For he was smitten with a sudden scourge of God in his whole body, and harassed by terrible pains and torments, he fell prostrate on the ground, wasted by hunger, while all his flesh was dissolved by an invisible and God-sent fire, so that the whole appearance of his frame was changed, and there was left only a kind of image wasted away by length of time to a skeleton of dry bones; so that those who were present could think of his body as nothing else than the tomb of his soul, which was buried in a body already dead and completely melted away. And as the 15 heat still more violently consumed him in the depths of his marrow, his eyes burst forth, and falling from their sockets left him blind. Thereupon still breathing and making free confession to the Lord, he invoked death, and at last, after acknowledging that he justly suffered these things on account of his violence against Christ, he gave up the ghost.

CHAPTER XI.

The Final Destruction of the Enemies of Religion.

THUS when Maximinus, who alone had 1 remained of the enemies of religion[1] and had appeared the worst of them all, was put out of the way, the renovation of the churches from their foundations was begun by the grace of God the Ruler of all, and the word of Christ, shining unto the glory of the God of the universe, obtained greater freedom than before,

---

of the persecutors, but in the present case exaggeration is hardly necessary, for it would seem from Lactantius' account, that he died not of poison, as he states, but of delirium tremens. As Mason remarks, "It is probable that Maximin died of nothing worse than a natural death. But the death which was natural to him was the most dreadful perhaps that men can die. Maximin was known as an habitual drunkard; and in his dying delirium he is said to have cried out that he saw God, with assessors, all in white robes, judging him." [10] See chap. 9, note 24.

[11] i.e. the epistle addressed to Sabinus, and quoted in the previous chapter, which was written toward the end of 312 (see that chapter, note 18).

[12] See above, chap. 7.

[1] Maximian died in 310 (see above, Bk. VIII. chap. 13, note 23), Galerius in 311 (see *ibid.* chap. 16, note 5), Maxentius in 312 (see above, chap. 9, note 7), and Diocletian early in 313 (see Bk. VIII. App. note 3).

while the impious enemies of religion were covered with extremest shame and dishonor.

2 For Maximinus himself, being first pronounced by the emperors a common enemy, was declared by public proclamations to be a most impious, execrable, and God-hating tyrant. And of the portraits which had been set up in every city in honor of him or of his children, some were thrown down from their places to the ground, and torn in pieces ; while the faces of others were obliterated by daubing them with black paint. And the statues which had been erected to his honor were likewise overthrown and broken, and lay exposed to the laughter and sport of those who wished to insult and **3** abuse them. Then also all the honors of the other enemies of religion were taken away, and all those who sided with Maximinus were slain, especially those who had been honored by him with high offices in reward for their flattery, and had behaved insolently toward **4** our doctrine. Such an one was Peucetius,[2] the dearest of his companions, who had been honored and rewarded by him above all, who had been consul a second and third time, and had been appointed by him chief minister ;[3] and Culcianus,[4] who had likewise advanced through every grade of office, and was also celebrated for his numberless executions of Christians in Egypt ;[5] and besides these not a few others, by whose agency especially the tyranny of Maximinus had been confirmed and ex- **5** tended. And Theotecnus[6] also was sum-

[2] Of this Peucetius (Rufinus *Peucedius*) we know only what is told us here. Valesius says : "The name is to be rendered *Picentius*, a name which was borne by a certain *calumniator* in the time of Constantine, as is stated by Zosimus at the end of his second book. The Latins, indeed, call them *Picentes* whom the Greeks call Πυκετίους."

[3] τῶν καθόλου λόγων ἔπαρχος, apparently equivalent to the phrase ἐπὶ τῶν καθόλου λόγων, used in Bk. VII. chap. 10, § 5. On its significance, see the note on that passage, and cf. Valesius' note *ad locum*.

[4] This same Culcianus appears in the *Acts of St. Phileas of Thmuis* (Ruinart, p. 434 sq.; see the extract printed in Mason, p. 290 sq.) as the magistrate or governor under whom Phileas suffered in Thebais. He is doubtless to be identified, as Valesius remarks, with Culeianus (Κουληιανός) mentioned by Epiphanius (*Hær.* LXVIII. 1) as governor of Thebais at the time of the rise of the Meletian schism, while Hierocles was governor of Alexandria.

[5] Culcianus seems to have been governor of Thebais (where Phileas suffered, according to Bk. VIII. chap. 9), not of Egypt. Possibly Eusebius employs the word Egypt in its general sense, as including Thebais.

[6] On Theotecnus, see above, chap. 2, note 4.

moned by justice which by no means overlooked his deeds against the Christians. For when the statue had been set up by him at Antioch,[7] he appeared to be in the happiest state, and was already made a governor by Maximinus. But Licinius, coming down to the city of **6** Antioch, made a search for impostors, and tortured the prophets and priests of the newly erected statue, asking them for what reason they practiced their deception. They, under the stress of torture, were unable longer to conceal the matter, and declared that the whole deceptive mystery had been devised by the art of Theotecnus. Therefore, after meting out to all of them just judgment, he first put Theotecnus himself to death, and then his confederates in the imposture, with the severest possible tortures. To all these were added also the **7** children[8] of Maximinus, whom he had already made sharers in the imperial dignity, by placing their names on tablets and statues. And the relatives of the tyrant, who before had been boastful and had in their pride oppressed all men, suffered the same punishments with those who have been already mentioned, as well as the extremest disgrace. For they had not received instruction, neither did they know and understand the exhortation given in the Holy Word : " Put not your trust in prin- **8** ces, nor in the sons of men, in whom there is no salvation ; his spirit shall go forth and return to his earth ; in that day all their thoughts perish." [9]

The impious ones having been thus **9** removed, the government was preserved firm and undisputed for Constantine and Licinius, to whom it fittingly belonged. They, having first of all cleansed the world of hostility to the Divine Being, conscious of the benefits which he had conferred upon them, showed their love of virtue and of God, and their piety and gratitude to the Deity, by their ordinance in behalf of the Christians.[10]

[7] See chap. 3.
[8] Lactantius (*De mort. pers.* chap. 50) tells us that Maximin left a wife and two children, a boy eight years old, named Maximus, and a daughter seven years old who was betrothed to Candidianus.
[9] Ps. cxlvi. 3, 4.
[10] See below, Bk. X. chap. 5.

BOOK X.

CHAPTER I.

The Peace granted us by God.

1   THANKS for all things be given unto God the Omnipotent Ruler and King of the universe, and the greatest thanks to Jesus Christ the Saviour and Redeemer of our souls, through whom we pray that peace may be always preserved for us firm and undisturbed by external troubles and by troubles of the mind.

2   Since in accordance with thy wishes, my most holy Paulinus,[1] we have added the tenth book of the Church History to those which have preceded,[2] we will inscribe it to thee, proclaiming thee as the seal of the whole

3   work; and we will fitly add in a perfect number the perfect panegyric upon the restoration of the churches,[3] obeying the Divine Spirit which exhorts us in the following words:

"Sing unto the Lord a new song, for he hath done marvelous things. His right hand and his holy arm hath saved him. The Lord hath made known his salvation, his righteousness hath he revealed in the presence of the nations."[4]

And in accordance with the utterance which   4 commands us to sing the new song, let us proceed to show that, after those terrible and gloomy spectacles which we have described,[5] we are now permitted to see and celebrate such things as many truly righteous men and martyrs of God before us desired to see upon earth and did not see, and to hear and did not hear.[6]

But they, hastening on, obtained far better   5 things,[7] being carried to heaven and the paradise of divine pleasure. But, acknowledging that even these things are greater than we deserve, we have been astonished at the grace manifested by the author of the great gifts, and rightly do we admire him, worshiping him with the whole power of our souls, and testifying to the truth of those recorded utterances, in which it is said, "Come and see the works   6 of the Lord, the wonders which he hath done upon the earth; he removeth wars to the ends of the world, he shall break the bow and snap the spear in sunder, and shall burn the shields with fire."[8]   Rejoicing in these things which have been clearly fulfilled in our day, let us proceed with our account.

The whole race of God's enemies was   7 destroyed in the manner indicated,[9] and was thus suddenly swept from the sight of men. So that again a divine utterance had its fulfillment: "I have seen the impious highly exalted and raising himself like the cedars of Lebanon; and I have passed by, and behold, he was not; and I have sought his place, and it could not be found."[10]   And finally a bright and   8 splendid day, overshadowed by no cloud, illuminated with beams of heavenly light the churches of Christ throughout the entire world. And not even those without our communion[11] were prevented from sharing in the same blessings, or at least from coming under their influ-

---

[1] Paulinus, bishop of Tyre, became afterward bishop of Antioch, as we are told by Eusebius, *Contra Marcellum*, I. 4, and by Philostorgius, *H. E.* III. 15. According to Jerome's *Chron.*, year of Abr. 2345, he was the successor of Philogonius and the predecessor of Eustathius in the episcopate of Antioch. He was still alive when Eusebius completed his *History*, that is, at least as late as 323 (see above, p. 45), but he was already dead when the Council of Nicæa met; for Eustathius was at that time bishop of Antioch (see e.g. Sozomen, *H. E.* I. 17, Theodoret, *H. E.* I. 7, and the Acts of the Council of Nicæa, ed. Labbei et Cossartii, I. p. 51), and Zeno, bishop of Tyre (see the Acts of the Nicene Council, *ibid.*). Philostorgius (*ibid.*) informs us that he became bishop of Antioch but six months before his death, and there is no reason to doubt the statement. Eusebius speaks of him in the highest terms, both here and in his *Contra Marcellum*, and it was at the dedication of his church in Tyre that he delivered the panegyric oration quoted in chap. 4, below. He is claimed as a sympathizer by Arius in his epistle to Eusebius of Nicomedia (Theodoret, *H. E.* I. 5), and that he accepted Arius' tenets is implied by Eusebius of Nicomedia, who, however, feels obliged to admonish him for not showing greater zeal in the support of the cause (see this epistle quoted by Theodoret, *H. E.* I. 6). This is the extent of our information in regard to him.

[2] On the date of the composition of the tenth book of the *History*, and its relation to the earlier books, see above, p. 45.

[3] εἰκότως δ' ἐν ἀριθμῷ τελείῳ τὸν τέλειον ἐνταῦθα καὶ πανηγυρικὸν τῆς τῶν ἐκκλησιῶν ἀνανεώσεως λόγον κατατάξομεν. The meaning of this sentence is very obscure. Valesius translates: *Nec absurde ut opinor, absolutam omnibus numeris orationem panegyricam de ecclesiarum instauratione hic in perfecto numero collocabimus.* Stroth, followed by Closs, renders: "Mit Recht werden wir hier auch eine vollständige feierliche Rede, von der Wiedererneuerung der Kirchen, als einen ordentlichen Theil miteinrücken." Crusè reads: "Justly, indeed, shall we here subjoin in a perfect number a complete discourse and panegyric on the renovation of the churches." The "perfect number" seems to refer to the number of the book (the number ten being commonly so called in ancient times), to which he has referred in the previous clause. Could we regard the "perfect panegyric" as referring to the book as a whole, as Crusè does, the sentence would be somewhat clearer; but the phrase seems to be a plain reference to the oration given in chap. 4, especially since Eusebius does not say τῆς ἐκκλησίας, but τῶν ἐκκλησιῶν, as in the title of that oration. I have preserved the play of words, τελείῳ — τέλειον, in order to bring out Eusebius' thought more clearly, but it must be remarked that the word τέλειον does not imply perfection of the quality of his oration on the author's part. It is used rather in the sense of complete or final, because it celebrates a completed work, as the tenth book completes his *History*, and thus crowns the whole.

[4] Psa. xcviii. 1, 2.

[5] Literally, "spectacles and narratives" (ὄψεις τε καὶ διηγήσεις).

[6] Cf. Matt. xiii. 17.   [7] Cf. Phil. i. 23.

[8] Psa. xlvi. 8, 9.

[9] See chaps. 10 and 11 of the preceding book.

[10] Psa. xxxvii. 35, 36.

[11] τοῖς ἔξωθεν τοῦ καθ' ἡμᾶς θιάσου.

ence and enjoying a part of the benefits bestowed upon us by God.[12]

CHAPTER II.

The Restoration of the Churches.

1 ALL men, then, were freed from the oppression of the tyrants, and being released from the former ills, one in one way and another in another acknowledged the defender of the pious to be the only true God. And we especially who placed our hopes in the Christ of God had unspeakable gladness, and a certain inspired joy bloomed for all of us, when we saw every place which shortly before had been desolated by the impieties of the tyrants reviving as if from a long and death-fraught pestilence, and temples again rising from their foundations to an immense height, and receiving a splendor far greater than that of the old ones which had been destroyed.

2 But the supreme rulers also confirmed to us still more extensively the munificence of God by repeated ordinances in behalf of the Christians ; and personal letters of the emperor were sent to the bishops, with honors and gifts of money. It may not be unfitting to insert these documents, translated from the Roman into the Greek tongue, at the proper place in this book,[1] as in a sacred tablet, that they may remain as a memorial to all who shall come after us.

CHAPTER III.

The Dedications in Every Place.

1 AFTER this was seen the sight which had been desired and prayed for by us all; feasts of dedication in the cities and consecrations of the newly built houses of prayer took place, bishops assembled, foreigners came together from abroad, mutual love was exhibited between people and people, the members of Christ's body were united in complete har-

2 mony. Then was fulfilled the prophetic utterance which mystically foretold what was to take place : " Bone to bone and joint to joint,"[1] and whatever was truly announced in enigmatic expressions in the inspired pas-

3 sage. And there was one energy of the

Divine Spirit pervading all the members, and one soul in all, and the same eagerness of faith, and one hymn from all in praise of the Deity. Yea, and perfect services were conducted by the prelates, the sacred rites being solemnized, and the majestic institutions of the Church observed,[2] here with the singing of psalms and with the reading of the words committed to us by God, and there with the performance of divine and mystic services ; and the mysterious symbols of the Saviour's passion were dispensed. At the same time people of every 4 age, both male and female, with all the power of the mind gave honor unto God, the author of their benefits, in prayers and thanksgiving, with a joyful mind and soul. And every one of the bishops present, each to the best of his ability, delivered panegyric orations, adding luster to the assembly.

CHAPTER IV.

Panegyric on the Splendor of Affairs.

1 A CERTAIN one of those of moderate talent,[1] who had composed a discourse, stepped forward in the presence of many pastors who were assembled as if for a church gathering, and while they attended quietly and decently, he addressed himself as follows to one who was in all things a most excellent bishop and beloved of God,[2] through whose zeal the temple in Tyre, which was the most splendid in Phœnicia, had been erected.

Panegyric upon the building of the churches, 2 *addressed to Paulinus, Bishop of Tyre.*

" Friends and priests of God who are clothed in the sacred gown and adorned with the heavenly crown of glory, the inspired unction and the sacerdotal garment of the Holy Spirit ; and thou,[3] oh pride of God's new holy temple, endowed by him with the wisdom of age, and yet exhibiting costly works and deeds of youthful and flourishing virtue, to whom God himself, who embraces the entire world, has granted the distinguished honor of building and renewing this earthly house to Christ, his only begotten and first-born Word, and to his holy and divine bride ;[4] — one might call thee a new Beseleel,[5] 3 the architect of a divine tabernacle, or Solomon, king of a new and much better Jerusalem,

---

[12] By the edict of Constantine and Licinius full religious liberty was granted, not only to the Christians, but to all men of whatever creed or cult.

[1] See below, chaps. 5–7.   [1] Ezek. xxxvii. 7.

[2] These sentences are excellent examples of Eusebius' rhetorical style, which marks the greater part of this tenth book. My endeavor has been to adhere as closely as possible to the original; and yet there are cases in which it is quite out of the question to give a literal translation without violating all grammatical laws, and in which the sense can be reproduced only by paraphrasing. The present sentence runs ναὶ μὴν καὶ τῶν προηγουμένων ἐντελεῖς θρησκείαι, ἱερουργίαι τε τῶν ἱερωμένων, καὶ θεοπρεπεῖς ἐκκλησίας θεσμοί.

[1] This person was clearly Eusebius himself (see above, p. 11). Upon the date of this dedicatory service, at which Eusebius delivered the oration given in full in this chapter, see *ibid.*

[2] Paulinus, bishop of Tyre. See above, chap. 1, note 1.
[3] i.e. Paulinus.   [4] Cf. Rev. xxi. 2.
[5] βεσελεήλ, which is the form found in the LXX. The Hebrew is בְּצַלְאֵל, which the R. V. renders " Bezalel." See Ex. xxxv. 30 sq.

or also a new Zerubabel, who added a much greater glory than the former to the temple
4 of God ;[6] — and you also, oh nurslings of the sacred flock of Christ, habitation of good words, school of wisdom, and august
5 and pious auditory of religion :[7] It was long ago permitted us to raise hymns and songs to God, when we learned from hearing the Divine Scriptures read the marvelous signs of God and the benefits conferred upon men by the Lord's wondrous deeds, being taught to say 'Oh God ! we have heard with our ears, our fathers have told us the work which thou didst in their
6 days, in days of old.'[8] But now as we no longer perceive the lofty arm[9] and the celestial right hand of our all-gracious God and universal King by hearsay merely or report, but observe so to speak in very deed and with our own eyes that the declarations recorded long ago are faithful and true, it is permitted us to raise a second hymn of triumph and to sing with loud voice, and say, 'As we have heard, so have we seen; in the city of the Lord of hosts, in the city of our God.'[10]
7 And in what city but in this newly built and God-constructed one, which is a 'church of the living God, a pillar and foundation of the truth,'[11] concerning which also another divine oracle thus proclaims, 'Glorious things have been spoken of thee, oh city of God.'[12] Since the all-gracious God has brought us together to it, through the grace of his Only-Begotten, let every one of those who have been summoned sing with loud voice and say, ' I was glad when they said unto me, we shall go unto the house of the Lord,'[13] and 'Lord, I have loved the beauty of thy house and the place
8 where thy glory dwelleth.'[14] And let us not only one by one, but all together, with one spirit and one soul, honor him and cry aloud, saying, 'Great is the Lord and greatly to be praised in the city of our God, in his holy mountain.'[15] For he is truly great, and great is his house, lofty and spacious and 'comely in beauty above the sons of men.'[16] 'Great is the Lord who alone doeth wonderful things' ;[17] 'great is he who doeth great things and things past finding out, glorious and marvelous things which cannot be numbered' ;[18] great is he 'who changeth times and seasons, who exalteth and debaseth kings' ;[19] 'who raiseth up the poor from the earth and lifteth up the needy from

the dunghill.'[20] 'He hath put down princes from their thrones and hath exalted them of low degree from the earth. The hungry he hath filled with good things and the arms of the proud he hath broken.'[21] Not only to
9 the faithful, but also to unbelievers, has he confirmed the record of ancient events ; he that worketh miracles, he that doeth great things, the Master of all, the Creator of the whole world, the omnipotent, the all-merciful, the one and only God. To him let us sing the new song,[22] supplying in thought,[23] 'To him who alone doeth great wonders : for his mercy endureth forever' ;[24] 'To him which smote great kings, and slew famous kings : for his mercy endureth forever' ;[25] 'For the Lord remembered us in our low estate and delivered us from our adversaries.'[26] And let us never cease to
10 cry aloud in these words to the Father of the universe. And let us always honor him with our mouth who is the second cause of our benefits, the instructor in divine knowledge, the teacher of the true religion, the destroyer of the impious, the slayer of tyrants, the reformer of life, Jesus, the Saviour of us who were in despair. For he alone, as the only all-
11 gracious Son of an all-gracious Father, in accordance with the purpose of his Father's benevolence, has willingly put on the nature of us who lay prostrate in corruption, and like some excellent physician, who for the sake of saving them that are ill, examines their sufferings, handles their foul sores, and reaps pain for himself from the miseries of another,[27] so us who were not only diseased and afflicted with terrible ulcers and wounds already mortified, but were even lying among the dead, he hath saved for himself from the very jaws of death. For none other of those in heaven had such

---

[20] 1 Sam. ii. 8 (Psa. cxiii. 7).
[21] Luke i. 52, 53.   [22] Cf. Psa. xcvi. 1.
[23] προσυπακούοντες. Eusebius seems to use this rather peculiar expression because the words of song which he suggests are not the words of the "new song" given by the Psalmist, but are taken from other parts of the book.   [24] Psa. cxxxvi. 4.
[25] Ibid. 17.   [26] Ibid. 23, 24.
[27] It is remarked by Valesius that these words are taken from some tragic poet. That they are quoted from an ancient writer is clear enough from the Ionic forms which occur (ὁρῇ, ἀλλοτριῇσι, ξυμφορῇσι), and if a few slight changes be made (καμνόντων to καμόντων, ἕνεκεν to εἵνεκεν, μὲν to τὰ, ἐπ' ἀλλοτριῇσι τε to ἀλλοτριῇσι) the words resolve themselves into iambic trimeters: —

τῆς τῶν καμόντων εἵνεκεν σωτηρίας
ὁρῇ τὰ δεινὰ, θιγγάνει δ' ἀηδέων,
ἀλλοτριῇσι συμφορῇσιν ἰδίας
καρποῦται λύπας.

According to Valesius, Gregory Nazianzen in his first Oratio quotes the last verse (καὶ τὸ ἐπ' ἀλλοτρίαις συμφοραῖς ἰδίας καρποῦσθαι λύπας, in which there is no trace of the poetical form) with the remark ὡς ἔφη τις τῶν παρ' ἐκείνοις σοφῶν; and Valesius adds: "Ad quem locum Elias Cretensis notat verba hæc esse Hippocratis quem Gregorius Nazianzenus sapientis cujusdam nomine designat." Moreover, Schwegler remarks that the words are taken from Hippocrates. In a note ad locum he says: "Hippocratis medici (cf. Hippocr. de Flat. init. p. 78, ed. Foes) quæ eadem laudantur et ab aliis Scriptoribus, veluti a Luciano in Bis. Accus. c. I. p. 49, ed. Bip. Cf. quæ interpretes adnotaverunt ad Luciani, l.c. Tom. VII. p. 400, ed. Bip." I have not examined these references, and can therefore form no judgment in the matter.

---

[6] See Hag. ii. 9.
[7] Eusebius addresses first the assembled clergymen in general, then Paulinus in particular, and finally the people, calling the latter "nurslings," "habitation," "school," "auditory." The significance of the words as used by him is plain enough, but their collocation is rather remarkable.
[8] Psa. xliv. 1.
[9] Cf. Ex. vi. 6 et al.
[10] Psa. xlviii. 8.
[11] 1 Tim. iii. 15.
[12] Psa. lxxxvii. 3.
[13] Psa. cxxii. 1.
[14] Psa. xxvi. 8.
[15] Psa. xlviii. 1.
[16] Psa. xlv. 2.
[17] Psa. cxxxvi. 4.
[18] Job ix. 10.
[19] Dan. ii. 21.

power as without harm [28] to minister to the salvation of so many. But he alone having reached our deep corruption, he alone having taken upon himself our labors, he alone having suffered the punishments due for our impieties, having recovered us who were not half dead merely, but were already in tombs and sepulchers, and altogether foul and offensive, saves us, both anciently and now, by his beneficent zeal, beyond the expectation of any one, even of ourselves, and imparts liberally of the Father's benefits, — he who is the giver of life and light, our great Physician and King and Lord, the Christ of God. For then when the whole human race lay buried in gloomy night and in depths of darkness through the deceitful arts of guilty demons and the power of God-hating spirits, by his simple appearing he loosed once for all the fast-bound cords of our impieties by the rays of his light, even as wax is melted. But when malignant envy and the evil-loving demon wellnigh burst with anger at such grace and kindness, and turned against us all his death-dealing forces, and when, at first, like a dog gone mad which gnashes his teeth at the stones thrown at him, and pours out his rage against his assailants upon the inanimate missiles, he leveled his ferocious madness at the stones of the sanctuaries and at the lifeless material of the houses, and desolated the churches, — at least as he supposed, — and then emitted terrible hissings and snake-like sounds, now by the threats of impious tyrants, and again by the blasphemous edicts of profane rulers, vomiting forth death, moreover, and infecting with his deleterious and soul-destroying poisons the souls captured by him, and almost slaying them by his death-fraught sacrifices of dead idols, and causing every beast in the form of man and every kind of savage to assault us, — then, indeed, the 'Angel of the great Council,' [29] the great Captain [30] of God, after the mightiest soldiers of his kingdom had displayed sufficient exercise through patience and endurance in everything, suddenly appeared anew, and blotted out and annihilated his enemies and foes, so that they seemed never to have had even a name. But his friends and relatives he raised to the highest glory, in the presence not only of all men, but also of celestial powers, of sun and moon and stars, and of the whole heaven and earth, so that now, as has never happened before, the su-

preme rulers, conscious of the honor which they have received from him, spit upon the faces of dead idols, trample upon the unhallowed rites of demons, make sport of the ancient delusion handed down from their fathers, and acknowledge only one God, the common benefactor of all, themselves included. And they confess Christ, the Son of God, universal King of all, and proclaim him Saviour on monuments, [31] imperishably recording in imperial letters, in the midst of the city which rules over the earth, his righteous deeds and his victories over the impious. Thus Jesus Christ our Saviour is the only one from all eternity who has been acknowledged, even by those highest in the earth, not as a common king among men, but as a true son of the universal God, and who has been worshiped as very God, [32] and that rightly. For what king that ever lived attained such virtue as to fill the ears and tongues of all men upon earth with his own name? What king, after ordaining such pious and wise laws, has extended them from one end of the earth to the other, so that they are perpetually read in the hearing of all men? Who has abrogated barbarous and savage customs of uncivilized nations by his gentle and most philanthropic laws? Who, being attacked for entire ages by all, has shown such superhuman virtue as to flourish daily, and remain young throughout his life? Who has founded a nation which of old was not even heard of, but which now is not concealed in some corner of the earth, but is spread abroad everywhere under the sun? Who has so fortified his soldiers with the arms of piety that their souls, being firmer than adamant, shine brilliantly in the contests with their opponents? What king prevails to such an extent, and even after death leads on his soldiers, and sets up trophies over his

---

[28] ἀβλαβῶς. The application of the word is not perfectly clear, but the meaning seems to be "without harm to himself," "unharmed." "He is the only one able to minister to our salvation without sinking under the weight of the burden, or suffering from his contact with us." Eusebius is perhaps thinking especially of Christ's absolute sinlessness and victory over all temptation; perhaps only in a more general way of the great strength needed for such a task, strength possessed by Christ alone in sufficient measure to prevent his own complete exhaustion under the immense task.
[29] Cf. Isa. ix. 6.   [30] μέγας ἀρχιστράτηγος; cf. Josh. v. 13.

[31] This seems to be simply a rhetorical expression of what is recorded in Bk. IX. chap. 9, in regard to the great statue of Constantine with a cross in his hand, erected in Rome after his victory over Maxentius. It is possible that other smaller monuments of a similar kind were erected at the same time.
[32] αὐτοθεόν. The exact sense in which Eusebius uses this word is open to dispute. That it asserts the Son to be possessed per se, in and of himself, of absolute deity, — that is, that he is self-existent, — can hardly be maintained, though Valesius does maintain it. The word admits some latitude of meaning, as Heinichen shows (in his edition of Eusebius, III. p. 736 sq., Melet. XX.), and its use does not forbid a belief in the subordination of the Son. In my opinion it clearly indicates a belief in an essential deity of the Son, but not a full and absolute deity. Stein, in his Eusebius, p. 138, remarks: "Eusebius wendet hier die platonischen Ausdrücke nach dem Vorbilde des Origenes auf das Wesen des Sohnes an. Nach Origenes bezeichnen diese Ausdrücke die Absolutheit die Sohnes, nach den Platonikern jedoch bedeuten sie nicht das höchste Wesen. Es ist nun Zweifelhaft, ob Eusebius mit diesen Begriffen den Sinn des Origenes, oder den der Platoniker verknüpft habe." There can be little doubt, in my opinion, that Eusebius followed Origen so far as he understood him, but that he never carried the essential deity of the Son so far as to cease to think of some kind of an essential subordination. See the discussion of Eusebius' position, on p. 11 sq. of this volume. I have translated the word αὐτοθεόν "very God," because there seems to be no other phrase which does not necessarily express more, or less, than Eusebius means by the word. It must be remembered, however, that in using the phrase which is commonly employed to translate the later Nicene ἀληθινὸν θεόν, I do not use it in the full sense thus ordinarily attached to it.

enemies, and fills every place, country and city, Greek and barbarian, with his royal dwellings, even divine temples with their consecrated oblations, like this very temple with its superb adornments and votive offerings, which are themselves so truly great and majestic, worthy of wonder and admiration, and clear signs of the sovereignty of our Saviour? For now, too, ' he spake, and they were made ; he commanded, and they were created.' [33] For what was there to resist the nod of the universal King and Governor and Word of God himself? [34]

21 "A special discourse would be needed accurately to survey and explain all this ; and also to describe how great the zeal of the laborers is regarded by him who is celebrated as divine, [35] who looks upon the living temple which we all constitute, and surveys the house, composed of living and moving stones, which is well and surely built upon the foundation of the apostles and prophets, the chief cornerstone being Jesus Christ himself, who has been rejected not only by the builders of that ancient building which no longer stands, but also by the builders — evil architects of evil works — of the structure, which is composed of the mass of men and still endures. [36] But the Father has approved him both then and now, and has made him the head of the corner 22 of this our common church. Who that beholds this living temple of the living God formed of ourselves — this greatest and truly divine sanctuary, I say, whose inmost shrines are invisible to the multitude and are truly holy and a holy of holies — would venture to declare it? Who is able even to look within the sacred enclosure, except the great High Priest of all, to whom alone it is permitted to fathom 23 the mysteries of every rational soul? But perhaps it is granted to another, to one only, to be second after him in the same work, namely, to the commander of this army whom the first and great High Priest himself has honored with the second place in this sanctuary, the shepherd of your divine flock who has

obtained your people by the allotment and the judgment of the Father, as if he had appointed him his own servant and interpreter, a new Aaron or Melchizedec, made like the Son of God, remaining and continually preserved by him in accordance with the united prayers of all of you. To him therefore alone let 24 it be granted, if not in the first place, at least in the second after the first and greatest High Priest, to observe and supervise the inmost state of your souls, — to him who by experience and length of time has accurately proved each one, and who by his zeal and care has disposed you all in pious conduct and doctrine, and is better able than any one else to give an account, adequate to the facts, of those things which he himself has accomplished with the Divine assistance. As to our first and great 25 High Priest, it is said, [37] ' Whatsoever he seeth the Father doing those things likewise the Son also doeth.' [38] So also this one, [39] looking up to him as to the first teacher, with pure eyes of the mind, using as archetypes whatsoever things he seeth him doing, produceth images of them, making them so far as is possible in the same likeness, in nothing inferior to that Beseleel, whom God himself ' filled with the spirit of wisdom and understanding ' [40] and with other technical and scientific knowledge, and called to be the maker of the temple constructed after heavenly types given in symbols. Thus this 26 one also bearing in his own soul the image of the whole Christ, the Word, the Wisdom, the Light, has formed this magnificent temple of the highest God, corresponding to the pattern of the greater as a visible to an invisible, it is impossible to say with what greatness of soul, with what wealth and liberality of mind, and with what emulation on the part of all of you, shown in the magnanimity of the contributors who have ambitiously striven in no way to be left behind by him in the execution of the same purpose. And this place, — for this deserves to be mentioned first of all, — which had been covered with all sorts of rubbish by the artifices of our enemies he did not overlook, nor did he yield to the wickedness of those who had brought about that condition of things, although he might have chosen some other place, for many other sites were available in the city, where he would have had less labor, and been free from trouble. But having first aroused himself 27 to the work, and then strengthened the whole people with zeal, and formed them all into one great body, he fought the first contest. For he thought that this church, which had been

---

[33] Psa. xxxiii. 9.

[34] τοῦ παμβασιλέως καὶ πανηγεμόνος καὶ αὐτοῦ θεοῦ λόγου. Valesius translates, *Verbi omnium regis ac principis ac per se Dei;* Closs, " des Wortes, das der König aller Könige, der oberste Fürst und selbst Gott ist "; Crusè, " The universal King, the universal Prince, and God, the Word himself." A conception is thus introduced which the clause as it stands, without the repetition of the article with λόγου, seems to me hardly to warrant. At any rate, the rendering which I have adopted seems more accurately to reproduce the original.

[35] θεολογουμένῳ. The use of the word θεολογέω in the sense of speaking of, or celebrating a person as divine, or attributing divinity to a person, was very common among the Fathers, especially in connection with Christ. See Suicer's *Thesaurus, s.v.* II. and Bk. V. chap. 28, § 4, above.

[36] Eusebius' reference to these various buildings is somewhat confusing. He speaks first of the Church of Christ, " the living temple which we all constitute"; then of the Jews, " the builders of that ancient temple which no longer stands"; and finally, as it seems, of the heathen, " builders of the structure which still endures and is composed of the mass of men " (τῶν πολλῶν ἀνθρώπων).

[37] Literally, " it says " (φησί), i.e. " the Scripture says."
[38] John v. 19.
[39] i.e. Paulinus.   [40] Ex. xxxv. 31.

especially besieged by the enemy, which had first suffered and endured the same persecutions with us and for us, like a mother bereft of her children, should rejoice with us in the signal 28 favor of the all-merciful God.   For when the Great Shepherd had driven away the wild animals and wolves and every cruel and savage beast, and, as the divine oracles say, 'had broken the jaws of the lions,'[41] he thought good to collect again her children in the same place, and in the most righteous manner he set up the fold of her flock, 'to put to shame the enemy and avenger,'[42] and to refute the impious daring of the enemies of God.[43] 29 And now they are not, — the haters of God, — for they never were.   After they had troubled and been troubled for a little time, they suffered the fitting punishment, and brought themselves and their friends and their relatives to total destruction, so that the declarations inscribed of old in sacred records have been proved true by facts.   In these declarations the divine word truly says among other things 30 the following concerning them : 'The wicked have drawn out the sword, they have bent their bow, to slay the righteous in heart ; let their sword enter into their own heart and their bows be broken.'[44]   And again : 'Their memorial is perished with a sound '[45] and 'their name hast thou blotted out forever and ever ';[46] for when they also were in trouble they 'cried out, and there was none to save : unto the Lord, and he heard them not.'[47]   But 'their feet were bound together, and they fell, but we have arisen and stand upright.'[48]   And that which was announced beforehand in these words, — 'O Lord, in thy city thou shalt set at naught their image,'[49] — has been shown to be true 31 to the eyes of all.   But having waged war like the giants against God,[50] they died in this way.   But she that was desolate and rejected by men received the consummation which we behold in consequence of her patience toward God, so that the prophecy of Isaiah 32 was spoken of her : 'Rejoice, thirsty desert, let the desert rejoice and blossom as the lily, and the desert places shall blossom and be glad.'[51]   'Be strengthened, ye weak hands and feeble knees.   Be of good courage, ye feeble-hearted, in your minds ; be strong, fear not. Behold our God recompenseth judgment and will recompense, he will come and save us.'[52]

'For,' he says, 'in the wilderness water has broken out, and a pool in thirsty ground, and the dry land shall be watered meadows, and in the thirsty ground there shall be springs of water.'[53]   These things which were 33 prophesied long ago have been recorded in sacred books ; but no longer are they transmitted to us by hearsay merely, but in facts. This desert, this dry land, this widowed and deserted one, 'whose gates they cut down with axes like wood in a forest, whom they broke down with hatchet and hammer,'[54] whose books also they destroyed,[55] 'burning with fire the sanctuary of God, and profaning unto the ground the habitation of his name,'[56] 'whom all that passed by upon the way plucked, and whose fences they broke down, whom the boar out of the wood ravaged, and on which the savage wild beast fed,'[57] now by the wonderful power of Christ, when he wills it, has become like a lily.   For at that time also she was chastened at his nod as by a careful father ; 'for whom the Lord loveth he chasteneth, and scourgeth every son whom he receiveth.'[58]   Then after 34 being chastened in a measure, according to the necessities of the case, she is commanded to rejoice anew ; and she blossoms as a lily and exhales her divine odor among all men.   'For,' it is said, 'water hath broken out in the wilderness,'[59] the fountain of the saving bath of divine regeneration.[60]   And now she, who a little before was a desert, 'has become watered meadows, and springs of water have gushed forth in a thirsty land.'[61]   The hands which before were 'weak' have become 'truly strong ';[62] and these works are great and convincing proofs of strong hands.   The knees, also, which before were 'feeble and infirm,' recovering their wonted strength, are moving straight forward in the path of divine knowledge, and hastening to the kindred flock[63] of the all-gracious Shepherd. And if there are any whose souls have been 35 stupefied by the threats of the tyrants, not even they are passed by as incurable by the saving Word ; but he heals them also and urges them on to receive divine comfort, saying, 'Be ye comforted, ye who are faint-hearted ; be ye strengthened, fear not.'[64]   This our new 36 and excellent Zerubabel, having heard the word which announced beforehand, that she who had been made a desert on account of God should enjoy these things, after the bitter cap-

---

[41] Psa. lviii. 6.   Eusebius agrees with the LXX, which reads τὰς μύλας τῶν λεόντων.
[42] Psa. viii. 2.   The LXX has καταλῦσαι instead of Eusebius' καταισχῦναι.
[43] Literally, "the God-fighting, daring deeds of the impious" (ταῖς θεομάχοις τῶν ἀσεβῶν τόλμαις).   [44] Psa. xxxvii. 14, 15.
[45] Psa. ix. 6.   Eusebius agrees with the LXX in reading μετ' ἤχου : "with a sound."
[46] Ibid. 5.   [48] Ibid. xx. 8.
[47] Psa. xviii. 41.   [49] Ibid. lxxiii. 20.
[50] Cf. Bk. I. chap. 2, § 19, above, and the note on that passage.
[51] Isa. xxxv. 1.   [52] Ibid. 3, 4.

[53] Ibid. 6, 7.   [54] Psa. lxxiv. 5, 6.
[55] Diocletian's first edict included the destruction of the sacred books of the Christians, as well as of their churches.   See above, Bk. VIII. chap. 2.
[56] Psa. lxxiv. 7.   [57] Ibid. lxxx. 12, 13.
[58] Heb. xii. 6, with which Eusebius agrees exactly, differing from Prov. iii. 12 in the use of παιδεύει instead of ἐλέγχει.
[59] Isa. xxxv. 6.
[60] τῆς θείας τοῦ σωτηρίου λουτροῦ παλιγγενεσίας.   Cf. Titus iii. 5.
[61] Isa. xxxv. 7.   [63] τὴν οἰκείαν ποίμνην.
[62] Ibid. 3.   [64] Isa. xxxv. 4.

tivity and the abomination of desolation, did not overlook the dead body; but first of all with prayers and supplications propitiated the Father with the common consent of all of you, and invoking the only one that giveth life to the dead as his ally and fellow-worker, raised her that was fallen, after purifying and freeing her from her ills. And he clothed her not with the ancient garment, but with such an one as he had again learned from the sacred oracles, which say clearly, 'And the latter glory of this house 37 shall be greater than the former.'[65] Thus, enclosing a much larger space, he fortified the outer court with a wall surrounding the whole, which should serve as a most secure 38 bulwark for the entire edifice.[66] And he raised and spread out a great and lofty vestibule toward the rays of the rising sun,[67] and furnished those standing far without the sacred enclosure a full view of those within, almost turning the eyes of those who were strangers to the faith, to the entrances, so that no one could pass by without being impressed by the memory of the former desolation and of the present incredible transformation. His hope was that such an one being impressed by this might be attracted and be induced to 39 enter by the very sight. But when one comes within the gates he does not permit him to enter the sanctuary immediately, with impure and unwashed feet; but leaving as large a space as possible between the temple and the outer entrance, he has surrounded and adorned it with four transverse cloisters, making a quadrangular space with pillars rising on every side, which he has joined with lattice-work screens of wood, rising to a suitable height; and he has left an open space[68] in the middle, so that the sky can be seen, and the free air bright in the rays 40 of the sun. Here he has placed symbols

of sacred purifications, setting up fountains opposite the temple which furnish an abundance of water wherewith those who come within the sanctuary may purify themselves. This is the first halting-place of those who enter; and it furnishes at the same time a beautiful and splendid scene to every one, and to those who still need elementary instruction a fitting station. But passing by this spectacle, he has 41 made open entrances to the temple with many other vestibules within, placing three doors on one side, likewise facing the rays of the sun. The one in the middle, adorned with plates of bronze, iron bound, and beautifully embossed, he has made much higher and broader than the others, as if he were making them guards for it as for a queen. In the same way, arrang- 42 ing the number of vestibules for the corridors on each side of the whole temple, he has made above them various openings into the building, for the purpose of admitting more light, adorning them with very fine wood-carving. But the royal house he has furnished with more beautiful and splendid materials, using unstinted liberality in his disbursements. It seems 43 to me superfluous to describe here in detail the length and breadth of the building, its splendor and its majesty surpassing description, and the brilliant appearance of the work, its lofty pinnacles reaching to the heavens, and the costly cedars of Lebanon above them, which the divine oracle has not omitted to mention, saying, 'The trees of the Lord shall rejoice and the cedars of Lebanon which he hath planted.'[69] Why need I now describe the 44 skillful architectural arrangement and the surpassing beauty of each part, when the testimony of the eye renders instruction through the ear superfluous? For when he had thus completed the temple, he provided it with lofty thrones in honor of those who preside, and in addition with seats arranged in proper order throughout the whole building, and finally placed in the middle[70] the holy of holies, the altar, and, that it might be inaccessible to the multitude, enclosed it with wooden lattice-work, accurately wrought with artistic carving, presenting a wonderful sight to the beholders. And not 45 even the pavement was neglected by him; for this too he adorned with beautiful marble of every variety. Then finally he passed on to the parts without the temple, providing spacious exedræ and buildings[71] on each side, which were

---

[65] Hag. ii. 9.

[66] The description of the church of Tyre which follows is very valuable, as being the oldest detailed description which we have of a Christian basilica. Eusebius mentions other churches in his *Vita Constantini*, III. 30–39, 41–43, 48, 50, 51–53, 58, IV. 58, and describes some of them at considerable length. We have a number of descriptions from later sources, but rely for our knowledge of early Christian architecture chiefly upon the extant remains of the edifices themselves. For a very full discussion of the present church, which was an excellent example of an ancient Christian basilica, and for a detailed description of its various parts, see Bingham's *Antiquities*, Bk. VIII. chap. 3 sq., and compare also the article *Basilika* in Kraus' *Real-Encyclopädie der Christ. Alterthümer*. The literature on the general subject of early Christian architecture is very extensive. See more particularly the works referred to in the articles in Smith and Cheetham's *Dict. of Christ. Antiq.* and in the *Encyclop. Britannica;* and cf. also Schaff's *Ch. Hist.* III. p. 538 sq.

[67] Bingham remarks that the ancient basilicas commonly faced the west, and that therefore the position of this church of Tyre was exceptional; but this is a mistake. It is true that from the fifth century on, the altar almost uniformly occupied the east end of the church, but previous to that time the position observed in the present case was almost universally followed, so that the present building was not at all exceptional in its position. See the article *Orientierung* in Kraus' *Real-Encyclopädie*. Although the common custom was to have the church stand east and west, yet the rule was often neglected, and there exist many notable examples of churches standing north and south, or quite out of line with the points of the compass.

[68] αἴθριον, the Latin *atrium*.

[69] Psa. civ. 16.

[70] i.e. in the apse, or chancel, not in the middle of the nave, or body of the church.

[71] ἐξέδρας καὶ οἴκους. Large basilicas were always provided with additional rooms, and adjacent buildings, such as baptisteries, diaconica, secretaria, &c., which were used for various ecclesiastical purposes, and which were often of considerable size, so that important synods frequently met in one or another of them. Cf. Bingham, *ibid.* chap. 7.

joined to the basilica, and communicated with the entrances to the interior of the structure. These were erected by our most peaceful [72] Solomon, the maker of the temple of God, for those who still needed purification and sprinkling by water and the Holy Spirit, so that the prophecy quoted above is no longer a word merely, but a fact; for now it has also come

46 to pass that in truth 'the latter glory of this house is greater than the former.' [73] For it was necessary and fitting that as her shepherd and Lord had once tasted death for her, and after his suffering had changed that vile body which he assumed in her behalf into a splendid and glorious body, leading the very flesh which had been delivered [74] from corruption to incorruption, she too should enjoy the dispensations of the Saviour. For having received from him the promise of much greater things than these, she desires to share uninterruptedly throughout eternity with the choir of the angels of light, in the far greater glory of regeneration, [75] in the resurrection of an incorruptible body, in the palace of God beyond the heavens, with Christ Jesus himself, the uni-

47 versal Benefactor and Saviour. But for the present, she that was formerly widowed and desolate is clothed by the grace of God with these flowers, and is become truly like a lily, as the prophecy says, [76] and having received the bridal garment and the crown of beauty, she is taught by Isaiah to dance, and to present her thank-offerings unto God the King in rever-

48 ent words. Let us hear her saying, 'My soul shall rejoice in the Lord; for he hath clothed me with a garment of salvation and with a robe of gladness; he hath bedecked me like a bridegroom with a garland, and he hath adorned me like a bride with jewels; and like the earth which bringeth forth her bud, and like a garden which causeth the things that are sown in it to spring forth, thus the Lord God hath caused righteousness and praise to

49 spring forth before all the nations.' [77] In these words she exults. And in similar words the heavenly bridegroom, the Word Jesus Christ himself, answers her. Hear the Lord saying, 'Fear not because thou hast been put to shame, neither be thou confounded because thou hast been rebuked; for thou shalt forget the former shame, and the reproach of thy widowhood shalt thou remember no more.' [78] 'Not [79] as a woman deserted and faint-hearted

hath the Lord called thee, nor as a woman hated from her youth, saith thy God. For a small moment have I forsaken thee, but with great mercy will I have mercy upon thee; in a little wrath I hid my face from thee, but with everlasting mercy will I have mercy upon thee, saith the Lord that hath re-deemed thee.' [80] 'Awake, awake, thou who **50** hast drunk at the hand of the Lord the cup of his fury; for thou hast drunk the cup of ruin, the vessel of my wrath, and hast drained it. And there was none to console thee of all thy sons whom thou didst bring forth, and there was none to take thee by the hand.' [81] 'Behold, I have taken out of thine hand the cup of ruin, the vessel of my fury, and thou shalt no longer drink it. And I will put it into the hands of them that have treated thee unjustly and have humbled thee.' [82] 'Awake, awake, put **51** on thy strength, put on thy glory. Shake off the dust and arise. Sit thee down, loose the bands of thy neck.' [83] 'Lift up thine eyes round about and behold thy children gathered together; behold they are gathered together and are come to thee. As I live, saith the Lord, thou shalt clothe thee with them all as with an ornament, and gird thyself with them as with the ornaments of a bride. For thy waste and corrupted and ruined places shall now be too narrow by reason of those that inhabit thee, and they that swallow thee up shall be far from thee. For thy sons whom thou hast lost **52** shall say in thine ears, The place is too narrow for me, give place to me that I may dwell. Then shalt thou say in thine heart, Who hath begotten me these? I am childless and a widow, and who hath brought up these for me? I was left alone, and these, where were they for me?' [84]

"These are the things which Isaiah fore- **53** told; and which were anciently recorded concerning us in sacred books; and it was necessary that we should sometime learn their truthfulness by their fulfillment. For when **54** the bridegroom, the Word, addressed such language to his own bride, the sacred and holy Church, this bridesman, [85] — when she was desolate and lying like a corpse, bereft of hope in the eyes of men, — in accordance with the united prayers of all of you, as was proper, stretched out your hands and aroused and raised her up at the command of God, the universal King, and at the manifestation of the power of Jesus Christ; and having raised her he established her as he had learned from the description given in the sacred oracles. This **55**

---

[72] The name Solomon (Heb. שְׁלֹמֹה) means "peaceful."
[73] Hag. ii. 9.
[74] λυθεῖσαν, which may mean also "dissolved, decayed." Crusè translates "dissolved"; Closs, "schon verwesend."
[75] Cf. Matt. xix. 28.   [77] Isa. lxi. 10, 11.
[76] See Isa. xxxv. 1.   [78] *Ibid.* liv. 4.
[79] The word "not" is omitted in the Hebrew (and consequently in our English versions), but is found in the LXX.

[80] Isa. liv. 6–8.   [82] *Ibid.* li. 22, 23.
[81] *Ibid.* li. 17, 18.   [83] *Ibid.* lii. 1, 2.
[84] *Ibid.* xlix. 18–21.
[85] νυμφοστόλος, referring to Paulinus.

is indeed a very great wonder, passing all admiration, especially to those who attend only to the outward appearance; but more wonderful than wonders are the archetypes and their mental prototypes and divine models; I mean the reproductions of the inspired and rational

56 building in our souls. This the Divine Son himself created after his own image, imparting to it everywhere and in all respects the likeness of God, an incorruptible nature, incorporeal, rational, free from all earthly matter, a being endowed with its own intelligence; and when he had once called her forth from non-existence into existence, he made her a holy spouse, an all-sacred temple for himself and for the Father. This also he clearly declares and confesses in the following words: ' I will dwell in them and will walk in them; and I will be their God, and they shall be my people.'[86] Such is the perfect and purified soul, so made from the beginning as to bear the image of the celestial Word.

57 But when by the envy and zeal of the malignant demon she became, of her own voluntary choice, sensual and a lover of evil, the Deity left her; and as if bereft of a protector, she became an easy prey and readily accessible to those who had long envied her; and being assailed by the batteries and machines of her invisible enemies and spiritual foes, she suffered a terrible fall, so that not one stone of virtue remained upon another in her, but she lay completely dead upon the ground, entirely divested of her natural ideas of God.

58 "But as she, who had been made in the image of God, thus lay prostrate, it was not that wild boar from the forest which we see that despoiled her, but a certain destroying demon and spiritual wild beasts who deceived her with their passions as with the fiery darts of their own wickedness, and burned the truly divine sanctuary of God with fire, and profaned to the ground the tabernacle of his name. Then burying the miserable one with heaps of earth, they destroyed every hope of deliverance.

59 But that divinely bright and saving Word, her protector, after she had suffered the merited punishment for her sins, again restored her, securing the favor of the all-merciful

60 Father. Having won over first the souls of the highest rulers, he purified, through the agency of those most divinely favored princes, the whole earth from all the impious destroyers, and from the terrible and God-hating tyrants themselves. Then bringing out into the light those who were his friends, who had long before been consecrated to him for life, but in the midst, as it were, of a storm of evils, had been concealed under his shelter, he honored them worthily

with the great gifts of the Spirit. And again, by means of them, he cleared out and cleaned with spades and mattocks — the admonitory words of doctrine[87] — the souls which a little while before had been covered with filth and burdened with every kind of matter and rubbish of impious ordinances. And when he had **61** made the ground of all your minds clean and clear, he finally committed it to this all-wise and God-beloved Ruler, who, being endowed with judgment and prudence, as well as with other gifts, and being able to examine and discriminate accurately the minds of those committed to his charge, from the first day, so to speak, down to the present, has not ceased to build. Now he has supplied the brilliant gold, again the refined and unalloyed silver, and the precious and costly stones in all of you, so that again is fulfilled for you in facts a sacred and mystic prophecy, which says, ' Behold **62** I make thy stone a carbuncle, and thy foundations of sapphire, and thy battlements of jasper, and thy gates of crystals, and thy wall of chosen stones; and all thy sons shall be taught of God, and thy children shall enjoy complete peace; and in righteousness shalt thou be built.'[88] Building therefore in righteousness, **63** he divided the whole people according to their strength. With some he fortified only the outer enclosure, walling it up with unfeigned faith; such were the great mass of the people who were incapable of bearing a greater structure. Others he permitted to enter the building, commanding them to stand at the door and act as guides for those who should come in; these may be not unfitly compared to the vestibules of the temple. Others he supported by the first pillars which are placed without about the quadrangular hall, initiating them into the first elements of the letter of the four Gospels. Still others he joined together about the basilica on both sides; these are the catechumens who are still advancing and progressing, and are not far separated from the inmost view of divine things granted to the faithful. Taking from **64** among these the pure souls that have been cleansed like gold by divine washing,[89] he then supports them by pillars, much better than those without, made from the inner and mystic teachings of the Scripture, and illumines them[90] by windows. Adorning the whole temple **65** with a great vestibule of the glory of the one universal King and only God, and placing

---

[87] ταῖς πληκτικαῖς τῶν μαθημάτων διδασκαλίας.
[88] Isa. liv. 11–14.
[89] θείῳ λουτρῷ; i.e. baptism.
[90] Heinichen, followed by Closs, reads τοὺς μὲν . . . τοὺς δέ: " *Some of them* he supports by pillars . . . *others of them* he illumines by windows." But all the MSS. read τοὺς μὲν . . . τοῖς δέ, which, in view of the general character of Eusebius' style throughout this oration, we are hardly justified in changing. I have therefore followed Valesius, Burton, and Crusè in retaining the reading of the MSS.

[86] 2 Cor. vi. 16.

on either side of the authority of the Father, Christ, and the Holy Spirit as second lights, he exhibits abundantly and gloriously throughout the entire building the clearness and splendor of the truth of the rest in all its details. And having selected from every quarter the living and moving and well-prepared stones of the souls, he constructs out of them all the great and royal house, splendid and full of light both within and without; for not only soul and understanding, but their body also is made glorious by the blooming ornament of purity and modesty.

66 And in this temple there are also thrones, and a great number of seats and benches, in all those souls in which sit the Holy Spirit's gifts, such as were anciently seen by the sacred apostles, and those who were with them, when there 'appeared unto them tongues parting asunder, like as of fire, and sat upon each one

67 of them.'[91] But in the leader of all it is reasonable to suppose[92] that Christ himself dwells in his fullness,[93] and in those that occupy the second rank after him, in proportion as each is able to contain the power of Christ and of the Holy Spirit.[94] And the souls of some — of those, namely, who are committed to each of them for instruction and care — may be

68 seats for angels. But the great and august and unique altar, what else could this be than the pure holy of holies of the soul of the common priest of all? Standing at the right of it, Jesus himself, the great High Priest of the universe, the Only Begotten of God, receives with bright eye and extended hand the sweet incense from all, and the bloodless and immaterial sacrifices offered in their prayers, and bears them to the heavenly Father and God of the universe. And he himself first worships him, and alone gives to the Father the reverence which is his due, beseeching him also to continue always kind and propitious to us all.

69 "Such is the great temple which the great Creator of the universe, the Word, has built throughout the entire world, making it an intellectual image upon earth of those things which lie above the vault of heaven, so that throughout the whole creation, including rational beings on earth, his Father might be honored and adored.

70 But the region above the heavens, with the models of earthly things which are there, and the so-called Jerusalem above,[95] and the heavenly Mount of Zion, and the supramundane city of the living God, in which innumerable choirs of angels and the Church of the first born, whose names are written in heaven,[96]

praise their Maker and the Supreme Ruler of the universe with hymns of praise unutterable and incomprehensible to us, — who that is mortal is able worthily to celebrate this? 'For eye hath not seen nor ear heard, neither have entered into the heart of men those things which God hath prepared for them that love him.'[97]

Since we, men, children, and women, small 71 and great, are already in part partakers of these things, let us not cease all together, with one spirit and one soul, to confess and praise the author of such great benefits to us, 'Who forgiveth all our iniquities, who healeth all our diseases, who redeemeth our life from destruction, who crowneth us with mercy and compassion, who satisfieth our desires with good things.'[98] 'For he hath not dealt with us according to our sins, nor rewarded us according to our iniquities;'[99] 'for as far as the east is from the west, so far hath he removed our iniquities from us. Like as a father pitieth his own children, so the Lord pitieth them that fear him.'[100]

Rekindling these thoughts in our memories, 72 both now and during all time to come, and contemplating in our mind night and day, in every hour and with every breath, so to speak, the Author and Ruler of the present festival, and of this bright and most splendid day, let us love and adore him with every power of the soul. And now rising, let us beseech him with loud voice to shelter and preserve us to the end in his fold, granting his unbroken and unshaken peace forever, in Christ Jesus our Saviour; through whom be the glory unto him forever and ever.[101] Amen."

CHAPTER V.

Copies of Imperial Laws.[1]

LET us finally subjoin the translations 1 from the Roman tongue of the imperial decrees of Constantine and Licinius.

---

[91] Acts ii. 3.   [92] ἴσως.
[93] αὐτὸς ὅλος ἐγκάθηται χριστός.
[94] Valesius remarks, "*Sic Hieronymus seu quis alius de ordinibus ecclesiæ : in illis esse partes et membra virtutem, in episcopo plenitudinem divinitatis habitare.*" From what source the quotation comes I do not know.
[95] Cf. Gal. iv. 26.   [96] Cf. Heb. xii. 22, 23.

[97] 1 Cor. ii. 9.
[98] Psa. ciii. 3–5.
[99] *Ibid.* 10.
[100] *Ibid.* 12, 13.
[101] εἰς τοὺς σύμπαντας αἰῶνας τῶν αἰώνων.
[1] Heinichen gives Ἀντίγραφα βασιλικῶν νόμων περὶ τῶν χριστιανοῖς προσηκόντων as the title of this chapter. All but three of the MSS., however, agree in limiting the title to the first three words, the last four being given by the majority of them as the title of chap. 6. The words are quite out of place at the head of that chapter, which in two important MSS., followed by Stroth, is made a part of chap. 5. Heinichen inserts the words at this point because they are out of place in the position in which they commonly occur; but the truth is, they are no better adapted to the present chapter than to that one, for only one of the edicts quoted in this chapter has reference to the property of Christians. It seems to me much more likely that the words were originally written in the margin of some codex opposite that particular rescript, and thence by an error slipped into the text at the head of a later one, which was then made a separate chapter. In view of the uncertainty, however, as to the original position of the words, I have followed Laemmer, Schwegler, Stroth, Closs, and Stigloher, in omitting them altogether.

2   *Copy of imperial decrees translated from the Roman tongue.*[2]

"Perceiving long ago that religious liberty ought not to be denied, but that it ought to be granted to the judgment and desire of each individual to perform his religious duties according to his own choice, we had given orders that every man, Christians as well as others, should preserve the faith of his own sect and re-
3   ligion.[3]   But since in that rescript, in which such liberty was granted them, many and various conditions[4] seemed clearly added, some of them, it may be, after a little retired from such
4   observance.   When I, Constantine Augustus, and I, Licinius Augustus, came under favorable auspices to Milan and took under consideration everything which pertained to the common weal and prosperity, we resolved among other things, or rather first of all, to make such decrees as seemed in many respects for the benefit of every one ; namely, such as should preserve reverence and piety toward the deity. We resolved, that is, to grant both to the Christians and to all men freedom to follow the religion which they choose, that whatever heavenly divinity exists[5] may be propitious to us and to all that live under our government.
5   We have, therefore, determined, with sound and upright purpose, that liberty is to be denied to no one, to choose and to follow the religious observances of the Christians, but that to each one freedom is to be given to devote his mind to that religion which he may think adapted to himself,[6] in order that the Deity may exhibit to us in all things his accustomed care and favor.   It was fitting that
6   we should write that this is our pleasure, that those conditions[7] being entirely left out which were contained in our former letter concerning the Christians which was sent to your devotedness, everything that seemed very severe and foreign to our mildness may be annulled, and that now every one who has the same desire to observe the religion of the Christians may do so without molestation. We have resolved to communicate this
7   most fully to thy care, in order that thou mayest know that we have granted to these same Christians freedom and full liberty to observe their own religion.   Since this has
8   been granted freely by us to them, thy devotedness perceives that liberty is granted to others also who may wish to follow their own religious observances ; it being clearly in accordance with the tranquillity of our times, that each one should have the liberty of choosing and worshiping whatever deity he pleases.   This has been done by us in order that we might not seem in any way to discriminate against any rank or religion.[8]   And we decree still
9   further in regard to the Christians, that their places, in which they were formerly accustomed to assemble, and concerning which in the former letter sent to thy devotedness a different command was given,[9] if it appear that any have bought them either from our treasury or from any other person, shall be restored to the said Christians, without demanding money or any other equivalent, with no delay or hesitation.   If any happen to have received the said places as a gift, they shall restore them as quickly as possible to these same Christians : with the understand-
10   ing that if those who have bought these places, or those who have received them as a gift, demand anything from our bounty, they may go to the judge of the district, that provision may be made for them by our clemency. All these things are to be granted to the society of Christians by your care immediately and

[2] This is the famous Edict of Milan, issued by Constantine and Licinius late in the year 312, after the former's victory over Maxentius (see above, Bk. IX. chap. 9, note 7).   The edict has a claim to be remembered as the first announcement of the great doctrine of complete freedom of conscience, and that not for one religion only, but for all religions.   In this respect it was a great advance upon the edict of Galerius, which had granted conditional liberty to a single faith.   The greater part of the edict (beginning with § 4) is extant in its original Latin form in Lactantius' *De mort. pers.* chap. 48.   The Greek translation is still less accurate than the translation of the edict of Galerius given in Bk. VIII. chap. 17, above, but the variations from the original are none of them of great importance. The most marked ones will be mentioned in the notes.

[3] The reference in this sentence is not, as was formerly supposed, to a lost edict of Constantine and Licinius, but to the edict of Galerius, as is proved by Mason (p. 327 sq.), who has completely exploded the old belief in three edicts of toleration, and has shown that there were only two; viz. that of Galerius, Constantine, and Licinius, published in 311, and the present one, issued by Constantine and Licinius in 312

[4] The Greek word is αἱρέσεις, which has been commonly translated " sects," and the reference has been supposed to be to various schismatic bodies included in the former edict, but, as Mason remarks, such an interpretation is preposterous, and introduces an idea in direct contradiction to the entire tenor of the present document. The fact is that, although " sects " is the natural translation of the word αἱρέσεις, we find the same word in § 6, below, used to translate *conditiones*, and it may be reasonably assumed — in fact, it may be regarded as certain in view of the context — that in the present case the same word stood in the Latin original.   I have no hesitation, therefore, in adopting the rendering which I have given in the text. These " conditions," then, to which the edict refers were enumerated, not in the former edict itself, but in the rescript which accompanied it (see above, Bk. VIII. chap. 17, note 9).   What these conditions were may be conjectured, as remarked in that note, from the provisions of the present edict (cf. Mason, p. 330 sq.).

[5] ὅ τι ποτέ ἐστι θειότης καὶ οὐρανίου πράγματος.   Latin: *quo quidem divinitas in sede cælesti.*   The Greek is by no means a reproduction of the sense of the Latin, and indeed, as it stands, is quite untranslatable.   I have contented myself with a paraphrase, which does not express what the Greek translator says, but perhaps is not entirely at variance with what he meant to say.

[6] In this sentence it is stated distinctly, not simply that Christians may remain Christians, but that anybody that pleases may become a Christian; that is, that the fullest liberty is granted to every man either to observe his ancestral religion or to choose another.

[7] Greek, αἱρέσεων; Latin, *conditionibus* (see note 4, above).

[8] μηδεμιᾷ τιμῇ μηδὲ θρησκείᾳ τινί.   Latin, *honori, neque cuiquam religioni.*   Mason concludes from this clause that in the rescript which accompanied the previous edict Christians had been excluded from certain official positions.

[9] That there was some condition attached in the last rescript to the restoration of their property to the Christians is clear from these words.   We may gather from what follows that the Christians were obliged to pay something for the restored property, either to the occupants or to the government.   Constantine states that henceforth the imperial treasury will freely bear all the expense involved in the transfer.

11 without any delay. And since the said Christians are known to have possessed not only those places in which they were accustomed to assemble, but also other places, belonging not to individuals among them, but to the society [10] as a whole, that is, to the society of Christians, you will command that all these, in virtue of the law which we have above stated, be restored, without any hesitation, to these same Christians; that is, to their society and congregation: the above-mentioned provision being of course observed, that those who restore them without price, as we have before said, may

12 expect indemnification from our bounty. In all these things, for the behoof of the aforesaid society of Christians, you are to use the utmost diligence, to the end that our command may be speedily fulfilled, and that in this also, by our clemency, provision may be made for

13 the common and public tranquillity.[11] For by this means,[12] as we have said before, the divine favor toward us which we have already experienced in many matters will continue

14 sure through all time. And that the terms of this our gracious ordinance may be known to all, it is expected that this which we have written will be published everywhere by you and brought to the knowledge of all, in order that this gracious ordinance of ours may remain unknown to no one."

15 *Copy of another imperial decree which they issued,[13] indicating that the grant was made to the Catholic Church alone.*

"Greeting to thee, our most esteemed Anulinus. It is the custom of our benevolence, most esteemed Anulinus, to will that those things which belong of right to another should not only be left unmolested, but should also be restored.[14] Wherefore it is our will that

16 when thou receivest this letter, if any such things belonged to the Catholic Church of the Christians, in any city or other place, but are now held by citizens [15] or by any others, thou shalt cause them to be restored immediately to the said churches. For we have already determined that those things which these same churches formerly possessed shall be restored to them. Since therefore thy devot-

17 edness perceives that this command of ours is most explicit, do thou make haste to restore to them, as quickly as possible, everything which formerly belonged to the said churches, — whether gardens or buildings or whatever they may be, — that we may learn that thou hast obeyed this decree of ours most carefully. Farewell, our most esteemed and beloved Anulinus."

Copy of an epistle in which the Emperor 18 *commands that a synod of bishops be held at Rome in behalf of the unity and concord of the churches.*[16]

---

[10] τῷ σωματίῳ. Latin, *corpori*. The use of this word (which we might almost translate "body corporate") is a distinct recognition of the full legal status of the Christian Church, and of their right as a corporation in the eyes of the law to hold property. The right did not on this occasion receive recognition for the first time, but more distinctly and in broader terms than ever before. Upon the right of the Church to hold property before the publication of this edict, see especially Hatch's *Constitution of the Early Christian Churches*, p. 152, note 25.

[11] Greek, τῆς κοινῆς καὶ δημοσίας ἡσυχίας. Latin, more simply, *quieti publicæ*.

[12] τούτῳ γὰρ τῷ λογισμῷ. Latin, *hactenus*.

[13] It would seem that this communication was sent to Anulinus soon after the issue of the Edict of Milan; for it gives directions for the carrying out of some of the provisions made in that edict, and is very likely but a sample of special letters sent in connection with that document to the governors of the various provinces. We know from the next chapter that Anulinus was proconsul of the Roman province of Africa, of which Carthage was the capital city, and which was very thickly populated with Christians. Of Anulinus himself we know only what we can learn from this and the next two chapters. The title of the rescript as given by Eusebius is somewhat misleading. There is no indication in the document itself that it was written with the distinct purpose of distinguishing the Catholic Church from schismatic bodies, and granting it privileges denied to them. If such had been its aim, it would certainly have stated it more clearly. The term " Catholic Church " (in § 16) seems in fact to be used in a general sense to indicate the Christian Church as a whole. It is, to be sure, possible that Constantine may already have had some knowledge of the schismatics whom he refers to in another epistle, quoted in the next chapter; but his omission of all reference to them in the present case shows that he did not intend at this time to draw lines between parties, or to pass judgment upon any society calling itself a Christian church.

[14] i.e. that if they *have* been molested, or taken from their owners, they should be restored.

[15] πολιτῶν. Valesius conjectures that πολιτευτῶν should be read instead of πολιτῶν, and therefore translates *a decurionibus*. Crusè, following him, reads "by the decurions." The correction, however, though an improvement, is not necessary, and I have not felt justified in adopting it.

[16] This and the next epistle were occasioned by the Donatist schism. This great schism arose after the close of the Diocletian persecution, and divided the church of North Africa for more than a century. Like the Novatian schism, it was due to the conflict of the more rigid and the more indulgent theories of discipline. In Novatianism, however, the burning question was the readmission of the lapsed; in Donatism, the validity of clerical functions performed by unholy or unfaithful clergymen. In the latter, therefore, the question was one of clerical, not lay, discipline, and there was involved in it a very important theological principle. The Donatists maintained that the validity of clerical functions depended upon the character of the administering clergyman; the Catholic party maintained that the validity of those functions depended solely upon Christ, and was quite independent of the character of the officiating clergyman, provided he had been duly qualified by the Church for the performance of such functions. Augustine, nearly a century after the rise of the sect, found it necessary to oppose it, and it was in the controversy with it that he developed his doctrine of the Church and the Sacraments. The immediate occasion of the schism was the election of Cæcilianus, who favored the milder principles of church discipline, to the bishopric of Carthage, in 311. His election was opposed by the entire rigoristic party in Carthage and throughout North Africa. It was claimed that the Bishop Felix of Aptunga, by whom he was ordained, had been a traditor during the persecution, and that therefore Cæcilian's ordination was not valid. As a consequence the bishops of Numidia, who had not been invited to assist in the choice and ordination of Cæcilian, held a synod in Carthage, and elected a counter-bishop, Majorinus. Thus the schism was definitely launched. The party called itself for a time by the name of its first bishop, but in 315 he was succeeded by Donatus, called the Great, to distinguish him from Donatus, bishop of Casæ Nigræ, who had been one of the original leaders of the movement. From him the sect took the name by which it was thenceforth known. Doubtless personal jealousies and enmities had considerable to do with the origin of the schism, but it is quite inaccurate to ascribe it wholly to such causes. The fundamental ground lay in the deep-seated difference in principles between the two parties in the Church, and it was inevitable that that difference should make itself felt in some such rupture, even had personal reasons not co-operated to such an extent as they did. Our chief sources for a knowledge of Donatism are the anti-Donatistic works of Augustine (see *The Nicene and Post-Nicene Fathers*, first series, Vol. IV. p. 369 sq.), together with a number of his epistles, and Optatus' *De Schismate Donatistarum*. The literature on the subject is very extensive. See especially Valesius' essay, *De Schismate Donat.*, appended to his edition of Eusebius (Reading's edition, p. 775 sq.); Ribbeck, *Donatus and Augustinus*, 1858; the articles *Cæcilianus* and *Donatism* in the *Dict. of Christ. Biog.* ;

"Constantine Augustus to Miltiades,[17] bishop of Rome, and to Marcus.[18] Since many such communications have been sent to me by Anulinus,[19] the most illustrious proconsul of Africa, in which it is said that Cæcilianus,[20] bishop of the city of Carthage, has been accused by some of his colleagues in Africa, in many matters; [21] and since it seems to me a very serious thing that in those provinces which Divine Providence has freely entrusted to my devotedness, and in which there is a great population, the multitude are found following the baser course, and dividing, as it were, into two parties, and the 19 bishops are at variance, — it has seemed good to me that Cæcilianus himself, with ten of the bishops that appear to accuse him, and with ten others whom he may consider necessary for his defense, should sail to Rome, that there, in the presence of yourselves and of Reticius [22] and Maternus [23] and Marinus,[24] your colleagues, whom I have commanded to hasten to Rome for this purpose,[25] he may be heard, as you may understand to be in accordance with the most holy law. But in order that 20 you may be enabled to have most perfect knowledge of all these things, I have subjoined to my letter copies of the documents sent to me by Anulinus, and have sent them to your above-mentioned colleagues. When your firmness has read these, you will consider in what way the above-mentioned case may be most accurately investigated and justly decided. For it does not escape your diligence that I have such reverence for the legitimate [26] Catholic Church that I do not wish you to leave schism or division in any place. May the divinity of the great God preserve you, most honored sirs, for many years."

Copy of an epistle in which the emperor 21 *commands another synod to be held for the purpose of removing all dissensions among the bishops.*

"Constantine Augustus to Chrestus,[27] bishop of Syracuse. When some began wickedly and perversely to disagree [28] among themselves in regard to the holy worship and celestial power and Catholic doctrine,[29] wishing to put an end to such disputes among them, I formerly gave command that certain bishops should be sent from Gaul, and that the opposing parties

---

Neander's *Church History*, Torrey's translation, II. p. 182 sq.; Hefele's *Conciliengesch.* 2d ed., I. p. 293 sq.; and Schaff's *Church History*, III. p. 360 sq. Constantine did not voluntarily meddle in the Donatistic controversy. He was first appealed to by the Donatists themselves, through the proconsul Anulinus, early in the year 313 (see Augustine, *Epistle* 88, for a copy of the letter in which Anulinus communicates their request to the emperor). In response to their appeal Constantine (in the present epistle) summoned the two parties to appear before a Roman synod, which was held in October, 313. The Donatists were unable to prove their charges, and the synod gave decision against them. Again, at their own request, their case was heard at a council held in Gaul the following year (the synod of Arles; see the next epistle of Constantine quoted in this chapter). This council also decided against them, and the Donatists appealed once more to the judgment of the emperor himself. He heard their case in Milan in 316, and confirmed the decisions of the councils, and soon afterward issued laws against them, threatening them with the banishment of their bishops and the confiscation of their property. He soon, however, withdrew his persecuting measures, and adopted a policy of toleration. During subsequent reigns their condition grew worse, and they were often obliged to undergo severe hardships; but they clung rigidly to their principles until the invasion of the Vandals in 428, when the entire North African Church was devastated.

[17] Miltiades (called also Melchiades) was bishop of Rome from July 2, 310, to Jan. 10 or 11, 314. See Lipsius, *Chron. der röm. Bischöfe*, p. 257 sq.

[18] Marcus is an otherwise unknown personage, unless Valesius' not improbable conjecture be accepted, that he was at this time a presbyter of Rome, and is to be identified with the Marcus who was bishop of Rome for some eight months in 336.

[19] χάρται. The reference, as remarked by Valesius, seems to be not to epistles of Anulinus, but to the communications of the Donatists forwarded to the emperor by Anulinus. In his epistle to the emperor, which was written April 15, 313 (see Augustine, *Ep.* 88), Anulinus speaks of two communications handed to him by the Donatists, which he forwards to the emperor with his own letter. The former of them, which is no longer extant, bore the title *Libellus ecclesiæ Catholicæ criminum Cæciliani.* The other, which is preserved by Optatus (Du Pin's edition, p. 22, and Routh, *Rel. Sac.* IV. 280) contained the request that the emperor would appoint some Gallic bishops to hear the case, because the church of that country had not been subjected to the same temptation as themselves during the persecution, and could therefore render an impartial decision. It was in consequence of this request that the Gallic bishops mentioned below were directed by the emperor to proceed to Rome to join with Miltiades in the adjudication of the case. Constantine speaks of receiving many such communications, but no others are preserved to us.

[20] Cæcilianus had been arch-deacon of the church of Carthage under the bishop Mensurius, and had been a diligent supporter of the latter in his opposition to the fanatical conduct and the extreme rigor of the stricter party during the persecution. In 311 he became bishop, and lived until about 345. We know nothing about his life after the first few years of the conflict. His title to the bishopric was universally acknowledged outside of North Africa, and by all there except the Donatists themselves.

[21] The chief charge brought against Cæcilian was that he had been ordained by a traditor, Felix of Aptunga, and that his ordination was therefore invalid. The charge against Felix was carefully investigated at the Council of Arles, and pronounced quite groundless. Many personal charges, such as cruelty to the martyrs in prison (which had its ground, doubtless, in his condemnation of the foolish fanaticism which was so common during the persecution in Africa), tyranny, bloodthirstiness, &c., were brought against Cæcilian, but were dismissed in every case as quite groundless.

[22] Reticius was bishop of Autun in Gaul (see Optatus, I. 22, and the references given below). An extended account of him, largely legendary, is given by Gregory of Tours (*De gloria Conf.* 75, according to the *Dict. of Christ. Biog.*). The dates of his accession and death are unknown to us. He attended the Council of Arles in 313 (see the list of those present, in Routh, IV. p. 312), and is spoken of in high terms by Augustine (*Contra Jul.* I. 7; *Opus imperf. cont. Jul.* I. 55), and also by Jerome, who informs us that he wrote a commentary on the Song of Songs and a work against Novatian (see his *de vir. ill.* 82, *Ep. ad Florentium*, and *ad Marcellam*, Migne, Nos. 5 and 37).

[23] Maternus was bishop of Cologne, the first one of that see known to us, but the date of his accession and death are unknown. He is mentioned by Optatus (*ibid.*), and was present at the Council of Arles (Routh, *ibid.*).

[24] Marinus, whose dates are likewise unknown, was bishop of Arles (see Optatus, *ibid.*), and was present at the Council in that city in 314 (see Routh, *ibid.* p. 313).

[25] This Roman Council convened in the house of Fausta, in the Lateran, on the second day of October, 313, and was attended by nineteen bishops, — the three from Gaul just mentioned, Miltiades himself, and fifteen Italian bishops (see Optatus, *ibid.*). The synod resulted in the complete victory of the party of Cæcilian, as remarked above (note 15).

[26] ἐνθέσμῳ.

[27] The name of Chrestus appears first in the list of those present at the Council of Arles (see Routh, IV. 312), and in consequence it has been thought that he presided at the Council, a conclusion which some have regarded as confirmed by Constantine's own words in § 24, below. But on the other hand, in the epistle of the synod addressed to Sylvester of Rome, and containing the canons of the Council, it is distinctly stated that Marinus, bishop of Arles, presided; and this in itself seems more probable, although the document in which the statement is found may not perhaps be genuine (see, for instance, Ffoulke's article *Marinus* in the *Dict. of Christ. Biog.*, which needs, however, to be taken with allowance, for the case against the genuineness of the extant canons of the Council is by no means so strong as he implies). Of Chrestus himself we know nothing more than can be gathered from this epistle.

[28] ἀποδιίστασθαι.   [29] τῆς αἱρέσεως τῆς καθολικῆς.

who were contending persistently and incessantly with each other, should be summoned from Africa ; that in their presence, and in the presence of the bishop of Rome, the matter which appeared to be causing the disturbance might be examined and decided with all care.[30]

22 But since, as it happens, some, forgetful both of their own salvation and of the reverence due to the most holy religion, do not even yet bring hostilities to an end, and are unwilling to conform to the judgment already passed, and assert that those who expressed their opinions and decisions were few, or that they had been too hasty and precipitate in giving judgment, before all the things which ought to have been accurately investigated had been examined, — on account of all this it has happened that those very ones who ought to hold brotherly and harmonious relations toward each other, are shamefully, or rather abominably,[31] divided among themselves, and give occasion for ridicule to those men whose souls are aliens to this most holy religion. Wherefore it has seemed necessary to me to provide that this dissension, which ought to have ceased after the judgment had been already given by their own voluntary agreement, should now, if possible, be brought to an end by the presence of

23 many. Since, therefore, we have commanded a number of bishops from a great many different places[32] to assemble in the city of Arles,[33] before the kalends of August, we have thought proper to write to thee also that thou shouldst secure from the most illustrious Latronianus,[34] corrector of Sicily,[35] a public vehicle, and that thou shouldst take with thee two others of the second rank,[36] whom thou thyself

shalt choose, together with three servants who may serve you on the way, and betake thyself to the above-mentioned place before the appointed day ; that by thy firmness, and 24 by the wise unanimity and harmony of the others present, this dispute, which has disgracefully continued until the present time, in consequence of certain shameful strifes, after all has been heard which those have to say who are now at variance with one another, and whom we have likewise commanded to be present, may be settled in accordance with the proper faith, and that brotherly harmony, though it be but gradually, may be restored. May the Almighty God preserve thee in health for many years."

CHAPTER VI.[1]

Copy of an Imperial Epistle in which Money is granted to the Churches.[2]

"CONSTANTINE AUGUSTUS to Cæcilianus,[3] 1 bishop of Carthage. Since it is our pleasure that something should be granted in all the provinces of Africa and Numidia and Mauritania to certain ministers of the legitimate[4] and most holy catholic religion, to defray their expenses, I have written to Ursus,[5] the illustrious finance minister[6] of Africa, and have directed him to make provision to pay to thy firmness three thousand folles.[7] Do thou there- 2

---

[30] See the previous epistle.

[31] αἰσχρῶς, μᾶλλον δὲ μυσερῶς.

[32] ἐκ διαφόρων καὶ ἀμυθήτων τόπων. Some old accounts give the number of bishops present at the Council as six hundred, but this is wild. Baronius gave the number as two hundred, and he has been followed by many others, but this rests upon a false reading in a passage in Augustine's works. The truth seems to be that there were not more than thirty-three bishops present, the number given in the only lists of the members of the synod which we have (see Routh, *ibid.*, and see also Hefele, *Conciliengesch.* I. p. 201).

[33] Arles (Latin *Arelate*), a city of Southern France, situated not far from the mouth of the Rhone. It was at this time one of the most prominent episcopal sees of Gaul, and was the seat of more than one important council, of which the present is the first known to us. The one summoned by Constantine convened, as we may gather from this passage, on the first of August, 314. We do not know how long its sessions continued, nor indeed any particulars in regard to it, though twenty-two canons are extant in an epistle addressed to Sylvester of Rome, which purport to be the genuine canons of the Council, and are commonly so regarded. Their genuineness, however, is by no means universally admitted (cf. e.g. the article in the *Dict. of Christ. Biog.* referred to in note 27). If the canons are genuine, we see that the Council busied itself with many other matters besides the Donatistic schism, especially with the Easter question and with various matters of church discipline. See Hefele, *Conciliengesch.* I. p. 201 sq. (2d ed.).

[34] According to Valesius the name of Latronianus is found (*teste Gualthero*) in an ancient Palermo inscription (*in tabulis Siculis, numero 164*). He is an otherwise unknown personage.

[35] The Greek τοῦ κορρήκτορος is evidently simply a transliteration of the original Latin *correctoris. Corrector*, in the time of the emperors, was " the title of a kind of land bailiff, a governor" (Andrews' Lexicon).

[36] τῶν ἐκ τοῦ δευτέρου θρόνου; i.e. presbyters. Valesius remarks *ad locum* that presbyters were commonly called "priests of the second order," as may be gathered from various authors. He refers

among others to Jerome, who says in his Epitaph on the blessed Paula, "There were present the bishops of Jerusalem and other cities, and an innumerable company of priests and Levites of the lower order (*inferioris gradus*)"; and to Gregory Nazianzen (*Carm. iambic. de vita sua,* p. 6), who says, "the bishops in the church sat on a higher throne, the presbyters on lower seats on either side, while the deacons stood by in white garments." Compare also Eusebius' description of the arrangement of the seats in the church of Tyre (chap. 4, § 67, above), and for other references see Valesius' note. Possibly the Latin phrase used by Constantine was similar to that employed by Jerome: *secundi gradus.*

[1] Upon the title of this chapter given in the majority of the MSS., see above, chap. 5, note 1.

[2] The accompanying epistle furnishes the first instance which we have of financial support furnished the clergy by the state. From this time on the old system of voluntary contributions fell more and more into disuse, and the clergy gained their support from the income upon the church property, which accumulated rapidly, in consequence of special grants by the state and voluntary gifts and legacies by pious Christians, or from imperial bounties, as in the present case. Chrysostom, however, complains that the clergy in his time were not as well supported as under the ancient voluntary system. The accuracy of his statement, however, is open to doubt, as is the accuracy of all such comparisons between an earlier age and our own, unless it be based upon exhaustive statistics. Upon the general subject of the maintenance of the clergy in the early Church, see Bingham's *Antiquities,* Bk. V. Compare also Hatch's *Constitution of the Early Christian Churches,* p. 150 sq. Upon the Montanistic practice of paying their clergy salaries, see above, Bk. V. chap. 18, note 8, for an example of the same thing among the Theodotians, see Bk. V. chap. 28, § 10.

[3] On Cæcilianus, see above, chap. 5, note 20.

[4] ἐνθέσμου.   [5] Ursus is an otherwise unknown personage.

[6] καθολικόν. Cf. Bk. VIII. chap. 11, note 3.

[7] φόλλεις. We learn from Epiphanius (*De pond. et mens.,* at the end of the work; Dindorf's ed. IV. p. 33) that there were two folles, one a small coin, and the other a sum of money of uncertain value. The latter is evidently referred to here. According to one computation it was worth 208 denarii. If this were correct, the present sum would amount to over ninety thousand dollars; but the truth is, we can reach no certainty in the matter. For an exhaustive discussion of the subject, see Petavius' essay in Dindorf's edition of Epiphanius, IV. p. 109 sq.

fore, when thou hast received the above sum of money, command that it be distributed among all those mentioned above, according to the brief[8] sent to thee by Hosius.[9] But if thou shouldst find that anything is wanting for the fulfillment of this purpose of mine in regard to all of them, thou shalt demand without hesitation from Heracleides,[10] our treasurer,[11] whatever thou findest to be necessary. For I commanded him when he was present that if thy firmness should ask him for any money, he should see to it that it be paid without delay. And since I have learned that some men of unsettled mind wish to turn the people from the most holy and catholic Church by a certain method of shameful corruption,[12] do thou know that I gave command to Anulinus, the proconsul, and also to Patricius,[13] vicar of the prefects,[14] when they were present, that they should give proper attention not only to other matters but also above all to this, and that they should not overlook such a thing when it happened. Wherefore if thou shouldst see any such men continuing in this madness, do thou without delay go to the above-mentioned judges and report the matter to them; that they may correct them as I commanded them when they were present.[15] The divinity of the great God preserve thee for many years."

3

4

5

---

8 βρεούϊον; probably for the Latin *breviarium*.
9 Doubtless to be identified with the famous Hosius, bishop of Cordova in Spain, who was for many years Constantine's most influential adviser and took a prominent part in all the great controversies of the first half of the fourth century, and who died shortly before 360, when he was upwards of a hundred years old. Upon his life, see especially the exhaustive article by Morse, in the *Dict. of Christ. Biog.*
10 Heracleides is, so far as I am aware, mentioned only here.
11 τοῦ ἐπιτρόπου τῶν ἡμετέρων κτημάτων.
12 This would seem to be a reference to the Donatists. If it is, it leads us to suppose that Constantine had heard about the troubles in Carthage before he received the communication from Anulinus referred to in the previous chapter; for we can hardly suppose that pending the trial of Cæcilian Constantine would show him such signal marks of favor, which would lay him at once open to the charge of partiality, and would be practically a prejudgment of the case. On the other hand, he could not have referred to the Donatists in this way after the trial of the case, for his words imply that he is referring, not to an already well-established and well-known party, but simply to individuals whom he has recently learned to be making some kind of trouble in the church. These considerations seem to me to lead to the conclusion that this epistle preceded the one to Miltiades quoted in the previous chapter, and also the one from Anulinus to Constantine (see notes 16 and 19 on that chapter). If this be so, it must have been written as early as April, 313, and therefore soon after the epistle to Anulinus quoted in the previous chapter, § 15 sq. We might then be led to suppose that it was in consequence of this grant made by Constantine solely to Cæcilian and the clergy under him that the Donatists decided to appeal to the emperor, his treatment of all who were opposed to Cæcilian showing them that he had heard reports of them by no means to their advantage, and thus impelling them to try and set themselves right in his eyes and in the eyes of the world by a public investigation of their cause. There are difficulties connected with the exact order of events at this point which beset any theory we may adopt, but the one just stated seems to me most in harmony with our sources and with the nature of the case. For a full, though not altogether satisfactory, discussion of the matter, which I cannot dwell upon here, see Walch's *Ketzergeschichte*, IV. p. 116 sq.
13 This Patricius is known to us, so far as I am aware, from this passage only.
14 τῷ οὐικαρίῳ τῶν ἐπάρχων, which doubtless represents the Latin *Vicarius Præfectorum*, the vicar or deputy of the prefects. See Valesius' note *ad locum* and the note of Heinichen (Vol. III. p. 463), with the additional references given by him.
15 This is the first instance we have of an effort on Constantine's

---

CHAPTER VII.

The Exemption of the Clergy.

Copy of an epistle in which the emperor commands that the rulers of the churches be exempted from all political duties.[1]

1

"Greeting to thee, our most esteemed Anulinus. Since it appears from many circumstances that when that religion is despised, in which is preserved the chief reverence for the most holy celestial Power, great dangers are brought upon public affairs; but that when legally adopted and observed[2] it affords the most signal prosperity to the Roman name and remarkable felicity to all the affairs of men, through the divine beneficence, — it has seemed good to me, most esteemed Anulinus, that those men who give their services with due sanctity and with constant observance of this law, to the worship of the divine religion, should receive recompense for their labors. Wherefore it is my will that those within the province entrusted to thee,[3] in the catholic Church, over which Cæcilianus presides,[4] who give their services to this holy religion, and who are commonly called clergymen, be entirely exempted from all public duties, that they may not by any error or sacrilegious negligence be drawn away from the service due to the Deity, but may devote themselves without any hindrance to their own law. For it seems that when they show greatest reverence to the Deity, the greatest benefits accrue to the state. Farewell, our most esteemed and beloved Anulinus."

2

---

part to suppress schismatics. In 316 he enacted a stringent law against the Donatists (see the previous chapter, note 16), which, however, he withdrew within a few years, finding the policy of repression an unwise one. The same was done later in connection with the Arians, whom he at first endeavored to suppress by force, but afterward tolerated. His successors were in the main far less tolerant than he was, and heretics and schismatics were frequently treated with great harshness during the fourth and following centuries.
1 Municipal offices and magistracies were a great burden under the later Roman empire. They entailed heavy expenses for those who filled them, and consequently, unless a man's wealth was large, and his desire for distinction very great, he was glad to be exempted, if possible, from the necessity of supporting such expensive honors, which he was not at liberty to refuse. The same was true of almost all the offices, municipal and provincial offices, high and low. Discharging the duties of an office was in fact practically paying a heavy tax to government, and of course the fewer there were that were compelled to pay this tax, the greater the burden upon the few. As a consequence, the exemption of any class of persons always aroused opposition from those who were not exempted. In granting this immunity to the clergy, however, Constantine was granting them only what had long been enjoyed by the heathen priesthood, and also by some of the learned professions. The privilege bestowed here upon the African clergy was afterward extended to those of other provinces, as we learn from the Theodosian Code, 16. 2 (A.D. 319). The direct result of the exemption was that many persons of means secured admission to the ranks of the clergy, in order to escape the burden of office-holding; and this practice increased so rapidly that within a few years the emperor was obliged to enact various laws restricting the privilege. See Hatch's *Constitution of the Early Christ. Churches*, p. 144 sq.
2 ἐνθέσμως ἀναληφθεῖσαν καὶ φυλαττομένην.
3 i.e. the proconsular province of Africa (see above, chap. 5, § 18).
4 i.e. the Church of the entire province; for the bishop of Carthage was the metropolitan of the province, and indeed was

CHAPTER VIII.

The Subsequent Wickedness of Licinius, and his Death.

1 SUCH blessings did divine and heavenly grace confer upon us through the appearance of our Saviour, and such was the abundance of benefits which prevailed among all men in consequence of the peace which we enjoyed. And thus were our affairs crowned 2 with rejoicings and festivities. But malignant envy, and the demon who loves that which is evil, were not able to bear the sight of these things; and moreover the events that befell the tyrants whom we have already mentioned were not sufficient to bring Licinius 3 to sound reason. For the latter, although his government was prosperous and he was honored with the second rank after the great Emperor Constantine, and was connected with him by the closest ties of marriage, abandoned the imitation of good deeds, and emulated the wickedness of the impious tyrants whose end he had seen with his own eyes, and chose rather to follow their principles than to continue in friendly relations with him who was better than they. Being envious of the common benefactor, he waged an impious and most terrible war against him, paying regard neither to laws of nature, nor treaties, nor blood, and giving 4 no thought to covenants.[1] For Constantine, like an all-gracious emperor, giving him

---

the leading bishop of North Africa, and thus recognized as in some sense at the head of the church of that entire section of country.
[1] To speak of Licinius as alone responsible for the civil war between himself and Constantine, which ended in his own downfall, is quite unjustifiable; indeed, this entire chapter is a painful example of the way in which prejudice distorts facts. The positions of the two emperors was such that a final struggle between them for the sole supremacy was inevitable. Already, in 314, a war broke out, which seems to have resulted from Licinius' refusal to deliver up a relative of his own, who had in some way been concerned in a conspiracy against Constantine. The occasion of the war is not perfectly plain, but it is certain that Constantine, not Licinius, was the aggressor. Constantine came off victorious, but was not able to overthrow his rival, and a treaty was concluded by which Illyricum, one of Licinius' most important provinces, was ceded to Constantine. The two emperors remained at peace, each waiting for a time when he could with advantage attack the other, until 323, when a second and greater war broke out, to which Eusebius, who omits all reference to the former, refers in these two chapters. The immediate occasion of this war, as of the former, is obscure, but it was certainly not due to Constantine's pity for the oppressed Christian subjects of Licinius, and his pious desire to avenge their sufferings, as Eusebius, who in his *Vita Const.* II. 3, in contradiction to this present passage, claims for his prince the honor of beginning the war without any other provocation, would have us believe. Doubtless the fact that Licinius was persecuting his Christian subjects had much to do with the outbreak of the war; for Constantine saw clearly that Licinius had weakened his hold upon his subjects by his conduct, and that therefore a good time had arrived to strike the decisive blow. A pretext—for of course Constantine could not go to war without some more material and plausible pretext than sympathy with oppressed Christian brethren—was furnished by some sort of a misunderstanding in regard to the respective rights of the two sovereigns in the border territory along the Danube frontier, and the war began by Constantine taking the initiative, and invading his rival's territory. Two battles were fought,—one at Adrianople in July, and the other at Chrysopolis in September, 323,—in both of which Constantine was victorious, and the latter of which resulted in the surrender of Licinius, and the accession of Constantine to the supreme sovereignty of both East and West. Cf. Gibbon, Harper's ed., I. p. 490 sq., and Burckhardt's *Zeit Constantins*, 2d ed., p. 328 sq. [1a] See below, p. 400.

---

evidences of true favor, did not refuse alliance with him, and did not refuse him the illustrious marriage with his sister, but honored him by making him a partaker of the ancestral nobility and the ancient imperial blood,[1a] and granted him the right of sharing in the dominion over all as a brother-in-law and co-regent, conferring upon him the government and administration of no less a portion of the Roman provinces than he himself possessed.[2] But Licinius, 5 on the contrary, pursued a course directly opposite to this; forming daily all kinds of plots against his superior, and devising all sorts of mischief, that he might repay his benefactor with evils. At first he attempted to conceal his preparations, and pretended to be a friend, and practiced frequently fraud and deceit, in the hope that he might easily accomplish the desired end.[3] But God was the friend, pro- 6 tector, and guardian of Constantine, and bringing the plots which had been formed in secrecy and darkness to the light, he foiled them. So much virtue does the great armor of piety possess for the warding off of enemies and for the preservation of our own safety. Protected by this, our most divinely favored emperor escaped the multitudinous plots of the abominable man. But when Licinius perceived 7 that his secret preparations by no means progressed according to his mind,—for God revealed every plot and wickedness to the God-favored emperor,—being no longer able to conceal himself, he undertook an open war.[4] And at the same time that he determined 8 to wage war with Constantine, he also proceeded to join battle with the God of the universe, whom he knew that Constantine worshiped, and began, gently for a time and quietly, to attack his pious subjects, who had never done his government any harm.[5] This he did under

---

[2] A more flagrant misrepresentation of facts could hardly be imagined. Licinius received his appointment directly from Galerius and owed nothing whatever to Constantine; in fact, he was an Augustus before the latter was, and held his half of the empire quite independently of the latter, and indeed by a far clearer title than Constantine held his. See above, Bk. VIII. chap. 13, notes 18 and 21.
[3] There is no reason to suppose that Licinius was any more guilty than Constantine in these respects.
[4] This is in direct contradiction to Eusebius' own statement in his *Vita Const.* II. 3 (see above, note 1), and is almost certainly incorrect.
[5] Licinius, as Görres has shown in his able essay *Die Licinianische Christenverfolgung*, p. 5 sq., did not begin to persecute the Christians until the year 319 (the persecution was formerly commonly supposed to have begun some three or four years earlier). The causes of his change of policy in this matter it is impossible to state with certainty, but the exceedingly foolish step seems to have been chiefly due to his growing hatred and suspicion of the Christians as the friends of Constantine. Though he had not hitherto been hostile to them, he had yet never taken any pains to win their friendship and to secure their enthusiastic support as Constantine had, and as a consequence they naturally looked with envy upon their brethren in the west, who were enjoying such signal marks of imperial favor. Licinius could not but be conscious of this; and as the relations between himself and Constantine became more and more strained, it was not unnatural for him to acquire a peculiar enmity toward them, and finally to suspect them of a conspiracy in favor of his rival. Whether he had any grounds for such a suspicion we do not know, but at any rate he began to show his changed attitude in 319 by clearing his palace of Christians (see § 10). No more foolish step can be imagined than the opening of a persecution

the compulsion of his innate wickedness
9 which drove him into terrible blindness. He
did not therefore keep before his eyes the
memory of those who had persecuted the Christians before him, nor of those whose destroyer
and executioner he had been appointed, on
account of the impieties which they had committed. But departing from sound reason, being
seized, in a word, with insanity, he determined
to war against God himself as the ally of Constantine, instead of against the one who was
10 assisted by him. And in the first place, he
drove from his house every Christian, thus
depriving himself, wretched man, of the prayers
which they offered to God in his behalf, which
they are accustomed, according to the teaching
of their fathers, to offer for all men. Then he
commanded that the soldiers in the cities should
be cashiered and stripped of their rank unless
they chose to sacrifice to the demons. And yet
these were small matters when compared
11 with the greater things that followed. Why
is it necessary to relate minutely and in
detail all that was done by the hater of God,
and to recount how this most lawless man invented unlawful laws?[6] He passed an ordinance
that no one should exercise humanity toward the
sufferers in prison by giving them food, and that
none should show mercy to those that were perishing of hunger in bonds; that no one should
in any way be kind, or do any good act, even
though moved by Nature herself to sympathize
with one's neighbors. And this was indeed an
openly shameful and most cruel law, calculated
to expel all natural kindliness. And in addition
to this it was also decreed, as a punishment, that
those who showed compassion should suffer the
same things with those whom they compassion-
ated; and that those who kindly ministered to

the suffering should be thrown into bonds and
into prison, and should endure the same punishment with the sufferers. Such were the decrees
of Licinius.

Why should we recount his innovations 12
in regard to marriage or in regard to the
dying — innovations by which he ventured to
annul the ancient laws of the Romans which
had been well and wisely formed, and to introduce certain barbarous and cruel laws, which
were truly unlawful and lawless?[7] He invented,
to the detriment of the provinces which were
subject to him, innumerable prosecutions,[8] and
all sorts of methods of extorting gold and silver,
new measurements of land[9] and injurious exactions from men in the country, who were
no longer living, but long since dead. Why 13
is it necessary to speak at length of the
banishments which, in addition to these things,
this enemy of mankind inflicted upon those
who had done no wrong, the expatriations of
men of noble birth and high reputation whose
young wives he snatched from them and consigned to certain baser fellows of his own, to be
shamefully abused by them, and the many married women and virgins upon whom he gratified
his passions, although he was in advanced age[10]
— why, I say, is it necessary to speak at length
of these things, when the excessive wickedness
of his last deeds makes the first appear
small and of no account? For, finally, he 14
reached such a pitch of madness that he
attacked the bishops, supposing that they — as
servants of the God over all — would be hostile to his measures. He did not yet proceed
against them openly, on account of his fear of
his superior, but as before, secretly and craftily,
employing the treachery of the governors for
the destruction of the most distinguished of
them. And the manner of their murder was
strange, and such as had never before been
heard of. The deeds which he performed 15

at this critical juncture. Just at a time when he needed the most
loyal support of all his subjects, he wantonly alienated the affections
of a large and influential portion of them, and in the very act gave
them good reason to become devoted adherents of his enemy. The
persecution of Licinius, as Görres has clearly shown (*ibid.* p. 29 sq.)
was limited in its extent and mild in its character. It began, as
Eusebius informs us, with the expulsion of Christians from the palace, but even here it was not universal; at least, Eusebius of Nicomedia and other prominent clergymen still remained Licinius' friends,
and were treated as such by him. In fact, he evidently punished only
those whom he thought to be his enemies and to be interested in the
success of Constantine, if not directly conspiring in his behalf. No
general edicts of persecution were issued by him, and the sufferings
of the Christians seem to have been confined almost wholly to occasional loss of property or banishment, or, still less frequently, imprisonment. A few bishops appear to have been put to death, but
there is no reason to suppose that they suffered at the command of
Licinius himself. Of course, when it was known that he was hostile to the Christians, fanatical heathen officials might venture, occasionally at least, to violate the existing laws and bring hated
bishops to death on one pretext or another. But such cases were
certainly rare, and there seem to have been no instances of execution on the simple ground of Christianity, as indeed there could not
be while the Edict of Milan remained unrepealed. Eusebius' statement that Licinius was about to proceed to severer measures, when
the war with Constantine broke out and put a stop to his plans, is
very likely true; but otherwise his report is rather highly colored,
as many other sources fully warrant us in saying. For a careful and
very satisfactory discussion of this whole subject, see Görres, *ibid.*
p. 32 sq.
 [6] Note the play on the word νόμος. νόμους ἀνόμους ὁ πανανομώ-
τατος.

[7] Another play upon the same word: νόμους, ἀνόμους ὡς ἀληθῶς καὶ παρανόμους.
[8] ἐπισκήψεις. The same word is used in connection with Maximinus in Bk. VIII. chap. 14, § 10, above. Valesius cites passages
from Aurelius Victor, and Libanius, in which it is said that Licinius
was very kindly disposed toward the rural population of his realm,
and that the cities flourished greatly under him. Moreover, Zosimus gives just such an account of Constantine as Eusebius gives of
Licinius. Allowance must undoubtedly be made on the one side for
Eusebius' prejudice against Licinius, as on the other for Zosimus'
well-known hatred of Constantine. Doubtless both accounts are
greatly exaggerated, though they probably contain considerable
truth, for there were few Roman emperors that did not practice
severe exactions upon their subjects, at times at least, if not continually, and it is always easy in a case of this kind to notice the dark
and to overlook the bright features of a reign. Licinius was certainly a cruel man in many respects, and one hardly cares to enter
the lists in his defense, but it should be observed that, until he became the enemy of Constantine and the persecutor of the Christians,
Eusebius uniformly spoke of him in the highest terms. Compare
Stroth's note *ad locum* (quoted also by Closs).
[9] i.e. for the purpose of making new assessments, which is always
apt to be looked upon as an oppressive act, whether unjust or not.
[10] ἐσχατόγηρως. Valesius remarks that, according to the epitomist of Victor, Licinius died in the sixtieth year of his age, so that
at the time of which Eusebius was speaking he was little more than
fifty years of age.

at Amaseia [11] and in the other cities of Pontus surpassed every excess of cruelty. Some of the churches of God were again razed to the ground, others were closed, so that none of those accustomed to frequent them could enter them and render the worship due to God.

16 For his evil conscience led him to suppose that prayers were not offered in his behalf; but he was persuaded that we did everything in the interest of the God-beloved emperor, and that we supplicated God for him.[12] Therefore he hastened to turn his fury against us.

17 And then those among the governors who wished to flatter him, perceiving that in doing such things they pleased the impious tyrant,[13] made some of the bishops suffer the penalties customarily inflicted upon criminals, and led away and without any pretext punished like murderers those who had done no wrong. Some now endured a new form of death: having their bodies cut into many pieces with the sword, and after this savage and most horrible spectacle, being thrown into the depths of

18 the sea as food for fishes. Thereupon the worshipers of God again fled, and fields and deserts, forests and mountains, again received the servants of Christ. And when the impious tyrant had thus met with success in these measures, he finally planned to renew the per-

19 secution against all. And he would have succeeded in his design, and there would have been nothing to hinder him in the work, had not God, the defender of the lives of his own people, most quickly anticipated that which was about to happen, and caused a great light to shine forth as in the midst of a dark and gloomy night, and raised up a deliverer for all, leading into those regions with a lofty arm, his servant, Constantine.

CHAPTER IX.

The Victory of Constantine, and the Blessings which under him accrued to the Subjects of the Roman Empire.

1 To him, therefore, God granted, from heaven above, the deserved fruit of piety, the trophies of victory over the impious, and he cast the guilty one with all his counselors and friends prostrate at the feet of Con-

2 stantine. For when Licinius carried his madness to the last extreme, the emperor, the friend of God, thinking that he ought no longer to be tolerated, acting upon the basis of sound judgment, and mingling the firm princi-

ples of justice with humanity, gladly determined to come to the protection of those who were oppressed by the tyrant, and undertook, by putting a few destroyers out of the way, to save the greater part of the human race.[1] For 3 when he had formerly exercised humanity alone and had shown mercy to him who was not worthy of sympathy, nothing was accomplished; for Licinius did not renounce his wickedness, but rather increased his fury against the peoples that were subject to him, and there was left to the afflicted no hope of salvation, oppressed as they were by a savage beast. Wherefore, 4 the protector of the virtuous, mingling hatred for evil with love for good, went forth with his son Crispus, a most beneficent prince,[2] and extended a saving right hand to all that were perishing. Both of them, father and son, under the protection, as it were, of God, the universal King, with the Son of God, the Saviour of all, as their leader and ally, drew up their forces on all sides against the enemies of the Deity and won an easy victory;[3] God having prospered them in the battle in all respects according to their wish. Thus, suddenly, and sooner 5 than can be told, those who yesterday and the day before breathed death and threatening were no more, and not even their names were remembered, but their inscriptions and their honors suffered the merited disgrace. And the things which Licinius with his own eyes had seen come upon the former impious tyrants he himself likewise suffered, because he did not receive instruction nor learn wisdom from the chastisements of his neighbors, but followed the same path of impiety which they had trod, and was justly hurled over the same precipice. Thus he lay prostrate. 6

But Constantine, the mightiest victor, adorned with every virtue of piety, together with his son Crispus, a most God-beloved prince, and in all respects like his father, recovered the East which belonged to them;[4] and they formed one united Roman empire as of old, bringing under their peaceful sway the whole world from the rising of the sun to the opposite quarter, both north and south, even to the extremities

---

[11] Amaseia, or Amasia, as it is more commonly called, was an important city of Pontus, situated on the river Iris.
[12] Eusebius makes it clear enough in this sentence that Licinius suspected a treasonable conspiracy on the part of the Christians. See above, note 1.
[13] See *ibid.*

---

[1] Eusebius speaks in the same way of the origin of the war in his *Vita Const.* II. 3. Cf. the previous chapter, note 1.
[2] Κρίσπῳ Βασιλεῖ φιλανθρωποτάτῳ. Crispus, the oldest son of Constantine, by his first wife Minervina, was born about the beginning of the fourth century, made Cæsar in 317, and put to death by Constantine in 326 on suspicion, whether justified or not we do not know, of conspiracy and treason. Our sources agree in pronouncing him a young man of most excellent character and marked ability; and indeed he proved his valor and military talents in the west in a campaign against the Franks, and also in the present war with Licinius, in which he won a great naval battle, and thus contributed materially to his father's victory. His execution is the darkest blot on the memory of Constantine, and however it may be palliated can never, as it seems, be excused. Eusebius prudently omits all reference to it in his *Vita Const.*
[3] The final battle was fought in September, 323. See the previous chapter, note 4.
[4] τὴν οἰκείαν ἑῴαν ἀπελάμβανον. Constantine's sole right to the East was the right of conquest.

7   of the declining day.   All fear therefore of those who had formerly afflicted them was taken away from men, and they celebrated splendid and festive days.   Everything was filled with light, and those who before were downcast beheld each other with smiling faces and beaming eyes.   With dances and hymns, in city and country, they glorified first of all God the universal King, because they had been thus taught, and then the pious emperor

8   with his God-beloved children.   There was oblivion of past evils and forgetfulness of every deed of impiety; there was enjoyment of present benefits and expectation of those yet to come.   Edicts full of clemency and laws containing tokens of benevolence and true piety were issued in every place by the victorious emperor.[5]   Thus after all tyranny had been

9   purged away, the empire which belonged to them was preserved firm and without a rival for Constantine and his sons alone.[6]   And having obliterated the godlessness of their predecessors, recognizing the benefits conferred upon them by God, they exhibited their love of virtue and their love of God, and their piety and gratitude to the Deity, by the deeds which they performed in the sight of all men.

---

[5] Some of these laws of Constantine have been preserved by Eusebius in his *Vita Const.* Bk. II.

[6] It is clear from this statement, as well as from the references to Crispus in the previous paragraphs, that the *History* was completed before his execution. See above, p. 45.

THE END, WITH GOD'S HELP, OF THE TENTH BOOK OF THE CHURCH
HISTORY OF EUSEBIUS PAMPHILI.

SUPPLEMENTARY NOTES AND TABLES.

On Bk. III. chap. 3, § 5 (note 17, continued).

Since this note was in type Dr. Gardiner's admirable and exhaustive essay on the authorship of the Epistle to the Hebrews (in the *Nicene and Post-Nicene Fathers*, First Series, Vol. XIV. p. 341 sq.) has come to hand, and I have been much pleased to see that the theory that Barnabas wrote the epistle is accepted and defended with vigor.

On Bk. III. chap. 3, § 6 (note 22, continued).

Upon the last chapter of Romans and its relation to the remainder of the epistle, see especially Farrar's *Life and Work of St. Paul*, p. 450 sq., Weiss' *Einleitung in das N. T.* p. 245 sq., Pfleiderer's *Urchristenthum*, p. 145, Renan's *Saint Paul*, p. 461 sq. (maintaining that an editor has combined four copies of the one encyclical letter of Paul, addressed severally to as many different churches), Lightfoot's *Commentary on Philippians*, p. 172 sq., and Schaff, *Ch. History*, I. p. 765.

On Bk. III. chap. 24, § 17 (note 18, continued).

In three places in the *Church History* (Bk. III. chap. 24, § 17, chap. 25, § 2, and chap. 39, § 16) John's "former" epistle is referred to, as if he had written only two. In the last passage the use of προτέρα instead of πρώτη might be explained as Westcott suggests (*Canon of the New Testament*, p. 77, note 2), by supposing Eusebius to be reproducing the words of Papias; but in the other passages this explanation will not do, for the words are certainly Eusebius' own. In the Muratorian Canon only two epistles of John are mentioned, and in Irenæus the second epistle is quoted as if it were the first (see Westcott, *ibid.* p. 384, note 1). These facts lead Westcott to ask : " Is it possible that the second epistle was looked upon as an appendix to the first? and may we thus explain the references to *two* epistles of John?" He continues : " The first epistle, as is well known, was called *ad Parthos* by Augustine and some other Latin authorities ; and the same title πρὸς Πάρθους is given to the second epistle in one Greek manuscript (62 Scholz). The Latin translation of Clement's *Outlines* (IV. 66) says : *Secunda Johannis epistola quæ ad virgines* (παρθένους) *scripta simplissima est.* Jerome, it may be added, quotes names from the *third* epistle as from the *second* (*De nom. Hebr.*)." On the other hand, in Bk. V. chap. 8, § 7, Eusebius speaks of the "first" (πρώτη) epistle of John, and in Bk. III. chap. 25, § 3, he expressly mentions a second and third epistle of John. It is evident, therefore, that whatever the use of προτέρα instead of πρώτη in connection with John's first epistle may mean as used by others, it does not indicate a knowledge of only a first and second as used by him. It is by no means impossible, however, that Westcott's suggestion may be correct, and that the first and second epistles were sometimes looked upon as but one, and it is possible that such use of them by some of his predecessors may account for Eusebius' employment of the word προτέρα in three separate passages.

On Bk. III. chap. 25, § 4 (note 18, continued).

The words ἡ φερομένη Βαρνάβα ἐπιστολή have been commonly translated "the so-called Epistle of Barnabas," or "the Epistle ascribed to Barnabas," implying a doubt in Eusebius' mind as to the authenticity of the work. This translation, however, is, in my opinion, quite unwarranted. There are passages in Eusebius where the word φέρομαι used in connection with writings cannot by any possibility be made to bear this meaning ; cases in which it can be interpreted only "to be extant" or "in circulation." Compare, for instance, Bk. II. chap. 15, § 1, Μάρκον οὗ τὸ εὐαγγέλιον φέρεται ; II. 18. 6, μονόβιβλα αὐτοῦ φέρεται ; III. 9. 4 ; III. 16 ; III. 25. 3, ἡ λεγομένη Ἰακώβου φέρεται; III. 37. 4; III. 39. 1; IV. 3. 1, εἰσέτι δὲ φέρεται παρὰ πλείστοις; IV. 14. 9, ἐν τῇ δηλωθείσῃ πρὸς φιλιππησίους αὐτοῦ γραφῇ φερομένῃ εἰς δεῦρο. Compare also IV. 15. 1; IV. 23. 4, 9, 12; IV. 24. 1; IV. 28; V. 5. 6; 19. 3; 23. 2; 24. 10; VI. 15. 1; VI. 20, &c. These passages, and many others which are cited by Heinichen (Vol. III. p. 91), prove that the word is frequently used in the sense of "extant" or "in circulation." But in spite of these numerous examples, Heinichen maintains that the word is also used by Eusebius in another and quite different sense; namely, "so-called" or "ascribed to," thus equivalent to λεγομένη. A careful examination, however, of all the passages cited by him in illustration of this second meaning will show that in them too the word may be interpreted in the same way as in those already referred to; in fact, that in many of them that is in itself the more natural interpretation. The passages to which we refer are Bk. III. chap. 25, §§ 2, 3, and 4; III. 3. 1, τὴν δὲ φερομένην αὐτοῦ δευτέραν; III. 39. 6 (where I ought to have translated "is extant under the name of John"). To draw a distinction between the meaning of the word as used in these and in the other passages is quite arbitrary, and therefore unwarranted. The sense in which, as we have found, Eusebius so commonly employs the word attaches also to the Latin word *fertur* in the Muratorian Canon. I have not endeavored to trace carefully the use of the word in other writers; but while many instances occur in which it is certainly used in this sense, others in which either interpretation is allowable, I have not yet found one in which this meaning is ruled out by the nature of the case or by the context. In view of these facts I believe we should be careful to draw a sharp distinction between λεγομένη or καλουμένη and φερομένη when used in connection with written works.

A considerable portion of my translation was in type before I had observed this distinction between the two words, which is commonly quite overlooked, and as a consequence in a few cases my rendering of the word φερομένη is inaccurate. All such cases I have endeavored to call attention to in these supplementary notes.

On Bk. III. chap. 28, § 1.

For *the Disputation which is ascribed to him*, read *his extant Disputation.*

On Bk. III. chap. 32, § 6 (note 14ᵃ).

The Greek reads πάσης ἐκκλησίας (without the article), and so, two lines below, ἐν πάσῃ ἐκκλησίᾳ. All the translators (with the exception of Pratten in the *Ante-Nicene Fathers*, Vol. VIII., who reads, "the churches") render "the whole church," as if reading πᾶς with the article. We have not, it is true, enough of Hegesippus' writings to be able to ascertain positively his use of πᾶς, and it is possible that he carelessly employed it indifferently with or without the article to signify the definite "all" or "the whole." In the absence of positive testimony, however, that he failed to draw the proper distinction between its use with and its use without the article, and in view of the fact that Eusebius himself (as well as other early Fathers so far as I am able to recall) is very consistent in making the distinction, I have not felt at liberty in my translation to depart from a strict grammatical interpretation of the phrases in question. Moreover, upon second thought, it seems quite as possible that Hegesippus meant to say "every" not "all"; for he can hardly have supposed these relatives of the Lord to have presided literally over the whole Church, while he might very well say that they presided each over the church in the city in which he lived, which is all that the words necessarily imply. The phrase just below, "in every church," is perhaps as natural as "in the whole church."

On Bk. III. chap. 36, § 13.

For *the Epistle to the Philippians which is ascribed to him*, read *his extant Epistle to the Philippians.*

On Bk. III. chap. 39, § 1 (note 1, continued).

Since the above note was in type Resch's important work on the *Agrapha* (von Gebhardt and Harnack's *Texte und Untersuchungen*, Bd. V. Heft 4) has come to hand. On p. 27 sq. he discusses at considerable length the sources of the Synoptic Gospels. He accepts the theory which is most widely adopted by New-Testament critics, that the synoptic tradition as contained in our Synoptic Gospels rests upon an original Gospel of Mark (nearly if not quite identical with our present Gospel of Mark) and a pre-canonical Hebrew Gospel. In agreement with such critics he draws a sharp distinction between this original Hebrew Gospel and our canonical Greek Matthew, while at the same time recognizing that the latter reproduces that original more fully than either of the other Gospels does. This original Hebrew he then identifies with the λόγια referred to by Papias as composed by Matthew in the Hebrew tongue (see Bk. III. chap. 39, § 16) ; that is, with the traditional Hebrew Gospel of Matthew (see *ibid.* chap. 24, note 5). The arguments which he urges in support of this position are very strong. Handmann regards the Gospel according to the Hebrews as the second original source of the synoptic tradition, along-side of the Ur-Marcus, and even suggests its identification with the λόγια of Papias, and yet denies its identity with the Hebrew Matthew. On the other hand, Resch regards the Hebrew Matthew, which he identifies with the λόγια of Papias, as the second original source of the synop-tic tradition, alongside of Mark or the Ur-Marcus, and yet, like Handmann, though on entirely different grounds, denies the identity of the Gospel according to the Hebrews with the Hebrew Matthew. Their positions certainly tend to confirm my suggestion that the Hebrew Matthew and the Gospel according to the Hebrews were originally identical (see above, Bk. III. chap. 27, note 8).

On Bk. III. chap. 39, § 6.

For *ascribed by name to John,* read *extant under the name of John.*

On Bk. III. chap. 39, § 16.

For *from the first epistle of John and from that of Peter likewise,* read *from the former epistle of John and from the epistle of Peter likewise.* See p. 388.

On Bk. IV. chap. 10.

For *the Pious,* read *Pius.*

On Bk. IV. chap. 18, § 2.

For *the Pious,* read *Pius.*

On Bk. V. Introd. § 1 (note 3, continued). *The Successors of Antoninus Pius.*

Antoninus Pius was succeeded in 161 by his adopted sons, Marcus Aurelius Antoninus Verus and Lucius Ceionius Ælius Aurelius Commodus Antoninus. Upon his accession to the throne the former transferred his name Verus to the latter, who was thenceforth called Lucius Aurelius Verus. In his *Chronicle* Eusebius keeps these two princes distinct, but in his *History* he falls into sad confusion in regard to them, and this confusion has drawn upon him the severe censure of all his critics. He knew of course, as every one did, that Antoninus Pius had two successors. In Bk. IV. chap. 14, § 10, he states this directly, and gives the names of the successors as " Marcus Aurelius Verus, who was also called Antoninus," and " Lucius." From that point on he calls the former of these princes simply Antoninus Verus, Antoninus, or Verus, dropping entirely the name Marcus Aurelius. In Bk. IV. chap. 18, § 2, he speaks of the emperor " whose times we are now recording," that is, the successor of Antoninus Pius, and calls him Antoninus Verus. In Bk. V. Introd. § 1 he refers to the same emperor as Antoninus Verus, and in Bk. V. chap. 4, § 3, and chap. 9, he calls him simply Antoninus, while in Bk. IV. chap. 13, § 8, he speaks of him as the " Emperor Verus." The death of this Emperor Antoninus is mentioned in Bk. V. chap. 9, and it is there said that he reigned nineteen years and was then succeeded by Commodus. It is evident that in all these passages he is referring to the emperor whom we know as Marcus Aurelius, but to whom he gives that name only once, when he records his accession to the empire. On the other hand, in Bk. V. chap. 5, § 1, Euse-bius speaks of Marcus Aurelius Cæsar and expressly distinguishes him from the Emperor Antoninus, to whom he has referred at the close of the previous chapter, and makes him the brother of that emperor. Again, in the same chapter, § 6, he calls this Marcus Aurelius Cæsar, just referred to, the " Emperor Marcus," still evidently distinguishing him from the Emperor Antoninus. In this chapter, therefore, he thinks of Marcus Aurelius as the younger of the two sons left by Antoninus Pius ; that is, he identifies him with the one whom we call Lucius Verus, and whom he himself calls Lucius in Bk. IV. chap. 14, § 10. Eusebius thus commits a palpable error. How are we to explain it?

The explanation seems to me to lie in the circumstance that Eusebius attempted to reconcile the tradition that Marcus Aurelius was not a persecutor with the fact known to him as a historian, that the emperor who succeeded Antoninus Pius was. It was the common belief in the time of Eusebius, as it had been during the entire preceding century, that all the good emperors had been friendly to the Christians, and that only the bad emperors had persecuted. Of course, among the good emperors was included the philosophical Marcus Aurelius (cf. e.g. Tertullian's *Apol.* chap. 5, to which Eusebius refers in Bk. V. chap. 5). It was of Marcus Aurelius, moreover, that the story of the Thundering Legion was told (see *ibid.*). But Eusebius was not able to overlook the fact that numerous martyrdoms occurred during the reign of the successor of Antoninus Pius. He had the documents recording the terrible persecution at Lyons and Vienne; he had an apology of Melito, describing the hardships which the Christians endured under the same emperor (see Bk. IV. chap. 26). He found himself, as an historian, face to face with two apparently contradictory lines of facts. How was the contradiction to be solved? He seems to have solved it by assuming that a confusion of names had taken place, and that the prince commonly known as Marcus Aurelius, whose noble character was traditional, and whose friendship to the Christians he could not doubt, was the younger, not the older of the two brothers, and therefore not responsible for the numerous martyrdoms which took place after the death of Antoninus Pius. And yet he is not consistent with himself even in his History; for he gives the two brothers their proper names when he first mentions them, and says nothing of an identification of Marcus Aurelius with Lucius. It is not impossible that the words Marcus Aurelius, which are used nowhere else of the older brother, are an interpolation; but for this there is no evidence, and it may be suggested as more probable that at the time when this passage was written the solution of the difficulty which he gives distinctly in Bk. V. chap. 5 had not yet occurred to him. That he should be able to fancy that Marcus Aurelius was identical with Lucius is perhaps not strange when we remember how much confusion was caused in the minds of other writers besides himself by the perplexing identity of the names of the various members of the Antonine family. To the two successors of Antoninus Pius, the three names, Aurelius, Verus, and Antoninus, alike belonged. It is not surprising that Eusebius should under the circumstances think that the name Marcus may also have belonged to the younger one. This supposition would seem to him to find some confirmation in the fact that the most common official designation of the older successor of Antoninus Pius was not Marcus Aurelius, but Antoninus simply, or M. Antoninus. The name Marcus Aurelius or Marcus was rather a popular than an official designation. Even in the *Chronicle* there seems to be a hint that Eusebius thought of a possible distinction between Antoninus the emperor and Marcus, or Marcus Aurelius; for while he speaks of the " Emperor Antoninus " at the beginning of the passages in which he recounts the story of the Thundering Legion (year of Abr. 2188), he says at the close: *literæ quoque exstant Marci regis* (the *M. Aureli gravissimi imperatoris* of Jerome looks like a later expansion of the simpler original) *quibus testatur copias suas iamiam perituras Christianorum precibus servatas esse.* But even when he had reached the solution pointed out, Eusebius did not find himself clear of difficulties; for his sources put the occurrence of the Thundering Legion after the date at which the younger brother was universally supposed to have died, and it was difficult on still other grounds to suppose the prince named Marcus Aurelius already dead in 169 (the date given by Eusebius himself in his *Chronicle* for the death of Lucius). In this emergency he came to the conclusion that there must be some mistake in regard to the date of his death, and possessing no record of the death of Marcus Aurelius as distinct from Antoninus, he simply passed it by without mention.

That Eusebius in accepting such a lame theory showed himself altogether too much under the influence of traditional views cannot be denied; but when we remember that the tradition that Marcus Aurelius was not a persecutor was supported by writers whose honesty and accuracy he could never have thought of questioning, as well as by the very nature of the case, we must, while we smile at the result, at least admire his effort to solve the contradiction which he, as an historian, felt more keenly than a less learned man, unacquainted with the facts on the other side, would have done.

On Bk. V. chap. 1, § 27 (note 26, continued).

See also Bk. VIII. chap. 10, note 5.

On Bk. VI. chap. 2 (note 1, continued). *Origen's Life and Writings.*

Origen Adamantius (on the second name, see Bk. VI. chap. 14, note 12) was of Christian parentage and probably of Greek descent on his father's side (as stated in the previous note), but whether born in Alexandria or not we do not know. Westcott suggests that his mother may have been of Jewish descent, because in an epistle of Jerome (*ad Paulam: Ep.* 39, § 1, Migne's ed.) he is said to have learned Hebrew so thoroughly that he " vied with his mother " in the singing of psalms (but compare the stricture of Redepenning on this passage, p. 187, note 1). The date of his birth may be gathered from the fact (stated in this chapter) that he was in his seventeenth year at the time of his father's death, which gives us 185 or 186 as the year of his birth (cf. Redepenning, I. p. 417–420, Erste Beilage). We learn from the present chapter that as a boy he was carefully trained by his father in the Scriptures and afterward in Greek literature, a training of which he made good use in later life. He was also a pupil of Clement in the catechetical school, as we learn from chaps. 6 and 14 (on the time, see chap. 6, note 4). He showed remarkable natural ability, and after the death of his father (being himself saved from martyrdom only by a device of his mother), when left in poverty with his mother and six younger brothers (see § 13 of this chapter), he was able, partly by the assistance of a wealthy lady and partly by teaching literature, to support himself (§ 14). Whether he supported the rest of the family Eusebius does not state, but his thoroughly religious character does not permit us to imagine that he left them to suffer. In his eighteenth year, there being no one at the head of the catechetical school in Alexandria, he was induced to take the school in charge and to devote himself to the work of instruction in the Christian faith. Soon afterward the entire charge of the work was officially committed to him by Demetrius, the bishop of Alexandria (see chap. 3). He lived at this time a life of rigid asceticism (ibid.), and even went so far as to mutilate himself in his zeal for the prosecution of his work (see chap. 8). His great influence naturally aroused the hostility of unbelievers against him; but though many of his pupils suffered martyrdom (see chap. 4), he himself escaped, we do not know how. Eusebius ascribes his preservation to the providence of God (ibid.). During these years in which he was at the head of the catechetical school, he devoted himself with vigor to the study of Greek philosophy, and was for a time a pupil of the Neo-Platonist Ammonius Saccas (chap. 19). He studied non-Christian thought, as he tells us, in order that he might be the better able to instruct his pagan and heretical pupils (ibid.). His labors in the school in time grew so heavy that he was obliged to associate with himself his friend and fellow-pupil Heraclas, to whom he committed the work of elementary instruction (chap. 15). It was during this time that he seems to have begun his *Hexapla*, having learned Hebrew in order to fit himself the better for his work upon the Old Testament (chap. 16). During this period (while Zephyrinus was bishop of Rome, i.e. before 217) he made a brief visit to Rome (chap. 14), and later he was summoned to Arabia, to give instruction to the governor of that country, and remained there a short time (chap. 19). Afterward, on account of a great tumult in Alexandria (see chap. 19, note 22), he left the city and went to Cæsarea in Palestine, where, although only a layman, he publicly expounded the Scriptures in the church (chap. 19). The bishop Demetrius strongly disapproved of this, and summoned him back to Alexandria (ibid.). Upon his return to Alexandria he entered upon the work of writing Commentaries on the Scriptures (see chap. 23). During this period he wrote also other important works (see chap. 24).

In the tenth year of Alexander Severus (A.D. 231) he left Alexandria (according to chap. 26) and took up his residence in Cæsarea, leaving his catechetical school in charge of his assistant, Heraclas. The cause of his departure is stated in chap. 23 to have been "some necessary affairs of the church" which called him to Greece. (For a statement of the reasons which lead me, contrary to the common opinion, to identify the departure mentioned in chap. 23 with that mentioned in chap. 26, see below, p. 395 sq.) Jerome (*de vir. ill.* c. 54) says that he went to Achaia on account of heresies which were troubling the churches there. His words are: *Et propter ecclesias Achaiæ, quæ pluribus hæresibus vexabantur, sub testimonio ecclesiasticæ epistolæ Athenas per Palæstinam pergeret.* He passed through Palestine on his way to Greece, and it was at this time that he was ordained a presbyter by the Palestinian bishops (chap. 23), Theoctistus of Cæsarea and Alexander of Jerusalem (according to Jerome, *l.c.*; cf. also Euseb. chap. 8). Whether he remained long in Palestine at this time, or went on at once to Greece, we do not know; but that a visit (to be distinguished from the second visit mentioned in chap. 32; see note 4 on that chapter) was made we know from a fragment of one of Origen's epistles written from Athens (printed in Lommatzsch's ed. of Origen's works, XXV. p. 388); with which are to be compared Epiphanius, *Hær.* LXIV. 1, and the remark made by Eusebius in chap. 16, § 2, in regard to the finding of a copy of a translation in Nicopolis. Origen's ordination resulted in the complete alienation of the bishop Demetrius (upon his earlier and later attitude toward Origen, and the causes of the change, see below, p. 394 sq.), and he called a council in Alexandria of bishops and presbyters (the council must have been held very soon after the receipt of the news of Origen's ordination, for Demetrius died in 232; see Bk. V. chap. 22, note 4) which decided that Origen should be required to leave Alexandria and not be allowed to reside or to teach there, but did not depose him from the priesthood. Afterward, however, Demetrius, combining with some bishops of like mind with himself, deposed Origen from his office, and the sentence was ratified by those who had before voted with him. Photius gives this account in *Cod.* 118, quoting from the lost *Defense* of Pamphilus and Eusebius. Eusebius himself tells us nothing about these proceedings in his History, but simply refers us (chap. 23) to the second book of his *Defense*, which he says contained a full account of the matter. (Upon the bearing of the words quoted by Photius from the *Defense*, see below, p. 395 sq.) Demetrius wrote of the result of the council "to the whole world" (according to Jerome's *de vir. ill.* c. 54), and the sentence was concurred in by the bishops of Rome and of all the other churches, except those of Palestine, Arabia, Phœnicia, and Achaia (see Jerome *ad Paul. Ep.* 33; and *Apol. adv. libros Ruf.* II. 18). Taking up his abode in Cæsarea, Origen made this place his headquarters for the rest of his life, and found there the most cordial sympathy and support (chap. 27). He carried on in Cæsarea a catechetical school, expounding the Scriptures, lecturing on theology, and at the same time continuing his literary labors in peace until the persecution of Maximinus (A.D. 235–237), during which some of his friends in Cæsarea suffered (see chaps. 27, 28, 30, 32, and 36). How Origen escaped and where he was during the persecution we do not know (see chap. 28, note 2). In 237 or 238, at any rate, he was (again) in Cæsarea, and at this time Gregory Thaumaturgus delivered his *Panegyric*, which is our best source for a knowledge of Origen's methods of teaching and of the influence which he exerted over his pupils. (Upon the date, see Draeseke, *Der Brief des Origenes an Gregorios* in the *Jabrbücher f. prot. Theologie*, 1887, p. 102 sq.) During this period he did considerable traveling, making another visit to Athens (see chap. 32) and two to Arabia (see chaps. 33 and 37). It was while in Cæsarea, and when he was over sixty years old, that he first permitted his discourses to be taken down by shorthand writers (see chap. 26). His correspondence with the Emperor Philip and his wife is mentioned by Eusebius in the same chapter. He was arrested during the Decian persecution and suffered terrible torments, but not martyrdom (chap. 39). He died not much more than a year after the close of the persecution, in the seventieth year of his age (see Bk. VII. chap. 1), at Tyre, and was buried there (Jerome, *de vir. ill.* c. 54).

Origen was without doubt the greatest scholar and the most original thinker of his age. He was at the same time a man of most devout piety, and employed all his wonderful talents in the service of what he believed to be the truth. His greatest labors were in the field of exegesis, and here his writings were epoch-making, although his results were often completely vitiated by his use of the allegorical method of interpretation and his neglect of the grammatical and historical sense. His services in the cause of scientific theology cannot be overestimated, and his thinking long stimulated the brightest minds of the Church, both orthodox and heretical. Both his natural predilections and his training in the philosophy which prevailed in Alexandria in that day led him in the direction of idealism, and to an excess of this, combined with his deep desire — common also to Clement — to reconcile Christianity with reason and to commend it to the minds of philosophers, are due most of his errors, nearly all of which are fascinating and lofty in conception. Those errors led the Church to refuse him a place among its saints and even among its Fathers in the stricter sense. Even before his death suspicions of his orthodoxy were widespread; and although he had many followers and warm defenders, his views were finally condemned at a home synod in Constantinople in 543 (?) (see Helele, II. 790). Into the bitter controversies which raged during the fourth and fifth centuries, and in which Jerome and Rufinus (the former against, the latter for, Origen) played so large a part we cannot enter here. See the article *Origenistic Controversies* in the *Dict. of Christ. Biog.*, or any of the Church histories and lives of Origen.

Origen was a marvelously prolific writer. Epiphanius (*Hær.* LXIV. 63) says that it was commonly reported that he had written 6000 works. Jerome reduces the number to less than a third (*adv. Ruf.* II. 22). But whatever the number, we know that he was one of the most voluminous — perhaps the most voluminous writer of antiquity. He wrote works of the most diverse nature, critical, exegetical, philosophical and theological, apologetic and practical, besides numerous epistles. (On his great critical work, the *Hexapla*, see chap. 16, note 8.) His exegetical works consisted of commentaries, *scholia* (or detached notes), and homilies. Of his commentaries on the Old Testament, which were very numerous, only fragments of those on Genesis, Exodus, the Psalms, and the Song of Solomon are preserved in the version of Rufinus, and a fragment of the commentary on Ezekiel in the *Philocalia*. Of the New Testament commentaries we have numerous fragments both in Greek and Latin (especially on Matthew and John), and the whole of Romans in the translation of Rufinus. Upon the commentaries composed by Origen while still in Alexandria, see chap. 24; on those written afterwards, see chaps. 32 and 36. No complete *scholia* are extant; but among the numerous exegetical fragments which are preserved there may be portions of these *scholia*, as well as of the commentaries and homilies. It is not always possible to tell to which a fragment belongs. Of the homilies, over 200 are preserved, the majority of them in the translation of Rufinus.

The philosophical and theological works known to us are the two books *On the Resurrection* (see chap. 24, note 5) : the *De principiis* (see *ibid.* note 6) ; and the *Stromata* (see *ibid.* note 7). Origen's great apologetic work is his *Contra Celsum* (see chap. 36, note 3).

Two works of a practical character are known to us : *On Martyrdom* (see chap. 28, note 3) ; and *On Prayer*. The latter work is not mentioned by Eusebius in his History, but is referred to in Pamphilus' *Apology for Origen*, Chap. VIII. (Lommatzsch, XXIV. p. 397). It is extant in the original Greek, and is printed by Lommatzsch, XVII. p. 79–297. It is addressed to two of his friends, Ambrosius and Tatiana, and is one of his most beautiful works. As to the date at which Origen wrote the work, we know (from chap. 23 of the work) only that it was written after the composition of the commentary on Genesis (see above, Bk. VI. chap. 24), but whether before or after his departure from Alexandria we cannot tell.

Of his epistles only two are preserved entire, one to Julius Africanus, and another to Gregory Thaumaturgus. On the former, see chap. 31, note 1. On the latter and on Origen's other epistles see chap. 36, note 7.

Finally must be mentioned the *Philocalia* (Lommatzsch, XXV. p. 1–278), a collection of judiciously selected extracts from Origen's works in twenty-seven books. Its compilers were Gregory Nazianzen and Basil.

The principal edition of Origen's works is that of the Benedictine Delarue in 4 vols. fol. ; reprinted by Migne in 8 vols. 8vo. A convenient edition is that of Lommatzsch, in 25 vols. small 8vo., a revision of Delarue's. Only his *De principiis, Contra Cels.*, and the epistles to Africanus and to Gregory have been translated into English, and are given in the *Ante-Nicene Fathers*, Vol. IV. p. 221 sqq. Of lives of Origen must be mentioned that of Huetius : *Origeniana* (Paris, 1679, in 2 vols.; reprinted in Delarue and Lommatzsch) ; also Redepenning's *Origenes. Eine Darstellung seines Lebens und seiner Lehre* (Bonn, 1841 and 1846, in 2 vols.). The respective sections in Lardner and Tillemont should be compared, and the thorough article of Westcott in the *Dict. of Christ. Biog.* IV. 96–142. For a good list of the literature on Origen, see Schaff, *Ch. Hist.* II. p. 785.

On Bk. VI. chap. 8, § 5 (note 4). *Origen and Demetrius.*

The friendship of Demetrius for Origen began early and continued, apparently without interruption, for many years. In 203 he committed to him the charge of the catechetical school (chap. 3) ; in the present chapter we find him encouraging him after learning of his rash deed ; some years afterward, upon Origen's return from a visit to Rome, where his fame as a teacher had already become very great, Demetrius still showed the very best spirit toward him (chap. 14) ; and a little later sent him into Arabia to give instruction to an officer in that country (chap. 19). It is soon after this that the first sign of a difference between the two men appears, upon the occasion of Origen's preaching in Cæsarea (*ibid.*). There seems, however, to have been no lasting quarrel, if there was any quarrel at all ; for in 231 we find Demetrius giving Origen letters of recommendation upon the occasion of his visit to Achaia (see below, p. 396). The fact that he gives him these letters, thus recognizing him as a member of his church in good standing, and sending him upon his important mission with his official approval, shows that no open break between himself and Origen can as yet have taken place. But in his commentary on John (Tom. VI. *præf.*) Origen shows us that his last years in Alexandria were by no means pleasant ones. He compares his troubles there to the waves of a stormy sea, and his final departure to the exodus of the children of Israel. We know that he had been engaged for some time in writing commentaries, and that the first five books of his commentary on John — epoch-making in their significance, and sure to cause a sensation in orthodox, conservative circles — had recently appeared. We know that his reputation for heterodoxy was already quite widespread and that the majority of the Egyptian clergy were by no means upon his side. The trials to which he refers, therefore, may well have been a result of this hostility to his teachings existing among the clergy about him, and Demetrius may have shared to an extent in the common feeling. At the same time his disapproval cannot have been very pronounced, or he could not have given his official sanction to Origen's important visit to Achaia. But now, things being in this condition, Origen set out upon his mission, leaving Heraclas in charge of his school, and undoubtedly with the expectation of returning again, for he left the unfinished sixth book of his commentary on John behind him (see preface to the sixth book). He stopped in Palestine on his way to Athens, and there was ordained a presbyter by the bishops of that country (upon the motives which prompted him in the matter, see below, p. 397). The result was a complete break between Demetrius and himself, and his condemnation by an Alexandrian synod. To understand Demetrius' action in the matter, we must remember that both Eusebius and Jerome attribute the change in his attitude to jealousy of

Origen. They may be too harsh in their judgment, and yet it is certainly not at all unnatural that the growing power and fame of his young catechumen should in time affect, all unconsciously, his attitude toward him. But we must not do Demetrius an injustice. There is no sign that his jealousy led him to attack Origen, or to seek to undermine his influence, and we have no right to accuse him, without ground, of such unchristian conduct. At the same time, while he remained, as he supposed, an honest friend of Origen's, the least feeling of jealousy (and it would have been remarkable had he never felt the least) would make him more suspicious of the latter's conduct, and more prone to notice in his actions anything which might be interpreted as an infringement of his own prerogatives, or a disregard of the full respect due him. We seem to see a sign of this over-sensitiveness (most natural under the circumstances) in his severe disapproval of Origen's preaching in Cæsarea, which surprised the Palestinian bishops, but which is not surprising when we realize that Demetrius might so easily construe it as a token of growing disrespect for his authority on the part of his rising young school principal. It is plain enough, if he was in this state of mind, that he might in all sincerity have given letters of recommendation to Origen and have wished him God speed upon his mission, and yet that the news of his ordination to the presbyterate by foreign bishops, without his own approval or consent, and indeed in opposition to his own principles and to ecclesiastical law, should at once arouse his ire, and, by giving occasion for what seemed righteous indignation, open the floodgates for all the smothered jealousy of years. In such a temper of mind he could not do otherwise than listen willingly to all the accusations of heresy against Origen, which were no doubt busily circulated in his absence, and it was inevitable that he should believe it his duty to take decided steps against a man who was a heretic, and at the same time showed complete disregard of the rules and customs of the Church, and of the rights of his bishop. The result was the definitive and final exclusion of Origen from communion with the Alexandrian church, and his degradation from the office of presbyter by decree of the Alexandrian synods described above, p. 392 sq. The two grounds of the sentence passed by these synods were plainly his irregular ordination to the priesthood when constitutionally unfit for it (cf. what Eusebius says in this chapter), and his heterodoxy (cf. e.g. the synodical epistle of the Egyptian bishops given in Mansi's *Collect. Concil.* IX. col. 524, and also Jerome's epistle *ad Pammachium et Oceanum*, § 10, and Rufinus' *Apologi in Hieron.* II. 21). That the ordination to the priesthood of one who had mutilated himself was not universally considered uncanonical in the time of Origen is proved by the fact that the Palestinian bishops (whom Origen cannot have allowed to remain ignorant of his condition) all united in ordaining him. But the very fact that they all *united* (which has perplexed some scholars) leads us to think that they realized that their action was somewhat irregular, and hence wished to give it sanction by the participation of a number of bishops. The first canon of the Council of Nicæa forbids such ordination, and the canon is doubtless but the repetition of an older one (cf. *Apost. Canons*, 21 to 24, and see Hefele, *Conciliengesch.* I. p. 377), and yet Origen's consent to his ordination makes it improbable that there was in force in his time, even in Alexandria, a canon placing absolute and unconditional clerical disabilities upon such as he. That the action, however, was considered at least irregular in Alexandria, is proved by the position taken in the matter by Demetrius; and the fact that he made so much of it leads us to believe that the synod, called by him, may now have made canon law of what was before only custom, and may have condemned Origen for violating that custom which they considered as binding as law. Certainly had there been no such custom, and had it not seemed to Demetrius absolutely binding, he would have ordained Origen to the priesthood long before. His ordination in Palestine was in violation of what was known to be Demetrius' own principle, and the principle of the Alexandrian church, even if the principle was not, until this time or later, formulated into a canon.

On Bk. VI. chap. 12, § 6.

Since this passage was printed, I have seen Westcott's translation of this fragment of Serapion's epistle in his *Canon of the New Testament*, 5th ed. p. 390 sq. (cf. especially p. 391, note), and am glad to note that his rendering of the words καταρξαμένων αὐτοῦ is the same as my own. His interpretation of one or two other points I am unable to adopt.

On Bk. VI. chap. 23, § 4 (note 6). *Origen's Visit to Achaia.*

Eusebius gives as the cause of Origen's visit to Greece simply "a pressing necessity in connection with ecclesiastical affairs," but Jerome (*de vir. ill.* c. 54) tells us that it was on account of heresies which were troubling the churches of Achaia (*propter ecclesias Achaiæ, quæ pluribus hæresibus vexabantur*). Photius (*Cod.* 118) reports that Origen went to Athens without the consent of Demetrius (χωρὶς τῆς τοῦ οἰκείου γνώμης ἐπισκόπου), but this must be regarded as a mistake (caused perhaps by his knowledge that it was Origen's ordination, which took place during this trip, that caused Demetrius' anger; for Photius does not say that this statement rests upon the authority of Pamphilus, but prefaces his whole account with the words ὁ τε Πάμφιλος μάρτυς καὶ ἕτεροι πλεῖστοι), for Jerome (de vir. ill. c. 54) says that Origen went to Athens by way of Palestine sub testimonio ecclesiasticæ epistolæ, and in chap. 62 he says that Alexander, bishop of Jerusalem wrote an epistle in which he stated that he had ordained Origen juxta testimonium Demetrii. We must therefore assume that Origen left Alexandria for Athens with Demetrius' approval, and with letters of recommendation from him. It is the common opinion that Origen left Alexandria this time about 228 A.D., and after his visit in Achaia returned to Alexandria, where he remained until excommunicated by the council called by Demetrius. Upon searching the sources, however, I can find absolutely no authority for the statement that he returned to Alexandria after his visit to Achaia; in fact, that he did seems by most scholars simply to be taken for granted without further investigation. The opinion apparently rests upon the inter-pretation of two passages, one in a report of the proceedings of the Alexandrian synod taken by Photius from Pamphilus' Apology, the other in the preface to the sixth book of Origen's commen-tary on the Gospel of John. In the former it is said that the synod voted to exile Origen from Alexandria, and forbade him to reside or to teach there (ψηφίζεται μεταστῆναι μὲν ἀπὸ Ἀλεξαν-δρείας τὸν Ὠριγένην, καὶ μήτε διατρίβειν ἐν αὐτῇ, μήτε διδάσκειν). But certainly such a decree is far from proving that Origen, at the time it was passed, was actually in Alexandria. It simply shows that he still regarded that city as his residence, and was supposed to be expecting to return to it after his visit was completed. In the preface to the sixth book of his commentary on John's Gospel, he speaks of the troubles and trials which he had been enduring in Alexandria before he finally left the city, and compares that departure to the exodus of the children of Israel. But certainly it is just as easy to refer these troubles to the time before his visit to Achaia, a time when in all probability the early books of his commentary on John, as well as others of his writings, had begun to excite the hostility of the Alexandrian clergy, and thus made his residence there uncomfortable. It is almost necessary to assume that this hostility had arisen some time before the synods were held, in order to account both for the hostility of the majority of the clergy, which cannot have been so seriously aroused in an instant, and also for the change in Demetrius' attitude, which must have found a partial cause in the already existing hostility of the clergy to Origen, hostility which led them to urge him on to take decisive steps against Origen when the fitting occasion for action came in the ordination of the latter (see above, p. 395). The only arguments which, so far as I am able to learn, have been or can be urged for Origen's return to Alexandria are thus shown to prove nothing. On the other hand, it is a fact that Origen was ordained on his way to Achaia, and then went on and did his business there, and it is difficult to imagine that Demetrius and the Alexandrian church would have waited so long before taking action in regard to this step, which appeared to them so serious. More than that, Origen reports that he had begun the sixth book of his com-mentary on John in Alexandria, but had left it there, and therefore began it anew in Palestine. It is difficult to imagine that his departure was so hasty that he could not take even his MSS. with him; but if he left only for his visit to Achaia, expecting to return again, he would of course leave his MSS. behind him, and when his temporary absence was changed by the synod into permanent exile, he might not have been in a position, or might not have cared, to send back for the unfinished work. Still further, it does not seem probable that, if he were leaving Alexandria an exile under the condemnation of the church, and in such haste as the leaving of his unfinished commentary would imply, he should be in a position to entrust the care of his catechetical school to his assistant Heraclas (as he is said in chap. 26 to have done). That matter would rather have been taken out of his hands by Demetrius and the rest of the clergy. But going away merely on a visit, he would of course leave the school in Heraclas' charge, and after his condem-nation the clergy might see that Heraclas was the man for the place, and leave him undisturbed in it. After having, upon the grounds mentioned, reached the conclusion, shared so far as I knew by no one else, that it is at least unlikely that Origen returned to Alexandria after his visit to Greece, I was pleased to find my position strengthened by some chronological considera-tions urged by Lipsius (Chronologie d. röm. Bischöfe, p. 195, note), who says that "we do not know whether Origen ever returned to Alexandria after his ordination," and who seems to think it probable that he did not. He shows that Pontianus did not become bishop of Rome until 230, and therefore, if Eusebius is correct in putting Origen's visit to Achaia in the time of Pontianus' episcopate, as he does in this passage, that visit cannot have taken place before 230 (the com-monly accepted date, which rests upon a false chronology of Pontianus' episcopate, is 228); while on the other hand, according to chap. 26, Origen's final departure from Alexandria took place in the tenth year of Alexander's reign (231 A.D.), shortly before Demetrius' death, which occurred not later than 232 (see Bk. V. chap. 22, note 4). Supposing, then, that Origen returned to Alexandria, we must assume his journey to Palestine, his ordination there, his visit to Achaia and settlement of the disputes there, his return to Alexandria, the composition of at least some part of his commentary on John, the calling of a synod, his condemnation and exile, — all within the space of about a year. These chronological considerations certainly increase the improbability of Origen's return to Alexandria. (It may be remarked that Redepenning, who accepts the commonly received chronology, assigns two years to the Cæsarean and Achaian visit.) Assuming, then, that this departure for Achaia is identical with that mentioned in chap. 26, we put it in the year 231. It must have been (as of course we should expect, for he stopped in Palestine only on his way to Achaia) very soon after his departure that Origen's ordination took place; and the synod must have been called very soon after that event (as we should likewise expect), for Demetrius died the following year.

As to the cause of Origen's ordination, it is quite possible, as Redepenning suggests, that when he went a second time to Palestine, his old friends, the bishops of Cæsarea, of Jerusalem, and of other cities, wished to hear him preach again, but that remembering the reproof of the bishop Demetrius, called forth by his preaching on the former occasion (see chap. 19), he refused, and that then the Palestinian bishops, in order to obviate that difficulty, insisted on ordaining him. It is not impossible that Origen, who seems never to have been a stickler for the exact observance of minor ecclesiastical rules and formalities, supposed that Demetrius, who had shown himself friendly in the past, and not hostile to him because of his youthful imprudence (see chap. 8), would concur willingly in an ordination performed by such eminent bishops, and an ordination which would prove of such assistance to Origen in the accomplishment of the work in Achaia which he was undertaking with the approval of Demetrius himself, even though the latter could not bring himself to violate what he considered an ecclesiastical canon against the ordination of eunuchs. We can thus best explain Origen's consent to the step which, when we consider his general character, it is difficult to suppose he would have taken in conscious opposition to the will of his bishop. (On Demetrius' view of the matter, see above, p. 394 sq.) He was ordained, according to Jerome's *de vir. ill.* c. 54 (cf. also chap. 8, above), by Theoctistus, bishop of Cæsarea, and Alexander, bishop of Jerusalem, together with "the most distinguished bishops of Palestine" (as Eusebius says in chap. 8).

On Bk. VII. chap. 25, § 11.

For *in the reputed second or third Epistle of John,* read *in the extant second and third Epistles of John* (ἐν τῇ δευτέρᾳ φερομένῃ Ἰωάννου καὶ τρίτῃ).

On Bk. VII. chap. 26, § 1 (note 4, continued).

On Dionysius' attitude toward Sabellianism and the occasion of the Apology (ἔλεγχος καὶ ἀπολογία) in four books, which he addressed to Dionysius of Rome, see Bk. VI. chap. 40, note 1. This work is no longer extant, but brief fragments of it have been preserved by Athanasius (in his *De Sent. Dionysii*) and by Basil (in his *De Spir. Sancto*). English translation in the *Ante-Nicene Fathers,* Vol. VI. p. 92 sq. The longer work was preceded by a shorter one, now lost, to which reference is made in one of the fragments of the longer work. We do not know the exact date of the work, but may assign it with considerable probability to the earlier part of the episcopate of Dionysius of Rome; that is, soon after 259. Upon this work and upon Dionysius' attitude toward Sabellianism, see especially Dittrich, *Dionysius der Grosse,* p. 91. sq.

On Bk. VIII. chap. 2, § 4 (note 3, continued). *The Causes of the Diocletian Persecution.*

The persecution of Diocletian, following as it did a period of more than forty years during which Christianity had been recognized as a *religio licita,* and undertaken as it was by a man who throughout the first eighteen years of his reign had shown himself friendly to the Christians, and had even filled his own palace with Christian servants, presents a very difficult problem to the historian. Why did Diocletian persecute? The question has taxed the ingenuity of many scholars and has received a great variety of answers. Hunziker (in his *Regierung und Christenverfolgung des Kaisers Diocletianus und seiner Nachfolger,* Leipzig, 1869), Burckhardt (in his *Zeit Constantins,* Basel, 1853, 2d and improved edition, Leipzig, 1880), and A. J. Mason (in his *Persecution of Diocletian,* Cambridge and London, 1876), not to mention other investigators, have treated the subject with great ability and at considerable length, and the student is referred to their works for a fuller examination of the questions involved. It is not my purpose here to discuss the various views that have been presented by others ; but inasmuch as I am unable fully to agree with any of them, I desire to indicate my own conception of the causes that led to the persecution. We are left almost wholly to conjecture in the matter ; for our only authority, Lactantius, makes so many palpably erroneous statements in his description of the causes which produced the great catastrophe that little reliance can be placed upon him (see Burckhardt's demonstration of these errors, *ibid.* p. 289 sq.). Nevertheless, he has preserved for us at least one fact of deep significance, and it is a great merit of Mason's discussion that he has proved so conclusively the correctness of the report. The fact I refer to is that the initiative came from Galerius, not from Diocletian himself. Lactantius states this very distinctly and repeatedly, but it has been argued by Hunziker and many others that the persecution had been in Diocletian's mind for a long time, and that it was but the culmination of his entire policy. Having settled political matters, it is said, he turned his attention to religious matters, and determined as a step toward the restoration of the old Roman religion in its purity to exterminate Christianity. But, as Mason shows, this is an entire misconception of Diocletian's policy. It had never been his intention to attack Christianity. Such an attack was opposed to all his principles, and was at length made only under the pressure of strong external reasons. But though Mason has brought out this important fact so clearly, and though he has shown that Galerius was the original mover in the matter, he has, in my opinion, gone quite astray in his explanation of the causes which led Diocletian to accede to the wishes of Galerius. According to Mason, Diocletian was induced against his will to undertake a course of action which his judgment told him was unwise. "But the Cæsar [Galerius] was the younger and the stronger man ; and a determination to do has always an advantage over the determination not to do. At length Diocletian broke down so far as to offer to forbid the profession of the faith within the walls of his palace and under the eagles of his legions. He was sure it was a mistaken policy. It was certainly distasteful to himself. The army would suffer greatly by the loss. Diocletian would have to part with servants to whom he was attached," &c. To my mind, it is impossible to believe that Diocletian — great and wise emperor as he had proved himself, and with an experience of over eighteen years of imperial power during which he had always shown himself master — can thus have yielded simply to the importunity of another man. Our knowledge of Diocletian's character should lead us to repudiate absolutely such a supposition. Feeling the difficulty of his own supposition, Mason suggests that Diocletian may have felt that it would be better for him to begin the persecution himself, and thus hold it within some bounds, than to leave it for Galerius to conduct when he should become emperor two years later. But certainly if, as Mason assumes, Diocletian was convinced that the measure was in itself vicious and impolitic, that was a most remarkable course to pursue. To do a bad thing in order to leave no excuse for a successor to do the same thing in a worse way — certainly that is hardly what we should expect from the strongest and the wisest ruler Rome had seen for three centuries. If he believed it ought not to be done, we may be sure he would not have done it, and that neither Galerius nor any one else could compel him to. He was not such a helpless tool in the hands of others, nor was he so devoid of resources as to be obliged to prevent a successor's folly and wickedness by anticipating him in it, nor so devoid of sense as to believe that he could. It is, in my opinion, absolutely necessary to assume that Diocletian was convinced of the necessity of proceeding against the Christians before he took the step he did. How then are we to account for this change in his opinions? Burckhardt attributes the change to the discovery of a plot among the Christians. But the question naturally arises, what motive can the Christians have had for forming a plot against an emperor so friendly to them and a government under which they enjoyed such high honors? Burckhardt gives no satisfactory answer to this very pertinent query, and consequently his theory has not found wide acceptance. And yet I believe he is upon the right track in speaking of a plot, though he has not formed the right conception of its causes and nature, and has not been able to urge any known facts in direct support of his theory. In my opinion the key to the mystery lies in the fact which Lactantius states and the truth of which Mason demonstrates, but which Burckhardt quite overlooks, that the initiative came from Galerius, not Diocletian, viewed in the light of the facts that Galerius had long been known to be a bitter enemy of the Christians, and that he was to succeed Diocletian within a couple of years. The course of events might be pictured somewhat as follows. Some of the Christian officials and retainers of Diocletian, fearing what might happen upon the accession of Galerius, who was known to be a deadly enemy of the Christians, and who might be expected, if not to persecute, at least to dismiss all the Christian officials that had enjoyed Diocletian's favor (Galerius himself had only heathen officials in his court), conceived the idea of frustrating in some way the appointed succession and secure it for some one who would be more favorable to them (possibly for the young Constantine, who was then at Diocletian's court, and who, as we know, was later so cordially hated by Galerius). It may have been hoped by some of them that it would be possible in the end to win Diocletian himself over to the side of Christianity, and then induce him to change the succession and transmit the power to a fitter prince. There may thus have been nothing distinctly treasonable in the minds of any of them, but there may have been enough to arouse the suspicions of Galerius himself, who was the one most deeply interested, and who was always well aware of the hatred which the Christians entertained toward him. We are told by Lactantius that Galerius spent a whole winter with Diocletian, endeavoring to persuade him to persecute. The latter is but a conclusion drawn by Lactantius from the events which followed ; for he tells us himself that their conferences were strictly private, and that no one knew to what they pertained. But why did the persecution of the Christians at this particular time seem so important a thing to Galerius that he should make this long and extraordinary visit to Nicomedia? Was it the result of a fresh accession of religious zeal on his part? I confess myself unable to believe that Galerius' piety lay at the bottom of the matter, and at any rate, knowing that he would himself be master of the empire in two years, why could he not wait until he could take matters into his own hands and carry them out after his own methods? No one, so far as I know, has answered this question ; and yet it is a very pertinent one. It might be said that Galerius was afraid that he should not be able to carry out such measures unless they had had the sanction of his great predecessor. But Galerius never showed, either as Cæsar or Augustus, any lack of confidence in himself, and I am inclined to think that he would have preferred to enjoy the glory of the great undertaking himself rather than give it all to another, had he been actuated simply by general reasons of hostility toward the Church. But if we suppose that he had conceived a suspicion of such a plan as has been suggested, we explain fully his remarkable visit and his long and secret interviews with Diocletian. There was no place in which he could discover more about the suspected plot (which he might well fancy to be more serious than it really was) than in Nicomedia itself; and if such a plot was on foot, it was of vital importance to unearth it and reveal it to Diocletian. We may believe then that Galerius busied himself during the whole winter in investigating matters, and that long after he had become thoroughly convinced of the existence of a plot Diocletian remained skeptical.

We may suppose that at the same time whatever vague plans were in the minds of any of the Christians were crystallizing during that winter, as they began to realize that Galerius' hold upon the emperor was such that the latter could never be brought to break with him. We may thus imagine that while Galerius was seeking evidence of a plot, the plot itself was growing and taking a more serious shape in the minds at least of some of the more daring and worldly minded Christians. Finally, sufficient proof was gathered to convince even Diocletian that there was some sort of a plot on foot, and that the plotters were Christians. The question then arose what course should be pursued in the matter. And this question may well have caused the calling together of a number of counsellors and the consultation of the oracle of Apollo of which Lactantius tells us. Galerius naturally wished to exterminate the Christians as a whole, knowing their universal hostility to him ; but Diocletian just as naturally wished to punish only such as were concerned in the plot, and was by no means convinced that the Christians as a whole were engaged in it. The decision which was reached, and which is exhibited in the edict of the 24th of February, 303, seems to confirm in a remarkable manner the theory which has been presented. Instead of issuing an edict against Christians in general, Diocletian directs his blows solely against Christians in governmental circles, — public officials and servants in official families (cf. the interpretation of the edict given above in Bk. VIII. chap. 2, note 6). This is certainly not the procedure of an emperor who is persecuting on religious grounds. The church officers should in that case have been first attacked as they had been by Decius and Valerian. The singling out of Christians in official circles — and the low as well as the high ones, the servants as well as the masters — is a clear indication that the motive was political, not religious. Moreover, that the edict was drawn in such mild terms is a confirmation of this. These men were certainly not all guilty, and it was not necessary to put them all to death. It was necessary to put an end to the plot in the most expeditious and complete way. The plotters should be shown that their plot was discovered, and the whole thing should be broken up by causing some of them to renounce their faith, by degrading and depriving of citizenship all that would not renounce it. It was a very shrewd move. Executions would but have increased the rebellious spirit and caused the plot to spread. But Diocletian was well aware that any one that renounced his faith would lose caste with his fellow-Christians, and even if he had been a plotter in the past, he could never hope to gain anything in the future from the accession of a Christian emperor. He was careful moreover to provide against any danger from those who refused to renounce their faith, by putting them into a position where it would be impossible for them to accomplish anything in that line in the future. He knew that a plot which had no support within official circles would be of no account and was not to be feared. The action, based on the grounds given, was worthy of Diocletian's genius ; explained in any other way it becomes, in my opinion, meaningless. A further confirmation of the view which has been presented is found in the silence of Lactantius and Eusebius. The former was in Nicomedia, and cannot have failed to know the ostensible if not the true cause of the great persecution. Diocletian cannot have taken such a step without giving some reason for it, and doubtless that reason was stated in the preambles of his edicts, as is the case in the edicts of other emperors ; but as it happens, while we know the substance of all the edicts, not a single preamble has been preserved. May it not be possible that the Christians, who preserved the terms of the edicts, found the preambles distasteful because derogatory to some of themselves and yet unfortunately not untrue? The reasons which Lactantius gives are palpable makeshifts, and indeed he does not venture to state them categorically. "I have learned," he says, "that the cause of his fury was as follows." Doubtless he had heard it thus in Christian circles ; but doubtless he had heard it otherwise from heathen or from the edicts themselves ; and he can hardly, as a sensible man, have been fully satisfied with his own explanation of the matter. Eusebius attempts no explanation. He tells us in chapter 1, above, that the Church just before the persecution was in an abominable state and full of unworthy Christians, and yet he informs us that he will pass by the unpleasant facts to dwell upon the brighter side for the edification of posterity. Was the cause of the persecution one of the unpleasant facts? He calls it a judgment of God. Was it a merited judgment upon some who had been traitors to their country? He gives us his opinion as to the causes of the persecution of Decius and Valerian ; why is he silent about the causes of this greatest of all the persecutions? His silence in the present case is eloquent.

The course of events after the publication of the First Edict is not difficult to follow. Fire broke out twice in the imperial palace. Lactantius ascribes it to Galerius, who was supposed to have desired to implicate the Christians ; but, as Burckhardt remarks, Diocletian was not the man to be deceived in that way, and we may dismiss the suspicion as groundless. That the fires were accidental is possible, but extremely improbable. Diocletian at least believed that they were kindled by Christians, and it must be confessed that he had some ground for his belief. At any rate, whether true or not, the result was the torture (for the sake of extorting evidence) and the execution of some of his most faithful servants (see Bk. VIII. chap. 6). It had become an earnest matter with Diocletian, and he was beginning to feel — as he had never had occasion to feel before — that a society within the empire whose claims were looked upon as higher than those of the state itself, and duty to which demanded, in case of a disagreement between it and the state, insubordination, and even treason, toward the latter, was too dangerous an institution to tolerate longer, however harmless it might be under ordinary circumstances. It was at about this time that there occurred rebellions in Melitene and Syria, perhaps in consequence of the publication of the First Edict ; at any rate, the Christians, who were regarded with ever increasing suspicion, were believed to be in part at least responsible for the outbreaks, and the result was that a second edict was issued, commanding that all the rulers of the churches should be thrown into prison (see above, Bk. VIII. chap. 6). Here Diocletian took the same step taken by Decius and Valerian, and instituted thereby a genuine religious persecution. It was now Christians as Christians whom he attacked ; no longer Christian officials as traitors. The vital difference between the first and second edicts is very clear. All that followed was but the legitimate carrying out of the principle adopted in the Second Edict, — the destruction of the Church as such, the extermination of Christianity.

On Bk. X. chap. 8, § 4 (note 1, a).

After Constantine's victory over Maxentius, his half-sister Constantia, daughter of Constantius Chlorus by his second wife, Theodora, was married to Licinius, and thus the alliance of the two emperors was cemented by family ties. Constantius Chlorus was a grandson of Crispus, brother of the Emperor Claudius II., and hence could claim to be, in a sense, of imperial extraction ; a fact which gave him a dignity beyond that of his colleagues, who were all of comparatively low birth. Constantine himself and his panegyrists always made much of his illustrious descent.

TABLE OF ROMAN EMPERORS.

Augustus	B.C. 27–A.D. 14	Maximin I.	235–238
Tiberius	A.D. 14–37	The Gordians, I. and II.	237–238
Caius Caligula	37–41	Maximus Pupiénus ⎱	
Claudius	41–54	Balbinus ⎰	238
Nero	54–68	Gordian III.	238–244
Galba	68–69	Philip	244–249
Otho	69	Decius	249–251
Vitellius	69	Gallus	251–252
Vespasian	69–79	Æmilian	253
Titus	79–81	Valerian	253–260
Domitian	81–96	Gallienus	260–268
Nerva	96–98	Claudius II.	268–270
Trajan	98–117	Aurelian	270–275
Hadrian	117–138	Tacitus	275–276
Antoninus Pius	138–161	Probus	276–282
Marcus Aurelius [Antoninus Verus] ⎱	161–180	Carus	282–283
Lucius Verus ⎰	161–169	Carinus ⎱	
Commodus	180–192	Numerian ⎰	283–284
Pertinax	193	Diocletian ⎱	
Didius Julianus	193	Maximian ⎰	284–305
Niger	193–194	Constantius ⎱	285–305
Septimius Severus	193–211	Galerius ⎰	305–306
Caracalla ⎱	211–217		305–311
Geta ⎰	211–212	Maxentius (not recognized by the others)	306–312
M. Opilius Macrinus	217–218	Licinius	307–323
Heliogabalus, or Elagabalus	218–222	Maximin II.	308–313
Alexander Severus	222–235	Constantine	308–337

The Bishops of Rome, Alexandria, Antioch, and Jerusalem, mentioned by Eusebius.

Bishops of Rome.

(Dates taken from the table given by Lipsius in his *Chronologie der röm. Bischöfe*, p. 263 sq.)

Linus.
Anencletus.
Clement.
Evarestus.
Alexander.
Xystus I., for about ten years; died between 124 and 126.
Telesphorus, 11 years; died between 135 and 137.
Hyginus, 4 years; died between 139 and 141.
Pius, 15–16 years; died between 154 and 156.
Anicetus, 11–12 years; died in 166 or 167.
Soter, 8–9 years; died in 174 or 175.
Eleutherus, 15 years; died in 189.
Victor, 9–10 years; 189–198 or 199.
Zephyrinus, 18–19 years; 198 or 199–217 (Aug. 26?).
Callistus, 5 years; 217–Oct. 14, 222.
Urbanus, 8 years; 222–230 (May 19?).
Pontianus, 5 years 2 months 7 days; (July 21?), 230–Sept. 28, 235.
Anteros, 1 month 12 days; Nov. 21, 235–Jan. 3, 236.
Fabianus, 14 years 10 days; 236–Jan. 20, 250. Vacancy from Jan. 21, 250–March, 251.
Cornelius, 2 years 3 months 10 days; beginning of March, 251–middle of June, 253.

Lucius, 8 months 10 days; June (25?), 253–March 5, 254.
Stephanus, 3 years 2 months 21 days; (May 12?), 254–Aug. 2, 257.
Xystus II., 11 months 12 (6?) days; Aug. 24 (31?), 257–Aug. 6, 258.
Dionysius, 9 years 5 months 2 days; July 22, 259–Dec. 27, 268.
Felix I., 5 years 11 months 25 days; Jan. 5, 269–Dec. 30, 274.
Eutychian, 8 years 11 months 3 days; (Jan. 5?) 275–Dec. 8, 283.
Caius, 12 years 4 months 6 days; Dec. 17, 283–April 22, 296.
Marcellinus, 8 years 3 months 25 days; June 30, 296–(Oct. 25?), 304. Vacancy until 307.
Marcellus, 1 year 7 months 21 days; (May 24?), 307–Jan. 15, 309.
Eusebius, 3 (4?) months 23 (16?) days; April 23 (16?), 309–Aug. 17, 309. Vacancy until 310.
Miltiades, 3 years 6 months 8 days; July 2, 310–Jan. 10 (11?), 314.

Bishops of Alexandria.

Annianus.	Justus.	Agrippinus.	Dionysius.
Abilius.	Eumenes.	Julian.	Maximus.
Cerdon.	Marcus.	Demetrius.	Theonas.
Primus.	Celadion.	Heraclas.	Peter.

Bishops of Antioch.

(Dates taken from the table given by Harnack in his *Zeit des Ignatius*, p. 62.)

Evodius.
Ignatius.
Hero.
Cornelius.
Eros.
Theophilus, died not earlier than 182.
Maximinus, died between 189 and 192.
Serapion, died about 209.
Asclepiades, died between 211 and 222.
Philetus, died not long before 229–231.
Zebinus, died between 238 and 249.

Babylas, died in 250, during the persecution of Decius.
Fabius, died toward the end of 252 or early in 253.
Demetrian, died between 257 and 260.
Paul, deposed between 266 and 269 (probably in 268).
Domnus.
Timæus, died about 280.
Cyril, sent to the mines in 303, and died probably toward the end of 306.
Tyrannus, succeeded Cyril probably in 303, possibly not until 306, and lived until the close of the persecution.

Bishops of Jerusalem.

James.
Symeon.
Justus.
Zacchæus.
Tobias.
Benjamin.
John.
Matthias.
Philip.
Seneca.

Justus.
Levi.
Ephres.
Joseph.
Judas.
Marcus.
Cassianus.
Publius.
Maximus I.
Julian I.

Gaius I.
Symmachus.
Gaius II.
Julian II.
Capito.
Maximus II. } [1]
Antoninus. }
Valens.
Dolichianus.
Narcissus.

Dius.
Germanio.
Gordius.
Narcissus, a second time.
Alexander.
Mazabanes.
Hymenæus.
Zambdas.
Hermon.

TABLE SHOWING THE ROMAN METHOD OF COUNTING THE DAYS OF THE MONTH.

(Taken from the *Encyclopædia Britannica*, article *Calendar*.)

DAYS OF THE MONTH.	MARCH. MAY. JULY. OCTOBER.	JANUARY. AUGUST. DECEMBER.	APRIL. JUNE. SEPTEMBER. NOVEMBER.	FEBRUARY.
1	Kalendæ.	Kalendæ.	Kalendæ.	Kalendæ.
2	6	4	4	4
3	5	3	3	3
4	4	Prid. Nonas.	Prid. Nonas.	Prid. Nonas.
5	3	Nonæ.	Nonæ.	Nonæ.
6	Prid. Nonas.	8	8	8
7	Nonae.	7	7	7
8	8	6	6	6
9	7	5	5	5
10	6	4	4	4
11	5	3	3	3
12	4	Prid. Idus.	Prid. Idus.	Prid. Idus.
13	3	Idus.	Idus.	Idus.
14	Prid. Idus.	19	18	16
15	Idus.	18	17	15
16	17	17	16	14
17	16	16	15	13
18	15	15	14	12
19	14	14	13	11
20	13	13	12	10
21	12	12	11	9
22	11	11	10	8
23	10	10	9	7
24	9	9	8	6
25	8	8	7	5
26	7	7	6	4
27	6	6	5	3
28	5	5	4	Prid. Kal. Mart.
29	4	4	3	
30	3	3	Prid. Kalen.	
31	Prid. Kalen.	Prid. Kalen.		

[1] These two names are omitted by Eusebius in his *History*, but are given in his *Chron.* and also by Epiphanius. See above, Bk. V. chap. 12, note 2.

"Instead of distinguishing the days by the ordinal numbers, first, second, third, etc., the Romans counted *backwards* from three fixed epochs; namely, the Kalends, the Nones, and the Ides. The Kalends were invariably the first day of the month, and were so denominated because it had been an ancient custom of the pontiffs to call the people together on that day, to apprise them of the festivals, or days that were to be kept sacred during the month. The Ides (from an obsolete verb *iduare*, to divide) were at the middle of the month, either the 13th or the 15th day; and the Nones were the *ninth* day before the Ides, counting inclusively. From these three terms the days received their denomination in the following manner: —

"Those which were comprised between the Kalends and the Nones were called *the days before the Nones;* those between the Nones and the Ides were called *the days before the Ides;* and, lastly, all the days after the Ides to the end of the month were called *the days before the Kalends* of the succeeding month.

"In the months of March, May, July, and October, the Ides fell on the 15th day, and the Nones consequently on the 7th: so that each of these months had six days named from the Nones. In all the other months the Ides were on the 13th and the Nones were on the 5th; consequently there were only four days named from the Nones. Every month had eight days named from the Ides. The number of days receiving their denomination from the Kalends depended on the number of days in the month and the day on which the Ides fell. For example, if the month contained 31 days, and the Ides fell on the 13th, as was the case in January, August, and December, there would remain 18 days after the Ides, which, added to the first of the following month, made 19 days of Kalends. In January, therefore, the 14th day of the month was called the *nineteenth before the Kalends of February* (counting inclusively), the 15th was the 18th before the Kalends, and so on to the 30th, which was called the third before the Kalends (*tertio Kalendas*), the last being the second of the Kalends, or the day before the Kalends (*pridie Kalendas*)."

TABLE OF MACEDONIAN MONTHS.

The months of the Macedonian year, as commonly employed in the time of Eusebius, corresponded exactly to the Roman months, but the year began with the first of September. The names of the months were as follows: —

MACEDONIAN.	ROMAN.		MACEDONIAN.	ROMAN.
1. Gorpiæus.	September.		7. Dystrus.	March.
2. Hyperberetæus.	October.		8. Xanthicus.	April.
3. Dius.	November.		9. Artemisius.	May.
4. Apellæus.	December.		10. Dæsius.	June.
5. Audynæus.	January.		11. Panemus.	July.
6. Peritius.	February.		12. Loüs.	August.

THE LIFE OF CONSTANTINE,

By EUSEBIUS,

TOGETHER WITH THE

ORATION OF CONSTANTINE TO THE ASSEMBLY OF THE SAINTS,

AND THE

ORATION OF EUSEBIUS IN PRAISE OF CONSTANTINE.

A REVISED TRANSLATION, WITH PROLEGOMENA AND NOTES, BY

ERNEST CUSHING RICHARDSON, Ph.D.,

LIBRARIAN AND ASSOCIATE PROFESSOR IN HARTFORD THEOLOGICAL SEMINARY.

PROLEGOMENA.

PREFACE.

In accordance with the instruction of the editor-in-chief the following work consists of a revision of the Bagster translation of Eusebius' " Life of Constantine," Constantine's " Oration to the Saints," and Eusebius' " Oration in Praise of Constantine," with somewhat extended Prolegomena and limited notes, especial attention being given in the Prolegomena to a study of the *Character* of Constantine. In the work of revision care has been taken so far as possible not to destroy the style of the original translator, which, though somewhat inflated and verbose, represents perhaps all the better, the corresponding styles of both Eusebius and Constantine, but the number of changes really required has been considerable, and has caused here and there a break in style in the translation, whose chief merit is that it presents in smooth, well-rounded phrase the generalized idea of a sentence. The work on the Prolegomena has been done as thoroughly and originally as circumstances would permit, and has aimed to present material in such way that the general student might get a survey of the man Constantine, and the various problems and discussions of which he is center. It is impossible to return special thanks to all who have given special facilities for work, but the peculiar kindness of various helpers in the *Bibliothèque de la Ville* at Lyons demands at least the recognition of individualized thanksgiving.

E. C. R.

HARTFORD, CONN., April 15, 1890.

TABLE OF CONTENTS.

PROLEGOMENA.

I.—CONSTANTINE THE GREAT.

CHAPTER I.

LIFE.[1]

§ 1. *Early Years.*

THE Emperor Flavius Valerius Constantinus, surnamed the Great,[2] born February 27, 272 or 274,[3] at Naïssus,[4] was son of Constantius Chlorus, afterwards Emperor,[5] and Helena his wife.[6] He was brought up at Drepanum, his mother's home,[7] where he remained until his father became

---

[1] This sketch of the life of Constantine is intended to give the thread of events, and briefly to supplement, especially for the earlier part of his reign, the life by Eusebius, which is distinctly confined to his religious acts and life.

[2] "Imperator Cæsar Augustus Consul Proconsul Pontifex Maximus, Magnus, Maximus, Pius, Felix, Fidelis, Mansuetus, Benificus, Clementissimus, Victor, Invictus, Triumphator, Salus Reip. Beticus, Alemanicus, Gothicus, Sarmarticus, Germanicus, Britannicus, Hunnicus, Gallicanus," is a portion of his title, as gathered from coins, inscriptions, and various documents.

[3] Calendarium Rom. in Petavius Uranal. p. 113. The date varies by a year or two, according to way of reckoning, but 274 is the date usually given. (Cf. Burckhardt, Manso, Keim, De Broglie, Wordsworth, etc.) Eutropius and Hieronymus say he died in his sixty-sixth year, Theophanes says he was sixty-five years old, and Socrates and Sozomen say substantially the same, while Victor, *Epit.* has sixty-three, and Victor, *Cæs.* sixty-two. Eusebius says he lived twice the length of his reign, i.e. 63 +.

Manso chose 274, because it agreed best with the representations of the two Victors as over against the "later church historians." But the two Victors say, one that he lived sixty-two years and reigned thirty-two, and the other that he lived sixty-three and reigned thirty; while Eutropius, secretary to Constantine, gives length of reign correctly, and so establishes a slight presumption in favor of his other statement. Moreover, it is supported by Hieronymus, whose testimony is not of the highest quality, to be sure, and is quite likely taken from Eutropius, and Theophanes, who puts the same fact in another form, and who certainly chose that figure for a reason. The statement of Eusebius is a very elastic generalization, and is the only support of Victor, *Epit.* Socrates, who, according to Wordsworth, says he was in his sixty-fifth year, uses the idiom ("mounting upon" (ἐπιβάς) sixty-five years, which at the least must mean nearly sixty-five years old, and unless there is some well-established usage to the contrary, seems to mean having lived already sixty-five years. In the interpretation of Sozomen (also given in *translation* "in his sixty-fifth year") he was "about" sixty-five years old. Now if he died in May, his following birthday would not have been as "about," and he must have been a little over sixty-five. This would make a strong consensus against Victor, against whom Eutropius alone would have a presumption of accuracy. On the whole it may be said that in the evidence, so far as cited by Manso, Wordsworth, Clinton, and the run of historians, there is no critical justification for the choice of the later date and the shorter life.

[4] Anon. Vales. p. 471. Const. Porphyr. (*De themat.* 2. 9), Stephanus Byzant. art. Ναϊσσός (ed. 1502, H. iii.), "Firmicus 1. 4." According to some it was Tarsus ("Julius Firmic. 1. 2"), or Drepanum (Niceph. Callist.), or in Britain (the English chroniclers, Voragine, and others, the mistake arising from one of the panegyrists (c. 4) speaking of his taking his origin thence), or Trèves (Voragine). Compare Vogt, who adds Rome ("Petr. de Natalibus"), or Roba (" Eutychius"), or Gaul ("Meursius"). Compare also monographs by Janus and by Schoepflin under *Literature.*

[5] For characterization of Constantius compare *V. C.* 1. 13 sq.

[6] It has been a much discussed question, whether Helena was legitimate wife or not. Some (Zosimus 2. 8; Niceph. Callist. 7. 18) have asserted that Helena was a woman "indifferent honest," and the birth of Constantine illegitimate. This view is simply psychologically impossible regarding a woman of so much and such strength of character. That she stood in the relation of legitimate concubinage (cf. Smith and Cheetham, *Dict.* 1. 422) is not improbable, since many (Hieron. Orosius, Zosimus 2. 8; Chron. Pasch. p. 516, and others) assert this lesser relationship. This would have been not unlike a modern morganatic marriage. The facts are: 1. That she is often spoken of as concubine (cf. above). 2. That she is distinctly called wife, and that by some of the most competent authorities (Eutrop. 10. 2; Anon. Vales. p. 471; Euseb. *H. E.* 8. 13; Ephraem p. 21, etc.), also in various inscriptions (compare collected inscriptions in Clinton 2. 81). 3. That she was divorced (Anon. Vales. p. 47). The weight of testimony is clearly in favor of word "wife," though with divorce so easy it seems to have been a name only. The view that she was married in the full legal sense, but only after the birth of Constantine, is plausible enough, and has a support more apparent than real, in the fact that he "first established that natural children should be made legitimate by the subsequent marriage of their parents" (Sandars *Inst. Just.* (1865) 113; cf. Cod. Just. V. xxvii. 1 and 5 ed. Krueger 2 (1877) 216).

Of course the story of her violation by and subsequent marriage to Constantius (Inc. auct. ed. Heydenreich) is purely legendary, and the same may be said of the somewhat circumstantial account of her relation as concubine, given by Nicephorus Callistus 7, 18. For farther account of Helena, compare the *V. C.* 3. 42 and notes.

[7] Helena was born probably at Drepanum, afterwards called Helenopolis, in her honor, by Constantine (Procopius *De ædif.* V. 2, p. 311, Chron. Pasch. etc.).

Cæsar (A.D. 292 acc. to Clinton) and divorced Helena (Anon. Vales. p. 471). He was then sent to the court of Diocletian, nominally to be educated (Praxagoras, in Müller, *Fragm.* 4 (1868); Zonar. 13. 1, &c.), but really as hostage,[1] and remained with Diocletian, or Galerius, until the year 306.[2] During this time he took part in various campaigns, including the famous Egyptian expedition of Diocletian in 296 (Euseb. *V. C.* 1. 19; Anon. Metroph., Theoph. p. 10).[3] Shortly after joining the emperor he contracted (296 or 297) his alliance with Minervina,[4] by whom he had a son, Crispus.[5] He was at Nicomedia when Diocletian's palace was struck by lightning (Const. *Orat.* 35), and was present at the abdication of Diocletian and Maximinus in 305 (Lact. *De M. P.* c. 18 sq.). This last event proved a crisis for Constantine. He had grown to be a man of fine physique (Lact. c. 18; Euseb. *V. C.* 1. 19), of proved courage and military skill (cf. remarks on physical characteristics under *Character*), and a general favorite (Lact. l.c.). He had already "long before" (Lact. c. 18) been created Tribune of the first order. It was both natural and fitting that at this time he should become Cæsar in the place of his father, who became Augustus. Every one supposed he would be chosen (c. 19), and Diocletian urged it (c. 18), but the princely youth was too able and illustrious to please Galerius, and Constantine was set aside for obscure, and incompetent men (cf. Lact.). His position was far from easy before. His brilliant parts naturally aroused the jealousy and suspicions of the emperors. They, or at least Galerius, even sought his death, it is said, by tempting him to fight wild beasts (a lion, Praxag. p. 3; cf. Zonaras 2, p. 623), or exposing him to special danger in battle (cf. Philistog. 1. 6; Lact. c. 24; Anon. Vales. p. 471; Theophanes p. 10-12, &c.). The situation, hard enough before, now became, we may well believe, intolerable. He was humiliated, handicapped, and even in danger of his life. He was practically a prisoner. The problem was, how to get away. Several times Constantius asked that his son might be allowed to join him, but in vain (Lact. c. 24; Anon. Vales. p. 471). Finally, however, Constantine gained a grudging permission to go. It was given at night, and the emperor intended to take it back in the morning (Lact. c. 24). But in the morning it was too late. Constantine had left at once to join his father. He lost no time either in starting or making the journey. Each relay of post horses which he left was maimed to baffle pursuit (Anon. Vales., Vict. *Epit.* p. 49; cf. Lact. c. 24, Praxag. p. 3). The rage of the emperor when he learned of the flight was great but vain. Constantine was already out of reach, and soon joined his father at Bononia (Boulogne, Anon. Vales.; cf. Eumen. *Paneg.* (310), c. 7),[6] just in time to accompany him on his final expeditions to Britain (Eumen. *Paneg.* (310) c. 7; cf. Anon. Vales. l.c.). Constantius died shortly after at York (Anon. Vales. p. 471; Eutrop. 10. 1), having named Constantine as his successor (Euseb. *V. C.* 1. 21; Eumen. *Paneg.* (310) c. 7.; Lact. c. 24).

---

[1] This appears from the disregard of his father's repeated requests that he be sent back to him (Lact., Anon. Vales. p. 471), and the whole story of his final flight. So also it is said by Anon. Vales. p. 471, and the two Victors (*Cæs.* p. 156, *Epit.* p. 49). Zonaras (12. 33, ed. Migne 1091), gives both reasons for sending, and is likely right. Nicephorus Callistus (7. 18) suggests that he was sent there for education, since Constantius could not take him himself on account of Theodora.

[2] He was with Diocletian still in 305 (cf. Lact. and note, below), and was with his father early in 306.

[3] Eusebius, who saw him on his way to Egypt in 296, gives the impression which he made on him at that time (l.c.). According to some he was also with Galerius in his Persian war, and this is possible (cf. Clinton 1. 338-40). Theophanes describes him as "already eminent in war" (p. 10), Anon. Vales. p. 471, as conducting himself "bravely."

[4] This was probably a morganatic marriage or concubinate (Victor, *Epit.* 41, Zosimus 2. 20; Zonaras 13. 2, &c.). "The improbability that Constantine should have marked out an illegitimate son as his successor" which Ramsay (Smith, *Dict.* 2. 1090) mentions as the only argument against, is reduced to a minimum in view of Constantine's law for the legitimization of natural children by rescript (Cod. Just. V. xxvii. ed. Krueger 2 (1877), 216-17; cf. notes of Sandars in his *Inst. Just.* (1865) 113). It would be uncritical, as in the case before mentioned, to lay stress on this as positive evidence, but over against a simple "improbability" it has a certain suggestiveness at least. The panegyrical praises of Constantine's continence hardly justify Clinton's claim that she was lawful wife; for to have a regular concubine would not have been considered in any sense immoral, and it would not have been particularly pertinent in a wedding oration to have introduced even a former wife. For what little is known of Minervina, compare Ramsay, in Smith *Dict.* 2. 1090, "Tillemont, *Hist. Emp.* IV. iv. p. 84," and Clinton, *Fasti Rom.* 2. (1850) 86, note *k*.

[5] Crispus was "already a young man" when made Cæsar in 317 (Zos. 2. 30).

[6] According to some (e.g. Victor, *Cæs.* p. 156; Victor, *Epit.* p. 51; Zos. 2. 8) his father was already in Britain.

§ 2. *The First Five Years of Reign.*

The will of the father was promptly ratified by the soldiers, who at once proclaimed Constantine Augustus.[1] Supported by them, and also by Erocus, king of the Allemanni (Vict. *Epit.* p. 49–50), he sent his portrait to Galerius, claiming the title of Augustus. This the emperor refused to grant, but, much against his will, allowed him to have the title of Cæsar (Lact. c. 25). Constantine did not insist on his right to the greater title, but waited his time, and in the interim contented himself with the lesser, — as the coins show.[2] There was enough to do. After his father's death he waged war against the Francs, and later against the Bructeri and others (Eutrop. 10. 3; *Paneg.* (307) c. 4; Eumen. *Paneg.* (310) cc. 10–12; Nazar. *Paneg.* (321) 18; Euseb. *V. C.* 1. 25, &c.; cf. Inscr. ap. Clinton 2. 93), and celebrated his victories by exposing his captives to the wild beasts (Eutrop. 10. 3; Eumen. *Paneg.* (310) c. 12; *Paneg.* (313) c. 23; cf. Nazar. *Paneg.* (321) c. 16).

Meanwhile affairs were marching at Rome, too. The same year (306) that Constantine was elected Augustus by the soldiers, Maxentius at Rome was proclaimed emperor by the Pretorian Guards (Eutrop. 10. 2; Vict. *Cæs.* p. 156; Anon. Vales. p. 472; Zos. 2. 9; Socr. 1. 2; Oros. c. 26, &c.; Lact. c. 26). He persuaded the willing (Eutrop. 10. 2) Maximian to resume the imperial purple (Lact. c. 26; Zos. 2. 10), but soon quarreled with him (Socr. 1. 2; Eutrop. 10. 3; Zos. 2. 11; Lact. c. 28).[3] In 307 Constantine and Maximinus were named "sons of the emperors," and the following year were reluctantly acknowledged as emperors by Galerius. Maximian, after he had quarreled with his son, betook himself to Gaul and made alliance with Constantine by giving his daughter Fausta in marriage (307). He proved an uncomfortable relative. The much-abused mother-in-law of fiction is not to be compared with this choice father-in-law of history. First he tried to supersede Constantine by corrupting his soldiers. At his persuasion Constantine had left behind the bulk of his army while he made a campaign on the frontier. As soon as he was supposably out of the way, the soldiers were won by largesses, and Maximian assumed the purple again. But he had reckoned without his host. Constantine acted with decisive promptness, returned by such rapid marches that he caught Maximian entirely unprepared (Lact. c. 29) and drove him into Marseilles, where the latter cursed him vigorously from the walls (Lact. c. 29), but was able to offer no more tangible resistance. The gates were thrown open (Lact. c. 29), and Maximian was in the power of Constantine, who this time spared his precious father-in-law.[4] Grateful for this mildness, Maximian then plotted to murder him. The plan was for Fausta to leave her husband's door open and for Maximian to enter and kill Constantine with his own hands. Fausta pretended to agree, but told her husband (Zos. 2. 11; Joh. Ant. p. 603; Oros. c. 28), who put a slave in his own place (but apparently did not "put himself in the place of" the slave), had the program been carried out, and catching Maximian in the act, granted him that supreme ancient mercy, — the right to choose how he would die (Lact. c. 30).[5]

Though in the midst of wars and plots, and liable at any time to have to run from one end of his province to the other to put down some insurrection, Constantine kept steadily at the work of internal improvement, organizing the interior, fortifying the boundaries, building bridges, restor-

---

[1] So Eusebius *H. E.* 8. 13; Lact. c. 25; Julian *Orat.* 1. p. 13. Eumenius (*Paneg.* 310, c. 7) says that he was elected "imperator," but in cc. 8–9 speaks of him as having become Cæsar. Eutropius (10. 2) also uses the word "imperator." Zosimus, on the other hand (2. 9), and Anonymous Vales. say he was elected "Augustus," but was only confirmed "Cæsar" by Galerius (see below). The elevation was in Britain (cf. Eutrop. 10. 2; Eumen. *Paneg.* (310) c. 9; Soz. 1. 5, &c.).

[2] See coins in Eckhel 8, p. 72, under the year. It is also expressly stated by *Paneg.* (307) c. 5.

[3] It is said by many that the quarrel was a feigned one, and that it was wholly for the purpose of getting rid of Constantine in behalf

of Maxentius that he betook himself to Gaul. That he went to Gaul with this purpose, at least, is mentioned by many (cf. Lact. c. 29; Oros. c. 28; Eutrop. 10. 2, "on a planned stratagem"). It seems curious, if he had attempted to supersede Maxentius by raising a mutiny (Eutrop. 10. 3), that he should now be working for him and planning to rejoin him (Eutrop. 10. 2), but it is no inconsistency in this man, who was consistent only in his unceasing effort to destroy others for his own advantage.

[4] Compare on all this Lact. c. 29; Eumen. *Paneg* c. 14.

[5] Socrates (1. 2) with many others (e.g. Zos. 2. 11) says he died at Tarsus, confusing him thus with Maximinus.

ing cities, building up educational institutions, &c.[1] At the end of five years' reign (July 24, 311) he had reduced the turbulent tribes, organized his affairs, and endeared himself to his people, especially to the Christians, whom he had favored from the first (Lact. c. 24), and who could hardly fail in those days of persecution to rejoice in a policy such as is indicated in his letter to Maximinus Daza in behalf of persecuted Christians (Lact. c. 37).

§ 3. *State of Affairs in 311.*

In the meantime, while the extreme west of the empire was enjoying the mild rule of Constantine, the other corners of the now quadrangular and now hexagonal world, over which during this time Maximinus, Galerius, Licinius, Maximian, and Maxentius had tried to reign, had had a much less comfortable time. Every emperor wanted a corner to himself, and, having his corner, wanted that of some one else or feared that some one else wanted his. In order clearly to understand Constantine, a glimpse of the state of affairs in these other parts of the empire, together with some idea of the kind of men with whom he had to deal is essential, and may be gotten from a brief view of (1) The rulers, (2) Characters of the rulers, (3) Condition of the ruled.

(1) *The Rulers.*

The intricate process of evolution and devolution of emperors, mysterious to the uninitiated as a Chinese puzzle, is briefly as follows : In 305 Diocletian and Maximian had abdicated (Lact. c. 18 ; Eutrop. 9. 27 ; Vict. *Cæs.*), Galerius and Constantius succeeding as Augusti and Severus, Maximinus Daza succeeding them as Cæsars (Lact. c. 19). In 306 Constantius died, Constantine was proclaimed Augustus by his army, Maxentius by the Pretorian Guards (cf. above), and Severus by Galerius (Lact. c. 25), while Maximian resumed the purple (see above) — four emperors, Galerius, Severus, Maximian, and Maxentius, with two Cæsars, Constantine and Maximinus, one with a pretty definite claim to the purple, and the other bound not to be left out in the cold. In 307 Licinius was appointed Augustus by Galerius (Lact. c. 29 ; Vict. *Cæs.;* Zos. 2. 11 ; Anon. Vales. ; Eutrop. 10. 4), who also threw a sop to Cerberus by naming Constantine and Maximin "sons of emperors" (Lact. c. 32 ; Coins in Eckhel 8 (1838) 52. 3). Constantine was given title of Augustus by Maximianus (?), and Maximinus about this time was forced, as he said, by his army to assume the title. Meantime the growing procession of emperors was reduced by one. Severus, sent against Maxentius, was deserted by his soldiers, captured, and slain in 307 (Lact. c. 26 ; Zos. 2. 10 ; Anon. Vales. ; Eutrop. 10. 2 ; Vict. *Cæs.* &c. &c.), leaving still six emperors or claimants, — Galerius, Licinius, Maxentius, Maximian, Maximinus, and Constantine. In 308, making the best of a bad matter, Galerius appointed Constantine and Maximin Augusti (see above), leaving the situation unchanged, and so it remained until the death of Maximian in 310 (see above), and of Galerius in May, 311 (Lact. c. 33 ; Vict. *Cæs.;* Vict. *Epit.;* Zos. 2. 11) reduced the number to four.

(2) *Characters of the Rulers.*

Constantine's own character has been hinted at and will be studied later. Severus was the least significant of the others, having a brief reign and being little mentioned by historians. Diocletian's characterization of him was, according to Lactantius (c. 18), as ejaculated to Galerius, "That dancing, carousing drunkard who turns night into day and day into night." The average character of the other emperors was that of the prisoners for life in our modern state prisons. Galerius, "that pernicious wild beast" (Lact. c. 25), was uneducated, drunken (Anon. Vales. p. 472); fond of boasting himself to be the illegitimate son of a dragon (Lact. 9 ; Vict. *Epit.* p. 49), and sanguinary and ferocious to an extraordinary degree (Lact. c. 9. 21, 22, &c.). Licinius, characterized by "ingratitude" and "cold-blooded ferocity," was "not only totally

---

[1] Notably at Autun. The city had been almost destroyed. Eumenius, whose oration of thanks in behalf of the people of Autun is extant, praises Constantine as the restorer, almost the founder. The work had been undertaken by Constantius, indeed, but was carried on by his son. Constantine's work of internal improvement was in many ways distinctly a continuation of the work begun by Constantius. Compare Eumen. *Paneg.* (especially c. 13, 22, &c.) and *Grat. act.*

indifferent to human life and suffering, and regardless of any principle of law or justice which might interfere with the gratification of his passions, but he was systematically treacherous and cruel, possessed of not one redeeming quality save physical courage and military skill " (Ramsay, in Smith *Dict.* 2, p. 784; compare Euseb. *H. E.* 10. 8; *V. C.* 1. 49–56), and " in avaricious cupidity worst of all " (Vict. *Epit.* p. 51). Maximinus' character " stands forth as pre-eminent for brutal licentiousness and ferocious cruelty — ' lust hard by hate ' " (Plumptre, in Smith & W. 3, p. 872), and according to Lactantius, c. 38, " that which distinguished his character and in which he transcended all former emperors was his desire of debauching women." He was cruel, superstitious, gluttonous, rapacious, and " so addicted to intoxication that in his drunken frolics he was frequently deranged and deprived of his reason like a madman " (Euseb. *H. E.* 8. 14). Maximianus has been thought to be on the whole the least outrageous, and his somewhat defective moral sense respecting treachery and murder has been noted (cf. above). He has been described as " thoroughly unprincipled . . . base and cruel " (Ramsay, in Smith *Dict.* 2, p. 981). He is described by Victor, (*Epit.* p. 48) as " ferus natura, ardens libidine," being addicted to extraordinary and unnatural lust (Lact. c. 8). Truly a choice " best " in this rogues' gallery. Of Maxentius it is said (Tyrwhitt, in Smith & W. 3, p. 865) : " His wickedness seems to have transcended description, and to have been absolutely unredeemed by any saving feature." He " left no impurity or licentiousness untouched " (Euseb. *H. E.* 8. 14; cf. Eutrop. 10. 4; Lact. 9). He was marked by " impiety," " cruelty," " lust," and tyranny (*Paneg.* [313] c. 4). He was the most disreputable of all, — unmitigatedly disreputable. With all due allowance for the prejudice of Christian historians, from whom such strong statements are mainly drawn, yet enough of the details are confirmed by Victor, *Epit.*, the Panegyrists, Eutropius, and other non-Christian writers to verify the substantial facts of the ferocity, drunkenness, lust, covetousness, and oppression of this precious galaxy of rulers.

(3) *Condition of the Ruled.*

Under such rulers there was a reign of terror during this period which contrasted strangely with the state of things under Constantine. Galerius was " driving the empire wild with his taxations " (cf. Lact. c. 23 and 26), affording in this also a marked contrast with the course of Constantine in Gaul. Maxentius led in the unbridled exercise of passion (Euseb. *H. E.* 8. 14; cf. Lact. c. 18), but in this he differed from the others little except in degree (compare Euseb. *V. C.* 1. 55 on Licinius), and according to Lactantius (c. 28) he was surpassed by Maximin. In brief, all did according to their own sweet wills, and the people had to stand it as best they could. The worst was that the oppression did not end with the emperors nor the friends and officials to whom they delegated power to satisfy their desires at the expense of the helpless. Their armies were necessary to them. The soldiers had to be conciliated and exactions made to meet their demands. They followed the examples of their royal leaders in all manner of excesses and oppressions. No property or life or honor was safe.

The persecution of the Christians reached a climax of horror in this period. The beginning of the tenth persecution was, to be sure, a little before this (303), but its main terror was in this time. Galerius and Maximian are said indeed to have persecuted less during this period, and Maxentius not at all; but Galerius was the real author and sanguinary promoter of the persecution which is ascribed to Diocletian (Lact. c. 11), while Maximian was, in 304, the author of the celebrated " Fourth Edict " which made death the penalty of Christianity, and Maxentius was only better because impartial — he persecuted both Christian and heathen (Euseb. *V. C.* 1. 33–6; *H. E.* 8. 14; Eutrop. 10. 4).[1] The persecution under Maximin was of peculiar atrocity (Euseb. *H. E.* 8. 17; 9. 6, &c.; Lact. c. 26–27), so that the whole of this period in the East, excepting a slight breathing space in 308, was a terror to Christians, and it is said that " these two years were the most prolific of bloodshed of any in the whole history of Roman persecu-

---

[1] " Raging against the nobles with every kind of destruction," Eutrop. 10. 4.

tions " (Marriott, in Smith & W. 2, p. 594). It was not until the very end of this period[1] that Galerius, in terror of death, issued the famous first edict of toleration.[2] Such was the condition of things in July, 311. The deaths of Severus in 307, Maximian in 310, and Galerius in 311, had cleared the stage so far as to leave but four Augusti, Licinius and Maximin in the East, Constantine and Maxentius in the West. The only well-ordered and contented section of the world was that of Constantine. In all the others there was oppression, excess, and discontent, the state of things at Rome being on the whole the most outrageous.

§ 4. *Second Five Years.*

This period was most momentous for the world's history. Maxentius, seeking an excuse for war against Constantine, found it in a pretended desire to avenge his father (Zos. 2. 14), and prepared for war.[3] Like his father before him, however, he did not know his man. Constantine's mind was prepared. He was alert and ready to act. He gathered all the forces, German, Gallic, and British (Zos. 2. 15) that he could muster, left a portion for the protection of the Rhine, entered Italy by way of the Alps (*Paneg.*), and marched to meet the much more numerous forces of Maxentius, — Romans, Italians, Tuscans, Carthagenians, and Sicilians (Zos. 2. 15).[4] First Sigusium was taken by storm (Naz. *Paneg.* [321] c. 17 and 21 ; *Paneg.* [313] c. 5) ; then the cavalry of Maxentius was defeated at Turin (Naz. *Paneg.* [321] c. 22 ; *Paneg.* [313] c. 6). After a few days' rest in Milan (*Paneg.* [313] c. 7) he continued his triumphant march, defeating the enemy again in a cavalry engagement at Brescia (Naz. *Paneg.* c. 25), and taking the strongly fortified Verona after a hard-fought battle before the walls (Anon. Vales. p. 473 ; *Paneg.* [313] ; Naz. *Paneg.* c. 25–26). This had taken him out of his way a little ; but now there were no enemies in the rear, and he was free to push on to Rome, on his way whither, if not earlier, he had his famous vision of the cross.[5] He reached the Tiber October 26. Maxentius, tempted by a dubious oracle[6] issued from Rome, crossed the Tiber, and joined battle. His apparently unwise action in staking so much on a pitched battle has its explanation, if we could believe Zosimus (2. 15), Eusebius (*V. C.* 1. 38), Praxagoras, and others. His object was, it is said, by a feigned retreat to tempt Constantine across the bridge of boats which he had built in such a way that it could be broken, and the enemy let into the river.[7] If it was a trick, he at least fell into his own pit. The dissipated soldiers of Maxentius gave way before the hardy followers of Constantine, fired by his own energy and the sight of the cross. The defeat was a rout. The bridge broke. Maxentius, caught in the jam, was cast headlong into the river (Anon. Val. p. 473 ; Lact. c. 44 ; Chron. Pasch. p. 521, &c.) ; and after a vain attempt to climb out on the steep bank opposite (*Paneg.* [313] c. 17), was swept away by the stream. The next day his body was found, the head cut off (Praxag. ; Anon. Vales. p. 473), and carried into the city (Anon. Vales. p. 473) on the point of a spear (*Paneg.* [313] c. 18 ; Zos. 2. 17 ; Praxag. p. 1). Constantine entered the city

---

[1] Edict of toleration was April 30; Constantine's anniversary, July 24.

[2] This edict was signed by Constantine and Licinius as well as by Galerius. The Latin text is found in Lactantius, *de mort. pers.* c. 24, and the Greek translation in Eusebius, *H. E.* 8. 17.

[3] Eusebius represents the occasion of Constantine's movement as a philanthropic compassion for the people of Rome (*V. C.* 1. 26; *H. E.* 9. 9).

Praxagoras (ed. Müller, p. 1) says distinctly that it was to avenge those who suffered under the tyrannical rule of Maxentius and Nazarius (*Paneg.* c. 19), that it was "for liberating Italy." So, too, Nazarius (*Paneg.* [321] c. 27), Zonaras (13. 1), Cedrenus, and Ephraem (p. 22) speak of a legation of the Romans petitioning him to go.

Undoubtedly he did pity them, and as to the legation, every Roman who found his way to Trèves must have been an informal ambassador asking help. The fact seems to be that he had long suspected Maxentius (Zos. 2. 15), and now, learning of his preparations for war, saw that his suspicions were well grounded. What-

ever underlying motive of personal ambition there may have been, it is probable that the philanthropic motive was his justification and pretext to his own conscience for the attempt to rid himself of this suspected and dangerous neighbor. Zosimus being Zosimus, it is probable that Maxentius was the aggressor if he says so.

[4] Constantine numbered, according to Zosimus, 90,000 foot, 8,000 horse; and Maxentius, 170,000 foot, and 18,000 horse. According to Panegyr. (313) c. 3, he left the major part of his army to guard the Rhine and went to meet a force of 100,000 men with less than 40,000 (c. 5).

[5] See note on Bk. I. c. 28.

[6] That " on the same day the enemy of the Romans should perish" (Lact. c. 44).

[7] The circumstance pronounced by Wordsworth "almost incredible" is witnessed to by Eusebius (*V. C.* 1. 38), Zosimus (2. 15), Praxagoras (ed. Müller, p. 1). The bridge certainly broke as mentioned by Lactantius (c. 44) and as represented on the triumphal arch, but whether the "plot" was an *ex post facto* notion or not is unclear.

in triumph amid rejoicings of the people,[1] exacted penalties from a few of those most intimate with Maxentius (Zos. 2. 17),[2] disbanded the Prætorian Guards (Vict. *Cæs.* p. 159 ; Zos. 2. 17), raised a statue to himself, and did many other things which are recorded ; and if he did as many things which are not recorded as there are recorded things which he did not do, he must have been very busy in the short time he remained there.[3]

Constantine was now sole emperor in the West, and the emperors were reduced to three. History was making fast. After a very brief stay in Rome he returned to Milan (Lact. c. 45), where Licinius met him (Anon. Vales. p. 473 ; Lact. c. 25 ; Vict. *Epit.* p. 50 ; Zos. 2. 17, &c.). It had become of mutual advantage to these emperors to join alliance. So a betrothal had been made, and now the marriage of Licinius to the sister of Constantine was celebrated (cf. refs. above Lact. ; Vict. ; Zos. ; Anon. Vales.). At the same time the famous Second Edict or Edict of Milan was drawn up by the two emperors (Euseb. *H. E.* 10. 5 ; Lact. c. 48), and probably proclaimed.[4] Constantine then returned to Gaul (Anon. Vales. p. 473 ; Zos. 11. 17), where he was forced into another sort of strenuous warfare — the ecclesiastical, taking a hand somewhat against his will in trying to settle the famous Donatist schism.[5]

Licinius had a more critical problem to meet. Maximin thought it a good time to strike while Licinius was off in Milan engaged in festivities (Lact. c. 45) ; but the latter, hastily gathering his troops and pushing on by forced marches, met near Heraclea and utterly defeated him (Lact. c. 46). Maximin fled precipitately, escaping the sword only to die a more terrible death that same summer (Lact. c. 49 ; Euseb. *V. C.* 1. 58 ; cf. Zos. 2. 17).[6] The death of Maximin cleared the field still farther. Through progressive subtractions the number of emperors had now been reduced to two, — one in the East and one in the West.

They, too, promptly fell out. The next year they were at war. Causes and pretexts were various ; but the pretext, if not the cause, was in general that Licinius proved an accomplice after the fact, at least, to a plot against Constantine.[7] Whatever the immediate cause, it was one of

---

[1] "Senate and people rejoiced with incredible rejoicing" (Vict. *Cæs.* p. 159). Cf. Euseb. *V. C.* 1. 39; *Paneg.* [313] c. 19; Naz. *Paneg.* c. 30; *Chron. Pasch.* p. 521, &c.

[2] It is said he put to death Romulus, son of Maxentius, but it lacks evidence, and the fact that Romulus was consul for two years (208-9) with Maxentius, and then Maxentius appears alone, seems to indicate that he died in 209 or 210 (cf. Clinton, under the years 208 and 209).

[3] For the churches he is said to have founded, compare note on Bk. I. ch. 42.

The curious patchwork triumphal arch which still stands in a state of respectable dilapidation near the Coliseum at Rome, was erected in honor of this victory. It is to be hoped that it was erected after Constantine had gone, and that his æsthetic character is not to be charged with this crime. It was an arch to Trajan made over for the occasion, — by itself and piecemeal of great interest. Apart from the mutilation made for the glory of Constantine, it is a noble piece of work. The changes made were artistic disfigurements; but art's loss is science's gain, and for the historian it is most interesting. The phrase "*instinctu divinitatis*" has its value in the "*Hoc signo*" discussion (cf. notes to the *V. C.*); and the sculptures are most suggestive.

[4] It has been maintained that there were three edicts of Constantine up to this time: 1. Galerius, Constantine, and Licinius in 311; 2. Constantine and Licinius in 312 (lost); 3. Constantine and Licinius in 313 (cf. Keim, p. 16 and 81-84; Zahn, p. 33). So Gass in Herzog, p. 201, Wordsworth (*Ch. Hist.*), and others. But, like most certain things, it seems to have been disproved. The "harder edict" seems to have been a product of Eusebius' rather slovenly historical method, and to refer to the first, or Galerian edict.

[5] The appeal of the Donatists to Constantine was first met by the appointment of a "court of enquiry," held at Rome, Oct. 2, 313. The result was unsatisfactory, and Constantine ordered an examination on the spot, which took place at Carthage, Feb. 15, 314 (Phil-

lott). The Donatists still urging, the Council of Arles was called, Aug. 1, 314, and some progress seemed to be made, but progress more satisfactory to the orthodox than to the schismatics, who urged again that Constantine hear the matter himself, as he finally did, November, 316 (Wordsworth; cf. Augustine, *Ep.* 43, ¶ 20). He confirmed the previous findings, and took vigorous but ineffective measures to suppress the Donatists, measures which he saw afterwards could not be carried out, and perhaps saw to be unjust. Compare Augustine, *Ep.* 43, ch. 2, and elsewhere, also various documents from Augustine, Lactantius, Eusebius, Optatus, &c., collected in Migne, *Patrol. Lat.* 8 (1844), 673-784. Compare also Fuller, *Donatism*, Phillott, *Felix*, — articles in Smith and W. *Dict.* &c.; and for general sources and literature, cf. *Donatist Schism*, Hartranft, in Schaff, *Nicene and Post-Nicene Fathers*, 4 (1887), 369-72; Völter, *Ursprung des Donatismus*, 1883; and Seeck in Brieger's *Zeitschrift f. Kirchengeschichte*, 10 (1889), 505-508.

[6] According to Lactantius (c. 49), an attempt at suicide by poison was followed by a wretched disease, bringing to a lingering and most painful death.

[7] Bassianus, who had married Anastasia, sister of Constantine, was incited by his brother, who was an adherent of Licinius, to revolt against Constantine. The attempt was nipped in the bud, and Constantine demanded from Licinius the author of the plot. His refusal, together with the throwing down of the statues of Constantine, was the direct occasion of the war (Anon. Vales. p. 473). Compare Eusebius, *V. C.* 1. 50-51, and Socr. 1. 3, where Licinius is charged with repeated treachery, perjury, and hypocrisy. Zosimus, on the other hand (2. 18), distinctly says that Licinius was not to blame, but that Constantine, with characteristic faithlessness to their agreement, tried to alienate some of Licinius' provinces. Here, however, notice that Zosimus would not count any movement *in behalf of Christians* as a proper motive, and sympathy for them was undoubtedly one of the underlying reasons.

the inevitabilities of fate. Another vigorous campaign followed, characterized by the same decisive action and personal courage on the part of Constantine which he had already shown, and which supplied his lack of soldiers.[1] First at Cibalis in Pannonia (Oct. 8),[2] then in a desperate battle at Mardia, Licinius was defeated and forced to make peace (Anon. Vales. p. 474; Zos. 2. 19–20). The world was re-divided between the affectionate brothers-in-law, and Constantine took Illyrium to his other possessions.[3] After this battle and the re-division there was a truce between the emperors for some years, during the early part of which (in 316 or 315) the Decennalia of Constantine were celebrated (Euseb. *V. C.* 1. 48).

§ 5. *Third Five Years.*

About the time of his decennial celebration,[4] his sons Crispus and Constantine, and Licinius, son of Licinius, were made Cæsars. The peace between the emperors continued during the whole of this period. There was more or less fighting with the frontier tribes, Crispus, e.g., defeating the Franks in 320 (Naz. *Paneg.* c. 3. 17?), but the main interest of the period does not lie in its wars. It was a period of legislation and internal improvement (cf. Laws of 319, 320, 321, collected in Clinton, 1, p. 9; also De Broglie, I. 1, 296–97). Early in the period he was at Milan, where the Donatist matter, which had been dragging along since 311, came up for final settlement (cf. note, above). He was also at one time or another at Arles and at Rome, but the latter and greater part of the period was spent mainly in Dacia and Pannonia (cf. Laws, as above). The close of his fifteen years was celebrated somewhat prematurely at Rome, in the absence of Constantine, by the oration of Nazarius (cf. Naz. *Paneg.*).

§ 6. *Fourth Five Years.*

If the third period was relatively quiet the fourth was absolutely stirring. There had undoubtedly been more or less fighting along the Danube frontier during the preceding years, but early in this period there was a most important campaign against the Sarmatians, in which they were defeated and their king taken prisoner.[5] In honor of this victory coins were struck (Eckhel, *Doct. Num. Vet.* 8 (1827) 87). But this was only skirmishing; afterwards came the tug of war. Nine years of peace proved the utmost limit of mutual patience, and Constantine and Licinius came to words, and from words to blows. For a long time Constantine had been vexed at the persecution of the Christians by Licinius (cf. Euseb. *H. E.* 10. 8, 9), persecutions waged perhaps with the express purpose of aggravating him.[6] Licinius, on the other hand, naturally chagrined over the previous loss of territory, knowing of Constantine's indignation over his persecutions, and perhaps suspecting him of further designs, was naturally suspicious when Constantine passed within his boundaries in pursuing the Sarmatians (Anon. Vales. p. 474). Mutual recriminations and aggravations followed. Licinius would not let the Sarmatian coins pass current and had them melted down (Anon. Contin. Dio. Cass., in Müller, *Fragm. Hist. Gr.* 4 [1868] 199). Altogether they soon came to blows. The steps were short, sharp, decisive. Constantine defeated Licinius by land (July 3, 323), and through Crispus, by sea (Soz. 1. 7; Anon. Vales. p. 474–5; Zos. 2. 22–3). After the defeat at Adrianople, Licinius retreated to Byzantium (Zos. 2. 23–5; Vict.

---

[1] Constantine at Cibalis had 20,000, Licinius 35,000 (Anon. Vales. p. 473).

[2] Zos. 2. 18; "by a sudden attack" (Eutrop. 10. 4); "by night" (Vict. *Epit.* p. 50). Cf. Orosius, c. 28.

[3] After the battle of Cibalis the Greeks and the Macedonians, the inhabitants of the banks of the Danube, of Achaia, and the whole nation of Illyrica became subject to Constantine (Soz. 1. 6; cf. Anon. Vales. p. 474; Zos. 2. 20; Oros. c. 28, &c.).

[4] Perhaps earlier and perhaps later. It is generally placed in 317 (cf. Clinton, p. 370).

[5] Zos. 2. 21. An exhaustive discussion of this is that by Bessell, *Gothen*, in Ersch u. Gruber, *Encykl.* I. 75 (Leipz. 1862), 132–33.

The same article (p. 133–35) discusses various relations of Goths and Sarmatians with Constantine.

[6] According to Sozomen, Licinius withdrew his favor from Christians and persecuted them, because "He was deeply incensed against the Christians on account of his disagreement with Constantine, and thought to wound him by their sufferings; and, besides, he suspected that they earnestly desired that Constantine should enjoy the sovereign rule" (1. 7). In this view of the case, it is easy to see how and why affairs marched as they did. Eusebius (*H. E.* 10. 9) makes this, like the war against Maxentius, a real crusade in behalf of the persecuted Christians.

Epit. p. 50), and then to Chalcedon (Anon. Vales. p. 475 ; Zos. 2. 25–6). Two months after the first victory (Sept. 18) a final and decisive battle was fought at Chrysopolis[1] (Anon. Vales. p. 475 ; Socr. 1. 4). Licinius surrendered on condition that his life should be spared (Zos. 2. 28), or rather Constantia secured from her brother the promise that his life should be spared (Anon. Vales. p. 475 ; Vict. *Epit.* p. 50 ; Pseudo-Leo, p. 85, &c.). He retired to Nicomedia, residing at Thessalonica (Soz. 1. 7 ; Pseudo-Leo, &c.), but was put to death the following year.[2] Constantine was now sole emperor. His first act (Soz. 1. 8) was to issue a proclamation in favor of the Christians (Soz. *l.c.*; *V. C.* 2. 24– , and 48–). This was followed by many other acts in their favor, — building of churches, &c. (cf. Euseb. *V. C.*, and notes). From this time on he was much identified with Christian affairs, and the main events are given *in extenso* by Eusebius (see various notes). In 325 (June 19–Aug. 25) the Council of Nicæa was held (cf. Euseb. *V. C.* 3. 6, and notes), and Constantine took an active part in its proceedings. The same year his Vicennalia were celebrated at Nicomedia (Euseb. *V. C.* 1. 1 ; Hieron.; Cassiod.) and the following year at Rome also (Hieron., Cassiod., Prosper., Idat.), Constantine being present at both celebrations,[3] being thus at Rome in July, and passing during the year as far as Arles, apparently spending some time at Milan (cf. the various laws in Clinton, v. 2, p. 92).

§ 7. *Fifth Five Years.*

The beginning of this period was the beginning of the series of acts which have taken most from the reputation of Constantine. Sometime in 326, perhaps while at Rome, he ordered the death of his son Crispus.[4] The same year (Hieron. *Chron.*) the Cæsar Licinius, his sister's son, was put to death (Eutrop. 10. 6 ; Hieron.; Prosper.), and shortly after[5] his wife Fausta died or was put to death.[6] But apart from this shadow, the period was hardly less brilliant, in its way, than preceding ones. It was a time of gigantic and, as some said, extravagant internal improvements. Among various enterprises was the refounding, in 327, of Drepanum, his mother's city, as Helenopolis (Hieron. An. 2343 ; *Chron. Pasch.* p. 283(?) ; Socr. *H. E.* 1. 18 ; Soz. 2. 2 ; Theoph. p. 41), and greatest of all, the transformation of the insignificant Byzantium into the magnificent Constantinople,[7] which was dedicated in 330 (Idatius ; *Chron. Pasch.* p. 285 ; Hesych. § 42 ; Hieron.; cf. Clinton).[8] It was probably during this period, too, that the work of improvement in Jerusalem was undertaken, and Helena made her famous visit thither (Euseb. *V. C.* 3. 42 ; Soz. 21 ; Socr. 1. 17 ; Ephraem. p. 24 : Theoph. 37–8, &c.).

§ 8. *Sixth Five Years.*

The main event of the last full five-year period of this reign was the Gothic war (Hieron. An. 2347 ; Idat.; Oros. c. 28 ; Anon. Vales. p. 476 ; Eutrop. 10. 7 ; Vict. *Cæs.* p. 352 ; cf. Soz. 1. 26), undertaken in behalf of the Sarmatians (Anon. Vales. *l.c.*), carried on by Constantine II., and brought to an end April 20, 332 (cf. Clinton). The following year (333) Constans was

---

[1] According to Zos. 2. 27, the final siege and surrender was at Nicomedia.

[2] Compare note on Bk. II. ch. 18.

[3] For his presence at Rome at this time, compare authorities above, and also law dated July, 326, given in Clinton (p. 380).

[4] Crispus was alive and in power March 1, 326, as appears from coins (cf. Eckhel, 8, p. 101–2). Whether he was put to death before the Vicennalia does not appear, but that he was is not probable. For death of Crispus and its date, compare Zos. 2. 29 ; Vict. *Cæs.*; Soz. 1. 5 ; Vict. *Epit.* p. 50 ; *Chron. Pasch.*; Eutrop. 10. 6, &c., and discussion under *Character*.

[5] The same year according to Greg. Tur. (1. 34). Cf. Eutrop. and Sidon. 327, and even 328, is the date given by some (cf. Clinton, v. 1, p. 382, and Wordsworth).

[6] Disputed, but generally allowed. On this series of deaths, compare the somewhat opposite views of Görres and Seeck in the articles mentioned under *Literature* for latest views.

[7] The date of the beginning of the work is curiously uncertain. Socrates (1. 6) puts it directly after the Council of Nicæa, and Philostorgius in 334, while there is almost equal variety among the modern historians. Burckhardt says Nov. 4, 326 ; De Broglie, 328 or 329 ; Wordsworth as early as 325. It is possible that the strangeness which he felt in visiting Rome in 326, and the hostility with which he was met there (Zos. 2. 29, 30), may have been a moving cause in the foundation of this "New Rome," and that it was begun soon after his visit there. He first began to build his capital near the site of Ilium (Soz. 2. 3 ; Zos. 2. 30), but "led by the hand of God" (Soz.), he changed his plan to that city whose site he so much admired (Soz.).

[8] For accounts of the founding of Constantinople, see Soz. 2. 3 ; Philostorgius, 2. 9 ; Malalas, 13. 5 ; Glycas, p. 462–64 ; Cedrenus, p. 495–98 ; Theoph. 41–42. Compare Zosimus, 2. 30 ; Anon. Vales. p. 475–76 ; Socrates, 1. 16 ; Orosius, c. 28 ; Praxagoras, Zononas, Codinus, Nicephoras Callistus, &c.

made consul (Idat.; Hieron.; Prosper has 332; cf. Zos. 2. 35; Vict. *Cæs.* p. 161, &c.), and in 334 the remarkable (Anon. Vales.) incorporation of 300,000 Sarmatians into the empire (Anon. Vales. p. 476; Idat.; Hieron.; cf. Ammian. 17. 12, 18; 17. 13; 19. 12; *V. C.* 4. 6). This same year Calocærus revolted in Crete and was defeated (Anon. Vales. p. 476; Vict. *Cæs.* p. 161; Oros. c. 28; Hieron.). The following year (335) Constantine celebrated his tricennalia, and Dalmatius was made Cæsar (Idat.; Hieron. An. 340; Vict. *Cæs.* p. 161; Anon. Vales. p. 476; Chron. Pasch. p. 532; Vict. *Epit.* p. 51; Oros. c. 28), making now four Cæsars and a nondescript (cf. Anon. Vales. p. 476), — Constantine II., Constantius, Constans, Dalmatius, and Hannibalianus, among whom the world was now partitioned (Anon. Vales. p. 476; Zos. 2. 39; Vict. *Epit.* p. 52).

§ 9. *Last Years.*

Later in this year, Constantine is known to have been at Jerusalem, where he dedicated a church (*V. C.* 4. 40; Chron. Pasch., but wrong year). It was also the year of the Synods of Tyre (Athanas. *c. Ar.* 1. p. 788; *V. C.* 4. 41; Theod. 1. 28). The same year, or early in the following one, Eusebius pronounced his tricennial oration (see *Special Prolegomena*). In 337 the Great Emperor died at Ancyrona, near Nicomedia, just as he was preparing for an expedition against the Persians, and was buried in the Church of the Apostles, at Constantinople (cf. notes on Eusebius' Life of Constantine).[1]

CHAPTER II.

CHARACTER.

§ 1. *Introduction.*

A man's character consists of an inherited personality enlarged, modified, or disfigured by his own repeated voluntary acts. A sufficiently exhaustive survey of such character may be made under the rubrics of: 1. Inherited characteristics. 2. Physical characteristics. 3. Mental characteristics. 4. Moral characteristics. 5. Religious characteristics.

The character of Constantine has been so endlessly treated, with such utter lack of agreement, that it seems hopeless to try to reach any clear results in a study of it. "Who shall decide when doctors disagree?" "How shall I go about it to find what sort of a man Constantine really was?" Certainly nothing can be gained by that method which chooses a few acts or characteristics to which shifting tests of various philosophies are applied. Nor can any haphazard selection and stringing together of traits give what is by its nature a synthesis of them all. Like any other scientific study, the first condition of method is that it be systematic. Then, a character generalization is worth just so much, no more, as the grounds on which it is based. To get a man's character from secondary sources, from other men's generalizations, is a hopelessly will-of-the-wisp effort. Again, another vice of characterization as usually practised is the interpretation of the whole by a part rather than the part by the whole. The individual act is thus made the standard of character. To get at what this personality called Constantine was therefore requires a systematic survey of the primary sources with a view to getting the *ensemble* that the eccentric may be judged by the normal. In such survey the main thing is the body of analyzed and grouped facts. The editor's summary, like any summary, is worth only what the facts are worth. This method, however imperfectly carried out, is at least better than rambling observations of incoherent phenomena; and has therefore been adopted in this attempt to find out what sort of a man this Constantine was; Physically, Mentally, Morally, Spiritually.

---

[1] The events and dates of these later periods have to do mainly with theological matters, — the "religious" activity of Constantine, to which Eusebius devotes his attention so fully, — and are treated in the *V. C.*

§ 2. *Inherited Characteristics.*

The fact of the inheritance of character, virtues or vices as the case may be, curiously recognized in various nations and ancient philosophies (cf. Ribot. *Heredity*, N.Y. 1875, p. 375–6), and even in the ten commandments, has received the clearer exposition of modern science. In view of it, a scientific study of character considers antecedent generations. Biography rests properly on genealogy. Constantine's father, Constantius Chlorus, was a man of great mildness, self-possession, and philosophic virtue, just, and a Neo-Platonist of the best type, a monotheist and philanthropist (cf. Sinclair, in Smith & W. 1. 661–2). Constantine is said to have inherited his father's strength, courage, personal appearance (Eumen. *Paneg.* c. 4), piety (Pseud.-Leo, p. 83; cf. Const. and Euseb. in *V. C.* 2. 49), and general virtues. The slur of Zosimus on the character of Constantine's mother seems to have been quite gratuitous. Her relation to Constantius was in nowise incompatible with virtue, and the honor afterwards paid her, along with the indisputable good early training of Constantine which was with her, indicate a woman of unusual character. The later enterprise and activity with the honors and responsibilities given her show her to have been of very considerable energy and ability.

§ 3. *Physical Characteristics.*

A graphic picture of his personal appearance is drawn by Cedrenus (p. 472–3). "Constantinus Magnus was of medium height, broad-shouldered, thick-necked, whence his epithet Bull-necked. His complexion was ruddy, his hair neither thick nor crisp curling, his beard scanty and not growing in many places, his nose slightly hooked, and his eyes like the eyes of a lion. He was joyous of heart and most cheery of countenance."[1] Many points in this description are confirmed by others, some apparently contradicted. Taken in detail, his *Height* was probably above medium. Over against this statement of Cedrenus (p. 472) that he was of middle height is that of the earlier Malalas (13. 1), who, while confirming the ruddiness of complexion, characterizes him as tall, and the explicit testimony of Eusebius, that among those with Diocletian "there was no one comparable with him for height" (*V. C.* 1. 19), and likewise among those present at Nicæa (*V. C.* 3. 10). But a "thick-necked" form hardly belongs to the strictly "tall" man, and a thick neck and broad shoulders would hardly belong to a form of "distinguished comeliness," if it were short (Lact. c. 18). It may be supposed therefore that he can be described as above medium height. Moreover, there would naturally have been more mention of height by Lactantius and Panegyrists if it had been very extraordinary. In respect of *Countenance* he was undoubtedly handsome. The "majestic beauty of his face" mentioned by Theophanes (p. 29; cf. *V. C.* 1. 19; 3. 10) is confirmed by suggestions in the Panegyrists (e.g. Eumen. c. 17; Naz. c. 24), and all general testimony, and not belied by the coins. His *Complexion* was ruddy; "reddish" in the expression of Cedrenus (p. 272), "fiery" in that of Malalas (13. 1). His *Hair*, rather thin and straight, scanty *Beard*, and "slightly hooked" *Nose* are shown also by the coins, where the nose varies from a pronounced Roman or ungraceful eagle's beak to a very proportionate, slightly aquiline member. His *Eyes* were lion-like (Cedren.), piercingly bright (Paneg. 313, c. 19; also Eumen.). His *Expression* was bright and joyous (Cedren.), characterized by "noble gravity mingled with hilarity" (Naz. *Paneg.* c. 24), by "serenity" and "cheerfulness" (cf. Euseb. *V. C.* 3. 11). In brief, he seems to have been a type of the sanguine temperament.

Added to his beauty of face was an unquestioned beauty of form. His distinguished comeliness of *Figure* (Lact. c. 18) is a favorite theme with his enthusiastic friend Eusebius, who says, "No one was comparable with him for grace and beauty of person" (cf. Eumen. c. 17; *V. C.* 1.

---

[1] Cf. Vict. *Epit.* p. 51, where "bull-necked" is rendered as equal to "scoffer," "such according to physiognomical writers being the character of stout men," Liddell and Scott, *Lex.* p. 1569. But the very proverb on which Victor bases this interpretation would seem to make it refer to energy and obstinate force of character, which is altogether better fitting the word and the physiognomical characteristic.

19 ; 3. 10), and that his figure was "manly and vigorous" (1. 20). The broad *Shoulders* and thick *Neck* prepare one for the testimony to his great bodily *Strength*. The feats of personal valor in combat with the Sarmatian champions and the wild beasts (cf. above), his personal energy in battle (e.g. before Verona ; cf. above), much special testimony (e.g. Eumen. *Paneg.* c. 4) and all the general testimony, show that the superlative language of Eusebius is well grounded, and interpreted with conservative imagination is to be taken as fact. According to him, " he so far surpassed his compeers in personal strength as to be a terror to them" (*V. C.* 1. 19), and in respect of *Vigor* of body was such that at the Council of Nicæa his very bearing showed that he surpassed all present in " invincible strength and vigor" ; while at the age of sixty or upwards, " he still possessed a sound and vigorous body, free from all blemish and of more than youthful vivacity ; a noble mien and strength equal to any exertion, so that he was able to join in martial exercises, to ride, endure the fatigues of travel, engage in battle," &c. (Vict. 4. 53). In *Bearing* he was " manly" (*V. C.* 1. 20), self-possessed, calm (*V. C.* 3. 11), dignified ("noble gravity," Naz. c. 24 ; cf. Eumen. &c.), with " majestic dignity of mien " (*V. C.* 3. 10) and serenity (*V. C.* 3. 10). In *Manners* he was " suave " (ἐπιεικής) (*V. C.* 3. 10) and " affable to all " (*V. C.* 3. 13). This singular affability was such, according to Lactantius (c. 18), as to endear him greatly to his soldiers. Over against this, however, must be set the statement of Victor, *Epit.* that he was " a scoffer [*irrisor*] rather than suave [*blandus*] " (Vict. *Epit.* 51). But this seems founded on a false exegesis (cf. above) and withal there is no absolute contradiction. Moreover, all his intercourse with bishops, deputies, soldiers, citizens, barbarians, seems to have generally made a favorable impression, and such success without affability of manner would have been marvelous. In *Dress* his taste, late in life at least, became somewhat gorgeous. If he were reigning to-day, the comic papers would undoubtedly represent him, like some other good and great men, with exaggerated red neckties and figured waistcoats. He " always wore a diadem," according to Victor, *Epit.* (p. 51), and according to many (Malal. 13. 7–8 ; Cedren. ; Pseudo-Leo, &c.) " none of the emperors before him " wore the diadem at all. Eusebius' description of his appearance at the Council of Nicæa would do credit to a Washington reporter on wedding-toilets ; he was " clothed in raiment which glittered, as it were, with rays of light, reflecting the glowing radiance of a purple robe, and adorned with the brilliant splendor of gold and precious stones " (*V. C.* 3. 10).

§ 4. *Mental Characteristics.*

According to his biographer-friend, Constantine was even more conspicuous for the excellence of his psychical qualities than his physical (*V. C.* 1. 19). Among these qualities are natural intelligence (*V. C.* 1. 19), sound judgment (*V. C.* 1. 19), well-disciplined power of thought (Theoph. p. 29), and peculiarly, as might be expected from his eye and general energy, penetration (Theoph. p. 29). In respect of *Education*, it is said on the one hand that he " reaped the advantages of a liberal education " (*V. C.* 1. 19), and particularly that he was thoroughly trained in the art of reasoning (*V. C.*) ; but according to Anonymous Vales. (p. 471), and also Cedrenus (p. 473), his literary education was scanty. If there was early lack, he made up for it afterwards with characteristic energy, for he attained very considerable erudition (of a sort) for an emperor, as is shown in his *Oration*. According to Eutropius he was devoted to liberal studies. According to Lydus he was skilled both in the science of letters and the science of arms ; for " if he had not excelled in both sciences, he would not have been made emperor of the Romans " (Lydus, *de Magist.* 3. 33), — a somewhat subjective ground. Such was his devotion to study that, according to Eusebius (*V. C.* 4. 29), " he sometimes passed sleepless nights in furnishing his mind with divine knowledge." The measure of his thoroughness may be gathered from the fact that his knowledge of Greek even, does not seem to have been very extensive — " with which he was not altogether unacquainted " (*V. C.* 3. 13). His learning, as shown in his orations, is the learning of a man of affairs, and has many elements of crudity and consequent pretentiousness; but he is not worse than many authors — much better than most royal authors.

His learning had at least the excellent quality that it was radiated with reference to expression, as all sound learning must be. According to Eusebius, much of his time was spent in composing discourses, many of which he delivered in public (*V. C.* 4. 29), and he continued to the last to compose discourses and to deliver frequent orations in public.

The description by Eusebius of the character of his orations (*V. C.* 4. 24) seems to forbid any assumption of pure vanity as his motive. It is the most natural thing in the world that an emperor should make speeches, and that he should speak on scholastic or religious themes, and with the use of classical philosophy, mythology, and literature, should be no surprise in the days of President Harrison, Mr. Gladstone, and the Emperor William. There is no doubt he wrote and spoke vigorously and effectively to his soldiers, and on political and judicial matters (witness his laws), and his learned literary production is very fair amateur work, considering. In the *Delivery* of his speeches he seems to have had self-possession and modesty of manner, as e.g. at the Council of Nicæa, where "he looked serenely around on the assembly with a cheerful aspect, and having collected his thoughts, in a calm and gentle tone . . . proceeded to speak" (*V. C.* 3. 11). His *Literary style* was somewhat inflated and verbose, but for this, compare *Special Prolegomena*. His *Patronage of learning* showed his interest in it. Following his father's example and continuing his work, he encouraged the schools in Gaul (cf. above). Hosius and Eusebius were his friends and counselors. He made Lactantius tutor to Crispus (Hieron. Chron.). He had copies of the Scriptures made and distributed (*V. C.* 3. 1). In short, he especially "encouraged the study of letters" (Vict. *Epit.* 51) in every way.

§ 5. *Moral Characteristics.*

(a) *In relations with events, things, or persons.* First of all, Constantine excelled in *Energy,* that fundamental of all developed character. He was pre-eminent for masculine strength of character (Theoph. p. 29), a man of energy (*vir ingens,* Eutrop. 10. 1). This was manifested at every turn, in his successful military activity under Diocletian, in the decisive acts at the time of leaving him, in the prosecution of campaigns against Maximian, Maxentius, Licinius, in the wholesale way in which he pushed internal improvements, the building of Constantinople, the multiplication of Christian houses of worship, in his studies, in his law-making; in short, in everything he touched there was the same teeming, resistless energy of the man. His *Determination* was "bent on effecting whatever he had settled in his mind" (Eutrop. 10. 5). His *Rapidity of action* when he rejoined his father is described by Lactantius as incredible (Lact. c. 24). He showed the same alacrity in his quick return and surprise of Maximian, in his first entry into Italy, and in his campaign against Licinius. This energy and activity rose to positive *Impetuosity,* which led him at Verona, before Rome, and at Cibalis to plunge into the midst of battle, communicating his own resistless, indomitable, alert will to do, to his soldiers. Closely linked with these qualities was that personal *Courage and Valor,* inherited from his father (Paneg. 307, c. 3), mentioned by Eusebius ·(*V. C.* 1. 11), and explicitly or implicitly by almost every one. This most indubitable of all his qualities was witnessed to even by the scoffing Julian as "inexpressibly" great (*Orat.* p. 13), and mentioned even in the work whose chief aim seems, almost, to detract from Constantine (*Cæs.* p. 23). United with all these characteristics of greatness was a far-reaching *Ambition.* This on the one hand is represented to be an ambition for power and glory. He was "exceedingly ambitious of military glory" (Eutrop. 10. 7); "aspiring to the sovereignty of the whole world" (Eutrop. 10. 5). According to Zosimus, at the time of the appointment of Severus and Maximin, already having his mind set on attaining royalty he was roused to a greater desire by the honor conferred on Severus and Maximin, and this eager desire of power was already well known to many. On the other hand, this ambition is represented to be a burning zeal for righting wrongs; his wars against Maxentius and Licinius real crusades, and his actual objective in all things the reform to be effected. If the fruit proves the motive, this was so ; for he consistently used or tried to use his power for what he thought public good. This he did in Gaul, after his victories, in his legislation, and in his internal improvements.

In view of all this powerfulness of personality, it may be said of all successes of this "man of power" (Eutrop. 10. 5) what Eutropius says of his success in war, that it was great, "but not more than proportioned to his exertions" (Eutrop.). With all this energy of personality, how- ever, he was far from being headstrong. On the contrary, he showed marked *Prudence*, resem- bling his father in this also (Paneg. 307, c. 3). Sustaining so long the delicate position at the court of Diocletian, all his provision for guarding the frontiers, his long-suffering in waiting to be confirmed Cæsar, in waiting his opportunity to meet Maxentius, in waiting and getting every- thing in hand before meeting Licinius, his wise moderation in demand on the conquered, and the not pressing forward until he had everything well arranged, show this, and a high degree of *Patience* withal. This latter virtue was peculiarly characteristic whether exercised in respect of things or plans or people, and his great patience in listening to complaints (Naz. c. 24) is only a part of the whole. As he was patient, so he was distinguished for *Perseverance*, and "firm and unshaken" (Theoph. p. 29) *Steadfastness*. So great energy united with these other qualities barely needs testimony to suggest great *Faithfulness* to his tasks in hand, as in that "strict atten- tion to his military duties" which Lactantius says (c. 18) characterized him as a young man. In brief, his whole personality was a marked example of that balance of power and the measuring of remote ends which is included under the word *Self-control*, in the use of the philosophy of which he, as well as his father, was a disciple. In this exercise of his great energy towards himself he was recognized to be remarkable. This self-control was manifested especially in his unusual *Chastity*. As a young man he was marked by correct moral habits (*probis moribus*, Lact. c. 18). The specific testimony of Eusebius to this (*V. C.*) would have comparatively little weight on a point like this, and the same might be said, in a measure, of the testimony of the Panegyrists (Naz. c. 24 ; 307, c. 4 ; 313, c. 4), who mention this virtue. But panegyrical art would forbid the laudation of what was conspicuously lacking ; rather it would not be mentioned, and the general testimony goes to show at least a contemporary reputation for extraordinary continence, considering his time and environment. His relationship with Minervina hardly touches this reputation, whether she was wife or only legitimate concubine. The accusations and innuendoes of Julian, *Cæsars*, have, in any fairly critical estimate, hardly more than the weight of some malignant gossip whose backbiting is from his own heart. "Honi soit qui mal y pense." Like Licinius, he seems to have been unable to understand that purity of heart which permitted the free companionship of women in social or religious life. Julian's general charge of luxuriousness and sensuousness (p. 43, 306, 25, 38, 42, &c.) must be regarded largely in the same light ; for this delight in soft garments, precious gems, games, and festivities was, if we can judge aright, in no sense "enervating pleasure and voluptuous indulgence" : for he was indefatigable in studies and works of all sorts, although it is perhaps to be referred to the vanity and love of display of which he is accused, and of which more later.

(b) *In relations with people.* In general he was *Amiable,* — popular with the soldiers, popular even with his subdued enemies (Eutrop. 10. 7). Diocletian reminded Galerius (Lact. c. 18) that he was "amiable," and he must have been so ; for he was "loved by soldiers" (Eumen. c. 16), and so "endeared to the troops" that in the appointment of Cæsar he was "the choice of every individual" (Lact. c. 18). This popularity he indeed "sought by every kind of liberality and obligingness" (Eutr. 10. 7.), but what he sought he found.

A very large element in this popularity was the universal *Mildness, Mercifulness,* and *Forbear- ance* which he showed. In these is found a class of characteristics which stand alongside his energy of character as peculiarly characteristic and great. "He whose familiar habit it was to save men's lives" (*V. C.* 4. 6), as a young man promised, in the opinion of Diocletian

(Lact. c. 18), to be "milder and more merciful than his father." Even in the opinion of Julian he was "far more humane (πραότερον), and in very many other respects superior to others, as I would demonstrate if there were opportunity" (Julian, *Orat.* p. 15) ; and he again (p. 96) speaks of him in laudatory terms as contrasted with the other emperors. Eusebius, as might be expected, is still stronger in expression, and sets Constantine "in contrast with tyrants who were stained with blood of countless numbers," saying that in Constantine's reign "the sword of justice lay idle," and men were "rather constrained by a paternal authority than governed by the stringent power of the laws" (*V. C.* 3. 1). This mercifulness he manifested on every occasion. "When Sigusium was on fire," he directed greater effort towards saving it than he had to capturing it (Naz. *Paneg.* c. 21). At the taking of Rome he punished a certain few only of those most intimate with Maxentius (Zos.), and even Zosimus notes the great joy and relief of people at the exchange of Constantine for Maxentius. It is noticeable that in the inscriptions the epithet "clementissimus," most rare of other emperors, is found a considerable number of times of him. So great was this mildness of conduct that he was "generally blamed for his clemency" (*V. C.* 4. 31), on the ground that crimes were not visited with their proper penalties. The testimony to this humaneness of character is almost unlimited and conclusive, but there is more or less evidence which is urged in qualification or contradiction. It is rather a common thing to say that he was at first mild, but later pride of prosperity caused him greatly to depart from this former agreeable mildness of temper (Eutrop.). Then the execution of the various members of his own family (cf. discussion below), the exposure of prisoners to the wild beasts (Eumen. *Paneg.* c. 12), his severe decree against those who should conceal copies of the works of Arius (Socr. 1. 9), his treatment of the Jews (Greg. Niceph., or at least his laws), and the severe penalties of some of his laws are among the points brought against him. But the remark of Eutropius is to be interpreted by the "former agreeable mildness of temper," to which he himself witnesses, and the fact that this latter period was that where the points of view of the two men had widely diverged. The exposure of prisoners to wild beasts was no evidence of cruelty in itself ; for under the customs then prevailing it might have been cruelty to his subjects not to have done this, and his treatment of the barbarian enemies is rather to be interpreted in the light of the testimony of Eutropius that he "left on the minds of the barbarians [Goths] a strong remembrance of his kindness" (10. 7). His treatment of his family is discussed elsewhere, but whatever its bearings may be, there is no just historico-psychological ground whatever for the use of the word which is so freely bandied, — cruelty. Cruel he was not in any sense. Even the extreme of the Panegyrist who says to him, "you are such by inheritance and destiny that you cannot be cruel" (Eumen. *Paneg.* c. 14), is nearer the truth. The penalties of his laws lay him open in a degree to a charge of growing severity ; but it was great, if sometimes mistaken and overzealous, regard for what he deemed the public welfare, and on quite a different plane from anything which we express as cruelty. Though with the growing conservatism of a man who finds his purposes of mercy continually perverted and his indulgences abused, he yet remained to the end of his life most merciful and mild compared with those who went before and who followed.

This fact becomes more clear in seeing how he excelled in kindred virtues. The *Patience* already mentioned, distinguished forbearance, and undoubted benevolence, or at least generosity, are traits which group with mercy and have no fellowship with cruelty. And these he had. He showed distinguished *Forbearance*, and that oftentimes, as in a disturbance at Antioch, where he "applied with much forbearance the remedy of persuasion" (*V. C.* 3. 59). The outrageous conduct of those who, in the Arian disturbances, dared "even to insult the statues of the emperor . . . had little power to excite his anger, but rather caused in him sorrow of spirit" (*V. C.* 3. 4), "and he endured with patience men who were exasperated against himself." These words are by Eusebius, to be sure ; but his conduct with Donatists, Arians, Maximinianus, and Licinius, in individual and on the whole, show that in fact he did habitually exercise great forbearance. To this was added much activity of positive *Kindness*. On first accession he "visited with much considerate kindness all those provinces" (*V. C.* p. 23). This kindness was shown throughout his reign, and brightly illustrated in his treatment of the persecuted Christians from the beginning, — in his acts in Gaul, in his famous toleration edict, in his letter to Maximin, and in his acts throughout. After his victory over Maxentius came the edict that those wrongfully deprived of their estates should be permitted to enjoy them again, . . . unjustly exiled were recalled and freed from imprisonment (Euseb. *V. C.* 1. 41). After the victory over Licinius he recalled Christian exiles, ordered restitution of property, released from labor in mines, from the solitude of islands, from toil in public works, &c., those who had been oppressed in these ways (*V. C.* p. 70–71). There is strong concensus of testimony to a very lovable habitual exercise of this trait in his "readiness to grant hearing," "patience in listening," and "kindness of response" to those whose complaints he had patiently listened to (Naz. 24). He was most excellent (*commodissimus*) to hear embassies and complaints of provinces (Vict. *Epit.* p. 51), — a testimony which is borne out by the facts. His *Generosity* is equally undoubted. His magnificent gifts and largesses to the army were still remembered in the time of Julian (*Orat.* p. 13). His constant and lavish giving to the Christians is Eusebius' unending theme : but it was not to the churches alone; for we read of his munificence to heathen tribes (*V. C.* 2. 22), his liberality to the poor (*V. C.* 1. 43) in giving money for clothing, provision for orphans and widows, marriage portions for virgins, compensation to losers in law suits (*V. C.* 4. 4). It was "scarcely possible to be near him without benefit" (*V. C.* 1. 43; cf. *V. C.* 3. 16; 3. 22; 4. 44).

Though slow to serve some friends through suspicion (i.e. *dubius* thus explained), he was "exceedingly generous towards others, neglecting no opportunity to add to their riches and honors" (Eutrop. 10. 7). "With royal magnificence he unlocked all his treasures and distributed his gifts with rich and high-souled liberality" (*V. C.* 3. 1). He seems to have carried it rather to excess, even on the showing of Eusebius. "No one could request a favor of the emperor, and fail of obtaining what he sought. . . . He devised new dignities, that he might invest a larger number with the tokens of his favor" (*V. C.* 4. 2). It is worth giving the account by Eusebius of this conduct in full here. He says (*V. C.* 4. 54) that this "was a virtue, however, which subjected him to censure from many, in consequence of the baseness of wicked men, who ascribed their own crimes to the emperor's forbearance. In truth, I can myself bear testimony to the grievous evils which prevailed during those times : I mean the violence of rapacious and unprincipled men, who preyed on all classes of society alike, and the scandalous hypocrisy of those who crept into the church. . . . His own benevolence and goodness of heart, the genuineness of his own faith, and his truthfulness of character induced the emperor to credit the professions of those reputed Christians who craftily preserved the semblance of sincere affection for his person. The confidence he reposed in such men sometimes forced him into conduct *unworthy of himself*, of which envy took advantage to cloud in this respect the luster of his character." There seems, therefore, some ground for the charge of *Prodigality*, that he "wasted public money in many useless buildings, some of which he shortly after destroyed because they were not built to stand" (Zos.), and (Zos. p. 104) "gave great largesses to ill-deserving persons, mistaking profusion for munificence" (τὴν γὰρ ἀσωτίαν ἡγεῖτο φιλοτιμίαν). Zosimus adds that to do this, he "imposed severe taxes on all, so severe that fathers were obliged to prostitute their daughters to raise the money, that tortures were employed, and in consequence whole villages depopulated." This testimony is, however, by one bitterly prejudiced, who regarded money spent on Christian houses of worship as worse than wasted, and indicates only what appears from Eusebius as well, that expenditures for cities, schools, and churches built, and for other matters, must have been enormous. But so, too, they were enormous under other emperors, and Constantine, at least, instead of spending on debauchery, seems to have had something to show for it. As to taxes, Zosimus would undoubtedly sympathize with the Kentucky moonshiners in their "oppression" by revenue officers, if he were here now and Constantine were President, and would fulminate in the daily papers against the wicked party which by its wicked tariff compels men to marry their daughters to rich husbands in order to get their taxes paid, — and incidental luxuries supplied. But that does not say that an exorbitant tariff, to supply "jobs" which shall furnish rich "spoils" for those who have "pulls" out of the pockets of the many, is good; yet this, in modern phrase, is about what Constantine did. Constantine's trust in his friends and generosity to the unworthy, with its consequences on the tax-payers, reminds strikingly of some of our own soldier-presidents, whom we love and admire without approving all their acts. And yet, on the other hand, much of the expenditure was for solid improvement, and could only be criticised by those who now oppose expenditures for navy, for improved postal service, public buildings, subsidies, &c.; though yet, again, his wholesale way of doing things also reminds one of the large generosity of some modern politicians in their race for popularity, with their Pension, Education, River and Harbor, and what not liberalities out of the pockets of the people. But whatever unwisdom may have been mingled, all this profusion shows in him a generosity of character which was at least amiable, and in the main genuine. His generosity took also the form of *Hospitality*, as shown by his entertainings at the Council of Nicæa (*V. C.* 4. 49). With all these qualities of amiable popularity there seems to have been joined a yet more fundamental element, of permanent influence among men, in a spirit of *Justice* so marked that the claim of the Panegyrist is hardly too sweeping when he says that "all who took refuge with him for whatever cause he treated justly and liberally" (Paneg. 307. 5) — if there is added "up to his light and ability." Closely linked with this again is that "*Unbending righteousness*" of which Theophanes (p. 29) speaks. And to all these qualities was added that synthesis of qualities, — a remarkable *Tact* in his intercourse with men, a trait typically exemplified in his conduct at the Council of Nicæa, where "the emperor gave patient audience to all alike, and reviewed every proposition with steadfast attention, and by occasionally assisting the arguments of each party in turn, he gradually disposed even the most vehement disputants to a reconciliation, . . . persuading some, convincing others by his reasonings, praising those who spoke well, and urging all to unity of sentiment, until at last he succeeded in bringing them to one mind and judgment respecting every disputed question" (*V. C.* 3. 13).

But success with men and popularity seem to have opened that pitfall of success, — *Vanity*, — and it is charged that he fell thereinto, although there is testimony to the exact contrary. According to Victor (*Epit.* p. 51) he was "immeasurably greedy of praise." This agrees with, and is at the same time modified by Eutropius' testimony to his ambition for glory and for honorable popularity (10. 7), and his apparently complacent reception of the outrageous flattery of Optatian (cf. his letter), seems at least to show some weakness in this direction. So again his tendency toward *Magnificence*, as shown in his assuming the diadem and his dress in general (cf. above), in the splendor of banquets as witnessed by his approving friend (*V. C.* 3. 15), his desire to do on a large scale whatever he did, whether in the building of cities or splendid houses of worship, or in book-binding ornamentations of pearls and gems. And yet again it is shown in what seems at this distance his *Conceit*, sublime in its unconsciousness in reckoning himself a sort of thirteenth, but, it would seem, a facile princeps apostle, in the disposition for his burial, "anticipating with extraordinary fervor of faith that his body would share their title with the apostles themselves. . . . He accordingly caused twelve coffins to be set up in this church, like sacred pillars, in honor and memory of the apostolic number, in the centre of which his own was placed, having six of theirs on either side of it" (*V. C.* 4. 60). One can seem to read in this a whole history of unblushing flattery, and it reminds that Eunapius (*Vic. ædes.* p. 41) has spoken of his pleasure in the stimulant of "intoxicating flattery." Still it is not to be supposed that this was a peculiarly weak vanity or an absorbing one. The testimony to his *Modesty* (*V. C.* 3. 10), though by Eusebius, is too circumstantial to be wholly unreal, and the testimony to his *Humility* in his "indignation at excessive praise" (*V. C.* 4. 48), and the records of Eusebius that he "was not rendered arrogant by these plaudits nor uplifted by the praises" (Euseb. *V. C.* 1. 39), and of the Chronicon Paschale (p. 521) that "he was not at all puffed up by the acclamations," evidently represent a genuine thing. This mixed character is too frequently met with to be incomprehensible. Real power, recognizing its own success, glad of the recognition of others, not at bottom because of cold vanity, but from warm appreciation of human friendliness, became through success in carrying out what seemed to him, and were, divine plans, fired with the thought that he was the especial and necessary minister of God, that his thoughts and will were directly touched by the Divine Will and thus that whatever he thought or willed was infallible. He is not unlike some modern rulers. The spirit, though one of real vanity, or egotism at least, has an element of nobleness in it, and in most of its manifestations commands respect along with the smile. The accusation of Zosimus of *Arrogance* " when he had attained to the sole authority," and that he "gave himself up to the unrestrained exercise of his power," must be interpreted like those of other un-Christian witnesses, in the light of the fact that his actions worked relative hardships to the non-Christians, and that very justice to the Christians would seem injustice to them, and if Constantine was more than just, his generosity was at some one's expense. His energy of execution and constant success, with his dominating idea of a Divine mission, would naturally engender this faith in his own infallibility ; for what is arrogance but this vanity joined with power? His action toward schismatics — Donatists, Arians, or orthodox troublers of his peace — was such as to suggest some degree of this vice. Yet his success in keeping the followers of the old religion fairly mollified, and his generally successful tact, showed that this was in no sense a dominating and unrelieved characteristic. Two other weaknesses closely allied with these are also imputed to Constantine : *Jealousy*, as illustrated by the statement that " wishing to minimize the deeds of his predecessors, he took pains to tarnish their virtues by giving them jocose epithets " (Dion. Cont. 2 [Müller, p. 199] ; cf. Vict. *Epit.* p. 51), and *Suspiciousness* (Eutrop. 10. 7) ; for which latter, a man who had survived as many plots as he had, might well be excused. Again and again and again he trusted men, and they deceived him. His conduct with Maximian shows that at least in the beginning, before he had had so much experience of untrustworthiness, he was remarkably free from this. A much more serious charge is that of *Faithlessness* preferred by Zosimus, who says (2. 28), " in violation of his oaths (for this was customary with him) " and twice repeats the charge. Eusebius, on the other hand, tells what great pains Constantine took not to be the one to break peace with Licinius (*V. C.*). One is worth as little as the other. The charge seems to rest mainly or wholly on his conduct towards Licinius, in beginning war and in putting him to death. A small boy once held a smaller boy in a firm grip, but agreed to spare him the cuffing he deserved because he was smaller. The smaller small boy promptly set his teeth in the leg of the larger small boy, and was properly cuffed for it. Thereupon the smaller small boy's big brother was filled with indignation, which he manifested by seeking and finding the same fate. The indignation in behalf of Licinius seems to be in large measure big brother indignation — indignation with the wrong party. He appears to have been one of those who held a compact to be binding on the other party only. It wasn't in the bargain that he should persecute the Christians, or in the other bargain that he should plot his benefactor's overthrow. That king in Scripture who took back his promise to forgive a debt of ten thousand talents was not faithless.

(c) *In relations with his family.* He was a filial *Son*, having the confidence of his father, as shown in his wish of succession, and showing his mother all honors when he came to power (cf. coins showing her position as empress, and *V. C.*). " And well may his character be styled blessed for his filial piety as well as on other grounds " (*V. C.* 3. 47).

It is in this relation to his family, however, that the most serious attacks on the character of Constantine have been made. Eutropius says : " But the pride of prosperity caused Constantine greatly to depart from his former agreeable mildness of temper. Falling first upon his own relatives, he put to death his son, an excellent man ; his sister's son, a youth of amiable disposition ; soon afterwards his wife ; and subsequently many of his friends." This has been a battle-ground of accusation or excusation in all the centuries. The testimony is very meagre and uncertain, but this much may be said : 1. That any jury would regard the fact of deaths as evidenced. It is witnessed by Eutrop. (10. 6), Zos., Vict., Hieron., &c. 2. That he was unjustifiable is not proven. In respect to the death of Fausta, at least, there was probably just cause; whether love intrigue or other intrigue, there seems to have been some real occasion. The death of Crispus, too, was from no mere suspicions, but on apparently definite grounds of distrust. It is historical assumption to say that he had no good grounds, whatever these may have been — illicit relationship with Fausta or more probably political intrigue. At the worst, he was put to death on false but, at the time, apparently true accusation: what has been done by judges and juries of the best intention.[1] Of Licinius, his sister's son, it can hardly be said that he had the same reason, as he was still a boy. But remembering the inherited character of Licinius, and noticing the curious fact that the cordiality between Constantia and Constantine was peculiarly great to the end, it seems as if there must have been some mitigating circumstance.[2] In all historical candor it looks as if there had been some general intrigue against Constantine which had been met in this way; but the fairest verdict to enter is "causes unknown."

In estimating the characteristic value of the acts it must be noted, 1. That it has in no sense the character of private execution. The emperor was judge. Even if he mistook evidence and put to death an innocent man, it was as when a judge does the same. 2. That the relative moral character of punishments inflicted is conditioned by the custom of punishment. An English judge of the past was not as cruel in hanging a man for theft, as a modern one in applying the extreme penalty of the law to an offense with mitigating circumstances, would be. 3. That all law of evidence, all rhyme and reason, says that any man's any act is to be interpreted in the light of his *general character*. Where evidence is lacking or doubtful, such evidence of general character has actual weight, and may be conclusive. In application to these acts note (a) The peculiar forbearance which Constantine exercised toward Maximian. (b) The conclusive universal testimony to the general mildness of his character and his habitual mercifulness. In view of this, it is to be judged that there was some real, or appearing, great ground of judicial wrath. 4. That Constantine had suffered from plots on the part of his own relatives over and over again, and spared, and been plotted against again, as in the cases of Maximian, Bassianus, and Licinius. 5. That they were not put to death "in a gust of passion" at once, but in successive acts. In view of these things it is fair and just to say that they were put to death on grounds which seemed just and for the welfare of society, and their deaths in no sense indicate cruelty or unnaturalness on the part of Constantine. Even the death of Licinius must be interpreted by the political ethics of the times and its circumstances. So long as sentimentalists continue to send bouquets to murderers and erect monuments to anarchists, they will regard execution, even legal execution, as *prima facie* evidence of cruelty, and the killing of a murderer in self-defense, or the hanging of a traitor, as crime. Constantine's whole character ensures that if he thought he could have spared them, or any one, with safety, he would have done so.[3]

In general he was a faithful *husband* as respects marital virtue, and a good *father*. He took care that his children should be well educated. Crispus was under Lactantius (Hieron.), and the others perhaps under Arborius ("Auson. de Prof. Burdig. 16"); at all events, he had the most accomplished teachers of secular learning to instruct in the art of war, and in political and legal science (*V. C.* 4. 51), and both by his own instruction and that of men of approved piety, took special pains with their religious training. He early appointed them to offices of authority, and distributed the empire among them.

---

[1] It is hardly necessary to say that the various tales of the remorse of Constantine for the death of Crispus are mythical. The tale of Sopater has been mentioned. That of Codinus (*De signo Cp.* p. 62–63), also that, "in regret for death of Crispus, he erected a statue of pure silver with the inscription, 'My unjustly treated son,' and did penance besides," falls into the same category.

[2] Seeck (*Ztschr. f. wiss. Theol.* 1890, p. 73) maintains that it is established ("urkundlich fest") that Licinius was still living in 336, in which case he would have been more than twenty years old. He maintains also that he was not the son of Constantine, but the illegitimate son of Licinius by a slave woman.

[3] On this question compare especially monographs of Görres and Seeck. See under *Literature*, where other titles, e.g. Hug and Wegnerus, will also be found. In general, the remark of Ludermann (Lipsius, *Theol. Jahrb.* 1886, p. 108) is valid, "The arguments against Constantine's Christianity, which are drawn from his moral character, have ever been the weakest."

(d) *In relations with friends.* His general conduct toward his friends was marked by very great liberality (cf. above). Eutropius speaks emphatically of this even while he uses the expression which has been such a puzzle to all, that "toward some of his friends he was double" (or dangerous), a phrase which is interpreted by Johannes Ant. as meaning "to some of friends false (unsound, ὑπούλως) and unsafe (unwholesome, οὐχ ὑγιῶς)" (ed. Müller 4. p. 602–3). His uniform effort to please his friends has been discussed above.

(e) *In relations with society.* 1. As *General* he seems to have been popular with his own soldiers (cf. above), inspiring them with enthusiasm and energy. Toward hostile soldiers he was merciful (cf. above), not following up an advantage further than was necessary, and toward conquered enemies unusually forbearing; e.g. at Sigusium, at Rome, with Maximian, with Licinius, and with the Goths (cf. above). His generalship is characterized by careful provision for the guarding of his rear, and by rapidity of movement and dash in actual conflict. 2. As *Legislator* he "enacted many laws, some good, but most of them superfluous, and some severe" (Eutrop. 10. 8). He seems to have had a weakness for law-making which, at all events, shows a characteristic respect for law little shared by his early contemporaries. Of course Eutropius would consider all laws in favor of Christians superfluous. Laws for the abolition of idolatrous practices, for the erection of Christian houses of worship, observance of the Lord's Day (*V. C.* 4. 23), permitting cases to be tried before bishops (Soz. 1. 9; Euseb. *H. E.* 10. 7; Cod. Theod. Tit. de episc. 2), &c., would surely seem so. But even in other laws Constantine seems to have had at times an abnormal zeal for law-making, when his energies were not occupied in war or church-building. The laws were generally wise and, at the least, benevolently or righteously meant. Such were the abolition of crucifixion (Vict. *Cæs.*) and of gladiatorial shows (*V. C.* 4. 25; Socr. 1. 8; C. Theod. 15. 12. 1), the law that the families of slaves were not to be separated (C. Theod. 2. 25), that forbidding the scourging of debtors (C. Theod. 7. 3), and that repressing calumny (Vict. *Epit.* 51). Among the "severe" laws were such as punished certain forms of illicit intercourse with death. 3. As *Statesman* his policy was broad and far-reaching. He fully organized and carefully established one section of his territory before he enlarged. He changed the whole constitution of the empire, both civil and military (cf. Wordsworth, in Smith & W.). He inaugurated reforms in finance, and especially was most assiduous in the matter of internal improvements, restoring and building from one end of the empire to the other. The great characteristic consummation of his reign was the union of Church and State, over which men are still divided as to whether it was a tremendous blessing or a tremendous curse. Tremendous it surely was in its shaping power on world history. (Compare numerous titles under *Literature.*) The general statement of Eutropius that "in the beginning of his reign he might have been compared to the best princes, in the latter part only to those of a middling character," must be interpreted by the fact that during the latter part of his reign he was so associated with Christianity, in itself a falling away in the eyes of the old religionists. His reign was one of order and justice such as few were, and an order out of chaos, a reign in which it could be peculiarly said that "chastity was safe and marriage protected" (Naz. c. 38), where a man's life and property were secure as under few of the Roman emperors. It is idle to refuse the title of Great to a man who, from the beginning, followed a consistent, though developing policy, organized the interior, and securely guarded the frontier of his empire at each enlargement, and finally unified the whole on such a basis as to secure large internal prosperity and development.

§ 6. *Religious Characteristics.*

Was Constantine a Christian? This vain question has to be considered, hardly discussed. The interminable opinions, one way or the other, are for the most part wise-seeming, meaningless generalizations. Like any generalized statement, it is conditioned by the point of view of the author. When ten men answered the question "What is a Christian?" in ten different ways, who shall say what any one is? This has been the difficulty. One does not conceive of Christianity apart from baptismal regeneration. The question has then narrowed to one of baptism. Constantine was not a Christian until just before his death. Another has some other test. Another is not a Christian himself, and so on. A good Biblical, Protestant starting-point is to say he was a Christian as soon as he believed in Christ, and that the evidence of faith is in confession and action. Already, before his campaign into Italy, he seems to have been in intimate contact with the Christians. Hosius was probably already one of his advisers. The young emperor had inherited his father's piety (Paneg. 307, c. 5), and was inclined to monotheism. The words of advisers must have made him think at least, and he seems to have made a sort of test of believing at the time of the famous "vision of the cross," whatever that may have been. Judging from the way men think and feel their way to faith, it seems psychologically probable that, feeling his way along to that point, he tried faith and, having success, he substantially believed from that time on. Certainly from a very early period after this, the evidences begin to be clear and increasingly so as presumably his faith itself became more clear and fixed. The account in Eusebius of the process of thought by which he inclined toward Christianity has the greatest plausibility. He says that "considering the matter of Divine assistance, it occurred to him that those who had relied on idols had been deceived and destroyed, while his father . . . had honored the one Supreme God, had found him Saviour, &c. . . . he judged it folly to join in the idle worship of those who were no gods . . . and felt it incumbent on him to honor no other than the God of his father." The nature of the vision of the cross, whether a miracle, a natural phenomenon, or only a dream, does not affect the probability of the account by Eusebius of what followed it (V. C. 1. 32). "At the time above specified, being struck with amazement at the extraordinary vision, and resolving to worship no other God save him who had appeared to him, he sent for those who were acquainted with the mysteries of his doctrines, and inquired also what God was. . . . They affirmed that he was God, the only begotten Son of the one and only God," and he thereupon "made the priests of God his counsellors and deemed it incumbent on him to honor the God who had appeared to him, with all devotion." According to Sozomen, "it is universally admitted Constantine embraced the religion of the Christians previous to his war with Maxentius and prior to his return to Rome and Italy; and this is evidenced by the dates of the laws which he enacted in favor of religion" (Soz. 1. 5; cf. 1. 3). Philostorgius (1. 6), "in conformity with all other writers," ascribes to the victory over Maxentius (Photius. *Epit.*). This is confirmed, too, by the remark of the Panegyrist (313, c. 4; cf. c. 2 and c. 11), that he conducted the war by Divine instruction, and the famous inscription on the triumphal arch, "*instinctu Divinitatis.*" According to Augustine he was at the time of the petition of the Donatists, "mindful of the hope which he maintained in Christ" (August. *contra litt. Petil.* Bk. II. c. 92, p. 205).

The tales of his baptism at this time, or by Sylvester at all, are pure fables (cf. under *The Mythical Constantine*), but it appears from antecedent probability, from testimony, and from his early subsequent identification with the Christians that he became fairly convinced at this time. His letters concerning the council at Arles, to be sure, have little direct evidence, but enough to show that he regarded the Christian religion as the worship of that one supreme God, and in them Hosius was already his trusted adviser. But in his letters to Chrestus (314) he speaks of those who are "forgetful of their own salvation and the reverence due to the most holy faith," and if his letter to the bishops after the council at Arles — a letter full of expressions like "Christ the Saviour," "brethren beloved," "I who myself await the judgment of Christ," "our Saviour"[1] — be genuine, Constantine was well advanced in his commitment in 314; but whether it is or not,

---

[1] It seems to have been frequently accepted as such — in the collections of councils, by the editor of Optatus, Ceillier, &c. It first appeared in the edition of Optatus, among the monuments relating to the Donatists gathered by him. These monuments are from one single though tolerably ancient MS., and no source for this is quoted, though the sources of others are given. In itself considered it is a surprise to find it at this stage of Constantine's life. Still, it is not unlike his later productions, and it is not impossible to think of its having been written in the enthusiasm of a successfully ended enterprise. It would seem (unless there be some confirmatory study of the letter, not now at hand) that a cautious criticism would base nothing on this letter alone.

the fact of his Christian advisers, of his laws in behalf of Christians, and various substantial favors to them, his recognition of their God as his one God, makes it almost idle to discuss the question. Was Constantine a Christian in 314? What is a Christian? He seems to have been. The type was that of many a business-man church-member of to-day — Christians, but neither over-well-instructed, nor dangerously zealous in the exercise of his faith. It must be remembered that during these earlier years his confession of his faith and identification of himself with the Christians was conditioned by his relation to the old religion. Such a change was a radical novelty. His position was not yet secure. He had to use his utmost tact to keep all elements in hand. He was conditioned just as a modern Christian emperor or president, a majority of whose political advisers and subjects or electors are non-religious. He had great problems of political organization to effect, and was immersed in these. The only matter of surprise is that he grew so rapidly. There is no ground whatever for supposing that he dissembled to the end, or even at all. To say that his retaining the title of pontifex maximus, or making concessions respecting the old worship, or allowing soothsayers to be consulted, or even the postponement of his baptism, indicate this, is critical absurdity in the face of evidence.[1] Testimony, both heathen and Christian, to the openness of his action is complete, and the testimony of his acts — such, e.g., as the law for the observance of Sunday — conclusive. Later, at least, he "most openly destroyed temple worship and built Christian houses of worship" (Eunap. *Vita Ædes.* 37, ed. Boiss. p. 20). From the defeat of Licinius on, edicts, letters, speeches, acts of all sorts, testify to a most unequivocal adoption of the Christian religion. Eusebius hardly overstates in saying that "he maintained a continual testimony to his Christianity, with all boldness and before all men, and so far was he from shrinking from an open profession of the Christian name, that he rather desired to make it manifest to all that he regarded this as his highest honor" (*V. C.* 3. 2). Really the question whether he considered himself, or was considered, a Christian at and after the time of the Council of Nicæa is too idle even to mention, if it had not been gravely discussed. In the opinion of the bishops there he was "most pious" and "dear to God" (*Ep. synod.* in Socr. 1. 9 ; Theodoret, 1. 8). On his part, letters are full of pious expression and usually begin or end or both with "beloved brethren." To the council itself he describes himself as "fellow-servant" of "Him who is our common Lord and Saviour." Another more considerable position is that all that indisputable external connection with Christianity was pure political expediency, that he was a shrewd politician who saw which way the wind was blowing, and had skill to take advantage of it. That Constantine was not a Christian in the strict sense even to the end of his life was the position of Keim. Burckhardt regards him as a pure politician, without a touch of Christian life. Brieger (1880) says we have not grounds to decide either way, whether he was "a godless egoistic fatalist or had a more or less warm religious or even Christian interest," but that the fixed fact is, that it was not because of his inner belief in the Christian religion that he showed favor to the Christians. In a brief attempt to get some basis in the sources, the enthusiastic testimony of Eusebius and other writers, explicit as it is, may be quite disregarded, even the testimony to facts, such as his practice of giving thanks (*V. C.* 1. 39), of invoking Divine aid (Euseb. *V. C.* 2, 4, 6, 13 ; Soz. 2. 34), of his erecting a place of prayer in his palace (Soz. 1. 8), of his fasting (*V. C.* 2. 41), of his having a stated hour of prayer (*V. C.* 4. 22), although all these are interesting. The documents, however, unless by supremely uncritical rejection, can be regarded as fundamental sources. A brief analysis of these, even though imperfect, will furnish grounds on the basis of which those who apply various tests may apply them. Starting from his faith in Christ, surely the center of Christianity, he believed Christ to be Son of God, "God and the Son of God the author of every blessing" (*S. C.*), the revealer of the 'Father, who has "revealed a pure light in the person of Thy Son . . . and hast thus given testimony concerning Thyself" (*S. C.* 1), proceeding from the Father (*S. C.*), and incarnate, his incarnation having been pre-

---

[1] His saying before baptism is discussed in the *V. C.* 4. 2, notes.

dicted also by the prophets. He believed this Son of God to be his Saviour (*Ad Tyr.*, *Ad Ant.*, *Ad Euseb.*, &c.) "our common Lord and Saviour" (*Ad Euseb.*), "our Saviour, our hope, and our life" (*Ad eccl. Al.*). He believed in his miraculous birth (*S. C.*) and in his death for our deliverance (*Ad Nic.*; cf. *Ad Mac.* &c.), "the path which leads to everlasting life" (*S. C.* 1), "a precious and toilsome" work (*Ad Euseb.*), and in his ascension into heaven (*S. C.* 1). He believed in "God the Father" (*Ad Euseb.* 2), "Almighty" (*Ad Euseb.*), Lord of all (*Ad Euseb.* 2), and the Holy Ghost (*Ad eccl. Al.*; cf. *S. C.*). He believed in "Divine Providence" (*Ad Eccl. Al.*; *Ad Alex. et Ar.*; *Ad. Euseb.* 1), God the preserver of all men (*Ad Alex. et Ar.*), who sees all things (*Ad Syn. Nic.*), who is near us and the observer of all our actions (*S. C.*), and "under the guidance of whose Almighty hand" he is (*Ad Prov. Pal.*), that all things are regulated by the determination of his will (*Ad Euseb.*). He believed in the existence of a personal devil (*Ad Eccl. Al.*). He believed in the future life (*Ad Prov. Pal.*), "the only true life" (*S. C.* 12), the "strife for immortality" (*Ad Euseb.*), to which those may aspire who know Him (*S. C.* 12). He believed in future rewards and punishments (*Ad Prov. Pal.*; *S. C.* 23). He believed in the inspiration of the Scriptures (*Ad Eccl. Al.*). He loved God (*Ad Euseb.* 2; *V. C.* 2. 55), and considered it his chief work in life to glorify Christ (*S. C.*). He loved his fellow-men, being disposed "to love you with an enduring affection" (*Ad Ant.*; *V. C.* 3. 60, &c.), and recognized it as virtue in others (8, c. 11). To him, God, in general, is the source of all blessings (*Ad Prov. Pal.*; *S. C.*, &c.). "I am most certainly persuaded," he says, "that I myself owe my life, my every breath, in short, my very inmost and secret thoughts to the favor of the Supreme God" (*Ad Prov. Pal.*). He recognizes contrition as a requisite for pardon (*Ad. Prov. Pal.*), and that it is the power of God which removes guilt (*Ad Euseb.*). In the conduct of life. "Our Saviour's words and precepts are a model, as it were, of what our life should be" (*Ad. Ant.*; *V. C.* 3. 60).

Expositions of his doctrinal and ethical positions might be multiplied almost without end from the many and fruitful sources, but a few specimens in his own expression will best show the spirit of his religious life. A most suggestive and beautiful sketch of Christ's ministry on earth too long to quote here may be found in his *Oration* (ch. 15), but the following selections will give the idea :

A description of the inner Christian life. "For the only power in man which can be elevated to a comparison with that of God is sincere and guiltless service and devotion of heart to Himself, with the contemplation and study of whatever pleases Him, the raising our affections above the things of earth, and directing our thoughts, as far as we may, to high and heavenly objects" (*S. C.* 14).

A description of the outer Christian life. "Compare our religion with your own. Is there not with us genuine concord, and unwearied love of others? If we reprove a fault, is not our object to admonish, not to destroy ; our correction for safety, not for cruelty? Do we not exercise not only sincere faith toward God, but fidelity in the relations of social life? Do we not pity the unfortunate? Is not ours a life of simplicity which disdains to cover evil beneath the mask of fraud and hypocrisy?" (*S. C.* 23).

A prayer. "Not without cause, O holy God, do I prefer this prayer to Thee, the Lord of all. Under Thy guidance have I devised and accomplished measures fraught with blessing : preceded by Thy sacred sign, I have led Thy armies to victory : and still on each occasion of public danger, I follow the same symbol of Thy perfections while advancing to meet the foe. Therefore have I dedicated to Thy service a soul duly attempered by love and fear. For Thy name I truly love, while I regard with reverence that power of which Thou hast given abundant proofs, to the confirmation and increase of my faith" (*Ad prov. Or.*).

A confession of faith in God and in Christ. "This God I confess that I hold in unceasing honor and remembrance ; this God I delight to contemplate with pure and guileless thoughts in the height of his glory." "His pleasure is in works of moderation and gentleness. He loves the meek and hates the turbulent spirit, delighting in faith. He chastises unbelief" (*Ad Sap.*).

" He is the supreme judge of all things, the prince of immortality, the giver of everlasting life "
(*S. C.* 36).

Was Constantine a Christian?   Let each one apply his own test.

§ 7. *General Characterizations.*

Before trying to gather into continuous statement the traits of character which have been examined, a few general characterizations must be mentioned at least.   Beginning at the bottom, the unfriendly, or hostile, or at the least unsympathetic, heathen testimonies generalize him as at least relatively and on the whole both great and good.   The general tendency of heathen testimony is to represent him as admirable in the early part of his reign, but execrable, or less admirable, in the latter part; that of Christian writers is to represent a growth of excellence, which raises him to saintship at the end.   This is most natural.   Favoring Christianity was itself a moral fall to a heathen, and bestowing money on Christians would be robbery.   The turning of his character was with his changing face towards Christianity, and culminated in the overthrow of Licinius.   Licinius fought really as the champion of heathenism.   The adherents of a lost cause are characterizing their victor.   It is like an ex-Confederate characterizing Lincoln or Grant.   The point of view is different.   Honest and true men in the South thought Lincoln a curse, and often in popular verdict his character was " black."   The popular proverb quoted by Victor (*Epit.* p. 51), " Bull-necked for ten years, for twelve a freebooter, and for ten a spend-thrift (immature child)," has just the value of a Southern popular opinion of Lincoln, or a rural Northerner's of " Jeff Davis."   Indeed, the first might summarize at times the Southern popular verdict of Grant; the second, a frequently expressed estimate of Lincoln's conduct in the emancipation of slaves; and the third, their view of the enormous expenditure for pensions of Union soldiers, even as it was fifteen years ago.   But even the rather severe Victor, who reports this proverb, finds Constantine " most excellent (*commodissimus*) in many respects," — in respect of certain laws, in his patronage of the arts, especially that of letters, as scholar, as author, in the hearing of delegations and complaints (p. 51).   Again, " Praxagoras, though a heathen, says that in all sorts of virtue and personal excellence and good fortune, Constantine outshone all the emperors who preceded him " (Photius, *Cod.* 62, ed. Müller, p. 1).   And finally, the heathen Eutropius, who characterizes from his standpoint so admirably,[1] though he naturally finds that " in the beginning of his reign he might have been compared to the best princes; in the latter part, only to those of middling character," nevertheless records " that innumerable good qualities of mind and body were present in him," and that he was " deservedly enrolled among the gods," — using the *meruit* which he uses also of Aurelian, but not generally, and not even of Constantius.   On purely heathen testimony, therefore, Constantine, taken by and large, was comparatively remarkable and admirable.   A moderate Christian characterization is that of Theophanes (p. 29): " Pre-eminent for masculine strength of character, penetration of mind, well-disciplined power of thought; for unbending righteousness, ready benevolence, thorough majestic beauty of countenance, mighty and successful in war, great in wars with the barbarians, invincible in domestic wars, and so firm and unshaken in faith that through prayer he obtained the victory in all his battles."

[1] " Constantine, being a man of great energy, bent upon effecting whatever he had settled in his mind. . . .   But the pride of prosperity caused Constantine greatly to depart from his former agreeable mildness of temper.   Falling first upon his own relatives, he put to death his son, an excellent man; his sister's son, a youth of amiable disposition; soon afterwards his wife; and subsequently many of his friends.

" He was a man who, in the beginning of his reign, might have been compared to the best princes; in the latter part of it, only to those of middling character.   Innumerable good qualities of mind and body were apparent in him; he was exceedingly ambitious of military glory, and had great success in his wars; a success, however, not more than proportioned to his exertions.   After he had terminated the Civil War, he also overthrew the Goths on various occasions, granting them at last peace, and leaving on the minds of the barbarians a strong remembrance of his kindness.   He was attached to the arts of peace and to liberal studies, and was ambitious of honorable popularity, which he, indeed, sought by every kind of liberality and obligingness.   Though he was slow, from suspicion, to serve some of his friends, yet he was exceedingly generous towards others, neglecting no opportunity to add to their riches and honors.   He enacted many laws, some good and equitable, but most of them superfluous, and some severe."

Remembering, therefore, that in order to understand a character in past centuries one must project himself into his time ; remembering again the circumstances of his time and its practice, we shall, without forgetting any of the acts on which he has been judged, find him on indisputable testimony superior to most of the other emperors in character, and as much above the circumstances of his times as would characterize a man of to-day as of peculiarly high moral character. In view of this, it is uncritical, and a violence to historical evidence, to approach one whom, at death, the heathen thought worthy to be enrolled among the gods, and the Christians canonized as saint (in the Greek calendar), as other than one who, taken all in all, was of unusual excellence of character. As in any synthesis, any organization, subordinate facts must be viewed in their relation to their center and whole, as by any law of criminal procedure acts must be judged in the light of general character, so any rational, legal, scientific, historical estimate of Constantine must be in view of this fact.

§ 8. *Summary.*

With this as center of perspective, we have a picture of Constantine with lights and shadows, to be sure, but in the main true in its drawing and coloring. He was a man of rather more than medium height, strongly built, with broad shoulders, thick neck, and generally athletic and well-formed figure. His piercing eye, slightly aquiline nose, scanty reddish beard, and florid complexion, together with his bright expression, made a countenance striking and even handsome. Of great physical strength and vigor, he carried himself in a manly, self-possessed, dignified, and serene manner, uniting a dignity which might rise at times even to *hauteur*, or even incipient arrogance, with a general and customary affability. His dress, like his complexion, was somewhat florid. His mind was active, alert, intense without being somber, penetrating, sound, fairly cultivated, and well exercised in expression by pen or word. He was animated, habile, and attentive in conversation, self-possessed, steady, and calm in formal address. He was pre-eminently a man of energy, intense and resistless, with a determination to accomplish whatever he attempted, which rose under opposition to irresistible impetuosity, and wrought a courage which, in action, was absolutely fearless. His ambition was limitless, but not wholly or even mainly selfish.

With his energy and ambition were united the ballast of marked prudence, patience, perseverance, faithfulness to details, steadfastness, and supreme self-control. He was amiable and tactful, popular with his soldiers, and careful to please. Toward those who came into his power he showed habitual mildness and forbearance, — a mildness so great that he was generally blamed for it ; and toward all he showed great kindness, justice, and a generosity which verged on the lavish. He was open to the charge of over-generosity, almost of prodigality, a good measure of real vanity, some over-insistence on his own will and thought as the final standard of right, and by no means free from mistakes or human weaknesses. He was a good son, husband, father, a remarkably successful general, a tolerable legislator, and a clear-sighted, firm-willed statesman. In his religious life he abounded in creed and confession — believing in the Trinity, the Divinity of Christ, the Atonement, the Resurrection, and Eternal Life, in Repentance and Faith, in love to God, and love to man. He preached his faith on all occasions ; he practiced thanksgiving and prayer abundantly. He regarded everything that he had or was as from God. The editor's brief judgment is that Constantine, for his time, made an astonishingly temperate, wise, and, on the whole, benevolent use of absolute power, and in morality, kindly qualities, and, at last, in real Christian character, greatly surpassed most nineteenth century politicians — standing to modern statesmen as Athanasius to modern theologians.

CHAPTER III.

WRITINGS.

§ 1. *Introduction.*

Quite a number of works by this emperor-author are extant.[1] They may be grouped under,
1. Oratorical writings; 2. Letters and decrees; 3. Laws; 4. Various.

§ 2. *Oratorical Writings.*

According to Eusebius (*V. C.* 4. 29; cf. 4. 55) these were very numerous, and it may well be
believed. He seems to have done much of everything he undertook at all — fighting, or learning, or building temples, or making laws, he was nothing if not incessant. He had a habit of
inflicting his orations on his court, and undoubtedly had plenty of enthusiastic hearers, as any
emperor would, and as Eusebius says he did. They seem to have been generally philosophical
with as much religion as possible worked in (*V. C.* 4. 9). Not many are extant, but we have
some account of the few following:

1. *Oration to the saints* (*Oratio ad sanctum cœtum*, S. C.). For this see the following
translation and Special Prolegomena.

2. *Address to the Council of Nicæa in praise of peace* (*Ad Syn. Nic.*), in Euseb. *V. C.* 3. 12.
Address of welcome. He rejoices in the assembly, and exhorts them to be united, that they may
thereby please God and do a favor to their emperor.

3. *Oration to the Council of Nicæa*, in Gelasius, *Hist. Coun. Nic.* 1. 7. Begins with rhetorical
comparison of the Church to a temple, and ends with injunctions to observe peace and to search
the Scriptures as the authority in all points of doctrine. Appears dubiously authentic.

4. *Address to the bishops on their departure from Nicæa.* Abstract in Euseb. *V. C.* 32. 1.
Exhorts them to keep peace, cautions against jealousy, &c.

5. *Funeral oration.* A description in Euseb. *V. C.* 4. 55. Dwells on the immortality of the
soul, the blessings laid up for those who love God, and the ruin of the ungodly.

His method of composition is spoken of by Eusebius (*V. C.* 4. 29), and his manner of
delivery may be gathered from Eusebius' description of his speech at the opening of the Council
of Nicæa (*V. C.* 3. 11). For the style of his oratorical discourses, compare remarks on the
Oration to the Saints in the Special Prolegomena.

§ 3. *Letters and Edicts.*

It is hard to separate between letters, edicts, and laws. A substantial autocrat, the form of
address was much the same, and the force. The extant letters are quite numerous, and those of
which we have definite or general mention, many. He seems to have been a most industrious
letter-writer. Of the extant letters a majority are undoubtedly or probably genuine. Some,
however, need more critical study than seems to have been given to them.[2] Following is the
roughly chronological list, the works being grouped by years. The dating is taken mainly from

---

[1] It is curious that there should be no critical edition of the collected works of so considerable a writer. A large portion of his works are, to be sure, included in Migne's *Patrologia Latina*, vol. 84, Paris, 1844; but this *Opera Universa* is neither wholly complete nor in any sense critical, and this seems to be the only attempt at a collection. The works enumerated here are mostly in the edition of Migne, but not all.

[2] There is of course more or less critical treatment of various letters in critical works on Donatism or Arianism or other special topics. Since writing the above, the exceedingly interesting analysis of sources for early Donatist history, by Seeck, in Briegers' *Ztschr. f. Kirchenges.*, 1889, has been examined. He has, like Völter and Deutsch before him, admirable critical studies of certain letters. But a systematic critical study of the Constantinian letters as a whole seem to be still lacking.

the Migne edition, Ceillier, and Valesius with slight original study. The descriptions are of course from the documents themselves.

1. (313 A.D.) *Edict of Constantine and Licinius for the restoration of the Church.* In Lact. *De M. P.* c. 48, and also in Euseb. *H. E.* 10. 5 (Op. Const. ed. Migne, 105–110). The second edict of toleration. The first edict (Euseb. 8. 17; Lact. *De M. P.* 34) can hardly be classed among the "writings" of Constantine. This famous second edict grants full religious liberty to the Christians and restoration of their property. Compare section on *Acts of Toleration* in Wordworth's *Constantinus.*

2. (313.) *First letter of Constantine and Licinius to Anulinus.* In Euseb. *H. E.* 10. 5 (Op. Const. ed. Migne, 479–480). Restores goods to the Catholic Christians; written about the same time as the edict of toleration, according to Ceillier.

3. (313.) *Second Letter of Constantine to Anulinus.* In Euseb. *H. E.* 10. 7 (Op. Const. 481–2). Ordering that the Catholic clergy be free from public service, that they might not be disturbed in their worship of God.

4. (313.) *Letter of Constantine to Cæcilianus.* In Euseb. *H. E.* 10. 6 (Op. Const. 481–4). Presents money — three thousand purses (folles) — to be distributed according to direction of Hosius.

5. (313.) *Letter of Constantine to Melchiades* (or *Miltiades*). In Euseb. *H. E.* 10. 5 (Op. Const. 477–). Having received various letters from Anulinus regarding Cæcilian and the Donatists, he summons a council at Rome to consider the matter.

6. (314.) *Letter of Constantine to Ablavius* (or *Ælafius*). In Optat. *Mon. vet.* p. 283–4 (Op. Const. 483–6). The result of the council at Rome not having proved final, he summons the Council of Arles.

7. (314.) *Letter of Constantine to Chrestus* (*Crescentius*), *bishop of Syracuse.* In Euseb. *H. E.* 10. 5 (Op. Const. 485–8). Invites to the Council of Arles.

8. (314.) *Letter of Constantine to the Bishops after the Council of Arles.* In Optat. *Mon. vet.* p. 287–8 (Op. Const. 487–90). Contains gratulations, reprobations of obstinate schismatists, and exhortations to patience with such obstinateness. It is full of religious expressions, and if genuine, is a most interesting exhibition of Constantine's religious position at this time, but it looks suspicious, and probably is not genuine.

9. (314.) *Letter of Constantine and Licinius to Probianus, the Proconsul of Africa.* In Augustine, *Ep.* 88 (ed. Migne 33 [1865] 3045), and also in *Contr. Cresc.* (43 [1861] 540, also in Op. Const. and tr. Engl. in Schaff, *Nicene and Post-Nicene Fathers*, i, p. 370). Orders that the Donatist Ingentius be brought to his court. One text adds Maximianus or Maximus in place of Maximus as epithet of Constantine.

10. (314 or 315.) *Letter of Constantine to the Donatist Bishops.* In Optat. *Mon. vet.* p. 290 (Op. Const. ed. Migne [1844] 490). As the Donatists were not yet satisfied, he summons them to meet Cæcilian, and promises if they convict him in one particular, it shall be as if in all.

11. (315.) *Letter of Constantine to Celsus.* In Optat. *Mon. vet.* p. 291 (Op. Const. 489–90). In reply to letter mentioning disturbances of the Donatists, he hints that he expects to go shortly to Africa and settle things summarily.

12. (315.) *Fragment of a Letter of Constantine to Eumalius Vicarius.* In Augustine's *Contr. Cresc.* 3. 71 (ed. Migne 43 [1861] 541; also Op. Const. 491–2). An extract of six lines, in which he says Cæcilianus was entirely innocent.

13. (316 or 317.) *Letter of Constantine to the bishops and people of Africa.* Optat. *Mon. vet.* p. 294 (Op. Const. 491–2). He has tried every way to settle the Donatist disturbances in vain, and now leaves them to God and advises patience.

14. (323.) *First Letter of Constantine to Eusebius.* In Euseb. *V. C.* 2. 46; Theodoret, 1. 14; Socr. 1. 9 (Op. Const. 491–4). Empowers the repairing, enlarging of old, and building of new churches.

15. (323 A.D.) *Law of Constantine respecting piety toward God and the Christian Religion* (Ad prov. Pal.). In Euseb. *V. C.* 2. 24–42 ; abstr. in Soz. 1. 8 (Op. Const. 253–282). This long edict, addressed to the inhabitants of Palestine, contains an exposition of the prosperity which attends the righteous and the adversity which comes to the wicked, followed by edict for the restitution of confiscated property, the recall of exiles, and various other rectifications of injustices. This is the copy, " or letter," sent to the heathen population of the empire.

16. (324.) *Constantine's edict to the people of the eastern provinces concerning the error of polytheism, &c.* (Ad. prov. Or). In Euseb. *V. C.* 48–. This letter, written in Latin and translated by Eusebius, begins with " some general remarks on virtue and vice," touches on the persecutions and the fate of the persecutors, expresses the wish that all would become Christians, praises God, and exhorts concord.

17. (323 or 324.) *Letter of Constantine to Alexander the Bishop and Arius the Presbyter.* In Euseb. *V. C.* 2. 64–72 ; Gelas. 2. 4 ; Socr. 1. 7 (Op. Const. 493–502). Expresses his desire for peace, his hope that they might have helped him in the Donatist troubles, his distress at finding that they, too, were in a broil, his opinion that the matters under discussion are of little moment, and what he thinks they are. He exhorts to unanimity, repeats his opinion that the matters are of little moment, mentions his " copious and constant tears," and finally gets through.

18. (324–5.) *Letter to Porphyrius* (Optatian). In Migne, *Patrol. Lat.* 19 [1846] 393–394 and in various editions of Optatian. This letter to Porphyrius or Optatian was on the occasion of the sending of a poem by the latter for his vicennalia. It expresses his pleasure and his disposition to encourage the cultivation of *belles lettres.* Compare note on Optatian under sources.

19. (325.) *Letter of Constantine the King, summoning the bishops to Nicæa.* In Cowper, *Syriac Misc.,* Lond. 1841, p. 5–6. This is translated from a Syriac MS. in the British Museum, written in 501. Gives as reason for the choice of Nicæa the convenience for the European bishops and " the excellent temperature of the air." This, if genuine, is the letter mentioned by Eusebius, *V. C.,* but it looks suspicious.

20. (325.) *Letter of Constantine to the churches after the Council of Nicæa.* In Euseb. *V. C.* 3. 17–20 ; Socr. 1. 9 (Op. Const. 501–506). Dwells on the harmonious result, especially respecting the Easter controversy, and commends to the bishops to observe what the Council has decreed.

21. (325.) *Letter of Constantine to the church of Alexandria.* In Socr. 1. 9 (Op. Const. 507–510). Expresses great horror of the blasphemy of Arius, and admiration for the wisdom of the more than three hundred bishops who condemned him.

22. (325.) *Letter of Constantine to Arius and the Arians.* In "Conc. 2. 269." A long and rather railing address against Arius.

23. (325.) *Letter of Constantine to the churches.* In Socr. *H. E.* 1. 9. A translation of a Syriac translation of this, written in 501, in Cowper, *Syriac Misc.,* Lond. 1861, p. 6–7. Against Arius and the Porphyrians, and threatens that any one who conceals a work of Arius shall be punished with death.

24. (325.) *Letter of Constantine to the Nicomedians against Eusebius and Theognis.* In Gelas. 3. 2 ; Theodoret, 1. 20 ; Soz. 1. 21 (Op. Const. 519–524). A theological discussion partly of the relation of Father and Son, and an attack on Eusebius of Nicomedia.

25. (325.) *Letter to Theodotus.* In Gelas. 3. 3 (Op. Const. 523–524). Counsels him to take warning by what has happened to Eusebius (of Nicomedia) and Theognis, i.e. banishment, and get rid of such evil influence, if any, as they may have had on him.

26. (325.) *Letter of Constantine to Macarius.* In Euseb. *V. C.* 3. 30–32 ; Theodoret, 1. 16. Directs the erection of a peculiarly magnificent church at the Holy Sepulcher in Jerusalem.

27. (330.) *Letter of Constantine to the Numidian Bishops.* In Optat. *Mon. vet.* p. 295 (Op. Const. 531–532). Concerns a church taken possession of by schismatics.

28. (332.) *Letter of Constantine to the Antiochians.* In Euseb. *V. C.* 3. 60 (Op. Const. 533–). Exhorts them not to persist in their effort to call Eusebius from Cæsarea to Antioch.

29. (332 A.D.) *Letter of Constantine to the Synod of Tyre deprecating the removal of Eusebius from Cæsarea.* In Euseb. *V. C.* 362 ; Theodoret, 1. 27 (Op. Const. 543–546).

30. (332.) *Second Letter of Constantine to Eusebius.* In Euseb. *V. C.* 3. 61 (Op. Const. 537–540). Commends Eusebius for having declined the call to Antioch.

31. (332.) *Second Letter of Constantine to Macarius and the rest of the Bishops in Palestine (to Eusebius).* In Euseb. *V. C.* 3. 52–53 (Op. Const. 539–544). Directs the suppression of idolatrous worship at Mamre.

32. (332.?) *Edict against the heretics.* In Euseb. *V. C.* 3. 64–5. Against Novatians, Valentinians, Marcionites, Paulians, Cataphrygians who are forbidden to assemble, and whose houses of worship are to be given to the Catholic party.

33. (333.) *Letter of Constantine to Sapor, King of the Persians.* In Euseb. 4. 9–13 ; Theodoret, 1. 24 (Op. Const. 545–552). Is mainly a confession of faith commending the Persian Christians to the special care of their king.

34. (333.) *Letters of Constantine to Antonius, the monk, and of Antonius to him* are mentioned in Athanasius, 1. 855 (Op. Const. 551–552). Constantine and his sons write as to a father. Antony grudgingly replies with some good advice for them to remember the day of judgment, regard Christ as the only emperor, and have a care for justice and the poor.

35. (333.) *Letter of Constantine to Eusebius in praise of his discourse concerning Easter.* Eusebius, *V. C.* 4. 35 (Op. Const. 551–554) praises the discourse and asks for more.

36. (333.) *Letter of Constantine to Eusebius on the preparation of the copies of the Scriptures.* In Euseb. *V. C.* 4. 36 ; Theod. 1. 15 ; Socr. 1. 9 (Op. Const. 553–554). Orders fifty copies with directions as to style.

37. (335.) *Fragment of the first letter of Constantine to Athanasius.* In Athan. *Apol.;* Socr. 1. 27 (Op. Const. 553–556 ; Tr. Engl. in Athan. *Hist. Tracts*, Oxf. 1843, p. 89). The letter summoning to the Council of Tyre, but only a half-dozen lines remain. This bids him admit all who wish to enter the church.

38. (335.) *Letter of Constantine to the people of the Alexandrian Church.* In Athan. *Apol. c. Ar.* c. 61 (Op. Const. 559–562 ; abstract in Soz. 2. 31 ; Tr. Engl. in Athan. *Hist. Tracts,* Oxf. 1850, p. 90–92). Is a general lamentation over the dissensions of the Church, with expression of confidence in Athanasius.

39. (335.) *Second Letter of Constantine to Athanasius.* Athan. *Apol.* (Op. Const. 555–558). Expresses his reprobation of the false accusations of the Meletians against Athanasius.

40. (335.) *Letter of Constantine to Joannes the Meletian.* Athan. *Apol.* (Op. Const. 557–560). Congratulates on his reconciliation with Athanasius.

41. (335.) *Letter of Constantine to Arius.* In Socr. 1. 25 (Op. Const. 561–562). Invites Arius to visit him — the famous visit where he presented a confession of faith claimed to be in conformity with that of Nicæa.

42. (335.) *A Letter to Dalmatius* is mentioned by Athanasius, *Apol.* 5. 13, but not preserved (Op. Const. 563–564 ; Tr. Engl. in Athan. *Hist. Tracts*, Oxf. 1850, p. 94). It required him to make judicial enquiry respecting the charge against Athanasius of the murder of Arsenius.

43. (335.) *Celebrated Letter of Constantine concerning the Synod of Tyre.* In Euseb. *V. C.* 3. 42 (Op. Const. 561–564). Exhorts the bishops to give zeal to fulfilling the purpose of the synod in the restitution of peace to the Church.

44. (335.) *Letter to the Bishops assembled at Tyre.* In Socr. *H. E.* 1. 34, and in Soz. *H. E.* 2. 28. Summons them to come to him at Constantinople and give account of their proceedings.

Besides these there are the clearly spurious :

1. *Letter of Helena to Constantine* (Op. Const. 529–530).

2. *Letter of Constantine in response to Helena* (Op. Const. 529–532).

3. *Treaty of peace between Constantine, Sylvester and Tiridates* (Op. Const. 579–582). On

Tiridates compare various sources in Langlois *Col. des historiens de . . . l'Arménie*, and for literature respecting their authenticity, his note on p. 103.

4. *Edict of Constantine to Pope Silvester* (Op. Const. 567–578). The famous Donatian which
first appeared in Pseudo-Isidore, and for which see under *The Mythical Constantine*, p. 442–3.

There are also quite a large number of letters mentioned with more or less description, and
a " multitude of letters " (*V. C.* 3. 24) of which there is no specific knowledge. Of the former
may be mentioned that *to the inhabitants of Heliopolis*, one to Valerius (or Valerianus or Verinus)
(Augustine, *Ad Donat. p. c.* c. 33) ; one *to the Council of Tyre*, asking them to hasten to Jerusalem (*V. C.* 4. 43 ; Soz. 2. 26) ; and one acknowledging the copies of the Scriptures prepared
at his order, through Eusebius (*V. C.* 4. 37).

§ 4. *Laws.*

The numerous laws are collected in the edition of Migne (*Patrol. Lat.* 8. p. 93–400), mainly
from the Theodosian code. They are in the opinion of Eutropius (10. 8) " many," " some
good and equitable, but most of them superfluous, and some severe " (cf. under *Character*).
Many of them show the author's tendency to declamation, but taken all in all they are business-
like and do credit, in the main, to their author's heart, and even, though less conspicuously, to his
head. For more specific account, compare the laws themselves as collected in Migne, the relating passages in Wordsworth and Ceillier, standard and annotated editions of the codes, and
special treatises, such as Balduin, *De leg. eccl. et civ.* 1737.

§ 5. *Various.*

Besides the more formal works mentioned above, various conversations, sayings, bon mots,
prayers, &c., are preserved, among which may be mentioned :

1. *Memoirs of himself*, of which no portion is extant. Writings of Constantine are mentioned
by Lydus (p. 194, 226), but whether the writings referred to deserve the title given by Burckhardt it is hard to say.

2. *A form of prayer* given by Constantine to his soldiers (*V. C.* 4. 20).

3. *His address* when the memorials of contendents, at Council of Nicæa, were brought to
him (Soz. 1. 17).

4. *The conversation with Acesius*, for which Socrates vouches, closing, " O Acesius, set up a
ladder, and do you alone climb up to heaven."

5. *His rebuke to the courtier* concerning covetousness (*V. C.* 4. 30).

6. *His answer* when told his statues had been stoned, " Strange, but I feel no wound "
(" Chrysost. *Ad Pop. Ant.*").

7. *His appeal to the bishops*, requesting them to confer upon him the rite of baptism (*V. C.*
4. 62).

8. *His Thanksgiving* after baptism *and testimony* (*V. C.* 4. 63).

In general, his writings were composed in Latin, and translated into Greek by those appointed
for this special purpose (*V. C.* 4. 32). His general style is rhetorical, rather profuse, and declam-
atory, abounding in pious allusion and exhortation, as well as philosophical quotation and reflection. His works are interesting to study and not without a touch here and there of genuine
literary interest. A remark on friendship, for example, unless it be a product of his habit of bor-
rowing the thoughts of other men more or less directly, is delightful and most quotable. " For
it often happens," he says, " that when a reconciliation is effected by the removal of the causes
of enmity, friendship becomes even sweeter than it was before " (Const. to Alex. and Ar. in
V. C. 2. 71).

CHAPTER IV.

THE MYTHICAL CONSTANTINE.

THE many legends which have attached themselves to the name of Constantine are valuable chiefly as curiosities, and can be treated here only in specimens. A few of the more interesting and important are the following :

1. *Constantine and his Mother Helena.*

A little anonymous work of some thirty pages, edited by Heydenreich from a fourteenth-century manuscript, was published under this title in 1879, and has drawn forth an astonishing amount of literature for so slight a thing. It has little value except as an illustration of mediæval romance, though Coen seems to think the honor of having introduced it into literature enough to warrant the expenditure of a good deal of pains in vindicating his claim to it. The story is written with tolerable art, and runs, abbreviated, something as follows :

Helena, daughter of a noble family of Trèves, came on a pious journey to Rome. The Emperor Constantius, crossing a bridge of the Tiber, saw Helena among other pilgrims. Struck with her beauty, he arranged that she should be detained by force at the inn where she stayed, when her fellow-pilgrims returned to Gaul. The emperor then constrained her by force, but, seeing the great grief which his act had caused, gave her a certain ornament of precious stones and his ring, as a sort of pledge, and went away. She did not venture to return to her country, but remained at Rome with the son who was born to her, representing that her Gallic husband was dead. This son, Constantine, grew up pleasing, handsome, and versatile. Certain merchants, seeing his excellent quality, formed a scheme of making money by palming him off on the emperor of the Greeks as a son-in-law, representing him to be a son of the Roman emperor.

The scheme was carried out, and the merchants after some time embarked again for Rome, with the Constantine and the princess, and much treasure. Toward the end of their journey they stopped over night at a little island. In the morning the young people awoke to find they had been deserted by the merchants, and Constantine in great grief confessed the deception which had been practiced. To this the princess replied that she cared little who he was or his family, since he was himself and her husband. After a few days of short rations they were taken by passing voyagers to Rome, where they joined Helena, and having purchased a house with the proceeds from the sale of certain valuables which the princess had kept with her, they went to hotel-keeping. Constantine took naturally to military life, and at tournaments surpassed every one else so far as to arouse astonishment and inquiry. The emperor would not believe him a poor and friendless man, and had his mother called. After much vigorous evasion the truth came out, confirmed by the ring which the emperor had given Helena. Constantius first had the merchants put to death, and gave all their property to Constantine. Then a treaty was made with the emperor of the East, and Constantine was recognized as heir to the empire.

A more wildly unhistorical historical novel could hardly have been written even by a Muhlbach. For further account, see under *Literature* especially articles by Heydenreich and by Coen.

2. *Constantine the Son of a British Princess.*

Duke Coel of Colchester, say the old chronicles, by an insurrection became king. The Senate, rejoiced at the overthrow of an enemy, sent Constantius to Britain. Coel, fearing, sent ambassadors to meet him, gave hostages, and shortly died. Constantius was crowned, married Helena, daughter of Coel, the most beautiful, cultivated, and educated woman of her time. By her he had a son, Constantine, afterwards called the Great. This is in substance the account of Geoffrey of Monmouth (5. 6) and Pierre de Langloft (1, p. 66–7). The story is mentioned by

Henry of Huntington (Bk. I. 37), who perhaps wrote before Geoffrey (in 1137 [?]), and Richard of Cirencester (2. 1. 33). Waurin (Vol. I. Bk. 2. 43) makes " Choel " Count of Leicester, but in general is identical with Geoffrey. The famous Brut of Layamon (ed. Madden, 2 [1847] p. 35) is translated with amplifications from Wace's Brut, and this in turn from Geoffrey. This makes Coel Earl of Gloucester. The Eulogium Hist. calls Helena (1. 337) daughter of a British king, but also concubine, though elsewhere (2, p. 267) she is wife according to the conventional story. It is also mentioned by many others ; e.g. Voragine, *Golden Legend.* It is interesting that this legendary father of Helena is supposed (Hayden, Index to Eulogium, p. 45, and Giles, note on Geoffrey, p. 162) to be the same as " Old King Cole, the merry old soul," making Constantine thus the grandson of the Mother Goose hero.

3. *Constantine's Leprosy; Healing and Baptism by Silvester.*

This tale is one of the most frequently found. The earliest account is said to be that of the Acts of Silvester. Some of the many who repeat it are Ephraem, Cedrenus, Zonaras. The following account is mainly from Glycas, p. 461–462.

When Constantine was fighting against Maxentius, after he had seen the sign of the cross, he was victorious. Then, forgetting, he was conquered, and grieving, he fell asleep and had a vision in which the blow of a switch on his nostrils brought blood which flowed down on his linen tunic in the form of a cross. Seeing this, he was filled with penitence, and became again victorious. Being led away a second time into idolatry through his wife Fausta, he was divinely afflicted with leprosy. The priests prescribed a bath in the blood of infants, and it was ordered ; but when he heard the lamentations of the mothers, he said it was better to suffer than that so many infants should perish. Therefore the apostles, Peter and Paul as some say, appeared to him and told him Silvester would cure him, as he did. There are many varieties of the story and various details as to baptism, but in general the whole series of stories regarding his baptism at Rome centers in this story, and gratitude for this cure is the supposed occasion of the famous donation of Constantine. In this the circumstances of the miracle are given at length, — the words of the apostles, Silvester's identification of them as apostles by portraits, the immersion, and subsequent instruction.

4. *Donation of Constantine.*

This most remarkable of forgeries for its practical effect on world-history has been the subject of endless discussion. It is, in brief, a supposed grant to the Pope of Rome, Silvester, of certain sweeping privileges in recognition of the miracle he has wrought. The edict gives a long confession of faith followed by an account of the miracle and mention of the churches he has built. Then follow the grants to Silvester, sovereign Pontiff and Pope of Rome, and all his successors until the end of the world, — the Lateran palace, the diadem, phryginus, the purple mantle and scarlet robe, imperial scepters, insignia, banners and the whole imperial paraphernalia, as well as various clerical privileges and pretty much the whole world to govern. It is impossible here even to represent in outline the history of this extraordinary fiction. Composed not earlier than the latter part of the eighth century (Martens et alt. 9 cent. ; Grauert, 840–850 ; Hauck, Bonneau, 752–757 ; Langen, 778, &c. ; Friedrich acc. to Seeberg, divides into an earlier [653] and a later [753] portion), it early came to be general, though not unquestioned, authority. In 1229–1230 a couple of unfortunates who ventured to doubt its authenticity were burned alive at Strasburg (Documents communicated by Ristelhuber to Bonneau p. 57–58). Not many years after, Dante seems (*Inf.* 19. 115) to have taken its authenticity for granted ; and although there is a possible doubting (*De Monarch.* 4. 10), he does not venture to dispute this. He denies, however, Constantine's power or right to give, if he did give. In modern times the fictitious character of the document is recognized by Protestants and Catholics alike, and the discussion, so vigorous formerly, over this authenticity has narrowed itself chiefly to a discussion of the place (France or Rome) and date (653–753, ninth century) and possible author. The discussion over these points has been lately renewed and is being carried on with animation. Among the later monographs are those of Martens (1889) and Friedrich (1889, not at hand). The latest treatise at hand is that of Seeberg in the Theol. Literaturbl. of Jan. 17. 24. 31 of the current year. For farther select literature, compare *Verzeichniss* in Martens ; for sources, the chapters of Martens and Preface of Bonneau ; for older literature, Muensch. p. 96–97, and in general the *Literature* of Constantine, in this volume, although no attempt has been made to exhaust the literature of this sub-topic there. Treatises on the Donation will be found under the names of Albani, Altus, Arrhenius, Bachmann, Bayet, Bonneau, Brunner, Chaulnes, Colombier, Cusa, Friedrich, Genelin, Grauert, Hauck, Hildebrand, Jacobatius, Kaufman, Krüger, Martens, Muench, Rallaye, Scheffer-Boichorst, Seeberg, Steuchus, Tacut, Valla, Walther, Wieland, Zeumer.

5. *Dream concerning the Founding of Constantinople.*

" As Constantine was sleeping in this city [Byzantium], he imagined that there stood before him an old woman whose forehead was furrowed with age ; but that presently, clad in an imperial robe, she became transformed into a beautiful girl, and so fascinated his eyes by the elegance of her youthful charms that he could not refrain from kissing her ; that Helena, his mother, being present, then said, 'She shall be yours forever ; nor shall she die till the end of time.' The solution of this dream, when he awoke, the emperor extorted from heaven, by fasting and almsgiving. And behold, within eight days, being cast again into a deep sleep, he thought he saw Pope Silvester, who died some little time before, regarding his convert with complacency, and saying, 'You have acted with your customary prudence in waiting for a solution from God of that enigma which was beyond the comprehension of man. The old woman you saw is this city, worn down by age, whose time-struck walls, menacing approaching ruin, require a restorer. But you, renewing its walls, and its affluence, shall signalize it also with your name ; and here shall the imperial progeny reign forever'" (William of Malmesbury, Chronicle, tr. English. Lond. 1847, p. 372–3. The final section, which instructs Constantine how to lay out the city, is omitted). This is taken by the Chronicler from Aldhelm's (d. 709) *de laudibus virginitatis* (c. 52, ed. Giles, 1844, p. 28–29), where, however, instead of kissing her, he much more appropriately " clothes her with his mantle, and puts his diadem adorned with pure gold and brilliant gems on her head." It is given also by Ralph de Diceto (ed. Stubbs, Lond. 1876), 74–75, and probably by many others.

6. *Voyage of Helena.*

A matter-of-fact account of things which are not so, given in Hakluyt's *Voyages*, 2 (1810), p. 34, is worth giving in the words of the translator :

" Helena Flavia Augusta, the heire and onely daughter of Cœlus, sometime the most excellent king of Britaine, by reason of her singular beautie, faith, religion, goodnesse, and godly Maiestie (according to the testimonie of Eusebius) was famous in all the world. Amongst all the women of her time there was none either in the liberall arts more learned, or in the instruments of musike more skilfull, or in the divers languages of nations more abundant than herselfe. She had a naturall quicknesse of wit, eloquence of speech, and a most notable grace in all her behaviour. She was seene in the Hebrew, Greeke, and Latin tongues. Her father (as Virumnius reporteth) had no other childe, . . . had by her a sonne called Constantine the great, while hee remained in Britaine . . . peace was granted to the Christian churches by her good meanes. After the light and knowledge of the Gospel, she grew so skilfull in divinity that she wrote and composed divers bookes and certaine Greeke verses also, which (as Ponticus reporteth) are yet extant . . . went to Jerusalem . . . lived to the age of fourscore years, and then died at Rome the fifteenth day of August, in the yeere of oure redemption 337. . . . Her body is to this day very carefully preserved at Venice."

7. *The Finding of the Cross.*

It is said in a certain "tolerably authentic chronicle," according to Voragine, that Constantine sent his mother Helena to Jerusalem to try to find the cross on which our Lord was crucified. When she arrived, she bade all the Jewish Rabbis of the whole land gather to meet her. Great was their fear. They suspected that she sought the wood of the cross, a secret which they had promised not to reveal even under torture, because it would mean the end of Jewish supremacy. When they met her, sure enough, she asked for the place of the crucifixion. When they would not tell, she ordered them all to be burned. Frightened, they delivered up Judas, their leader and instigator, saying that he could tell. She gave him his choice of telling or dying by starvation. At first he was obstinate, but six days of total abstinence from food brought him to terms, and on the seventh he promised. He was conducted to the place indicated, and in response to prayer, there was a sort of earthquake, and a perfume filled the air which converted Judas. There was a temple of Venus on the spot. This the queen had destroyed. Then Judas set to digging vigorously, and at the depth of twenty feet, found three crosses, which he brought to Helena. The true cross was tested by its causing a man to rise from the dead, or according to others, by healing a woman, or according to others, by finding the inscription of Pilate. After an exceedingly vigorous conversation between the devil and Judas, the latter was baptized and became Bishop Cyriacus. Then Helena set him hunting for the nails of the cross. He found them shining like gold and brought them to the queen, who departed, taking them and a portion of the wood of the cross. She brought the nails to Constantine, who put them on his bridle and helmet, or according to another account, two were used in this way, and one was thrown into the Adriatic Sea.

It is interesting to trace the melancholy consequences of this particular enterprise of Constantine's in the sad death of St. Cyriacus née Judas. The Emperor Julian, the apostate, "invited" him to sacrifice to idols. When he refused, melted lead was poured into his mouth; then an iron bedstead was brought, on which he was stretched, while a fire was built underneath and the body of the martyr larded with salt and fat. The saint did not budge, and Julian had a deep well dug, which was filled with venomous serpents. But contact with the saint killed the serpents, and a cauldron of boiling oil succeeded. Julian was so angry at the alacrity and cheerfulness of the saint's preparations for this bath, that he killed him with a blow of his sword. There is some consolation in the thought of this premature death, in the fact that, unless his claim that he was nephew to Stephen, the Proto-martyr, be disallowed, he had reached a ripe old age of two hundred and fifty years or thereabouts.

The literature on this legend is very great. The finding of the cross is mentioned as early as Cyril of Jerusalem (ab. 347–350), within twenty-five years of the visit of Helena recorded by Eusebius (*V. C.* 3. 26), and with great frequency afterwards. The failure of any mention by Eusebius seems, however, conclusive against any finding, or pretended finding, at the time of Helena's famous visit, though the contrary is acutely argued by Newman. The finding and use of the nails is often separated from the other, and is found in many of the sources on Constantine. But even those who believe in the miracle of the finding of the cross will hardly vouch for the story in the above form, which is substantially that of Voragine.

Compare Sinker's article, *Cross, Finding of,* in Smith and Cheetham, *Dict.* 1 (1880), 503–506; Jameson, *Hist. of Our Lord,* 2 (1872) 385–391; Newman, *Essays on Miracles* (Lond. 1875) 287–326; and especially Voragine, whom see under *Sources.* Under the article *Helena,* in Smith & W. is a sub-article by Argles on the *Invention of the Cross,* which gives an admirable abstract of the sources in order.

These examples of the stories which have gathered around the name of Constantine do not begin to exhaust the list. The interesting tales of the sword of Constantine presented to Athelstan (*Reg. Malms.* 1, 1879, p. 55, 468; *Eul. Hist.* 3, 1863, p. 12), his conversion through remorse, and the whole series of allusions and stories in mediæval fiction and poetry must be passed here. If any one has the curiosity to follow them up, he will find the references in the articles of Heydenreich a good guide to literature. A few stories, like that of Constantine and Tiridates, one hesitates to class among the wholly fictitious (compare, under *Sources*, Agathangelos, Zenobius, and Faustus).

CHAPTER V.

Sources and Literature.

§ 1. *Introduction.*

THE insertion in such a work as this of what seems almost technical in its character has this twofold purpose : first, to give a glimpse of the grounds of our knowledge of Constantine, with a view of how far and in what directions it has been worked out through literature ; second, to serve the expressed purpose of this series, of encouraging farther study in its lines. The very knowledge of what the sources are, and their character, apart from any special study of them, gives a width of horizon and definiteness of conception to the general student, which can hardly be gotten in any other way ; while for any one who plans farther study in any line, it is of first importance to find the what and where of his material.

§ 2. *Sources.*

Remembering the class of students for which the series is chiefly intended, effort has been made to refer to translations of sources where they are at hand, and to refer to the best accessible English authorities on them. But the plan has been to refer to the source itself in the edition actually used, and for literature on them to choose the best for ready reference. Both editions and authorities on sources are therefore selections, usually from many, of such as seem most directly useful. The intention has been to guide to all frequently mentioned sources, whether they were of great value or not, since a useless one costs often quite as much trouble to hunt up and find useless, as a good one to use. It is hardly to be hoped that all the sources often referred to have been gathered, but the following list represents pretty much all that are worth mentioning, and some which are not.

1. *Inscriptions, coins, medals, &c.*

In some sense these are the most reliable of sources, in spite of counterfeits. A large number will be found collected in Clinton. For farther critical study, compare the collections, great and small; for which, with the matter of inscriptions in general, see Hicks, E. L., and Hübner, E., in the *Encyclopædia Britannica*, 13 (1881) 121–133; and Babington, in Smith and Cheetham, 1 (1880) 841–862. Monographs on those relating to Constantine will be found under the names, Cavedoni, Cigola, Eltz, Freherus, Garucci, Harduin, Penon, Revellot, Valois, Westphalen, Werveke, in the *Literature* of this volume.

2. *Laws.*

These, with their dates, their official nature, their fullness and variety, are primary, and are the only sources recognized by some. They are embodied in the Theodosian and Justinian Codes, and collected from these are edited in Migne, *Patrol. Latina*, Vol. 8. See under *Writings* of Constantine, above.

3. *Other Writings by Constantine.*

See under *Writings*, above, p. 436. With this might perhaps be included also writings *to* Constantine, like that of Anulinus in Augustinus, *Ep.* 88.

4. *General Literary Sources.*

Taking in general chronological order, without attempting the impossibility of fixing the exact chronological place, the first group of contemporary sources is that of the Panegyrists (for collected editions, see Engelmann).

It was a serious mistake, now recognized, to pass them by as worthless. Like all authentic documents, they have a minimum residuum of undoubted material, which is larger or smaller according to the critical acumen of the investigator. In the case of these, however inflated or eulogistic they may be, the circumstances under which they were spoken give a considerable value.

(1) *Incerti auctoris Panegyricus Maximiano et Constantino dictus* (*Paneg.* 307). In Migne, *Patrol. Lat.* 8 (1844), 609–620. Pronounced at celebration of marriage of Constantine and Fausta, A.D. 307. Besides having the great value of being contemporary evidence, the author shows a certain ingenuity in enlarging on the virtues of the young Constantine, who had few deeds to show, and on the deeds of Maximian, who had few virtues, and has therefore a certain discernible modicum of truth.

Compare the *Monitum* in Migne, Ramsay's article on *Drepanius*, in Smith, *Dict.* 1073-4, and references under Eumenius.

(2) EUMENIUS (310–311). (*a*) *Panegyric* (*Panegyricus Constantino Augusto*). In Migne, *Patrol. Lat.* 8 (1884), 619–640. (*b*) *Thanksgiving Oration* (*Gratiarum Actio Constantino Augusto*). In Migne, *Patrol. Lat.* 8 (1844), 641–654. Eumenius flourished during the reigns of Constantius, with whom he was in high favor, and Constantine. He was head of the school at Autun. The *Panegyric* was delivered at Treves, in 310. The authorship of Eumenius has been unwarrantably questioned, on the ground that the flattery and exaggeration of the work are not consistent with his taste and sense; but it would seem that both his exaggeration and his taste have been themselves exaggerated. His praise is hardly more " outrageous " than panegyrics were wont to be, — or are, for that matter; and so far from being " worthless," there is a peculiar deal of interesting, unquestionable, and primary historical evidence. Still, his taste and veracity are not much above that of modern eulogists of living or dead emperors and politicians. The *Gratiarum Actio* is the official oration of thanks to Constantine in behalf of the citizens of Autun, on account of favors shown them. It was pronounced at Treves in 311.

Compare Ramsay, in Smith, *Dict.* 2 (1859), 92; the Procœmium, in ed. Migne, 619–622; also for editions, Ramsay, article *Drepanius*, in Smith, *Dict.* 1. 1073-4; and for literature, Chevalier. For general account of the Panegyrists, see this article on Drepanius.

(3) *Incerti Panegyricus Constantino Augusto* (Paneg. 313). In Migne, *Patrol. Lat.* 8 (1844), 653– This is usually ascribed to Nazarius, on the ground of style. It was spoken at Treves in 313, and relates mainly to the war with Maxentius. Various details relating to this are of such nature and form as to suggest again that the author is the same as that of the 321 Paneg., — Nazarius.

Compare Ramsay, in Smith, *Dict.* 2 (1859), 1145; the Procœmium in ed. Migne, &c., and literature as under EUMENIUS, above.

(4) NAZARIUS. (321) *Panegyric* (*Panegyricus Constantino Augusto dictus*). In ed. Migne, *Patrol. Lat.* 8 (1844), 581–608. Nazarius is mentioned by Jerome as a distinguished rhetorician. This oration was delivered at Rome in 321. Constantine was not present. It is superlatively eulogistic, but like the related panegyrics contains many historical facts of greatest value.

Compare Ramsay, in Smith, *Dict.* 2 (1859), 1145, the *Monitum*, in Migne, and references under EUMENIUS.

In the midst of the period which these cover comes one of the two great Christian sources, and he is followed by a considerable row of great and small Christians during the century.

(5) LACTANTIUS (ab. 313–314). *On the Deaths of the Persecutors* (*De M. P.*). Ed. Fritsche (Lips. 1842), 248–286; ed. Migne, *Patrol. Lat.* 7 (Par. 1844), 157–276; tr. in *T. & T. Clark Library*, 22 (Edinb. 1871), 164–211, and in *Ante-Nicene Fathers* (Buffalo and N. Y.), 300–326 [Lord Hailes' translation]. There are many editions in collected works, and about a dozen separate, and many translations, — in all a hundred or more editions and translations. There has been much controversy regarding the author of this work, but there is little doubt that it was Lactantius. Ebert (*Gesch. chr. Lat. Lit.* 1. 83) claims to have demonstrated the fact, and most of the later writers agree. The work was composed after the edict of Constantine and Licinius, and before the break between the two, i.e. 313–314. It was written thus in the midst of things, and has the peculiar historical value of a contemporary document, unprejudiced by later events. It is a sort of psalm of triumph, colored by the passionate rejoicing of one persecuted over the Divine vengeance which has come upon the persecutors. " In the use of the work the historian must employ great critical discernment " (Ebert, in Herzog, 8 [1881], 365). But granted all his prejudice, the facts he witnesses are of first value.

Compare Ffoulkes, in Smith and Wace, 3 (1882), 613–617; Teuffel, *Hist. Rom. Lit.* 2 (1873), 334; Ebert, in Herzog, *Encyk.* 8 (1881), 364–366, and *Gesch. chr. Lat. Lit.* 1 (1874), 83; and for farther literature, *Bibliog. Synops.* in *Ante-Nicene Fathers Suppl.* (1887), 77–81.

(6) EUSEBIUS (ab. 260–340). 1. *Ecclesiastical History.* 2. *Constantine.* 3. *Chronicle.*
For 1 and 3 compare Prolegomena of Dr. McGiffert at the beginning of this volume, and for 2, *Special Prolegomena*, p. 466.

(7) OPTATIAN (fl. ab. 326). *Panegyric*, in Migne, *Patrol. Lat.* 19 (1846), 395–432; Letter to Constantine, do. 391–392. Optatian, Porfirius, or Porphyrius, as he is variously called, is dubiously Christian, composed this

poem, or series of poems, while in exile, on the occasion of the Vicennalia of Constantine. It dates, therefore, from 325 or 326. It is a most extraordinary aggregation of acrostics, pattern poems, and every possible device of useless, mechanical variety of form, of little value, excepting as a sort of dime-museum exhibition of patience and ingenuity. It consists mainly in calling Constantine flattering names, but contains here and there an historical suggestion. It was accompanied by a letter to Constantine, and drew one from him, and a pardon as well (Hieronymus, *Chron.*).

Compare Wilson, article *Porfirius*, in Smith & W. 4 (1887), 440; article *Porphyrius*, in Smith, *Dict.* 3 (1859), 502; and for editions and literature, Engelmann.

(8) ATHANASIUS (296–373). *Apology against the Arians*, and various works, ed. Bened. (1698), 2 v. in 3, f°; ed. Migne, *Patrol. Gr.* 25–28 (1857), 4 v.; translated in part in Newman, *Library of the Fathers*, and in Schaff-Wace, *Nicene and Post-Nicene Fathers* (announced). The works of Athanasius contain various letters of Constantine (see under *Works*) and much of primary historical value for the latter part of Constantine's reign. So far as it goes, the matter is almost equal to official documents as source.

Compare Bright, in Smith & W. 1 (1877), 179–203; Schaff, *Hist. of Church*, 23 (1884), 884–893; and for extensive literature and editions, Chevalier and Graesse.

(9) CYRIL OF JERUSALEM (ab. 315–386). *Catechetical Lectures*. In Migne, *Patrol. Gr.* 33 (1857), especially 830. English translations in Newman, *Library of Fathers*, 2 (1838), one ref. p. 178. *Letter to Constantine II. concerning the sign of the cross seen at Jerusalem*, c. 3. In Migne, *Patrol. Gr.* 33 (1857), 1165–1176, ref. on 1167–1168. Two or three references only to excavation of the cross and building of churches, &c., at Jerusalem. They take significance only in the fact that Cyril is so near the time (the letter was 351[?], or not many years later), and delivered his lectures in the very church which Constantine had built (sect. 14, 22).

Compare Schaff, *Hist. of Church*, 3 (1884), 923–925; Venables, in Smith & W. 1 (1877), 760–763; and literature in Chevalier, Schaff, &c.; also editions in Graesse, Hoffmann, &c.

(10) AMBROSIUS OF MILAN (ab. 340–397). *Oration on the Death of Theodosius*. In Migne, *Patrol. Lat.* 16 (1866), portion relating to Constantine especially, 1462–1465. Relates chiefly to the Finding of the Cross.

Compare Davies, in Smith & W. 1 (1877), 91–99; also Chevalier, Engelmann, Schoenemann, &c.

(11) HIERONYMUS (JEROME) (331–420). *Chronicle*. In Migne, *Patrol. Lat.* 27 (1866). Part relating to Constantine, 493 (497)–500. A translation and continuation of the *Chronicle* of Eusebius, who ends with the death of Licinius. An indispensable but aggravating authority.

Compare Salmon, *Eusebius, Chronicle of*, in Smith & W. 2 (1880), 348–355.

(12) AUGUSTINUS (354–430). *Ep.* 43, ed. Migne, 33 (1865), 159– , §§ 4, 5, 20, &c. He gives account of the various Donatist hearings, and speaks of having read aloud from various original documents, including the petition to Constantine, the proconsular acts, the proceedings of the court at Rome, and the letters of Constantine. He speaks of the hearing at Milan. *Ep.* 88, ed. Migne, *Patrol. Lat.* 33 (1865), 302–309. This has the text of letter of Anulinus to Constantine, and Constantine to Probianus. *Eps.* 76. 2; 93. 13–14, 16 (which contains account of decree of Constantine that property of obstinate Donatists should be confiscated); 105. 9, 10 (not translated); 141. 8–10 (not translated), in ed. Migne, and tr. English ed. Schaff, contain various matter on the Donatist acts of Constantine. *Ad Donatistas post collationem*, c. 33, § 56; ed. Migne, 43 (1861), 687 (important for *dates* given). *Contra litt. Petil.* Bk. II. ch. 92, § 205; ed. Migne, 45 (1861), 326. Tr. in Schaff, *Nicene and Post-Nicene Fathers*, 4 (1887), 580–581. *Contr. Epist. Parmen.* Bk. I. chs. 5–6, § 10–11; ed. Migne, 43 (1861), 40–41. Augustine as a source is of primary value, because of the otherwise unknown sources which he uses and quotes.

Compare Schaff, *Hist. of Church*, 3 (1884), 988–1028; Maclear, in Smith & W. *Dict.* 1 (1877), 216–228. For literature, see Schaff, Chevalier, Engelmann, and for particular literature of the Donatist portions, Hartranft, in Schaff, *Nicene and Post-Nicene Fathers*, 4 (1887), 369–372; and for editions, see Schoenemann, Graesse, Brunet, Engelmann, Schaff, Hartranft, &c.

The equally numerous series of non-Christian writers is headed, in value at least, though not in time, by Constantine's secretary.

(13) EUTROPIUS (4th cent.). *Abridgment of Roman History*, Bk. 10. Multitudes of editions and translations; the ones used are: (Paris, 1539), 63–68; transl. by Watson, (Bohn, 1853), 527–535. Eutropius was secretary to Constantine, and afterwards the intimate of Julian. His testimony, though brief, is of peculiar weight from his position for knowing and from a certain flavor of fairness. It was early remarked (Nicephorus Gregoras) that his praise of Constantine had peculiar force, coming from a heathen and friend of Julian. His dispraise, on the other hand, is conditioned by the fact that he applies it only to the period after Constantine began peculiarly to favor the Christians. He seems to be a cool, level-headed man of the world, unsympathetic with Constantine's religion, and, writing *from this standpoint*, presents a just, candid, reliable account of him.

Compare Ramsay, in Smith, *Dict.* 2 (1859), 126–127; Watson, *Notice*, in his translations; also for multitudinous editions and translations, and relatively scanty though considerable literature, Chevalier, Engelmann, Graesse.

(14) SCRIPTORES HISTORIÆ AUGUSTÆ (? 2–324).   Ed. Jordan and Eyssenhardt, Berol. 1864, 2 v.   Contains a few dedications to and mentions of Constantine, for which see Index.

Compare Teuffel, *Hist. of Rom. Lit.* tr. Wagner, 2 (Lond. 1873), 320–324.

(15) VICTOR, SEXTUS AURELIUS (fl. 350–400).   *Cæsars.*   In ed. Schottius, Antv. Plantin, 1579, p. 97–167. Section on Constantine chiefly, 157–162.   *Epitome,* Antv. 1579.   Section on Constantine, p. 49–52.   These works, by different authors, have been associated since the time of the above edition with the name of Victor.   The former is by him, the latter probably by a slightly later Victor.   They use the same sources with Zosimus, but supplement him (Wordsworth).   Both are interesting and important, and in Manso's judgment, final where they agree.

Compare Ramsay, in Smith, *Dict.* 3 (1859), 1256–1257; Thomas, article *Aurelius,* in *Biog. Dict.* (1886), 228; Manso, *Leben Const.* p. 215; and scanty references in Chevalier.   For editions and farther literature, see Engelmann.

(16) PRAXAGORAS ATHENIENSIS (4th cent.).   In Photius, *Cod.* 62; Ed. Bekker, p. 20; ed. Müller, *Fragm.* 4 (1868), 2–3.   Lived in reign of Constantine (Müller, p. 2).   Although a heathen (Photius, *Cod.* 62), he lauds Constantine above all his predecessors.   He wrote various works in the Ionic dialect, among others a "history of the deeds of Constantine the Great, in two books," composed at the age of twenty-two.   The fragments or *resumé* are preserved by Photius, as above.   Though brief (three columns), it is a concise mass of testimony.

Compare Smith, *Dict.* 3. 517; also for literature, Chevalier; and for editions, the various editions of Photius in Graesse, Hofmann, Engelmann, &c.

(17) CALENDARIUM ROMANUM CONSTANTINI MAGNI (350).   In Petavius, *Uranologium* (1630), 112–119. Written after 337, and in or before 355, probably in 355.   It is authority for the birthday of Constantine, Constantius, &c.

Compare Greswell, *Origines Kalendariæ Italicæ,* 4 (Oxf. 1854), 388–392.

(18) JULIAN THE APOSTATE (331–363).   *Cæsars. Orations on Constantius and Constantinus, et pass.*   Ed. Paris, 1630, p. 12–96, 422; Vol. 2, 1–54, *passim.*   Compare also ed. Hertlein, Lips. 1875–76, 2 v. 8vo.   Editions and translations are very numerous.   (Compare arts. of Wordsworth and Graves; also Engelmann, Graesse, &c.   The orations which are panegyrical were delivered (Wordsworth) 355 and 358, and the *Cæsars* dates from shortly after his accession (in 361).   The latter is a satire which has found literary favor, the substantial purpose of which is thought to be a suggestion that he (Julian) is much superior to all the great emperors; but which if one were to venture a guess at its real motive, is quite as much a systematic effort to minimize by ridicule the lauded Constantine.   The laudatory words of Julian himself in his orations are quite overshadowed by the bitter sarcasms of the Cæsars.   As a matter of estimate of the value of this source, there is to be remembered the bitterness of Julian's hostility to Christianity.   What to Eusebius was a virtue would to Julian be a vice.   In view of his prejudice, everything which he concedes is of primary weight, while his ill-natured gossip carries a presumption of slanderousness.

Compare Schaff, *Hist. of Church,* 2. 40–59; Wordsworth, in Smith & W. 3. 484–525; Graves, in Smith, *Dict.* 644–655.   Compare for endless literature, Wordsworth, Chevalier, Engelmann, 1 (1880), 476–477.

(19) LIBANIUS, (314 or 316–391 +).   *Orations.*   Ed. Morellus, Par. 1606–1627.   Contain a few allusions of more or less interest and historical value, for which, see ed. Morellus, Index volume 2, fol. Qqqvᵇ.

Compare Schmitz, in Smith, *Dict.* 2 (1859), 774–776; and for editions and literature, Chevalier, Engelmann, &c.

(21) AMMIANUS MARCELLINUS (d. ab. 395).   *Histories.*   There are many editions, for which compare Engelmann, Graesse, and Wordsworth.   Among editions are ed. Valesius (1636) and ed. Eyssenhardt, Berol. 1871. The work was a continuation of Tacitus, but the first thirteen books (including Constantine's period) are best.   He says (Bk. 15, ed. Valesius, 1636, p. 56–57) that Constantine investigated the Manichæans and like sects through Musonius, and gives account of the bringing of his obelisk to Rome, perhaps by Constantine (Bk. 17, p. 92–93; compare Parker, *Twelve Egypt. Obelisks in Rome,* Oxf. 1879, p. 1), and makes other mention, for which see Index to ed. Eyssenhardt, p. 566.

Compare Wordsworth, in Smith & W. 1 (1879), 99–101, and for literature, Chevalier (scanty) and Engelmann, 2 (1882), 43–45 (Rich).

(22) EUNAPIUS (Anti-Christian) (ab. 347–414).   *Lives of the Philosophers and Sophists; Ædesius.*   Ed. Boissonade (Amst. 1822), 19–46 *passim.*   Eunapius was born at Sardis about 347, and died after 414 A.D. (cf. Müller, *Fragm.* 87).   He was a teacher of rhetoric, and besides this work wrote a continuation of the history of Dexippus, extending from 270–404 A.D.   Fragments of this are preserved, but none relating to Constantine. Photius (*Cod.* 77) says that he calumniated the Christians, especially Constantine.   With the fragments in Müller, *Fragm.* 4 (1868), 11–56, is included also (14–15) a fragment from the *Vita Ædes.,* relating to Sopater.   The death of Sopater and the relation of Ablavius to it is given more fully in the *Vita Ædes.* with various suggestive allusions.   Much of his history is supposed to be incorporated in Zosimus, and this gives importance to his name, weight to Zosimus, and light on the hostile position of Zosimus towards Constantine.

Cf. Photius, *Cod.* 77; Müller, *Fragm.* 4 (1868), 7–9; Mozley, in Smith & W. 2 (1880), 285–286; Schmitz, in Smith, *Dict.* 2 (1859), 93; also for further literature and editions, Chevalier and Engelmann.

(23) BEMARCHIUS (4th cent.) was of Cæsarea in Cappadocia; wrote the *Acts of Constantine* in ten books (Suidas, s.v. Βήμαρχιος; cf. Zonaras, p. 386). No portion is preserved. Wrote under Constantius, on whom he is said (Libanius, *Orat.* ed. Reiske, p. 24) to have delivered a panegyric.

Cf. Müller, *Fragm.* 4 (1868), 3; Smith, *Dict.* 1 (1859), 482, &c.

An early but as yet valueless group is that of Syriac and Armenian sources on the (apocryphal) treaty of Constantine with Tiridates.

(24) ZENOBIUS OF KLAG (fl. ab. 324). *History of Daron.* French translation from Armenian in Langlois, *Coll. Hist. Arm.* 1 (1867), 353–355. Like the works of the other Armenian historians, the text of this writer has suffered more or less from corruption. He has two mentions (p. 344 and 351) of Constantine, the latter being an account of the treaty with Tiridates.

Compare introduction of Langlois, and literature in Chevalier.

(25) AGATHANGELUS (ab. 330). *History of the Reign of Tiridates and of the Preaching of St. Gregory the Illuminator,* c. 125–127, § 163–169; in *Acta SS. Boll.* Sept. VIII. 320– ; also with French translation from Armenian in Langlois, *Coll. d. hist. de l'Arm.* p. 97–. The work extends for 226–330 A.D. The author was secretary to Tiridates, but the work as we have it is a redaction made, however, not long after, as it was used by Moses of Khorene. This was in turn later (seventh century?) retouched by some Greek hagiographer. This Greek form is extant in MSS. at Florence and Paris (cf. editions above), and there is reason to suppose that the extant Armenian is a version from this Greek form. But with its additions of arrantly apocryphal matter, it is hard to tell what is what, and so all considerable mention of the relation of Constantine and Tiridates has been left out of the account of Constantine's life. Yet we must hesitate to put it all down under the mythical; for Tiridates certainly had intercourse with the Romans, and the original form of this life was certainly by a competent hand, and the matter relating to Constantine is in part soberly historical enough.

For farther information, compare Davidson on Gregorius Illuminator, in Smith & W., *Dict.* 2. 737–739; Introduction, Langlois, p. 99–103.

(26) FAUSTUS OF BYZANTIUM (320–392). *Historical Library.* French translation from the Armenian in Langlois, *Coll. d. hist. Arm.* 1. 201–310. There are mentions of Constantine and Tiridates in Bk. 3, chaps. 10 and 21. The work is open to some suspicions of having been tampered with, but Langlois inclines to give it a fairly good character. If genuine, the mention of the treaty with Tiridates would nearly establish it as historical fact.

Compare Beauvois in *Nouv. biog. gén.* 17 (1856), 203, and Introduction of Langlois; also, literature in Chevalier.

The writers of the following centuries are for the most part Christian, uncertain or religiously unknown, excepting the very pronounced non-Christian who heads the list.

(27) ZOSIMUS (fl. ab. 400–450). *History.* Ed. Bekker (Bonn, 1837), 8vo. Section on Constantine occupying Bk. 2. 8– , p. 72–106. The date of this writer has been put as early as the fourth century and as late as the end of the fifth. It will be safe to divide extremes. He is a heathen who, on the period of Constantine, draws from an anti-Christian and anti-Constantinian source, and who regards the introduction of Christianity as a chief cause of the decline of the Roman Empire (cf. various passages cited by Milligan). He is prejudiced against Christianity with the bitter prejudice of one who finds himself in a steadily narrowing minority, and he is occasionally credulous. But he wrote in a clear, interesting style, without intentional falsifications, and was quite as moderate as the Christian writer (Evagrius, 3. 41) who calls Zosimus himself a "fiend of hell." His extended account is therefore of great value among the sources, and especially as it is probably drawn in large measure from the earlier lost work of Eunapius.

Compare Milligan, in Smith & W., 4 (1887), 1225–1227: Mason, in Smith, *Dict.* 3 (1859), 1334–1335; also, for literature, Chevalier and Engelmann, and for editions, Engelmann.

ANONYMUS VALESIANUS (fifth century). Ed. Valesius (Paris, 1636), p. 471–476. This fragment, first published by Valesius in the above editions of Ammianus, is of the highest value for the life of Constantine. It is evidently drawn from various sources, many of which are now lost. The compiler or writer shows a judiciousness and soberness which commends his statements as peculiarly trustworthy.

Compare the exhaustive examination by Ohnesorge, *Der Anonymus Valesii de Constantino.* Kiel, 1885. 8vo.

(27) STEPHEN OF BYZANTIUM (ab. 400). *Greek Cities.* Venet. Aldus, 1502, fol. H. iii. s.v. Ναϊσσὸς. The work is a dictionary of geography, and the fact in these few lines is of first value.

Compare Smith, in Smith, *Dict.* 3 (1859), 904–906. Chevalier, Hoffmann, etc.

(28) SOZOMEN (b. ab. 400). *Ecclesiastical History.* Ed. Hussey, English translation, London, Bohn, 1855; newly edited by Hartranft in Schaff, *Nicene and Post-Nicene Fathers,* 2 (1890) [in press]. This history covers the period 323–423 (not 439). He draws largely from Eusebius. He has been described rightly (Dowling,

Study of Eccl. Hist. p. 31) as relatively inaccurate, rhetorical and credulous. But he works from sources, though mainly from extant ones. For farther discussion, compare Hartranft in volume 2 of this series.

Compare also Milligan, in Smith & W. 4 (1887), 722–723, and literature in Chevalier.

(29) SOCRATES (b. ab. 408). *Ecclesiastical History.* Ed. Hussey, reprinted with Introduction by Bright, Oxf. 1878. English translation, London, Bohn, newly edited by Zenos in volume 2 of this series [in press]. This history covers the period 306–439. It is written with general good judgment, but for Constantine adds little to Eusebius of which it professes to be a continuation.

For farther description and discussion, compare Zenos, Milligan, in Smith & W. 4 (1887), 709–711, and literature in Chevalier.

(30) THEODORET (b. ab. 393?–457?). *Ecclesiastical History.* In Migne, *Patrol. Gr.* 82 (1859), 879–1280. English translation, London, Bohn, 1854. The birth of Theodoret has been placed at various dates, 386, 387, 393, &c., and the exact time of his death (453–458) is equally uncertain. This work reaches from 324 to 429, and is generally regarded as learned and impartial. It gives much concerning Constantine's relations to the Arian controversy and incorporates many documents, which appear to be taken mainly from Eusebius' *Life of Constantine.* A chief value is, it would seem, for the text of Eusebius. But his very use of documents shows care and gives value.

Compare Venables, in Smith & W. 4 (1887), 904–919; Newman, *Hist. Sketches,* 2 (1876), 303–362; Schaff, *Hist. of Church,* 3 (1884), 881–882; and literature in Chevalier; also for editions, Graesse and Hoffmann.

(31) OROSIUS, PAULUS (ab. 417). *Histories,* Bk. 7, chaps. 26–28. Ed. Migne *Patrol. Lat.* 31 (1846), 635–1174; section relating to Constantine occupies 1128–1137. For many editions and MSS. compare Schoenemann, *Bibl. Patr. Lat.* 2 (1794), 481–507, and Engelmann, 2 (1882), 441–. It is said (Manso) that Orosius adds nothing to existing material. This is only in part true. At all events, his value as corroboratory evidence is considerable, brief as the work is.

Compare Phillott, in Smith & W. 4 (1887), 157–158; Ebert, *Gesch. d. chr. Lat. Lit.* 1 (1874), 323–330, and literature in Chevalier and Engelmann.

(32) PROSPER AQUITANUS (403–463 +). *Chronicle.* Ed. Migne, *Patrol. Lat.* 51 (1861), 535–606 (8). Portion relating to Constantine, 574–576. The *Chronicle* extends to 444 or 455. To 326 he depends mainly on Eusebius' *Chronicle,* and for the rest of our period on the continuation of Hieronymus.

Compare Phillott, in Smith & W. 3 (1882), 492–497; Teuffel, *Hist. of Rom. Lit.* 2 (Lond. 1873), 482–484; and for literature, editions, &c., Chevalier, Engelmann, &c.

(33) IDATIUS (468+). *List of Consuls* (Fasti Idatiani). In Migne, *Patrol. Lat.* 51 (1861), 891–914; portion relating to Constantine, 907–908. Idatius lived until after 469. This work, which is not generally acknowledged to be his, although quoted under his name, ends in 468. It contains brief statements of some events under the most significant years.

Compare Ramsay, in Smith, *Dict.* 2 (1859), and literature under "Idace de Lamego," in Chevalier.

(34) GELASIUS OF CYZICUS (ab. 450–). *History of the Council of Nicæa.* In Labbe, *Concilia,* 2 (1671), 103–286. There is also an abstract in Photius, *Bibl. Cod.* 88, ed. Migne, *Patrol. Gr.* 103 (1860), 293–296. Venables is probably just when he says: "His work is little more than a compilation from the ecclesiastical histories of Eusebius, Socrates, Sozomen, and Theodoret, to which he has added little but what is very doubtful or manifestly untrue." There is a little on Constantine not in those sources, but to try to fix on any of it as authoritative quite baffles one. Still, it is not wholly clear that he did not use sources, as well as his own imagination, in adding to the other sources. It may be said to be " of doubtful value," as source. It is not easy to see what Venables means in saying that the third book, as we have it, gives only three letters of Constantine. This is true; but the second book, " as we have it," gives several more.

Compare Venables, in Smith & W. 2 (1880), 621–623.

(35) JACOBUS OF SARUG (452–521). *Homily on the Baptism of Constantine.* Ed. Frothingham, Roma, 1882. For further information consult the extended study of Frothingham.

(25) PHILOSTORGIUS (b. ab. 468). English translation by Walford (Lond. Bohn, 1855), 425–528. The original work covered the period between 300 and 425. The fragments preserved contain several interesting facts, or fictions, relating to Constantine, some not found elsewhere. Photius and all the orthodox have always called him untrustworthy or worse, and a very unorthodox critic (Gibbon) finds him passionate, prejudiced, and ignorant; but it seems to be agreed that he used some sources not availed of by others.

Compare Milligan, in Smith & W. 4 (1587), 390; Dowling, *Study of Eccl. Hist.* p. 26–27; and literature in Chevalier.

(26) HESYCHIUS MILESIUS (ab. 500? —). *Origins of Constantinople.* In Müller, *Fragm.* 4 (1868), 146–155; also in ed. Orelli (Lips. 1820), 59–73. Hesychius, surnamed Illustris, of Miletus lived in the early part of the sixth century. This work contains several allusions to the founding of the city of Constantine. It seems to have been taken almost word for word in parts by Codinus.

Compare Venables, in Smith & W. 3 (1882), 12–13; Means, in Smith, *Dict.* 2 (1859), 447–448; Müller, *Fragm.* 4 (1868), 143–145; also literature in Chevalier, and editions and literature in Engelmann.

(27) CASSIODORUS (ab. 468–561 +). *Tripartite History.* In Opera, ed. Garetius, 1 (Rotom. 1679, fol.), b 1–b 372. On Constantine, especially p. 207–243. (Same ed. in Migne, *Patrol. Lat.* 69 [1865], 879–1214.) Cassiodorus was born about 468 and lived to be more than ninety-three years old. This work is an epitome of Socrates, Sozomen, and Theodoret, and has no additional value as source. A work on the Goths has been preserved to us only in an epitome by Jordanes. See Jordanes.

Compare Young, in Smith & W. 1 (1877), 416–418, or (better for this work) Ramsay, in Smith, 1 (1859), 623–625; and for literature and editions, Chevalier, Engelmann, Graesse, etc.

(28) LYDUS, JOANNES (LAURENTIUS) (490–550 +). *De Mensibus; De Magistratibus; De Ostentis, passim.* Ed. Bekker, in *Corp. Hist. Byz.* (1837). Other editions of the various works may be found noticed in Graesse, *Trésor,* 4 (1863), 122; Brunet, *Manuel,* 3 (1862), 880; Engelmann, *Bibl. scr. class.* 1 (1880), 478–479; Hoffmann, *Lex.* He was born at Philadelphia in 490, and lived some time after 550. He was a heathen, but respectful toward Christianity (Photius, Cod. 180). He mentions Constantine ten or a dozen times; e.g. his foundation of Constantinople (*De O.* 21. 5), Constantine's learning and military skill (*De mag.* 3. 53), and quotes (*De magistr.* 3. 33, ed. Bonn., p. 226), Constantine's own writings.

Compare Photius, Cod. 180; Means, in Smith, *Dict.* 2 (1859), 600; Hase, Pref. and in ed. Bekker; Joubert, in *Nouv. biog. gén.* (Hoefer), 32 (1860), 388–391; and for farther literature, Chevalier and the article of Joubert, and Engelmann, *Bibl. scr. class.* 1 (1880), 479.

(29) JORDANES (or JORNANDES) (–551 ?). *History of the Goths,* (*De Getarum origine et rebus gestis*). In Cassiodorus, Opera, ed. Garetius, 1 (Rotom. 1679), 397–425; same ed. in Migne, *Patrol. Lat.* 69 (1865), 1251–1296. This work on the Goths is said by its author to be an epitome of the work of Cassiodorus. It says (p. 406–407) that Constantine employed Goths in his campaign against Licinius, and also in the building of Constantinople. It was composed in 551 or 552 (cf. Wattenbach, *Deutschland's Geschichtsq.* 1 [1877], 66).

Compare Hodgkin, in *Encycl. Brit.* 13 (1881), 747–749; Acland, in Smith & W. 3 (1882), 431–438 (exhaustive); and abundant literature in Chevalier, Engelmann, Wattenbach, &c.; also editions in Engelmann, "Potthast. *Bibl. hist. med. æv.* 1862, p. 102," &c.

(30) ANONYMOUS, QUI DIONIS CASSII HISTORIAS CONTINUAVIT (sixth century ?). 14. Licinius (18 lines); 15. Constantinus (9 lines). In Müller, *Fragm.* 4 (1868), 199; cf. especially Introd. in Müller, p. 191–192. These were first published by Ang. Mai in *Script. Vet. Nov. Call.* 2, 135–, 527–, and are found also in various editions of Dion Cassius; e.g. ed. Sturz. 9 (Spz. 1843). Mai strongly inclines to suspect that Johannes Antiochenus is the author, but this Müller (p. 191) argues to be impossible. They are sometimes referred to as Excerpta Vaticana. Petrus Patricius and various others have been suggested as authors, but all that is affirmed with any assurance is that the author was a Christian. This is on the ground of Diocletianus, 1 (p. 198). The fragments are very brief, but contain several little facts and turns not found elsewhere.

(31) EVAGRIUS (536?–594+). *Ecclesiastical History,* 3. 40–41. English translation (1709), 472–474. A violent invective against and disproval of the charges of Zosimus against Constantine and adds nothing to historical facts.

Compare Milligan, in Smith & W. 2 (1880), 423–424.

(32) PROCOPIUS CÆSARIENSIS (fl. 547–565). *Histories.* Ed. Dindorf, Bonn, 1833–1838, 3 v. Two or three slight mentions, of which the nearest to any account is the division of the empire by Constantine, and the founding of Constantinople (*De bel. Vand,* 1. 1). He flourished from about 547 to 565. Whether he was Christian or heathen is uncertain. He is characterized by peculiar truthfulness (cf. his *De ædif.* 1; Praf. ed. Bonn, v. 3, 170–, and Milligan).

Compare Milligan, in Smith & W. 4 (1887), 487–488; Plate, in Smith, *Dict.* 3, 538–540; also for literature, Chevalier and Engelmann, 1. 655; and for editions, Milligan, Plate, and the various bibliographies.

(33) PETRUS PATRICIUS (fl. 550–562). *Fragments.* In Müller, *Fragm.* 4 (1868), 189. Gives account of an embassy of Licinius to Constantine.

Compare Means, in Smith, *Dict.* 3 (1859), 226–227; also Chevalier and Hoffmann.

(34) GREGORY OF TOURS (ab. 573–594). *History of the Franks,* 1. 34. Ed. Ruinart (Paris, 1699), 27, &c. (?) *History of the Seven Sleepers,* do. 1272–1273, &c. *Liber miraculorum,* do. 725–729. The edition of Ruinart is reprinted in Migne, *Patrol. Lat.* vol. 71 (1867). In the first of these he quotes as authorities, Eusebius and Junius; the latter are full of legendary matter.

Compare Buchanan, in Smith & W. 2 (1880), 771–776; also for editions and literature, Engelmann, Chevalier, and Graesse.

(35) CHRONICON PASCHALE (ab. 630 A.D.). Ed. Dindorf, Bonn, 1832, 2 v.; section relating to Constantine occupies vol. 1, p. 516–533. Ed. Migne, *Patrol. Gr.* 92 (Paris, 1865). The work is a chronicle of the world from the creation until 630. It has been thought, but on insufficient grounds (cf. Salmon), that the first part ended with A.D. 354 and was written about that time. It is really a homogeneous work and written probably not long after 630 A.D. (Salmon). It is frequently quoted, unfortunately, as Alexandrian Chronicle (e.g. M'Clintock and Strong Cycl.). The chief value is the chronological, but the author has used good sources and presumably some not now extant. It has something the value of a primary source of second rate.

Compare Salmon, In Smith & W. 1. (1877), 509–513; Clinton, *Fasti. Rom.* 2 (1850), 169; Ideler, *Handb. d. Chron.* 2 (1826), 350–351, 462–463; and for literature and editions, Salmon.

(36) *Anonymous Acts of Metrophanes and Alexander* (seventh century ?), "in which is contained also a life of the emperor Constantine the Great." In Photius, Cod. 256; ed. Migne, *Patrol. Gr.* 104 (1860), 105–120. A more complete recension of this anonymous piece was edited by Combefis, who regards it as the work of a contemporary, written therefore in the middle of the fourth century (cf. his *Hist. Mon.* p. 573, teste Fabricius). The authentic details can be traced word for word, according to Tillemont, in other historians, while impossible statements show it to be not the work of a contemporary. It seems to fall under the class of works where "What is true is not new, and what is new is not true," but it can hardly be regarded as sufficiently determined whether or no it is worthless.

Compare Tillemont, *Mém.* 7 (1732), 657; Fabricius, *Bibl. Gr.* 9 (1737), 124 and 498; *Acta. SS.* Nov. 1.

(37) Johannes Antiochenus (fl. 610–650). *Chronological History.* Fragments in Müller, 4 (1868), 535(8)–622; *Fragm.* 168–169, on Constantius and Galerius, and 170–171a, on Constantine, p. 602–603. This writer is to be distinguished from Johannes Malalas, also known as Johannes Antiochenus. He flourished somewhere between 610–650 (Müller, p. 536). The sections relating to Constantine are in the main exactly correspondent to Eutropius. It has been conjectured (Müller, p. 1538) that Eutropius and Johannes copied from a common Greek source; but the curious error in the section on Constantine (p. 603), by which "commodæ" is converted into a proper name, and becomes the name of the sister whose son Constantine put to death, shows it to have been translated from the Latin. The work of Johannes has, however, some interesting suggestions and additions; e.g. its paraphrase of the word "dubius" in the characterization of Constantine's conduct towards his friends.

Compare Müller, p. 535–538; Means, in Smith, *Dict.* 2 (1859), 587; also article of Stokes, and other literature under Malalas.

(38) Malalas (= John of Antioch) (ab. 700). *Chronography*, Bk. 13, 1–11. Ed. Dindorf (Bonnæ, 1831); in *Corp. scr. hist. Byz.* (section on Constantine, p. 316–324); also in Migne, *Patrol. Gr.* 97 (Par. 1865), 1–70. Earlier editions are, Oxf. 1691, 8°; Venice, 1733, fol. [reprint of 1691, "quite useless"]. Lived about 700 (Müller, *Fragm.* 4 [1868], 536), or about 650 (Chevalier, 1205). He has been placed as late as ninth century (Hody), and as early as 601 (Cave.). Nothing is known of his personal history. He is to be distinguished from the John of Antioch in Müller's *Fragm.* who is earlier than Malalas. He is very credulous and inaccurate and the section on Constantine is no exception to the rule.

Compare Prolegomena of Hody and Dindorf; Stokes, in Smith & W. 3 (1882), 787–788, &c.; and farther literature in Chevalier, *Rép.* 1205; Hoefer, *Nouv. biog. gén.* 32 (1060), 1007, and the article of Stokes.

(39) Pseudo-Isidore (eighth cent.?). *Decretals.* In Migne, *Patrol. Lat.* 130 (1853), 245–252. The famous "Donation of Constantine," which appears here for the first time. See under *The Mythical Constantine.*

Compare Schaff, *Hist. of Church,* 4 (1885), 268–733; and for literature, Chevalier under Isidore Mercator; also the literature of the *Donation.*

(40) Theophanes (758–818). *Chronography.* Ed. Classen, Bonn. 1839–41, 2 v. Section on Constantine occupying vol. 1, p. 10–51; also in Migne, *Patrol. Gr.* 108 (186). This work "is justly regarded as one of the most important in the whole series of Byzantine historians" (Dowling, p. 69). Theophanes was friend of Georgius Syncellus; and at his request (Prœm. p. 5) took up the latter work at the point where he left off (Diocletian), extending it to 811. He is an authority of judgment and weight for matters relating to his own times, and on quite a different level of historical character from Cedrenus and Zonaras. Although of very much less value for Constantine, he shows even here a certain historical judgment and discrimination. His book is an intelligent work from various sources, one of which is Eusebius. He says that he has diligently examined many works, and reports nothing on his own authority, but on the authority of ancient historiographers and "logographers" (Prœm. p. 5).

Compare Dowling, *Introd.* (Lond. 1838), 69–70; Smith, in Smith, *Dict.* 3. 1082–1083; Gass, in Herzog, *Real Enc.* 15 (1885), 536–537; *Acta sanctorum Boll.* March 12; and for (extensive) literature, Chevalier.

(41) Anastasius Bibliothecarius (d. 879). *Lives of the Roman Pontiffs.* In Migne, *Patrol. Lat.* 127–128 (1852). 34. S. Silvester, vol. 127, 1511–1527. Small use.

Compare Schaff, *Hist. of the Church,* 4 (1885), 774–776; and for literature and editions, Chevalier and Graesse.

(42) Photius (ninth cent.). *Bibliotheca.* In Migne, *Patrol. Gr.* vols. 103–104 (1860). Contains excerpts from and comments on Praxagoras, Eunapius, Gelasius, Anon. Metroph., and Eusebius, which see.

Compare Schaff, *Hist. of Church,* 4 (1885), 636–642; Means, in Smith, *Dict.* 3 (1859), 347–355.

(43) Constantinus Porphyrogenitus (c. VII.) (fl. 911–959). *De thematibus.* Ed. Bekker (Bonn. 1840), 1–64, in *Corp. scr. hist. Byz.;* and in ed. Migne, *Patrol. Gr.* 113 (1864), 63–140. Gives (2. 8, ed. Bonn. p. 57–58) account of division of the empire among his sons by Constantine. He also mentions in his *De cer. aul. Byz.* (ed. Reiske, Bonn. 1829; ed. Migne, *Patrol. Gr.* 112); e.g. the "cross of Constantine" several times mentioned, and gives a few facts of archæological interest. Constantinus VII. was emperor 911–959.

Compare Plate, in Smith, *Dict.* 1. 349-351; Ceillier, 12 (1862), 811-813; and for farther literature, Chevalier and Engelmann, 1 (1880), 249; also for editions, Plate, who has admirable survey.

(44) LEO DIACONUS (tenth century). *Histories*, 5. 9 and 8. 8. In ed. Hase (Bonn. 1828), p. 91 and 138. Mentions the foundation of a city, the vision of the cross, the Scythian wars, and burial in the Church of the Apostles at Constantinople, and characterizes him as "among emperors the one renowned in story" (8. 8). For other editions, compare Brunet, Graesse, Hoffmann, and Engelmann. He lived from about 950 to at least 993. He was used by Scylitzes (cf. Cedrenus) and perhaps Zonaras. "Style vicious," and "knowledge . . . of ancient history is slight" (Means).

Compare Means, in Smith, *Dict.* 2 (1859), 743-744; M'Clintock and Strong, *Encycl.* 5 (1875), 351; Hase, Præf.; and for literature, Chevalier.

It is by some stretching of the term that many of those dating before the year 1000 are admitted as sources. Some contribute hardly a single fact not in other sources. This is still more true of the period following, but this period is especially rich in sources of historical fictions — and these must be considered. So the Byzantine historians to the invention of printing are given, and some Western writings, which contain relevant matter.

(45) ZONARAS, JOHANNES (1042-1130?). *Chronicle.* Ed. Migne, *Patrol. Gr.* 134-135 (Par. 1864). The section relating to Constantine occupies Vol. 1. 1097-1118, Bk. 13, chs. 1-4; cf. also end of Bk. 12. The ed. Pinder, Bonn. 1841-1844, 2 v., is unfinished, containing only twelve books. It has since been edited by Dindorf, Lips. 1868-1875, 6 v. Bk. 13 is in Vol. 3 (1870). This work consists of eighteen books extending from the beginning of the world until 1118. Zonaras draws, for Christian period, from Eusebius, Philostorgius, &c., with some discernment, and so deserves a tolerably high place among the Byzantine historians (Zöckler). He incorporates a choice variety of fables, but gives more or less facts which seem to be facts. He actually adds almost nothing to the sources of Constantine, though there are certain facts over which one lingers a little before relegating to the great class of "interesting, if true."

Compare Smith, *Dict.* 3. 1331; Zöckler, in Herzog, *Real Enc.* 17 (1886), 555-556; and for (rich) literature, Zöckler, Chevalier, and Engelmann, 1 (1880), 798.

(46) CEDRENUS, GEORGIUS (ab. 1057). *Compendium of History.* Ed. Bekker, Bonn. 1838-1839, 2 v., the section relating to Constantine occupying Vol. 1, p. 472-520 *et pass.* Also in Migne, *Patrol. Gr.* 121-122 (Par. 1864). Nothing is known of his personal history. The work is a chronicle from the beginning of the world until 1057 A.D. He mentions as his chief sources Georgius Syncellus, "until the time of Maximianus and Maximinus," and from this point Theophanes, Siculus, Psellus, and others (cf. p. 4; cf. also Glycas. *Chron.*, ed. Bonn. p. 457), and claims to have collected facts not in these sources. He mentions the work of Joannes Thracesius, or Curopalates, who is probably Scylitzes, whose work corresponds so exactly with that of Cedrenus in parts as to suggest the one or the other a better copier than compiler. The statement of Ceillier is that Cedrenus copied the work of Scylitzes for the period 811-1057, and that Scylitzes afterwards continued his work to 1081; i.e. there was a double edition of the work of Scylitzes, and Cedrenus wrote between. But Means (p. 760) thinks otherwise, and gives good reasons, making one edition and placing Cedrenus' work later, i.e. after 1081. The "additional facts" are few, the compilation is uncritical and credulous; but the work is recognized as a source to be consulted, though with greatest critical care.

Compare Plate, in Smith, *Dict.* 1. 658; Ceillier, 13 (1863), 560; Means, *Scylitzes*, in Smith, *Dict.* 3. 759-762; and for literature, Chevalier, under the words *Cedrene* and *Scylitzes.*

(47) PSEUDO-LEO. *Chronography*, under *Constantius Chlorus* and *Constantinus Magnus.* Ed. Bekker (Bonn. 1842), p. 83-90. In *Corp. scr. hist. Byz.* from Cramer, *Anecd. gr. bibl. reg. Par.* 2 (1839), 243-379. It is published as the first part of the *Chronography* of Leo Grammaticus, because assigned to him by the catalogues of the MS. at Paris. It is thought by Cramer, however, not to be by him, but to be "compiled from various writers, — Cedrenus, Joannes Antiochenus, *Chronicon Paschali*, and perhaps others which are lost" (cf. Cramer, *Anecd. gr.* 2. 243-379, quoted by Bekker, Præf. iii.-iv.). In this section the author quotes Socrates and Eusebius, but uses other and some unusual sources. While one hesitates to lay much weight on an author of such unknown age and personality, and which contains obvious errors, yet it carries the conviction of a certain moderate weight. Many passages are identical, almost word for word, with Cedrenus. In one of these passages the author refers to Socrates as his authority, while there is no such mention in Cedrenus. They may have taken from the same source. At all events, this work appears on its face much more like sober history than do Cedrenus and Zonaras. Its absolute value as source is very slight.

Compare Preface of Bekker.

(48) ATTALIATA, MICHAEL (ab. 1072). *History.* Ed. De Presle and Bekker, Bonn. 1853. 8°. He mentions (p. 217, also p. 222) half a dozen things relating to Constantine; that he was reckoned among the apostles, the sign of the cross, &c., but nothing of value, unless (p. 222) the transposition of a colony from Iberia to Assyria (?). Compare Præf. of De Presle, also Graves, in Smith, *Dict.* 1. 409, who, however, does not mention this work; and for literature, Chevalier and De Presle, p. 7-8.

(49) ANNA COMNENA (1083–1148). *Alexias.* Ed. Schopen-Reifferscheid, Bonn. 1839–1878. Mentions among two or three other deeds, a statue which this "father and lord of the city" had made over for him (12. 4), and that he has been counted among the apostles (14. 8).

Compare Plate, in Smith, *Dict.* 1. 179; Klippel, in Herzog, 1 (1877), 427–429, &c.

(50) GLYCAS, MICH (after 1118). *Chronicle* (or *Annals*). Ed. Bekker, Bonn. 1836; the section relating to Constantine occupies p. 460–468, ed. Migne, 158 (Par. 1866), 1–958. This work of Glycas extends from the beginning of the world to A.D. 1118. Though "justly placed among the better Byzantine historians" (Plate), for the period of Constantine he is one of the worst. His critical judgment seems to incline to the selection of the most unhistoric. He gives at end of preceding section a description of the work of Scylitzes (cf. Cedrenus), and quotes in it a work of Alexander on the Invention of the Cross.

Compare Plate, in Smith, *Dict.* 2. 277; Joubert. in *Nouv. biog. gén.* (Hoefer), 20 (1857), 845–846; and for literature, Chevalier; also for editions, Hoffmann.

(51) NICETAS CHONIATAS (Acominatus) (1150–1216 +). *History.* Ed. Bekker, in *Corp. scr. hist. Byz.* Bonn. 1835, 8°; ed. Migne, *Patrol. Gr.* 139 (1865), 282–1088 (= Mai, *Bibl. nov. patr.* 6. ?). *Thesaurus*, in Migne, *Patrol. Gr.* 139–140 (1865), 1087–1443, 1–282 (= Mai, *Spicil. Rom.* v. 4). Born about 1150, and lived until 1216 at least. Gives in his *History* two or three things which relate to "the first and mightiest among Christian emperors" (*De Is. Aug.* 3. 7, ed. Bonn. p. 583); e.g. the tale of the nails from the cross (do. p. 584), and the despoiling of his tomb (*De Al. Is. Aug.* 1. 7, p. 632); also a few in the *Thesauri*, e.g. his conciliation to Arianism through his sister and her friend, the Arian presbyter (6. 3 and 6), and various matters relating to the Arian controversy (mainly in Bk. 5), where he uses the familiar sources, — Eusebius, Socrates, Sozomen, Theodoret, Philostorgius, &c., but also some other less familiar ones.

Compare Worman, in M'Clintock and Strong, *Cyclop.* 7 (1877), 54–55; Plate, in Smith, *Dict.* 2. 1182–1183; Ullmann, in *Stud. u. Krit.* (1833), 674–700; Gass, in Herzog, 10 (1882), 540–541, and abridged in Schaff-Herz. 2. 1652. Compare for literature, the above and Chevalier; and for editions, Worman, Plate, Brunet, Graesse, Hoffmann, &c.

(52) GREGORAS, NICEPHORAS (1295–1359). *Byzantine History*, Bks. 1–37. Ed. Shopen (v. 1–2) and Bekker (v. 3), Bonn. 1829, 1830, and 1855. In *Corp. scr. hist. Byz.*; ed. Migne, *Patrol. Lat.* 148–149 (1865). Mentions incidentally half a dozen facts relating to foundation of Constantinople (10. 1; 14. 3, &c.), his destruction of idolatry (19. 1), treatment of the Jews (26. 15), and enlargement of empire (26. 37). He was born 1295, and died after 1359. Was more learned but less judicious than Cantacuzenus (Plate).

Compare Plate, in Smith, *Dict.* 2. 304–306; Joubert, in *Nouv. biog. gén.* 21 (1857), 889–891; also for literature, Chevalier, and for editions, Plate and Joubert.

(53) EPHRÆMIUS (fourteenth century). *Cæsars* (?). Constantinus. Ed. Bekker, Bonn. 1840, 8°; section on Constantine occupies p. 21–25; ed. Migne, 143 (Par. 1865), 1–380. It was first edited by Mai, *Scr. vet. nov. coll.* 3 (1828), 1–225 (Dowl.). This metrical chronicle introduces one or two fables, but is in the main at least semi-historical, but its additional facts give no impression of having special sources, — in brief, it is scarcely a source, rather literature.

Compare Smith, *Dict.* 2. 28; Bonneau, in *Nouv. biog. gén.* (Hoefer) 16 (1856), 127; Mai, *Præf.* in ed. Bekker, also ed. Migne. Compare for literature, Chevalier.

(54) CANTACUZENUS, JOANNES. ANGELUS COMNENUS PALÆOLOGUS (d. 1375 +). *Histories.* Ed. Schopen, Bonn. 1828–1832, 3 v.; also in Migne, *Patrol. Gr.* 153–154 (Dowl. 1866). Speaks of Constantine as a model of clemency (4. 2; ed. Bonn. v. 3, p. 18) worthy to be compared with the apostles (3. 92), and as led by the spirit of God like David (4. 48; ed. Bonn. v. 3, p. 351), and mentions the time (in May) when his memory is celebrated (4. 4; 3. 92), but has hardly a half-dozen mentions and fewer facts of interest or value. He reigned 1342–1355, abdicated, and lived until after 1375.

Compare Plate, in Smith, *Dict.* 579–581; and for farther literature, Chevalier and Engelmann, also for editions.

(55) NICEPHORUS CALLISTUS (d. ab. 1450). *Ecclesiastical History*, 7. 17–18, 55. In Migne, *Patrol. Gr.* 145–147. Bk. 7 is in 145, and Bk. 8 in 146. This late history, not so bad as some in style, but full of legendary matter, was compiled from the standard existing historians, and perhaps some others. The portions on Constantine are taken almost wholly from Eusebius, Socrates, Sozomen, and other existing historians.

Compare Schaff, *Church Hist.* 3 (1884), 883–884; Plate, in Smith, *Dict.* 2 (1859), 1180–1181; Dowling, *Introd.* (1838), 91–93.

(56) *Monody on the Younger Constantine* (ab. 1450). Ed. Frotscher, *Anon. Græci oratio funebris*, Freiberg i. S., 1855. This work has not been seen, but according to Seeck (*Ztschr. f. Wiss. Theol.* 1890, p. 64) and Wordsworth (p. 630) this edition contains the result of a study by Wesseling, which shows that this work, referring to an anonymous emperor, does not refer to Constantine II. at all, but to some ruler who belongs in the fifteenth century.

Compare Seeck and Wordsworth for editions.

(57) CODINUS (d. ab. 1453 ?). *Excerpts on the origins of Constantinople.* Ed. Bekker (Bonn. 1843). For

other editions, compare articles of Plate and the *Nouv. biog. gén.* Contains considerable relating to Constantine, especially respecting the founding of Constantinople, and the buildings and statues in it. Mainly compilation, or compilation from compilation, but is from partly lost sources and far from unnecessary. He died about 1453 (?).

Compare Plate, in Smith, *Dict.* 1 (1859), 810–811; *Nouv. biog. gén.* 11 (1855), 24–25; and for literature, Chevalier.

(58) DUCAS (fl. 1450–1460 A.D.) gives "From the incarnation until Constantine the Great, 318 years," and speaks of a church restored by him. Ed. Bekker, in *Corp. scr. hist. Byz.* (1834), p. 13 and 48.

(59) GEOFFREY OF MONMOUTH (d. 1154). *British History.* English translation (Lond. Bohn, 1848), 162–. The passage relating to Constantine covers a number of pages, and is ninety-five per cent fiction, five per cent fact.

Compare Tedder, in Stephen, *Dict. of Nat. Biog.* 21 (1890), 133–135.

Various of the old chronicles are only translations or paraphrases of this; e.g. the *Chronicle* of Pierre de Langtoft (ed. Wright, Lond. 1866, p. 76–78), various Welsh, Anglo-Saxon, and French chronicles, Waurin's *Recueil des Chroniques* (ed. Hardy, Lond. 1864), although Hardy maintains that neither Waurin or any of the other versions are real translations, but says there is some lost common source.

(60) HENRY OF HUNTINGDON (1135). *History of the English.* Ed. Arnold, Lond. 1879, 8°, p. 29–31. Engl. translation, Lond. Bohn, 1853, p. 28–29. This is written from generally good sources, notably Eutropius, and means to be historical; but its mythical details — e.g. Helena, a British princess, Constantine cured of leprosy — make it useless.

Compare Forester, Preface to translation; Wright, *Biog. Brit. Lit.* 2 (1846), 167–173.

(61) WILLIAM OF MALMESBURY (1137). *Chronicle of England.* English translation, Giles (Lond. Bohn, 1847), 6. Mentioned as a source because often quoted in literature. He ascribes to Constantine the introduction of the British settlement in France.

Compare Wright, *Biog. Brit. Lit.* 2 (1846), 134–142.

(62) DICETO, RALPH DE (d. 1202?). *Abbreviated Chronicles.* Ed. Stubbs, Lond. 1876; section on Constantine, p. 73–76. This work was composed before 1188. It consists in the main of abstracts from Eutropius, Eusebius, Jerome, and Rufinus, with various mythical details from William of Malmesbury and other sources.

Compare Poole, in Stephen, *Dict. of Nat. Biog.* 15 (1888), 12–14. This is taken from Stubbs, Introduction, q.v.

(63) *Eulogium Historiarum* (ab. 1366). Ed. Haydon, Lond. 1858, 3 v.; section on Constantine, 1. 337–339; 2. 267–268, 332–333; 3. 12, 265. This was probably written by Peter, a monk of Malmesbury (Haydon), about 1366. Compiled from various sources, has familiar facts, but is of no value except for legends.

Compare Preface of Haydon.

(64) VORAGINE (1230–1298). *Golden Legend. Legend concerning the Invention of the Cross.* Ed. Graesse (Lips. 1846, repr. Vratisl. 1890). French translation by Brunet, 2 (1843), 118–116. Early English translation printed by Caxton. A curious mixture of fact and fable, in which legendary is gathered, but all facts are expressed with a curious conscientiousness, or pretended conscientiousness, in quoting authorities. But on Constantine, however, his authorities do not always come to the test of containing what he quotes from them.

Compare article *Varaggio*, in M'Clintock and Strong, *Cyclop.* 10 (1881), 719, Brunet's *Preface* and the Proceedings of the American Soc. of Ch. Hist. for 1889.

Besides the above-mentioned sources there are many mentions which may be found in the various collections of mediæval documents, such, e.g., as Pertz, *Monumenta Germaniæ Historica,* which has various interesting chronicles covering the period of Constantine.

§ 3. *Literature.*

In making the following thread to the rich literature on Constantine the plan has been to confine almost wholly to *Monographs,* since to refer to all histories, encyclopædias, and the like which treat of him would be endless. Only such few analyzed references are introduced as have special reasons. Even with this limit it cannot be at all hoped that the list is exhaustive. Considerable pains has been taken, however, to make it full, as there is no really extended modern list of works on Constantine, excepting, perhaps, Chevalier (*Rép. des sources hist. du Moyen Age*). The effort was made to see each work referred to personally, but the libraries of London, Oxford, Berlin, Paris, could not supply them, and after a good deal of search in other libraries and more or less successful effort to purchase, there is still a considerable portion which has not been seen. The editor has tried in vain to decide in various instances whether præses or respondent is author in certain dissertations. Following is the list :

ALBANI, JO. HIER. *Liber pro oppugnata R. pontif. dignitate & Constantini donatione.* Colon. Agrip. 1535, fol.; Romæ, 1547, 4°; Venetiis, 1584, fol.

ALEXANDER, NATALIS. *Hist. eccles.* IV. (1778), 345-351 (= Zaccaria, Thes. theolog. VII. 886-900), 431-451.

ALFORD, MICH. *Brittania illustrata, s. liber de Lucii, Helenæ, et Constantini patria et fide.* Antwerpiæ, 1641. 4°.

ALTUS, HENRICUS. *Donatio Constantini imperatoris facto (ut aiunt) Sylvestro papæ (præs. Joach. Hilde-brando).* Helmstadii, 1661. 4° (p. 56). *Not* Hildebrand?

ALZOG, J. *Manual of Universal Church History.* Tr. Pabisch and Byrne. Cincinnati, O., 1874. 3 v. 8°, p. 462-476. Relations of Constantine the Great to the Catholic Church. Very Roman Catholic.

ANDLAU, FR. VON. *Die byz. Kaiser. Hist.-stud.* Mainz, 1865, 8°.

ANTONIADES, CRYSANTHOS. *Kaiser Licinius, eine historische Untersuchung nach dem bestern alten und neueren Quellen.* München, 1884. 8°. Unfortunately not at hand, but often mentioned with greatest respect by Görres and others.

ARBELLOT. *Mémoire sur les statues équestres de Constantin placées dans les églises de l'ouest de la France.* Limoges, 1885. 8°, 34 pp. (Cf. Audiat, Louis, in Bull. soc. arch. Saintonge, 1885. II. v. 186-193, 280-292.) Contains a history of the long archæological discussion on the subject of the equestrian statue on the façades of various churches in the west of France. Some say it represents Charles Martel, Charlemagne, the *founder* of the church, the rider who appeared to Heliodorus, Rider of the Apocalypse, St. Martin, St. George or the Church Triumphant. Consult for many titles on the discussion, which it is not worth while to give here. Arrives at the result that the "*greater part*" represent Constantine.

ARENDT. *Ueber Constantin und sein Verhältniss zum Christenthum.* In Theolog. Quartalschr. Tübing. 1834. III. 387.

ARRHENIUS, LAUR. *Dissertatio historica de Constantino Magno.* Upsal. 1719. 4°.

—— —— *Refutatio commenti de donatione Constantini Magni.* Upsal. 1729. 8°.

AUBÉ, B. *De Constantino imperatore, pontifice maximo dissertatio.* Lutetiæ, 1861. 8°, 108 pp. Examines Constantine's attitude toward (1) Pagans, (2) Christians; concludes that, as a matter of fact, he exercised the office of Pontifex Maximus over both.

AUDIAT, LOUIS. *Les statues au portail des églises.* In Bull. de la soc. des arch. de la Saintogne. 5 (1884-1885) (1885), 186, 193. Starts out from Arbellot. Gives ten various theories. Mentions various works. This with Arbellot a sufficient apparatus for this topic.

BACHMANN, P. *Wider die Natterzungen, . . . Dabey ein Antwort auff Constantini Donation, welche der Luther spöttlich nennet den Hohen Artickel des allerheyligisten Bebstlichen glaubens* (Dresden), 1538, 4°, (45). p. Examines whether the Donation is "ein Teuffelische lügen und Gottes lasterung (wie sie der Luther nennet)."

BAIER, JOH. DAV. *Disputatio de erroribus quibusdam politicis Constantino Magno imputatis.* Jenæ, 1705, 4°.

BALDUINUS, FRANC. *Constantinus Magnus, sive de Constantini imperatoris legibus ecclesiasticis atque civilibus commentariorum libri 2.* Basileæ, 1556, 8°; Argent, 1612, 8°; præf. Nic. Hier. Gundling, Lipsiæ-Halæ, 1727, 8°, 235 (23) pp.

BANG, A. CHRS. *Kirchen og Romerstaten indtil Constantin den Stre.* Christiana, 1879, 8°.

BARING, NICOL. *Dissertatio epistolica de crucis signo a Constantino Magno conspecto.* Hannov. 1645, 8°.

BARONIUS, *Annales* (1590), 306, 16-18, 3-25; 307, 3-15; 312, 7-337, 37; 358, 27. Cf. Pagi, *Crit.* (1689), 306, 5-307, 14; 311, 9-337, 6; 547, 12.

BARTOLINI, DOMENICO. *Come Costantini Augusti imperatore innalzasse in Roma i primi sacri edifici del culto cristiano.* Dissertazione in Atti Accad. Rom. archeol. 12 (1852) I. 281-308. Opposes the idea that these belong to a period not before Honorius. Separately printed. "Dissertazione . . . letta nell' Adunanza tenuta. il di 16 di marzo, *1843*." pp. 30 (1).

BAUDOT. *Dissertation critique sur la famille de Constantin, & en particulier sur Constantin le Jeune.* In Magas. encyclop. 6 (1812), 241-274. Under head of *Numismatique* opposes Valois in Acad. Inscr. 1740. The medals do refer to Constantine. Includes a discussion of Constantine's family.

BAUNE, J. DE LA. *Vita Constantini Magni, herausgegeben von A. Jäger.* Norimb. 1779, 8°.

BAYET, C. *La fausse donation de Constantini, examen de quelques théories récentes.* In Ann. fac. lett. Lyon, 1884, I. 3 (1884), 12-44. The donation belongs in second half of eighth century, or first half of ninth.

BERTHELÉ, JOS. In Bibl. ec. des Chartes, 46 (1885), 330-331. [Review of Arbellot.] Gives brief analysis, and mentions one statue omitted by Arbellot.

BEUSTE, JOACH. V. *Oratio de Constantino Magno.* Witteb. 1569, 8°. "Extat Tom VI. Orationum Vitem-burgensium."

βίος καὶ πολιτεία τῶν ἁγίων θεοστέπτων μεγάλων βασιλέων καὶ ἰσαποστόλων Κωνσταντίνου καὶ Ἑλένης [Mnemeia hagiologica, p. 164] Βενετία, 1884, la. 8°.

BOEHRINGER. *Athanasius u. Arius.* 1874, p. 1-53.

BOISSIER. *Essais d'histoire religieuse, I. un dernier mot sur les persecutions; II. la conversion de Constantin.* In Rev. d. deux mondes (Feb. 1886), p. 790-818, (July) p. 51-72.

BONNEAU, ALCIDE. *Étude historique.* In his edition-translation of Valla's Donation of Constantine. Interesting, and gathers much of what one wants to know first about the Donation.

BONNETTY, A. *De la donation de Constantin et de la protection qu'il accorda au christianisme.* In Annal de Philos. chrèt. (1831), 125–136. Personal conversion a secondary question. It is sufficient to have proved that it was no longer possible for paganism to occupy the throne of the world.

BORCHMANN, JAC. FRID. *Dissertatio historico-critica de labaro Constantini Magni.* Hafniæ, 1700. 4°.

BOTT, THEOD. *Constantin le Grand et sa position entre le paganisme et le christianisme, essai historico-critique.* Colmar, 1874. 8°, 51 pp.

BRIEGER, THEOD. *Constantine der Grosse als Religions-politicker. Kirchengeschichtlicher Beitrag.* Gotha, 1880. 8°, 48 pp. Cf. Grisar, in Zeitschr. kath. Theol. 1882, vi. 554–562.

BRIDGES, MATTH. *Roman Empire under Constantine the Great.* London, 1828. 8°, 467 pp.

BROGLIE, A. DE. *L'Eglise et L'Empire Romaine au IV. siècle. I. Régne de Constantin.* Paris, 1856. 8°. One of the best and most frequently cited.

BRUNNER, H. In the Festgabe für R. v. Gneist, Berlin, 1888, p. 5 (1)–35. Donation.

BUCHHOLZ, SAM. *Constantin der Grosse in seiner wahren Grösse wirderhergestellt.* Berlin, 1772. 4°.

BUDDEUS. *Observ. sel. liter.* I. (1700), 370–440.

BURCKHARDT, JAK. *Die Zeit Constantin's des Grossen.* Basel, 1853. 8°, 222 pp. Leipzig, 1880. 8°. For a long time the standard work on Constantine. Unsympathetic, and in a measure unjust.

DE BURIGNEY. *Hist. des Revolutions de l'empire le Constantinople depuis le fondation.* . . . Paris, 1750; tr. German, Hamb. 1754.

BUSÆUS, JOH. *Disputatio theolog. de baptismo Constantini Magni.* 4°. Moguntiæ, 1589.

CANONICI, MATT. ALOIS. *Proposizioni storico-critiche intorno alla vita dell' imperatore Costantino.* . . . 4°. Parma, 1760. Compare Cigola, Vincenzo.

CASTELLI, IGN. *Intorno al battesimo di Costantino imper. dissertazione.* In La scienza e la fede. 11 (Nap. 1870), 201–219.

CAUSSIN, NICOLAS. *Eques christianus, s. Constantius Magnus.* Trad. du franç. par Henri Lamormain. Vienn. 1637, 8°.

CAVE. *Scr. Eccl.* I. (1741), 183–185.

CAVEDONI, C. *Disamina della nuova edizione della Numismatica Costantiniana del P. Raffaele Garrucci d. C. d. G.* 19 pp. Extr. dalla Rivista della Numismatica (Olivieri), 2 (1864).

CAVEDONI. " *Recherches critique sur les médailles de Constantin le Grand et de son fils ornées de types et de symboles chrétiens.*" Modena, 1858.

CEILLIER. *Histoire des auteurs sac. et eccl.* 3 (1865), 118–148.

CHAULNES, GABRIEL DE. In Ann. philos. chrét. 5 ser. E. XVI. (1867), 261–271. On the donation of Constantine.

CHAUNER. *Influence of Christianity upon the Legislation of Constantine.* 1874, 8°.

CHIFFLETUS, PETR. FRANC. *Dissert.* . . . *De loco, tempore & cæteris adjunctis conversionis magni Constantini ad fidem christianam.* . . . Paris, 1676, 8°.

Church Policy of Constantine the Great. In North British Rev. 1870, LII. I.

CIAMPINI, JOAN. *De sacris ædificiis a Constantino Magno constructis synopsis historica.* Romæ, 1693, la. 4° (or fol.), 8 f.–218 p.

CIGOLA, VINCENZO. *Proposizioni storico-critiche intorno alla vita dell' Imperatore Costantino (praes. Madama Isabella di Spagna) Vincenzo Cigola Bresciano Convittore nel Regio-Ducal ecclegio de' Nobili ei Parma.* Parma, 1760, 4°, 44 pp. Three plates of coins and medals of Constantine and (2) various theses. At end sixteen pages of inscriptions, and three pages of coins and medals (60 pages in all).

Civiltà Cattolica. Ser. 5, Vol. 10 (1864), 601–609. 1. La frase *instinctu Divinitatis* nell' arco trionfale di Costantino. 2. Le monete di Costantino, posteriori alla vittoria sopra Massenzio.

CLINTON, H. F. *Fasti Romani,* 1 (Oxf. 1845), 348–397; 2 (1850), 86–94. This is a most convenient massing of sources, including groupings of laws and inscriptions. One of the most thoroughly useful of works.

COEN, ACH. *Di una leggenda relativa alla nascità e alla gioventù di Costantino Magno.* In Arch. soc. Romana stor. patria, 1880-1882, IV. 1–55, 293–316, 535–561; V. 33–66, 489–541. Roma, 1882. 8°, 191 pp. Cf. Rev. d. Quest. hist. 33. 682; Vesselofsky, A. in Romania, 14 (1885), 137–143.

COLOMBIER, H. M. *La donation de Constantin.* In Études relig. hist. litt. (1877), 31 year, 5 ser. Vol. II. 801–829. Is worth looking over, as it gathers many of the facts which bear on date. Thinks he has " exact date." " L'origine Romaine n'est guère douteuse " " vers l'an 687," by " clecs mécontents du pape."

COMBES, FRANCOIS. *Les liberateurs des nations.* Paris, 1874. 8°, p. 208–229. *Constantin Liberateur des Chrétiens.*

Considérations générales sur le christianisme (iv. s.). *L'empereur Constantin.* St. Etiénne, 1884. 16°, 136 pp.

Constantin Imp. Byzantini Numismatis argentei Expositio, 1600.

Die Constantinische Schenkungsurkunde. I. BRUNNER, H. *Das Constitutum Constantini.* II. ZEUMER, K. *Der älteste Text.* Berlin, Springer, 1888. 8°, 60 pp. "Aus Festgabe f. Rud. v. Gneist."

Constantinus Magnus Romanorum imperator Joanne Reuchline Phorcensi interprete. Tubingæ, 1513. 4°, 23 pp. *Contin. Monthly*, 6 (1864), 161 (Schaff?).

CRACKENTHORPE, RICHARD. *The Defense of Constantine: with a treatise of the Popes temporall monarchie. Wherein, besides divers passages, touching other Counsels, both General and Proviciall, the second Roman Synod, under Sylvester, is declared to be a meere Fiction and Forgery.* London, 1621. 4°, pp. (16), 283(1). Ch. 1–7. Seven reasons proving the Synod to be a forgery. Ch. 8. That Constantine made no such donation, and Gretser refuted. Ch. 9. Three reasons to prove that Constantine never made donation. Ch. 10–15. Seven witnesses, four popes, sixteen other witnesses, thirty lawyers, and eight emperors alleged by Marta as witnesses of Constantine's donation examined; also four reasons brought by Marta and Albanus. Consult for older literature relating to the Donation.

La crueldad, y Sinrazon | La venuce auxilio y valor, Maxencio y Constantino (coloph.). Barcelona per Carlo Gilbert y Tuto, Impressor y Librerio. Historical drama. Introduces character of Constantine, the younger Constantine, Fausta, &c.

CURTON, A. DE. In Nouv. biog. gén. 11 (1855), 581–595.

CUSA, NICOLAUS DE. *De Concordantia Catholica. Judicium de donatione Constantini.* Basil, 1568.

CUTTS, EDW. L. *Constantine the Great, the union of the State and the Church.* London and New York, 1881. 12°, XIV. 422 pp. For general, not especially scholarly use.

DALHUS. *Dissertatio de baptismo Constantini Magni.* Hafniæ, 1696 (1698, Vogt.).

DEMETRIADES, KALLIOP. *Die christliche Regierung und Orthodoxie Kaiser Constantin d. Grossen, eine histor. Studie.* München, 1878, 8°, IV. 47 pp.

DIEZE, JOH. ANDR. *Dissertatio de forma imperii Romani Constantino Magno recte atque sapienter mutata.* Lipsiæ, 1752, 4°, 34 pp.

DÖLLINGER, J. V. *Die Papst–Fabeln des Mittelalters.* 1863. Cf. Civiltà cattol., ser. 5, v. 10 (1864), 303–330; tr. Ger. Mainz, 1867. gr. 8°, 34 pp.

DÖLLINGER. In Münchener Hist. Jahrb. (1865), 337–.

DUDLEY, DEAN. *History of the First Council of Nice: A world's Christian convention, A.D. 325; with a life of Constantine.* Boston, Dean Dudley & Co., 1879, 120 pp.

DUERR, JOAN. FRID. *Dissertatio historica de Constantino Magno.* Jenæ, 1684, 4°.

DU PIN. *Nov. Bibl. Aut. Eccl.* 2, p. 16–.

DURUY, VICT. *Les premières années du règne de Constantin* (305–323). In Compte rendu acad. scien. mor. polit. (1881). F. XVI. 737–765. Speaks of his "cold cruelty." He was convinced that "the future was victory to Christians, and political wisdom counselled to go with them."

——— ——— *La politique religieuse de Constantin* (312–337). In Compte rendu acad. scien. mor. polit. (1882), XVII. 185–227. Orleans, 1882, 8°, 47 pp. = Rev. archæolog., 1882, B. XLIII. 96–110, pl. 155–175. Cf. Allard, P., in Lettres chrét. (1882), V. 244–249. "Fragment de son Histoire des Romains." Treats: I. La vision miraculeuse. II. Le lavarum. III. Popularité croissante du culte du Soleil. IV. Constantin à Rome en 312: son arc de triomphe. V. L'édit de Milan (313). VI. Mesures pour l'éxecution de l'édit de Milan. VIII. Monnaies de Constantin; Constantinople. IX. Resumé.

——— ——— *Les conditions sociales au temps de Constantin.* In Compte rendu acad. scien. mor. polit. (1882), XVIII. 729–772. Treats: La cour, La noblesse, La bourgeoisie, La plèbe, Les corporations réglementées, L'armée.

DU VOISIN, J. B. *Dissertation critique sur la vision de Constantin.* Paris, 1774. 12°, 331 pp. Cf. Journ. d. sçavans (1774), 452–459.

ECKHEL. *Doctrina numerum veterum.* 8 (Vindob. 1828), 71–95.

ELTZ, H. In Public. hist. Inst. Luxembourg (1874–1875), XXIX. 225–236. In this paper, p. 215–236, p. 225–235, are occupied with coins of Constantine and his sons.

EWYCK, FLORENTIUS OB. *Oratio in laudem Constantini Magni habitu a . . . Tempore Exanimis Huberni Gandæ a. d. XII. Cal. Januar. MDCXCIII.* Gandæ, 1692, pp. 11(1). Draws nice little moral of the "good example" from Constantine.

FABRICIUS, JOAN. ALB. *Dissertatio de cruce Constantini Magni qua probatur eam fuisse phænomenon in halone solari, quo Deus usus, sit ad Constantini Magni animum promovendum.* Hamburgi, 1706. 40 (or Woltereck, who is resp.?). Cf. "Bibl. gr. VI. (1714–1749), 1–29; IX. 68 (2a, IV. 882; VI. 693–718)."

FARLATI. *Illyric. sac.* VIII. (1819), 25–27.

FLETCHER, JOS. *Life of Constantine the Great.* London, 1852. 12mo.

FREHERUS. "Diss. Const. Imp. Numis." 1600. Evidently = Const. Imp. Byz. Numism. cf. above.

FINCKIUS, CASP. *De disput. de Baptismo.* T. V. p. 313, disp. XIII.

FRICK, JOH. *Dissertatio de fide Constantini Magni haud dubie christiana.* Ulmæ, 1713. 4°. Not Frick (who is præses), but Miller(?).

FRIEDRICH, J. *Die Konstantinische Schenkung.* Nördlingen, 1889. 8°. VII. 197 pp. Reviewed in Theol. Literaturblatt, 1890, Nos. 3–5; in Evang. Kirch-ztng, No. 18 (1889); by Schultze, in Theol. Litt. Ber. 1889; Liter. Centralblatt, 1889, No. 33; by Bloch, in Mttlgn. a. d. histor. Litt. (1890), No. 1; by Löwenfeld, in Deutsche Ltzng. (1890), No. 3.

FRIMELIUS, JOANNIS. *De Constantini Magni Religione, Baptismo & rerum sacrarum apparatu.* Mentioned by Kunardus, in a " Disputationum Catalogus," p. (8).

FROMMANN, E. A. *De codicibus s. jussu Constantini ab Eusebio curatis.* Coburgi, 1761. 4°.

FROTHINGHAM, ARTHUR. Compare edition of Jacobus of Sarug.

FUHRMANN, MATTHIAS. *Historia sacra de baptismo Constantino Max. Augusti.* I. Romæ, 1742; II. Viennæ in Austria, 1747, 4°, fig.

GARRUCCI, RAFF. *Esame critico e cronologico della numismatica Costantiniana portante segni di cristianesimo.* Roma, 1858, 8°, 72 pp.

—— In Vetri cimit. crist. Roma (1884), append. 1858. Croce greca sulle monete di Costantino e sua famiglia, 89, 90, 91. Croce latina sulle . . . Costantino padre e figlio e di Costanzo, 95. Vario modo di figuriale ai tempi di Costantino, 103.

—— —— *Verres ornés de figures en or, trouvés dans les Catacombes Romaines.* 2d ed. 1864. Has at end discussion of symbols of Constantine. Compare Anal. Jur. Pout. 1873.

GASPARIN, AG. DE. *Innocent III., le siècle apostolique, Constantin.* Paris, 1873, 12°, p. 75–193.

—— —— *Constantin.* In *Le christianisme au quatrième siècle.* Genéve, 1858, 8°, p. 1–139. The question of church and state. The present problem of the churches is to undo the work of Constantine. Lectures to Y. M. C. A. of Geneva.

GENELIN. *Das Schenkungsversprechen und die Schenkung Pippins.* Wien und Leipzig, 1880.

GENGEL, GEORG. *De Constantino Magno, primo Christianorum imperatore, dissertatio* . . . Calissii, 1726, 8°, 14–89–6 pp.

GIBBON. *Decline and Fall of the Roman Empire.* Many editions. Furnishes later historians of Constantine with almost unlimited material for adoring quotation.

GIRAULT, CL. XAV. *Dissertation histor. & critique sur le lieu où la croix miraculeuse apparut à Constantin & à son armée.* In Magas. encyclop. Paris, 1810, 8°.

GÖRRES, FRANZ. *Die Verwandtenmorde Constantin's des Grossen.* In Ztschr. f. wiss. Theol. 30 (1887), 343–377. Reaches, with Hilgenfeld, the rather severe judgment that, on the whole, the bloodguiltiness of Licinius is less than that of Constantine. There are also various other interesting reviews or treatises by Görres.

GRAETZ, H. *Die Herrschaft des Christenthums durch Constantin's Bekehrung.* In Monatsschrift f. gesch. u. wiss. Judenthum (1887), 416–421.

GRAUERT, HERM. *Die Konstantinische Schenkung.* In Görres-Ges. Histor. Jahrb. 1882–84, III. p. 3–30; IV. (1883), 45–95, 525–617, 674–680; V. 117–120. Reaches result that it arose not in Rome, but in France, from the cloister of St. Denis, shortly before or at the same time with the Pseudo-Isidore, and shortly after 840. (Weiland, p. 142.)

GRETSER. *De sancta cruce.* In Opera, v. 2. Ratisbonæ, 1734, fol.

GRISAR, HARTM. *Die vorgeblichen Beweise gegen die Christlichkeit Constantins des Grossen.* In Zeitschr. f. kathol. Theolog. VI. (1882), 585–607. Cf. La Controverse, 1882, III. 693–702.

GROSSIUS, MATTH. *Dissertatio de donatione Constantini Magni.* Lipsiæ, 1620. 4°.

GUALTHERIUS. See Walther.

GUIDI, IGN. *Il battesimo di Costantino imperatore.* In Nuova Antologia, B. XLI. (1883), 41–52. Starts from Frothingham's work. Consult for list of authors who repeat the story. Mentions some who still believe in the fable.

GUSTA, FRANC. *Vita di Costantino il grande, 1° imperat. christiano.* Foligno, 1786; 2 v. 4°. ediz. 2, rev. ricorr. ed. accresc. 1790; ed. 3. 2 v. 320 and 282 pp. 8°. 1816. 2 v. 332 and 296 pp. 8°. In Zaccaria, *Raccolta di dissertazioni,* 13. (1795), 172–189.

HAENISIUS, GOTTLIEB. *Dissertatio de Constantino Magno non ex rationibus politicis christiano. Vulgo Ob Constantinus Magnus ohngeachtet seiner späten Tauffe, ein wahrer Christ zu nennen.* (Praes. Gott. Chr. Lentnerus.) 1714, Lipsiæ. p. 76. Usually referred to under Lentner, but B. M. correctly gives Haenisius (?)

HAKLUYT. *Voyages,* 2 (1810), 34–35. 1. The voyage of Helena. Latin and English. The author of Latin not given. He quotes as authorities, *Eusebius, Virumnius,* and *Ponticus.* 2. The voyage of Constantine the Great, emperor and king of Britaine, to Greece, Ægypt, Persia, and Asia, Anno 339. Latin and English. Rather phenomenal energy on the part of a man two years dead.

HALLERN (Heller?), GODOFREDUS (Vratisl.). *Disputatio theologica quanta de religione Constantini Magni. . . . Jodoci Kedii* . . . (Praes. And. Kunardo [19 Maji, A.O.K. MDLIIX.], Wittenbergæ [1658]. 4°, p. 123–172. Kunardus?)

HALLOIX, PETR. *Epistola de baptismo Constantini.* In Morin, *Antiq. eccl. orient.* (1682).

HARDUIN, J. *Chronologia sæculi Constantiniani ex solis numis antiquis.* In his *Op. sel.* p. 442–.

HARTMANN, J. A. *Dissertatio historica de Helena, Constantini Magni matre.* Marb. 1723. 4°.

HAUCK, A. *Zur donatio Constantini.* In Ztschr. f. kirchl. Wissensch. u. kirchl. Leben (1888), 201–207.

HEBENSTREIT, G. E. (= Hofmann, C. F.). *Histoire de Constantin le Grand.* Limoges, 1866. 12°. 148 pp..

HECKENHOEK, ADR. *Oratio in laudem Constantini Magni primi christianorum imperatoris.* (viii. Aprilis. MDCCXVI.), Dordrechti. (4) 23 pp.

HELMKE. *De Constantini Magni ita moribus et legibus penitus ex fontibus repetita disputatio.* Pars I, Progr.. Stargard, 1827. 4°.

HESSE, JOANN. CHRISTIANUS. *Dissertatio Historico-Pragmatica qua Constantinum Magnum ex rationibus politicis Christianum.* (Præs. B. G. Struvius) [" autor respondens," Hesse]. May, MDCCXIII. Jenæ, (4) 76 pp. *Not* Struve? Pref. is by Struve, to be sure, but seems to be congratulatory letter to Hesse on his work? But Haenisius(?) (1714), the following year, ascribes to Struve.

HEUMANN, CHPH. A. *De cruce cœlesti a Constantino Magno conspecta.* In his *Poecile*, 2. 50–.

HEYDENREICH, EDUARD. *Ueber einen neu gefundenen Roman von der Jugendgeschichte Constantins des Grossen und von der Kaiserin Helena.* In Verhandll. d. Philologenversammlung in Trier, p. 177 ff.; Repr. in d. Berliner Zeitschr. f. d. Gymnasialwesen, 34 (1880), 271–.

——— ——— *Der libellus de Constantino Magno ejusque matre Helena und die übrigen Berichte über Constantins des Grossen Geburt und Jugend. Eine kritische Untersuchung von* . . . In Archiv für Litteraturgeschichte hrsg. Fr. Schnorr. Carolsfeld. X (1881), 319–363.

HILDEBRAND, JOACH. *Dissertatio de donatione Constantini Magni.* Helmstad, 1661, 4°; 1703; 1739; 1761. Altus or Hildebrand?

HOFMANN, CAR. FRID. ET HEBENSTREIT, GEO. ERN. *Disputatio Historico-Critica de Constantini Magni sepulchro.* Lipsiæ, 1759, 4°, 48 pp.

HOJER, J. C. *Quæ Constantino Magno favoris in Christian. fuerunt caussæ.* Jenæ, 1758, 16 pp.

HAUTE, THEODORUS VAN DER. *Oratio prior de Constantino Magno,* dicta a . . . Delfis. Apud Joannem Speyers, Bibliopolam, 1702, 14 pp. Spoken at the same time with Rouille's Oration. Cf. Rouille for estimate.

[HUG] *Denkschrift zur Ehrenrettung Constantin's des Grossen.* In Zeitschrift Geistlichkeit Erzbisth. Freiburg, III. Heft. (Freib. 1829.) 1–104. Treats various charges. The death of Crispus a plot of Fausta for the sake of her children, she causing it to seem to Constantine that Crispus and his nephew were plotting against the empire.

HUNCKLER. *Constantin le Grand et son règne.* Limoges, 1843 and 1846. 12°. ("1843, 12°; do. 1846, 12°.")

HYNITZSCH, ADOLF. *Die Taufe Constantins des Grossen nach Geschichte und Sage.* 1870. Progr. des Gymnasium in Stendel.

Incerti auctoris de Constantino Magno ejusque matre Helena libellus. E codicibus primus edidit Eduardus Heydenreich. Lips., Teubner, 1879. 12°. p. vii. [1], 30. See under *The Mythical Constantine.*

JACOBATIUS. *De concilio tractatus.* Romæ, 1538, lib. X. art. 8, p. 780–783. *De donatione Constantini.*

JACOBUS OF SARUG. *L' omilia di Giacomo di Sarúg sul Battesimo di Costantino imperatore,* trad. ed annot. da Arthur L. Frothingham, Jr. Roma, 1882. Fol. (From Reale Accad. dei Lincei. CCLXXIX [1881–82].) Consult for various sources and writers where story is found.

JACUTIUS, MATTH. *Syntagma quo ad parentis magno Constantino crucis historia complexa est universa.* . . . Romæ, 1755. 4°.

JANUS, JOH. W. *Schediasma historicum de patria Constantini Magni.* Witteb. 1716. 4°.

"JANUS." *Der Pabst und das Concil.* Leipzig, 1869. 8°, xix, 451 pp.

JEEP, LUDW. *Zur Gesch. Constantins.* Festschrift f. E. Curtius. (Berlin, 1884. 8°.) p. 79.

Journal des Sçavants. (1774), p. 451–459. Review and analysis of Du Voisin.

KAUFMANN, GEORG. *Eine neue Theorie über die Entstehung u. Tendenz der angeblichen Schenkung Constantins.* In Allgem. Zeitung (1884), 194–196, 211–212. Valuable. Weiland, p. 146–147.

KEDD, JOD. *Constantinus Magnus Romano-catholicus, ecclesia catholicus, s. Stephanus & primi Hungariæ reges Romano catholici* . . . Viennæ Austriæ, 1655. 4°, 145 pp.

KEIM. *Die röm Toleranz-Edickte.* In "Theol. Jahrb. 1852 II."

KEIM, THEODOR. *Der Uebertritt Constantins des Grossen zum Christenthum,* academ. Vortrag . . . Zürich, 1862, 8°. viij.–106 pp. "A Christian in its strict sense Constantine was certainly not, even up to the end of his life," and yet he was inwardly touched by Christianity.

KERI, FRANCISC. BORG. *Imperatores orientes* . . . *a Constantio Magno ad Constantini ultimum.* . . . Tyrnaviæ, 1774. Fol.

KIST, N. C. *De commutatione quam, Constantino auctore societas subiit christiana.* Trajecti ad Rh. 1818, 120 pp. 8°.

KORMART, CHRPH. *Dissertatio politica de Constantino Magno.* Lipsiæ, 1665. 4°.

KRUG. *Byz. Chron.* St. Petersb. 1810. 8°.

KRÜGER, G. *Zur Frage nach der Entstehungszeit der Konstantinschen Schenkung.* In Theol. Literaturzeitung, 14 (1889), 429-435, 455-460.

KUNADUS, AND. *Constantinus Magnus Evangelicus Constantino Romano-Catholico 'Jodoci Keddii 'Jesuitæ oppositus.* Ed. second, Witteb. 1666. 4°, p. (8) 224.

LANDUCCI. *Una celebre costituzione dell' imperatore Costantino, saggio esegetico.* Padova, 1886. 8°, 30 pp.

LANGEN, HENRICUS. *Constantinus Magnus Intentu Utriusque Maximiani, et Herculii et Galerii in regimine confirmatus.* (Præs. J. J. Weidner.) 8 Sept. 1703. Rostochii (p. 48). (By Langen, NOT *Weidner* ?)

LANGEN, J. *Entstehung und Tendenz der Konstantinischen Schenkungsurkunde.* In Sybel, Hist. Zeitschr. (1883), p. 413-435. "Erweitete Ausführung e. Aufsatze in deutschen Merkur, 1881, Nr. 34."

LANGEN. In *Geschichte d. römischen Kirche.* Bonn, 1885, p. 726-.

LA SALLE. In Biografia universale, XIII. (Venezia, 1823), 363-370.

LE BEAU. *Hist. du Bas-Emp. en commenç. a Constantin.* T. 1-21, Par. 1757-1781, Cont. par (H. P.) Ameiltron. T. 22-26, Par. 1781-1807. T. 271,2. do. 1811. 8° (28 vols.). Nouv. ed. ed. St. Martin. T. 1-13, Par. 1824-1832. Cont. Brosset, T. 14-21, Par. 1833-1836. 8°.

(LEFORT DE LA MORINIÈRE, ADRIEN CLAUDE.) *Histoire abrégée du règne de Constantin empereur d'Orient et d'Occident.* Par. 1756. 12°.

LENTNER, GOTTFR. CHRIST. *Dissertatio de Constantino Magno non ex rationibus politicis christiano.* 4°. Lipsiæ, 1714. Cf. note under Haenisius. Yet the author regards the *præses* of a preceding dissertation as author, and the *præses* here is printed in capitals, so *Lentner* is real author?

Life of Constantine the Great. In Christ. Rev. 4 (1839), 201.

Literary and Theological Review (1839), 541.

LUPI, ANT. MAR. *Theses historicæ, chronolog., crictica, philolog., &c., ad vitam s. Constantini Magni imper. aug.* Panormi, 1736. 4°.

—— —— *Dissertaz. lett. ed. alt. oper.* 1 (1785), 267-292, in Gori, Symbolæ litter. IX. (Florent. 1752), 133-176.

MABRUN. *Constantinus Magnus sive idolatria debellata.* Par. 1658. 4°. Latin poem.

MAMACHI, THOM. MAR. *De cruce Constantino visa & de evangelica chronotaxi.* Florentiæ, 1738. 8°.

MANSO, JOH. CASP. FRDR. *Leben Constantins des Grossen, nebst einigen Abhandlungen geschichtlichen Inhalts.* Breslau, 1817, 8°; Wien, 1819. 8°.

MARÇAY, DE. *Histoire de Constantin le Grand.* Limoges, 1873, 8°, 126 pp.

MARTENS. *Die falsche General-Konzession Konstantins.* München (Leipzig), 1889, 8°. Contains especially convenient reprint, with commentary.

——. *Die römische Frage unter Pipin und Karl dem Grossen*, p. 327 sq. Says donation arose after 800, in last years of Charlemagne or beginning of Louis. *Wieland*, p. 141.

——. *Die drei unechten Kapitel der Vita Hadrian.* In Tübingen Theol. Quartalschrift (1886), 601.

——. *Heinrich IV. und Gregor VII. nach der Schilderung von Ranke's Weltgeschichte.* Kritische Betrachtungen. Danzig, 1887.

MARTINI, E. D. A. *Ueber die Einführung der christlichen Religion als Staatsreligion im römischen Reiche durch den Kaiser Constantin.* München, 1813. 4°, 48 pp.

MAS, AUGUSTE. *L'empereur d'Arles.* In Mém, de l'acad. de Vaucluse, IV. (1885), 197-213. Rev. of Alex. Mouzin's "drama in verse." Treats early events. Very full description and analysis of poem.

Mercersburg Review, 12 (1850), 173.

MEYER, P. In Festschrift d. Gymn. Adolfinum zu Moers. Bonn, 1882. 4°. So noted; but the editor's copy of this Festschrift contains nothing by Meyer, while the separately printed *De Vita Constantini Eusebiana*, by Meyer, paged 23-28, which is at hand, has no indication of its origin and may be from Program.

MILLERUS, JOANN. MARTINUS. *De fide Constantini Magni haud dubie christiana.* Dissertatio (præs. Jo. Frickii) e fontibus genuinis . . . Ulmæ (1613), 4°, p. (4) 62. (*Not* Frick?)

MOLINET, CL. In Ephemer. erudit. Parisien. (1681), Eph. XI. Dissertatio de veritate Crucis a Constantino visæ ex numis antiquis confirmata.

MOLLER, DAN. GUIL. *Disputatio de labaro Constantiniano.* Altorf, 1696. 4°.

MONOD, PAUL. *La politique religieuse de Constantin.* Montaubon, 1886. 8°.

MORIN, JEAN. *Histoire de la délivrance de l'église chrétienne par l'empereur Constantin et de la grandeur et souveraineté temporelle donnée à l'église Romaine par les roys de France.* Par. 1630. Fol. A translation of Eusebius' Life of Constantine.

MOUZIN, ALEX. Cf. Mas, Aug., in Mém, acad. Vaucluse, 1885, IV. 197-213.

MÜHLBACHER, E. In Mitth. Inst. öster. Geschforsch (1881), 2. 115-116.

MÜNCH, ERNST. JOS. HERM. *Uber die Schenkung Constantin's, beitrag zur Literatur u. Kritik der Quellen des kanonischen Rechts u. der Kirchengeschichte.* Freiburg im Breisgau, 1824. 8°, 102 pp. Also in *Vermischte Schriften*, Ludwigsburg, 1828, p. 185-.

MUSSET, GEORGES. *Encore les statues équestres au portail des églises.* In Rev. Poitev. et Saint. (1886), 71–76. Thinks Arbellot has not solved the question.

NESTIUS, JACOB. *Apologia pro Constantino Magno.* In Miscell. Lipsien. nova (1716), II. 471–476.

NÈVE, FELIX. *Constantin et Théodose devant les églises orientales, étude tirée des sources grecques et arméniennes,* in Rev. catholiq. E. III. (1857), 356–364, 401–414, 507–521. Louvain, 1857. 8°.

NICOLAI, JOAN. *De Constantini baptismo, ubi, quando et a quo fuerit celebratus, historica dissertatio.* Paris, 1680. 12°, 266 pp. (1690, Vogt.)

OHNESORGE, W. *Der Anonymus Valesii de Constantino.* 1885. 8°, 112 pp. Reviewed at length by Fr. Görres, in Ztschr. f. wiss. Theol. 29 (1886), 504–512. It is, in fact, a most interesting and exhaustive study of the document.

ONGARONI, FRANC. *Dissertationes III. de moribus et religione Constantini Magni, de Juliani religione et gestis, deque templi Hierosolymitani instauratione ab eodem Juliano attentata et divinitus impedita.* Mediolani, 1778. 4°.

OORDT, J. W. G. VAN. *Constantijn de Groote en zijne voorgangers, eine studie over den Romeinschen keizertijde.* I Deel. Haarlem, 1868. 8°, x, 383 pp. This first part takes only to Antoninus Pius.

Origine della Donazione di Costantino secundo il Döllinger. In Civiltà cattolica, Ser. 5, v. 10 (1864), 303–330.

PAPEBROCHIUS. *Comment. histor.* In Acta s. s. Bolland. Maii V. (1685), 12–27 pl. Cf. Jun. p. 16–.

PENON. *Des monnaies de Constantin-le-Grand relatives à la Provence.* In Rep. trav. soc. statist. Marseille. 28 (1866), 176–182. Such as relate to coinage at Arles.

PFAHLER. Trad. fr. *Histoire de Constantin le Grand et de son siècle.* 1862. 8°, 202 pp.

(PILATI, C. ANT.) *Gesch. d. Veränderungen in d. Regierungu d. Gesetzen u. d. menschl. Geiste von Constantins Bekehrung an bis auf d. Untergang d. weström-Reichs.* A. d. Franz. Leipz. 1784.

PLATE, W. *Constantinus I.* In Smith, Dict. of Gr. and Rom. Biog. 1 (1859), 831–837.

POLUS, REGIN. . . . *De baptismo Constantini Magni imper.* . . . Romæ, Paul Manut, 1562, 4°; Dilingæ, 1562, 8°; Venet. 1563, 4°; Lovanii, 1567, fol.

Prologue and epilogue to the last new play, Constan the Great [by N. Lee]. s. e. (1683), one leaf, fol.

RALLAYE, LÉONCE DE LA. *De la donation de Constantin d'après le Dr. Doellinger* [i.e. *Papst leg.*]. In Le Monde (1864), Juillet, 3, p. 3–4; Juillet, 7, p. 3–4. Review, but has value of an original article. Origin in France.

La rappresentatione di Costantino imperatore et di San Silvestro Papa, et di Santa Elena Imperatrice. Stampata in Siena, con licenza de' superiori, et ristampata in Orvieto. [1550?? B. M. Catal.; Fierenze, 1562, 4°; do. 1588. 4°.]

Reign of Constantine the Great. In Dublin Rev. 1857. XLII. 490.

REISKIUS, JOANNES. (Program.) 1681. 4°.

REUMONT, ALFRED VON. *Constantin der Grosse.* In his Gesch. d. Stadt Rom, 1 (Berlin, 1867), B. 3, Abschn. 2 = p. 595–646. p. 859–860 has a *Chronological table* of reign of Constantine.

REVELLAT, J. P. *Notice sur une remarquable particularité que présente toute une série de milliaires de Constantin le Grand.* In Rev. archéolog. 1883, c. 11. 39–48, 69–78, 148–155; Par. 188–. 8°. Cf. Thédenat, H. in Bull. critiq. 1885, vi. 69–73. The name of Maximian removed.

RICHARDSON, SAMUEL. *The necessity of toleration in matters of religion . . . Here also is the copy of the Edict of the Emperors Constantine and Licinius.* Lond. 1647, p. (2) 21 (1). Edict, p. 1–3.

RICHTER, HEINRICH. *Das weströmische Reich.* Berlin, 1865. 8°, p. 31–101, "Die römischen Kaiser und die christliche Kirche von Diocletian bis zum Tode Constantins I."

ROMANE, ALFRED. *Essai sur Constantin et ses rapports avec l'église chrétienne.* Thèse présentée à la Faculté de théologie protestante de Strasbourg. Strasbourg, 1867. 8°, p. (2) 114. Study of relation of church and state in fourth century. Does not find one solitary evidence of regenerate life in Constantine. He had no religion but his policy.

ROSSIGNOL, JEAN. PIERRE. *Virgile et Constantin le Grand.* 1° p. Paris, 1845. 8°. Première partie, p. (2) xxxvi, 351 (1). Examines Eclogue of Virgil found in C.'s Oration and arrives at conclusion that "beyond a doubt" Constantine did not write the oration, but Eusebius "le coupable c'est Eusèbe."

ROUILLE, JOANNES LUDOVICUS DU. *Orat. posterior de Constantino Magno dicta . . .* III. Nonas. Februarii, No. c/ɔ, iocii. Delfis. . . . 4°, 14 pp. Brief, rhetorical, eulogistic, worthless.

ROYON, JAS. C. *Hist. du Bas-Empire depuis Constantin.* v. 1–4. Paris, xii–1803. 8°.

SAGITTARIUS, JOH. CHRISTFRIED. *Dissertatio histor. de Constantino Magno.* Jenæ, 1650. 4°.

SANDINUS, ANT. *Disput. histor.* (1742), 135–149.

ST. VICTOR, LÉONARD DE. *Fondation de Constantinople.* In Anal. Jur. Pontif. XII. (1873), col. 402–414.

——— ———. *Apparition de la croix à l'emper. Constantin.* In Anal. juris pontif. XII. (1873), 389–401. Moyen d'accorder Lactance avec Eusèbe. Written middle of last century; MSS. in Bibl. Nat.

SCHAFF, P. *Constantine the Great and the Downfall of Paganism in the Roman Empire.* In Biblioth. Sac. 1863; XX. 778. Review of Burckhardt, Keim, and Stanley's Eastern Church.

SCHEFFER-BOICHORST, P. *Neuere Forsuchungen über die konstantinische Schenkung.* In Mtthlgn. des Inst. f. oesterreich. Geschichtsforschg. 10 (1889), 302–325.

SCHELSTRATE, EMANUEL. *Antiq. illust. circa Concil Gen., etc., et præcipua tr. Hist. Eccles. Cog.* Antv. 1678, p. 11, diss III. c. VI. De baptismo Constantini num Romæ a S. Silvestro num Nicomediæ ab Eusebio collatus fuit, an potius et Romæ et Nicomediæ.

Die Schenkung Constantin's. Mainz, 1866. 8°. Translated from Civiltà Cattolica.

SCHMIDIUS, JO. ANDR. In hist. Ser. IV. fabulis Variorum, etc. Helmst. 1712. 4° (Conradus resp.).

SCHMIDT, O. *Zur Beurtheilung Constantins des Grossen.* Duisberg, 1863. 4°. Progr.

SCHOEPFLIN. *Constantinus Magnus non fuit britannus.* In Commentationes historicæ. Basil, 1741. 4°.

SCHROECKH, J. M. *Leben des Kaisers Constantin des Grossen.* In his Allgemeine Biographie. Cf. Num. 66.

SCHULTZE, VIKTOR. *Untersuchungen zur Geschichte Konstantin's des Gr.* In Ztschr. f. Kirchengeschichte, 7 (1885), 343–371; 8 (1886), 517–542. 1. Die römische Bildsäule mit dem Kreuze. 2. Die Tempelbauten in Konstantinopel. 3. Die Inschrift von Hispellum. 4. Konstantin und die Haruspicen. 5. Der Staat und das Osferwesen. 6. Der Untergang des Licinius.

SCHURZFLEISCH, CONR. SAM. *Quæ sit vera origo imperii Rom. christiani.* In his Controverss, XXXV.

——. *Dissertatio de primo christianorum imperatore.* Wittebergæ, 1679. 4°, 52 pp. (præs. M. Difenbach).

SCHWARZ. *Colleg. histor.* 8 (1737), 436–715.

SCULTETUS, ABRAH. *Confutatio Cæs. Baronii de baptismo Constantini Magni.* Neustadii, 1607. 4°.

SEEBERG. *Zur konstantinischen Schenkung.* In Theol. Literaturblatt, 1890, cols. 25–27, 33–36, 41–45. Rev. of Friedrich.

SEECK, OTTO. *Quellen und Urkunden über die Aufänge des Donatismus.* In Ztschr. f. Kirchenges. 10 (1889), 505–568. A very systematic and interesting examination of sources.

—— ——. *Die Verwandtenmorde Constantin's des Grossen.* In Zeitschr. f. Wiss. Theol. 33 (1890), 63–77. While disclaiming any attempt to whitewash Constantine, he finds his conduct not incompatible with being a good Christian.

SEVESTRE. *Dict. patrol.* I. (1861), 1137–1148.

SIMONIDES, CONSTANT. *Panegyric of that holy and apostolic heaven-crowned King Constantine the Great.* London, 1854. 8°.

SMITH, W. BROWNING. *Constantine.* In Enc. Brit. 6 (1878), 298–301.

SOLIKOV, I. I. Moscow, 1810. In Russian.

STAPFER, EDM. *Constantin I.* In Lichtenberger, Encycl. des. sciences rel. 3 (1878), 388–393.

STEUCHUS, AUGUST. Contra Laurent Valla. *De falsa donatione Constantini . . .* Lugduni Bat. 1545, 8°; 1547, 4°.

STRESO, J. A. *Konstantijn de Groote en Karel de Groote.* Arnhem, 1836. 8°.

STRUVE, BERN. GOTTH. *Bibl. hist.* V. (1790), I, 178–207.

—— ——. *Dissertatio de Constantino Magno ex rationibus politicis christiano.* Jenæ, 1713. 4°. See HESSE.

SUCHIER. *Disputationis de Zosimi et Eusebii, historiarum scriptorum in Constantini Magni imperatoris rebus exponendis fide et auctoritate, part I.* Hersfeld, 1856. 4°. 25 pp. Gymn. Progr.

——. *Qualem Eusebius Constantinum Magnum imperatorem adumbraverat, paucis exponitur.* Hersfeld, 1857. 4°, 36 pp.

SUHR, BALTHUS. JOACHIM. *Constantini Magni signo crucis Christi in nubibus viso, ad Christianismum inauguratus* (præs. J. J. Weidner). Rostochii, 1703. (Suhr, *not* Weidner?)

TACUT, GULIELMUS. *Oratio in Donationem Constantini Magni nomine falso jactatam.* Delphis, 1726. 4°. Do. Rom. 1755. No use.

TENTZEL, GUIL. ERN. *Examen fabulæ Romanæ de duplici baptismo Constantini Magni.* Witteberge, 1683. 4°.

THIELMANN. *Ueber Sprache und Kritik des libellus de Constantino Magno ejusque matre Helena.* In Blätter f. d. bayerische Gymnasialwesen, 16 (1880), 124–

THIERRY, AMADÉE. *Constantin en Gaule.* In Acad. d. sciences mor. et polit., 9 (1846), 349–364. Pleasantly written resumé of the period, with not very exact characterization of Constantine in very attractive style.

—— ——. XI. (1847), 374–387. *Fragment d'histoire sur la politique chrétienne de Constantin.* Takes the heathen side. Neat rhetorically.

THOMASIUS, CHRIST. *De fide scriptorum Constantini Magni.* In Observatt Hallens. XXII. 1. Treats especially Zosimus. Cf. Vogt. p. 15–16.

—— ——. *In fabulas de parentibus Constantini Magni.* In Obs. Hall. T. 1, n. 23, p. 377–388.

TILLEMONT. *Histoire des empereurs,* 4 (1697), 76–381, 613–664.

TIRABOSCHI. *Stor. lett. Ital.* II. (1806), 373–377, 457.

TOBLER, ADOLF. *Kaiser Constantinus als betrogner Ehemann.* In Jahrb. Roman. Engl. Lit. 13 (= N.F.I.) (1874), 104–108. Various allusions in old French poetry.

TODERINI, GIAMBATT. *La Costantiniana apparizione della croce difesa contro . . . G. A. Fabrico.* Venezia, 1773. 4°.

TRESCHO, LEB. F. *Beitr. üb. einige Vorwürfe wider d. Ksr. Constantin d. Gr.* In his Brr. üb. d. neueste theol. Literat. II. 360–.

UNGER, FRIEDRICH WILHELM. *Die Bauten Constantin's des Grossen am heiligen Grabe zu Jerusalem.* Göttingen, 1866. 8°. iv, 128 pp. Abdruck aus Benfey, Th., Orient. u. Occid. II. 177–232, 385–466. He thinks to demonstrate that a part of the *Haram* in Jerusalem has indisputable evidences of Constantinian origin. He seems to build dangerously much on Fergusson (Lond. 1847).

VALENTINI. *Il codice di Eusebio della Biblioteca Queriniana di Brescia illustrato.* In Commentari dell' Ateneo di Brescia, 1885, p. 20–32 (?).

VALLA, LAURENTIUS. *De falso credita et ementita donatione Constantini.* For various editions, see Graesse, vol. 6. 2, p. 249, and the Étude of Bonneau. The edition of 1520 is usually cited as princeps, for the first edition was published clandestinely by Ulrich von Hutten in 1517. A convenient one is that with translation by Bonneau, Paris, 1879. It was written in the middle of the fifteenth century, and for venturing to deny the authority of the Donation, the author was obliged to flee in disguise from Rome.

VARENNE, BERNARD DE. *Histoire de Constantin le Grand, 1er empereur chrétien.* Par. 1728. 4°.

VALOIS, CHARLES DE. *Discours dans lequel on prétend faire voir que les médailles qui portent pour légende : F. Cl. Constantinus Jun N. C. n'apartiennent point à Constantin le jeune fils de Constantin le Grand.* In Soc. trav. Acad. inscr. et belles let. 4°. V. 3. Maintains that all such medals belong to a brother of Constantine, and not to his son.

VEDELIUS, NICOLAUS. *De episcopatu Constantini Magni seu de potestate magistratuum Reformatorum circa res Ecclesiasticas dissertatio.* Repetita cum responsione ad interrogata quædam. Franekenæ, Apud Uldericum Balck, 1642. p. (48) 143. Nature indicated by sub-title. Takes as text Constantine's remark that he, too, was a bishop. (V. c. 4, 24.)

VINCENTIUS BELVACENSIS. *Spec. hist.* XIV. 1, 43–44, 47–58, 102.

VISCONTI. *Sopra la cristianità di Costantino Magno, dimonstrata co monumenti e con le medaglie. . . .* In Atti Accad. Rom. Archeol. VI. (1835), 207–228. "Sopra il nimbo usato ne' ritiatti di esso imperatore."

VOGT, JOH. *Historia litteraria Constantini Magni, plus centum et quinquaginta rerum Constantinianarum Scriptores sistens.* Hamburgi, Apud Viduam B. Schilleri & J. C. Kisnerum, 1720. Compare for older literature on Constantine. There is long account of literature by topics.

VOIGT, GOTTFR. *Vita Constantini Magni disputatione historica descripta.* Rostochii, 1675. 4°.

VOIGT, MORITZ. *Drei epigraphische Constitutionen Constantin's des Grossen und ein epigraphisches Rescript des præf. Præt. Ablavius. . . .* Leipzig, 1860. 8°. ix. (1) 242. The documents occupy to p. 42. The remainder of the work taken up with an essay on the Pagi and Vici of the Roman Empire.

WALCH, CHR. GUIL. FRANC. *De τοις εισω της εκκλησιας et τοις εκτος Constantini Magni Commentatio.* D. II. August, MCCDLXXXIII. lecta. In Comment. Soc. Reg. Sci. Gotting. vi. 2, 1783–84 (Got. 1785), 81–106. Separate title-page to part 2, dated 1784. Is a discussion of Constantin's famous saying. Gives *passim* many references to writers who have discussed the question.

WALTHER, BALTHAS. *Diatribe elenchetica de imperatoris Constantini Magni baptismo, donatione et legatione ad concilium Nicænum.* Jenæ, 1816. 12°.

WEGNERUS, JOH. ERNESTUS. *Constantinus Magnus Imperator, Maximorum postulatus criminum, sed potiori parte absolutus ex Judiciali Gen.* (Præs. Georgi Casp. Kirchmaieri.) Wittenbergæ, 1698, 16 pp. Note title.

WEIDNER, JOHAN. JOACH. (resp. Johannes Goethe). *Dissertatio historica de Constantino Magno qua illum honeste & ex legitimo matrimonio natum contra G. Arnoldum vindicatur ac defenditur.* Rostochii, 1702. 4°, p. (2) 34. Weidner is *præses*. The dedication is by Goethe to his father, and Goethe is called author by the British Museum Catalogue.

—— ——. *Constantinus Magnus superatis juventæ discriminibus legitimus tandem patris Constantii successor.* 1702; ib. 1703, p. (4) 40. Accorded to Weidner by *Vogt.* "Burck" is respondant, and seems by preface to be author, but ?

—— ——. *Dissertatio de Constantino Magno Signo crucis Christi in nubibus viso ad Christianismum inaugurato.* ib. 1703. 4°.

WEILAND, L. *Die constantinische Schenkung.* In Ztschr. f. Kirchenrecht, 22₁ (1887), 137–160; 22₂ (1888), 185–210. Origin was between 813 and 875 and was by contemporary of Hadrian I.

WERNSDORF, JO. CHR. *D. de visu Constantini Magni locus Eumenii Rhetoris capite xxi. Panegyrici Constantini dictus explicatus.* In Stosch. Ferd., Museum Crit. II II. (Lemgoviae, 1778), 131–187. Shows that the "appearance related by Eumenius (as taking place in Gaul) is the same as that referred to by Eusebius."

WERNSDORF, E. F. *De Constantini Magni religione Paschali ad Euseb. de vita Const. M. b. iv. c. 22.* Wittebergæ, 1758. 4°, pp. 24. Constantine's piety exemplified in his paschal observance.

WERVEKE, N. VAN. *Trouvaille d'Ermsdorf. Médailles romaines de l'époque de Constantin.* p. 440–498.

Descriptive catalogue of coins and medals found at Emsdorf in 1880, intermingled with discussion. Large number. Interesting. Also something "In Public. hist. Instit. Luxembourg (1881–1882), XXXV. 450–476"?

WESSELOFSKY, ALEX. *Le dit de l'empereur Constant.* In Romania, 6 (Paris, 1877), 161–198 (cf. G. Paris, 588–596), VII. 331. Poem from MS. in Copenhagen. Records three redactions of the story.

WESTPHALEN, COMTE DE. *La date de l'avènement au trône de Constantin le Grand, d'après Eusèbe et les médailles.* In Revue numismatique (1877), 26–42.

WEYTINGH, JOANNES HENRICUS ARNOLDUS. *Disquisitio historica de Constantino Magno.* Daventriæ, 1826. 8°. (4) 74 (2). Treats: 1. State of empire to death of Augustus; 2. State of empire to death of Constantius Chlorus; 3. Constantine and his acts; 4. Critical estimate of Constantine.

WITHOF, FRID. THEOD. *Dissertatio histor. de ficta Constantini Magni lepra.* Lingen, 1767. 4°.

WOLFF, JOH. CHRTPH. *Disputatio de visione crucis Constantino Magno in cælo oblatæ.* Witteb. 1706. 4°. " 1707" (*Danz*); "also in *Oeirichs* German liter. opusce, II. 303–" (*Danz*).

WOLTERECK, CHR. *Exercitatio critica qua disputatur crucem quam in cælis vidisse se juravit Constantinus Magnus Imperator, fuisse naturalem, in Halone Solari.* (Praes. J. A. Fabricius.) Hamburgi, 1706, pp. 32 and plate. (*Not* Fabricus?)

WORDSWORTH. *Constantine the Great and his sons: Constantinus I.* In Smith & Wace. *Dict.* I (1877), 624–649. Treats Authorities, Life, in three periods, Legislation and Policy, Character and Writings, Vision of the Cross, and Coins.

ZAHN, THDR. *Constantin der Grosse und die Kirche.* Hannover, 1876. Gr. 8°, 35 pp.

ZEUMER, K. *Der älteste Text des Constitutum Constantini.* Berlin, 1888. In Festgabe für Gneist.

NOTE 1. — The number of works which have suggested themselves as really necessary to complete a working list for the student of Constantine is very great. Some works like HEFELE'S *Conciliengeschichte* seem indispensable, others like HARNACK'S article in Herzog, *Encykl.* on the *Konstantinopolitanisches Symbol* have a very important correlative bearing, and ought really to be especially mentioned because the general student would not readily find them out. Several works on the historical value of Eusebius' Life of Constantine, also should really have been inserted. The latest of these is :

CRIVELLUCCI, A. *Della fede storica di Eusebio nella vita di Costantino:* appendice al volume I. della Storia delle relazioni tra lo stato e la chiesa. Livorno, tip. di Raffaelo Giusti edit. 1888. 8°, 145 pp. Reviewed in Nuova Antologia, Ser. 3, vol. 21, 1 Maggio, 1889; by F. Görres, in Ztschr. f. wiss. Theol. 33. 1 (1890); by V. Schultze, Theol. Litbl. (1889), Nos. 9, 10. Says that the life of Constantine is no better than an historical novel.

For farther literature on special points compare references in the notes.

NOTE 2. — The attempt to secure accuracy in the above list has proved one of great difficulty. All references could not be verified, and as "conjectural emendation" is even more dangerous in bibliography than in textual criticism, readings have not generally been changed excepting on what seemed actual evidence. The only way to avoid laying oneself open to criticism in making a bibliography is not to make it. The editor can only say for this that a great deal of pains has been expended on improving accuracy as well as in gathering titles and annotating. The difficulty is shown in the fact that the work quoted on the double authority of Oettinger and of Chevalier as by Janus, proves on securing the work itself, after the list is in plate, to be really by Vogt and dedicated to Janus.

II.—SPECIAL PROLEGOMENA.

§ 1. THE LIFE OF CONSTANTINE.

1. Editions.

THE Life is found in the editions of Eusebius (compare list in Dr. McGiffert's Prolegomena) of 1544 (p. 117ᵃ-), 1612 (p. 301-), 1659, 1672, 1678, 1720 (p. 583-) and 1822 at least. The edition of Heinichen first published in 1830 (p. 1-332, 333-406, 407-500) and republished in 1869 : *Eusebius Pamphili Vita Constantini et Panegyricus atque Constantini ad sanctorum Coetum oratio. Recensuit cum annotatione critica atque indicibus denuo edidit . . . Lipsiæ, Hermann Mendelssohn, 1869.* 8° is the latest and best.

2. Translations.

The editions of *Latin* translations are very numerous. Basil. 1549, Portesius (V. C. 650-698, O. C. 698-715, no L. C.) ; Basil, 1557, Musculus (V. C. 158-215, O. C. 217-231, no L. C.) ; Basil, 1559 (V. C. 650-698, O. C. 698-715) ; Par. 1562, Musculus (V. C. 160-218, O. C. 218-234) ; Antv. 1568 (?), Christophorson (V. C. 224-306ᵃ, O. C. 306ᵇ-326ᵃ, L. C. 326ᵇ-361) ; Basil, 1570, Portesius (V. C. 862-914, O. C. 915-932) and Christophorson (L. C. 932-971) ; Paris, 1571, Christophorson (258-341, 341-362, 362-397) ; Basil, 1579, Portesius (V. C. 862-914, O. C. 915-932), and Christophorson (L. C. 923-971) ; Paris, 1581 (V. C. p. 214-297, O. C. 297-317, L. C. 317-355) ; Colon. 1581, Christophorson (V. C. 195-268, O. C. 269-286, L. C. 287-317) ; "1591 (Grynæus)" ; Basil, 1611 (Grynæus), Christophorson (V. C. 118-170, O. C. 171-184, no L. C.) ; Paris, 1677, Valesius (V. C. 164-232, O. C. 233-248 ; L. C. 249-275) ; Frf. ad M. 1695, Valesius (328-465, 466-497, 498-549) ; Cambr. 1720 (Reading) Valesius ; Cambr. 1746 (Reading) Valesius ; 1822 (Zimmermann), Valesius (772-1046, 1047-1117, 1118-1232) ; Par. 1842 (Cailleau). The editions of 1612, 1659, and 1672 at least also have Latin translations. There is a *French* translation by J. Morin, *Histoire de la délivrance de l'Église, &c., Par. 1630,* fol., and another by Cousin, *Par. 1675,* 4°, and *1686,* 4°. There is a *German* translation by Stroth, Quedlinb. 1799, v. 2, p. 141-468, and one by Molzberger. Kempten, 1880. For English translations, see the following paragraph.

3. English translations.

The first English translation of Eusebius was by Merideth Hanmer (compare Prolegomena of Dr. McGiffert). The first editions of Hanmer did not contain the Life of Constantine. It is a little hard to distinguish the early editions, but there were at least three, and perhaps four, editions (1577 (76), 1585 (84), 1607, 1619 ?), before there was added in 1637 to the 1636 edition ("fourth edition" not "fifth edition 1650," as Wood, *Athenæ Oxon.*), a translation by Wye Saltonstall as follows :

Eusebius | *His life of Constantine,* | *in foure* | *bookes.* | *With Constantine's Oration to the Clergie* | *. . .* | *London.* | *Printed by Thomas Cotes, for Michael Sparke, and are to be* | *sold at the blue Bible in greene Arbour* | *1637 ;* fol. pp. (2) 1-106 (E), 107-132 (C), 133-163(4) (L. C.). The dedication by the "translator" is signed *Wye Saltonstall.* This was reprinted : *London.*

Printed by Abraham Miller, dwelling in Black Friers, 1649. fol., and is probably the same as that quoted often (e.g. Hoffmann) as 1650. The Life occupies p. 1–74. It was again reprinted, *London, 1656,* fol., it is said, revised and enlarged. The former editions having become exhausted, it was proposed to re-edit and republish Hanmer's (Saltonstall's) version, but the editor found it " a work of far greater labor to bring *Dr. Hanmer's Translation* to an agreement with the *Greek Text* of *Valesius' Edition,* than to make a *New One,*" which latter thing he accordingly did and did well. It was published in 1682, with the following title :

The | *Life* | of | *Constantine* | *in four books,* | *Written in Greek, by Eusebius Pamphilus, Bishop of Cæsarea in* | *Palestine; done into English from that edition set forth by* | *Valesius, and Printed at Paris in the Year 1659.* | *Together with* | *Valesius's Annotations on the said Life, which are made* | *English, and set at their proper places in the margin.* | *Hereto is also annext the Emperour Constantine's Oration to the* | *Convention of the Saints, and Eusebius Pamphilus's Speech concerning the praises of Constantine,* | *spoken at his tricennalia.* | *Cambridge,* | *Printed by John Hayes, Printer to the University, 1682,* fol. This was published with the 1683 edition of the History, and so is properly 1683 in spite of title-page. In 1692 this was reprinted with new general title-page, but otherwise identically the same edition with same sub-titles and same paging. In 1709 a new edition was published, also with the History, having substantially the same matter on the title-page but *The second edition. London. Printed for N. and J. Churchill, in the Year 1709.* In this paging is the same (527–633), but there is preliminary matter added before the History. This version is said by Crusé (compare also Dr. McGiffert's Prolegomena) to be by T. Shorting. Whoever it was by, it was well done and most interesting. In the course of time, however, it became antiquated in form, and there was added in 1845 to the Bagster edition of the ecclesiastical historians an anonymous translation :

The | *Life* | of | *the Blessed Emperor* | *Constantine,* | *in four books.* | *From 306–337 A.D.* | *By* | *Eusebius Pamphilus* | *...* | *London :* | *Samuel Bagster and Sons ;* | *...* | *MDCCCXLV.* 8°. p. xx, 380. This translation is in somewhat inflated style, which perhaps represents Eusebius and Constantine better than a simpler one, but which sometimes out-Herods Herod, as, e.g. in the oration of Constantine, p. 279, where it takes fourteen English words to express seven Greek ones, " Far otherwise has it been during the corrupt and lawless period of human life " for " It was not thus in lawless times." A quotation from Matthew (xxvi. 52) on p. 267 takes eight words in the original, twelve in the 1881 Revised Version, sixteen in the phrase of Constantine, and twenty-two in this translation. The translation is made from the edition of Valesius, not the first of Heinichen, as appears from the division of Bk. 1, chap. 10, and similar peculiarities. The present edition (1890) is a revision of the translation of 1845 founded on the edition of Heinichen.

4. *Author and date.*

Almost no fact of history is unquestioned ; therefore the unquestionable authorship of Eusebius has been questioned. Some have made the author Macarius (compare Vogt. Hist. lit. p. 12), evidently on the ground of the letter (3. 52) which the author says was addressed to himself, but which is to Macarius and others, but there is no real doubt of the Eusebian authorship. It was written after the death of Constantine (337), and therefore between 337 and 340, when Eusebius died. The interesting hypothesis of Meyer (p. 28) that it was perhaps written mainly in Constantine's lifetime, at the suggestion and under the direction of Constantine, to defend him against charges brought, or which might be brought, against him, is worth mentioning, although it is more ingenious than probable. The headings of the chapters are by another, though probably not much later, and a competent hand (cf. Lightfoot).

5. *Trustworthiness of Eusebius.*

The value of a writer is determined by (1) His sources of knowledge, (2) His own intellectual and moral ability. Again, the criticism of a given work seeks whether the aim proposed for that work has been truly fulfilled.   A man who attempts a treatise on Geometry is not to be criticised because he omits mention of sulphuric acid, or if he purposes a description of Wagner's music, because he does not produce a Helmholtz on Sound.   The application of these principles to Eusebius' Life of Constantine requires brief examination of 1. The proposed scope of the work.   2. The character of the sources.   3. The intellectual and moral competency of Eusebius in the premises.

(1) *The Scope of the Work.*   This is quite definitely outlined (1. 11).   In contrast with those who have recorded the evil deeds of other emperors and thus have "become to those who by some favor had been kept apart from evil, teachers not of good, but of what should be silenced in oblivion and darkness," he proposes to record the noble actions of this emperor.   He proposes, however, to pass over many things, — his wars, personal bravery, victories, and successes, his legislative acts, and many other things, and confine himself to such things as have reference to his religious character.   His aim, therefore, is distinctly limited to his religious acts, and it is not stretching his meaning too far to say, expressly limited to his virtuous actions.

(2) *Character of the Sources.*   The advantages which Eusebius had for knowing of the life of Constantine, especially of his religious acts, could hardly be surpassed.   He lived in the midst of the events which he records, was personal friend of the emperor, received letters from him directly, and had every opportunity to gather the other letters and documents which form so large a part of his history (cf. *V. C.* 1. 10).

(3) *Competency of Eusebius.*   Respecting this there is endless controversy.   The fullness of material is unquestionable, the intellectual competency of Eusebius is almost equally so, and the questionings regard mainly whether the author has made a proper use of material.   Opinions are various, but this does not mean that they are equally well grounded and valuable.   Some of the latest judgments are the most severe.   Crivellucci (Livorno, 1888) calls it an historical novel, and Görres, in a review of Crivellucci, agrees that it is worth less than the Panegyrics of Eumenius and Nazarius, which is certainly milder than Manso's (p. 222) "more shameless and lying" than these.   Right or wrong, this is a frequently repeated view.   Some (Hely, p. 141) cannot speak too strongly of the "contempt" which he "deserves," and accuse of "pious fraud" or the next thing to it (Kestner, 1816, p. 67).   For farther criticisms consult the works cited by Dr. McGiffert under *Literature*, and the special works on Eusebius cited in the *Literature* to Constantine above, *passim*.   The criticisms group generally around 1. The suppression of the facts respecting the deaths of Crispus, &c., and various others derogatory to Constantine.   2. The eulogistic tone and coloring of the work, especially the very pietistic saintly sort of flavor given to Constantine.

As to the suppression of facts, note (1) That he gives entire warning of his plan.   It would have been artistically and ethically improper, in a work which distinctly sets out with such purpose, to admit that class of facts.   It takes more or less from the value of the work, but it does not reflect on the general trustworthiness of what is said.   (2) No similar judgment is passed on Eutropius, the Victors, Anonymous Valesianus or Zosimus, for not mentioning his pious acts.   (3) A comparison of most biographies of living or recently dead presidents, kings, and emperors will be greatly to the advantage, even, of this fourth century eulogist over those of our boasted critical age.

As to eulogistic and exaggerated tone, observe (1) That it was more or less justified.   That is, the premises of the criticism which are substantially that Constantine was not saintly or pietistic and was non-committal toward Christianity, are false.   His extreme testimony is backed by very general testimony in the election of Constantine to technical saintship.   (2) That it compares well with modern eulogists and extremely well with the contemporary Panegyrists of Constantine.   (3) That Eusebius takes care frequently to guard his statements by quoting his source, as in the matter of the vision of the cross, or by ascribing to hearsay.

In general, the work stands very much on the same level as the biographies of generals in the late civil war, or of presidents, written by admiring members of their staffs or cabinets, incorporating authentic documents, intending to be truthful, and generally succeeding, but yet full of the enthusiasm of admiring friendship and inclined not to see, or to extenuate or even suppress, faults and mistakes. Nevertheless, they are valuable on the positive side as the real testimony to genuinely believed excellency by those in the position to know intimately. Eusebius is, substantially, genuine. Such supreme hypocrisy as would produce this work, without admiring respect and *after its subject was dead*, is inconceivable in him. All the unconscious turns of phrase show at least a consistent attitude of mind. The work is, in brief, by a competent author, from ample sources and without intentional falsification or misrepresentation. It probably represents the current Christian view of the man as accurately and honestly as any biography of Lincoln or the Emperor William written within a year or two of their deaths has done. As we now think of these two men whom doubtless inquisitive criticism might find to have faults, so the Christians in general and his friend Eusebius in particular probably thought of the Great Emperor. Compare discussion and literature of the trustworthiness of Eusebius as a historical writer in the Prolegomena of Dr. McGiffert in this volume.

6. *Value of the work.*

That the work on any basis but the untenable one of out-and-out forgery should be characterized as "worthless" or "a mere romance" or "of less value than the heathen panegyrists" is a curious bit of psychological performance, for it does precisely what it grounds its contempt for Eusebius on, — suppresses and exaggerates. Taking the minimum residuum of the most penetrating criticism, and the work is yet a source of primary value for understanding the man Constantine. This residuum includes (1) The documents which the work contains. These amount at the very least estimate to more than one-fourth of the whole matter, and the appended oration of Constantine is nearly as much more. (2) Many facts and details where there could be no possibility of motive for falsifying. (3) Much which critical care can draw out of the over-statements of eulogy.

§ 2. ORATION OF CONSTANTINE.

The *Editions* and *Translations* of this work are substantially identical with those of the Life. See above, under *Life*. The *Authenticity* of the work has been doubted, and its composition ascribed to Eusebius or some other Christian writer, but without sufficient reason. It was appended by Eusebius to his Life of Constantine as specimens of the latter's style (cf. *V. C.* 4. 32). As such it shows a man of some learning, though learning taken at second hand, it is thought, from Lactantius and others (cf. Wordsworth's Constantine I.). It was composed in Latin, and translated into Greek by the special officials appointed for such work (*V. C.* 4. 32). It was delivered on Good Friday, but in what year or where is not known. It has been placed before the year 324 (Ceiller, 130), but the mention of events and the character of the work itself suggest a considerably later date.

§ 3. ORATION OF EUSEBIUS.

The *Editions* and *Translations* are substantially as those of the Life, above, but some of the earlier ones do not contain this work. It was delivered in the year 336 (or possibly 335) at Constantinople, in celebration of the thirtieth anniversary of Constantine's accession, Constantine himself being present (cf. *V. C.* 4. 46 and O. C. 1). It gave the emperor lively satisfaction, from which one may safely infer a peculiar taste for combined panegyric and philosophical theology unless the hypothesis of a double work be true. According to this hypothesis the work consists of two separate orations, spoken perhaps at different times, the first including chapters 1–10, which are panegyrical in character, and the other chapters 11–18, which are theological (compare Lightfoot, Eusebius, p. 343 ; also McGiffert, Prolegomena, p. 43). It is like the oration of Constantine, a proper part of the Life of Constantine being appended according to his promise in Bk. 4, ch. 46.

The special points relating to these works are treated in the notes.

CONSTANTINE.

THE TABLE OF CONTENTS.

THE LIFE OF CONSTANTINE.

BOOK I.

BOOK II.

BOOK III.

BOOK IV.

THE ORATION OF CONSTANTINE.

THE ORATION OF EUSEBIUS.

THE LIFE

OF THE

BLESSED EMPEROR CONSTANTINE,

BY

EUSEBIUS PAMPHILUS.

—◦◦◦—

BOOK I.

CHAPTER I.

Preface. — Of the Death of Constantine.

ALREADY[1] have all mankind united in celebrating with joyous festivities the completion of the second and third decennial period of this great emperor's reign; already have we ourselves received him as a triumphant conqueror in the assembly of God's ministers, and greeted him with the due meed of praise on the twentieth anniversary of his reign:[2] and still more recently we have woven, as it were, garlands of words, wherewith we encircled his sacred head in his own palace on his thirtieth anniversary.[3]

But now, while I desire[4] to give utterance to some of the customary sentiments, I stand perplexed and doubtful which way to turn, being wholly lost in wonder at the extraordinary spectacle before me. For to whatever quarter I direct my view, whether to the east, or to the west, or over the whole world, or toward heaven itself, everywhere and always I see the blessed one yet administering the self-same empire. On earth I behold his sons, like some new reflectors of his brightness, diffusing everywhere the luster of their father's character,[5] and himself still living and powerful, and governing all the affairs of men more completely than ever before, being multiplied in the succession of his children. They had indeed had previously the dignity of Cæsars;[6] but now, being invested with his very self, and graced by his accomplishments, for the excellence of their piety they are proclaimed by the titles of Sovereign, Augustus, Worshipful, and Emperor.

CHAPTER II.

The Preface continued.

AND I am indeed amazed, when I consider that he who was but lately visible and present with us in his mortal body, is still, even after death, when the natural thought disclaims everything superfluous as unsuitable, most marvelously endowed with the same imperial dwellings, and honors, and praises as heretofore.[1] But farther,

---

[1] Literally " recently " or " not long since," and so it is rendered by Tr. 1709, Stroth, Molzberger, Valesius (" nuper "), and Portesius. Christophorson and Cousin avoid the awkwardness by circumlocution or simple omission, while our translator shows his one characteristic excellence of hitting nearly the unliteral meaning in a way which is hard to improve.

[2] The assembly referred to was the Council of Nicæa. Constantine's vicennial celebration was held at Nicomedia during the session of the Council at Nicæa (July 25), according to Hieronymus and others, but celebrated again at Rome the following year. The speech of Eusebius on this occasion is not preserved. Valesius thinks the one spoken of in the *V. C.* 3. 11, as delivered in the presence of the council, is the one referred to.

[3] This oration is the one appended by Eusebius to this *Life of Constantine*, and given in this translation (cf. *V. C.* 4. 46).

[4] [In the text it is ὁ λόγος, " my power of speech, or of description, much desires," and so throughout this preface: but this kind of personification seems scarcely suited to the English idiom. — *Bag.*] This usage of Logos is most interesting. Both he and his 'friend, the emperor, are fond of dwelling on the circles of philosophical thought which center about the word Logos (cf. the Oration of Constantine, and especially the Vicennial Oration of Eusebius). " My Logos desires " seems to take the place in ancient philosophical slang which " personality " or " self " does in modern. In ancient usage the word includes " both the ratio and the oratio " (Liddell and Scott), both the thought and its expression, both reasoning and saying, — the " internal " and " expressed " of the Stoics, followed by Philo and early Christian theology. He seems to use it in the combined sense, and it makes a pretty good equivalent for " personality," " my personality desires," &c. The idiom is kept up through the chapter.

[5] Constantine II., Constantius, and Constans proved on the whole sorry reflectors of glory.

[6] The first had been Cæsar more than twenty years; the second, ten; and the third, less than five.

[1] Referring to special honors paid after death, as mentioned in Bk. 4.

when I raise my thoughts even to the arch of heaven, and there contemplate his thrice-blessed soul in communion with God himself, freed from every mortal and earthly vesture, and shining in a refulgent robe of light, and when I perceive that it is no more connected with the fleeting periods and occupations of mortal life, but honored with an ever-blooming crown, and an immortality of endless and blessed existence, I stand as it were without power of speech or thought[2] and unable to utter a single phrase, but condemning my own weakness, and imposing silence on myself, I resign the task of speaking his praises worthily to one who is better able, even to him who, being the immortal God and veritable Word, alone has power to confirm his own sayings.[3]

CHAPTER III.

How God honors Pious Princes, but destroys Tyrants.

HAVING given assurance that those who glorify and honor him will meet with an abundant recompense at his hands, while those who set themselves against him as enemies and adversaries will compass the ruin of their own souls, he has already established the truth of these his own declarations, having shown on the one hand the fearful end of those tyrants who denied and opposed him,[1] and at the same time having made it manifest that even the death of his servant, as well as his life, is worthy of admiration and praise, and justly claims the memorial, not merely of perishable, but of immortal monuments.

Mankind, devising some consolation for the frail and precarious duration of human life, have thought by the erection of monuments to glorify the memories of their ancestors with immortal honors. Some have employed the vivid delineations and colors of painting[2]; some have carved statues from lifeless blocks of wood; while others, by engraving their inscriptions deep on tablets[3] and monuments, have thought

to transmit the virtues of those whom they honored to perpetual remembrance. All these indeed are perishable, and consumed by the lapse of time, being representations of the corruptible body, and not expressing the image of the immortal soul. And yet these seemed sufficient to those who had no well-grounded hope of happiness after the termination of this mortal life. But God, that God, I say, who is the common Saviour of all, having treasured up with himself, for those who love godliness, greater blessings than human thought has conceived, gives the earnest and first-fruits of future rewards even here, assuring in some sort immortal hopes to mortal eyes. The ancient oracles of the prophets, delivered to us in the Scripture, declare this; the lives of pious men, who shone in old time with every virtue, bear witness to posterity of the same; and our own days prove it to be true, wherein CONSTANTINE, who alone of all that ever wielded the Roman power was the friend of God the Sovereign of all, has appeared to all mankind so clear an example of a godly life.

CHAPTER IV.

That God honored Constantine.

AND God himself, whom Constantine worshiped, has confirmed this truth by the clearest manifestations of his will, being present to aid him[1] at the commencement, during the course, and at the end of his reign, and holding him up to the human race as an instructive example of godliness. Accordingly, by the manifold blessings he has conferred on him, he has distinguished him alone of all the sovereigns of whom we have ever heard as at once a mighty luminary and most clear-voiced herald of genuine piety.

CHAPTER V.

That he reigned above Thirty Years, and lived above Sixty.

WITH respect to the duration of his reign, God honored him with three complete periods of ten years, and something more, extending the whole term of his mortal life to twice this number of years.[1] And being pleased to make him a representative of his own sovereign power, he displayed him as the conqueror of the whole race of tyrants, and the destroyer of those God-defying giants[2] of the earth who madly raised

---

[2] Here there is play on the word Logos. My logos stands voiceless and a-logos, "un-logosed." If the author meant both to refer to expression, the first relates to the sound, and the second to the power of construction or composition. The interchangeableness of the weaving of consecutive thought in the mind, and the weaving it in expressed words, is precisely the question of the "relation of thought and language," so warmly contested by modern philosophers and philologians (cf. Müller, *Science of Thought*, Shedd's *Essays*, &c.). The old use of logos for both operations of "binding together" various ideas into one synthetical form has decided advantages.

[3] Here there is again the play on the word Logos. For Eusebius' philosophy of the logos, and of Christ as the Logos or Word, see the second half of his tricennial oration and notes.

[1] Compare Lactantius, *De mortibus persecutorum*, which doubtless the author had in mind.

[2] [Κηροχύτου γραφῆς, properly encaustic painting, by means of melted wax. — *Bag.*] Compare admirable description of the process in the Century Dictionary, ed. Whitney, N.Y. 1889, v. 2.

[3] Κύβεις, at first used of triangular tablets of wood, brass, or stone, but afterwards of any inscribed "pillars or tablets." Cf. Lexicons.

[1] Whether δεξιῶς is read or δεξιός, with Valesius, "present to aid," covers the idea better than "graciously present" (Molz).

[1] Compare discussion of length of reign and life under *Life* in Prolegomena, p. 411.

[2] [Γιγάντων. The persecuting emperors appear to be meant, of whom there is more mention hereafter. — *Bag.*] Refers of course

their impious arms against him, the supreme King of all. They appeared, so to speak, for an instant, and then disappeared : while the one and only true God, when he had enabled his servant, clad in heavenly panoply, to stand singly against many foes, and by his means had relieved mankind from the multitude of the ungodly, constituted him a teacher of his worship to all nations, to testify with a loud voice in the hearing of all that he acknowledged the true God, and turned with abhorrence from the error of them that are no gods.

CHAPTER VI.

That he was the Servant of God, and the Conqueror of Nations.

THUS, like a faithful and good servant, did he act and testify, openly declaring and confessing himself the obedient minister of the supreme King. And God forthwith rewarded him, by making him ruler and sovereign, and victorious to such a degree that he alone of all rulers pursued a continual course of conquest, unsubdued and invincible, and through his trophies a greater ruler than tradition records ever to have been before. So dear was he to God, and so blessed ; so pious and so fortunate in all that he undertook, that with the greatest facility he obtained the authority over more nations than any who had preceded him,[1] and yet retained his power, undisturbed, to the very close of his life.

CHAPTER VII.

Comparison with Cyrus, King of the Persians, and with Alexander of Macedon.

ANCIENT history describes Cyrus, king of the Persians, as by far the most illustrious of all kings up to his time. And yet if we regard the end of his days,[1] we find it but little corresponded with his past prosperity, since he met with an inglorious and dishonorable death at the hands of a woman.[2]

Again, the sons of Greece celebrate Alexander the Macedonian as the conqueror of many and diverse nations ; yet we find that he was removed by an early death, before he had reached maturity, being carried off by the effects of revelry and drunkenness.[3] His whole life embraced but the space of thirty-two years, and his reign extended to no more than a third part of that period. Unsparing as the thunderbolt, he advanced through streams of blood and reduced entire nations and cities, young and old, to utter slavery. But when he had scarcely arrived at the maturity of life, and was lamenting the loss of youthful pleasures, death fell upon him with terrible stroke, and, that he might not longer outrage the human race, cut him off in a foreign and hostile land, childless, without successor, and homeless. His kingdom too was instantly dismembered, each of his officers taking away and appropriating a portion for himself. And yet this man is extolled for such deeds as these.[4]

CHAPTER VIII.

That he conquered nearly the Whole World.

BUT our emperor began his reign at the time of life at which the Macedonian died, yet doubled the length of his life, and trebled the length of his reign. And instructing his army in the mild and sober precepts of godliness, he carried his arms as far as the Britons, and the nations that dwell in the very bosom of the Western ocean. He subdued likewise all Scythia, though situated in the remotest North, and divided into numberless diverse and barbarous tribes. He even pushed his conquests to the Blemmyans and Ethiopians, on the very confines of the South ; nor did he think the acquisition of the Eastern nations unworthy his care. In short, diffusing the effulgence of his holy light to the ends of the whole world, even to the most distant Indians, the nations dwelling on the extreme circumference of the inhabited earth, he received the submission of all the rulers,[1] governors,[2] and satraps of barbarous nations, who cheerfully welcomed and saluted him, sending embassies and presents, and setting the highest value on his acquaintance and friendship ; insomuch that they honored him with pictures and statues in their respective countries, and Constantine alone of all emperors was acknowledged and celebrated by all. Notwithstanding, even among these distant na-

---

to the mythical Gigantes who fought against the gods. It is used in the same sense in which Æschylus uses it of Capaneus (Theb. 424), who defied Zeus in declaring that even his thunderbolts should not keep him out of Thebes.

[1] Compare the various wars against Franks, Bructerians, Goths, Sarmatians and others mentioned in *Life* in Prolegomena. Compare also chapter 8 of this book.

[1] [Such seems to be the probable meaning of this passage, which is manifestly corrupt, and of which various emendations have been proposed. — *Bag.*] Perhaps better paraphrased, " But since the test of blessedness lies not in this, but in his end, we look and find that this." The key to the idea is found in the remark near the end of chapter 11. Cf. also note.

[2] This is the account of Diodorus, who says he was taken prisoner and crucified by the queen of the " Scythians " (3. 11, ed. 1531, f. 80^h). Herodotus says that he was slain in battle, but his head cut off afterwards and dipped in a sack of blood by the queen Tomyris, who had rejected his suit, the death of whose son he had caused,

and who had sworn to " give him his fill of blood " (Herod. Bk. 1, §§ 205–214). Xenophon says he died quietly in bed (*Cyrop.* 8. 7).

[3] A malarial fever, but made fatal by drinking at a banquet (cf. Plut. chaps. 75 and 76, Arrian, Bk. 7).

[4] Eusebius' rhetorical purpose makes him unfair to Alexander, who certainly in comparison with others of his time brought relative blessing to the conquered (cf. Smith, *Dict.* 1, p. 122).

[1] Toparchs or prefects.   [2] Ethnarchs.

tions, he proclaimed the name of his God in his royal edicts with all boldness.

CHAPTER IX.

That he was the Son of a Pious Emperor, and bequeathed the Power to Royal Sons.

NOR did he give this testimony in words merely, while exhibiting failure in his own practice, but pursued every path of virtue, and was rich in the varied fruits of godliness. He ensured the affection of his friends by magnificent proofs of liberality; and inasmuch as he governed on principles of humanity, he caused his rule to be but lightly felt and acceptable to all classes of his subjects; until at last, after a long course of years, and when he was wearied by his divine labors, the God whom he honored crowned him with an immortal reward, and translated him from a transitory kingdom to that endless life which he has laid up in store for the souls of his saints, after he had raised him up three sons to succeed him in his power. As then the imperial throne had descended to him from his father, so, by the law of nature, was it reserved for his children and their descendants, and perpetuated, like some paternal inheritance, to endless generations. And indeed God himself, who distinguished this blessed prince with divine honors while yet present with us, and who has adorned his death with choice blessings from his own hand, should be the writer of his actions; since he has recorded his labors and successes on heavenly monuments.[1]

CHAPTER X.

Of the Need for this History, and its Value for Edification.

HOWEVER, hard as it is to speak worthily of this blessed character, and though silence were the safer and less perilous course, nevertheless it is incumbent on me, if I would escape the charge of negligence and sloth, to trace as it were a verbal portraiture, by way of memorial of the pious prince, in imitation of the delineations of human art. For I should be ashamed of myself were I not to employ my best efforts, feeble though they be and of little value, in praise of one who honored God with such surpassing devotion. I think too that my work will be on other grounds both instructive and necessary, since it will contain a description of those royal and noble actions which are pleasing to God, the Sovereign of all. For would it not be dis-

graceful that the memory of Nero, and other impious and godless tyrants far worse than he, should meet with diligent writers to embellish the relation of their worthless deeds with elegant language, and record them in voluminous histories, and that I should be silent, to whom God himself has vouchsafed such an emperor as all history records not, and has permitted me to come into his presence, and enjoy his acquaintance and society?[1]

Wherefore, if it is the duty of any one, it certainly is mine, to make an ample proclamation of his virtues to all in whom the example of noble actions is capable of inspiring the love of God. For some who have written the lives of worthless characters, and the history of actions but little tending to the improvement of morals, from private motives, either love or enmity, and possibly in some cases with no better object than the display of their own learning, have exaggerated unduly their description of actions intrinsically base, by a refinement and elegance of diction.[2] And thus they have become to those who by the Divine favor had been kept apart from evil, teachers not of good, but of what should be silenced in oblivion and darkness. But my narrative, however unequal to the greatness of the deeds it has to describe, will yet derive luster even from the bare relation of noble actions. And surely the record of conduct that has been pleasing to God will afford a far from unprofitable, indeed a most instructive study, to persons of well-disposed minds.

CHAPTER XI.

That his Present Object is to record only the Pious Actions of Constantine.

IT is my intention, therefore, to pass over the greater part of the royal deeds of this thrice-blessed prince; as, for example, his conflicts and engagements in the field, his personal valor, his victories and successes against the enemy, and the many triumphs he obtained: likewise his provisions for the interests of individuals, his legislative enactments for the social advantage of his subjects, and a multitude of other imperial labors which are fresh in the memory of all; the design of my present undertaking being to speak and write of those circumstances only which have reference to his religious character.

And since these are themselves of almost infinite variety, I shall select from the facts

---

[1] "The pillars of heaven." — *Molz* (?).

[1] The Bagster translation, following Valesius, divides the tenth chapter, making the eleventh begin at this point.
[2] It looks as if there might perhaps be a direct hit at Lactantius here, as having, through "enmity," described actions intrinsically base in peculiarly elegant diction; but Lactantius' descriptions are hardly more realistic than Eusebius' own.

which have come to my knowledge such as are most suitable, and worthy of lasting record, and endeavor to narrate them as briefly as possible. Henceforward, indeed, there is a full and free opportunity for celebrating in every way the praises of this truly blessed prince, which hitherto we have been unable to do, on the ground that we are forbidden to judge any one blessed before his death,[1] because of the uncertain vicissitudes of life. Let me implore then the help of God, and may the inspiring aid of the heavenly Word be with me, while I commence my history from the very earliest period of his life.

CHAPTER XII.

That like Moses, he was reared in the Palaces of Kings.

ANCIENT history relates that a cruel race of tyrants oppressed the Hebrew nation; and that God, who graciously regarded them in their affliction, provided that the prophet Moses, who was then an infant, should be brought up in the very palaces and bosoms of the oppressors, and instructed in all the wisdom they possessed. And when in the course of time he had arrived at manhood, and the time was come for Divine justice to avenge the wrongs of the afflicted people, then the prophet of God, in obedience to the will of a more powerful Lord, forsook the royal household, and, estranging himself in word and deed from the tyrants by whom he had been brought up, openly acknowledging his true brethren and kinsfolk. Then God, exalting him to be the leader of the whole nation, delivered the Hebrews from the bondage of their enemies, and inflicted Divine vengeance through his means on the tyrant race. This ancient story, though rejected by most as fabulous, has reached the ears of all. But now the same God has given to us to be eye-witnesses of miracles more wonderful than fables, and, from their recent appearance, more authentic than any report. For the tyrants of our day have ventured to war against the Supreme God, and have sorely afflicted His Church.[1] And in the midst of these, Constantine, who was shortly to become their destroyer, but at that time of tender age, and blooming with the down of early youth, dwelt, as that other servant of God had done, in the very home of the tyrants,[2] but young as he was did not share the manner of

life of the ungodly : for from that early period his noble nature, under the leading of the Divine Spirit, inclined him to piety and a life acceptable to God. A desire, moreover, to emulate the example of his father had its influence in stimulating the son to a virtuous course of conduct. His father was Constantius[3] (and we ought to revive his memory at this time), the most illustrious emperor of our age ; of whose life it is necessary briefly to relate a few particulars, which tell to the honor of his son.

CHAPTER XIII.

Of Constantius his Father, who refused to imitate Diocletian, Maximian, and Maxentius,[1] in their Persecution of the Christians.

AT a time when four emperors[2] shared the administration of the Roman empire, Constantius alone, following a course of conduct different from that pursued by his colleagues, entered into the friendship of the Supreme God.

For while they besieged and wasted the churches of God, leveling them to the ground, and obliterating the very foundations of the houses of prayer,[3] he kept his hands pure from their abominable impiety, and never in any respect resembled them. They polluted their provinces by the indiscriminate slaughter of godly men and women ; but he kept his soul free from the stain of this crime.[4] They, involved in the mazes of impious idolatry, enthralled first themselves, and then all under their authority, in bondage to the errors of evil demons, while he at the same time originated the profoundest peace throughout his dominions, and secured to his subjects the privilege of celebrating without hindrance the worship of God. In short, while his colleagues oppressed all men by the most grievous exactions, and rendered their lives intolerable, and even worse than death, Constantius alone governed his people with a mild and tranquil sway, and exhibited towards them a truly parental and fostering care.

Numberless, indeed, are the other virtues of this man, which are the theme of praise to all ; of these I will record one or two instances, as specimens of the quality of those which I must pass by in silence, and then I will proceed to the appointed order of my narrative.

---

[1] [Alluding probably to Ecclesiastes xi. 28, " Judge none blessed before his death; for a man shall be known in his children." Or, possibly, to the well-known opinion of Solon to the same effect. Vide Herod. i. 32; Aristot. Eth. Nicom. i. 11.—*Bag.*] Compare also above, chapter 7.
[1] The persecuting emperors. Compare Prolegomena, *Life.*
[2] He was brought up with Diocletian and Galerius. Compare Prolegomena, *Life.*

[3] Constantius Chlorus, Neo-Platonist and philanthropist. Compare following description.
[1] The author of the chapter heading means of course Galerius. Maxentius was not emperor until after the death of Constantius.
[2] [Diocletian, Maximian, Galerius, and Constantius. — *Bag.*]
[3] For account of these persecutions, see *Church History*, Bk. 8, and notes of McGiffert.
[4] Compare the *Church History*, 8. 13, and Lactantius, *De mort. pers.* 15. The latter says he allowed buildings to be destroyed, but spared human life.

CHAPTER XIV.

How Constantius his Father, being reproached with Poverty by Diocletian, filled his Treasury, and afterwards restored the Money to those by whom it had been contributed.

IN consequence of the many reports in circulation respecting this prince, describing his kindness and gentleness of character, and the extraordinary elevation of his piety, alleging too, that by reason of his extreme indulgence to his subjects, he had not even a supply of money laid up in his treasury; the emperor who at that time occupied the place of supreme power sent to reprehend his neglect of the public weal, at the same time reproaching him with poverty, and alleging in proof of the charge the empty state of his treasury. On this he desired the messengers of the emperor to remain with him awhile, and, calling together the wealthiest of his subjects of all nations under his dominion, he informed them that he was in want of money, and that this was the time for them all to give a voluntary proof of their affection for their prince.

As soon as they heard this (as though they had long been desirous of an opportunity for showing the sincerity of their good will), with zealous alacrity they filled the treasury with gold and silver and other wealth; each eager to surpass the rest in the amount of his contribution: and this they did with cheerful and joyous countenances. And now Constantius desired the messengers of the great emperor[1] personally to inspect his treasures, and directed them to give a faithful report of what they had seen; adding, that on the present occasion he had taken this money into his own hands, but that it had long been kept for his use in the custody of the owners, as securely as if under the charge of faithful treasurers. The ambassadors were overwhelmed with astonishment at what they had witnessed: and on their departure it is said that the truly generous prince sent for the owners of the property, and, after commending them severally for their obedience and true loyalty, restored it all, and bade them return to their homes.

This one circumstance, then, conveys a proof of the generosity of him whose character we are attempting to illustrate: another will contain the clearest testimony to his piety.

---

[1] Or the senior Augustus. "Diocletian is thus entitled in the ancient panegyrists and in inscriptions." — *Heinichen*.

It was "towards the end of the second century of the Christian era" that there began to be a plurality of *Augusti*, but "from this time we find two or even a greater number of *Augusti;* and though in that and in all similar cases the persons honored with the title were regarded as participators of the imperial power, still the one who received the title first was looked upon as the head of the empire." — Smith, *Dict. Gr. and Rom. Ant.*

CHAPTER XV.

Of the Persecution raised by his Colleagues.

BY command of the supreme authorities of the empire, the governors of the several provinces had set on foot a general persecution of the godly. Indeed, it was from the imperial courts themselves that the very first of the pious martyrs proceeded, who passed through those conflicts for the faith, and most readily endured both fire and sword, and the depths of the sea; every form of death, in short, so that in a brief time all the royal palaces were bereft of pious men.[1] The result was, that the authors of this wickedness were entirely deprived of the protecting care of God, since by their persecution of his worshipers they at the same time silenced the prayers that were wont to be made on their own behalf.

CHAPTER XVI.

How Constantius, feigning Idolatry, expelled those who consented to offer Sacrifice, but retained in his Palace all who were willing to confess Christ.

ON the other hand, Constantius conceived an expedient full of sagacity, and did a thing which sounds paradoxical, but in fact was most admirable.

He made a proposal to all the officers of his court, including even those in the highest stations of authority, offering them the following alternative: either that they should offer sacrifice to demons, and thus be permitted to remain with him, and enjoy their usual honors; or, in case of refusal, that they should be shut out from all access to his person, and entirely disqualified from acquaintance and association with him. Accordingly, when they had individually made their choice, some one way and some the other, and the choice of each had been ascertained, then this admirable prince disclosed the secret meaning of his expedient, and condemned the cowardice and selfishness of the one party, while he highly commended the other for their conscientious devotion to God. He declared, too, that those who had been false to their God must be unworthy of the confidence of their prince; for how was it possible that they should preserve their fidelity to him, who had proved themselves faithless to a higher power? He determined, therefore, that such persons should be removed altogether from the imperial court, while, on the other hand, declaring that those men who, in bearing witness for the truth, had proved them-

---

[1] Compare accounts of martyrs in the palaces, in the *Church History*, 8. 6.

selves to be worthy servants of God, would manifest the same fidelity to their king, he entrusted them with the guardianship of his person and empire, saying that he was bound to treat such persons with special regard as his nearest and most valued friends, and to esteem them far more highly than the richest treasures.

CHAPTER XVII.

Of his Christian Manner of Life.

THE father of Constantine, then, is said to have possessed such a character as we have briefly described. And what kind of death was vouchsafed to him in consequence of such devotion to God, and how far he whom he honored made his lot to differ from that of his colleagues in the empire, may be known to any one who will give his attention to the circumstances of the case. For after he had for a long time given many proofs of royal virtue, in acknowledging the Supreme God alone, and condemning the polytheism of the ungodly, and had fortified his household by the prayers of holy men,[1] he passed the remainder of his life in remarkable repose and tranquillity, in the enjoyment of what is counted blessedness, — neither molesting others nor being molested ourselves.

Accordingly, during the whole course of his quiet and peaceful reign, he dedicated his entire household, his children, his wife, and domestic attendants, to the One Supreme God : so that the company assembled within the walls of his palace differed in no respect from a church of God ; wherein were also to be found his ministers, who offered continual supplications on behalf of their prince, and this at a time when, with most,[2] it was not allowable to have any dealings with the worshipers of God, even so far as to exchange a word with them.

CHAPTER XVIII.

That after the Abdication of Diocletian and Maximian, Constantius became Chief Augustus, and was blessed with a Numerous Offspring.

THE immediate consequence of this conduct was a recompense from the hand of God, insomuch that he came into the supreme authority of the empire. For the older emperors, for some unknown reason, resigned their power ;

and this sudden change took place in the first year after their persecution of the churches.[1]

From that time Constantius alone received the honors of chief Augustus, having been previously, indeed, distinguished by the diadem of the imperial Cæsars,[2] among whom he held the first rank ; but after his worth had been proved in this capacity, he was invested with the highest dignity of the Roman empire, being named chief Augustus of the four who were afterwards elected to that honor. Moreover, he surpassed most of the emperors in regard to the number of his family, having gathered around him a very large circle of children both male and female. And, lastly, when he had attained to a happy old age, and was about to pay the common debt of nature, and exchange this life for another, God once more manifested His power in a special manner on his behalf, by providing that his eldest son Constantine should be present during his last moments, and ready to receive the imperial power from his hands.[3]

CHAPTER XIX.

Of his Son Constantine, who in his Youth accompanied Diocletian into Palestine.

THE latter had been with his father's imperial colleagues,[1] and had passed his life among them, as we have said, like God's ancient prophet. And even in the very earliest period of his youth he was judged by them to be worthy of the highest honor. An instance of this we have ourselves seen, when he passed through Palestine with the senior emperor,[2] at whose right hand he stood, and commanded the admiration of all who beheld him by the indications he gave even then of royal greatness. For no one was comparable to him for grace and beauty of person, or height of stature ; and he so far surpassed his compeers in personal strength as to be a terror to them. He was, however, even more conspicuous for the excellence of his mental[3] qualities than for his superior physical endowments ; being gifted in the first place with a sound judgment,[4] and having also reaped the advantages of a liberal education. He was

---

[1] "Is said to have" is added conjecturally here by an earlier editor, but Heinichen omits, as it would seem Eusebius himself did.
[2] Other readings are "with the others," or "with the rest," but in whatever reading it refers to all the other emperors.

[1] The persecution was in 303 or 304. Compare discussion of date in Clinton, *Fasti Rom.* ann. 303–305. The abdication was in 305.
[2] Eusebius uses the terms Augustus, king, autocrat, and Cæsar with a good deal of interchangeableness. It is hard to tell sometimes whether king (βασιλεύς) means emperor or Cæsar. In general, Augustus has been transferred in translations, and king and autocrat both rendered emperor, which seems to be his real usage.
[3] Constantine reached him just before his death, though possibly some weeks before. Compare Prolegomena.
[1] Diocletian and Galerius.
[2] Diocletian. He was on his way to Egypt in the famous campaign against Achilleus in 296–297.
[3] Or "psychical," meaning more than intellectual.
[4] Rather, perhaps, "self-control."

also distinguished in no ordinary degree both by natural intelligence and divinely imparted wisdom.

CHAPTER XX.

Flight of Constantine to his Father because of the Plots of Diocletian.[1]

THE emperors then in power, observing his manly and vigorous figure and superior mind, were moved with feelings of jealousy and fear, and thenceforward carefully watched for an opportunity of inflicting some brand of disgrace on his character. But the young man, being aware of their designs, the details of which, through the providence of God, more than once came to him, sought safety in flight;[2] in this respect again keeping up his resemblance to the great prophet Moses. Indeed, in every sense God was his helper; and he had before ordained that he should be present in readiness to succeed his father.

CHAPTER XXI.

Death of Constantius, who leaves his Son Constantine Emperor.[1]

IMMEDIATELY, therefore, on his escape from the plots which had been thus insidiously laid for him, he made his way with all haste to his father, and arrived at length at the very time that he was lying at the point of death.[2] As soon as Constantius saw his son thus unexpectedly in his presence, he leaped from his couch, embraced him tenderly, and, declaring that the only anxiety which had troubled him in the prospect of death, namely, that caused by the absence of his son, was now removed, he rendered thanks to God, saying that he now thought death better than the longest life,[3] and at once completed the arrangement of his private affairs. Then, taking a final leave of the circle of sons and daughters by whom he was surrounded, in his own palace, and on the imperial couch, he bequeathed the empire, according to the law of nature,[4] to his eldest son, and breathed his last.

CHAPTER XXII.

How, after the Burial of Constantius, Constantine was proclaimed Augustus by the Army.

NOR did the imperial throne remain long unoccupied: for Constantine invested himself with his father's purple, and proceeded from his father's palace, presenting to all a renewal, as it were, in his own person, of his father's life and reign. He then conducted the funeral procession in company with his father's friends, some preceding, others following the train, and performed the last offices for the pious deceased with an extraordinary degree of magnificence, and all united in 'honoring this thrice blessed prince with acclamations and praises, and while with one mind and voice, they glorified the rule of the son as a living again of him who was dead, they hastened at once to hail their new sovereign by the titles of Imperial and Worshipful Augustus, with joyful shouts.[1] Thus the memory of the deceased emperor received honor from the praises bestowed upon his son, while the latter was pronounced blessed in being the successor of such a father. All the nations also under his dominion were filled with joy and inexpressible gladness at not being even for a moment deprived of the benefits of a well ordered government.

In the instance of the Emperor Constantius, God has made manifest to our generation what the end of those is who in their lives have honored and loved him.

CHAPTER XXIII.

A Brief Notice of the Destruction of the Tyrants.

WITH respect to the other princes, who made war against the churches of God, I have not thought it fit in the present work to give any account of their downfall,[1] nor to stain the memory of the good by mentioning them in connection with those of an opposite character. The knowledge of the facts themselves will of itself suffice for the wholesome admonition of those who have witnessed or heard of the evils which severally befell them.

---

[1] Eusebius himself speaks in the plural, and other writers speak of plots by both Diocletian and Galerius. Compare Prolegomena.

[2] Compare detailed account in Lactantius, *De M. P.* c. 24.

[1] Βασιλεύς. The writer of the chapter headings uses this word here and Augustus in the following chapter, but it does not seem to mean technically "Cæsar," and so the rendering emperor is retained.

[2] This seems to imply that Constantine reached him only after he was sick in bed, i.e. at York in Britain; but other accounts make it probable that he joined him at Boulogne before he sailed on this last expedition to Britain. Compare Prolegomena.

[3] Literally, "than immortality [on earth]."

[4] It will hardly be agreed that imperial succession is a law of nature anyway. Rather, "the succession [where it exists] is established by the express will or the tacit consent of the nation," and the "pretended proprietary right . . . is a chimera" (Vattell,

Law of Nations, Phila., 1867, p. 24, 25). That primogeniture is a natural law has been often urged, but it seems to be simply the law of first come first served. The English custom of primogeniture is said to have risen from the fact that in feudal times the eldest son was the one who, at the time of the father's death, was of an age to meet the duties of feudal tenure (compare Kent, *Commentaries*, Boston, 1867, v. 4, p. 420, 421). This is precisely the fact respecting Constantine. His several brothers were all too young to be thought of.

[1] The verdict was not confirmed at once. Galerius refused him the title of emperor, and he contented himself with that of Cæsar for a little. Compare Prolegomena.

[1] But he has done this himself in his *Church History.* Compare also Lactantius, *De mortibus persecutorum.*

CHAPTER XXIV.

It was by the Will of God that Constantine became possessed of the Empire.

THUS then the God of all, the Supreme Governor of the whole universe, by his own will appointed Constantine, the descendant of so renowned a parent, to be prince and sovereign: so that, while others have been raised to this distinction by the election of their fellow-men, he is the only one to whose elevation no mortal may boast of having contributed.

CHAPTER XXV.

Victories of Constantine over the Barbarians and the Britons.

As soon then as he was established on the throne, he began to care for the interests of his paternal inheritance, and visited with much considerate kindness all those provinces which had previously been under his father's government. Some tribes of the barbarians who dwelt on the banks of the Rhine, and the shores of the Western ocean, having ventured to revolt, he reduced them all to obedience, and brought them from their savage state to one of gentleness. He contented himself with checking the inroads of others, and drove from his dominions, like untamed and savage beasts, those whom he perceived to be altogether incapable of the settled order of civilized life.[1] Having disposed of these affairs to his satisfaction, he directed his attention to other quarters of the world, and first passed over to the British nations,[2] which lie in the very bosom of the ocean. These he reduced to submission, and then proceeded to consider the state of the remaining portions of the empire, that he might be ready to tender his aid wherever circumstances might require it.

CHAPTER XXVI.

How he resolved to deliver Rome from Maxentius.

WHILE, therefore, he regarded the entire world as one immense body, and perceived that the head of it all, the royal city of the Roman empire, was bowed down by the weight of a tyrannous oppression; at first he had left the task of liberation to those who governed the other divisions of the empire, as being his superiors in point of age. But when none of these proved able to afford relief, and those who had attempted it had experienced a disastrous termination of their enterprise,[1] he said that life was without enjoyment to him as long as he saw the imperial city thus afflicted, and prepared himself for the overthrowal of the tyranny.

CHAPTER XXVII.

That after reflecting on the Downfall of those who had worshiped Idols, he made Choice of Christianity.

BEING convinced, however, that he needed some more powerful aid than his military forces could afford him, on account of the wicked and magical enchantments which were so diligently practiced by the tyrant,[1] he sought Divine assistance, deeming the possession of arms and a numerous soldiery of secondary importance, but believing the co-operating power of Deity invincible and not to be shaken. He considered, therefore, on what God he might rely for protection and assistance. While engaged in this enquiry, the thought occurred to him, that, of the many emperors who had preceded him, those who had rested their hopes in a multitude of gods, and served them with sacrifices and offerings, had in the first place been deceived by flattering predictions, and oracles which promised them all prosperity, and at last had met with an unhappy end, while not one of their gods had stood by to warn them of the impending wrath of heaven; while one alone who had pursued an entirely opposite course, who had condemned their error, and honored the one Supreme God during his whole life, had found him to be the Saviour and Protector of his empire, and the Giver of every good thing. Reflecting on this, and well weighing the fact that they who had trusted in many gods had also fallen by manifold forms of death, without leaving behind them either family or offspring, stock, name, or memorial among men: while the God of his father had given to him, on the other hand, manifestations of his power and very many tokens: and considering farther that those who had already taken arms against the tyrant, and had marched to the battle-field under the protection of a multitude of gods, had met with a dishonorable end (for one of them[2] had shamefully retreated from the contest without a blow, and the other,[3] being slain in the midst of

---

[1] The Franci, Bructeri, &c.
[2] [Eusebius here speaks of a *second* expedition of Constantine to Britain, which is not mentioned by other ancient writers; or he may have been forgetful or ignorant of the fact that Constantine had received the imperial authority in Britain itself, Constantius having died in his palace at York, A.D. 306. Vide Gibbon's *Decline and Fall*, chap. 14.—*Bag.*] It seems to be a part of the confusion about his crossing to Britain in the first place.

[1] Referring to the unsuccessful expeditions of Severus and Galerius.
[1] Compare chapters 36 and 37; also Lactantius, *De M. P.* chap. 44. [2] Galerius. [3] Severus.

his own troops, became, as it were, the mere sport of death[4]) ; reviewing, I say, all these considerations, he judged it to be folly indeed to join in the idle worship of those who were no gods, and, after such convincing evidence, to err from the truth ; and therefore felt it incumbent on him to honor his father's God alone.

CHAPTER XXVIII.

How, while he was praying, God sent him a Vision of a Cross of Light in the Heavens at Mid-day, with an Inscription admonishing him to conquer by that.

ACCORDINGLY he called on him with earnest prayer and supplications that he would reveal to him who he was, and stretch forth his right hand to help him in his present difficulties. And while he was thus praying with fervent entreaty, a most marvelous sign appeared to him from heaven, the account of which it might have been hard to believe had it been related by any other person. But since the victorious emperor himself long afterwards declared it to the writer of this history,[1] when he was honored with his acquaintance and society, and confirmed his statement by an oath, who could hesitate to accredit the relation, especially since the testimony of after-time has established its truth? He said that about noon, when the day was already beginning to decline, he saw with his own eyes the trophy of a cross of light in the heavens, above the sun, and bearing the inscription, CONQUER BY THIS. At this sight he himself was struck with amazement, and his whole army also, which followed him on this expedition, and witnessed the miracle.[2]

---

[4] This last phrase has exercised the ingenuity of translators greatly. This translation does well enough, though one might hazard " was easily overcome by death," or " was an easy victim to death."

[1] Note here the care Eusebius takes to throw off the responsibility for the marvelous. It at the same time goes to show the general credibility of Eusebius, and some doubt in his mind of the exact nature and reality of what he records.

[2] This very circumstantial account has met with doubters from the very beginning, commencing with Eusebius himself. There are all sorts of explanations, from that of an actual miracle to that of pure later invention. The fact of some, at least supposed, special divine manifestation at this time can hardly be denied. It is mentioned vaguely by *Paneg.* 313, on the triumphal arch shortly after. It is reported as a dream by Lactantius about the same time with the erection of the arch, and alluded to in general, but hardly to be doubted, terms by Nazarius in 321. Moreover, it is witnessed to by the fact of the standard of the cross which was made. As to the real nature of the manifestation, it has been thought to be as recorded by Constantine, and if so, as perhaps some natural phenomenon of the sun, or to have been a simple dream, or an hallucination. It is hardly profitable to discuss the possibilities. The lack of contemporary evidence to details and the description of Lactantius as a dream to any idea of a miraculous image with inscriptions clearly seen by all. Some cross-like arrangement of the clouds, or a " parahelion," or some sort of a suggestion of a cross, may have been seen by all, but evidently there was no definite, vivid, clear perception, or it would have been in the mouths of all, and certainly recorded, or at least it would not have been recorded as *something else* by Lactantius. It seems probable that the emperor, thinking intensely, with all the weight of his great problem resting on his energetic mind, wondering if the Christian God was perhaps the God who could help, saw in some suggestive shape of

CHAPTER XXIX.

How the Christ of God appeared to him in his Sleep, and commanded him to use in his Wars a Standard made in the Form of the Cross.

HE said, moreover, that he doubted within himself what the import of this apparition could be. And while he continued to ponder and reason on its meaning, night suddenly came on ; then in his sleep the Christ of God appeared to him with the same sign which he had seen in the heavens, and commanded him to make a likeness of that sign which he had seen in the heavens, and to use it as a safeguard in all engagements with his enemies.

CHAPTER XXX.

The Making of the Standard of the Cross.

AT dawn of day he arose, and communicated the marvel to his friends : and then, calling together the workers in gold and precious stones, he sat in the midst of them, and described to them the figure of the sign he had seen, bidding them represent it in gold and precious stones. And this representation I myself have had an opportunity of seeing.

CHAPTER XXXI.

A Description of the Standard of the Cross, which the Romans now call the Labarum.[1]

Now it was made in the following manner. A long spear, overlaid with gold, formed the

---

the clouds or of sunlight the form of a cross, and there flashed out in his mind in intensest reality the vision of the words, so that for the moment he was living in the intensest reality of such a vision. His mind had just that intense activity to which such a thing is possible or actual. It is like Goethe's famous meeting of his own self. It is that genius power for the realistic representation of ideal things. This is not the same exactly as " hallucination," or even " imagination." The hallucination probably came later when Constantine gradually represented to himself and finally to Eusebius the vivid idea with its slight ground, as an objective reality,—a common phenomenon. When the emperor went to sleep, his brain molecules vibrating to the forms of his late intense thought, he inevitably dreamed, and dreaming naturally confirmed his thought. This does not say that the suggestive form seen, or the idea itself, and the direction of the dream itself, were not providential and the work of the Holy Spirit, for they were, and were special in character, and so miraculous (or why do ideas come?) ; but it is to be feared that Constantine's own spirit or something else furnished some of the later details. There is a slight difference of authority as to when and where the vision took place. The panegyrist seems to make it before leaving Gaul, and Malalas is inaccurate as usual in having it happen in a war against the barbarians. For fuller discussion of the subject see monographs under *Literature* in the Prolegomena, especially under the names: BARING, DU VOISIN, FABRICIUS, GIRAULT, HEUMANN, JACUTIUS MAMACHI, MOLINET, ST. VICTOR, SUHR, TODERINI, WEIDENER, WERNSDORF, WOLTERECK. The most concise, clear, and admirable supporter of the account of Eusebius, or rather Constantine, as it stands, is Newman, *Miracles* (Lond. 1875), 271–286.

[1] [From the Bretagnic *lab*, to raise, or from *labarva*, which, in the Basque language, still signifies a standard. — Riddle's *Lat. Dict.* voc. *Labarum.* Gibbon declares the derivation and meaning of the word to be " totally unknown, in spite of the efforts of the critics, who have ineffectually tortured the Latin, Greek, Spanish, Celtic, Teutonic, Illyric, Armenian, &c., in search of an etymology." — *Decline and Fall*, chap. 22, note 33. — *Bag.*] Compare the full

figure of the cross by means of a transverse bar laid over it. On the top of the whole was fixed a wreath of gold and precious stones; and within this,[2] the symbol of the Saviour's name, two letters indicating the name of Christ by means of its initial characters, the letter P being intersected by X in its centre:[3] and these letters the emperor was in the habit of wearing on his helmet at a later period. From the cross-bar of the spear was suspended a cloth,[4] a royal piece, covered with a profuse embroidery of most brilliant precious stones; and which, being also richly interlaced with gold, presented an indescribable degree of beauty to the beholder. This banner was of a square form, and the upright staff, whose lower section was of great length,[5] bore a golden half-length portrait[6] of the pious emperor and his children on its upper part, beneath the trophy of the cross, and immediately above the embroidered banner.

The emperor constantly made use of this sign of salvation as a safeguard against every adverse and hostile power, and commanded that others similar to it should be carried at the head of all his armies.

CHAPTER XXXII.

How Constantine received Instruction, and read the Sacred Scriptures.

THESE things were done shortly afterwards. But at the time above specified, being struck with amazement at the extraordinary vision, and resolving to worship no other God save Him who had appeared to him, he sent for those who were acquainted with the mysteries of His doctrines, and enquired who that God was, and what was intended by the sign of the vision he had seen.

They affirmed that He was God, the only begotten Son of the one and only God: that the sign which had appeared was the symbol of immortality,[1] and the trophy of that victory over death which He had gained in time past when sojourning on earth. They taught him also the causes of His advent, and explained to him the true account of His incarnation. Thus he was instructed in these matters, and was impressed with wonder at the divine manifestation which had been presented to his sight. Comparing, therefore, the heavenly vision with the interpretation given, he found his judgment confirmed; and, in the persuasion that the knowledge of these things had been imparted to him by Divine teaching, he determined thenceforth to devote himself to the reading of the Inspired writings.

Moreover, he made the priests of God his counselors, and deemed it incumbent on him to honor the God who had appeared to him with all devotion. And after this, being fortified by well-grounded hopes in Him, he hastened to quench the threatening fire of tyranny.

CHAPTER XXXIII.

Of the Adulterous Conduct of Maxentius at Rome.[1]

FOR he who had tyrannically possessed himself of the imperial city,[2] had proceeded to great lengths in impiety and wickedness, so as to venture without hesitation on every vile and impure action.

For example: he would separate women from their husbands, and after a time send them back to them again, and these insults he offered not to men of mean or obscure condition, but to those who held the first places in the Roman senate. Moreover, though he shamefully dishonored almost numberless free women, he was unable to satisfy his ungoverned and intemperate desires. But[3] when he assayed to corrupt Christian women also, he could no longer secure success to his designs, since they chose rather to submit their lives[4] to death than yield their persons to be defiled by him.

---

article of Venables, in Smith and Cheetham, *Dict.* 1 (1880), 908–911, with its references and cuts.

[2] Thus rather than "on." Compare cuts in article of Venables. "It [the monogram of Christ] is often set within a crown or palm branch."—*Wolcott, Sacred Archæology*, p. 390.

[3] [Χιαζομένου τοῦ ρ κατὰ τὸ μεσαίτατον. The figure ☧ would seem to answer to the description in the text. Gibbon gives two specimens, ☧ and ☧ as engraved from ancient monuments. Chap. 20, note 35.—*Bag.*] The various coins given by Venables all have the usual form of the monogram ☧. Compare also Tyrwhitt, art. *Monogram*, in Smith and Cheetham; also the art. *Monogramme du Christ*, in Martigny, *Dict. d. ant.* (1877), 476–483.

[4] That this was no new invention of Constantine may be seen by comparing the following description of an ordinary Roman standard, ". . . each cohort had for its own ensign the serpent or dragon, which was woven on a square piece of cloth, elevated on a gilt staff, to which a cross-bar was adapted for the purpose . . . under the eagle or other emblem was often placed a head of the reigning emperor." Yates, art. *Signa militaria*, in Smith, *Dict. Gr. and Rom. Ant.* (1878), 1044–1045.

[5] "Which in its full extent was of great length."—*Bag.*, according to suggestion of Valesius of a possible meaning, but better as above, meaning the part below the cross-bar. So *Valesius, Christophorson*, 1709, *Molzberger*.

[6] "Medallions."—*Venables*.

---

[1] Both Socrates (5. 17) and Sozomen (7. 15) relate that symbols of the cross found in a temple of Serapis, on its destruction by Theodosius, were explained by the Christians of the time as symbols of immortality. Cf. also Suidas (ed. Gasiford, 2 (1834), 3398), s. v. Σταυροι; Valesius on Socrates and Sozomen; Jablonski, *Opuscula*, 1, p. 156–. The study of the pre-christian use of the cross is most suggestive. It suggests at least that in some way the passion of our Lord was the realization of some world-principle or "natural Law."

[1] Compare the *Church History*, 8. 14.

[2] Maxentius, made emperor by an uprising of the Prætorian Guards in 306.

[3] "For" seems to express the author's real meaning, but both punctuation of editors and renderings of translators insist on "but."

[4] Various readings of text add "lawfully married" women, and send them back again "grievously dishonored," and so *Bag.*, but Heinichen has this reading. Compare note of Heinichen.

CHAPTER XXXIV.

How the Wife of a Prefect slew herself for Chastity's Sake.[1]

Now a certain woman, wife of one of the senators who held the authority of prefect, when she understood that those who ministered to the tyrant in such matters were standing before her house (she was a Christian), and knew that her husband through fear had bidden them take her and lead her away, begged a short space of time for arraying herself in her usual dress, and entered her chamber. There, being left alone, she sheathed a sword in her own breast, and immediately expired, leaving indeed her dead body to the procurers, but declaring to all mankind, both to present and future generations, by an act which spoke louder than any words, that the chastity for which Christians are famed is the only thing which is invincible and indestructible. Such was the conduct displayed by this woman.

CHAPTER XXXV.

Massacre of the Roman People by Maxentius.

ALL men, therefore, both people and magistrates, whether of high or low degree, trembled through fear of him whose daring wickedness was such as I have described, and were oppressed by his grievous tyranny. Nay, though they submitted quietly, and endured this bitter servitude, still there was no escape from the tyrant's sanguinary cruelty. For at one time, on some trifling pretense, he exposed the populace to be slaughtered by his own body-guard; and countless multitudes of the Roman people were slain in the very midst of the city by the lances and weapons, not of Scythians or barbarians, but of their own fellow-citizens. And besides this, it is impossible to calculate the number of senators whose blood was shed with a view to the seizure of their respective estates, for at different times and on various fictitious charges, multitudes of them suffered death.

CHAPTER XXXVI.

Magic Arts of Maxentius against Constantine; and Famine at Rome.

BUT the crowning point of the tyrant's wickedness was his having recourse to sorcery: sometimes for magic purposes ripping up women with child, at other times searching into the

bowels of new-born infants. He slew lions also, and practiced certain horrid arts for evoking demons, and averting the approaching war, hoping by these means to get the victory. In short, it is impossible to describe the manifold acts of oppression by which this tyrant of Rome enslaved his subjects: so that by this time they were reduced to the most extreme penury and want of necessary food, a scarcity such as our contemporaries do not remember ever before to have existed at Rome.[1]

CHAPTER XXXVII.

Defeat of Maxentius's Armies in Italy.

CONSTANTINE, however, filled with compassion on account of all these miseries, began to arm himself with all warlike preparation against the tyranny. Assuming therefore the Supreme God as his patron, and invoking His Christ to be his preserver and aid, and setting the victorious trophy, the salutary symbol, in front of his soldiers and body-guard, he marched with his whole forces, trying to obtain again for the Romans the freedom they had inherited from their ancestors.

And whereas, Maxentius, trusting more in his magic arts than in the affection of his subjects, dared not even advance outside the city gates,[1] but had guarded every place and district and city subject to his tyranny, with large bodies of soldiers,[2] the emperor, confiding in the help of God, advanced against the first and second and third divisions of the tyrant's forces, defeated them all with ease at the first assault,[3] and made his way into the very interior of Italy.

CHAPTER XXXVIII.

Death of Maxentius on the Bridge of the Tiber.[1]

AND already he was approaching very near Rome itself, when, to save him from the necessity of fighting with all the Romans for the tyrant's sake, God himself drew the tyrant, as it were by secret cords, a long way outside the gates.[2] And now those miracles recorded in

---

[1] This chapter is found almost word for word in the *Church History*, 8. 14.

[1] *1709, Molz.* &c., add "nor anywhere else," but *Bag.* is undoubtedly right in translating simply "ever before." The chapter is found substantially and in part word for word in the *Church History*, 8. 14.
[1] "Because the soothsayers had foretold that if he went out of it, he should perish." Lact. *De M. P.*
[2] *Bag.* adds "and numberless ambuscades," following *Valesius* and *1709*. The word so rendered is the word for "companies of soldiers." The rather awkward "multitude of heavy-armed soldiers and myriads of companies of soldiers" may be rendered as above, although "larger bodies of soldiers and limitless supplies" suggested by the translation is perhaps the real meaning. He had both "men and means."
[3] At Sigusium, Turin, Brescia, and Verona.
[1] The Milvian, the present Ponte Molle.
[2] The present Ponte Molle is nearly 2½ kilometers (say 1½ miles)

Holy Writ, which God of old wrought against the ungodly (discredited by most as fables, yet believed by the faithful), did he in every deed confirm to all alike, believers and unbelievers, who were eye-witnesses of the wonders. For as once in the days of Moses and the Hebrew nation, who were worshipers of God, " Pharaoh's chariots and his host hath he cast into the sea, and his chosen chariot-captains are drowned in the Red Sea,"[3] —so at this time Maxentius, and the soldiers and guards[4] with him, " went down into the depths like stone,"[5] when, in his flight before the divinely-aided forces of Constantine, he essayed to cross the river which lay in his way, over which, making a strong bridge of boats, he had framed an engine of destruction, really against himself, but in the hope of ensnaring thereby him who was beloved by God. For his God stood by the one to protect him, while the other, godless,[6] proved to be the miserable contriver of these secret devices to his own ruin. So that one might well say, " He hath made a pit, and digged it, and is fallen into the ditch which he made. His mischief shall return upon his own head, and his violence shall come down upon his own pate."[7] Thus, in the present instance, under divine direction, the machine erected on the bridge, with the ambuscade concealed therein, giving way unexpectedly before the appointed time, the bridge began to sink, and the boats with the men in them went bodily to the bottom.[8] And first the wretch himself, then his armed attendants and guards, even as the sacred oracles had before described, " sank as lead in the mighty waters."[9] So that they who thus obtained victory from God might well, if not in the same words, yet in fact in the same spirit as the people of his great servant Moses, sing and speak as they did concerning the impious tyrant of old : " Let us sing unto the Lord, for he hath been glorified exceedingly : the horse and his rider hath he thrown into the sea. He is become my helper and my shield unto salvation." And again, " Who is like unto thee, O Lord, among the gods? who is like thee, glorious in holiness, marvelous in praises, doing wonders? "[10]

from the Porta del Popolo (at the Mons Pincius). The walls at that time were the ones built by Aurelian, and are substantially the same as the present ones. This Pons Milvius was first built 100 years B.C., and " some part of the first bridge is supposed to remain" (Jenkin, p. 329). Compare Jenkin, art. *Bridges*, in *Enc. Brit.* 4 (1878), 329, for cut and description.
[3] Ex. xv. 15, 16, Septuagint translation.
[4] " Heavy armed and light armed."   [5] Ex. xv. 5.
[6] " Godless," or if ἄνευ is to be read, " destitute of his aid," as *Bag.* Much conjecture has been expended on this reading. Heinichen has ἀθεεί.
[7] Ps. vii. 15, 16, Septuagint translation.
[8] This matter is discussed in the Prolegomena.
[9] Ex. xv. 10.
[10] Ex. xv. 1, 2, 11, Septuagint version. This whole chapter with the last paragraph of the preceding are in the *Church History*, 9. 9.

CHAPTER XXXIX.

Constantine's Entry into Rome.

HAVING then at this time sung these and such-like praises to God, the Ruler of all and the Author of victory, after the example of his great servant Moses, Constantine entered the imperial city in triumph. And here the whole body of the senate, and others of rank and distinction in the city, freed as it were from the restraint of a prison, along with the whole Roman populace, their countenances expressive of the gladness of their hearts, received him with acclamations and abounding joy ; men, women, and children, with countless multitudes of servants, greeting him as deliverer, preserver, and benefactor, with incessant shouts. But he, being possessed of inward piety toward God, was neither rendered arrogant by these plaudits, nor uplifted by the praises he heard :[1] but, being sensible that he had received help from God, he immediately rendered a thanksgiving to him as the Author of his victory.

CHAPTER XL.

Of the Statue of Constantine holding a Cross, and its Inscription.

MOREOVER, by loud proclamation and monumental inscriptions he made known to all men the salutary symbol, setting up this great trophy of victory over his enemies in the midst of the imperial city, and expressly causing it to be engraven in indelible characters, that the salutary symbol was the safeguard of the Roman government and of the entire empire. Accordingly, he immediately ordered a lofty spear in the figure of a cross to be placed beneath the hand of a statue representing himself, in the most frequented part of Rome, and the following inscription to be engraved on it in the Latin language : BY VIRTUE OF THIS SALUTARY SIGN, WHICH IS THE TRUE TEST OF VALOR, I HAVE PRESERVED AND LIBERATED YOUR CITY FROM THE YOKE OF TYRANNY. I HAVE ALSO SET AT LIBERTY THE ROMAN SENATE AND PEOPLE, AND RESTORED THEM TO THEIR ANCIENT DISTINCTION AND SPLENDOR.[1]

[1] Compare Prolegomena under *Character*, and also for other accounts of the universal joy under *Life*.
[3] Compare the *Church History*, 9. 9.
[4] So Heinichen. This reading is an emendation from the Oration of Eusebius, 9. 8, supported by one MS. The reading Γραφῇ would be translated with *Bag.* " many writings."
[1] Compare the *Church History*, 9. 9.
If it be true, as Crusè says, that in this inscription there are traces of the Latin original, it gives a strong presumption that Eusebius was quoting a really existing inscription and accordingly that it is genuine. If so, of course the probability of the vision of the cross is greatly increased.

CHAPTER XLI.

Rejoicings throughout the Provinces; and Constantine's Acts of Grace.

THUS the pious emperor, glorying in the confession of the victorious cross, proclaimed the Son of God to the Romans with great boldness of testimony. And the inhabitants of the city, one and all, senate and people, reviving, as it were, from the pressure of a bitter and tyrannical domination, seemed to enjoy purer rays of light, and to be born again into a fresh and new life. All the nations, too, as far as the limit of the western ocean, being set free from the calamities which had heretofore beset them, and gladdened by joyous festivals, ceased not to praise him as the victorious, the pious, the common benefactor: all, indeed, with one voice and one mouth, declared that Constantine had appeared by the grace of God as a general blessing to mankind. The imperial edict also was everywhere published, whereby those who had been wrongfully deprived of their estates were permitted again to enjoy their own, while those who had unjustly suffered exile were recalled to their homes. Moreover, he freed from imprisonment, and from every kind of danger and fear, those who, by reason of the tyrant's cruelty, had been subject to these sufferings.

CHAPTER XLII.

The Honors conferred upon Bishops, and the Building of Churches.

THE emperor also personally inviting the society of God's ministers, distinguished them with the highest possible respect and honor, showing them favor in deed and word as persons consecrated to the service of his God. Accordingly, they were admitted to his table, though mean in their attire and outward appearance; yet not so in his estimation, since he thought he saw not the man as seen by the vulgar eye, but the God in him. He made them also his companions in travel, believing that He whose servants they were would thus help him. Besides this, he gave from his own private resources costly benefactions to the churches of God, both enlarging and heightening the sacred edifices,[1] and embellishing the august sanctuaries[2] of the church with abundant offerings.

---

[1] " Oratories," or chapels.
[2] Variously rendered, but seems to say that the smaller buildings were enlarged and the larger ones enriched. The number of buildings which Constantine is claimed to have erected in Rome alone is prodigious. One meets at every turn in the modern city churches which were, it is said, founded or remodeled by him. For interesting monograph which claims to have established the Constantinian foundation of many of these, see CIAMPINI in Prolegomena, under *Literature.*

CHAPTER XLIII.

Constantine's Liberality to the Poor.

HE likewise distributed money largely to those who were in need, and besides these showing himself philanthropist and benefactor even to the heathen, who had no claim on him;[1] and even for the beggars in the forum, miserable and shiftless, he provided, not with money only, or necessary food, but also decent clothing. But in the case of those who had once been prosperous, and had experienced a reverse of circumstances, his aid was still more lavishly bestowed. On such persons, in a truly royal spirit, he conferred magnificent benefactions; giving grants of land to some, and honoring others with various dignities. Orphans of the unfortunate he cared for as a father, while he relieved the destitution of widows, and cared for them with special solicitude. Nay, he even gave virgins, left unprotected by their parents' death, in marriage to wealthy men with whom he was personally acquainted. But this he did after first bestowing on the brides such portions as it was fitting they should bring to the communion of marriage.[2] In short, as the sun, when he rises upon the earth, liberally imparts his rays of light to all, so did Constantine, proceeding at early dawn from the imperial palace, and rising as it were with the heavenly luminary, impart the rays of his own beneficence to all who came into his presence. It was scarcely possible to be near him without receiving some benefit, nor did it ever happen that any who had expected to obtain his assistance were disappointed in their hope.[3]

CHAPTER XLIV.

How he was present at the Synods of Bishops.

SUCH, then, was his general character towards all. But he exercised a peculiar care over the church of God: and whereas, in the several provinces there were some who differed from each other in judgment, he, like some general bishop constituted by God, convened synods of his ministers. Nor did he disdain to be present and sit with them in their assembly, but bore a share in their deliberations, ministering to all that pertained to the peace of God. He took

---

[1] So usually rendered literally, " to those who came to him from without," but it might rather mean " foreigners." His generosity included not only the worthy poor citizens, but foreigners and beggars.
[2] The word used is the κοινωνία, familiar in the doctrine of the " communion" or " fellowship" of the saints. It has the notion of reciprocity and mutual sharing.
[3] The popular proverb that at the end of his life he was a spendthrift, as given by Victor, represents the other side of this liberality. Compare Prolegomena, under *Character.*

his seat, too, in the midst of them, as an individual amongst many, dismissing his guards and soldiers, and all whose duty it was to defend his person; but protected by the fear of God, and surrounded by the guardianship of his faithful friends. Those whom he saw inclined to a sound judgment, and exhibiting a calm and conciliatory temper, received his high approbation, for he evidently delighted in a general harmony of sentiment; while he regarded the unyielding with aversion.[1]

CHAPTER XLV.

His Forbearance with Unreasonable Men.

MOREOVER he endured with patience some who were exasperated against himself, directing them in mild and gentle terms to control themselves, and not be turbulent. And some of these respected his admonitions, and desisted; but as to those who proved incapable of sound judgment, he left them entirely at the disposal of God, and never himself desired harsh measures against any one. Hence it naturally happened that the disaffected in Africa reached such a pitch of violence as even to venture on overt acts of audacity;[1] some evil spirit, as it seems probable, being jealous of the present great prosperity, and impelling these men to atrocious deeds, that he might excite the emperor's anger against them. He gained nothing, however, by this malicious conduct; for the emperor laughed at these proceedings, and declared their origin to be from the evil one; inasmuch as these were not the actions of sober persons, but of lunatics or demoniacs; who should be pitied rather than punished; since to punish madmen is as great folly as to sympathize with their condition is supreme philanthropy.[2]

CHAPTER XLVI.

Victories over the Barbarians.

THUS the emperor in all his actions honored God, the Controller of all things, and exercised an unwearied[1] oversight over His churches. And God requited him, by subduing all barbarous nations under his feet, so that he was able every-

where to raise trophies over his enemies: and He proclaimed him as conqueror to all mankind, and made him a terror to his adversaries: not indeed that this was his natural character, since he was rather the meekest, and gentlest, and most benevolent of men.

CHAPTER XLVII.

Death of Maximin,[1] who had attempted a Conspiracy, and of Others whom Constantine detected by Divine Revelation.

WHILE he was thus engaged, the second of those who had resigned the throne, being detected in a treasonable conspiracy, suffered a most ignominious death. He was the first whose pictures, statues, and all similar marks of honor and distinction were everywhere destroyed, on the ground of his crimes and impiety. After him others also of the same family were discovered in the act of forming secret plots against the emperor; all their intentions being miraculously revealed by God through visions to His servant.

For he frequently vouchsafed to him manifestations of himself, the Divine presence appearing to him in a most marvelous manner, and according to him manifold intimations of future events. Indeed, it is impossible to express in words the indescribable wonders of Divine grace which God was pleased to vouchsafe to His servant. Surrounded by these, he passed the rest of his life in security, rejoicing in the affection of his subjects, rejoicing too because he saw all beneath his government leading contented lives; but above all delighted at the flourishing condition of the churches of God.

CHAPTER XLVIII.

Celebration of Constantine's Decennalia.

WHILE he was thus circumstanced, he completed the tenth year of his reign. On this occasion he ordered the celebration of general festivals, and offered prayers of thanksgiving to God, the King of all, as sacrifices without flame or smoke.[1] And from this employment he derived much pleasure: not so from the tidings he received of the ravages committed in the Eastern provinces.

---

[1] Constantine, like Eusebius himself, would be a distinct "tolerationist" in modern theological controversy. One may imagine that Eusebius entered into favor with Constantine in this way. It commends itself to our feeling; but after all, the unyielding Athanasius was a greater man than Eusebius.

[1] Compare Prolegomena, under *Life* and *Works*.

[2] [This passage in the text is defective or corrupt. — *Bag.*] What is given is substantially the conventional translation of *Valesius, Heinichen, Molzberger,* and with some variation, *1709* and *Bag.* It is founded, however, on a conjectural reading, and reluctating against this, a suggestion may be hazarded — "an excessive philanthropy for the folly of the insane, even to the point of sympathy for them."

[1] Some read "unbroken" or "perfect."

[1] There is long discussion of whether Maximian or Maximin is intended. To any one who compares the order of narration in the *Church History,* 9. 9, 11, the discussion will seem idle, though it is curious that the one most jealous and greedy of power should have been mistaken for one of the abdicators. It seems as if there had been some confusion in the mind of Eusebius himself.

[1] Unburnt offerings, meat offerings.

CHAPTER XLIX.

How Licinius oppressed the East.

For he was informed that in that quarter a certain savage beast was besetting both the church of God and the other inhabitants of the provinces, owing, as it were, to the efforts of the evil spirit to produce effects quite contrary to the deeds of the pious emperor : so that the Roman empire, divided into two parts, seemed to all men to resemble night and day; since darkness overspread the provinces of the East, while the brightest day illumined the inhabitants of the other portion. And whereas the latter were receiving manifold blessings at the hand of God, the sight of these blessings proved intolerable to that envy which hates all good, as well as to the tyrant who afflicted the other division of the empire ; and who, notwithstanding that his government was prospering, and he had been honored by a marriage connection[1] with so great an emperor as Constantine, yet cared not to follow the steps of that pious prince, but strove rather to imitate the evil purposes and practice of the impious ; and chose to adopt the course of those whose ignominious end he had seen with his own eyes, rather than to maintain amicable relations with him who was his superior.[2]

CHAPTER L.

How Licinius attempted a Conspiracy against Constantine.

Accordingly he engaged in an implacable war against his benefactor, altogether regardless of the laws of friendship, the obligation of oaths, the ties of kindred, and already existing treaties. For the most benignant emperor had given him a proof of sincere affection in bestowing on him the hand of his sister, thus granting him the privilege of a place in family relationship and his own ancient imperial descent, and investing him also with the rank and dignity of his colleague in the empire.[1] But the other took the very opposite course, employing himself in machinations against his superior, and devising various means to repay his benefactor with injuries. At first, pretending friendship, he did all things by guile and treachery, expecting thus to succeed in concealing his designs ; but God enabled his servant to detect the schemes thus devised in darkness. Being discovered, however,

in his first attempts, he had recourse to fresh frauds ; at one time pretending friendship, at another claiming the protection of solemn treaties. Then suddenly violating every engagement, and again beseeching pardon by embassies, yet after all shamefully violating his word, he at last declared open war, and with desperate infatuation resolved thenceforward to carry arms against God himself, whose worshiper he knew the emperor to be.

CHAPTER LI.

Intrigues of Licinius against the Bishops, and his Prohibition of Synods.

And at first he made secret enquiry respecting the ministers of God subject to his dominion, who had never, indeed, in any respect offended against his government, in order to bring false accusations against them. And when he found no ground of accusation, and had no real ground of objection against them, he next enacted a law, to the effect that the bishops should never on any account hold communication with each other, nor should any one of them absent himself on a visit to a neighboring church ; nor, lastly, should the holding of synods, or councils for the consideration of affairs of common interest,[1] be permitted. Now this was clearly a pretext for displaying his malice against us. For we were compelled either to violate the law, and thus be amenable to punishment, or else, by compliance with its injunctions, to nullify the statutes of the Church ; inasmuch as it is impossible to bring important questions to a satisfactory adjustment, except by means of synods. In other cases also this God-hater, being determined to act contrary to the God-loving prince, enacted such things. For whereas the one assembled the priests of God in order to honor them, and to promote peace and unity of judgment ; the other, whose object it was to destroy everything that was good, used all his endeavors to destroy the general harmony.

CHAPTER LII.

Banishment of the Christians, and Confiscation of their Property.

And whereas Constantine, the friend of God, had granted to His worshipers freedom of access to the imperial palaces ; this enemy of God, in a spirit the very reverse of this, expelled thence all Christians subject to his authority. He banished those who had proved themselves his most

---

[1] Licinius married in 313 Constantia, sister of Constantine.
[2] Thus generally following the *Church History* (10. 8).
[1] This rendering of *Bag.* is really a gloss from the *Church History*, 10. 8. Compare rendering of McGiffert. Molzberger renders "and left him in complete possession of the portions of the kingdom which had fallen to his lot."

[1] Perhaps "synods or councils and conferences on economic matters."

faithful and devoted servants, and compelled others, on whom he had himself conferred honor and distinction as a reward for their former eminent services, to the performance of menial offices as slaves to others ; and at length, being bent on seizing the property of all as a windfall, for himself, he even threatened with death those who professed the Saviour's name. Moreover, being himself of a nature hopelessly debased by sensuality, and degraded by the continual practice of adultery and other shameless vices, he assumed his own worthless character as a specimen of human nature generally, and denied that the virtue of chastity and continence existed among men.

CHAPTER LIII.

Edict that Women should not meet with the Men in the Churches.

ACCORDINGLY he passed a second law, which enjoined that men should not appear in company with women in the houses of prayer, and forbade women to attend the sacred schools of virtue, or to receive instruction from the bishops, directing the appointment of women to be teachers of their own sex. These regulations being received with general ridicule, he devised other means for effecting the ruin of the churches. He ordered that the usual congregations of the people should be held in the open country outside the gates, alleging that the open air without the city was far more suitable for a multitude than the houses of prayer within the walls.

CHAPTER LIV.

That those who refuse to sacrifice are to be dismissed from Military Service, and those in Prison not to be fed.

FAILING, however, to obtain obedience in this respect also, at length he threw off the mask, and gave orders that those who held military commissions in the several cities of the empire should be deprived of their respective commands, in case of their refusal to offer sacrifices to the demons. Accordingly the forces of the authorities in every province suffered the loss of those who worshiped God ; and he too who had decreed this order suffered loss, in that he thus deprived himself of the prayers of pious men. And why should I still further mention how he directed that no one should obey the dictates of common humanity by distributing food to those who were pining in prisons, or should even pity the captives who perished with hunger ; in short, that no one should perform a virtuous action, and that those whose natural

feelings impelled them to sympathize with their fellow-creatures should be prohibited from doing them a single kindness? Truly this was the most utterly shameless and scandalous of all laws, and one which surpassed the worst depravity of human nature : a law which inflicted on those who showed mercy the same penalties as on those who were the objects of their compassion, and visited the exercise of mere humanity with the severest punishments.[1]

CHAPTER LV.

The Lawless Conduct and Covetousness of Licinius.

SUCH were the ordinances of Licinius. But why should I enumerate his innovations respecting marriage, or those concerning the dying, whereby he presumed to abrogate the ancient and wisely established laws of the Romans, and to introduce certain barbarous and cruel institutions in their stead, inventing a thousand pretenses for oppressing his subjects? Hence it was that he devised a new method of measuring land, by which he reckoned the smallest portion at more than its actual dimensions, from an insatiable desire of acquisition. Hence too he registered the names of country residents who were now no more, and had long been numbered with the dead, procuring to himself by this expedient a shameful gain. His meanness was unlimited and his rapacity insatiable. So that when he had filled all his treasuries with gold, and silver, and boundless wealth, he bitterly bewailed his poverty, and suffered as it were the torments of Tantalus. But why should I mention how many innocent persons he punished with exile ; how much property he confiscated ; how many men of noble birth and estimable character he imprisoned, whose wives he handed over to be basely insulted by his profligate slaves, and to how many married women and virgins he himself offered violence, though already feeling the infirmities of age? I need not enlarge on these subjects, since the enormity of his last actions causes the former to appear trifling and of little moment.[1]

CHAPTER LVI.

At length he undertakes to raise a Persecution.

FOR the final efforts of his fury appeared in his open hostility to the churches, and he directed his attacks against the bishops themselves,

---

[1] Compare *Church History*, 10. 9.
[1] Compare *Church History*, 10. 9, and the same for the following chapters, in parts or whole.

whom he regarded as his worst adversaries, bearing special enmity to those men whom the great and pious emperor treated as his friends. Accordingly he spent on us the utmost of his fury, and, being transported beyond the bounds of reason, he paused not to reflect on the example of those who had persecuted the Christians before him, nor of those whom he himself had been raised up to punish and destroy for their impious deeds: nor did he heed the facts of which he had been himself a witness, though he had seen with his own eyes the chief originator of these our calamities (whoever he was), smitten by the stroke of the Divine scourge.

CHAPTER LVII.

That Maximian,[1] brought Low by a Fistulous Ulcer with Worms, issued an Edict in Favor of the Christians.

For whereas this man had commenced the attack on the churches, and had been the first to pollute his soul with the blood of just and godly men, a judgment from God overtook him, which at first affected his body, but eventually extended itself to his soul. For suddenly an abscess appeared in the secret parts of his person, followed by a deeply seated fistulous ulcer; and these diseases fastened with incurable virulence on the intestines, which swarmed with a vast multitude of worms, and emitted a pestilential odor. Besides, his entire person had become loaded, through gluttonous excess, with an enormous quantity of fat, and this, being now in a putrescent state, is said to have presented to all who approached him an intolerable and dreadful spectacle. Having, therefore, to struggle against such sufferings, at length, though late, he came to a realization of his past crimes against the Church; and, confessing his sins before God, he put a stop to the persecution of the Christians, and hastened to issue imperial edicts and rescripts for the rebuilding of their churches, at the same time enjoining them to perform their customary worship, and to offer up prayers on his behalf.[2]

CHAPTER LVIII.

That Maximin, who had persecuted the Christians, was compelled to fly, and conceal himself in the Disguise of a Slave.

Such was the punishment which he underwent who had commenced the persecution. He,[1] however, of whom we are now speaking, who had been a witness of these things, and known them by his own actual experience, all at once banished the remembrance of them from his mind, and reflected neither on the punishment of the first, nor the divine judgment which had been executed on the second persecutor.[2] The latter had indeed endeavored to outstrip his predecessor in the career of crime, and prided himself on the invention of new tortures for us. Fire nor sword, nor piercing with nails, nor yet wild beasts or the depths of the sea sufficed him. In addition to all these, he discovered a new mode of punishment, and issued an edict directing that their eyesight should be destroyed. So that numbers, not of men only, but of women and children, after being deprived of the sight of their eyes, and the use of the joints of their feet, by mutilation or cauterization, were consigned in this condition to the painful labor of the mines. Hence it was that this tyrant also was overtaken not long after by the righteous judgment of God, at a time when, confiding in the aid of the demons whom he worshiped as gods, and relying on the countless multitudes of his troops, he had ventured to engage in battle. For, feeling himself on that occasion destitute of all hope in God, he threw from him the imperial dress which so ill became him, hid himself with unmanly timidity in the crowd around him, and sought safety in flight.[3]

He afterwards lurked about the fields and villages in the habit of a slave, hoping he should thus be effectually concealed. He had not, however, eluded the mighty and all-searching eye of God: for even while he was expecting to pass the residue of his days in security, he fell prostrate, smitten by God's fiery dart, and his whole body consumed by the stroke of Divine vengeance; so that all trace of the original lineaments of his person was lost, and nothing remained to him but dry bones and a skeleton-like appearance.

CHAPTER LIX.

That Maximin, blinded by Disease, issued an Edict in Favor of the Christians.

And still the stroke of God continued heavy upon him, so that his eyes protruded and fell from their sockets, leaving him quite blind: and thus he suffered, by a most righteous retribution, the very same punishment which he had been

---

1 [Galerius Maximian. The description of his illness and death in the next chapter is repeated from the author's *Ecclesiastical History*, Bk. 8, c. 16. — *Bag.*] Compare translation of McGiffert, p. 338. and note; also Lactantius, *De M. P.* c. 33.
2 Compare edict in the *Church History*, 8. 17.

1 Licinius.
2 [Maximin, ruler of the Eastern provinces of the empire. — *Bag.*]
3 He was defeated by Licinius, who had much inferior forces. Compare Prolegomena, under *Life*, and references.

the first to devise for the martyrs of God. At length, however, surviving even these sufferings, he too implored pardon of the God of the Christians, and confessed his impious fighting against God : he too recanted, as the former persecutor had done ; and by laws and ordinances explicitly acknowledged his error in worshiping those whom he had accounted gods, declaring that he now knew, by positive experience, that the God of the Christians was the only true God. These were facts which Licinius had not merely received on the testimony of others, but of which he had himself had personal knowledge : and yet, as though his understanding had been obscured by some dark cloud of error, persisted in the same evil course.

BOOK II.

CHAPTER I.

Secret Persecution by Licinius, who causes Some Bishops to be put to Death at Amasia of Pontus.

IN this manner, he of whom we have spoken continued to rush headlong towards that destruction which awaits the enemies of God; and once more, with a fatal emulation of their example whose ruin he had himself witnessed as the consequence of their impious conduct, he re-kindled the persecution of the Christians, like a long-extinguished fire, and fanned the unhallowed flame to a fiercer height than any who had gone before him.

At first, indeed, though breathing fury and threatenings against God, like some savage beast of prey, or some crooked and wriggling serpent, he dared not, from fear of Constantine, openly level his attacks against the churches of God subject to his dominion; but dissembled the virulence of his malice, and endeavored by secret and limited measures to compass the death of the bishops, the most eminent of whom he found means to remove, through charges laid against them by the governors of the several provinces. And the manner in which they suffered had in it something strange, and hitherto unheard of. At all events, the barbarities perpetrated at Amasia of Pontus surpassed every known excess of cruelty.

CHAPTER II.

Demolition of Churches, and Butchery of the Bishops.

FOR in that city some of the churches, for the second time since the commencement of the persecutions, were leveled with the ground, and others were closed by the governors of the several districts, in order to prevent any who frequented them from assembling together, or rendering due worship to God. For he by whose orders these outrages were committed was too conscious of his own crimes to expect that these services were performed with any view to his benefit, and was convinced that all we did, and all our endeavors to obtain the favor of God, were on Constantine's behalf.

These servile governors[1] then, feeling assured that such a course would be pleasing to the impious tyrant, subjected the most distinguished prelates of the churches to capital punishment. Accordingly, men who had been guilty of no crime were led away, without cause[2] punished like murderers: and some suffered a new kind of death, having their bodies cut piecemeal; and, after this cruel punishment, more horrible than any named in tragedy, being cast, as a food to fishes, into the depths of the sea. The result of these horrors was again, as before, the flight of pious men, and once more the fields and deserts received the worshipers of God. The tyrant, having thus far succeeded in his object, he farther determined to raise a general persecution of the Christians:[3] and he would have accomplished his purpose, nor could anything have hindered him from carrying his resolution into effect, had not he who defends his own anticipated the coming evil, and by his special guidance conducted his servant Constantine to this part of the empire, causing him to shine forth as a brilliant light in the midst of the darkness and gloomy night.

CHAPTER III.

How Constantine was stirred in Behalf of the Christians thus in Danger of Persecution.

HE, perceiving the evils of which he had heard to be no longer tolerable, took wise counsel, and tempering the natural clemency of his character with a certain measure of severity, hastened to succor those who were thus grievously oppressed. For he judged that it would rightly be deemed a pious and holy task to secure, by the removal of an individual, the safety of the greater part of the human race. He judged too, that if he listened to the dictates of clemency only, and bestowed his pity on one utterly unworthy of it, this would, on the one hand, confer no real benefit on a man whom nothing would induce to abandon his evil practices, and whose fury against his subjects would only be likely to in-

---

1 Literally, "the flatterers and time-servers about him."
2 Or "openly."
3 [The reading in the text is τούτων, but should be πάντων, of *all* Christians, as it is in *Hist. Eccles.* Bk. 10, c. 8, from which this passage is almost verbally taken. — *Bag.*]

crease;[1] while, on the other hand, those who suffered from his oppression would thus be forever deprived of all hope of deliverance.

Influenced by these reflections, the emperor resolved without farther delay to extend a protecting hand to those who had fallen into such an extremity of distress. He accordingly made the usual warlike preparations, and assembled his whole forces, both of horse and foot. But before them all was carried the standard which I have before described, as the symbol of his full confidence in God.

CHAPTER IV.

That Constantine prepared himself for the War by Prayer: Licinius by the Practice of Divination.

HE took with him also the priests of God, feeling well assured that now, if ever, he stood in need of the efficacy of prayer, and thinking it right that they should constantly be near and about his person, as most trusty guardians of the soul.

Now, as soon as the tyrant understood that Constantine's victories over his enemies were secured to him by no other means than the co-operation of God, and that the persons above alluded to were continually with him and about his person; and besides this, that the symbol of the salutary passion preceded both the emperor himself and his whole army; he regarded these precautions with ridicule (as might be expected), at the same time mocking and reviling the emperor with blasphemous words.

On the other hand, he gathered round himself Egyptian diviners and soothsayers, with sorcerers and enchanters, and the priests and prophets of those whom he imagined to be gods. He then, after offering the sacrifices which he thought the occasion demanded, enquired how far he might reckon on a successful termination of the war. They replied with one voice, that he would unquestionably be victorious over his enemies, and triumphant in the war: and the oracles everywhere held out to him the same prospect in copious and elegant verses. The soothsayers certified him of favorable omens from the flight of birds; the priests[1] declared the same to be indicated by the motion of the entrails of their victims. Elevated, therefore, by these fallacious assurances, he boldly advanced at the head of his army, and prepared for battle.

CHAPTER V.

What Licinius, while sacrificing in a Grove, said concerning Idols, and concerning Christ.

AND when he was now ready to engage, he desired the most approved of his body-guard[1] and his most valued friends to meet him in one of the places which they consider sacred. It was a well-watered and shady grove, and in it were several marble statues of those whom he accounted to be gods. After lighting tapers and performing the usual sacrifices in honor of these, he is said to have delivered the following speech:

"Friends and fellow-soldiers! These are our country's gods, and these we honor with a worship derived from our remotest ancestors. But he who leads the army now opposed to us has proved false to the religion of his forefathers, and adopted atheistic sentiments, honoring in his infatuation some strange and unheard-of Deity, with whose despicable standard he now disgraces his army, and confiding in whose aid he has taken up arms, and is now advancing, not so much against *us* as against those very gods whom he has forsaken. However, the present occasion shall prove which of us is mistaken in his judgment, and shall decide between our gods and those whom our adversaries profess to honor. For either it will declare the victory to be ours, and so most justly evince that our gods are the true saviours and helpers; or else, if this God of Constantine's, who comes we know not whence, shall prove superior to our deities (who are many, and in point of numbers, at least, have the advantage), let no one henceforth doubt which god he ought to worship, but attach himself at once to the superior power, and ascribe to him the honors of the victory. Suppose, then, this strange God, whom we now regard with ridicule, should really prove victorious; then indeed we must acknowledge and give him honor, and so bid a long farewell to those for whom we light our tapers in vain. But if our own gods triumph (as they undoubtedly will), then, as soon as we have secured the present victory, let us prosecute the war without delay against these despisers of the gods."

Such were the words he addressed to those then present, as reported not long after to the writer of this history by some who heard them spoken.[2] And as soon as he had concluded his speech, he gave orders to his forces to commence the attack.

---

[1] This seems to intend some exoneration of Constantine, explaining why he was what the heathen called "faithless" towards Licinius.

[1] Soothsayers and priests. These were technically "augurs" and "haruspices." Compare for their functions the articles *Augur*, *Divinatio*, and *Haruspices*, in Smith, *Dict. Gr. and Rom. Ant.*

[1] Literally, "shield-bearers," but here relates to a chosen body of guards, as in the Macedonian army. Compare Liddell and Scott, *Lex.* s.v. ὑπασπιστής.

[2] The whole passage seems altogether too appropriate to receive ready credence; but it is worth noting here how Eusebius "quotes his authors," and seems to give the thing for what it is worth, keeping perhaps the same modicum of reservation for the hearers' rela-

CHAPTER VI.

An Apparition seen in the Cities subject to Licinius, as of Constantine's Troops passing through them.

WHILE these things were taking place a supernatural appearance is said to have been observed in the cities subject to the tyrant's rule. Different detachments of Constantine's army seemed to present themselves to the view, marching at noonday through these cities, as though they had obtained the victory. In reality, not a single soldier was anywhere present at the time, and yet this appearance was seen through the agency of a divine and superior power, and foreshadowed what was shortly coming to pass. For as soon as the armies were ready to engage, he who had broken through the ties of friendly alliance[1] was the first to commence the battle; on which Constantine, calling on the name of "God the Supreme Saviour," and giving this as the watchword to his soldiers, overcame him in this first conflict: and not long after in a second battle he gained a still more important and decisive victory, the salutary trophy preceding the ranks of his army.

CHAPTER VII.

That Victory everywhere followed the Presence of the Standard of the Cross in Battle.

INDEED, wherever this appeared, the enemy soon fled before his victorious troops. And the emperor perceiving this, whenever he saw any part of his forces hard pressed, gave orders that the salutary trophy should be moved in that direction, like some triumphant charm[1] against disasters: at which the combatants were divinely inspired, as it were, with fresh strength and courage, and immediate victory was the result.

CHAPTER VIII.

That Fifty Men were selected to carry the Cross.

ACCORDINGLY, he selected those of his bodyguard who were most distinguished for personal strength, valor, and piety, and intrusted them with the sole care and defense of the standard. There were thus no less than fifty men whose only duty was to surround and vigilantly defend

the standard, which they carried each in turn on their shoulders. These circumstances were related to the writer of this narrative by the emperor himself in his leisure moments, long after the occurrence of the events: and he added another incident well worthy of being recorded.

CHAPTER IX.

That One of the Cross-bearers, who fled from his Post, was slain: while Another, who faithfully stood his Ground, was preserved.

FOR he said that once, during the very heat of an engagement, a sudden tumult and panic attacked his army, which threw the soldier who then bore the standard into an agony of fear, so that he handed it over to another, in order to secure his own escape from the battle. As soon, however, as his comrade had received it, and he had withdrawn, and resigned all charge of the standard, he was struck in the belly by a dart, which took his life. Thus he paid the penalty of his cowardice and unfaithfulness, and lay dead on the spot: but the other, who had taken his place as the bearer of the salutary standard, found it to be the safeguard of his life. For though he was assailed by a continual shower of darts, the bearer remained unhurt, the staff of the standard receiving every weapon. It was indeed a truly marvelous circumstance, that the enemies' darts all fell within and remained in the slender circumference of this spear, and thus saved the standard-bearer from death; so that none of those engaged in this service ever received a wound.

This story is none of mine, but for this,[1] too, I am indebted to the emperor's own authority, who related it in my hearing along with other matters. And now, having thus through the power of God secured these first victories, he put his forces in motion and continued his onward march.

CHAPTER X.

Various Battles, and Constantine's Victories.

THE van, however, of the enemy, unable to resist the emperor's first assault, threw down their arms, and prostrated themselves at his feet. All these he spared, rejoicing to save human life. But there were others who still continued in arms, and engaged in battle. These the emperor endeavored to conciliate by friendly

---

tive imagination and memory, when relating after the events, that the modern reader does.

　[1] [Licinius was suspected of having secretly countenanced Bassianus (who had married Constantine's sister Anastasia, and received the rank of Cæsar) in a treasonable conspiracy. Vide Gibbon, *Decline and Fall*, chap. 14. — *Bag.*] Compare Prolegomena, under *Life.*
　[1] Or "**remedy**"; i.e. that which keeps off harm.

　[1] [Πάλιν, "again," alluding to the former miracle, the vision of the cross, which Eusebius does not venture to attest himself, but relates on the word and oath of Constantine. Vide Bk. 1, cc. 28 and 30. — *Bag.*]

overtures, but when these were not accepted he ordered his army to commence the attack. On this they immediately turned and betook themselves to flight; and some were overtaken and slain according to the laws of war, while others fell on each other in the confusion of their flight, and perished by the swords of their comrades.

CHAPTER XI.

Flight, and Magic Arts of Licinius.

In these circumstances their commander, finding himself bereft of the aid of his followers,[1] having lost his lately numerous array, both of regular and allied forces, having proved, too, by experience, how vain his confidence had been in those whom he thought to be gods, ignominiously took to flight, by which indeed he effected his escape, and secured his personal safety, for the pious emperor had forbidden his soldiers to follow him too closely,[2] and thus allowed him an opportunity for escape. And this he did in the hope that he might hereafter, on conviction of the desperate state of his affairs, be induced to abandon his insane and presumptuous ambition, and return to sounder reason. So Constantine, in his excessive humanity, thought and was willing patiently to bear past injuries, and extend his forgiveness to one who so ill deserved it; but Licinius, far from renouncing his evil practices, still added crime to crime, and ventured on more daring atrocities than ever. Nay, once more tampering with the detestable arts of magic, he again was presumptuous: so that it might well be said of him, as it was of the Egyptian tyrant of old, that God had hardened his heart.[3]

CHAPTER XII.

How Constantine, after praying in his Tabernacle, obtained the Victory.

But while Licinius, giving himself up to these impieties, rushed blindly towards the gulf of destruction, the emperor on the other hand, when he saw that he must meet his enemies in a second battle, devoted the intervening time to his Saviour. He pitched the tabernacle of the cross[1] outside and at a distance from his camp, and there passed his time in a pure and holy manner, offering up prayers to God; following thus the example of his ancient prophet, of whom the sacred oracles testify, that he pitched the tabernacle without the camp.[2] He was attended only by a few, whose faith and pious devotion he highly esteemed. And this custom he continued to observe whenever he meditated an engagement with the enemy. For he was deliberate in his measures, the better to insure safety, and desired in everything to be directed by divine counsel. And making earnest supplications to God, he was always honored after a little with a manifestation of his presence. And then, as if moved by a divine impulse, he would rush from the tabernacle, and suddenly give orders to his army to move at once without delay, and on the instant to draw their swords. On this they would immediately commence the attack, fight vigorously, so as with incredible celerity to secure the victory, and raise trophies of victory over their enemies.

CHAPTER XIII.

His Humane Treatment of Prisoners.

Thus the emperor and his army had long been accustomed to act, whenever there was a prospect of an engagement; for his God was ever present to his thoughts, and he desired to do everything according to his will, and conscientiously to avoid any wanton sacrifice of human life. He was anxious thus for the preservation not only of his own subjects, but even of his enemies. Accordingly he directed his victorious troops to spare the lives of their prisoners, admonishing them, as human beings, not to forget the claims of their common nature. And whenever he saw the passions of his soldiery excited beyond control, he repressed their fury by a largess of money, rewarding every man who saved the life of an enemy with a certain weight of gold. And the emperor's own sagacity led him to discover this inducement to spare human life, so that great numbers even of the barbarians were thus saved, and owed their lives to the emperor's gold.

CHAPTER XIV.

A Farther Mention of his Prayers in the Tabernacle.

Now these, and a thousand such acts as these, were familiarly and habitually done by the emperor. And on the present occasion he retired, as his custom was before battle, to the privacy of his tabernacle, and there employed his time in prayer to God. Meanwhile he strictly ab-

---

[1] "Slaves," a word which has frequently been used by Eusebius in this literal sense.
[2] This idiom here is nearly the English, "followed on the heels" of any one.   [3] Ex. ix. 12.
[1] [This tabernacle, which Constantine always carried with him in his military expeditions, is described by Sozomen, Bk. 1, c. 8; see English translation. — Bag.]

[2] [Alluding to Ex. xxxiii. 7, &c. — Bag.]

stained from anything like ease, or luxurious living, and disciplined himself by fasting and bodily mortification, imploring the favor of God by supplication and prayer, that he might obtain his concurrence and aid, and be ready to execute whatever he might be pleased to suggest to his thoughts. In short, he exercised a vigilant care over all alike, and interceded with God as much for the safety of his enemies as for that of his own subjects.

CHAPTER XV.

Treacherous Friendship, and Idolatrous Practices of Licinius.

AND inasmuch as he who had lately fled before him now dissembled his real sentiments, and again petitioned for a renewal of friendship and alliance, the emperor thought fit, on certain conditions, to grant his request,[1] in the hope that such a measure might be expedient, and generally advantageous to the community. Licinius, however, while he pretended a ready submission to the terms prescribed, and attested his sincerity by oaths, at this very time was secretly engaged in collecting a military force, and again meditated war and strife, inviting even the barbarians to join his standard,[2] and he began also to look about him for other gods, having been deceived by those in whom he had hitherto trusted. And, without bestowing a thought on what he had himself publicly spoken on the subject of false deities, or choosing to acknowledge that God who had fought on the side of Constantine, he made himself ridiculous by seeking for a multitude of new gods.

CHAPTER XVI.

How Licinius counseled his Soldiers not to attack the Standard of the Cross.

HAVING now learned by experience the Divine and mysterious power which resided in the salu-

tary trophy, by means of which Constantine's army had become habituated to victory, he admonished his soldiers never to direct their attack against this standard, nor even incautiously to allow their eyes to rest upon it; assuring them that it possessed a terrible power, and was especially hostile to him; so that they would do well carefully to avoid any collision with it. And now, having given these directions, he prepared for a decisive conflict with him whose humanity prompted him still to hesitate, and to postpone the fate which he foresaw awaited his adversary. The enemy, however, confident in the aid of a multitude of gods, advanced to the attack with a powerful array of military force, preceded by certain images of the dead, and lifeless statues, as their defense. On the other side, the emperor, secure in the armor of godliness, opposed to the numbers of the enemy the salutary and life-giving sign, as at once a terror to the foe, and a protection from every harm. And for a while he paused, and preserved at first the attitude of forbearance, from respect to the treaty of peace to which he had given his sanction, that he might not be the first to commence the contest.

CHAPTER XVII.

Constantine's Victory.

BUT as soon as he perceived that his adversaries persisted in their resolution, and were already drawing their swords, he gave free scope to his indignation, and by a single charge[1] overthrew in a moment the entire body of the enemy, thus triumphing at once over them and their gods.

CHAPTER XVIII.

Death of Licinius, and Celebration of the Event.

HE then proceeded to deal with this adversary of God and his followers according to the laws of war, and consign them to fitting punishment. Accordingly the tyrant himself, and they whose counsels had supported him in his impiety, were together subjected to the just punishment of death. After this, those who had so lately been deceived by their vain confidence in false deities, acknowledged with unfeigned sincerity the God of Constantine, and openly professed their belief in him as the true and only God.

---

1 [" He consented to leave his rival, or, as he again styled Licinius, his friend and brother, in the possession of Thrace, Asia Minor, Syria, and Egypt; but the provinces of Pannonia, Dalmatia, Dacia, Macedonia, and Greece, were yielded to the Western empire, and the dominions of Constantine now extended from the confines of Caledonia to the extremity of Peloponnesus." — Gibbon, *Decline and Fall*, chap. XIV. — *Bag.*]

2 [Gibbon (chap. XIV.) says that the reconciliation of Constantine and Licinius maintained, *above eight years*, the tranquillity of the Roman world. If this be true, it may be regarded as one proof that our author's work is rather to be considered as a general sketch of Constantine's life and character than as a minutely correct historical document. — *Bag.*] There is either a strange lack of perspective in this account, or else Eusebius omits all account of the first wars with Licinius (314) which resulted in the division of territory mentioned in the above note. This latter view is plausible on comparison with the account in the *Church History*. In this view the conditions referred to above relate to the terms on which Licinius was spared on Constantia's request, and what follows is the explanation of the alleged oath-breaking of Constantine in putting Licinius to death.

---

1 "With one shout and charge." This does not agree with the account of the final struggle by which Licinius came into Constantine's power, as generally given, and lends some probability to the view that after he had been captured he again revolted.

CHAPTER XIX.

Rejoicings and Festivities.

AND now, the impious being thus removed, the sun once more shone brightly after the gloomy cloud of tyrannic power. Each separate portion of the Roman dominion became blended with the rest; the Eastern nations united with those of the West, and the whole body of the Roman empire was graced as it were by its head in the person of a single and supreme ruler, whose sole authority pervaded the whole. Now too the bright rays of the light of godliness gladdened the days of those who had heretofore been sitting in darkness and the shadow of death. Past sorrows were no more remembered, for all united in celebrating the praises of the victorious prince, and avowed their recognition of his preserver as the only true God. Thus he whose character shone with all the virtues of piety, the emperor VICTOR, for he had himself adopted this name as a most fitting appellation to express the victory which God had granted him over all who hated or opposed him,[1] assumed the dominion of the East, and thus singly governed the Roman empire, re-united, as in former times, under one head. Thus, as he was the first to proclaim to all the sole sovereignty of God, so he himself, as sole sovereign of the Roman world, extended his authority over the whole human race. Every apprehension of those evils under the pressure of which all had suffered was now removed; men whose heads had drooped in sorrow now regarded each other with smiling countenances, and looks expressive of their inward joy. With processions and hymns of praise they first of all, as they were told, ascribed the supreme sovereignty to God, as in truth the King of kings; and then with continued acclamations rendered honor to the victorious emperor, and the Cæsars, his most discreet and pious sons. The former afflictions were forgotten, and all past impieties forgiven: while with the enjoyment of present happiness was mingled the expectation of continued blessings in the future.

CHAPTER XX.

Constantine's Enactments in Favor of the Confessors.

MOREOVER, the emperor's edicts, permeated with his humane spirit, were published among us also, as they had been among the inhabitants of the other division of the empire; and his laws, which breathed a spirit of piety toward God, gave promise of manifold blessings, since they secured many advantages to his provincial subjects in every nation, and at the same time prescribed measures suited to the exigencies of the churches of God. For first of all they recalled those who, in consequence of their refusal to join in idol worship, had been driven to exile, or ejected from their homes by the governors of their respective provinces. In the next place, they relieved from their burdens those who for the same reason had been adjudged to serve in the civil courts, and ordained restitution to be made to any who had been deprived of property. They too, who in the time of trial had signalized themselves by fortitude of soul in the cause of God, and had therefore been condemned to the painful labor of the mines, or consigned to the solitude of islands, or compelled to toil in the public works, all received an immediate release from these burdens; while others, whose religious constancy had cost them the forfeiture of their military rank, were vindicated by the emperor's generosity from this dishonor: for he granted them the alternative either of resuming their rank, and enjoying their former privileges, or, in the event of their preferring a more settled life, of perpetual exemption from all service. Lastly, all who had been compelled by way of disgrace and insult to serve in the employments of women,[1] he likewise freed with the rest.

CHAPTER XXI.

His Laws concerning Martyrs, and concerning Ecclesiastical Property.

SUCH were the benefits secured by the emperor's written mandates to the persons of those who had thus suffered for the faith, and his laws made ample provision for their property also.

With regard to those holy martyrs of God who had laid down their lives in the confession of His name, he directed that their estates should be enjoyed by their nearest kindred; and, in default of any of these, that the right of inheritance should be vested in the churches. Farther, whatever property had been consigned to other parties from the treasury, whether in the way of sale or gift, together with that retained in the treasury itself, the generous mandate of the emperor directed should be restored to the original owners. Such benefits did his bounty, thus widely diffused, confer on the Church of God.

---

[1] Like very many other things which Eusebius tells of Constantine, that which was entirely customary with other emperors as well as Constantine has the appearance of being peculiar to him. Victor is a common title of various emperors.

[1] [In the gynæcia (γυναικεῖα), or places where women, and subsequently slaves of both sexes, were employed in spinning and weaving for the emperor. *Vide infra*, ch. 34. — *Bag.*] See note on ch. 34.

CHAPTER XXII.

How he won the Favor of the People.

BUT his munificence bestowed still further and more numerous favors on the heathen peoples and the other nations of his empire. So that the inhabitants of our [Eastern] regions, who had heard of the privileges experienced in the opposite portion of the empire, and had blessed the fortunate recipients of them, and longed for the enjoyment of a similar lot for themselves, now with one consent proclaimed their own happiness, when they saw themselves in possession of all these blessings ; and confessed that the appearance of such a monarch to the human race was indeed a marvelous event, and such as the world's history had never yet recorded. Such were their sentiments.

CHAPTER XXIII.

That he declared God to be the Author of his Prosperity : and concerning his Rescripts.

AND now that, through the powerful aid of God his Saviour, all nations owned their subjection to the emperor's authority, he openly proclaimed to all the name of Him to whose bounty he owed all his blessings, and declared that He, and not himself, was the author of his past victories. This declaration, written both in the Latin and Greek languages, he caused to be transmitted through every province of the empire. Now the excellence of his style of expression[1] may be known from a perusal of his letters themselves, which were two in number ; one addressed to the churches of God ; the other to the heathen population in the several cities of the empire. The latter of these I think it well to insert here, as connected with my present subject, in order on the one hand that a copy of this document may be recorded as matter of history, and thus preserved to posterity, and on the other that it may serve to confirm the truth of my present narrative. It is taken from an authentic copy of the imperial statute in my own possession ; and the signature in the emperor's own handwriting attaches as it were the impress of truth to the statement I have made.

CHAPTER XXIV.

Law of Constantine respecting Piety towards God, and the Christian Religion.[1]

" VICTOR CONSTANTINUS, MAXIMUS AUGUSTUS, to the inhabitants of the province of Palestine.

" To all who entertain just and sound sentiments respecting the character of the Supreme Being, it has long been most clearly evident, and beyond the possibility of doubt, how vast a difference there has ever been between those who maintain a careful observance of the hallowed duties of the Christian religion, and those who treat this religion with hostility or contempt. But at this present time, we may see by still more manifest proofs, and still more decisive instances, both how unreasonable it were to question this truth, and how mighty is the power of the Supreme God : since it appears that they who faithfully observe His holy laws, and shrink from the transgression of His commandments, are rewarded with abundant blessings, and are endued with well-grounded hope as well as ample power for the accomplishment of their undertakings. On the other hand, they who have cherished impious sentiments have experienced results corresponding to their evil choice. For how is it to be expected that any blessing would be obtained by one who neither desired to acknowledge nor duly to worship that God who is the source of all blessing ? Indeed, facts themselves are a confirmation of what I say.

CHAPTER XXV.

An Illustration from Ancient Times.

" FOR certainly any one who will mentally retrace the course of events from the earliest period down to the present time, and will reflect on what has occurred in past ages, will find that all who have made justice and probity the basis of their conduct, have not only carried their undertakings to a successful issue, but have gathered, as it were, a store of sweet fruit as the produce of this pleasant root. Again, whoever observes the career of those who have been bold in the practice of oppression or injustice ; who have either directed their senseless fury against God himself, or have conceived no kindly feelings towards their fellow-men, but have dared to afflict them with exile, disgrace, confiscation, massacre, or other miseries of the like kind, and all this without any sense of compunction, or wish to direct thoughts to a better course, will find that such men have received a recompense proportioned to their crimes. And these are results which might naturally and reasonably be expected to ensue.[1]

---

[1] " The value of our narrative " is the rendering of Molzberger. " The powerfulness of his language." — *1709.*
[1] Compare Epitome in Sozomen, i. 8.

[1] There is a curious unanimity of effort on the part of theological amateurs, ancient and modern, to prove that those upon whom the tower in Siloam fell were guiltier than others. This was the spirit of Lactantius and it is not to be wondered at that Constantine should adopt such a peculiarly self-satisfying doctrine.

CHAPTER XXVI.

Of Persecuted and Persecutors.

"For whoever have addressed themselves with integrity of purpose to any course of action, keeping the fear of God continually before their thoughts, and preserving an unwavering faith in him, without allowing present fears or dangers to outweigh their hope of future blessings — such persons, though for a season they may have experienced painful trials, have borne their afflictions lightly, being supported by the belief of greater rewards in store for them ; and their character has acquired a brighter luster in proportion to the severity of their past sufferings. With regard, on the other hand, to those who have either dishonorably slighted the principles of justice, or refused to acknowledge the Supreme God themselves, and yet have dared to subject others who have faithfully maintained his worship to the most cruel insults and punishments ; who have failed equally to recognize their own wretchedness in oppressing others on such grounds, and the happiness and blessing of those who preserved their devotion to God even in the midst of such sufferings : with regard, I say, to such men, many a time have their armies been slaughtered, many a time have they been put to flight ; and their warlike preparations have ended in total ruin and defeat.

CHAPTER XXVII.

How the Persecution became the Occasion of Calamities to the Aggressors.

"From the causes I have described, grievous wars arose, and destructive devastations. Hence followed a scarcity of the common necessaries of life, and a crowd of consequent miseries : hence, too, the authors of these impieties have either met a disastrous death of extreme suffering, or have dragged out an ignominious existence, and confessed it to be worse than death itself, thus receiving as it were a measure of punishment proportioned to the heinousness of their crimes.[1] For each experienced a degree of calamity according to the blind fury with which he had been led to combat, and as he thought, defeat the Divine will : so that they not only felt the pressure of the ills of this present life, but were tormented also by a most lively apprehension of punishment in the future world.[2]

CHAPTER XXVIII.

That God chose Constantine to be the Minister of Blessing.

"AND now, with such a mass of impiety oppressing the human race, and the commonwealth in danger of being utterly destroyed, as if by the agency of some pestilential disease, and therefore needing powerful and effectual aid ; what was the relief, and what the remedy which the Divinity devised for these evils ? (And by Divinity is meant the one who is alone and truly God, the possessor of almighty and eternal power : and surely it cannot be deemed arrogance in one who has received benefits from God, to acknowledge them in the loftiest terms of praise.) I myself, then, was the instrument whose services He chose, and esteemed suited for the accomplishment of his will. Accordingly, beginning at the remote Britannic ocean, and the regions where, according to the law of nature, the sun sinks beneath the horizon, through the aid of divine power I banished and utterly removed every form of evil which prevailed, in the hope that the human race, enlightened through my instrumentality, might be recalled to a due observance of the holy laws of God, and at the same time our most blessed faith might prosper under the guidance of his almighty hand.

CHAPTER XXIX.

Constantine's Expressions of Piety towards God; and Praise of the Confessors.

"I SAID,[1] under the guidance of his hand ; for I would desire never to be forgetful of the gratitude due to his grace. Believing, therefore, that this most excellent service had been confided to me as a special gift, I proceeded as far as the regions of the East, which, being under the pressure of severer calamities, seemed to demand still more effectual remedies at my hands. At the same time I am most certainly persuaded that I myself owe my life, my every breath, in short, my very inmost and secret thoughts, entirely to the favor of the Supreme God. Now I am well aware that they who are sincere in the pursuit of the heavenly hope, and have fixed this hope in heaven itself as the peculiar and predominant principle of their lives, have no need to depend on human favor, but rather have enjoyed higher honors in proportion as they have separated themselves from the inferior and evil things of this earthly existence. Nevertheless I deem it

---

[1] Compare Lactantius, *On the deaths of the persecutors* (De M. P.), and the *Church History* of Eusebius.
[2] Literally "beneath the earth," referring of course to the Græco-Roman conception of Hades.

[1] [" I said, under the guidance," &c. It seems necessary to supply some expression of this kind, in order to preserve the sense, which is otherwise interrupted by the division (in this instance, at least, manifestly improper) into chapters. — *Bag.*]

incumbent on me to remove at once and most completely from all such persons the hard necessities laid upon them for a season, and the unjust inflictions under which they have suffered, though free from any guilt or just liability. For it would be strange indeed, that the fortitude and constancy of soul displayed by such men should be fully apparent during the reign of those whose first object it was to persecute them on account of their devotion to God, and yet that the glory of their character should not be more bright and blessed, under the administration of a prince who is His servant.

CHAPTER XXX.

A Law granting Release from Exile, from Service in the Courts, and from the Confiscation of Property.

" LET all therefore who have exchanged their country for a foreign land, because they would not abandon that reverence and faith toward God to which they had devoted themselves with their whole hearts, and have in consequence at different times been subject to the cruel sentence of the courts ; together with any who have been enrolled in the registers of the public courts, though in time past exempt from such office ; let these, I say, now render thanks to God the Liberator of all, in that they are restored to their hereditary property, and their wonted tranquility. Let those also who have been despoiled of their goods, and have hitherto passed a wretched existence, mourning under the loss of all that they possessed, once more be restored to their former homes, their families, and estates, and receive with joy the bountiful kindness of God.

CHAPTER XXXI.

Release likewise granted to Exiles in the Islands.

" FURTHERMORE, it is our command that all those who have been detained in the islands against their will should receive the benefit of this present provision ; in order that they who till now have been surrounded by rugged mountains and the encircling barrier of the ocean, being now set free from that gloomy and desolate solitude, may fulfill their fondest wish by revisiting their dearest friends. Those, too, who have prolonged a miserable life in the midst of abject and wretched squalor, welcoming their restoration as an unlooked-for gain, and discarding henceforth all anxious thoughts, may pass their lives with us in freedom from all fear. For that any one could live in a state of fear under our government, when we boast and believe

ourselves to be the servants of God, would surely be a thing most extraordinary even to hear of, and quite incredible ; and our mission is to rectify the errors of the others.

CHAPTER XXXII.

And to those ignominiously employed in the Mines and Public Works.

" AGAIN, with regard to those who have been condemned either to the grievous labor of the mines, or to service in the public works, let them enjoy the sweets of leisure in place of these long-continued toils, and henceforth lead a far easier life, and more accordant with the wishes of their hearts, exchanging the incessant hardships of their tasks for quiet relaxation. And if any have forfeited the common privilege of liberty, or have unhappily suffered dishonor,[1] let them hasten back every one to the country of his nativity, and resume with becoming joy their former positions in society, from which they have been as it were separated by long residence abroad.

CHAPTER XXXIII.

Concerning those Confessors engaged in Military Service.

" ONCE more, with respect to those who had previously been preferred to any military distinction, of which they were afterwards deprived, for the cruel and unjust reason that they chose rather to acknowledge their allegiance to God than to retain the rank they held ; we leave them perfect liberty of choice, either to occupy their former stations, should they be content again to engage in military service, or after an honorable discharge, to live in undisturbed tranquillity. For it is fair and consistent that men who have displayed such magnanimity and fortitude in meeting the perils to which they have been exposed, should be allowed the choice either of enjoying peaceful leisure, or resuming their former rank.

CHAPTER XXXIV.

The Liberation of Free Persons condemned to labor in the Women's Apartments, or to Servitude.

" LASTLY, if any have wrongfully been deprived of the privileges of noble lineage, and subjected to a judicial sentence which has consigned them

[1] Glossed by Molzberger as " political dishonor."

to the women's apartments[1] and to the linen making, there to undergo a cruel and miserable labor, or reduced them to servitude for the benefit of the public treasury, without any exemption on the ground of superior birth; let such persons, resuming the honors they had previously enjoyed, and their proper dignities, henceforward exult in the blessings of liberty, and lead a glad life. Let the free man,[2] too, by some injustice and inhumanity, or even madness, made a slave, who has felt the sudden transition from liberty to bondage, and ofttimes bewailed his unwonted labors, return to his family once more a free man in virtue of this our ordinance, and seek those employments which befit a state of freedom; and let him dismiss from his remembrance those services which he found so oppressive, and which so ill became his condition.

CHAPTER XXXV.

Of the Inheritance of the Property of Martyrs and Confessors, also of those who had suffered Banishment or Confiscation of Property.

"Nor must we omit to notice those estates of which individuals have been deprived on various pretenses. For if any of those who have engaged with dauntless and resolute determination in the noble and divine conflict of martyrdom have also been stripped of their fortunes; or if the same has been the lot of the confessors, who have won for themselves the hope of eternal treasures; or if the loss of property has befallen those who were driven from their native land because they would not yield to the persecutors, and betray their faith; lastly, if any who have escaped the sentence of death have yet been despoiled of their worldly goods; we ordain that the inheritances of all such persons be transferred to their nearest kindred. And whereas the laws expressly assign this right to those most nearly related, it will be easy to ascertain to whom these inheritances severally belong. And it is evidently reasonable that the succession in these cases should belong to those who would have stood in the place of nearest affinity, had the deceased experienced a natural death.

CHAPTER XXXVI.

The Church is declared Heir of those who leave no Kindred; and the Free Gifts of such Persons Confirmed.

"But should there be no surviving relation to succeed in due course to the property of those above-mentioned, I mean the martyrs, or confessors, or those who for some such cause have been banished from their native land; in such cases we ordain that the church locally nearest in each instance shall succeed to the inheritance. And surely it will be no wrong to the departed that that church should be their heir, for whose sake they have endured every extremity of suffering. We think it necessary to add this also, that in case any of the above-mentioned persons have donated any part of their property in the way of free gift, possession of such property shall be assured, as is reasonable, to those who have thus received it.

CHAPTER XXXVII.

Lands, Gardens, or Houses, but not Actual Produce from them, are to be given back.

"And that there may be no obscurity in this our ordinance, but every one may readily apprehend its requirements, let all men hereby know that if they are now maintaining themselves in possession of a piece of land, or a house, or garden, or anything else which had appertained to the before-mentioned persons, it will be good and advantageous for them to acknowledge the fact, and make restitution with the least possible delay. On the other hand, although it should appear that some individuals have reaped abundant profits from this unjust possession, we do not consider that justice demands the restitution of such profits. They must, however, declare explicitly what amount of benefit they have thus derived, and from what sources, and entreat our pardon for this offense; in order that their past covetousness may in some measure be atoned for, and that the Supreme God may accept this compensation as a token of contrition, and be pleased graciously to pardon the sin.

CHAPTER XXXVIII.

In what Manner Requests should be made for these.

"But it is possible that those who have become masters of such property (if it be right or possible to allow them such a title) will assure us by way of apology for their conduct, that it was not in their power to abstain from this appropriation at a time when a spectacle of misery in all its forms everywhere met the view; when men were cruelly driven from their homes, slaughtered without mercy, thrust forth without remorse: when the confiscation of the property of innocent persons was a common thing, and

---

[1] In the Greek houses there were separate suites for men and women. Compare article *Domus*, in Smith, *Dict. of Gr. and Rom. Antiq.*

[2] [That is, the free subject of inferior rank, accustomed to labor for his subsistence, but not to the degradation of slavery.]

when persecutions and property seizures were unceasing. If any defend their conduct by such reasons as these, and still persist in their avaricious temper, they shall be made sensible that such a course will bring punishment on themselves, and all the more because this correction of evil is the very characteristic of our service to the Supreme God. So that it will henceforth be dangerous to retain what dire necessity may in time past have compelled men to take; especially because it is in any case incumbent on us to discourage covetous desires, both by persuasion, and by warning examples.

CHAPTER XXXIX.

The Treasury must restore Lands, Gardens, and Houses to the Churches.

" NOR shall the treasury itself, should it have any of the things we have spoken of, be permitted to keep them; but, without venturing as it were to raise its voice against the holy churches, it shall justly relinquish in their favor what it has for a time unjustly retained. We ordain, therefore, that all things whatsoever which shall appear righteously to belong to the churches, whether the property consist of houses, or fields and gardens, or whatever the nature of it may be, shall be restored in their full value and integrity, and with undiminished right of possession.

CHAPTER XL.

The Tombs of Martyrs and the Cemeteries to be transferred to the Possession of the Churches.

" AGAIN, with respect to those places which are honored in being the depositories of the remains of martyrs, and continue to be memorials of their glorious departure; how can we doubt that they rightly belong to the churches, or refrain from issuing our injunction to that effect? For surely there can be no better liberality, no labor more pleasing or profitable, than to be thus employed under the guidance of the Divine Spirit, in order that those things which have been appropriated on false pretenses by unjust and wicked men, may be restored, as justice demands, and once more secured to the holy churches.

CHAPTER XLI.

Those who have purchased Property belonging to the Church, or received it as a Gift, are to restore it.

" AND since it would be wrong in a provision intended to include all cases, to pass over those who have either procured any such property by right of purchase from the treasury, or have retained it when conveyed to them in the form of a gift; let all who have thus rashly indulged their insatiable thirst of gain be assured that, although by daring to make such purchases they have done all in their power to alienate our clemency from themselves, they shall nevertheless not fail of obtaining it, so far as is possible and consistent with propriety in each case. So much then is determined.

CHAPTER XLII.

An Earnest Exhortation to worship God.

" AND now, since it appears by the clearest and most convincing evidence, that the miseries which erewhile oppressed the entire human race are now banished from every part of the world, through the power of Almighty God, and at the same time the counsel and aid which he is pleased on many occasions to administer through our agency; it remains for all, both individually and unitedly, to observe and seriously consider how great this power and how efficacious this grace are, which have annihilated and utterly destroyed this generation, as I may call them, of most wicked and evil men; have restored joy to the good, and diffused it over all countries; and now guarantee the fullest authority both to honor the Divine law as it should be honored, with all reverence, and pay due observance to those who have dedicated themselves to the service of that law. These rising as from some dark abyss and, with an enlightened knowledge of the present course of events, will henceforward render to its precepts that becoming reverence and honor which are consistent with their pious character.
Let this ordinance be published in our Eastern provinces." [1]

CHAPTER XLIII.

How the Enactments of Constantine were carried into Effect.

SUCH were the injunctions contained in the first letter which the emperor addressed to us. And the provisions of this enactment were speedily carried into effect, everything being conducted in a manner quite different from the atrocities which had but lately been daringly perpetrated during the cruel ascendancy of the tyrants. Those persons also who were legally entitled to it, received the benefit of the emperor's liberality.

---

[1] [This seems to be the subscription or signature in the emperor's own handwriting, which is referred to at the end of ch. 23. — *Bag.*]

CHAPTER XLIV.

That he promoted Christians to Offices of Government, and forbade Gentiles in Such Stations to offer Sacrifice.

AFTER this the emperor continued to address himself to matters of high importance, and first he sent governors to the several provinces, mostly such as were devoted to the saving faith ; and if any appeared inclined to adhere to Gentile worship, he forbade them to offer sacrifice. This law applied also to those who surpassed the provincial governors in rank and dignity,[1] and even to those who occupied the highest station, and held the authority of the Prætorian Præfecture.[2] If they were Christians, they were free to act consistently with their profession ; if otherwise, the law required them to abstain from idolatrous sacrifices.

CHAPTER XLV.

Statutes which forbade Sacrifice, and enjoined the Building of Churches.

SOON after this, two laws were promulgated about the same time ; one of which was intended to restrain the idolatrous abominations which in time past had been practiced in every city and country ; and it provided that no one should erect images, or practice divination and other false and foolish arts, or offer sacrifice in any way.[1] The other statute commanded the heightening of the oratories, and the enlargement in length and breadth of the churches of God ; as though it were expected that, now the madness of polytheism was wholly removed, pretty nearly all mankind would henceforth attach themselves to the service of God. His own personal piety induced the emperor to devise and write these instructions to the governors of the several provinces : and the law farther admonished them not to spare the expenditure of money, but to draw supplies from the imperial treasury itself. Similar instructions were written also to the bishops of the several churches ; and the emperor was pleased to transmit the same to myself, being the first letter which he personally addressed to me.

CHAPTER XLVI.

Constantine's Letter to Eusebius and Other Bishops, respecting the Building of Churches, with Instructions to repair the Old, and erect New Ones on a Larger Scale, with the Aid of the Provincial Governors.

" VICTOR CONSTANTINUS, MAXIMUS AUGUSTUS, to Eusebius.

" Forasmuch as the unholy and willful rule of tyranny has persecuted the servants of our Saviour until this present time, I believe and have fully satisfied myself, best beloved brother, that the buildings belonging to all the churches have either become ruinous through actual neglect, or have received inadequate attention from the dread of the violent spirit of the times.

" But now, that liberty is restored, and that serpent[1] driven from the administration of public affairs by the providence of the Supreme God, and our instrumentality, we trust that all can see the efficacy of the Divine power, and that they who through fear of persecution or through unbelief have fallen into any errors, will now acknowledge the true God, and adopt in future that course of life which is according to truth and rectitude. With respect, therefore, to the churches over which you yourself preside, as well as the bishops, presbyters, and deacons of other churches with whom you are acquainted, do you admonish all to be zealous in their attention to the buildings of the churches, and either to repair or enlarge those which at present exist, or, in cases of necessity, to erect new ones.

" We also empower you, and the others through you, to demand what is needful for the work, both from the provincial governors and from the Prætorian Præfect. For they have received instructions to be most diligent in obedience to your Holiness's orders. God preserve you, beloved brother." A copy of this charge was transmitted throughout all the provinces to the bishops of the several churches : the provincial governors received directions accordingly, and the imperial statute was speedily carried into effect.

---

[1] [That is, the proconsuls, the vicars (or vice-præfects), and counts, or provincial generals. — *Bag.*]

[2] [The power of the four Prætorian Præfects in the time of Constantine is thus described by Gibbon : " 1. The Præfect of the East stretched his ample jurisdiction into the three parts of the globe which were subject to the Romans, from the cataracts of the Nile to the banks of the Phasis, and from the mountains of Thrace to the frontiers of Persia. 2. The important provinces of Pannonia, Dacia, Macedonia, and Greece once acknowledged the authority of the Præfect of Illyricum. 3. The power of the Præfect of Italy was not confined to the country from whence he derived his title ; it extended over the additional territory of Rhætia as far as the banks of the Danube, over the dependent islands of the Mediterranean, and over that part of the continent of Africa which lies between the confines of Cyrene and those of Tingitania. 4. The Præfect of the Gauls comprehended under that plural denomination the kindred provinces of Britain and Spain, and his authority was obeyed from the wall of Antoninus to the fort of Mount Atlas." — *Decline and Fall*, chap. 17. — *Bag.*]

[1] [That is, private sacrifices : for it appears that the idolatrous temples were allowed to be open for *public* worship. — *Bag.*]

[1] [Licinius, thus designated for the subtlety of his character. — *Bag.*] More probably for his wickedness, and perhaps with thought of the " dragon " of the Book of Revelation. The word is δράκων, not ὄφις. It is the latter which is used in the LXX, where the English version speaks of the serpent as the " subtlest." For historical and symbolical use of the words, compare Fergusson, *Tree and Serpent Worship* (Lond., 1874), and Conway, *Demorology and Devil Lore* (N.Y., 1879, 2 v.).

CHAPTER XLVII.

That he wrote a Letter in Condemnation of Idolatry.

MOREOVER, the emperor, who continually made progress in piety towards God, dispatched an admonitory letter to the inhabitants of every province, respecting the error of idolatry into which his predecessors in power had fallen, in which he eloquently exhorts his subjects to acknowledge the Supreme God, and openly to profess their allegiance to his Christ as their Saviour. This letter also, which is in his own handwriting, I have judged it necessary to translate from the Latin for the present work, in order that we may hear, as it were, the voice of the emperor himself uttering these sentiments in the audience of all mankind.

CHAPTER XLVIII.

Constantine's Edict to the People of the Provinces concerning the Error of Polytheism, commencing with Some General Remarks on Virtue and Vice.

"VICTOR CONSTANTINUS, MAXIMUS AUGUSTUS, to the people of the Eastern provinces.

"Whatever is comprehended under the sovereign[1] laws of nature, seems to convey to all men an adequate idea of the forethought and intelligence of the divine order. Nor can any, whose minds are directed in the true path of knowledge to the attainment of that end, entertain a doubt that the just perceptions of sound reason, as well as those of the natural vision itself, through the sole influence of genuine virtue, lead to the knowledge of God. Accordingly no wise man will ever be surprised when he sees the mass of mankind influenced by opposite sentiments. For the beauty of virtue would be useless[2] and unperceived, did not vice display in contrast with it the course of perversity and folly. Hence it is that the one is crowned with reward, while the most high God is himself the administrator of judgment to the other.

"And now I will endeavor to lay before you all as explicitly as possible, the nature of my own hopes of future happiness.[3]

CHAPTER XLIX.

Concerning Constantine's Pious Father, and the Persecutors Diocletian and Maximian.

"THE former emperors I have been accustomed to regard as those with whom I could have no sympathy,[1] on account of the savage cruelty of their character. Indeed, my father was the only one who uniformly practiced the duties of humanity, and with admirable piety called for the blessing of God the Father on all his actions, but the rest, unsound in mind, were more zealous of cruel than gentle measures; and this disposition they indulged without restraint, and thus persecuted the true doctrine during the whole period of their reign. Nay, so violent did their malicious fury become, that in the midst of a profound peace, as regards both the religious and ordinary interests of men, they kindled, as it were, the flames of a civil war.[2]

CHAPTER L.

That the Persecution originated on Account of the Oracle of Apollo, who, it was said, could not give Oracles because of "the Righteous Men."

"ABOUT that time it is said that Apollo spoke from a deep and gloomy cavern, and through the medium of no human voice, and declared that *the righteous men* on earth were a bar to his speaking the truth, and accordingly that the oracles from the tripod were fallacious. Hence it was that he suffered his tresses to droop in token of grief,[1] and mourned the evils which the loss of the oracular spirit would entail on mankind. But let us mark the consequences of this.

CHAPTER LI.

That Constantine, when a Youth, heard from him who wrote the Persecution Edict that "the Righteous Men" were the Christians.

"I CALL now on thee, most high God, to witness that, when young, I heard him who at that time was chief among the Roman emperors, unhappy, truly unhappy as he was, and laboring under mental delusion, make earnest enquiry as to who these righteous ones on earth were, and that one of the Pagan priests then

---

[1] Or "fixed," "appointed."
[2] By a conjectural reading Stroth makes this "fools," instead of "useless," and renders, "For fools would not otherwise recognize the charm of virtue."
[3] [The remark of Valesius in reference to the difficulty of this chapter appears probable; viz. that it is partly to be attributed to Constantine's own want of clearness, and partly to his translator, who has rendered obscure Latin into still more obscure Greek. — *Bag.*]

[1] The word means "having no share with," and sometimes "disinherited." It may perhaps mean, "I have been accustomed to think of the former emperors as having been deprived of their possessions on account," &c.
[2] [The persecution of the Christians, with its attendant horrors, being the act, not of foreign enemies, but of their countrymen and fellow-citizens. — *Bag.*]
[1] This is translated by Molzberger, "Therefore the priests let their hair hang down," &c.

present replied that they were doubtless the Christians. This answer he eagerly received, like some honeyed draught, and unsheathed the sword which was ordained for the punishment of crime, against those whose holiness was beyond reproach. Immediately, therefore, he issued those sanguinary edicts, traced, if I may so express myself, with a sword's point dipped in blood; at the same time commanding his judges to tax their ingenuity for the invention of new and more terrible punishments.

CHAPTER LII.

The Manifold Forms of Torture and Punishment practiced against the Christians.

"THEN, indeed, one might see with what arrogance those venerable worshipers of God were daily exposed, with continued and relentless cruelty, to outrages of the most grievous kind, and how that modesty of character[1] which no enemy had ever treated with disrespect, became the mere sport of their infuriated fellow-citizens. Is there any punishment by fire, are there any tortures or forms of torment, which were not applied to all, without distinction of age or sex? Then, it may be truly said, the earth shed tears, the all-encircling compass of heaven mourned because of the pollution of blood; and the very light of day itself was darkened in grief at the spectacle.

CHAPTER LIII.

That the Barbarians kindly received the Christians.

"BUT what is the consequence of this? Why, the barbarians themselves may boast now of the contrast their conduct presents to these cruel deeds; for they received and kept in gentlest captivity those who then fled from amongst us, and secured to them not merely safety from danger, but also the free exercise of their holy religion. And now the Roman people bear that lasting stain which the Christians, at that time driven from the Roman world, and taking refuge with the barbarians, have branded on them.

CHAPTER LIV.

What Vengeance overtook those who on Account of the Oracle raised the Persecution.

"BUT why need I longer dwell on these lamentable events, and the general sorrow which in consequence pervaded the world? The perpetrators of this dreadful guilt are now no more: they have experienced a miserable end, and are consigned to unceasing punishment in the depths of the lower world. They encountered each other in civil strife, and have left neither name nor race behind. And surely this calamity would never have befallen them, had not that impious deliverance of the Pythian oracle exercised a delusive power over them.[1]

CHAPTER LV.

Constantine gives Glory to God, makes Grateful Acknowledgment of the Sign of the Cross, and prays for the Churches and People.

"AND now I beseech thee, most mighty God, to be merciful and gracious to thine Eastern nations, to thy people in these provinces, worn as they are by protracted miseries; and grant them healing through thy servant. Not without cause, O holy God, do I prefer this prayer to thee, the Lord of all. Under thy guidance have I devised and accomplished measures fraught with blessings: preceded by thy sacred sign I have led thy armies to victory: and still, on each occasion of public danger, I follow the same symbol of thy perfections while advancing to meet the foe. Therefore have I dedicated to thy service a soul duly attempered by love and fear. For thy name I truly love, while I regard with reverence that power of which thou hast given abundant proofs, to the confirmation and increase of my faith. I hasten, then, to devote all my powers to the restoration of thy most holy dwelling-place, which those profane and impious men have defiled by the contamination of violence.

CHAPTER LVI.

He prays that All may be Christians, but compels None.

"MY own desire is, for the common good of the world and the advantage of all mankind, that thy people should enjoy a life of peace and undisturbed concord. Let those, therefore, who still delight in error, be made welcome to the same degree of peace and tranquillity which they have who believe. For it may be that this restoration of equal privileges to all will prevail to lead them into the straight path. Let no one molest another, but let every one do as his soul desires. Only let men of sound judgment be assured of this, that those only can live a life of holiness and purity, whom thou callest to a reli-

---

[1] σωφροσύνη.

[1] Compare, on all this, the *Church History* and notes, and also the Prolegomena to this work.

ance on thy holy laws. With regard to those who will hold themselves aloof from us, let them have, if they please, their temples[1] of lies : *we have the glorious edifice of thy truth, which thou hast given us as our native home.*[2] We pray, however, that they too may receive the same blessing, and thus experience that heartfelt joy which unity of sentiment inspires.

CHAPTER LVII.

He gives Glory to God, who has given Light by his Son to those who were in Error.

" And truly our worship is no new or recent thing, but one which thou hast ordained for thine own due honor, from the time when, as we believe, this system of the universe was first established. And, although mankind have deeply fallen, and have been seduced by manifold errors, yet hast thou revealed a pure light in the person of thy Son, that the power of evil should not utterly prevail, and hast thus given testimony to all men concerning thyself.

CHAPTER LVIII.

He glorifies him again for his Government of the Universe.

" The truth of this is assured to us by thy works. It is thy power which removes our guilt, and makes us faithful. The sun and the moon have their settled course. The stars move in no uncertain orbits round this terrestrial globe. The revolution of the seasons recurs according to unerring laws. The solid fabric of the earth was established by thy word : the winds receive their impulse at appointed times ; and the course of the waters continues with ceaseless flow,[1] the ocean is circumscribed by an immovable barrier, and whatever is comprehended within the compass of earth and sea, is all contrived for wondrous and important ends.

---

[1] Or " groves."
[2] ['Ονπερ κατὰ φύσιν δέδωκας. The clause is thus rendered by Valesius: " Nos splendidissimam domum veritatis tuæ, quam nascentibus nobis donasti, retinemus." This seems almost as unintelligible as the original. The translation above attempted yields, perhaps, a sense not inconsistent with the general scope of the passage. — *Bag.*] *1709* renders " according to nature." Molzberger has " through no merit on our part." Stroth renders " characteristically " or " as our own natural possession" (i.e. eigenthümlich); and is confirmed by Heinichen, while Christophorson has " natura " and Portesius " a natura." The last is the best *translation* " by nature." As a matter of *interpretation* Bagster is probably wrong and Stroth substantially right. Whether Constantine had the Epistle to the Romans in mind or not, he had the same thought as Paul that men " by nature " have the " truth of God," but exchange this for a lie (Rom. i. 25; ii. 14; cf. xi. 21 and 24). This suggests, however, another possible meaning, that the truth is known " through the things that are made " (Rom. i. 20). For various philosophical usages of φύσις, compare interesting note in Grant, *Ethics of Aristotle*, 1 (Lond. 1885), 483, 484.
[1] Probably meaning rains.

" Were it not so, were not all regulated by the determination of thy will, so great a diversity, so manifold a division of power, would unquestionably have brought ruin on the whole race and its affairs. For those agencies which have maintained a mutual strife[2] would thus have carried to a more deadly length that hostility against the human race which they even now exercise, though unseen by mortal eyes.

CHAPTER LIX.

He gives Glory to God, as the Constant Teacher of Good.

" Abundant thanks, most mighty God, and Lord of all, be rendered to thee, that, by so much as our nature becomes known from the diversified pursuits of man, by so much the more are the precepts of thy divine doctrine confirmed to those whose thoughts are directed aright, and who are sincerely devoted to true virtue. As for those who will not allow themselves to be cured of their error, let them not attribute this to any but themselves. For that remedy which is of sovereign and healing virtue is openly placed within the reach of all. Only let not any one inflict an injury on that religion which experience itself testifies to be pure and undefiled. Henceforward, therefore, let us all enjoy in common the privilege placed within our reach, I mean the blessing of peace, endeavoring to keep our conscience pure from all that is contrary.

CHAPTER LX.

An Admonition at the Close of the Edict, that No One should trouble his Neighbor.

" Once more, let none use that to the detriment of another which he may himself have received on conviction of its truth ; but let every one, if it be possible, apply what he has understood and known to the benefit of his neighbor ; if otherwise, let him relinquish the attempt. For it is one thing voluntarily to undertake the conflict for immortality, another to compel others to do so from the fear of punishment.

" These are our words ; and we have enlarged on these topics more than our ordinary clemency would have dictated, because we were unwilling to dissemble or be false to the true faith ; and the more so, since we understand there are some who say that the rites of the heathen temples, and the power of darkness, have been entirely removed. We should indeed have earnestly

---

[2] [Constantine seems here to allude to the Gentile deities as powers of evil, capable, if unrestrained by a superior power, of working universal ruin. — *Bag.*]

recommended such removal to all men, were it not that the rebellious spirit of those wicked errors still continues obstinately fixed in the minds of some, so as to discourage the hope of any general restoration of mankind to the ways of truth."[1]

CHAPTER LXI.

How Controversies originated at Alexandria through Matters relating to Arius.[1]

In this manner the emperor, like a powerful herald of God, addressed himself by his own letter to all the provinces, at the same time warning his subjects against superstitious[2] error, and encouraging them in the pursuit of true godliness. But in the midst of his joyful anticipations of the success of this measure, he received tidings of a most serious disturbance which had invaded the peace of the Church. This intelligence he heard with deep concern, and at once endeavored to devise a remedy for the evil. The origin of this disturbance may be thus described. The people of God were in a truly flourishing state, and abounding in the practice of good works. No terror from without assailed them, but a bright and most profound peace, through the favor of God, encompassed his Church on every side. Meantime, however, the spirit of envy was watching to destroy our blessings, which at first crept in unperceived, but soon revelled in the midst of the assemblies of the saints. At length it reached the bishops themselves, and arrayed them in angry hostility against each other, on pretense of a jealous regard for the doctrines of Divine truth. Hence it was that a mighty fire was kindled as it were from a little spark, and which, originating in the first instance in the Alexandrian church,[3] overspread the whole of Egypt and Libya, and the further Thebaid. Eventually it extended its ravages to the other provinces and cities of the empire; so that not only the prelates of the churches might be seen encountering each other in the strife of words, but the people themselves were completely divided, some adhering to one faction and others to another. Nay, so notorious did the scandal of these proceedings become, that the sacred matters of inspired teaching were exposed to the most shameful ridicule in the very theaters of the unbelievers.

CHAPTER LXII.

Concerning the Same Arius, and the Melitians.[1]

Some thus at Alexandria maintained an obstinate conflict on the highest questions. Others throughout Egypt and the Upper Thebaid, were at variance on account of an earlier controversy: so that the churches were everywhere distracted by divisions. The body therefore being thus diseased, the whole of Libya caught the contagion; and the rest of the remoter provinces became affected with the same disorder. For the disputants at Alexandria sent emissaries to the bishops of the several provinces, who accordingly ranged themselves as partisans on either side, and shared in the same spirit of discord.

CHAPTER LXIII.

How Constantine sent a Messenger and a Letter concerning Peace.

As soon as the emperor was informed of these facts, which he heard with much sorrow of heart, considering them in the light of a calamity personally affecting himself, he forthwith selected from the Christians in his train one whom he well knew to be approved for the sobriety and genuineness of his faith,[1] and who had before this time distinguished himself by the boldness of his religious profession, and sent him to negotiate peace[2] between the dissentient parties at Alexandria. He also made him the bearer of a most needful and appropriate letter to the original movers of the strife: and this letter, as exhibiting a specimen of his watchful care over God's people, it may be well to introduce into this our narrative of his life. Its purport was as follows.

CHAPTER LXIV.

Constantine's Letter to Alexander the Bishop, and Arius the Presbyter.

"Victor Constantinus, Maximus Augustus, to Alexander and Arius.

"I call that God to witness, as well I may, who is the helper of my endeavors, and the Preserver of all men, that I had a twofold reason for undertaking that duty which I have now performed.

---

[1] The editorial "we" used by *Bag.* throughout these edicts has been retained, although the first person singular is employed throughout in the original.

[1] For literature relating to Arianism, compare *Literature* at the end of article by Schaff, in Smith and Wace, *Dict.* I (1877), 159, and in the Schaff-Herzog *Encyclopædia*, I, p. 137.

[2] "Demoniacal." *1709* renders "diabolical."

[3] It was at Alexandria that the controversy with Arius arose. He was called to account by Alexander of Alexandria who summoned one council and then another, at which Arius and his followers were excommunicated.

[1] [The Melitians, or Meletians, an obscure Egyptian sect, of whom little satisfactory is recorded. — *Bag.*] Compare Blunt, *Dict. of Sects, Heresies,* &c. (1874), 305-308.

[1] [Hosius, bishop of Cordova. — *Bag.*] Hosius had already been for some time a trusted adviser, having acted for Constantine also in the Donatist matters. Compare on Hosius the full article of Morse in Smith and Wace.

[2] By "acting as umpire."

CHAPTER LXV.

His Continual Anxiety for Peace.

" My design then was, first, to bring the diverse judgments formed by all nations respecting the Deity to a condition, as it were, of settled uniformity; and, secondly, to restore to health the system of the world, then suffering under the malignant power of a grievous distemper. Keeping these objects in view, I sought to accomplish the one by the secret eye of thought, while the other I tried to rectify by the power of military authority. For I was aware that, if I should succeed in establishing, according to my hopes, a common harmony of sentiment among all the servants of God, the general course of affairs would also experience a change correspondent to the pious desires of them all.

CHAPTER LXVI.

That he also adjusted the Controversies which had arisen in Africa.

" FINDING, then, that the whole of Africa was pervaded by an intolerable spirit of mad folly, through the influence of those who with heedless frivolity had presumed to rend the religion of the people into diverse sects; I was anxious to check this disorder, and could discover no other remedy equal to the occasion, except in sending some of yourselves to aid in restoring mutual harmony among the disputants, after I had removed that common enemy[1] of mankind who had interposed his lawless sentence for the prohibition of your holy synods.

CHAPTER LXVII.

That Religion began in the East.

" FOR since the power of Divine light, and the law of sacred worship, which, proceeding in the first instance, through the favor of God, from the bosom, as it were, of the East, have illumined the world, by their sacred radiance, I naturally believed that you would be the first to promote the salvation of other nations, and resolved with all energy of thought and diligence of enquiry to seek your aid. As soon, therefore, as I had secured my decisive victory and unquestionable triumph over my enemies, my first enquiry was concerning that object which I felt to be of paramount interest and importance.

---

[1] [Licinius, whose prohibition of synods is referred to in Bk. 1, ch. 51. The disputes here mentioned are those between the Catholic Christians and the Donatists, a very violent sect which sprung up in Africa after the persecution by Diocletian. — *Bag.*]

CHAPTER LXVIII.

Being grieved by the Dissension, he counsels Peace.

" BUT, O glorious Providence of God ! how deep a wound did not my ears only, but my very heart receive in the report that divisions existed among yourselves more grievous still than those which continued in that country![1] so that you, through whose aid I had hoped to procure a remedy for the errors of others, are in a state which needs healing even more than theirs. And yet, having made a careful enquiry into the origin and foundation of these differences, I find the cause to be of a truly insignificant character, and quite unworthy of such fierce contention. Feeling myself, therefore, compelled to address you in this letter, and to appeal at the same time to your unanimity[2] and sagacity, I call on Divine Providence to assist me in the task, while I interrupt your dissension in the character of a minister of peace. And with reason : for if I might expect, with the help of a higher Power, to be able without difficulty, by a judicious appeal to the pious feelings of those who heard me, to recall them to a better spirit, even though the occasion of the disagreement were a greater one, how can I refrain from promising myself a far easier and more speedy adjustment of this difference, when the cause which hinders general harmony of sentiment is intrinsically trifling and of little moment ?

CHAPTER LXIX.

Origin of the Controversy between Alexander and Arius, and that these Questions ought not to have been discussed.

" I UNDERSTAND, then, that the origin of the present controversy is this. When you, Alexander, demanded of the presbyters what opinion they severally maintained respecting a certain passage in the Divine law,[1] or rather, I should say, that you asked them something connected with an unprofitable question, then you, Arius, inconsiderately insisted on[2] what ought never to have been conceived at all, or if conceived, should have been buried in profound silence. Hence it was that a dissension arose between you, fellowship was withdrawn,[3] and

---

[1] [Africa: alluding to the schism of the Donatists. — *Bag.*]
[2] Or " mutual."
[1] [The word νόμος seems to be commonly used by Eusebius as a general term for Divine revelation; as we employ the word " Scripture." — *Bag.*]
[2] The plain English " stuck to " represents the idea of Heinichen (*animo infixisses infixumque teneres*) followed by *Molz* (*mit unkluger Hartnäckigkeit festhieltest*). *Bag.* had " gave utterance to," and with this *Vales., 1709,* and *Str.* correspond.
[3] *Bag.,* " The meeting of the synod was prohibited."

the holy people, rent into diverse parties, no longer preserved the unity of the one body. Now, therefore, do ye both exhibit an equal degree of forbearance,[4] and receive the advice which your fellow-servant righteously gives. What then is this advice? It was wrong in the first instance to propose such questions as these, or to reply to them when propounded. For those points of discussion which are enjoined by the authority of no law, but rather suggested by the contentious spirit which is fostered by misused leisure, even though they may be intended merely as an intellectual exercise, ought certainly to be confined to the region of our own thoughts, and not hastily produced in the popular assemblies, nor unadvisedly intrusted to the general ear. For how very few are there able either accurately to comprehend, or adequately to explain subjects so sublime and abstruse in their nature? Or, granting that one were fully competent for this, how many people will he convince? Or, who, again, in dealing with questions of such subtle nicety as these, can secure himself against a dangerous declension from the truth? It is incumbent therefore on us in these cases to be sparing of our words, lest, in case we ourselves are unable, through the feebleness of our natural faculties, to give a clear explanation of the subject before us, or, on the other hand, in case the slowness of our hearers' understandings disables them from arriving at an accurate apprehension of what we say, from one or other of these causes the people be reduced to the alternative either of blasphemy or schism.

CHAPTER LXX.

An Exhortation to Unanimity.

" Let therefore both the unguarded question and the inconsiderate answer receive your mutual forgiveness.[1] For the cause of your difference has not been any of the leading doctrines or precepts of the Divine law, nor has any new heresy respecting the worship of God arisen among you. You are in truth of one and the same judgment:[2] you may therefore well join in communion and fellowship.

---

[4] On "forgiveness."
[1] Rendered "forbearance" above.
[2] [The emperor seems at this time to have had a very imperfect knowledge of the errors of the Arian heresy. After the Council of Nice, at which he heard them fully explained, he wrote of them in terms of decisive condemnation in his letter to the Alexandrian church. Vide Socrates' *Eccles. Hist.*, Bk. 1, ch. 9. — *Bag.*] Neither at this time nor at any time does Constantine seem to have entered very fully into an appreciation of doctrinal niceties. Later he was more than tolerant of semi-Arianism. He seems to have depended a good deal on the "explanations" of others, and to have been led in a somewhat devious path in trying to follow all.

CHAPTER LXXI.

There should be no Contention in Matters which are in themselves of Little Moment.

" For as long as you continue to contend about these small and very insignificant questions, it is not fitting that so large a portion of God's people should be under the direction of your judgment, since you are thus divided between yourselves. I believe it indeed to be not merely unbecoming, but positively evil, that such should be the case. But I will refresh your minds by a little illustration, as follows. You know that philosophers, though they all adhere to one system, are yet frequently at issue on certain points, and differ, perhaps, in their degree of knowledge: yet they are recalled to harmony of sentiment by the uniting power of their common doctrines. If this be true, is it not far more reasonable that you, who are the ministers of the Supreme God, should be of one mind respecting the profession of the same religion? But let us still more thoughtfully and with closer attention examine what I have said, and see whether it be right that, on the ground of some trifling and foolish verbal difference between ourselves, brethren should assume towards each other the attitude of enemies, and the august meeting of the Synod be rent by profane disunion, because of you who wrangle together on points so trivial and altogether unessential? This is vulgar, and rather characteristic of childish ignorance, than consistent with the wisdom of priests and men of sense. Let us withdraw ourselves with a good will from these temptations of the devil. Our great God and common Saviour of all has granted the same light to us all. Permit me, who am his servant, to bring my task to a successful issue, under the direction of his Providence, that I may be enabled, through my exhortations, and diligence, and earnest admonition, to recall his people to communion and fellowship. For since you have, as I said, but one faith, and one sentiment respecting our religion, and since the Divine commandment in all its parts enjoins on us all the duty of maintaining a spirit of concord, let not the circumstance which has led to a slight difference between you, since it does not affect the validity of the whole, cause any division or schism among you. And this I say without in any way desiring to force you to entire unity of judgment in regard to this truly idle question, whatever its real nature may be. For the dignity of your synod may be preserved, and the communion of your whole body maintained unbroken, however wide a difference may exist among you as to unimportant matters. For we are not all of us like-minded on every subject, nor is there such a thing as one disposition and judgment common to all alike. As far, then, as regards the Divine Providence, let there be one faith, and one understanding among you, one united judgment in reference to God. But as to your subtle disputations on questions of little or no significance, though you may be unable to harmonize in sentiment, such differences should be consigned to the secret custody of your own minds and thoughts. And now, let the preciousness of common affection, let faith in the truth, let the honor due to God and to the observance of his law continue immovably among you. Resume, then, your mutual feelings of friendship, love, and regard : restore to the people their wonted embracings ; and do ye yourselves, having purified your souls, as it were, once more acknowledge one another. For it often happens that when a reconciliation is effected by the removal of the causes of enmity, friendship becomes even sweeter than it was before.

CHAPTER LXXII.

The Excess of his Pious Concern caused him to shed Tears ; and his Intended Journey to the East was postponed because of These Things.

" RESTORE me then my quiet days, and untroubled nights, that the joy of undimmed light, the delight of a tranquil life, may henceforth be my portion. Else must I needs mourn, with constant tears, nor shall I be able to pass the residue of my days in peace. For while the people of God, whose fellow-servant I am, are thus divided amongst themselves by an unreasonable and pernicious spirit of contention, how is it possible that I shall be able to maintain tranquillity of mind ? And I will give

you a proof how great my sorrow has been on this behalf. Not long since I had visited Nicomedia, and intended forthwith to proceed from that city to the East. It was while I was hastening towards you, and had already accomplished the greater part of the distance, that the news of this matter reversed my plan, that I might not be compelled to see with my own eyes that which I felt myself scarcely able even to hear. Open then for me henceforward by your unity of judgment that road to the regions of the East which your dissensions have closed against me, and permit me speedily to see yourselves and all other peoples rejoicing together, and render due acknowledgment to God in the language of praise and thanksgiving for the restoration of general concord and liberty to all."

CHAPTER LXXIII.

The Controversy continues without Abatement, even after the Receipt of This Letter.

IN this manner the pious emperor endeavored by means of the foregoing letter to promote the peace of the Church of God. And the excellent man [1] to whom it was intrusted performed his part not merely by communicating the letter itself, but also by seconding the views of him who sent it ; for he was, as I have said, in all respects a person of pious character. The evil, however, was greater than could be remedied by a single letter, insomuch that the acrimony of the contending parties continually increased, and the effects of the mischief extended to all the Eastern provinces. These things jealousy and some evil spirit who looked with an envious eye on the prosperity of the Church, wrought.

---

[1] [Hosius of Cordova, mentioned above, ch. 63. — *Bag.*]

BOOK III.

CHAPTER I.

A Comparison of Constantine's Piety with the Wickedness of the Persecutors.

IN this manner that spirit who is the hater of good, actuated by envy at the blessing enjoyed by the Church, continued to raise against her the stormy troubles of intestine discord, in the midst of a period of peace and joy. Meanwhile, however, the divinely-favored emperor did not slight the duties befitting him, but exhibited in his whole conduct a direct contrast to those atrocities of which the cruel tyrants had been lately guilty,[1] and thus triumphed over every enemy that opposed him. For in the first place, the tyrants, being themselves alienated from the true God, had enforced by every compulsion the worship of false deities: Constantine convinced mankind by actions as well as words,[2] that these had but an imaginary existence, and exhorted them to acknowledge the only true God. They had derided his Christ with words of blasphemy: he assumed that as his safeguard[3] against which they directed their blasphemies, and gloried in the symbol of the Saviour's passion. They had persecuted and driven from house and home the servants of Christ: he recalled them every one, and restored them to their native homes. They had covered them with dishonor: he made their condition honorable and enviable in the eyes of all. They had shamefully plundered and sold the goods of godly men: Constantine not only replaced this loss, but still further enriched them with abundant presents. They had circulated injurious calumnies, through their written ordinances, against the prelates of the Church: he, on the contrary, conferred dignity on these individuals by personal marks of honor, and by his edicts and statutes raised them to higher distinction than before. They had utterly demolished and razed to the ground the houses of prayer: he commanded that those which still existed should be enlarged, and that new ones should be raised on a magnificent scale at the expense of the imperial treasury. They had ordered the inspired records to be burnt and utterly destroyed: he decreed that copies of them should be multiplied, and magnificently adorned[4] at the charge of the imperial treasury. They had strictly forbidden the prelates, anywhere or on any occasion, to convene synods; whereas he gathered them to his court from every province, received them into his palace, and even to his own private apartments and thought them worthy to share his home and table. They had honored the demons with offerings: Constantine exposed their error, and continually distributed the now useless materials for sacrifice, to those who would apply them to a better use. They had ordered the pagan temples to be sumptuously adorned: he razed to their foundations those of them which had been the chief objects of superstitious reverence. They had subjected God's servants to the most ignominious punishments: he took vengeance on the persecutors, and inflicted on them just chastisement in the name of God, while he held the memory of his holy martyrs in constant veneration. They had driven God's worshipers from the imperial palaces: he placed full confidence in them at all times, and knowing them to be the better disposed and more faithful than any beside. They, the victims of avarice, voluntarily subjected themselves as it were to the pangs of Tantalus: he with royal magnificence unlocked all his treasures, and distributed his gifts with rich and high-souled liberality. They committed countless murders, that they might plunder or confiscate the wealth of their victims; while throughout the reign of Constantine the sword of justice hung idle everywhere, and both people and municipal magistrates[5] in every provence were governed rather by paternal authority than by any constraining.[6] Surely

---

[1] Compare contrast with the other emperors in Prolegomena, under *Life*.
[2] Eusebius expressly states that Constantine's words had little result in conversion. It is meant here that the success of one who relied on God itself proved the vanity of idols.
[3] This may perhaps mean "ordered to be inscribed" or "wrote it to be his safeguard." This form of *Bag.* is a satisfactory paraphrase.

[4] Their bindings were adorned with precious stones according to Cedrenus. Compare Prolegomena, *Character, Magnificence*.
[5] [Πολιτευτῶν ἀνδρῶν, here, apparently, the Decurions, who formed the *corporations* of the cities, and were subject to responsible and burdensome offices. Vide Gibbon, *Decline and Fall*, chap. 17. — *Bag.*] So Valesius maintains, and has been generally if not universally followed. Though it might be overventuresome to change the translation therefore, it befits the sense better and suits the words admirably to apply to the different classes, Peregrini and Cives. This distinction did not fully pass away until the time of Justinian (Long, art. *Civitas*, in Smith, *Dict. Gr. and Rom. Ant.*), and it seems certain that Eusebius meant this.
[6] This above is a sort of resumé of the life of Constantine. For illustration of the various facts mentioned, compare the latter part of the *Church History* and the various acts and documents in this Life. Compare also Prolegomena, under *Life*, and especially under *Character*. It seems now and then to be like a little homily on.

it must seem to all who duly regard these facts, that a new and fresh era of existence had begun to appear, and a light heretofore unknown suddenly to dawn from the midst of darkness on the human race : and all must confess that these things were entirely the work of God, who raised up this pious emperor to withstand the multitude of the ungodly.

CHAPTER II.

Farther Remarks on Constantine's Piety, and his Open Testimony to the Sign of the Cross.

AND when we consider that their iniquities were without example, and the atrocities which they dared to perpetrate against the Church such as had never been heard of in any age of the world, well might God himself bring before us something entirely new, and work thereby effects such as had hitherto been never either recorded or observed. And what miracle was ever more marvelous than the virtues of this our emperor, whom the wisdom of God has vouchsafed as a gift to the human race? For truly he maintained a continual testimony to the Christ of God with all boldness, and before all men ; and so far was he from shrinking from an open profession of the Christian name, that he rather desired to make it manifest to all that he regarded this as his highest honor, now impressing on his face the salutary sign, and now glorying in it as the trophy which led him on to victory.[1]

CHAPTER III.

Of his Picture surmounted by a Cross and having beneath it a Dragon.

AND besides this, he caused to be painted on a lofty tablet, and set up in the front of the portico of his palace, so as to be visible to all, a representation of the salutary sign placed above his head, and below it that hateful and savage adversary of mankind, who by means of the tyranny of the ungodly had wasted the Church of God, falling headlong, under the form of a dragon, to the abyss of destruction. For the sacred oracles in the books of God's prophets have described him as a dragon and a crooked serpent ;[1] and for this reason the emperor thus publicly displayed a painted[2] resemblance of the dragon beneath his own and his children's

feet, stricken through with a dart, and cast headlong into the depths of the sea.

In this manner he intended to represent the secret adversary of the human race, and to indicate that he was consigned to the gulf of perdition by virtue of the salutary trophy placed above his head. This allegory, then, was thus conveyed by means of the colors of a picture : and I am filled with wonder at the intellectual greatness of the emperor, who as if by divine inspiration thus expressed what the prophets had foretold concerning this monster, saying that " God would bring his great and strong and terrible sword against the dragon, the flying serpent ; and would destroy the dragon that was in the sea."[3] This it was of which the emperor gave a true and faithful representation in the picture above described.

CHAPTER IV.

A Farther Notice of the Controversies raised in Egypt by Arius.

IN such occupations as these he employed himself with pleasure : but the effects of that envious spirit which so troubled the peace of the churches of God in Alexandria, together with the Theban and Egyptian schism, continued to cause him no little disturbance of mind. For in fact, in every city bishops were engaged in obstinate conflict with bishops, and people rising against people ; and almost like the fabled Symplegades,[1] coming into violent collision with each other. Nay, some were so far transported beyond the bounds of reason as to be guilty of reckless and outrageous conduct, and even to insult the statues of the emperor. This state of things had little power to excite his anger, but rather caused in him sorrow of spirit ; for he deeply deplored the folly thus exhibited by deranged men.

CHAPTER V.

Of the Disagreement respecting the Celebration of Easter.

BUT before this time another most virulent disorder had existed, and long afflicted the

---

the glory of having the shoe on the other foot — the glory of having done to others what others had done to them.
[1] Note the explicit testimony of Eusebius here, and compare *Prolegomena,* under *Religious Characteristics.*
[1] Especially the book of Revelation, and Isaiah as quoted below.
[2] [Literally, by encaustic painting. See Bk. 1, ch. 3, note. — *Bag.*]

[3] Isa. xxvii. 1. This is not taken from the Septuagint translation, as it corresponds with the Hebrew against the LXX. It differs in the word used for " terrible," and none of the editions (or at least not the Vatican, Holmes and Parsons, Van Ess, or Tischendorf) and none of the MSS. cited by Holmes and Parsons, have the phrase " in the sea " as the Hebrew. Grabe has this latter as various reading (ed. Bagster, 16°, p. 74), but there is hardly a possibility that it is the true reading.
[1] The famous rocks in the Euxine which were wont to close against one another and crush all passing ships, and by which the Argo was said (*Od.* 12. 69) to be the only ship which ever passed in safety.

Church; I mean the difference respecting the salutary feast of Easter.[1] For while one party asserted that the Jewish custom should be adhered to, the other affirmed that the exact recurrence of the period should be observed, without following the authority of those who were in error, and strangers to gospel grace.

Accordingly, the people being thus in every place divided in respect of this,[1] and the sacred observances of religion confounded for a long period (insomuch that the diversity of judgment in regard to the time for celebrating one and the same feast caused the greatest disagreement between those who kept it, some afflicting themselves with fastings and austerities, while others devoted their time to festive relaxation), no one appeared who was capable of devising a remedy for the evil, because the controversy continued equally balanced between both parties. To God alone, the Almighty, was the healing of these differences an easy task; and Constantine appeared to be the only one on earth capable of being its minister for this good end. For as soon as he was made acquainted with the facts which I have described, and perceived that his letter to the Alexandrian Christians had failed to produce its due effect, he at once aroused the energies of his mind, and declared that he must prosecute to the utmost this war also against the secret adversary who was disturbing the peace of the Church.

CHAPTER VI.

How he ordered a Council to be held at Nicæa.

THEN as if to bring a divine array against this enemy, he convoked a general council, and invited the speedy attendance of bishops from all quarters, in letters expressive of the honorable estimation in which he held them. Nor was this merely the issuing of a bare command, but the emperor's good will contributed much to its being carried into effect: for he allowed some the use of the public means of conveyance, while he afforded to others an ample supply of horses[1] for their transport. The place, too, selected for the synod, the city Nicæa in Bithynia (named from *"Victory"*), was appropriate to the occasion.[2] As soon then as the imperial injunction was generally made known, all with

the utmost willingness hastened thither, as though they would outstrip one another in a race; for they were impelled by the anticipation of a happy result to the conference, by the hope of enjoying present peace, and the desire of beholding something new and strange in the person of so admirable an emperor. Now when they were all assembled, it appeared evident that the proceeding was the work of God, inasmuch as men who had been most widely separated, not merely in sentiment, but also personally, and by difference of country, place, and nation, were here brought together, and comprised within the walls of a single city, forming as it were a vast garland of priests, composed of a variety of the choicest flowers.

CHAPTER VII.

Of the General Council, at which Bishops from all Nations were Present.[1]

IN effect, the most distinguished of God's ministers from all the churches which abounded in Europe, Lybia,[2] and Asia were here assembled. And a single house of prayer, as though divinely enlarged, sufficed to contain at once Syrians and Cilicians, Phœnicians and Arabians, delegates from Palestine, and others from Egypt; Thebans and Libyans, with those who came from the region of Mesopotamia. A Persian bishop too was present at this conference, nor was even a Scythian found wanting to the number.[3] Pontus, Galatia, and Pamphylia, Cappadocia, Asia, and Phrygia, furnished their most distinguished prelates; while those who dwelt in the remotest districts of Thrace and Macedonia, of Achaia and Epirus, were notwithstanding in attendance. Even from Spain itself, one whose fame was widely spread took his seat as an individual in the great assembly.[4] The prelate of the imperial city[5] was prevented from attending by extreme old age; but his presbyters were present, and supplied his place. Constantine is the first prince of any age who bound together such a garland as this with the bond of peace, and presented it to his Saviour as a thank-offering for the victories he had obtained over every foe, thus exhibiting in our own times a similitude of the apostolic company.

---

[1] For endless literature of the Paschal controversy, compare articles in all the religious encyclopædias, especially perhaps Steitz, in the Schaff-Herzog; and for history and discussion of the question itself, see Hensley's art. *Easter*, in Smith and Cheetham, *Dict.*
[1] By some this phrase is joined to the preceding paragraph, — strangers . . . "in this as in other respects," and so *Bag.* translates, but the division followed here is that of *Hein.*
[1] "Beasts of burden."
[2] The probably apocryphal version of the summoning letter given by Cowper (*Syr. Misc.*) from the Syriac gives the reason of the choice of Nicæa, "the excellent temperature of the air" there.

[1] The standard work on councils is Hefele, *Conciliengeschichte*, available to the English reader in the translation of Clark, Oxenham, &c. (Edinb. 1872 sq.), a work so thoroughly fundamental that a general reference to it will serve as one continuous note to matters relating to the councils held under Constantine.
[2] = Africa.
[3] It is noted that this evidence of the presence of foreign bishops — "missionary bishops," so to speak — is confirmed by Gelasius and also by the roll of the members.
[4] [Hosius of Cordova. — *Bag.*]
[5] [It has been doubted whether Rome or Constantinople is here intended. The authority of Sozomen and others is in favor of the former. See English translation, published as one volume of this series. — *Bag.*] Also in this series.

CHAPTER VIII.

That the Assembly was composed, as in the Acts of the Apostles, of Individuals from Various Nations.

FOR it is said[1] that in the Apostles' age, there were gathered " devout men from every nation under heaven " ; among whom were Parthians, and Medes, and Elamites, and the dwellers in Mesopotamia, in Judea, and Cappadocia, in Pontus and Asia, in Phrygia and Pamphylia, in Egypt, and the parts of Libya about Cyrene ; and sojourners from Rome, both Jews and proselytes, Cretans and Arabians. But that assembly was less, in that not all who composed it were ministers of God ; but in the present company, the number of bishops exceeded two hundred and fifty,[2] while that of the presbyters and deacons in their train, and the crowd of acolytes and other attendants was altogether beyond computation.

CHAPTER IX.

Of the Virtue and Age of the Two Hundred and Fifty Bishops.

OF these ministers of God, some were distinguished by wisdom and eloquence, others by the gravity of their lives, and by patient fortitude of character, while others again united in themselves all these graces.[1] There were among them men whose years demanded veneration : others were younger, and in the prime of mental vigor ; and some had but recently entered on the course of their ministry. For the maintenance of all ample provision was daily furnished by the emperor's command.

CHAPTER X.

Council in the Palace. Constantine, entering, took his Seat in the Assembly.

Now when the appointed day arrived on which the council met for the final solution of the questions in dispute, each member was present for this in the central building of the palace,[1] which appeared to exceed the rest in magnitude. On each side of the interior of this were many seats disposed in order, which were occupied by those who had been invited to attend, according to their rank. As soon, then, as the whole assembly had seated themselves with becoming orderliness, a general silence prevailed, in expectation of the emperor's arrival. And first of all, three of his immediate family entered in succession, then others also preceded his approach, not of the soldiers or guards who usually accompanied him, but only friends in the faith. And now, all rising at the signal which indicated the emperor's entrance, at last he himself proceeded through the midst of the assembly, like some heavenly messenger of God, clothed in raiment which glittered as it were with rays of light, reflecting the glowing radiance of a purple robe, and adorned with the brilliant splendor of gold and precious stones. Such was the external appearance of his person ; and with regard to his mind, it was evident that he was distinguished by piety and godly fear. This was indicated by his downcast eyes, the blush on his countenance, and his gait. For the rest of his personal excellencies, he surpassed all present in height of stature and beauty of form, as well as in majestic dignity of mien, and invincible strength and vigor. All these graces, united to a suavity of manner, and a serenity becoming his imperial station, declared the excellence of his mental qualities to be above all praise.[2] As soon as he had advanced to the upper end of the seats, at first he remained standing, and when a low chair of wrought gold had been set for him, he waited until the bishops had beckoned to him, and then sat down, and after him the whole assembly did the same.

CHAPTER XI.

Silence of the Council, after Some Words by the the Bishop Eusebius.

THE bishop who occupied the chief place in the right division of the assembly[1] then rose, and, addressing the emperor, delivered a concise speech, in a strain of thanksgiving to Almighty God on his behalf. When he had resumed his seat, silence ensued, and all regarded the emperor with fixed attention ; on which he looked serenely round on the assembly with a cheerful aspect, and, having collected his thoughts, in a calm and gentle tone gave utterance to the following words.

---

[1] Acts ii. 5 sqq.
[2] The number present is given variously as three hundred (Socrates), three hundred and eighteen (Athanasius, &c.), two hundred and seventy (Theodoret), or even two thousand (cf. Hefele). It has been conjectured that the variation came from the omission of names of the Arians (cf. note of Heinichen, Vol. 3, p. 506–507), or that it varied during the two months and more.
[1] This is the way it is interpreted by Sozomen, 1, 17. The phrase, which is literally " of middling character," is translated by *Molz.* and others as if it meant " mild " or " modest," as if it referred in some way to the doctrine of the mean.
[1] [Hence it seems probable that this was the last day of the Council; the entire session of which occupied more than two

months, and which was originally held in a church. — *Bag.*] The exact dates of the Council are controverted, but it seems that it ended August 25, having probably begun June 14.
[2] Compare Prolegomena, under *Physical and Mental Characteristics.*
[1] [The authority of Sozomen and other writers seems to decide that this was Eusebius himself. — *Bag.*]

CHAPTER XII.

Constantine's Address to the Council concerning Peace.[1]

" IT was once my chief desire, dearest friends, to enjoy the spectacle of your united presence ; and now that this desire is fulfilled, I feel myself bound to render thanks to God the universal King, because, in addition to all his other benefits, he has granted me a blessing higher than all the rest, in permitting me to see you not only all assembled together, but all united in a common harmony of sentiment. I pray therefore that no malignant adversary may henceforth interfere to mar our happy state ; I pray that, now the impious hostility of the tyrants has been forever removed by the power of God our Saviour, that spirit who delights in evil may devise no other means for exposing the divine law to blasphemous calumny ; for, in my judgment, intestine strife within the Church of God is far more evil and dangerous than any kind of war or conflict ; and these our differences appear to me more grievous than any outward trouble. Accordingly, when, by the will and with the co-operation of God, I had been victorious over my enemies, I thought that nothing more remained but to render thanks to him, and sympathize in the joy of those whom he had restored to freedom through my instrumentality ; as soon as I heard that intelligence which I had least expected to receive, I mean the news of your dissension, I judged it to be of no secondary importance, but with the earnest desire that a remedy for this evil also might be found through my means, I immediately sent to require your presence. And now I rejoice in beholding your assembly ; but I feel that my desires will be most completely fulfilled when I can see you all united in one judgment, and that common spirit of peace and concord prevailing amongst you all, which it becomes you, as consecrated to the service of God, to commend to others. Delay not, then, dear friends : delay not, ye ministers of God, and faithful servants of him who is our common Lord and Saviour : begin from this moment to discard the causes of that disunion which has existed among you, and remove the perplexities of controversy by embracing the principles of peace. For by such conduct you will at the same time be acting in a manner most pleasing to the supreme God, and you will confer an exceeding favor on me who am your fellow-servant."

[1] The earnest desire of Constantine to promote peace in the church makes one judge with leniency the rather arbitrary and very mechanical method he often took to secure it. As over against the unity of form or the unity of compromise, there is one only real unity — a unity in the truth, being one in *the* Truth. The secret of peace is reason with right.

CHAPTER XIII.

How he led the Dissentient Bishops to Harmony of Sentiment.

As soon as the emperor had spoken these words in the Latin tongue, which another interpreted, he gave permission to those who presided in the council to deliver their opinions. On this some began to accuse their neighbors, who defended themselves, and recriminated in their turn. In this manner numberless assertions were put forth by each party, and a violent controversy arose at the very commencement. Notwithstanding this, the emperor gave patient audience to all alike, and received every proposition with steadfast attention, and by occasionally assisting the argument of each party in turn, he gradually disposed even the most vehement disputants to a reconciliation. At the same time, by the affability of his address to all, and his use of the Greek language, with which he was not altogether unacquainted, he appeared in a truly attractive and amiable light, persuading some, convincing others by his reasonings, praising those who spoke well, and urging all to unity of sentiment, until at last he succeeded in bringing them to one mind and judgment respecting every disputed question.

CHAPTER XIV.

Unanimous Declaration of the Council concerning Faith, and the Celebration of Easter.

THE result was that they were not only united as concerning the faith, but that the time for the celebration of the salutary feast of Easter was agreed on by all. Those points also which were sanctioned by the resolution of the whole body were committed to writing, and received the signature of each several member.[1] Then the emperor, believing that he had thus obtained a second victory over the adversary of the Church, proceeded to solemnize a triumphal festival in honor of God.

CHAPTER XV.

How Constantine entertained the Bishops on the Occasion of his Vicennalia.

ABOUT this time he completed the twentieth year of his reign.[1] On this occasion public festivals were celebrated by the people of the provinces generally, but the emperor himself invited and feasted with those ministers of God

[1] The extant signatures are of doubtful authenticity. Compare Hefele, p. 269.
[1] Compare Prolegomena, *Life*.

whom he had reconciled, and thus offered as it were through them a suitable sacrifice to God. Not one of the bishops was wanting at the imperial banquet,[2] the circumstances of which were splendid beyond description. Detachments of the body-guard and other troops surrounded the entrance of the palace with drawn swords, and through the midst of these the men of God proceeded without fear into the innermost of the imperial apartments, in which some were the emperor's own companions at table, while others reclined on couches arranged on either side.[3] One might have thought that a picture of Christ's kingdom was thus shadowed forth, and a dream rather than reality.

CHAPTER XVI.

Presents to the Bishops, and Letters to the People generally.

AFTER the celebration of this brilliant festival, the emperor courteously received all his guests, and generously added to the favors he had already bestowed by personally presenting gifts to each individual according to his rank. He also gave information of the proceedings of the synod to those who had not been present, by a letter in his own hand-writing. And this letter also I will inscribe as it were on some monument by inserting it in this my narrative of his life. It was as follows :

CHAPTER XVII.

Constantine's Letter to the Churches respecting the Council at Nicæa.

" CONSTANTINUS AUGUSTUS, to the Churches.

" Having had full proof, in the general prosperity of the empire, how great the favor of God has been towards us, I have judged that it ought to be the first object of my endeavors, that unity of faith, sincerity of love, and community of feeling in regard to the worship of Almighty God, might be preserved among the highly favored multitude who compose the Catholic Church. And, inasmuch as this object could not be effectually and certainly secured, unless all, or at least the greater number of the bishops were to meet together, and a discussion of all particulars relating to our most holy religion to take place ; for this reason as numerous an assembly as possible has been convened, at which I myself was present, as one among yourselves (and far be it from me to deny that which is my greatest joy, that I am your fellow-servant), and every question received due and full examination, until that judgment which God, who sees all things, could approve, and which tended to unity and concord, was brought to light, so that no room was left for further discussion or controversy in relation to the faith.

CHAPTER XVIII.

He speaks of their Unanimity respecting the Feast of Easter, and against the Practice of the Jews.

" AT this meeting the question concerning the most holy day of Easter was discussed, and it was resolved by the united judgment of all present, that this feast ought to be kept by all and in every place on one and the same day. For what can be more becoming or honorable to us than that this feast from which we date our hopes of immortality, should be observed unfailingly by all alike, according to one ascertained order and arrangement ? And first of all, it appeared an unworthy thing that in the celebration of this most holy feast we should follow the practice of the Jews, who have impiously defiled their hands with enormous sin, and are, therefore, deservedly afflicted with blindness of soul. For we have it in our power, if we abandon their custom, to prolong the due observance of this ordinance to future ages, by a truer order, which we have preserved from the very day of the passion until the present time. Let us then have nothing in common with the detestable Jewish crowd ; for we have received from our Saviour a different way. A course at once legitimate and honorable lies open to our most holy religion. Beloved brethren, let us with one consent adopt this course, and withdraw ourselves from all participation in their baseness.[1] For their boast is absurd indeed, that it is not in our power without instruction from them to observe these things. For how should they be capable of forming a sound judgment, who, since their parricidal guilt in slaying their Lord, have been subject to the direction, not of reason, but of ungoverned passion, and are swayed by every impulse of the mad spirit that is in them ? Hence it is that on this point as well as others they have no perception of the truth, so that, being altogether ignorant of the true adjustment of this question, they sometimes celebrate

---

[2] At the risk of seeming trivial in sober and professedly condensed annotation, one cannot help noting that the human nature of ancient and modern councils is the same, — much controversy and more or less absenteeism, but all present at dinner.

[3] For notice of these couches, see Smith, *Dict. Gr. and Rom. Ant.*, article *Lectica*.

[1] [The idea seems to be (as explained by Valesius) that if they joined the Jews in celebrating this feast, they would seem to consent to their crime in crucifying the Lord. — *Bag.*] He carried out his reprobation of the Jews in his actions in discriminating laws at least, and perhaps in actual persecution.

Easter twice in the same year. Why then should we follow those who are confessedly in grievous error? Surely we shall never consent to keep this feast a second time in the same year. But supposing these reasons were not of sufficient weight, still it would be incumbent on your Sagacities[2] to strive and pray continually that the purity of your souls may not seem in anything to be sullied by fellowship with the customs of these most wicked men. We must consider, too, that a discordant judgment in a case of such importance, and respecting such religious festival, is wrong. For our Saviour has left us one feast in commemoration of the day of our deliverance, I mean the day of his most holy passion; and he has willed that his Catholic Church should be one, the members of which, however scattered in many and diverse places, are yet cherished by one pervading spirit, that is, by the will of God. And let your Holinesses' sagacity reflect how grievous and scandalous it is that on the self-same days some should be engaged in fasting, others in festive enjoyment; and again, that after the days of Easter some should be present at banquets and amusements, while others are fulfilling the appointed fasts. It is, then, plainly the will of Divine Providence (as I suppose you all clearly see), that this usage should receive fitting correction, and be reduced to one uniform rule.

CHAPTER XIX.

Exhortation to follow the Example of the Greater Part of the World.

"SINCE, therefore, it was needful that this matter should be rectified, so that we might have nothing in common with that nation of parricides who slew their Lord: and since that arrangement is consistent with propriety which is observed by all the churches of the western, southern, and northern parts of the world, and by some of the eastern also: for these reasons all are unanimous on this present occasion in thinking it worthy of adoption. And I myself have undertaken that this decision should meet with the approval of your Sagacities,[1] in the hope that your Wisdoms[1] will gladly admit that practice which is observed at once in the city of Rome, and in Africa; throughout Italy, and in Egypt, in Spain, the Gauls, Britain, Libya, and the whole of Greece; in the dioceses of Asia and Pontus, and in Cilicia, with entire unity of judgment. And you will consider not only that the number of churches is far greater in the regions I have enumerated than in any other, but also that it is most fitting that all should unite in desiring that which sound reason appears to demand, and in avoiding all participation in the perjured conduct of the Jews.[2] In fine, that I may express my meaning in as few words as possible, it has been determined by the common judgment of all, that the most holy feast of Easter should be kept on one and the same day. For on the one hand a discrepancy of opinion on so sacred a question is unbecoming, and on the other it is surely best to act on a decision which is free from strange folly and error.

CHAPTER XX.

Exhortation to obey the Decrees of the Council.

"RECEIVE, then, with all willingness this truly Divine injunction, and regard it as in truth the gift of God. For whatever is determined in the holy assemblies of the bishops is to be regarded as indicative of the Divine will. As soon, therefore, as you have communicated these proceedings to all our beloved brethren, you are bound from that time forward to adopt for yourselves, and to enjoin on others the arrangement above mentioned, and the due observance of this most sacred day; that whenever I come into the presence of your love, which I have long desired, I may have it in my power to celebrate the holy feast with you on the same day, and may rejoice with you on all accounts, when I behold the cruel power of Satan removed by Divine aid through the agency of our endeavors, while your faith, and peace, and concord everywhere flourish. God preserve you, beloved brethren!"

The emperor transmitted a faithful copy[1] of this letter to every province, wherein they who read it might discern as in a mirror the pure sincerity of his thoughts, and of his piety toward God.

CHAPTER XXI.

Recommendation to the Bishops, on their Departure, to Preserve Harmony.

AND now, when the council was on the point of being finally dissolved, he summoned all the bishops to meet him on an appointed day, and on their arrival addressed them in a farewell

---

[2] ['Αγχίνοια. This word is one of a class of expressions frequently used by Eusebius, and which, being intended as *titles of honor*, like "Excellency," &c., should, where possible, be thus rendered. In the present instance it is applied to the heads of the churches collectively. — *Bag.*] More probably in this case it is *not* the title, but means "your sagacity."
[1] Rather "sagacity" and "wisdom."

[2] [Valesius explains this as referring to the conduct of the Jews in professing to acknowledge God as their king, and yet denying him by saying, "We have no king but Cæsar." — *Bag.*]
[1] This *Hein.* regards as the correct meaning, although "equally valid," or "authoritative," has been regarded as possible.

speech, in which he recommended them to be diligent in the maintenance of peace, to avoid contentious disputations, amongst themselves, and not to be jealous, if any one of their number should appear pre-eminent for wisdom and eloquence, but to esteem the excellence of one a blessing common to all. On the other hand he reminded them that the more gifted should forbear to exalt themselves to the prejudice of their humbler brethren, since it is God's prerogative to judge of real superiority. Rather should they considerately condescend to the weaker, remembering that absolute perfection in any case is a rare quality indeed. Each, then, should be willing to accord indulgence to the other for slight offenses, to regard charitably and pass over mere human weaknesses ; holding mutual harmony in the highest honor, that no occasion of mockery might be given by their dissensions to those who are ever ready to blaspheme the word of God : whom indeed we should do all in our power to save, and this cannot be unless our conduct seems to them attractive. But you are well aware of the fact, that testimony is by no means productive of blessing to all, since some who hear are glad to secure the supply of their mere bodily necessities, while others court the patronage of their superiors ; some fix their affection on those who treat them with hospitable kindness, others again, being honored with presents, love their benefactors in return ; but few are they who really desire the word of testimony, and rare indeed is it to find a friend of truth. Hence the necessity of endeavoring to meet the case of all, and, physician-like, to administer to each that which may tend to the health of the soul, to the end that the saving doctrine may be fully honored by all. Of this kind was the former part of his exhortation ;[1] and in conclusion he enjoined them to offer diligent supplications to God on his behalf. Having thus taken leave of them, he gave them all permission to return to their respective countries ; and this they did with joy, and thenceforward that unity of judgment at which they had arrived in the emperor's presence continued to prevail, and those who had long been divided were bound together as members of the same body.

CHAPTER XXII.

How he dismissed Some, and wrote Letters to Others; also his Presents.

FULL of joy therefore at this success, the emperor presented as it were pleasant fruits in the way of letters to those who had not been present at the council. He commanded also that ample gifts of money should be bestowed on all the people, both in the country and the cities, being pleased thus to honor the festive occasion of the twentieth anniversary of his reign.

CHAPTER XXIII.

How he wrote to the Egyptians, exhorting them to Peace.

AND now, when all else were at peace, among the Egyptians alone an implacable contention still raged,[1] so as once more to disturb the emperor's tranquillity, though not to excite his anger. For indeed he treated the contending parties with all respect, as fathers, nay rather, as prophets of God ; and again he summoned them to his presence, and again patiently acted as mediator between them, and honored them with gifts, and communicated also the result of his arbitration by letter. He confirmed and sanctioned the decrees of the council, and called on them to strive earnestly for concord, and not to distract and rend the Church, but to keep before them the thought of God's judgment. And these injunctions the emperor sent by a letter written with his own hand.

CHAPTER XXIV.

How he wrote Frequent Letters of a Religious Character to the Bishops and People.

BUT besides these, his writings are very numerous on kindred subjects, and he was the author of a multitude of letters, some to the bishops, in which he laid injunctions on them tending to the advantage of the churches of God ; and sometimes the thrice blessed one addressed the people of the churches generally, calling them his own brethren and fellow-servants. But perhaps we may hereafter find leisure to collect these despatches in a separate form, in order that the integrity of our present history may not be impaired by their insertion.

CHAPTER XXV.

How he ordered the Erection of a Church at Jerusalem, in the Holy Place of our Saviour's Resurrection.

AFTER these things, the pious emperor addressed himself to another work truly worthy of record, in the province of Palestine. What

---

[1] Or " such were the injunctions which the emperor laid especially on their consciences."

[1] Continuation of the Arian controversy.

then was this work? He judged it incumbent on him to render the blessed locality of our Saviour's resurrection an object of attraction and veneration to all. He issued immediate injunctions, therefore, for the erection in that spot of a house of prayer: and this he did, not on the mere natural impulse of his own mind, but being moved in spirit by the Saviour himself.

CHAPTER XXVI.

That the Holy Sepulchre had been covered with Rubbish and with Idols by the Ungodly.

FOR it had been in time past the endeavor of impious men (or rather let me say of the whole race of evil spirits through their means), to consign to the darkness of oblivion that divine monument of immortality to which the radiant angel had descended from heaven, and rolled away the stone for those who still had stony hearts, and who supposed that the living One still lay among the dead; and had declared glad tidings to the women also, and removed their stony-hearted unbelief by the conviction that he whom they sought was alive. This sacred cave, then, certain impious and godless persons had thought to remove entirely from the eyes of men, supposing in their folly that thus they should be able effectually to obscure the truth. Accordingly they brought a quantity of earth from a distance with much labor, and covered the entire spot; then, having raised this to a moderate height, they paved it with stone, concealing the holy cave beneath this massive mound. Then, as though their purpose had been effectually accomplished, they prepare on this foundation a truly dreadful sepulchre of souls, by building a gloomy shrine of lifeless idols to the impure spirit whom they call Venus, and offering detestable oblations therein on profane and accursed altars. For they supposed that their object could not otherwise be fully attained, than by thus burying the sacred cave beneath these foul pollutions. Unhappy men! they were unable to comprehend how impossible it was that their attempt should remain unknown to him who had been crowned with victory over death, any more than the blazing sun, when he rises above the earth, and holds his wonted course through the midst of heaven, is unseen by the whole race of mankind. Indeed, his saving power, shining with still greater brightness, and illumining, not the bodies, but the souls of men, was already filling the world with the effulgence of its own light. Nevertheless, these devices of impious and wicked men against the truth had prevailed for a long time, nor had any one of the governors, or military command-ers, or even of the emperors themselves ever yet appeared, with ability to abolish these daring impieties, save only that one who enjoyed the favor of the King of kings. And now, acting as he did under the guidance of the divine Spirit, he could not consent to see the sacred spot of which we have spoken, thus buried, through the devices of the adversaries, under every kind of impurity, and abandoned to forgetfulness and neglect; nor would he yield to the malice of those who had contracted this guilt, but calling on the divine aid, gave orders that the place should be thoroughly purified, thinking that the parts which had been most polluted by the enemy ought to receive special tokens, through his means, of the greatness of the divine favor. As soon, then, as his commands were issued, these engines of deceit were cast down from their proud eminence to the very ground, and the dwelling-places of error, with the statues and the evil spirits which they represented, were overthrown and utterly destroyed.

CHAPTER XXVII.

How Constantine commanded the Materials of the Idol Temple, and the Soil itself, to be removed at a Distance.

NOR did the emperor's zeal stop here; but he gave further orders that the materials of what was thus destroyed, both stone and timber, should be removed and thrown as far from the spot as possible; and this command also was speedily executed. The emperor, however, was not satisfied with having proceeded thus far: once more, fired with holy ardor, he directed that the ground itself should be dug up to a considerable depth, and the soil which had been polluted by the foul impurities of demon worship transported to a far distant place.

CHAPTER XXVIII.

Discovery of the Most Holy Sepulchre.[1]

THIS also was accomplished without delay. But as soon as the original surface of the ground, beneath the covering of earth, appeared, immediately, and contrary to all expectation, the venerable and hallowed monument of our Saviour's resurrection was discovered. Then indeed did this most holy cave present a faithful simili-

---

[1] On the site of the sepulchre, compare Besant, *Sepulchre, the Holy,* in Smith and Cheetham, 2 (1880), 1881–1888. He discusses (*a*) Is the present site that fixed upon by the officers of Constantine? and (*b*) Was that site certainly or even probably the true spot where our Lord was buried? Compare also reports of the Palestine Exploration Fund Survey, *Jerusalem,* 1884, p. 429–435 (Conder).

tude of his return to life, in that, after lying buried in darkness, it again emerged to light, and afforded to all who came to witness the sight, a clear and visible proof of the wonders of which that spot had once been the scene, a testimony to the resurrection of the Saviour clearer than any voice could give.

CHAPTER XXIX.

How he wrote concerning the Erection of a Church, both to the Governors of the Provinces, and to the Bishop Macarius.

IMMEDIATELY after the transactions I have recorded, the emperor sent forth injunctions which breathed a truly pious spirit, at the same time granting ample supplies of money, and commanding that a house of prayer worthy of the worship of God should be erected near the Saviour's tomb on a scale of rich and royal greatness. This object he had indeed for some time kept in view, and had foreseen, as if by the aid of a superior intelligence, that which should afterwards come to pass. He laid his commands, therefore, on the governors of the Eastern provinces, that by an abundant and unsparing expenditure they should secure the completion of the work on a scale of noble and ample magnificence. He also despatched the following letter to the bishop who at that time presided over the church at Jerusalem, in which he clearly asserted the saving doctrine of the faith, writing in these terms.

CHAPTER XXX.

Constantine's Letter to Macarius respecting the Building of the Church of our Saviour.

" VICTOR CONSTANTIUS, MAXIMUS AUGUSTUS, to Macarius.

" Such is our Saviour's grace, that no power of language seems adequate to describe the wondrous circumstance to which I am about to refer. For, that the monument of his most holy Passion, so long ago buried beneath the ground, should have remained unknown for so long a series of years, until its reappearance to his servants now set free through the removal of him[1] who was the common enemy of all, is a fact which truly surpasses all admiration. For if all who are accounted wise throughout the world were to unite in their endeavors to say somewhat worthy of this event, they would be unable to attain their object in the smallest degree. Indeed, the nature of this miracle as far transcends the capacity of human reason as

heavenly things are superior to human affairs. For this cause it is ever my first, and indeed my only object, that, as the authority of the truth is evincing itself daily by fresh wonders, so our souls may all become more zealous, with all sobriety and earnest unanimity, for the honor of the Divine law. I desire, therefore, especially, that you should be persuaded of that which I suppose is evident to all beside, namely, that I have no greater care than how I may best adorn with a splendid structure that sacred spot, which, under Divine direction, I have disencumbered as it were of the heavy weight of foul idol worship ; a spot which has been accounted holy from the beginning in God's judgment, but which now appears holier still, since it has brought to light a clear assurance of our Saviour's passion.

CHAPTER XXXI.

That the Building should surpass all the Churches in the World in the Beauty of its Walls, its Columns, and Marbles.

" IT will be well, therefore, for your sagacity to make such arrangements and provision of all things needful for the work, that not only the church itself as a whole may surpass all others whatsoever in beauty, but that the details of the building may be of such a kind that the fairest structures in any city of the empire may be excelled by this. And with respect to the erection and decoration of the walls, this is to inform you that our friend Dracilianus, the deputy of the Prætorian Præfects, and the governor of the province, have received a charge from us. For our pious directions to them are to the effect that artificers and laborers, and whatever they shall understand from your sagacity to be needful for the advancement of the work, shall forthwith be furnished by their care. And as to the columns and marbles, whatever you shall judge, after actual inspection of the plan, to be especially precious and serviceable, be diligent to send information to us in writing, in order that whatever quantity or sort of materials we shall esteem from your letter to be needful, may be procured from every quarter, as required, for it is fitting that the most marvelous place in the world should be worthily decorated.

CHAPTER XXXII.

That he instructed the Governors concerning the Beautifying of the Roof; also concerning the Workmen, and Materials.

" WITH respect to the ceiling[1] of the church,

---

[1] [Licinius appears to be meant, whose death had occurred A.D. 326, in which year the alleged discovery of the Lord's sepulchre took place. — *Bag.*]

[1] The word used is the technical " camera," meaning properly a

I wish to know from you whether in your judgment it should be panel-ceiled,[2] or finished with any other kind of workmanship. If the panel ceiling be adopted, it may also be ornamented with gold. For the rest, your Holiness will give information as early as possible to the beforementioned magistrates how many laborers and artificers, and what expenditure of money is required. You will also be careful to send us a report without delay, not only respecting the marbles and columns, but the paneled ceiling also, should this appear to you to be the most beautiful form. God preserve you, beloved brother !"

CHAPTER XXXIII.

How the Church of our Saviour, the New Jerusalem prophesied of in Scripture, was built.

THIS was the emperor's letter; and his directions were at once carried into effect. Accordingly, on the very spot which witnessed the Saviour's sufferings, a new Jerusalem was constructed, over against the one so celebrated of old, which, since the foul stain of guilt brought on it by the murder of the Lord, had experienced the last extremity of desolation, the effect of Divine judgment on its impious people. It was opposite this city that the emperor now began to rear a monument to the Saviour's victory over death, with rich and lavish magnificence. And it may be that this was that second and new Jerusalem spoken of in the predictions of the prophets,[1] concerning which such abundant testimony is given in the divinely inspired records.

First of all, then, he adorned the sacred cave itself, as the chief part of the whole work, and the hallowed monument at which the angel radiant with light had once declared to all that regeneration which was first manifested in the Saviour's person.

CHAPTER XXXIV.

Description of the Structure of the Holy Sepulchre.

THIS monument, therefore, first of all, as the chief part of the whole, the emperor's zealous

magnificence beautified with rare columns, and profusely enriched with the most splendid decorations of every kind.

CHAPTER XXXV.

Description of the Atrium and Porticos.

THE next object of his attention was a space of ground of great extent, and open to the pure air of heaven. This he adorned with a pavement of finely polished stone, and enclosed it on three sides with porticos of great length.

CHAPTER XXXVI.

Description of the Walls, Roof, Decoration, and Gilding of the Body of the Church.

FOR at the side opposite to the cave, which was the eastern side, the church itself was erected; a noble work rising to a vast height, and of great extent both in length and breadth. The interior of this structure was floored with marble slabs of various colors; while the external surface of the walls, which shone with polished stones exactly fitted together, exhibited a degree of splendor in no respect inferior to that of marble. With regard to the roof, it was covered on the outside with lead, as a protection against the rains of winter. But the inner part of the roof, which was finished with sculptured panel work, extended in a series of connected compartments, like a vast sea, over the whole church;[1] and, being overlaid throughout with the purest gold, caused the entire building to glitter as it were with rays of light.

CHAPTER XXXVII.

Description of the Double Porticos on Either Side, and of the Three Eastern Gates.

BESIDES this were two porticos on each side, with upper and lower ranges of pillars,[1] corresponding in length with the church itself; and these also had their roofs ornamented with gold. Of these porticos, those which were exterior to the church were supported by columns of great size, while those within these rested on piles[2] of

---

certain style of vaulted ceiling, but here it is perhaps the generic ceiling if the specific word below means panel ceiling.
[2] This is the word for the Lacunaria or panel ceilings, a style of ceiling where "planks were placed across these beams at certain intervals leaving hollow spaces," "which were frequently covered with gold and ivory, and sometimes with paintings." Compare article *Domus*, in Smith, *Dict. Gr. and Rom. Ant.* The passage may mean either "with respect to the ceiling . . . whether . . . wainscoted" or "with respect to the Camera . . . whether panel ceiled."
[1] [Apparently referring (says Valesius) to Rev. xxi. 2: "And I, John, saw the holy city, new Jerusalem, coming down from God,

out of heaven," &c.; an extraordinary, nay, almost ludicrous application of Scripture, though perhaps characteristic of the author's age. — *Bag.*] And it may be said characteristic of Eusebius himself, for it is not his only sin in this regard.
[1] It would seem from this description that the paneling was like that of Santa Maria Maggiore at Rome, a horizontal surface rather than the pointed roof paneled.
[1] Whether this means two series, one underground and one above (*Molz.* and many), or not, is fully discussed by Heinichen in a separate note (*Eusebius*, vol. 3, p. 520–521).
[2] [These inner porticos seem to have rested on massy piles, because they adjoined the sides of the church, and had to bear its

stone beautifully adorned on the surface. Three gates, placed exactly east, were intended to receive the multitudes who entered the church.

CHAPTER XXXVIII.

Description of the Hemisphere, the Twelve Columns, and their Bowls.

OPPOSITE these gates the crowning part of the whole was the hemisphere,[1] which rose to the very summit of the church. This was encircled by twelve columns (according to the number of the apostles of our Saviour), having their capitals embellished with silver bowls of great size, which the emperor himself presented as a splendid offering to his God.

CHAPTER XXXIX.

Description of the Inner Court, the Arcades, and Porches.

IN the next place he enclosed the atrium, which occupied the space leading to the entrances in front of the church. This comprehended, first the court, then the porticos on each side, and lastly the gates of the court. After these, in the midst of the open market-place,[1] the general entrance-gates, which were of exquisite workmanship, afforded to passers-by on the outside a view of the interior which could not fail to inspire astonishment.

CHAPTER XL.

Of the Number of his Offerings.

THIS temple, then, the emperor erected as a conspicuous monument of the Saviour's resurrection, and embellished it throughout on an imperial scale of magnificence. He further enriched it with numberless offerings of inexpressible beauty and various materials, — gold, silver, and precious stones, the skillful and elaborate arrangement of which, in regard to their magnitude, number, and variety, we have not leisure at present to describe particularly.[1]

CHAPTER XLI.

Of the Erection of Churches in Bethlehem, and on the Mount of Olives.

IN the same country he discovered other places, venerable as being the localities of two sacred caves : and these also he adorned with lavish magnificence. In the one case, he rendered due honor to that which had been the scene of the first manifestation of our Saviour's divine presence, when he submitted to be born in mortal flesh ; while in the case of the second cavern he hallowed the remembrance of his ascension to heaven from the mountain top. And while he thus nobly testified his reverence for these places, he at the same time eternized the memory of his mother,[1] who had been the instrument of conferring so valuable a benefit on mankind.

CHAPTER XLII.

That the Empress Helena,[1] Constantine's Mother, having visited this Locality for Devotional Purposes, built these Churches.

FOR she, having resolved to discharge the duties of pious devotion to the God, the King of kings, and feeling it incumbent on her to render thanksgivings with prayers on behalf both of her own son, now so mighty an emperor, and of his sons, her own grandchildren, the divinely favored Cæsars, though now advanced in years, yet gifted with no common degree of wisdom, had hastened with youthful alacrity to survey this venerable land ; and at the same time to visit the eastern provinces, cities, and people, with a truly imperial solicitude. As soon, then, as she had rendered due reverence to the ground which the Saviour's feet had trodden, according to the prophetic word which says [2] "Let us worship at the place whereon his feet have stood," she immediately bequeathed the fruit of her piety to future generations.

CHAPTER XLIII.

A Farther Notice of the Churches at Bethlehem.

FOR without delay she dedicated two churches to the God whom she adored, one at the grotto which had been the scene of the Saviour's birth ; the other on the mount of his ascension. For

---

roof, which was loftier than any of the rest. — *Bag.*] Translated by *Molz.* "Quadrangular supports." "In Architecture *a cubic mass of building,* to serve for bearings." — *Liddell and Scott.*

[1] [Apparently, the altar, which was of a hemispherical, or rather hemicylindrical form. — *Bag.*] Also a much-discussed question. Compare Heinichen, vol. 3, p. 521-522.

[1] [In front of the larger churches there was generally a street, or open space, where a market was held on the festival of the Martyr to whom the church was dedicated. Regard was also had, in this arrangement, to architectural effect, the object being that nothing should interfere with the view of the front of the church. *Vide* Valesius *in loc.* — *Bag.*]

[1] Some idea of various features of this building may be gathered from the cuts and descriptions of other basilicas in Fergusson, *History of Architecture,* i (1874), 400 sq.; Lübke, *Geschichte der Architektur,* i (Lpg. 1875), 229 sq.; Langl.'s series of *Bilder zur Geschichte,* &c.

[1] Compare Prolegomena, p. 411.
[1] Compare Wordsworth, *Helena,* in Smith and Wace, *Dict.* 2 (1880), 881 sq. That she was made empress is shown also by the coins. Cf. coins in Eckhel.
[2] [Ps. cxxxi. 7. Septuagint. — *Bag.*] Engl. Vers. cxxxii. 7, "We will worship at his footstool."

he who was "God with us" had submitted to be born even in a cave[1] of the earth, and the place of his nativity was called Bethlehem by the Hebrews. Accordingly the pious empress honored with rare memorials the scene of her travail who bore this heavenly child, and beautified the sacred cave with all possible splendor. The emperor himself soon after testified his reverence for the spot by princely offerings, and added to his mother's magnificence by costly presents of silver and gold, and embroidered hangings. And farther, the mother of the emperor raised a stately structure on the Mount of Olives also, in memory of his ascent to heaven who is the Saviour of mankind, erecting a sacred church and temple on the very summit of the mount. And indeed authentic history informs us that in this very cave the Saviour imparted his secret revelations to his disciples.[2] And here also the emperor testified his reverence for the King of kings, by diverse and costly offerings. Thus did Helena Augusta, the pious mother of a pious emperor, erect over the two mystic caverns these two noble and beautiful monuments of devotion, worthy of everlasting remembrance, to the honor of God her Saviour, and as proofs of her holy zeal, receiving from her son the aid of his imperial power. Nor was it long ere this aged woman reaped the due reward of her labors. After passing the whole period of her life, even to declining age, in the greatest prosperity, and exhibiting both in word and deed abundant fruits of obedience to the divine precepts, and having enjoyed in consequence an easy and tranquil existence, with unimpaired powers of body and mind, at length she obtained from God an end befitting her pious course, and a recompense of her good deeds even in this present life.

CHAPTER XLIV.

Of Helena's Generosity and Beneficent Acts.

FOR on the occasion of a circuit which she made of the eastern provinces, in the splendor of imperial authority, she bestowed abundant proofs of her liberality as well on the inhabitants of the several cities collectively, as on individuals who approached her, at the same time that she scattered largesses among the soldiery with a liberal hand. But especially abundant were the gifts she bestowed on the naked and unprotected poor. To some she gave money, to others an ample supply of clothing: she liberated some from imprisonment, or from the bitter servitude of the mines; others she delivered from unjust oppression, and others again, she restored from exile.

CHAPTER XLV.

Helena's Pious Conduct in the Churches.

WHILE, however, her character derived luster from such deeds as I have described, she was far from neglecting personal piety toward God.[1] She might be seen continually frequenting his Church, while at the same time she adorned the houses of prayer with splendid offerings, not overlooking the churches of the smallest cities. In short, this admirable woman was to be seen, in simple and modest attire, mingling with the crowd of worshipers, and testifying her devotion to God by a uniform course of pious conduct.

CHAPTER XLVI.

How she made her Will, and died at the Age of Eighty Years.

AND when at length at the close of a long life, she was called to inherit a happier lot, having arrived at the eightieth year of her age, and being very near the time of her departure, she prepared and executed her last will in favor of her only son, the emperor and sole monarch of the world, and her grandchildren, the Cæsars his sons, to whom severally she bequeathed whatever property she possessed in any part of the world. Having thus made her will, this thrice blessed woman died in the presence of her illustrious son, who was in attendance at her side, caring for her and held her hands: so that, to those who rightly discerned the truth, the thrice blessed one seemed not to die, but to experience a real change and transition from an earthly to a heavenly existence, since her soul, remoulded as it were into an incorruptible and angelic essence,[1] was received up into her Saviour's presence.[2]

---

[1] [Literally, beneath the earth. It seems to have been characteristic of the age of Eusebius to invest the more prominent circumstances connected with the Lord's life on earth with a degree of romance and mystery equally inconsistent with Scripture and with probability. It is obvious that Scripture furnishes no authority for the caves either of the nativity or ascension. See ch. 41, supra.— Bag.] Compare discussion by Andrews, Cave of the Nativity in his Life of our Lord (N. Y.), 77-83.
[2] [Alluding, probably, to the discourse in Matt. xxiv., delivered by our Lord to the disciples on the Mount of Olives.— Bag.]

[1] According to some apocryphal accounts Constantine owed his conversion to his mother (compare the apocryphal letters mentioned under Writings, in the Prolegomena), but Eusebius, below (ch. 47), seems to reverse the fact.
[1] [These words seem to savor of Origen's doctrine, to which Eusebius was much addicted. Origen believed that, in the resurrection, bodies would be changed into souls, and souls into angels, according to the testimony of Jerome. See Valesius in loc.— Bag.]
[2] The date of Helena's death is usually placed in 327 or 328. Compare Wordsworth, l.c. Since she was eighty years old at the time of her death she must have been about twenty-five when Constantine was born.

CHAPTER XLVII.

*How Constantine buried his Mother, and how
he honored her during her Life.*

HER body, too, was honored with special
tokens of respect, being escorted on its way to
the imperial city by a vast train of guards, and
there deposited in a royal tomb. Such were
the last days of our emperor's mother, a person
worthy of being had in perpetual remembrance,
both for her own practical piety, and because
she had given birth to so extraordinary and admirable an offspring. And well may his character be styled blessed, for his filial piety as well
as on other grounds. He rendered her through
his influence so devout a worshiper of God,
(though she had not previously been such,)
that she seemed to have been instructed from
the first by the Saviour of mankind : and besides
this, he had honored her so fully with imperial
dignities, that in every province, and in the very
ranks of the soldiery, she was spoken of under
the titles of Augusta and empress, and her likeness was impressed on golden coins.[1] He had
even granted her authority over the imperial
treasures, to use and dispense them according
to her own will and discretion in every case :
for this enviable distinction also she received at
the hands of her son. Hence it is that among
the qualities which shed a luster on his memory,
we may rightly include that surpassing degree of
filial affection whereby he rendered full obedience to the Divine precepts which enjoin due
honor from children to their parents. In this
manner, then, the emperor executed in Palestine
the noble works I have above described : and
indeed in every province he raised new churches
on a far more imposing scale than those which
had existed before his time.

CHAPTER XLVIII.

*How he built Churches in Honor of Martyrs,
and abolished Idolatry at Constantinople.*

AND being fully resolved to distinguish the
city which bore his name with especial honor,
he embellished it with numerous sacred edifices,
both memorials of martyrs on the largest scale,
and other buildings of the most splendid kind,
not only within the city itself, but in its vicinity :
and thus at the same time he rendered honor
to the memory of the martyrs, and consecrated
his city to the martyrs' God. Being filled, too,
with Divine wisdom, he determined to purge

the city which was to be distinguished by his
own name from idolatry of every kind, that
henceforth no statues might be worshiped there
in the temples of those falsely reputed to be
gods, nor any altars defiled by the pollution of
blood : that there might be no sacrifices consumed by fire, no demon festivals, nor any of
the other ceremonies usually observed by the
superstitious.

CHAPTER XLIX.

*Representation of the Cross in the Palace, and
of Daniel at the Public Fountains.*

ON the other hand one might see the fountains in the midst of the market place graced
with figures representing the good Shepherd,
well known to those who study the sacred oracles, and that of Daniel also with the lions,
forged in brass, and resplendent with plates of
gold. Indeed, so large a measure of Divine
love possessed the emperor's soul, that in the
principal apartment of the imperial palace itself,
on a vast tablet[1] displayed in the center of its
gold-covered paneled ceiling, he caused the symbol of our Saviour's Passion to be fixed, composed
of a variety of precious stones richly inwrought
with gold. This symbol he seemed to have
intended to be as it were the safeguard of the
empire itself.

CHAPTER L.

*That he erected Churches in Nicomedia, and in
Other Cities.*

HAVING thus embellished the city which bore
his name, he next distinguished the capital of
Bithynia[1] by the erection of a stately and magnificent church, being desirous of raising in this
city also, in honor of his Saviour and at his
own charges, a memorial of his victory over his
own enemies and the adversaries of God. He
also decorated the principal cities of the other
provinces with sacred edifices of great beauty ;
as, for example, in the case of that metropolis
of the East which derived its name from Antiochus, in which, as the head of that portion
of the empire, he consecrated to the service of
God a church of unparalleled size and beauty.
The entire building was encompassed by an enclosure of great extent, within which the church
itself rose to a vast elevation, being of an octagonal form, and surrounded on all sides by

---

[1] Compare note above. It is said (Wordsworth) that while silver and copper coins have been found with her name, none of gold
have yet come to light.

[1] Perhaps the largest " panel." The restored church of St. Paul,
outside the walls at Rome, has a paneled ceiling with a very large
central panel.

[1] [Nicomedia, where Constantine had besieged Licinius, and
compelled him to surrender; in memory of which event he built this
church. — *Bag.*]

many chambers, courts, and upper and lower apartments; the whole richly adorned with a profusion of gold, brass, and other materials of the most costly kind.

CHAPTER LI.

That he ordered a Church to be built at Mambre.

SUCH was the principal sacred edifices erected by the emperor's command. But having heard that the self-same Saviour who erewhile had appeared on earth[1] had in ages long since past afforded a manifestation of his Divine presence to holy men of Palestine near the oak of Mambre,[2] he ordered that a house of prayer should be built there also in honor of the God who had thus appeared. Accordingly the imperial commission was transmitted to the provincial governors by letters addressed to them individually, enjoining a speedy completion of the appointed work. He sent moreover to the writer of this history an eloquent admonition, a copy of which I think it well to insert in the present work, in order to convey a just idea of his pious diligence and zeal. To express, then, his displeasure at the evil practices which he had heard were usual in the place just referred to, he addressed me in the following terms.

CHAPTER LII.

Constantine's Letter to Eusebius concerning Mambre.

"VICTOR CONSTANTINUS, MAXIMUS AUGUSTUS, to Macarius, and the rest of the bishops in Palestine.[1]

"One benefit, and that of no ordinary importance, has been conferred on us by my truly pious mother-in-law,[2] in that she has made known to us by letter that abandoned folly of impious men which has hitherto escaped detection

by you: so that the criminal conduct thus overlooked may now through our means obtain fitting correction and remedy, necessary though ardy. For surely it is a grave impiety indeed, that holy places should be defiled by the stain of unhallowed impurities. What then is this, dearest brethren, which, though it has eluded your sagacity, she of whom I speak was impelled by a pious sense of duty to disclose?

CHAPTER LIII.

That the Saviour appeared in this Place to Abraham.

"SHE assures me, then, that the place which takes its name from the oak of Mambre, where we find that Abraham dwelt, is defiled by certain of the slaves of superstition in every possible way. She declares that idols[1] which should be utterly destroyed have been erected on the site of that tree; that an altar is near the spot; and that impure sacrifices are continually performed. Now since it is evident that these practices are equally inconsistent with the character of our times, and unworthy the sanctity of the place itself, I wish your Gravities[2] to be informed that the illustrious Count Acacius, our friend, has received instructions by letter from me, to the effect that every idol which shall be found in the place above-mentioned shall immediately be consigned to the flames; that the altar be utterly demolished; and that if any one, after this our mandate, shall be guilty of impiety of any kind in this place, he shall be visited with condign punishment. The place itself we have directed to be adorned with an unpolluted structure, I mean a church; in order that it may become a fitting place of assembly for holy men. Meantime, should any breach of these our commands occur, it should be made known to our clemency without the least delay by letters from you, that we may direct the person detected to be dealt with, as a transgressor of the law, in the severest manner. For you are not ignorant that the Supreme God first appeared to Abraham, and conversed with him, in that place. There it was that the observance of the Divine law first began; there first the Saviour himself, with the two angels, vouchsafed to Abraham a manifestation of his presence; there God first appeared to men; there he gave promise to Abraham concerning his future seed, and straightway fulfilled that promise; there he foretold that he should be the father of a multitude of nations.

---

[1] This doctrine, which appears again and again in Eusebius and in Constantine, has a curiously interesting bearing at present theological controversies in America, and England for that matter. It may be called the doctrine of the "eternal Christ," as over against the doctrine of the "essential Christ," or that which seems to make his existence begin with his incarnation — the "historical Christ." He had historical existence from the beginning, both as the indwelling and as the objective, and one might venture to think that advocates of these two views could find a meeting-ground, or solution of difficulty at least, in this phrase which represents him who was in the beginning with God and is and ever shall be, who has made all things which have been made, and is in all parts of the universe and the world, among Jews and Gentiles.

[2] [The English version in this passage (Gen. xviii. 1), and others, has "plains," though the Septuagint and ancient interpreters generally render it, as here, by "oak," some by "terebinth" (turpentine tree), the Vulgate by "convallis." — *Bag.*] The Revised Version (1881–1885) has "oaks."

[1] The writer of this history says the letter was addressed to him, while it is really to Macarius. On this ground the Eusebian authorship of the book has been challenged, but of course Eusebius is among "the rest of the bishops."

[2] [Eutropia, mother of his empress Fausta. — *Bag.*]

[1] [These objects of idolatrous worship were probably figures intended to represent the angels who had appeared to Abraham. — *Bag.*] More probably they were some form of images obscenely worshiped.

[2] Better "Reverences," and so throughout.

For these reasons, it seems to me right that this place should not only be kept pure through your diligence from all defilement, but restored also to its pristine sanctity ; that nothing hereafter may be done there except the performance of fitting service to him who is the Almighty God, and our Saviour, and Lord of all. And this service it is incumbent on you to care for with due attention, if your Gravities be willing (and of this I feel confident) to gratify my wishes, which are especially interested in the worship of God. May he preserve you, beloved brethren ! "

CHAPTER LIV.

Destruction of Idol Temples and Images everywhere.

ALL these things the emperor diligently performed to the praise of the saving power of Christ, and thus made it his constant aim to glorify his Saviour God. On the other hand he used every means to rebuke the superstitious errors of the heathen. Hence the entrances of their temples in the several cities were left exposed to the weather, being stripped of their doors at his command ; the tiling of others was removed, and their roofs destroyed. From others again the venerable statues of brass, of which the superstition of antiquity had boasted for a long series of years, were exposed to view in all the public places of the imperial city : so that here a Pythian, there a Sminthian Apòllo, excited the contempt of the beholder : while the Delphic tripods were deposited in the hippodrome and the Muses of Helicon in the palace itself. In short, the city which bore his name was everywhere filled with brazen statues of the most exquisite workmanship, which had been dedicated in every province, and which the deluded victims of superstition had long vainly honored as gods with numberless victims and burnt sacrifices, though now at length they learnt to renounce their error, when the emperor held up the very objects of their worship to be the ridicule and sport of all beholders. With regard to those images which were of gold, he dealt with them in a different manner. For as soon as he understood that the ignorant multitudes were inspired with a vain and childish dread of these bugbears of error, wrought in gold and silver, he judged it right to remove these also, like stumbling-stones thrown in the way of men walking in the dark, and henceforward to open a royal road, plain and unobstructed to all. Having formed this resolution, he considered no soldiers or military force of any sort needful for the suppression of the evil : a few of his own friends sufficed for this service, and these

he sent by a simple expression of his will to visit each several province. Accordingly, sustained by confidence in the emperor's pious intentions and their own personal devotion to God, they passed through the midst of numberless tribes and nations, abolishing this ancient error in every city and country. They ordered the priests themselves, amidst general laughter and scorn, to bring their gods from their dark recesses to the light of day : they then stripped them of their ornaments, and exhibited to the gaze of all the unsightly reality which had been hidden beneath a painted exterior. Lastly, whatever part of the material appeared valuable they scraped off and melted in the fire to prove its worth, after which they secured and set apart whatever they judged needful for their purpose, leaving to the superstitious worshipers that which was altogether useless, as a memorial of their shame. Meanwhile our admirable prince was himself engaged in a work similar to what we have described. For at the same time that these costly images of the dead were stripped, as we have said, of their precious materials, he also attacked those composed of brass ; causing those to be dragged from their places with ropes and as it were carried away captive, whom the dotage of mythology had esteemed as gods.

CHAPTER LV.

Overthrow of an Idol Temple, and Abolition of Licentious Practices, at Aphaca in Phœnicia.

THE emperor's next care was to kindle, as it were, a brilliant torch, by the light of which he directed his imperial gaze around, to see if any hidden vestiges of error might still exist. And as the keen-sighted eagle in its heavenward flight is able to descry from its lofty height the most distant objects on the earth, so did he, while residing in the imperial palace of his own fair city, discover as from a watch-tower a hidden and fatal snare of souls in the province of Phœnicia. This was a grove and temple, not situated in the midst of any city, nor in any public place, as for splendor of effect is generally the case, but apart from the beaten and frequented road, at Aphaca, on part of the summit of Mount Lebanon, and dedicated to the foul demon known by the name of Venus. It was a school of wickedness for all the votaries of impurity, and such as destroyed their bodies with effeminacy. Here men undeserving of the name forgot the dignity of their sex, and propitiated the demon by their effeminate conduct ; here too unlawful commerce of women and adulterous intercourse, with other horrible and infamous practices, were perpetrated in this temple as in a place beyond the scope and restraint of law. Meantime these evils remained unchecked by the presence of any observer, since no one of fair character ventured to visit such scenes. These proceedings, however, could not escape the vigilance of our august emperor, who, having himself inspected them with characteristic forethought, and judging that such a temple was unfit for the light of heaven, gave orders that the building with its offerings should be utterly destroyed. Accordingly, in obedience to the imperial command, these engines of an impure superstition were immediately abolished, and the hand of military force was made instrumental in purging the place. And now those who had heretofore lived without restraint learned self-control through the emperor's threat of punishment, as likewise those superstitious Gentiles wise in their own conceit, who now obtained experimental proof of their own folly.

CHAPTER LVI.

Destruction of the Temple of Æsculapius at Ægæ.[1]

FOR since a wide-spread error of these pretenders to wisdom concerned the demon worshiped in Cilicia, whom thousands regarded with reverence as the possessor of saving and healing power, who sometimes appeared to those who passed the night in his temple, sometimes restored the diseased to health, though on the contrary he was a destroyer of souls, who drew his easily deluded worshipers from the true Saviour to involve them in impious error, the emperor, consistently with his practice, and desire to advance the worship of him who is at once a jealous God and the true Saviour, gave directions that this temple also should be razed to the ground. In prompt obedience to this command, a band of soldiers laid this building, the admiration of noble philosophers, prostrate in the dust, together with its unseen inmate, neither demon nor god, but rather a deceiver of souls, who had seduced mankind for so long a time through various ages. And thus he who had promised to others deliverance from misfortune and distress, could find no means for his own security, any more than when, as is told in myth, he was scorched by the lightning's stroke.[2] Our emperor's pious deeds, however, had in them nothing fabulous or feigned; but by virtue of the manifested power of his Saviour, this temple as well as others was so utterly overthrown, that not a vestige of the former follies was left behind.

CHAPTER LVII.

How the Gentiles abandoned Idol Worship, and turned to the Knowledge of God.

HENCE it was that, of those who had been the slaves of superstition, when they saw with their own eyes the exposure of their delusion, and beheld the actual ruin of the temples and images in every place, some applied themselves to the saving doctrine of Christ; while others, though they declined to take this step, yet reprobated the folly which they had received from their fathers, and laughed to scorn what they had so long been accustomed to regard as gods. Indeed, what other feelings could possess their minds, when they witnessed the thorough uncleanness concealed beneath the fair exterior of the objects of their worship? Beneath this were found either the bones of dead men or dry skulls, fraudulently adorned by the arts of magicians,[1] or filthy rags full of abominable impurity, or a bundle of hay or stubble. On seeing all these things heaped together within their lifeless images, they denounced their fathers' extreme folly and their own, especially when neither in the secret recesses of the temples nor in the statues themselves could any inmate be found; neither demon, nor utterer of oracles, neither god nor prophet, as they had heretofore supposed: nay, not even a dim and shadowy phantom could be seen. Accordingly, every gloomy cavern, every hidden recess, afforded easy access to the emperor's emissaries: the inaccessible and secret chambers, the innermost shrines of the temples, were trampled by the soldiers' feet; and thus the mental blindness which had prevailed for so many ages over the gentile world became clearly apparent to the eyes of all.

CHAPTER LVIII.

How he destroyed the Temple of Venus at Heliopolis, and built the First Church in that City.

SUCH actions as I have described may well be reckoned among the emperor's noblest achievements, as also the wise arrangements which he made respecting each particular province. We may instance the Phœnician city Heliopolis, in which those who dignify licentious pleasure with a distinguishing title of honor, had permitted their wives and daughters to commit shameless fornication. But now a new statute, breathing the very spirit of modesty, proceeded from the emperor, which peremptorily forbade the con-

---

1 [On the coast of Cilicia, near Issus. — *Bag.*]
2 [By Jupiter, for restoring Hippolytus to life, at Diana's request. — *Bag.*]

1 Through another reading translated by *Val.*, *1709*, *Bag.*, "stolen by impostors." Stroth has "impiously employed for magicians' arts."

tinuance of former practices. And besides this, he sent them also written exhortations, as though he had been especially ordained by God for this end, that he might instruct all men in the principles of chastity. Hence, he disdained not to communicate by letter even with these persons, urging them to seek diligently the knowledge of God. At the same time he followed up his words by corresponding deeds, and erected even in this city a church of great size and magnificence: so that an event unheard of before in any age, now for the first time came to pass, namely, that a city which had hitherto been wholly given up to superstition now obtained the privilege of a church of God, with presbyters and deacons, and its people were placed under the presiding care of a bishop consecrated to the service of the supreme God. And further, the emperor, being anxious that here also as many as possible might be won to the truth, bestowed abundant provision for the necessities of the poor, desiring even thus to invite them to seek the doctrines of salvation, as though he were almost adopting the words of him who said, "Whether in pretense, or in truth, let Christ be preached."[1]

CHAPTER LIX.

Of the Disturbance at Antioch by Eustathius.

IN the midst, however, of the general happiness occasioned by these events, and while the Church of God was every where and every way flourishing throughout the empire, once more that spirit of envy, who ever watches for the ruin of the good, prepared himself to combat the greatness of our prosperity, in the expectation, perhaps, that the emperor himself, provoked by our tumults and disorders, might eventually become estranged from us. Accordingly, he kindled a furious controversy at Antioch, and thereby involved the church in that place in a series of tragic calamities, which had well-nigh occasioned the total overthrow of the city. The members of the Church were divided into two opposite parties; while the people, including even the magistrates and soldiery, were roused to such a pitch, that the contest would have been decided by the sword, had not the watchful providence of God, as well as dread of the emperor's displeasure, controlled the fury of the multitude. On this occasion, too, the emperor, acting the part of a preserver and physician of souls, applied with much forbearance the remedy of persuasion to those who needed it. He gently pleaded, as it were by an embassy, with his people, sending among them one

of the best approved and most faithful of those who were honored with the dignity of Count;[1] at the same time that he exhorted them to a peaceable spirit by repeated letters, and instructed them in the practice of true godliness. Having prevailed by these remonstrances, he excused their conduct in his subsequent letters, alleging that he had himself heard the merits of the case from him on whose account the disturbance had arisen.[2] And these letters of his, which are replete with learning and instruction of no ordinary kind, I should have inserted in this present work, were it not that they might affix a mark of dishonor to the character of the persons accused. I will therefore omit these, being unwilling to revive the memory of past grievances, and will only annex those to my present narrative which he wrote to testify his satisfaction at the re-establishment of peace and concord among the rest. In these letters, he cautioned them against any desire to claim the ruler of another district,[3] through whose intervention peace had been restored, as their own, and exhorted them, consistently with the usage of the Church, to choose him as their bishop, whom the common Saviour of all should point out as suited for the office. His letter, then, is addressed to the people and to the bishops, severally, in the following terms.

CHAPTER LX.

Constantine's Letter to the Antiochians, directing them not to withdraw Eusebius from Cæsarea, but to seek some one else.

"VICTOR CONSTANTINUS, MAXIMUS AUGUSTUS, to the people of Antioch.

"How pleasing to the wise and intelligent portion of mankind is the concord which exists among you! And I myself, brethren, am disposed to love you with an enduring affection, inspired both by religion, and by your own manner of life and zeal on my behalf. It is by the exercise of right understanding and sound discretion, that we are enabled really to enjoy our blessings. And what can become you so well as this discretion? No wonder, then, if I affirm that your maintenance of the truth has tended rather to promote your security than to draw on you the hatred of others. Indeed, amongst brethren, whom the selfsame disposition to walk

---

[1] Phil. i. 18. But "is preached," not "let Christ be preached."

[1] "Believed to have been Strategus Musonius" (*Venables*).
[2] [Eustathius, bishop of Antioch, whose deposition, on the ground of a charge of immorality, by the partisans of Eusebius of Nicomedia, had occasioned the disturbances alluded to in the text. —*Bag.*] There is a view that this whole trouble was the result of an intrigue of Eusebius to get the better of Eustathius, who was in a sense a rival. Compare for very vigorous expression of this view, Venables, *Eustathius of Antioch*, in Smith and Wace, *Dict.*
[3] This is rather literal, and the paraphrase of *Molz.* may be better, "no foreign bishops."

in the ways of truth and righteousness promises, through the favor of God, to register among his pure and holy family, what can be more honor-able than gladly to acquiesce in the prosperity of all men? Especially since the precepts of the divine law prescribe a better direction to your proposed intention, and we ourselves desire that your judgment should be confirmed by proper sanction.[1] It may be that you are surprised, and at a loss to understand the meaning of this introduction to my present address. The cause of it I will not hesitate to explain without re-serve. I confess, then, that on reading your records I perceived, by the highly eulogistic testimony which they bear to Eusebius, bishop of Cæsarea, whom I have myself long well known and esteemed for his learning and moderation, that you are strongly attached to him, and de-sire to appropriate him as your own. What thoughts, then, do you suppose that I entertain on this subject, desirous as I am to seek for and act on the strict principles of right? What anxiety do you imagine this desire of yours has caused me? O holy faith, who givest us in our Saviour's words and precepts a model, as it were, of what our life should be, how hardly wouldst thou thyself resist the sins of men, were it not that thou refusest to subserve the purposes of gain! In my own judgment, he whose first ob-ject is the maintenance of peace, seems to be superior to Victory herself; and where a right and honorable course lies open to one's choice, surely no one would hesitate to adopt it. I ask then, brethren, why do we so decide as to in-flict an injury on others by our choice? Why do we covet those objects which will destroy the credit of our own reputation? I myself highly esteem the individual whom ye judge worthy of your respect and affection: notwithstanding, it cannot be right that those principles should be entirely disregarded which should be authorita-tive and binding on all alike, so that each should not be content with his own circumstances, and all enjoy their proper privileges: nor can it be right, in considering the claims of rival candi-dates, to suppose but that not one only, but many, may appear worthy of comparison with this person. For as long as no violence or harshness are suffered to disturb the dignities of the church, they continue to be on an equal footing, and worthy of the same consideration everywhere. Nor is it reasonable that an in-quiry into the qualifications of this one should be made to the detriment of others; since the judgment of all churches, whether reckoned of greater or less importance in themselves, is equally capable of receiving and maintaining the divine ordinances, so that one is in no way in-ferior to another, if we will but boldly declare the truth, in regard to that standard of practice which is common to all. If this be so, we must say that you will be chargeable, not with retain-ing this prelate, but with wrongfully removing him; your conduct will be characterized rather by violence than justice; and whatever may be generally thought by others, I dare clearly and boldly affirm that this measure will furnish ground of accusation against you, and will pro-voke factious disturbances of the most mischiev-ous kind: for even timid flocks can show the use and power of their teeth, when the watchful care of their shepherd declines, and they find themselves bereft of his accustomed guidance. If this then be really so, if I am not deceived in my judgment, let this, brethren, be your first consideration, for many and important consid-erations will immediately present themselves, whether, should you persist in your intention, that mutual kindly feeling and affection which should subsist among you will suffer no dimi-nution? In the next place, remember that he, who came among you for the purpose of offering disinterested counsel,[2] now enjoys the reward which is due to him in the judgment of heaven; for he has received no ordinary recom-pense in the high testimony you have borne to his equitable conduct. Lastly, in accordance with your usual sound judgment, do ye exhibit a becoming diligence in selecting the person of whom you stand in need, carefully avoiding all factious and tumultuous clamor; for such clamor is always wrong, and from the collision of dis-cordant elements both sparks and flame will arise. I protest, as I desire to please God and you, and to enjoy a happiness commensurate with your kind wishes, that I love you, and the quiet haven of your gentleness, now that you have cast from you that which defiled,[3] and re-ceived in its place at once sound morality and concord, firmly planting in the vessel the sacred standard, and guided, as one may say, by a helm of iron in your course onward to the light of heaven. Receive then on board that merchan-dise which is incorruptible, since, as it were, all

---

[1] To the various and controverted translations of this passage it may be ventured to add one, "we ourselves desire your judgment to be fortified by good counsels."

[2] The other point of view has been alluded to. It seems on the face of it, in this unanimous endorsement by the church, as if Euse-bius had had the right of it in his quarrel with Eustathius; but on the other hand, it is to be remembered that this wonderful harmony in the church had come about from the fact that Eustathius and all who sympathized with him had withdrawn, and only the party of Eusebius was left. It would be like a "unanimous" vote in Parlia-ment with all the opposition benches empty. The endorsement of his own party does not count for much.

[3] [Alluding to the deposition of Eustathius, who had been charged with the crime of seduction. The reader who consults the original of this chapter, especially the latter part of it, may judge of the difficulty of eliciting any tolerable sense from an obscure, and possibly corrupted, text.— *Bag.*] The translator (*Bag.*) shows ingenuity in this extracting of the general sense from the involved Greek of the writing of Constantine or the translation as it suppos-ably is. But the very fact of the obscurity shown in this and in his oration alike is conclusive against any thought that the literary work ascribed to Constantine was written by Eusebius.

bilge water has been drained from the vessel; and be careful henceforth so to secure the enjoyment of all your present blessing, that you may not seem at any future time either to have determined any measure on the impulse of inconsiderate or ill-directed zeal, or in the first instance rashly to have entered on an inexpedient course. May God preserve you, beloved brethren ! "

CHAPTER LXI.

The Emperor's Letter to Eusebius praising him for refusing the Bishopric of Antioch.

The Emperor's Letter to me on my refusing the Bishopric of Antioch.

" Victor Constantinus, Maximus Augustus, to Eusebius.

" I have most carefully perused your letter, and perceive that you have strictly conformed to the rule enjoined by the discipline of the Church. Now to abide by that which appears at the same time pleasing to God, and accordant with apostolical tradition, is a proof of true piety. You have reason to deem yourself happy on this behalf, that you are counted worthy, in the judgment, I may say, of all the world, to have the oversight of any church. For the desire which all feel to claim you for their own, undoubtedly enhances your enviable fortune in this respect. Notwithstanding, your Prudence, whose resolve it is to observe the ordinances of God and the apostolic canon of the Church,[1] has done excellently well in declining the bishopric of the church at Antioch, and desiring to continue in that church of which you first received the oversight by the will of God. I have written on this subject to the people of Antioch, and also to your colleagues in the ministry who had themselves consulted me in regard to this question ; on reading which letters, your Holiness will easily discern, that, inasmuch as justice itself opposed their claims, I have written to them under divine direction. It will be necessary that your Prudence should be present at their conference, in order that this decision may be ratified in the church at Antioch. God preserve you, beloved brother ! "

CHAPTER LXII.

Constantine's Letter to the Council, deprecating the Removal of Eusebius from Cæsarea.

" Victor Constantinus, Maximus Augustus, to Theodotus, Theodorus, Narcissus, Aëtius, Alpheus, and the rest of the bishops who are at Antioch.

---

[1] Canon 15 (or 14) of the " Apostolical Canons." Cf. ed. Bruns. i (Berol. 1839), 3.

" I have perused the letters written by your Prudences, and highly approve of the wise resolution of your colleague in the ministry, Eusebius. Having, moreover, been informed of the circumstances of the case, partly by your letters, partly by those of our illustrious counts,[1] Acacius and Strategius, after sufficient investigation I have written to the people of Antioch, suggesting the course which will be at once pleasing to God and advantageous for the Church. A copy of this I have ordered to be subjoined to this present letter, in order that ye yourselves may know what I thought fit, as an advocate of the cause of justice, to write to that people : since I find in your letter this proposal, that, in consonance with the choice of the people, sanctioned by your own desire, Eusebius the holy bishop of Cæsarea should preside over and take the charge of the church at Antioch. Now the letters of Eusebius himself on this subject appeared to be strictly accordant with the order prescribed by the Church. Nevertheless it is expedient that your Prudences should be made acquainted with my opinion also. For I am informed that Euphronius the presbyter, who is a citizen of Cæsarea in Cappadocia, and George of Arethusa, likewise a presbyter, and appointed to that office by Alexander at Alexandria,[2] are men of tried faith. It was right, therefore, to intimate to your Prudences, that in proposing these men and any others whom you may deem worthy the episcopal dignity, you should decide this question in a manner conformable to the tradition of the apostles. For in that case, your Prudences will be able, according to the rule of the Church and apostolic tradition, to direct this election in the manner which true ecclesiastical discipline shall prescribe. God preserve you, beloved brethren ! "

CHAPTER LXIII.

How he displayed his Zeal for the Extirpation of Heresies.

Such were the exhortations to do all things to the honor of the divine religion which the emperor addressed to the rulers of the churches. Having by these means banished dissension, and

---

[1] The word has thus generally been rendered by *Bag.*, and does probably refer to their official title, although in this case and occasionally he translates " friends."

[2] [George (afterwards bishop of Laodicea) appears to have been degraded from the office of presbyter on the ground of impiety, by the same bishop who had ordained him. Both George and Euphronius were of the Arian party, of which fact it is possible that Constantine was ignorant. — *Bag.*] Georgius was at one time or another Arian, semi-Arian, and Anomoean, and is said to have been called by Athanasius " the most wicked of all the Arians " (Venables in Smith and Wace, *Dict.* 2. 637). He was constantly pitted against Eustathius, which accounts for his appearance at this time. Euphronius was the one chosen at this time. Compare Bennett, *Euphronius*, in Smith and Wace, *Dict.* 2. 297.

reduced the Church of God to a state of uniform harmony, he next proceeded to a different duty, feeling it incumbent on him to extirpate another sort of impious persons, as pernicious enemies of the human race. These were pests of society, who ruined whole cities under the specious garb of religious decorum; men whom our Saviour's warning voice somewhere terms false prophets and ravenous wolves: "Beware of false prophets, which will come to you in sheep's clothing, but inwardly are ravening wolves. By their fruits ye shall know them." [1] Accordingly, by an order transmitted to the governors of the several provinces, he effectually banished all such offenders. In addition to this ordinance he addressed to them personally a severely awakening admonition, exhorting them to an earnest repentance, that they might still find a haven of safety in the true Church of God. Hear, then, in what manner he addressed them in this letter.

CHAPTER LXIV.

Constantine's Edict against the Heretics.

"Victor Constantinus, Maximus Augustus, to the heretics.

"Understand now, by this present statute, ye Novatians, Valentinians, Marcionites, Paulians, ye who are called Cataphrygians,[1] and all ye who devise and support heresies by means of your private assemblies, with what a tissue of falsehood and vanity, with what destructive and venomous errors, your doctrines are inseparably interwoven; so that through you the healthy soul is stricken with disease, and the living becomes the prey of everlasting death. Ye haters and enemies of truth and life, in league with destruction! All your counsels are opposed to the truth, but familiar with deeds of baseness; full of absurdities and fictions: and by these ye frame falsehoods, oppress the innocent, and withhold the light from them that believe. Ever trespassing under the mask of godliness, ye fill all things with defilement: ye pierce the pure and guileless conscience with deadly wounds, while ye withdraw, one may almost say, the very light of day from the eyes of men. But why should I particularize, when to speak of your criminality as it deserves demands more time and leisure than I can give? For so long and unmeasured is the catalogue of your offenses, so hateful and altogether atrocious are they, that a single day would not suffice to recount them all. And, indeed, it is well to turn one's ears and eyes from such a subject, lest by a description of each particular evil, the pure sincerity and freshness of one's own faith be impaired. Why then do I still bear with such abounding evil; especially since this protracted clemency is the cause that some who were sound are become tainted with this pestilent disease? Why not at once strike, as it were, at the root of so great a mischief by a public manifestation of displeasure?

CHAPTER LXV.

The Heretics are deprived of their Meeting Places.

"Forasmuch, then, as it is no longer possible to bear with your pernicious errors, we give warning by this present statute that none of you henceforth presume to assemble yourselves together.[1] We have directed, accordingly, that you be deprived of all the houses in which you are accustomed to hold your assemblies: and our care in this respect extends so far as to forbid the holding of your superstitious and senseless meetings, not in public merely, but in any private house or place whatsoever. Let those of you, therefore, who are desirous of embracing the true and pure religion, take the far better course of entering the catholic Church, and uniting with it in holy fellowship, whereby you will be enabled to arrive at the knowledge of the truth. In any case, the delusions of your perverted understandings must entirely cease to mingle with and mar the felicity of our present times: I mean the impious and wretched double-mindedness of heretics and schismatics. For it is an object worthy of that prosperity which we enjoy through the favor of God, to endeavor to bring back those who in time past were living in the hope of future blessing, from all irregularity and error to the right path, from darkness to light, from vanity to truth, from death to salvation. And in order that this remedy may be applied with effectual power, we have commanded, as before said, that you be positively deprived of every gathering point for your superstitious meetings, I mean all the houses of prayer, if such be worthy of the name, which belong to

---

[1] [Matt. vii. 15, 16.] Quoted perhaps from memory, or else this text is defective, for this reads, "will come" where all N. T. MSS. have "come."

[1] Sufficiently good general accounts of these various heresies may be found in Blunt. *Dict. of Sects, Heresies, Ecclesiastical Parties, and Schools of Religious Thought*, Lond. 1874, p. 382-389, Novatians; p. 612-614, Valentinians; p. 296-298, Marcionites; p. 515-517, Samosatenes (Paulians); p. 336-341, Montanists (Cataphrygians). Or see standard Encyclopædias.

[1] There is throughout this Life a curious repetition in the details of action against heretics of precisely the same things which Christians complained of as having been done to them. The idea of toleration then seems to have been much as it was in pre-reformation times, or, not to judge other times when there is a beam in our own eye, as it is in America and England to-day, — the largest toleration for every one who thinks as we do, and for the others a temporary suspension of the rule to "judge not," with an amended prayer, "Lord, condemn them, for they know not what they do," and a vigorous attempt to force the divine judgment.

heretics, and that these be made over without delay to the catholic Church; that any other places be confiscated to the public service, and no facility whatever be left for any future gathering; in order that from this day forward none of your unlawful assemblies may presume to appear in any public or private place. Let this edict be made public."

CHAPTER LXVI.

How on the Discovery of Prohibited Books among the Heretics, Many of them return to the Catholic Church.

THUS were the lurking-places of the heretics broken up by the emperor's command, and the savage beasts they harbored (I mean the chief authors of their impious doctrines) driven to flight. Of those whom they had deceived, some, intimidated by the emperor's threats, disguising their real sentiments, crept secretly into the Church. For since the law directed that search should be made for their books, those of them who practiced evil and forbidden arts were detected, and these were ready to secure their own safety by dissimulation of every kind.[1] Others, however, there were, who voluntarily

and with real sincerity embraced a better hope. Meantime the prelates of the several churches continued to make strict inquiry, utterly rejecting those who attempted an entrance under the specious disguise of false pretenses, while those who came with sincerity of purpose were proved for a time, and after sufficient trial numbered with the congregation. Such was the treatment of those who stood charged with rank heresy: those, however, who maintained no impious doctrine, but had been separated from the one body through the influence of schismatic advisers, were received without difficulty or delay. Accordingly, numbers thus revisited, as it were, their own country after an absence in a foreign land, and acknowledged the Church as a mother from whom they had wandered long, and to whom they now returned with joy and gladness. Thus the members of the entire body became united, and compacted in one harmonious whole; and the one catholic Church, at unity with itself, shone with full luster, while no heretical or schismatic body anywhere continued to exist.[2] And the credit of having achieved this mighty work our Heaven-protected emperor alone, of all who had gone before him, was able to attribute to himself.

---

[1] Here again it is worth noting, for history and for edification, that books were prohibited and heretics treated just as the Christians did not like to "be done by," by the heathen.

[2] This famous "church unity," for which Constantine has been blessed or execrated, as the case might be, in all the ages since, was hardly more complete than modern unified churches where all the members held different pet doctrines and are prepared to fight for them to the bitter end.

BOOK IV.

CHAPTER I.

How he honored Many by Presents and Promotions.

WHILE thus variously engaged in promoting the extension and glory of the Church of God, and striving by every measure to commend the Saviour's doctrine, the emperor was far from neglecting secular affairs; but in this respect also he was unwearied in bestowing benefits of every kind and in quick succession on the people of every province. On the one hand he manifested a paternal anxiety for the general welfare of his subjects; on the other he would distinguish individuals of his own acquaintance with various marks of honor; conferring his benefits in every instance in a truly noble spirit. No one could request a favor from the emperor, and fail of obtaining what he sought: no one expected a boon from him, and found that expectation vain.[1] Some received presents in money, others in land; some obtained the Prætorian præfecture, others senatorial, others again consular rank: many were appointed provincial governors: others were made counts of the first, second, or third order: in numberless instances the title of Most Illustrious, and many other distinctions were conferred; for the emperor devised new dignities, that he might invest a larger number with the tokens of his favor.

CHAPTER II.

Remission of a Fourth Part of the Taxes.

THE extent to which he studied the general happiness and prosperity may be understood from a single instance, most beneficial and universal in its application, and still gratefully remembered. He remitted a fourth part of the yearly tribute paid for land, and bestowed it on the owners of the soil; so that if we compute this yearly reduction, we shall find that the cultivators enjoyed their produce free of tribute every fourth year.[1] This privilege being established by law, and secured for the time to come,

has given occasion for the emperor's beneficence to be held, not merely by the then present generation, but by their children and descendants, in perpetual remembrance.

CHAPTER III.

Equalization of the More Oppressive Taxes.

AND whereas some persons found fault with the surveys of land which had been made under former emperors, and complained that their property was unduly burdened; acting in this case also on the principles of justice, he sent commissioners to equalize the tribute, and to secure immunity to those who had made this appeal.

CHAPTER IV.

His Liberality, from his Private Resources, to the Losers in Suits of a Pecuniary Nature.

IN cases of judicial arbitration, in order that the loser by his decision might not quit his presence less contented than the victorious litigant, he himself bestowed, and from his own private means, in some cases lands, in other money, on the defeated party. In this manner he took care that the loser, as having appeared in his presence, should be as well satisfied as the gainer of the cause; for he considered that no one ought in any case to retire dejected and sorrowful from an interview with such a prince.[1] Thus it happened that both parties returned from the scene of trial with glad and cheerful countenances, while the emperor's noble-minded liberality excited universal admiration.

CHAPTER V.

Conquest of the Scythians defeated through the Sign of Our Saviour.

AND why should I relate even briefly and incidentally, how he subjected barbarous nations to the Roman power; how he was the first who

---

[1] Compare Prolegomena, under *Character*, for the criticism of this conduct from those who viewed it from another point of view.
[1] For directly contrary account of his taxations, compare Prolegomena, under *Character*.

[1] In reality it may have been less childish than Eusebius makes it appear, for it probably refers to cases where it was a matter of just equalization of claims, where each party thought his claim just.

subjugated the Scythian[1] and Sarmatian tribes, which had never learned submission, and compelled them, how unwilling soever, to own the sovereignty of Rome? For the emperors who preceded him had actually rendered tribute to the Scythians: and Romans, by an annual payment, had confessed themselves servants to barbarians; an indignity which our emperor could no longer bear, nor think it consistent with his victorious career to continue the payment his predecessors had made. Accordingly, with full confidence in his Saviour's aid, he raised his conquering standard against these enemies also, and soon reduced them all to obedience; coercing by military force those who fiercely resisted his authority, while, on the other hand, he conciliated the rest by wisely conducted embassies, and reclaimed them to a state of order and civilization from their lawless and savage life. Thus the Scythians at length learned to acknowledge subjection to the power of Rome.

CHAPTER VI.

Conquest of the Sarmatians, consequent on the Rebellion of their Slaves.

WITH respect to the Sarmatians, God himself brought them beneath the rule of Constantine, and subdued a nation swelling with barbaric pride in the following manner. Being attacked by the Scythians, they had entrusted their slaves with arms, in order to repel the enemy. These slaves first overcame the invaders, and then, turning their weapons against their masters, drove them all from their native land. The expelled Sarmatians found that their only hope of safety was in Constantine's protection: and he, whose familiar habit it was to save men's lives, received them all within the confines of the Roman empire.[1] Those who were capable of serving he incorporated with his own troops: to the rest he allotted lands to cultivate for their own support: so that they themselves acknowledged that their past misfortune had produced a happy result, in that they now enjoyed Roman liberty in place of savage barbarism. In this manner God added to his dominions many and various barbaric tribes.

CHAPTER VII.

Ambassadors from Different Barbarous Nations receive Presents from the Emperor.

INDEED, ambassadors were continually arriving from all nations, bringing for his acceptance their most precious gifts. So that I myself have sometimes stood near the entrance of the imperial palace, and observed a noticeable array of barbarians in attendance, differing from each other in costume and decorations, and equally unlike in the fashion of their hair and beard. Their aspect truculent and terrible, their bodily stature prodigious: some of a red complexion, others white as snow, others again of an intermediate color. For in the number of those I have referred to might be seen specimens of the Blemmyan tribes, of the Indians, and the Ethiopians,[1] "that widely-divided race, remotest of mankind." All these in due succession, like some painted pageant, presented to the emperor those gifts which their own nation held in most esteem; some offering crowns of gold, others diadems set with precious stones; some bringing fair-haired boys, others barbaric vestments embroidered with gold and flowers: some appeared with horses, others with shields and long spears, with arrows and bows, thereby offering their services and alliance for the emperor's acceptance. These presents he separately received and carefully laid aside, acknowledging them in so munificent a manner as at once to enrich those who bore them. He also honored the noblest among them with Roman offices of dignity; so that many of them thenceforward preferred to continue their residence among us, and felt no desire to revisit their native land.

CHAPTER VIII.

That he wrote also to the King of Persia,[1] who had sent him an Embassy, on Behalf of the Christians in his Realm.

THE king of the Persians also having testified a desire to form an alliance with Constantine, by sending an embassy and presents as assurances of peace and friendship, the emperor, in negotiating this treaty, far surpassed the monarch who had first done him honor, in the magnificence with which he acknowledged his gifts. Having heard, too, that there were many churches of God in Persia, and that large numbers there were gathered into the fold of Christ, full of joy at this intelligence, he resolved to extend his anxiety for the general welfare to that country also, as one whose aim it was to care for all alike in every nation.

---

[1] [Probably the Goths are meant, as in Socrates' *Eccles. Hist.* Bk. I. ch. 18. — *Bag.*] Compare for his Gothic wars, references in Prolegomena, under *Life.*
[1] To the number of 300,000, according to *Anonymus Valesianus.* This was in the year 334.

[1] [Αἰθίοπας, τοὶ διχθὰ δεδαίαται, ἔσχατοι ἀνδρῶν,
Οἱ μὲν δυσομένου ὑπερίονος, οἱ δ᾽ ἀνιόντος.
— *Odyss.* 1. 23, 24. — *Bag.*]

[1] Sapor II. (310–381) called the Great, one of the Sassanidæ and afterwards the persistent enemy of the sons of Constantine. He was at various times a bitter persecutor of the Christians, and it is said (Plate) that "no Persian king had ever caused such terror to Rome as this monarch." Compare article by Plate on the Sassanidæ in Smith, *Dict. of Gr. and R. Biog. and Mythol.*

CHAPTER IX.

Letter of Constantine Augustus to Sapor, King of the Persians, containing a truly Pious Confession of God and Christ.

Copy of his Letter to the King of Persia.

"By keeping the Divine faith, I am made a partaker of the light of truth: guided by the light of truth, I advance in the knowledge of the Divine faith. Hence it is that, as my actions themselves evince, I profess the most holy religion; and this worship I declare to be that which teaches me deeper acquaintance with the most holy God; aided by whose Divine power, beginning from the very borders of the ocean, I have aroused each nation of the world in succession to a well-grounded hope of security; so that those which, groaning in servitude to the most cruel tyrants, and yielding to the pressure of their daily sufferings, had well nigh been utterly destroyed, have been restored through my agency to a far happier state. This God I confess that I hold in unceasing honor and remembrance; this God I delight to contemplate with pure and guileless thoughts in the height of his glory.

CHAPTER X.

The Writer denounces Idols, and glorifies God.

"This God I invoke with bended knees, and recoil with horror from the blood of sacrifices, from their foul and detestable odors, and from every earth-born magic fire:[1] for the profane and impious superstitions which are defiled by these rites have cast down and consigned to perdition many, nay, whole nations of the Gentile world. For he who is Lord of all cannot endure that those blessings which, in his own loving-kindness and consideration of the wants of men, he has revealed for the use of all, should be perverted to serve the lusts of any. His only demand from man is purity of mind and an undefiled spirit; and by this standard he weighs the actions of virtue and godliness. For his pleasure is in works of moderation and gentleness: he loves the meek, and hates the turbulent spirit: delighting in faith, he chastises unbelief: by him all presumptuous power is broken down, and he avenges the insolence of the proud. While the arrogant and haughty are utterly overthrown, he requites the humble and forgiving with deserved rewards: even so does he highly honor and strengthen with his special help a kingdom justly governed, and

maintains a prudent king in the tranquillity of peace.

CHAPTER XI.

Against the Tyrants and Persecutors; and on the Captivity of Valerian.

"I cannot, then, my brother, believe that I err in acknowledging this one God, the author and parent of all things: whom many of my predecessors in power, led astray by the madness of error, have ventured to deny, but who were all visited with a retribution so terrible and so destructive, that all succeeding generations have held up their calamities as the most effectual warning to any who desire to follow in their steps. Of the number of these I believe him[1] to have been, whom the lightning-stroke of Divine vengeance drove forth from hence, and banished to your dominions, and whose disgrace contributed to the fame of your celebrated triumph.

CHAPTER XII.

He declares that, having witnessed the Fall of the Persecutors, he now rejoices at the Peace enjoyed by the Christians.

"And it is surely a happy circumstance that the punishment of such persons as I have described should have been publicly manifested in our own times. For I myself have witnessed the end of those who lately harassed the worshipers of God by their impious edicts. And for this abundant thanksgivings are due to God that through his excellent Providence all men who observe his holy laws are gladdened by the renewed enjoyment of peace. Hence I am fully persuaded that everything is in the best and safest posture, since God is vouchsafing, through the influence of their pure and faithful religious service, and their unity of judgment respecting his Divine character, to gather all men to himself.

CHAPTER XIII.

He bespeaks his Affectionate Interest for the Christians in his Country.

"Imagine, then, with what joy I heard tidings so accordant with my desire, that the fairest districts of Persia are filled with those men on whose behalf alone I am at present speaking, I

---

[1] [Referring to the luminous appearances produced by the Pagan priests in the celebration of their mysteries. — *Bag.*]

[1] [Valerian, who had been a persecutor of the Christians, and whose expedition against the Persians had terminated in his own captivity, and subjection to every kind of insult and cruelty from the conquerors. — *Bag.*]

mean the Christians. I pray, therefore, that both you and they may enjoy abundant prosperity, and that your blessings and theirs may be in equal measure ;[1] for thus you will experience the mercy and favor of that God who is the Lord and Father of all. And now, because your power is great, I commend these persons to your protection; because your piety is eminent, I commit them to your care. Cherish them with your wonted humanity and kindness; for by this proof of faith you will secure an immeasurable benefit both to yourself and us."

CHAPTER XIV.

How the Zealous Prayers of Constantine procured Peace to the Christians.

THUS, the nations of the world being everywhere guided in their course as it were by the skill of a single pilot, and acquiescing in the administration of him who governed as the servant of God, the peace of the Roman empire continued undisturbed, and all classes of his subjects enjoyed a life of tranquillity and repose. At the same time the emperor, who was convinced that the prayers of godly men contributed powerfully to the maintenance of the public welfare, felt himself constrained zealously to seek such prayers, and not only himself implored the help and favor of God; but charged the prelates of the churches to offer supplications on his behalf.

CHAPTER XV.

He causes himself to be represented on his Coins, and in his Portraits, in the Attitude of Prayer.

How deeply his soul was impressed by the power of divine faith may be understood from the circumstance that he directed his likeness to be stamped on the golden coin of the empire with the eyes uplifted as in the posture of prayer to God: and this money became current throughout the Roman world. His portrait also at full length was placed over the entrance gates of the palaces in some cities, the eyes upraised to heaven, and the hands outspread as if in prayer.

CHAPTER XVI.

He forbids by Law the Placing his Likeness in Idol Temples.

IN this manner he represented himself, even through the medium of painting, as habitually engaged in prayer to God. At the same time he forbade, by an express enactment, the setting up of any resemblance of himself in any idol temple, that not even the mere lineaments of his person might receive contamination from the error of forbidden superstition.

CHAPTER XVII.

Of his Prayers in the Palace, and his Reading the Holy Scriptures.

STILL nobler proofs of his piety might be discerned by those who marked how he modeled as it were his very palace into a church of God, and himself afforded a pattern of zeal to those assembled therein: how he took the sacred scriptures into his hands, and devoted himself to the study of those divinely inspired oracles; after which he would offer up regular prayers with all the members of his imperial court.

CHAPTER XVIII.

He enjoins the General Observance of the Lord's Day, and the Day of Preparation.

HE ordained, too, that one day should be regarded as a special occasion for prayer: I mean that which is truly the first and chief of all, the day of our Lord and Saviour. The entire care of his household was entrusted to deacons and other ministers consecrated to the service of God, and distinguished by gravity of life and every other virtue: while his trusty body guard, strong in affection and fidelity to his person, found in their emperor an instructor in the practice of piety, and like him held the Lord's salutary day in honor, and performed on that day the devotions which he loved. The same observance was recommended by this blessed prince to all classes of his subjects: his earnest desire being gradually to lead all mankind to the worship of God. Accordingly he enjoined on all the subjects of the Roman empire to observe the Lord's day, as a day of rest, and also to honor the day which precedes the Sabbath; in memory, I suppose, of what the Saviour of mankind is recorded to have achieved on that day.[1] And since his desire was to teach his whole army zealously to honor the Saviour's day (which derives its name from light, and from the sun),[2] he freely granted to those

---

doritus and Nicephorus. — *Bag.*] Stroth translates (*Hein.*), " So I desire for you the greatest prosperity; and for them, too, I wish that it may prosper as with you."
[1] [That is, Friday. The passage is not very intelligible. Does it mean that Constantine ordered this day to be distinguished in some way from others, as the day of the Lord's crucifixion? — *Bag.*]
[2] [The decree of Constantine for the general observance of Sun-

[1] [The sense given above of this passage (which in the text is corrupt), is founded on the reading restored by Valesius from Theo-

among them who were partakers of the divine faith, leisure for attendance on the services of the Church of God, in order that they might be able, without impediment, to perform their religious worship.

CHAPTER XIX.

That he directed even his Pagan Soldiers to pray on the Lord's Day.

WITH regard to those who were as yet ignorant of divine truth, he provided by a second statute that they should appear on each Lord's day on an open plain near the city, and there, at a given signal, offer to God with one accord a prayer which they had previously learnt. He admonished them that their confidence should not rest in their spears, or armor, or bodily strength, but that they should acknowledge the supreme God as the giver of every good, and of victory itself; to whom they were bound to offer their prayers with due regularity, uplifting their hands toward heaven, and raising their mental vision higher still to the King of heaven, on whom they should call as the Author of victory, their Preserver, Guardian, and Helper. The emperor himself prescribed the prayer to be used by all his troops, commanding them to pronounce the following words in the Latin tongue:

CHAPTER XX.

The Form of Prayer given by Constantine to his Soldiers.

"WE acknowledge thee the only God: we own thee, as our King, and implore thy succor. By thy favor have we gotten the victory: through thee are we mightier than our enemies. We render thanks for thy past benefits, and trust thee for future blessings. Together we pray to thee, and beseech thee long to preserve to us, safe and triumphant, our emperor Constantine and his pious sons."

Such was the duty to be performed on Sunday by his troops, and such the prayer they were instructed to offer up to God.

CHAPTER XXI.

He orders the Sign of the Saviour's Cross to be engraven on his Soldiers' Shields.

AND not only so, but he also caused the sign of the salutary trophy to be impressed on the very shields of his soldiers; and commanded that his embattled forces should be preceded in their march, not by golden images, as heretofore,[1] but only by the standard of the cross.

CHAPTER XXII.

Of his Zeal in Prayer, and the Honor he paid to the Feast of Easter.

THE emperor himself, as a sharer in the holy mysteries of our religion, would seclude himself daily at a stated hour in the innermost chambers of his palace; and there, in solitary converse with his God, would kneel in humble supplication, and entreat the blessings of which he stood in need. But especially at the salutary feast of Easter, his religious diligence was redoubled; he fulfilled as it were the duties of a hierophant with every energy of his mind and body, and outvied all others in the zealous celebration of this feast. He changed, too, the holy night vigil into a brightness like that of day, by causing waxen tapers of great length to be lighted throughout the city: besides which, torches everywhere diffused their light, so as to impart to this mystic vigil a brilliant splendor beyond that of day.[1] As soon as day itself returned, in imitation of our Saviour's gracious acts, he opened a liberal hand to his subjects of every nation, province, and people, and lavished abundant bounties on all.

CHAPTER XXIII.

How he forbade Idolatrous Worship, but honored Martyrs and the Church Festivals.

SUCH were his sacred ministrations in the service of his God. At the same time, his subjects, both civil and military, throughout the empire, found a barrier everywhere opposed against idol worship, and every kind of sacrifice forbidden.[1] A statute was also passed, enjoining the due observance of the Lord's day, and transmitted to the governors of every province, who undertook, at the emperor's command, to respect the days commemorative of martyrs, and duly to honor the festal seasons in the churches:[2] and all these intentions were fulfilled to the emperor's entire satisfaction.

---

day appears to have been issued A.D. 321, before which time both "the old and new sabbath" were observed by Christians.

"Constantine (says Gibbon, ch. 20, note 8) styles the Lord's day *Dies solis*, a name which could not offend the ears of his Pagan subjects."— *Bag.*] This has been urged as ground for saying that Constantine did not commit himself to Christianity until the end of life, but it only shows his tact and care in treating the diverse elements of his empire.

[1] Compare for these, Yates, article *Signa Militaria* in Smith, *Dict. Gr. and Rom. Ant.*, where there is given cut of the arch of Constantine showing such standards.

[1] Compare Venables, *Easter, Ceremonies of,* in Smith and Cheetham, *Dict.*, for account of the customs of the day.

[1] [This prohibition must be limited to private sacrifices. See Bk. II., ch. 45, note.— *Bag.*]

[2] " *Str.* rightly translates ' and honored the festal days by public gatherings,' while *Val.* [and *Bag.*] falsely renders ' duly honored the festival seasons of the church.' "— *Hein.*

CHAPTER XXIV.

That he described himself to be a Bishop, in Charge of Affairs External to the Church.

HENCE it was not without reason that once, on the occasion of his entertaining a company of bishops, he let fall the expression, "that he himself too was a bishop," addressing them in my hearing in the following words: "You are bishops whose jurisdiction is within the Church: I also am a bishop, ordained by God to overlook whatever is external to the Church."[1] And truly his measures corresponded with his words; for he watched over his subjects with an episcopal care, and exhorted them as far as in him lay to follow a godly life.

CHAPTER XXV.

Prohibition of Sacrifices, of Mystic Rites, Combats of Gladiators, also the Licentious Worship of the Nile.

CONSISTENTLY with this zeal he issued successive laws and ordinances, forbidding any to offer sacrifice to idols, to consult diviners, to erect images, or to pollute the cities with the sanguinary combats of gladiators.[1] And inasmuch as the Egyptians, especially those of Alexandria, had been accustomed to honor their river through a priesthood composed of effeminate men, a further law was passed commanding the extermination of the whole class as vicious, that no one might thenceforward be found tainted with the like impurity. And whereas the superstitious inhabitants apprehended that the river would in consequence withhold its customary flood, God himself showed his approval of the emperor's law by ordering all things in a manner quite contrary to their expectation. For those who had defiled the cities by their vicious conduct were indeed seen no more; but the river, as if the country through which it flowed had been purified to receive it, rose higher than ever before, and completely overflowed the country with its fertilizing streams: thus effectually admonishing the deluded people to turn from impure men, and ascribe their prosperity to him alone who is the Giver of all good.

---

[1] This saying of Constantine has occasioned a deal of exegesis and conjecture. Compare monograph of Walch mentioned under *Literature* in the Prolegomena for discussion and references to other older literature.

[1] The most accessible reference for getting a glimpse of the legislation of Constantine in these and similar regards is the section, *The alteration in general and penal legislation* in Wordsworth's Constantinus I., in Smith and Wace, *Dict.* 1 (1877). This section is on p. 636–7. Compare also the laws themselves as gathered in Migne, *Patrol. lat.* vol. 8. Compare also Prolegomena for general statement of the value of his legislation and his reputation as legislator.

CHAPTER XXVI.

Amendment of the Law in Force respecting Childless Persons, and of the Law of Wills.

So numerous, indeed, were the benefits of this kind conferred by the emperor on every province, as to afford ample materials to any who might desire to record them. Among these may be instanced those laws which he entirely remodelled, and established on a more equitable basis: the nature of which reform may be briefly and easily explained. The childless were punished under the old law with the forfeiture of their hereditary property, a merciless statute, which dealt with them as positive criminals. The emperor annulled this, and decreed that those so circumstanced should inherit. He regulated the question on the principles of equity and justice, arguing willful transgressors should be chastised with the penalties their crimes deserve. But nature herself denies children to many, who long, perhaps, for a numerous offspring, but are disappointed of their hope by bodily infirmity. Others continue childless, not from any dislike of posterity, but because their ardent love of philosophy[1] renders them averse to the conjugal union. Women, too, consecrated to the service of God, have maintained a pure and spotless virginity, and have devoted themselves, soul and body, to a life of entire chastity and holiness. What then? Should this conduct be deemed worthy of punishment, or rather of admiration and praise; since to desire this state is in itself honorable, and to maintain it surpasses the power of unassisted nature? Surely those whose bodily infirmity destroys their hope of offspring are worthy of pity, not of punishment: and he who devotes himself to a higher object calls not for chastisement, but especial admiration. On such principles of sound reason did the emperor rectify the defects of this law. Again, with regard to the wills of dying persons, the old laws had ordained that they should be expressed, even at the latest breath, as it were, in certain definite words, and had prescribed the exact form and terms to be employed. This practice had occasioned many fraudulent attempts to hinder the intentions of the deceased from

---

[1] [The word "philosophy," here and in the 28th chapter, plainly indicates that virginity which was so highly honored in the earlier ages of Christianity, and the undue exaltation of which was productive, necessarily, of evils which it is scarcely possible to estimate at their full extent. — *Bag.*] On the growing prevalence of the practice of virginity compare Hatch, *Virgins*, in Smith and Cheetham, *Dict.* But this note belongs rather to the paragraph below; for the author does not refer to Christian virginity, but primarily to philosophical celibacy in this instance. The Neo-Platonic philosophy of the times, through its doctrine of the purification of the soul by its liberation from the body or sensuous things, taught celibacy and ascetic practices generally. So Plotinus (d. 270 A.D.) practiced and taught to a degree, and Porphyry (d. 301+) more explicitly. Compare rich literature on Neo-Platonism, and conveniently Zeller, *Outlines of Gr. Philos.* Lond., 1886, p. 326–43, *passim.*

being carried into full effect. As soon as our emperor was aware of these abuses, he reformed this law likewise, declaring that a dying man ought to be permitted to indicate his last wishes in as few words as possible, and in whatever terms he pleased; and to set forth his will in any written form; or even by word of mouth, provided it were done in the presence of proper witnesses, who might be competent faithfully to discharge their trust.

CHAPTER XXVII.

Among Other Enactments, he decrees that no Christian shall slave to a Jew, and affirms the Validity of the Decisions of Councils.

He also passed a law to the effect that no Christian should remain in servitude to a Jewish master, on the ground that it could not be right that those whom the Saviour had ransomed should be subjected to the yoke of slavery by a people who had slain the prophets and the Lord himself. If any were found hereafter in these circumstances, the slave was to be set at liberty, and the master punished by a fine.

He likewise added the sanction of his authority to the decisions of bishops passed at their synods, and forbade the provincial governors to annul any of their decrees: for he rated the priests of God at a higher value than any judge whatever. These and a thousand similar provisions did he enact for the benefit of his subjects; but there is not time now to give a special description of them, such as might convey an accurate idea of his imperial wisdom in these respects: nor need I now relate at length, how, as a devoted servant of the Supreme God, he employed himself from morning until night in seeking objects for his beneficence, and how equally and universally kind he was to all.

CHAPTER XXVIII.

His Gifts to the Churches, and Bounties to Virgins and to the Poor.

His liberality, however, was most especially exercised on behalf of the churches of God. In some cases he granted lands, in others he issued supplies of food for the support of the poor, of orphan children, and widows; besides which, he evinced much care and forethought in fully providing the naked and destitute with clothing. He distinguished, however, with most special honor those who had devoted their lives to the practice of Divine philosophy. Hence his respect, little short of veneration, for God's most holy and ever virgin choir: for he felt assured

that the God to whom such persons devoted themselves was himself an inmate of their souls.

CHAPTER XXIX.

Of Constantine's Discourses and Declamations.[1]

For himself, he sometimes passed sleepless nights in furnishing his mind with Divine knowledge: and much of his time was spent in composing discourses, many of which he delivered in public; for he conceived it to be incumbent on him to govern his subjects by appealing to their reason, and to secure in all respects a rational obedience to his authority. Hence he would sometimes himself evoke an assembly, on which occasions vast multitudes attended, in the hope of hearing an emperor sustain the part of a philosopher. And if in the course of his speech any occasion offered of touching on sacred topics, he immediately stood erect, and with a grave aspect and subdued tone of voice seemed reverently to be initiating his auditors in the mysteries of the Divine doctrine: and when they greeted him with shouts of acclamation, he would direct them by his gestures to raise their eyes to heaven, and reserve their admiration for the Supreme King alone, and honor him with adoration and praise. He usually divided the subjects of his address, first thoroughly exposing the error of polytheism, and proving the superstition of the Gentiles to be mere fraud, and a cloak for impiety. He then would assert the sole sovereignty of God: passing thence to his Providence, both general and particular. Proceeding next to the dispensation of salvation, he would demonstrate its necessity, and adaptation to the nature of the case; entering next in order on the doctrine of the Divine judgment.[2] And here especially he appealed most powerfully to the consciences of his hearers, while he denounced the rapacious and violent, and those who were slaves to an inordinate thirst of gain. Nay, he caused some of his own acquaintance who were present to feel the severe lash of his words, and to stand with downcast eyes in the consciousness of guilt, while he testified against them in the clearest and most impressive terms that they would have an account to render of their deeds to God. He reminded them that God himself had given him the empire of the world, portions of which he himself, acting on the same Divine principle, had intrusted to their government; but that all would in due time be alike summoned to give account of their actions to the Supreme Sovereign of all. Such was his constant testimony;

---

[1] Compare Prolegomena, under *Character* and *Writings*.
[2] Compare Prolegomena, and the Oration appended to this work.

such his admonition and instruction. And he himself both felt and uttered these sentiments in the genuine confidence of faith : but·his hearers were little disposed to learn, and deaf to sound advice ; receiving his words indeed with loud applause, but induced by insatiable cupidity practically to disregard them.

CHAPTER XXX.

That he marked out before a Covetous Man the Measure of a Grave, and so put him to Shame.

ON one occasion he thus personally addressed one of his courtiers : " How far, my friend, are we to carry our inordinate desires ? " Then drawing the dimensions of a human figure with a lance which he happened to have in his hand, he continued : " Though thou couldst obtain the whole wealth of this world, yea, the whole world itself, thou wilt carry with thee at last no more than this little spot which I have marked out, if indeed even that be thine." [1] Such were the words and actions of this blessed prince ; and though at the time he failed to reclaim any from their evil ways, yet notwithstanding the course of events afforded evident proof that his admonitions were more like Divine prophecies than mere words.

CHAPTER XXXI.

That he was derided because of his Excessive Clemency.[1]

MEANTIME, since there was no fear of capital punishment to deter from the commission of crime, for the emperor himself was uniformly inclined to clemency, and none of the provincial governors visited offenses with their proper penalties, this state of things drew with it no small degree of blame on the general administration of the empire ; whether justly or not, let every one form his own judgment : for myself, I only ask permission to record the fact.

CHAPTER XXXII.

Of Constantine's Oration which he wrote to the Assembly of the Saints.[1]

THE emperor was in the habit of composing his orations in the Latin tongue, from which they were translated into Greek by interpreters appointed for this special service. One of the discourses thus translated I intend to annex, by way of specimen, to this present work, that one, I mean, which he inscribed " To the assembly of the saints," and dedicated to the Church of God, that no one may have ground for deeming my testimony on this head mere empty praise.

CHAPTER XXXIII.

How he listened standing to Eusebius' Declamation in Honor of our Saviour's Sepulchre.

ONE act, however, I must by no means omit to record, which this admirable prince performed in my own presence. On one occasion, emboldened by the confident assurance I entertained of his piety, I had begged permission to pronounce a discourse on the subject of our Saviour's sepulchre in his hearing. With this request he most readily complied, and in the midst of a large number of auditors, in the interior of the palace itself, he stood and listened with the rest. I entreated him, but in vain, to seat himself on the imperial throne which stood near : he continued with fixed attention to weigh the topics of my discourse, and gave his own testimony to the truth of the theological doctrines it contained. After some time had passed, the oration being of considerable length, I was myself desirous of concluding ; but this he would not permit, and exhorted me to proceed to the very end. On my again entreating him to sit, he in his turn was displeased and said that it was not right to listen in a careless manner to the discussion of doctrines relating to God ; and again, that this posture was good and profitable to himself, since it was reverent to stand while listening to sacred truths. Having, therefore, concluded my discourse, I returned home, and resumed my usual occupations.

CHAPTER XXXIV.

That he wrote to Eusebius respecting Easter, and respecting Copies of the Holy Scriptures.

EVER careful for the welfare of the churches of God, the emperor addressed me personally in a letter on the means of providing copies of the inspired oracles, and also on the subject of the most holy feast of Easter. For I had myself dedicated to him an exposition of the mystical import of that feast ; and the manner in which he honored me with a reply may be understood by any one who reads the following letter.

[1 Since it is uncertain whether thou wilt be buried in the ground, or consumed by fire, or drowned in the sea, or devoured by wild beasts (Valesius in loc.). — *Bag.*]

1 Compare Prolegomena, under *Character*.

1 Compare the Oration itself following this work.

CHAPTER XXXV.

Constantine's Letter to Eusebius, in praise of his Discourse concerning Easter.

"Victor Constantinus, Maximus Augustus, to Eusebius.

"It is indeed an arduous task, and beyond the power of language itself, worthily to treat of the mysteries of Christ, and to explain in a fitting manner the controversy respecting the feast of Easter, its origin as well as its precious and toilsome accomplishment.[1] For it is not in the power even of those who are able to apprehend them, adequately to describe the things of God. I am, notwithstanding, filled with admiration of your learning and zeal, and have not only myself read your work with pleasure, but have given directions, according to your own desire, that it be communicated to many sincere followers of our holy religion. Seeing, then, with what pleasure we receive favors of this kind from your Sagacity, be pleased to gladden us more frequently with those compositions, to the practice of which, indeed, you confess yourself to have been trained from an early period, so that I am urging a willing man, as they say, in exhorting you to your customary pursuits. And certainly the high and confident judgment we entertain is a proof that the person who has translated your writings into the Latin tongue is in no respect incompetent to the task, impossible though it be that such version should fully equal the excellence of the works themselves. God preserve you, beloved brother." Such was his letter on this subject: and that which related to the providing of copies of the Scriptures for reading in the churches was to the following purport.

CHAPTER XXXVI.

Constantine's Letter to Eusebius on the Preparation of Copies of the Holy Scriptures.

"Victor Constantinus, Maximus Augustus, to Eusebius.

"It happens, through the favoring providence of God our Saviour, that great numbers have united themselves to the most holy church in the city which is called by my name. It seems, therefore, highly requisite, since that city is rapidly advancing in prosperity in all other respects, that the number of churches should also be increased. Do you, therefore, receive with all readiness my determination on this behalf. I have thought it expedient to instruct your Prudence to order fifty copies of the sacred Scriptures, the provision and use of which you know to be most needful for the instruction of the Church, to be written on prepared parchment in a legible manner, and in a convenient, portable form, by professional transcribers thoroughly practiced in their art.[1] The catholicus[2] of the diocese has also received instructions by letter from our Clemency to be careful to furnish all things necessary for the preparation of such copies; and it will be for you to take special care that they be completed with as little delay as possible.[3] You have authority also, in virtue of this letter, to use two of the public carriages for their conveyance, by which arrangement the copies when fairly written will most easily be forwarded for my personal inspection; and one of the deacons of your church may be intrusted with this service, who, on his arrival here, shall experience my liberality. God preserve you, beloved brother!"

CHAPTER XXXVII.

How the Copies were provided.

Such were the emperor's commands, which were followed by the immediate execution of the work itself, which we sent him in magnificent and elaborately bound volumes of a threefold and fourfold form.[1] This fact is attested by another letter, which the emperor wrote in acknowledgment, in which, having heard that the city Constantia in our country, the inhabitants of which had been more than commonly devoted to superstition, had been impelled by a sense of religion to abandon their past idolatry, he testified his joy, and approval of their conduct.

---

[1] [i.e. through the sufferings and resurrection of Christ. — *Bag.*]

[1] *Molz.* in a note regards these as lectionaries, but they are usually thought to have been regular copies of the Scriptures in Greek — Septuagint and N. T., and the Codex Sinaiticus has been thought to be one of them. It dates from not earlier than the time of Eusebius, as it contains the Eusebian Canons, but yet from the fourth century. Altogether it is not impossible that it was one of these, and at all events a description of it, extracted from Scriveners (*Introduction*, 1883, p. 88 sq.), will be a fair illustration. "13½ inches in length by 14⅞ inches high." . "Beautiful vellum." "Each page comprises four columns, with 48 lines in each column." "Continuous noble uncials." "Arranged in quires of four or three sheets." It is evident from comparison of several quotations of Eusebius that the copy of the New Testament which he himself used was not closely related with the Sinaitic text, unless the various readings headed by this MS. are all mistakes originating with it. Compare allusions in the notes to such different readings. The last clause, although in the text of Heinichen, is of doubtful authority.

[2] This word is a transcription, rendered "Procurator" by *Bag.*, and is perhaps corresponding to that official (cf. Long. article *Fiscus*, in Smith, *Dict. Gr. and R. Ant.*). But this transcription is recognized (cf. Ffoulkes, *Catholicus*, in Smith and Cheetham, *Dict.*).

[3] The fact that the Sinaiticus exhibits two or three hands suggests that it was prepared with rapidity, and the having various scribes was a way to speed.

[1] [The parchment copies were usually arranged in quaternions, i.e. four leaves made up together, as the ternions consisted of three leaves. The quaternions each contained sixteen pages, the ternions twelve (Valesius in loc.). — *Bag.*] So probably, although the three-columned form of the Sinaiticus and the four of the Vaticanus suggest a possible other meaning.

CHAPTER XXXVIII.

How the Market-town of Gaza was made a City for its Profession of Christianity, and received the Name of Constantia.

FOR in fact the place now called Constantia, in the province of Palestine, having embraced the saving religion, was distinguished both by the favor of God, and by special honor from the emperor, being now for the first time raised to the rank of a city, and receiving the more honored name of his pious sister in exchange for its former appellation.

CHAPTER XXXIX.

That a Place in Phœnicia also was made a City, and in Other Cities Idolatry was abolished, and Churches built.

A SIMILAR change was effected in several other cities; for instance, in that town of Phœnicia which received its name from that of the emperor, and the inhabitants of which committed their innumerable idols to the flames, and adopted in their stead the principles of the saving faith. Numbers, too, in the other provinces, both in the cities and the country, became willing inquirers after the saving knowledge of God; destroyed as worthless things the images of every kind which they had heretofore held most sacred; voluntarily demolished the lofty temples and shrines which contained them; and, renouncing their former sentiments, or rather errors, commenced and completed entirely new churches. But since it is not so much my province to give a circumstantial detail of the actions of this pious prince, as it is theirs who have been privileged to enjoy his society at all times, I shall content myself with briefly recording such facts as have come to my own personal knowledge, before I proceed to notice the last days of his life.

CHAPTER XL.

That having conferred the Dignity of Cæsars on his Three Sons at the Three Decennial Periods of his Reign, he dedicated the Church at Jerusalem.

BY this time the thirtieth year of his reign was completed. In the course of this period, his three sons had been admitted at different times as his colleagues in the empire. The first, Constantinus, who bore his father's name, obtained this distinction about the tenth year of his reign. Constantius, the second son, so called from his grandfather, was proclaimed Cæsar about the twentieth, while Constans, the third, whose name expresses the firmness and stability of his character, was advanced to the same dignity at the thirtieth anniversary of his father's reign.[1] Having thus reared a threefold offspring, a Trinity,[2] as it were, of pious sons, and having received them severally at each decennial period to a participation in his imperial authority, he judged the festival of his Tricennalia to be a fit occasion for thanksgiving to the Sovereign Lord of all, at the same time believing that the dedication of the church which his zealous magnificence had erected at Jerusalem might advantageously be performed.

CHAPTER XLI.

That in the meantime he ordered a Council to be convened at Tyre, because of Controversies raised in Egypt.

MEANWHILE that spirit of envy which is the enemy of all good, like a dark cloud intercepting the sun's brightest rays, endeavored to mar the joy of this festivity, by again raising contentions to disturb the tranquillity of the Egyptian churches. Our divinely favored emperor, however, once more convened a synod composed of many bishops, and set them as it were in armed array, like the host of God, against this malignant spirit, having commanded their presence from the whole of Egypt and Libya, from Asia, and from Europe, in order, first, to decide the questions in dispute, and afterwards to perform the dedication of the sacred edifice above mentioned. He enjoined them, by the way, to adjust their differences at the capital city of Phœnicia, reminding them that they had no right, while harboring feelings of mutual animosity, to engage in the service of God, since his law expressly forbids those who are at variance to offer their gift until they have first become reconciled and mutually disposed to peace. Such were the salutary precepts which the emperor continually kept vividly before his own mind, and in accordance with which he admonished them to undertake their present duties in a spirit of perfect unanimity and concord, in a letter to the following purport.

CHAPTER XLII.

Constantine's Letter to the Council at Tyre.

"VICTOR CONSTANTINUS, MAXIMUS AUGUSTUS, to the holy Council at Tyre.

---

[1] These are general dates; "about" the tenth, etc., would have been more exact. Compare Prolegomena, under *Life*.

[2] [Τριάδος λόγῳ. Well may the old English Translator remark on this, "An odd expression." We may go further, and denounce it as an instance of the senseless and profane adulation to which our author, perhaps in the spirit of his age, seems to have been but too much inclined. — *Bag.*]

"Surely it would best consist with and best become the prosperity of these our times, that the Catholic Church should be undivided, and the servants of Christ be at this present moment clear from all reproach. Since, however, there are those who, carried away by a baleful and furious spirit of contention (for I will not charge them with intentionally leading a life unworthy of their profession), are endeavoring to create that general confusion which, in my judgment, is the most pernicious of all evils ; I exhort you, forward as you already are, to meet together and form a synod without delay : to defend those who need protection ; to administer remedies to your brethren who are in peril ; to recall the divided members to unity of judgment ; to rectify errors while opportunity is yet allowed : that thus you may restore to so many provinces that due measure of concord which, strange and sad anomaly ! the arrogance of a few individuals has destroyed. And I believed that all are alike persuaded that this course is at the same time pleasing to Almighty God (as well as the highest object of my own desires), and will bring no small honor to yourselves, should you be successful in restoring peace. Delay not, then, but hasten with redoubled zeal to terminate the present dissensions in a manner becoming the occasion, by assembling together in that spirit of true sincerity and faith which the Saviour whom we serve especially demands from us, I may almost say with an audible voice, on all occasions. No proof of pious zeal on my part shall be wanting. Already have I done all to which my attention was directed by your letters. I have sent to those bishops whose presence you desired, that they may share your counsels. I have despatched Dionysius, a man of consular rank, who will both remind those prelates of their duty who are bound to attend the Council with you, and will himself be there to superintend the proceedings, but especially to maintain good order. Meantime should any one, though I deem it most improbable, venture on this occasion to violate my command, and refuse his attendance, a messenger shall be despatched forthwith to banish that person in virtue of an imperial edict, and to teach him that it does not become him to resist an emperor's decrees when issued in defense of truth. For the rest, it will be for your Holinesses, unbiased either by enmity or favor, but consistently with ecclesiastical and apostolic order, to devise a fitting remedy whether it be for positive offenses or for unpremeditated errors ; in order that you may at once free the Church from all reproach, relieve my anxiety, and, by restoring the blessings of peace to those who are now divided, procure the highest honor for yourselves. God preserve you, beloved brethren ! " [1]

CHAPTER XLIII.

Bishops from all the Provinces attended the Dedication of the Church at Jerusalem.

No sooner had these injunctions been carried into effect, than another emissary arrived with despatches from the emperor, and an urgent admonition to the Council to hasten their journey to Jerusalem without delay.[1] Accordingly they all took their departure from the province of Phœnicia, and proceeded to their destination, availing themselves of the public means of transport. Thus Jerusalem became the gathering point for distinguished prelates from every province, and the whole city was thronged by a vast assemblage of the servants of God. The Macedonians had sent the bishop of their metropolis ; [2] the Pannonians and Mœsians the fairest of God's youthful flock among them. A holy prelate from Persia too was there, deeply versed in the sacred oracles ; while Bithynian and Thracian bishops graced the Council with their presence ; nor were the most illustrious from Cilicia wanting, nor the chief of the Cappadocians, distinguished above all for learning and eloquence. In short, the whole of Syria and Mesopotamia, Phœnicia and Arabia, Palestine, Egypt, and Libya, with the dwellers in the Thebaid, all contributed to swell the mighty concourse of God's ministers, followed as they were by vast numbers from every province. They were attended by an imperial escort,[3] and officers of trust had also been sent from the palace itself, with instructions to heighten the splendor of the festival at the emperor's expense.

CHAPTER XLIV.

Of their Reception by the Notary Marianus ; the Distribution of Money to the Poor ; and Offerings to the Church.

THE director and chief of these officers was a most useful servant of the emperor, a man eminent for faith and piety, and thoroughly acquainted with the Divine word, who had been honorably conspicuous by his profession of godliness during the time of the tyrants' power, and therefore was deservedly entrusted with the arrangement of the present proceedings. Accordingly, in faithful obedience to the emperor's commands, he received the assembly with courteous hospitality, and entertained them with

[1] Compare on the Synod of Tyre (held 335 A.D.), Hefele, *Hist. of Councils*, 2 (1876), 17–26.
[1] Compare Hefele, 2. 26–7.
[2] [Alexander, bishop of Thessalonica. By the Pannonian and Mœsian bishops are meant Ursacius and Valens, leaders of the Arian party ; by the Bithynian and Thracian, Theogonius of Nicæa, and Theodorus of Perinthus (Valesius).—*Bag.*]
[3] "The emperor showed himself very attentive to them."—*Molz.*

feasts and banquets on a scale of great splendor. He also distributed lavish supplies of money and clothing among the naked and destitute, and the multitudes of both sexes who suffered from want of food and the common necessaries of life. Finally, he enriched and beautified the church itself throughout with offerings of imperial magnificence, and thus fully accomplished the service he had been commissioned to perform.

CHAPTER XLV.

Various Discourses by the Assembled Bishops; also by Eusebius, the Writer of this History.

MEANTIME the festival derived additional luster both from the prayers and discourses of the ministers of God, some of whom extolled the pious emperor's willing devotion to the Saviour of mankind, and dilated on the magnificence of the edifice which he had raised to his memory. Others afforded, as it were, an intellectual feast to the ears of all present, by public disquisitions on the sacred doctrines of our religion. Others interpreted passages of holy Scripture, and unfolded their hidden meaning; while such as were unequal to these efforts presented a bloodless sacrifice and mystical service to God in the prayers which they offered for general peace, for the Church of God, for the emperor himself as the instrumental cause of so many blessings, and for his pious sons. I myself too, unworthy as I was of such a privilege, pronounced various public orations in honor of this solemnity, wherein I partly explained by a written description the details of the imperial edifice, and partly endeavored to gather from the prophetic visions apt illustrations of the symbols it displayed.[1] Thus joyfully was the festival of dedication celebrated in the thirtieth year of our emperor's reign.

CHAPTER XLVI.

That Eusebius afterwards delivered his Description of the Church of the Saviour, and a Tricennial Oration before Constantine himself.

THE structure of the church of our Saviour, the form of his sacred cave, the splendor of the work itself, and the numberless offerings in gold,

and silver, and precious stones, I have described to the best of my ability, and dedicated to the emperor in a separate treatise, which on a fitting opportunity I shall append to this present work. I shall add to it also that oration on his Tricennalia which shortly afterwards, having traveled to the city which bears his name, I delivered in the emperor's own presence.[1] This was the second opportunity afforded me of glorifying the Supreme God in the imperial palace itself: and on this occasion my pious hearer evinced the greatest joy, as he afterwards testified, when he entertained the bishops then present, and loaded them with distinctions of every kind.

CHAPTER XLVII.

That the Council at Nicæa was held in the Twentieth, the Dedication of the Church at Jerusalem in the Thirtieth, Year of Constantine's Reign.

THIS second synod the emperor convened at Jerusalem, being the greatest of which we have any knowledge, next to the first which he had summoned at the famous Bithynian city. That indeed was a triumphal assembly, held in the twentieth year of his reign, an occasion of thanksgiving for victory over his enemies in the very city which bears the name of victory.[1] The present meeting added luster to the thirtieth anniversary, during which the emperor dedicated the church at the sepulchre of our Saviour, as a peace-offering to God, the giver of all good.

CHAPTER XLVIII.

That Constantine was displeased with one who praised him excessively.

AND now that all these ceremonies were completed, and the divine qualities of the emperor's character continued to be the theme of universal praise, one of God's ministers presumed so far as in his own presence to pronounce him blessed, as having been counted worthy to hold absolute and universal empire in this life, and as being destined to share the empire of the Son of God in the world to come. These words, however, Constantine heard with indignation, and forbade the speaker to hold such language, exhorting him rather to pray earnestly on his behalf, that whether in this life or in that which is to come, he might be found worthy to be a servant of God.[1]

---

[1] [Eusebius gives us no example of his application of Scripture in this case. His commentator Valesius refers to Zeph. iii. 8 (LXX), Διά τοῦτο ὑπόμεινόν με, λέγει Κύριος, εἰς ἡμέραν ἀναστάσεώς μου εἰς μαρτύριον, and tells us that Cyril of Jerusalem, in his fourth Homily, explains this passage in Zephaniah of the Martyrium, or Basilica, which Constantine built on the spot of the Lord's resurrection. Let any one examine the whole passage (allowing for the mistake of one Hebrew word for another by the LXX), and say, if this be a fair specimen, what we are to think of the Fathers of the fourth century as interpreters of Scripture. See also Bk. 3, ch. 33, note. — *Bag.*] " Interpreted pertinent passages from the prophets." — *Str.* and *Molz.*

[1] The Oration is appended to this work.
[1] Nicæa.
[1] Yet Eusebius himself in his Oration uses language almost as obnoxious, and records that Constantine was much pleased with it. The difference was probably one of gracefulness.

CHAPTER XLIX.

Marriage of his Son Constantius Cæsar.

ON the completion of the thirtieth year of his reign he solemnized the marriage of his second son,[1] having concluded that of his first-born long before. This was an occasion of great joy and festivity, the emperor himself attending on his son at the ceremony, and entertaining the guests of both sexes, the men and women in distinct and separate companies, with sumptuous hospitality. Rich presents likewise were liberally distributed among the cities and people.

CHAPTER L.

Embassy and Presents from the Indians.

ABOUT this time ambassadors from the Indians, who inhabit the distant regions of the East, arrived with presents consisting of many varieties of brilliant precious stones, and animals differing in species from those known to us. These offerings they presented to the emperor, thus allowing that his sovereignty extended even to the Indian Ocean, and that the princes of their country, who rendered homage to him both by paintings and statues, acknowledged his imperial and paramount authority. Thus the Eastern Indians now submitted to his sway, as the Britons of the Western Ocean had done at the commencement of his reign.

CHAPTER LI.

That Constantine divided the Empire between his Three Sons, whom he had instructed in Politics and Religion.

HAVING thus established his power in the opposite extremities of the world, he divided the whole extent of his dominions, as though he were allotting a patrimonial inheritance to the dearest objects of his regard, among his three sons. To the eldest he assigned his grandfather's portion; to the second, the empire of the East; to the third, the countries which lie between these two divisions.[1] And being desirous of furnishing his children with an inheritance truly valuable and salutary to their souls, he had been careful to imbue them

with true religious principles, being himself their guide to the knowledge of sacred things, and also appointing men of approved piety to be their instructors. At the same time he assigned them the most accomplished teachers of secular learning, by some of whom they were taught the arts of war, while they were trained by others in political, and by others again in legal science. To each moreover was granted a truly royal retinue, consisting of infantry, spearmen, and body guards, with every other kind of military force; commanded respectively by captains, tribunes, and generals,[2] of whose warlike skill and devotion to his sons the emperor had had previous experience.

CHAPTER LII.

That after they had reached Man's Estate he was their Guide in Piety.

As long as the Cæsars were of tender years, they were aided by suitable advisers in the management of public affairs; but on their arrival at the age of manhood their father's instructions alone sufficed. When present he proposed to them his own example, and admonished them to follow his pious course: in their absence he furnished them by letter with rules of conduct suited to their imperial station, the first and greatest of which was an exhortation to value the knowledge and worship of the Sovereign Lord of all more than wealth, nay, more than empire itself. At length he permitted them to direct the public administration of the empire without control, making it his first request that they would care for the interests of the Church of God, and boldly profess themselves disciples of Christ. Thus trained, and excited to obedience not so much by precept as by their own voluntary desire for virtue, his sons more than fulfilled the admonitions of their father, devoting their earnest attention to the service of God, and observing the ordinances of the Church even in the palace itself, with all the members of their households.[1] For their father's forethought had provided that all the attendants of his sons should be Christians. And not only so, but the military officers of highest rank, and those who had the control of public business, were professors of the same faith: for the emperor placed confidence in the fidelity of men devoted to the service of God, as in a strong and sure defense. When our thrice blessed prince had completed these arrangements, and thus secured order and tranquillity throughout the empire, God, the dispenser of all blessings, judged it to be the fitting

---

[1] His second son by Fausta. Crispus seems now to be counted out. This was not the famous Eusebia who was his second wife.

[1] ["The younger Constantine was appointed to hold his court in Gaul; and his brother Constantius exchanged that department, the ancient patrimony of their father, for the more opulent, but less martial, countries of the East. Italy, the Western Illyricum, and Africa, were accustomed to revere Constans, the third of his sons, as the representative of the great Constantine" (Gibbon, *Decline and Fall*, ch. 18).— *Bag.*] Compare Prolegomena, under *Life*.

[2] Centurions, generals, tribunes.
[1] The expression is over strong. Constantius, e.g., was not baptized until just before his death.

time to translate him to a better inheritance, and summoned him to pay the debt of nature.

CHAPTER LIII.

Having reigned about Thirty-two Years, and lived above Sixty, he still had a Sound Body.

HE completed the time of his reign in two and thirty years, wanting a few months and days,[1] and his whole life extended to about twice that period. At this age he still possessed a sound and vigorous body, free from all blemish, and of more than youthful vivacity ; a noble mien, and strength equal to any exertion ; so that he was able to join in martial exercises, to ride, endure the fatigues of travel, engage in battle, and erect trophies over his conquered enemies, besides gaining those bloodless victories by which he was wont to triumph over those who opposed him.[2]

CHAPTER LIV.

Of those who abused his Extreme Benevolence for Avarice and Hypocrisy.

IN like manner his mental[1] qualities reached the highest point of human perfection. Indeed he was distinguished by every excellence of character, but especially by benevolence ; a virtue, however, which subjected him to censure from many, in consequence of the baseness of wicked men, who ascribed their own crimes to the emperor's forbearance. In truth I can myself bear testimony to the grievous evils which prevailed during these times ; I mean the violence of rapacious and unprincipled men, who preyed on all classes of society alike, and the scandalous hypocrisy of those who crept into the Church, and assumed the name and character of Christians. His own benevolence and goodness of heart, the genuineness of his own faith, and his truthfulness of character, induced the emperor to credit the profession of these reputed Christians, who craftily preserved the semblance of sincere affection for his person. The confidence he reposed in such men sometimes forced him into conduct unworthy of himself, of which envy took advantage to cloud in this respect the luster of his character.[2]

CHAPTER LV.

Constantine employed himself in Composition of Various Kinds to the Close of his Life.

THESE offenders, however, were soon overtaken by divine chastisement. To return to our emperor. He had so thoroughly trained his mind in the art of reasoning that he continued to the last to compose discourses on various subjects, to deliver frequent orations in public, and to instruct his hearers in the sacred doctrines of religion. He was also habitually engaged in legislating both on political and military questions ;[1] in short, in devising whatever might be conducive to the general welfare of the human race. It is well worthy of remark, that, very shortly before his departure, he pronounced a funeral oration before his usual auditory, in which he spoke at length on the immortality of the soul, the state of those who had persevered in a life of godliness, and the blessings which God has laid up in store for them that love him. On the other hand he made it appear by copious and conclusive arguments what the end of those will be who have pursued a contrary career, describing in vivid language the final ruin of the ungodly. His powerful testimony on these subjects seemed so far to touch the consciences of those around him, that one of the self-imagined philosophers, of whom he asked his opinion of what he had heard, bore testimony to the truth of his words, and accorded a real, though reluctant, tribute of praise to the arguments by which he had exposed the worship of a plurality of gods. By converse such as this with his friends before his death, the emperor seemed as it were to smooth and prepare the way for his transition to a happier life.

CHAPTER LVI.

How he took Bishops with him on an Expedition against the Persians, and took with him a Tent in the Form of a Church.

IT is also worthy of record that about the time of which I am at present writing, the emperor, having heard of an insurrection of some barbarians in the East, observed that the conquest of this enemy was still in store for him, and resolved on an expedition against the Persians. Accordingly he proceeded at once to put his forces in motion, at the same time communicating his intended march to the bishops who happened to be at his court, some of whom he judged it right to take with him as compan-

---

[1] [In his *Chronicon*, Eusebius gives the more correct period of thirty years and ten months. Constantine's reign began A.D. 306, and his death took place A.D. 337. — *Bag.*] Compare Prolegomena, also Clinton, *Fasti Rom.* an. 337.
[2] Compare Prolegomena, under *Character*.
[1] "Psychical qualities" — including more than intellectual.
[2] Compare Prolegomena, *Character*. There is a striking touch of naturalness in this passage which tells for the historical trustworthiness of the biographer, and though exposing the fault of the emperor yet gives a rather pleasing glimpse of his character.

[1] Compare remarks in Prolegomena, under *Writings* and *Character*.

ions, and as needful coadjutors in the service of God. They, on the other hand, cheerfully declared their willingness to follow in his train, disclaiming any desire to leave him, and engaging to battle with and for him by supplication to God on his behalf. Full of joy at this answer to his request, he unfolded to them his projected line of march;[1] after which he caused a tent of great splendor, representing in shape the figure of a church, to be prepared for his own use in the approaching war. In this he intended to unite with the bishops in offering prayers to the God from whom all victory proceeds.

CHAPTER LVII.

How he received an Embassy from the Persians and kept the Night Vigil with others at the Feast of Easter.

In the meanwhile the Persians, hearing of the emperor's warlike preparations, and not a little terrified at the prospect of an engagement with his forces, dispatched an embassy to pray for conditions of peace. These overtures the emperor, himself a sincere lover of peace, at once accepted, and readily entered on friendly relations with that people. At this time, the great festival of Easter was at hand; on which occasion he rendered the tribute of his prayers to God, and passed the night in watching with the rest.

CHAPTER LVIII.

Concerning the Building of a Church in Honor of the Apostles at Constantinople.

After this he proceeded to erect a church in memory of the apostles, in the city which bears his name. This building he carried to a vast height, and brilliantly decorated by encasing it from the foundation to the roof with marble slabs of various colors. He also formed the inner roof of finely fretted work, and overlaid it throughout with gold. The external covering, which protected the building from the rain, was of brass instead of tiles; and this too was splendidly and profusely adorned with gold, and reflected the sun's rays with a brilliancy which dazzled the distant beholder. The dome was entirely encompassed by a finely carved tracery, wrought in brass and gold.

CHAPTER LIX.

Farther Description of the same Church.

Such was the magnificence with which the emperor was pleased to beautify this church.

The building was surrounded by an open area of great extent, the four sides of which were terminated by porticos which enclosed the area and the church itself. Adjoining these porticos were ranges of stately chambers, with baths and promenades, and besides many apartments adapted to the use of those who had charge of the place.

CHAPTER LX.

He also erected his own Sepulchral Monument in this Church.

All these edifices the emperor consecrated with the desire of perpetuating the memory of the apostles of our Saviour. He had, however, another object in erecting this building: an object at first unknown, but which afterwards became evident to all. He had in fact made choice of this spot in the prospect of his own death, anticipating with extraordinary fervor of faith that his body would share their title with the apostles themselves, and that he should thus even after death become the subject, with them, of the devotions which should be performed to their honor in this place. He accordingly caused twelve coffins to be set up in this church, like sacred pillars in honor and memory of the apostolic number, in the center of which his own was placed, having six of theirs on either side of it. Thus, as I said, he had provided with prudent foresight an honorable resting-place for his body after death, and, having long before secretly formed this resolution, he now consecrated this church to the apostles, believing that this tribute to their memory would be of no small advantage to his own soul. Nor did God disappoint him of that which he so ardently expected and desired. For after he had completed the first services of the feast of Easter, and had passed this sacred day of our Lord in a manner which made it an occasion of joy and gladness to himself and to all; the God through whose aid he performed all these acts, and whose zealous servant he continued to be even to the end of life, was pleased at a happy time to translate him to a better life.

CHAPTER LXI.

His Sickness at Helenopolis, and Prayers respecting his Baptism.

At first he experienced some slight bodily indisposition, which was soon followed by positive disease. In consequence of this he visited the hot baths of his own city; and thence proceeded to that which bore the name of his mother. Here he passed some time in the church of the

---

[1] From this point to the end of the first sentence in ch. 58 is bracketed by Heinichen.

martyrs, and offered up supplications and prayers to God. Being at length convinced that his life was drawing to a close, he felt the time was come at which he should seek purification from sins of his past career, firmly believing that whatever errors he had committed as a mortal man, his soul would be purified from them through the efficacy of the mystical words and the salutary waters of baptism.[1] Impressed with these thoughts, he poured forth his supplications and confessions to God, kneeling on the pavement in the church itself, in which he also now for the first time received the imposition of hands with prayer.[2] After this he proceeded as far as the suburbs of Nicomedia, and there, having summoned the bishops to meet him, addressed them in the following words.

CHAPTER LXII.

Constantine's Appeal to the Bishops, requesting them to confer upon him the Rite of Baptism.

"THE time is arrived which I have long hoped for, with an earnest desire and prayer that I might obtain the salvation of God. The hour is come in which I too may have the blessing of that seal which confers immortality; the hour in which I may receive the seal of salvation. I had thought to do this in the waters of the river Jordan, wherein our Saviour, for our example, is recorded to have been baptized: but God, who knows what is expedient for us, is pleased that I should receive this blessing here. Be it so, then, without delay:[1] for should it be his will who is

Lord of life and death, that my existence here should be prolonged, and should I be destined henceforth to associate with the people of God, and unite with them in prayer as a member of his Church, I will prescribe to myself from this time such a course of life as befits his service." After he had thus spoken, the prelates performed the sacred ceremonies in the usual manner, and, having given him the necessary instructions, made him a partaker of the mystic ordinance. Thus was Constantine the first of all sovereigns who was regenerated and perfected in a church dedicated to the martyrs of Christ; thus gifted with the Divine seal of baptism, he rejoiced in spirit, was renewed, and filled with heavenly light: his soul was gladdened by reason of the fervency of his faith, and astonished at the manifestation of the power of God. At the conclusion of the ceremony he arrayed himself in shining imperial vestments, brilliant as the light,[2] and reclined on a couch of the purest white, refusing to clothe himself with the purple any more.

CHAPTER LXIII.

How after his Baptism he rendered Thanks to God.

HE then lifted his voice and poured forth a strain of thanksgiving to God; after which he added these words. "Now I know that I am truly blessed: now I feel assured that I am accounted worthy of immortality, and am made a partaker of Divine light." He further expressed his compassion for the unhappy condition of those who were strangers to such blessings as he enjoyed: and when the tribunes and generals of his army appeared in his presence with lamentations and tears at the prospect of their bereavement, and with prayers that his days might yet be prolonged, he assured them in reply that he was now in possession of true life; that none but himself could know the value of the blessings he had received; so that he was anxious rather to hasten than to defer his departure to God. He then proceeded to complete the needful arrangement of his affairs, bequeathing an annual donation to the Roman inhabitants of his imperial city; apportioning the inheritance of the empire, like a patrimonial estate, among his own children; in short, making every disposition according to his own pleasure.[1]

[1] Literally "salutary word of cleansing," but the paraphrase of *Bag.* will stand well whichever of the readings, "salutary cleansing," or "salutary word of cleansing," is adopted.
[2] [These words seem to prove that the emperor now first became a catechumen. His postponement of baptism until his last illness (after having stood forward so long as the public advocate and protector of the Christian religion), and the superstitious reliance which he was encouraged to place on the late performance of this "mysterious" rite, afford an evidence of the melancholy obscuration of Christian truth at the very time when Christianity was ostensibly becoming the religion of the Roman Empire. There is probably too much truth in the following remarks of Gibbon: "The pride of Constantine, who refused the privileges of a catechumen, cannot easily be explained or excused: but the delay of his baptism may be justified by the maxims and practice of ecclesiastical antiquity. The sacrament of baptism was supposed to contain a full and absolute expiation of sin; and the soul was instantly restored to its original purity, and entitled to the promise of eternal salvation. Among the proselytes of Christianity, there were many who judged it imprudent to precipitate a salutary rite, which could not be repeated; to throw away an inestimable privilege, which could never be recovered," &c. (*Decline and Fall*, ch. 20). — *Bag.*] On the forms of admission to the catechumenate, compare Marriott, *Baptism*, in Smith and Cheetham, *Dict.*
[1] Or "no hesitation." On this clause a deal of controversy has hinged. "No hesitation shall longer prevail" is the rendering of *Molz.*, and Keim (Uebertritt C. p. 1) similarly gives "let all duplicity be banished." In the view of this translation, Constantine had been hedging all his life, trying to be Christian to Christians and heathen to heathen. The basis of the hypothesis is too slight for it to have any weight in view of the overwhelming documentary evidence of the frequent public professions of Christianity by Constantine, for which see Prolegomena, under *Character*. Discussion of various points relating to his baptism will be found under *Literature*, under the names Busaeus, Castelli, Dalhus, Frimelius Fuhrmann, Guidi, Halloix, Hynitzsch, Jacobus of Sarug, Nicolai, Polus, Schelstrate, Scultetus, Tentzel, Walther, Withof.

[2] [It was customary for neophytes to wear white garments, which they laid aside on the eighth day from their baptism. — *Bag.*]
[1] The idea of ownership in empire which seems so strange in these days of republics, and is disallowed even by theoretical monarchists, seems to have been a most matter-of-course one in the mind of Constantine, and Eusebius was a true imperialist regarding "tyranies" and "republics" as in the same category. Whether it was by "divine right" or "natural right" they were quite sure it was a "right," and one to be freely exercised.

CHAPTER LXIV.

Constantine's Death at Noon on the Feast of Pentecost.

ALL these events occurred during a most important festival, I mean the august and holy solemnity of Pentecost, which is distinguished by a period of seven weeks, and sealed with that one day on which the holy Scriptures attest the ascension of our common Saviour into heaven, and the descent of the Holy Spirit among men. In the course of this feast the emperor received the privileges I have described ; and on the last day of all, which one might justly call the feast of feasts, he was removed about mid-day to the presence of his God, leaving his mortal remains to his fellow mortals, and carrying into fellowship with God that part of his being which was capable of understanding and loving him.[1] Such was the close of Constantine's mortal life. Let us now attend to the circumstances which followed this event.

CHAPTER LXV.

Lamentations of the Soldiery and their Officers.

IMMEDIATELY the assembled spearmen and body-guard rent their garments, and prostrated themselves on the ground, striking their heads, and uttering lamentations and cries of sorrow, calling on their imperial lord and master, or rather, like true children, on their father, while their tribunes and centurions addressed him as their preserver, protector, and benefactor. The rest of the soldiery also came in respectful order to mourn as a flock the removal of their good shepherd. The people meanwhile ran wildly throughout the city, some expressing the inward sorrow of their hearts by loud cries, others appearing confounded with grief : each mourning the event as a calamity which had befallen himself, and bewailing his death as though they felt themselves bereft of a blessing common alike to all.

CHAPTER LXVI.

Removal of the Body from Nicomedia to the Palace at Constantinople.

AFTER this the soldiers lifted the body from its couch, and laid it in a golden coffin, which they enveloped in a covering of purple, and removed to the city which was called by his own name. Here it was placed in an elevated

---

[1] Compare Prolegomena, *Life, Last Years ;* also for age at time of death, Prolegomena, p. 411, *note.*

position in the principal chamber of the imperial palace, and surrounded by candles burning in candlesticks of gold, presenting a marvelous spectacle, and such as no one under the light of the sun had ever seen on earth since the world itself began. For in the central apartment of the imperial palace, the body of the emperor lay in its elevated resting-place, arrayed in the symbols of sovereignty, the diadem and purple robe, and encircled by a numerous retinue of attendants, who watched around it incessantly night and day.

CHAPTER LXVII.

He received the same Honors from the Counts and other Officers as before his Death.

THE military officers, too, of the highest rank, the counts, and the whole order of magistrates, who had been accustomed to do obeisance to their emperor before, continued to fulfill this duty without any change, even after his death entering the chamber at the appointed times, and saluting their coffined sovereign with bended knee, as though he were still alive. After them the senators appeared, and all who had been distinguished by any honorable office, and rendered the same homage. These were followed by multitudes of every rank, who came with their wives and children to witness the spectacle. These honors continued to be rendered for a considerable time, the soldiers having resolved thus to guard the body until his sons should arrive, and take on themselves the conduct of their father's funeral. No mortal had ever, like this blessed prince, continued to reign even after death, and to receive the same homage as during his life : he only, of all who have ever lived, obtained this reward from God : a suitable reward, since he alone of all sovereigns had in all his actions honored the Supreme God and his Christ, and God himself accordingly was pleased that even his mortal remains should still retain imperial authority among men ; thus indicating to all who were not utterly devoid of understanding the immortal and endless empire which his soul was destined to enjoy. This was the course of events here.

CHAPTER LXVIII.

Resolution of the Army to confer thence-forward the Title of Augustus on his Sons.

MEANWHILE the tribunes selected from the troops under their command those officers whose fidelity and zeal had long been known to the emperor, and dispatched them to the Cæsars with intelligence of the late event. This service they accordingly performed. As soon, however, as the soldiery throughout the provinces received the tidings of the emperor's decease, they all, as if by a supernatural impulse, resolved with one consent, as though their great emperor had been yet alive, to acknowledge none other than his sons as sovereigns of the Roman world: and these they soon after determined should no longer retain the name of Cæsar, but should each be honored with the title of Augustus, a name which indicates the highest supremacy of imperial power. Such were the measures adopted by the army; and these resolutions they, communicated to each other by letter, so that the unanimous desire of the legions became known at the same point of time throughout the whole extent of the empire.

CHAPTER LXIX.

Mourning for Constantine at Rome; and the Honor paid him there through Paintings after his Death.

ON the arrival of the news of the emperor's death in the imperial city, the Roman senate and people felt the announcement as the heaviest and most afflictive of all calamities, and gave themselves up to an excess of grief. The baths and markets were closed, the public spectacles, and all other recreations in which men of leisure are accustomed to indulge, were interrupted. Those who had erewhile lived in luxurious ease, now walked the streets in gloomy sadness, while all united in blessing the name of the deceased, as the one who was dear to God, and truly worthy of the imperial dignity. Nor was their sorrow expressed only in words: they proceeded also to honor him, by the dedication of paintings to his memory, with the same respect as before his death. The design of these pictures embodied a representation of heaven itself, and depicted the emperor reposing in an ethereal mansion above the celestial vault. They too declared his sons alone to be emperors and Augusti, and begged with earnest entreaty that they might be permitted to receive the body of their emperor, and perform his obsequies in the imperial city.

CHAPTER LXX.

His Burial by his Son Constantius at Constantinople.

THUS did they there testify their respect for the memory of him who had been honored by God. The second of his sons, however, who had by this time arrived, proceeded to celebrate his father's funeral in the city which bears his name, himself heading the procession, which was preceded by detachments of soldiers in military array, and followed by vast multitudes, the body itself being surrounded by companies of spearmen and heavy armed infantry. On the arrival of the procession at the church dedicated to the apostles of our Saviour, the coffin was there entombed. Such honor did the youthful emperor Constantius render to his deceased parent, both by his presence, and by the due performance of this sacred ceremony.

CHAPTER LXXI.

Sacred Service in the Church of the Apostles on the Occasion of Constantine's Funeral.

As soon as [Constantius] had withdrawn himself with the military train, the ministers of God came forward, with the multitude and the whole congregation of the faithful, and performed the rites of Divine worship with prayer. At the same time the tribute of their praises was given to the character of this blessed prince, whose body rested on a lofty and conspicuous monument, and the whole multitude united with the priests of God in offering prayers for his soul, not without tears, — nay, rather with much weeping; thus performing an office consonant with the desires of the pious deceased.[1] In this respect also the favor of God was manifested to his servant, in that he not only bequeathed the succession of the empire to his own beloved sons, but that the earthly tabernacle of his thrice blessed soul, according to his own earnest wish, was permitted to share the monument of the apostles; was associated with the honor of their name, and with that of the people of God; was honored by the performance of the sacred ordinances and mystic service; and enjoyed a participation in the prayers of the saints. Thus, too, he continued to possess imperial power even after death, controlling, as though with renovated life, a universal dominion, and retaining in his own name, as Victor, Maximus, Augustus, the sovereignty of the Roman world.[2]

CHAPTER LXXII.

Of the Phœnix.

WE cannot compare him with that bird of Egypt, the only one, as they say, of its kind, which dies,

---

[1] [Alluding to his desire of being buried in the church of the apostles, and sharing their honors, as noticed in ch. 60. — *Bag.*]
[2] [It appears that an interregnum of about three months took place, during which all the laws and edicts continued to be issued in the name of Constantine, as before his death. — *Bag.*]

self-sacrificed, in the midst of aromatic perfumes, and, rising from its own ashes with new life, soars aloft in the same form which it had before. Rather did he resemble his Saviour, who, as the sown corn which is multiplied from a single grain, had yielded abundant increase through the blessing of God, and had overspread the whole world with his fruit. Even so did our thrice blessed prince become multiplied, as it were, through the succession of his sons. His statue was erected along with theirs in every province ; and the name of Constantine was owned and honored even after the close of his mortal life.

CHAPTER LXXIII.

How Constantine is represented on Coins in the Act of ascending to Heaven.

A COINAGE was also struck which bore the following device. On one side appeared the figure of our blessed prince, with the head closely veiled : the reverse exhibited him sitting as a charioteer, drawn by four horses, with a hand stretched downward from above to receive him up to heaven.

CHAPTER LXXIV.

The God whom he had honored deservedly honored him in Return.

SUCH are the proofs by which the Supreme God has made it manifest to us, in the person of Constantine, who alone of all sovereigns had openly professed the Christian faith, how great a difference he perceives between those whose privilege it is to worship him and his Christ, and those who have chosen the contrary part, who provoked his enmity by daring to assail his Church, and whose calamitous end, in every instance, afforded tokens of his displeasure, as manifestly as the death of Constantine conveyed to all men an evident assurance of his Divine love.

CHAPTER LXXV.

He surpassed all Preceding Emperors in Devotion to God.

STANDING, as he did, alone and pre-eminent among the Roman emperors as a worshiper of God ; alone as the bold proclaimer to all men of the doctrine of Christ ; having alone rendered honor, as none before him had ever done, to his Church ; having alone abolished utterly the error of polytheism, and discountenanced idolatry in every form : so, alone among them both during life and after death, was he accounted worthy of such honors as none can say have been attained to by any other ; so that no one, whether Greek or Barbarian, nay, of the ancient Romans themselves, has ever been presented to us as worthy of comparison with him.[1]

---

[1] The sharp sarcasms of Julian's *Cæsars* seem almost to have taken their text from this challenge. He marshals the great emperors before the gods, where each presents his claim to greatness. Constantine is greatly ridiculed, and yet to choose between Julian and Eusebius, if regard is had to Constantine's real effect on world history, Eusebius is the truer judge, and is at least not so far wrong that his superlative enthusiasm for his imperial friend cannot be readily pardoned.

THE ORATION

OF

THE EMPEROR CONSTANTINE,

WHICH HE ADDRESSED

"TO THE ASSEMBLY OF THE SAINTS."

—◦—

CHAPTER I.

Preliminary Remarks on the Feast of Easter: and how the Word of God, having conferred Manifold Benefits on Mankind, was betrayed by his Beneficiaries.

THAT light which far outshines the day and sun, first pledge of resurrection, and renovation of bodies long since dissolved,[1] the divine token[2] of promise, the path which leads to everlasting life — in a word, the day of the Passion — is arrived, best beloved doctors, and ye, my friends who are assembled here, ye blessed multitudes, who worship him who is the author of all worship, and praise him continually with heart and voice, according to the precepts of his holy word. But thou, Nature,[3] parent of all things, what blessing like to this hast thou ever accomplished for mankind? Nay rather, what is in any sense thy workmanship, since he who formed the universe is himself the author of thy being? For it is he who has arrayed thee in thy beauty; and the beauty of Nature is life according to Nature's laws. But principles quite opposed to Nature have mightily prevailed; in that men have agreed in withholding his rightful worship from the Lord of all, believing that the order of the universe depended, not on his providence, but on the blind uncertainty of chance: and this notwithstanding the clearest announcement of the truth by his inspired prophets, whose words should have claimed belief, but were in every way resisted by that impious wickedness which hates the light of truth, and loves the ob-scure mazes of darkness. Nor was this error unaccompanied by violence and cruelty, especially in that the will of princes encouraged the blind impetuosity of the multitude, or rather itself led the way in the career of reckless folly. Such principles as these, confirmed by the practice of many generations, became the source of terrible evils in those early times : but no sooner had the radiance of the Saviour's presence appeared, than justice took the place of wrong, a calm succeeded the confusion of the storm, and the predictions of the prophets were all fulfilled. For after he had enlightened the world by the glorious discretion and purity of his character, and had ascended to the mansions of his father's house, he founded his Church on earth, as a holy temple of virtue, an immortal, imperishable temple, wherein the worship due to the Supreme Father and to himself should be piously performed. But what did the insane malice of the nations hereupon devise? Their effort was to reject the grace of Christ, and to ruin that Church which was ordained for the salvation of all, though they thus ensured the overthrow of their own superstition.[4] Once more then unholy sedition, once more war and strife prevailed, with stiff-neckedness, luxurious riot, and that craving for wealth which now soothes its victims with specious hope, now strikes them with groundless fear; a craving which is contrary to nature, and the very characteristic of Vice herself. Let her, however, lie prostrate in the dust, and own the victorious power of Virtue ; and let her rend and tear herself, as well she may, in the bitterness of repentance. But let us now proceed to speak of topics which pertain to the Divine doctrine.

---

[1] Or "once suffering."

[2] ἕρμαιον, "gift of Hermes"; i.e. providential good-fortune. Valesius wrongly conjectures ἕρμα, "foundation" of promise.

[3] Valesius, followed by various translators, substitutes "God" for "Nature." But all MS. authority, and the context as well, is against.

[4] 1709, *Molz., Vales., Cous.*, render "substitute in place thereof their own superstition."

CHAPTER II.

An Appeal to the Church and to his Hearers to pardon and correct the Errors of his Speech.

HEAR then, thou master[1] of the ship, possessor of virgin purity, and thou Church, the cherisher of tender and inexperienced age, guardian of truth and gentleness, through whose perennial fountain the stream[2] of salvation flows! Be ye also indulgent, my hearers, who worship God sincerely, and are, therefore, the objects of his care: attending, not to the language, but to the truth of what is said; not to him who speaks, but rather to the pious zeal which hallows his discourse! For what will be the use of words when the real purpose of the speaker remains unknown? It may be, indeed, that I essay great things; the love of God which animates my soul, a love which overpowers natural reserve, is my plea for the bold attempt. On you, then, I call, who are best instructed in the mysteries of God, to aid me with your counsel, to follow me with your thoughts, and correct whatever shall savor of error in my words, expecting no display of perfect knowledge, but graciously accepting the sincerity of my endeavor. And may the Spirit of the Father and the Son accord his mighty aid, while I utter the words which he shall suggest to speech or thought.[3] For if any one, whether in the practice of eloquence, or any other art, expects to produce a finished work without the help of God, both the author and his efforts will be found alike imperfect; while he has no cause to fear, no room for discouragement,[4] who has once been blessed with the inspiration of Heaven. Wherefore asking your indulgence for the length of this preface, let us attempt the theme in its utmost scope.[5]

CHAPTER III.

That God is the Father of the Word, and the Creator of all Things; and that Material Objects could not continue to exist, were their Causes Various.

GOD, who is ever above all existence, and the good which all things desire, has no origin, and therefore no beginning, being himself the originator[1] of all things which receive existence.

But he who proceeds from him is again united to him; and this separation from and union with him is not local, but intellectual in its character. For this generation was accompanied by no diminution of the Father's substance (as in the case of generation by seed); but by the determining act of foreknowledge God manifested a Saviour presiding over[2] this sensible world, and all created things therein.[3] From hence, then, is the source of existence and life to all things which are within the compass of this world; hence proceed the soul, and every sense;[4] hence those organs through which the sense-perceptions are perfected. What, then, is the object of this argument? To prove that there is One director of all things that exist, and that all things, whether in heaven or on earth, both natural and organized bodies,[5] are subject to his single sovereignty. For if the dominion of these things, numberless as they are, were in the hands, not of one but of many, there must be a partition and distribution of the elements, and the old fables would be true;[6] jealousy, too, and ambition, striving for superior power, would destroy the harmonious concord of the whole, while each of the many masters would regulate in a manner different from the rest the portion subject to his control. The fact, however, that this universal order is ever one and the same, is the proof that it is under the care of a superior power, and that its origin cannot be ascribed to chance. Else how could the author of universal nature ever be known? To whom first, or last, could prayers and supplications be addressed? Whom could I choose[7] as the object of my worship, without being guilty of impiety towards the rest? Again, if haply I desired to obtain some temporal blessing, should I not, while expressing my gratitude to the Power who favored my request, convey a reproach to him who opposed it? Or to whom should I pray, when desiring to know the cause of my calamity, and to obtain deliverance? Or let us suppose that the answer is given by oracles and prophecies,

---

[1] [The bishop who is thus metaphorically addressed as the guide and controller of the Church. — *Bag.*]
[2] Some MSS. read πόμα, "draught."
[3] "I read αὐτῇ φράσει . . . but regarding φράσει as derived not from the verb φράζειν, but from the noun φράσις." — *Hein.*
[4] "Ought not to shrink or to be neglectful."
[5] Valesius, followed by *1709* and substantially by *Bag.*, omitting πρός, renders "enter upon the head and principal matter of our design." *Hein.* retains πρός, and like *Molz.* renders "proceed, as well as I may, to my theme." He means rather that having God's help he will not fear to "essay great things."
[1] "Beginning."

[2] Presiding "overseer," "president," or "ruler." It is the one who has charge of games or ships or public works, &c.
[3] Cf. John i. 3, 13, 14, and Eph. i. 10. There is the greatest variety in the rendering of this passage, of which *Bag.'s* is the worst. The writer draws here on a philosophy of the Logos, which recognizes the second person of the Trinity as the creator and head of created things. The free version of Cousin gives the best flavor of the idea. "He was produced by the inexhaustible fecundity of his eternal mind to preside over the creation and government of this visible world." A better translation waits on a better exposition of the doctrine of the Logos and its history.
[4] *Molz.* renders "und die Organe, mit Hilfe derer das Wahrgenommene innerlich zur Idee erhoben wird."
[5] *Chr.* substantially "natural and artificial"; *Molz.* "lifeless and live"; perhaps "inorganic and organic" is meant.
[6] [Alluding to the fabulous division of the world between the brothers Jupiter, Neptune, and Pluto. Valesius *in loc.* — *Bag.*] Or rather Zeus, Poseidon, and Hades. Zeus had the heavens, Poseidon the sea, and Hades the underworld, while the earth remained "with high Olympus, common to us all" — a fruitful source of dissension. Cf. Homer, *Il.* XV. 184–195, ed. Doederlein, 2 (1864), p. 64–65; tr. Bryant, XV. ll. 227–245.
[7] A possible reading here is ἐξαιρετως, i.e. take as the chief object, &c. — *Vales.* and *Hein.*

but that the case is not within the scope of their authority, being the province of some other deity.[8] Where, then, is mercy? where is the provident care of God for the human race? Unless, indeed, some more benevolent Power, assuming a hostile attitude against another who has no such feeling, be disposed to accord me his protection. Hence anger, discords, mutual censure, and finally universal confusion, would ensue, while each departed from his proper sphere of action, dissatisfied, through ambitious love of power, with his allotted portion. What, then, would be the result of these things? Surely this discord among the heavenly powers would prove destructive to the interests of earth : the orderly alternation of times and seasons would disappear ; the successive productions of the earth would be enjoyed no more : the day itself, and the repose of night which follows it, would cease to be. But enough on this subject : let us once more resume that species of reasoning which admits of no reply.

CHAPTER IV.

On the Error of Idolatrous Worship.

WHATEVER has had a beginning, has also an end. Now that which is a beginning in respect of time, is called a generation : and whatever is by generation is subject to corruption, and its beauty[1] is impaired by the lapse of time. How, then, can they whose origin is from corruptible generation, be immortal? Again, this supposition has gained credit with the ignorant multitude, that marriages, and the birth of children, are usual among the gods. Granting, then, such offspring to be immortal, and continually produced, the race must of necessity multiply to excess : and if this were so, where is the heaven, or the earth, which could contain so vast and still increasing a multitude of gods? But what shall we say of those men who represent these celestial beings as joined in incestuous union with their sister goddesses, and charge them with adultery and impurity?[2] We declare, further, with all confidence, that the very honors and worship which these deities receive from men are accompanied by acts of wantonness and profligacy. Once more ; the experienced and skillful sculptor, having formed the conception of his design, perfects his work according to the rules of art ; and in a little while, as if forgetful of himself, idolizes his own creation, and adores it as an immortal god, while yet he

admits that himself, the author and maker of the image, is a mortal man. Nay, they even show the graves and monuments of those whom they deem immortal, and bestow divine honors on the dead : not knowing that that which is truly blessed and incorruptible needs no distinction which perishable men can give : for that Being, who is seen by the mental eye, and conceived by the intellect alone, requires to be distinguished by no external form, and admits no figure to represent its character and likeness. But the honors of which we speak are given to those who have yielded to the power of death : they once were men, and tenants, while they lived, of a mortal body.

CHAPTER V.

That Christ, the Son of God, created All Things, and has appointed to Every Thing the Term of its Existence.

BUT why do I defile my tongue with unhallowed words, when my object is to sound the praises of the true God? Rather let me cleanse myself, as it were, from this bitter draught by the pure stream which flows from the everlasting fountain of the virtue[1] of that God who is the object of my praise. Be it my special province to glorify Christ, as well by the actions of my life, as by that thanksgiving which is due to him for the manifold and signal blessings which he has bestowed. I affirm, therefore, that he[2] has laid the foundations of this universe ; and conceived the race of men, ordaining these things by his word. And immediately he transferred our newly created parents (ignorant at first, according to his will, of good and evil) to a happy region, abounding in flowers and fruits of every kind.[3] At length, however, he appointed them a seat on earth befitting creatures endued with reason ; and then unfolded to their faculties, as intelligent beings, the knowledge of good and evil. Then, too, he bade the race increase ; and each healthy region of the world, as far as the bounds of the circumambient ocean, became the dwelling-place of men ; while with this increase of numbers the invention of the useful arts went hand in

---

[8] Valesius remarks that many instances are recorded where the oracle of Apollo replied to those who consulted him that Bacchus or Saturn must be placated in order to their liberation.

[1] "Form."

[2] A favorite theme of the Christian apologists. Cf. long list given in the *Clementine Recognitions*, X. 22.

[1] Or "perfections."

[2] "To be referred not to the preceding 'Christ' but . . . the supreme God."—*Hein.* (?).

[3] [Constantine seems to have supposed the Paradise of our first parents to be somewhere apart from this earth. In this fanciful idea, which is obviously indefensible from Scripture he is countenanced by the opinions of Tertullian, Tatian, Clement of Alexandria, Origen, Valentinian, and Jerome, some of whom placed it in or above the third heaven, others in the fourth, others again in a world superior to the present, &c. See the note of Valesius, who quotes from some of these Fathers. In reference to what follows, we may ask, Was Constantine acquainted with, or does he avoid noticing, the circumstances of the fall?—*Bag.*] *Ans.* Constantine like many another to our own day seems to regard the "fall" as a fall upwards—that complacent optimism which ignores Scripture and Schopenhauer alike.

hand. Meantime the various species of inferior[4] animals increased in due proportion, each kind discovering some characteristic quality, the special gift of nature : the tame distinguished by gentleness and obedience to man ; the wild by strength and swiftness, and an instinctive foresight which warned them to escape from peril. The gentler animals he placed entirely beneath man's protecting care, but entailed on him the necessity of strife with those of fiercer nature. He next created the feathered race, manifold in number, diverse in character and habits ; brilliant with every variety of color, and endued with native powers of melody. Finally, having arranged with wise discrimination whatever else the compass of this world contains, and having assigned to every creature the stated term of its existence, he thus completed the beautiful order of the perfect whole.

CHAPTER VI.

The Falsity of the General Opinion respecting Fate[1] is proved by the Consideration of Human Laws, and by the Works of Creation, the Course of which is not Fortuitous, but according to an Orderly Arrangement which evinces the Design of the Creator.

THE great majority, however, in their folly, ascribe the regulation of the universe to nature, while some imagine fate, or accident,[2] to be the cause. With regard to those who attribute the control of all things to fate, they know not that in using this term they utter a mere word, but designate no active power, nor anything which has real and substantial existence. For what can this fate be, considered in itself, if nature be the first cause of all things? Or what shall we suppose nature itself to be, if the law of fate be inviolable? Indeed, the very assertion that there is a law of fate implies that such law is the work of a legislator : if, therefore, fate itself

be a law, it must be a law devised by God. All things, therefore, are subject to God, and nothing is beyond the sphere of his power. If it be said that fate is the will[3] of God, and is so considered, we admit the fact. But in what respect do justice,[4] or self-control,[5] or the other virtues, depend on fate? From whence, if so, do their contraries, as injustice and intemperance, proceed? For vice has its origin from nature, not from fate ; and virtue is the due regulation of natural character and disposition. But, granting that the varied results of actions, whether right or erroneous in themselves, depend on fortune or fate : in what sense can the general principle of justice,[6] the principle of rendering to every one his due, be ascribed to fate?[7] Or how can it be said that laws, encouragements to virtue and dissuasives from what is evil, praise, blame, punishment, in short whatever operates as a motive to virtue, and deters from the practice of vice, derive their origin from fortune or accident, and not rather from that of justice,[8] which is a characteristic attribute of the God of providence? For the events which befall men are consequent upon the tenor of their lives. Hence pestilence or sedition, famine and plenty, succeed in turn, declaring plainly and emphatically that all these things are regulated with reference to our course of life. For the Divine Being delights in goodness, but turns with aversion from all impiety ; looks with acceptance on the humble spirit, but abhors presumption, and that pride which exalts itself above what becomes a creature. And though the proofs of these truths are clear and manifest to our sight, they appear in a still stronger light, when we collect, and as it were concentrate our thoughts within ourselves, and ponder their causes with deep attention. I say, then, that it becomes us to lead a life of modesty and gentleness, not suffering our thoughts to rise proudly above our natural condition, and ever mindful that God is near us,

---

[4] Without the λόγος, i.e. inarticulate or (as here) irrational.

[1] For a full discussion of various definitions and usage of the word Fate (ἡ εἱαρμένη) in Greek philosophy, compare Zeller, *Stoics, Epicureans, and Sceptics* (Lond. 1880), p. 170-171, notes.

[2] αὐτόματον. The usual word for chance or accident is τύχη. These may be here, as is often the case, simple synonyms, but both words are used in the same phrase later in such way as to suggest that τύχη is parallel with "fate" rather than "chance" in the author's mind. αὐτόματον seems to be used of "self-originating," τύχη of originating from some unknown cause or without any cause. The former is the modern, self-energized, "lift-yourselves-by-your-own-boot-straps" evolution. The latter is a form of agnosticism. Aristotle (*Metaph.* 10. 8) defines chance (τύχη) as a "cause by accident" (συμβεβηκός), or more literally "coincidence," which is substantially what Janet (*Final Causes*, 1878, p. 19) means by defining chance as the coïncidence of causes. At the end of the same chapter Aristotle uses αὐτόματον in contrast with τύχη — "τύχη or even αὐτόματον," which has been rendered (M'Mahon) "chance or even spontaneity." In modern phrase those who hold these three various views of the universe might be characterized as "material evolutionists," "transcendental idealists," and "philosophical (or perhaps 'agnostic') evolutionists."

[3] i.e. "plan."

[4] δικαιοσύνη, better "righteousness," "correctness of thinking, feeling, and acting" (Thayer, *Lex.* p. 149). So its opposite mentioned below (ἀδικία) is better "unrighteousness," as generally in the revised English version of the N. T., "mammon of unrighteousness" (Luke xvi. 9, e.g.). The word means more than our "just," "more," as Socrates said (Plat. *Rep.* 1. 331), "than to speak the truth and pay your debts." Righteousness is the better translation, but we are met with the difficulty that it has generally been rendered justice in translations of the philosophers.

[5] σωφροσύνη, temperance, *vs.* ἀκολασία, intemperance, below ; soundness of mind *vs.* insanity (cf. use in Acts xxvi. 25, and of verb in Mark v. 15; Luke viii. 35; also use in Plato, *Rep.* 332, &c.); self-control *vs.* unbridled desire. This same contrast of σωφροσύνη and ἀκολασία is found in Aristotle, *Eth.* 2, vii. 3; 7, vii. 1; and especially 7, ix. 5.

[6] τὶ δίκαιον, not δικαιοσύνη.

[7] This is very free, and follows translation of Valesius and *1709* text. *1709* marg. translates more literally, "But either crimes, or, on the other hand, brave performances, which are [the property] of a good and right purpose of mind, if they happen sometimes one way, at others another," and *Molz.* somewhat similarly. It is possible that it should read: "Granted that either evil actions proceeding from a good and upright will, or contrariwise, good actions [from an evil will] which issue directly contrary [to their own nature or to just expectation] may be ascribed to chance or fate, how can the right," &c.   [8] δικαιοσύνη.

and is the observer of all our actions. But let us still farther test the truth of the proposition, that the order of the universe depends on chance[9] or accident.[1] Are we then to suppose that the stars and other heavenly bodies, the earth and sea, fire and wind, water and air, the succession of the seasons, the recurrence of summer and winter, that all these have an undesigned and fortuitous existence, and not rather that they proceed from the creative hand of God? Some, indeed, are so senseless as to say that most of these things have been devised by mankind because of their need of them. Let it be admitted that this opinion has a semblance of reason in regard to earthly and corruptible things (though Nature herself supplies every good with a lavish hand); yet can we believe that things which are immortal and unchangeable are the inventions of men? These, indeed, and all things else which are beyond the reach of our senses, and comprehended by the intellect[11] alone, receive their being, not from the material life of man, but from the intellectual and eternal essence of God. Again, the orderly arrangement of these things is the work of his providence: for instance, that the day, deriving radiance from the sun, is bright; that night succeeds his setting, and the starry host[12] by which night itself is redeemed from total darkness. And what shall we say of the moon, which when most distant from, and opposite to the sun, is filled with light, but wanes in proportion to the nearness of her approach to him? Do not these things manifestly evince the intelligence[13] and sagacious wisdom of God? Add to this that needful warmth of the solar rays which ripens the fruits of the earth; the currents of wind, so conducive to the fertility of the seasons; the cool and refreshing showers; and the harmony of all these things in accordance with which all are reasonably and systematically conducted: lastly, the everlasting order of the planets, which return to the selfsame place at their appointed times: are not all these, as well as the perfect ministry of the stars, obedient to a divine law, evident proofs of the ordinance[14] of God? Again, do the mountain heights, the deep and hollow valleys, the level and extensive plains, useful as they are, as well as pleasing to the eye, appear to exist independently of the will of God? Or do not the proportion and alternate succession of land and water, serviceable, the one for husbandry, the other for the transport of such foreign products

as we need, afford a clear demonstration of his exact and proportionate providential care? For instance, the mountains contain a store of water, which the level ground receives, and after imbibing sufficient for the renovation of the soil, sends forth the residue into the sea, and the sea in turn passes it onward to the ocean. And still we dare to say that all these things happen by chance[15] and accident; unable though we be to show by what shape or form this chance is characterized; a thing which has no foundation either in intellect or sense existence; which rings in our ears as the mere sound of an unsubstantial name!

CHAPTER VII.

In regard to Things above our Comprehension, we should glorify the Creator's Wisdom, and attribute their Causes to him alone, and not to Chance.

IN fact, this word "chance" is the expression of men who think in haphazard and illogical fashion; who are unable to understand the causes of these things, and who, owing to the feebleness of their own apprehensions, conceive that those things for which they cannot assign a reason, are ordered without reason. There are, unquestionably, some things which possess wonderful natural properties, and the full apprehension of which is very difficult: for example, the nature of hot springs. For no one can easily explain the cause of so powerful a fire; and it is indeed surprising that though surrounded on all sides by a body of cold water, it loses none of its native heat. These phenomena appear to be of rare occurrence throughout the world, being intended, I am persuaded, to afford to mankind convincing evidence of the power of that Providence which ordains that two directly opposite natures, heat and cold, should thus proceed from the self-same source. Many indeed, yea, numberless, are the gifts which God has bestowed for the comfort and enjoyment of man; and of these the fruit of the olive-tree and the vine deserve especial notice; the one for its power of renovating and cheering the soul,[1] the other because it ministers to our enjoyment, and is likewise adapted for the cure of bodily disease. Marvelous, too, is the course of rivers, flowing night and day with unceasing motion, and presenting a type of ever-flowing, never-ceasing life: and equally wonderful is the alternate succession of day and night.

---

[9] τύχη.   [10] αὐτόματον.
[11] νόος was not narrowed to the mere intellectual functions. "Intellectual" is not to be taken of brain function only, but of brain and heart, — real knowing, as against the "intellectuation" which men nowadays try to force the word "know" to mean.
[12] 'Quire of the stars," 1709.
[13] The "λόγος ἐνδιάθετος" of Philo, frequent in Alexandrian theologians. It is the unuttered thought *vs.* the expressed word.
[14] Fore-ordination, or plan.

[15] αὐτόματον.
[1] ψυχῆς = "soul." In the absence of a proper Biblical psychology the word has been most sadly abused in translations. The only way back to a proper conception of the words "spirit" and "soul" and "life," &c., is to re-establish a uniform rendering for them. It is as bad as the rendering of our English version, where *nephesh* (= ψυχή) is rendered "life."

CHAPTER VIII.

That God bestows an Abundant Supply of whatever is suited to the Wants of Man, and ministers but sparingly to his Pleasures; in Both Cases with a View to his Advantage.

LET what has been said suffice to prove that nothing exists without reason and intelligence, and that reason itself and providence are of God. It is he who has also distributed the metals, as gold, silver, copper, and the rest, in due proportion; ordaining an abundant supply of those which would be most needed and generally employed, while he dispensed those which serve the purposes merely of pleasure in adornment of luxury with a liberal and yet a sparing hand, holding a mean between parsimony and profusion. For the searchers for metals, were those which are employed for ornament procured in equal abundance with the rest, would be impelled by avarice to despise and neglect to gather those which, like iron or copper, are serviceable for husbandry, or house-building, or the equipment of ships; and would care for those only which conduce to luxury and a superfluous excess of wealth. Hence it is, as they say, that the search for gold and silver is far more difficult and laborious than that for any other metals, the violence of the toil thus acting as a counterpoise to the violence of the desire. And how many instances might still further be enumerated of the workings of that Divine Providence which, in all the gifts which it has so unsparingly conferred upon us, plainly urges us to the practice of self-control and all other virtues, and leads us away from unbefitting covetousness! To trace the secret reasons of all these things is indeed a task which exceeds the power of human faculties. For how can the intellect of a frail and perishable being arrive at the knowledge of perfect truth, or apprehend in its purity the counsel of God from the beginning?

CHAPTER IX.

Of the Philosophers, who fell into Mistaken Notions, and Some of them into Danger, by their Desire of Universal Knowledge. — Also of the Doctrines of Plato.

WE ought, therefore, to aim at objects which are within our power, and exceed not the capacities of our nature. For the persuasive influence of argument has a tendency to draw most of us away from the truth of things, which has happened to many philosophers, who have employed themselves in reasoning, and the study of natural science, and who, as often as the magnitude of the subject surpasses their powers of investigation, adopt various devices for obscuring the truth. Hence their diversities of judgment, and contentious opposition to each others' doctrines, and this notwithstanding their pretensions to wisdom. Hence, too, popular commotions have arisen, and severe sentences, passed by those in power, apprehensive of the overthrow of hereditary institutions, have proved destructive to many of the disputants themselves. Socrates, for example, elated by his skill in argumentation, indulging his power of making the worse appear the better reason,[1] and playing continually with the subtleties of controversy, fell a victim to the slander of his own countrymen and fellow-citizens. Pythagoras, too, who laid special claim to the virtues of silence and self-control, was convicted of falsehood. For he declared to the Italians that the doctrines which he had received during his travels in Egypt, and which had long before been divulged by the priests of that nation, were a personal revelation to himself from God. Lastly, Plato himself, the gentlest and most refined of all, who first essayed to draw men's thoughts from sensible to intellectual and eternal objects, and taught them to aspire to sublimer speculations, in the first place declared, with truth, a God exalted above every essence, but to him he added also a second, distinguishing them numerically as two, though both possessing one perfection, and the being of the second Deity proceeding from[2] the first. For he is the creator and controller of the universe, and evidently supreme: while the second, as the obedient agent of his commands, refers the origin of all creation to him as the cause. In accordance, therefore, with the soundest reason, we may say that there is one Being whose care and providence are over all things, even God the Word, who has ordered all things; but the Word being God himself is also the Son of God. For by what name can we designate him except by this title of the Son, without falling into the most grievous error? For the Father of all things is properly considered the Father of his own Word. Thus far, then, Plato's sentiments were sound; but in what follows he appears to have wandered from the truth, in that he introduces a plurality of gods, to each of whom he assigns specific forms. And this has given occasion to still greater error among the unthinking portion of

---

[1] This is almost identically the form of what Socrates (*Apol.* c. 2) declared to be the falsehood circulated by his enemies to his prejudice. "But far more dangerous are those who began when you were children and took possession of your minds with their falsehoods, telling of one Socrates, a wise man who . . . made the worse appear the better cause" (λόγον, "reason"), Tr. Jowett, i (1874), 316. This example does peculiar discredit either to the learning or the mental honesty of the author.

[2] Rather "deriving existence from," "proceeding from," gives strict idea, but may be confounded with the technical "proceeding from" of the "filioque" controversy, which is quite another phrase.

mankind, who pay no regard to the providence of the Supreme God, but worship images of their own devising, made in the likeness of men or other living beings. Hence it appears that the transcendent nature and admirable learning of this philosopher, tinged as they were with such errors as these, were by no means free from impurity and alloy. And yet he seems to me to retract, and correct his own words, when he plainly declares that a rational soul is the breath[3] of God, and divides all things into two classes, intellectual and sensible : [the one simple, the other][4] consisting of bodily structure ; the one comprehended by the intellect alone, the other estimated by the judgment and the senses. The former class, therefore, which partakes of the divine spirit, and is uncompounded and immaterial, is eternal, and inherits everlasting life ; but the latter, being entirely resolved into the elements of which it is composed, has no share in everlasting life. He farther teaches the admirable doctrine, that those who have passed a life of virtue, that is, the spirits of good and holy men, are enshrined, after their separation from the body, in the fairest mansions of heaven. A doctrine not merely to be admired, but profitable too.[5] For who can believe in such a statement, and aspire to such a happy lot, without desiring to practice righteousness and temperance, and to turn aside from vice? Consistently with this doctrine he represents the spirits of the wicked as tossed like wreckage on the streams of Acheron and Pyriphlegethon.

CHAPTER X.

Of those who reject the Doctrines of Philosophers, as well as those of Scripture : and that we ought to believe the Poets in All Things, or disbelieve them in All.

THERE are, however, some persons so infatuated, that when they meet with such sentiments as these, they are neither converted or alarmed : nay, they even treat them with contempt and scorn, as if they listened to the inventions of fable ; applauding, perhaps, the beauty of the eloquence, but abhorring the severity of the precepts. And yet they give credence to the fictions of the poets, and make both civilized and barbarous[1] countries ring with exploded and false tales. For the poets assert that the judgment of souls after death is committed to men whose parentage they ascribe to the gods,[2] extolling their righteousness and impartiality and represent them as guardians of the dead. The same poets describe the battles of the gods and certain usages of war among them, and speak of them as subject to·the power of fate. Some of these deities they picture to us as cruel, others as strangers to all care for the human race, and others again as hateful in their character. They introduce them also as mourning the slaughter of their own children, thus implying their inability to succor, not strangers merely, but those most dear to them. They describe them, too, as subject to human passions, and sing of their battles and wounds, their joys and sorrows. And in all this they appear worthy of belief.[3] For if we suppose them to be moved by a divine impulse to attempt the poetic art, we are bound to believe them and to be persuaded of what they utter under this inspiration. They speak, then, of the calamities to which their divinities are subject ; calamities which of course are altogether true ! But it will be objected that it is the privilege of poets to lie, since the peculiar province of poetry is to charm[4] the spirits of the hearers, while the very essence of truth is that things told be in reality exactly what they are said to be.[5] Let us grant that it is a characteristic of poetry occasionally to conceal the truth. But they who speak falsehood do it not without an object ; being influenced either by a desire of personal gain or advantage, or possibly, being conscious of some evil conduct, they are induced to disguise the truth by dread of the threatening vengeance of the laws. But surely it were possible for them (in my judgment), by adhering faithfully to truth at least while treating of the nature of the Supreme Being, to avoid the guilt at once of falsehood and impiety.

---

[3] " Spirit."
[4] " The one simple " is not in the text, but is a conjectural addition of Valesius, followed by most translators. " Consisting of bodily structure " seems possibly to be an epexegetical phrase relating to the " all things " which he divides into intellectual and sensible, making the intellectual as well as the sensible to have bodily (somatic) structure. " All things," or " the universe," a plural technical term, is regarded as his mind passes to the explanation as " the all." This psychological probability appears a simpler solution than the various textual conjectures.
[5] Heinichen suspects that there has been an inversion of words here, and that it should have been, " He further teaches the admirable and profitable doctrine," and " a doctrine not merely to be admired " omitted.

[1] " All the Greek-speaking world, and foreign lands as well."
[2] Rhadamanthus was a son of Jove (or Vulcan) and Europa. Cf. Hom. *Il.* 14. 322; *Od.* 4. 564, 7. 323.
[3] [There can be no doubt (though the fact is not immediately apparent from the wording of the text), that the spirit of this passage is ironical. — *Bag.*]
[4] Rather " cheat," or " delude." Mr. Charles Dudley Warner, essayist and novelist, says in an interesting essay on the relation of fiction to life, that the object of fiction is to produce illusions, and the test of its art is its power to produce such illusion.
[5] There is a temptation here to adopt the translation of *Molz.* " Truth lies in the fiction, however, when what is told corresponds to reality." Mr. Warner, in his lecture, goes on to say that the object of fiction is to reveal what is, — not the base and sordid things only or peculiarly, but the best possibilities, and gives an exquisite exposition of the fact that the idealism of true fiction is simply the realism of the nobler characteristics and truths. The truth is, that the object of fiction or poetry as art is to produce the image, — fill the whole personality with a picture. This is only gained in its highest form when every detail exactly corresponds to truth or reality. The function of fiction is not illusion, but realization. Its object is the reproduction of truth. *Molz.* makes Constantine say that fiction is true when it corresponds to reality, though the forms be not historical or actual. This is a true observation, but not what Constantine says. He says in substance, with Mr. Warner, that the

CHAPTER XI.

On the Coming of our Lord in the Flesh; its Nature and Cause.[1]

WHOEVER, then, has pursued a course unworthy of a life of virtue, and is conscious of having lived an irregular and disorderly life, let him repent, and turn with enlightened spiritual vision to God; and let him abandon his past career of wickedness, content if he attain to wisdom even in his declining years. We, however, have received no aid from human instruction; nay, whatever graces of character are esteemed of good report by those who have understanding, are entirely the gift of God. And I am able to oppose no feeble buckler against the deadly weapons of Satan's armory; I mean the knowledge I possess of those things which are pleasing to him: and of these I will select such as are appropriate to my present design, while I proceed to sing the praises of the Father of all. But do thou, O Christ, Saviour of mankind, be present to aid me in my hallowed task! Direct the words which celebrate thy virtues,[2] and instruct me worthily to sound thy praises. And now, let no one expect to listen to the graces of elegant language: for well I know that the nerveless eloquence of those who speak to charm the ear, and whose aim is rather applause than sound argument, is distasteful to hearers of sound judgment. It is asserted, then, by some profane and senseless persons, that Christ, whom we worship, was justly condemned to death, and that he who is the author of life to all, was himself deprived of life. That such an assertion should be made by those who have once dared to enter the paths of impiety, who have cast aside all fear, and all thought of concealing their own depravity, is not surprising. But it is beyond the bounds of folly itself that they should be able, as it seems, really to persuade themselves that the incorruptible God yielded to the violence of men, and not rather to that love alone which he bore to the human race: that they should fail to perceive that divine magnanimity and forbearance is changed by no insult, is moved from its intrinsic steadfastness by no revilings; but is ever the same, breaking down and repelling, by the spirit of wisdom and greatness of soul, the savage fierceness of those who assail it. The gracious kindness of God had determined to abolish iniquity, and to exalt order and justice. Accordingly, he gathered a company of the wisest among men,[3] and ordained that most noble and useful doctrine, which is calculated to lead the good and blessed of mankind to an imitation of his own providential care. And what higher blessing can we speak of than this, that God should prescribe the way of righteousness, and make those who are counted worthy of his instruction like himself; that goodness might be communicated to all classes of mankind, and eternal felicity be the result? This is the glorious victory: this the true power: this the mighty work, worthy of its author, the restoration of all people to soundness of mind: and the glory of this triumph we joyfully ascribe to thee, thou Saviour of all! But thou, vile and wretched blasphemy, whose glory is in lies and rumors and calumny; thy power is to deceive and prevail with the inexperience of youth, and with men who still retain the folly of youth. These thou seducest from the service of the true God, and settest up false idols as the objects of their worship and their prayers; and thus the reward of their folly awaits thy deluded victims: for they calumniate Christ, the author of every blessing, who is God, and the Son of God. Is not the worship of the best and wisest of the nations of this world worthily directed to that God, who, while possessing boundless power, remains immovably true to his own purpose, and retains undiminished his characteristic kindness and love to man? Away, then, ye impious, for still ye may while vengeance on your transgressions is yet withheld; begone to your sacrifices, your feasts, your scenes of revelry and drunkenness, wherein, under the semblance of religion, your hearts are devoted to profligate enjoyment, and pretending to perform sacrifices, yourselves are the willing slaves of your own pleasures. No knowledge have ye of any good, nor even of the first commandment of the mighty God, who both declares his will to man, and gives commission to his Son to direct the course of human life, that they who have passed a career of virtue and self-control may obtain, according to the judgment of that Son, a second, yea, a blessed and happy existence.[4] I have now declared the decree of God respecting the life which he prescribes to man, neither ignorantly, as many have done, nor

---

object is to produce illusion or deceive, while the idea of truth is just the reverse.

[1] One MS. adds, "and concerning those who did not know this mystery." In another the chapter is divided, and this is the heading of the second part.

[2] Or "this discourse concerning virtue."

[3] [Alluding to the apostles, who are called in the beginning of ch. 15, "the best men of their age." Were it our province to criticise, we might notice the contrariety of such expressions as these to the account which Scripture gives us of those "unlearned and ignorant men," the feeble, and, in themselves, fallible instruments, whom God selected to further his wondrous designs of mercy to a ruined world. — *Bag.*] Were it in our province to criticise the critic, we might notice that the fear of the Lord is the beginning of wisdom, and refer to the whole Book of Proverbs. Any just conception of wisdom or true learning says the same thing. The man who knows that God and not φύσις or τύχη manages the universe, is more learned than the wisest of those learned in things which are not so.

[4] Christophorson extends ch. 10 to this point, and here introduces ch. 11, with the heading "On the coming of Our Lord in the flesh; its nature and cause."

resting on the ground of opinion or conjecture. But it may be that some will ask, Whence this title of Son? Whence this generation of which we speak, if God be indeed only One, and incapable of union with another? We are, however, to consider generation as of two kinds; one in the way of natural birth, which is known to all; the other, that which is the effect of an eternal cause, the mode of which is seen by the prescience of God, and by those among men whom he loves. For he who is wise will recognize the cause which regulates the harmony of creation. Since, then, nothing exists without a cause, of necessity the cause of existing substances preceded their existence. But since the world and all things that it contains exist, and are preserved,[5] their preserver must have had a prior existence; so that Christ is the cause of preservation, and the preservation of things is an effect:[6] even as the Father is the cause of the Son, and the Son the effect of that cause. Enough, then, has been said to prove his priority of existence. But how do we explain his descent to this earth, and to men? His motive in this,[7] as the prophets had foretold, originated in his watchful care for the interests of all: for it needs must be that the Creator should care for his own works. But when the time came for him to assume a terrestrial body, and to sojourn on this earth, the need requiring, he devised for himself a new mode[8] of birth. Conception was there, yet apart from marriage: childbirth, yet pure virginity: and a maiden became the mother of God! An eternal nature received a beginning of temporal existence: a sensible form of a spiritual essence, a material manifestation of incorporeal brightness,[9] appeared. Alike wondrous were the circumstances which attended this great event. A radiant dove, like that which flew from the ark of Noah,[10] alighted on the Virgin's bosom:

and accordant with this impalpable union, purer than chastity, more guileless than innocence itself, were the results which followed. From infancy possessing the wisdom of God, received with reverential awe by the Jordan, in whose waters he was baptized, gifted with that royal unction, the spirit of universal intelligence; with knowledge and power to perform miracles, and to heal diseases beyond the reach of human art; he yielded a swift and unhindered assent to the prayers of men, to whose welfare, indeed, his whole life was devoted without reserve. His doctrines instilled, not prudence only,[11] but real wisdom: his hearers were instructed, not in the mere social virtues,[12] but in the ways which conduct to the spiritual world; and devoted themselves to the contemplation of immutable and eternal things, and the knowledge of the Supreme Father. The benefits which he bestowed were no common blessings: for blindness, the gift of sight; for helpless weakness, the vigor of health; in the place of death, restoration to life again. I dwell not on that abundant provision in the wilderness, whereby a scanty measure of food became a complete and enduring supply[13] for the wants of a mighty multitude.[14] Thus do we render thanks to thee, our God and Saviour, according to our feeble power; unto thee, O Christ, supreme Providence of the mighty Father, who both savest us from evil, and impartest to us thy most blessed doctrine: for I say these things, not to praise, but to give thanks. For what mortal is he who shall worthily declare thy praise, of whom we learn that thou didst from nothing call creation into being, and illumine it with thy light; that thou didst regulate the confusion of the elements by the laws of harmony and order? But chiefly we mark thy loving-kindness,[15] in that thou hast caused those

---

[5] Preserved, preserver, and preservation = saved, saviour, and salvation. This represents the N. T. idea better than the popular conception which confuses Christ our Saviour with Christ our Redeemer. Redemption was a necessary part of his effort for our salvation, but the salvation itself was a saving, in literal English preserving. We have been redeemed; we are being saved.

[6] *Bag.* follows here Valesius' translation and note where he makes the word "preservation" a conjectural emendation of Scaliger, inconsistent with the meaning of the passage, and omits translating "the cause of all things that exist." But *Hein.* does not even hint such reading, and his text (followed also by *Molz.*), so far from tending to disturb the whole meaning, gives much the more intelligent conception. Christ is the preserver (saviour) of things. Preservation of things is the effect of that cause, just as the Father is the cause of the Son, and the Son the effect of that cause. Therefore the preserver precedes created things as a cause precedes its effect.

[7] Valesius expresses a preference for the reading καθόδου (advent) here instead of καθόλου (universal), but the latter is the reading of Heinichen, and undoubtedly correct. *Bag.* has followed Valesius.

[8] "New mode" is a paraphrase supported by only one MS. The real meaning of νόθην is well expressed by *Chr.*, "alienam quandam a communi hominum natura nascendi rationem sibi excogitavit." Its usual meaning is "illegitimate."

[9] This is supposed to refer to Heb. i. 3, although a different Greek word is used.

[10] Various suggestions have been made regarding the dove which according to the literal rendering "flew from the ark of Noah." Christophorson (according to Valesius) supposes it to be that dove

which Noah formerly sent out of the ark, this dove being a figure of the Holy Spirit which was afterward to come in the Virgin. Jerome, *Ep. ad Oc.*, also regards the Noachic dove as a symbol of the Holy Spirit. Vales., followed by *1711* and *Bag.*, prefer to translate as if it were "like that," &c. This form of the story, according to which the Holy Spirit descends in the form of a dove, is according to Valesius from the Apochrypha; perhaps, he suggests, from the "Gospel to the Hebrews." In later art the dove is the constant symbol of the Holy Spirit, and is often found in pictures of the annunciation, e.g. in pictures by Simeone Memmi, Dürer, Andrea del Sarto, and many others. It is found in six of the pictures of the annunciation given by Mrs. Jameson (*Legends of the Madonna*, p. 165 sq.).

[11] The author seems to have here a reference to the Aristotelian distinction between prudence and wisdom (cf. *Ethics*, 6. 3; 7. 8, &c.). It reminds of that passage (vi. 7, ed. Grant ad. ii. 165-166), where the two are distinguished and defined, wisdom being "concerned with the immutable, and prudence with the variable"; and a little farther along wisdom is distinguished from "statesmanship," i.e. the "social" of *Bag.*, which is a form of "prudence" (tr. Williams, p. 160), and indeed (vi. 8. 1) generically identical with prudence. So again (1, 2) "political art" is identified with ethics.

[12] Social virtues or "political" virtues. Cf. the "political art" or "statesmanship" of Aristotle.

[13] [Πολλοῦ χρόνου, "for a considerable time." This seems to be a rhetorical addition to the circumstances of the miracle, scarcely to be justified by the terms of the inspired narrative.—*Bag.*]

[14] At this point Christophorson begins his chapter xii., "of those who did not know the mystery," &c.

[15] The translator takes most extraordinary liberties with the word "philanthropy"; now it is "loving-kindness," now "love of their

whose hearts inclined to thee to desire earnestly a divine and blessed life, and hast provided that, like merchants of true blessings, they might impart to many others the wisdom and good fortune they had received ; themselves, meanwhile, reaping the everlasting fruit of virtue. Freed from the trammels of vice, and imbued with the love of their fellow-men, they keep mercy ever before their eyes, and hoping for the promises of faith ; [16] devoted to modesty, and all those virtues which the past career of human life had thrown aside [but which were now restored by him whose providence is over all].[17] No other power could be found to devise a remedy for such evils, and for that spirit of injustice which had heretofore asserted its dominion over the race of men. Providence, however, could reach the circumstances even here, and with ease restored whatever had been disordered by violence and the licentiousness of human passion. And this restoring power he exercised without concealment. For he knew that, though there were some whose thoughts were able to recognize and understand his power, others there were whose brutish and senseless nature led them to rely exclusively on the testimony of their own senses. In open day, therefore, that no one, whether good or evil, might find room for doubt, he manifested his blessed and wondrous healing power ; restoring the dead to life again, and renewing with a word the powers of those who had been bereft of bodily sense.[18] Can we, in short, suppose, that to render the sea firm as the solid ground, to still the raging of the storm, and finally to ascend to heaven, after turning the unbelief of men to steadfast faith by the performance of these wondrous acts, demanded less than almighty power, was less than the work of God ? Nor was the time of his passion unaccompanied by like wonders : when the sun was darkened, and the shades of night obscured the light of day. Then terror everywhere laid hold upon the people, and the thought that the end of all things was already come, and that chaos, such as had been ere the order of creation began, would once more prevail. Then, too, the cause was sought of so terrible an evil, and in what respect the trespasses of men had provoked the wrath of Heaven ; until God himself, who surveyed with calm dignity the arrogance of the ungodly, renewed the face of heaven, and

adorned it with the host of stars. Thus the beclouded face of Nature was again restored to her pristine beauty.

CHAPTER XII.

Of those who are Ignorant of this Mystery ; and that their Ignorance is Voluntary. The Blessings which await those who know it, especially such as die in the Confession of the Faith.[1]

BUT it will be said by some, who love to blaspheme, that it was in the power of God to ameliorate and soften the natural will of man. What better way, I ask, what better method could be devised, what more effectual effort put forth for reclaiming evil man, than converse with God himself? Was not he visibly present to teach them the principles of virtuous conduct? And if the personal instructions of God were without effect, how much more, had he continued absent and unheard? What, then, had power to hinder this most blessed doctrine? The perverse folly of man. For the clearness of our perceptions is at once obscured, as often as we receive with angry impatience those precepts which are given for our blessing and advantage. In truth, it was the very choice of men to disregard these precepts, and to turn a deaf ear to the commandments so distasteful to them ; though had they listened, they would have gained a reward well worthy such attention, and that not for the present only, but the future life, which is indeed the only true life. For the reward of obedience to God is imperishable and everlasting life, to which they may aspire who know him,[2] and frame their course of life so as to afford a pattern to others, and as it were a perpetual standard for the imitation of those who desire to excel in virtue. Therefore was the doctrine committed to men of understanding, that the truths which they communicated might be kept with care and a pure conscience by the members of their households, and that thus a truthful and steadfast observance of God's commands might be secured, the fruit of which is that boldness in the prospect of death which springs from pure faith and genuine holiness before God. He who is thus armed can withstand the tempest of the world, and is sustained even to martyrdom by the invincible power of God, whereby he boldly overcomes the greatest terrors, and is accounted worthy of a crown of glory by him to whom he has thus nobly testi-

---

fellow-men," and so on in picturesque variety, and yet as appropriate as it is lacking in uniformity.
[16] Cf. Rom. viii. 25 ; Gal. v. 5.
[17] [The text, in the last clause of this passage, is undoubtedly corrupt. The above is an attempt to supply a probable sense. — *Bag.*] This is omitted by *Hein.* from his text.
[18] i.e. healing the paralytics. This paraphrased passage reads more literally, " bidding those bereft of sense [i.e. sensation, feeling] to feel again." Still it may be that *Molz.* is right in thinking it refers to the senses — seeing, hearing, &c. — as well as feeling, though his translation will hardly stand ; " and to such as lacked any of the senses he granted the full use of all their senses again."

[1] Literally and better, " through the confession." It refers to those who are technically known as confessors. Although in general the distinction prevails by which those who have suffered, but not unto death, are called " confessors," while those who lost their lives are called " martyrs " (cf. Pseud-Cypr. *de dupl. Mart.* c. 31), yet its use for martyrs is not uncommon (cf. Ambrose, *ad Gratian,* c. 2). Later the term was used of all, especially faithful professors of Christ. [2] Cf. John xvii. 3 ; 1 John v. 19–20.

fied.[3] Nor does he himself assume the praise, knowing full well that it is God who gives the power both to endure, and to fulfill with ready zeal the Divine commands. And well may such a course as this receive the meed of never-failing remembrance and everlasting honor. For as the martyr's life is one of sobriety and obedience to the will of God, so is his death an example of true greatness and generous fortitude of soul. Hence it is followed by hymns and psalms, words and songs of praise to the all-seeing God : and a sacrifice of thanksgiving is offered in memory of such men, a bloodless, a harmless sacrifice, wherein is no need of the fragrant frankincense, no need of fire ; but only enough of pure light[4] to suffice the assembled worshipers. Many, too, there are whose charitable spirit leads them to prepare a temperate banquet for the comfort of the needy, and the relief of those who had been driven from their homes : a custom which can only be deemed burdensome[5] by those whose thoughts are not accordant with the divine and sacred doctrine.

CHAPTER XIII.

That there is a Necessary Difference between Created Things. That the Propensity to Good and Evil depends on the Will of Man ; and that, consequently, Judgment is a Necessary and Reasonable Thing.

THERE are, indeed, some who venture with childish presumption to find fault with God in respect of this also, and ask why it is that he has not created one and the same natural disposition for all, but rather has ordained the existence of many things different, nay, contrary in their nature, whence arises the dissimilarity of our moral conduct and character. Would it not (say they) have been better, both as regards obedience to the commands of God, and a just apprehension of himself, and for the confirmation of individual faith, that all mankind should be of the same moral character? It is indeed ridiculous to expect that this could be the case, and to forget that the constitution of the world is different from that of the things that are in the world ; that physical and moral objects are not identical in their nature, nor the affections of the body the same as those of the soul. [For the immortal soul far exceeds the material world

in dignity, and is more blessed than the perishable and terrestrial creation, in proportion as it is noble and more allied to God.[1]] Nor is the human race excluded from participation in the divine goodness ; though this is not the lot of all indiscriminately, but of those only who search deeply into the Divine nature, and propose the knowledge of sacred things as the leading object of their lives.

CHAPTER XIV.

That Created Nature differs infinitely from Uncreated Being ; to which Man makes the Nearest Approach by a Life of Virtue.

SURELY it must be the very height of folly to compare created with eternal things, which latter have neither beginning nor end, while the former, having been originated and called into being, and having received a commencement of their existence at some definite time, must consequently, of necessity have an end. How then can things which have thus been made, bear comparison with him who has ordained their being? Were this the case,[1] the power to command their existence could not rightly be attributed to him. Nor can celestial things be compared to him, any more than the material[2] with the intellectual[3] world, or copies with the models from which they are formed. Nay, is it not absurd thus to confound all things, and to obscure the honor of God by comparing him with men, or even with beasts? And is it not characteristic of madmen, utterly estranged from a life of sobriety and virtue, to affect a power equivalent to that of God? If indeed we in any sense aspire to blessedness like that of God, our duty is to lead a life according to his commandments : so shall we, having finished a course consistent with the laws which he has prescribed, dwell for ever superior to the power of fate, in eternal and undecaying mansions. For the only power in man which can be elevated to a comparison with that of God, is sincere and guileless service and devotion of heart to himself, with the contemplation and study of whatever pleases him, the raising our affections above the things of earth, and directing our thoughts, as far as we may, to high and heavenly objects : for from such endeavors, it is said, a victory accrues to us more valuable than

---

[3] This translation " to whom " accords with the reading of Valesius, followed by *1611, Mols.*, " *Zimmermann,*" *Cous.* (" whose cause he has sustained "), but *Hein.* adopts the reading " who," preceded by *Chr.*, who translates " who himself bravely endured martyrdom."

[4] [Alluding to the tapers, &c., lighted at the tombs of martyrs on the anniversary of their death. — *Bag.*] Compare Scudamore, *Lights, The Ceremonial Use of,* in Smith and Cheetham, *Dict.* i (1880), 993 sq.

[5] " Vulgar."

[1] [The text of this passage is defective. The conjectural restoration of Valesius, which seems probable, is chiefly followed. — *Bag.*] Heinichen, like Christophorson and Savil before him, " does not hesitate," with one of the MSS., to omit this passage.

[1] This is following with Heinichen, and meets the conjecture of Valesius as over against the MSS. and other conjectures, which, substituting μανία for ὅμοια, read " for if it be madness to liken these things to him," &c.

[2] Or " sensible " ; i.e. world of sense or perception.

[3] This is the word often rendered by *Bag.* as " spiritual."

many blessings.[4] The cause, then, of that difference which subsists, as regards the inequality both of dignity and power in created beings, is such as I have described. In this the wise acquiesce with abundant thankfulness and joy: while those who are dissatisfied, display their own folly, and their arrogance will reap its due reward.

CHAPTER XV.

Of the Saviour's Doctrines and Miracles; and the Benefits he confers on those who own Subjection to him.

THE Son of God invites all men to the practice of virtue, and presents himself to all who have understanding hearts, as the teacher of his saving precepts.[1] Unless, indeed, we will deceive ourselves, and remain in wretched ignorance of the fact, that for our advantage, that is, to secure the blessing of the human race, he went about upon earth; and, having called around him the best men of their age, committed to them instructions full of profit, and of power to preserve them in the path of a virtuous life; teaching them the faith and righteousness which are the true remedy against the adverse power of that malignant spirit whose delight it is to ensnare and delude the inexperienced. Accordingly he visited the sick, relieved the infirm from the ills which afflicted them, and consoled those who felt the extremity of penury and want. He commended also sound and rational sobriety of character, enjoining his followers to endure, with dignity and patience, every kind of injury and contempt; teaching them to regard such as visitations permitted by their Father, and the victory is ever theirs who nobly bear the evils which befall them. For he assured them that the highest strength of all consisted in this steadfastness of soul, combined with that philosophy which is nothing else than the knowledge of truth and goodness, producing in men the generous habit of sharing with their poorer brethren those riches which they have themselves acquired by honorable means. At the same time he utterly forbade all proud oppression, declaring that, as he had come to associate with the lowly, so those who despised the lowly would be excluded from his favor. Such and so great was the test whereby he proved the faith of those who owned allegiance to his authority, and thus he not only prepared them for the contempt of danger and

terror, but taught them at the same time the most genuine confidence in himself. Once, too, his rebuke was uttered to restrain the zeal of one of his companions, who yielded too easily to the impulse of passion, when he assaulted with the sword, and, eager to protect his Saviour's life, exposed his own. Then it was that he bade him desist, and returned his sword to its sheath, reproving him for his distrust of refuge and safety in himself, and declaring solemnly that all who should essay to retaliate an injury by like aggression, or use the sword, should perish by a violent death.[2] This is indeed heavenly wisdom, to choose rather to endure than to inflict injury, and to be ready, should necessity so require, to suffer, but not to do, wrong. For since injurious conduct is in itself a most serious evil, it is not the injured party, but the injuring, on whom the heaviest punishment must fall. It is indeed possible for one who is subject to the will of God to avoid the evil both of committing and of suffering injury, provided his confidence be firm in the protection of that God whose aid is ever present to shield his servants from harm. For how should that man who trusts in God attempt to seek for resources in himself? In such a case he must abide the conflict with uncertainty of victory: and no man of understanding could prefer a doubtful to a certain issue. Again, how can that man doubt the presence and aid of God, who has had experience of manifold dangers, and has at all times been easily delivered, at his simple nod, from all terrors: who has passed, as it were, through the sea which was leveled by the Saviour's word, and afforded a solid road for the passage of the people? This is, I believe, the sure basis of faith, the true foundation of confidence, that we find such miracles as these performed and perfected at the command of the God of Providence. Hence it is that even in the midst of trial we find no cause to repent of our faith, but retain an unshaken hope in God; and when this habit of confidence is established in the soul, God himself dwells in the inmost thoughts. But he is of invincible power: the soul, therefore, which has within it him who is thus invincible, will not be overcome by the perils which may surround it. Likewise,[3] we learn this truth from the victory of God himself, who, while intent on providing for the blessing of mankind, though grievously insulted by the malice of the ungodly, yet passed unharmed through the sufferings of his passion, and gained a mighty conquest, an everlasting crown of triumph, over all

---

[4] This is supposed to refer to Rev. ii. 7–10; iii. 11, &c. It might well have in mind Col. iii. 2–4, or best of all Rev. xxi. 7, as containing the thought of victory (νικάω = " overcome ").

[1] This accords with the " margin of the Geneva Edition," and mentioned by Valesius, who gives also " in the Saviour's commands " and " in the Father's commands," which latter is adopted by Heinichen.

[2] Matt. xxvi. 52; for " all they that take the sword shall perish by the sword." Note the characteristic inflation of style. Matthew takes eight words, the English translators twelve, Constantine sixteen, and his translator twenty-two ponderous words.

[3] Val. prefers πρὸς (" besides ") to παρὰ (" likewise, at the same time "), and is followed by *Bag.*

iniquity; thus accomplishing the purpose of his own providence and love as regards the just, and destroying the cruelty of the impious and unjust.

CHAPTER XVI.

The Coming of Christ was predicted by the Prophets; and was ordained to be the Overthrow of Idols and Idolatrous Cities.

LONG since had his passion, as well as his advent in the flesh, been predicted by the prophets. The time, too, of his incarnation had been foretold, and the manner in which the fruits of iniquity and profligacy, so ruinous to the works and ways of righteousness, should be destroyed, and the whole world partake of the virtues of wisdom and sound discretion, through the almost universal prevalence of those principles of conduct which the Saviour should promulgate, over the minds of men; whereby the worship of God should be confirmed, and the rites of superstition utterly abolished. By these not the slaughter of animals alone, but the sacrifice of human victims, and the pollutions of an accursed worship, had been devised : as, for example, by the laws of Assyria and Egypt, the lives of innocent men were offered up in images of brass or earth. Therefore have these nations received a recompense worthy so foul a worship. Memphis and Babylon [it was declared][1] shall be wasted, and left desolate with their fathers' gods. Now these things I speak not from the report of others, but having myself been present, and actually seen the most wretched of these cities, the unfortunate Memphis.[2] Moses desolated, at the Divine command, the land of the once mighty Pharaoh, whose arrogance was his destruction,[3] and destroyed his army (which had proved victorious over numerous and mighty nations, an army strong in defenses and in arms), not by the flight of arrows or the hurling of hostile weapons, but by holy prayer alone, and quiet supplication.

CHAPTER XVII.

Of the Wisdom of Moses, which was an Object of Imitation to the Wise among Heathen Nations. Also concerning Daniel, and the Three Children.

No nation has ever been more highly blessed than that which Moses led : none would have continued to enjoy higher blessings, had they not willingly withdrawn themselves from the guidance of the Holy Spirit. But who can worthily describe the praises of Moses himself; who, after reducing to order an unruly nation, and disciplining their minds[1] to habits of obedience and respect, out of captivity restored them to a state of freedom, turned their mourning into gladness, and so far elevated their minds,[1] that, through the excess of contrast with their former circumstances, and the abundance of their prosperity, the spirit of the people was elated with haughtiness and pride? So far did he surpass in wisdom those who had lived before him, that even the wise men and philosophers[2] who are extolled by heathen nations aspired to imitate his wisdom. For Pythagoras, following his wisdom, attained to such a pitch of self-control, that he became to Plato, himself a model of discretion, the standard of his own self-mastery. Again, how great and terrible the cruelty of that ancient Syrian king, over whom Daniel triumphed, the prophet who unfolded the secrets of futurity, whose actions evinced transcendent greatness of soul, and the luster of whose character and life shone conspicuous above all? The name of this tyrant was Nebuchadnezzar, whose race afterward became extinct, and his vast and mighty power was transferred to Persian hands. The wealth of this tyrant was then, and is even now, celebrated far and wide, as well as his ill-timed devotion to unlawful worship, his idol statues, lifting their heads to heaven, and formed of various metals, and the terrible and savage laws ordained to uphold this worship. These terrors Daniel, sustained by genuine piety towards the true God, utterly despised, and predicted that the tyrant's unseasonable zeal would be productive of fearful evil to himself. He failed, however, to convince the tyrant (for excessive wealth is an effectual barrier to true soundness of judgment), and at length the monarch displayed the savage cruelty of his character, by commanding that the righteous prophet should be exposed to the fury of wild beasts. Noble, too, indeed was the united spirit exhibited by those brethren[3] (whose example others have since followed, and

---

[1] Not in text. This parenthesis is the least obnoxious of various proposed paraphrases.
[2] Probably refers to its destruction by Diocletian, whom Constantine accompanied. See Prolegomena, *Life, Early Years.*
[3] The text of this passage is most dubious. *Bag.,* following Valesius, translates: "And an actual witness of the wretched fate which has befallen these cities. Memphis lies desolate; that city which was the pride of the once mighty Pharaoh whose power Moses crushed at the Divine command." This has been changed to accord with the text and punctuation of Heinichen. The change makes Constantine declare himself an eye-witness of the fate of Memphis alone, which is thought to accord with the facts; for while he was in fact in Egypt with Diocletian, there is no evidence that he ever saw Babylon. And yet it is possible he did.
[1] "Souls."
[2] The sage commentators on this passage have thought it incumbent to explain and, as it were, apologize for the apparent tautology, "wise men or philosophers, — whichever you choose to call them" (*Val.* and *Hein.*). Colloquially speaking, there is a vast difference between being a philosopher and being a wise man. Probably this is no slip of style nor gracious option of language such as the editors impute, but some more or less clear distinction of technical terms.
[3] "Spirit exhibited by these brethren in suffering martyrdom."

have won surpassing glory by their faith in the Saviour's name),[4] those, I mean, who stood unharmed in the fiery furnace, and the terrors appointed to devour them, repelling by the holy touch of their bodies the flame by which they were surrounded. On the overthrow of the Assyrian Empire, which was destroyed by thunderbolts from Heaven,[5] the providence of God conducted Daniel to the court of Cambyses the Persian king. Yet envy followed him even here ; nor envy only, but the deadly plots of the magians against his life, with a succession of many and urgent dangers, from all which he was easily delivered by the providential care of Christ,[6] and shone conspicuous in the practice of every virtue. Three times in the day did he present his prayers to God, and memorable were the proofs of supernatural power which he displayed : and hence the magians, filled with envy at the very efficacy of his petitions, represented the possession of such power to the king as fraught with danger, and prevailed on him to adjudge this distinguished benefactor of the Persian people to be devoured by savage lions. Daniel, therefore, thus condemned, was consigned to the lions' den (not indeed to suffer death, but to win unfading glory) ; and though surrounded by these ferocious beasts of prey, he found them more gentle than the men who had enclosed him there. Supported by the power of calm and steadfast prayer, he was enabled to subdue all these animals, ferocious as, by nature, they were. Cambyses, on learning the event (for so mighty a proof of Divine power could not possibly be concealed), amazed at the marvelous story, and repenting the too easy credence he had given to the slanderous charges of the magians, resolved, notwithstanding, to be himself a witness of the spectacle. But when he saw the prophet with uplifted hands rendering praises to Christ, and the lions crouching, and as it were worshiping, at his feet, immediately he adjudged the magians, to whose persuasions he had listened, to perish by the self-same sentence, and shut them up in the lions' den.[7] The beasts, erewhile so gentle, rushed at once upon their victims, and with all the fierceness of their nature tore and destroyed them all.[8]

---

[4] *Molz.* remarks that to get any intelligent meaning out of this mass of sounding words, the translator often has to guess and translate very freely.

[5] ['Αναιρεθείσης κεραυνῶν βολαῖς. This must be regarded as a *rhetorical* rather than *historical* allusion to the extinction of the Assyrian Empire. The critical reader will not fail to mark occasional instances of inaccuracy and looseness of statement in this chapter, and generally in the course of the oration. — *Bag.*] Valesius objects to this passage as follows in the language of *1711:* "Neither do I well understand that. For Men, Towns, and Cities may be destroyed by Thunder-bolts, . . . But, truly I can't see how a kingdom could be ruined by Thunder."

[6] Constantine evidently believed in an eternal Christ.

[7] "He adjudged to perish by the self-same sentence, and shut them up in the lions' den," is bracketed by Valesius and the second clause omitted by *Bag.*

CHAPTER XVIII.

Of the Erythræan Sibyl, who pointed in a Prophetic Acrostic at our Lord and his Passion. The Acrostic is "Jesus Christ, Son of God, Saviour, Cross."

My desire, however, is to derive even from foreign sources a testimony to the Divine nature of Christ. For on such testimony it is evident that even those who blaspheme his name must acknowledge that he is God, and the Son of God if indeed they will accredit the words of those whose sentiments coincided with their own.[1] The Erythræan Sibyl, then, who herself assures us that she lived in the sixth generation after the flood, was a priestess of Apollo, who wore the sacred fillet in imitation of the God she served, who guarded also the tripod encompassed with the serpent's folds, and returned prophetic answers to those who approached her shrine ; having been devoted by the folly of her parents to this service, a service productive of nothing good or noble, but only of indecent fury, such as we find recorded in the case of Daphne.[2] On one occasion, however, having rushed into the sanctuary of her vain superstition, she became really filled with inspiration from above, and declared in prophetic verses the future purposes of God ; plainly indicating the advent of Jesus by the initial letters of these verses, forming an acrostic in these words : JESUS CHRIST, SON OF GOD, SAVIOUR, CROSS. The verses themselves are as follows :

Judgment ! Earth's oozing pores[3] shall mark the day;
Earth's heavenly king his glories shall display:
Sovereign of all, exalted on his throne,
Unnumbered multitudes their God shall own;
Shall see their Judge, with mingled joy and fear,
Crowned with his saints, in human form appear.
How vain, while desolate earth's glories lie,
Riches, and pomp, and man's idolatry !
In that dread hour, when Nature's fiery doom
Startles the slumb'ring tenants of the tomb,
Trembling all flesh shall stand; each secret wile,
Sins long forgotten, thoughts of guilt and guile,
Open beneath God's searching light shall lie :
No refuge then, but hopeless agony.
O'er heaven's expanse shall gathering shades of night
From earth, sun, stars, and moon, withdraw their light;
God's arm shall crush each mountain's towering pride;
On ocean's plain no more shall navies ride.
Dried at the source, no river's rushing sound
Shall soothe, no fountain slake the parched ground.
Around, afar, shall roll the trumpet's blast,
Voice of wrath long delayed, revealed at last.
In speechless awe, while earth's foundations groan,
On judgment's seat earth's kings their God shall own.

---

[8] "Eliminated them all." Valesius calls attention to the characteristic slight inaccuracies of our author! e.g. in the Biblical account (1) it was not the magi; (2) it was not Cambyses.

[1] "Of their own selves."

[2] [Daughter of Tiresias, and priestess at Delphi. She was called Sibyl, on account of the wildness of her looks and expressions when she delivered oracles (Lempriere in voc.). — *Bag.*]

[3] ['Ιδρώσει γὰρ χθὼν, κ.τ.λ. — *Bag.*]

Uplifted then, in majesty divine,
Radiant with light, behold Salvation's Sign!
Cross of that Lord, who, once for sinners given,
Reviled by man, now owned by earth and heaven,
O'er every land extends his iron sway.
Such is the name these mystic lines display;
Saviour, eternal king, who bears our sins away.[4]

It is evident that the virgin uttered these verses under the influence of Divine inspiration. And I cannot but esteem her blessed, whom the Saviour thus selected to unfold his gracious purpose towards us.

CHAPTER XIX.

That this Prophecy respecting our Saviour was not the Fiction of any Member of the Christian Church, but the Testimony of the Erythræan Sibyl, whose Books were translated into Latin by Cicero before the coming of Christ. Also that Virgil makes mention of the same, and of the Birth of the Virgin's Child: though he spoke obscurely of this Mystery from Fear of the Ruling Powers.

---

[4] [It can scarcely be necessary to observe that the acrostic, the general sense of which has been aimed at in the above translation, must be regarded as the pious fiction of some writer, whose object was to recommend the truth of Christianity to heathens by an appeal to the authority of an (alleged) ancient heathen prophecy. — *Bag.*] The quotation is found in the edition of Alexandre, Bk. VIII. ch. 219-250. (Cf. translation in Augustin, *De civ. Dei.*) The translation of *Bag.*, giving the "general sense" and reproducing the acrostic, stands unchanged. The translation of 1709, much more vigorous and suggestive of the "Dies Iræ," is as follows:

"When the Great Day of Judgment shall appear,
  The melting Earth shall then dissolve with fear;
A King Immortal shall from Heav'n descend,
  At whose Tribunal the whole world attend.
Both Just and Wicked shall, when Time grows old,
  Their mighty God in flesh array'd behold;
Armies of Saints on His Right hand shall come,
  Whilst Humane Souls expect their final doom.
Th' Universe shall be a dry, Barren Strand,
  And Thorns shall flourish on the scorched land;
Men shall with indignation cast away
  Their Wealth and Idols in that dreadful day.
The parching Earth, and Heaven in flames shall fry,
  And searching fire drain the Ocean dry:
All flesh which in the Grave imprison'd lay,
  Shake off their Fetters, and return to Day.
Fire 'twixt Good and Bad shall diff'rence make,
  And filthy Dross from purer Metal take.
Man's secret Deeds shall all be open lay'd,
  And th' obscure Mazes of their Hearts displayed;
Gnashing their Teeth, they shall their Fate bewail:
  The stars harmonious daunce, and th' Sun shall fail.
The Orbs roll'd up, shrink into darkest night,
  The Labouring Moon shall lose her borrowed light.
Mountains with Plains on the same Level lye;
  Vallies shall gape no more, nor Hills be high.
On the proud Billows Ships shall ride no more:
  And Lightning the Earth's Face shall shrivel sore.
The crackling Rivers with fierce Fire shall burn,
  Which shall their streams to solid Crystal turn.
The Heav'nly Trump shall blow a doleful sound,
  And th' world's destruction, and its sin resound.
The yawning Earth Hell's vast Abyss shall shew;
  All Kings before God's just Tribunal go.
Then Liquid Sulphur from the Sky shall stream,
  God shall pour down Rivers of vengeful flame;
All men shall then the Glorious Cross descry,
  That wished-for sign unto a faithful eye:
The Life of pious Souls, their chief delight;
  To Sinners an Offence, a dismal sight!
Enlightening the called with its beams,
  When cleansed from sin in twice six limpid streams.
His Empire shall be boundless, and that God
  Shall Rule the Wicked with an Iron Rod;
This God, Immortal King, describ'd in Verse,
  Our Saviour, dying, shall man's doom Reverse."

MANY, however, who admit that the Erythræan Sibyl was really a prophetess, yet refuse to credit this prediction, and imagine that some one professing our faith, and not unacquainted with the poetic art, was the composer of these verses. They hold, in short, that they are a forgery, and alleged to be the prophecies of the Sibyl on the ground of their containing useful moral sentiments, tending to restrain licentiousness, and to lead man to a life of sobriety and decorum. Truth, however, in this case is evident, since the diligence of our countrymen[1] has made a careful computation of the times; so that there is no room to suspect that this poem was composed after the advent and condemnation of Christ, or that the general report is false, that the verses were a prediction of the Sibyl in an early age. For it is allowed that Cicero was acquainted with this poem, which he translated into the Latin tongue, and incorporated with his own works.[2] This writer was put to death during the ascendancy of Antony, who in his turn was conquered by Augustus, whose reign lasted fifty-six years. Tiberius succeeded, in whose age it was that the Saviour's advent enlightened the world, the mystery of our most holy religion began to prevail, and as it were a new race of men commenced: of which, I suppose, the prince of Latin poets thus speaks:

Behold, a new, a heaven-born race appears.[3]

And again, in another passage of the Bucolics:

Sicilian Muses, sound a loftier strain.

What can be clearer than this? For he adds,

The voice of Cuma's oracle is heard again.[4]

Evidently referring to the Cumæan Sibyl. Nor was even this enough: the poet goes further, as if irresistibly impelled to bear his testimony. What then does he say?

Behold! the circling years new blessings bring:
The virgin comes, with her the long-desired king.[5]

---

[1] "Our men," i.e. Christians rather than "countrymen."
[2] [The passage in Cicero (*De Divinatione*, Bk. II. ch. 54) clearly does not refer to *this* acrostic, and contains in itself a plain denial of prophetic truth in the Sibylline prediction (whatever it was) which the writer had in view. "Non esse autem illud carmen furentis, cum ipsum poema declaret (est enim magis artis et diligentiæ, quam incitationis et motus), tum verò ea, quæ ἀκροστιχίς dicitur, cum deinceps ex primis versuum litteris aliquid connectitur, ut in quibusdam Cumanis, id certe magis est attenti animi, quam furentis," &c. — *Bag.*]
[3] This and following quotations are found in the fourth eclogue of Virgil — the *Pollio*. The version of *Bag.* is allowed to stand. If farther variety of rendering and interpretation is desired, it can be found in charming profusion in the various English translations of Virgil of which the few at hand give ample promise. Those at hand are Ogilby, Lond., 1675, p. 41-49; Warton, Lond., 1763, p. 76-82; Trapp, Lond., 1755, p. 37-46; Kennedy, Lond., 1849, p. 25-29; Wilstach, Bost., 1884, p. 154-161; Bowen, Lond., 1887, p. 24-28. Compare Henley, *Observations on the Subject of the Fourth Eclogue*, etc., Lond., 1788. 8vo.
[4] Here is variety indeed. *1711* renders, "Last times are come Cumæa's prophecy," — whatever that may mean. *Molz.* has "Now the voice of the famed oracle of Cumæ is dumb."
[5] Constantine takes large liberty with the poet here in order to

Who, then, is the virgin who was to come? Is it not she who was filled with, and with child of, the Holy Spirit? And why is it impossible that she who was with child of the Holy Spirit should be, and ever continue to be a virgin? This king, too, will return, and by his coming lighten the sorrows of the world. The poet adds,

> Thou, chaste Lucina, greet the new-born child,
> Beneath whose reign the iron offspring ends,
> A golden progeny from heaven descends;
> His kingdom banished virtue shall restore,
> And crime shall threat the guilty world no more.

We perceive that these words are spoken plainly and at the same time darkly, by way of allegory. Those who search deeply for the import of the words, are able to discern the Divinity of Christ. But lest any of the powerful in the imperial city might be able to accuse the poet of writing anything contrary to the laws of the country, and subverting the religious sentiments which had prevailed from ancient times, he intentionally obscures the truth. For he was acquainted, as I believe, with that blessed mystery which gave to our Lord the name of Saviour : [6] but, that he might avoid the severity of cruel men, he drew the thoughts of his hearers to objects with which they were familiar, saying that altars must be erected, temples raised, and sacrifices offered to the new-born child. His concluding words also are adapted to the sentiments of those who were accustomed to such a creed ; for he says :

CHAPTER XX.

A Farther Quotation from Virgilius Maro respecting Christ, with its Interpretation, showing that the Mystery was indicated therein darkly, as might be expected from a Poet.

> A life immortal he shall lead, and be
> By heroes seen, himself shall heroes see;

evidently meaning the righteous.

> The jarring nations he in peace shall bind,
> And with paternal virtues rule mankind.
> Unbidden earth her earliest fruits shall bring,
> And fragrant herbs, to greet her infant king.

Well indeed was this admirably wise and accomplished man acquainted with the cruel character of the times. He proceeds :

> The goats, uncall'd, full udders home shall bear;
> The lowing herds no more fierce lions fear.

Truly said : for faith will not stand in awe of the mighty in the imperial palace.

> His cradle shall with rising flowers be crown'd :
> The serpent's brood shall die; the sacred ground
> Shall weeds and poisonous plants refuse to bear;
> Each common bush th' Assyrian rose [1] shall wear.

Nothing could be said more true or more consistent with the Saviour's excellency than this. For the power of the Divine Spirit presents the very cradle of God, like fragrant flowers, to the new-born race.[2] The serpent, too, and the venom of that serpent, perishes, who originally beguiled our first parents, and drew their thoughts from their native innocence [3] to the enjoyment of pleasures, that they might experience [4] that threatened death. For before the Saviour's advent, the serpent's power was shown in subverting the souls of those who were sustained by no well-grounded hope, and ignorant of that immortality which awaits the righteous. But after that he had suffered, and was separated for a season from the body which he had assumed, the power of the resurrection was revealed to man through the communication of the Holy Spirit : and whatever stain of human guilt might yet remain was removed by the washing of sacred lustrations.

Then indeed could the Saviour bid his followers be of good cheer, and, remembering his adorable and glorious resurrection, expect the like for themselves. Truly, then, the poisonous race may be said to be extinct. Death himself is extinct, and the truth of the resurrection sealed. Again, the Assyrian race is gone, which first led the way to faith in God.[5] But when he speaks of the growth of amomum every where, he alludes to the multitude of the true worshipers of God.[6] For it is as though a multitude of branches, crowned with fragrant flowers, and fitly watered, sprung from the self-same root. Most justly said, Maro, thou wisest of poets ! and with this all that follows is consistent.

> But when heroic worth his youth shall hear,
> And learn his father's virtues to revere.

By the praises of heroes, he indicates the works of righteous men : by the virtues of his Father he speaks of the creation and everlasting structure of the world : and, it may be, of those laws by which God's beloved Church is guided, and ordered in a course of righteousness and virtue. Admirable, again, is the advance to higher

---

make him say what he would like to have had him say. The latest translation at hand (Bowen) renders:

"Now is the world's grand cycle begun once more from of old;
Justice the Virgin comes, and the Saturn Kingdom again."

[6] "The blessed and salutary mystery of our Saviour." — *1709.*
"Mystery of salvation." — *Molz.*

[1] [Amomum. — *Bag.*] "Assyrian cinnamon," Kennedy, p. 28; "the cardamon's spice shall grow, That from Assyria's gardens," Wilstach, I, p. 157; "Syrian spices," Trapp, I, p. 92; "Assyria's rich perfume," Warton, I, p. 78; "Assyrian roses," Ogilby, p. 42.
[2] [i.e. the Christians. — *Bag.*]
[3] Self-control.
[4] "Might *not* experience," according to some, including Heinichen, who rejects in first, but accepts in text of his *second* edition.
[5] [Referring, apparently, to Abraham. This passage is founded on a misconstruction of Virgil's line by Constantine, which is followed by the Greek verse itself according to one edition. — *Bag.*]
[6] [By a kind of play on the word amomum, he alludes to the Christians as ἄμωμοι, or blameless persons. — *Bag.*]

things of that state of life which is intermediate, as it were, between good and evil, and which seldom admits a sudden change:

Unlabored harvests shall the fields adorn,[7]

that is, the fruit of the Divine law springs up for the service of men.

And clustered grapes shall blush on every thorn.

Far otherwise has it been during the corrupt and lawless period of human life.

The knotted oaks shall showers of honey weep.[8]

He here describes the folly and obduracy of the men of that age; and perhaps he also intimates that they who suffer hardships in the cause of God, shall reap sweet fruits of their own endurance.

Yet, of old fraud some footsteps shall remain;
The merchant still shall plough the deep for gain:
Great cities shall with walls be compassed round,
And sharpened shares shall vex the fruitful ground:
Another Tiphys shall new seas explore,
Another Argo land the chiefs upon the Iberian shore;
Another Helen other wars create,
And great Achilles urge the Trojan fate.

Well said, wisest of bards! Thou hast carried the license of a poet precisely to the proper point. For it was not thy purpose to assume the functions of a prophet, to which thou hadst no claim. I suppose also he was restrained by a sense of the danger which threatened one who should assail the credit of ancient religious practice. Cautiously, therefore, and securely, as far as possible, he presents the truth to those who have faculties to understand it; and while he denounces the munitions and conflicts of war[9] (which indeed are still to be found in the course of human life), he describes our Saviour as proceeding to the war against Troy, understanding by Troy the world itself.[10] And surely he did maintain the struggle against the opposing powers of evil, sent on that mission both by the designs of his own providence and the commandment of his Almighty Father. How, then, does the poet proceed?

But when to ripen'd manhood he shall grow,

that is, when, having arrived at the age of manhood, he shall utterly remove the evils which

encompass the path of human life, and tranquilize the world by the blessings of peace:

The greedy sailor shall the seas forego;
No keel shall cut the waves for foreign ware,
For every soil shall every product bear.
The laboring hind his oxen shall disjoin;
No plough shall hurt the glebe, no pruning-hook the vine;
Nor wool shall in dissembled colors shine:
But the luxurious father of the fold,
With native purple, and unborrow'd gold,
Beneath his pompous fleece shall proudly sweat;
And under Tyrian robes the lamb shall bleat.
Mature in years, to ready honors move,
O of celestial seed, O foster son of Jove!
See, laboring nature calls thee to sustain
The nodding frame of heaven, and earth, and main!
See to their base restored, earth, seas, and air;
And joyful ages, from behind, in crowding ranks appear.
To sing thy praise, would heaven my breath prolong,
Infusing spirits worthy such a song,
Not Thracian Orpheus should transcend my lays,
Nor Linus, crown'd with never-fading bays;
Though each his heavenly parent should inspire;
The Muse instruct the voice, and Phœbus tune the lyre.
Should Pan contend in verse, and thou my theme,
Arcadian judges should their God condemn.[11]

Behold (says he) how the mighty world and the elements together manifest their joy.

CHAPTER XXI.

That these Things cannot have been spoken of a Mere Man: and that Unbelievers, owing to their Ignorance of Religion, know not even the Origin of their own Existence.

IT may be some will foolishly suppose that these words were spoken of the birth of a mere ordinary mortal. But if this were all, what reason could there be that the earth should need neither seed nor plough, that the vine should require no pruning-hook, or other means of culture? How can we suppose these things to be spoken of a mere mortal's birth? For nature is the minister of the Divine will, not an instrument obedient to the command of man. Indeed, the very joy of the elements indicates the advent of God, not the conception of a human being. The prayer, too, of the poet that his life might be prolonged is a proof of the Divinity of him whom he invoked; for we desire life and preservation from God, and not from man. Indeed, the Erythræan Sibyl thus appeals to God: "Why, O Lord, dost thou compel me still to foretell the future, and not rather remove me from this earth to await the blessed day of thy coming?" And Maro adds to what he had said before:

---

7 "The fields shall mellow wax with golden grain."
8 *Bag.* adds:
  "And through the matted grass the liquid gold shall creep."
1709 translates:
  "And th' hardened oaks with dewy honey sweat."
While *Molz.* has
  "Forth from the hard oak stems the lovely honey flows."
These all approach Virgil closer than they do Constantine. With all allowance for poetic license, "pine" should hardly be translated "oak."
9 Literally, "times and wars." — *1709*.
10 This, bad as it is, is hardly worse than the subjective interpretation of Scripture by modern allegorizers, and certainly no worse than some of the Scripture interpretations of Eusebius.

11 [The reader will perceive that the foregoing verses, with but little exception, and very slight alteration, are taken from Dryden's translation of the fourth eclogue of Virgil. — *Bag.*]

Begin, sweet boy! with smiles thy mother know,
Who ten long months did with thy burden go.
No mortal parents smiled upon thy birth:
No nuptial joy thou know'st, no feast of earth.

How could his parents have smiled on him? For his Father[1] is God, who is a Power without sensible quality,[2] existing, not in any definite shape, but as comprehending other beings,[3] and not, therefore, in a human body. And who knows not that the Holy Spirit has no participation in the nuptial union? For what desire can exist in the disposition of that good which all things else desire? What fellowship, in short, can wisdom hold with pleasure? But let these arguments be left to those who ascribe to him a human origin, and who care not to purify themselves from all evil in word as well as deed. On thee, Piety, I call to aid my words, on thee who art the very law of purity, most desirable of all blessings, teacher of holiest hope, assured promise of immortality! Thee, Piety, and thee, Clemency, I adore. We who have obtained thine aid[4] owe thee everlasting gratitude for thy healing power. But the multitudes whom their innate hatred of thyself deprives of thy succor, are equally estranged from God himself, and know not that the very cause of their life and being, and that of all the ungodly, is connected with the rightful worship of him who is Lord of all: for the world itself is his, and all that it contains.

CHAPTER XXII.

The Emperor thankfully ascribes his Victories and all other Blessings to Christ; and condemns the Conduct of the Tyrant Maximin, the Violence of whose Persecution had enhanced the Glory of Religion.

To thee, Piety, I ascribe the cause of my own prosperity, and of all that I now possess. To this truth the happy issue of all my endeavors bears testimony: brave deeds, victories in war, and triumphs over conquered foes. This truth the great city itself allows with joy and praise. The people, too, of that much-loved city accord in the same sentiment, though once, deceived by ill-grounded hopes, they chose a ruler unworthy of themselves,[1] a ruler who speedily received the chastisement which his audacious deeds deserved. But be it far from me now to recall the memory of these events, while holding converse with thee, Piety, and essaying with earnest endeavor to address thee with holy and gentle words. Yet will I say one thing, which haply shall not be unbefitting or unseemly. A furious, a cruel, and implacable war was maintained by the tyrants against thee, Piety, and thy holy churches: nor were there wanting some in Rome itself who exulted at a calamity so grievous to the public weal. Nay, the battle-field was prepared; when thou didst stand forth,[2] and present thyself a voluntary victim, supported by faith in God. Then indeed it was that the cruelty of ungodly men, which raged incessantly like a devouring fire, wrought for thee a wondrous and ever memorable glory. Astonishment seized the spectators themselves, when they beheld the very executioners who tortured the bodies of their holy victims wearied out, and disgusted at the cruelties;[3] the bonds loosened, the engines of torture powerless, the flames extinguished, while the sufferers preserved their constancy unshaken even for a moment. What, then, hast thou gained by these atrocious deeds, most impious of men?[4] And what was the cause of thy insane fury? Thou wilt say, doubtless, these acts of thine were done in honor of the gods. What gods are these? or what worthy conception hast thou of the Divine nature? Thinkest thou the gods are subject to angry passions as thou art? Were it so indeed, it had been better for thee to wonder at their strange determination than obey their harsh command, when they urged thee to the unrighteous slaughter of innocent men. Thou wilt allege, perhaps, the customs of thy ancestors, and the opinion of mankind in general, as the cause of this conduct. I grant the fact: for those customs are very like the acts themselves, and proceed from the self-same source of folly. Thou thoughtest, it may be, that some special power resided in images formed and fashioned by human art; and hence thy reverence, and diligent care lest they should be defiled: those mighty and highly exalted gods, thus dependent on the care of men!

CHAPTER XXIII.

Of Christian Conduct. That God is pleased with those who lead a Life of Virtue: and that we must expect a Judgment and Future Retribution.

COMPARE our religion with your own. Is

---

[1] "Father" is emendation of Valesius embodied in his translation (1659), but not his text (1659). It is bracketed by *Molz.* "His God [and Father]."
[2] "Pure force."
[3] In this form it sounds much like Pantheism, but in translation of *Molz.* this reads, "but determinable through the bounds of other [existences]."
[4] So Valesius conjectures it should read, but the text of *Val.* and *Hein.* read, "We needy ones owe," &c.
[1] [Maxentius (W. Lowth in loc.). — *Bag.*]

[2] This passage clearly refers to the voluntary sufferings of the martyrs. See the note of Valesius.
[3] "At a loss to invent fresh cruelties," *Bag.*; "And perplexed at the labor and trouble they met with," *1709*; "And reluctantly pursuing their terrible work," *Molz.*
[4] Alluding to Maximin, the most bitter persecutor of the Christians, as appears from the title of this chapter.

there not with us genuine concord, and un-wearied love of others? If we reprove a fault, is not our object to admonish, not to destroy; our correction for safety, not for cruelty? Do we not exercise, not only sincere faith towards God, but fidelity in the relations of social life? Do we not pity the unfortunate? Is not ours a life of simplicity, which disdains to cover evil beneath the mask of fraud and hypocrisy? Do we not acknowledge the true God, and his un-divided sovereignty? This is real godliness: this is religion sincere and truly undefiled: this is the life of wisdom; and they who have it are travelers, as it were, on a noble road which leads to eternal life. For he who has entered on such a course, and keeps his soul pure from the pollutions of the body, does not wholly die: rather may he be said to complete the service appointed him by God, than to die. Again, he who confesses allegiance to God is not easily overborne by insolence or rage, but nobly stands under the pressure of necessity and the trial of his constancy is, as it were, a passport to the favor of God. For we cannot doubt that the Deity is pleased with excellence in human con-duct. For it would be absurd indeed if the powerful and the humble alike acknowledge gratitude to those from whose services they re-ceive benefit, and repay them by services in return, and yet that he who is supreme and sovereign of all, nay, who is Good itself, should be negligent in this respect. Rather does he follow us throughout the course of our lives, is near us in every act of goodness, accepts, and at once rewards our virtue and obedience; though he defers the full recompense to that future period, when the actions of our lives shall pass under his review, and when those who are clear in that account shall receive the reward of everlasting life, while the wicked shall be visited with the penalties due to their crimes.

CHAPTER XXIV.

Of Decius, Valerian, and Aurelian, who expe-rienced a Miserable End in consequence of their Persecution of the Church.

To thee, Decius,[1] I now appeal, who has trampled with insult on the labors of the right-eous: to thee, the hater of the Church, the punisher of those who lived a holy life: what is now thy condition after death? How hard and wretched thy present circumstances! Nay, the interval before thy death gave proof enough of thy miserable fate, when, overthrown with all thine army on the plains of Scythia, thou didst

expose the vaunted power of Rome to the con-tempt of the Goths. Thou, too, Valerian, who didst manifest the same spirit of cruelty towards the servants of God, hast afforded an example of righteous judgment. A captive in the ene-mies' hands, led in chains while yet arrayed in the purple and imperial attire, and at last thy skin stripped from thee, and preserved by com-mand of Sapor the Persian king, thou hast left a perpetual trophy of thy calamity. And thou, Aurelian, fierce perpetrator of every wrong, how signal was thy fall, when, in the midst of thy wild career in Thrace, thou wast slain on the public highway, and didst fill the furrows of the road with thine impious blood!

CHAPTER XXV.

Of Diocletian, who ignobly abdicated[1] the Impe-rial Throne, and was terrified by the Dread of Lightning for his Persecution of the Church.

DIOCLETIAN, however, after the display of re-lentless cruelty as a persecutor, evinced a con-sciousness of his own guilt, and, owing to the affliction of a disordered mind, endured the confinement of a mean and separate dwelling.[2] What, then, did he gain by his active hostility against our God? Simply this, I believe, that he passed the residue of his life in continual dread of the lightning's stroke. Nicomedia attests the fact; eyewitnesses, of whom I my-self am one, declare it. The palace, and the emperor's private chamber were destroyed, con-sumed by lightning, devoured by the fire of heaven. Men of understanding hearts had in-deed predicted the issue of such conduct; for they could not keep silence, nor conceal their grief at such unworthy deeds; but boldly and openly expressed their feeling, saying one to another: "What madness is this? and what an insolent abuse of power, that man should dare to fight against God; should deliberately insult the most holy and just of all religions; and plan, without the slightest provocation, the destruc-tion of so great a multitude of righteous per-sons? O rare example of moderation to his subjects! Worthy instructor of his army in the care and protection due to their fellow-citizens! Men who had never seen the backs of a retreat-ing army plunged their swords into the breasts of their own countrymen!" So great was the effusion of blood shed, that if shed in battle with barbarian enemies, it had been sufficient to pur-

---

[1] [*Vide* Euseb. *Hist. Eccles.* Bk. VI. ch. 39. Gibbon (ch. 16) notices very leniently the persecution of Decius. — *Bag.*]

[1] Cf. Prolegomena, *Life.*
[2] [The derangement of Diocletian appears to have been tem-porary only. The causes of his abdication are not very clearly ascertained; but he seems to have meditated the step a considerable time previously. See Gibbon, ch. 13, and the note of Valesius. — *Bag.*]

chase a perpetual peace.[3] At length, indeed, the providence of God took vengeance on these unhallowed deeds; but not without severe damage to the state. For the entire army of the emperor of whom I have just spoken, becoming subject to the authority of a worthless person,[4] who had violently usurped the supreme authority at Rome (when the providence of God restored freedom to that great city), was destroyed in several successive battles. And when we remember the cries with which those who were oppressed, and who ardently longed for their native liberty, implored the help of God; and their praise and thanksgiving to him on the removal of the evils under which they had groaned, when that liberty was regained, and free and equitable intercourse restored: do not these things every way afford convincing proofs of the providence of God, and his affectionate regard for the interests of mankind?

CHAPTER XXVI.

The Emperor ascribes his Personal Piety to God; and shows that we are bound to seek Success from God, and attribute it to him; but to consider Mistakes as the Result of our own Negligence.

WHEN men commend my services, which owe their origin to the inspiration of Heaven, do they not clearly establish the truth that God is

the cause of the exploits I have performed? Assuredly they do: for it belongs to God to do whatever is best, and to man, to perform the commands of God. I believe, indeed, the best and noblest course of action is, when, before an attempt is made, we provide as far as possible for a secure result: and surely all men know that the holy service in which these hands have been employed has originated in pure and genuine faith towards God; that whatever has been done for the common welfare has been effected by active exertion combined with supplication and prayer; the consequence of which has been as great an amount of individual and public benefit as each could venture to hope for himself and those he holds most dear. They have witnessed battles, and have been spectators of a war in which the providence of God has granted victory to this people:[1] they have seen how he has favored and seconded our prayers. For righteous prayer is a thing invincible; and no one fails to attain his object who addresses holy supplication to God: nor is a refusal possible, except in the case of wavering faith;[2] for God is ever favorable, ever ready to approve of human virtue. While, therefore, it is natural for man occasionally to err, yet God is not the cause of human error. Hence it becomes all pious persons to render thanks to the Saviour of all, first for our own individual security, and then for the happy posture of public affairs: at the same time intreating the favor of Christ with holy prayers and constant supplications, that he would continue to us our present blessings. For he is the invincible ally and protector of the righteous: he is the supreme judge of all things, the prince of immortality, the Giver of everlasting life.

---

[3] *Valesius* and *Hein.*, in his first edition, and *Bag.* read this transposed thus, ". . . severe damage to the state, and an effusion of blood, which, if shed," etc. But *Val.* suggests, and Heinichen adopts in his second edition, that the whole sentence should be transposed as above.

[4] ["He means Maxentius, as appears from what follows. How Diocletian's army came under the command of Maxentius, it is not difficult to understand. After Diocletian's abdication, Galerius Maximian took the command of his forces, giving part to Severus Cæsar for the defence of Italy. Shortly afterwards, Maxentius having usurped the Imperial power at Rome, Galerius sent Severus against him with his forces. Maxentius, however, fraudulently and by promises corrupted and drew to his own side Severus's army. After this, Galerius, having marched against Maxentius with a more numerous force, was himself in like manner deserted by his troops. Thus the army of Diocletian came under the power of Maxentius" (Valesius ad loc.). — *Bag.*]

---

[1] i.e. the Roman. So *Val.* and *Hein.*, but *Val.* thinks it may perhaps rather be "to my army."

[2] Better, literally, "slackening faith." There is somewhat of loss from the primitive and real conception of faith in the fixing of the word "wavering" as the conventional expression for weak. Faith is the steadfast current of personality towards an object, and poverty of faith is more often the abatement or slackening of that steady, insistent activity than the wavering of doubt. There is more unbelief than disbelief.

THE ORATION

OF

EUSEBIUS PAMPHILUS,

IN PRAISE OF

THE EMPEROR CONSTANTINE.

PRONOUNCED ON THE THIRTIETH ANNIVERSARY OF HIS REIGN.

1
Prologue to the Oration.[1]

I COME not forward prepared with a fictitious narrative, nor with elegance of language to captivate the ear, desiring to charm my hearers, as it were, with a siren's voice; nor shall I present the draught of pleasure in cups of gold decorated with lovely flowers (I mean the graces of style) to those who are pleased with such things. Rather would I follow the precepts of the wise, and admonish all to avoid and turn aside from the beaten road, and keep themselves from

2 contact with the vulgar crowd. I come, then, prepared to celebrate our emperor's praises in a newer strain; and, though the number be infinite of those who desire to be my companions in my present task, I am resolved to shun the common track of men,[2] and to pursue that untrodden path which it is unlawful to enter on with unwashed feet. Let those who admire a vulgar style, abounding in puerile subtleties, and who court a pleasing and popular muse, essay, since pleasure is the object they have in view, to charm the ears of men by a narrative of merely human merits. Those, however, who are initiated into the universal science,[3] and have attained to Divine as well as human

knowledge, and account the choice of the latter as the real excellence, will prefer those virtues of the emperor which Heaven itself approves, and his pious actions, to his merely human accomplishments; and will leave to inferior encomiasts the task of celebrating his lesser merits. For since our emperor is gifted as 3 well with that sacred wisdom which has immediate reference to God, as with the knowledge which concerns the interests of men; let those who are competent to such a task describe his secular acquirements, great and transcendent as they are, and fraught with advantage to mankind (for all that characterizes the emperor is great and noble), yet still inferior to his diviner qualities, to those who stand without the sacred precincts. Let those, however, who 4 are within the sanctuary, and have access to its inmost and untrodden recesses, close the doors against every profane ear, and unfold, as it were, the secret mysteries of our emperor's character to the initiated alone. And let those who have purified their ears in the streams of piety, and raised their thoughts on the soaring wing of the mind itself, join the company which surrounds the Sovereign Lord of all, and learn in silence the divine mysteries. Mean- 5 while let the sacred oracles, given, not by the spirit of divination (or rather let me say of madness and folly), but by the inspiration of Divine truth,[4] be our instructors in these mysteries; speaking to us of sovereignty, generally: of him who is the Supreme Sovereign of all, and the heavenly array which surrounds the Lord of all; of that exemplar of imperial power which

---

[1] The conventional heading has been retained. Literally it is "Tricennial oration of Eusebius, addressed to the Emperor Constantine. Prologue to the praises addressed to Constantine."

The translation of this oration shows, even more than that of the *Life* or Constantine's *Oration*, a sympathy on the part of the translator with the florid style of Eusebius, and, trying as the style itself is, the success of *Bag.* in presenting the spirit of the original with, on the whole, very considerable accuracy of rendering has been a constant matter of surprise during the effort to revise.

[2] Cf. Hom. *Il.* 6. 202, tr. Bryant, 6. 263-4, "shunning every haunt of human-kind."

[3] Eusebius seems to use this phrase much as the modern phrases "The final philosophy," "The science of sciences," "The queen of sciences," when applied to theology.

[4] "Divine light."

is before us, and that counterfeit coin: and, lastly, of the consequences which result from both. With these oracles, then, to initiate us in the knowledge of the sacred rites, let us essay, as follows, the commencement of our divine mysteries.

CHAPTER I.

The Oration.

1 To-day is the festival of our great emperor: and we his children rejoice therein, feeling the inspiration of our sacred theme. He who presides over our solemnity is the Great Sovereign himself; he, I mean, who is truly great; of whom I affirm (nor will the sovereign who hears me be offended, but will rather approve of this ascription of praise to God), that HE is above and beyond all created things, the Highest, the Greatest, the most Mighty One; whose throne is the arch of heaven, and the earth the footstool of his feet.[1] His being none can worthily comprehend; and the ineffable splendor of the glory which surrounds him repels the gaze of every eye from his

2 Divine majesty. His ministers are the heavenly hosts; his armies the supernal powers, who own allegiance to him as their Master, Lord, and King. The countless multitudes of angels, the companies of archangels, the chorus of holy spirits, draw from and reflect his radiance as from the fountains of everlasting light. Yea, every light, and specially those divine and incorporeal intelligences whose place is beyond the heavenly sphere, celebrate this august Sovereign with lofty and sacred strains of praise. The vast expanse of heaven, like an azure veil, is interposed between those without, and those who inhabit his royal mansions: while round this expanse the sun and moon, with the rest of the heavenly luminaries (like torch-bearers around the entrance of the imperial palace), perform, in honor of their sovereign, their appointed courses; holding forth, at the word of his command, an ever-burning light to those whose lot is cast in the darker regions without the pale of heaven. And surely when

3 I remember that our own victorious emperor renders praises to this Mighty Sovereign, I do well to follow him, knowing as I do that to him alone we owe that imperial power under which we live. The pious Cæsars, instructed by their father's wisdom, acknowledge him as the source of every blessing: the soldiery, the entire body of the people, both in the country and in the cities of the empire, with the governors of the several provinces, assembling together in accordance with the precept of their great Saviour and Teacher, worship him. In short, the whole family of mankind, of every nation, tribe, and tongue, both collectively and severally, however diverse their opinions on other subjects, are unanimous in this one confession; and, in obedience to the reason implanted in them, and the spontaneous and uninstructed impulse of their own minds, unite in calling on the One and only God.[2] Nay, does not the

4 universal frame of earth acknowledge him her Lord, and declare, by the vegetable and animal life which she produces, her subjection to the will of a superior Power? The rivers, flowing with abundant stream, and the perennial fountains, springing from hidden and exhaustless depths, ascribe to him the cause of their marvellous source. The mighty waters of the sea, enclosed in chambers of unfathomable depth, and the swelling surges, which lift themselves on high, and menace as it were the earth itself, shrink back when they approach the shore, checked by the power of his Divine law. The duly measured fall of winter's rain, the rolling thunder, the lightning's flash, the eddying currents of the winds, and the airy courses of the clouds, all reveal his presence to those to whom his Person is invisible. The

5 all-radiant sun, who holds his constant career through the lapse of ages, owns him Lord alone, and obedient to his will, dares not depart from his appointed path. The inferior splendor of the moon, alternately diminished and increased at stated periods, is subject to his Divine command. The beauteous mechanism of the heavens, glittering with the hosts of stars, moving in harmonious order, and preserving the measure of each several orbit, proclaims him the giver of all light: yea, all the heavenly luminaries, maintaining at his will and word a grand and perfect unity of motion, pursue the track of their ethereal career, and complete in the lapse of revolving ages their distant course. The alternate recurrence of day and night, the changing seasons, the order and proportion of the universe, all declare the manifold wisdom of [his boundless power]. To him the unseen agencies which hold their course throughout the expanse of space, render the due tribute of praise. To him this terrestrial globe itself, to him the heavens above, and the choirs beyond the vault of heaven, give honor as to their mighty Sovereign: the angelic hosts greet him with ineffable songs of Praise; and the spirits which draw their being from incorporeal light, adore him as their Creator. The

---

[1] Paraphrased from Is. lxvi. 1.

[2] [We must be content here (and probably in other passages of this *Oration*) to tolerate as rhetorical embellishment that which, regarded literally, is in every sense palpably untrue. — *Bag.*] The intention of the passage is probably like that of those who say now that there is no nation where, in some form, God is not worshipped.

everlasting ages which were before this heaven and earth, with other periods beside them, infinite, and antecedent to all visible creation, acknowledge him the sole and supreme
6 Sovereign and Lord. Lastly, he who is in all, before, and after all,[3] his only begotten, pre-existent Word, the great High Priest of the mighty God, elder than all time and every age, devoted to his Father's glory, first and alone makes intercession with him for the salvation of mankind.[4] Supreme and pre-eminent Ruler of the universe, he shares the glory of his Father's kingdom : for he is that Light, which, transcendent above the universe, encircles the Father's Person, interposing and dividing between the eternal and uncreated Essence and all derived existence : that Light which, streaming from on high, proceeds from that Deity who knows not origin or end, and illumines the super-celestial regions, and all that heaven itself contains, with the radiance of wisdom bright beyond the splendor of the sun. This is he who holds a supreme dominion over this whole world,[5] who is over and in all things, and pervades all things[6] visible and invisible; the Word of God. From whom and by whom our divinely favored emperor, receiving, as it were, a transcript of the Divine sovereignty, directs, in imitation of God himself, the administration of this world's affairs.

CHAPTER II.

1 THIS only begotten Word of God reigns, from ages which had no beginning, to infinite and endless ages, the partner of his Father's kingdom. And [our emperor] ever beloved by him, who derives the source of imperial authority from above, and is strong in the power of his sacred title,[1] has controlled the empire of
2 the world for a long period of years. Again, that Preserver of the universe orders these heavens and earth, and the celestial kingdom, consistently with his Father's will. Even so our emperor whom he loves, by bringing those whom he rules on earth to the only begotten Word and Saviour renders them fit subjects of his
3 kingdom. And as he who is the common Saviour of mankind, by his invisible and Divine power as the good shepherd, drives far

away from his flock, like savage beasts, those apostate spirits which once flew through the airy tracts above this earth, and fastened on the souls of men;[2] so this his friend, graced by his heavenly favor with victory over all his foes, subdues and chastens the open adversaries of the truth in accordance with the usages of war. He who is the pre-existent Word, the 4 Preserver of all things, imparts to his disciples the seeds of true wisdom and salvation, and at once enlightens and gives them understanding in the knowledge of his Father's kingdom. Our emperor, his friend, acting as interpreter to the Word of God, aims at recalling the whole human race to the knowledge of God ; proclaiming clearly in the ears of all, and declaring with powerful voice the laws of truth and godliness to all who dwell on the earth. Once 5 more, the universal Saviour opens the heavenly gates of his Father's kingdom to those whose course is thitherward from this world. Our emperor, emulous of his Divine example, having purged his earthly dominion from every stain of impious error, invites each holy and pious worshiper within his imperial mansions, earnestly desiring to save with all its crew that mighty vessel of which he is the appointed pilot. And he alone of all who have wielded the imperial power of Rome, being honored by the Supreme Sovereign with a reign of three decennial periods, now celebrates this festival, not, as his ancestors might have done, in honor of infernal demons, or of the apparitions of seducing spirits, or of the fraud and deceitful arts of impious men ; but as an act of thanksgiving to him by whom he has thus been honored, and in acknowledgment of the blessings he has received at his hands. He does not, in imitation of ancient usage, defile his imperial mansions with blood and gore, nor propitiate the infernal deities with fire and smoke, and sacrificial offerings ; but dedicates to the universal Sovereign a pleasant and acceptable sacrifice, even his own imperial soul, and a mind truly fitted for the service of God. For this sacrifice alone 6 is grateful to him : and this sacrifice our emperor has learned, with purified mind and thoughts, to present as an offering without the intervention of fire and blood, while his own piety, strengthened by the truthful doctrines with which his soul is stored, he sets forth in magnificent language the praises of God, and

---

[3] [Referring possibly to Rev. i. 8. "I am Alpha and Omega, the beginning and the ending saith the Lord, which is, and which was, and which is to come, the Almighty." —*Bag.*] Or, possibly, refers to Eph. iv. 6, as it seems to be simply some verbal suggestion.
[4] [The Arianism implied in this passage, if referred to the Word as God, disappears if we regard it as spoken of Christ as the Word manifested in human nature. See the note of Valesius ad loc. — *Bag.*] [5] Universe.
[6] This is directly from Eph. iv. 6: " Who is over all and through all and in all." It is thus directly referred to the Father, and on the basis of the above note of *Bag.* seems to convict of Arianism, but in reality the conception of a pre-existing Word is distinctly orthodox.
[1] [It is difficult to know precisely what is meant here. Possibly the name of Christian. — *Bag.*]

[2] This is an allusion to what was afterwards known as Vampirism, — a belief of unknown antiquity, and especially prevalent in various forms in the East. Rydberg (*Magic of the Middle Ages*, p. 207) describes the mediæval form thus: " The vampires, according to the belief of the Middle Ages, are disembodied souls which clothe themselves again in their buried bodies, steal at night into houses, and suck from the nipple of the sleeping all their blood." (Cf. Perty, *d. myst. Ersch.* 1 [1872], 383. 91; Görres' *Chr. myst.* Vol. 3, etc.) Similar in nature was that notion of the spirits who sucked away the breath of sleeping persons, which has left its trace in the modern superstition that cats suck away the breath of sleeping children.

imitates his Divine philanthropy by his own imperial acts. Wholly devoted to him, he dedicates himself as a noble offering, a first-fruit of that world, the government of which is intrusted to his charge. This first and greatest sacrifice our emperor first dedicates to God ; and then, as a faithful shepherd, he offers, not " famous hecatombs of firstling lambs," but the souls of that flock which is the object of his care, those rational beings whom he leads to the knowledge and pious worship of God.

CHAPTER III.

1   AND gladly does he accept and welcome this sacrifice, and commend the presenter of so august and noble an offering, by protracting his reign to a lengthened period of years, giving larger proofs of his beneficence in proportion to the emperor's holy services to himself. Accordingly he permits him to celebrate each successive festival during great and general prosperity throughout the empire, advancing one of his sons, at the recurrence of each decennial period, to a share of his own imperial

2   power.[1] The eldest, who bears his father's name, he received as his partner in the empire about the close of the first decade of his reign : the second, next in point of age, at the second ; and the third in like manner at the third decennial period, the occasion of this our present festival. And now that the fourth period has commenced, and the time of his reign is still further prolonged, he desires to extend his imperial authority by calling still more of his kindred to partake his power ; and, by the appointment of the Cæsars,[2] fulfills the predictions of the holy prophets, according to what they uttered ages before: " And the saints of the

3   Most High shall take the kingdom."[3] And thus the Almighty Sovereign himself accords an increase both of years and of children to our most pious emperor, and renders his sway over the nations of the world still fresh and flourishing, as though it were even now springing up in its earliest vigor. He it is who appoints him this present festival, in that he has made him victorious over every enemy that disturbed his peace : he it is who displays him as an example of

4   true godliness to the human race. And thus our emperor, like the radiant sun, illuminates the most distant subjects of his empire

---

[1] A general statement, such as Eusebius is fond of making. The elevation of his sons was about these times, but not on them exactly. Compare Prolegomena, *Life.*
[2] [Dalmatius and Hanniballianus. — *Bag.*]
[3] [Dan. vii. 18. It is surely needless to remark on so singular and vicious an application of Scripture as this, further than that it is either a culpable rhetorical flourish, or else an indication of a lamentable defect of spiritual intelligence in the most learned writer of the fourth century. — *Bag.*] " But the saints of the Most High shall receive the kingdom." — *Revised Version.*

through the presence of the Cæsars, as with the far piercing rays of his own brightness. To us who occupy the eastern regions he has given a son worthy of himself ;[4] a second and a third respectively to other departments of his empire, to be, as it were, brilliant reflectors of the light which proceeds from himself. Once more, having harnessed, as it were, under the self-same yoke the four most noble Cæsars[5] as horses in the imperial chariot, he sits on high and directs their course by the reins of holy harmony and concord ; and, himself every where present, and observant of every event, thus traverses every region of the world. Lastly, invested as he   5 is with a semblance of heavenly sovereignty, he directs his gaze above, and frames his earthly government according to the pattern of that Divine original, feeling strength in its conformity to the monarchy of God. And this conformity is granted by the universal Sovereign to man alone of the creatures of this earth : for he only is the author of sovereign power, who decrees that all should be subject to the rule of one. And surely monarchy far transcends every   6 other constitution and form of government : for that democratic equality of power, which is its opposite, may rather be described as anarchy and disorder. Hence there is one God, and not two, or three, or more : for to assert a plurality of gods is plainly to deny the being of God at all. There is one Sovereign ; and his Word and royal Law is one : a Law not expressed in syllables and words, not written or engraved on tablets, and therefore subject to the ravages of time ; but the living and self-subsisting Word, who himself is God, and who administers his Father's kingdom on behalf of all who are after him and subject to his power. His attendants are   7 the heavenly hosts ; the myriads of God's angelic ministers ; the super-terrestrial armies, of unnumbered multitude ; and those unseen spirits within heaven itself, whose agency is employed in regulating the order of this world. Ruler and chief of all these is the royal Word, acting as Regent of the Supreme Sovereign. To him the names of Captain, and great High Priest, Prophet of the Father, Angel of mighty counsel, Brightness of the Father's light, Only begotten Son, with a thousand other titles, are ascribed in the oracles of the sacred writers. And the Father, having constituted him the living Word, and Law, and Wisdom, the fullness of all blessing, has presented this best and greatest gift to all who are the subjects of his sovereignty. And he himself, who pervades   8 all things, and is every where present, unfolding his Father's bounties to all with unsparing hand, has accorded a specimen of his sov-

---

[4] [Constantius Cæsar. — *Bag.*]
[5] Compare Prolegomena, under *Life.*

ereign power even to his rational creatures of this earth, in that he has provided the mind of man, who is formed after his own image, with Divine faculties, whence it is capable of other virtues also, which flow from the same heavenly source. For he only is wise, who is the only God: he only is essentially good: he only is of mighty power, the Parent of justice, the Father of reason and wisdom, the Fountain of light and life, the Dispenser of truth and virtue: in a word, the Author of empire itself, and of all dominion and power.

CHAPTER IV.

1   BUT whence has man this knowledge, and who has ministered these truths to mortal ears? Or whence has a tongue of flesh the power to speak of things so utterly distinct from fleshly or material substance? Who has gazed on the invisible King, and beheld these perfections in him? The bodily sense may comprehend elements and their combinations, of a nature kindred to its own: but no one yet has boasted to have scanned with corporeal eye that unseen kingdom which governs all things; nor has mortal nature yet discerned the beauty of perfect wisdom. Who has beheld the face of righteousness through the medium of flesh? And whence came the idea of legitimate sovereignty and imperial power to man? Whence the thought of absolute dominion to a being composed of flesh and blood? Who declared those ideas which are invisible and undefined, and that incorporeal essence which has no external form, to the mortals of this earth?

2   Surely there was but one interpreter of these things; the all-pervading Word of God.[1] For he is the author of that rational and intelligent being which exists in man; and, being himself one with his Father's Divine nature, he sheds upon his offspring the out-flowings of his Father's bounty. Hence the natural and untaught powers of thought, which all men, Greeks or Barbarians, alike possess: hence the perception of reason and wisdom, the seeds of integrity and righteousness, the understanding of the arts of life, the knowledge of virtue, the precious name of wisdom, and the noble love of philosophic learning. Hence the knowledge of all that is great and good: hence apprehension of God himself, and a life worthy of his worship: hence the royal authority of man, and his invincible lordship over the creatures of this world.

3   And when that Word, who is the Parent of rational beings, had impressed a character on the mind of man according to the

image and likeness of God,[2] and had made him a royal creature, in that he gave him alone of all earthly creatures capacity to rule and to obey (as well as forethought and foreknowledge even here, concerning the promised hope of his heavenly kingdom, because of which he himself came, and, as the Parent of his children, disdained not to hold converse with mortal men); he continued to cherish the seeds which himself had sown, and renewed his gracious favors from above; holding forth to all the promise of sharing his heavenly kingdom. Accordingly he called men, and exhorted them to be ready for their heavenward journey, and to provide themselves with the garment which became their calling. And by an indescribable power he filled the world in every part with his doctrine, expressing by the similitude of an earthly kingdom that heavenly one to which he earnestly invites all mankind, and presents it to them as a worthy object of their hope.

CHAPTER V.

AND in this hope our divinely-favored   1 emperor partakes even in this present life, gifted as he is by God with native virtues, and having received into his soul the out-flowings of his favor. His reason he derives from the great Source of all reason: he is wise, and good, and just, as having fellowship with perfect Wisdom, Goodness, and Righteousness: virtuous, as following the pattern of perfect virtue: valiant, as partaking of heavenly strength. And   2 truly may he deserve the imperial title, who has formed his soul to royal virtues, according to the standard of that celestial kingdom. But he who is a stranger to these blessings, who denies the Sovereign of the universe, and owns no allegiance to the heavenly Father of spirits; who invests not himself with the virtues which become an emperor, but overlays his soul with moral deformity and baseness; who for royal clemency substitutes the fury of a savage beast; for a generous temper, the incurable venom of malicious wickedness; for prudence, folly; for reason and wisdom, that recklessness which is the most odious of all vices, for from it, as from a spring of bitterness, proceed the most pernicious fruits; such as inveterate profligacy of life, covetousness, murder, impiety and defiance of God; surely one abandoned to such vices as these, however he may be deemed powerful through despotic violence, has no true title to the name of Emperor. For how should he whose soul   3 is impressed with a thousand absurd images of

---

[1] " And no one knoweth who the Son is, save the Father; and who the Father is, save the Son, and he to whomsoever the Son willeth to reveal him." — Luke x. 22.

[2] Eusebius, in making it the Word who impresses the image of God on men, shows good philosophy and good theology.

false deities,[1] be able to exhibit a counterpart of the true and heavenly sovereignty? Or how can he be absolute lord of others, who has subjected himself to the dominion of a thousand cruel masters? a slave of low delights and ungoverned lust, a slave of wrongfully-extorted wealth, of rage and passion, as well as of cowardice and terror; a slave of ruthless

4 demons, and soul-destroying spirits? Let, then, our emperor, on the testimony of truth itself, be declared alone worthy of the title; who is dear to the Supreme Sovereign himself; who alone is free, nay, who is truly lord: above the thirst of wealth, superior to sexual desire; victorious even over natural pleasures; controlling, not controlled by, anger and passion.[2] He is indeed an emperor, and bears a title corresponding to his deeds; a Victor in truth, who has gained the victory over those passions which overmaster the rest of men: whose character is formed after the Divine original[3] of the Supreme Sovereign, and whose mind reflects, as in a mirror, the radiance of his virtues. Hence is our emperor perfect in discretion, in goodness, in justice, in courage, in piety, in devotion to God: he truly and only is a philosopher, since he knows himself, and is fully aware that supplies of every blessing are showered on him from a source quite external to himself, even from heaven itself. Declaring the august title of supreme authority by the splendor of his vesture, he alone worthily wears that imperial purple which so well becomes

5 him. He is indeed an emperor, who calls on and implores in prayer the favor of his heavenly Father night and day, and whose ardent desires are fixed on his celestial kingdom. For he knows that present things, subject as they are to decay and death, flowing on and disappearing like a river's stream, are not worthy to be compared with him who is sovereign of all; therefore it is that he longs for the incorruptible and incorporeal kingdom of God. And this kingdom he trusts he shall obtain, elevating his mind as he does in sublimity of thought above the vault of heaven, and filled with inexpressible longing for the glories which shine there, in comparison with which he deems the precious things of this present world but darkness. For he sees earthly sovereignty to be but a petty and fleeting dominion over a mortal and temporary life, and rates it not much higher than the goatherd's, or shepherd's, or herdsman's power: nay, as more burdensome than theirs, and exercised over more stubborn subjects. The acclamations of the people, and the voice of flattery, he reckons rather troublesome than pleasing, because of the steady constancy of his character, and genuine discipline of his mind. Again, when he beholds the mili-

6 tary service of his subjects, the vast array of his armies, the multitudes of horse and foot, entirely devoted to his command, he feels no astonishment, no pride at the possession of such mighty power; but turns his thoughts inward on himself, and recognizes the same common nature there. He smiles at his vesture, embroidered with gold and flowers, and at the imperial purple and diadem itself, when he sees the multitude gaze in wonder, like children at a bugbear, on the splendid spectacle.[4] Himself superior to such feelings, he clothes his soul with the knowledge of God, that vesture, the broidery of which is temperance, righteousness, piety, and all other virtues; a vesture such as truly becomes a sovereign. The

7 wealth which others so much desire, as gold, silver, or precious gems, he regards to be, as they really are, in themselves mere stones and worthless matter, of no avail to preserve or defend from evil. For what power have these things to free from disease, or repel the approach of death? And knowing as he does this truth by personal experience in the use of these things, he regards the splendid attire of his subjects with calm indifference, and smiles at the childishness of those to whom they prove attractive. Lastly, he abstains from all excess in food and wine, and leaves superfluous dainties to gluttons, judging that such indulgences, however suitable to others, are not so to him, and deeply convinced of their pernicious tendency, and their effect in darkening the intellectual powers of the soul. For all these reasons, 8

---

[1] There seems to be a clear hint of Philonism here, or Philonism as developed by the Neo-Platonists and the Christian Theologians. The history of the thought seems to begin in the Platonic ideas. These self-existing forms which impress themselves on the soul naturally become personalities to which the soul submits, and whose images are impressed on the soul. These personalized ideas are in the thought of Philo the thoughts or ideas of God, " powers " who do his will, like the Valkyr of the Northern mythology, — the personified thoughts or will of Odin. These objective ideas in organized whole were the Word.

The objectivity of ideas, placed in relation with " mind reading," " thought transference," and the like, and with the modern conceptions of the conservation of energy and transmission of force by vibrations, give an interesting suggestion of a material basis for the conception. If thought is accompanied by vibration of brain molecules, it is of course quite conceivable that that vibration be projected through any medium which can transmit vibration, whether the nerves of another person or the air. A person of supreme energy of will would make these vibrations more intense, and an Infinite personality would make tangible even perhaps to the point of that resistance which we call matter. The conception of one great central Personality issuing an organized related system of thoughts in various stages of embodiment, in one massive, constant forth-streaming of will, is most interesting. According to it, all will forms of the individual are true as they are in harmony with these norms. Where, however, the lesser wills project incongruous will forms, they are in conflict with the greater. According to it, the human soul is beaten upon by all ideas which have ever been projected, either in individual or in some combined total of force, and is formed according to what it submits itself to, whether to the lesser and mal-organized or to the Great Norm.

[2] Compare Prolegomena, *Character*. This peculiar self-control, it is to be remembered, was characteristic also of his father, and in a measure the product of the Neo-Platonic philosophy.

[3] Literally, the " archetypal idea," — the same phrase as that used by Philo, 1. 4 (ed. Lips., 1828, I. p. 7); i.e. that incorporeal model or image of God on which the corporeal world was formed.

[4] This may be true; but compare Prolegomena, *Character*, for his practice, at least.

our divinely taught and noble-minded emperor, aspiring to higher objects than this life affords, calls upon his heavenly Father as one who longs for his kingdom; exhibits a pious spirit in each action of his life; and finally, as a wise and good instructor, imparts to his subjects the knowledge of him who is the Sovereign Lord of all.

CHAPTER VI.

1   And God himself, as an earnest of future reward, assigns to him now as it were tricennial crowns[1] composed of prosperous periods of time; and now, after the revolution of three circles of ten years, he grants permission to all mankind to celebrate this general, nay 2   rather, this universal festival. And while those on earth thus rejoice, crowned as it were with the flowers of divine knowledge, surely, we may not unduly suppose that the heavenly choirs, attracted by a natural sympathy, unite their joy with the joy of those on earth: nay, that the Supreme Sovereign himself, as a gracious father, delights in the worship of duteous children, and for this reason is pleased to honor the author and cause of their obedience through a lengthened period of time; and, far from limiting his reign to three decennial circles of years, he extends it to the remotest 3   period, even to far distant eternity. Now eternity[2] in its whole extent is beyond the power of decline or death: its beginning and extent alike incapable of being scanned by mortal thoughts. Nor will it suffer its central point to be perceived, nor that which is termed its present duration to be grasped by the inquiring mind. Far less, then, the future, or the past: for the one is not, but is already gone; while the future has not yet arrived, and therefore is not. As regards what is termed the present time, it vanishes even as we think or speak, more swiftly than the word itself is uttered. Nor is it possible in any sense to apprehend this time as present; for we must either expect the future, or contemplate the past; the present slips from us, and is gone, even in the act of thought. Eternity, then, in its whole extent, resists and refuses subjection to mortal reason. 4   But it does not refuse to acknowledge its own Sovereign and Lord,[3] and bears him as it were mounted on itself, rejoicing in the

fair trappings which he bestows.[4] And he himself, not binding it, as the poet imagined, with a golden chain,[5] but as it were controlling its movements by the reins of ineffable wisdom, has adjusted its months and seasons, its times and years, and the alterations of day and night, with perfect harmony, and has thus attached to it limits and measures of various kinds. For eternity, being in its nature direct, and stretching onward into infinity, and receiving its name, eternity, as having an everlasting existence,[6] and being similar in all its parts, or rather having no division or distance, progresses only in a line of direct extension. But God, who has distributed it by intermediate sections, and has divided it, like a far extended line, in many points, has included in it a vast number of portions; and though it is in its nature one, and resembles unity itself, he has attached to it a multiplicity of numbers, and has given it, though formless in itself, an endless variety of forms 5   For first of all he framed in it formless matter, as a substance capable of receiving all forms. He next, by the power of the number two, imparted quality to matter, and gave beauty to that which before was void of all grace. Again, by means of the number three, he framed a body compounded of matter and form, and presenting the three dimensions of breadth, and length, and depth. Then, from the doubling of the number two, he devised the quaternion of the elements, earth, water, air, and fire, and ordained them to be everlasting sources for the supply of this universe. Again, the number four produces the number ten. For the aggregate of one, and two, and three, and four, is ten.[7] And three multiplied with ten discovers the period of a month: and twelve successive months complete the course of the sun. Hence the revolutions of years, and changes of the seasons, which give grace, like variety of color in painting, to that eternity which before was formless and devoid of beauty, for the refreshment and delight of those whose lot it is to traverse therein the course of life. For as the ground 6   is defined by stated distances for those who run in hope of obtaining the prize; and as the road of those who travel on a distant journey is marked by resting-places and measured intervals, that the traveler's courage may not fail at the interminable prospect; even so the Sovereign of the universe, controlling eternity itself within

---

[1] [Alluding (says Valesius) to the crowns of gold which the people of the several provinces were accustomed to present to the Roman emperors on such occasions as the present. — *Bag.*] In his prologue to the *Life*, Eusebius calls this very oration a weaving of tricennial crowns (or garlands). These crowns had their historical origin in the triumphal crowns under the Roman system. Cf. Rich, in Smith, *Dict. Gr. and Rom. Ant.* p. 361.

[2] [It is perhaps difficult to find a better word to express the original αἰών. — *Bag.*]

[3] Compare 1 Tim. i. 17 (*marg.*), "King of the ages" (" æons," or according to this translation " eternity").

[4] [Days, months, years, seasons, &c., are here intended. Valesius, ad loc. — *Bag.*]

[5] Hom. *Il.* 8, 19.

[6] [Αἰών, ὥσπερ ἀεὶ ὤν. — *Bag.*]

[7] From what source Eusebius draws this particular application of the Pythagorean principle is uncertain. This conception of the derivation of ten from four is found in Philo, *de Mund. Opif.* ch. 15, and indeed it is said (*Ueberweg*) that with the earliest Pythagoreans four and ten were the especially significant numbers in creation. This mixture of Neo-Pythagoreanism with Platonism and Philonism was characteristic of the time.

the restraining power of his own wisdom, directs and turns its course as he judges best. The same God, I say, who thus clothes the once undefined eternity as with fair colors and blooming flowers, gladdens the day with the solar rays; and, while he overspreads the night with a covering of darkness, yet causes the glittering stars, as golden spangles, to shine therein. It is he who lights up the brilliancy of the morning star, the changing splendor of the moon, and the glorious companies of the starry host, and has arrayed the expanse of heaven, like some vast mantle, in colors of varied beauty. Again, having created the lofty and profound expanse of air, and caused the world in its length and breadth to feel its cooling influence, he decreed that the air itself should be graced with birds of every kind, and left open this vast ocean of space to be traversed by every creature, visible or invisible, whose course is through the tracts of heaven. In the midst of this atmosphere he poised the earth, as it were its center, and encompassed it with the ocean as with a beautiful azure vesture. Having ordained this earth to be at once the home, the nurse, and the mother of all the creatures it contains, and watered it both with rain and water-springs, he caused it to abound in plants and flowers of every species, for the enjoyment of life. And when he had formed man in his own likeness, the noblest of earthly creatures, and dearest to himself, a creature gifted with intellect and knowledge, the child of reason and wisdom, he gave him dominion over all other animals which move and live upon the earth. For man was in truth of all earthly creatures the dearest to God: man, I say, to whom, as an indulgent Father, he has subjected the brute creation; for whom he has made the ocean navigable, and crowned the earth with a profusion of plants of every kind; to whom he has granted reasoning faculties for acquiring all science; under whose control he has placed even the creatures of the deep, and the winged inhabitants of the air; to whom he has permitted the contemplation of celestial objects, and revealed the course and changes of the sun and moon, and the periods of the planets and fixed stars. In short, to man alone of earthly beings has he given commandment to acknowledge him as his heavenly Father, and to celebrate his praises as the Supreme

8 Sovereign of eternity itself. But the unchangeable course of eternity the Creator has limited by the four seasons of the year, terminating the winter by the approach of spring, and regulating as with an equal balance that season which commences the annual period. Having thus graced the eternal course of time with the varied productions of spring, he added the summer's heat; and then granted as it were

a relief of toil by the interval of autumn: and lastly, refreshing and cleansing the season by the showers of winter, he brings it, rendered sleek and glossy, like a noble steed, by these abundant rains, once more to the gates of spring.

As soon, then, as the Supreme Sovereign 9 had thus connected his own eternity by these cords of wisdom with the annual circle, he committed it to the guidance of a mighty Governor, even his only begotten Word, to whom, as the Preserver of all creation, he yielded the reins of universal power. And he, receiving this inheritance as from a beneficent Father, and uniting all things both above and beneath the circumference of heaven in one harmonious whole, directs their uniform course; providing with perfect justice whatever is expedient for his rational creatures on the earth, appointing its allotted limits to human life, and granting to all alike permission to anticipate even here the commencement of a future existence. For he has taught them that beyond this present world there is a divine and blessed state of being, reserved for those who have been supported here by the hope of heavenly blessings; and that those who have lived a virtuous and godly life will remove hence to a far better habitation; while he adjudges to those who have been guilty and wicked here a place of punishment according to their crimes. Again, as in the 10 distribution of prizes at the public games, he proclaims various crowns to the victors, and invests each with the rewards of different virtues: but for our good emperor, who is clothed in the very robe of piety, he declares that a higher recompense of his toils is prepared; and, as a prelude to this recompense, permits us now to assemble at this festival, which is composed of perfect numbers, of decades thrice, and triads ten times repeated. The first of 11 these, the triad, is the offspring of the unit, while the unit is the mother of number itself, and presides over all months, and seasons, and years, and every period of time. It may, indeed, be justly termed the origin, foundation, and principle of all number, and derives its name from its abiding character.[8] For, while every other number is diminished or increased according to the subtraction or addition of others, the unit alone continues fixed and steadfast, abstracted from all multitude and the numbers which are formed from it, and resembling that indivisible essence which is distinct from all things beside, but by virtue of participation in which the nature of all things else subsists. For the unit is 12 the originator of every number, since all

---

8 [Μονὰς, παρὰ τὸ μένειν ὠνομασμένη. The analogies from number in this chapter (which the reader will probably consider puerile enough) seem to be an imitation of some of the mystical speculations of Plato. — Bag.]

multitude is made up by the composition and addition of units; nor is it possible without the unit to conceive the existence of number at all. But the unit itself is independent of multitude, apart from and superior to all number; form-

13 ing, indeed, and making all, but receiving no increase from any. Kindred to this is the triad; equally indivisible and perfect, the first of those sums which are formed of even and uneven numbers. For the perfect number two, receiving the addition of the unit, forms the triad, the first perfect compound number. And the triad, by explaining what equality is, first taught men justice, having itself an equal beginning, and middle, and end. And it is also an image of the mysterious, most holy, and royal Trinity, which, though itself without beginning or origin, yet contains the germs, the reasons, and causes of the existence of all created

14 things. Thus the power of the triad may justly be regarded as the first cause of all things. Again, the number ten, which contains the end of all numbers, and terminates them in itself, may truly be called a full and perfect number, as comprehending every species and every measure of numbers, proportions, concords, and harmonies. For example, the units by addition form and are terminated by the number ten; and, having this number as their parent, and as it were the limit of their course, they round this as the goal of their career.

15 Then they perform a second circuit, and again a third, and a fourth, until the tenth, and thus by ten decades they complete the hundredth number. Returning thence to the first starting point, they again proceed to the number ten, and having ten times completed the hundredth number, again they recede, and perform round the same barriers their protracted course, proceeding from themselves back to themselves again, with revolving motion.

16 For the unit is the tenth of ten, and ten units make up a decade, which is itself the limit, the settled goal and boundary of units: it is that which terminates the infinity of number; the term and end of units. Again, the triad combined with the decade, and performing a threefold circuit of tens, produces that most natural number, thirty. For as the triad is in respect to units, so is the number thirty in

17 respect to tens. It is also the constant limit to the course of that luminary which is second to the sun in brightness. For the course of the moon from one conjunction with the sun to the next, completes the period of a month; after which, receiving as it were a second birth, it recommences a new light, and other days, being adorned and honored with thirty

18 units, three decades, and ten triads. In the same manner is the universal reign of our

victorious emperor distinguished by the giver of all good, and now enters on a new sphere of blessing, accomplishing, at present, this tricennalian festival, but reaching forward beyond this to far more distant intervals of time, and cherishing the hope of future blessings in the celestial kingdom; where, not a single sun, but infinite hosts of light surround the Almighty Sovereign, each surpassing the splendor of the sun, glorious and resplendent with rays derived from the everlasting source of light. There

19 the soul enjoys its existence, surrounded by fair and unfading blessings; there is a life beyond the reach of sorrow; there the enjoyment of pure and holy pleasures, and a time of unmeasured and endless duration, extending into illimitable space; not defined by intervals of days and months, the revolutions of years, or the recurrence of times and seasons, but commensurate with a life which knows no end. And this life needs not the light of the sun, nor the lustre of the moon or the starry host, since it has the great Luminary himself, even God the Word, the only begotten Son of the Almighty Sovereign. Hence it is that the

20 mystic and sacred oracles reveal him to be the Sun of righteousness, and the Light which far transcends all light. We believe that he illumines also the thrice-blessed powers of heaven with the rays of righteousness, and the brightness of wisdom, and that he receives truly pious souls, not within the sphere of heaven alone, but into his own bosom, and confirms indeed the assurances which he himself has given. No

21 mortal eye has seen, nor ear heard, nor can the mind in its vesture of flesh understand what things are prepared for those who have been here adorned with the graces of godliness; blessings which await thee too, most pious emperor, to whom alone since the world began has the Almighty Sovereign of the universe granted power to purify the course of human life: to whom also he has revealed his own symbol of salvation, whereby he overcame the power of death, and triumphed over every enemy. And this victorious trophy, the scourge of evil spirits, thou hast arrayed against the errors of idol worship, and hast obtained the victory not only over all thy impious and savage foes, but over equally barbarous adversaries, the evil spirits themselves.

CHAPTER VII.

1 FOR whereas we are composed of two distinct natures, I mean of body and spirit, of which the one is visible to all, the other invisible, against both these natures two kinds of barbarous and savage enemies, the one invisibly, the other openly, are constantly arrayed.

The one oppose our bodies with bodily force : the other with incorporeal assaults besiege
2 the naked soul itself.   Again, the visible barbarians, like the wild nomad tribes, no better than savage beasts, assail the nations of civilized men, ravage their country, and enslave their cities, rushing on those who inhabit them like ruthless wolves of the desert, and destroying all who fall under their power. But those unseen foes, more cruel far than barbarians, I mean the soul-destroying demons whose course is through the regions of the air, had succeeded, through the snares of vile polytheism, in enslaving the entire human race, insomuch that they no longer recognized the true God, but wandered in the mazes of atheistic error. For they procured, I know not whence, gods who never anywhere existed, and set him aside who is the only and the true God, as though he were not.
3   Accordingly the generation of bodies was esteemed by them a deity, and so the opposite principle to this, their dissolution and destruction, was also deified. The first, as the author of generative power, was honored with rites under the name of Venus :[1] the second, as rich, and mighty in dominion over the human race, received the names of Pluto, and Death. For men in those ages, knowing no other than naturally generated life, declared the cause and origin of that life to be divine : and again, believing in no existence after death, they proclaimed Death himself a universal conqueror and a mighty god. Hence, unconscious of responsibility, as destined to be annihilated by death, they lived a life unworthy of the name, in the practice of actions deserving a thousand deaths. No thought of God could enter their minds, no expectation of Divine judgment, no recollection of, no reflection on, their spiritual existence : acknowledging one dread superior, Death, and persuaded that the dissolution of their bodies by his power was final annihilation, they bestowed on Death the title of a mighty, a wealthy god, and hence the name of Pluto.[2] Thus, then, Death became to them a god ; nor only so, but whatever else they accounted precious in comparison with death, whatever contributed to
4   the luxuries of life. Hence animal pleasure became to them a god ; nutrition, and its production, a god ; the fruit of trees, a god ; drunken riot, a god ; carnal desire and pleasure, a god. Hence the mysteries of Ceres and Proserpine, the rape of the latter, and her subsequent restoration, by Pluto : hence the orgies of Bacchus, and Hercules overcome by drunkenness as by a mightier god : hence the adulterous rites of Cupid and of Venus : hence Jupiter himself infatuated with the love of women, and of Ganymede :[3] hence the licentious legends of deities abandoned to effeminacy and pleasure. Such were the weapons of superstition 5 whereby these cruel barbarians and enemies of the Supreme God afflicted, and indeed entirely subdued, the human race ; erecting everywhere the monuments of impiety, and rearing in every corner the shrines and temples of their false religion. Nay, so far were the 6 ruling powers of those times enslaved by the force of error, as to appease their gods with the blood of their own countrymen and kindred ; to whet their swords against those who stood forward to defend the truth ; to maintain a ruthless war and raise unholy hands, not against foreign or barbarian foes, but against men bound to them by the ties of family and affection, against brethren, and kinsmen, and dearest friends, who had resolved, in the practice of virtue and true piety, to honor and worship God. Such was the spirit of madness with 7 which these princes sacrificed to their demon deities men consecrated to the service of the King of kings. On the other hand their victims, as noble martyrs in the cause of true godliness, resolved to welcome a glorious death in preference to life itself, and utterly despised these cruelties. Strengthened, as soldiers of God, with patient fortitude, they mocked at death in all its forms ; at fire, and sword, and the torment of crucifixion ; at exposure to savage beasts, and drowning in the depths of the sea ; at the cutting off and searing of limbs, the digging out of eyes, the mutilation of the whole body ; lastly, at famine, the labor of the mines, and captivity : nay, all these sufferings they counted better than any earthly good or pleasure, for the love they bore their heavenly King. In like manner women also evinced a spirit of constancy and courage not inferior to that of men. Some endured the same conflicts 8 with them, and obtained a like reward of their virtue : others, forcibly carried off to be the victims of violence and pollution, welcomed death rather than dishonor ; while many, very many more, endured not even to hear the same threats wherewith they were assailed by the provincial governors, but boldly sustained every variety of torture, and sentence of death in every form.[4] Thus did these valiant soldiers of the Almighty Sovereign maintain the conflict with steadfast fortitude of soul against the hostile forces of polytheism : and thus did these enemies of God and adversaries of man's salvation, more cruel far than the ferocious savage, delight in libations of human blood : thus did

---

¹ Or Aphrodite.

² [Μέγαν θεὸν καὶ πλούσιον, παρα καὶ Πλούτωνα, τὸν θάνατον ἀνηγόρευον. — Bag.]

³ On these various names, compare Smith, *Dict. of Gr. and Rom. Biog.*

⁴ For account of the various details of persecution mentioned, compare the *Church History.*

their ministers drain as it were the cup of un-righteous slaughter in honor of the demons whom they served, and prepare for them this dread and impious banquet, to the ruin of
9 the human race. In these sad circum-stances, what course should the God and King of these afflicted ones pursue? Could he be careless of the safety of his dearest friends, or abandon his servants in this great extremity? Surely none could deem him a wary pilot, who, without an effort to save his fellow-mariners, should suffer his vessel to sink with all her crew: surely no general could be found so reckless as to yield his own allies, without resistance, to the mercy of the foe: nor can a faithful shepherd regard with unconcern the straying of a single sheep from his flock, but will rather leave the rest in safety, and dare all things for the wan-derer's sake, even, if need be, to contend
10 with savage beasts. The zeal, however, of the great Sovereign of all was for no uncon-scious[5] sheep: his care was exercised for his own faithful host, for those who sustained the battle for his sake: whose conflicts in the cause of godliness he himself approved, and hon-ored those who had returned to his presence with the prize of victory which he only can bestow, uniting them to the angelic choirs. Others he still preserved on earth, to commu-nicate the living seeds of piety to future gene-rations; to be at once eye-witnesses of his vengeance on the ungodly, and narrators
11 of the events. After this he outstretched his arm in judgment on the adversaries, and utterly destroyed them with the stroke of Divine wrath, compelling them, how reluctant soever, to confess with their own lips and recant their wickedness, but raising from the ground and exalting gloriously those who had long been
12 oppressed and disclaimed by all. Such were the dealings of the Supreme Sover-eign, who ordained an invincible champion to be the minister of his heaven-sent vengeance (for our emperor's surpassing piety delights in the title of Servant of God), and him he has proved victorious over all that opposed him, having raised him up, an individual against many foes. For they were indeed numberless, being the friends of many evil spirits (though in reality they were nothing, and hence are now no more); but our emperor is one, appointed by, and the representative of, the one Almighty Sovereign. And they, in the very spirit of impiety, destroyed the righteous with cruel slaughter: but he, in imitation of his Saviour, and knowing only how to save men's lives, has spared and instructed in godliness the im-
13 pious themselves. And so, as truly worthy the name of VICTOR, he has subdued the

[5] "ἀλόγου."

twofold race of barbarians; soothing the savage tribes of men by prudent embassies, compelling them to know and acknowledge their superiors, and reclaiming them from a lawless and brutal life to the governance of reason and humanity; at the same time that he proved by the facts themselves that the fierce and ruthless race of unseen spirits had long ago been vanquished by a higher power. For he who is the preserver of the universe had punished these invisible spirits by an invisible judgment: and our em-peror, as the delegate of the Supreme Sovereign, has followed up the victory, bearing away the spoils of those who have long since died and mouldered into dust, and distributing the plun-der with lavish hand among the soldiers of his victorious Lord.[6]

CHAPTER VIII.

For as soon as he understood that the 1 ignorant multitudes were inspired with a vain and childish dread of these bugbears of error, wrought in gold and silver, he judged it right to remove these also, like stumbling-stones thrown in the path of men walking in the dark, and henceforward to open a royal road, plain and unobstructed, to all. Hav- 2 ing formed this resolution, he considered that no soldiers or military force of any sort was needed for the repression of the evil: a few of his own friends sufficed for this service, and these he sent by a simple expression of his will to visit each several province. Ac- 3 cordingly, sustained by confidence in the emperor's piety and their own personal devo-tion to God, they passed through the midst of numberless tribes and nations, abolishing this ancient system of error in every city and coun-try. They ordered the priests themselves, in the midst of general laughter and scorn, to bring their gods from their dark recesses to the light of day. They then stripped them of their ornaments, and exhibited to the gaze of all the unsightly reality which had been hidden beneath a painted exterior: and lastly, whatever part of the material appeared to be of value they scraped off and melted in the fire to prove its worth, after which they secured and set apart whatever they judged needful for their purposes, leaving to the superstitious worshipers what was alto-gether useless, as a memorial of their shame. Meanwhile our admirable prince 4 was himself engaged in a work similar to that we have described. For at the same time that these costly images of the dead were stripped, as we have said, of their precious

[6] [That is, stripping the images of those whose temples he de-stroyed, and apportioning the spoils among his Christian followers. See the next chapter, which is mostly a transcript of the 54th and 55th chapters of the Third Book of the *Life of Constantine.* — *Bag.*]

materials, he also attacked those composed of brass; causing those to be dragged from their places with ropes, and, as it were, carried away captive, whom the dotage of mythology had esteemed as gods. The next care of our august emperor was to kindle, as it were, a brilliant torch, by the light of which he directed his imperial gaze around, to see if any hidden 5 vestiges of error might yet exist. And as the keen-sighted eagle in its heavenward flight is able to descry from its lofty height the most distant objects on the earth : so did he, whilst residing in the imperial palace of his own fair city, discover, as from a watch-tower, a hidden and fatal snare of souls in the province of Phœnicia. This was a grove and temple, not situated in the midst of any city, or in any public place, as for splendor of effect is gener-6 ally the case, but apart from the beaten and frequented road, on part of the summit of Mount Lebanon, and dedicated to the foul demon known by the name of Venus. It was a school of wickedness for all the abandoned votaries of impurity and such as destroyed their bodies with effeminacy. Here men undeserving the name forgot the dignity of their sex, and propitiated the demon by their effeminate conduct : here too unlawful commerce of women, and adulterous intercourse, with other horrible and infamous practices, were perpetrated in this temple as in a place beyond the scope and restraint of law.

Meantime these evils remained unchecked by the presence of any observer, since no one of fair character ventured to visit such scenes. 7 These proceedings, however, could not escape the vigilance of our august emperor, who, having himself inspected them with characteristic forethought, and judging that such a temple was unfit for the light of heaven, gave orders that the building with its offerings should be utterly destroyed. Accordingly, in obedience to the imperial edict, these engines of an impure superstition were immediately abolished, and the hand of military force was made instrumental in purging the place. And now those who had heretofore lived without restraint, learned, through the imperial threat of punishment, 8 to practice self-control. Thus did our emperor tear the mask from this system of delusive wickedness, and expose it to the public gaze, at the same time proclaiming openly his Saviour's name to all. No advocate appeared ; neither god nor demon, prophet nor diviner, could lend his aid to the detected authors of the imposture. For the souls of men were no longer enveloped in thick darkness : but enlightened by the rays of true godliness, they deplored the ignorance and pitied the blindness of their forefathers, rejoicing at the same time in their

own deliverance from such fatal error.[1] Thus speedily, according to the counsel 9 of the mighty God, and through our emperor's agency, was every enemy, whether visible or unseen, utterly removed : and henceforward peace, the happy nurse of youth, extended her reign throughout the world. Wars were no more, for the gods were not : no more did warfare in country or town, no more did the effusion of human blood, distress mankind, as heretofore, when demon-worship and the madness of idolatry prevailed.

CHAPTER IX.

AND now we may well compare the pres-1 ent with former things, and review these happy changes in contrast with the evils that are past, and mark the elaborate care with which in ancient times porches and sacred precincts, groves and temples, were prepared in every city for these false deities, and how their shrines were enriched with abundant offerings. The 2 sovereign rulers of those days had indeed a high regard for the worship of the gods. The nations also and people subject to their power honored them with images both in the country and in every city, nay, even in their houses and secret chambers, according to the religious practice of their fathers. The fruit, however, of this devotion, far different from the peaceful concord which now meets our view, appeared in war, in battles, and seditions, which harassed them throughout their lives, and deluged their countries with blood and civil slaughter. Again, the objects of their worship could 3 hold out to these sovereigns with artful flattery the promise of prophecies, and oracles, and the knowledge of futurity : yet could they not predict their own destruction, nor forewarn themselves of the coming ruin : and surely this was the greatest and most convincing proof of their imposture. Not one of those whose 4 words once were heard with awe and wonder, had announced the glorious advent of the Saviour of mankind,[1] or that new revelation of divine knowledge which he came to give. Not Pythius himself, nor any of those mighty gods, could apprehend the prospect of their approaching desolation ; nor could their oracles point at him who was to be their conqueror and destroyer. What prophet or diviner could 5 foretell that their rites would vanish at the presence of a new Deity in the world, and that the knowledge and worship of the Almighty Sovereign should be freely given to all mankind?

[1] " The Pharisee stood and prayed thus with himself, God, I thank thee that I am not as the rest of men."
[1] He seems to disagree with the view of the heathen prophecy which his imperial hearer maintained in his *Oration to the Saints.*

Which of them foreknew the august and pious reign of our victorious emperor, or his triumphant conquests everywhere over the false demons, or the overthrow of their high places?

6 Which of the heroes has announced the melting down and conversion of the lifeless statues from their useless forms to the necessary uses of men? Which of the gods have yet had power to speak of their own images thus melted and contemptuously reduced to fragments?

7 Where were the protecting powers, that they should not interpose to save their sacred memorials, thus destroyed by man? Where, I ask, are those who once maintained the strife of war, yet now behold their conquerors abiding securely in the profoundest peace? And where are they who upheld themselves in a blind and foolish confidence, and trusted in these vanities as gods; but who, in the very height of their superstitious error, and while maintaining an implacable war with the champions of the truth, perished by a fate proportioned to their

8 crimes? Where is the giant race whose arms were turned against heaven itself; the hissings of those serpents whose tongues were pointed with impious words against the Almighty King? These adversaries of the Lord of all, confident in the aid of a multitude of gods, advanced to the attack with a powerful array of military force, preceded by certain images of the dead, and lifeless statues, as their defense. On the other side our emperor, secure in the armor of godliness, opposed to the numbers of the enemy the salutary and life-giving Sign, as at the same time a terror to the foe, and a protection against every harm; and returned victorious at once over the enemy and the demons whom they served.[2] And then, with thanksgiving and praise, the tokens of a grateful spirit, to the Author of his victory, he proclaimed this triumphant Sign, by monuments as well as words, to all mankind, erecting it as a mighty trophy against every enemy in the midst of the imperial city, and expressly enjoining on all to acknowledge this imperishable symbol of salvation as the safeguard of the power of Rome and of the

9 empire of the world. Such were the instructions which he gave to his subjects generally; but especially to his soldiers, whom he admonished to repose their confidence, not in their weapons, or armor, or bodily strength, but to acknowledge the Supreme God as the giver of every good, and of victory itself.

10 Thus did the emperor himself, strange and incredible as the fact may seem, become the instructor of his army in their religious exercises, and teach them to offer pious prayers in

accordance with the divine ordinances, uplifting their hands towards heaven, and raising their mental vision higher still to the King of heaven, on whom they should call as the Author of victory, their preserver, guardian, and helper. He commanded too, that one day should be regarded as a special occasion for religious worship; I mean that which is truly the first and chief of all, the day of our Lord and Saviour; that day the name of which is connected with light, and life, and immortality, and every good.

11 Prescribing the same pious conduct to himself, he honored his Saviour in the chambers of his palace, performing his devotions according to the Divine commands, and storing his mind with instruction through the hearing of the sacred word. The entire care of his household was intrusted to ministers devoted to the service of God, and distinguished by gravity of life and every other virtue; while his trusty body-guards, strong in affection and fidelity to his person, found in their emperor an instructor in the practice of a godly life.

12 Again, the honor with which he regards the victorious Sign is founded on his actual experience of its divine efficacy. Before this the hosts of his enemies have disappeared: by this the powers of the unseen spirits have been turned to flight: through this the proud boastings of God's adversaries have come to nought, and the tongues of the profane and blasphemous been put to silence. By this Sign the Barbarian tribes were vanquished: through this the rites of superstitious fraud received a just rebuke: by this our emperor, discharging as it were a sacred debt, has performed the crowning good of all, by erecting triumphant memorials of its value in all parts of the world, raising temples and churches on a scale of royal costliness, and commanding all to unite in constructing the sacred houses of prayer.

13 Accordingly these signal proofs of our emperor's magnificence forthwith appeared in the provinces and cities of the empire, and soon shone conspicuously in every country; convincing memorials of the rebuke and overthrow of those impious tyrants who but a little while before had madly dared to fight against God, and, raging like savage dogs, had vented on unconscious buildings that fury which they were unable to level against him; had thrown to the ground and upturned the very foundations of the houses of prayer, causing them to present the appearance of a city captured and abandoned to the enemy. Such was the exhibition of that wicked spirit whereby they sought as it were to assail God himself, but soon experienced the result of their own madness and folly. But a little time elapsed, when a single blast of the storm of Heaven's displeasure swept

[2] For details respecting the following enumeration, compare the *Life of Constantine*, of which this is a résumé. This sentence and the preceding are taken almost word for word from ch. 16 of Bk. II.

them utterly away, leaving neither kindred, nor offspring, nor memorial of their existence among men : for all, numerous as they were, disap- peared as in a moment beneath the stroke 14 of Divine vengeance. Such, then, was the fate which awaited these furious adversaries of God : but he who, armed with the salutary Trophy, had alone opposed them (nay rather, not alone, but aided by the presence and the power of him who is the only Sovereign), has replaced the ruined edifices on a greater scale, and made the second far superior to the first. For example, besides erecting various churches to the honor of God in the city which bears his name, and adorning the Bithynian capital with another on the greatest and most splendid scale, he has distinguished the principal cities of the other provinces by structures of a similar 15 kind. Above all, he has selected two places in the eastern division of the empire, the one in Palestine (since from thence the life- giving stream has flowed as from a fountain for the blessing of all nations), the other in that me- tropolis of the East which derives its name from that of Antiochus ; in which, as the head of that portion of the empire, he has consecrated to the service of God a church of unparalleled size and beauty. The entire building is encom- passed by an enclosure of great extent, within which the church itself rises to a vast elevation, of an octagonal form, surrounded by many chambers and courts on every side, and dec- orated with ornaments of the richest kind.[3] 16 Such was his work here. Again, in the province of Palestine, in that city which was once the seat of Hebrew sovereignty, on the very site of the Lord's sepulchre, he has raised a church of noble dimensions, and adorned a temple sacred to the salutary Cross with rich and lavish magnificence, honoring that everlasting monument, and the trophies of the Saviour's victory over the power of death, with a splendor which no language can describe. 17 In the same country he discovered three places venerable as the localities of three sacred caves : and these also he adorned with costly structures, paying a fitting tribute of rev- erence to the scene of the first manifestation of the Saviour's presence ; while at the second cavern he hallowed the remembrance of his final ascension from the mountain top ; and celebrated his mighty conflict, and the victory which crowned it, at the third.[4] All these places our emperor thus adorned in the hope of proclaiming the symbol of redemption to

---

[3] Almost word for word from the *Life*, Bk. III. ch. 50.
[4] [In the *Life of Constantine* (vide [Bk. III. ch. 41] supra), Eusebius mentions two caves only, and speaks of the churches built by Helena at Bethlehem and on the Mount of Olives. He here al- ludes to the magnificent church erected by Constantine at the Lord's sepulchre, and ascribes to him those of Helena also, as having been raised at the emperor's expense. Valesius, ad loc.—*Bag.*]

all mankind ; that Cross which has in- 18 deed repaid his pious zeal ; through which his house and throne alike have prospered, his reign has been confirmed for a lengthened series of years, and the rewards of virtue bestowed on his noble sons, his kindred, and their de- scendants. And surely it is a mighty evi- 19 dence of the power of that God whom he serves, that he has held the balances of justice with an equal hand, and has apportioned to each party their due reward. With regard to the destroyers of the houses of prayer, the penalty of their impious conduct followed hard upon them : forthwith were they swept away, and left neither race, nor house, nor family behind. On the other hand, he whose pious devotion to his Lord is conspicuous in his every act, who raises royal temples to his honor, and proclaims his name to his subjects by sacred offerings throughout the world, he, I say, has de- servedly experienced him to be the preserver and defender of his imperial house and race. Thus clearly have the dealings of God been manifested, and this through the sacred efficacy of the salutary Sign.

CHAPTER X.

MUCH might indeed be said of this salu- 1 tary Sign, by those who are skilled in the mysteries of our Divine religion. For it is in very truth the symbol of salvation, wondrous to speak of, more wondrous still to conceive ; the appearance of which on earth has thrown the fictions of all false religion from the beginning into the deepest shade, has buried superstitious error in darkness and oblivion, and has revealed to all that spiritual light which enlightens the souls of men, even the knowledge of the only true God. Hence the universal change 2 for the better, which leads men to spurn their lifeless idols, to trample under foot the lawless rites of their demon deities, and laugh to scorn the time-honored follies of their fathers. Hence, too, the establishment in every place of those schools of sacred learning, wherein men are taught the precepts of saving truth, and dread no more those objects of creation which are seen by the natural eye, nor direct a gaze of wonder at the sun, the moon, or stars ; but acknowledge him who is above all these, that invisible Being who is the Creator of them all, and learn to worship him alone. Such 3 are the blessings resulting to mankind from this great and wondrous Sign, by virtue of which the evils which once existed are now no more, and virtues heretofore unknown shine every- where resplendent with the light of true godliness. Discourses, and precepts, and 4 exhortations to a virtuous and holy life, are proclaimed in the ears of all nations. Nay, the emperor himself proclaims them : and it is indeed a marvel that this mighty prince, raising his voice in the hearing of all the world, like an interpreter of the Almighty Sovereign's will, invites his subjects in every country to the 5 knowledge of the true God. No more, as in former times, is the babbling of impious men heard in the imperial palace ; but priests and pious worshipers of God together celebrate his majesty with royal hymns of praise. The name of the one Supreme Ruler of the universe is proclaimed to all : the gospel of glad tidings connects the human race with its Almighty King, declaring the grace and love of the heavenly Father to his children on the earth. His praise is everywhere sung in triumphant strains : the voice of mortal man is blended with the har- 6 mony of the angelic choirs in heaven ; and the reasoning soul employs the body which invests it as an instrument for sounding forth a fitting tribute of praise and adoration to his name. The nations of the East and the West are instructed at the same moment in his precepts : the people of the Northern and Southern regions unite with one accord, under the influence of the same principles and laws, in the pursuit of a godly life, in praising the one Supreme God, in acknowledging his only begotten Son their Saviour as the source of every blessing, and our emperor as the one ruler on the earth, together with his pious sons. 7 He himself, as a skillful pilot, sits on high at the helm of state, and directs the vessel with unerring course, conducting his people as it were with favoring breeze to a secure and tranquil haven. Meanwhile God himself, the great Sovereign, extends the right hand of his power from above for his protection, giving him victory over every foe, and establishing his empire by a lengthened period of years : and he will bestow on him yet higher blessings, and confirm in every deed the truth of his own promises. But on these we may not at present dwell ; but must await the change to a better world : for it is not given to mortal eyes or ears of flesh, fully to apprehend the things of God.[1]

CHAPTER XI.

1   AND now, victorious and mighty Constantine, in this discourse, whose noble argument is the glory of the Almighty King, let me lay before thee some of the mysteries of his sacred truth : not as presuming to instruct thee, who art thyself taught of God ; nor to disclose to thee those secret wonders which he himself, not through the agency of man, but through our common Saviour, and the frequent light of his Divine presence has long since revealed and unfolded to thy view : but in the hope of leading the unlearned to the light, and displaying before those who know them not the causes and motives of thy pious deeds. True it is 2 that thy noble efforts for the daily worship and honor of the Supreme God throughout the habitable world, are the theme of universal praise. But those records of gratitude to thy Saviour and Preserver which thou hast dedicated in our own province of Palestine, and in that city from which as from a fountain-head the Saviour Word[1] has issued forth to all mankind ; and again, the hallowed edifices and consecrated temples which thou hast raised as trophies of his victory over death ; and those lofty and noble structures, imperial monuments of an imperial spirit, which thou hast erected in honor of the everlasting memory of the Saviour's tomb ; the cause, I say, of these things is not equally obvious to all. Those, indeed, who are en- 3 lightened in heavenly knowledge by the power of the Divine Spirit, well understand the cause, and justly admire and bless thee for that counsel and resolution which Heaven itself inspired. On the other hand the ignorant and spiritually blind regard these designs with open mockery and scorn, and deem it a strange and unworthy thing indeed that so mighty a prince should waste his zeal on the graves and monuments of the dead. " Were it not 4 better," such a one might say, " to cherish those rites which are hallowed by ancient usage ; to seek the favor of those gods and heroes whose worship is observed in every province ; instead of rejecting and disclaiming them, because subject to the calamities incident to man ? Surely they may claim equal honors with him who himself has suffered : or, if they are to be rejected, as not exempt from the sorrows of humanity, the same award would justly be pronounced respecting him." Thus, with important and contracted brow, might he give utterance in pompous language to his self-imagined wisdom. Filled with compassion for this 5 ignorance, the gracious Word of our most beneficent Father freely invites, not such a one alone, but all who are in the path of error, to receive instruction in Divine knowledge ; and has ordained the means of such instruction throughout the world, in every country and village, in cultivated and desert lands alike, and in every city : and, as a gracious Saviour and Physician of the soul, calls on the Greek and the Barbarian, the wise and the unlearned, the rich

---

[1] At this point, according to some (compare Special Prolegomena), one oration ends and another begins.

[1] Here the author seems to speak doubly of the Word and the word.

and the poor, the servant and his master, the subject and his lord, the ungodly, the profane, the ignorant, the evil-doer, the blasphemer, alike to draw near, and hasten to receive his heavenly cure. And thus in time past had he clearly announced to all the pardon of former transgressions, saying, "Come unto me, all ye that labor and are heavy laden, and I will give you rest."[2] And again, "I am not come to call the righteous, but sinners, to repentance."[3] And he adds the reason, saying, "For they that are whole need not a physician, but they that are sick."[4] And again, "I desire not the death of a sinner, but rather that he

6 should repent."[5] Hence it is only for those who are themselves instructed in Divine things and understand the motives of that zeal of which these works are the result, to appreciate the more than human impulse by which our emperor was guided, to admire his piety toward God, and to believe his care for the memorial of our Saviour's resurrection to be a desire imparted from above, and truly inspired by that Sovereign, to be whose faithful servant and minister for good is his proudest boast.

7 In full persuasion, then, of thy approval, most mighty emperor, I desire at this present time to proclaim to all the reasons and motives of thy pious works. I desire to stand as the interpreter of thy designs, to explain the counsels of a soul devoted to the love of God. I propose to teach all men, what all should know who care to understand the principles on which our Saviour God employs his power, the reasons for which he who was the pre-existent Controller of all things at length descended to us from heaven: the reasons for which he assumed our nature, and submitted even to the power of death. I shall declare the causes of that immortal life which followed, and of his resurrection from the dead. Once more, I shall adduce convincing proofs and arguments, for the sake of those who yet need such

8 testimony: and now let me commence my appointed task.

Those who transfer the worship due to that God who formed and rules the world to the works of his hand; who hold the sun and moon, or other parts of this material system, nay, the elements themselves, earth, water, air, and fire, in equal honor with the Creator of them all; who give the name of gods to things which

never would have had existence, or even name, except as obedient to that Word of God who made the world: such persons in my judgment resemble those who overlook the master hand which gives its magnificence to a royal palace; and, while lost in wonder at its roofs and walls, the paintings of varied beauty and coloring which adorn them, and its gilded ceilings and sculptures, ascribe to them the praise of that skill which belongs to the artist whose work they are: whereas they should assign the cause of their wonder, not to these visible objects, but to the architect himself, and confess that the proofs of skill are indeed manifest, but that he alone is the possessor of that skill who has made them what they are. Again, well 9 might we liken those to children, who should admire the seven-stringed lyre, and disregard him who invented or has power to use it: or those who forget the valiant warrior, and adorn his spear and shield with the chaplet of victory: or, lastly, those who hold the squares and streets, the public buildings, temples, and gymnasia of a great and royal city in equal honor with its founder; forgetting that their admiration is due, not to lifeless stones, but to him whose wisdom planned and executed these mighty works. Not less absurd is it for 10 those who regard this universe with the natural eye to ascribe its origin to the sun, or moon, or any other heavenly body. Rather let them confess that these are themselves the works of a higher wisdom, remember the Maker and Framer of them all, and render to him the praise and honor above all created objects. Nay rather, inspired by the sight of these very objects, let them address themselves with full purpose of heart to glorify and worship him who is now invisible to mortal eye, but perceived by the clear and unclouded vision of the soul, the supremely sovereign Word of God. To take the instance of the human body: no one has yet conferred the attribute of wisdom on the eyes, or head, the hands, or feet, or other members, far less on the outward clothing, of a wise and learned man: no one terms the philosopher's household furniture and utensils, wise: but every rational person admires that invisible and secret power, the mind of the man himself. How much more, then, is our admiration 11 due, not to the visible mechanism of the universe, material as it is, and formed of the selfsame elements; but to that invisible Word who has moulded and arranged it all, who is the only-begotten Son of God, and whom the Maker of all things, who far transcends all being, has begotten of himself, and appointed Lord and Governor of this universe? For since it 12 was impossible that perishable bodies, or the rational spirits which he had created, should

---

[2] Matt. xi. 28.
[3] Matt. xi. 13. R. V.: "For I came not to call the righteous, but sinners." The text here has the reading εισμετανοιαν, omitted by Tischendorf and the revisers with אB, etc., but supported by CEGKL, sab. cop., etc. It is worth noting that it is not in the Sinaitic, and if this text reading is correct it would nearly overthrow the possibility that this MS. was one of those prepared under the direction of Eusebius.   [4] Matt. xi. 12.
[5] Ezek. xviii. 23. R. V.: "Have I any pleasure in the death of the wicked, saith the Lord God: and not rather that he should return from his way and live?"

approach the Supreme God, by reason of their immeasurable distance from his perfections, for he is unbegotten, above and beyond all creation, ineffable, inaccessible, unapproachable, dwelling, as his holy word assures us,[6] in the light which none can enter; but they were created from nothing, and are infinitely far removed from his unbegotten Essence; well has the all-gracious and Almighty God interposed as it were an intermediate Power[7] between himself and them, even the Divine omnipotence of his only-begotten Word. And this Power, which is in perfect nearness and intimacy of union, with the Father, which abides in him, and shares his secret counsels, has yet condescended, in fullness of grace, as it were to conform itself to those who are so far removed from the supreme majesty of God. How else, consistently with his own holiness, could he who is far above and beyond all things unite himself to corruptible and corporeal matter? Accordingly the Divine Word, thus connecting himself with this universe, and receiving into his hands the reins, as it were, of the world, turns and directs it as a skillful charioteer according to his own will and pleasure. The 13 proof of these assertions is evident. For supposing that those component parts of the world which we call elements, as earth, water, air, and fire, the nature of which is manifestly without intelligence, are self-existent; and if they have one common essence, which they who are skilled in natural science call the great receptacle, mother, and nurse of all things; and if this itself be utterly devoid of shape and figure, of soul and reason; whence shall we say it has obtained its present form and beauty? To what shall we ascribe the distinction of the elements, or the union of things contrary in their very nature? Who has commanded the liquid water to sustain the heavy element of earth? Who has turned back the waters from their downward course, and carried them aloft in clouds? Who has bound the force of fire, and caused it to lie latent in wood, and to combine with substances most contrary to itself? Who has mingled the cold air with heat, and thus reconciled the enmity of opposing principles? Who has devised the continuous suc-

cession of the human race, and given it as it were an endless term of duration? Who has moulded the male and female form, adapted their mutual relations with perfect harmony, and given one common principle of production to every living creature? Who changes the character of the fluid and corruptible seed, which in itself is void of reason, and gives it its prolific power? Who is at this moment working these and ten thousand effects more wonderful than these, nay, surpassing all wonder, and with invisible influence is daily and hourly perpetuating the production of them all? Surely 14 the wonder-working and truly omnipotent Word of God may well be deemed the efficient cause of all these things: that Word who, diffusing himself through all creation, pervading height and depth with incorporeal energy, and embracing the length and breadth of the universe within his mighty grasp, has compacted and reduced to order this entire system, from whose unreasoned and formless matter he has framed for himself an instrument of perfect harmony, the nicely balanced chords and notes of which he touches with all-wise and unerring skill. He it is who governs the sun, and moon, and the other luminaries of heaven by inexplicable laws, and directs their motions for the service of the universal whole. It 15 is this Word of God who has stooped to the earth on which we live, and created the manifold species of animals, and the fair varieties of the vegetable world. It is this same Word who has penetrated the recesses of the deep, has given their being to the finny race, and produced the countless forms of life which there exist. It is he who fashions the burden of the womb, and informs it in nature's laboratory with the principle of life. By him the fluid and heavy moisture is raised on high, and then, sweetened by a purifying change, descends in measured quantities to the earth, and at stated seasons in more profuse supply. Like a skillful husbandman, 16 he fully irrigates the land, tempers the moist and dry in just proportion, diversifying the whole with brilliant flowers, with aspects of varied beauty, with pleasant fragrance, with alternating varieties of fruits, and countless gratifications for the taste of men. But why do I dare essay a hopeless task, to recount the mighty works of the Word of God, and describe an energy which surpasses mortal thought? By some, indeed, he has been termed the Nature of the universe, by others, the World-Soul, by others, Fate. Others again have declared him to be the most High God himself, strangely confounding things most widely different; bringing down to this earth, uniting to a corruptible and material body, and assigning to that supreme and unbegotten Power who is Lord of all an intermediate place between

---

[6] 1 Tim. vi. 16.

[7] [This whole passage (which is defended by Valesius) appears, if rigidly interpreted, to lie under suspicion of a tinge of Arianism. — *Bag.*] It savors directly of Philo. His doctrine was of an ineffable God, above and separate from matter, and defiled by any contact with it. To bring him into connection with created things he introduced intermediate beings, or "powers," the universal power including all the rest being the Logos. Compare brief account in Zeller's *Outlines of Greek Philosophy*, p. 320-325; Siegfried, *Philo von Alexandria* (Jena, 1875), especially p. 199 sq., 219 sq., and p. 362-364, where he treats very inadequately of Eusebius' dependence on Philo; also works of Philo and Eusebius' *Præp.* and *Demonst. Ev.* There is a chance of viewing the Word thus as created, but if this is guarded against (as it is by him in the use of "begotten"), there is nothing intrinsically heterodox in making the Word the Creator of the world and only Revealer of the Father. The direct Philonian influence is seen in the phraseology of the following sentences.

irrational animals and rational mortals on the one hand, and immortal beings on the other.[8]

CHAPTER XII.

1 ON the other hand, the sacred doctrine teaches that he who is the supreme Source of good, and Cause of all things, is beyond all comprehension, and therefore inexpressible by word, or speech, or name ; surpassing the power, not of language only, but of thought itself. Uncircumscribed by place, or body ; neither in heaven, nor in ethereal space, nor in any other part of the universe ; but entirely independent of all things else, he pervades the depths of unexplored and secret wisdom. The sacred oracles teach us to acknowledge him as the only true God,[1] apart from all corporeal essence, distinct from all subordinate ministration. Hence it is said that all things are from him, but
2 not through him.[2] And he himself dwelling as Sovereign in secret and undiscovered regions of unapproachable light, ordains and disposes all things by the single power of his own will. At his will whatever is, exists ; without that will, it cannot be. And his will is in every case for good, since he is essentially Goodness itself. But he through whom are all things, even God the Word, proceeding in an ineffable manner from the Father above, as from an everlasting and exhaustless fountain, flows onward like a river with a full and abundant stream of power for the preservation of the universal whole.
3 And now let us select an illustration from our own experience. The invisible and undiscovered mind within us, the essential nature of which no one has ever known, sits as a monarch in the seclusion of his secret chambers, and alone resolves on our course of action. From this proceeds the only-begotten word from its father's bosom, begotten in a manner and by a power inexplicable to us ; and is the first mes-

senger of its father's thoughts, declares his secret counsels, and, conveying itself to the ears of others, accomplishes his designs. And
4 thus the advantage of this faculty is enjoyed by all : yet no one has ever yet beheld that invisible and hidden mind, which is the parent of the word itself.[3] In the same manner, or rather in a manner which far surpasses all likeness or comparison, the perfect Word of the Supreme God, as the only-begotten Son of the Father (not consisting in the power of utterance, nor comprehended in syllables and parts of speech, nor conveyed by a voice which vibrates on the air ; but being himself the living and effectual Word of the most High, and subsisting personally as the Power and Wisdom of God),[4] proceeds from his Father's Deity and kingdom.[5] Thus, being the perfect Offspring of a perfect Father, and the common Preserver of all things, he diffuses himself with living power throughout creation, and pours from his own fullness abundant supplies of reason,[6] wisdom, light, and every other blessing, not only on objects nearest to himself, but on those most remote, whether in earth, or sea, or any other sphere of being. To all these
5 he appoints with perfect equity their limits, places, laws, and inheritance, allotting to each their suited portion according to his sovereign will. To some he assigns the super-terrestrial regions, to others heaven itself as their habitation : others he places in ethereal space, others in air, and others still on earth. He it is who transfers mankind from hence to another sphere, impartially reviews their conduct here, and bestows a recompense according to the life and habits of each. By him provision is made for the life and food, not of rational creatures only, but also of the brute creation, for the service of men ; and while to the latter he
6 grants the enjoyment of a perishable and fleeting term of existence, the former he invites to a share in the possession of immortal life. Thus universal is the agency of the Word of God : everywhere present, and pervading all things by the power of his intelligence, he looks upward to his Father, and governs this lower creation, inferior to and consequent upon himself, in accordance with his will, as the common Preserver of all things. Interme-
7

---

[8] [Of this somewhat obscure passage, a translator can do no more than give as nearly as possible a literal version. The intelligent reader will not fail to perceive that the author, here and in the following chapter, has trodden on very dangerous ground. — *Bag.*] Compare above notes on the relations of Eusebius and Philo.

[1] [Referring, apparently, to John xvii. 3, " And this is life eternal, that they might know thee the only true God, and Jesus Christ whom thou hast sent : " a passage which has been called a stronghold of the impugners of the Deity of Christ ; but which, simply considered with its context, cannot fairly be understood to indicate any inferiority of the Son to the Father ; but rather appears to speak of the mission of the former as the manifestation of the grace of him who is called " the only true God " in contradistinction to the polytheism of the heathen world. In other words, the knowledge of " the only true God," in connection with that of " Jesus Christ whom he has sent," constitutes " eternal life " ; the one being ineffectual, and indeed impossible, without the other. — *Bag.*] Compare 1 John v. 20-21 : " That we know him that is true and we are in him that is true, even in his Son Jesus Christ. This is the true God and eternal life," which seems to show that John had no idea of any subordination in essence in this matter.

[2] [But see, for a refutation of this statement, Rom. xi. 36, and Heb. ii. 10. — *Bag.*] Yet the second of these references clearly refers to the Son. Eusebius, speaking of God the Father, has in mind the truth that all things were made by the Son, " and without him was not anything made that hath been made." John i. 3.

[3] The author is now speaking especially of the spoken or " expressed " word.

[4] Compare 1 Cor. i. 24.

[5] This conception that the Divine Word stands in something the same relation with the Father that the human word (internal and external) does to the human spirit has, at least, an interesting suggestion towards the unraveling of this curious mystery, which, for lack of a better word, it is the fashion just now to call a human personality, and which certainly is made in the image and likeness of God. Unless there lurks in the idea some subtle heresy, one may venture to accept as an interesting analogy this relation of invisible self, self expressed to self (internal word), self revealed (external word), and an expression carried to the point of embodiment (incarnation).

[6] " Logos " again, — here the internal word.

diate, as it were, and attracting the created to the uncreated Essence, this Word of God exists as an unbroken bond between the two, uniting things most widely different by an inseparable tie. He is the Providence which rules the universe; the guardian and director of the whole: he is the Power and Wisdom of God, the only-begotten God, the Word begotten of God himself. For "In the beginning was the Word, and the Word was with God, and the Word was God. All things were made by him; and without him was not anything made that hath been made"; as we learn from the words of the sacred writer.[7] Through his vivifying power all nature grows and flourishes, refreshed by his continual showers, and invested 8 with a vigor and beauty ever new. Guiding the reigns of the universe, he holds its onward course in conformity to the Father's will; and moves, as it were, the helm of this mighty ship. This glorious Agent, the only-begotten Son of the Supreme God, begotten by the Father as his perfect Offspring, the Father has given to this world as the highest of all goods; infusing his word, as spirit into a lifeless body, into unconscious nature; imparting light and energy to that which in itself was a rude, inanimate, and formless mass, through the Divine power. Him therefore it is ours to acknowledge and regard as everywhere present, and giving life to matter and the elements of nature:[8] in him we see Light, even the spiritual offspring of inexpressible Light: one indeed in essence, as being the Son of one Father; but possessing in himself many and varied 9 powers. The world is indeed divided into many parts; yet let us not therefore suppose that there are many independent Agents: nor, though creation's works be manifold, let us thence assume the existence of many gods. How grievous the error of those childish and infatuated advocates of polytheistic worship, who deify the constituent parts of the universe, and divide into many that system which is only 10 one! Such conduct resembles theirs who should abstract the eyes of an individual man, and term them the man himself, and the ears, another man, and so the head: or again, by an effort of thought should separate the neck, the breast and shoulders, the feet and hands, or other members, nay, the very powers of sense, and thus pronounce an individual to be a multitude of men. Such folly must surely be rewarded with contempt by men of sense. Yet such is he who from the component parts of a single world can devise for himself a multitude of gods, or even deem that world which is the

work of a Creator, and consists of many parts, to be itself a god:[9] not knowing that the Divine Nature can in no sense be divisible into parts; since, if compounded, it must be so through the agency of another power; and that which is so compounded can never be Divine. How indeed could it be so, if composed of unequal and dissimilar, and hence of worse and better elements? Simple, indivisible, uncompounded, the Divine Nature exists at an infinite elevation above the visible constitution of this world. And hence we are assured by the 11 clear testimony of the sacred Herald,[10] that the Word of God, who is before all things, must be the sole Preserver of all intelligent beings: while God, who is above all, and the Author of the generation of the Word, being himself the Cause of all things, is rightly called the Father of the Word, as of his only-begotten Son, himself acknowledging no superior Cause. God, therefore, himself is One, and from him proceeds the one only-begotten Word, the omnipresent Preserver of all things. And as the many-stringed lyre is composed of different chords, both sharp and flat, some slightly, others tensely strained, and others intermediate between the two extremes, yet all attuned according to the rules of harmonic art; even so this material world, compounded as it is of many elements, containing opposite and antagonist principles, as moisture and dryness, cold and heat, yet blended into one harmonious whole, may justly be termed a mighty instrument framed by the hand of God: an instrument on which the Divine Word, himself not composed of parts or opposing principles, but indivisible and uncompounded, performs with perfect skill, and produces a melody at once accordant with the will of his Father the Supreme Lord of all, and glorious to himself. Again, as there are manifold external and internal parts and members comprised in a single body, yet one invisible soul, one undivided and incorporeal mind pervades the whole; so is it in this creation, which, consisting of many parts, yet is but one: and so the One mighty, yea, Almighty Word of God, pervading all things, and diffusing himself with undeviating energy throughout this universe, is the Cause of all things that exist therein. Survey the com- 12 pass of this visible world. Seest thou not how the same heaven contains within itself the countless courses and companies of the stars?

---

[7] John i. 1-3.

[8] One on the scent for heresy might prick up his ears, and sound the alarm of "Gnosticism."

[9] A curious work just issued (anonymous), under the authority of the Bureau of Education, very complacently evolves the truth of existence out of the author's pure, untrammeled consciousness,—for he has never read any works either on science or on theology,—and arrives at the condescending conclusion that there is a God; or rather, in the words of Eusebius, the author comes to "deem that world . . . to be itself God."

[10] [Referring (says Valesius) to St. John, whose words Eusebius had lately cited, "In the beginning was the Word," &c., and now explains paraphrastically. The reader will decide for himself on the merits of the paraphrase. — Bag.]

Again, the sun is one, and yet eclipses many, nay all other luminaries, by the surpassing glory of his rays. Even so, as the Father himself is One, his Word is also One, the perfect Son of that perfect Father. Should any one object because they are not more, as well might he complain that there are not many suns, or moons, or worlds, and a thousand things beside; like the madman, who would fain subvert the fair and perfect course of Nature herself. As in the visible, so also in the spiritual world: in the one the same sun diffuses his light throughout this material earth; in the other the One Almighty Word of God illumines all things with in-
13 visible and secret power. Again, there is in man one spirit, and one faculty of reason, which yet is the active cause of numberless effects. The same mind, instructed in many things, will essay to cultivate the earth, to build and guide a ship, and construct houses: nay, the one mind and reason of man is capable of acquiring knowledge in a thousand forms: the same mind shall understand geometry and astronomy, and discourse on the rules of grammar, and rhetoric, and the healing art. Nor will it excel in science only, but in practice too: and yet no one has ever supposed the existence of many minds in one human form, nor expressed his wonder at a plurality of being in man, because he is thus capable of varied knowl-
14 edge. Suppose one were to find a shapeless mass of clay, to mould it with his hands, and give it the form of a living creature; the head in one figure, the hands and feet in another, the eyes and cheeks in a third, and so to fashion the ears, the mouth and nose, the breast and shoulders, according to the rules of the plastic art. The result, indeed, is a variety of figure, of parts and members in the one body; yet must we not suppose it the work of many hands, but ascribe it entirely to the skill of a single artist, and yield the tribute of our praise to him who by the energy of a single mind has framed it all. The same is true of the universe itself, which is one, though consisting of many parts: yet surely we need not suppose many creative powers, nor invent a plurality of gods. Our duty is to adore the all-wise and all-perfect agency of him who is indeed the Power and the Wisdom of God, whose undivided force and energy pervades and penetrates the universe, creating and giving life to all things, and furnishing to all, collectively and severally, those manifold supplies of which he is himself the
15 source. Even so one and the same impression of the solar rays illumines the air at once, gives light to the eyes, warmth to the touch, fertility to the earth, and growth to plants. The same luminary constitutes the course of time, governs the motions of the stars, performs the circuit of the heavens, imparts beauty to the earth, and displays the power of God to all: and all this he performs by the sole and unaided force of his own nature. In like manner fire has the property of refining gold, and fusing lead, of dissolving wax, of parching clay, and consuming wood; producing these varied effects by one and the same burning power. 16 So also the Supreme Word of God, pervading all things, everywhere existent, everywhere present in heaven and earth, governs and directs the visible and invisible creation, the sun, the heaven, and the universe itself, with an energy inexplicable in its nature, irresistible in its effects. From him, as from an everlasting fountain, the sun, the moon, and stars receive their light: and he forever rules that heaven which he has framed as the fitting emblem of his own greatness. The angelic and spiritual powers, the incorporeal and intelligent beings which exist beyond the sphere of heaven and earth, are filled by him with light and life, with wisdom and virtue, with all that is great and good, from his own peculiar treasures. Once more, with one and the same creative skill, he ceases not to furnish the elements with substance, to regulate the union and combinations, the forms and figures, and the innumerable qualities of organized bodies; preserving the varied distinctions of animal and vegetable life, of the rational and the brute creation; and supplying all things to all with equal power: thus proving himself the Author, not indeed of the seven-stringed lyre,[11] but of that system of perfect harmony which is the workmanship of the One world-creating Word.[12]

CHAPTER XIII.

AND now let us proceed to explain the 1 reasons for which this mighty Word of God descended to dwell with men. Our ignorant and foolish race, incapable of comprehending him who is the Lord of heaven and earth, proceeding from his Father's Deity as from the supreme fountain, ever present throughout the world, and evincing by the clearest proofs his providential care for the interests of man; have ascribed the adorable title of Deity to the sun, and moon, the heaven and the stars of heaven. Nor did they stop here, but deified the earth itself, its products, and the various substances by which animal life is sustained, and devised

---

[11] [In reference, singularly enough, to the illustration of the lyre in the preceding chapter. — *Bag.*]
[12] It is idle to treat as philosophically or theologically unworthy of consideration a system of thought so definitely unified, and with such Scriptural basis as the above. It may not be profound or original, but is definite and clear.

images of Ceres, of Proserpine, of Bacchus,[1] and many such as these. Nay, they shrank not from giving the name of gods to the very conceptions of their own minds, and the speech by which those conceptions are expressed; calling the mind itself Minerva, and language Mercury,[2] and affixing the names of Mnemosyne and the Muses to those faculties by means of which science is acquired. Nor was even this enough: advancing still more rapidly in the career of impiety and folly, they deified their own evil passions, which it behooved them to regard with aversion, or restrain by the principles of self-control. Their very lust and passion and impure disease of soul, the members of the body which tempt to obscenity, and even the very uncontrol[3] in shameful pleasure, they described under the titles of Cupid, Priapus, Venus,[4] and other kindred terms. Nor did they stop even here. Degrading their thoughts of God to this corporeal and mortal life, they deified their fellow-men, conferring the names of gods and heroes on those who had experienced the common lot of all, and vainly imagining that the Divine and imperishable Essence could frequent the tombs and monuments of the dead. Nay, more than this: they paid divine honors to animals of various species, and to the most noxious reptiles: they felled trees, and excavated rocks; they provided themselves with brass, and iron, and other metals, of which they fashioned resemblances of the male and female human form, of beasts, and creeping things; and these they made the objects of their worship. Nor did this suffice. To the evil spirits themselves which lurked within their statues, or lay concealed in secret and dark recesses, eager to drink their libations, and inhale the odor of their sacrifices, they ascribed the same divine honors. Once more, they endeavored to secure the familiar aid of these spirits, and the unseen powers which move through the tracts of air, by charms of forbidden magic, and the compulsion of unhallowed songs and incantations. Again, different nations have adopted different persons as objects of their worship. The Greeks have rendered to Bacchus, Hercules, Æsculapius, Apollo, and others who were mortal men, the titles of gods and heroes. The Egyptians have deified Horus and Isis, Osiris, and other mortals such as these. And thus they who boast of the wondrous skill whereby they have discovered geometry, astronomy, and the science of number, know not, wise as they are in their own conceit, nor understand how to estimate the measure of the power of God, or calculate his exceeding greatness above the nature of irrational and mortal beings. Hence they shrank not from applying the name of gods to the most hideous of the brute creation, to venomous reptiles and savage beasts. The Phœnicians deified Melcatharus, Usorus,[5] and others; mere mortals, and with little claim to honor: the Arabians, Dusaris[6] and Obodas: the Getæ, Zamolxis: the Cicilians, Mopsus: and the Thebans, Amphiaraus:[7] in short, each nation has adopted its own peculiar deities, differing in no respect from their fellow-mortals, being simply and truly men. Again, the Egyptians with one consent, the Phœnicians, the Greeks, nay, every nation beneath the sun, have united in worshiping the very parts and elements of the world, and even the produce of the ground itself. And, which is most surprising, though acknowledging the adulterous, unnatural, and licentious crimes of their deities, they have not only filled every city, and village, and district with temples, shrines, and statues in their honor, but have followed their evil example to the ruin of their own souls. We hear of gods and the sons of gods described by them as heroes and good genii, titles entirely opposed to truth, honors utterly at variance with the qualities they are intended to exalt. It is as if one who desired to point out the sun and the luminaries of heaven, instead of directing his gaze thitherward, should grope with his hands on the ground, and search for the celestial powers in the mud and mire. Even so mankind, deceived by their own folly and the craft of evil spirits, have believed that the Divine and spiritual Essence which is far above heaven and earth could be compatible with the birth, the affections, and death, of mortal bodies here below. To such a pitch of madness did they proceed, as to sacrifice the dearest objects of their affection to their gods, regardless of all natural ties, and urged by frenzied feeling to slay their only and best beloved children. For what can be a greater proof of madness, than to offer human sacrifice, to pollute every city, and even their own houses, with kindred blood? Do not the Greeks themselves attest this, and is not all history filled with records of the same impiety? The Phœnicians devoted their best beloved and only children as an annual sacrifice to Saturn. The Rhodians, on the sixth day of the month Metageitnion,[8] offered human victims to the same god. At Salamis, a man was pursued in

---

[1] " Of Demeter, of Cora, of Dionysius."
[2] " Athene . . . Hermes."
[3] The word used here, ἀκράτεια, is the opposite of the famous philosophical word for self-control — ἐγκράτεια.
[4] " Eros, Priapus, Aphrodite."

[5] It is probably that " Melkathros " and " Usous " referred to in the *Præp. Evang.* 1. 10 (ed. Gaisford, Oxon. 1843, 1. p. 77 and 84). The same passage may be found with English translation in Cory's *Ancient Fragments*, Lond. 1832, p. 6–7, 13.
[6] Dusaris was, it is said, equivalent to Bacchus.
[7] All the above names, excepting those specially noted, may be found in Smith, *Dict. of Greek and Roman Biog. and Mythol.*
[8] Corresponding nearly to our August. Key. *Calendarium*, in Smith, *Dict. Gr. and R. Ant.* p. 223.

the temple of Minerva Agraulis and Diomede, compelled to run thrice round the altar, afterwards pierced with a lance by the priest, and consumed as a burnt offering on the blazing pile. In Egypt, human sacrifice was most abundant. At Heliopolis three victims were daily offered to Juno, for whom king Amoses, impressed with the atrocity of the practice, commanded the substitution of an equal number of waxen figures. In Chios, and again in Tenedos, a man was slain and offered up to Omadian Bacchus. At Sparta they immolated human beings to Mars. In Crete they did likewise, offering human sacrifices to Saturn. In Laodicea of Syria a virgin was yearly slain in honor of Minerva, for whom a hart is now the substitute. The Libyans and Carthaginians appeased their gods with human victims. The Dumateni of Arabia buried a boy annually beneath the altar. History informs us that the Greeks without exception, the Thracians also, and Scythians, were accustomed to human sacrifice before they marched forth to battle. The Athenians record the immolation of the virgin children of Leus,[9] and the daughter of Erechtheus.[10] Who knows not that at this day a human victim is offered in Rome itself at the festival of Jupiter Latiaris? And these facts are confirmed by the testimony of the most approved philosophers. Diodorus, the epitomizer of libraries,[11] affirms that two hundred of the noblest youths were sacrificed to Saturn by the Libyan people, and that three hundred more were voluntarily offered by their own parents. Dionysius, the compiler of Roman history,[12] expressly says that Jupiter and Apollo demanded human sacrifices of the so-called Aborigines, in Italy. He relates that on this demand they offered a proportion of all their produce to the gods; but that, because of their refusal to slay human victims, they became involved in manifold calamities, from which they could obtain no release until they had decimated themselves, a sacrifice of life which proved the desolation of their country. Such and so great were the evils which of old afflicted the whole human race. Nor was this the full extent of their misery: they groaned beneath the pressure of other evils equally numerous and irremediable. All nations, whether civilized or barbarous, throughout the world, as if actuated by a demoniac frenzy, were infected with sedition as with some fierce and

8

9

terrible disease: insomuch that the human family was irreconcilably divided against itself; the great system of society was distracted and torn asunder; and in every corner of the earth men stood opposed to each other, and strove with fierce contention on questions of law and government. Nay, more than this: with passions aroused to fury, they engaged in mutual conflicts, so frequent that their lives were passed as it were in uninterrupted warfare. None could undertake a journey except as prepared to encounter an enemy · in the very country and villages the rustics girded on the sword, provided themselves with armor rather than with the implements of rural labor, and deemed it a noble exploit to plunder and enslave any who belonged to a neighboring state. Nay, more than this: from the fables they had themselves devised respecting their own deities, they deduced occasions for a vile and abandoned life, and wrought the ruin of body and soul by licentiousness of every kind. Not content with this, they even overstepped the bounds which nature had defined, and together committed incredible and nameless crimes, " men with men (in the words of the sacred writer) working unseemliness, and receiving in themselves that recompense of their error which was due." Nor did they stop even here; but perverted their natural thoughts of God, and denied that the course of this world was directed by his providential care, ascribing the existence and constitution of all things to the blind operation of chance, or the necessity of fate. Once more: believing that soul and body were alike dissolved by death, they led a brutish life, unworthy of the name: careless of the nature or existence of the soul, they dreaded not the tribunal of Divine justice, expected no reward of virtue, nor thought of chastisement as the penalty of an evil life. Hence it was that whole nations, a prey to wickedness in all its forms, were wasted by the effects of their own brutality: some living in the practice of most vile and lawless incest with mothers, others with sisters, and others again corrupting their own daughters. Some were found who slew their confiding guests; others who fed on human flesh; some strangled, and then feasted on, their aged men; others threw them alive to dogs. The time would fail me were I to attempt to describe the multifarious symptoms of the inveterate malady which had asserted its dominion over the whole human race. Such, and numberless others like these, were the prevailing evils, on account of which the gracious Word of God, full of compassion for his human flock, had long since, by the ministry of his prophets, and earlier still, as well as later, by that of men distinguished by

10

11

12

13

14

15

9 [Leus is said to have offered his three daughters, Phasithea, Theope, and Eubule; the oracle at Delphi having declared that the relief of the city from famine could only be effected by the shedding of the blood of his daughters by one of the citizens. — Bag.]

10 [Alluding to the sacrifice of his daughter Chthonia by Erechtheus, son of Pandion; the Athenians having been promised victory, by the oracle, over the Eleusinians and their Thracian allies, on the condition of the death of a daughter of Erechtheus. — Bag.]

11 Diodorus Siculus, whose work is mentioned elsewhere (Præp. Evang. i. 6, ed. Gaisford, p. 40) as a " historical library."

12 Dionysius of Halicarnassus.

pious devotion to God, invited those thus desperately afflicted to their own cure; and had, by means of laws, exhortations, and doctrines of every kind, proclaimed to man the principles and elements of true godliness. But when for mankind, distracted and torn as I have said, not indeed by wolves and savage beasts, but by ruthless and soul-destroying spirits of evil, human power no longer sufficed, but a help was needed superior to that of man; then it was that the Word of God, obedient to his all-gracious Father's will, at length himself appeared, and most willingly made his abode amongst us.

16 The causes of his advent I have already described, induced by which he condescended to the society of man; not in his wonted form and manner, for he is incorporeal, and present everywhere throughout the world, proving by his agency both in heaven and earth the greatness of his almighty power, but in a character new and hitherto unknown. Assuming a mortal body, he deigned to associate and converse with men; desiring, through the medium of their own likeness, to save our mortal race.

CHAPTER XIV.

1   AND now let us explain the cause for which the incorporeal Word of God assumed this mortal body as a medium of intercourse with man. How, indeed, else than in human form, could that Divine and impalpable, that immaterial and invisible Essence manifest itself to those who sought for God in created and earthly objects, unable or unwilling otherwise to discern the Author and Maker of all things?

2   As a fitting means, therefore, of communication with mankind, he assumed a mortal body, as that with which they were themselves familiar; for like, it is proverbially said, loves its like. To those, then, whose affections were engaged by visible objects, who looked for gods in statues and lifeless images, who imagined the Deity to consist in material and corporeal substance, nay, who conferred on men the title of divinity, the Word of God presented himself in this form.

3   Hence he procured for himself this body as a thrice-hallowed temple, a sensible habitation of an intellectual power; a noble and most holy form, of far higher worth than any lifeless statue. The material and senseless image, fashioned by base mechanic hands, of brass or iron, of gold or ivory, wood or stone, may be a fitting abode for evil spirits: but that Divine form, wrought by the power of heavenly wisdom, was possessed of life and spiritual being; a form animated by every excellence, the dwelling-place of the Word of God,

4   a holy temple of the holy God. Thus

the indwelling Word[1] conversed with and was known to men, as kindred with themselves; yet yielded not to passions such as theirs, nor owned, as the natural soul, subjection to the body. He parted not with aught of his intrinsic greatness, nor changed his proper Deity. For as the all-pervading radiance of the sun receives no stain from contact with dead and impure bodies; much less can the incorporeal power of the Word of God be injured in its essential purity, or part with any of its greatness, from spiritual contact with a human body.

Thus, I say, did our common Saviour prove   5 himself the benefactor and preserver of all, displaying his wisdom through the instrumentality of his human nature, even as a musician uses the lyre to evince his skill. The Grecian myth tells us that Orpheus had power to charm ferocious beasts, and tame their savage spirit, by striking the chords of his instrument with a master hand: and this story is celebrated by the Greeks, and generally believed, that an unconscious instrument could subdue the untamed brute, and draw the trees from their places, in obedience to its melodious power. But he who is the author of perfect harmony, the all-wise Word of God, desiring to apply every remedy to the manifold diseases of the souls of men, employed that human nature which is the workmanship of his own wisdom, as an instrument by the melodious strains of which he soothed, not indeed the brute creation, but savages endued with reason; healing each furious temper, each fierce and angry passion of the soul, both in civilized and barbarous nations, by the remedial power of his Divine doctrine. Like a physician of perfect skill, he met the diseases of their souls who sought for God in nature and in bodies, by a fitting and kindred remedy, and showed them God in human form. And then, with no less care for the   6 body than the soul, he presented before the eyes of men wonders and signs, as proofs of his Divine power, at the same time instilling into their ears of flesh the doctrines which he himself uttered with a corporeal tongue. In short, he performed all his works through the medium of that body which he had assumed for the sake of those who else were incapable of apprehending his Divine nature. In all   7 this he was the servant of his Father's will, himself remaining still the same as when with the Father; unchanged in essence, unimpaired in nature, unfettered by the trammels of mortal flesh, nor hindered by his abode in a human body from being elsewhere present.[2]

---

[1] All these various conceptions of the Word are strictly Biblical: (1) The Word the only revealer of the Father, who otherwise could not be known; (2) The human body the temple of God; (3) The indwelling Word.

[2] This ought to relieve Eusebius from any charge of Arianism in

8 Nay, at the very time of his intercourse with men, he was pervading all things, was with and in the Father, and even then was caring for all things both in heaven and earth. Nor was he precluded, as we are, from being present everywhere, or from the continued exercise of his Divine power. He gave of his own to man, but received nothing in return: he imparted of his Divine power to mortality, but derived no accession from mortality itself.

9 Hence his human birth to him brought no defilement; nor could his impassible Essence suffer at the dissolution of his mortal body. For let us suppose a lyre to receive an accidental injury, or its chord to be broken; it does not follow that the performer on it suffers: nor, if a wise man's body undergo punishment, can we fairly assert that his wisdom, or the soul within him, are maimed or burned.

10 Far less can we affirm that the inherent power of the Word sustained any detriment from his bodily passion, any more than, as in the instance we have already used, the solar rays which are shot from heaven to earth contract defilement, though in contact with mire and pollution of every kind. We may, indeed, assert that these things partake of the radiance of the light, but not that the light is contaminated, or the sun defiled, by this contact

11 with other bodies. And indeed these things are themselves not contrary to nature; but the Saviour, the incorporeal Word of God, being Life and spiritual Light itself, whatever he touches with Divine and incorporeal power must of necessity become endued with the intelligence of light and life. Thus, if he touch a body, it becomes enlightened and sanctified, is at once delivered from all disease, infirmity, and suffering, and that which before was lacking is

12 supplied by a portion of his fullness. And such was the tenor of his life on earth; now proving the sympathies of his human nature with our own, and now revealing himself as the Word of God: wondrous and mighty in his works as God; foretelling the events of the far distant future; declaring in every act, by signs, and wonders, and supernatural powers, that Word whose presence was so little known; and finally, by his Divine teaching, inviting the souls of men to prepare for those mansions which are above the heavens.

CHAPTER XV.

1 WHAT now remains, but to account for those which are the crowning facts of all; I mean his death, so far and widely known, the

this relation, however "dangerous" the ground he has trodden on may be.

manner of his passion, and the mighty miracle of his resurrection after death: and then to establish the truth of these events by the clearest testimonies? For the reasons detailed above he used the instrumentality of a 2 mortal body, as a figure becoming his Divine majesty, and like a mighty sovereign employed it as his interpreter in his intercourse with men, performing all things consistently with his own Divine power. Supposing, then, at the end of his sojourn among men, he had by any other means suddenly withdrawn himself from their sight, and, secretly removing that interpreter of himself, the form which he had assumed, had hastened to flee from death, and afterwards by his own act had consigned his mortal body to corruption and dissolution: doubtless in such a case he would have been deemed a mere phantom by all. Nor would he have acted in a manner worthy of himself, had he who is Life, the Word, and the Power of God, abandoned this interpreter of himself to corruption and death. Nor, again, would 3 his warfare with the spirits of evil have received its consummation by conflict with the power of death. The place of his retirement must have remained unknown; nor would his existence have been believed by those who had not seen him for themselves. No proof would have been given that he was superior to death; nor would he have delivered mortality from the law of its natural infirmity. His name had never been heard throughout the world; nor could he have inspired his disciples with contempt of death, or encouraged those who embraced his doctrine to hope for the enjoyment of a future life with God. Nor would he have fulfilled the assurances of his own promise, nor have accomplished the predictions of the prophets concerning himself. Nor would he have undergone the last conflict of all; for this was to be the struggle with the power of death. For all these reasons, then, and 4 inasmuch as it was necessary that the mortal body which had rendered such service to the Divine Word should meet with an end worthy its sacred occupant, the manner of his death was ordained accordingly. For since but two alternatives remained: either to consign his body entirely to corruption, and so to bring the scene of life to a dishonored close, or else to prove himself victorious over death, and render mortality immortal by the act of Divine power; the former of these alternatives would have contravened his own promise. For as it is not the property of fire to cool, nor of light to darken, no more is it compatible with life, to deprive of life, or with Divine intelligence, to act in a manner contrary to reason. For how would it be consistent, with reason, that he who had promised life to others, should permit his own body, the form which he had chosen, to perish beneath the power of corruption? That he who had inspired his disciples with hopes of immortality, should yield this exponent of his Divine counsels to be destroyed by death? The second alternative was therefore needful: I mean, that he should assert his dominion over the power of death. But how? should this be a furtive and secret act, or openly performed and in the sight of all? So mighty an achievement, had it remained unknown and unrevealed, must have failed of its effect as regards the interests of men; whereas the same event, if openly declared and understood, would, from its wondrous character, redound to the common benefit of all. With reason, therefore, since it was needful to prove his body victorious over death, and that not secretly but before the eyes of men, he shrank not from the trial, for this indeed would have argued fear, and a sense of inferiority to the power of death, but maintained that conflict with the enemy which has rendered mortality immortal; a conflict undertaken for the life, the immortality, the salvation of all.

6 Suppose one desired to show us that a vessel could resist the force of fire; how could he better prove the fact than by casting it into the furnace and thence withdrawing it entire and unconsumed? Even thus the Word of God, who is the source of life to all, desiring to prove the triumph of that body over death which he had assumed for man's salvation, and to make this body partake his own life and immortality, pursued a course consistent with this object. Leaving his body for a little while,[1] and delivering it up to death in proof of its mortal nature, he soon redeemed it from death, in vindication of that Divine power whereby he has manifested the immortality which he has promised to be utterly beyond the sphere of death. The

7 reason of this is clear. It was needful that his disciples should receive ocular proof of the certainty of that resurrection on which he had taught them to rest their hopes as a motive for rising superior to the fear of death. It was indeed most needful that they who purposed to pursue a life of godliness should receive a clear impression of this essential truth: more needful still for those who were destined to declare his name in all the world, and to communicate to mankind that knowledge of God which he had before ordained for all nations. For

8 such the strongest conviction of a future life was necessary, that they might be able with fearless and unshrinking zeal to maintain the conflict with Gentile and polytheistic error: a conflict the dangers of which they would never

have been prepared to meet, except as habituated to the contempt of death. Accordingly, in arming his disciples against the power of this last enemy, he delivered not his doctrines in mere verbal precepts, nor attempted to prove the soul's immortality, by persuasive and probable arguments; but displayed to them in his own person a real victory over death. Such 9 was the first and greatest reason of our Saviour's conflict with the power of death, whereby he proved to his disciples the nothingness of that which is the terror of all mankind, and afforded a visible evidence of the reality of that life which he had promised; presenting as it were a first-fruit of our common hope, of future life and immortality in the presence of God.

The second cause of his resurrection was, 10 that the Divine power might be manifested which dwelt in his mortal body. Mankind had heretofore conferred Divine honors on men who had yielded to the power of death, and had given the titles of gods and heroes to mortals like themselves. For this reason, therefore, the Word of God evinced his gracious character, and proved to man his own superiority over death, recalling his mortal body to a second life, displaying an immortal triumph over death in the eyes of all, and teaching them to acknowledge the Author of such a victory to be the only true God, even in death itself. I may 11 allege yet a third cause of the Saviour's death. He was the victim offered to the Supreme Sovereign of the universe for the whole human race: a victim consecrated for the need of the human race, and for the overthrow of the errors of demon worship. For as soon as the one holy and mighty sacrifice, the sacred body of our Saviour, had been slain for man, to be as a ransom for all nations, heretofore involved in the guilt of impious superstition, thenceforward the power of impure and unholy spirits was utterly abolished, and every earth-born and delusive error was at once weakened and destroyed. Thus, then, this salutary victim 12 taken from among themselves, I mean the mortal body of the Word, was offered on behalf of the common race of men. This was that sacrifice delivered up to death, of which the sacred oracles speak: "Behold the Lamb of God, which taketh away the sin of the world."[2] And again, as follows: "He was led as a sheep to the slaughter, and as a lamb before the shearer is dumb." They declare also the cause, saying: "He bears our sins, and is pained for us: yet we accounted him to be in trouble, and in suffering, and in affliction. But he was wounded on account of our sins, and bruised because of our iniquities: the chastisement of our peace was

---

[1] [These words (as Valesius observes) need not be too rigidly interpreted. — *Bag.*]

[2] John i. 29.

upon him; *and* by his bruises we were healed. All we as sheep have gone astray; every one has gone astray in this way; and the Lord gave him up for our sins."[3]

13 Such were the causes which led to the offering of the human body of the Word of God. But forasmuch as he was the great high priest, consecrated to the Supreme Lord and King, and therefore more than a victim, the Word, the Power, and the Wisdom of God; he soon recalled his body from the grasp of death, presented it to his Father as the first-fruit of our common salvation, and raised this trophy, a proof at once of his victory over death and Satan, and of the abolition of human sacrifices, for the blessing of all mankind.

CHAPTER XVI.

1 AND now the time is come for us to proceed to the demonstration of these things; if indeed such truths require demonstration, and if the aid of testimony be needful to confirm the certainty of palpable facts. Such testimony, however, shall be here given; and let it be received with an attentive and gracious ear.

2 Of old the nations of the earth, the entire human race, were variously distributed into provincial, national, and local governments,[1] subject to kingdoms and principalities of many kinds. The consequences of this variety were war and strife, depopulation and captivity, which raged in country and city with unceasing fury. Hence, too, the countless subjects of history, adulteries, and rapes of women; hence the woes of Troy, and the ancient tragedies, so known

3 among all peoples. The origin of these may justly be ascribed to the delusion of polytheistic error. But when that instrument of our redemption, the thrice holy body of Christ, which proved itself superior to all Satanic fraud, and free from evil both in word and deed, was raised, at once for the abolition of ancient evils, and in token of his victory over the powers of darkness; the energy of these evil spirits was at once destroyed. The manifold forms of government, the tyrannies and republics, the siege of cities, and devastation of countries caused thereby, were now no more, and one God

4 was proclaimed to all mankind. At the same time one universal power, the Roman empire, arose and flourished, while the enduring and implacable hatred of nation against nation was now removed: and as the knowledge of

one God, and one way of religion and salvation, even the doctrine of Christ, was made known to all mankind; so at the self-same period, the entire dominion of the Roman empire being vested in a single sovereign, profound peace reigned throughout the world. And thus, by the express appointment of the same God, two roots of blessing, the Roman empire, and the doctrine of Christian piety, sprang up together for the benefit of men. For before 5 this time the various countries of the world, as Syria, Asia, Macedonia, Egypt, and Arabia, had been severally subject to different rulers. The Jewish people, again, had established their dominion in the land of Palestine. And these nations, in every village, city, and district, actuated by some insane spirit, were engaged in incessant and murderous war and conflict. But two mighty powers, starting from the same point, the Roman empire, which henceforth was swayed by a single sovereign, and the Christian religion, subdued and reconciled these contending elements. Our Saviour's mighty 6 power destroyed at once the many governments and the many gods of the powers of darkness, and proclaimed to all men, both rude and civilized, to the extremities of the earth, the sole sovereignty of God himself. Meantime the Roman empire, the causes of multiplied governments being thus removed, effected an easy conquest of those which yet remained; its object being to unite all nations in one harmonious whole; an object in great measure already secured, and destined to be still more perfectly attained, even to the final conquest of the ends of the habitable world, by means of the salutary doctrine, and through the aid of that Divine power which facilitates and smooths its way. And surely this must appear a wondrous 7 fact to those who will examine the question in the love of truth, and desire not to cavil at these blessings.[2] The falsehood of demon superstition was convicted: the inveterate strife and mutual hatred of the nations was removed: at the same time One God, and the knowledge of that God, were proclaimed to all: one universal empire prevailed; and the whole human race, subdued by the controlling power of peace and concord, received one another as brethren, and responded to the feelings of their common nature. Hence, as children of one God and Father, and owning true religion as their common mother, they saluted and welcomed each other with words of peace. Thus the whole world appeared like one well-ordered and united family: each one might journey unhindered as far as and whithersoever he pleased: men might

---

[3] [Isaiah liii. 4, 5, 6, 7. Septuagint, English translation, p. 728. —*Bag.*] P. 889 of the Bagster ed., 1879. Though the first reasons make one feel as if the author had been in danger of slighting the atoning work of the Word, he here very clearly comes up, as usual, to the Biblical position.

[1] Eparchies, ethnarchies, and toparchies.

[2] This is a fair appeal, applicable to his present hearers. It at least was true of Constantine's reign, that it produced a state of relative peace and prosperity.

securely travel from West to East, and from East to West, as to their own native country : in short, the ancient oracles and predictions of the prophets were fulfilled, more numerous than we can at present cite, and those especially which speak as follows concerning the saving Word. "He shall have dominion from sea to sea, and from the river to the ends of the earth." And again, "In his days shall righteousness spring up ; and abundance of peace." "And they shall beat their swords into plough-shares, and their spears into sickles : and nation shall not take up sword against nation, neither shall 8 they learn to war any more."[3] These words, predicted ages before in the Hebrew tongue, have received in our own day a visible fulfillment, by which the testimonies of the ancient oracles are clearly confirmed. And now, if thou still desire more ample proof, receive it, not in words, but from the facts themselves. Open the eyes of thine understanding ; expand the gates of thought ; pause awhile, and consider ; inquire of thyself as though thou wert another, and thus diligently examine the nature of the case. What king or prince in any age of the world, what philosopher, legislator, or prophet, in civilized or barbarous lands, has attained so great a height of excellence, I say not after death, but while living still, and full of mighty power, as to fill the ears and tongues of all mankind with the praises of his name? Surely none save our only Saviour has done this, when, after his victory over death, he spoke the word to his followers, and fulfilled it by the event, saying to them, "Go ye, and make disciples of all nations in my name."[4] He it was who gave the distinct assurance, that his gospel must be preached in all the world for a testimony to all nations, and immediately verified his word : for within a little time the world 9 itself was filled with his doctrine. How, then, will those who caviled at the commencement of my speech be able to reply to this? For surely the force of ocular testimony is superior to any verbal argument. Who else than he, with an invisible and yet potent hand, has driven from human society like savage beasts that ever noxious and destructive tribe of evil spirits who of old had made all nations their prey, and by the motions of their images had practiced many a delusion among men? Who else, beside our Saviour, by the invocation of his name, and by unfeigned prayer addressed through him to the Supreme God, has given power to banish from the world the remnant of

those wicked spirits to those who with genuine and sincere obedience pursue the course of life and conduct which he has himself prescribed? Who else but our Saviour has taught his followers to offer those bloodless and reasonable sacrifices which are performed by prayer and the secret worship of God? Hence is 10 it that throughout the habitable world altars are erected, and churches dedicated, wherein these spiritual and rational sacrifices are offered as a sacred service by every nation to the One Supreme God. Once more, who but he, with invisible and secret power, has suppressed and utterly abolished those bloody sacrifices which were offered with fire and smoke, as well as the cruel and senseless immolation of human victims ; a fact which is attested by the heathen historians themselves? For it was not till after the publication of the Saviour's Divine doctrine, about the time of Hadrian's reign, that the practice of human sacrifice was universally abandoned. Such and so manifest are the 11 proofs of our Saviour's power and energy after death. Who then can be found of spirit so obdurate as to withhold his assent to the truth, and refuse to acknowledge his life to be Divine? Such deeds as I have described are done by the living, not the dead ; and visible acts are to us as evidence of those which we cannot see. It is as it were an event of yesterday that an impious and godless race disturbed and confounded the peace of human society, and possessed mighty power. But these, as soon as life departed, lay prostrate on the earth, worthless as dung, breathless, motionless, bereft of speech, and have left neither fame nor memorial behind. For such is the condition of the dead ; and he who no longer lives is nothing : and how can he who is nothing be capable of any act? But how shall his existence be called in question, whose active power and energy are greater than in those who are still alive? And though he be invisible to the natural eye, yet the discerning faculty is not in outward sense. We do not comprehend the rules of art, or the theories of science, by bodily sensation ; nor has any eye yet discerned the mind of man. Far less, then, the power of God : and in such cases our judgment is formed from apparent results. Even thus 12 are we bound to judge of our Saviour's invisible power, and decide by its manifest effects whether we shall acknowledge the mighty operations which he is even now carrying on to be the works of a living agent ; or whether they shall be ascribed to one who has no existence ; or, lastly, whether the inquiry be not absurd and inconsistent in itself. For with what reason can we assert the existence of one who is not? Since all allow that that which has no existence

---

[3] [Psalm lxxi. 7, 8; Isaiah ii. 4. Septuagint. — *Bag.*] Psalm lxxii., English version.
[4] Matt. xxviii. 19. There is an interesting various reading here, where Eusebius, with B. as against Aleph, adds something; but where B. and others have ουν, and D. and others have νυν, Eusebius has γουν.

is devoid of that power, and energy, and action, for these are characteristics of the living, but the contrary is characteristic of the dead.

CHAPTER XVII.

1   AND now the time is come for us to consider the works of our Saviour in our own age, and to contemplate the living operations of the living God. For how shall we describe these mighty works save as living proofs of the power of a living agent, who truly enjoys the life of God? If any one inquire the nature 2   of these works, let him now attend. But recently a class of persons, impelled by furious zeal, and backed by equal power and military force, evinced their enmity against God, by destroying his churches, and overthrowing from their foundations the buildings dedicated to his worship. In short, in every way they directed their attacks against the unseen God, and assailed him with a thousand shafts of impious words. But he who is invisible 3   avenged himself with an invisible hand. By the single fiat of his will his enemies were utterly destroyed, they who a little while before had been flourishing in great prosperity, exalted by their fellow men as worthy of divine honor, and blessed with a continued period of power and glory,[1] so long as they had maintained peace and amity with him whom they afterwards opposed. As soon, however, as they dared openly to resist his will, and to set their gods in array against him whom we adore; immediately, according to the will and power of that God against whom their arms were raised, they all received the judgment due to their audacious deeds. Constrained to yield and flee before his power, together they acknowledged his Divine nature, and hastened to reverse the measures which they had before essayed. 4   Our Saviour, therefore, without delay erected trophies of this victory everywhere, and once more adorned the world with holy temples and consecrated houses of prayer; in every city and village, nay, throughout all countries, and even in barbaric wilds, ordaining the erection of churches and sacred buildings to the honor of the Supreme God and Lord of all. Hence it is that these hallowed edifices are deemed worthy to bear his name, and receive not their appellation from men, but from the Lord himself, from which circumstances they are called churches (or houses of the 5   Lord).[2] And now let him who will stand

forth and tell us who, after so complete a desolation, has restored these sacred buildings from foundation to roof? Who, when all hope appeared extinct, has caused them to rise on a nobler scale than heretofore? And well may it claim our wonder, that this renovation was not subsequent to the death of those adversaries of God, but whilst the destroyers of these edifices were still alive; so that the recantation of their evil deeds came in their own words and edicts.[3] And this they did, not in the sunshine of prosperity and ease (for then we might suppose that benevolence or clemency might be the cause), but at the very time that they were suffering under the stroke of Divine vengeance. Who, again, has been able to retain in   6 obedience to his heavenly precepts, after so many successive storms of persecution, nay, in the very crisis of danger, so many persons throughout the world devoted to philosophy, and the service of God and those holy choirs of virgins who had dedicated themselves to a life of perpetual chastity and purity? Who taught them cheerfully to persevere in the exercise of protracted fasting, and to embrace a life of severe and consistent self-denial? Who has persuaded multitudes of either sex to devote themselves to the study of sacred things, and prefer to bodily nutriment that intellectual food which is suited to the wants of a rational soul?[4] Who has instructed barbarians and peasants, yea, feeble women, slaves, and children, in short, unnumbered multitudes of all nations, to live in the contempt of death; persuaded of the immortality of their souls, conscious that human actions are observed by the unerring eye of justice, expecting God's award to the righteous and the wicked, and therefore true to the practice of a just and virtuous life? For they could not otherwise have persevered in the course of godliness. Surely these are the acts which our Saviour, and he alone, even now performs. And now let us pass from these topics, and endeavor by inquiries such as   7 these that follow to convince the objector's obdurate understanding. Come forward, then, whoever thou art, and speak the words of reason: utter, not the thoughts of a senseless heart, but those of an intelligent and enlightened mind: speak, I say, after deep solemn converse with thyself. Who of the sages whose names have yet been known to fame, has ever been foreknown and proclaimed from the remotest ages, as our Saviour was by the prophetic oracles to the once divinely-favored Hebrew nation? But

---

[1] [Referring to Diocletian, and others of the persecuting emperors. — *Bag.*]
[2] [Κυριακὸν ἠξίωνται τῶν ἐπωνυμιῶν. The German "Kirche," the Scotch "Kirk," and the English "Church" are said, probably enough, to derive their origin from this Greek word. — *Bag.*]

[3] Compare literature on the edicts of toleration.
[4] [There is nothing which need surprise us in the praises of virginity, monkery, and asceticism, in a writer of the fourth century. The intelligent Christian will surely shrink from the thought of ascribing, with Eusebius, these fruitful sources of corruption to the Lord himself. — *Bag.*]

his very birth-place, the period of his advent, the manner of his life, his miracles, and words, and mighty acts, were anticipated and recorded in the sacred volumes of these prophets.

8 Again, who so present an avenger of crimes against himself; so that, as the immediate consequence of their impiety, the entire Jewish people were scattered by an unseen power, their royal seat utterly removed, and their very temple with its holy things levelled with the ground? Who, like our Saviour, has uttered predictions at once concerning that impious nation and the establishment of his church throughout the world, and has equally verified both by the event? Respecting the temple of these wicked men, our Saviour said: " Your house is left unto you desolate " :[5] and, " There shall not be left one stone upon another in this place, that shall not be thrown down."[6] And again, of his church he says : " I will build my church upon a rock, and the gates of hell

9 shall not prevail against it."[7] How wondrous, too, must that power be deemed which summoned obscure and unlettered men from their fisher's trade, and made them the legislators and instructors of the human race ! And how clear a demonstration of his deity do we find in the promise so well performed, that he would make them fishers of men : in the power and energy which he bestowed, so that they composed and published writings of such authority that they were translated into every civilized and barbarous language,[8] were read and pondered by all nations, and the doc-

10 trines contained in them accredited as the oracles of God ! How marvelous his predictions of the future, and the testimony whereby his disciples were forewarned that they should be brought before kings and rulers, and should endure the severest punishments, not indeed as criminals, but simply for their confession of his name ! Or who shall adequately describe the power with which he prepared them thus to suffer with a willing mind, and enabled them, strong in the armor of godliness, to maintain a constancy of spirit indomitable in the midst

11 of conflict? Or how shall we enough admire that steadfast firmness of soul which strengthened, not merely his immediate followers, but their successors also, even to our present age, in the joyful endurance of every infliction, and every form of torture, in proof of their devotion to the Supreme God? Again, what monarch has prolonged his government through so vast a series of ages? Who else has power

to make war after death, to triumph over every enemy, to subjugate each barbarous and civilized nation and city, and to subdue his adversaries with an invisible and secret hand?

Lastly, and chief of all, what slanderous 12 lip shall dare to question that universal peace to which we have already referred, established by his power throughout the world?[9] For thus the mutual concord and harmony of all nations coincided in point of time with the extension of our Saviour's doctrine and preaching in all the world : a concurrence of events predicted in long ages past by the prophets of God. The day itself would fail me, gracious emperor, should I attempt to exhibit in a single view those cogent proofs of our Saviour's Divine power which even now are visible in their effects ; for no human being, in civilized or barbarous nations, has ever yet exhibited such power of Divine virtue as our Saviour.

But why do I speak of men, since of the 13 beings whom all nations have deemed divine, none has appeared on earth with power like to his ? If there has, let the fact now be proved. Come forward, ye philosophers, and tell us what god or hero has yet been known to fame, who has delivered the doctrines of eternal life and a heavenly kingdom as he has done who is our Saviour ? Who, like him, has persuaded multitudes throughout the world to pursue the principles of Divine wisdom, to fix their hope on heaven itself, and look forward to the mansions there reserved for them that love God ? What god or hero in human form has ever held his course from the rising to the setting sun, a course co-extensive as it were with the solar light, and irradiated mankind with the bright and glorious beams of his doctrine, causing each nation of the earth to render united worship to the One true God ? What god or hero yet, as he has done, has set aside all gods and heroes among civilized or barbarous nations; has ordained that divine honors should be withheld from all, and claimed obedience to that command : and then, though singly conflicting with the power of all, has utterly destroyed the opposing hosts ; victorious over the gods and heroes of every age, and causing himself alone, in every region of the habitable world, to be acknowledged by all people as the only Son of God ? Who else has commanded the 14 nations inhabiting the continents and islands of this mighty globe to assemble weekly on the Lord's day, and to observe it as a festival, not indeed for the pampering of the body, but for the invigoration of the soul by instruction in Divine truth ? What god or hero, exposed, as our Saviour was, to so sore a conflict, has raised

---

[5] Matt. xxiii. 38.
[6] Matt. xxiv. 2, — apparently a paraphrase from memory.
[7] Matt. xvi. 18.
[8] The Syriac, Peschito, and possibly the Curetonian, the old Latin (Itala), probably both the Thebaic and Memphitic Coptic versions, at least, had been made at this time.

[9] [The peace which Christ, at his birth, bestowed on the Roman world (Valesius). — Bag.]

the trophy of victory over every foe? For they indeed, from first to last, unceasingly assailed his doctrine and his people: but he who is invisible, by the exercise of a secret power, has raised his servants and the sacred houses of their worship to the height of' glory.

But why should we still vainly aim at detailing those Divine proofs of our Saviour's power which no language can worthily express; which need indeed no words of ours, but themselves appeal in loudest tones to those whose mental ears are open to the truth? Surely it is a strange, a wondrous fact, unparalleled in the annals of human life; that the blessings we have described should be accorded to our mortal race, and that he who is in truth the only, the eternal Son of God, should thus be visible on earth.

CHAPTER XVIII.

THESE words of ours, however, [gracious] Sovereign, may well appear superfluous in your ears, convinced as you are, by frequent and personal experience, of our Saviour's Deity; yourself also, in actions still more than words, a herald of the truth to all mankind. Yourself, it may be, will vouchsafe at a time of leisure to relate to us the abundant manifestations which your Saviour has accorded you of his presence, and the oft-repeated visions of himself which have attended you in the hours of sleep. I speak not of those secret suggestions which to us are unrevealed: but of those principles which he has instilled into your own mind, and which are fraught with general interest and benefit to the human race. You will yourself relate in worthy terms the visible protection which your Divine shield and guardian has extended in the hour of battle; the ruin of your open and secret foes; and his ready aid in time of peril. To him you will ascribe relief in the midst of perplexity; defence in solitude; expedients in extremity; foreknowledge of events yet future; your forethought for the general weal; your power to investigate uncertain questions; your conduct of most important enterprises; your administration of civil affairs;[1] your military arrangements, and correction of abuses in all departments; your ordinances respecting public right; and, lastly, your legislation for the common benefit of all. You will, it may be, also detail to us those particulars of his favor which are secret to us, but known to you alone, and treasured in your royal memory as in secret storehouses. Such, doubtless, are the reasons, and such the convincing proofs of your Saviour's power, which caused you to raise that sacred edifice which presents to all, believers and unbelievers alike, a trophy of his victory over death, a holy temple of the holy God: to consecrate those noble and splendid monuments of immortal life and his heavenly kingdom: to offer memorials of our Almighty Saviour's conquest which well become the imperial dignity of him by whom they are bestowed. With such memorials have you adorned that edifice which witnesses of eternal life: thus, as it were in imperial characters, ascribing victory and triumph to the heavenly Word of God: thus proclaiming to all nations, with clear and unmistakable voice, in deed and word, your own devout and pious confession of his name.

---

[1] Literally, "Your political economies."

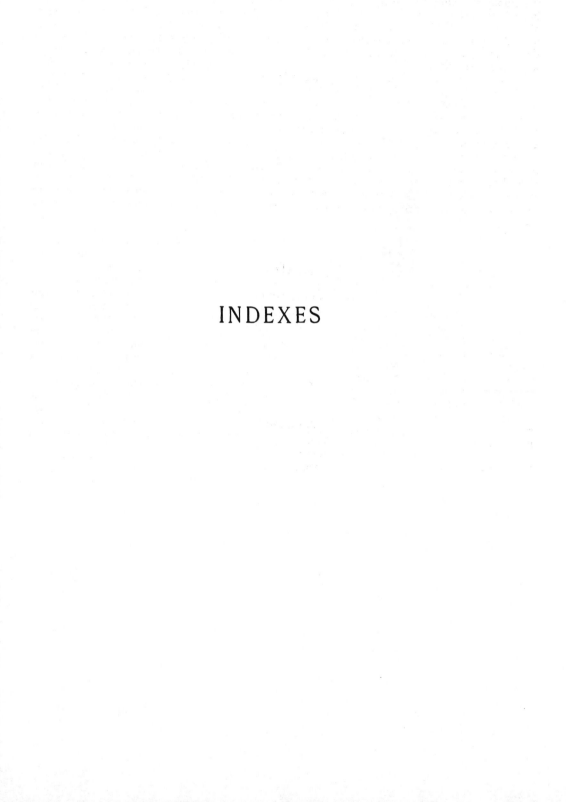

INDEXES

THE CHURCH HISTORY OF EUSEBIUS.

INDEX OF SUBJECTS.

THE CHURCH HISTORY OF EUSEBIUS.

INDEX OF TEXTS.

* Passages marked with an asterisk are simply referred to in text or notes, not quoted.

GENERAL INDEX.

NOTE. — The references to prolegomena and notes are in italics.